Lecture Notes in Artificial Intelligence 9112

Subseries of Lecture Notes in Computer Science

LNAI Series Editors

Randy Goebel
University of Alberta, Edmonton, Canada
Yuzuru Tanaka
Hokkaido University, Sapporo, Japan
Wolfgang Wahlster
DFKI and Saarland University, Saarbrücken, Germany

LNAI Founding Series Editor

Joerg Siekmann
DFKI and Saarland University, Saarbrücken, Germany

More information about this series at http://www.springer.com/series/1244

Cristina Conati · Neil Heffernan
Antonija Mitrovic · M. Felisa Verdejo (Eds.)

Artificial Intelligence in Education

17th International Conference, AIED 2015
Madrid, Spain, June 22–26, 2015
Proceedings

 Springer

Editors
Cristina Conati
University of British Columbia
Vancouver, BC
Canada

Neil Heffernan
Computer Science Department
Worcester Polytechnic Institute
Worcester, MA
USA

Antonija Mitrovic
Department of Computer Science
and Software Engineering
University of Canterbury
Christchurch
New Zealand

M. Felisa Verdejo
E.T.S.I. Informática
Universidad National de Educacion
a Distancia
Madrid
Spain

ISSN 0302-9743   ISSN 1611-3349   (electronic)
Lecture Notes in Artificial Intelligence
ISBN 978-3-319-19772-2   ISBN 978-3-319-19773-9   (eBook)
DOI 10.1007/978-3-319-19773-9

Library of Congress Control Number: 2015940412

LNCS Sublibrary: SL7 – Artificial Intelligence

Printed on acid-free paper

Springer International Publishing AG Switzerland is part of Springer Science+Business Media
(www.springer.com)

Preface

The 17th International Conference on Artificial Intelligence in Education (AIED 2015) joined the longstanding series of biennial international conferences for high-quality research in intelligent systems and cognitive science for educational computing applications. The conference provides opportunities for the cross-fertilization of approaches, techniques, and ideas from the many fields that comprise AIED, including computer science, cognitive and learning sciences, education, game design, psychology, sociology, linguistics, as well as many domain-specific areas. Since the first AIED meeting over 30 years ago, both the breadth of the research and the reach of the technologies have expanded in dramatic ways.

There were 170 submissions as full papers to AIED 2015, of which 50 were accepted as long papers (10 pages) with oral presentation at the conference (for an acceptance rate of 29%), and 65 were accepted for poster presentation with four pages in the proceedings. Of the 20 papers directly submitted as posters, 13 were accepted. Each submission was reviewed by at least three members of the Program Committee, including one senior member. In addition, submissions underwent a discussion period to ensure that all reviewers' opinions would be considered and leveraged to generate a group recommendation to the program chairs.

Three distinguished researchers from industry and academia gave plenary invited talks illustrating prospective directions for the field: Vania Dimitrova (University of Leeds, UK), Pierre Dillenbourg (École Polytechnique Fédérale de Lausanne and Center for Digital Education at the Swiss Federal Institute of Technology), and Bror Saxberg, Chief Learning Officer at Kaplan, Inc. (USA).

The conference also included:

- A Doctoral Consortium that provided 12 doctoral students with the opportunity to present their ongoing doctoral research at the conference and receive invaluable feedback from the AIED community.
- An Interactive Events session during which AIED attendees could experience first-hand eight new and emerging intelligent learning environments via interactive demonstrations.
- An Industry and Innovation Track intended to support connections between industry (both for-profit and non-profit) and the research community. The seven companies that participated in this track presented their need of and involvement with educational technologies and engaged with AIED researchers to learn about some of the most promising new developments in the field and connect with academic partners.

On the first and last day of the conference, AIED 2105 hosted eight workshops focused on providing in-depth discussion of current and emerging topics of interest to the AIED community, including: Intelligent Support for Learning in Groups (ISLG); Culturally Aware Tutoring Systems (CATS 2015); Intelligent Support in Exploratory and

Open-Ended Learning Environments; Learning Analytics for Project-Based and Experiential Learning Scenarios; Should AI Stay Married to Ed?; Simulated Learners; Developing a Generalized Intelligent Framework for Tutoring (GIFT); Informing Design Through a Community of Practice; and Affect, Meta-Affect, Data and Learning (AMADL 2015).

We give our most heartfelt thanks to the Universidad National de Educacion a Distancia (UNED) for hosting AIED 2015, and to our sponsors for their support: Pearson, Carnegie Learning, and Carney Inc. We also want to acknowledge the amazing work of the AIED 2015 Organizing Committee and of the Program Committee members (listed herein), who with their enthusiastic contributions gave us invaluable support in putting this conference together.

April 2015   Cristina Conati
                                                                    Neil Heffernan
                                                                 Antonija Mitrovic
                                                                 M. Felisa Verdejo

Organization

International Artificial Intelligence in Education Society

Management Board

Tanja Mitrovic	University of Canterbury, New Zealand - President
Jack Mostow	Carnegie Mellon University, USA - Secretary / Treasurer
Ben du Boulay	University of Sussex, UK - President-Elect
Vincent Aleven	Carnegie Mellon University, USA - Journal Editor
Judy Kay	University of Sydney, Australia - Journal Editor

IAIED Society Executive Committee

Vincent Aleven	Carnegie Mellon University, USA
Ryan S.J.D. Baker	Columbia University Teacher's College, USA
Tiffany Barnes	North Carolina State University, USA
Joseph E. Beck	Worcester Polytechnic Institute, USA
Gautam Biswas	Vanderbilt University, USA
Benedict du Boulay (Emeritus)	University of Sussex, UK
Susan Bull	University of Birmingham, UK
Ricardo Conejo	University of Malaga, Spain
Vania Dimitrova	University of Leeds, UK
Sidney D'Mello	University of Notre Dame, USA
Art Graesser	University of Memphis, USA
Neil Heffernan	Worcester Polytechnic Institute, USA
H. Chad Lane	Institute for Creative Technologies, University of Southern California, USA
Chee-Kit Looi	Nanyang Technological University, Singapore
Rosemary Luckin	University of London, UK
Bruce McLaren	Carnegie Mellon University, USA
Antonija (Tanja) Mitrovic	University of Canterbury, New Zealand
Riichiro Mizoguchi	Osaka University, Japan
Zachary Pardos	University of California at Berkeley, USA
Ido Roll	University of British Columbia, Canada
Carolyn Penstein Rose	Carnegie Mellon University, USA
Julita Vassileva	University of Saskatchewan, Canada

Erin Walker   Arizona State University, USA
Kalina Yacef   University of Sydney, Australia

Organizing Committee

General Chair

Antonija (Tanja)   Head of the University of Canterbury Computer
  Mitrovic   Science and Software Engineering Department
                                       and the Research Leader of the Intelligent
                                       Computer Tutoring Research Group

Organization Chair

M. Felisa Verdejo   Universidad Nacional de Educación a Distancia
                                       (UNED), Spain

Program Committee Chairs

Cristina Conati   University of British Columbia, Canada
Neil Heffernan   Worcester Polytechnic Institute, USA

Tutorial and Workshop Chairs

Jesus G. Boticario   Artificial Intelligence Department, UNED, Spain
Kasia Muldner   Carleton University, Canada

Industry Track Chairs

Steve Ritter   Carnegie Learning Incorporated, USA
Paola Rizzo   Interagens s.r.l., Italy

Doctoral Consortium Chairs

Tiffany Barnes   North Carolina State University, USA
Bert Bredeweg   University of Amsterdam, The Netherlands
Beverly Park Woolf   University of Massachusetts (UMASS) Amherst,
                                       USA

Poster Chairs

Matt Easterday   Northwestern University, USA
Kaska Porayska-Pomsta   Institute of Education, University of London, UK

Interactive Events Chairs

Ilya Goldin   Pearson, USA
Olga C. Santos   Artificial Intelligence Department, UNED, Spain

Panel Chair

Judy Kay   University of Sydney, Australia

Publicity Chair

Sebastien Lalle   University of British Columbia, Canada

Senior Program Committee

Vincent Aleven   Carnegie Mellon University, USA
Ivon Arroyo   University of Massachusetts Amherst, USA
Kevin Ashley   University of Pittsburgh, USA
Roger Azevedo   North Carolina State University, USA
Gautam Biswas   Vanderbilt University, USA
Bert Bredeweg   University of Amsterdam, The Netherlands
Vania Dimitrova   University of Leeds, UK
Sidney D'Mello   University of Notre Dame, USA
Benedict Du Boulay   University of Sussex, UK
Art Graesser   University of Memphis, USA
Jim Greer   University of Saskatchewan, Canada
W. Lewis Johnson   Alelo Inc., USA
Akihiro Kashihara   The University of Electro-Communications, Japan
Judy Kay   University of Sydney, Australia
Kenneth Koedinger   Carnegie Mellon University, USA
H. Chad Lane   University of Southern California, USA
James Lester   North Carolina State University, USA
Gordon McCalla   University of Saskatchewan, Canada
Bruce Mclaren   Carnegie Mellon University, USA
Alessandro Micarelli   Roma Tre University, Italy
Tanja Mitrovic   University of Canterbury, New Zealand
Riichiro Mizoguchi   Japan Advanced Institute of Science and Technology
Jack Mostow   Carnegie Mellon University, USA
Helen Pain   University of Edinburgh, UK
Niels Pinkwart   Humboldt Universität zu Berlin, Germany
Ido Roll   University of British Columbia, Canada
Ryan S.J.D. Baker   Columbia University, USA
Peter Sloep   Open Universiteit Nederland, The Netherlands
Pierre Tchounikine   University of Grenoble, France
Wouter Van Joolingen   University of Twente, The Netherlands
Kurt Vanlehn   Arizona State University, USA
Julita Vassileva   University of Saskatchewan, Canada
Felisa Verdejo   Universidad Nacional de Educación a Distancia, Spain
Beverly Park Woolf   University of Massachusetts, USA
Kalina Yacef   The University of Sydney, Australia

Program Committee

Esma Aimeur   University of Montreal, Canada
Fabio Akhras   Renato Archer Center of Information Technology, Brazil

Local Committee

Co-organizers (Liaison with AIED Organizing Chair)

Jesus G. Boticario   Artificial Intelligence Department, UNED
Olga C. Santos   Artificial Intelligence Department, UNED

Student Volunteer Chair

Sergio Salmeron-Majadas   Artificial Intelligence Department, UNED

Website Chair

Emmanuelle Gutiérrez y   Artificial Intelligence Department, UNED
  Restrepo

Financial Issues

Pilar Muñoz   Director of Training and Projects,
                            UNED Foundation

Dissemination Activities

Elena Bárcena   Foreign Philology and Linguistics Department,
                              UNED
Raúl Cabestrero   Basic Psychology II Department, UNED
Manuel Castro   Electrical Engineering, Electronics
                              and Control Department, UNED
Elena Gaudioso   Artificial Intelligence Department, UNED
Catalina Martínez-Mediano   Department of Research Methods and Diagnosis
                              in Education I, UNED
Pilar Quirós   Basic Psychology II Department, UNED
Tim Read   Computer Systems and Languages Department,
                              UNED
Miguel Rodríguez-Artacho   Computer Systems and Languages Department,
                              UNED
Rosa Carro   Computer Science Department, Universidad
                              Autónoma de Madrid
Carlos Delgado Kloos   Universidad Carlos III de Madrid
Baltasar Fernández-Manjón   Department of Software Engineering and Artificial
                              Intelligence, Universidad Complutense de Madrid
Diana Pérez Marín   Computer Systems and Languages Department,
                              Universidad Rey Juan Carlos de Madrid

Sponsors

Universidad Nacional de Educación a Distancia (UNED), Spain

Universidad Complutense de Madrid, Spain

Pearson

Carnegie Learning

Carney Inc. (Mari)

Keynote Speakers Abstracts

Orchestration Graphs: How to Scale up Rich Pedagogical Scenarios?

Pierre Dillenbourg

CHILI Lab., Center for Digital Education,
Swiss Federal Institute of Technology,
RLC D1 740, Station 20, CH-1015 Lausanne, Switzerland
pierre.dillenbourg@epfl.ch

The goal of orchestration graphs is to describe how rich learning activities, often designed for small classes, can be scaled up to thousands of participants, as in MOOCs. A sequence of learning activities is modeled as a graph with specific properties. The vertices or nodes of the graph are the learning activities. Learners perform some of these activities individually, some in teams and other ones with the whole class. The graph has a geometric nature, time being represented horizontally and the social organization (individual, teams, class) vertically. These activities can be inspired by heterogeneous learning theories: a graph models the integration of heterogeneous activities into a coherent pedagogical scenario. The edges of the graph connect activities. They represent the two-fold relationship between activities: how they relate to each other from a pedagogical and from an operational viewpoint. From the operational viewpoint, edges are associated to operators that transform the data structures produced during a learning activity into the data structures needed to run the next activity.

From the pedagogical viewpoint, an edge describes why an activity is necessary for the next activity: it can for instance be a cognitive pre-requisite, a motivational trick, an advanced organizer or an organizational constraint. The extent to which an activity is necessary for the next one is encompassed in the weight of an edge. The transition between two activities is stored as a matrix: the cell (m,n) of a transition matrix stores the probability that a learner in cognitive state m will evolve to state n in the next activity. The transition matrix can be summarized by a parameter that constitutes the edge weight: an edge between two activities has a heavy weight if the learner performance in an activity is very predictive of his success of the connected activity. The graph also constitutes a probabilistic network that allows predicting the future state of a learner. An orchestation graph describes how the scenario can be modified, stretched, cut, extended.

Open, Interactive, Social: Intelligent Mentors that Embrace Diversity of Real World Experiences

Vania Dimitrova

School of Computing, University of Leeds, Leeds LS2 9JT, UK
v.g.dimitrova@leeds.ac.uk

This talk will draw lessons from a journey in designing and developing intelligent learning environments for adult learners. Early work on interactive open learner modelling showed potential for computer tutors that help learners to understand themselves. While this is necessary for effective adult learning systems, it is not sufficient. Intelligent learning environments have to consider the way adults learn: self-directed, experienced-based, goal- and relevancy oriented.

A key factor is how well the learner connects their learning with the real world, which brings forth the key challenge of modelling real world experiences. Crowdwisdom - digital traces left in social media - can offer a cost-effective, scalable and reusable way to 'sense' the real world. I will show how we leverage semantic technologies to gain deeper insights into social content and to model different view-points. This paves the way towards intelligent mentoring that harnesses diversity by leveraging the interaction in socio-cyber-physical systems.

Learning Engineering: The Art and Science of Improving Learning Performance

Bror Saxberg

Kaplan Inc.
6301 Kaplan University Avenue, Fort Lauderdale, FL 33309, USA
bror.saxberg@kaplan.com

There's a ton of research out about how learning can be enhanced by the right kinds of learning experiences, including how technology can help. However, very little of that is getting to students at scale, compared with random walks with technology (e.g., "Video is great, right? Must have more"). This talk is about what is being done at Kaplan to try to be "learning engineers," applying learning science at scale in practical circumstances. Kaplan is trying to work in Pasteur's Quadrant for the domain of learning sciences: to see what works and doesn't at scale with careful data collection, and to become a test-bed and a source of new questions about lifting student performance in the field.

Contents

Posters

Doctoral Consortium Paper

Workshop Abstracts

Industry Track Papers

Interactive Events

Full Papers

Is a Dialogue-Based Tutoring System that Emulates Helpful Co-constructed Relations During Human Tutoring Effective?

Patricia Albacete[✉], Pamela Jordan, and Sandra Katz

Learning Research and Development Center, University of Pittsburgh,
Pittsburgh, PA 15260, USA
palbacet@pitt.edu

Abstract. We present an initial field evaluation of Rimac, a natural-language tutoring system which implements decision rules that simulate the highly interactive nature of human tutoring. We compared this rule-driven version of the tutor with a non-rule-driven control in high school physics classes. Although students learned from both versions of the system, the experimental group outperformed the control group. A particularly interesting finding is that the experimental version was especially beneficial for female students.

Keywords: ITS · Natural-language tutoring systems · Physics education

1   Introduction

Research on one-on-one human tutoring has shown that its highly interactive nature largely accounts for its effectiveness (e.g. [5], [8], [16]). However, machine-learning driven analyses of automated tutoring indicate that neither the amount of interaction during tutoring (e.g., the frequency of exchanges, such as question-answer exchanges), nor the granularity of the interaction (e.g., whether an exchange addresses a problem-solving goal or its sub-goals) predict how much students learn from tutoring. Instead, they point to *what content* is addressed and *how* it is addressed in a particular context ([6], [14]) as key features of tutorial dialogue. This research, in turn, highlights the need to further specify what these features are, so that they can be more generally simulated in natural-language tutoring systems.

Since tutoring is carried out through language, some developers of dialogue-based tutoring systems have stressed the need for more research aimed at identifying particular linguistic mechanisms that support learning during tutoring (e.g., [3], [15]). Several research teams, including ours, have responded to this call through various approaches, including machine learning driven analyses of annotated interactions between students and an automated tutor, and statistical analyses of annotated human tutorial dialogue corpora (e.g., [3, 4], [12], [17]). The tie that binds these studies is their focus on the *interactions* between the student and the tutor, instead of on the contributions of either party, the student or the tutor. Correspondingly, this research is grounded in linguistic theories that can help describe the relationships between

© Springer International Publishing Switzerland 2015
C. Conati et al. (Eds.): AIED 2015, LNAI 9112, pp. 3–12, 2015.
DOI: 10.1007/978-3-319-19773-9_1

speaker turns. For example, Speech Act Theory is well-suited for classifying one intention associated with each speaker's utterances during an instructional dialogue (e.g., to ask a question, make an assertion) and for highlighting interaction patterns, but is inadequate for capturing how information in the tutor's turn relates to information in the student's turn, and vice versa; in other words, for highlighting where in the interactions *knowledge* co-construction may be taking place.

Rhetorical Structure Theory (RST) captures both informational and intentional relationships between parts of a discourse (spoken or written text, and dialogue) and is generalizable across domains ([13]). For these reasons, we used RST to identify potentially effective rhetorical relationships during live physics tutorial dialogues and to express these relationships as decision rules that could be explicitly encoded within a natural-language tutoring system for physics, Rimac. This work on specifying a set of dialogue decision rules is summarized in the next section; a more detailed description can be found in [11]. The current paper focuses on an initial evaluation of an experimental version of Rimac that deliberately incorporates these decision rules, as compared with a control version of the tutor that does not.

2   Rimac and the Decision Rules that Simulate Interactivity

Rimac is a web-based natural-language tutoring system that scaffolds students in acquiring a deeper understanding of the physics concepts and principles associated with quantitative physics problems. It performs this task through automated reflective dialogues that students engage in after solving quantitative physics problems on paper. Rimac's dialogues were developed following a common framework for generating automated dialogues known as a *directed line of reasoning*, or DLR ([7]). During a DLR, the tutor presents a series of carefully ordered questions to the student. If the student answers a question correctly, he advances to the next question in the DLR. Otherwise, the system launches a remedial sub-dialogue and then returns to the main line of reasoning after the sub-dialogue has completed.

In order to simulate the interactivity of human tutoring in Rimac, we first used RST to characterize the co-constructed discourse relations that took place during live physics tutoring sessions, by manually annotating a large corpus of reflective discussions between human tutors and students. We focused on inter-speaker relationships that implement abstraction and specification (e.g., part:whole, step:process) since these relationships have been shown to promote learning (e.g., [17]) and on other relationships that are common in the domain of physics, such as comparison and conditional reasoning (e.g., Louwerse et al., 2008; cited in [11]). For example, the student says, "The acceleration would be positive" and the tutor follows up with "Right, the x component of the acceleration would be positive." According to RST, this exchange would be classified as a whole:part relation, since the student names a vector (acceleration) and the tutor refers to a specific component of that vector. To take another example, a student says, "the velocity is 14" and the tutor specifies, "it is 14 m/s." This is a co-constructed object:attribute relation in which the student provides a value for velocity and the tutor specifies its units. After we tagged each student-tutor and tutor-student dialogue exchange according to the types of discourse relations that they embodied, we searched for correlations between the frequency of each type of relation and learning, as measured by students' gain scores from pretest to posttest. We found that the frequency of several types of co-constructed relations in the tagged corpus predicted learning and, moreover, that these correlations varied according to student ability level [11]. In order to express these potentially beneficial tutorial interactions as decision rules that could guide dialogue authoring, we needed to specify the discourse contexts, or "triggering conditions", under which they occurred—for example, if they tended to take place at the beginning, middle, or end of a dialogue; if they were triggered by particular types of student errors, etc. The 11 decision rules that stemmed from this process guide dialogue authoring by specifying how the tutor should respond to different types of student input, at each step of the dialogue—that is, after a student's response to each question in the main line of reasoning, or during a remedial sub-dialogue.

Table 1 presents an example of one of the 11 tutoring decision rules that stemmed from this process. Along with related rules, the decision rule shown in Table 1 drives Rimac's implementation of co-constructed condition reasoning relations, which we found predicted learning especially among low pretest scorers [11].

Table 1. A conditional reasoning exchange during human tutoring and associated decision rule

Reflection Question: A bungee jumper of mass 80 kg just had an exciting ride from the center of a bridge. Unfortunately, the bungee, fully stretched, leaves him 18 meters above the ground. What is the tension in the bungee as he is hanging there? ***Student:*** Tension = weight *(student assertion of physical situation)* ***Tutor:*** Why does the tension equal the weight in this problem? *(tutor prompt for condition(s))* ***Student:*** Because there are no other outside forces acting on the bungee/jumper system. *(condition)* Discourse Relation: *T-S: situation:condition* Decision rule that stemmed from conditional relationships such as this: *If the student does not provide an explanation to support a claim, especially at the beginning of a reflective dialogue, prompt the student to explain why this claim is true in the given situation.*

Would a version of Rimac that deliberately implements this suite of dialogue decision rules outperform a more traditional version of the system, which does not? To address this question, we conducted an experiment to compare two versions of reflective dialogues in Rimac. For the control version, dialogue authors, who were experienced physics tutors or teachers, were instructed to write the best dialogues that they could, by following the standard authoring framework (i.e., DLRs, with embedded remedial sub-dialogues). For the experimental version, the same authors were asked to revise the dialogues they had produced for the control version by applying the decision rules in appropriate contexts as frequently as possible, and without altering the content discussed during the control version of the dialogues.

Table 2 illustrates these two versions of Rimac's dialogues. They were produced using the TuTalk dialogue development toolkit [10]. To keep accuracy of automatic recognition of student input high, most questions posed by the tutor require a short answer. However, implementation of some decision rules, such as the one shown in Table 1, invite an explanation from the student. Given the complexity of interpreting such responses, and the frustration that students experience when the system misinterprets them, we bypassed this problem by presenting a menu of responses for students to map theirs to, as shown in the first dialogue excerpt in Table 2.

It is important to note that some dialogue rules were unintentionally incorporated within the control dialogues. This is not surprising, given that the decision rules stem from analyses of naturally occurring human tutorial interaction. In other words, it would have been unnatural for dialogue authors to completely avoid employing the interaction patterns embodied in the decision rules while generating the control dialogues. Nonetheless, we verified that the frequency of each rule was significantly lower in the control version of each dialogue than in its experimental counterpart.

Table 2. Dialogue excerpts from the experimental (rule-driven) and control versions of Rimac

Rule-driven Tutor (T=Tutor; S=Student)	Control Tutor (T=Tutor; S=Student)
Example1: Decision rule: *If the student does not provide an explanation to support a claim, especially at the beginning of a reflective dialogue, prompt the student to explain why this claim is true, in the given situation.*	A correct answer from the student moves him on to the next step in the line of reasoning.
T: Is the direction of the acceleration in the same direction or the opposite direction of the motion? S: Opposite. T: Why do you think this? S: Because there is deceleration so the acceleration has to be opposite the motion. T: Please select the best match below for the answer you just gave: o The problem said so • Because when an object is slowing down acceleration opposes its motion o Because when there is deceleration the acceleration is always negative o Another reason. T: I agree. Let's now step through the reasoning.	T: Is the direction of the acceleration in the same direction or the opposite direction of the motion? S: Opposite. T: Very good. Let's now step through the reasoning.
Example 2: Decision rule: *When the student answers a question incorrectly, if possible, state the condition(s) under which the answer would be correct.*	When the student answers a question incorrectly he receives a remediation.
S: The final velocity is larger. T: *If the supertanker were speeding up the final velocity would be larger.* But the supertanker is slowing down hence the final velocity is smaller than the initial velocity.	S: The final velocity is larger. T: Not quite. The supertanker is slowing down hence the final velocity is smaller than the initial velocity.

3   System Evaluation

Participants. The study was conducted in high school physics classes at four schools in the Pittsburgh PA area, following the course unit on kinematics, with 256 students participating; 117 females and 137 males. (Two students in the experimental condition did not report gender.) Students were randomly assigned to conditions: experimental (decision rule-based version; N= 125, 54 females, 69 males) and control (standard DLR version; N= 131, 63 females, 68 males).

Materials. After consulting with high school physics teachers, we selected three quantitative kinematics problems and developed several reflective dialogues per problem which addressed their associated concepts. Students engaged in these dialogues after solving the problems. Also with teachers' advice, we developed tests that would allow us to measure students' learning gains after using the tutor. The pretest was isomorphic to the posttest. The tests consist of 14 items; 8 multiple-choice and 6 open-response problems. We developed a rubric to promote consistent scoring across graders, who were experts in the physics content. Tests were scored by one grader and reviewed by another to ensure fidelity to the rubric; adjustments were made when necessary.

Procedure. On the first day of data collection, the teacher gave the pretest in class and assigned four homework problems: the three problems mentioned in the materials section for which we had developed reflective dialogues, plus an extra problem. The purpose of the extra problem was to control for time on task, since we expected the experimental dialogues to take longer to work through than the control dialogues. This problem was isomorphic to one other assigned problem, to control for content. During the next one or two days (depending on whether classes were 45 min. or 80 min. long), students used Rimac in class. For each homework problem, students watched a video "walkthrough" of a sample solution and then engaged in the problem's reflective dialogues. The videos focused on procedural/problem-solving knowledge, while the dialogues focused on conceptual knowledge. Finally, at the next class meeting, teachers administered the posttest.

Results. Data analysis addressed four objectives—namely, to determine whether: a) students who interacted with the tutor learned, as measured by amount of gain from pretest to posttest, regardless of treatment condition, b) there was a difference in amount of gain between conditions, c) there was an aptitude-treatment interaction d) there were gender differences in learning from one or both versions of the system.

The data was first analyzed considering all problems together; then multiple-choice and open-response problems were considered separately. We expected that students' ability to verbalize physics concepts and reasoning would be better fostered by the experimental version of the system, and open-response items would detect this better than multiple-choice test items. Moreover, open-response problems do not allow for guessing the correct answer to the extent that multiple-choice items do.

Did students learn from the tutoring system? To determine whether students' interaction with Rimac, irrespective of condition, promoted learning, we compared pretest scores with posttest scores by performing paired samples t-tests. The results are shown in Table 3. When all students were considered together, we found a statistically significant difference between pretest and posttest for multiple-choice problems, open-response problems, and all problems combined. When students were considered by condition, we found a statistically significant difference between pretest and posttest for all problems and for multiple-choice problems. However, for open-response problems, we found a significant difference only in the experimental group.

Taken together, these findings suggest that students in both conditions learned from the system; on average, they could solve a half to one more problem correctly on the posttest than on the pretest. However, the experimental version of the system was perhaps more effective in helping students express the physics reasoning required to solve the open-response problems.

Did one version of the tutor promote learning better than the other? Before testing our hypothesis that students who used the experimental version of Rimac would out-perform students who used the control version, we compared pretest scores and time on task between conditions. There were no statistically significant between-group differences in pretest scores considering all problems combined, multiple-choice problems or open-response problems. However, we found that the mean time on task in the experimental condition (M=48.2 minutes SD=13.5 minutes) was significantly higher than in the control condition (M=45.04 minutes SD=12.18 minutes), ($t(254)=$ 1.963, $p=0.05$) which prompted us to perform an ANCOVA to test the effect of condition on gain score, using time on task as a covariate to control for its possible effects. [Before performing the ANCOVA we verified that there was no interaction between condition and time on task. None was present; $F(1,252)=.001$, $p=.977$]. Controlling for time on task, we found a significant effect of condition on gains for all problems combined ($F(1,252)=4.478$, $p=.035$), but not for multiple-choice problems or open-response problems considered separately.

Table 3. Learning from interacting with the system

Problems considered	Condition	Pretest Mean SD (normalized Mean SD)	Posttest Mean SD (normalized Mean SD)	t (n)	p
All problems	All Students	M=5.04 SD=2.48 (M=0.36 SD=0.18)	M=5.87 SD=2.61 (M=0.42 SD=0.19)	$t(255)=7.55$	< 0.01
	Experimental	M=4.95 SD=2.55 (M=0.35 SD=0.18)	M=6.00 SD=2.65 (M=0.43 SD=0.19)	$t(124)= 6.92$	< 0.01
	Control	M=5.13 SD=2.42 (M=0.37 SD=0.17)	M=5.74 SD=2.57 (M=0.41 SD=0.18)	$t(130)= 3.92$	< 0.01
Multiple choice	All Students	M=3.53 SD=1.73 (M=0.44 SD=0.22)	M=4.19 SD=1.69 (M=0.52 SD=0.21)	$t(255)= 6.78$	< 0.01
	Experimental	M=3.52 SD=1.80 (M=0.44 SD=0.23)	M=4.33 SD=1.72 (M=0.54 SD=0.22)	$t(124)= 5.94$	< 0.01
	Control	M=3.55 SD=1.67 (M=0.44 SD=0.21)	M=4.05 SD=1.66 (M=0.51 SD=0.21)	$t(130)= 3.72$	< 0.01
Open response	All Students	M=1.51 SD=1.12 (M=0.25 SD=0.19)	M=1.68 SD=1.28 (M=0.28 SD=0.21)	$t(255)= 2.80$	0.01
	Experimental	M=1.43 SD=1.11 (M=0.24 SD=0.19)	M=1.68 SD=1.33 (M=0.28 SD=0.22)	$t(124)= 2.79$	0.01
	Control	M=1.58 SD=1.14 (M=0.26 SD=0.19)	M=1.68 SD=1.24 (M=0.28 SD=0.21)	$t(130)= 1.19$	0.24

The results of further between-group comparisons using t-tests are presented in Table 4. Gains were defined as (posttest – pretest) and their normalized versions as (posttest / #problems) – (pretest / #problems). Consistent with the ANCOVA results, when all problems were considered together, the mean gain of the experimental condition was significantly higher than the mean gain of the control condition. However, no significant difference between conditions was found when considering multiple-choice problems and open-response problems individually.

Overall, even though the practical difference between gain score was very modest—on average, about .5 items or about a 4% increase in correct number of problems solved—these findings suggest that the experimental version of the system has the potential to outperform its control counterpart.

Table 4. Comparing learning between conditions

Problems Considered	Condition	Gain = Posttest-Pretest (normalized Gain)	$t(n)$	p
All problems	Experimental	M=1.06 SD=1.71 (M=0.08 SD=0.12)	$t(254)=2.078$	0.04
	Control	M=0.60 SD=1.76 (M=0.04 SD=0.13)		
Multiple choice	Experimental	M=0.81 SD=1.53 (M=0.10 SD=0.19)	$t(254)=1.600$	0.11
	Control	M=0.50 SD=1.55 (M=0.06 SD=0.19)		
Open re-sponse	Experimental	M=0.24 SD=0.98 (M=0.04 SD=0.16)	$t(254)=1.173$	0.24
	Control	M=0.10 SD=0.97 (M=0.02 SD=0.16)		

Did the effect of condition on learning vary depending on student ability? In other words, was there an aptitude-treatment interaction (ATI)? Using course grade as a measure of aptitude, we found no significant interaction between condition and aptitude in their effect on overall gain ($F(1,251)=.586$, $p=.45$), multiple-choice gain ($F(1,251)=1.751$, $p=.19$), or open-response gain ($F(1,251)=.553$, $p=.46$) (the grade of one student was not reported by her teacher). Since grading can vary across schools and teachers, we also investigated ATI using pretest score (i.e., prior knowledge) as a measure of aptitude. Similarly, we did not find a significant interaction between condition and aptitude in their effect on overall gain score ($F(1,252)=.048$, $p=.83$), gains on multiple-choice problems ($F(1,252)=.096$, $p=.76$), or gains on open-response problems ($F(1,252)=1.002$, $p=.32$).

These results suggest that the effect of condition on learning does not vary depending on students' ability in physics. Correspondingly, given that students in the decision rule-based condition significantly outperformed students in the control condition, the ATI analyses indicate that students using the decision rule-guided dialogues learned more across ability levels.

Did the effectiveness of each version of the tutor depend on gender? To investigate possible gender differences, we first performed a t-test comparing gains of females with gains of males, for both conditions combined. We found no statistically significant differences between mean gains for all problems combined and for multiple-choice items. However, females' mean gains on open-response items (M=0.37, SD=0.91) were significantly higher than males' mean gains (M=0.001 SD=1.01), $t(252)=3.025$, $p<0.001$.

To investigate if this gender difference would apply to each version of the system considered separately, we performed a t-test comparing gains of females with gains of males by condition. In the experimental condition, we found no statistically significant gender differences for all problems combined or for multiple-choice problems. However, for open-response problems, females' mean gains (M=0.55 SD=0.90; normalized M=0.09 SD=0.15) were statistically significantly higher than males' mean gains (M=0.002 SD=0.99; normalized M=0.0003 SD=0.16), t(121)=3.190, p<0.01. In the control condition, we did not find a statistically significant difference between males' and females' gains when all problems were considered together or when multiple-choice and open-response items were considered separately. These findings indicate that the decision rule-based dialogues may have benefited more females than males, especially in their ability to express the physics reasoning invoked by open-response problems.

Given the possible effects that time on task and prior knowledge could have on learning gains, we investigated gender differences in time on task and pretest scores. We found no statistically significant gender differences for either factor for any grouping of problems, when we considered all students combined and students grouped according to condition. Additionally we tested for gender differences in PSAT reading scores to consider whether gender-based differences in ability to read through the dialogues might account for the observed gender differences in learning gains. (We only had PSAT scores from 196 students; 94 females, 101 males, out of 256 participants.) But no significant differences were found. This suggests that there is a true gender difference in the effectiveness of the system, particularly for solving open-response problems.

We then further examined gender differences in gain scores by considering each gender separately. For females, the mean gain in the experimental condition for all problems considered together (M=1.39 SD=1.71) was significantly higher than the mean gain in the control condition (M=0.65 SD=1.57), t(115)=2.410, p=0.02. Consistent with our prior findings, we found that females' mean gain on open-response items in the experimental condition (M=0.55 SD=0.90) was significantly higher than in the control condition (M=0.21 SD=0.89), t(115)=2.062, p=0.04, and we did not find this between-condition difference for females' gains on multiple-choice items (t(115)=1.337, p=0.39). In contrast, for males, we did not find any between-condition differences in gain scores—not when we considered all problems combined (t(135)=0.844, p=0.40), multiple-choice problems (t(135)=0.995, p=0.32), or open-response problems (t(135)=0.009, p=0.99).

These results provide additional evidence that the decision rule-based version of Rimac outperformed the control version in supporting learning, especially of the concepts and reasoning skills required to solve the open-response items, and that this effect was more pronounced for female students. These findings corroborate those of prior research indicating that younger female students performed best when using a tutor that delivered more interactive hints compared to a less interactive control [1].

4   Conclusions and Future Work

Our preliminary evaluation of Rimac revealed that students learned across conditions and suggested that a decision rule-guided version of the dialogues has the potential to outperform a control version developed according to standard DLR practices. Given the brevity of the intervention, this test of our hypothesis is inconclusive. To validate our findings, we plan to conduct future field trials in which students use the tutor for a longer period of time.

Our analyses also indicated that the experimental version of Rimac benefited female physics students more than male students, at least in acquiring the physics knowledge and reasoning skills needed to solve the open-response problems. If this finding is supported by future trials, it could have important implications for physics education—in particular, for improving female high school students' performance in physics courses and willingness to enroll in more advanced courses. Prior research indicates that poor retention of young women in physics after high school is indeed a problem and suggests possible causes. One contributing factor might be gender differences in how students study physics. As reported in [9], female high school physics students state that they tend to memorize facts rather than strive for understanding. Even though female high school students sometimes outperform their male peers in physics, their awareness of a shaky grasp of physics concepts might prevent them from enrolling in college-level physics courses. A high percentage of women who do take physics in college perform poorly, scoring in the lowest quartile on qualitative physics assessments [2]. This might be due, in part, to a fact-oriented approach to learning the material. Hence, it is possible that we observed higher learning gains for female students because they needed a tutoring system that emphasizes understanding more so than their male peers. If so, an expanded and enhanced version of Rimac might help to close the gender gap in physics enrollment in college and promote conceptual understanding—especially among women, who seem to need this most.

The experimental version of Rimac that we assessed in this study incorporated the full set of (11) decision rules that implement discourse relations whose frequency predicted learning in [11]. Although the rule-driven system as a whole seems promising, the current study cannot tell us which decision rules, in particular, promote learning. In our current work, we are assessing selected rules individually. We also plan to test the generalizability of these rules to another domain.

Acknowledgements. The authors thank the Rimac project team for their contributions: Stefani Allegretti, Michael Ford, Kevin Krost, Michael Lipschultz, Diane Litman, Scott Silliman, and Christine Wilson. This research was supported by the Institute of Education Sciences, U.S. Dept. of Education, through Grant R305A10063 to the University of Pittsburgh. The opinions expressed are those of the authors and do not necessarily represent the views of the Institute or the U.S. Dept. of Education.

References

1. Arroyo, I., Beck, J.E., Woolf, B.P., Beal, C.R., Schultz, K.: Macroadapting animalwatch to gender and cognitive differences with respect to hint interactivity and symbolism. In: Gauthier, G., VanLehn, K., Frasson, C. (eds.) ITS 2000. LNCS, vol. 1839, pp. 574–583. Springer, Heidelberg (2000)

2. Bates, S., Donnely, R., MacPhee, C., Sands, D., Birch, M., Walet, N.R.: Gender Differences in Conceptual Understanding of Newtonian Mechanics: a UK Cross-institution Comparison. European Journal of Physics **34**, 421–434 (2013)

3. Boyer, K.E., Phillips, R., Ingram, A., Ha, E.Y., Wallis, M., Vouk, M., Lester, J.: Characterizing the effectiveness of tutorial dialogue with hidden markov models. In: Aleven, V., Kay, J., Mostow, J. (eds.) ITS 2010, Part I. LNCS, vol. 6094, pp. 55–64. Springer, Heidelberg (2010)

4. Chi, M.T.H., Roy, M., Hausmann, R.G.: Observing Tutorial Dialogues Collaboratively: Insights About Human Tutoring Effectiveness From Vicarious Learning. Cognitive Science **32**(2), 301–341 (2008)

5. Chi, M.T.H., Siler, S., Jeong, H., Yamauchi, T., Hausmann, R.G.: Learning from Human Tutoring. Cognitive Science **25**, 471–533 (2001)

6. Chi, M., VanLehn, K., Litman, D., Jordan, P.: An Evaluation of Pedagogical Tutorial Tactics for a Natural Language Tutoring System: A Reinforcement Learning Approach. International Journal of Artificial Intelligence in Education **21**, 83–113 (2011)

7. Evens, M., Michaels, J.: One-on-one Tutoring by Humans and Computers. Lawrence Erlbaum Associates, New Jersey (2006)

8. Graesser, A.C., Person, N.K., Magliano, J.P.: Collaborative Dialogue Patterns in Naturalistic One-on-one Tutoring. Applied Cognitive Psychology **9**, 495–522 (1995)

9. Hazari, Z., Sadler, P.M., Tai, R.H.: Gender Differences in the High School and Affective Experiences of Introductory College Physics Students. The Physics Teacher **46**, 423 (2008)

10. Jordan, P., Hall, B., Ringenberg, M., Cui, Y., Rose, C.: Tools for authoring a dialogue agent that participates in learning studies. In: Proceedings of the 13th International Conference of AI in Education (2007)

11. Katz, S., Albacete, P.: A Tutoring System That Simulates the Highly Interactive Nature of Human Tutoring. Journal of Educational Psychology **105**(4), 1126–1141 (2013)

12. Litman, D., Forbes-Riley, K.: Correlations Between Dialogue Acts and Learning in Spoken Tutoring Dialogues. Natural Language Engineering **12**, 161–176 (2006)

13. Mann, W.C., Thompson, S.: Rhetorical Structure Theory: Toward a Functional Theory of Text Organization. Text **8**, 243–281 (1988)

14. Murray, R.C., VanLehn, K.: A comparison of decision-theoretic, fixed-policy and random tutorial action selection. In: Ikeda, M., Ashley, K.D., Chan, T.-W. (eds.) ITS 2006. LNCS, vol. 4053, pp. 114–123. Springer, Heidelberg (2006)

15. Ravenscroft, A., Pilkington, R.M.: Investigation by Design: Developing Models to Support Reasoning and Conceptual Change. International Journal of Artificial Intelligence in Education **11**, 273–298 (2000)

16. Van de Sande, C., Greeno, J.G.: A Framing of Instructional Explanations: Let's explain with you. In: Stein, M.K., Kucan, L. (eds.) Instructional Explanations in the Disciplines, pp. 69–82. Springer, New York (2010)

17. Ward, A., Litman, D.: Adding abstractive reflection to a tutorial dialogue system. In: Proceedings of the 24th International Florida Artificial Intelligence Research Society Conference FLAIRS (2011)

Educational Question Answering Motivated by Question-Specific Concept Maps

Thushari Atapattu$^{(\boxtimes)}$, Katrina Falkner, and Nickolas Falkner

School of Computer Science, University of Adelaide, Adelaide, Australia
{thushari.atapattu,katrina.falkner,
nickolas.falkner}@adelaide.edu.au

Abstract. Question answering (QA) is the automated process of answering general questions submitted by humans in natural language. QA has previously been explored within the educational context to facilitate learning, however the majority of works have focused on text-based answering. As an alternative, this paper proposes an approach to return answers as a concept map, which further encourages meaningful learning and knowledge organisation. Additionally, this paper investigates whether adapting the returned concept map to the specific question context provides further learning benefit. A randomised experiment was conducted with a sample of 59 Computer Science undergraduates, obtaining statistically significant results on learning gain when students are provided with the question-specific concept maps. Further, time spent on studying the concept maps were positively correlated with the learning gain.

Keywords: Concept mapping · Educational question answering · NLP

1 Introduction

Question answering (QA) is a modern application of information retrieval where exact answers are returned as a result of questions submitted by humans in natural language. This is in contrast to the more typical approach in information retrieval systems or search engines, in returning a ranked list of relevant documents. QA systems have been developed for a range of contexts, including open-domain to answer general questions [1], and closed-domains such as medicine, sports (e.g. BASEBALL) and geology (e.g. LUNAR).

QA systems are well suited to the educational context [2], providing assistance where learners struggle to find answers or in addressing common misconceptions. According to Novak and Canas [3], text-based short answers have been shown to support short-term learning. There are concerns as to the effectiveness of text answers in achieving long-term learning goals, including meaningful learning. Concepts included in both the question expressed by the learner, and the text answer are not explicitly related to other concepts within the domain, meaning that 'obtaining text answers' through typical QA systems do not support effective construction of knowledge structures [3]. Additionally, the majority of the QA systems are supportive only of 'factoid' question types (e.g. list, definition) [1, 4] which aid lower levels of educational objectives [5].

© Springer International Publishing Switzerland 2015
C. Conati et al. (Eds.): AIED 2015, LNAI 9112, pp. 13–22, 2015.
DOI: 10.1007/978-3-319-19773-9_2

As an alternative, this paper focuses on returning knowledge organisation techniques, particularly concept maps as answers. To achieve this, a framework capable of automatically extracting concept maps from lecture slides was developed using natural language processing (NLP) techniques, enabling the use of auto-generated concept maps as a positive alternative to expert concept maps [6, 7]. Concept maps are effective educational tools which consists of concepts, connected by directed edges to form relations, employing a hierarchical organisation scheme with the most general concept at the top, and more specific concepts arranged below. This aids meaningful learning, as relevant prior knowledge is able to be integrated with new information [3].

Additionally, this paper investigates whether adapting the returned concept map to the specific question context provides further learning benefits. This research develops a framework enabling the automated extraction of question-specific concept maps to answer learner questions using NLP and graph theory techniques. These concept maps assist the learner to understand the interrelationships between concepts for parallel processing in contrast to the sequential nature of text-based answers.

2   Related Works

Question answering systems can be classified based on several factors including *question types* (e.g. factoid, opinion, casual) [8], *input type* (e.g. natural language text, spoken natural language), *expected answer type* (short text answers, paragraphs, semantic graphs) and *supporting context* (open-domain or closed-domain) [9]. Among them, this work focuses on *question type* and *expected answer type*, which we consider to be most useful within educational question answering (EQA).

Within the educational context, 'question type' is the category of the question to measure various skills of the learner, defined by the question stem (e.g. *what, why*) [8, 9]. Questions are commonly constructed according to learning objectives defined by taxonomies like Bloom's taxonomy [5]. A computer model for question answering called *Quest* was proposed by Graesser et al. [8] which simulates psychological aspects of human question answering. The validation of model using convergence score (close to 0) suggested that very few nodes of conceptual graphs are good answers to the given question.

AnswerArt [4] is among the few systems, apart from ours, which utilises knowledge organisation techniques to formulate answers. This provides text answers along with the lists of facts associated with the answer, a summarised paragraph and visual representation of the *knowledge source* using semantic graphs [4]. AnswerArt is not restricted to a specific domain, however is limited to a number of question types with *pre-defined question templates* such as Yes/No, list, and reason (why). This restricts the flexibility of formulating questions, however, their system not possess restrictions on vocabulary. Although semantic networks are effective in knowledge organisation, their familiarity among learners is relatively low. Our own study found that 82% ($n=56$) of participants have heard, previously used or currently using knowledge organisation techniques, however, among them, only 1 student (out of 56) has experience in semantic networks, while 91% have experience in either concept maps or mind maps.

3 Question-Specific Concept Map Extraction

This section presents the framework for extracting question-specific concept maps (QSCMap). Figure 1 illustrates an example of the process.

Question: Compare and contrast <u>system testing</u> and <u>release testing</u>

Sample text answers:

1. Release testing is a form of system testing

2. System testing focuses on discovering bugs while release testing checks that the system meets its requirement

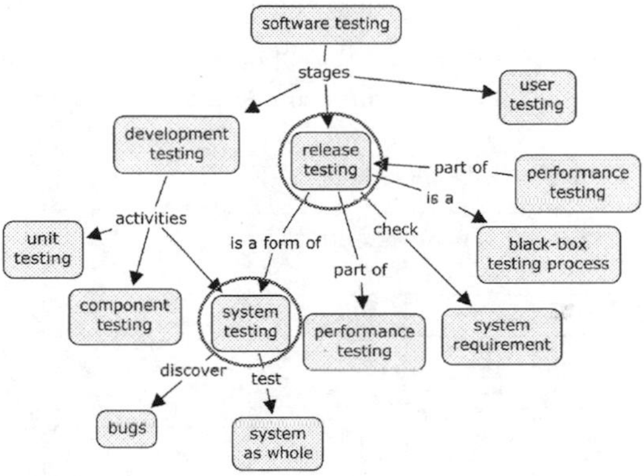

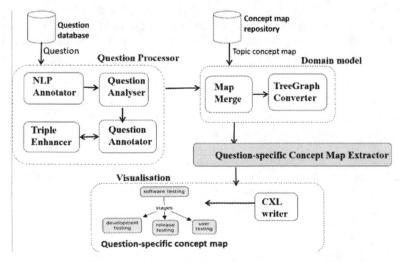

(a)   (b)

Fig. 1. Example question a) text-based answer b) question-specific concept map

QSCMap (Figure 1(b)) provides additional information for the learner to effectively comprehend the relations between the concepts under assessment, and further, illustrates how these concepts are connected to the topic and other concepts.

Figure 2 illustrates the architecture of the framework including four main components: question processor, domain model, QSCMap extractor and visualisation.

Fig. 2. Architecture of the question-specific concept map framework

Question Processor. identifies the 'question type' and converts the input question into 'triple' form. Within this work, we defined two question types: 'descriptive' and 'comparison', supported by a background study which analysed Software Engineering examination questions from year 2000 to 2012. The examinations consisted of 60 broad questions, the majority of which consisted of approximately 100 sub-questions. The study considered only the lecture material-based questions, with other types such as scenario-based eliminated.

NLP Annotator. parses the input question using Stanford NLP tools [10] and obtains part-of-speech tags, lemma annotations and parser tree (Table 1 and Figure 3).

Table 1. NLP annotations

Question	Part-of -speech	Lemma
What	WP	What
is	VBZ	be
the	DT	the
purpose	NN	purpose
of	IN	of
regrssion	NN	regression
testing	NN	testing

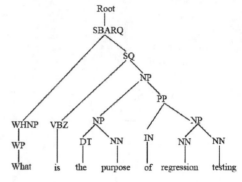

Fig. 3. Parser tree

Question Annotator. converts the question into 'triple' form (e.g. *what is white-box testing?* => (*white-box testing, is, ?*)) by considering the grammatical structure (Figure 3). This work reused some of the algorithms proposed to extract concept-relation-concept triples from English sentence in our own work [6] and other heuristics proposed by Dali et al. [4]. Unlike converting 'sentences' into triples which contains all the three elements (subject-verb-object), question triples can have one or more known elements, while other elements can be returned as the answer to the question.

Triple Enhancer. utilises the Synset library of WordNet [11] to find synonyms of non-terminological words (e.g. '*stage*' and '*phase*'). This arises when vocabulary used to write the questions is different from the terminology used in knowledge source of domain model (e.g. lecture slides).

Domain Model. consists of a repository of concept maps extracted from lecture slides [6, 7]. **Map merge** component automatically combines concept maps of related topics to create a richer domain model by reading the CXL (Concept Map Extensible Language) files [12] of each concept maps.

Due to the hierarchical nature of concept maps (i.e. taxonomic relations) and the inclusion of directed labelled edges between arbitrary pair of nodes (i.e. non-taxonomic relations and cross-links), a suitable data structure to store concept maps is a graph with a tree skeleton. **TreeGraph converter** reuses and customises the 'Tree-

Graph' data structure implemented by Stanford NLP group to store grammar trees [10].

Question-Specific Concept Map Extractor. is the core of the framework which extracts concept maps correspond to the input question. The process of QSCMap extraction is identified as a problem of 'sub graph matching' [13];

A data graph $G = (V, E)$, composed of a set of vertices V and a set of edges E. Each e ϵ E is a pair (v_i, v_j) where $v_i, v_j \epsilon$ V.

A pattern ('question triple') $P = (Vp, Ep)$, which specifies the structural and semantic requirements that a sub graph of G must satisfy in order to match the pattern P.

The task is to find the set M of sub graphs of G that 'match' the pattern P. A graph G' $= (V', E')$ is a sub graph of G if and only if $V' \subseteq V$ and $E' \subseteq E$.

This work utilises the 'similarity-based exact sub graph' matching technique. This process is supported through a lemmatisation technique [10] where labels of concepts and relations in both question triple and domain model are mapped to their base form. Additionally, synonyms of the labels of relations are utilised [11]. This process maintains a threshold of 15 concepts based on the suggestions by Novak and Canas [3] and the feedback received from domain experts.

When determining the boundary of a sub graph, our algorithm considered the features listed in Table 2.

Table 2. Features for question-specific concept map extraction

Feature	Description
Question type	'Descriptive' or 'comparison'
In-degree and out-degree	Number of incoming and outgoing links of each node. This determines the importance of each node
Root	Most general node of the map
Leaf nodes	Nodes without children, generally these are the most specific nodes of the map
Number of over-lapping nodes	This determines the boundary of the sub graph; Overlapping nodes should always be greater than 0. If this number is greater than 1, the boundary of the sub graph needs to accommodate all the overlapping nodes and its common parents, children and siblings
Number of over-lapping relations	If relations in the question triple are not overlapping with the relations in the TreeGraph, synonyms are considered. The overlapping of relations are not mandatory, particularly in 'comparison' type questions
Distance between overlapping nodes	This considers the distance in every path including cross-links

The extracted sub graphs are converted to CXL format for **visualisation** using IHMC CMap Tools (see Figure 1 (b)) [12].

The benefits for learners who utilise this framework include the support for both interrogative (i.e. starts with *wh*-clause) and imperative (i.e. starts with words like *identify*) questions without restrictions in the grammatical structure. Additionally, this work derived two question types (descriptive and comparison) correspond to three objective levels of Bloom's taxonomy (i.e. knowledge, comprehension and analysis) [5].

Concept Map Mining Framework
Our system models the domain using concept maps generated from lecture slides (known as topic concept maps – TCMap) using the *concept map mining framework (CMMF)* [6, 7]. CMMF includes automated noise elimination (e.g. *course announcements, references*), resolution of syntactically and semantically missing and ambiguous sentences (e.g. pronouns, incomplete sentence fragments), useful knowledge acquisition in the form of concept-relation-concept triples using NLP-based algorithms, arrangement of extracted knowledge in a hierarchy, and ranking of concepts using structural and graph-based features (e.g. *term frequency, degree centrality, proximity*). The design and validation of CMMF is described further in [6, 7].

4   Evaluation

4.1   Method

A study was conducted with a sample of 59 second year Undergraduates in the University of Adelaide, who had enrolled in the Software Engineering (SE) course in Semester 1, 2014. A randomised experimental design was used with three treatment groups and a control group based on the *answer type* received by the participants. The Control group (LS) received text-based answers through a selected lecture slide segments. Treatment group 1 (TCMap) received a customised version of topic concept map with those concepts necessary for question answering, in addition to other related concepts. Treatment group 2 (HLCMap) received the same concept maps as group 1; however, in their maps, the context to answer the question is emphasised (manually using CMap tools [12]). Treatment group 3 (QSCMap) received the question-specific maps extracted from the proposed framework. The extracted QSCmaps were reviewed by two domain experts. Their feedback included manually removing some of the concepts from QSCmaps which did not illustrate a 'relation label'. This was an issue reported in CMMF, which occurred due to the point-based nature of lecture slides [7].

Ten multiple-choice questions (MCQs) were constructed by the researchers with the use of previous examinations and a text book of SE. These questions were provided to the participants in order to reduce the issues arise from forming questions by learners including incorrect terminology and grammatical issues. These questions covered 68% of the important concepts included in the 'software testing' topic.

A web-based prototype was developed for the experiments. Participants attempted each MCQ once before getting the answers through the QA system. This score was recorded as students' prior knowledge on the subject matter (pre-test). If the answers to the first attempt is incorrect, participants are expected to learn the required knowledge through the resources allocated for them and re-attempt any number of times within the allocated time for the study. Their scores, time spent on each resources (i.e. time spent between '*getting help*' and '*go back to question*') and attempts were collected for a quantitative data analysis.

After two week gap, a post-test was conducted to measure the learning outcome. Post-test was paper-based, consisting 10 questions with a combination of MCQs, fill-in-the-blanks and open-ended questions in order to minimise the memorisation of answers from previous study. These questions were constructed from similar topic, covering similar concepts; however, with a different presentation. Among the 59 participants of the main study, only 30 students were able to participate to the post-tests.

After the experiments, participants were requested to complete a questionnaire consisted of open-ended and close-ended questions.

4.2   Quantitative Analysis

The results of Table 3 illustrates that the QSCMap group has the numerically highest mean for *learning gain* ($M = 5.0$, $SD = 1.5$, $n = 9$) while the control group (LS) has the smallest mean ($M = 2.5$, $SD = 2.0$, $n = 7$)

Table 3. Descriptive statistics of pre-test and learning gain

Group	Pre-test M (SD)	Learning gain M (SD)	n
LS	2.9 (1.9)	2.5 (2.0)	7
TCMap	1.8 (1.5)	3.2 (1.4)	7
HLCMap	2.6 (1.5)	3.6 (2.0)	7
QSCMap	2.5 (1.5)	5.0 (1.5)	9
Total	2.4 (1.6)	4.0 (1.9)	30

Analysis of Variance (one-way ANOVA) was conducted to compare means of learning gain. Prior to that three assumptions of ANOVA were evaluated. The homogeneity of variances, $F (3,26) = .698$, $p = .562 (>.05)$ was not violated. Shapiro-Wilk test indicated that the dependent variable was normally distributed around means. Due to the randomised assign of participants into groups, there was no influence of the performance of an individual in one group to the others in the same group. Results of the one-way ANOVA (Table 4) indicated that the means between groups were significant; $F(3,26) = 3.103$, $p = .044 (< .05)$, $\eta^2 = .263$.

Table 4. Summary results of one-way ANOVA

	Sum of Squares	df	Mean square	F	Sig.
Between Groups	28.292	3	9.431	3.103	.044
Within Groups	79.008	26	3.039		
Total	107.300	29			

Table 5. Summary of Tukey HSD post-hoc test

(I) Group	(J) Group	Mean Difference (I-J)	Std. error	Sig.	95% Confidence Interval	
					Lower Bound	Upper Bound
LS	TCMap	-.71429	.93178	.450	-2.6296	1.2020
	HLCMap	-1.14286	.93178	.231	-3.0582	.7724
	QSCMap	-2.55556*	.87849	.007	-4.3613	-.7498
TCMap	HLCMap	-.42857	.93178	.649	-2.3439	1.4867
	QSCMap	-1.84127*	.87849	.046	-3.6470	-.0355
HLCMap	QSCMap	-1.41270	.87849	.120	-3.2185	.3931

*. The mean difference is significant at the 0.05 level

Tukey HSD post-hoc test was conducted to compare the mean differences (Table 5). According to the results, means between QSCMap and LS groups are statistically significant; $p = .007$ ($< .05$). This suggests that the use of question-specific concept map-based answers is beneficial for learners in contrast to text-based answers. However, due to the smaller sample size in each group ($n = 9$ in QSCMap and $n = 7$ in LS), these findings cannot be generalised to a wider population [14]. Even though the effect of QSCMap has not been studied previously within EQA, utilising knowledge organisation techniques such as concept maps or knowledge maps over text-representations proved to be beneficial in many studies [15].

The means between QSCMap and TCMap groups are also statistically significant; $p = .046$ ($< .05$). This suggests that the use of *question-specific concept map*-based answers have higher learning gain than the topic concept map-based answers. The primary reason for this could be the amount of information included in each answers and their relevancy to the context. According to Novak & Canas [3], concept maps constructed to answer a question is more effective than a concept map which represent a domain/topic. The former involves more dynamic thinking and a deeper understanding.

However, the means between QSCMap and HLCMap are not statistically significant. This could be due to the fact that students in the HLCMap group might only have looked at the highlighted area of the map without being overloaded by the number of concepts and relations provided in the *topic concept map*. The idea of highlighting the relevant context is further supported in the feedback of students.

Pearson correlation analysis was conducted to measure the correlation between the time spent on each form of resource and the learning gain. There was a positive correlation between time spent on concept maps and learning gain; QSCMap ($\gamma = .801, p < .05$) and TCMap ($\gamma = .594, p < .05$). However, control group had a negative correlation. This could have occurred if the students in the control group spent more time scrolling the lecture slides to formulate an answer when the relevant information is scattered throughout the slides.

4.3   Qualitative Analysis

Participants were questioned about the issues and suggestions about the system. Students in the TCMap group mentioned that *"too much of information in concept maps"*, *"they were kind of bland, it is difficult to navigate when more and more information added to the map"*. Similarly, they suggested *"use colors to help identifying important sections"*, *"improve appearance by providing partial concept maps that applies to the topic"*, *"need colors and switches"*, *"less concepts"*, *"a way to toggle between maps of higher and lower densities of information"*, *"color codes or smaller maps"*. Since the participants of this group had no idea about maps in HLCMap or QSCMap groups, they repeatedly mentioned the requirement of colors to differentiate information or smaller maps to focus more relevant information.

The participants in the HLCMap group had minor issues or suggestions such as *"concept maps were useful for hints"*, *"useful if ability to search within the map"*, *"a feature in which you can click on a concept to retrieve more information"*, *"more details in relation labels"*.

Some students in the QSCMap group reported that *"not enough information provided in the concept map"*, *"it was quite good"*. However, similar to HLCMap group, they suggested to have more explanations in the concept map by allowing them to click the concepts to retrieve further information.

5   Conclusion

The use of question answering systems to automatically answer questions is a widespread area of research in NLP and information retrieval. The adoption of the QA to facilitate learning requires wide focus in the AIED research. This paper presented an approach to utilise concept maps in contrast to text-based answers for the questions presented to EQA. Additionally, this paper investigated whether adapting the returned concept map to the specific question context provides further learning benefit. We have obtained significant results on learning gain when presenting question-specific concept maps in contrast to lecture slides or topic concept maps. Further, time spent on concept maps were positively correlated with the learning gain.

The future works include expanding the system to support more question types with higher-level of learning objectives [5, 8]. In addition, questions and their corresponding QSCmaps generated from our framework are expected to evaluate using different dimensions (e.g. *coverage, correctness, pedagogy*) in multiple CS subjects with the use of two to three domain experts in order to calculate *inter-rater reliability*. More sophisticated natural language understanding techniques are required to accept questions from learners or integration of question generation is necessary in contrast to expert-constructed questions utilised in the study. Based on the results and the feedback obtained from the students, it is uncertain whether the students' preferred type of concept maps are QSCMaps or HLCMaps. Therefore, the current study can be expanded using a larger student cohort to find the answer to this.

Although the research discussed here does not support adaptive question answering through student modeling, the concept maps adapted to the context of questions improved the learning experience. Therefore, future research within the AIED community can be focused on adaptive question answering with the use of suitable form of concept maps.

References

1. Katz, B. Annotating the world wide web using natural language. In: Fifth RIAO Conference on Computer Assisted Information Searching on the Internet (1997)
2. Gurevych, I., et al., Educational question answering based on social media content. In: Proceedings of the 2009 conference on Artificial Intelligence in Education, p. 133-140 (2009)
3. Novak, J.D., Canas, A.J.: The Theory underlying Concept maps and How to construct and use them. Florida Institute for Human and Machine Cognition (2006)
4. Dali, L., et al.: Question answering based on semantic graphs. In: Language and Technology Conference, Poznan (2009)
5. Bloom, B., et al., Taxonomy of educational objectives: the classification of educational goals. In: Handbook I: Cognitive Domain, New York, Toronto (1956)
6. Atapattu, T., Falkner, K. Falkner, N.: Acquistion of triples of knowledge from lecture notes: a natural langauge processing approach. In: 7th International Conference on Educational Data Mining, London (2014)
7. Atapattu, T., Falkner, K., Falkner, N.: Evaluation of Concept Importance in Concept Maps Mined from Lecture Notes: Computer vs Human. In 6th International Conference on Computer Supported Education, Barcelona (2014)
8. Graesser, A., Gordon, S., Brainerd, L.: QUEST: A model of question answering. Computers & Mathematics with Applications **23**(6–9), 733–745 (1992)
9. Kolomiyets, O., Moens, M.: A survey on question answering technology from an information retrieval perspective. Information Sciences **181**(24) (2011)
10. Manning, C., et al.: The stanford CoreNLP natural language processing toolkit. In: 52nd Annual Meeting of the Association for Computational Linguistics: System Demonstrations, Baltimore (2014)
11. Miller, G.A., et al.: Introduction to WordNet: An On-line Lexical Database. International Journal of Lexicography **3**(4), 235–244 (1990)
12. Canas, A.J., et al.: CmapTools: a knowledge modeling and sharing environment. In: First International Conference on Concept Mapping, Pamplona (2004)
13. Gallagher, B.: Matching structure and semantics: A survey on graph-based pattern matching. AAAI FS **6**, 45–53 (2006)
14. Kenny, D.A.: Statistics for the Social and Behavioural Sciences (1987)
15. O'Donnell, A.M., et al.: Knowledge Maps as Scaffolds for Cognitive Processing. Educational Psychology Review **14**(1), 71–86 (2002)

A Study of Automatic Speech Recognition in Noisy Classroom Environments for Automated Dialog Analysis

Nathaniel Blanchard[1(✉)], Michael Brady[1], Andrew M. Olney[2], Marci Glaus[3], Xiaoyi Sun[3], Martin Nystrand[3], Borhan Samei[2], Sean Kelly[4], and Sidney D'Mello[1]

[1] University of Notre Dame, Notre Dame, USA
nblancha@nd.edu
[2] University of Memphis, Memphis, USA
[3] University of Wisconsin-Madison, Madison, USA
[4] University of Pittsburgh, Pittsburgh, USA

Abstract. The development of large-scale automatic classroom dialog analysis systems requires accurate speech-to-text translation. A variety of automatic speech recognition (ASR) engines were evaluated for this purpose. Recordings of teachers in noisy classrooms were used for testing. In comparing ASR results, Google Speech and Bing Speech were more accurate with word accuracy scores of 0.56 for Google and 0.52 for Bing compared to 0.41 for AT&T Watson, 0.08 for Microsoft, 0.14 for Sphinx with the HUB4 model, and 0.00 for Sphinx with the WSJ model. Further analysis revealed both Google and Bing engines were largely unaffected by speakers, speech class sessions, and speech characteristics. Bing results were validated across speakers in a laboratory study, and a method of improving Bing results is presented. Results provide a useful understanding of the capabilities of contemporary ASR engines in noisy classroom environments. Results also highlight a list of issues to be aware of when selecting an ASR engine for difficult speech recognition tasks.

Keywords: Google speech · Bing speech · Sphinx 4 · Microsoft speech · ASR engine evaluation

1   Introduction

Dialogic instruction, a form of classroom discourse focusing on the free exchange of ideas and open-ended discussion between teachers and students, has been linked to key constructs of learning such as student engagement [1] and deep comprehension [2]. Although classroom discussion is generally considered beneficial, actual use of appropriate dialogic instructional strategies in classrooms varies widely. Recent research in teacher education has demonstrated the importance of careful measurement and assessment of dialogic practices in promoting changes in teacher practice [3]. A long-term goal of the present research is to facilitate fast and efficient assessment of classroom discourse processes and outcomes for use in teacher professional development.

© Springer International Publishing Switzerland 2015
C. Conati et al. (Eds.): AIED 2015, LNAI 9112, pp. 23–33, 2015.
DOI: 10.1007/978-3-319-19773-9_3

Motivation. Previously, large-scale efforts to improve classroom discourse have been conducted using complex, labor-intensive, and expensive excursions into classrooms. Nystrand and Gamoran [4, 5] studied thousands of students across hundreds of classroom observations of middle and high school English Language Arts classes. They found positive effects on student learning from the overall dialogic quality of discourse. However, the sheer number of human coders required makes such studies cost prohibitive. The feasibility of such large-scale deployment has been stretched to its limits. With modern technology, a new approach consisting of the transcription of recorded in-class audio through automatic speech recognition (ASR), in combination with data mining and natural language understanding to automate the coding of classroom discourse, might finally be feasible.

We are addressing automated classroom dialogic analysis with CLASS 5. CLASS 5 is intended to automate dialogic instructional feedback through a large-scale implementation of Nystrand's coding scheme [4, 5], which focuses on the nature of questions involved in classroom discussion. Specifically, five properties of question events are coded: authenticity, uptake, level of evaluation, cognitive level, and question source. Nystrand et al. reported that among these variables, authenticity and uptake are the most important properties affecting student achievement [5, 6]. Previously, coders would begin by sitting in classrooms and recording when and what types of questions were asked followed by revision in the lab. CLASS 5 is intended to automate this task with an emphasis on recognizing different question events.

ASR is an important first step in recognizing question events from classroom audio because it enables the application of text-based machine learning techniques. However, speech recognition in noisy environments remains a challenging research problem, and most available ASR technologies are designed for desktop dictation in a quiet office environment. To determine the suitability of existing ASR technologies for CLASS 5, we analyze several out-of-the-box ASR solutions that do not require training on speakers and do not require any domain-specific knowledge. We focus on dialogic questions asked by teachers because they are highly correlated with student achievement [4]. This paper looks to identify which ASR systems are best suited for large-scale implementation of audio transcription in classrooms.

Related Work. Wang et. al. [7] experimented with real classroom audio in a way that could be adapted to provide feedback for teachers. They built classifiers to identify if 30-second segments of audio corresponded to discussion, lecture, or group work. Audio data was collected using LENA [8], which was adapted to report when either teachers are speaking, students are speaking, speech is overlapping, or there is silence; there was no attempt at ASR. Although Wang et. al. [7] reported success classifying classroom discourse at course-grained levels, their audio solution only provided information on *who was speaking*, while coding of question events requires knowing *what was said*.

Within the AIED community, much of the work on spoken-language technologies has focused on one-on-one interactions in intelligent tutoring systems (ITSs). For example, Litman and Silliman [9] developed ITSPOKE, a physics tutor that engages students in spoken discussion to correct errors and prompt student self-explanation.

Mostow and Aist [10] built a reading tutor called Project LISTEN to improve oral reading and comprehension. Schultz et. al. [11] created a spoken conversational tutor architecture called SCoT. Ward et. al. [12] has developed a conversational ITS called My Science Tutor (MyST) for 3rd, 4th, and 5th grade students. Finally, Johnson and Valente [13] created a spoken dialog tutor to teach language and cultural skills. Despite impressive advances in conversational tutoring, the focus of these systems has been one-on-one human-computer interactions with customized domain-specific desktop oriented ASR approaches. The question of whether these ASR solutions generalize in noisy classroom environments remains unanswered.

There have been some efforts to quantify contemporary ASR systems, albeit outside of classroom contexts. Morbini et al. [14] recently reviewed some of today's freely available ASR engines. They tested five ASR engines including Google Speech, Pocketsphinx, Apple, AT&T Watson, and Otosense-Kaldi. Tests were based on recordings obtained from six different spoken dialog systems, or systems where computers converse with humans in a variety of settings. These settings range from casual museum visitors speaking into a mounted directional microphone to trained demonstrators speaking into headset microphones. Their analyses focused on the strengths and weaknesses of the ASR engine's performance across different dialog systems. While their results provided a useful table of features associated with each engine, the authors concluded there was no single best ASR engine for all dialog systems. Their results did not address variable conditions that are often out of the developer's control, such as vocabulary domain. Furthermore, although the methods used to record audio were documented the quality and clarity of this audio were unreported. Thus, no inference can be drawn about which ASR engine would perform best for untested applications, such as transcribing naturalistic classroom discourse, thereby motivating the present study.

Contribution and Novelty. The present study provides, for the first time, a comparative evaluation and analysis of contemporary ASR engines for audio recordings from noisy classroom environments. The emphasis is on studying the accuracy of ASR engines on recordings of mic'ed teacher audio as they go about their normal classroom routines. We focus on teacher audio because dialogic instruction can be automatically coded using only teacher questions [15]. In addition to comparing transcription accuracy of five ASR systems, detailed analyses are performed on the two best-performing systems. The most effective ASR engine from the classroom study is validated in a follow-up laboratory study with more speaker variability. Although this work is done within the context of a specific research project (the development of CLASS 5), accurate ASR is important for many tasks. Taking a foundational look at what is possible for today's ASR systems in noisy classroom environments has implications for AIED researchers interested in developing other classroom-based spoken-language technologies or scaling up existing projects.

2   Classroom Recording Study

2.1   Method

Data Collection. Audio recordings were collected at a rural Wisconsin middle school during literature, language arts, and civics classes. The recordings were of three different teachers: two males – Speaker 1 and Speaker 2 – and one female – Speaker 3. The recordings span classes of about 45 minutes each on 9 separate days over a period of 3-4 months. Due to the occasional missed session, classroom change, or technical problem, a total of 21 of these classroom recordings were available for analysis here. During each class session, teachers wore a Samson AirLine 77 'True Diversity' UHF wireless headset unidirectional microphone that recorded their speech, with the headset hardware gain adjusted to maximum. Audio files were saved in 16 kHz, 16-bit mono .wav format. Teachers were recorded naturalistically as they taught their class as usual.

Two observers trained in Nystrand et. al.'s dialogic coding technique for audio annotation and classification [4, 16] were present in the classroom during recording. Observers marked teacher's dialogic questions with start and stop times as the class progressed, and later reviewed the questions for accuracy. Audio of teacher questions was then extracted from the recordings and saved as individual .wav files by sectioning the audio using the observers' labeled start and stop times. In total, there were 530 questions obtained from teacher speech. Table 1 presents information about the amount of time teachers spent asking questions (in seconds), mean verbosity (number of words in a question), mean duration (number of seconds taken to ask a question), mean speech rate (number of words per second), and maximum silence (longest pause in the middle of the speech). In general, Speaker 1 and Speaker 2 asked more questions than Speaker 3 and were more verbose. Speaker 3 had the slowest speech rate, while Speaker 2 tended to pause for the shortest amount of time when speaking.

Table 1. Means of question characteristics (standard deviations in parentheses)

Speaker	N	Verbosity (words)	Question Duration (secs)	Speech Rate(words/sec)	Maximum Silence (secs)
1	189	8.82 (6.06)	4.29 (2.29)	2.05 (0.79)	1.12 (0.52)
2	250	10.93 (6.82)	4.10 (2.30)	2.88 (1.25)	0.86 (0.60)
3	91	3.07 (2.48)	3.62 (1.60)	1.11 (0.89)	1.20 (0.64)

ASR Engines. We evaluated five ASR engines: Google Speech [17], Bing Speech [18], AT&T Watson [19], Microsoft Speech SDK 5.1, and two variants of Sphinx 4 [20]. Google Speech, Bing Speech, and AT&T Watson are query-oriented, cloud-based recognition systems primarily intended for web-queries on mobile devices (typically noisy conditions). Google Speech includes twenty-seven languages and dialects, Bing Speech includes seven languages, and AT&T Watson includes nineteen languages and has recognition contexts. Sphinx 4 is a flexible ASR that allows developers to incorporate their own custom models; however, we limited our analysis to prebuilt acoustic models derived from the Wall Street Journal (Sphinx-WSJ), trained on people reading the WSJ, and the English Broadcast News Speech (Sphinx-HUB4), trained on speech from real broadcast news. Microsoft Speech, integrated with Windows since Vista, associates a speech profile with a user and adapts to that user's speaking style and audio environment. We eliminated this adaptive bias by creating a new untrained speech profile for each recording date. We focus our efforts on these systems because they are freely available, except for Microsoft Speech (which requires a copy of Windows).

Evaluation Procedure. We processed all recorded questions through the ASR engines. We then compared the transcriptions that were output by the engines with observer-generated transcriptions. Performance metrics were word accuracy (WAcc) and simple word overlap (SWO). WAcc is the complement of the standard ASR metric of word error rate (WER). (WAcc = 1 − WER). WER is calculated by dynamically aligning the ASR engine's hypothesized transcript with the coder's transcript and dividing the number of substitutions, insertions, and deletions required to transform the transcript into the hypothesis divided by the number of words in the transcript. SWO is the number of words that appear in both the computer-recognized speech and the human-recognized speech divided by the total number of words in the human-recognized speech. WAcc preserves word order while SWO ignores it. WAcc is bounded on (-∞, 1] while SWO is bounded on [0, 1]. For both metrics higher numbers indicate better performance.

2.2 Results

Overall ASR Accuracy Rates. Table 2 presents the mean WAcc and SWO by ASR. Here, the cloud-based ASR engines Google Speech and Bing Speech clearly outperformed the other engines. Google Speech performed 7.69% better than Bing Speech when word order was considered (WAcc metric), but Bing performed 3.33% better than Google when word order was ignored (SWO metric). Bing and Google WAcc was, respectively, 26.8% and 36.6%, higher than AT&T Watson. The Sphinx HUB4 model did show improvements over the WSJ model, but overall HUB4 accuracy was lower than Bing and Google, with a performance similar to Microsoft.

Given their superior performance on the two key metrics, we focus subsequent analyses on Google and Bing. Because WAcc was strongly correlated with SWO for both Bing (Pearson's r = 0.792) and Google (r = 0.908), we focus on WAcc.

Table 2. Mean accuracy by ASR (standard deviations in parentheses)

ASR	WAcc	SWO
Google Speech	0.56 (0.35)	0.60 (0.31)
Bing Speech	0.52 (0.41)	0.62 (0.31)
AT&T Watson	0.41 (0.48)	0.53 (0.31)
Sphinx (HUB4)	0.14 (0.61)	0.32 (0.30)
Microsoft	0.08 (0.70)	0.33 (0.31)
Sphinx (WSJ)	0.00 (0.67)	0.27 (0.27)

Error Types. On average, for Bing, 40% (SD = 36%) of the errors were substitutions (ASR substituted one word for another), 30% (SD = 36%) were deletions (ASR missed words), and 15% (SD = 26%) were insertions (ASR inserted words). For Google, 44% (SD = 36%) of errors were substitutions, 35% (SD = 36%) were deletions, and 8% (SD = 20%) were insertions. Thus, there were modest differences across ASR engines for substitution and deletion errors, and larger differences for insertion errors.

WAcc by Individual Speaker. Small differences were found between speakers. The mean difference in average WAcc across pairs of speakers (i.e., average of Speaker 1 vs. Speaker 2, Speaker 1 vs. Speaker 3, and Speaker 2 vs. Speaker 3) were quite small – 0.12 for Bing and 0.06 for Google. This suggests that these ASRs were mostly unaffected by speaker variability, at least with respect to the teachers in our sample.

WAcc by Class Session. To quantify the consistency of the ASRs across class sessions, we conducted a decomposition of variance in error rates within and between class observations [21]. For Bing, 3.8% of the variance in error rates lies between class sessions; the vast majority of the variance in error rates was within-observations, across utterances. For Google, a similarly small percentage of variance lies between observations, only about 3.3% in these data. Thus, automatic speech recognition is largely invariant to the differences in instructional topic, etc. occurring in these data.

WAcc by Speech Characteristics. We investigated the relationship between WAcc and the four speech characteristics listed in Table 1. Models that regressed WAcc on these four speech characteristics (using a stepwise feature selection method) explained 2.6% of the variance for Google and 4.2% of the variance for Bing. The negligible variance explained in these models indicates Google and Bing were mostly immune to variation in speech characteristics.

Confidence of ASR Hypotheses. Bing provides confidence estimates with its output, thereby affording an additional analysis of Bing. We note mean WAcc scores of 0.00, 0.35, 0.48, 0.65 for confidence levels of: rejected ($N = 4$), low ($N = 59$), medium ($N = 284$), and high ($N = 183$), respectively. Removing the rejections and the low confidence questions resulted in a mean WAcc of 0.55 for the remaining 467 utterances, which reflects a small improvement over the overall WAcc of 0.52 reported in Table 1. The results were not more notable because confidence estimation itself was imperfect.

Comparing Google and Bing. Table 3 provides a cross tabulation for questions recognized perfectly (WAcc = 1), completely incorrectly (WAcc <= 0), and in between (0 < WAcc < 1) across both ASRs. Bing and Google completely failed and succeeded for the same 28 and 30 questions, respectively. Interestingly, Google perfectly transcribed 10 of the 78 questions that Bing completely failed to recognize, while Bing perfectly transcribed 16 of the 73 questions that Google completely failed to recognize. In general, Bing and Google's WAcc scores were only modestly correlated (Pearson's r = 0.306), which suggests that there may be advantages to combining them.

Table 3. Cross tabulation of Bing and Google WAcc

		Google		
		WAcc <= 0	0 < WAcc < 1	WAcc = 1
Bing	WAcc <= 0	28	40	10
	0 < WAcc <1	29	325	29
	WAcc = 1	16	23	30

Qualitative Analysis of Complete Failures. We performed a qualitative analysis on the questions for which both ASRs completely failed (WAcc <= 0) by listening to each audio file and noting potential causes of errors (See Table 4). The most common failure involved the teacher questioning a student by calling his or her name (e.g., "Marty?") – both ASRs were equally susceptible to this issue. Another common failure, more so for Google than for Bing, occurred when the teacher was quizzing a student on specific vocabulary words that were either not in the ASR dictionaries or were rare enough to be unrecognizable without context (e.g., cacophony, despot). Bing often failed when audio was not perfectly segmented (e.g. the segmented audio file began in the middle of loud student speech), an inevitable byproduct of collecting audio in a noisy environment. Both ASRs experienced failure when questions were only one word, which typically occurred when students were quizzed on vocabulary. Google faltered when teachers rushed through questions. Bing experienced 19 complete failures when the teacher began a question but paused for a long interval before continuing with the question. Both recognizers failed when teachers asked implicit questions, such as where the teacher began a statement and paused for the student to complete the utterance ("speaker one is…"). The recognizers struggled when teachers over-enunciated syllables, which occurred when presenting unfamiliar vocabulary to students.

Table 4. Failure Analysis (Number of errors by category and ASR)

Error	Bing	Google	Error	Bing	Google
Student name	26	25	Rushed	5	18
Vocabulary	11	21	Long Pause	19	0
Imperfect Segmentation	23	12	Implicit question	4	6
One word	12	13	Over enunciate	6	3

WAcc Improvements by Eliminating Pauses for Bing. We identified 113 instances with imperfect WAcc likely attributed to a long teacher pause, which negatively affected Bing but not Google, as indicated by the analysis of complete failures (see Table 4). To mitigate these failures, pauses were automatically identified and removed, and the resulting modified audio was rerun through Bing. Eliminating the silences raised mean WAcc from 0.30 (SD = 0.41) to 0.34 (SD = 0.58), eliminated all rejections, and raised the overall WAcc for Bing from 0.52 (SD = 40.1) to 0.53 (0.46) and SWO from 0.62 (SD = 0.31) to 0.65 (SD = 0.30). Removing the remaining low confidence instances increased Bing's WAcc to 0.58 (SD = 0.43) and Bing's SWO increased to 0.71 (SD = 0.25). Thus, Bing's WAcc was higher than Google's overall WAcc.

3   Laboratory Study on Reliability Across Speakers Using Bing

Due to the logistics of data collection, the original classroom study only involved 3 speakers. We therefore conducted a laboratory study with 28 speakers to test the reliability of Bing across a larger number of speakers. We focused on Bing instead of Google because it has an easier to use application programming interface (API – details of which are not discussed here), it provides confidence scores, it resulted in WAcc performance equal to Google (after eliminating pauses and low confidence scores), and exhibits a SWO well above Google.

Method. 13 male and 15 female for a total of 28 English-speaking undergraduate students were recruited. These participants were instructed to play the part of a teacher leading a discussion in a classroom. Participants read the teacher's lines from transcripts of classroom speech displayed on a computer screen. The students' portions of the scripts were pre-recorded by an actor and automatically played in response to the participant's speech. Participants proceeded through three scripts constructed from transcripts of three separate teachers. Script order was balanced across participants with a Latin Square. Participant speech was recorded using the same headset microphone as was used to record teachers in classrooms.

Results. In total, 3057 recordings of dialog turns were obtained and submitted to Bing for recognition. Utterance-level mean WAcc was 0.60 (SD = 0.32), considerably higher than the previously reported Bing WAcc of 0.52 (SD 0.41), presumably because of the controlled laboratory environment. We performed a decomposition of variance analysis to quantify the variation in word error rates for Bing across participants. We found a small but non-trivial proportion of variance at the speaker level (ICC=.096). The standard deviation of the word error rates across speakers was 0.10 (about the grand mean of 0.61). The estimated confidence interval for the ICC suggests that as much as 15% of the variance in word error rates is a function of speaker-level speech attributes.

4   Discussion

We tested five implementations of ASR engines on 530 spontaneous spoken dialogic questions from 3 different teachers recorded with a headset microphone in noisy classrooms, and conducted a follow-up laboratory study. Google Speech and Bing Speech largely outperformed AT&T Watson, Microsoft Speech, and two implementations of Sphinx. A summary of results yields seven key insights:

1. Google ASR performed slightly better than Bing when word order was considered, but Bing performed slightly better than Google when word order was disregarded. The WAcc of Google and Bing was only moderately correlated, indicating different strengths and weaknesses, thereby raising the possibility of combining the two.
2. The majority of Bing and Google errors were substitution errors. Furthermore, deletion errors were more frequent than insertion errors.
3. Differences in speakers and sessions had little impact on WAcc. This conclusion was further validated for Bing using 28 English speakers in a laboratory study.
4. Bing was susceptible to failure when speech had long pauses. We corrected this by removing long pauses. Doing so, along with removing low confidence results, resulted in Bing having a higher WAcc than Google.
5. Speech characteristics (i.e. speech duration, speech verbosity, speech length, and maximum silence) were found to have very small effects on ASR accuracy. This indicates Google Speech and Bing Speech were largely unaffected by these factors.
6. Bing provides useful confidence scores that are relatively representative of the accuracy of the hypothesis, along with multiple alternative hypotheses about what was spoken. This is a major advantage of using Bing over Google.
7. Both Bing and Google completely failed or perfectly succeeded for a roughly 14% of utterances, and these instances of complete failure and success did not always overlap. Combining these two recognizers to avoid these failures may be strategic.

Limitations. Our results suggest that Bing and Google were the best out-of-the-box ASR engines for automatically transcribing teacher speech in noisy classrooms with a specific emphasis on questions. However, other applications may have different ASR needs. The engines we selected for evaluation were limited to free engines requiring no training or optimizing in any way. Furthermore, our study focused only on dialogic questions. We note the possibility that the strict use of questions in our study may somehow have influenced our results (though we have no reason to believe this is the case). Since we were able to collect recordings from only three teachers from one school, there is a chance that our results will not be corroborated across regions or speakers. However, considering the versatility of the ASRs thus far, a significant change in our results in response to a larger data set is not anticipated, but this awaits empirical verification. Finally, we did not test all possible ASR engines and we acknowledge that some ASR engines could perform better than the engines we tested.

Concluding Remarks. Our results give us some confidence that ASR technologies have matured to the point that they can be useful for the automatic transcriptions of speech from classrooms and other noisy environments. To be clear, these technologies are still fopar from perfect. However, the goal is not to obtain perfect transcription of speech, but to obtain a reasonable representation of spoken dialog to serve as input to language processing techniques that should be uninfluenced by ambiguities in speech recognition (see [22] for further discussion). Furthermore, our analysis of where these systems succeed and fail on recordings from the classroom environments should benefit researchers who have been working with educational dialog in on-one-one settings, but who are interested in testing spoken-language technologies in the classroom.

Acknowledgements. This research was supported by the Institute of Education Sciences (IES) (R305A130030). Any opinions, findings and conclusions, or recommendations expressed in this paper are those of the author and do not represent the views of the IES.

References

1. Kelly, S.: Classroom discourse and the distribution of student engagement. Soc. Psychol. Educ. **10**, 331–352 (2007)
2. Sweigart, W.: Classroom Talk, Knowledge Development, and Writing. Res. Teach. Engl. **25**, 469–496 (1991)
3. Juzwik, M.M., Borsheim-Black, C., Caughlan, S., Heintz, A.: Inspiring Dialogue: Talking to Learn in the English Classroom. Teachers College Press (2013)
4. Nystrand, M., Gamoran, A., Kachur, R., Prendergast, C.: Opening dialogue. Teachers College, Columbia University, New York (1997)
5. Gamoran, A., Kelly, S.: Tracking, instruction, and unequal literacy in secondary school English. In: Stab. Change Am. Educ. Struct. Process Outcomes, pp. 109–126 (2003)
6. Nystrand, M., Gamoran, A.: The big picture: Language and learning in hundreds of English lessons. In: Open. Dialogue., pp. 30–74 (1997)
7. Wang, Z., Pan, X., Miller, K.F., Cortina, K.S.: Automatic classification of activities in classroom discourse. Comput. Educ. **78**, 115–123 (2014)
8. Ford, M., Baer, C.T., Xu, D., Yapanel, U., Gray, S.: The LENA Language Environment Analysis System. Technical Report LTR-03-2. Boulder, CO: LENA Foundation (2008)
9. Litman, D.J., Silliman, S.: ITSPOKE: An intelligent tutoring spoken dialogue system. In: Demonstration Papers at HLT-NAACL 2004, Association for Computational Linguistics, pp. 5–8 (2004)
10. Mostow, J., Aist, G.: Evaluating tutors that listen: An overview of Project LISTEN (2001)
11. Schultz, K., Bratt, E.O., Clark, B., Peters, S., Pon-Barry, H., Treeratpituk, P.: A scalable, reusable spoken conversational tutor: Scot. In: Proceedings of the AIED 2003 Workshop on Tutorial Dialogue Systems: With a View toward the Classroom, pp. 367–377 (2003)
12. Ward, W., Cole, R., Bolaños, D., Buchenroth-Martin, C., Svirsky, E., Vuuren, S.V., Weston, T., Zheng, J., Becker, L.: My science tutor: A conversational multimedia virtual tutor for elementary school science. ACM Trans. Speech Lang. Process. TSLP. **7**, 18 (2011)
13. Johnson, W.L., Valente, A.: Tactical Language and Culture Training Systems: using AI to teach foreign languages and cultures. AI Mag. **30**, 72 (2009)
14. Morbini, F., Audhkhasi, K., Sagae, K., Artstein, R., Can, D., Georgiou, P., Narayanan, S., Leuski, A., Traum, D.: Which ASR should I choose for my dialogue system? In: Proceedings of the SIGDIAL 2013 Conference, Metz, pp. 394–403 (2013)
15. Samei, B., Olney, A., Kelly, S., Nystrand, M., D'Mello, S., Blanchard, N., Sun, X., Glaus, M., Graesser, A.: Domain independent assessment of dialogic properties of classroom discourse. In: Stamper, J., Pardos, Z., Mavrikis, M., McLaren, B.M., (Eds.) Proceedings of the 7th International Conference on Educational Data Mining, London, pp. 233–236 (2014)
16. Nystrand, M., Wu, L.L., Gamoran, A., Zeiser, S., Long, D.A.: Questions in time: Investigating the structure and dynamics of unfolding classroom discourse. Discourse Process. **35**, 135–198 (2003)
17. Schalkwyk, J., Beeferman, D., Beaufays, F., Byrne, B., Chelba, C., Cohen, M., Kamvar, M., Strope, B.: Your word is my command: google search by voice: a case study. In: Advances in Speech Recognition, pp. 61–90. Springer (2010)

18. Microsoft: The Bing Speech Recognition Control (2014). http://www.bing.com/dev/en-us/speech. (accessed January 14, 2015)
19. Goffin, V., Allauzen, C., Bocchieri, E., Hakkani-Tür, D., Ljolje, A., Parthasarathy, S., Rahim, M.G., Riccardi, G., Saraclar, M.: The AT&T WATSON speech recognizer. In: ICASSP (1), pp. 1033–1036 (2005)
20. Walker, W., Lamere, P., Kwok, P., Raj, B., Singh, R., Gouvea, E., Wolf, P., Woelfel, J.: Sphinx-4: A flexible open source framework for speech recognition (2004)
21. Kelly, S., Majerus, R.: School-to-school variation in disciplined inquiry. Urban Educ. 0042085911413151 (2011)
22. D'Mello, S.K., Graesser, A., King, B.: Toward Spoken Human-Computer Tutorial Dialogues. Human-Computer Interact. **25**, 289–323 (2010)

Teachable Agents with Intrinsic Motivation

Ailiya Borjigin[✉], Chunyan Miao, Su Fang Lim, Siyao Li[✉], and Zhiqi Shen

Nanyang Technological University, Singapore, Singapore
{ailiya,ascymiao,sflim2,lisi0010,zqshen}@ntu.edu.sg

Abstract. Dynamic communication between Teachable Agents (TA) and students is crucial for educational effectiveness of the TA, as dynamic interaction is the vital part throughout the teaching and learning processes. Existing TA design mainly focuses on the functions and features to ensure the TA to be taught by students rather than bi-directional interaction. However, according to reciprocity theory in social psychology, if the TA can offer friendly actions, students in response will be much more cooperative and motivated. In order to improve quality of communication and seize the interest of students, we propose a need modeling approach to enable TAs to have "intrinsic motivations". In this way, the TA can proactively carry out dynamic communication with students so that the TA can adapt to students' changing behaviors and sustain a good human-agent relationship. Our field study showed that students were highly attracted by the TA with dynamic needs. They statistically completed more tasks. Also, better results were obtained on students' learning efficiency and attitude towards TA's informational usefulness and affective interactions.

Keywords: Teachable Agent · Intrinsic motivation · Dynamic communication

1 Introduction

Teachable Agent (TA) is a type of computer agent which is designed to be taught by students. According to Learning-by-Teaching Theory, the bi-directional interaction between TA and students can induce students to take the learning responsibility and achieve better learning outcomes [1]. The communication quality of TAs influences the educational value of the entire learning system [2], since students need to be convinced that their teaching is important and valuable for the "naïve" TA. Without effective interactions, a TA cannot persuade students to teach it even if the TA has the best student model and teaching knowledge. Moreover, according to reciprocity theory in social psychology, if the TA can offer friendly actions, students in response will be much more cooperative and motivated. Therefore, TA should spontaneously take actions and proactively interact with students to enlighten students' deep learning through teaching the TA.

To pursue agent's proactivity, we look into the field of Intrinsically Motivated Agent (IMA). IMA are based on the concept of "intrinsic motivation" from psychology. An agent is considered as intrinsically motivated when its behavior is "for its own sake", other than driven by an external stimulus [3]. If a TA could have intrinsic motivation, it

© Springer International Publishing Switzerland 2015
C. Conati et al. (Eds.): AIED 2015, LNAI 9112, pp. 34–43, 2015.
DOI: 10.1007/978-3-319-19773-9_4

can be designed to proactively interact with students by means such as asking questions related to students prior problems, asking for further explanation, looking into something new, etc. In light of this idea, our group has proposed the Intrinsically Motivated Teachable Agent (IMTA) in [4], which is motivated by psychological needs defined in Self-Determination Theory (SDT) [5]. SDT stated that three psychological needs elicit intrinsically motivated behaviors, namely Competence, Relatedness, and Autonomy. Actions are generated in order to avoid any dissatisfaction of these three innate needs. IMTA is designed to associate the innate needs with TA's educational requirements to facilitate students' learning experience.

Despite the proactive interaction and more interesting learning scenario provided by IMTA, the system design lacks a crucial part, the dynamic matching between IMTA's needs and motivated behaviors. As a result, the IMTA lacks of dynamic changes and generates monotonic reactions. In order to solve this problem and improve the quality of communication between IMTA and students, we aim to propose a new approach to model TA's psychological needs, and integrate the proposed need model into a real IMTA system. With the new model, the TA in our system can generate dynamic interactions with students and seize their attention throughout the learning process. To sum up, the objectives of this paper include: 1) model IMTA's needs and integrating into a TA-enhanced virtual learning environment; 2) evaluate students' interest in learning, learning efficiency, and attitude towards the refined IMTA.

In the following section, we will introduce the educational project where IMTA is embedded in, and discuss why a psychological need model is important. We propose the need model in Section 3, and report the field study results in Section 4. After the discussion on the experiment results, we end the paper in Section 5 with conclusions and future work.

2   Virtual Singapura Project and Related Work

An E-learning project, Virtual Singapura (VS), is applied to demonstrate the use of improved IMTA in practice. The VS platform is a 3D virtual learning environment, which allows secondary school students in Singapore to learn science lessons (especially the knowledge about the transport in living things). Two types of teachable agents "Little Water Molecules" and "Little Mineral Salt Molecules" were developed in the project, as in Fig.1a. VS project brings students to a journey together with water molecules to explore the inside of a running down banana tree (Fig. 1b), and to find out the problems. Students can teach the TAs through Concept Map panel (Fig. 1c) and experiment panels (Fig. 1d).

To improve the learning experience of students, TAs should adapt to students' dynamic behaviors and establish human-like interactions. Some researchers have worked in this area. For instance, Matsuda et al. [6] studied how to implement adaptive help of TA to facilitate student's learning. Biswas et al. [7] discussed the interactive action patterns with agent responses. Roger et al. [8] studied how to design dynamic prompting and feedback to improve students' learning efficiency. James et al. [9] investigated the relationship between dialogue responsiveness and learning with TA. These studies focus on how to appropriately design TA's responses to student, but they did not highlight the importance of TA's proactiveness. In this paper, the proposed IMTA are expected to spontaneously take actions and proactively interact with students, driven by its intrinsic motivation.

Fig. 1. (a) Water and menarial salt molecules in underground. (b) 3D example demostration of sick banana tree. (c) Draw concept map in teaching panel by drag and drop. (d) teaching panel 2 expriments.

How to bring agents with intrinsic motivation? Several researchers from computer agents discussed their opinions: (1) Singh, from an evolutionary perspective, considered "reproductive success" as the drive for agents to behave proactively [10]; (2) Baranès & Oudeyer designed robots to pursue activities for which "learning progress is maximal" [11]; (3) Merrick considered agent's self-motivated exploration as seeking for "novelty, interest, and competence" [12]. Although the focus of exploration and learning new knowledge are paramount to motivated agents, they did not discuss how to design the intrinsic motivation for educational agents to improve students' learning. Thus, the proposed IMTA focuses on combining the motivation design with the pedagogical requirements and synthesizes the various behaviors into a unified sense of "self-willing", which may improve TA's dynamic interaction with students and enhance the believability.

3   Need Modelling in IMTA

This section discusses an improved system design incorporating a model of psychological needs and details of the model used in IMTA. To incorporate the educational requirements into TA's intrinsic motivation, we have designed three types of need of the proposed IMTA. The *Need of Novelty* let TA learn new knowledge from students, which provide opportunity for students to reflect on their knowledge; the *Need of Performance* let TA practice the learnt knowledge in learning environment, which help students to examine their teaching effect by observing TA's behaviors; the *Need of Relatedness* let TA keep tight relationship with students and more effectively attract students to perform as a good teacher. In our previous research, we have developed the mapping among ability of TA, needs of TA, and motivation of TA based on SDT. The mapping is given in Table 1 below, and this mapping continues to hold in this paper.

Table 1. Mapping among Ability, Needs, and Motivation of IMTA [2]

Ability	Need	Motivation
Teachability	Need of novelty	Pursuit of new knowledge
Practicability	Need of performance	Pursuit of performance
Affectivability	Need of relatedness	Pursuit of relatedness

In order to incorporate a model of psychological need and reflect the relationship between psychological needs and motivation, the architecture of IMTA is given in Figure 1 below.

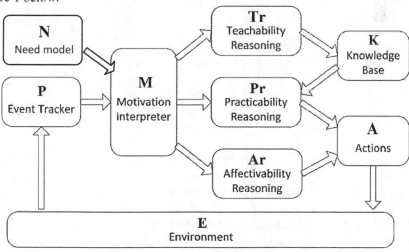

Fig. 2. IMTA's Architecture

In this architecture, Tr, Pr, Ar are the three reasoning entity that achieves teachability, practicability, and affectivability. M, Motivation Interpreter, provides motivation so that agent knows which goal to pursue. The most significant improvement is the introduction of N, need model, as another input to motivation interpreter in additional to event tracker. It simulates the real-life scenario where individual's motivation is affected not only by external stimuli in environment, but also by internal psychological needs. By linking output of need model to motivation interpreter, this architecture of IMTA resembles more closely to real-life learning behaviors.

In discussion below, the need model will be firstly introduced, followed by the model interpretation which uses need model as input to select motivation. Finally, a way to model the effect of past events on current need is discussed.

3.1   Intrinsic Need Functions

IMTA's different needs are modelled as different innate functions. Different needs have different relationships between need strength and time. At any given time, an IMTA may be challenged by the combination of different needs with different levels of activation.

An impulse signaling is used for generating peeks of needs across times. The impulse represents the internal tendency towards the pursuit of a need. Three impulse frequencies, $freq_{lo}$, $freq_{me}$, $freq_{hi}$, are used. In this paper, pursuit of performance is assigned with the highest frequency to stimulate the process adopted by the IMTA to reinforce concepts with students; pursuit of relatedness is with lowest to reduce nonnecessary communication cost. Other agent designers can assign frequencies differently to reflect their own use case.

However, needs vary across time more closely to waves rather than impulses. Therefore, a set of smooth functions is further proposed to simulate need changes over time. The set of soft-windowing functions is defined as Equation (1) below.

$$
\begin{aligned}
\text{Duration}_i &= {}^{1}\!/_{freq_i} \\
\text{Win}_i &= (t, t + \text{Duration}_i) \\
\mu_i &= {}^{1}\!/_{2} \, \text{Duration}_i \\
\sigma_i &= \frac{1}{factor_i} \text{Duration}_i \\
\text{WinFun}_i(t) &= \exp\left(-\frac{(t - \mu_i)^2}{2\sigma_i}\right).
\end{aligned}
\tag{1}
$$

where t is the current time; $i \in \{$"low", "mediate", "high"$\}$ denotes each of the three different need frequencies; Win_i refers to window i spanning from t (impulse firing time) to $t + \text{Duration}_i$; Duration_i is the time span of window i; μ_i and σ_i are the center and spread of the ith windowing function respectively; $factor_i$ is a predefined constant; and WinFun_i is the Gaussian membership function defining the ith window.

Equation (1) above is used in functions that describe need of novelty and need of performance. Need of relatedness does not fit Equation (1) because relatedness is less frequently needed, but once it emerges, the need function should excite itself immediately. This does not correspond to the smooth tails on both sides of Equation (1). To model the rapid emergence of need of relatedness, a Rayleigh distribution is used as below in Equation (2).

$$\text{WinFun}_i(t, \varsigma) = \frac{t}{\varsigma^2} e^{-t^2/2\varsigma^2} . \tag{2}$$

From definition of Rayleigh distribution,

$$\mu_i = \varsigma\sqrt{\frac{\pi}{2}} \approx 1.253\varsigma$$

$$\sigma = \frac{4 - \pi}{2}\varsigma^2 \approx 0.429\varsigma^2 \tag{3}$$

An illustration of need functions is shown in Fig 3. The horizontal axis is time, and the vertical axis is need level. Three need functions are represented in Figure 2. Curve A represents need modelled by Rayleigh distribution; curve B and curve C represent needs modelled by Gaussian distribution.

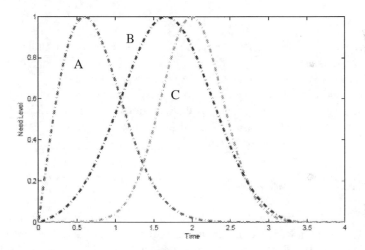

Fig. 3. Representation of Need Functions in Equation (1) and (2)

3.2   Motivation Interpretation

Based on SDT and our model, motivation arises because of intrinsic needs and external stimuli from environment. Motivation Interpreter is the entity that synthesizes information from external environment and intrinsic need to dynamically determine IMTA's current motivation. It takes values of intrinsic need functions discussed above to calculate motivation intensities. Intensity of motivation represents IMTA's eagerness to pursue that motivation. Different weights are also assigned to intrinsic need functions to represent the relationship between needs and motivations. In our model, IMTA's motivation intensity is calculated as follows:

$$V^{M_i} = w_i \times V^{N_i}, \forall i . \tag{4}$$

Where w_i denotes the need weight of need N_i, and V denotes the intensity of motivation and level of need.

IMTA will then proactively select motivation with highest intensity and tries to accomplish it by triggering one of the reasoning entities, Tr, Ar, or Pr. Each of the entities will have a set of well-defined goals. Once the goal can be achieved by IMTA given the stimuli from external environment, the motivation will be accomplished. The selection of current motivation resembles trade-offs in real life.

3.3   Weight Adjustment in Motivation Interpretation

In real-life learning, current learning need and target are also affected by what happened in the past. For example, if need of performance is not satisfied previously, the eagerness to satisfy this need will increase. IMTA's behavior should also be affected by outcome of past event. In this paper, the effect of past events on IMTA's needs is modelled by a simple weight adjustment in Equation (5) below,

$$w_i = w_i + \beta^n - \beta^p \tag{5}$$

where w_i denotes the need weight of need N_i, β denotes an updating rate in range (0, 1], and n or p denotes the number of times that the need is satisfied negatively or positively. Weights are always normalized to be bound within range [0, 1].

Using Equation (5), needs that are not previously satisfied will have higher weight in subsequent valuation, and motivations that can satisfy this need will be more likely to be selected. The needs that are satisfied previously will be less prominent in the next round of motivation interpretation.

4   Field Study and Results

The study was conducted in Xinmin Secondary School, Singapore. It aimed to examine if TAs with and without dynamic needs pursue may have different impact on students' learning. It was designed as "intervention versus ablated intervention" [2].

Students are randomly selected from the same grade. All students had not been taught about the subject and therefore deemed to have the same level of knowledge on the subject. They were divided into two groups; the treatment group consisting of 14 students used IMTA with intrinsic need model, while the control group consisting of 11 students used IMTA without intrinsic need model. The tests were deployed during student's Co-curricular Activities. Students were required to teach the IMTA in VS virtual environment on how water molecules and mineral molecules are transported from the root to the leaves, and among parts of the plant. There were 5 teaching tasks in 5 game scenes within the 3D sick banana tree, which are 1) Root, 2) Stem, 3) Xylem, 4) Leaf, and 5) Phloem. VS system automatically collected the number of tasks completed by each student and the time student spent in each scene. At the end of the study, the communication effectiveness of IMTA was measured by a questionnaire derived from the Agent Persona Instrument (API). It provides a holistic approach that takes into account different perspectives such as look and behavior, as well as computer-based aspects of the agent [13]. API includes 4 sub-measures – 1) facilitating learning, 2) credible, 3) human-like, and 4) engaging. The questionnaires were in 5-point scale, from 1 (strongly disagree) to 5 (strongly agree).

To sum up, we compare the treatment group and control group through:

(i)   The number of teaching tasks students completed: to depict students' willingness to interact with TA. In our experiment, it was not compulsory for students to complete all tasks. Students could stop whenever they felt bored.

(ii)   The average time spent of students in each teaching task: to indicate the learning efficiency of students

(iii)   The questionnaire scores on students' judgments about the communication effectiveness of TAs

4.1   Number of Tasks Completion

Through analyzing students' data collected by TA system, we found that students in treatment group completed 3.57 tasks on average, and students in control group completed 2.58 tasks on average. We did a t-test and there was a significant difference of the tasks completed by two groups of students (p = 0.02). In order to find the cause of the difference, we did short interviews among the two groups of students. We found that students felt fun when TA's behaviors are less predictable. This made students in treatment group continue playing with the TA and see what the TA will perform next. We can conclude that students were motivated by IMTA with dynamic behaviors. They are interested in IMTA, and would like to teach IMTA more topics.

4.2   Average Time Spent on Each Task

There is also a significant difference (p = 0.06) in average time spent by student in each task. In treatment group, each student spent 346 seconds in one scene on average, while students in control group spent 624 seconds in one scene on average. This means IMTA with intrinsic need can increase learning efficiency. The improvement may derive from two perspectives. First, the generation of TA's needs, especially the need of novelty may easily cover all the knowledge points and quickly find students' problems. This can increase the learning speed of students. Second, according to students' feedback through the interview, they "want to teach more" so that they "planed the time to finish all the tasks" in their Co-Curricular Activities lessons.

4.3   Students' Attitude Towards IMTA

Students' attitudes towards the communication effectiveness of TAs further confirmed our analysis above. The IMTA with need model were better received by students. The differences in the self-report questionnaire results between two groups are summarized in table below. Each value pair follows Mean/Variance format.

Students in treatment group reported significantly better results in all of the four areas related to informational usefulness and emotive interaction. We can also find that the scores of Credible, Human-like, and Engaging in control group are much lower than the scores in treatment group. This may because that the dynamic need changes affect much more on TA's "personality" related factors, which make it more believable and interesting. Thus, the latter three factors improved much more on the

IMTA with need model. On the other side, the factor Facilitate Learning of IMTA without need model reached 3.15, which has the smallest differences from the IMTA with need model. This may be indicated that students still think the IMTA without need model is useful although it is not very interesting. Therefore, based on our study, IMTA with intrinsic needs model did interact with students more effectively, and stimulate student's learning interests.

Table 2. Comparison of Student's Attitude towards IMTA

Perspective	Factors	IMTA with Need Model	IMTA without Need Model	$P_{one-tail}$
Informational	Facilitate Learning	3.66/0.244	3.15/0.191	0.006
Usefulness	Credible	3.63/0.308	2.33/0.739	6.22E-5
Affective	Human-like	3.84/0.275	2.74/0.506	6.39E-5
Interaction	Engaging	3.43/0.371	2.82/0.160	0.004

There is also a quite interesting phenomenon that, for the IMTA without need model, we received lower scores from the self-reported questionnaires from secondary school students comparing with the results we collected in primary school grade four [2]. Though the survey questions are not exactly the same, there are still several similar questions in common. In our opinions, this may be because the students in secondary school are teenagers who are more critical. Their standards of a good educational game become higher than the younger ones. Therefore, our suggestion on this situation is that we can use 7 or 9 point scales rather than 5 point scales to collect more precise results from secondary students. Nevertheless, we will not compare the students from different age range.

5   Conclusion and Future Work

In this paper, we proposed a psychological need modeling approach to enhance the dynamic interactions of TAs with intrinsic motivations. The model has been used in VS, a 3D virtual learning environment. The TA in VS can proactively carry out dynamic communication with students so that it may adapt to students' changing behaviors. Positive results have been collected from the field study in secondary school. First, students in treatment group statistically completed more tasks than control group. Second, better results were obtained on students' learning efficiency in treatment group. Third, students reported higher scores towards TA's informational usefulness and affective interactions. Therefore, we conclude that the proposed model has been better received in communication with students and also enhanced students' learning experience.

There are also limitations of this study. First, the student sample size is limited. In the future we will conduct studies with larger data size so the statistical results will be more significant. Second, we have collected some but not rich enough behavioral data of students in the 3D learning environment. Those students' behavioral data may reveal much more first-hand student information and improve the analysis towards students' experience and preferences. Therefore, we plan to incorporate new functions into the existing system to record all types of user behavior data in the virtual learning environment. The data will then be analyzed to assess students' learning competencies, such as self-regulation, learning motivation, reflective thinking skills, etc.

Acknowledgement. This research is supported in part by Interactive and Digital Media Programme Office (IDMPO), National Research Foundation (NRF). We also thank Dr. Zhao Guopeng as this work is partially extended based on his Ph.D.thesis.

References

1. Biswas, G., Leelawong, K., Schwartz, D., Vye, N., Vanderbilt, T.: Learning by teaching: A new agent paradigm for educational software. Applied Artificial Intelligence **19**, 363–392 (2005)
2. Woolf, B.P.: Building intelligent interactive tutors: Student-centered strategies for revolutionizing e-learning. Morgan Kaufmann (2010)
3. Singh, S., Barto, A.G., Chentanez, N.: Intrinsically motivated reinforcement learning. Paper presented at the In: Proc. of the 18th Annual Conf. on Neural Information Processing Systems (NIPS 2004) (2005)
4. Zhao, G., Borjigin, A., Shen, Z.: Learning-by-Teaching: Designing Teachable Agents with Intrinsic Motivation. Educational Technology & Society **15**, 62–74 (2010)
5. Singh, S., Lewis, R.L., Barto, A.G., Sorg, J.: Intrinsically motivated reinforcement learning: An evolutionary perspective. IEEE Transactions on Autonomous Mental Development **2**(2), 70–82 (2010)
6. Matsuda, N., Yarzebinski, E., Keiser, V., Raizada, R., Cohen, W.W., Stylianides, G.J., Koedinger, K.R.: Cognitive anatomy of tutor learning: Lessons learned with SimStudent. Journal of Educational Psychology **105**(4) (2013)
7. Biswas, G., et al.: Measuring Self-Regulated Learning Skills through Social Interactions in a teachable Agent Environment. Research and Practice in Technology Enhanced Learning **5**(2), 123–152 (2010)
8. Azevedo, R., et al.: The Effectiveness of Pedagogical Agents' Prompting and Feedback in Facilitating Co-adapted Learning with MetaTutor. In: Cerri, S.A., Clancey, W.J., Papadourakis, G., Panourgia, K. (eds.) ITS 2012. LNCS, vol. 7315, pp. 212–221. Springer, Heidelberg (2012)
9. Segedy, J.R., Kinnebrew, J.S., Biswas, G.: Investigating the relationship between dialogue responsiveness and learning in a teachable agent environment. In: Biswas, G., Bull, S., Kay, J., Mitrovic, A. (eds.) AIED 2011. LNCS, vol. 6738, pp. 547–549. Springer, Heidelberg (2011)
10. Baranès, A., Oudeyer, P.Y.: R-IAC: Robust intrinsically motivated exploration and active learning. IEEE Transactions on Autonomous Mental Development **1**(3), 155–169 (2009)
11. Merrick, K.E.: A comparative study of value systems for self-motivated exploration and learning by robots. IEEE Transactions on Autonomous Mental Development **2**(2), 119–131 (2010)
12. Baylor, A., Ryu, J.: The API (Agent Persona Instrument) for assessing pedagogical agent persona In: World Conference on Educational Multimedia, Hypermedia and Telecommunications, pp. 448–451 (2003)

Temporal Generalizability of Face-Based Affect Detection in Noisy Classroom Environments

Nigel Bosch[1(✉)], Sidney D'Mello[1,2], Ryan Baker[3], Jaclyn Ocumpaugh[3], and Valerie Shute[4]

[1] Departments of Computer Science, University of Notre Dame, Notre Dame, IN 46556, USA
{pbosch1,sdmello}@nd.edu
[2] Psychology, University of Notre Dame, Notre Dame, IN 46556, USA
sdmello@nd.edu
[3] Department of Human Development, Teachers College, Columbia University,
New York, NY 10027, USA
baker2@exchange.tc.columbia.edu, jocumpaugh@wpi.edu
[4] Department of Educational Psychology and Learning Systems,
Florida State University, Tallahassee, FL 32306-4453, USA
vshute@fsu.edu

Abstract. The goal of this paper was to explore the possibility of generalizing face-based affect detectors across multiple days, a problem which plagues physiological-based affect detection. Videos of students playing an educational physics game were collected in a noisy computer-enabled classroom environment where students conversed with each other, moved around, and gestured. Trained observers provided real-time annotations of learning-centered affective states (e.g., boredom, confusion) as well as off-task behavior. Detectors were trained using data from one day and tested on data from different students on another day. These cross-day detectors demonstrated above chance classification accuracy with average Area Under the ROC Curve (AUC, .500 is chance level) of .658, which was similar to within-day (training and testing on data collected on the same day) AUC of .667. This work demonstrates the feasibility of generalizing face-based affect detectors across time in an ecologically valid computer-enabled classroom environment.

1 Introduction

Students experience various affective states that influence learning in striking ways [1, 2]. For example, boredom has been shown to be negatively related to learning in multiple computerized learning environments [3, 4], while engagement has been shown to be positively associated with learning [4]. Affect has also been shown to influence learning by modulating cognitive and motivational processes in striking ways (see [5] for a review). Given the importance of affect to learning, researchers have been creating computerized learning environments that automatically detect and respond to students' affective states [6]. For example, one experiment comparing an affect-sensitive intelligent tutoring system (ITS) to the same ITS without affect sensitivity found that learners with low prior knowledge learned significantly more ($d = .713$) from the affect-sensitive version compared to the plain version of the ITS

© Springer International Publishing Switzerland 2015
C. Conati et al. (Eds.): AIED 2015, LNAI 9112, pp. 44–53, 2015.
DOI: 10.1007/978-3-319-19773-9_5

[7]. Despite the success of such affect-sensitive learning environments, work remains to be done to enable affect-sensitivity to function in contexts outside of a laboratory study, such as a noisy classroom. One key challenge involves the development of accurate affect detectors that can function in computer-enabled classrooms. Some work is being done in this area ([4, 8]).

Another important issue is temporal generalizability (generalization over time), which seeks to ascertain whether a detector trained on data from one day will still work well when classifying data from a different day. Such a detector might not work well because the features it uses may be influenced by factors specific to a day. Physiology-based sensors have been shown to suffer from such differences [9]. For example, a student's average skin conductance (a physiological feature) may change from one day to the next. Thus, detectors created using skin conductance data from one day may not work well on a different day unless specific measures are taken to compensate for the day-to-day differences.

In this paper we focus on face-based affect detection. Potential causes of day differences in face-based affect detection include lighting in the classroom (which can change how well computer vision algorithms detect facial features), students' mood (which might alter their affect and facial expressions), number of students (which might influence how distracted students are by their friends and how much they converse with each other), and perhaps other factors. However, whether day-to-day differences impact face-based affect detection accuracy (as they do physiology-based detectors) is currently unknown, and is the central focus the current paper.

Related Work. Many different modalities (e.g., facial features, physiology, audio) have been proposed and evaluated for affect detection [10]. To keep the scope manageable, we focus on affect detection efforts in educational contexts and those testing differences across days.

Interaction data from log-files has shown promise for building affect detectors that generalize across time. Pardos et al. [4] used interaction data collected over the span of a few days in 2010 to build affect detectors. These detectors were then applied to a separate, previously collected dataset from two school years (Fall 2004-Spring 2006). The detectors' predictions were correlated with students' scores on a standardized test. Several of these correlations demonstrated the consistency of detectors across two school years. Predicted boredom ($r = -.119$ for year 1, $r = -.280$ for year 2), confusion ($r = -.165$, $r = -.089$), and gaming the system ($r = -.431$, $r = -.301$) negatively correlated with test score in both school years, while engaged concentration ($r = .449$, $r = .258$) positively correlated in both years. However, they did not directly test cross-year generalization by building detectors on one year of data and testing on the other.

Physiology has been used for affect detection with channels such as skin conductance and heart rate [8, 11]. However, multiple studies have observed degraded affect detection performance using physiological data when models trained using data from one day are tested using data from another day [9, 11]. In a classic study, Picard et al. [11] found that physiological data were more tightly clustered by affective state within data from the same day than were data from another day. The data distribution parameters become less reliable due to changing factors like mood and attention, and the decision boundaries for classifiers became less effective for discriminating instances of affect from a later day.

Cameras are a ubiquitous part of modern computers, from tablets to laptops to webcams, so face-based affect detection is an attractive option compared to modalities that require special equipment like skin conductance sensors or heart rate monitors. A variety of approaches have been used for face-based affect detection [10, 12]. Frustration [13, 14], engagement [13, 15], confusion [16], and other learning-centered affective states can be detected using facial features. However, many of these and other studies have taken place in a lab environment where data were collected one or two students at a time over the course of a few months. The conditions in lab-based studies are typically tightly controlled in an effort to reduce outside influences on the outcomes of studies. Changes like lighting and mood, and differences in classes (e.g., number of students, teaching strategies) that could influence affect detection may not be salient, unlike in a more ecological data collection setting such as a computer-enabled classroom. Thus, temporal generalizability of face-based affect detectors is currently an open question with important practical implications.

Current Study. To assess the ability of face-based affect detection to generalize over time in the ecologically valid setting of a computer-enabled classroom, the current paper attempts to answer three novel questions: 1) how does performance change when affect detectors are trained on one day and tested on another? (*cross-day*) compared to training and testing on data collected on the same day (*within-day*); 2) how do model and data parameters differ between the best-performing models built using data from different days? and 3) how much do different cross-day models rely on the same features for affect detection? The novelty of our contribution is that, to the best of our knowledge, this is the first paper to attempt to explore the possibility of face-based affect detection generalizing across time.

This paper uses a dataset that has been used for previous work on face-based affect detection [17]. Face videos were recorded in a noisy computer-enabled classroom environment where up to thirty students at a time played an educational physics game. Students talked to others and themselves, gestured, and occasionally left for bathroom breaks. Factors such as number of students in a class, lighting, and time of day varied as well. A subset of learning-centered affective states (boredom, confusion, delight, engagement, frustration, and off-task behavior) were detected using in a student-independent fashion to ensure generalization to new students. Detection was successful with average Area Under the ROC Curve (AUC) of .709. Data were collected over two days (with a 3-day interval). However, data from two days were pooled together for building detectors, and thus there was no evidence of generalization across days. In the current study we compare results of generalization against the baseline standards established in this previous work by training detectors on data collected on one day and testing them on data collected on a second day [17].

2   Method

A more thorough treatment of the data collection procedure and the model building method used in this study can be obtained by examining [17]. In this paper, we focus on only the most important aspects and those closely related to the goals of this paper.

2.1   Data

The data were collected from 137 8th and 9th grade students (57 male, 80 female) who were enrolled in a public school in a medium-sized city in the Southeastern U.S. Students were tested in groups of about 20 students per class period (55 minutes per period). The study took place in one of the school's computer-enabled classrooms, which was equipped with about 30 desktop computers. Inexpensive webcams ($30) were affixed at the top of the monitor on each computer.

Students played Physics Playground [18], a two-dimensional game that requires the player to apply principles of Newtonian physics in an attempt to guide a green ball to a red balloon (key goal) in many challenging configurations. Fig. 1 illustrates a configuration requiring a ramp drawn to build up speed before launching up to red balloon. Everything in the game obeys the basic laws of physics relating to gravity and Newton's three laws of motion. Students' affective states and on-task vs. off-task behaviors were coded using the Baker-Rodrigo Observation Method Protocol (BROMP) field observation system [19]. The affective states of interest were boredom, confusion, delight, engaged concentration, and frustration. This list of states was selected based on previous reviews on affect during learning with technology [1] and from observing students during pilot data collection (these data were not used in the current models). Delight was only added to the list of affective states on the second day, so cross-day generalization testing could not be performed for delight. In addition to affect, students were coded as being: *on task* when working on their own computer, *on-task conversation* when conversing with other students about the task, and *off task* in other situations (e.g., task-unrelated conversation, watching other students without conversation, using a cellphone).

Fig. 1. Ramp solution in Physics Playground

We consider data from two days of game-play (Day 1 and Day 2). Day 2 data were collected three days after Day 1. We obtained 1,767 observations of affective states and 1,899 observations of on-task/off-task behavior across these two days. Engaged concentration occurred most frequently (73.0% Day 1, 78.6% Day 2), followed by frustration (16.4%, 11.3%), boredom (6.7%, 2.7%), and confusion (3.9%, 1.2%), after removing instances of delight. Despite slightly increased off-task behavior on Day 2 (5.3% vs. 4.3% on Day 1), there appeared to be a general trend toward more engagement and less of the other affective states on Day 2.

2.2   Building the Affect Detectors

Machine learning methods, used to build the affect detectors, proceeded in three phases: feature engineering, supervised classification, and detector validation.

Feature Engineering. The Computer Expression Recognition Toolbox (CERT) [20] is a computer vision tool used to automatically detect the likelihood of 19 different action units (AUs, facial muscle movements; [21]) in any given frame of a video stream. Estimates of head pose and head position information are given by CERT as well. CERT has been tested with databases of both posed facial expressions and spontaneous facial expressions, achieving accuracy of 90.1% and 79.9%, respectively, when discriminating between instances of the AU present vs. absent [20].

We used FACET SDK (no longer available as standalone software), a commercialized version of the CERT computer vision software, for facial feature extraction. Features were created by computing the median, and standard deviation for the frame-level likelihood values of AUs and head position obtained from FACET in a window of time leading up to each observation. For example, we created two features from the AU4 channel (brow lower) by taking the median, and standard deviation of AU4 likelihoods within a six second window leading up to an affect observation. Window sizes of 3, 6, 9, and 12 seconds were explored. We also used two features (median and standard deviation) computed from gross body movement in the videos. Body movement was calculated as the proportion of pixels in each video frame that differed from a continuously updated estimate of the background image generated from the four previous frames using a motion silhouette algorithm [22].

Poor lighting, extreme head pose or position, occlusions from hand-to-face gestures, and rapid movements can all cause face registration errors; these issues were not uncommon due to the game-like nature of the software and the active behaviors of the students in this study. A third (34%) of the instances were discarded because FACET was not able to register the face for at least one second (13 frames) during an observation (a common problem in face-based affect detection), and thus the presence of AUs could not be estimated.

Tolerance analysis was used to eliminate features with high multicollinearity (variance inflation factor > 5) [23]. RELIEF-F feature selection [24] was used to obtain a sparser, more diagnostic set of features for classification. Feature selection was performed using 10 iterations of leave-33%-of-students-out nested cross-validation within the training data only.

Supervised Learning. A two-class approach was used for each affective state, where that affective state was discriminated from all others. For example, engaged was discriminated from all frustrated, bored, delighted, and confused instances combined (referred to as "all other"). Behaviors were similarly grouped into two classes: off-task and both on-task and on-task conversation. Weka, a popular machine learning tool, was used to train supervised classifiers [25]. Bayes net, updateable naïve Bayes, classification via clustering, and logistic regression classifiers were chosen based on our prior results [17]. Synthetic oversampling (with SMOTE; [26]) was used to equalize class sizes on the training data only. The distributions in the testing data were not changed, to preserve the validity of the results.

Model Validation to Test Generalization. Testing the generalization of models across days was performed with a nested cross validation approach to ensure generalization to new students and new days. First, data from one day were chosen as training data. Then, 67% of students were randomly selected from that day and their data were used to build a model using a repeated random sub-sampling approach with 150 iterations for model selection and evaluation. This model was tested using data from the remaining 33% of students in the same day (same-day generalization: e.g., train on Day 1, test on Day 1) or on the opposite day (cross-day generalization: e.g., train on Day 1, test Day 2). Student-level independence was thus ensured for both testing on the same day and on a different day. Fig. 2 illustrates the validation process.

The process of randomly selecting students for training and testing was repeated 150 times for each model (train-test: Day 1-Day 1; Day 1-Day 2; Day 2-Day 1; Day 2-Day 2) and the results were averaged across iterations.

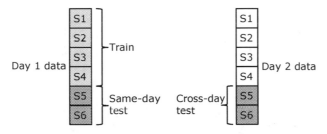

Fig. 2. Example of same-day and cross-day testing with student-level independence

3   Results and Discussion

Results are organized with respect to the research questions listed in the Introduction.

Research Question 1: Cross-Day Generalization. To explore the performance of models trained on one day and tested on another, we compared performance against the model trained and tested on data from the same day. The same-day results were averaged across both of the same-day models (e.g., train on Day 1, test on Day 1; train on Day 2, test on Day 2). Likewise, the cross-day results were obtained by averaging both cross-day models (train Day 1, test Day 2; train Day 2, test Day 1) for each affective state. Table 1 contains the results for each affective state. Previous work with both days of data combined is also provided as a reference point [17].

Table 1. Results of cross-day compared to same-day detection

Classification	Cross-day AUC	Same-day AUC	Change (Cross-day - Same-day)	Combined-days AUC	Change (Cross-day - Combined-days)
Boredom	.577	.574	0.23%	.610	-3.34%
Confusion	.639	.665	-2.61%	.649	-1.02%
Engagement	.662	.679	-1.72%	.679	-1.70%
Frustration	.631	.643	-1.21%	.631	0.02%
Off Task	.781	.774	0.72%	.816	-3.48%
Mean	**.658**	**.667**	**-0.92%**	**.677**	**-1.90%**

Note. Cross-day change is percentage of change in AUC, which is bounded on [0, 1].

The key result is that the cross-day models performed with similar accuracy (average AUC = .658) to same-day models (average AUC = .667). Though there was a slight decrease overall in classification accuracy (< 1%), no detector suffered notably. The largest drop (2.61% drop in AUC) occurred for confusion.

Compared to previous work with combined-days models, same-day models had 0.99% lower performance and cross-day models had 1.90% lower performance. Decreased performance may be attributable to the fact that the combined-days models have the advantage of twice as much training data. With more data, cross-day model performance might improve and approach the combined-days models' performance.

Research Question 2: Comparison of Model Parameters. In addition to number of instances, we compared other data and model parameters to illustrate potential differences between the individual day models. Window size (3, 6, 9, or 12 seconds), feature selection (yes or no), and classifier were compared. Table 2 shows the differences in the best-performing Day 1 and Day 2 models.

Table 2. Differences between Day 1 and Day 2 models

Classification	Window Size		Feature Selection		Classifier	
	Day 1	Day 2	Day 1	Day 2	Day 1	Day 2
Boredom	12 sec	12 sec	Yes	Yes	CVC	CVC
Confusion	12 sec	12 sec	Yes	Yes	**BN**	**UNB**
Engagement	9 sec	9 sec	No	No	BN	BN
Frustration	**9 sec**	**6 sec**	No	No	BN	BN
Off Task	12 sec	12 sec	Yes	Yes	UNB	UNB

Note. Bold indicates parameters that differed between models. Classifiers listed were Classification Via Regression (CVC), Bayes Net (BN), and Updateable Naïve Bayes (UNB).

Of the 15 parameters for each individual day model, only two differed (denoted in bold in Table 2). The close similarities between the data and model parameters of the best-performing detectors suggest that the particular day does not make a notable difference in parameters, and thus the chosen parameters are not the result of overfitting models to day-specific attributes.

Research Question 3: Comparison of Feature Selection Rankings. We examined correlations of feature rankings between the Day 1 models and Day 2 models to determine how similar the set of selected features might be on different days. Feature rankings were recorded during each iteration of RELIEF-F feature selection [24] in each model of the three that used feature selection (boredom, confusion, and off-task). RELIEF-F uses L1 distance to rank a feature based on within-class distance vs. between-class distance, so rankings are subject to substantial variation unless data are tightly clustered within that feature. Thus, correlations were expected to be modest provide a measure of how similar the data clustering is within features between days.

The correlation between Day 1 and Day 2 feature rankings was lower for the affective states than for off-task behavior. Confusion was correlated least ($r = .248$), followed by boredom ($r = .270$). However, feature rankings for both affective state models were correlated between days in the positive direction, demonstrating that at least some of the same clustering present in the features was detected by RELIEF-F in both days. Off-task behavior was correlated more highly and in the expected direction between days ($r = .402$).

We also examined the correlations between each feature rankings from each individual day and the combined-days models. Both affective states' feature rankings correlated with the combined-days models ($r = .595$ for boredom, $r = .654$ for confusion). Off-task feature rankings were also correlated ($r = .613$). The comparatively large magnitude of these correlations was not surprising given that half of the data in the combined-days models matches the data in each individual day model.

4   General Discussion

Creating affect detectors that generalize across time is important if intelligent education environments are going to be useful for learning across multiple sessions. We tested if affect detection models built using facial features and machine learning techniques could be generalized across days with reasonable accuracy for several affective states (boredom, confusion, engagement, and frustration) that are important to learning, as well as off-task behavior.

Main Findings. We built student-independent cross-day affect detection models and compared them to same-day and combined-days models. Cross-day detection was successful using training data from one day and testing data from another day with AUC = .658. Compared to performance of the same-day models (AUC = .667) and combined-days models (AUC = .677) for these affective states, the cross-day generalization models show similar performance, though marginally lower for some affective states. We also found some similarity (and difference) in the feature selection rankings between days of data (average $r = .249$ for affective states, $r = .402$ for off-task behavior). Cross-day models could still successfully classify data from a different day at levels well above chance despite differences in feature selection rankings.

Limitations and Future Work. This study is not without its limitations, particularly with regards to the breadth of data used. Though we collected data from multiple class periods and two days, all data were collected in the same computer-enabled classroom and learning environment. Lighting conditions and the students who participated varied somewhat between days, but more variation (such as could be obtained from different learning environments at multiple schools) might make the task even more difficult and produce new insights on generalization of face-based affect detection to new contexts. Similarly, the amount of time represented in this study (two different days) is enough to explore the first steps of cross-day generalization, but not enough to explore larger differences such as cross-seasonal generalization (i.e., train models in fall test in spring). Future work will address these issues by expanding data collection to encompass more geographical areas and extended periods of time.

Concluding Remarks. We took the first steps in studying the temporal generalizability of face-based affect detectors in classroom contexts. With affect detectors that generalize well across time and work in noisy school environments, affect-sensitive computerized education environments can respond to the affective needs of students with confidence that detections are not simply the result of factors specific to a particular day. The next step is to study temporal generalization across extended time frames, such as months or years, so that seasonal differences can be better understood.

Acknowledgment. This research was supported by the National Science Foundation (NSF) (ITR 0325428, HCC 0834847, DRL 1235958) and the Bill & Melinda Gates Foundation. Any opinions, findings and conclusions, or recommendations expressed in this paper are those of the authors and do not necessarily reflect the views of NSF.

References

1. D'Mello, S.: A selective meta-analysis on the relative incidence of discrete affective states during learning with technology. Journal of Educational Psychology. **105**, 1082–1099 (2013)
2. Schutz, P., Pekrun, R. (eds.): Emotion in Education. Academic Press, San Diego, CA (2007)
3. Bosch, N., D'Mello, S., Mills, C.: What emotions do novices experience during their first computer programming learning session? In: Lane, H.C., Yacef, K., Mostow, J., Pavlik, P. (eds.) AIED 2013. LNCS, vol. 7926, pp. 11–20. Springer, Heidelberg (2013)
4. Pardos, Z.A., Baker, R.S.J.D., San Pedro, M.O.C.Z., Gowda, S.M., Gowda, S.M.: Affective states and state tests: investigating how affect throughout the school year predicts end of year learning outcomes. In: Proceedings of the Third International Conference on Learning Analytics and Knowledge, pp. 117–124. ACM, New York (2013)
5. Fiedler, K., Beier, S.: Affect and cognitive processes in educational contexts. International handbook of emotions in education, pp. 36–56 (2014)
6. D'Mello, S., Blanchard, N., Baker, R., Ocumpaugh, J., Brawner, K.: I feel your pain: a selective review of affect-sensitive instructional strategies. In: Sottilare, R., Graesser, A., Hu, X., and Goldberg, B. (eds.) Design Recommendations for Intelligent Tutoring Systems – vol. 2: Instructional Management, pp. 35–48 (2014)
7. D'Mello, S., Lehman, B., Sullins, J., Daigle, R., Combs, R., Vogt, K., Perkins, L., Graesser, A.: A time for emoting: when affect-sensitivity is and isn't effective at promoting deep learning. In: Aleven, V., Kay, J., Mostow, J. (eds.) Intelligent Tutoring Systems. Lecture Notes in Computer Science, vol. 6094, pp. 245–254. Springer, Heidelberg (2010)
8. Arroyo, I., Cooper, D.G., Burleson, W., Woolf, B.P., Muldner, K., Christopherson, R.: Emotion sensors go to school. AIED, pp. 17–24 (2009)
9. Alzoubi, O., Hussain, M., D'Mello, S., Calvo, R.A.: Affective Modeling from Multichannel Physiology: Analysis of Day Differences. In: D'Mello, S., Graesser, A., Schuller, B., Martin, J.-C. (eds.) ACII 2011, Part I. LNCS, vol. 6974, pp. 4–13. Springer, Heidelberg (2011)
10. D'Mello, S., Kory, J.: Consistent but modest: a meta-analysis on unimodal and multimodal affect detection accuracies from 30 studies. In: Proceedings of the 14th ACM international conference on Multimodal interaction, pp. 31–38. ACM, New York (2012)

11. Picard, R.W., Vyzas, E., Healey, J.: Toward machine emotional intelligence: analysis of affective physiological state. IEEE Transactions on Pattern Analysis and Machine Intelligence. **23**, 1175–1191 (2001)
12. Zeng, Z., Pantic, M., Roisman, G.I., Huang, T.S.: A survey of affect recognition methods: Audio, visual, and spontaneous expressions. IEEE Transactions on Pattern Analysis and Machine Intelligence. **31**, 39–58 (2009)
13. Grafsgaard, J.F., Wiggins, J.B., Boyer, K.E., Wiebe, E.N., Lester, J.C.: Automatically recognizing facial expression: predicting engagement and frustration. In: Proceedings of the 6th International Conference on Educational Data Mining (2013)
14. Kapoor, A., Burleson, W., Picard, R.W.: Automatic prediction of frustration. International Journal of Human-Computer Studies. **65**, 724–736 (2007)
15. Whitehill, J., Serpell, Z., Lin, Y.-C., Foster, A., Movellan, J.R.: The faces of engagement: Automatic recognition of student engagement from facial expressions. IEEE Transactions on Affective Computing. **5**, 86–98 (2014)
16. Bosch, N., Chen, Y., D'Mello, S.: It's written on your face: detecting affective states from facial expressions while learning computer programming. In: Trausan-Matu, S., Boyer, K.E., Crosby, M., Panourgia, K. (eds.) ITS 2014. LNCS, vol. 8474, pp. 39–44. Springer, Heidelberg (2014)
17. Bosch, N., D'Mello, S., Baker, R., Ocumpaugh, J., Shute, V.J., Ventura, M., Wang, L., Zhao, W.: Automatic detection of learning-centered affective states in the wild. In: Proceedings of the 2015 International Conference on Intelligent User Interfaces (IUI 2015). ACM, New York, NY, USA (in Press)
18. Shute, V.J., Ventura, M., Kim, Y.J.: Assessment and learning of qualitative physics in Newton's Playground. The Journal of Educational Research. **106**, 423–430 (2013)
19. Ocumpaugh, J., Baker, R., Rodrigo, M.M.T.: Baker-Rodrigo observation method protocol (BROMP) 1.0. Training manual version 1.0. Technical Report. New York, NY: EdLab. Manila, Philippines: Atenco Laboratory for the Learning Sciences (2012)
20. Littlewort, G., Whitehill, J., Wu, T., Fasel, I., Frank, M., Movellan, J., Bartlett, M.: The computer expression recognition toolbox (CERT). In: 2011 IEEE International Conference on Automatic Face Gesture Recognition and Workshops (FG 2011), pp. 298–305 (2011)
21. Ekman, P., Friesen, W.V.: Facial action coding system. Consulting Psychologist Press, Palo Alto, CA (1978)
22. Kory, J., D'Mello, S., Olney, A.: Motion Tracker: Cost-effective, non-intrusive, fully-automated monitoring of bodily movements using motion silhouettes. Presented at the (in review)
23. Allison, P.D.: Multiple regression: a primer. Pine Forge Press (1999)
24. Kononenko, I.: Estimating attributes: analysis and extensions of RELIEF. In: Bergadano, F., Raedt, L.D. (eds.) Machine Learning: ECML-94. Lecture Notes in Computer Science, vol. 784, pp. 171–182. Springer, Heidelberg (1994)
25. Holmes, G., Donkin, A., Witten, I.H.: WEKA: a machine learning workbench. In: Proceedings of the Second Australian and New Zealand Conference on Intelligent Information Systems, pp. 357–361 (1994)
26. Chawla, N.V., Bowyer, K.W., Hall, L.O., Kegelmeyer, W.P.: SMOTE: synthetic minority over-sampling technique. Journal of Artificial Intelligence Research. **16**, 321–357 (2011)

Transfer Learning for Predictive Models in Massive Open Online Courses

Sebastien Boyer and Kalyan Veeramachaneni[⊠]

Computer Science and Artificial Intelligence Laboratory,
Massachusetts Institute of Technology, Cambridge, USA
{sebboyer,kalyan}@csail.mit.edu

Abstract. Data recorded while learners are interacting with Massive Open Online Courses (MOOC) platforms provide a unique opportunity to build predictive models that can help anticipate future behaviors and develop interventions. But since most of the useful predictive problems are defined for a real-time framework, using knowledge drawn from the past courses becomes crucial. To address this challenge, we designed a set of processes that take advantage of knowledge from both previous courses and previous weeks of the same course to make real time predictions on learners behavior. In particular, we evaluate multiple transfer learning methods. In this article, we present our results for the stopout prediction problem (predicting which learners are likely to stop engaging in the course). We believe this paper is a first step towards addressing the need of transferring knowledge across courses.

1 Introduction

Data recorded while learners are interacting with the Massive Open Online Courses (MOOC) platform provide a unique opportunity to learn about the efficacy of the different resources, build predictive models that can help develop interventions and propose/recommend strategies for the learner. Consider for example a model built to predict *stopout*, that is, how likely is the learner to stop engaging with the course in the coming weeks. One can learn the model retrospectively on data generated from a finished course by following a typical data mining procedure: splitting the data into *test-train*, learning the model and tuning its parameters *via* cross validation using the *training* data, and testing the models accuracy on *test* data which is a proxy for how model may perform on unseen data.

In this paper, we focus on operationalization of the predictive models for real time use. We raise a fundamental question: whether models *trained* on previous courses would perform well on a new course (perhaps a subsequent offering of the same course). This question is of utmost importance in MOOCs due to the following observations:

Offerings could be subtly different: Due to the very nascent nature of the online learning platforms, many aspects of the course evolve. Learners are thus placed in a different environment each time, so they may interact and behave differently.

© Springer International Publishing Switzerland 2015
C. Conati et al. (Eds.): AIED 2015, LNAI 9112, pp. 54–63, 2015.
DOI: 10.1007/978-3-319-19773-9_6

Offerings have a different learner/instructor population: Subsequent offeringsof
a course have a different population of students, teaching assistants, and in
some cases, different instructors.

Some variables may not transfer: Some of the variables developed for one offering may not exist in the subsequent offering. For example, if a variable is the
time spent on a specific tutorial, the variable may not be computed if the
tutorial is not offered in subsequent offering.

To develop methods for operationalization of models for real time predictions,
in this paper we study three different offerings of a course offered by MIT via
edX called *Circuits and Electronics*. We formulate two versions of the prediction
problem. One version of the problem, in a very limited number of prediction
scenarios, allows us to use data gathered in an on-going course to make predictions in the same course. We call this *in-situ* learning. In the second version
we employ multiple transfer learning methods and examine their performance.
In our models we rely on a set of variables that we consider are universal, and
employ techniques to overcome the differences in their ranges.

The paper is organized as follows. In next section we present the datasets
we are working with, and the features/variables we defined and extracted. In
Section 3 we define the *stopout* prediction problem and multiple versions of
the problem formulation. In Section 4 we present different transfer learning
approaches we employ. Section 5 presents the results. Section 6 presents the
related work in this area. Section 7 concludes.

2   Dataset

In a MOOC every mouse click learners make on the course website is recorded,
their submissions are collected, and their interactions on forums are stored. In
this paper, our data is from three consecutive offerings of an MITx course called
6.002x : Circuits and Electronics offered *via* edX platform. We chose three
offerings of this course as an ideal test case for transfer learning since we
expect that different offerings of the same course may have statistically similar learner-behavior data. We name the offerings as A (offered in spring 2012),
B (offered in fall 2012) and C (offered in spring 2013). The number of learners
who registered/certified in these three offerings were 154753/7157, 51394/2987
and 29,050/1099 respectively.

Per Learner Longitudinal Variables. Even though each course could be
different in terms of content, student population and global environment, the
data gathered during the student's interaction with the platform allows us to
extract a common set of longitudinal variables as shown in table 1 (more details
about these features are presented in [12]).

3   Stopout Prediction in MOOCs

We consider the problem of predicting *stopout* (a.k.a *dropout*) for learners in
MOOCs. The prediction problem is described as: considering a course of duration

Table 1. Features derived per learner per week for the above-mentioned courses

x_1	Total time spent on all resources
x_2	Number of distinct problems attempted
x_3	Number of submissions
x_4	Number of distinct correct problems
x_5	Average number of submissions per problem
x_6	Ratio of total time spent to number of distinct correct problems
x_7	Ratio of number of problems attempted to number of distinct correct problems
x_8	Duration of longest observed event
x_9	Total time spent on lecture resources
x_{10}	Total time spent on book resources
x_{11}	Total time spent on wiki resources
x_{12}	Number of correct submissions
x_{13}	Percentage of the total submissions that were correct
x_{14}.	Average time between a problem submission and problem due date

k weeks, given a set of longitudinal observations (*covariates*) that describe the learner *behavior* and *performance* in a course up until a week i predict whether or not the learner will persist in week $i + j$ to k where $j \in \{1 \ldots k - i\}$ is the *lead* [10]. A learner is said to *persist* in week i if s/he attempts at least *one* problem presented in the course during the week. In the context of MOOC's, making real time predictions about *stopout* would give a tremendous opportunity to make interventions, collect surveys and improve course outcomes.

3.1   Problem Formulation and Learning Possibilities

Given the learner interactions data up until week i, we formulate two different types of prediction problems. These different formulations have implications on how training data could be assembled and how model learning could incorporate information from a previous course.

Formulations

- **Entire history**: In this formulation, we use all the information available regarding the learner up until week i for making predictions beyond week i.
- **Moving window**: In this formulation, we use a fixed amount of historical information (parameterized by `window size`) of the learner to make predictions. That is, if the `window size` is set to 2 then for any week i we only use information from weeks $i - 1$ and $i - 2$.

Learning

- **In-situ learning**: In-situ learning attempts to learn a predictive model from the data from the on-going course itself. To be able to do so we have to assemble data corresponding to learners that *stopped* out (negative exemplars) along with learners who are *persisting* (positive exemplars). This is only possible for the moving window formulation. Under the formulation, when the course is at week i and the `window size` is w, *lead* is j, and $w + j < i$, we can assemble training examples by following a sliding window protocol over the data up until i.

- **Transfer learning**: Through transfer learning we attempt to transfer information (training data samples or models) from a previous course to establish a predictive model for an ongoing course.

Performance Metric: We note that the positive examples in our dataset (learners that don't *stopout*) only represent around 10% of the total amount of learners. A simple baseline could lead to very high accuracy (e.g. predicting that every learner dropped out for all the test samples gives an accuracy of nearly 90%). We use Area Under the Curve as a metric to capture and compare the discriminatory performance of our models.

4 Transfer Learning

Notationally we call *source offering S* (for past source offering) and *target offering T* (for current on-going course). n_S and n_T respectively are the number of samples in the source and target offering and $D_S = \{x_{Si}, y_{Si}\}_{i=1}^{n_s}$ represents the data from the source. We distinguish two main scenarios for transfer learning as defined in [8] and [13]: **inductive transfer** learning where some labels are available for the target course given by $D_T = \{x_{Ti}, y_{Ti}\}_{i=1}^{n_t}$ and **transductive transfer** where no labels are available for the target course data, given by $D_T = \{x_{Ti}\}_{i=1}^{n_t}$.

4.1 A Naive Approach

When using samples from a previous course to help predict in a new course, we first wonder if the two tasks (predicting in the first course and predicting in the second course) are similar enough so that applying a model learnt on the first course to the second one would give satisfying results. To answer this question we train a logistic regression model with optimized ridge regression parameter on S and apply it to T. We call this *naive* transfer method.

4.2 Inductive Learning Approach

Multi-task Learning Method. In the multi-task learning method (MT)[2], two sets of weights are learnt for samples from source and target. The weights are coupled by having a common component that is shared between a weight for a covariate from source and target. This sharing is represented by:

$$\begin{cases} w_S = v_S + c_0 \\ w_T = v_T + c_0 \end{cases}$$

where $v_S, v_T \in \Re^d$, $d = m + 1$ for m covariates. From a logistic regression perspective, this method requires learning two coupled weight vectors, while regularizing the two components separately:

$$(w_S^*, w_T^*) = \arg \min_{v_S, v_T, w_0} \sum_{i=1:n_S} l(x_{Si}, y_{Si}, w_S) +$$

$$\sum_{i=1:n_T} l(x_{Ti}, y_{Ti}, w_T) + \frac{\lambda_1}{2}(||v_s||^2 + ||v_T||^2) + \lambda_2 ||c_0||^2$$

where $l(x, y, w) = \log(\frac{1}{1+\exp(-y(w^0+x^T.w))})$. Regularization allows us to set the degree of similarity between courses via parameter $\frac{\lambda_2}{\lambda_1}$ stands for relative significance of the independent part over the common part of the weights. For small values of $\frac{\lambda_2}{\lambda_1}$ we expect the two models to have very common weight vectors (regularization constraints are higher on the distinct part v_S and v_T than on the common part c_0). In our experiments we set $\lambda_1 = 0.2$ and $\lambda_2 = 0.8$.

Logistic Regression with Prior Method. In MT method, the regularization parameters impose the same common/particular penalization ratio to all the components of the weight vector that correspond to different covariates. However, in most cases we would like to differentiate between covariates as their importance is likely to vary between source and the target course.

Hence we resort to a method that uses Prior distribution on the weights of the target model [3]. The Logistic Regression with Prior method, PM, first estimates the prior distribution (assumed to be Gaussian) on the weights by splitting the data from source course into $D = 10$ sub-samples (without replacement). For each sub-sample, we fit the usual logistic regression classifier using ridge regularization. We obtain D sets of weights $\{\{w_i^k\}_{i=1:d}\}_{k=1:D}$ and use them to compute our prior belief on the weights we expect to derive from any new course as follows:

$$\begin{cases} \mu_j = \dfrac{1}{D} \displaystyle\sum_{k=1:D} w_j^k & \text{for } j = 1:d \\[4mm] \sigma_j = \sqrt{\dfrac{1}{D-1} \displaystyle\sum_{k=1:D} (w_j^k - \mu_j)^2} & \text{for } j = 1:d \end{cases}$$

When building a model for the target domain, in this formulation, the usual logistic regression cost function $NLL(w_0, w) = \sum_{i=1:N} l(x_{Ti}, y_{Ti}, w_T) + \frac{1}{2}\lambda \sum_{j=1:d} w_j^2$ becomes $NLL(w_0, w) = \sum_{i=1:N} l(x_{Ti}, y_{Ti}, w_T) + \frac{1}{2}\lambda \sum_{j=0:d} \frac{(w_j-\mu_j)^2}{\sigma_j^2}$, where $\mu = [\mu_1, \ldots, \mu_d], \sigma = [\sigma_1, \ldots, \sigma_d]$ and $l(x_i, y_i, w) = \log(\frac{1}{1+\exp(-y_i(w^0+x_i^T.w))})$ is the log-likelihood of the i th data point for a multivariate gaussian prior on the distributions. The effect of such strategy is to allow higher flexibility (less constraints) for weights which vary significantly across source sub-domains and constrain more the weights whose variation across source sub-domains are smaller. In our experiments, we set $\lambda = 1$.

4.3   Transductive Learning Approach

In this section we focus on the scenario where no labeled samples are available in the target course. This is the case when considering a *entire history* setting (no labeled samples from the ongoing course are available because the week of the prediction is in the future). To transfer the model from source to target, we follow our belief that the covariates from the two courses may overlap to a significant degree and we use a sample correction bias [5]. This importance sampling, or IS, method is equivalent to assuming that the covariates are drawn from a common distribution and that their difference comes from a selection bias during the sampling process (out of this general common distribution). In order to correct this sample selection bias, the idea is to give more weight to the learners in the source course that are "close" to the learners in the target course. Doing so, the classification algorithm takes advantage of the similar learners of the source course and barely considers the significantly different ones. For each target sample we predict: $\hat{y}_{Ti} = \arg \max_{y \in \{+1,-1\}} l(x_{Ti}, y, w^*)$. The weights are estimated from the source data by optimizing:

$$\text{where } w^* = \arg \min_{w} \sum_{i=1:n_S} \beta_i \, l(x_{Si}, y_{Si}, w)$$

Note that each learner's data is reweighted using a parameter β_i in the log likelihood objective function. Finding the optimal β_i for such a reweighting procedure would be straigthforward if we knew the two distributions from which the source and the target learners data are drawn. To find these in practice, we use a gaussian kernel $k(x, z) = \exp(-\frac{\|x-z\|^2}{\sigma^2}) \, \forall x, z \in S \cup T$ to measure the distance between data points. In our experiments $\sigma = 1$. We then compute for each source data point an average importance to the target domain: $\kappa_i = \frac{1}{n_T} \sum_{j=1:n_T} k(x_{Si}, x_{Tj})$ and use a quadratic formulation found in [5] to evaluate the optimal coefficients β_i^*.

$$\beta^* \sim \arg \min_{\beta} \frac{1}{2}\beta^T K \beta - n_S \, \kappa^T \beta \, s.t. \, \beta_i \in [0, B] \text{ and } \left| \sum_{i=1:n_S} \beta_i - n_S \right| \leq n_S \epsilon$$

where $K_{ij} = k(x_{Si}, x_{Sj})$. The second term in the optimization problem makes sure we choose β_i high when the average distance of X_{S_i} to all the X_{T_*} is low.

5   Experimental Settings and Results

Problem Settings: As per Figure 1 there are number of ways a prediction problem can be solved. For inductive transfer learning, we have two methods - *prior* and *multi-task*. In total the same prediction problem can be solved *via* 7 different methods. As a reminder, we denote the courses as follows: *6.002x* spring 2012 as A, *6.002x* fall 2012 as B, and *6.002x* spring 2013 as C. First we consider the *entire history* setting and then present results for *moving window* setting. For comparison we define an *a-posteriori* model.

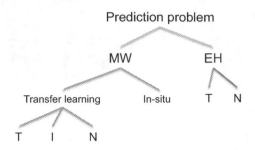

Fig. 1. Different ways we can learn and execute a model depending on the formulation we choose. MW stands for *Moving Window*, EH stands for *Entire History*, T stands for *Transductive model*, I stands for *Inductive model* and N stands for *Naive* model.

Definition 1. *a-posteriori model: It is the model built retrospectively using the labeled data from the target course itself. That is, the data from the target course is split into train and test and a model is trained on the training data and AUC is reported on the test data. We note that this is typically how results on dropout prediction are reported in several papers up until now.*

Entire History Formulation: Within the entire history setting, two different methods can be applied - *naive* and *importance sampling*. When applying these two methods we normalize features (using *min-max* normalization) independently within each course. Intuitively this makes sense, as normalizing all data using the normalization parameters calculated on the training set/previous course could induce misrepresentation of variables. For example, the variable *number of correct problems* could have different ranges as the total number of problems offered during a particular week may vary from offering to offering. Course-wise normalization allows us to compare learners to their peers thus making variables across courses comparable.

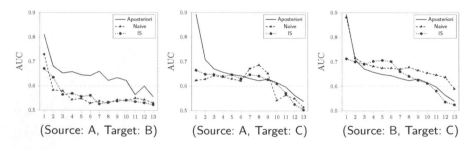

Fig. 2. Performance of transfer learning models for the *Entire History* formulation. Solid black line plots stands for the AUC obtained for the hypothetical case where we could access data from the future of the ongoing course (*a-posteriori* model). *Naive* method stands for the AUC obtained by naively using the source course as a training dataset and the target course as a test set. *IS* stands for *importance sampling* method.

Figure 2 shows the results achieved for three different transfer learning scenarios. On *x-axis* is the *lead* for the prediction problem and the *y-axis* is the average AUC across different amounts of history (same *lead* at different weeks). For example, at lead= 1, the *y-axis* value is the average of AUC values for 13 prediction problems defined at week 1-to-13. To summarize our results we use a question-answer format.

Is the Performance of an a-Posteriori Model a Good Indicator of Real Time Prediction Performance?: The a-posteriori model performance in most cases presents an optimistic estimate. Models trained on a previous offering struggle to achieve the same performance when transferred. This is especially true for one week ahead prediction. In two out of three cases in Figure 2 we notice a drop of 0.1 or more in AUC value when a model from previous offering is used. Hence, we argue that when developing *stopout* models for MOOCs for real time use, one *must* evaluate the performance of the model on successive offerings and report its performance.

Which is Better: Naive or Importance Sampling Based Transfer?: Based on our experiments we are not able to conclusively say whether *naive* transfer or the *importance sampling* based transfer is better. In some prediction problems one is better than the other and vice-versa. We hypothesize that the performance of *importance sampling* based approach can be further improved by tuning its parameters and perhaps fusing the predictions of both the methods can yield a better/robust performance.

What Could Explain the Slightly Better Performance of Transferred Models on C?: Number of learners in course C are significantly less than that in B or A. We posit that perhaps having more data in A or B enabled development of models that transferred well to C. This is specially true for B-to-C transfer. Additionally, since chronologically B is closer to C we hypothesize that not much may have changed in the platform or the course structure between these two offerings. This, together with the fact that B has more data enabled models trained on B to perform well on C (when compared to the *a-posteriori* model developed on C).

Moving Window Formulation. We next consider the *moving window* formulation. We consider that the target course is at week 4 and our goal is to predict whether or not learners who are in week 4 will stopout or will stay in the course. Fixing the `window size` to be 2 we can generate training examples for lead 1 by assembling covariates from week 1 and 2 and week 2 and 3. For lead 2 we can form training examples by assembling covariates from week 1 and 2. This allows us to generate labeled exemplars as we have knowledge about *stopouts* for week 3 and 4 in the ongoing course. Thus we are able to perform *in-situ* learning and inductive transfer learning methods. However, we are only able to solve two prediction problems - lead 1 and lead 2. We present the results achieved via multiple methods in Figure 3. We present the summary of our results.

How Did In-situ Learning Do?: In-situ learning did surprisingly well when compared to transfer learning methods under the *moving window* formulation.

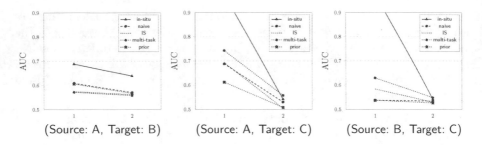

Fig. 3. Performance of transfer learning models for the *Moving Window* formulation

For both B and C the performance for lead 1 and 2 is between 0.6 -0.7 AUC (at week 4). This performance is also comparable to the *entire history* version of the same problem. In our subsequent work we intend to evaluate *in-situ* learning for a wide variety of prediction problems and not just at week 4.

6   Related Work

Dropout prediction and analysis of reasons for dropout are of great interest to the educational research community in a variety of contexts: e-learning, distance education, and online courses offered by community colleges. However, most studies focus on the identifying aspects of student's behavior, progress, and performance that correlate with dropout. These studies inform policy or give a broader understanding as to why students dropout [9,11]. Real-time predictions are rarely studied [6,7], but to the best of our knowledge, we have not found studies that examine whether models transfer well or if they could be deployed. Perhaps, MOOCs provide an ideal use case for transfer learning; with multiple offerings of the same course during a year, it is paramount that we use what we learned from the previous course to make predictions and design interventions in the next course. Within MOOC literature, there is an increasing amount of interest in predicting *stopout* [1,4]. In most cases, methods have focused on predicting one-week ahead and have not attempted to use trained on one course on another. Through this study, we are taking the first steps toward understanding different situations in which one can transfer models/data samples from one course to another. We have succeeded in (a) defining different ways real-time predictions can be achieved for a new offering, (b) multiple ways in which transfer learning can be achieved, and (c) demonstration of transfer learning performance.

7   Conclusion

In this paper we presented different methods that allow us to make real time predictions for learners in MOOCs. Particularly, we emphasized on transfer learning techniques that form the foundation for using models in real time. The key ideas of these methods were to formulate two different settings for a same prediction problem (using aggregate data from previous course or partial data form the ongoing course) and implement advanced machine learning techniques for both.

From an engineering and scientific perspective, we believe these are first steps towards building high fidelity predictive systems for MOOC's (beyond retrospectively analyzing *stopout* prediction problem). To complete the model, we expect further work to designing new transfer learning methods, designing methodologies to tune the parameters for the current transfer learning approaches, evaluating the methods systematically on a number of courses, defining more covariates for learners and deploying the predictive system in an actual course.

References

1. Balakrishnan, G., Coetzee, D.: Predicting student retention in massive open online courses using hidden markov models. In: Technical report No. UCB/EECS-2013-109. EECS, University of California, Berkeley (2013)
2. Caruana, R.: Multitask Learning. Springer (1998)
3. Chelba, C., Acero, A.: Adaptation of maximum entropy capitalizer: Little data can help a lot. Computer Speech & Language **20**(4), 382–399 (2006)
4. Halawa, S., Greene, D., Mitchell, J.: Dropout prediction in moocs using learner activity features. In: Proceedings of the European MOOC Summit, EMOOCs (2014)
5. Huang, J., Gretton, A., Borgwardt, K.M., Schölkopf, B., Smola, A.J.: Correcting sample selection bias by unlabeled data. In: Advances in neural information processing systems, pp. 601–608 (2006)
6. Lauría, E.J.M., Baron, J.D., Devireddy, M., Sundararaju, V., Jayaprakash, S.M.: Mining academic data to improve college student retention: an open source perspective. In: Proceedings of the 2nd International Conference on Learning Analytics and Knowledge, pp. 139–142. ACM (2012)
7. Lykourentzou, I., Giannoukos, I., Nikolopoulos, V., Mpardis, G., Loumos, V.: Dropout prediction in e-learning courses through the combination of machine learning techniques. Computers & Education **53**(3), 950–965 (2009)
8. Pan, S.J., Yang, Q.: A survey on transfer learning. IEEE Transactions on Knowledge and Data Engineering **22**(10), 1345–1359 (2010)
9. Street, H.D.: Factors influencing a learners' decision to drop-out or persist in higher education distance learning. Online Journal of Distance Learning Administration **13**(4) (2010)
10. Taylor, C., Veeramachaneni, K., O'Reilly, U.-M.: Likely to stop? predicting stopout in massive open online courses (2014). arXiv preprint arXiv:1408.3382
11. Tyler-Smith, K.: Early attrition among first time elearners: A review of factors that contribute to drop-out, withdrawal and non-completion rates of adult learners undertaking elearning programmes. Journal of Online learning and Teaching **2**(2), 73–85 (2006)
12. Veeramachaneni, K., O'Reilly, U.-M., Taylor, C.: Towards feature engineering at scale for data from massive open online courses (2014). arXiv preprint arXiv:1407.5238
13. Yang, Q., Pan, S.J.: Transfer learning and applications. In: Intelligent Information Processing, p. 2 (2012)

Mind the Gap: Improving Gender Equity in Game-Based Learning Environments with Learning Companions

Philip Sheridan Buffum[1(✉)], Kristy Elizabeth Boyer[1], Eric N. Wiebe[2],
Bradford W. Mott[1], and James C. Lester[1]

[1] Department of Computer Science, North Carolina State University, North Carolina, USA
{psbuffum,keboyer,bwmott,lester}@ncsu.edu
[2] Department of STEM Education, North Carolina State University Raleigh,
North Carolina, USA
wiebe@ncsu.edu

Abstract. Game-based learning environments hold great promise for engaging learners. Yet game mechanics can initially pose barriers for students with less prior gaming experience. This paper examines game-based learning for a population of middle school learners in the US, where female students tend to have less gaming experience than male students. In a pilot study with an early version of ENGAGE, a game-based learning environment for middle school computer science education, female students reported higher initial frustration. To address this critical issue, we developed a prototype learning companion designed specifically to reduce frustration through the telling of autobiographical stories. In a pilot study of two 7th grade classrooms, female students responded especially positively to the learning companion, eliminating the gender gap in reported frustration. The results suggest that introducing learning companions can directly contribute to making the benefits of game-based learning equitable for all learners.

Keywords: Learning companions · Game-based learning · Gender

1 Introduction

Game-based learning environments can be highly engaging [1] and can effectively support student learning [2–4]. Research has shown that adding game-based features to existing educational software can increase motivation and mastery achievement if the given software supports long-term interactions [5]. However, among some learner populations, subgroups of students have less gaming experience than others, posing a barrier to the less experienced students' initial engagement within the game-based learning environment. For example, prior studies have found that male students tend to score higher on certain dimensions of engagement within game-based learning, perhaps due to their greater familiarity with gameplay mechanics [4]. Additionally, students who have low expectations upon beginning to interact with a game-based learning environment tend to learn less [6]. These findings indicate that great care must be taken to avoid disadvantaging students who enter with less prior gameplay

© Springer International Publishing Switzerland 2015
C. Conati et al. (Eds.): AIED 2015, LNAI 9112, pp. 64–73, 2015.
DOI: 10.1007/978-3-319-19773-9_7

experience. Indeed, fine-grained analysis of many educational interventions, particularly for disciplines in STEM or computing, have found equity to be an issue on some level [7, 8].

Rather than dissuade the community from the merits of game-based learning environments, these findings should compel us to investigate ways to improve the equity of our systems. This paper focuses on a method to improve the *gender equity* of a game-based learning environment for middle school computer science. In this paper, we use the term "gender equity" specifically in regard to our efforts to make a system that does not disadvantage female students *due to its gameplay* (other dimensions of gender equity, such as efforts to ensure equal representation of female and male students playing the game, are crucial as well, but beyond the scope of this paper). Pilot data with the ENGAGE game-based learning environment revealed gender disparities in the early gameplay, likely due to female students feeling frustrated with gameplay mechanics. To counteract this, we looked to the success of animated pedagogical agents at improving attitudes among middle school students towards similar fields as computer science [9]. Specifically, we built a learning companion [10] designed to counteract the negative frustration that female students may encounter with gameplay mechanics early in gameplay. We hypothesized that the affective scaffolding provided by the learning companion would have a positive impact on female students, thus bringing more gender equity to the overall game-based learning environment.

2 Related Work

Animated pedagogical agents have long been found to have positive affective impact on young students, due to the well-documented *persona effect* [11]. Although some research has raised questions about whether the persona effect extends to a broader age range of learners (such as college students) [12], there is strong evidence as to the affective benefits of these agents on middle school students. More specifically, an animated pedagogical agent can be designed to take on any one of a number of different roles. *Intelligent tutors* generally operate as a knowledge expert, motivator, or mentor, all of which have demonstrated benefits [13]. *Teachable agents*, conversely, are designed to appear less knowledgeable than the student, requiring the student to learn for the sake of "teaching" the agent [14, 15]. Similarly, *learning companions* also play a non-authoritative role, providing a social peer alongside the student within an interactive learning environment [10].

Research on learning companions has featured gender as a focal point. The gender of the learning companion has been found to have an impact on students' attitudes and learning [16], as well as the relative likelihood of the agent receiving counterproductive, abusive behavior from the student [17]. Critically, learning companions have been found to have especially positive affective results for female students, such as improving female students' confidence in mathematics and reducing the gender gap in frustration in that field [18], as well as improving self-efficacy among female students [19]. There is strong evidence in support of tailoring the behavior of such agents based on the gender (as well as achievement level) of the learner [20–22]. In addition to their gender-specific impact, learning companions have also been found to have especially great impacts for low-achieving students [23, 24].

3   ENGAGE Pilot Study: The No-Companion Condition

We have been developing a game-based learning environment, ENGAGE, to teach middle school students about computer science. In the game, students take on the role of computer scientists as they embark upon an adventure revolving around a socially relevant challenge, developing their computational thinking [25] skills along the way. The game has been piloted in multiple middle schools with diverse learner popula-tions, and initial studies have provided promising results about the game's effective-ness for supporting students who enter with varying prior experiences and abilities [26]. The entire ENGAGE game-based learning experience includes gameplay and complementary out-of-game classroom activities. It has been integrated within a quar-terly oceanography elective for middle school students that was initially offered in two public middle schools. Within this pilot study, data were collected from a total of 50 students at the two schools, in grades six through eight. The participants were 23 female and 27 male students. These students used a version of the ENGAGE game-based learning environment that did not include a learning companion.

While conducting classroom observations, the project team noticed (via qualitative interpretation of observational behavior) a potential trend of female students exhibit-ing frustration during early gameplay sessions, particularly with gameplay mechanics. As such, we looked to the survey data to confirm if such a trend existed. Table 1 shows the responses to a 5-point Likert scale item, in which students were asked to agree/disagree with the statement, "I felt frustrated while playing the game." (We will refer to this as *Frustration* for the sake of clarity). Students answered this question at the end of each session as part of the validated User Engagement Scale (UES) [27].

Differences were found *between female and male* students for Frustration on both of the first two gameplay sessions (over the academic term, students took an average of ten gameplay sessions to complete the entire game). In Session 1, female students reported an average Frustration of 2.91, compared to an average of 2.04 by their male classmates. In Table 1, this is the row labeled "Frustration – Session 1". We ran a One-Way ANOVA, and the results showed a statistically significant difference $(F(1, 48) = 7.53, p < .01)$.

Table 1. No-Companion Condition: Frustration on Two Post-Surveys, on 5-point Likert Scale. (Higher Numbers Indicate More Frustration).

	Female (n = 23)	Male (n = 27)	Overall (n = 50)
Frustration – Session 1	2.91 (SD = 1.125)	2.04 (SD = 1.125)	2.44 (SD = 1.198)
Frustration – Session 2	3.48 (SD = 1.275)	2.63 (SD = 1.182)	3.02 (SD = 1.286)

Additionally, Frustration rose overall for all students from Session 1 to Session 2 (shown in the third column of Table 1), from an overall average of 2.44 to an overall average of 3.02. A Repeated Measures ANOVA found this also to be statistically significant $(F(1, 49) = 9.35, p < .01)$. Moreover, as one can see in the Table 1 row labeled "Frustration – Session 2", the gender gap persisted ($F(1, 48) = 5.96$, $p < .05$), with frustration levels for both genders rising as students confronted a gameplay challenge that, although not designed to be frustrating, proved to require skill with gameplay mechanics. A common problem in this 'Tri-Level Room' challenge was students accidentally falling in the water due to their struggles with navigating their avatar (Figure 1). The character in this scene is the student's avatar.

Fig. 1. Screenshot of Game at 'Tri-Level Room'

4   The ENGAGE with Learning Companion Condition

Having noted this gender gap, we sought to design a timely intervention that could mitigate frustration in the gameplay for female students, as they overcame the initial obstacle of becoming familiar with gameplay mechanics. We consequently used Unity 3D to develop a prototype of an animated pedagogical agent, named Adriana. Adriana is a six-year-old girl whose sister lives in the underwater research station where the learner has been interacting in the game-based learning environment. In crafting Adriana's utterances, we aimed to design empathetic dialogue that would parallel the behaviors and resulting emotions that students might experience at this stage of the gameplay. We furthermore were guided by research on the value of agents' autobiographical stories and social conversation [28, 29], and particularly by research indicating that such agents can improve students' attitudes towards STEM fields [30]. Adriana tells the learner about her older sister, an expert computer scientist whom the player will meet later in the game. She also tells the learner about how she herself has visited the underwater research station and how she fell in the water many times. Adriana reassures the player that falling in the water in these challenging rooms is not abnormal, and that moving around the station will become easier with experience. Students respond to Adriana with typed, natural language replies. The interaction with Adriana is designed to last approximately five minutes. Figure 2 shows an excerpt of interaction with Adriana.

Adriana:	"Um, falling in the water is not fun, especially when it happens over and over. Guess how many times I fell in. Do you know?"
Student:	"I dunno, maybe 2 or 3 times?"
Adriana:	"A million times. That's what [my sister] said – I can't count very well, but she said I fell in a million times. She says I'm clumsy. Do you think I'm clumsy?"
Student:	"Maybe a little."
Adriana:	"Haha! Anyways, don't feel bad if you fall in the water, too. It's only really a problem in the part of the station where you are. Other than that, how do you like it?"
Student:	"It is very nice."

Fig. 2. Excerpt of Student Interaction with Learning Companion

After developing a prototype of the learning companion, we conducted a study to test the agent's effectiveness, with particular interest in her ability to reduce frustration in female students during early gameplay. The study was conducted with two seventh-grade classes at an urban middle school. This was a different school than had been used in the No-Companion pilot study in order to ensure that the students had no prior exposure to the game-based learning environment. The school is in the same district as the prior schools and its demographics are similar. A total of 39 students participated in the study. We report results from the 28 students who completed the post-survey and who gave consent for participation in research. Of those 28 students (ages 12-13), 14 were female and 14 were male.[1]

Each participant attended two hour-long sessions, which were held on back-to-back days. In Session 1, students individually played the game up to a pre-defined stopping point. All students were able to reach this stopping point within fifty minutes of gameplay. Immediately upon reaching the stopping point, each student completed the Session 1 post-survey. We determined the stopping point based on the pilot data, which indicated that the next challenge, the 'Tri-Level Room', was particularly frustrating. Adriana's dialogue utterances were crafted to avert preemptively the frustration arising at this particular point in the game.

At the start of Session 2 on the second day, students first interacted with Adriana. Figure 3 shows a screen-capture from the beginning of an interaction. As with the rest of the gameplay, each student interacted with Adriana individually. We tested two versions of Adriana, one with dialogue and one with monologue, and participants were evenly distributed across the two versions. These interactions lasted an average of 5 minutes, with the shortest lasting just under one minute and the longest lasting almost 10 minutes. The agent's dialogue moves were pre-scripted, with each student receiving a similar progression of textual utterances from Adriana. As students finished their interactions with Adriana, they then proceeded with gameplay in ENGAGE, where they immediately encountered the 'Tri-Level Room'. Students continued playing the game until five minutes before the end of the session (resulting in approximately 40-50 minutes of gameplay for Session 2). Students then completed the Session 2 post-survey.

---

[1] Eleven of these 28 students interacted with a monologue version of Adriana. The monologue and dialogue data were aggregated into the Companion condition described in this paper.

Fig. 3. Adriana the Learning Companion

As in the No-Companion condition, the post-surveys for both Session 1 and Session 2 included the Frustration item, "I felt frustrated while playing the game." The Session 2 post-survey for this Companion condition also included four items about the student's affective response to Adriana, which we will refer to as *Reaction to Adriana*, as well as three demographic questions at the end. In the following section, we examine the results of Frustration and Reaction to Adriana.

5   Results

To analyze the success of Adriana the learning companion, we first examined the self-reported student Frustration. Table 2 summarizes the results of this survey item, broken down by gender and session.

Table 2. Companion Condition: Frustration on Two Post-Surveys, on 5-point Likert Scale

	Female (n = 14)	Male (n = 14)	Overall (n = 28)
Frustration – Session 1	2.39 (SD = 0.87)	1.58 (SD = 0.67)	2.00 (SD = 0.87)
Frustration – Session 2	2.21 (SD = 1.25)	2.07 (SD = 1.27)	2.14 (SD = 1.24)

As with the No-Companion study, a gender gap was evident after Session 1 (before students interacted with the learning companion). In Table 2, this is the row labeled "Frustration – Session 1". Female students reported at this stage an average Frustration of 2.39 on a 5-point Likert Scale, compared to 1.58 for their male classmates. A One-Way ANOVA found this to be statistically significant ($F(1,23) = 6.585$, $p < .05$). However, this gender gap was no longer observed after students interacted with Adriana and then played more of the game (including the part that had previously been found particularly frustrating for students). On the post-survey for Session 2 (in Table 2, this is the row labeled "Frustration – Session 2"), female students reported Frustration at an average of 2.21, statistically equivalent to the 2.07 average for male students (F(1, 26) = 0.09, p = .77). Moreover, there was *not* a significant increase in Frustration overall among all students from Session 1 to Session 2 (as shown in the third column in Table 2), which is noteworthy given the increased complexity of the Session 2 gameplay challenges. However, Frustration did rise for male students from Session 1 to Session 2 (which was also true for the No-Companion version of the game, as seen in Table 1).

In order to better understand these results, we examined the Reaction to Adriana items. There were four such items in which students were asked to agree/disagree with statements on a 5-point Likert scale. Table 3 displays the results for these items. Female students generally responded with higher ratings on all these items compared to their male classmates. While none of the differences is statistically significant, these results echo other findings on gender and learning companions [18] that have shown female students respond favorably to this type of pedagogical agent.

Table 3. Student Responses to Learning Companion, on 5-point Likert Scale

	Female (n = 14)	Male (n = 14)
I enjoyed interacting with Adriana.	3.71 (SD = 1.14)	3.2 (SD = 1.03)
I would enjoy interacting with Adriana again in the future.	3.64 (SD = 1.28)	3.27 (SD = 1.12)
Interacting with Adriana helped me to enjoy playing the game.	3.79 (SD = 1.25)	3.27 (SD = 1.19)
Interacting with Adriana helped me to feel less frustrated while playing the game.	3.36 (SD = 1.08)	2.64 (SD = 1.01)

6   Discussion

Data from pilot studies of the ENGAGE game-based learning environment without a learning companion suggested that female students experienced more frustration. We developed a learning companion designed to mitigate this frustration. We hypothesized that in the version of the game with a learning companion, a gender gap in frustration would be observed after Session 1 (before the learning companion was present), but that this gender gap would no longer be observed after Session 2 when the learning companion was introduced. The results confirmed this hypothesis.

The learning companion Adriana effectively "leveled the playing field" for female students regarding frustration. Notably, female students in the Companion condition actually reported slightly less average frustration after Session 2 than Session 1, in contrast to the reverse finding in the No-Companion condition. While frustration still rose for male students from Session 1 to Session 2, classroom observations suggest that this frustration stems from several other causes including the increased difficulty of the challenges in Session 2. Female students also still face these same alternative sources of frustration, but Adriana's intervention here mitigated the *additional* burden of being frustrated with gameplay mechanics. While not all frustration necessarily inhibits learning [31], these results suggest that the learning companion did improve gender equity in this game-based learning experience.

It is important to note that the two conditions described in this paper were not designed simultaneously as part of a controlled experiment. The larger ENGAGE study, which this paper refers to as the No-Companion condition, was conducted as an authentic classroom study in which students played the game in pairs. The study of the learning companion, referred to as the Companion condition, was conducted in a controlled manner, with students playing the game individually. An additional limitation is that there were two versions of the learning companion tested in the Companion condition, as part of an original study design to compare monologue with dialogue for the agent. However, there were no significant differences in student survey responses between the two versions of the learning companion, although interactions with the monologue version were several minutes shorter on average than those with the dialogue version. The Companion condition data were therefore aggregated together.

7   Conclusion and Future Work

Support for underrepresented populations, including underrepresentation based on gender, is of central concern in the design of interactive learning environments. For game-based learning environments, overcoming initial differences in gameplay experience is a particularly promising area for improving equity for learners. This paper has presented results demonstrating the success of a learning companion specifically crafted to mitigate the frustration that comes along with developing proficiency in gameplay mechanics. The learning companion in this study succeeded with female students, who were previously more frustrated than male students.

More broadly, this paper highlights the complex issue of gender equity in game-based learning environments. In designing the ENGAGE game, the research team conducted focus groups with diverse middle school students, created an array of avatars from which students could choose to represent themselves, and adopted best practices from the research community on broadening participation. Even with these careful steps taken, early versions of the game still revealed gender disparities in the level of frustration. The positive results with this prototype learning companion indicate that we need nuanced understanding of where individual game-based learning environments struggle with equity.

This naturally leads to a number of important directions for future research. One important area of investigation is how to create a learning companion with whom students will enjoy conversing many times over a period of time, which is vital for the success of game-based learning environments designed to support long-term interventions. Research on relational agents [32] will guide this future line of inquiry. Another line of future research should examine how to support equity at a finer granularity. Categorizing students in binary fashion as "female" or "male" is a natural distinction, but ultimately we will need to consider all dimensions of a student's identity. Finally, a study of how learning companions can support collaborative game-based learning is an important direction, as related research on pedagogical agents that support collaboration within intelligent tutoring systems has shown promise [33]. With continued research and appropriate interventions, we as a research community can design game-based learning environments that equitably serve all students.

Acknowledgments. The authors wish to thank colleagues from the Center for Educational Informatics for their assistance. This work is supported in part by the National Science Foundation through Grants CNS-113897, CNS-1042468, and IIS-1409639. Any opinions, findings, conclusions, or recommendations expressed in this report are those of the participants, and do not necessarily represent the official views, opinions, or policy of the National Science Foundation.

References

1. Sabourin, J.L., Lester, J.C.: Affect and engagement in game-based learning environments. IEEE Trans Affect Comput **5**, 45–56 (2014)
2. Johnson, W.L.: Serious use of a serious game for language learning. Int J Artif Intell Educ **20**, 175–195 (2010)
3. Kim, J.M., Hill, R.W., Technologies, C., Lane, H.C., Forbell, E., Core, M., Marsella, S., Pynadath, D., Hill Jr, R.W., Durlach, P.J., Hart, J.: BiLAT: A game-based environment for practicing negotiation in a cultural context. Int J Artif Intell Educ **19**, 289–308 (2009)
4. Rowe, J.P., Shores, L.R., Mott, B.W., Lester, J.C.: Integrating Learning, Problem Solving, and Engagement in Narrative-Centered Learning Environments. Int J Artif Intell Educ **21**, 115–133 (2011)
5. Jackson, G.T., McNamara, D.S.: Motivation and performance in a game-based intelligent tutoring system. J Educ Psychol **105**, 1036–1049 (2013)
6. Snow, E.L., Jackson, G.T., Varner, L.K., McNamara, D.S.: Expectations of technology: a factor to consider in game-based learning environments. In: Lane, H., Yacef, K., Mostow, J., Pavlik, P. (eds.) AIED 2013. LNCS, vol. 7926, pp. 359–368. Springer, Heidelberg (2013)
7. Jenson, J., de Castell, S., Bryson, M.: "Girl talk": gender, equity, and identity discourses in a school-based computer culture. Womens Stud Int Forum **26**, 561–573 (2003)
8. Shah, N., Lewis, C., Caires, R.: Analyzing Equity in Collaborative Learning Situations: A Comparative Case Study in Elementary Computer Science. Int. Conf. Learn. Sci. Conf. pp 495–502 (2014)
9. Plant, E.A., Baylor, A.L., Doerr, C.E., Rosenberg-Kima, R.B.: Changing Middle-School Students' Attitudes and Performance Regarding Engineering With Computer-Based Social Models. Comput Educ **53**, 209–215 (2009)
10. Chou, C.-Y., Chan, T.-W., Lin, C.-J.: Redefining the Learning Companion: The Past, Present, and Future of Educational Agents. Comput Educ **40**, 255–269 (2003)
11. Lester, J.C., Converse, S.A., Kahler, S.E., Barlow, S.T., Stone, B.A., Bhogal, R.S.: The persona effect: affective impact of animated pedagogical agents. In: Proc. SIGCHI Conf. Hum. Factors Comput. Syst. - CHI 1997. pp 359–366 (1997)
12. Miksatko, J., Kipp, K.H., Kipp, M.: The persona zero-effect: evaluating virtual character benefits on a learning task with repeated interactions. In: Safonova, A. (ed.) IVA 2010. LNCS, vol. 6356, pp. 475–481. Springer, Heidelberg (2010)
13. Baylor, A.L., Kim, Y.: Validating Pedagogical Agent Roles: Expert, Motivator, and Mentor, pp. 463–466. World Conf. Educ. Multimedia, Hypermedia Telecommun (2003)
14. Biswas, G., Leelawong, K., Schwartz, D., Vye, N.: Learning by Teaching: A New Agent Paradigm for Educational Software. Appl Artif Intell **19**, 363–392 (2005)

15. Chase, C.C., Chin, D.B., Oppezzo, M.A., Schwartz, D.L.: Teachable Agents and the Protégé Effect: Increasing the Effort Towards Learning. J Sci Educ Technol **18**, 334–352 (2009)
16. Arroyo, I., Woolf, B.P., Royer, J.M., Tai, M.: Affective gendered learning companions. In: Proc. of AIED 2009. pp 41–48 (2009)
17. Silvervarg, A., Raukola, K., Haake, M., Gulz, A.: The effect of visual gender on abuse in conversation with ECAs. In: Nakano, Y., Neff, M., Paiva, A., Walker, M. (eds.) IVA 2012. LNCS, vol. 7502, pp. 153–160. Springer, Heidelberg (2012)
18. Arroyo, I., Woolf, B.P., Cooper, D.G., Burleson, W., Muldner, K.: The impact of animated pedagogical agents on girls' and boys' emotions, attitudes, behaviors and learning. In: 2011 IEEE 11th Int. Conf. Adv. Learn. Technol. IEEE, pp 506–510 (2011)
19. Kim, Y., Wei, Q., Xu, B., Ko, Y., Ilieva, V.: MathGirls: toward developing girls' positive attitude and self-efficacy through pedagogical agents. In: Proc. of AIED 2007. pp. 119–126 (2007)
20. Kim, D.Y., Baylor, A.L.: Pedagogical Agents as Learning Companions: The Role of Agent Competency and Type of Interaction. Educ Technol Res Dev **54**, 223–243 (2014)
21. Burleson, W., Picard, R.: Evidence for Gender Specific Approaches to the Development of Emotionally Intelligent Learning Companions. IEEE Intell Syst J **22**, 62–69 (2007)
22. Arroyo, I., Burleson, W., Tai, M., Muldner, K., Woolf, B.P.: Gender differences in the use and benefit of advanced learning technologies for mathematics. J Educ Psychol **105**, 957–969 (2013)
23. Woolf, B.P., Arroyo, I., Muldner, K., Burleson, W., Cooper, D.G., Dolan, R., Christopherson, R.M.: The effect of motivational learning companions on low achieving students and students with disabilities. In: Aleven, V., Kay, J., Mostow, J. (eds.) ITS 2010, Part I. LNCS, vol. 6094, pp. 327–337. Springer, Heidelberg (2010)
24. Rader, E., Echelbarger, M., Cassell, J.: Brick by brick: iterating interventions to bridge the achievement gap with virtual peers. In: Proc. 2011 Annu. Conf. Hum. factors Comput. Syst. - CHI 2011. pp. 2971–2974 (2011)
25. Wing, J.M.: Computational Thinking. Commun ACM **49**, 33 (2006)
26. Frankosky, M.H., Wiebe, E.N., Buffum, P.S., Boyer, K.E.: Spatial Ability and Other Predictors of Gameplay Time: Understanding Barriers to Learning in Game-based Virtual Environments. AERA Appl. Res. Immersive Environ. Learn. SIG (2015). to appear
27. O'Brien, H.L.O., Toms, E.G.: The Development and Evaluation of a Survey to Measure User Engagement. J Am Soc Inf Sci **61**, 50–69 (2010)
28. Bickmore, T., Schulman, D., Yin, L.: Engagement vs. deceit: virtual humans with human autobiographies. In: Ruttkay, Z., Kipp, M., Nijholt, A., Vilhjálmsson, H.H. (eds.) IVA 2009. LNCS, vol. 5773, pp. 6–19. Springer, Heidelberg (2009)
29. Gulz, A., Haake, M., Silvervarg, A.: Extending a teachable agent with a social conversation module – effects on student experiences and learning. In: Biswas, G., Bull, S., Kay, J., Mitrovic, A. (eds.) AIED 2011. LNCS, vol. 6738, pp. 106–114. Springer, Heidelberg (2011)
30. Ogan, A., Aleven, V., Jones, C., Kim, J.: Persistent effects of social instructional dialog in a virtual learning environment. In: Biswas, G., Bull, S., Kay, J., Mitrovic, A. (eds.) AIED 2011. LNCS, vol. 6738, pp. 238–246. Springer, Heidelberg (2011)
31. Baker, R.S.J., D'Mello, S.K.D., Rodrigo, M.M.T., Graesser, A.C.: Better to be frustrated than bored: The incidence, persistence, and impact of learners' cognitive–affective states during interactions with three different computer-based learning environments. Int J Hum Comput Stud **68**, 223–241 (2010)
32. Bickmore, T.W., Picard, R.W.: Establishing and maintaining long-term human-computer relationships. ACM Trans Comput Interact **12**, 293–327 (2005)
33. Kumar, R., Ai, H., Beuth, J.L., Rosé, C.P.: Socially capable conversational tutors can be effective in collaborative learning situations. In: Aleven, V., Kay, J., Mostow, J. (eds.) ITS 2010, Part I. LNCS, vol. 6094, pp. 156–164. Springer, Heidelberg (2010)

Comparing Representations for Learner Models in Interactive Simulations

Cristina Conati[✉], Lauren Fratamico, Samad Kardan, and Ido Roll

University of British Columbia, V6T1Z4, Vancouver, Canada
{conati,fratamic,skardan}@cs.ubc.ca, ido.roll@ubc.ca

Abstract. Providing adaptive support in Exploratory Learning Environments is necessary but challenging due to the unstructured nature of interactions. This is especially the case for complex simulations such as the DC Circuit Construction Kit used in this work. To deal with this complexity, we evaluate alternative representations that capture different levels of detail in student interactions. Our results show that these representations can be effectively used in the user modeling framework proposed in [2], including behavior discovery and user classification, for student assessment and providing real-time support. We discuss trade-offs between high and low levels of detail in the tested interaction representations in terms of their ability to evaluate learning and inform feedback.

Keywords: Educational data mining · Clustering · User modeling · Interactive simulations · Exploratory learning environments

1 Introduction

Interactive simulations are educational tools that can foster student-driven, exploratory learning by allowing students to proactively experiment with concrete examples of concepts and processes they have learned in theory. There is increasing research in Intelligent Tutoring System (ITS) to endow these interactive simulations and other types of Exploratory Learning Environments (ELE from now on) with the ability to provide student-adaptive support for those students who may not learn effectively from these rather unstructured, open-ended activities [2–5]. Providing this support entails building a user-model that can estimate the learner's proficiency in learning via exploration and need for help during interaction. However, building such a model is especially challenging because it is relatively unclear how to operationalize exploration skills and difficult to define a priori which behaviors are conductive to learning.

Some previous work has dealt with the challenge by limiting the exploratory nature of the interaction [4, 6]. In contrast, Kardan and Conati [2] proposed a student modeling framework that learns from action logs which student behaviors should trigger help during interaction with an ELE. *Clustering* is used to identify students who behave and

---

Cristina Conati, Lauren Fratamico, Samad Kardan, Ido Roll—All authors have contributed equally to this work and are listed alphabetically.

C. Conati et al. (Eds.): AIED 2015, LNAI 9112, pp. 74–83, 2015.
DOI: 10.1007/978-3-319-19773-9_8

learn similarly from the interaction. Asso*ciation rule mining* is applied to derive distinguishing interaction behaviors from the clusters, and these behaviors are leveraged to drive the provision of adaptive support in real time during interaction. This student modeling framework was successfully applied to provide adaptive support in the CSP applet, an ELE for a constraint satisfaction algorithm [7]. The part of the CSP applet used in [7] involves a limited number of actions and thus it was sufficient to represent student behaviors in terms of raw actions. This simple representation did not scale up when we tried to apply the framework to a more complex simulation that provides over a hundred types of actions for exploring concepts related to electricity, the PhET DC Circuit Construction Kit (CCK). Thus, in [5] we proposed a richer, multi-layer representation of *action-events* that includes information on individual actions (e.g., join), as well as the manipulated components (e.g., light bulbs), the relevant family of actions (e.g., revise), and the observed outcome (e.g., changes to light intensity). We showed that clustering interaction behaviors based on this representation succeeds in identifying students with different learning outcomes in CCK.

In this paper, we provide a comprehensive evaluation of this multi-layer representation as the basis to apply the student modeling framework proposed in [2] to CCK. The evaluation is in terms of ability to *identify learners* with high- or low- learning gains, suitability for *user modeling* (i.e. to classify new students in terms of their learning performance as they work with CCK), and for *defining the content of adaptive support* during interaction. Furthermore, we use these evaluation dimensions to compare alternative representations derived from the multi-layer structure in [5], which capture different aspects of interaction behaviors at different levels of granularity. Our results show both classification accuracies comparable to those reported in [7], as well as that the approach succeeds in discovering association rules that can be leveraged to design interactive support, thus providing evidence on the generality of this student modeling framework across representations. We further discuss tradeoffs between evaluation dimensions that need to be considered when choosing the most suitable representation for assessing and supporting students during interaction with ELE as complex as CCK.

In the rest of the paper we first discuss related work. Then, we describe the CCK simulation and the study used for collecting data. Next, we present the different representations we evaluated, and summarize the user modeling approach we used. After presenting the evaluation results, we conclude with a general discussion of findings, contributions, limitations, and future work.

2   Related Work

Most of the work done so far on providing adaptive feedback in interactive simulations has dealt with the challenge of how to identify when and how a student needs support by limiting the exploratory nature of the interaction. For instance, the simulations developed by Hussain et al. [8] provide feedback on how to behave in pre-defined cultural/language-related scenarios with clear definition of correct answers/behaviors. The Chemistry VLab [9] provides help on well-defined steps required to run a scientific experiment. Science ASSISTments [4] provides feedback on the specific problem of controlling for variables in experimental design. Work on designing adaptive support for more open-ended exploratory interactions has relied either on expert knowledge (e.g., [10] and [3]) or on data-mining (e.g. [7] and [11]) to identify suitable feedback strategies. The work in [11], which provides scaffolding to students using an environment that supports learning by teaching an artificial student, relies on knowing a priori which students learned or not from the system to mine the relevant feedback strategies. In contrast, the approach successfully evaluated in [7], and adopted in this paper, groups learners via clustering on their interaction behaviors alone (with little processing), without using additional information.

3   The CCK Simulation and User Study

The CCK simulation is part of PhET [12], a freely-available and widely-used suite of simulations in different science and math topics. CCK includes 124 different types of actions to build and test DC circuits by connecting different components including wires, light bulbs, resistors, batteries, and measurement instruments (Figure 1). The available actions include adding, moving, joining, splitting, and removing components, as well as changing the attributes of components (such as resistance). Additional actions relate to the interface (such as changing views) or the simulation itself (such as resetting the simulation). CCK provides animated responses with regard to the state of the circuits on the testbed. For instance, when a light bulb is connected to the circuit, the light intensity and speed of electrons change with variation of the current.

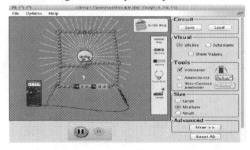

Fig. 1. The CCK simulation

CCK is a tool and instructors define activities outside the environment. Being an inquiry environment, not all students make optimal use of the simulation. Our long-term goal is to assess the effectiveness of students' behaviors in CCK and provide explicit support to foster learning.

Data used in this paper was collected from 96 first-year physics students who participated in a laboratory user study described in [5, 13] and who had less-than-perfect pre-test scores. In the study, participants completed two 25-minute activities. The first activity, on the topic of light bulbs, had different conditions of external scaffolding (using tables and prompts). In contrast, the second activity, on the topic of resistors, was identical for all learners, and included only minimal guidance. Thus, here we focus on data only from the second activity. Students were told to "investigate how resistors affect the behaviors of circuits" and were given advice to combine resistors with different resistances. The students were expected to use CCK to help them explore this learning goal. As this was their second activity with the simulation, all students were proficient with the testbed. Students were assessed on their conceptual knowledge before and after the activities, with the pre-test being a subset of the post-test. To avoid priming students, the pre-test only included questions not related to specific circuits (e.g., comparing the current in two different resistors with different resistances), whereas the post-test also included questions on specific circuit diagrams.

4   Representing the User Actions

Clustering students based on their actions requires a representation that captures important aspects of these actions. However, the large variety of actions available in CCK, together with their contextual nature, makes clustering challenging. Notably, action outcomes depend on the state of the simulation. For example, connecting a wire leads to different outcomes based on the state of the circuit (e.g., existence of a battery) and testing instruments (e.g., how they are connected). The CCK logs information on the type of action, the component used, and the response of the physical model. In addition, actions with one component often affect other components (e.g., changes to batteries affect existing light bulbs).

As described in [5], we created a structured representation that can capture these "action-events" – i.e., user actions and their relevant contextual information - at different levels of granularity. The structure contains four layers: "actions" describe the action that students took, e.g., *join* (25 types). "Components", describe the manipulated component, e.g., *wire* (22 different types). "Family" denotes the general type of action, and there are 8 families in the structure. Common families include: *Build* (describes actions such as adding, removing, and joining components, before the circuit is live), *Test* (describes actions with the measurement instruments), *Organize* (describe actions that re-arrange circuit components without making any structural changes), and *Revise* (describe all build actions that take place on a working circuit). Finally, "outcomes" capture what happens in the circuit after an action is performed. There are 6 types of outcomes, including: *None*, *Deliberate-measure* (the value displayed on a measurement device is updated as a result of using it), *Current-change* (a change in the current reflected in the speed of movement of electrons), and *Light-intensity-change* (the light intensity of a light bulb changes). One action-event may cause more than one outcome. By creating this structure we have added contextual information to the data. For example the action-event current_change.revise.join.wire describes *joining* (action) a *wire* (component) that led to a *current-change* (outcome) when *revising* a circuit (family). In addition, we captured "pauses" longer than 15 seconds as an additional family of actions, with a single type of (in)action.

While in [5] all 4 layers of the structure were used to represent actions-events, subsets of the layers can represent events at different levels of granularity. In turn, each representation can be used to generate different feature sets based on the types of measures used to summarize the action-events for each user. These measures include: (i) frequency of the action-event, i.e., the proportion of each type of action-event over total action-events (denoted by _f); (ii) mean; and (iii) standard deviation of the time spent before each action-event.

In [5], we described the performance of the action-event feature set using all 4 layers when used to cluster students who learn similarly with CCK. Here, we investigate the effect of levels of granularity in feature set representation on both generating meaningful clusters, as well as on building effective user models and informing feedback, as in [7]. Thus, we generated feature sets that use different subsets of layers in the action-event structure. For each representation, we also experimented with using only frequencies vs. adding time-related summative measures, for a total of 22 different feature sets.

We also tested a feature set that goes beyond actions as units of operation by grouping consecutive actions of the same type into entities called a *block*. We have 6 different blocks, including *Test* (all actions related to using measurement devices), *Construct* (any action that changes the circuit before testing), *Modify* (any action that changes the circuit after testing it), and *Reset* (removing the whole circuit). Each block has two kinds of features: summative features about the block (frequency, average duration and average number of actions within), and specific features about each outcome within the block (for instance, frequency of light-intensity-changes within a construct block).

Of the 23 feature sets described above, only 3 generated meaningful clusters that group students in terms of their learning:

1) *OFAC_f*: Set including all action-events elements (Outcome, Family, Action, Component) with frequency information (210 features)
2) *FAC_f*: Same as the first set, but without Outcome. (202 features)
3) OAC_f: Same as the first feature set, but without the Family layer (90 features).

It should be noted that OAC_f is a feature set that requires less feature engineering, as all the three layers included (outcomes, actions and components) were available in the log files with only minor modifications (e.g., calculation of pauses). The Family layer included in the other two feature sets, on the other hand, was defined via extensive discussion among the authors in terms of how best to conceptualize the various actions available in CCK.

Interestingly, all three feature sets include only information on action frequency, indicating that summative statistics capturing how much time student spend before actions are not contributing to identify different learning outcomes. This can be explained by the fact that we capture significant pauses before actions via a specific action and family (Pauses). Alternatively, there may be important timing information over sequences of actions (e.g., planning a certain circuit or running a series of tests), but not in individual actions [9].

5   Evaluating Representations for Assessment and Support

We applied the user modeling framework for ELE, first proposed in [2], to evaluate how well the three feature sets identified above support building user models. The framework consists of two main phases: *Behavior Discovery* and *User Classification*.

In *Behavior Discovery,* each user's interaction data is first pre-processed into feature vectors. Students are then clustered using these vectors in order to identify users with similar interaction behaviors. The resulting clusters are then analyzed to see whether they identify groups of students with different learning outcomes. If they are, the distinctive interaction behaviors in each cluster are identified via association rule mining. This process extracts the common behavior patterns in terms of class association rules in the form of $X \rightarrow c$, where X is a set of feature-value pairs and c is the predicted class label for the data points where X applies. During the association rule mining process, the values of features are discretized into bins [2].

In *User Classification*, the labeled clusters and the corresponding association rules extracted in Behavior Discovery are used to train a classifier student model. As new users interact with the system, they would be classified in real-time into one of the identified clusters, based on a membership score that summarizes how well the user's behaviors match the association rules for each cluster. Thus, in addition to classifying students in terms of learning, this phase returns the specific association rules describing the learner's behaviors that caused the classification. These behaviors can then be used to trigger real-time interventions designed to encourage productive behaviors and discourage detrimental ones, as described in [7].

Based on this framework, the three measures we use to evaluate the feature sets described in the previous section are: (i) *Quality of the generated clusters*, measured by effect size of difference in learning performance between students in the different clusters. (ii) *Classification accuracy* of user models trained on the obtained clusters. (iii) *Usefulness* of the generated association rules in identifying behavior patterns that can be used to design and trigger support to students.

6 Results

6.1 Quality of the Clusters

Table 1 shows the outcome of clustering on the three feature sets. Each row describes one cluster in the optimal number of clusters for that representation. Clusters are named based on their learning performance. The table also reports cluster size (after removing clustering outliers) and the average learning performance of a cluster's members (measured as corrected post-test scores). The last two columns report the p-value and effect size of the difference in learning performance between clusters, obtained via an ANCOVA on the post-test scores, controlling for pre-test. Thus, a larger effect-size suggests a representation that better separates students with different learning levels.

Table 1. Summary statistics for the clustering results

Feature Sets	Cluster	#Members	Average Corrected Post-test	p-value	Effect Size (partial eta squared)
FAC_f	High	67	.596	.048	.041
	Low	29	.534		
OAC_f	High	66	.609	.007	**.076**
	Low	30	.509		
OFAC_f	High	61	.613	.013	.065
	Low	35	.516		

All feature sets generated two clusters, identifying groups of students with high vs. low learning. Effect sizes of the difference in learning performance varied for different feature sets, ranging from small effect size (for *FAC_f*) to medium-small effect (for *OAC_f* and *OFAC_f*). Interestingly, *OAC_f* achieves the highest effect size, showing that the addition of more feature-engineered information (the Family) reduced the differences in learning between the two clusters.

6.2   Classification Accuracy

For each of the three feature sets, a classifier user model is trained on the generated clusters, using 8-fold nested cross validation to set the model's parameters and find its cross-validated accuracy[1]. Table 2 reports classification performance of each classifier in terms of overall accuracy, class accuracy for high and low learners, and kappa scores. The classifiers achieved moderate-to-good kappa values between 0.56 and 0.7. All accuracies are significantly above the baseline, indicating that our user-modeling framework can effectively classify students working with CCK with all three feature-sets. The feature set based on the most detailed representation, *OFAC_f*, is superior to the other 2 sets on all accuracy measures, including being the most balanced classifier. This indicates that the additional level of representation added by the Family level is beneficial for classifier accuracy when all information (action, outcome, component) is leveraged. Also, both feature sets that include Outcome show higher accuracy compared with *FAC_f*, suggesting that the outcome of students' actions, rather than the actions themselves, are most beneficial to identify low vs. high learners.

Table 2. Classifier accuracy measures for different feature sets. Baseline is the accuracy of the most likely classifier.

Feature Sets	Baseline	Overall Accuracy % (Std. dev.)	High Learner Class Accuracy	Low Learner Class Accuracy	Kappa
FAC_f	.698	83.3 (5.9)	.851	.724	.564
OAC_f	.688	84.4 (9.4)	.909	.700	.626
OFAC_f	.653	86.5 (8.8)	**.918**	**.771**	**.702**

6.3   Usefulness for Providing Adaptive Support

Association rules identify behavioral patterns that are representative of what students in a given cluster do with CCK (see [14] for a discussion of how patterns are derived from rules). These patterns are useful if they are associated with low (or high) learning performance that can inform adaptive interventions. Specifically, if a student is classified as a "Low Learner" (LL) at any given point of working with CCK, adaptive interventions can be provided to discourage the LL patterns he is showing and to encourage the HL patterns he is not showing. The number of identified patterns varies greatly among feature sets, ranging from 15 in *OAC_f* to 17 in *FAC_f* to 23 in *OFAC_f*, showing that the most complex representation captures finer grained variations in learner behaviors. Example patterns are shown in Table 3.

While the patterns produced by all three feature sets varied, we identified 4 trends that occurred in at least two feature sets each. This shows that our general approach for

---

[1] The accuracies reported are calculated at the end of the interaction, which presents an upper bound for the accuracy of the model during the interaction.

behavior discovery is able to uncover core behaviors that are stable across representations. One of these trends is related to addition of light bulbs and changes in light intensity. High Leaners (HL) both add light bulbs infrequently and make infrequent changes in light intensity. Since this activity was focused on understanding how resistors work in circuits, light bulbs were likely distractors at best, and possibly interfered with observing the behavior of other resistors. We see the adding light bulb behavior associated with HL in both the *FAC_f* feature set (*Build.add.lightBulb_f = Low*) as well as in the *OFAC_f* feature set further qualified with the outcome (None.*Build.add.lightBulb_f = Low*), as shown in Table 3. We also see HL making changes to light intensity with low frequency in both *OFAC_f* (*light_intensity.Revise.split.junction_f = Low*) and *OAC_f* (*light_intensity.join.wire_f = Low*). The other trends across feature sets show that high leaners do the following actions more frequently: i) use testing devices (to examine the circuit configuration), ii) change the resistance of resistors (possibly to experiment with a range of resistors, as suggested by the activity), and iii) pause (possibly to plan, reflect, and take notes). The first two are intuitively effective behaviors for understanding how resistors work in a circuit. The last one is an indication of learners taking time to best leverage the learning activity.

Table 3. Sample patterns for each feature set (raw form and English description)

Feature Sets	Cluster	Pattern [Description]
FAC_f	HL	Build.add.lightBulb_f = Low [When building, they added light bulbs with low frequency]
	LL	Build.changeResistance.resistor_f = Low [When building, they changed the resistance of resistors with low frequency]
OAC_f	HL	light_intensity.join.wire_f = Low [They joined wires resulting in light intensity change with lower frequency]
	LL	deliberate_measure.traceMeasure.nonContactAmmeter_f = Low [They used the non contact ammeter by tracing with low frequency]
OFAC_f	HL	None.Build.add.lightBulb_f = Low [When building, they added light bulbs resulting in no outcome with low frequency]
	LL	deliberate_measure.Test.startMeasure.voltmeter_f = Low [When testing, they used the voltmeter with low frequency]

Next we evaluate the usefulness of these patterns to inform support. One criterion for doing so is level of detail. Naturally, this depends on the granularity of the corresponding feature set in the different representations. Thus, behaviors in *OFAC_f* give the most contextual information about timing and can be used to give students feedback with regard to the *outcome* of desired actions, *what* to do to achieve that outcome in terms of a high level behavior, and *how* to achieve it using specific action and component. For example, a hint based on the pattern in Table 3 for LL in *OFAC_f* could suggest students to do more deliberate measurements (*outcome*), achieve this by testing more (*what* to do), and, if necessary, give an even more specific suggestion to use the voltmeter (*how*). In contrast, both of the other two feature sets cannot give one of those layers of hints. *OAC_f* can only tell students the *outcome* of what they need to do and the specifics of *how* to do it, but a more general level of information is missing. For example, based on the LL rule for OAC_f, students can be told to trace with the non-contact ammeter more often, but there is no general "test more" hint. *FAC_f* can only tell students *what* to do and the specifics of *how* to do it, but cannot tell them the *outcome* to achieve. For example, students can be told to change the resistance of their resistors more often, but without emphasizing the desired outcomes.

The richer level of detail available due to the nature of the $OFAC\_f$ representation lends itself well to provide sequences of hints with narrowing specificity (a well-established approach to hint provision in ITS). For instance, a first level of hint could tell the student the *outcome* that they should try to achieve, then, if needed a second level of hint could suggest the family (*what* to do at the high level), followed by a hint on *how* to do it. The OAC_f and FAC_f feature sets do not support this hint progression, though missing levels could be inferred. For example, if the detailed hint suggests to trace more with the non-contact ammeter, a hint could still first suggest general testing.

7   Discussion and Conclusion

To summarize our results, we found the OAC_f feature set to be the best for identifying high versus low learners. This feature set does not include the knowledge-engineered Family layer. However, it was the feature set based on the most complex representation, $OFAC\_f$, that scored highest in terms of classifier accuracy. It was also the set that identified the largest number of behavioral patterns, 23, and that can provide richer levels of feedback to the students. In summary, our comparison of representations that differ in the level of granularity has identified a trade-off between suitability to provide support and quality of the clusters: hints generated by the most complex representation in $OFAC\_f$ would target the right students due to a high classification accuracy, can give detailed support, and can provide the largest number of hints. On the other hand, the representation with the least amount of feature engineering, OAC_f, generates rules that come from higher quality clusters, albeit offers fewer hints, with fewer levels of support. These hints may also be given inappropriately due to lower model accuracy. An experimental evaluation is required to see how this tradeoff impacts the effectiveness of interventions in an adaptive version of CCK. Thus, generating different adaptive versions of CCK based on the classifiers and behavior patterns identified in this paper is one of the next steps of this research.

More importantly, the results in this paper provides evidence on the generality of the user-modeling framework we used for our evaluation. This framework had already been successfully applied for modeling students and providing support in a rather simple simulation for an AI algorithm [7]. Here we show that it can transfer to more complex ELE such as CCK, at least in terms of successfully classifying student learning at the end of the interaction (all classifiers discussed in this paper achieved respectable kappa values, higher than 0.55) and identifying interaction behaviors intuitively associated with more/less effective learning. One of the next steps of this research is investigating how to design real-time hints that can foster the productive patterns and discourage the others as we did in [7]. This includes investigating the overtime accuracy of the classifier user model. Another step of future work is to further test the generality of this modeling framework by applying it to another simulation of the PhET family. This will allow us to identify productive patterns across simulations and domains and bring us closer to addressing the challenge of a general modeling framework for interactive simulations.

References

1. Perera, D., Kay, J., Koprinska, I., Yacef, K., Zaiane, O.R.: Clustering and Sequential Pattern Mining of Online Collaborative Learning Data. IEEE Transactions on Knowledge and Data Engineering. **21**, 759–772 (2009)
2. Kardan, S., Conati, C.: A framework for capturing distinguishing user interaction behaviours in novel interfaces. In: Proc. of the 4th Int. Conf. on Educational Data Mining. pp. 159–168. Eindhoven, the Netherlands (2011)
3. Mavrikis, M., Gutierrez-Santos, S., Geraniou, E., Noss, R.: Design requirements, student perception indicators and validation metrics for intelligent exploratory learning environments. Personal and Ubiquitous Computing, pp. 1–16
4. Gobert, J.D., Pedro, M.A.S., Baker, R.S.J.D., Toto, E., Montalvo, O.: Leveraging Educational Data Mining for Real-time Performance Assessment of Scientific Inquiry Skills within Microworlds. JEDM - Journal of Educational Data Mining. **4**, 111–143 (2012)
5. Kardan, S., Roll, I., Conati, C.: The usefulness of log based clustering in a complex simulation environment. In: Trausan-Matu, S., Boyer, K.E., Crosby, M., Panourgia, K. (eds.) ITS 2014. LNCS, vol. 8474, pp. 168–177. Springer, Heidelberg (2014)
6. Westerfield, G., Mitrovic, A., Billinghurst, M.: Intelligent augmented reality training for assembly tasks. In: Lane, H., Yacef, K., Mostow, J., Pavlik, P. (eds.) AIED 2013. LNCS, vol. 7926, pp. 542–551. Springer, Heidelberg (2013)
7. Kardan, S., Conati, C.: Providing adaptive support in an interactive simulation for learning. an experimental evaluation. In: Proceedings of CHI 2015, (to appear)
8. Hussain, T.S., Roberts, B., Menaker, E.S., Coleman, S.L., Pounds, K., Bowers, C., Cannon-Bowers, J.A., Murphy, C., Koenig, A., Wainess, R. et al.: Designing and developing effective training games for the US Navy. In: The Interservice/Industry Training, Simulation & Education Conference (I/ITSEC). NTSA (2009)
9. Borek, A., McLaren, B.M., Karabinos, M., Yaron, D.: How much assistance is helpful to students in discovery learning? In: Cress, U., Dimitrova, V., Specht, M. (eds.) EC-TEL 2009. LNCS, vol. 5794, pp. 391–404. Springer, Heidelberg (2009)
10. Roll, I., Aleven, V., Koedinger, K.R.: The invention lab: using a hybrid of model tracing and constraint-based modeling to offer intelligent support in inquiry environments. In: Intelligent Tutoring Systems, pp. 115–124. Springer (2010)
11. Leelawong, K., Biswas, G.: Designing Learning by Teaching Agents: The Betty's Brain System. International Journal of Artificial Intelligence in Education. **18**, 181–208 (2008)
12. Wieman, C.E., Adams, W.K., Perkins, K.K.: PhET: Simulations That Enhance Learning. Science. **322**, 682–683 (2008)
13. Roll, I., Yee, N., Cervantes, A.: Not a magic bullet: the effect of scaffolding on knowledge and attitudes in online simulations. In: Proc. of Int. Conf. of the Learning Sciences, pp. 879–886 (2014)
14. Kardan, S., Conati, C.: Evaluation of a data mining approach to providing adaptive support in an open-ended learning environment: a pilot study. In: AIED 2013 Workshops Proceedings vol. 2, pp. 41–48 (2013)

Games Are Better than Books: In-Situ Comparison of an Interactive Job Interview Game with Conventional Training

Ionut Damian[1]([✉]), Tobias Baur[1], Birgit Lugrin[1], Patrick Gebhard[2], Gregor Mehlmann[1], and Elisabeth André[1]

[1] Augsburg University, Augsburg, Germany
{damian,baur,lugrin,mehlmann,andre}@hcm-lab.de
[2] DFKI GmbH - Saarbrücken, Saarbrücken, Germany
gebhard@dfki.de

Abstract. Technology-enhanced learning environments are designed to help users practise social skills. In this paper, we present and evaluate a virtual job interview training game which has been adapted to the special requirements of young people with low chances on the job market. The evaluation spanned three days, during which we compared the technology-enhanced training with a traditional learning method usually practised in schools, i.e. reading a job interview guide. The results are promising as professional career counsellors rated the pupils who trained with the system significantly better than those who learned with the traditional method.

Keywords: Technology-enhanced training · Serious game · Social coaching · Job interview · NEET · User study · Virtual agent

1 Introduction

As a consequence of worldwide economical and financial crisis throughout the last decade, many countries are facing a rising number of people who are not in employment, education or training (NEETs). Especially young adults with low socio-emotional and interaction skills [8,12], such as a lack of self-confidence or sense of their own strengths struggle to convince recruiters of their fit in a company during job interviews. To address this issue, governments take action by introducing job interview training early in graduation years of school as well as support various organisations which coach youngsters in finding jobs and improving social skills pertinent for job interviews.

Compared to classical learning approaches (e.g. coaching), technology-enhanced solutions such as serious games present themselves as viable and advantageous alternatives [16]. Their automated nature gives users access to personalized feedback without the need for human coaches, improving scalability and repeatability. This reduces the running costs of such systems making them a viable solution for a larger user group.

© Springer International Publishing Switzerland 2015
C. Conati et al. (Eds.): AIED 2015, LNAI 9112, pp. 84–94, 2015.
DOI: 10.1007/978-3-319-19773-9_9

From a recruiters point of view, the goal of a job interview is to determine the fit of the candidate to a particular position in the company by evaluating the candidate's verbal (i.e. content of utterance) and nonverbal behaviour (e.g. use of voice, gestures, postures, facial expressions). Nonverbal behaviour is particularly critical as research shows it takes a significant role during interpersonal interaction [4,13]. Furthermore, studies [5,9] show that nonverbal behaviour has a large impact on the outcome of a job interview. Training such behaviour can therefore be very beneficial to improving ones chances for employment.

In this paper we investigate the potential of a virtual job interview game for training young adults. The application was developed in scope of a larger research project [1] that aims at creating a scenario-based simulation platform for young people to explore, practise and improve their social skills in the domain of job interviews. We build upon this application by adapting it to a narrower target group, i.e. 13 to 16 year old pupils from a German school of lower education.

In the resulting system, the user takes part in a gamified job interview led by a virtual character. Using social signal processing techniques, the system records and analyses the user's nonverbal behaviours which are used to trigger actions for the virtual characters in realtime, but also as material for the debriefing phase.

The system is evaluated in a three day study during which we measured the impact of the system on the pupils' job interview performance and compared it to a conventional learning method commonly used by the school (learning from a written job interview guide). We were able to measure statistical significant improvements for the pupils who interacted with the system but not for those who used the written job interview guide. Furthermore, after the final day, professional practitioners rated the overall performance of the pupils who used the system significantly better than of those who used the written job interview guide.

2   Related Work

A variety of methodologies have been developed for training social behaviour. Most common techniques involve the learner memorizing certain behavioural patterns either from a written source or from audio or video tutorials. More advanced forms rely on human coaches who help the learner practise the learned behaviours through the use of various exercises such as role-plays [7,11] and video feedback.

Computerized social skill training tools have seen rapid evolution in the recent years due to advances in the areas of social signal processing as well as improving virtual characters. Such tools are meant to complement or even substitute traditional training approaches [2,10,14].

The effectiveness of such technology-enhanced learning systems has been the focus of various studies in the recent years. Investigations conducted by Pan et al. [14], for example, suggest that a party simulation involving a virtual female agent can help reduce social anxiety in young adult males. Sapouna et al. [15] studied the effect of a virtual learning system to reduce the bullying victimisation rate of children in schools. Their results show that the system had a positive effect on the children's abilities to cope with bullying. Hoque et al. [10] explored the impact of a job interview training environment on MIT students. They conclude that students who used the system to train, experienced a larger performance increase than students who used conventional methods. These results are encouraging for our research. However, while Hoque et al. recruited MIT students as participants, our target group was job-seeking youths who have been categorized as being at risk of exclusion. The ambition of our work was to perform an in-situ study at a local school to investigate the impact of a job interview training game on underprivileged youngsters. Furthermore, the study was embedded in the existing curriculum of the school. This specific situation raised high expectations from teachers and pupils which had to be met by the software.

To sum up, while related work points out the great potential of technology-enhanced training, to the best of our knowledge none managed to ecologically validate the effectiveness of such tools in the domain of job interviews in-situ, i.e. in a school with real job seekers at risk of exclusion.

3   User Group

The aim of the present contribution is to test a job interview training system, which was developed as part of our previous work [1], in-situ and evaluate it with final year pupils in the age range of 13 to 16 of a school in Bavaria, Germany. Unlike schools in most other countries, the Bavarian school system foresees the same education for all children only for the first four years of education. Afterwards, children are split up to join different school types based on the grades in the fourth grade and their parents intention, and are assigned to either *Mittelschule* (preparing for vocational education), *Realschule* (providing a broader range of education for intermediate pupils) and *Gymnasium* (prepares pupils to study at a university). One of the effects of this structure is that pupils who join a *Mittelschule* receive a lower level of education and thus have fewer chances to find a qualified job, especially as they have to compete with pupils of a higher education due to the current situation on the job market.

Regarding the overall aim of our project (to help youngsters that are in danger of not finding a job), pupils in the final grades of the *Mittelschule* are best suited for our target user group. Their lack of job interview pertinent skills is also known to their teachers. To help their pupils prepare to find a job, eight-graders of a *Mittelschule* are given lectures on writing applications and curricula vitae as well as instructions on job interviews. "Many of our pupils are having a hard time preparing to find a job and many have no assistance from their parents." says the deputy headmaster of our cooperating *Mittelschule*. "A technical system that puts pupils into prototypical situations in job interviews would be very helpful for their preparation."

4   Technology-Enhanced Training System

The training system was developed as part of the European Project TARDIS [1]. The aim of the project was to help young adults improve their nonverbal

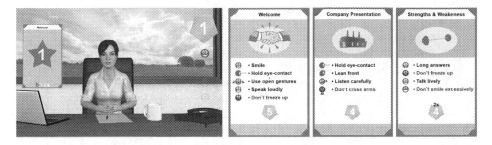

Fig. 1. The virtual character playing the role of an interviewer (left). The game cards give hints to the pupils regarding appropriate behaviour for upcoming interview phases (right).

behaviour during job interviews. The system enables users to take part in a job interview simulation where a virtual character plays the role of the recruiter (Figure 1 (left)). The virtual character is able to perform both proactive and reactive behaviour.

The proactive behaviour consists of a series of questions asked by the virtual character. After each question, the virtual character waits for the user to answer while displaying backchanneling behaviour, such as nodding, head tilting, maintaining or breaking eye gaze. To facilitate such reactive behaviour the system analyses the nonverbal behaviour (gestures, postures, body expressivity, facial expressions and use of voice) of the user in realtime during the interaction using social signal processing techniques and various sensors [2,6].

Besides impacting the behaviour of the virtual character, the results of the behaviour analysis are also stored for later use in a semi-automatic debriefing phase. During this phase, the user's recorded behaviour is displayed side-by-side with the virtual character's behaviour to facilitate an easy analysis of the interaction [3]. This supports the identification of critical incidents which might have an impact on the outcome of a real interview. Furthermore, various metrics are extracted from the behaviour of the user to enable between-session comparison and improvement tracking.

To ensure the system was suitable for deployment in the learning environment of our cooperating *Mittelschule*, we conducted workshops with the teachers at different stages of the prototype. Due to their long experience in working with the pupils, the teachers were able to provide us with detailed feedback regarding teaching pitfalls and motivation techniques. Based on their recommendations, the system was incrementally adapted to meet the requirements and abilities of the pupils. The largest concern the teachers had regarded the system's ability to keep the pupils engaged and motivated. Thus, various game-like elements have been added to the system. More precisely, we introduced physical game cards (Figure 1 (right)) which are similar in appearance to those of classic board games and give hints on how to behave during the interview. A scoring system keeps track of how well a pupil follows these hints. For example, if the pupil smiles at an appropriate moment, the score will get incremented by one.

Fig. 2. Mock job interview with professional career trainers (left) and interaction with job interview training system (right)

The score is meant to act as an incentive to replay the game in order to achieve a better score.

Further, we implemented two job interview scenarios which teachers characterized as most appealing for the pupils of our cooperating *Mittelschule*: electromechanical engineer and trained retail salesman. The interview simulation has been split up into three phases (*Welcome, Company Presentation,* and *Strengths and Weaknesses*) to give the training exercise more structure. For each phase, a specific game card has been designed as illustrated in Figure 1 (right). Prior to each phase, the virtual character instructs the pupil to pick up the corresponding game card, read it carefully and put it back on the table. After each phase, the virtual character gives the user feedback on how she or he performed.

5   Evaluation

In order to test our adapted system with the target user group, we conducted a user study in a cooperating *Mittelschule* (Parkschule in Stadtbergen/Germany). The objective of the user study was twofold: On the one hand we wanted to investigate whether pupils' skills are rated better by practitioners after using the interactive job training game compared to before. On the other hand, we wanted to evaluate whether their skills are rated better, or at least equally well, in comparison with pupils who trained using conventional teaching methods.

Participants. In total, 20 pupils (10 male and 10 female) from the eight and ninth grade (final and second to last years) have been recruited to take part in the study. Participants were aged between 13 and 16 (mean = 14.37; SD = 0.94). The data of one participant had to be removed due to extraordinary circumstances resulting in nervous and unfocused behaviour (she accompanied her friend to the hospital after a minor accident).

Additionally, two career counsellors participated in the study as professional practitioners. The career counsellors are employed full time at Career Service - Augsburg University, where they advise students on choosing suitable

Table 1. Procedure of user study over three days

	experimental group	control group
day 1	mock job interview	mock job interview
day 2	interaction with training system	training with book
day 3	mock job interview	mock job interview

jobs, preparing their application documents such as CV, and training for job interviews.

Procedure and Apparatus. The user study was conducted over the course of three days. An overview of the procedure can be seen in Table 1. On the first day, all pupils participated in mock job interviews led by a practitioner (see Figure 2 (left)). The purpose of these mock interviews on the first day was to establish a baseline regarding the job interview performance of the pupils prior to additional training. Furthermore, as the system's goal is to help the users improve their nonverbal behaviour, the practitioners were also asked to focus on the nonverbal behaviour, i.e. how the participants answer rather than what they say. Two interviews were carried out in parallel in separate rooms whilst each lasted for approximately 7 minutes. This duration was deemed sufficient by the practitioners to get an objective measurement of the pupils' job interview performance. After each mock interview, both pupils and practitioners filled in questionnaires *A* and *B* respectively.

In *Questionnaire A*, practitioners rated 1) the pupil's overall performance, 2) whether they would recommend the pupil for employment, 3) appropriate usage of smiles, 4) appropriate usage of eye contact, 5) appropriate usage of gestures, as well as whether the pupil seemed 6) nervous 7) interested and 8) focused. In *Questionnaire B*, pupils self-reported on whether they thought they 1) performed well in the interview, 2) were nervous, 3) used a lot of filler words such as "er" or "uhm", 3) were focused, 4) were aware of their non-verbal behaviour and 5) performed appropriate non-verbal behaviour. Both Questionnaires used Likert scales ranging from 1 to 7, with a higher value indicating a better performance. The only exception is the dimension nervousness, where a lower score is considered being better.

On the second day, pupils were randomly divided into experimental group (EG) and control group (CG), resulting in four females and six males for the EG and five females and four males for the CG.

The EG interacted with the interactive training system adapted for the school. Figure 2 (right) shows a sample interaction with the system where a pupil analyses one of the game cards, before starting the interaction phase. The participant was seated at a school desk with a Microsoft Kinect and a webcam positioned to face her or him. During the interaction, the participant was also wearing a close-talk microphone. Each training lasted for about 15 minutes, split between game interaction and debriefing. During the training session, the pupils' nonverbal behaviour was recorded and analysed by the system. In the

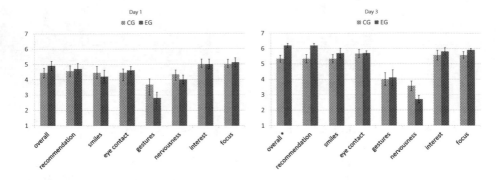

Fig. 3. Practitioners' ratings of day one (left) and day three (right) comparing CG and EG. Dimensions marked with * present significant differences between the two groups.

debriefing phase, a researcher assisted the pupils in reviewing their performance using the debriefing mode of the training system. However, the researcher only provided technical support with the system and helped the pupils understand the interface.

Pupils of the CG were reading a job interview guide[1] for the same amount of time. The written guide is published by a local youth advisory institution and regularly used by our cooperating school to prepare their pupils for job trainings.

On the third day, a second round of mock job interviews was conducted with each participant. Pupils of both groups (EG and CG) were brought to the practitioners in random order, who were unaware of which condition the pupils have been assigned to during the second day. After each mock interview, pupils and practitioners filled in the same questionnaire they filled in during day one (questionnaires A and B respectively). This allowed us to compare the pupils' performance between day one and three.

5.1   Results

To determine the quality of the results we used independent two-tailed t-tests when comparing between groups, and paired two-tailed t-tests when comparing between days. In both cases we apply the Bonferroni-Holm error correction method to adjust the significance levels. Analysing the first day of our experimental setup, no significant differences were found in questionnaires A and B comparing pupils that were later assigned to either join EG or CG, using the independent two-tailed t-test (see Figure 3 (left)).

Comparing the two groups again after the third day (after either having used the system or the written guide on the second day and performing a second mock interview on the third day) revealed interesting insights. We found statistically significant differences for the practitioners' ratings on overall performance

---

[1] https://www.aok-on.de/bayern/berufseinsteiger/beruf-zukunft/
koerpersprache-im-vorstellungsgespraech/

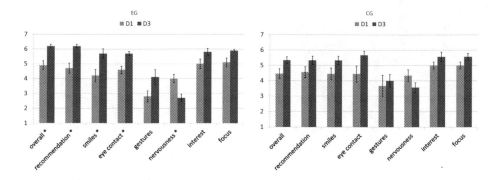

Fig. 4. Practitioners' ratings of EG (left) and CG (right) across day one and three. Dimensions marked with * present significant differences between the two days.

($p = 0.004$, $\alpha = 0.006$), indicating that pupils of the EG were rated better compared to pupils of the CG. A strong trend was also found for the recommendation dimension ($p = 0.012$, $\alpha = 0.007$). All other dimensions were also rated better for the EG than for the CG, albeit not significant. Figure 3 (right) illustrates these results.

In order to evaluate the improvement of performance for each group individually, we compared the results within groups between day one and three. Our tests revealed significant differences for the EG for the dimensions recommendation ($p = 0.005$, $\alpha = 0.006$), overall performance ($p = 0.006$, $\alpha = 0.007$), nervousness ($p = 0.006$, $\alpha = 0.007$), eye contact ($p = 0.007$, $\alpha = 0.010$) and smiles ($p = 0.012$, $\alpha = 0.013$) (Figure 4 (left)). No significant improvements in the practitioners' ratings have been found for the CG when comparing day three to day one (Figure 4 (right)). However, trends have been found for smiles ($p = 0.021$, $\alpha = 0.006$), overall performance ($p = 0.035$, $\alpha = 0.007$) and eye contact ($p = 0.047$, $\alpha = 0.007$).

Regarding the pupils' self-assessment, no significant differences were found between the two groups on the first and third day. However on the third day, a strong trend was found for the nervousness dimension ($p = 0.030$, $\alpha = 0.008$), with pupils of the EG rating themselves as less nervous than pupils of the CG. Comparing the two days for each group separately, reveals a significant difference on the nervousness dimension ($p = 0.001$, $\alpha = 0.008$) for the EG only, with participants rating themselves being less nervous on the third day compared to the first day.

Table 2 gives an overview of the mean ratings from both questionnaires on the first and on the third day for both conditions.

5.2 Discussion

The analysis of the questionnaire data on the first day of our experiment revealed no significant differences, suggesting that the pupils were performing equally well

Table 2. Mean values of control group (CG) and experimental group (EG) on first and third day. Significant differences between groups on a particular day are written in bold and marked with *. Significant differences within groups between days are written in italic and marked with ‡.

Questionnaire A	day 1 CG	EG	day 3 CG	EG	Questionnaire B	day 1 CG	EG	day 3 CG	EG
overall performance	4.44	*4.9‡*	**5.33***	***6.2‡****	overall performance	4.66	4.6	5.33	5.2
recommendation	4.55	*4.7‡*	5.33	*6.2‡*	nervousness	4.77	*4.2‡*	4.33	*2.2‡*
smiles	4.44	*4.2‡*	5.33	*5.7‡*	use of filler words	4.88	3.4	4.22	3.0
eye contact	4.44	*4.6‡*	5.66	*5.7‡*	focus	4.23	3.9	4.56	4.6
gestures	3.6	2.8	4.0	4.1	aware of n.v. behaviour	5.0	5.0	5.77	5.4
nervousness	4.33	*4.0‡*	3.55	*2.7‡*	n.v. behaviour	5.22	4.7	5.77	5.1
interest	5.0	5.0	5.55	5.8					
focus	5.0	5.1	5.55	5.9					

in their job interviews. We can thus consider differences observed on the third day between the groups to be caused by the training completed on the second day. In general, both groups improved from the first day to the third. This is not surprising considering the fact that all participants preoccupied themselves with the topic of job interviews over the course of three days. However, only for the pupils of the EG were we able to observe significant differences (for the dimensions overall performance, recommendation for the job, smiles, eye contact and nervousness). Furthermore, when comparing the two groups on the third day, practitioners rated the overall job interview performance of the EG significantly better by than that of the CG.

This suggests that the technology-enhanced training had a greater effect on the pupils' job interview performance than the traditional method. We consider this very encouraging, especially since the reading material that the CG was using on the second day is issued by a respectable local youth organisation and is regularly used by our cooperating school.

The only statistical difference found in the pupils' ratings was the self-reported nervousness of the EG between day one and three. This is also interesting as it indicates that the virtual job training environment might help users feel more comfortable during job interviews.

The system also left a good impression on the school teachers who stated that "using the system, pupils seem to be highly motivated and able to learn how to improve their behaviour [...] they usually lack such motivation during class." As a possible reason for this they mentioned the technical nature of the system, which "transports the experience into the youngster's own world" and that the technology-enhanced debriefing phase "makes the feedback be much more believable." Pupils also seemed to enjoy interacting with the system. Most of them asked questions regarding how the score was computed, and which of their behaviours contributed to the final score. This suggests that the scoring functionality had a positive effect on the pupils' engagement in the exercise. Furthermore, the game cards were also received well. One participant even asked for permission to photograph the game cards so she would be able to study them at home.

6 Conclusion

In this paper we explored the use of a technology-enhanced training system to aid youngsters at risk of exclusion in improving social skills pertinent to job interviews. The system combines game elements with job interview simulation mechanics and debriefing techniques in an attempt to achieve a maximum impact on the youngsters. Following a three day user study, we found that pupils who work with the training system improve more than those who use traditional learning methods, i.e. reading a written job interview guide. More precisely, professional practitioners rated the overall performance of the pupils who trained with the system significantly better than of those who did not. Further, only for the pupils who trained with the system were we able to measure statistically significant improvements.

A major contribution of our work is the in-situ study that shows clear benefits of computer-based job training systems for underprivileged pupils. To the best of our knowledge, no other virtual job training system achieved such a result in a similar ambitious setting. Despite the time- and resource-consuming nature of our three day evaluation, the school was very supportive in embedding our study into the school curriculum. We are convinced that virtual environments have a great potential to be used as job interview training instruments on a large scale, extending current teaching practices. Currently, additional studies in other European countries with different school types are being conducted.

Acknowledgments. This work was partially funded by the EC within FP7-ICT-2011-7 (Project TARDIS, grant agreement no. 288578). We thank the teachers Bernhard Pietzowski and Richard Endraß from the Parkschule Stadtbergen for helping organize the study and the pupils for their participation. We also thank Julia Brombach and Claudia Lange-Hetmann from the Career Service of the Augsburg University for volunteering as practitioners.

References

1. Anderson, K., André, E., Baur, T., Bernardini, S., Chollet, M., Chryssafidou, E., Damian, I., Ennis, C., Egges, A., Gebhard, P., Jones, H., Ochs, M., Pelachaud, C., Porayska-Pomsta, K., Rizzo, P., Sabouret, N.: The TARDIS framework: intelligent virtual agents for social coaching in job interviews. In: Reidsma, D., Katayose, H., Nijholt, A. (eds.) ACE 2013. LNCS, vol. 8253, pp. 476–491. Springer, Heidelberg (2013)
2. Baur, T., Damian, I., Gebhard, P., Porayska-Pomsta, K., André, E.: A job interview simulation: Social cue-based interaction with a virtual character. In: Proc. SocialCom, pp. 220–227. IEEE (2013)

3. Baur, T., Damian, I., Lingenfelser, F., Wagner, J., André, E.: NovA: automated analysis of nonverbal signals in social interactions. In: Salah, A.A., Hung, H., Aran, O., Gunes, H. (eds.) HBU 2013. LNCS, vol. 8212, pp. 160–171. Springer, Heidelberg (2013)

4. Birdwhistell, R.L.: Kinesics and Context: Essays on Body Motion Communication. University of Pennsylvania press (2011)

5. Carl, H.: Nonverbal communication during the employment interview. ABCA Bulletin **44**(4), 14–19 (1980)

6. Gebhard, P., Baur, T., Damian, I., Mehlmann, G., Wagner, J., André, E.: Exploring interaction strategies for virtual characters to induce stress in simulated job interviews. In: Proc. AAMAS. pp. 661–668 (2014)

7. Greene, J., Burleson, B.: Handbook of Communication and Social Interaction Skills. LEA's Communication Series. L. Erlbaum Associates (2003)

8. Hammer, T.: Mental health and social exclusion among unemployed youth in scandinavia. a comparative study. Intl. Social Welfare **9**(1), 53–63 (2000)

9. Hollandsworth, J.G., Kazelskis, R., Stevens, J., Dressel, M.E.: Relative contributions of verbal, articulative, and nonverbal communication to employment decisions in the job interview setting. Personnel Psychology **32**(2), 359–367 (1979)

10. Hoque, M.E., Courgeon, M., Martin, J., Mutlu, B., Picard, R.W.: Mach: my automated conversation coach. In: Proc. UbiComp. ACM (2013)

11. Kelly, J.A., Wildman, B.G., Berler, E.S.: Small group behavioral training to improve the job interview skills repertoire of mildly retarded adolescents. Applied Behavior Analysis **13**(3), 461–471 (1980)

12. MacDonald, R.: Disconnected youth? social exclusion, the underclass and economic marginality. Social Work and Society **6**(2), 236–247 (2008)

13. Mehrabian, A.: Silent messages: Implicit Communication of Emotions and Attitudes. Wadsworth Publishing Co Inc, Belmont (1981)

14. Pan, X., Gillies, M., Barker, Clark, D.M.C.M., Slater, M.: Socially anxious and confident men interact with a forward virtual woman: An experiment study. PLoS ONE **7**(4) (2012)

15. Sapouna, M., Wolke, D., Vannini, N., Watson, S., Woods, S., Schneider, W., Enz, S., Hall, L., Paiva, A., André, E., et al.: Virtual learning intervention to reduce bullying victimization in primary school: a controlled trial. Child Psychology and Psychiatry **51**(1), 104–112 (2010)

16. Stapleton, A.J., Taylor, P.C.: Why videogames are cool & school sucks! In: Proc. AGDC 2003. vol. 20, p. 23 (2003)

Predicting Comprehension from Students' Summaries

Mihai Dascalu[1(✉)], Larise Lucia Stavarache[1], Philippe Dessus[2],
Stefan Trausan-Matu[1], Danielle S. McNamara[3], and Maryse Bianco[2]

[1] Computer Science Department, University Politehnica of Bucharest, Bucharest, Romania
{mihai.dascalu,stefan.trausan}@cs.pub.ro,
larise.stavarache@ro.ibm.com
[2] LSE, University Grenoble Alpes, Grenoble, France
{philippe.dessus,maryse.bianco}@upmf-grenoble.fr
[3] LSI, Arizona State University, Tempe, USA
dsmcnama@asu.edu

Abstract. Comprehension among young students represents a key component of their formation throughout the learning process. Moreover, scaffolding students as they learn to coherently link information, while organically constructing a solid knowledge base, is crucial to students' development, but requires regular assessment and progress tracking. To this end, our aim is to provide an automated solution for analyzing and predicting students' comprehension levels by extracting a combination of reading strategies and textual complexity factors from students' summaries. Building upon previous research and enhancing it by incorporating new heuristics and factors, Support Vector Machine classification models were used to validate our assumptions that automatically identified reading strategies, together with textual complexity indices applied on students' summaries, represent reliable estimators of comprehension.

Keywords: Reading strategies · Textual complexity · Summaries assessment · Comprehension prediction · Support vector machines

1 Introduction

The challenges in helping readers understand discourse and achieving coherent underlying mental representations push educators to devise alternative and novel techniques, beyond focusing on classical cognitive reading processes. Devising instruction on reading comprehension strategies emerged from the need to facilitate continuous learning and enable readers to enhance their understanding levels without eliminating or giving up traditional learning methods. For example, *SERT* (Self-Explanation Reading Training) [1] was designed to support readers in self-monitoring their understanding while engaging in effective comprehension strategies. The principal assumption underlying SERT is that, in order to fully understand a text, readers must be able to provide an answer to the basic question "What does this mean?". iSTART [2], the first automated system that scaffolds self-explanations, has demonstrated that SERT is a successful complementary strategy for learning, particularly for high school stu-

© Springer International Publishing Switzerland 2015
C. Conati et al. (Eds.): AIED 2015, LNAI 9112, pp. 95–104, 2015.
DOI: 10.1007/978-3-319-19773-9_10

dents. Psychological and pedagogical research has demonstrated that individuals better understand challenging text if they attempt to explain to themselves what they have read [3], and students do so more effectively if they have been provided training and practice in using comprehension strategies [4, 5]. In addition, by using self-explanation, readers tend to more effectively structure the content and step away from rote learning (which usually results in more rapid memory loss) and towards more organic learning. This process in turn results in more connections between concepts, helping the reader to construct coherent and long lasting mental representations [6].

Based on our previous work [7, 8], this study is focused on comprehension assessment for elementary school students derived from their summaries, by identifying metacognitive comprehension strategies [9] and by applying specific textual complexity factors on their summaries. In terms of building technologies to assess the use of strategies within summaries, primary school students represent a different category of learners than the ones addressed thus far, as they possess less knowledge compared with adult or experienced readers. Hence, their ability to interconnect information based on previous experience is clearly lower. The current work builds on previous research by using refined mechanisms for identifying reading strategies and a comprehensive set of textual complexity indices incorporating classic surface indices derived from automatic essay grading techniques, morphology and syntax [10], as well as semantics and discourse [7, 11]. In addition, Support Vector Machine classification models [12] use combined subsets of reading strategies and textual complexity factors, which are applied on the analyzed summaries, in order to predict students' comprehension levels.

The primary research question addressed in this study is the following: Are reading strategies identified from students' summaries, combined with textual complexity factors also extracted from their summaries, reliable predictors for evaluating the students' comprehension levels? The following sections include an overview of techniques used to identify reading strategies, textual complexity categories from our multi-layered approach, the proposed classification model used to combine the identified reading strategies and textual complexity factors for predicting the comprehension level from students' summaries, ending with conclusions and future work.

2   Reading Strategies Identification

Readers, although sometimes not fully aware, frequently make use of reading strategies to improve their understanding and to interconnect information out of which four main categories are distinguishable [1]: 1 *paraphrasing*, 2) *text-based inferences* consisting of *causality* and *bridging*, 3) *knowledge-based inferences* or elaboration, and 4) monitoring or *control. Paraphrasing* enables users to express their current understanding on the topic by reusing words and concepts from the initial text, which can be considered a first step in building a coherent representation of discourse. *Text-based inferences* build explicit relationships between two or more textual segments of the initial text. On the other hand, *knowledge-based inferences* connect the information from the presented text to the learner's personal knowledge, this being essential for building the situation model [13]. Last but not least, *control strategies* grant balance during the actual monitoring process, as readers explicitly express what they have or have not understood.

The use and identification of reading strategies as described above on a large scale can be problematic, considering the disproportion between the number of students and tutors. Moreover, assessing the content of a summary is a demanding and a subjectivity-laden activity, which can benefit by being assisted by automated techniques. These are the main motives behind the idea of using a computer program instead of or as support for a human tutor. Additionally, an automated comprehension assessment tool helps learners by enabling them to better track their progress and develop more rapidly.

Starting from the identification strategies previously proposed and validated [14] that were applied to students' self-explanations given at predefined breakpoints in the narration of the reading material, our aim was to adapt the automated extraction methods to better match the processing of summaries, following the previous categories. Causal and bridging strategies had to be separated due to the underlying computational complexity and their corresponding approaches. However, causal inferences can be considered a particular case of bridging, as well as a reference resolution. Altogether, reading strategies highlight inferences made by learners and the connection between the summaries and the referential material.

Causality is identified by using cue phrases or discourse markers such as "*parce que*" (the experiments were performed in French, the translation is "because"), "*pour*" (for), "*donc*" (thus), "*alors*" (then), "*à cause de*" (because of), whereas for *control* different markers are used such as "*je me souviens*" (I remember), "*je crois*" (I believe that), "*j'ai rien compris*" (I haven't understood anything) and are enforced in the pattern matching process. Subsequently, *paraphrases* are extracted through lexical similarities by identifying identical lemmas, stems, or synonyms from lexicalized ontologies – *WordNet* or *WOLF* [15, 16] – with words from the initial text. Adjacent words from students' summaries are clustered into segments of paraphrasing concepts, highlighting contiguous zones strongly related to the initial text.

Further on, an *inferred concept* is considered to be a non-paraphrased word, not present in the original text, yet maintains a high cohesion value with it. Cohesion plays a central role in our discourse representation and analysis [8] and its corresponding value is determined as an aggregated score of semantic similarity measures [8] applied on lexicalized ontologies [15], more specifically Wu-Palmer distance applied on WOLF [16], cosine similarity from Latent Semantic Analysis (LSA) [17] vector spaces, and Jensen-Shannon dissimilarity applied on Latent Dirichlet Allocation (LDA) [18] topic distributions. Both LSA and LDA semantic models were trained on "Le Monde" corpora (French newspaper, approx. 24M words) after applying stop words elimination and lemmatization.

Finally, the measure for *bridging* considers the connections between different textual segments from the initial text and the summary. Therefore, for each sentence in the summary, the sentence with the highest cohesion with the initial text is identified and marked as being linked to the summary if the corresponding cohesion value exceeds a threshold. The imposed threshold is used to limit the linkage of off-topic sentences from the summary with the initial text. Subsequently, a similar aggregation of contiguous sentences from the initial reading material with the bridging segments is performed, which highlights the sections of the reading material that are actually recalled within the summary.

3   Textual Complexity Assessment

Automated evaluation of textual complexity represents a key focus for the linguistic research field; it emphasizes the evolution of technology's facilitator role in educational processes. *E-Rater* [19] can be considered one of the first systems which automatically measures essay complexity by extracting a set of features representing facets of writing quality. The *E-Rater* analyzer supports a multi-layered textual complexity evaluation based on the centering theory about building a model for assessing the complexity of inferences within the discourse [20]. In addition, various indices are considered for measuring complexity [19] such as spelling errors, content analysis based on vocabulary measures, lexical complexity/diction, proportion of grammar and of style comments, organization, and development scores and features rewarding idiomatic phraseology.

Multiple systems were implemented and were widely adopted in various educational programs [21]: *Lexile* (MetaMetrics), *ATOS* (Renaissance Learning), Degrees of Reading Power: *DRP Analyzer* (Questar Assessment, Inc.), *REAP* (Carnegie Mellon University), *SourceRater* (Educational Testing Service), *Coh-Metrix* (University of Memphis) and *Dmesure* (Université Catholique de Louvain). Our implemented system, *ReaderBench* [7, 8], integrates the most common indices from the previous systems as baseline and is centered on semantics and discourse analysis by including additional indices for evaluating textual cohesion and discourse connectivity, described later on in detail.

As presented in [22], there are three main categories of factors considered in the textual complexity analysis of the French language that also include the most common and frequently used indices from the previous solutions. Firstly, the *surface* category is comprised of quantitative measures and the analysis of individual elements (words, phrases, paragraphs) by extracting simple or combined indices (e.g., Page's grading technique for automated scoring including number of words, sentences or paragraphs, number of commas, average word length or words per sentence) [23], as well as word and character entropy [10]. A particular set of factors from surface analysis handles *word complexity,* which consist of the distance between the inflected form, lemma and stem, specificity of a concept reflected in its inverse document frequency from the training corpora (in our case, articles from "Le Monde" corpora), the distance in the hypernym tree from the lexicalized ontology WOLF [16], or the word senses count from the same ontology.

Secondly, the *syntactic* category handles the parsing tree by considering the maximum height and size of the tree, as well as the distributions of specific parts of speech. Balanced CAF (Complexity, Accuracy, and Fluency) [24] techniques also add their contribution to the analysis of the previous category through the introduction of lexical/syntactic diversity and sophistication.

Thirdly, whereas the first two categories are more representative for writing ability, the *semantics* and *discourse analysis* category is more comprehension centered by identifying the underlying cohesive links [7, 8, 11]. This category makes use of lexical chains, semantic distances, and discourse connectives, all centered on cohesion, a key feature in terms of discourse representation [8] and textual complexity analysis. This category is particularly appealing as it addresses the internal structure of the summary and provides clear insights on whether the learner has achieved a coherent representation of the text or if (s)he is facing problems in terms of cohesion when expressing impressions and thoughts within the summary.

4   Validation of the Comprehension Prediction Model

Model validation of learner's comprehension level has been performed using several scenarios comprising of different combinations between reading strategies, textual complexity factors applied to students' summaries, cohesion between each summary and the initial reading material, as well as external factors (e.g., students' oral fluency). Firstly, comprehension prediction based on reading strategies and cohesion has been computed in order to shape the baseline of our approach. Secondly, multiple textual complexity factors employed on the students' summaries were combined, clearly revealing that using all indices together cannot be an accurate predictor of textual complexity and that surface indices are not reliable for the task at hand. The next scenario only used the best matching factors, from both previous scenarios, which proved successful and increased both the average and the individual agreements. Finally, oral fluency has been added as an external factor –one highly related to comprehension–, which in return provided a significant increase in prediction accuracy.

Our experiments [25] have been conducted with students between the ages of 8 and 11 years old (3rd–5th grade), uniformly distributed in terms of their age, and who produced 149 summaries of the two French stories of approximately 450 words (*The Cloud Swallower* and *Matilda*). After their lecture, students explained what they understood by verbally summarizing their impressions and thoughts about the initial text. These summaries were recorded and later on transcribed. Students were also administered a posttest comprising of 28 questions used to assess their comprehension of the reading materials. Predefined rules and patterns were used to automatically clean the transcribed verbalizations. With regards to the proposed textual complexity factors applied on students' summaries, the same factors were used in [22] to predict the difficulty of the selected French stories. As a result, both texts were classified as being optimal for 3rd graders, making them appropriate in terms of reading ease for all the students participating in our experiments. Because the materials were presented to adjacent elementary classes, their levels were adequate for both 4th and 5th graders who did not consider them to be boring, nor childish.

With regards to comprehension prediction, we opted to create three comprehension classes (noted C1, C2, and C3 in the following tables) with a distribution of 30%, 40% and 30% of student posttest scores sorted in ascending order and to apply 3-fold cross-validations for the SVM training process. This distribution created an equitable split of students per comprehension classes and also marked significant differences in terms of covered scores per class from the [0; 28] scale for all questions from the posttest. Multiclass SVMs have been trained to predict the appropriate comprehension class based on the selected factors applied on students' summaries. We opted to use RBF kernels as the corresponding hyperparameters (the regularization constant C and the kernel hyperparameter γ) were optimized through Grid Search [26]. In addition, we must emphasize that average accuracy is quite low as there are some high discrepancies between summaries with similar comprehension scores in terms of structure and complexity, which ultimately misleads the SVM training process.

As expected, reading strategies, paraphrases, control and causality occurrences were much easier to identify than information coming from students' experience. Nevertheless, if we consider each strategy separately, the prediction rate is low, whereas the combination dramatically increases accuracy (see Table 1). Also, for some strategies it was impossible to differentiate among comprehension classes because rather few occurrences exist in the training dataset, or because students equitably use that specific strategy. We also noticed small prediction rates for the first and second classes due to rather small differentiations between adjacent classes and to conflicting instances. The previous instances consisted of encountered cases in which students with a high number of potentially involuntarily used reading strategies pertained to a low comprehension class based on their posttest, although all textual indices from their summary pointed to a higher degree of comprehension.

In order to increase the strength of the link between the summary and the original reading material, cohesion between the entire texts was introduced. However as a singular effect, the overall agreement decreased.

Table 1. Comprehension prediction agreement based on reading strategies and cohesion

Factors	C1	C2	C3	Average agreement
Paraphrasing	.214	.235	.804	*.418*
Text-based inferences	.524	.431	.647	*.534*
Knowledge-based inferences	.095	.020	1	*.372*
Control	0	0	1	*.333*
All reading strategies	.595	.451	.608	*.551*
All reading strategies plus the cohesion value with the initial document	.571	.451	.549	*.524*

Results presented in Table 1 are encouraging based on the limited number of training instances, the reduced number of classification attributes, and the fact that a lot of noise existed within the transcriptions. Nevertheless, additional factors were introduced in order to increase the accuracy of comprehension prediction.

Table 2. Comprehension prediction accuracy based on textual complexity factors

Factors	C1	C2	C3	Average
All textual complexity indices	.167	.137	.941	.415
Surface factors and CAF	0	.294	.863	.386
Morphology and semantics	.524	.275	.725	.508
Morphology, semantics, all reading strategies and cohesion with initial document	.524	.49	.529	.514

Table 3. Average prediction accuracy for the best matching indices

Most relevant factors	M	Most relevant factors	M
(C) Causal relation	.587	(B) Syntactic Sophistication - CAF	.433
(D) Text-based inferences	.540	(B) Avg. tree depth	.429
(A) Word entropy	.509	(D) Cohesion with initial text	.429
(B) Avg. number of adverbs	.494	(D) Paraphrasing	.429
(A) No. words in summary	.488	(B) Avg. no. pronouns	.427
(A) Avg. word length	.486	(A) Mean word polysemy count	.427
(C) All connectives	.474	(A) Lexical Diversity	.426
(C) Logical relation	.470	(C) Overall document score	.424
(A) Mean distance between words and corresponding stems	.463	(A) Avg. no. sentences per paragraph	.423
(C) Avg. intra-paragraph cohesion	.461	(A) Total no. sentences	.423
(A) Avg. sentence length	.455	(C) Avg. sentence-block cohesion	.421
(A) Avg. words in sentence	.452	(A) Normalized no. sentences	.420
(A) Standard deviation for words (letters)	.447	(B) Third Person Singular Pronouns Count	.415
(C) Avg. paragraph score	.443	(B) Avg. no. adjectives	.412
(A) Normalized no. of commas	.441	(B) Avg. tree size	.411
(B) Second Person Singular Pronouns Count	.441	(B) First Person Singular Pronouns Count	.410
(B) Avg. no. prepositions	.436	(B) Lexical Sophistication - CAF	.409
(A) Normalized no. words	.435	(A) Mean word distance in hypernym tree	.400

*(A) - surface factors; (B) - syntactic and morphological factors, including CAF;
(C) - semantics, discourse analysis and connectives; (D) - reading strategies.

As it can be observed from Table 2, the integration of surface indices collectively has a low prediction rate. Moreover, the use of too many factors (out of which some proved to be inadequate) is also detrimental to the overall classification: the use of all textual complexity indices or of only the surface factors predicted that all summaries were in the highest comprehension class, clearly a problem in the classification due to the structure similarities between all summaries. Therefore, it turned out to be most appropriate to rely only on complementary and stable factors of textual complexity. Moreover, a slight improvement could be observed after considering the adapted reading strategies extracted from the summary and the cohesion with the initial reading material.

In addition, the best matching individual factors from Table 3 represent a balanced and representative mixture of the previously identified analysis categories and their integration marks a significant improvement in the prediction rate: C1: *.571*; C2: *.608*; C3: *.804*, with an average agreement of .661.

Table 4. Comprehension prediction accuracy after introducing oral fluency

Factors	C1	C2	C3	Average
All reading strategies, cohesion with initial document and oral fluency	.667	.529	.784	*.660*
Morphology, semantics, all reading strategies, cohesion with initial document and oral fluency	.714	.549	.784	*.683*

In the end, the addition of external, non-textual factors (e.g., students' oral fluency determined manually as the number of spoken words per minute) improved the overall results (see Table 4), whereas the problems of using all textual complexity indices remain in the identification of the first two comprehension classes. Overall, the combination of morphology, semantics, reading strategies, cohesion with the initial document, and oral fluency turned out to be one of the most reliable predictors of comprehension for students at the given age. In addition, the semantics category of textual complexity factors, corroborated with the semantic similarity between the summary and the original text, emphasize the importance of cohesion, both internally within the summary, but also between the summary and the initial reading material.

5   Conclusion and Future Research Directions

The integration of the two different approaches applied to summaries resulted in a promising direction for improving comprehension prediction among students. Neither of the two approaches by itself is sufficient to obtain a reliable estimation of comprehension, whereas the combination represents leverage for improving the assessment process. Nevertheless, we can state that reading strategies by themselves are good predictors for assessing comprehension, while morphology and semantics provide a solid ground for evaluations that surpass surface factors commonly used in other automated systems. Moreover, we must emphasize the complementarity of the approaches, as reading strategies and cohesion reflect the link with the initial reading material, whereas textual complexity factors are centered on analyzing the summary's internal structure. Furthermore, the performed measurements and validations indicate that reading strategies, mixed with textual complexity factors [21] and essay scoring techniques [27] increase the accuracy of the predictions related to a student's comprehension level.

As described above, students are a special category of learners who pass through an increasingly difficult process of where they constantly receive more and more information that they must assimilate. This transition along with the inspection of the summaries has emphasized the need for introducing additional techniques to improve understanding and to facilitate both their activity and their tutor's. The main goal of this paper was to expand the research path of assessing comprehension, while the overall scope our system, *ReaderBench,* remained to support tutors through a regularized and predictable process of prediction as an alternative to the subjectivity-laden task of manual evaluation.

Our future aims consist of expanding the experimental components further, by adding the possibility to automatically assess students' reading fluency and by deploying *ReaderBench* in classroom settings in order to analyze student's comprehension levels on a regular basis and to infer possible comprehension issues, more accurately and in a timely manner.

Acknowledgements. This research was partially supported by the ANR DEVCOMP 10-BLAN-1907-01 and the 2008-212578 LTfLL FP7 projects, by the NSF grants 1417997 and 1418378 to Arizona State University, as well as by the POSDRU/159/1.5/S/132397 and 134398 projects. We would also like to thank Aurélie Nardy and Françoise Toffa who helped us to gather the experimental data, as well as the teachers and students who participated in our experiments.

References

1. McNamara, D.S.: SERT: Self-Explanation Reading Training. Discourse Processes **38**, 1–30 (2004)
2. McNamara, D.S., Levinstein, I., Boonthum, C.: iSTART: Interactive strategy training for active reading and thinking. Behavior Research Methods, Instruments, & Computers **36**(2), 222–233 (2004)
3. Millis, K., Magliano, J.P., Wiemer-Hastings, K., Todaro, S., McNamara, D.S.: Assessing and improving comprehension with latent semantic analysis. In: Landauer, T.K., McNamara, D., Dennis, S., Kintsch, W. (eds.) Handbook of Latent Semantic Analysis, pp. 207–225. Erlbaum, Mahwah (2007)
4. McNamara, D.S., O'Reilly, T.P., Best, R.M., Ozuru, Y.: Improving adolescent students' reading comprehension with iSTART. Journal of Educational Computing Research **34**(2), 147–171 (2006)
5. Jackson, G.T., McNamara, D.S.: Motivation and performance in a game-based intelligent tutoring system. Journal of Educational Psychology **105**, 1036–1049 (2013)
6. McNamara, D.S., Magliano, J.P.: Self-explanation and metacognition. In: Hacher, J.D., Dunlosky, J., Graesser, A.C. (eds.) Handbook of metacognition in education, pp. 60–81. Erlbaum, Mahwah (2009)
7. Dascalu, M., Dessus, P., Bianco, M., Trausan-Matu, S., Nardy, A.: Mining texts, learners productions and strategies with *ReaderBench*. In: Peña-Ayala, A. (ed.) Educational Data Mining: Applications and Trends. SCI, vol. 524, pp. 345–377. Springer, Heidelberg (2014)
8. Dascălu, M.: Analyzing Discourse and Text Complexity for Learning and Collaborating. SCI, vol. 534. Springer, Heidelberg (2014)
9. Nash-Ditzel, S.: Metacognitive Reading Strategies Can Improve Self-Regulation. Journal of College Reading and Learning **40**(2), 45–63 (2010)

10. Dascălu, M., Trausan-Matu, S., Dessus, P.: Towards an integrated approach for evaluating textual complexity for learning purposes. In: Popescu, E., Li, Q., Klamma, R., Leung, H., Specht, M. (eds.) ICWL 2012. LNCS, vol. 7558, pp. 268–278. Springer, Heidelberg (2012)

11. Dascalu, M., Dessus, P., Trausan-Matu, Ş., Bianco, M., Nardy, A.: *ReaderBench*, an environment for analyzing text complexity and reading strategies. In: Lane, H.C., Yacef, K., Mostow, J., Pavlik, P. (eds.) AIED 2013. LNCS, vol. 7926, pp. 379–388. Springer, Heidelberg (2013)

12. Cortes, C., Vapnik, V.N.: Support-Vector Networks. Machine Learning **20**(3), 273–297 (1995)

13. van Dijk, T.A., Kintsch, W.: Strategies of discourse comprehension. Academic Press, New York (1983)

14. Dascalu, M., Dessus, P., Bianco, M., Trausan-Matu, S.: Are automatically identified reading strategies reliable predictors of comprehension? In: Trausan-Matu, S., Boyer, K.E., Crosby, M., Panourgia, K. (eds.) ITS 2014. LNCS, vol. 8474, pp. 456–465. Springer, Heidelberg (2014)

15. Budanitsky, A., Hirst, G.: Evaluating WordNet-based Measures of Lexical Semantic Relatedness. Computational Linguistics **32**(1), 13–47 (2006)

16. Sagot, B.: WordNet Libre du Francais (WOLF) (2008). http://alpage.inria.fr/~sagot/wolf.html

17. Landauer, T.K., Dumais, S.T.: A solution to Plato's problem: the Latent Semantic Analysis theory of acquisition, induction and representation of knowledge. Psychological Review **104**(2), 211–240 (1997)

18. Blei, D.M., Ng, A.Y., Jordan, M.I.: Latent Dirichlet Allocation. Journal of Machine Learning Research **3**(4–5), 993–1022 (2003)

19. Powers, D.E., Burstein, J., Chodorow, M., Fowles, M.E., Kukich, K.: Stumping e-rater®: Challenging the validity of automated essay scoring. ETS, Princeton (2001)

20. Grosz, B.J., Weinstein, S., Joshi, A.K.: Centering: a framework for modeling the local coherence of discourse. Computational Linguistics **21**(2), 203–225 (1995)

21. Nelson, J., Perfetti, C., Liben, D., Liben, M.: Measures of text difficulty Council of Chief State School Officers, Washington, DC (2012)

22. Dascalu, M., Stavarache, L.L., Trausan-Matu, S., Dessus, P., Bianco, M.: Reflecting comprehension through french textual complexity factors. In: ICTAI 2014, pp. 615–619. IEEE, Limassol (2014)

23. Page, E.: The imminence of grading essays by computer. Phi Delta Kappan **47**, 238–243 (1966)

24. Housen, A., Kuiken, F.: Complexity, Accuracy, and Fluency in Second Language Acquisition. Applied Linguistics **30**(4), 461–473 (2009)

25. Nardy, A., Bianco, M., Toffa, F., Rémond, M., Dessus, P.: Contrôle et régulation de la compréhension. In: David, J., Royer, C. (eds.) L'apprentissage de la Lecture: Convergences, Innovations, Perspectives, p. 16. Peter Lang, Bern-Paris (in press)

26. Bergstra, J., Bengio, Y.: Random Search for Hyper-Parameter Optimization. The Journal of Machine Learning Research **13**, 281–305 (2012)

27. Todd, R.W., Khongput, S., Darasawang, P.: Coherence, cohesion and comments on students' academic essays. Assessing Writing **12**(1), 10–25 (2007)

A Tutorial Dialogue System for Real-Time Evaluation of Unsupervised Dialogue Act Classifiers: Exploring System Outcomes

Aysu Ezen-Can[✉] and Kristy Elizabeth Boyer

Department of Computer Science,
North Carolina State University, Raleigh, USA
{aezen,keboyer}@ncsu.edu

Abstract. Dialogue act classification is an important step in understanding students' utterances within tutorial dialogue systems. Machine-learned models of dialogue act classification hold great promise, and among these, unsupervised dialogue act classifiers have the great benefit of eliminating the human dialogue act annotation effort required to label corpora. In contrast to traditional evaluation approaches which judge unsupervised dialogue act classifiers by accuracy on manual labels, we present results of a study to evaluate the performance of these models with respect to their performance within end-to-end system evaluation. We compare two versions of the tutorial dialogue system for introductory computer science: one that relies on a supervised dialogue act classifier and one that depends on an unsupervised dialogue act classifier. A study with 51 students shows that both versions of the system achieve similar learning gains and user satisfaction. Additionally, we show that some incoming student characteristics are highly correlated with students' perceptions of their experience during tutoring. This first end-to-end evaluation of an unsupervised dialogue act classifier within a tutorial dialogue system serves as a step toward acquiring tutorial dialogue management models in a fully automated, scalable way.

Keywords: Dialogue act classification · Unsupervised machine learning · Tutorial dialogue systems

1 Introduction

Today's tutorial dialogue systems are effective [22], yet they still aspire to improve by supporting the flexible natural language interactions of the most effective human tutors [1,9]. However, improving natural language interactions is a challenging task because there is extensive engineering effort required to build a full natural language dialogue pipeline [5]. We have seen an upsurge of interest in improving natural language understanding in tutorial dialogue for a variety of domains such as physics (AutoTutor [17], Why2Atlas [23], Andes [24], ITSPOKE [16] and Rimac [13]), the circulatory system (CIRCSIM-Tutor [6]), electricity and electronics (BEETLE-II [5]), and programming (ProPL [14], iList [8]).

© Springer International Publishing Switzerland 2015
C. Conati et al. (Eds.): AIED 2015, LNAI 9112, pp. 105–114, 2015.
DOI: 10.1007/978-3-319-19773-9_11

Dialogue act classification is one of the most useful mechanisms for understanding student utterances. Dialogue acts aim to capture the "act" underlying an utterance such as asking a question, making a statement, and acknowledgement [19]. Classifying student dialogue acts accurately may support more effective tutoring, as the whole pipeline of dialogue management depends on them. For example, a negative feedback from the student such as "I am not following" may be followed by remedial help from the tutor, in contrast to a statement of plan such as "I am not working on that method yet" which may be followed by an acknowledgment from the tutor.

The task of automatic dialogue act classification has been studied extensively in the literature, mostly within supervised machine learning [3,19]. However, supervised classification is labor-intensive as it requires engineering dialogue act taxonomies and labeling corpora before training classifiers. As an alternative, unsupervised classifiers have gained attention recently. These models build groupings of student utterances directly from the data. However, to date, no deployed dialogue system has utilized an unsupervised dialogue act classifier; rather, researchers have evaluated the performance of unsupervised models as standalone components by comparing to manual labels [7,18]. The downside of this approach is that expecting a fully data-driven model to replicate a human annotation scheme may not capture how well that data-driven model will perform in an end-to-end deployment. Therefore, evaluating unsupervised dialogue act models without comparing to manual annotations and within their usage environment is of the utmost importance.

We have implemented a tutorial dialogue system that can be utilized to compare the performance of two different dialogue act classifiers within a real-time system. We trained an unsupervised dialogue act model on a corpus of human tutorial dialogue in the domain of introductory computer science, and for comparison we trained a supervised model. We hypothesized that the unsupervised dialogue act model, which relies on hierarchical clustering and uses no manual labels during model training, would support equal or better student learning than the supervised dialogue act model, which relies on a decision tree classifier and represents a state-of-the-art, highly accurate dialogue act classifier that agrees with human annotations 89.6% of the time. Experimental results with 51 students show that unsupervised and supervised dialogue act models indeed achieved similar performance for supporting learning gains and user satisfaction.

Additionally, we conduct a PARADISE dialogue analysis in which the relative contribution of various factors to a system's overall performance is investigated [25]. We conduct regression analyses to determine factors affecting the outcomes of the system. The results show that students' perceptions are significantly associated with system outcomes such as how involved students become during the tutoring session and how difficult students feel that the tasks are.

2 System Design

The primary goal of the study is to evaluate an unsupervised dialogue act classifier in its intended usage environment and to compare it to a supervised classifier within a tutorial dialogue system. This section describes two versions of a tutorial dialogue system: one that implements an *unsupervised* dialogue act classifier and one that uses a *supervised* dialogue act classifier. A screenshot is shown in Fig. 1.

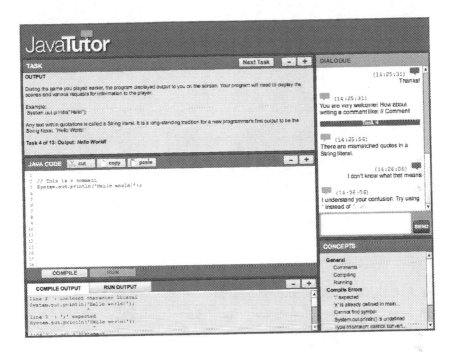

Fig. 1. Screenshot from the tutorial dialogue system

2.1   System Architecture Overview

Both versions of the tutorial dialogue system depend on the same pipeline. First, dialogue act classification takes place to interpret student's words. Then, a code analysis module utilizes regular expressions to identify errors in student's code. The output of these modules is used in the generation module, where the tutor move is determined. Fig. 2 presents the architecture diagram of the dialogue system.

2.2   Dialogue Act Classification

In this section, we explain how the dialogue act classification task is handled within the system. Both dialogue act classifiers were trained on a corpus of 2,417 student utterances collected in a computer-mediated environment for teaching Java programming language within a study which has been detailed in previous publications [10]. First, the features are extracted, which are then used as inputs to the dialogue act classifiers (supervised or unsupervised).

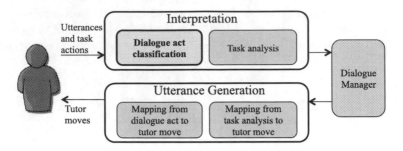

Fig. 2. System architecture diagram

Features. For classification of dialogue acts, we extract two sets of features: textual and task-related. These are the same set of features extracted both for training (building the dialogue act classifiers) and testing (real-time classification of dialogue acts). The textual features are solely extracted from the student utterances. These include unigrams and bigrams of both tokens (words and punctuation) and part-of-speech tags.

While experimenting with the dialogue interactions, students are asked to complete the tasks provided. To satisfy the requirements, the students write and test their programming code. The task-related features are extracted from the task events that occur in real-time throughout the tutoring. There are three task-related features used within the system. Two of them are utilized within dialogue act classification, and one of them is used to provide remedial help. We use the latest task action (compile, run, writing a message to the tutor) and its result (success, error, begin, stop) to improve the dialogue act classification task. In addition, we use regular expressions to compare the student's code to the solutions of previous students to understand whether the student's code has an error.

Supervised Dialogue Act Classification. For supervised dialogue act classification, we use an off-the-shelf decision tree classifier from Weka [11] and train it on dialogue act tags [20]. This tagging scheme consists of 18 student dialogue act labels for the portion of the task that the system implements (*Greeting, Extra-Domain Question, Ready Question, Confirmation Question, Direction Question, Information Question, Observation, Correction, Understanding Feedback, Not Understanding Feedback, Explanation, Other, Yes-No Answer, Extra-Domain Answer, Answer, Positive Feedback, Ready Answer, Acknowledgement*), with Cohen's Kappa of $\kappa = 0.87$ (89.6 % agreement) showing high reliability [20].

Unsupervised Dialogue Act Classification. As for the unsupervised dialogue act classification, we utilize a hierarchical clustering approach that assigns utterances to individual clusters initially and merges the most similar two clusters in each iteration until the hierarchy is completed by having one large cluster. By examining the whole hierarchy, we qualitatively chose the stopping point where the groupings of utterances make sense. The number of clusters determined at this stopping point would have been the number of clusters to be used if no comparison with a supervised classifier were to take place. However, our goal is to provide similar conditions to both of the supervised and unsupervised classifiers. In order to make sure that the number of clusters are not different from the number of manual labels, we merged the clusters that are sparse and used the same number of clusters (18) as the number of manual tags. The details of this unsupervised framework are beyond the scope of this paper due to space limitations but have been fully described in a prior publication [7].

2.3   Tutorial Policies and Utterance Generation

Having obtained the machine-learned models, we authored policies which govern system moves given the output of the classifier. For the supervised version, we authored moves for each manual label (e.g., Question; Negative Feedback) and for the unsupervised version, we crafted tutor moves to each cluster (with clusters interpreted qualitatively). These policies were created to be as similar as possible while providing contextually appropriate responses to the dialogue act.

When students interact with the system, it calls upon the trained dialogue act classifier to classify each new student utterance. Then based upon the dialogue policy, the system chooses tutor moves on the fly. Additional features provided for generating tutorial moves include the output of automated code analysis using regular expressions, which compares student's code to previous correct student solutions to understand if there are any errors. The output of this code analysis is used to fill slots within the tutorial move templates. Example tutor moves are depicted in Fig. 3.

In addition to the dialogue act classifiers' support, the system takes initiative to provide feedback when needed; that is, it is not constrained to respond to student requests [10]. This task-based feedback is the same across both the supervised and unsupervised versions of the system.

In cases where there are multiple code errors returned by the regular expression module, we apply prioritization of errors. We provide the tutor move that corresponds to the latest error, which is determined by the line number of the

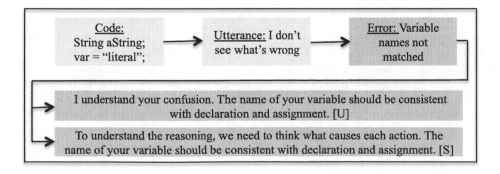

Fig. 3. Sample tutor moves with sample code and utterance. [U] indicates the unsupervised dialogue act classifier move and [S] indicates the supervised classifier move.

error. In addition, less priority is given to the task errors, such as variable declaration not found although the task description asks for a variable description, than syntax errors such as trying to declare a variable but could not successfully do so syntactically.

In addition to the classifiers, we incorporate a hybrid approach which makes use of simple rules. The motivation for utilizing rules is that for some phenomena such as greetings and thanking, the responses are clear; therefore the classifiers do not need to be run. If a student utterance falls into one of these categories, the approach returns the corresponding moves from the rules. For more complex utterances, we run the dialogue act classifiers.

3   Evaluation

We have hypothesized that our unsupervised dialogue act classifier will support equal or better student learning and satisfaction compared to a state-of-the-art supervised dialogue act classifier. To test this hypothesis, we conducted a study with two conditions: 24 participants were in the supervised condition and 27 participants were in the unsupervised condition. The students (12 female, 39 male) were drawn from a university-level first-year-engineering class and participated as part of an in-class activity.

The students were randomly assigned to the different versions of the system. Their interactions with the system were logged. They took a pre-test and pre-survey, and after tutoring completed a post-survey and post-test identical to the pre-test. The pre-survey consisted of several widely used measures including goal orientation [21], general self-efficacy [2], and confidence in learning computer science and programming [15]. We investigate contributions of these measures to system outcomes in Section 4.

Students in both conditions received a statistically equivalent number of tutor messages: 35.2 in the supervised condition and 38.7 in the unsupervised condition. To compare the effectiveness of the two systems, we use multiple metrics from the surveys and tests. First, we consider usability as indicated by a set of ten items on the post-survey (e.g., 'The tutoring system was knowledgeable about programming.', 'The tutoring system was supportive.'). There was no significant difference between two versions of the system with respect to usability, with both sets of users rating the system 2.99 out of 5 ($p=0.5$; stdev=0.8). The second metric we compare is students' perception of how effective the tutor feedback was. This measure is taken from fourteen post-survey questions (e.g., 'It was easy to learn from the tutor's feedback.','I paid attention to the tutor's feedback.'). Similar to the usability questions, the tutor feedback ratings in supervised and unsupervised versions were not significantly different ($p=0.4$; stdev=0.9).

Finally, we compare the systems in terms of learning gain. The learning gains were significantly positive in both conditions ($mean_{sup}=0.12$, $p=0.05$, stdev=0.21; $mean_{unsup}=0.14$, $p=0.0009$, stdev=0.18) and these means were not significantly different ($p=0.3$). As hypothesized, the results indicate that the unsupervised dialogue act classifier supported statistically equivalent learning gain and user satisfaction as the state-of-the-art supervised models, while the unsupervised model required only a small fraction of the manual labor (for interpreting clusters) compared to the supervised model (for which extensive labeling of the corpus was required). Next we build descriptive regression models to examine the relationships between pre-measures and post-measures.

4   Evaluating System Outcomes

Since the unsupervised and supervised dialogue act classifiers produced comparable tutorial dialogue interactions, we aggregated the data from the two conditions in order to explore the factors affecting the outcome of the system. We leveraged the dialogue system evaluation framework PARADISE [25] and built multiple regression to reveal relationships between student characteristics and fine-grained logs from the tutorial dialogue interactions (the predictors), and students' perceptions of the tutorial dialogue (the response variables).

We built one multiple regression model for predicting each post-measure of interest from the surveys or tests (endurability, curiosity, felt involvement, focused attention, task difficulty and post-test score), with the same set of independent variables each time that include pre-survey, pre-test, number of utterances written by the student, number of total logged activities, number of compile/run events, number of program content changes logged, number of compile errors and number of tutor messages received. The goal was not to obtain accurate predictive models necessarily, but to investigate *descriptive* models that indicate the aspects of the learners or of the interactions that are significantly associated with outcomes.

As shown in Fig. 4, the outcomes of the system were related not only to the effectiveness of the tutoring, but also heavily to incoming perceptions of the students. We present features with significance $p < 0.05$ and the post-measures they predict. The endurability category had four post-survey items which measure the extent to which the students considered the tutoring session worthwhile and rewarding. The felt involvement category consisted of three survey items measuring how much the students were involved in the task, and the focused attention category involved seven questions about how much the students were focused on the task. Finally, the curiosity category measured how interested the students were with the system using three questions.

The results show that some predictors were correlated with multiple system outcomes. For example, the confidence that students have in computer science was significantly predictive of endurability, curiosity, felt involvement and task difficulty. Similarly, the extent to which students find computer science useful was significantly associated with all presented post-measures except task difficulty, highlighting the fact that the perceptions of students are related to how they feel about the tutoring system. Learning goal orientation (mastery vs. performance) was measured with twelve pre-survey questions, and the models showed that students that were willing to face challenging tasks also felt more involved with the learning task. Finally, students who aimed to score higher than other students felt that the tasks were more difficult.

Descriptive Linear Regression Models

Endurability *My learning experience was rewarding.*	= 0.4028 * CS confidence + 0.4279 * CS usefulness - 0.7784 * self-efficacy
Curiosity *The content of the tutoring system incited my curiosity.*	= 0.5480 * CS confidence + 0.3681 * CS usefulness
Felt involvement *I was really drawn into my learning task.*	= 0.4724 * CS confidence + 0.3171 * CS usefulness - 1.5409 * self-efficacy[†] + 0.7083 * learning goal orientation
Focused attention *I blocked out things around me when I was working.*	= 0.4744 * CS usefulness[†]
Task difficulty *How mentally demanding was the task?*	= -9.6884 * CS confidence + 9.0752 * achievement goal orientation[†] - 0.1358 * number of compile/run events + 0.4956 * number of tutor moves[†]

Fig. 4. Multivariate linear regression analyses for describing the outcomes of the system using measures from pre-survey and from tutorial interaction. CS stands for computer science, [†] represents $p < 0.005$, all others are $p < 0.05$. Task difficulty has a range from 0-100, all others 1-5.

In addition to these student characteristics or attitudes, several aspects of the tutorial interaction were correlated with outcomes. The number of logged activities, code changes and compile/run events were all positively correlated with the number of utterances written by students throughout the session. One might argue that these measures are correlated with the outcomes because they are also correlated with pre-test scores, which affects the system outcome. However, pre-test score was not significantly correlated with any of the predictors in the regression analyses.

The results suggest that the perceptions of students even before starting the tutoring session are indicative of the outcomes of the system. Such observations are harmonious with those from prior studies [4,12]. The findings highlight the importance not only of honing the tutorial dialogue within interaction to be as effective as possible, but to adapting to the characteristics and attitudes that students bring in to the tutoring session. In fact, an important limitation of this work arises from students' attitudes and preferences: namely, as students participated as part of an in-class activity and knew that their final product would not be graded for quality, they typically tried to finish as quickly as possible and made fewer than desired utterances to the system. Accounting for and mitigating these types of issues with tutorial dialogue systems is a crucial area for the field as we aim to provide one-on-one adaptive tutoring to very broad populations of students with varying levels of intrinsic motivation toward the task.

5   Conclusion

Tutorial dialogue systems have traditionally required tremendous hand authoring. If we can acquire effective unsupervised dialogue act classifiers from the increasingly vast corpora available, we can transform the way tutorial dialogue systems are built. This paper has described a tutorial dialogue system that relies on a fully unsupervised dialogue act model, and the results demonstrate that it supports student learning and satisfaction as well as a comparable system that relies on a state-of-the-art supervised dialogue act model.

Motivated by the promise of unsupervised models, both in suggesting fully data-driven classification schemes and eliminating human labor, it is very promising to explore them further for tutorial dialogue systems. Another important area of research involves integrating more sophisticated natural language generation with these dialogue act models to increase the flexibility of system utterances. Finally, because incoming motivation of students has such a strong correlation with outcomes, adaptive systems that adjust their strategies according to student motivation are a promising direction for improving tutorial dialogue systems.

References

1. Bloom, B.S.: The 2 sigma problem: the search for methods of group instruction as effective as one-to-one tutoring, p. 4–16. Educational Researcher (1984)
2. Chen, G., Gully, S.M., Eden, D.: Validation of a new general self-efficacy scale. Organizational Research Methods 4(1), 62–83 (2001)
3. Chen, L., Eugenio, B.D.: Multimodality and dialogue act classification in the Robo Helper project. In: Proceedings of the Annual SIGDIAL Meeting, pp. 183–192 (2013)
4. DMello, S., Williams, C., Hays, P., Olney, A.: Individual differences as predictors of learning and engagement. In: Proceedings of the Annual Meeting of the Cognitive Science Society pp. 308–313 (2009)
5. Dzikovska, M., Steinhauser, N., Farrow, E., Moore, J., Campbell, G.: BEETLE II: Deep natural language understanding and automatic feedback generation for intelligent tutoring in basic electricity and electronics. IJAIED 24(3), 284–332 (2014)
6. Evens, M.W., Chang, R.-C., Lee, Y. H., Shim, L.S., Woo, C.W., Zhang, Y., Michael, J.A., Rovick, A.A.: CIRCSIM-Tutor: An intelligent tutoring system using natural language dialogue. In: Proceedings of Applied Natural Language Processing, pp. 13–14 (1997)
7. Ezen-Can, A., Boyer, K.E.: Combining task and dialogue streams in unsupervised dialogue act models. In: Proceedings of the Annual SIGDIAL Meeting, pp. 113–122 (2014)
8. Fossati, D., Di Eugenio, B., Brown, C., Ohlsson, S.: Learning linked lists: experiments with the iList system. In: Woolf, B.P., Aïmeur, E., Nkambou, R., Lajoie, S. (eds.) ITS 2008. LNCS, vol. 5091, pp. 80–89. Springer, Heidelberg (2008)
9. Graesser, A.C., Person, N.K., Magliano, J.P.: Collaborative dialogue patterns in naturalistic one-to-one tutoring. Applied Cognitive Psychology 9(6), 495–522 (1995)

10. Ha, E.Y., Grafsgaard, J.F., Mitchell, C.M., Boyer, K.E., Lester, J.C.: Combining verbal and nonverbal features to overcome the 'information gap' in task-oriented dialogue. In: Proceedings of the Annual SIGDIAL Meeting on Discourse and Dialogue, pp. 247–256 (2012)
11. Hall, M., National, H., Frank, E., Holmes, G., Pfahringer, B., Reutemann, P., Witten, I.H.: The WEKA data mining software: An update. ACM SIGKDD Explorations Newsletter **11**(1), 10–18 (2009)
12. Jackson, G.T., Graesser, A.C., McNamara, D.S.: What students expect may have more impact than what they know or feel. In: Proceedings of AIED, pp. 73–80 (2009)
13. Jordan, P., Albacete, P., Ford, M.J., Katz, S., Lipschultz, M., Litman, D., Silliman, S., Wilson, C.: Interactive event: the Rimac tutor - a simulation of the highly interactive nature of human tutorial dialogue. In: Lane, H.C., Yacef, K., Mostow, J., Pavlik, P. (eds.) AIED 2013. LNCS, vol. 7926, pp. 928–929. Springer, Heidelberg (2013)
14. Lane, H.C., VanLehn, K.: Teaching the tacit knowledge of programming to novices with natural language tutoring. Computer Science Education **15**(3), 183–201 (2005)
15. Lee, C., Bobko, P.: Self-efficacy beliefs: Comparison of five measures. Journal of Applied Psychology **79**(3), 364 (1994)
16. Litman, D., Silliman, S.: ITSPOKE: An intelligent tutoring spoken dialogue system. Demonstration Papers at HLT-NAACL **2004**, 5–8 (2004)
17. Nye, B.D., Graesser, A.C., Hu, X.: AutoTutor and family: A review of 17 years of natural language tutoring. IJAIED **24**(4), 427–469 (2014)
18. Rus, V., Moldovan, C., Niraula, N., Graesser, A.C.: Automated discovery of speech act categories in educational games. In: Proceedings of EDM, pp. 25–32 (2012)
19. Stolcke, A., Ries, K., Coccaro, N., Shriberg, E., Bates, R., Jurafsky, D., Taylor, P., Martin, R., Van Ess-Dykema, C., Meteer, M.: Dialogue act modeling for automatic tagging and recognition of conversational speech. Computational Linguistics **26**(3), 339–373 (2000)
20. Vail, A.K., Boyer, K.E.: Identifying effective moves in tutoring: on the refinement of dialogue act annotation schemes. In: Trausan-Matu, S., Boyer, K.E., Crosby, M., Panourgia, K. (eds.) ITS 2014. LNCS, vol. 8474, pp. 199–209. Springer, Heidelberg (2014)
21. VandeWalle, D., Cron, W.L., Slocum Jr, J.W.: The role of goal orientation following performance feedback. Journal of Applied Psychology **86**(4), 629 (2001)
22. VanLehn, K., Graesser, A.C., Jackson, G.T., Jordan, P., Olney, A., Rosé, C.P.: When are tutorial dialogues more effective than reading? Cognitive Science **31**(1), 3–62 (2007)
23. VanLehn, K., Jordan, P.W., Penstein Rosé, C., Bhembe, D., Böttner, M., Gaydos, A., Makatchev, M., Pappuswamy, U., Ringenberg, M.A., Roque, A.C., Siler, S., Srivastava, R.: The architecture of Why2-Atlas: a coach for qualitative physics essay writing. In: Cerri, S.A., Gouardéres, G., Paraguaçu, F. (eds.) ITS 2002. LNCS, vol. 2363, p. 158. Springer, Heidelberg (2002)
24. VanLehn, K., Lynch, C., Schulze, K., Shapiro, J.A., Shelby, R., Taylor, L., Treacy, D., Weinstein, A., Wintersgill, M.: The Andes physics tutoring system: Lessons learned. IJAIED **15**(3), 147–204 (2005)
25. Walker, M.A., Litman, D.J., Kamm, C.A., Abella, A.: PARADISE: a framework for evaluating spoken dialogue agents. In: Proceedings of the European Chapter of the Association for Computational Linguistics, pp. 271–280 (1997)

Positive Impact of Collaborative Chat Participation in an edX MOOC

Oliver Ferschke[✉], Diyi Yang, Gaurav Tomar, and Carolyn Penstein Rosé

Carnegie Mellon University, 5000 Forbes Ave., Pittsburgh, PA, USA
{ferschke,diyiy,gtomar,cprose}@cs.cmu.edu

Abstract. A major limitation of the current generation of MOOCs is a lack of opportunity for students to make use of each other as resources. Analyses of attrition and learning in MOOCs both point to the importance of social engagement for motivational support and overcoming difficulties with material and course procedures. In this paper we evaluate an intervention that makes synchronous collaboration opportunities available to students in an edX MOOC. We have implemented a Lobby program that students can access via a live link at any time. Upon entering the Lobby, they are matched with other students that are logged in to it. Once matched, they are provided with a link to a chat room where they can work with their partner students on a synchronous collaboration activity, supported by a conversational computer agent. Results of a survival model in which we control for level of effort suggest that having experienced a collaborative chat is associated with a slow down in the rate of attrition over time by a factor of two. We discuss implications for design, limitations of the current study, and directions for future research.

Keywords: Collaborative reflection · Survival analysis · Massive open online courses

1 Introduction

The rise of Massive Open Online Courses (MOOCs) has been the subject of a great deal of hype followed by almost as much disappointment. Some of the biggest limitations are related to the human side of effective educational experiences. In contrast, the field of Computer Supported Collaborative Learning (CSCL) has a rich history extending for nearly two decades, covering a broad spectrum of research related to learning in groups, especially in computer mediated environments. In this paper we describe the initial stages of a research program designed to import findings from a history of successful classroom research in the field of CSCL to the challenging environment of MOOCs.

Effective collaborative learning experiences are known to provide many benefits to learners in terms of cognitive, metacognitive, and social impact (Kirschner, Paas, & Kirschner, 2009; Webb & Palinscar, 1996). These experiences offer a potentially valuable resource for MOOCs, if affordances can be provided that facilitate high quality collaborative learning interactions in the absence of human facilitators that can

© Springer International Publishing Switzerland 2015
C. Conati et al. (Eds.): AIED 2015, LNAI 9112, pp. 115–124, 2015.
DOI: 10.1007/978-3-319-19773-9_12

keep up with the high enrolment in such courses. In this paper, we build on a paradigm for dynamic support for group learning that has proven effective for improving interaction and learning in a series of online group learning studies conducted in classroom settings. In particular we refer to using tutorial dialogue agent technology to provide interactive support within a synchronous collaborative chat environment (Kumar et al., 2007; Chaudhuri et al., 2008; Chaudhuri et al., 2009; Kumar et al., 2010; Ai et al., 2010; Kumar & Rosé, 2011). Introduction of such technology in a classroom setting has consistently led to significant improvements in student learning (Adamson et al., 2014), and even positive impacts on the classroom environment outside of the collaborative activities (Clarke et al., 2013). While it would seem to be desirable to import such technology into a MOOC setting to provide a learning experience that is both more instructionally valuable and socially supportive, such an introduction comes with it technical, methodological, and theoretical challenges. In this paper we present an early design for integration of this technology with the edX platform and results from a first deployment study. We provide an analysis of findings, which culminates in a vision for an ongoing research program.

2   Motivating Synchronous Collaboration in MOOCs

Tutorial dialogue agents have already achieved substantial impact in the field of CSCL. In that context, it has been noted that in order to support the growth of student discussion skills, it is necessary to design environments with affordances that encourage transactive discussion behaviors and other valuable learning behaviors. The most popular approach to providing such affordances in the past decade has been that of script-based collaboration (Dillenbourg, 2002; Kollar et al., 2006; Kobbe et al., 2007). The early non-adaptive scripting approaches described above can sometimes result in both over-scripting and in interference between multiple scripts (Weinberger et al., 2007), both of which have been shown to be detrimental to student performance. More dynamic approaches can trigger scripted support in response to the automatic analysis of participant activity (Soller & Lesgold, 2000; Erkens & Janssen, 2008; Rosé et al., 2008; McLaren et al., 2007; Mu et al., 2012). This sort of analysis can occur at a macro-level, following the state of the activity as a whole, or it can be based on the micro-level classification of individual user contributions.

The collaborative tutoring agents described by Kumar and colleagues (Kumar & Rosé, 2011; Kumar et al., 2007) were among the first to implement dynamic scripting in a CSCL environment. In that work, the role of the support was to increase the conceptual depth of discussions by occasionally engaging students in directed lines of reasoning called Knowledge Construction Dialogues (KCDs) (Rosé & VanLehn, 2005) that lead students step by step to construct their understanding of a concept and how it applies to the collaborative problem solving context. These encounters were triggered in the midst of collaborative discussions by detection that students were discussing an issue that is associated with one of the pre-authored interactive directed lines of reasoning. Thus, these interventions had the ability to be administered when appropriate given the discussion, rather than being triggered in a one-size-fits-all fashion. In an initial evaluation (Kumar et al., 2007), this form of dynamic support was associated with higher learning gains than a control condition where students had access to the same lines of reasoning, but in a static form. In a subsequent study, students were found to gain significantly more if they had the option to choose whether or not to participate in the directed line of reasoning when it was triggered (Chaudhuri et al., 2009). Scripting such as this offers the potential for minimal interventions to be used more precisely and to greater effect, with the hope of greater likelihood of students internalizing the support's intended interaction patterns. Further, the benefits of fading support over time (Wecker & Fischer, 2007) might be more fully realized, as the frequency of intervention could be tuned to the students' demonstrated competence.

Now that this positive impact of tutorial dialogue agents within the field of CSCL has been established, a valuable next step could be to import this positive effect in the context of MOOCs. A particular challenge of this transfer is the relatively high attrition rate in MOOCs. If students drop out before they have the chance to experience a valuable learning experience, then they will not have the opportunity to benefit from the offered materials. Thus, in this work, we ask the question of whether experience of a collaborative chat supported by a tutorial dialogue agent has the effect of slowing down attrition over time in a MOOC.

The MOOC environment presents a number of challenges that must be addressed in order to introduce synchronous collaboration opportunities, but chief among them is the tremendous coordination challenge. In a MOOC, students may come and go as they please, and since they may be logging in from anywhere, any number of events could interfere with the task proceeding as planned: some students may have different preferences regarding which activities within a task to spend more or less time on, or a student may be called away from the computer, the internet connection may drop, or a student may give up and drop out in the middle of the activity. Furthermore, the sheer numbers of students make it challenging to coordinate plans for meeting times.

3   Technical Approach

As a first step towards achieving a positive impact of CSCL technology in MOOCs, we integrated a collaborative chat environment with interactive agent support in a recent 9-week long MOOC on learning analytics (DALMOOC) that was hosted on the edX platform from October to December 2014. Overall, 21,941 students enrolled in the course. The median age was 31 with 24.8% of the students 25 and under, 50.4% between 26 and 40 and 19.2% over 40. 180 countries were represented in the course with the majority of students from the USA (26%) and India (19%). A self-selected subset of students attempted participation in collaborative reflection activities that were offered each week as enrichment activities subsequent to individual learning activities.

In the following, we will describe the integration of our chat environment in DALMOOC. In order to facilitate the formation of ad-hoc study groups for the chat activity, we make use of a simple setup referred to as a Lobby. The Lobby introduces an intermediate layer between the edX platform and the synchronous chat tool. Even though the Lobby allows groups of arbitrary sizes to be formed, we decided that agent-guided discussions in groups of two students are the most suitable setup. Students enter the Lobby with a clearly labeled button integrated with the edX platform. In order to increase the likelihood of a critical mass of students being assigned to pairs, we suggested but did not enforce a couple of two hour time slots during each week of the MOOC when students might engage in the collaborative activities. These timeslots were advertised in weekly newsletters.

Upon entering the Lobby, students were asked to enter their screen name. Once logged into the lobby, the student waited to be matched with another participant. If they were successfully matched with another learner who arrived at the Lobby within 10 minutes, they and their partner were presented with a link to a chat room created for them in real time. Otherwise they were requested to come back later. A visualization was presented to them that illustrated the frequency of student clicks on the button at different times of the day on the various days of the week across a variety of time zones so that they would be able to gauge when would be a convenient time for them to come back when the likelihood of a match would be higher.

The chat setup had been used in earlier classroom research (Adamson et al., 2014). It provides opportunities for students to interact with one another through chat as well as to share images. The chat environment furthermore has built-in support for conversational agents who appear as regular users in the chat. In DALMOOC, the tutorial dialogue agents led the pairs of students through collaborative reflection activities that prompted them to share their thoughts about the learning activities they had engaged in individually before entering the collaborative reflection. A separate Lobby and chat instance was set up for each week of the course, and in each chat instance the agent was configured to scaffold discussion about the central topic of the respective week. Both the Lobby software and the chat tool logged any interactions that occurred between the students or between the students and the system. Overall, 371 unique students participated in the chat activities during the first two weeks of the course. They posted 4,624 messages in 215 chat sessions with a total of 58,325 tokens. The average duration of a chat was 15 minutes.

Integrating a synchronous collaborative activity in an inherently asynchronous learning environment that is used by students in different time zones from all over the world was one of the greatest organizational challenges to overcome. As mentioned earlier, we attempted to alleviate the problem by introducing dedicated chat hours to increase the likelihood of students getting matched with each other. Nevertheless, frequently students who entered the Lobby could not be matched with a chat partner within 10 minutes. The high percentage of students who waited until the Lobby asked them to return at a later point in time is however a good indicator that the students are motivated to participate. 257 students returned at least once to the Lobby while individual students logged in up to 15 times in a given week.

4   Evaluating the Impact of Participation on Attrition

In order to measure the strength of association between participation in a collaborative chat and attrition, we use a survival analysis. Survival analysis is a statistical modeling technique used to model the effect of one or more indicator variables at a time point on the probability of an event occurring on the next time point. In our case, we are modeling the effect of participation in a collaborative chat on probability that a student ceases to participate actively in the course on the next time point. In DALMOOC, students participated in chat sessions that were offered in each of the first 6 weeks of the course.

4.1   Methodology

Survival models are a form of proportional odds logistic regression, and they are known to provide less biased estimates than simpler techniques (e.g., standard least squares linear regression) that do not take into account the potentially truncated nature of time-to-event data (e.g., users who had not yet ceased their participation at the time of the analysis but might at some point subsequently). The survival models we employ in this study make a prediction about the probability of an event at each time point based on the presence of some set of predictors. The estimated weights on the predictors are referred to as hazard ratios. The hazard ratio of a predictor indicates how the relative likelihood of the failure (in our case, student dropout) occurring increases or decreases with an increase or decrease in the associated predictor in the case of a numeric predictor, or presence vs. absence of the factor in the case of a binary variable. A hazard ratio of 1 means the factor has no effect.

If the hazard ratio is a fraction, then the factor decreases the probability of the event. For example, if the hazard ratio was a number of value .4, it would mean that for every standard deviation greater than average the predictor variable is, the event is 60% less likely to occur (i.e., 1 - n). If the hazard ratio is instead greater than 1, that would mean that the factor has a positive effect on the probability of the event. In particular, if the hazard ratio is 1.25, then for every standard deviation greater than average the predictor variable is, the event is 25% more likely to occur (i.e., n - 1).

Survival analyses are correlational analyses, and as such they do not provide causal evidence for an effect. However, lack of an effect in a survival analysis would suggest that the data fail to provide causal evidence as well. A positive effect in a survival analysis would suggest that it makes sense as a next step to manipulate the associated factor so that causal evidence for a positive effect could be measured.

4.2   Specifying the Model

In our survival model we include control variables, independent variables, and a dependent variable. Our primary interest is in how the independent variables related to participation in collaborative chats make predictions about the dependent variable, which indicates course dropout. However, control variables are essential. They allow us to account for factors other than the factors of interest that may influence attrition so they do not bias the results. For example, some students start the course with a greater commitment to active participation, and factors associated with higher a priori commitment are typically associated with slower attrition over time (Wen et al., 2014; Wang et al., 2012). If we do not account for this in control variables, then the independent variables that differ in value depending on the a priori commitment level of students will have results that confound the factors of interest with a priori commitment.

Unit of Analysis. In order to assess the impact of measured factors at each time point during a student's trajectory through the course, it is necessary to decide what the unit of analysis is. In other words, it is necessary to determine how much time each time point should represent. Even the most active participants in the course did not participate every day. However, very active participants returned to the course more than once within a week. Thus we adopted a span of two days as the length of each time point. Since our analysis spans 6 weeks of time, we estimate the probability of retention in the course at each of 21 time points in our analysis.

Student Population. In order to participate in a chat, a student had to attempt to be matched for a chat by clicking on the button to enter the Lobby. In DALMOOC, while there were over 20,000 students who enrolled in the course, most of these students were not active participants. In any given week, only between 1,181 and 6,379 students logged into the course with a median of 1,920 over the full 9-week runtime of the course. The collaborative chat activities were positioned as enrichment activities after the individual work for the week was completed. Thus, students who attempted to be matched for a chat were on average more active and more committed to the course than students who did not. We would expect a variable that indicates that a student made at least one attempt to be matched during a time period would be associated with lower attrition. As discussed above, however, these attempts did not always result in a successful match due to a lack of critical mass of students at many times. Frequently in order to be successfully matched for a chat, students had to click to enter the Lobby at many different times. Failing to be matched for a chat was discouraging to students, as evidenced by complaints mentioned in the discussion forums. And we would expect that larger numbers of attempts would be associated with more and more frustration, and therefore, higher attrition. Thus, we expect these two potential independent variables of interest to be associated with opposite effects, although the variables themselves would necessarily be correlated. In survival models it is important not to include multiple independent variables that are highly correlated. But including only one or the other is also problematic, since we expect that these are both important effects. In order to address these issues we only include in the survival analysis presented here the subset of students who during at least one time point clicked to enter the Lobby at least once. In that way we control for the elevated level of a priori commitment associated with the set of students who clicked to enter the Lobby at least once. Only 815 students attempted to be matched for a collaborative chat at least once during the 6 weeks when collaborative chats took place. Thus, the survival analysis we present in this paper is focused on these 815 students. To test the implications of this choice over the whole set of students who clicked in the course materials at least once, we verified that clicking to enter the Lobby at least once was associated with lower attrition whereas the number of clicks to enter the Lobby was associated with higher attrition.

Control Variables. Other indicators of commitment to active engagement were the number of clicks on course videos or number of clicks to access the discussion forums. We present the estimates for the model computed over the selected 815 students below using number of *Video Clicks* and number of *Forum Clicks* as control variables. Over the whole set of students, number of video clicks did not make a significant prediction about attrition, and number of forum clicks was associated with lower attrition.

Independent Variables. Since only the 815 students who clicked to enter the Lobby at least once were included in the analysis, it was not necessary to include that binary variable in the model as an independent variable. So we were able to include number of Lobby clicks, which we refer to as *Match Attempts*, as an independent variable, in order to quantify its hypothesized association with higher attrition. We also included a binary variable called *Match Success* that was true for students who were successfully matched for a chat during a time period in order to measure the hypothesized association between the experience of being matched for a chat and lower attrition. In order to measure a hypothesized mitigating effect on the negative impact of having to click many times to be matched if one is finally matched successfully, we included the interaction between these two variables in the model as well.

Dependent variable. The dependent variable we referred to as drop. This was a binary variable that was 1 during the last time point of a student's active participation in the MOOC and 0 otherwise. All of the continuous variables in the model were standardized in order to enhance the interpretability of the model estimates. In other words, the range of continuous variables was scaled so that the range had a mean value of 0 and a standard deviation of 1.

4.3   Survival Model Results

We hypothesized that we would find evidence that the experience of collaborative chats would be associated with lower attrition over time, and the results of the survival analysis support this hypothesis.

Table 1 presents the hazard ratios computed from the survival analysis. First we examine the estimated hazard ratios on control variables to make sure those effects make sense. The hazard ratio on Video Clicks indicates that elevated numbers of video clicks are associated with higher attrition rather than lower attrition, which was a surprise. When we examined the logfiles for the students included in the survival analysis, we noticed that virtually all of them had viewed all of the videos. Thus, elevated numbers of video clicks could distinguish students who were having trouble following the videos and needed to backtrack multiple times. The hazard ratio on Forum Clicks, .51, suggests that students with elevated numbers of clicks on the discussion forums, which occur either when students are reading the discussions or posting to the forums, was associated with a substantial reduction in attrition. In particular, it suggests attrition is reduced by half when students have a standard deviation higher number of forum clicks than average.

Now we turn to an examination of the hazard ratios on our independent variables. As hypothesized, elevated numbers of Match Attempts are associated with higher attrition. In particular, a hazard ratio of 2.33 indicates that students who have an elevated level of Match Attempts at a time point are 133% or 2.33 times more likely to drop out at the next time point. This suggests a substantial negative effect of the frustration at sometimes having to try multiple times to get matched for a chat. However, the hazard ratio on Match Success suggests a substantial reduction of attrition when a student experiences a match with another student. In particular, a hazard ratio of .44 suggests that students who experience a match are 56% less likely to drop out at the next time point than students who did not experience a match success. The interaction term is also associated with a fractional hazard ratio. In particular, a hazard ratio of .76 suggests that over and above the generally positive effect of experiencing a match, the experience of a match after having made multiple attempts partly mitigates the negative effect of the multiple attempts, in particular, reducing attrition by 24%. The survival curves that display visually the difference in attrition over time of students who experience a match vs. students who do not experience a match is displayed in Figure 1.

Table 1. Survival table with estimates that measure the impact of control variables (Video Clicks and Forum Clicks), and independent variables (Match Attempts, Match Success, and the interaction between the two) on probability of survival from one time point to the next

Independent Variable	Hazard Ratio	p-Value
Video Clicks	2.38	$p < .0001$
Forum Clicks	0.51	$p < .0001$
Match Attempts	2.33	$p < .0001$
Match Success	0.44	$p < .01$
Interaction between Attempts and Success	0.76	$p < .05$

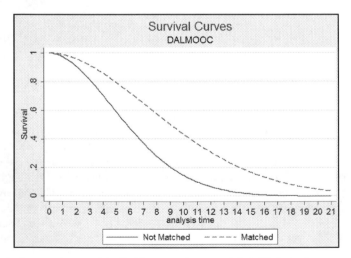

Fig. 1. Survival curve that graphically illustrates how much less likely to drop out at each time point a student is if they experience a match for a synchronous collaboration at that time point

5   Discussion and Conclusions

In this paper we have evaluate an intervention that makes synchronous collaboration opportunities available to students in an edX MOOC. The results suggest a substantial reduction in attrition over time when students experience a match for a synchronous collaborative reflection exercise. Nevertheless, these results must be treated with some caution as we experienced significant difficulty in managing the logistics of matches. Even with 20,000 students enrolled in the course, some students had to make as many as 15 attempts to be matched with a partner before a match was made. Because the results suggest that students found value in the experience, it appears to be worth the effort to address this challenge in future work. One potential direction is to form matches during other course activities that extend over time, such as a video lecture. Students could simultaneously be waiting for a match and watching a video. In that case, students may experience more success at matches since the wait time would be longer on average. And furthermore, there may be less negative impact of not getting matched on an attempt since students would be doing something productive while waiting.

Acknowledgement. This research was supported in part by NSF grant SBE-0836012 and funding from Google and Bosch.

References

1. Adamson, D., Dyke, G., Jang, H.J., Rosé, C.P.: Towards an Agile Approach to Adapting Dynamic Collaboration Support to Student Needs. International Journal of AI in Education **24**(1), 91–121 (2014)
2. Ai, H., Kumar, R., Nguyen, D., Nagasunder, A., Rosé, C.P.: Exploring the effectiveness of social capabilities and goal alignment in computer supported collaborative learning. In: Aleven, V., Kay, J., Mostow, J. (eds.) ITS 2010, Part II. LNCS, vol. 6095, pp. 134–143. Springer, Heidelberg (2010)
3. Chaudhuri, S., Kumar, R., Joshi, M., Terrell, E., Higgs, F., Aleven, V., Penstein Rosé, C.: It's not easy being green: supporting collaborative "green design" learning. In: Woolf, B.P., A\"ımeur, E., Nkambou, R., Lajoie, S. (eds.) ITS 2008. LNCS, vol. 5091, pp. 807–809. Springer, Heidelberg (2008)
4. Chaudhuri, S., Kumar, R., Howley, I., Rosé, C.P.: Engaging collaborative learners with helping agents. In: Proceedings of the 2009 conference on Artificial Intelligence in Education: Building Learning Systems that Care: From Knowledge Representation to Affective Modeling, pp. 365–372. IOS Press (2009)
5. Clarke, S., Chen, G., Stainton, K., Katz, S., Greeno, J., Resnick, L., Howley, H., Adamson, D., Rosé, C.P.: The impact of CSCL beyond the online environment. In: Proceedings of Computer Supported Collaborative Learning (2013)
6. Dillenbourg, P.: Over-scripting CSCL: The risks of blending collaborative learning with instructional design. In: Three worlds of CSCL - Can we support CSCL? pp. 61–91 (2002)
7. Erkens, G., Janssen, J.: Automatic Coding of Dialogue Acts in Collaboration Protocols. International Journal of Computer Supported Collaborative Learning **3**, 447–470 (2008)

8. Kirschner, F., Paas, F., Kirschner, P.A.: A cognitive load approach to collaborative learning: United brains for complex tasks. Educational Psychology Review **21**, 31–42 (2009)
9. Kobbe, L., Weinberger, A., Dillenbourg, P., Harrer, A., Hämäläinen, R., Häkkinen, P., Fischer, F.: Specifying computer-supported collaboration scripts. International Journal of Computer-Supported Collaborative Learning **2**(2), 211–224 (2007)
10. Kollar, I., Fischer, F., Hesse, F.W.: Collaborative scripts - a conceptual analysis. Educational Psychology Review **18**(2), 159–185 (2006)
11. Kumar, R., Rosé, C.P., Wang, Y.C., Joshi, M., Robinson, A.: Tutorial dialogue as adaptive collaborative learning support. In: Proceedings of Artificial Intelligence in Education (2007)
12. Kumar, R., Ai, H., Beuth, J.L., Rosé, C.P.: Socially Capable Conversational Tutors Can Be Effective in Collaborative Learning Situations. In: Aleven, V., Kay, J., Mostow, J. (eds.) ITS 2010, Part I. LNCS, vol. 6094, pp. 156–164. Springer, Heidelberg (2010)
13. Kumar, R., Rosé, C.P.: Architecture for Building Conversational Agents that Support Collaborative Learning. IEEE Transactions on Learning Technologies 4(1) (2011)
14. McLaren, B., Scheuer, O., De Laat, M., Hever, R., de Groot, R., Rosé, C.P.: Using machine learning techniques to analyze and support mediation of student e-discussions. In: Proceedings of Artificial Intelligence in Education, pp. 331–338. IOS Press (2007)
15. Mu, J., Stegmann, K., Mayfield, E., Rosé, C.P., Fischer, F.: The ACODEA Framework: Developing Segmentation and Classification Schemes for Fully Automatic Analysis of Online Discussions. International Journal of Computer Supported Collaborative Learning **7**(2), 285–305 (2012)
16. Rosé C.P., VanLehn, K.: An Evaluation of a Hybrid Language Understanding Approach for Robust Selection of Tutoring Goals. International Journal of AI in Education 15(4) (2005)
17. Rosé, C.P., Wang, Y.C., Cui, Y., Arguello, J., Stegmann, K., Weinberger, A., Fischer, F.: Analyzing collaborative learning processes automatically: Exploiting the advances of computational linguistics in computer-supported collaborative learning. The International Journal of Computer-Supported Collaborative Learning **3**(3), 237–271 (2008)
18. Soller, A., Lesgold, A.: Modeling the process of collaborative learning. In: Proceedings of the International Workshop on New Technologies in Collaborative Learning. Japan: Awaiji–Yumebutai (2000)
19. Webb, N.M., Palinscar, A.S.: Group processes in the classroom. In: Berliner, D.C., Calfee, R.C. (eds.) Handbook of educational psychology, pp. 841–873. Prentice Hall, New York (1996)
20. Wecker, C., Fischer, F.: Fading scripts in computer-supported collaborative learning: the role of distributed monitoring. In: CSCL 2007 Proceedings of the 8th International Conference on Computer Supported Collaborative Learning, pp. 764–772 (2007)
21. Weinberger, A., Stegmann, K., Fischer, F., Mandl, H.: Scripting argumentative knowledge construction in computer-supported learning environments. In: Scripting Computer-Supported Collaborative Learning, CSCL Book Series vol. 6, ch. 6, pp. 191–211 (2007)
22. Wen, M., Yang, D., Rosé, D.: Linguistic reflections of student engagement in massive open online courses. In: Proceedings of the International Conference on Weblogs and Social Media (2014)

Who Needs Help? Automating Student Assessment Within Exploratory Learning Environments

Mark Floryan[1]([⊠]), Toby Dragon[2], Nada Basit[1], Suellen Dragon[2], and Beverly Woolf[3]

[1] University of Virginia, Charlottesville, USA
{mfloryan,basit}@virginia.edu
[2] Ithaca College, Ithaca, USA
{tdragon,sdragon}@ithaca.edu
[3] University of Massachusetts Amherst, Amherst, USA
bev@cs.umass.edu

Abstract. This article describes efforts to offer automated assessment of students within an exploratory learning environment. We present a regression model that estimates student assessments in an ill-defined medical diagnosis tutor called Rashi. We were pleased to find that basic features of a student's solution predicted expert assessment well, particularly when detecting low-achieving students. We also discuss how expert knowledge bases might be leveraged to improve this process. We suggest that developers of exploratory learning environments can leverage this technique with relatively few extensions to a mature system. Finally, we describe the potential to utilize this information to direct teachers' attention towards students in need of help.

1 Introduction

The field of computer supported education is continually growing and shaping our educational landscape. With this growth, we see computer systems designed to offer more authentic learning experiences, and less rote educational techniques such as lecture, textbook reading, and multiple choice questions. Instead, Exploratory Learning Environments (ELEs) offer users the potential to engage more deeply through interaction and experimentation. This increased autonomy also comes with a price, namely that many students require support in order to succeed in open-ended spaces [7]. This problem is exacerbated by the subject matter often presented in these ELEs, which is ill-defined [5]. Engaging with ELEs and ill-defined problem spaces can offer interesting, authentic learning situations, as students face realistic challenges and have the opportunity to approach and situate the knowledge in their own way. However, supporting students is crucial, as students can become lost or stuck more easily in such complex scenarios [8].

We argue that there is a straight-forward method of offering some automated assessment without a large investment of resources, given that the system has

© Springer International Publishing Switzerland 2015
C. Conati et al. (Eds.): AIED 2015, LNAI 9112, pp. 125–134, 2015.
DOI: 10.1007/978-3-319-19773-9_13

already been used, that data have been collected, and that the student solutions have been graded. In this scenario, supervised machine learning techniques can be applied to estimate new grades from old data. By using the model created from previous data, the system can offer automated assessment on the fly, to help teachers decide which students may be in need of assistance.

2   Related Work

Although assessment in exploratory learning environments is largely unexplored, several attempts at doing so exist. The researchers involved with RomanTutor[2] compared user actions to a learned model to profile learners as experts, inter-mediates, etc.. In addition to this, several researchers have focused on using natural language approaches to assess learners. Walker et al. analyzed student contributions to a discussion of inter-cultural awareness to provide feedback to both students and moderators [4]. This system used a simple keyword analysis along with a model of dimensions of strong forum posts to categorize student contributions. In a somewhat similar analysis, Latent-Semantic Analysis was used within AutoTutor to assess learners into broad categories (good, vague, erroneous, etc.) [6].

Some systems analyze user actions within ELEs to categorize learners, as is done in Betty's Brain [10][11]. Additionally, Davoodi et. al. used unsupervised machine learning to cluster students by behavior oriented features in the game Prime Climb [9]. They discovered that such features helps distinguish between students with various understandings of the underlying domain knowledge and imply that this information might be used to provide feedback early on in the interaction.

Probably most similar to our work however, Ting et al. examined the design of dynamic decision networks to evaluate student inquiry skills [1]. The researchers evaluated several models specifically designed to support scientific inquiry skills. The model was validated against the opinions of six domain experts. However, their work was focused specifically on inquiry behavior, and did not attempt to explicitly measure content knowledge.

3   Setting/Motivation

To study automated assessment techniques, we consider one exploratory learning environment for ill-defined domains that has been used continually in classrooms since 2007. The system, called Rashi, is a domain-independent inquiry learning system that invites students to explore, create hypotheses, and investigate dif-ferent real-life phenomena within the given domain [3]. Various data collection methods (interactive images, interview interfaces, etc.) acquaint students with methods commonly used by professionals to access and filter information.

For the data related to this research, we consider the domain of Biology, where students use Rashi to step into the role of a doctor, evaluating patients and generating hypotheses about their medical condition. Students can interview the virtual patients, perform a physical examination, or run lab tests (see figure 1, right). The central collection of student work is a tool called the notebook, which is represented by two different portions, the data table (figure 1 left-bottom) and the argument editor (figure 1 left-top). Students explore and collect data, which is automatically logged in the data table from the various sources. They use this notebook to explicate their hypotheses, and connect these hypotheses with the data they have collected. In this way, the end result of student work on a given case is a notebook that represents the data collected, the hypothesis formed, and the relationships (supporting or refuting) between data and hypotheses.

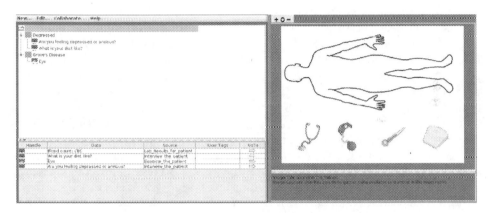

Fig. 1. A subset of the Rashi environment. Students can perform a physical examination on the patient (right) and organize their inquiry argument in their notebook (left).

The system is often used in large introductory science courses, with hundreds of students. On this scale, the teachers and teaching assistants (TAs) are unable to work individually with each student. Instead, the students are graded based on the final state of their notebook, and this single grade is the only feedback that a student receives. While the system has been met with praise from both teachers and students alike, this lack of feedback does lead to certain problems. Specifically, some subset of students often seem to miss the point of the exercise, or to have little to no skill at the inquiry process. These students often do not seek assistance and therefore can be overlooked until their final grade, when it is too late to offer assistance.

The overarching goal of this work is to support teachers working with large groups of students in Rashi. The pressing need is for teachers to be able to quickly identify students that are in need of support or teacher intervention. Therefore, our intermediate goal, and the subject of this paper, is to define a method of using the data already available to create an on-the-spot assessment of general student performance. This can be used by teachers and TAs to note a subset of students that are clearly in need of assistance.

4   Feature Selection

For the purpose of our study, we planned to utilize specific features of logged student solutions in order to predict assessments made by teachers about these solutions. To choose features, we first worked with several individuals involved in grading biology reports to obtain insight as to important aspects of student activity that warrant a high assessment. These discussions lead us to collect basic statistics regarding the breadth and depth of a student argument created within Rashi. These features include the number of hypotheses the student considered, the amount of observable data collected, and the number of relationships established between data and hypotheses. These features are intuitively necessary for any assessment because they represent the building blocks of students solutions. Slightly more complex features address the percentage of collected observations from various data sources, motivated by the observation that students should be performing less laboratory testing and more non-invasive inquiry (e.g., speaking with the patient, physical examination, etc.). Finally, our experts also mentioned that students should be performing simple data collection early in the process and more advanced (i.e., ordering lab tests) later in the inquiry process. We thus calculated, for each possible data type in Rashi, the average percentage along a relative inquiry timeline (0.0 representing the beginning of inquiry and 1.0 representing the end of inquiry) when data of that type was collected by the student. For example, 0.25 for physical examinations represents that the student mostly performed physical examinations one quarter of the way through the diagnosis process. Notice that this is a relative timeline and not dependent on exact timestamps, offering a basic measure of the ordering of inquiry behavior tasks. Collectively, we refer to all of these features as the basic features (see figure 2, top).

Moving beyond the basic features, we also sought to utilize Rashis expert knowledge base (ekb), built previously to support adaptive hints and feedback [3]. We posited that features taking advantage of this ekb might provide the contextual information necessary to distinguish student assessments based on the specific biology content involved. The ekb supports a simple text matching scheme to detect when students are utilizing biology concepts that experts have agreed are related to the case at hand. We thus pulled features representing how a students work matches the expert knowledge base in various ways (figure 2, bottom).

5   Experimental Design

To employ supervised machine learning to automate assessment, we need both a data set from which to pull the features discussed in the previous section, and information about the relative success of the students associated with this data set. In this way, we can investigate how well an automated system can predict actual teachers assessments in Rashi, with a particular focus on detecting low-achieving students.

Table 1. Basic features used to assess students (left) along with features requiring an expert knowledge base (right)

BASIC FEATURES	
Feature Name	Description
Num Hypos	Number of hypotheses the student considered
Num Rels	Number of relationships the student created
Num Data	Number of data observations collected by the student
Relations Per Hypothesis	Number of relations divided by num. of hypotheses
Percent Exam	Percent of data collected through physical examination of the patient
Percent Interview	Percent of data collected by interviewing the patient
Percent Lab	Percent of data collected by running lab tests
Time Examination	Percent along time scale in which student primarily performed physical examinations
Time Interview	Percent along time scale in which student primarily interviewed the patient
Time Lab	Percent along time scale in which student primarily requested laboratory tests

EKB FEATURES	
Feature Name	Description
Hypo. Match Score	How well student hypotheses match nodes in the ekb
Rel. Match Score	Score for how well student relationships match the ekb
Num. Data Associated	Amount of data collected related to a hypothesis but not connected by student
Lab. Justification Matches	How well justifications for ordering lab tests match to the ekb
Scratch Pad Matches	How well contents of student scratch pad match the ekb

To gather features from logged data, we utilized data collected during the Fall term of 2012 at a large university in the Northeast United States. The participants were all college students taking the introductory biology course and used our system for approximately 1.5 hours during one of the weekly laboratory sessions. The students were given a single case (i.e., one patient to diagnose) and worked in small teams (2-3 students) on the case. Each group submitted a single argument in Rashi. For this reason, the analysis in this paper treats small groups of students as a single entity, not necessarily predicting the assessment of individuals but rather individual Rashi accounts. The students were required to submit a lab report the following week describing their work and thus some students logged into the system to continue working outside of the designated lab time. We acquired the data described for 93 student solutions, representing most of the students in the class described above. Accounts that produced no data (appeared to be no work done at all) were removed, as well as several accounts from which we were unable to gather the required features (corrupted data).

To gather data about the quality of student solutions, a subject matter expert (SME) graded each students solution by logging into the tutor and observing the students work directly. Our SME is an adjunct faculty in Biology and has used Rashi in the classroom previously. However, she was not involved with the classrooms associated with these experiments, and was not involved in the choice of feature selection. We are thus confident that she was qualified to grade these student lab reports, and that she was not involved enough with the project to be overfitting grades to our decisions about features.

The SME graded each of the students as she would for her own purpose as a teacher, on a five point scale (A-F, which we then mapped to the integers five through one, respectively). In this way, we argue that this data could be readily available for any case in Rashi where the students were graded by a teacher in this manner. The SME provided two grades per student, one for display of proper inquiry behavior (we call this the Investigative grade) and the other for proper application of medical knowledge (we call this the Medical grade). Both sets of grades contained a negative skew (towards poor grades), though the medical grades were less so.

Table 2. Distribution of grades given by the domain expert

	F	D	C	B	A	Total
MEDICAL	28	16	24	13	12	93
INVESTIGATIVE	30	36	8	9	10	93

With both features and grades for the dataset in hand, we fit a linear regression model with only the basic features, with only the ekb features, and with both. We also fit models for the medical grades as well as the investigative grades separately. Some of our features, by visual inspection, were quadratic or logarithmic in nature and were thus scaled to an appropriate polynomial. In addition, all features were normalized. We used four-fold cross validation for each of the conditions described above. The four results from the folds were averaged (see Results section). The advantage of this method over repeated random subsampling is that all observations are used for both training and validation, and each observation is used for validation exactly once.

As we are particularly interested in detecting low-achieving students, we also consider a binary decision of low vs. high achieving. For this analysis, we counted the number of students graded at a 1 or 2 (D or F), for both investigative and medical scores. We then simply calculate the percentage with which our model also predicts a low score (2.5 or less) for those same students. In addition, we count the number of false positives presented by our model, defined as a student predicted as a low-achiever that was actually given a high score (3 or higher) by the SME. Our hope is that our model does particularly well detecting low-achieving students, as the greatest benefit to teachers would be the identification of students in need of support.

6   Results and Discussion

The table below displays the individual results of each fold of the four-fold cross validation. We present both the average error rates for all test data points along with the average error squared values. In particular, when the expert knowledge base features are used alone, the models tend to do poorly. The ekb features do seem more predictive when measuring medical grades rather than investigative grades.

Table 3. Results of four-fold analysis. Average error rates (left) are shown as well as average error squared rates (right).

INVESTIGATIVE					INVESTIGATIVE			
Fold	Basic	EKB	Both		Fold	Basic	EKB	Both
1	0.54	0.75	0.42		1	0.67	0.83	0.39
2	0.48	0.73	0.47		2	0.38	0.81	0.40
3	0.48	1.06	0.47		3	0.49	1.63	0.46
4	0.64	0.93	0.50		4	0.57	1.42	0.38
Error:	0.54	0.87	0.46		Squared Error:	0.53	1.17	0.41

MEDICAL					MEDICAL			
Fold	Basic	EKB	Both		Fold	Basic	EKB	Both
1	0.72	0.58	0.62		1	0.66	0.52	0.52
2	0.61	0.76	0.55		2	0.61	0.84	0.55
3	0.60	0.89	0.57		3	0.56	1.18	0.55
4	0.81	0.82	0.75		4	0.90	0.98	0.80
Error:	0.69	0.76	0.62		Squared Error:	0.68	0.88	0.60

The basic features tend to predict grades fairly well, averaging around half of a point error rate for investigative grades and somewhat more than this (0.69) for medical grades. This again is intuitive because our basic features do not capture domain knowledge and thus are worse predictors, though it still seems that good investigative skills tend to correlate with display of domain knowledge. When both types of features are combined, we achieve slightly better results, which is expected. The features utilizing the ekb provide some extra contextual information that leads to better predictions. Our best case for predicting investigative scores uses both sets of features together, which yielded an average error rate of 0.46.

The graphs in figure 2 show our models predictions on two sample sets of test data. One can see visually that our predictions do fairly well, and while they may not be adequate to assign grades, they should be adequate for judging relative student performance to support teachers. We discuss this potential usage in the conclusions section below.

Additionally, figure 3 shows the top five features (by weight) discovered by each model. We include only results for the model's fit with both sets of features (basic and EKB features) for simplicity.

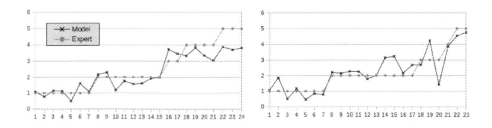

Fig. 2. Example assessments given by our model along with the domain expert's assessments

	Feature Name:	Feature Type:	Weight:		Feature Name:	Feature Type:	Weight:
Investigative:	Rels Per Hypo	Basic	1.62	*Medical:* Rels Per Hypo	Basic	1.14
	Num Rels	Basic	1.36	Hypo Match Score	EKB	1.10
	Hypo Match Score	EKB	0.95	Num Rels	Basic	1.05
	Lab Just. Matches	EKB	0.66	Lab Just. Matches	EKB	0.60
	Num Data	Basic	0.41	Num Hypos	Basic	0.58

Fig. 3. Top features by weight for both our investigative and medical models

As the foreseen use of this model is to provide an instructor with information during the tutors usage, giving the instructor broad assessment and the ability to intervene with specific students when necessary. To accomplish this specific goal, we also performed an analysis on detecting a binary decision between low and high achieving students(see experimental design section above). The results of this analysis can be seen below:

Table 4. Analysis of our model's ability to detect students who are not progressing well through the tutor's exercise

INVESTIGATIVE				
Fold	Num Low-Achievers	Num Detected	Correct Rate	False Positives
1	19	18	0.947	0
2	17	14	0.824	1
3	16	15	0.938	0
4	14	14	1.000	0
Total	66	61	0.924	1

MEDICAL				
Fold	Num Low-Achievers	Num Detected	Correct Rate	False Positives
1	12	10	0.833	0
2	11	6	0.545	0
3	9	7	0.778	0
4	12	8	0.667	0
Total	44	31	0.705	0

Our model succeeds in predicting low-achieving students (those earning a grade of D or F) for the investigative scores. We see a 92.4 success rate for detecting low-achieving students with only one false positive. Our predictions for medical scores are more conservative and less accurate. However, we still see a 70.5 percent detection rate, which in practice is still useful to a teacher. As before, we believe we see less accuracy for medical grades as the contextual information is harder to detect than the structure of a students argument.

7   Conclusions

While exploratory learning environments provide greater freedom and ability to practice in ill-defined domains, automated assessment in these environments is difficult. In addition, such systems are often meant to teach general learning skills (e.g., inquiry) and not only domain specific knowledge (e.g., biology). We argue that there is unharnessed power in data collected by these computer systems and those that use them. We demonstrate that even basic machine learning techniques can provide enough insight to offer broad assessment and help direct teacher attention to students most in need. Providing a sample training set for grading and using basic regression models over readily-available features is a low-cost way to quickly provide any system lacking other automated assessment. The (potentially rough) assessment can be useful in a variety of ways. For large classes, a tool might use this model to suggest students that teachers (or teaching assistants) should seek out for personal attention. Additionally, student assessments could be fed into a coaching module [3] to provide adaptive support to students.

Obviously, more accurate predictions would be more useful. We believe that the ekb is one key element improving these predictions. In particular, we would expect the ekb to improve predictions on domain knowledge (represented as medical above), as it potentially offers a clear distinction between process and content. While the ekb-related features offered slight improvement, it was not a significant effect. We consider underlying reasons methods for improvement in the following section.

8 Future Work

Our immediate intentions are to incorporate this model into the Rashi tutor and do real-time assessment. We do not intend, at least initially, for this to be student facing, but rather to manifest itself as a tool for alerting teachers of students requiring attention. The specific implementation details of such a tool can range from quite simplistic (a list of students with detected low scores) to quite complicated (student assessments with details and meta-data provided). We hope to prototype and pilot test simple versions of this tool in schools using Rashi in the Spring of 2015. Thus, future studies will focus on whether this tool can, in the hands of teachers, lead to improved inquiry behavior, increased domain knowledge, etc.

While our larger goals involve using predictions to support teachers and students, we also must consider methods of improving the current predictor. One attempt would be to employ Stratified Cross-Validation because the distribution of grades were not equal. This involves taking care, when creating the folds, to ensure cross-validation is operating on folds that are identical in grade distribution. Beyond improving the statistical method, we can also improve the predictive power of the features used in the regression. We see the ekb as a crucial component in this effort, even as our current experiment indicates that the ekb was not overly helpful. We theorize that the lack of predictive power might actually lie in a weak connection mechanism between actual student work and the ekb (done only with automated keyword matching [3]). We plan to test this theory and implement a more robust identification mechanism should it prove to be potentially useful.

References

1. Ting, C.-Y., Phon-Amnuaisuk, S.: Optimal dynamic decision network model for scientific inquiry learning environment. Applied Intelligence **33**(3), 387–406 (2010)
2. Fournier-Viger, P., Nkambou, R., Nguifo, E.M.: Exploiting Partial Problem Spaces Learned to Provide Key Tutoring Services in Procedural and Ill-Defined Domains. Artificial Intelligence in Education: Building Learning Systems that Care: From Knowledge Representation to Affective Modelling **200**, 383 (2009)
3. Dragon, T., Park Woolf, B., Marshall, D., Murray, T.: Coaching within a domain independent inquiry environment. In: Ikeda, M., Ashley, K.D., Chan, T.-W. (eds.) ITS 2006. LNCS, vol. 4053, pp. 144–153. Springer, Heidelberg (2006)
4. Walker, Erin, et al.: Two approaches for providing adaptive support for discussion in an ill-defined domain. Intelligent Tutoring Systems for Ill-Defined Domains: Assessment and Feedback in Ill-Defined Domains, 1 (2008)
5. Mitrovic, A., Weerasinghe, A.: Revisiting ill-denedness and the consequences for ITSs. Artificial intelligence in Education: Building Learning Systems that Care from Knowledge Representation to Affective Modelling, 375–382 (2009)
6. Graesser, A.C., et al.: Using latent semantic analysis to evaluate the contributions of students in AutoTutor. Interactive Learning Environments **8**(2), 129–147 (2000)
7. Mavrikis, M., et al.: Design requirements, student perception indicators and validation metrics for intelligent exploratory learning environments. Personal and Ubiquitous Computing **17**(8), 1605–1620 (2013)
8. Lynch, C., et al.: Defining ill-defined domains; a literature survey. In: Proceedings of the Workshop on Intelligent Tutoring Systems for Ill-Defined Domains at the 8th International Conference on Intelligent Tutoring Systems (2006)
9. Davoodi, A., Kardan, S., Conati, C.: Understanding Users Interaction Behavior with an Intelligent Educational Game: Prime Climb. In: AIED 2013 Workshops Proceedings Volume 2 Scaffolding in Open-Ended Learning Environments (OELEs), p. 9 (2013)
10. Kinnebrew, J.S., Segedy, J.R., Biswas, G.: Analyzing the temporal evolution of students behaviors in open-ended learning environments. Metacognition and learning **9**(2), 187–215 (2014)
11. Segedy, J., Biswas, G., Sulcer, B.: A Model-Based Behavior Analysis Approach for Open-Ended Environments. Educational Technology and Society **17**(1), 272–282 (2014)

Moody Agents: Affect and Discourse During Learning in a Serious Game

Carol M. Forsyth[1,2(✉)], Arthur Graesser[2], Andrew M. Olney[2], Keith Millis[3], Breya Walker[2], and Zhiqiang Cai[2]

[1] Educational Testing Services, Rosedale Rd., Princeton, NJ 08648, New Jersey
cforsyth@ets.org
[2] The University of Memphis, Institute for Intelligent Systems, Innovation Drive, Memphis, TN 38152, USA
cforsyth@ets.org
[3] Northern Illinois University, Psychology Building, Dekalb, IL 60115, USA

Abstract. The current study investigated teacher emotions, student emotions, and discourse features in relation to learning in a serious game. The experiment consisted of 48 subjects participating in a 4-condition within-subjects counter-balanced pretest-interaction-posttest design. Participants interacted with a serious game teaching research methodology with natural language conversations between the human student and two artificial pedagogical agents. The discourse of the artificial pedagogical agents was manipulated to evoke student affective states. Student emotion was measured via affect grids and discourse features were measured with computational linguistics techniques. Results indicated that learner's arousal levels impacted learning and that language use is correlated with learning.

Keywords: Discourse · Serious game · Emotion · Intelligent tutoring systems · Learning

1 Introduction

The goal of the current investigation is to discover both affective and cognitive- discourse components influencing learner's experiences in a serious game known as *Operation ARIES!* (ARA, in the commercial web version; [1]). The game teaches students critical thinking in the domain of research methodology using natural language conversations between a human student and two or more artificial agents. In previous research, the system has been used to investigate both discourse and affect during learning [2,3] as it provides an atmosphere of learning tasks that are easily manipulated and controlled by researchers. The current investigation was designed to measure the impact of teacher (an artificial pedagogical agent) mood, or more generalized emotion, on student learning, human student emotions on learning, and the relationship between student discourse features with learning during interaction with this serious game.

© Springer International Publishing Switzerland 2015
C. Conati et al. (Eds.): AIED 2015, LNAI 9112, pp. 135–144, 2015.
DOI: 10.1007/978-3-319-19773-9_14

1.1   Emotions and Learning

Recently, emotions have been studied on a moment-to-moment basis during the learning process with Intelligent Tutoring Systems, including but not limited to *OperationARIES!* [3,4]. Many previous studies focus on transient and discrete learning-centered emotions (e.g. confusion or surprise) whereas the current investigation focused on a broader and longer-lasting category of emotions, categorized by two separate dimensions of valence and arousal [5]. Valence describes the polarity of emotion, whereas arousal defines the intensity. Accordingly, learning-centered emotions can be categorized as having either a negative valence (i.e., frustration and boredom), a positive valence (flow/engagement and delight), or somewhere in-between, depending on context (e.g., confusion and surprise).

Affective states of teachers may influence student emotions, and therefore learning gains [6-8]. Some research suggests enthusiasm and other positive emotions increase teachers' effectiveness by increasing the efficiency of the instruction [7-8]. However, Sullins and colleagues [6] found teachers, in this case artificial agents, displaying negative affect, to be most conducive to learning. Thus, contradictory empirical evidence exists as to whether it is positively- or negatively- valenced teacher emotions that best facilitate learning [6-7].

Regardless of the teacher, recent studies suggest student emotions play a role in learning [3-4,7]. Students in a positive affective state may have greater cognitive flexibility, global processing capacities, creativity, and attention. Conversely, students in a negatively- valenced affective state have more analytical and focused processing (for a review,see [7]). These findings are supported by *the broaden and build theory* [9] that draws on a Darwinian evolutionary perspective. The broaden and build theory is based on the idea that negative emotions tend to require immediate reactions, whereas positive emotions allow one to view the surroundings (broaden) and accrue more resources in order to increase the probability of survival (build). Another possibility is that valence itself does not affect the functioning of cognitive processes. The *arousal theory* suggests that only the intensity (not the valence) of an emotional trigger is important [10]. However these findings may only be true for simple tasks [11], but not more intricate tasks such as creative problem-solving [7]. Simple vs. complex tasks may evoke shallow vs. deep learning, a characteristic that can be captured by discourse features.

1.2   Discourse Comprehension

Psychological theories of comprehension have identified multiple representations and strategies corresponding to multiple levels of discourse comprehension ([14] for a review). In the current investigation, we use a taxonomy developed by Graesser and colleagues [15, 16] including five levels of discourse processes ranging from shallow to deep level comprehension. These levels can be captured in a computational linguistic tool known as Coh-Metrix [16,17]. The 5 levels measure comprehension on a continuum of shallow to deep comprehension include *word concreteness* (words), *syntactic simplicity* (syntax), *referential cohesion* (textbase), *deep cohesion* (situation model), and *narrativity* (genre). These 5 measures are derived from a principal component analysis of over 100 discourse features measured in Coh-Metrix [18]. In addition to these 5 measures corresponding to the framework, a composite measure of formality may potentially be indicative of cognitive strategies and comprehension. All scores are represented on a scale from 0 to 1 indicating presence of the corresponding features within the text. For example, a score of 0 for word concreteness would imply that many abstract words such as "imagine" were used whereas a score of 1 means that many concrete words (e.g. "participant") are present in the text. In the current study, the discourse features corresponding to these levels of comprehension, along with both the teacher and student emotions, are investigated in relation to learning.

2　Experiment

The purpose of the current experiment is to investigate the relationships between teacher emotions, student emotions, and discourse features with learning in the environment of a serious game. Specifically, we were testing the hypothesis that teacher emotion (positive or negative) affect student learning gains. The second hypothesis was that student emotions impact learning gains. Finally, we predicted that student discourse features associated with shallow (e.g. repeating concrete words) vs. deep comprehension (e.g. conceptual understanding) may correlate with learning and provide insight to findings from the analyses on emotions.

2.1　Design

The emotions-oriented hypotheses were tested using a 4 condition, within-subjects, counter-balanced pretest-interaction-posttest design. Participants interacted with *OperationARIES!* by reading an e-book, answering multiple-choice questions, and conversing in natural language dialog about four topics on scientific methodology with two artificial agents. Three of the conditions were created by manipulating the affective language (i.e. positive, negative, or neutral) used by the pedagogical agents during the natural language conversations, and a fourth served as a control where learners only read the e-book. The assignment of condition (i.e. positive, negative, neutral or control) was counter-balanced across participants. However, the order of the topics remained constant across all 4 conditions. Thus, each participant received each mood condition for one of the topics (counterbalanced across participants and topics) and one chapter served as a control (i.e., text only). Students were asked to report affect 5 times throughout the experiment to gauge the students' affective states. The initial report was obtained before interaction to gain a baseline, followed by sequential reports after each of the 4 topics within the system. Learning gains were assessed using a pretest and posttest consisting of multiple-choice and open-ended questions. Finally, discourse features of the student input during interaction with *OperationARIES!* were analyzed using the computational linguistic tool, Coh-Metrix.

2.2   Participants

The study included 48 (N=48) undergraduate and graduate students at a state universi-ty in Tennessee. Out of the total number of participants, 4 were graduate students and the other 44 were undergraduate students. Subjects were recruited using the university subject pool as well as through flyers and word of mouth. Two types of compensation were offered: A monetary reward ($15 for completion of the entire experiment) or course credit (2 hours course credit towards an Introduction to Psychology course). Only 13% of the students requested the monetary compensation ($15), whereas the others preferred 2 hours of credit towards an Introduction to Psychology course.

2.3   Materials

Agent-Human Interaction. *Operation ARIES!* [1] is an adaptive Intelligent Tutoring System with game-like features that teaches students the scientific method through natu-ral language conversations. Throughout the game, a narrative about aliens invading the world and propagating bad science is delivered via e-mails, conversation, and videos. There are three interactive modules of ARIES, each focusing on a different type of knowledge acquisition (i.e. didactic, applied, applied question generation). However, the current experiment only focused on the first module, the Training module, which teach-es the basic declarative knowledge about the definition, importance, and an example of each of 21 topics of research methodology. In the current experiment, students only interacted with the system across 4 topics of research methodology.

Students completed interaction with this module in 4 distinct phases. For each chapter, students first read an e-book (Phase 1), then answered 6 multiple-choice (MC) questions (Phase 2), and then conversed with the two pedagogical agents in a trialog, or three-way conversation (Phase 3) immediately after each of the final three MC items. Although the original game adaptively places students into one of three pedagogical modes (vicarious learning, standard tutoring, teachable agent) depending on their prior-knowledge, the game was altered in the current experiment to force all students regardless of prior-knowledge level into the intermediate mode of standard tutoring for the sake of consistency. Therefore we will only address the standard tu-toring mode in relation to the current study. This mode of standard tutoring consisted of the pedagogical agents asking the student a specific question about the current topic and scaffolding the students to help them articulate a pre-determined ideal answer referred to as an expectation.

In the standard tutoring mode, the pedagogical conversation with the artificial agents was launched after the MC questions by asking an initial question to students. If the student gave an answer to the initial question that was very close to the expecta-tion, then the tutor gave positive feedback and moved forward in the conversation. However, if the student's answer was vague or incomplete, the tutor launched into a scaffolding dialogue consisting of pumps ("Tell me more"), feedback, hints, prompts, and correcting misconceptions if necessary. When all else failed, *OperationARIES!* simply told the student the right answer with an assertion.

Every question asked by the pedagogical agents had a corresponding expectation or ideal answer (the two terms are used interchangeably within the game).

For example, a question requiring such an answer could be, "Why are operational definitions important?" The expectation is "Operational definitions are important because they allow a particular variable to be reliably recognized, measured and understood by all researchers." The human students' input is compared to the expectation using a combination of Latent Semantic Analysis [19], regular expressions [20], and word overlap metrics that adjusts for word frequency. This method of computing semantic matches in *OperationARIES!* is not significantly different from semantic similarity judgments between two humans [21].

For the purposes of this experiment, the affective display of the generalized mood of the agents was altered by changing the curriculum scripts, which is the predetermined speech of the two pedagogical agents. Both the teacher agent and student agent displayed the same valence of emotional content (i.e. positive, negative, or neutral) at the same time. So, during a "positive" chapter within the learning session, both the teacher and student agents exhibited a positively-valenced affective state. During a "negative" chapter, both displayed a negatively-valenced affective state. For each chapter, the emotional display or mood of the agents remained either positive, negative, or neutral for both agents throughout an entire chapter.

The affectively-valenced discourse of the artificial agents were changed using the Linguistic Inquiry and Word Count lexicon (LIWC; [12]) which has been used to measure persistent affective states[13]. This lexicon has numerous words associated with positive and negative affective states. For example, words with positive- valence include "happy", "curious", and "awesome" whereas negatively-valenced words include "bored" and "sad." Therefore, with *OperationARIES!* an example statement in the negative condition would be, "No. You are incorrect. Let's just go over the importance of these dull things one more time. Why do we need to have operational definitions?" As the reader may notice, the manipulation did not include a change in feedback as the goal of the study was not to provide false feedback but rather to manipulate the affective expression of the teacher agents.

The altered agent speech covered three chapters of material with three separate chapters each designated to one mood condition (i.e., positive, negative, or neutral). The participants were exposed to a fourth chapter of content through the E-book only. This chapter served as a control for the counter-balanced conversations with the artificial agents. In order to return the student to a baseline of emotion between the within-subjects conditions, each chapter began with the student answering 6 multiple-choice questions about the topic and reading a summarized chapter of the E-book within *OperationARIES!*.

Assessment of Learning Gains. Two similar, but not identical, versions of a learning gains assessment were developed using multiple-choice and short answer questions. The learning gains assessments were counter-balanced, so both versions of the assessment were used as a pretest or a posttest that assessed learning gains. Each test consisted of a total of 32 questions, 8 questions per topic. Both the pretest and the posttest were manually graded in accordance with the associated rubric. Inter-rater reliability was established on a by-item basis for the short-answer questions ($r > .70$). Then proportional learning gains (PLG) were calculated using the formula [(posttest-prettest)/(1-pretest)], [22]. This value was used to measure initial learning gains from interaction with the game. However, in conducting linear mixed effects models, the posttest was the dependent variable and the pretest was treated as a covariate. This was a necessary compromise as proportional learning gains often produce highly negative values when calculated on the item level.

2.4   Procedure

After completing an informed consent, all participants were randomly assigned to different materials that varied: 2 tests (pre/post) x 4 pedagogical agent moods (e.g., positive, negative, neutral, neutral text only) in a counterbalancing scheme. The assignment of the two tests (version A and version B) was counter-balanced as pretest and posttest. Thus, within the four possible mood conditions (e.g., positive, negative, neutral, neutral text only) and the counter-balanced learning gains assessments, there were 48 cells in this within-subjects design. After being randomly assigned to a specific group, each subject was first given a pretest followed by instructions on how to complete the affect grid which is a self-report measure of valence and arousal on a 2 dimensional grid. The researcher then gained a baseline affective state for each participant by asking each individual participant, "How do you feel participating in this experiment?" Students verbally replied and were asked to denote this emotion on the first affect grid. After completing the baseline affect grid, each participant interacted with *Operation ARIES!* in the respective assigned condition. During interaction with *Operation ARIES!*, students read an e-book on each chapter as well as answered multiple-choice questions before engaging in a natural language dialogue with the two pedagogical agents. In accordance with the given condition, the participants conversed with the agents displaying the information in a specific mood, i.e. positive, negative, or neutral. In the control condition, participants only read the e-book and answered multiple-choice questions but did not participate in a tutorial conversation with the agents. After completion of each topic, participants were asked to fill out the subsequent affect grid. This process occurred iteratively across the chapters. Upon completion of the interaction with *OperationARIES!,* the participants completed the posttest and were debriefed.

3   Analyses

Before testing our hypotheses, we first conducted a paired samples t-test to confirm that learning actually occurred. Students' proportional learning gains were significantly higher for the topics covered in conversational conditions when compared to those covered in the control (t (1,47)=1.85, p <.05, *Cohen's d* = .55). Next, a series of linear mixed models were conducted to assess the three main hypotheses. The mixed model approach allows for calculation of differences based on observations not participants, thus leveraging the within-subjects power of the design. Recall, the first hypothesis was that the affective state of the pedagogical agents would affect learning. The second hypothesis was that the human students' affective state would affect learning. The third hypothesis was that the student's discourse features would correlate with learning gains. For all three hypotheses, we wanted to generalize across individual differences between participants, topics taught in *OperationARIES!*, and the counter-balanced order of the tests. Thus, these three variables were treated as random factors in all of the following analyses.

A mixed effect model was conducted to determine whether differences in learning existed between the three conversational moods and the control. The model included four conditions and pretest as fixed effects, with participant, topic, and test version held as random factors was used to evaluate posttest scores. The model was not significantly different from the null model including pretest as a fixed factor and participant, topic, and test as random factors(X^2(3, N=192) = .50, p = .92). This result indicates that student learning was not altered by the artificial teacher's mood.

Next, a manipulation check was performed to ensure that the mood displayed by the pedagogical agents transferred to the participant so that analyses about student emotions and learning could be conducted. Before analyses were conducted, the values from the affect grid were computed from the baseline and standardized so that interactions between valence and arousal could be analyzed. Using a model including the four conditions as a fixed effect and participant, topic and test as random factors, the manipulation appeared to have indeed induced student affect. Specifically, the condition of the tutor (i.e., positive, negative, neutral, or control) had a significant main effect on self-reported valence of the student (F (3,189) = 5.63, p < .01). The model was significantly different from the null model including the random factors of participant, topic and test (X^2(3, N = 192) = 16.30, p < .001) with a difference in variance accounted for of 8% (R^2 = .076). Therefore, the pedagogical agent's mood accounts for 8% of the variance in student reported affective valence.

Post hoc analyses with a Tukey correction showed significant mood contagion for the negative and positive tutorial conditions, with a marginally significant difference from the neutral condition. Specifically, the negative condition showed an increase in negatively-valenced affect compared to the text (or control) condition (z (1,192) = -3.987, p < .001). The positive condition showed a significant increase in positively-valenced affect compared to the negative tutorial condition (z (1,191) = 2.65, p < .05), and the neutral tutorial condition showed a marginally significant increase in negative affect (z (1,191) = 2.310, p < .1).

The second hypothesis investigated was the relationships between the students' valence, arousal, the interaction between the two, and learning gains. A series of additive models were conducted to assess whether any relationships were additive or interactive. Models testing the fixed factors of valence and the interaction of valence and arousal along with the three random factors were non-significant compared to the null model (X^2 (1, N = 293) = .02, p = .88); (X^2(1, N = 192) = .54, p = .46), respectively. However, a full model of arousal, valence and pretest as fixed factors with participant, topic, and test as random factors was significantly different from the previous model (X^2 (1, N = 192) = 3.72, p = .05). This model suggests that arousal, not valence, significantly contributed to learning (F (1,191) = 4.20, p < .05); (F (1.191) = .14, p = .71), respectively. Specifically, valence to contributed near 0% of the variance (R^2 = .001) whereas arousal accounted for 1.2% of the variance (R^2 = .012).This relationship between arousal and learning was negative (t (1,191) = -2.02, p = .04). Therefore, the lower the intensity of affect reported by the student, the higher the learning gains.

Discourse Features. The analyses on the discourse of the students only applied to the conditions where students had tutorial conversations with the agents, thus excluding the control condition and reducing the number of observations (N = 144). In evaluating learning gains, first a model with pretest and the composite metric of formality as fixed factors and participant, topic and test version A or B (referred to as "test") as random factors was compared to a null model including just pretest and the three random factors, and found to be non-significant ($X^2(7,N =144)= .46$, $p =.50$). Next, a model with all five of the components and pretest as fixed factors with participant, topic, and test as random factors was not significantly different from a null model including pretest and the random factors of participant, topic, and test (X^2 (11, N =144) = 8.29, $p =.14$). Although the full model with all 5 components was not significant, one of the components known as the word concreteness significantly correlated with learning. This component is indicative of words evoking a mental representation and more meaningful than abstract words. Therefore a trimmed model was tested with the fixed factors of word concreteness and pretest and topic, test, and participant as random factors was tested for effects on learning. This model was significantly different from a null model of pretest and the three random factors (X^2 (8, N= 144) = 4.69, $p =.03$). The component of word concreteness had a significant main effect (F (1,143) = 4.88, $R^2 =.02$, $p <.05$) with a positive relationship with learning (t (1,143) = 2.209, $p < .05$). The principal component of concreteness might best represent the most shallow level of comprehension compared to the other components. This makes sense in the current context as students were learning the basic didactic knowledge [23].

4   Conclusions

Results indicated that there was no direct impact of the mood of the pedagogical agents on learning. On the other hand, student emotions did impact learning gains. Indeed students with lower arousal levels showed higher learning gains. Finally, the discourse analysis revealed word concreteness, which is indicative of shallow comprehension, is related to learning.

Teacher mood did not affect student learning. However, teacher mood did affect student affective state. Previous research has found contradictory yet significant findings as to the nature of the relationship between teacher moods and learning [6,7]. In fact, it may be the case that teacher mood can only have an indirect effect on learning via student affect. A future study may address this issue by examining moderators and mediators as well as exploring the impact of having a stronger manipulation such as altered feedback, body posture of the agent, or speech.

The result that arousal, not valence, impacts student learning may best be explained by the arousal theory. The theory suggests that intensity of emotions rather than valence contributes to learning on certain tasks [10], especially those shallow in nature [11]. The Training module of *OperationARIES!*, the module used in the current study, teaches shallow knowledge whereas subsequent modules within the game are required for deeper conceptual learning [23].The discourse analyses suggests that students were learning shallow knowledge during the interaction with the altered version of the game as well. Specifically, the component representing the use of meaningful, concrete words (a shallow level of comprehension) is the only component that significantly contributed to learning in this study. The corresponding comprehension framework suggests that this is indicative of didactic knowledge only. Therefore, it seems likely that a sweet spot of intensity, in accordance with the arousal theory, may be important for learning within this module of the game.

The nature and contributing factors while learning through interaction with an Intelligent Tutoring System such as *OperationARIES!* are varied and complex. Many factors not tested in this study may contribute to learning gains in such an environment. However, this study definitively shows a relationship between arousal and discourse features related to learning.

Acknowledgements. This research was supported by the Institute for Education Sciences, U.S. Department of Education, through Grant R305B070349 to Northern Illinois University. The opinions expressed are those of the authors and do not represent views of the Institute or the U.S. Department of Education.

References

1. Millis, K., Forsyth, C., Butler, H., Wallace, P., Graesser, A.C., Halpern, D.: Operation ARIES! a serious game for teaching scientific inquiry: serious games and edutainment applications. In: Ma, M., Oikonomou, A., Lakhmi, J. (eds.), pp. 169–196. Springer-Verlag, London (2011)
2. Forsyth, C.M., Graesser, A.C., Pavlik, P., Cai, Z., Butler, H., Halpern, D.F., Millis, K.: Operation ARIES! methods, mystery and mixed models: Discourse features predict affect in a serious game. J. Ed. D. Min. **5,** 147–189 (2013)
3. D'Mello, S., Graessar, A.C.: Emotions during learning with AutoTutor: adaptive technologies for training and education. In: Durlach, P.J., Lesgold, A. (eds.). Cambridge University Press (2012)
4. Conati, C., Maclaren, H.: Empirically building and evaluating a probabilistic model of user affect. User Mod. User-Ad. Inter. **19**, 267–303 (2009)
5. Russell, J., Weiss, A., Mendelsohn, J.A.: Affect grid: A single-item scale of pleasure and arousal. J. of Pers. and Soc. Psych. **57**, 493–5029 (1989)
6. Sullins, J., Craig, S., Graesser, A.C.: Tough love: the influence of an agent's negative affect on students' learning. In: Dimitrova, V., Mizoguchi, R., Du Boulay, B., Graesser, A.C. (eds.) Artificial Intelligence in Education: Building Learning Systems that Care: From Knowledge Representation to Affective Modeling, pp. 677–679. IOS Press, Am-sterdam (2009)
7. Isen, A.M.: Positive affect and decision processes: some recent theoretical developments with practical implications: handbook of consumer psychology. In: Haugdevedt, C., Herr, P.M., Kardes, F.R. (eds.), pp. 273–296. Psychology Press, New York (2008)
8. Franzel, A.C., Goetz, T., Ludtke, O., Pekrun, R., Sutton, R.E.: Emotion transmission in the classroom: Exploring the relationship between teacher and student enjoyment. J. Ed. Psy. **101**, 705–716 (2009)
9. Frederickson, B.L.: The role of positive emotions in positive psychology: The broaden-and-build theory of positive emotions. Amer. Psy. **56**, 218–226 (2001)

10. Lang, P.J.: The emotion probe: Studies of motivation and attention. Amer. Psy. **50**, 372–385 (1995)
11. Martindale, C.: Cognition and Consciousness. Dorsey Press, Illinois (1981)
12. Pennebaker, J., Francis, M.E., Booth R.J.: Linguistic inquiry and word count (LIWC): LIWC2001, Mahwah, New Jersey (2001)
13. Rude, S.S., Gortner, E., Pennebaker, J.: Language use of depressed and depression-vulnerable college students. Cog. & Emot. **18**, 1121–1133 (2004)
14. Graesser, A.C., Forsyth, C.: Discourse comprehension: oxford handbook of cognitive psychology. In: Reisberg, D. (ed.). Oxford University Press (2014)
15. Graesser, A.C., Millis, K.K., Zwaan, R.A.: Discourse comprehension. Annual Review of Psychology **48**, 163–189 (1997)
16. Graesser, A.C., McNamara, D.S.: Computational analyses of multilevel discourse comprehension. Top. Cog. Sci. (2011)
17. Graesser, A.C., McNamara, D.S., Louwerse, M.M., Cai, Z.: Coh-Metrix: Analysis of text on cohension and language. Beh. Res. Meth., Instru., and Comp. **36**, 193–202 (2004)
18. Graesser, A.C., McNamara, D.S., Kulikowich, J.: Coh-Metrix: Providing multilevel analyses of text characteristics. Ed. Res. **40**, 223–234 (2011)
19. Landauer, T., McNamara, D.S., Dennis, S., Kintsch, W.: Handbook of Latent Semantic Analysis, Mahwah, New Jersey (2007)
20. Jurafsky, D., Martin, J.: Speech and language processing. Prentice Hall, New Jersey (2008)
21. Cai, Z., Graesser, A.C., Forsyth, C., Burkett, C., Millis, K., Wallace, P., Halpern, D., Butler: Trialog in ARIES: user input assessment in an intelligent tutoring system. In: 3rd IEEE International Conference on Intelligent Computing and Intelligent Systems, pp. 429–433. IEEE Press, China (2011)
22. Jackson, G.T., Graesser, A.C., McNamara, D.S.: What students expect may have more impact than what they know or feel: artificial intelligence in education; building learning systems that care; from knowledge representation to affective modeling. In: Dimitrova, V., Mizoguchi, R., Du Boulay, B., Graesser, A.C. (eds.), pp. 73–80. IOS Press (2009)
23. Forsyth, Carol, Graesser, Arthur, Walker, Breya, Millis, Keith, Pavlik Jr., Philip I., Halpern, Diane: Didactic galactic: types of knowledge learned in a serious game. In: Lane, HChad, Yacef, Kalina, Mostow, Jack, Pavlik, Philip (eds.) AIED 2013. LNCS, vol. 7926, pp. 832–835. Springer, Heidelberg (2013)

Examining the Predictive Relationship Between Personality and Emotion Traits and Learners' Agent-Direct Emotions

Jason M. Harley[1,2(✉)], Cassia C. Carter[3], Niki Papaionnou[3], François Bouchet[4,5], Ronald S. Landis[3], Roger Azevedo[6], and Lana Karabachian[2]

[1] Computer Science and Operations Research, Université de Montréal, Montréal, QC, Canada
jason.harley@umontreal.ca
[2] Educational and Counselling Psychology, McGill University, Montréal, QC, Canada
[3] Illinois Institute of Technology, Psychology, Chicago, IL, USA
[4] Sorbonne Universités, UPMC University Paris 06, UMR 7606, LIP6, 75005 Paris, France
[5] CNRS, UMR 7606, LIP6, 75005 Paris, France
[6] North Carolina State University, Psychology, Raleigh, NC, USA

Abstract. The current study examined the relationships between learners' ($N = 124$) personality traits, the emotions they experience while typically studying (trait studying emotions), and the emotions they reported experiencing as a result of interacting with two Pedagogical Agents (PAs - agent-directed emotions) in MetaTutor, an advanced multi-agent learning environment. Overall, significant relationships between a subset of trait emotions (trait anger, trait anxiety) and personality traits (agreeableness, conscientiousness, and neuroticism) were found for three agent-directed emotions (pride, boredom, and neutral) though the relationships differed between the two PAs. These results demonstrate that some trait emotions and personality traits can be used to predict learners' emotions toward specific PAs (with different roles). Suggestions are provided for adapting PAs to support learners' (with certain characteristics) experience of positive emotions (e.g., enjoyment) and minimize their experience of negative emotions (e.g., boredom). Such an approach presents a scalable and easily implemented method for creating emotionally-adaptive, agent-based learning environments, and improving learner-PA interactions to support learning.

Keywords: Emotions · Agent-directed emotions · Trait emotions · Personality traits · Pedagogical agents · Intelligent tutoring systems

1 Introduction

Emotions can critically impact how students learn with agent-based learning environments (ABLEs; [1-3]). ABLEs [4] are distinct from other computer-based learning environments (e.g., multi-agent systems, intelligent tutoring systems, serious games) because of their use of pedagogical agents (PAs); animated characters designed to provide several functions such as immediate and tailored prompts and feedback to

© Springer International Publishing Switzerland 2015
C. Conati et al. (Eds.): AIED 2015, LNAI 9112, pp. 145–154, 2015.
DOI: 10.1007/978-3-319-19773-9_15

support student learning. Despite research that examines emotions in these environments, very little is known in terms of why students experience different emotions during their interactions with these computer-based systems. For example, do students experience frustration because of the PA's feedback or because they are unable to locate multimedia material relevant to their current learning goal? Furthermore, there are contextual and individual difference variables, such as personality traits and trait emotions that can also contribute to the complexity of understanding the impact of emotions on learning with ABLEs. As such, the current study examined the relationships between learners' personality traits (five factor model; [5]), the emotions they experience while typically studying (trait studying emotions; [6]), and the emotions they reported experiencing as a result of the PAs (agent-directed emotions).

At present, research concerning students' agent-directed emotions is scarce. Studies also demonstrate that PAs have a range of different functions and features, such as deploying strategies to help students regulate their emotions, different dynamic facial expressions, gender, and race [1-4,7-8]. In addition to the characteristics of the PA, a number of learner characteristics (gender, prior knowledge, personality traits) have also been shown to influence learner-PA interactions [1,2,8]. However, the paucity of research on this topic makes any conclusions or recommendations tentative. This study contributes to the literature by evaluating the predictive utility of two sets of learner characteristics and how this information can be used to provide individually-tailored, user-system adaptation [8]. User-system adaptation involves changing features of the ABLE (e.g., PAs) to optimize them for different types of learners. In this study, MetaTutor, an ABLE for learning about the human circulatory system and fostering self-regulated learning (SRL) was used to examine learner-PA interactions.

1.1   Learner Characteristics

Trait emotions. Trait emotions represent one set of individual differences that are related to what students typically experience while learning with respect to the behaviours they engage in while learning and their learning outcomes [9]. Specifically, trait emotions are habitual, re-occurring emotions experienced in a particular achievement context, such as feeling anxiety during tests or boredom while studying algebra. Pekrun [9] contrasts trait emotions with state emotions, which are emotions experienced in response to a particular situation (e.g., academic achievement situation). The relationship between trait studying emotions and agent-directed emotions as experienced during a studying task with an ABLE has not yet been examined. In addition to learners' trait emotions, personality traits are examined as a second source of individual differences.

Personality Traits. Personality traits reflect individual differences in stable dispositions, which determine one's pattern of thought, emotionality, and behaviour [5,10]. Although several models of personality have been developed, the most comprehensive framework and consistent findings have derived from the five-factor model (FFM; [5]). These factors include Neuroticism (tendency to be temperamental and experience negative moods and feelings; e.g., Anxiety, and Depression), Conscientiousness (associated with efficiency, determination, responsibility, and persistence), Agreeableness (tendency to be more friendly, considerate of others, altruistic, sympathetic), Extraversion (associated with high physical and verbal activity, assertiveness, sociability), and Openness to Experience (tendency to prefer novel and broader ideas and experiences, intellectual activities, creativity). The FFM represents the highest level of the personality hierarchy, encompassing most of personality elements into five dimensions, thus providing order to various measures of personality. Numerous studies have empirically shown that personality is an important predictor of academic performance [10].

1.2   The Current Study

The purpose of the current study was to examine the relationship between learners' trait emotions as well as personality traits and their agent-directed emotions while interacting with MetaTutor. Given the novelty of the study, no suitable theoretical frameworks or corpus of prior research offered a compelling conceptual foundation upon which to formulate strong hypotheses. As a result, we identified our main research questions as follows: *What are the predictive effects of personality traits and trait emotions on participants' agent-directed emotions (i.e., how participants reported the agents made them feel during the learning session), and does the quality of prompts and feedback provided by the PA (i.e., experimental condition) moderate these associations?* Given space constraints, we report the results of two of the four PAs in MetaTutor, the ones that are the most consistently active throughout the learning session (see 2.2 and 2.3).

2   Methods

2.1   Participants

One hundred and twenty four undergraduate students from two North American Universities (one large, public institution and one small, private institution) participated in this study. Participants (65.3% female; 64.5% Caucasian) had a mean age of 21 and mean GPA of 3.07 and were randomly assigned to either an experimental or control condition (see 2.3 for details).

2.2   MetaTutor Learning Environment

MetaTutor was developed to teach students about the circulatory system and how to regulate their learning. MetaTutor is an adaptive, multi-agent hypermedia learning environment which presents 38 digital pages of human circulatory-system content (including text and diagrams) organized in a table of contents. The main interface of MetaTutor includes a timer that indicates how much time remains in the learning session, and an SRL palette where participants can initiate interactions with one of four PAs depending on the action chosen. Participants' subgoals are displayed during the learning session directly below their overall learning goal (*to learn all they could about the human circu-*

latory system; located in the upper-center portion of the screen) within progress bars automatically filled as learners navigate through pages relevant to the currently active subgoal. One of the four PAs is always visible in the upper right-hand corner of the learning environment. Each is responsible for specific tasks during the learning session, such as certain self-regulatory processes, and provides audible assistance through the use of a text-to-speech engine. Specifically, *Gavin the Guide* provides guidance for participants in the learning environment and administers pretest and posttest knowledge assessments and self-report measures, *Pam the Planner* prompts and scaffolds planning processes primarily at the beginning of the learning session (e.g., prior knowledge activation, setting subgoals), *Mary the Monitor* prompts and supports participants in their monitoring processes (e.g., judgment of learning), and *Sam the Strategizer* prompts participants to engage in learning strategies and ensures their use (e.g., note-taking, summarizing). Mary and Sam are the PAs examined in this study because they provide (1) interventions (2) throughout the learning session.

2.3   Experimental Design and Learning Conditions

Participants were randomly assigned to either an experimental Prompt and Feedback (PF; n = 59) condition or Control (n = 65) condition. The strategies used in each condition differed in nature, detail, and amount of scaffolding provided by the PAs. Table 1 summarizes the two PA's behavior by condition that this paper examines.

Table 1. Summary of PA behaviour by condition and learning context

Context	Summary of PA Behaviour	
	Prompt and Feedback Condition	Control Condition
Self-regulated Learning Behaviour	**Prompts**: Sam and Mary provide prompts to students to engage in SRL behaviours, such as making summaries and content evaluations.	**Prompts**: Sam and Mary do not provide any SRL prompts.
	Feedback: Sam and Mary provide feedback regarding students' use of SRL processes. E.g. whether students have written an appropriate summary; Mary agrees that the content of a page is relevant. Feedback irrespective of whether they are prompted by the agent or self-initiated (through the SRL palette) by the learner.	**Feedback**: Sam and Mary do not provide any feedback.
Administration of assessments	Mary administers page and subgoal quizzes to participants. Provides feedback on how learners did on them; helps them decide whether to move on or revisit learning material.	Mary gives page and subgoal quizzes. No feedback provided.

2.4   Experimental Procedure

The experiment consisted of two sessions (Session 1 lasted approximately 30 minutes and Session 2 lasted approximately three hours), separated by a maximum of three days or a minimum of one hour to avoid participant fatigue. During Session 1, participants read and signed an informed consent form and were administered several self-report questionnaires (e.g., demographics, mini-IPIP, AEQ-trait emotions – cf. section 2.5) and a content pretest. All participants completed the session individually on a desktop computer. Participants were compensated up to $10 at the end of session 1 ($10/hr.) or given course credit (depending on availability of a subject pool).

During session 2, participants were shown an introductory video presenting information regarding the MetaTutor learning environment, including training on how to use different components and navigate through the system. Participants were also provided with instructions on how to set and create their own subgoals. Each participant was given an hour to learn as much as possible about the circulatory system using MetaTutor. Halfway through the learning session, participants were given the opportunity to take a five-minute break. At the end of session 2, participants were asked to complete a posttest followed by a series of self-report questionnaires. Lastly, all participants were debriefed and received up to $40 for participating in the study.

2.5   Measures and Materials

Achievement Emotions Questionnaire (AEQ-Trait). The AEQ [6] was used to assess the cognitive, motivational, and physiological components of emotions. The measure consists of 24 scales that assess three classes of emotions: class-related, learning-related, and test-related emotions. Only the 75-item learning-related emotions scale, consisting of eight learning-related emotions (Enjoyment, Hope, Pride, Anger, Shame, Anxiety, Hopelessness, and Boredom) was used in the current study. Items were grouped into three sections that assessed how participants usually felt before, during, and after studying in an academic setting. The AEQ uses a 5-point Likert response scale, ranging from 1 (strongly disagree) to 5 (strongly agree). A sample item from the before studying section is "I look forward to studying." A mean score was derived for each learning-related trait emotion. Coefficient alphas for the learning-related scales ranged from .53 to .93.

Mini-International Personality Item Pool (mini-IPIP). The mini-IPIP is a 20-item version of the 50-item International Personality Item Pool-Five-Factor Model measure. The mini-IPIP [11] was used to assess the personality dimensions of the FFM. Participants were asked to respond to each item using a 5-point Likert response scale ranging from 1 (very inaccurate) to 5 (very accurate). A sample item is "I get upset easily." Mean scores were generated for each personality dimension. This measure demonstrated adequate internal consistencies for all dimensions ($\alpha = .71-.77$).

Agent Response Inventory (ARI). The ARI consists of 76 items assessing the extent to which each of the four PAs made them feel 19 different discrete emotions (Happiness, Enjoyment, Hope, Pride, Curiosity, Eureka, Anger, Frustration, Anxiety, Shame, Fear, Contempt, Disgust, Boredom, Hopelessness, Sadness, Surprise, Confusion, and Neutral). Participants were asked to respond to each item using a 5-point Likert response scale ranging from 1 (strongly disagree) to 5 (strongly agree). A sample item was "SAM made me feel that I was enjoying myself." The ARI and the digital definition handout (provided in a side panel to participants while they filled out the self-report) were based on a similar, single-item self-report measure that had good agreement rates with emotions obtained from automatic facial expression recognition software (the emotion-value questionnaire: EV; [7]).

3   Results

3.1   Data Cleaning and Descriptive Statistics

Prior to addressing our research questions, we first examined all of our predictor and dependent variables for skewness, kurtosis, and outliers. There were a large number of highly skewed variables, especially in the ARI emotions for various agents. Many of the negative emotions, such as Disgust, Frustration, or Anger, were rarely or simply not elicited by any of the agents and were removed from subsequent analyses; this does not mean, however, that learners never experienced these emotions (see [7]), only that they did not identify the agents as the cause of those emotions. We set the threshold for identifying significant skew or kurtosis at $z = +/- 3.35$.

Descriptive statistics for the personality scales, the trait emotion scales, and the agent-directed emotions are reported in Tables 2 and 3 (skewed variables that were not included in further analyses are italicized). The AEQ trait emotion means ranged from 2.01 to 3.93 on a five-point scale. The mini-IPIP scale means ranged from 2.74 to 4.06 on a five-point scale. The ARI emotions that were left as dependent variables were Happy, Enjoyment, Hopeful, Proud, Bored, and Neutral for both agents. The emotion of Curiosity was also analyzed for Mary, but not Sam. The means on these variables ranged from 2.28 to 3.44 on a 1-5 scale.

3.2   Personality Traits, Trait Emotions, Condition, and Agent-Directed Emotions

The research question was evaluated with a series of moderated regression analyses, one for Sam and one for Mary, which tested for the presence of significant effects of two sets of predictor variables (personality traits and trait emotions) on agent-directed emotions while considering the moderating effect of Condition. For each of the moderated multiple regression analyses, the predictor variables, along with Condition, were entered as main effects into the first step while the variables and their interactions with Condition were entered into the second step. Higher-order (e.g., 3-way) interaction effects were not included. These regressions were run for each ARI emotion for each agent. Results for significant models are discussed below (cf. Tables 2 and 3).

Sam the Strategizer. We examined whether participants felt more or less Happiness, Enjoyment, Hopefulness, Pride, Boredom, or Neutrality due to their interactions with him. The model for Step 1 of the moderated regression on Happiness was statistically significant ($R^2 = .20$, $p < .05$). Specifically, a statistically significant main effect was found for Condition ($\beta = -0.30$, $p < .01$), such that participants in the Control condition experienced higher levels of Happiness with Sam. However, the change in R^2 was not statistically significant for the model of the second step, and there were no statistically significant interactions.

For Neutral emotion expression as the outcome measure, the models for both step 1 ($R^2 = .19$, $p < .05$) and step 2 ($R^2 = .33$, $p < .01$) were statistically significant. A main effect was found for Condition ($\beta = -0.33$, $p < .01$), where participants in the Control condition felt significantly more Neutral towards Sam. Interaction effects were found for Anxiety and Condition (β = -0.54, p < .05), Anger and Condition (β = 0.53, p < .01), and Conscientiousness and Condition (β = -0.24, p < .05).

Table 2. Descriptive Stats. for AEQ and IPIP

	Variables	M	SD
	Shame	2.63	0.87
	Anxious	2.93	0.80
	Anger	2.26	0.70
AEQ	Pride	3.93	0.60
	Hope	3.67	0.69
	Enjoyment	3.52	0.55
	Bored	2.58	0.85
	Hopelessness	*2.01*	*0.82*
	Agreeableness	4.06	0.63
	Conscientiousness	3.74	0.76
IPIP	Extraversion	3.21	0.89
	Openness	*3.88*	*0.75*
	Neuroticism	2.74	0.85

Table 3. Descriptive Stats. for ARI

ARI Emotions	Sam		Mary	
	M	SD	M	SD
happiness	2.69	1.06	3.00	1.10
enjoyment	2.49	1.07	2.76	1.16
hopefulness	2.71	1.07	2.96	1.18
pride	2.56	1.07	2.76	1.18
anger	*1.97*	*1.30*	*1.89*	*1.20*
frustration	*2.14*	*1.38*	*2.05*	*1.25*
anxiety	*1.95*	*1.25*	*2.08*	*1.28*
fear	*1.48*	*0.86*	*1.53*	*0.95*
shame	*1.55*	*0.97*	*1.54*	*0.91*
hopelessness	*1.51*	*0.94*	*1.49*	*0.86*
boredom	2.49	1.29	2.37	1.27
surprise	*1.85*	*1.15*	*1.93*	*1.19*
contempt	*2.02*	*1.31*	*1.93*	*1.20*
disgust	*1.26*	*0.63*	*1.21*	*0.59*
confusion	*1.81*	*1.24*	*1.65*	*0.95*
curiosity	1.98	1.15	2.28	1.31
sadness	*1.29*	*0.66*	*1.27*	*0.62*
eureka	*1.46*	*0.87*	*1.80*	*1.18*
neutral	3.25	1.43	3.24	1.34

Note. Variables in italics were beyond the skewness cutoff and were not used in further analyses

Examining the visual representation of the significant interactions for Sam, Figure 1 shows that participants in the Control condition with lower levels of trait Anger experienced lower levels of Neutral feelings than those with higher levels of trait Anger. In contrast, participants in the PF condition mirrored these differences, but at lower levels of Neutral elicited from Sam. Figure 2 shows a pattern of interaction results with Condition moderating the effects of trait Anxiety on the Neutral emotion outcome. Participants in the Control condition experienced more Neutral feelings at higher trait Anxiety levels, where participants in the PF condition experienced more Neutral feelings at lower Anxiety levels. The moderation of Condition and Conscientiousness for Sam predicting Neutral follows the same pattern as Figure 2. Participants in the Control condition experienced more Neutral feelings toward Sam when they had high levels of Conscientiousness, whereas participants in the PF condition experienced more Neutral feelings toward Sam when they had low levels of Conscientiousness.

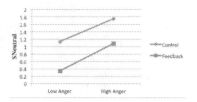

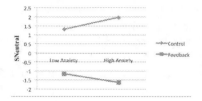

Fig. 1. Interaction results for Anger and Condition predicting Neutral for Sam

Fig. 2. Interaction results for Anxiety and Condition predicting Neutral for Sam

Mary the Monitor. The criterion of Pride yielded statistically significant results. The model for Step 1 ($R^2 = .21$, $p < .01$) showed a statistically significant main effect of Condition ($\beta = 0.25$, $p < .01$), such that participants in the PF condition experienced significantly more feelings of Pride with Mary. The model for Step 2 ($R^2 = .35$, $p < .01$) yielded a statistically significant interaction of Anger and Condition ($\beta = -0.48$, $p < .05$) and of Conscientiousness and Condition ($\beta = -0.29$ $p < .05$). Figure 2 shows the pattern of interaction results for both of these interactions. For the Anger and Condition interaction, participants in the Control condition experienced higher levels of Pride with Mary at higher levels of trait Anger, whereas participants in the PF condition experienced higher levels of Pride at lower levels of trait Anger. For the Conscientiousness interaction with Condition, participants in the Control condition reported higher levels of Pride for higher levels of Conscientiousness; participants in the PF condition experienced higher levels of Pride for lower levels of Conscientiousness.

The analyses on Boredom did not have a statistically significant model for Step 1, but the model for Step 2 was statistically significant ($R^2 = .30$, $p < .05$). Specifically, the model from Step 2 yielded a statistically significant main effects for Neuroticism ($\beta = 0.50$, $p < .05$) and Condition ($\beta = -0.22$, $p < .05$), and a statistically significant interaction between Neuroticism and Condition ($\beta = -0.44$, $p < .01$). Figure 2 shows the graph of the pattern of this interaction. Participants in the Control condition reported higher levels of Boredom at higher levels of Neuroticism and participants in the PF condition reported higher levels of Boredom when they had low Neuroticism.

4   Discussion

4.1   Sam

Our results revealed that participants were more likely to feel more Neutral toward Sam in the Control condition. Students in the PF condition were more likely to experience lower mean levels of Neutral toward Sam than in the Control condition, in particular those low in Trait Anger. Given that Neutral is assumed to be an adaptive state in which learners are not distracted by negative emotions, such as Boredom or Frustration, it can be seen as an appropriate agent-directed emotional classification, albeit not as adaptive as the positively-valenced, activating emotions of Enjoyment and Curiosity. Therefore, our results for Sam indicate an area for further examination, specifically to see what emotions students in the PF condition, in particular those low in trait Anger, experienced instead of Neutral. A preliminary review of the differences in the means between agent-directed emotions indicates that learners experienced higher levels of negative activating emotions, such as Anxiety and Frustration, in the PF condition than in the Control condition. It is possible that this could be due to certain prompts (e.g., mandatory summaries) that Sam gives which some students (e.g., those low in trait anger) may find disruptive rather than helpful. Therefore, if students are identified as being low in trait anger the system could reduce the number of prompts Sam provides to help minimize learners' experience of negative emotions.

4.2   Mary

Results revealed that students high in Agreeableness were more likely to feel Proud when interacting with Mary and those high in Neuroticism were more likely to feel more Bored. When considering Condition, learners were more likely to report feeling more Proud and less Bored in terms of their interactions with Mary when in the PF condition (and vice versa for the Control condition). Students high in trait Anger and Conscientiousness were more likely to experience higher levels of Pride when interacting with Mary in the Control condition, while students high in Neuroticism were more likely to feel Bored on account of Mary in the Control condition. These results suggest that Mary's interactions with students elicited the most positive responses from students in the PF condition, where she helped students monitor their learning rather than play a passive role until they self-initiated monitoring behaviors. They may have also felt more proud in the PF condition on account of Mary congratulating them when they accurately assessed their level of knowledge regarding a page of content. It is possible that students who are used to experiencing Anger while studying may have felt Proud and considered Mary partially responsible for this emotion, even though her role was minimal in the Control condition. Students high in Conscientiousness may have felt that Mary gave them more autonomy in the Control condition and therefore felt more Pride.

A preliminary review of the differences in frequencies between students' use of self- vs. PA-initiated SRL behaviors indicates that learners in the Control condition engaged in more self-initiated SRL behavior than learners in the PF condition. Therefore, if students were identified as being high in conscientiousness, they may benefit from fewer prompts by experiencing more Pride, in addition to engaging in more self-initiated SRL behaviors. Although students high in Neuroticism were more Bored with Mary in the Control condition, Mary's interactions with them were minimal and informational at most when they didn't self-initiate monitoring behaviors. Therefore, more Neurotic students may have reported that Mary made them feel Bored in the Control condition if they were Bored to begin with in MetaTutor, and therefore expected her to interact with them more. Therefore, it is not necessary to adapt behavior.

4.3   Conclusions, Limitations, and Future Directions

This study examined the predictive effects of learners' trait emotions and personality traits on agent-directed emotions. Overall, significant relationships between a subset of trait emotions and personality traits were found, though the relationships differed between PAs. These results demonstrate that some trait emotions (trait Anger and trait Anxiety) and personality traits (Agreeableness, Conscientiousness, and Neuroticism) can be used to predict learners' agent-directed emotions toward specific PAs (Pride, Boredom, and Neutral). The skewed distribution of the majority of the agent-directed emotion measures (low levels) was a limitation of this study. Low levels of emotions and higher levels of Neutral have, however, been previously identified with other measures and studies with MetaTutor. The size of our sample is also a limitation of this study, which resulted in weaker statistical power than would have been ideal for the number of predictive variables examined. This study is novel in exploring these affective relationships, however, further research is required to draw conclusions regarding the relationship between agent-directed emotions, trait emotions, personality traits, and learning. More research is also needed in order to make further instructional prescriptions for PAs regarding how their prompts and feedback can be adapted to learners' individual characteristics, though this study provides a number of insights. Such an approach could present a scalable and easily implemented means for creating more emotionally-adaptive ABLEs and improving learner-PA interactions.

Acknowledgements. The research presented in this paper has been supported by a doctoral and postdoctoral fellowship from the Fonds Québécois de recherche – Société et culture (FQRSC) and a Joseph-Armand Bombardier Canada Graduate Scholarship for Doctoral research from the Social Sciences and Humanities Research Council (SSHRC) of Canada awarded to the first author. This research has also been supported by funding awarded to the sixth author from the National Science Foundation (IIS 1008282), SSHRC, and the Canada Research Chairs program.

References

1. D'Mello, S., Graesser, A.: AutoTutor and Affective Autotutor. ACM Transactions on Interactive Intelligent Systems **2**(4), 1–39 (2013)
2. Arroyo, I., Woolf, B.P., Royer, J.M., Tai, M.: Affective gendered learning companions. Artificial Intelligence in Education, pp. 41–48. IOS Press, Amsterdam (2009)
3. Conati, C., Maclaren, H.: Empirically building and evaluating a probabilistic model of user affect. User Modeling and User-Adapted Interaction **19**, 267–303 (2009)
4. Harley, J.M., Azevedo, R.: Toward a feature-driven understanding of students' emotions during interactions with ABLEs. Int. J. of Games & Comp. Med. Sim. **6**(3), 17–34 (2014)
5. Costa, P.T., McCrae, R.R.: Normal personality assessment in clinical practice: The NEO Personality Inventory. Psychological Assessment **4**(1), 5–13 (1992)
6. Pekrun, R., Goetz, T., Titz, W., Perry, R.: Academic achievement emotions in students' self-regulated learning and achievement. Educational Psychologist **37**, 91–206 (2002)
7. Harley, J.M., Bouchet, F., Hussain, S., Azevedo, R., Calvo, R.: A multi-componential analysis of emotions during complex learning with an intelligent multi-agent system. Computers in Human Behavior **48**, 615–625 (2015)
8. Sabourin, Jennifer, Mott, Bradford, Lester, James C.: Modeling learner affect with theoretically grounded dynamic bayesian networks. In: D'Mello, Sidney, Graesser, Arthur, Schuller, Björn, Martin, Jean-Claude (eds.) ACII 2011, Part I. LNCS, vol. 6974, pp. 286–295. Springer, Heidelberg (2011)
9. Pekrun, R.: The control-value theory of achievement emotions: assumptions, corollaries, and implications for ed. research and practice. Ed. Psych. Review **18**, 315–341 (2006)
10. Chamorro-Premuzic, T., Furnham, A.: Personality and intellectual competence. Erlbaum, Mahwah, NJ (2005)
11. Donnellan, M.B., Oswald, F.L., Baird, B.M., Lucas, R.E.: The mini-IPIP scales. Psychological Assessment **18**, 192–203 (2006)

Evaluating Human and Automated Generation of Distractors for Diagnostic Multiple-Choice Cloze Questions to Assess Children's Reading Comprehension

Yi-Ting Huang[1,2] and Jack Mostow[2(✉)]

[1] National Taiwan University, Taipei, Taiwan
d97008@im.ntu.edu.tw
[2] Carnegie Mellon University, Pittsburgh, PA, USA
mostow@cs.cmu.edu

Abstract. We report an experiment to evaluate DQGen's performance in generating three types of distractors for diagnostic multiple-choice cloze (fill-in-the-blank) questions to assess children's reading comprehension processes. Ungrammatical distractors test syntax, nonsensical distractors test semantics, and locally plausible distractors test inter-sentential processing. 27 knowledgeable humans rated candidate answers as correct, plausible, nonsensical, or ungrammatical without knowing their intended type or whether they were generated by DQGen, written by other humans, or correct. Surprisingly, DQGen did significantly better than humans at generating ungrammatical distractors and slightly better than them at generating nonsensical distractors, albeit worse at generating plausible distractors. Vetting its output and writing distractors only when necessary would take half as long as writing them all, and improve their quality.

Keywords: Question generation · Reading comprehension · Cloze · Distractors

1 Introduction

Traditionally, generation of questions to assess reading comprehension relied on humans – either teachers (and students) during instruction, or materials developers beforehand. More recently, the less labor-intensive approach of automated question generation has been used for multiple tasks, such as inserting comprehension checks in a reading tutor [1], generating comprehension instruction [2], testing vocabulary [3], recognizing children's spoken questions [4], assessing closed-domain knowledge [5, 6], evaluating language proficiency [7-10], and assisting academic writing [11].

One type of question especially conducive to automated generation is the multiple choice cloze (fill-in-the-blank) question, in which one word in a sentence is replaced with a blank. Answering without guessing requires having relevant background knowledge and understanding the context in order to select the best word from a list of options for completing the sentence. Cloze questions are used in many standardized tests, such as SAT (Scholastic Aptitude Test), TOEFL (Test of English as a Foreign Language), and TOEIC (Test of English for International Communication). Research has explored automated generation of cloze questions for various purposes, for

© Springer International Publishing Switzerland 2015
C. Conati et al. (Eds.): AIED 2015, LNAI 9112, pp. 155–164, 2015.
DOI: 10.1007/978-3-319-19773-9_16

example to test comprehension of important concepts in textbooks [5]. In the domain of language learning, a growing number of studies explain how to generate such questions to test English language proficiency with verbs [7], prepositions [8], adjectives [9], and grammar patterns [10]. Especially in language learning, cloze questions can test the ability to decide which word is consistent with the surrounding context. Thus they tap comprehension processes that judge various types of consistency, such as syntactic, semantic, and inter-sentential, in the course of constructing a situation model that represents "the content or microworld that the text is about" [12]. In brief, these processes encode sentences, integrate them into an overall representation of meaning, notice gaps and inconsistencies, and repair them [13, 14].

DQGen (Diagnostic Question Generator) [15] generates cloze questions for diagnostic assessment of a child's comprehension while reading a given text. As Fig. 1 illustrates, DQGen's questions have four components. The *stem* is the truncated sentence, "That helps your body find and kill _____." The *context* is the text preceding the stem. The *correct answer* is by definition the deleted original word "germs." The *distractors* are the other candidate completions.

Some of those cells patrol your body. They are hungry, and they eat germs! Some stop the trouble germs make. Others make antibodies. They stick to germs. That helps your body find and kill _____.

1. are   – **ungrammatical**
2. intestines – **nonsensical** (but grammatical)
3. terrorists – **plausible** (meaningful by itself but incorrect given the preceding text)
4. germs   – **correct**

Fig. 1. Annotated example of a multiple-choice cloze question generated by DQGen

To detect failures in different comprehension processes, DQGen uses three types of distractors. Each type of distractor indicates a different type of comprehension failure when chosen by a child instead of the correct answer. DQGen classifies the word "are" as ungrammatical because it has the wrong part of speech. DQGen classifies "intestines" as nonsensical because "find and kill intestines ." does not occur in the Google N-grams corpus. DQGen classifies "terrorists" as plausible only locally because "find and kill terrorists ." occurs in the Google N-grams corpus, but "terrorists" is topically unrelated to the preceding paragraph. DQGen classifies "germs" as correct because it was the last word of the original sentence. Aggregating children's performance over questions with these three types of distractors should not only assess their comprehension, but profile the difficulties faced by a given child or posed by a given text. For instance, a child who processes syntax and semantics but not the relation of a sentence to the context preceding it would reject the ungrammatical and nonsensical distractors, but pick the plausible distractor as often as the correct answer.

DQGen uses a generate-and-test approach. It chooses a candidate at random from a source of candidates for that type of distractor, and rejects the candidate if it does not satisfy the constraints for that type, e.g. that ungrammatical distractors must have the wrong part of speech. Mostow and Jang [15] evaluated DQGen by itself; here we evaluate the current (2014) version of DQGen against human performance. Section 2 describes our experiment. Section 3 reports results. Section 4 concludes.

2   Experimental Design

To evaluate DQGen against human performance, we had to specify the task being performed and the criteria by which to evaluate it. Given a text with some sentences selected to turn into stems by deleting the last word, the task was to generate a distractor of each type – ungrammatical, nonsensical, and plausible.

Our principal evaluation criterion was whether a generated distractor achieved its purpose according to human judges blind to its source (DQGen or human), its intended type (ungrammatical, nonsensical, or plausible), and the correct (original) answer. An additional evaluation criterion was time: we wanted to know how long it took humans to rate or write each type of distractor. Besides quantifying the relative difficulty of rating vs. writing the three types of distractors, the practical purpose of this information was to predict which would be faster – writing distractors by hand, or hand-vetting distractors generated by DQGen.

MATERIALS: To enable controlled evaluation of distractors, we gave DQGen and humans the same 7 texts from Project LISTEN's Reading Tutor [16], containing a total of 16 cloze stems and chosen to ensure that DQGen could generate each type of distractor for each stem.

APPARATUS: To run the experiment, we implemented a website in PHP and connected it to a MySQL database server that logged a timestamped event for each page entrance or exit, keyboard input, or menu selection. The database also kept track of each participant's position in the protocol in order to continue at the same point after an interruption, and to avoid repeating any of the protocol.

PARTICIPANTS: To recruit human experts proficient in English and sufficiently knowledgeable about reading comprehension to rate and write distractors, we posted a request to Carnegie Mellon's doctoral Program in Interdisciplinary Research (www.cmu.edu/pier) and to the Society for the Scientific Study of Reading (triplesr.org). The request directed participants to the website for the experiment.

After data cleaning to filter out data from in-house software testing, failed attempts to log in, unfinished protocols, and two null ratings, we had data for 27 participants.

PROCEDURE: The experimental protocol consisted of logging into the experiment website, a brief introduction, the two main tasks (first rating, then writing), and finally a survey with a series of optional typed-input questions about various aspects of the experiment.

The introduction thanked participants for "helping our research by doing two tasks: rating (the first task) and designing (the second task) multiple choice cloze (fill-in-the-blank) items to assess children's reading comprehension." It explained that in the first task, they would read texts containing a total of 8 cloze stems, see different candidate completions of each stem, and classify each completion as **Correct, Plausible, Nonsensical,** or **Ungrammatical.**   It showed the annotated example in Fig. 1 and:

> Please classify each choice on its own merits, independently of the others.
> Your responses will be timed as a measure of the effort they require.
> Therefore you will not get an opportunity to revise them.
> Also, please try to avoid interruptions during a text.
> However, pausing between texts is fine.

In the rating task, participants read 3-4 texts containing a total of 8 stems.   Stems appeared on a new screen with this note: "If you need to reread the text first, please click on the *Previous* button above. Otherwise, click on one of the 4 buttons below to classify the following completion (independently of the others)." The button for each rating included its description shown in Fig. 1.   Participants rated seven candidate single-word completions, one at a time, for each stem, e.g., "*The next morning, Silly Pilly was ready to go to* ____." The seven candidates, reordered randomly for each participant, consisted of the correct answer ("*school*"), the three distractors generated by DQGen ("*along*", "*slang*", and "*breakfast*"), and three authored by humans (e.g. "*blue*", "*slip*", and "*home*").   The writing task was similar:

> In the second task, you will read texts that contain cloze items. You will be prompted to type in four **1-word** completions of each cloze item, one completion of each kind. **These words should be no harder for a child than the reading level of the text.**

To avoid problematic input such as null responses, typos, and non-words, we included code to reject them and prompt for a replacement, but these events, averaging 25 seconds, occurred for only 11 of the 504 human-written distractors in our data.

ASSIGNMENT TO CONDITIONS: All participants did rating before writing, which we considered harder and in fact averaged about 3 times as long per completion.   To avoid text-specific bias, we counter-balanced the study design so that half the participants (the "AB" group) rated completions for the 8 stems in set A and then wrote completions for the 8 stems in set B, and the other half (the "BA" group) rated completions for the stems in set B and then wrote completions for the stems in set A.

Participants in each group rated the same distractors generated by DQGen, but they rated different distractors authored by humans, so as to give us a more diverse sample. To limit the protocol duration, each participant rated distractors authored by only one participant from the other group.   Accordingly, we used the following algorithm to assign participants to rate human-authored distractors.

The first participants saw distractors written by staff experienced with cloze questions.   However, as soon as participants completed the protocol, the distractors written by these protocol completers became available for subsequent participants to rate. Once a participant completed the protocol by writing distractors for set B, another participant was assigned to rate them, and to write distractors for set A.   Similarly, those distractors were eventually (if ever) rated by some subsequent participant assigned to rate set A and write distractors for set B, and so on.

This "daisy-chaining" algorithm assigned each new participant to rate cloze items from whichever set (A or B) had been rated so far by fewer participants who had finished the protocol. It chose human-authored distractors not yet rated by anyone who had finished the protocol.   Consequently, all 27 participants rated distractors generated by DQGen for either set A or set B.   21 participants' distractors got rated – 16 participants with one rating per distractor, and the other five with two. Our data set contains no ratings for the remaining six participants' distractors, either because nobody rated them, or because we discarded data from other participants who may have rated them but didn't finish the rest of the protocol.

3   Results

Table 1 shows the percentage of ratings of each intended distractor type as Ungrammatical, Nonsensical, Plausible, or Correct, based on 1486 ratings by 27 raters of 16 correct answers, 48 distractors generated by DQGen, and 504 distractors written by 21 humans. Inter-rater reliability was substantial on distractors generated by DQGen (Fleiss' Kappa = 0.66). Only 40 human-authored distractors were rated by more than one rater, namely 5 sets of 8 distractors rated by a pair of raters. Cohen's Kappa for each pair of raters averaged 0.46 (N = 5, SD 0.25), i.e., only moderate agreement, vs. 0.60 (SD 0.09), close to substantial agreement, on the 8 DQGen-generated distractors they both rated, but the two means did not differ reliably on a paired T-test (p=0.31).

Table 1. Confusion matrix for ratings of DQGen's and human distractors and correct answers

Rating:	Ungrammatical		Nonsensical		Plausible		Correct	
Intended type:	DQGen	Human	DQGen	Human	DQGen	Human	DQGen	Human
Ungrammatical	93% > 81% [a]		4%	16%	3%	1%	0%	2%
Nonsensical	14%	5%	81% > 74% [b]		5%	20%	0%	1%
Plausible	2%	2%	23%	23%	54% < 63% [c]		21%	13%
Correct	0%		2%		18%		80%	

a. Chi-square $p < 0.001$; b. $p = 0.089$; c. $p = 0.053$

The **boldfaced** diagonal entries in Table 1 compare the percentages of ratings that agreed with the intended types of DQGen- and human-generated distractors. To determine which differences were not only reliable but likely to generalize to unseen data from similar cloze stems and raters, we used a logistic mixed-effects model. Like logistic regression, it predicted a binary outcome – whether the rating of a distractor will agree with its intended type – as the log odds ratio of the probability of agreement over the probability of disagreement. It used random effects to model variation in cloze stems or raters. To find the model that fit the data best, we used backward model selection, starting with five predictors we expected could affect the outcome. Three were fixed effects: distractor source, intended type, and their interaction. Two were random effects: stem and rater (just their intercepts, not their slopes, which our data was too sparse to estimate). We kept removing the weakest predictor (the one with the highest p-value) until doing so stopped improving model fit in a Likelihood Ratio Test. We now relate the resulting model in Table 2 to the ratings in Table 1:

Main Effect of Intended Distractor Type: Compared to their nonsensical distractors, both DQGen and humans generated significantly worse ($p < 0.02$) plausible distractors, with a trend ($p < 0.1$) toward better ungrammatical distractors.

No Main Effect of Source: Surprisingly, DQGen's distractor quality did not differ significantly overall from humans'.

Interaction of Source with Distractor Type: Although DQGen and humans did not differ significantly overall, they differed for some distractor types after adjusting for the fixed effect of distractor type and the random effect of stem.   DQGen's ungrammatical distractors were significantly ($p < 0.001$) better than humans', its plausible distractors were probably ($p \sim 0.05$) worse than humans', and there was a trend ($p < 0.1$) for its nonsensical distractors to be better than humans'.

No Random Effect of Individual Rater: We would have expected a rater effect if some raters were systematically worse, e.g., rated at random.   The absence of such an effect reassuringly suggests the results are likely to generalize to future similar raters.

Random Effect of Stem: Performance differed reliably by stem (SD = 0.35), i.e., the best-fitting model had a (1 | stem) $\sim N(0, 0.35^2)$ distribution of random per-stem intercepts.   For some stems, raters could not tell correct answers from plausible distractors, as the error analysis in Section 3.2 below will discuss further.

Table 2. Best-fitting model of agreement; reference base for distractor_type is Nonsensical

Model: *agreement ~ distractor_type + source × distractor_type + (1 | stem)*		
Random effects:	**Variance:**	**SD:**
stem	0.12	0.35
Fixed effects:	**β coefficient:**	***p*-value:**
intercept	1.08	<0.001
distractor_type = Ungrammatical	0.40	0.098
distractor_type = Plausible	-0.53	0.014
distractor_type = Ungrammatical × source = DQGen	1.11	<0.001
distractor_type = Nonsensical × source = DQGen	0.41	0.082
distractor_type = Plausible × source = DQGen	-0.39	0.053

Time Analysis: To see whether DQGen could speed up human authoring, we compared the time for humans to rate versus write distractors.   They averaged about 5 seconds to rate a choice and about 19 seconds to write any type of distractor.   Based on Table 1, rating a distractor generated by DQGen and rewriting it only if unacceptable would average (5 seconds) + (1 − agreement rate) × (19 seconds) = about 10 seconds, barely half of the 19 seconds to write it by hand.   Moreover, 92% of distractors would match their intended type if vetting is perfect, i.e. rates DQGen-generated distractors properly by definition.   Only 73% of human-authored distractors do so.

   To analyze effects on the time to rate a choice, we used mixed-effects linear regression starting with source, type, rating agreement and their interaction as fixed effects, and stem and rater as random effects.   Backward model selection led to the model in Table 3:

No Main Effects: Rating time didn't differ reliably by source, type, or agreement.

Random Effects: Rating time differed reliably by both stem and rater.

Interaction of Agreement with Intended Type (p < 0.001):   Rating was significantly faster when it agreed with choices intended to be correct (4.6 s < 8.7 s), ungrammatical (4.3 s < 7.2 s), or nonsensical (5.2 s < 5.7 s).   For plausible distractors, rating was slower (6.6 s > 5.8 s) (albeit not significantly) when it agreed with intended type, perhaps because confirming that a distractor is plausible requires additional thought.

Table 3. Best-fitting model of time to rate a choice

Model: *duration ~ intended_type × agreement + (1 | stem) + (1 | rater)*		
Random effects:	**Variance:**	**SD:**
stem	3.48	1.87
rater	1.92	1.38
Fixed effects:	**β coefficient:**	***t*-value:**
intercept	6.26	10.32
intended_type = Ungrammatical × agreement = agree	-1.89	-4.76
intended_type = Nonsensical × agreement = agree	-0.97	-2.37
intended_type = Plausible × agreement = agree	0.14	0.33
intended_type = Correct × agreement = agree	-1.61	-3.24

Error Analysis: To shed light on which distractors were rated differently than their intended type, and why, we now discuss the off-diagonal cases in Table 1, most frequent first:

Distractors Intended to be Plausible but Rated as Nonsensical: One possibility is that the raters disregarded "meaningful by itself" in our definition of plausible and took context into account in rating some distractors as nonsensical.

Distractors Intended to be Plausible but Rated as Correct, or Vice Versa: For instance, raters performed below or near chance on two sentences from a speech by Bill Clinton where his actual word fit no better than the plausible distractor:

- our people have always mustered the determination to construct from these crises the pillars of our _____.   [history]

Only 21% of the ratings of "history" classified it as correct, vs. 86% for "democracy."

- Clearly America must continue to lead the world we did so much to __.   [make]

Only half of the ratings for "make" classified it as correct.

DQGen assumes that the correct answer fits better than topically unrelated distractors. This assumption fails when lack of topicality fails to disqualify a plausible distractor.

Distractors Generated by DQGen to be Nonsensical, but Rated as Ungrammatical: For instance, 13 of 14 raters classified the distractor "share" as ungrammatical here:

- We nip if they stray too far from ____.   [home]

DQGen chooses nonsensical distractors to have the same part of speech as the correct answer, in this case the noun "home".   The word "share" can be a noun, but evidently raters perceived it here as a verb and hence ungrammatical.

Distractors Written by Humans to be Ungrammatical, but Rated as Nonsensical: 6 of 13 raters classified "brave," "flows," "light," "politics," or "run" as nonsensical in:

-   Now, the sights and sounds of this ceremony are broadcast instantaneously to billions around the ____.   [world]

Perhaps the raters parsed them as nouns, but their authors did not (except "politics"). In generating ungrammatical distractors, DQGen considers alternative parts of speech.

Distractors Written by Humans to be Nonsensical, but Rated as Plausible: For instance, of the supposedly nonsensical distractors written by humans for the sentence "We nip if they stray too far from ____.", "Bananas," "beaches," "beans," "England," "heaven," "muscle," "pizza, " and "sheep" were indeed classified as nonsensical (each by a different rater), but "England," "heaven, "rivers", "sheep," and "water" were classified as plausible (each by some other rater).   The last three distractors could be attributed to authors taking context into account, and therefore considering them nonsensical even though they're plausible out of context.   Apparently they were unable to disregard context in deciding whether a word is nonsensical.   The disagreement on "England" and "heaven" suggests that it's less clear-cut how to rate them, or perhaps that their plausibility or lack thereof depends on the extent to which the rater ignores context.   Evidently writing or judging nonsensical distractors is a difficult task for human raters who know the context, because they have trouble disregarding it.   Depriving humans of the context would make both tasks easier for humans.   In contrast, DQGen by its very design disregards the context when generating nonsensical or ungrammatical distractors.

4   Conclusion

This paper contributes to automated diagnostic assessment of children's reading comprehension by comparing the 2014 version of DQGen against human performance in generating ungrammatical, nonsensical, and plausible distractors for cloze stems. We had assumed that human performance was a gold standard to aspire to, and an existence proof of the level of performance possible; the gap would show where further progress was possible and needed.

Surprisingly, DQGen did not differ significantly overall from human performance, and actually beat humans at generating ungrammatical and nonsensical distractors. Its plausible distractors were too plausible, i.e. rated as correct answers 18% of the time. Error analysis elucidated the performance differences: DQGen considers all parts of speech and distinguishes local from contextual plausibility, but needs stronger heuristics than topicality to reliably generate distractors implausible in the larger context.

We projected that vetting DQGen's output and writing distractors only if needed, rather than writing them all, would take only half the time and yield better distractors.

Previous evaluations of automatically generated cloze questions relied on expert critiques or crowdsourced human performance at answering them. We found one study [5] in which three experts compared their estimated time to write cloze questions for different texts with vs. without automated assistance. Our study was much more tightly controlled, evaluating DQGen-generated vs. human-authored distractors for the same 16 cloze stems by what percentage of ratings by knowledgeable judges agreed with the distractors' intended types, and by the exact logged time to write or rate them. To gauge the generalizability of our results to similar stems and raters, we used mixed-effects models to analyze 1486 ratings by 27 raters of 16 correct answers, 48 distractors generated by DQGen, and 504 distractors authored by 21 humans.

Small-scale crowd-sourced expert rating and writing of distractors enabled controlled comparison of both the quality of each type of distractor and the time to write or rate them. It exposed the influence of the preceding text on raters' ability to distinguish nonsensical from plausible distractors. Future studies should eliminate this influence by having humans rate or write distractors for cloze stems before seeing their context, and only then decide which plausible distractors do not fit the context.

Limitations of this study leave ample room for future work. We used 16 cloze stems from just seven stories. To enable controlled comparison of distractors, we took these stems as givens, so we did not evaluate the percentage of sentences turned into cloze stems (yield), and we evaluated just the distractors, not the cloze stems, nor the overall quality of the resulting questions in diagnostic comprehension assessment. We used education and reading researchers blind to intended type to rate distractors, rather than validate them against expert diagnostic assessments of children. Finally, distractors based on deeper models of comprehension processes such as inter-sentential inference may enable more reliable and informative diagnostic assessments.

Acknowledgements. This research was funded in part by the National Science Foundation through Grant IIS1124240, and by the Taiwan National Science Council's Overseas Project for Post Graduate Research NSC103-2917-I-002-017. We thank everyone who rated and wrote distractors; reviewers and H. Jang for their comments; and Prof. Y.S. Sun at National Taiwan University and Dr. M.C. Chen at Academia Sinica for supporting the first author. The opinions expressed are those of the authors and do not necessarily represent the views of the National Science Foundation or the National Science Council.

References

1. Mostow, J., Beck, J.E., Bey, J., Cuneo, A., Sison, J., Tobin, B., Valeri, J.: Using Automated Questions to Assess Reading Comprehension, Vocabulary, and Effects of Tutorial Interventions. Technology, Instruction, Cognition and Learning 2(1-2), 97–134 (2004)
2. Mostow, J., Chen, W.: Generating instruction automatically for the reading strategy of self-questioning. In: Proceedings of the 14th International Conference on Artificial Intelligence in Education, pp. 465–472. IOS Press, Brighton, UK (2009)

3. Gates, D., Aist, G., Mostow, J., Mckeown, M., Bey, J.: How to generate cloze questions from definitions: a syntactic approach. In: Proceedings of the AAAI Symposium on Question Generation 2011. AAAI Press, Arlington, VA

4. Chen, W., Mostow, J., Aist, G.S.: Recognizing Young Readers' Spoken Questions. International Journal of Artificial Intelligence in Education 21(4), 255–269 (2013)

5. Mitkov, R., Ha, L.A., Karamanis, N.: A Computer-aided Environment for Generating Multiple Choice Test Items. Natural Language Engineering 12(2), 177–194 (2006)

6. Agarwal, M., Mannem, P.: Automatic gap-fill question generation from text books. In: Proceedings of the 6th Workshop on Innovative Use of NLP for Building Educational Applications, pp. 56–64. Association for Computational Linguistics (2011)

7. Sumita, E., Sugaya, F., Yamamoto, S.: Measuring non-native speakers' proficiency of English by using a test with automatically-generated fill-in-the-blank questions. In: Proceedings of the Second Workshop on Building Educational Applications Using NLP, pp. 61–68. Association for Computational Linguistics, Ann Arbor, MI (2005)

8. Lee, J., Seneff, S.: Automatic generation of cloze items for prepositions. In: INTERSPEECH, pp. 2173–2176 (2007)

9. Lin, Y.-C., Sung, L.-C., Chen, M.C.: An automatic multiple-choice question generation scheme for english adjective understanding. In: Workshop on Modeling, Management and Generation of Problems/Questions in eLearning, the 15th International Conference on Computers in Education (ICCE 2007), pp. 137–142 (2007)

10. Huang, Y.-T., Chen, M.C., Sun, Y.S.: Personalized automatic quiz generation based on proficiency level estimation. In: 20th International Conference on Computers in Education (ICCE 2012), Singapore (2012)

11. Ming, L., Calvo, R.A., Aditomo, A., Pizzato, L.A.: Using Wikipedia and Conceptual Graph Structures to Generate Questions for Academic Writing Support. IEEE Transactions on Learning Technologies 5(3), 251–263 (2012)

12. Graesser, A.C., Bertus, E.L.: The Construction of Causal Inferences While Reading Expository Texts on Science and Technology. Scientific Studies of Reading 2(3), 247–269 (1998)

13. van den Broek, P., Everson, M., Virtue, S., Sung, Y., Tzeng, Y.: Comprehension and memory of science texts: Inferential processes and the construction of a mental representation. In: Otero, J.L.J., Graesser, A.C. (eds.) The Psychology of Science Text Comprehension. Erlbaum, Mahwah, NJ (2002)

14. Kintsch, W.: An Overview of Top-Down and Bottom-Up Effects in Comprehension: The CI Perspective. Discourse Processes A Multidisciplinary Journal 39(2&3), 125–128 (2005)

15. Mostow, J., Jang, H.: Generating diagnostic multiple choice comprehension cloze questions. NAACL-HLT 2012 7th Workshop on Innovative Use of NLP for Building Educational Applications, pp. 136–146. Association for Computational Linguistics, Montréal (2012)

16. Mostow, J.: Lessons from project LISTEN: what have we learned from a reading tutor that listens? In: Lane, H.C., Yacef, K., Mostow, J., Pavlik, P. (eds.) AIED 2013. LNCS, vol. 7926, pp. 557–558. Springer, Heidelberg (2013)

Machine Learning for Holistic Evaluation of Scientific Essays

Simon Hughes[1]([✉]), Peter Hastings[1], Mary Anne Britt[2],
Patricia Wallace[2], and Dylan Blaum[2]

[1] DePaul University, Chicago, IL, USA
simonhughes22@hotmail.com
[2] Northern Illinois University, Dekalb, IL, USA

Abstract. In the US in particular, there is an increasing emphasis on
the importance of science in education. To better understand a scientific topic, students need to compile information from multiple sources
and determine the principal causal factors involved. We describe an approach for automatically inferring the quality and completeness of causal
reasoning in essays on two separate scientific topics using a novel, two-
phase machine learning approach for detecting causal relations. For each
core essay concept, we initially trained a window-based tagging model to
predict which individual words belonged to that concept. Using the predictions from this first set of models, we then trained a second stacked
model on all the predicted word tags present in a sentence to predict
inferences between essay concepts. The results indicate we could use such
a system to provide explicit feedback to students to improve reasoning
and essay writing skills.

Keywords: Reading · Argumentation · Causal relation · Natural language inference · Machine learning · Natural language processing · NLP

1 Introduction

Educational standards in the US have increased considerably in accordance with
the Common Core standards and Next-Generation science standards [15,19].
These standards call for a focus on comprehending and evaluating science models, theories, explanations, and evidence, and learning from multiple documents
and representation formats. However, middle and high school students and even
many undergraduates have difficulty learning from multiple documents in science or history [4,25]. One explanation is students fail to develop an adequate
schema for this genre to guide their reasoning. According to Kintsch and Van

D. Blaum—The research reported here was supported by the Institute of Education
Sciences, U.S. Department of Education, through Grant R305F100007 to University
of Illinois at Chicago. The opinions expressed are those of the authors and do not
represent views of the Institute or the U.S. Department of Education.

© Springer International Publishing Switzerland 2015
C. Conati et al. (Eds.): AIED 2015, LNAI 9112, pp. 165–175, 2015.
DOI: 10.1007/978-3-319-19773-9_17

Dijk [16], effective integration and summarization requires learning genre-specific macro-rules that differentiate the more salient information from the less.

To explain scientific phenomena, one must explain how a sequence of causal factors leads to an outcome via a sequence of intervening concepts — a causal chain. For example, in Figure 1 we can see how the 2 separate initiating factors of DECREASE IN TRADE WINDS and STORMS/RAINFALL lead via two different causal chains to the outcome of CORAL BLEACHING. A schema for such a process would thus involve slots for the initiating factors, concepts, the final outcome and for the causal links by which the factors and concepts drive the outcome.

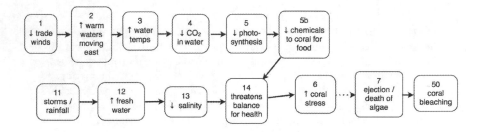

Fig. 1. Causal model for coral bleaching

Essay writing is an important learning skill, and has been shown to promote deeper understanding and integration of information from different sources [3, 26]. Thus, as part of a much larger project[1] [7], we are examining student comprehension of scientific explanations (e.g., explain how and why coral bleaching rates vary at different times) from multiple documents of a variety of types (e.g., descriptive texts, images, graphs and maps) as measured primarily from an essay written with the available documents. A complete and coherent explanation requires integrating information from the entire document set to form a causal model of the phenomena. To improve reading and writing skills in this domain, students need practice developing schemas for understanding this sort of material. This study investigates the use of machine learning to map written essays to a complete causal model of the essay topic. This technique can then lead to the creation of tools that can help guide students in the development of such schemas to aid comprehension and develop better writing and reasoning skills.

2   Related Work

Explaining causality has long been a focus in science education [5, 24, for example]. However, little research has been carried out to automatically detect causal

---

[1] The assessment was created by the READI science design team which includes D. Blaum, M. A. Britt, W. Brown, C. Burkett, M. George, S. R. Goldman, C. Greenleaf, K. James, M. Ko, K. Lawless, S. Marple, U. Sexton, P. Wallace, & M. Yukhymenko.

inference in essays. In 1987, Cohen [6] described a theoretical framework detailing the different problems that need to be addressed to understand argumentative discourse.

Most work in this area has focused on the use of surface lexical features and syntactic patterns to extract causal relations from open domain text. Previous work was mostly restricted to certain sub-types of causal relations involving noun phrases [2], such as between nominals, and between nouns and verbs only. In 2002, Girju and Moldovan [8] used lexico-syntactic patterns to detect a particular form of causal relation between two noun phrases of the form <NP1 Verb NP2>, where the verb was a simple causative. They achieved an accuracy of 65.6% compared to the average of two human annotators. In Semeval 2007, Task 4 focused on "the classification of semantic relations between nominals" [9], which included the detection of causal relations. The highest F_1 score on this category was 0.82 with an accuracy of 77.5% on a system that used features based on WordNet, VerbNet, lexico-syntactic features and parse features. To move beyond surface lexical features, in 2014 Riaz and Girju [21], used Integer Linear Programming to combine verb and noun semantics with the predictions of a supervised machine-learning model trained only on linguistic features. They focused on detecting only causal relations between noun and verbs, achieving an F_1 score of 0.41 and an accuracy of 80.73%, a 15% improvement over using linguistic features alone. In a very different approach, Rink et al [22] built a system to detect the presence or absence of causality only in sentences containing verbal events joined with a conjunction. They created graphical models of causal sentences encoding syntactic and hypernymy information, and dependencies from a dependency parser. They then extracted sub-graph patterns that occurred in causal sentences and used a constraint satisfaction solver to detect these patterns from new sentences, attaining an F_1 score of 0.39.

In contrast, our work does not restrict the type of causal relation based on the syntactic categories involved. However, we only concern ourselves with the causal relations defined in the causal model, which can take the form of any combination of syntactic categories observed in the essays, but are restricted to relations relevant to the essay topics. We also investigate automatic inference of full causal chains, a topic that has received little attention in the literature.

3   The Essay Annotation Procedure

Two document sets assess students abilities to integrate information and develop an understanding about two scientific phenomena: coral bleaching and skin cancer. The documents were prepared from reputable sources (e.g. the NASA earth observatory, the US Geological Survey, and online science textbooks), and each started with some short background material to provide framing, necessary vocabulary, and relevant background knowledge. The sources were compiled such that the students needed to combine information from multiple sources to fully answer the question.

In conjunction with the development of the document sets, a causal model of each scientific phenomenon was created (see Figure 1) that represents the relevant scientific phenomena in the source documents and the causal connections between them, from initiating factors (e.g., decreased trade winds, storms and rainfall, decreased salinity) via various intervening concepts to the final outcome (coral bleaching, or increased skin cancer rates). This can be thought of as a representation of the causal structure of the ideal essay according to the viewpoint of the researchers. There are 2 possible full causal chains in each model, each starting with a different initiating factor but resulting in the same final outcome.

Each student was provided with the essay prompt (e.g. explain the causes of coral bleaching), and asked to answer using the source material. 105 middle and high-school students were assigned 2 essay questions. The essays were then annotated by two different annotators according to how well they aligned with the corresponding causal model. Inter-rater reliability was high ($\kappa = 0.85$). Words or phrases indicating concepts from the model were tagged, and causal links were made between them where it was explicitly stated in the essay. For example "How coral are bleaching because the water temperature is increasing, the solubility of carbon dioxide (CO_2) in water decreases" was coded as concept 3 (INCREASING WATER TEMPS) causing concept 4 (DECREASING CO_2 IN WATER), which causes concept 50 (CORAL BLEACHING). Here the student missed the intervening concepts in the chain, going straight from concept 4 to 50.

4   The Tagging Problem: Identifying Concept Codes

4.1   Previous Work

In previous work, we experimented with a number of different machine learning techniques to detect the core concepts and claims in student essays, [10,12,14], including a support vector machine (SVM), a regular expression learning algorithm [10,14], and the k-nearest neighbor algorithm run on Latent Semantic Analysis (LSA) projections of the sentences. Under this approach, we found that training a separate binary classifier per code was more effective than a multi-class classifier trained on all codes due to the degree of semantic overlap between concept codes in the domain.

In some of these previous studies, we were only able to utilize annotations on individual sentences, although many of the concept codes only covered a few words or short phrases within each sentence. For instance, in the coral bleaching domain, the most common concept code is the concept CORAL BLEACHING, which is most often referred to using exactly those terms, or "coral whitening", or similar. When such a phrase occurs in a sentence with 10 or 20 other words, it is difficult for the algorithm to learn which words denote the particular phrase. Another limitation to our previous work was the use of a bag of word representation for the sentences fed to the SVM and k-nearest neighbor classifiers. This ignores word order, and means the classifier cannot distinguish between individual words and phrases. The regular expression learner was able to learn multi-word phrases over the sentences, but that had lower accuracy on most tasks. In this work, we use a tagging model which overcomes these 2 limitations.

Curriculum learning is the technique of training machine learning models on gradually harder training examples, and lowers the generalization error in some problems [1]. We take a similar approach for detecting causality. We first train a set of tagging models, one per concept, to learn tags for individual words. We then feed the predicted tags into a second set of classification algorithms to solve a much harder problem, detecting inferences within a sentence. We use the same approach to detect concept codes at the sentence level, as this allows the classifier to utilize information about the presence of other tags in the sentence.

4.2 A Window-Based Tagger

Tagging models are commonly used in natural language processing to tag words with one or more labels, such as in identifying parts of speech tags such as nouns or verbs, or in named entity recognition. To effectively determine the concept code of a word in this domain, it's important to include the surrounding context of the word as that denotes the word's meaning and can disambiguate its word sense. For this reason, we feed a window of words around the target word to an SVM to predict the concept code for the individual word. Each word and position forms a separate feature, so if the word 'melanin' occurs in window position 1 and in position 5, those are treated as separate features. We experimented with a range of window sizes, 1, 3, 5, 7 and 9 and found 7 to be optimal. In addition, we used all bi-grams (consecutive word pairs) appearing in the window as additional features, again encoded with their relative window position. We experimented with trigrams, but that lowered tagging accuracy. Table 1 shows the recall, precision, F_1 score and classification accuracy for the word-level tagging task on the validation data using 5 fold cross-validation. The mean values were computed over all the concept codes, the weighted mean was weighted by the number of occurrences of each code.

Table 1. Word tagging results

	Coral Bleaching			Skin Cancer		
	Recall	Precision	F_1	Recall	Precision	F_1
Mean	0.57	0.67	0.58	0.62	0.72	0.66
Weighted Mean	0.70	0.80	0.73	0.70	0.75	0.72

In preparing the data, we replaced words occurring only once in each document set with a special token, padded the start and ends of the sentence with special start and stop tokens, and used a spelling corrector based on [18] to correct typos. We used stemming only on the coral bleaching data as it reduced accuracy on the skin cancer data set. We did not remove stop words as they can aid classification accuracy when tagging words based on their context. In previous work [11] we compared the performance of Linear Discriminant Analysis, an SVM, Random Forest and a Decision Tree on this task and found the SVM to be superior in terms of F_1 score, and so that technique was used in this paper.

In addition to training the tagging model to detect concept codes, we also trained it on 3 additional tags, "Causal Tags", associated with the causal chains - CAUSER, RESULT and EXPLICIT. CAUSER was an additional tag applied to concepts denoted as causal. Similarly, RESULT was applied to concepts denoted as the result of a causal link. EXPLICIT describes words or phrases that link CAUSE concepts with RESULT concepts and often includes terms denoting causality, such as "can cause", "because of" and "affects". Predictions for these 3 tags, along with the other concept codes from the tagger were then used to build a predictive model to predict which sentences contained causal links.

5   Sentence-Level Concepts and Causality

Causal links within the essays occur within a sentence, and as such cannot be detected using a tagging model alone, as they occur between concepts. To detect causal links, we used a form of stacking, or "stacked generalization" [27], to train a binary classifier on the output of the tagging models. Having trained a different tagging model for each of the codes, including the Causal Tags, we first aggregated the word-level predictions at the sentence level in 3 different ways to produce 3 sets of features. (1) For each code, we took the maximum distance either side of the margin (positive and negative) learned by the SVM classifier over all words in the sentence. This measures how strongly parts of each sentence are positive and negative exemplars of each code. (2) We created a binary feature for each code that was true if any of the words were tagged with that code. (3) We took all the unique codes predicted over the sentence and created a feature for each unique pairwise combination of codes. We experimented with several other sets of features, including computing the mean distance from the margin per word, computing 3-way combinations of predicted codes, and features representing the order in which pairs of codes appeared in the sentence. However, these three feature sets proved optimal in terms of classification accuracy. A separate binary SVM classifier was then trained using these three feature sets as input to predict three types of causal relation for each sentence: Cause-Explicit-Result, Cause-Explicit and Explicit-Result, as well as the individual concept codes at the sentence level. The last two causal relationships represent incomplete cause-effect relations. Table 2 shows the classification accuracy at the sentence level for the three relations and the average classification accuracy over all the non-causal concept codes on the validation data using 5-fold cross-validation.

6   Evaluating Writing Quality

In prior work, we have used tools to automatically identify core concepts [10,12,14], and, starting with human scoring of core concepts, automatically

Table 2. Sentence level classification accuracy

	Coral Bleaching			Skin Cancer		
	Recall	Precision	F_1	Recall	Precision	F_1
Cause-Explicit	0.64	0.66	0.65	0.66	0.61	0.61
Explicit-Result	0.61	0.65	0.63	0.68	0.62	0.63
Cause-Explicit-Res.	0.63	0.68	0.65	0.67	0.62	0.62
Concept Mean	0.74	0.72	0.71	0.81	0.77	0.78
Concept Weighted	0.88	0.84	0.85	0.88	0.84	0.85

identify causal chains [11]. As the logical next step, we identified four levels of explanation quality that capture general goals for an explanation (e.g., accuracy, completeness, coherence). When reading, especially multiple documents, readers' goals determine what is relevant which, in turn, influences how information is processed [17,23]. Therefore, we selected categories that could point to feedback that could be used to help students refine the goals for the task.

The four quality levels were (1) No core content, (2) No causal chains, (3) Causal chain with no intervening factors, (4) Chain with intervening. The "No core content" essays did not have any core concepts other than the final outcome of the causal chain that was given. Students who received no credit for core concepts generally focused on statements that were supporting but not part of the explanation, or were too vague. Feedback for these students could encourage them to begin to identify elements of the explanation and to make their statement of the concept more explicit and complete. For example, merely saying that "wind affects the water" does not help the reader distinguish wind conditions that would lead to coral bleaching from those that would lead to healthy coral. Students may not understand the importance of attending to directional modifiers. In the "No causal chains" essays, students focused on at least one important element of the causal model but did not explicitly connect this information to the final outcome. These students are reproducing some correct concepts but could be instructed how to connect these concepts via intervening concepts to the final outcome. The final two types of essays actually have some degree of structure that is required in the essay question. The difference is whether there is some success in connecting initiating factors and intervening concepts. Students' writing that included a causal chain but with no intervening concepts could be encouraged to examine whether concepts across documents could be connected as intervening causes.

To assess entire essays and for the pedagogically appropriate categories, we had to convert binary causal predictions into predictions for specific concepts, and aggregate the predictions over all the sentences in each essay. For this, we employed simple heuristics. For each sentence in which a causal connection was predicted, we assumed that it was between the first two codes (numerically) identified in the sentence. When there are exactly two concepts in the sentence, this heuristic works well. If there are 1 or 0 codes identified, it results in a partial chain (which also happens in student essays). If there are more than two concepts, this results in additional, unconnected concept codes. For example, if the system predicted a causal connection and codes 1, 2 and 50, this was identified by the heuristics as a causal chain between 1 and 2 with an extra 50.

Aggregating the sentence codes for an essay required resolving vague concepts and linking chains together. For each of the concept codes, the human coders could mark it as "vague" if it only partially matched the concept. But we only want to give an essay credit for claims which are fully specified. Because many writers start out general and get more specific, when aggregating, we converted vague concepts to non-vague if they were specified fully elsewhere in the essay.

Multiple metrics were defined to evaluate the relative completeness of each student's essay, and to compute the quality level defined above. The evaluation of the inferred causal chains with respect to these pedagogically useful attributes is shown in Table 3. The first four numerical columns show the correspondence between four measures computed from the human coders and those from the machine learning approach: the number of unique codes in the essay, the number of unique causal chains, the maximum chain length, and the number of distinct paths leading to the final outcome. The Quality column shows the correspondence between the explanation quality level assigned by the coders and by the system. Because these attributes are interval and ordinal (Quality) we measured correspondence with accuracy, adjacent accuracy (which includes misses by 1), and Krippendorff's alpha (agreement), instead of Recall, Precision, and F_1.

Table 3. Essay-level accuracy and correlations

	Codes	Chains	Length	Paths	Quality
	Coral Bleaching				
Accuracy	0.57	0.62	0.63	0.63	0.51
Adjacent	0.91	0.90	0.85	0.91	0.85
Agreement	0.89	0.37	0.20	0.36	0.56
	Skin Cancer				
Accuracy	0.38	0.41	0.48	0.45	0.43
Adjacent	0.87	0.90	0.81	0.93	0.88
Agreement	0.82	0.34	0.27	0.33	0.47

It is important to note that each of these measures has a relatively wide range of values (0–9, 0–4, 0–5, 0–3, and 1–4, respectively), so the expected accuracy of random guessing for any of them would be from 0.1 to 0.25. As these results show, the aspects of the classification that rely only on inference of codes are fairly reliable. Even if the machine learning identification of codes doesn't exactly match the human calculation, the agreement is high. The rest of the attributes and the quality level rely on identifying the causal connections, which is notoriously hard, and that is reflected in our results. Nevertheless, the high adjacent accuracies make us confident that feedback generated on the basis of these evaluations would be helpful for the students.

7   Conclusions and Further Work

Prior work in this area [2,8,9,20–22] has demonstrated the difficulty of automatically inferring causality from text, and has primarily focused on detecting sub-types of causal relations. Instead we focused on a particular domain, and our approach was able to detect partial and full causal chains, a topic without much precedence in the literature. Furthermore, we presented a novel scoring rubric for assessing the accuracy, completeness and coherence of the explanations present in the essays. We then demonstrated reasonable accuracy in automating this assessment task. This approach has the potential to be used to develop intelligent tutoring systems to assist students with the development of mental schema to help them refine their goals for this task, and thus aid comprehension, reasoning skills and writing ability. For example, if a student skips a section of the causal chain, such as going from concept 4 to 50 as described in section 3, a tutoring system could show the graph of the causal model, highlighting the missing inferences to guide the student to produce a more complete essay.

There are a few limitations to our approach that could be addressed in future work. A limitation of the window-based tagging model is that it can only consider relationships between words that occur together within a window, and cannot consider longer-term dependencies. Long-Short-Term-Memory Recurrent Neural Networks can learn long-term dependencies between sequential items [13], and could be a promising future direction for this work. We also plan to explore the use of coreference resolution to help identify causal connections that are linked anaphorically across sentences. Finally, it would be interesting to investigate whether the causal patterns learned by our system could predict causal relations in open domain text.

References

1. Bengio, Y., Louradour, J., Collobert, R., Weston, J.: Curriculum learning. In: Proceedings of the 26th Annual International Conference on Machine Learning, pp. 41–48. ACM (2009)
2. Blanco, E., Castell, N., Moldovan, D.: Causal relation extraction. In: LREC (2008)
3. Britt, M.A., Wiemer-Hastings, P., Larson, A., Perfetti, C.: Using intelligent feedback to improve sourcing and integration in students' essays. International Journal of Artificial Intelligence in Education **14**, 359–374 (2004)
4. Britt, M.A., Aglinskas, C.: Improving students' ability to identify and use source information. Cognition and Instruction **20**(4), 485–522 (2002)
5. Chi, M., Roscoe, R., Slotta, J., Roy, M., Chase, C.: Misconceived causal explanations for emergent processes. Cognitive Science **36**, 1–61 (2012)
6. Cohen, R.: Analyzing the structure of argumentative discourse. Computational Linguistics **13**(1–2), 11–24 (1987)
7. Institute for Education Sciences. Reading for understanding across grades 6 through 12: Evidence-based argumentation for disciplinary learning. washington, d.c.: National center for education research (2010). http://www.ies.ed.gov/ncer/projects/results.asp?ProgID=62&NameID-351 (last accessed January 20, 2015)

8. Girju, R., Moldovan, D.: Mining answers for causation questions. In: Proc. The AAAI Spring Symposium on Mining Answers from Texts and Knowledge Bases (2002)
9. Girju, R., Nakov, P., Nastase, V., Szpakowicz, S., Turney, P., Yuret, D.: Semeval-2007 task 04: classification of semantic relations between nominals. In: Proceedings of the 4th International Workshop on Semantic Evaluations, p. 1318 (2007)
10. Hastings, P., Hughes, S., Magliano, J., Goldman, S., Lawless, K.: Text categorization for assessing multiple documents integration, or john henry visits a data mine. In: Biswas, G., Bull, S., Kay, J., Mitrovic, A. (eds.) AIED 2011. LNCS, vol. 6738, pp. 115–122. Springer, Heidelberg (2011)
11. Hastings, P., Hughes, S., Britt, A., Blaum, D., Wallace, P.: Toward automatic inference of causal structure in student essays. In: Trausan-Matu, S., Boyer, K.E., Crosby, M., Panourgia, K. (eds.) ITS 2014. LNCS, vol. 8474, pp. 266–271. Springer, Heidelberg (2014)
12. Hastings, P., Hughes, S., Magliano, J., Goldman, S., Lawless, K.: Assessing the use of multiple sources in student essays. Behavior Research Methods **44**(3), 622–633 (2012)
13. Hochreiter, S., Schmidhuber, J.: Long short-term memory. Neural Computation **9**(8), 1735–1780 (1997)
14. Hughes, S., Hastings, P., Magliano, J., Goldman, S., Lawless, K.: Automated approaches for detecting integration in student essays. In: Cerri, S.A., Clancey, W.J., Papadourakis, G., Panourgia, K. (eds.) ITS 2012. LNCS, vol. 7315, pp. 274–279. Springer, Heidelberg (2012)
15. Achieve Inc. Next Generation Science Standards. Achieve Inc. (2013)
16. Kintsch, W., Van Dijk, T.A.: Toward a model of text comprehension and production. Psychological Review **85**(5), 363–394 (1978)
17. Lehman, S., McCrudden, M., Schraw, G., Poliquin, A.: The effect of causal diagrams on text learning. Contemporary Educational Psychology **33**, 367–388 (2007)
18. How to write a spelling corrector. http://norvig.com/spell-correct.html
19. The Council of Chief State School Officers. The common core standards for english language arts and literacy in history/social studies and science and technical subjects. Washington, DC: National Governors Association for Best Practices (2010). http://www.corestandards.org
20. Riaz, M., Girju, R.: In-depth exploitation of noun and verb semantics to identify causation in verb-noun pairs. In: 15th Annual Meeting of the Special Interest Group on Discourse and Dialogue, p. 161 (2014)
21. Riaz, M., Girju, R.: Recognizing causality in verb-noun pairs via noun and verb semantics. In: EACL 2014, p. 48 (2014)
22. Rink, B., Bejan, C.A., Harabagiu, S.M.: Learning textual graph patterns to detect causal event relations. In: Guesgen, H.W., Murray, R.C. (eds.) FLAIRS Conference. AAAI Press (2010)
23. Rouet, J.F., Britt, M.A.: Relevance processes in multiple document comprehension. In : McCrudden, M.T., Magliano, J.P., Schraw, G. (eds.) Text Relevance and Learning from Text. Information Age Publishing, Greenwich, CT (in press)
24. White, B., Frederiksen, J.: Causal model progressions as a foundation for intelligent learning environments. Artificial Intelligence **42**, 99–157 (1990)

25. Wiley, J., Goldman, S.R., Graesser, A., Sanchez, C., Ash, I., Hemmerich, J.: Source evaluation, comprehension, and learning in internet science inquiry tasks. American Educational Research Journal **46**(4), 1060–1106 (2009)
26. Wiley, J., Voss, J.F.: Constructing arguments from multiple sources: Tasks that promote understanding and not just memory for text. Journal of Educational Psychology **91**, 301–311 (1999)
27. Wolpert, D.H.: Stacked generalization. Neural Networks **5**(2), 241–259 (1992)

Learning to Diagnose a Virtual Patient: An Investigation of Cognitive Errors in Medical Problem Solving

Amanda Jarrell[1(✉)], Tenzin Doleck[1], Eric Poitras[2], Susanne Lajoie[1], and Tara Tressel[1]

[1] Department of Educational and Counselling Psychology, McGill University,
Montreal, QC, Canada
amanda.jarrell@mail.mcgill.ca
[2] Department of Educational Psychology, University of Utah, Salt Lake City, UT, USA

Abstract. Although cognitive errors (i.e., premature closure, faulty data gathering, and faulty knowledge) are the main reasons for making diagnostic mistakes, the mechanisms by which they occur are difficult to isolate in clinical settings. Computer-based learning environments (CBLE) offer the opportunity to train medical students to avoid cognitive errors by tracking the onset of these errors. The purpose of this study is to explore cognitive errors in a CBLE called Bio-World. A logistic regression was fitted to learner behaviors that characterize premature closure in order to predict diagnostic performance. An ANOVA was used to assess if participants who were highly confident in their wrong diagnosis engaged in more faulty data gathering via confirmation bias. Findings suggest that diagnostic mistakes can be predicted from faulty knowledge and faulty data gathering and indicate poor metacognitive awareness. This study supports the notion that to improve diagnostic performance medical education programs should promote metacognitive skills.

Keywords: Cognitive errors · Metacognition · Computer-based learning environment

1 Introduction

Providing a correct diagnosis is crucial to the health of individuals within any population. However, doctors do not always make the correct diagnosis because medical reasoning is a complex and ill-defined task. It has been suggested that in clinical settings, 15% of diagnoses result in a diagnostic error [1]. Diagnostic errors made in clinical practice cause unnecessary harm to patients and costs to the healthcare system. Specifically, diagnostic error is the leading cause of malpractice claims against hospitals in the United States [2]. Types of diagnostic error include: (1) when a diagnosis is delayed even though sufficient information is available, (2) a wrong diagnosis is provided before the correct diagnosis, or (3) a diagnosis is not provided at all [3]. Although the mechanisms for making a diagnostic error are complex, one of the main reasons is cognitive error [4]. In addition, there is evidence that overconfidence is also related to diagnostic error in clinical practice. In one study, physicians who were "completely certain" of their diagnosis before the death of a patient were wrong 40%

© Springer International Publishing Switzerland 2015
C. Conati et al. (Eds.): AIED 2015, LNAI 9112, pp. 176–184, 2015.
DOI: 10.1007/978-3-319-19773-9_18

of the time, as confirmed by an autopsy [5]. Computer-based learning environments (CBLE) offer the opportunity to train students to avoid cognitive errors, track confidence levels and foster metacognitive skills by mapping the onset of these errors. Early detection of cognitive errors and inflated confidence levels can allow the system to respond with appropriate scaffolding such as individualized feedback and hints. The purpose of this research is to investigate the influence of cognitive errors and confidence levels on the diagnostic performance of medical students in the context of BioWorld [6]. BioWorld is a CBLE that allows students to practice diagnostic reasoning and receive feedback on their diagnoses. The findings obtained from this study will inform the future development of BioWorld by tailoring the feedback to the specific needs of different students.

1.1   Cognitive Errors in Diagnostic Reasoning

Cognitive errors that lead to a diagnostic error can result from faulty knowledge, data gathering, or synthesis [3]. However, not all of these factors equally lead to diagnostic mistakes. Research suggests that the reason for making a diagnostic error in clinical practice is primarily due to faulty synthesis (i.e., incorrect processing of the available information) and secondarily due to faulty data gathering   (i.e. collecting information that only supports the hypothesis) [3]. Faulty synthesis and data gathering can be manifested in many ways, most notably in premature closure and confirmation bias. Premature closure occurs when a physician fails to consider other possible diagnoses once an initial diagnosis has been identified. Confirmation bias occurs when a physician has the tendency to interpret information in a way that supports his or her current diagnosis and does not search for disconfirming evidence [4,7, 3]. Expectedly, both types of cognitive errors can cause physicians to make a diagnostic mistake. For example, in a case where a patient presents symptoms of a rare disease, such as pheochromocytoma, a physician might incorrectly interpret the patient's increased heart rate to support a more common disease, such as arrhythmia. The physician might then order laboratory tests that confirm arrhythmia but consequently fail to consider alternative diagnoses that are also characterized by increased heart rate. In this example, the physician is subject to both premature closure, by settling on his or her initial diagnosis of arrhythmia without exploring alternatives, as well as confirmation bias, by interpreting the symptoms in a way that supported his or her initial hypothesis while also failing to consider other evidence that would have ruled out arrhythmia.

1.2   Metacognition and Cognitive Errors

Premature closure and faulty data gathering might be appropriately attributed to dysregulation. Dysregulation refers to instances when learners do not adaptively regulate their cognitive and metacognitive behaviors [8]. Dysregulation occurs when individuals do not correct their behavior in response to the task, fail to metacognitively monitor their strategy use, or fail to make accurate metacognitive judgments. To reduce cognitive errors resulting from dysregulation, medical education programs should promote metacognition and self-regulation strategies [9, 3, 10]. Metacognitive skills in medical problem solving include the ability to orient the problem space, plan and execute actions, monitor outcomes, evaluate one's overall progress, and elaborate on a solution [11]. One way to promote these skills is to compare the actions of medical students with those of expert physicians and tailor instruction to the specific needs of the learner. Expert models can promote metacognition by supporting the formulation of plans and monitoring progress [10]. Cultivating metacognitive skills is thought to enable medical students to develop an awareness of their thinking and reasoning processes, and the ability to evaluate if these processes are effective. It has been suggested that these skills will reduce the occurrence of cognitive errors and improve diagnostic performance by encouraging medical students to consider more hypotheses and evaluate evidence in a flexible manner [9].

1.3 Overconfidence and Cognitive Errors

Another important factor that can cause some physicians to be more vulnerable to cognitive errors than others is overconfidence. Overconfidence during diagnostic reasoning occurs when a physician thinks he or she has made a correct diagnosis but the diagnosis is in fact wrong. Berner and Garber [7] propose two reasons why overconfidence can lead to a diagnostic error. First, physicians tend to generate hypotheses almost immediately after hearing a patient's symptoms. Second, even if more information is needed, physicians who are confident with their initial hypothesis often seek information that only confirms their initial hypothesis. In other words, confidence in an early hypothesis influences subsequent cognitive activities and plans of action. Although in the majority of cases this leads to the identification of the correct diagnosis and rapid treatment, in other cases this leads to a diagnostic error.

One important limitation of previous research on cognitive errors in clinical reasoning is that the majority of these studies rely on retrospective self-evaluations of errors. This is because cognitive errors are difficult to observe in clinical settings, as different types of errors can overlap and there is no process data that can be used to identify if a particular cognitive error has occurred [4]. These limitations make it difficult to reliably isolate diagnostic errors and identify the mechanisms by which they occur. Without this information, it remains unclear which type of cognitive errors (i.e., faulty knowledge, faulty data gathering, or faulty synthesis) are made during diagnostic reasoning, or the cause of the error and how best to support medical students as they learn to diagnose a patient. CBLEs can uniquely track the onset of these errors and respond appropriately to foster metacognition and reduce dysregulation.

1.4 Research Objectives

The purpose of this study is to address this gap by analyzing process data to evaluate the impact of premature closure and confirmation bias, as well as overconfidence on the diagnostic performance of medical students. To address this aim we focus on two research questions: (1) Can diagnostic performance be predicted from premature closure?; and (2) Do participants who are highly confident in their wrong diagnosis engage in more faulty data gathering via confirmation bias?

With regard to the first question, it is expected that if participants engage in premature closure, they will be more likely to select an incorrect diagnosis and take less time to solve the case. With regard to the second question, it is expected that participants who are confident in their wrong diagnosis will engage in more faulty data gathering when compared to other participants. The analyses presented within this paper represent a preliminary exploration of cognitive errors as medical students diagnose a virtual patient in a CBLE.

2   Methods

2.1   Participants

This study consisted of 30 first and second year medical students from a North American university. The sample consisted of 11 men and 19 women, with an average age of 23 ($SD = 2.60$).

2.2   BioWorld

BioWorld [6] is a computer-based learning environment (CBLE) that simulates clinical reasoning and is designed to support the metacognitive activities of medical students as they learn to diagnose a patient (see Figure 1). Each case begins with a patient history where medical students can gather evidence by highlighting relevant symptoms and save them to the evidence palette. Medical students use this evidence to propose possible diagnoses and report their confidence on each diagnosis. Students can access and change their diagnoses and the associated confidence levels at any point during the session. The students can obtain further evidence by a) ordering laboratory tests to confirm or disconfirm a particular diagnosis, b) searching the online library for information about a particular disease, diagnostic test, or medical term, or by c) requesting help using the consultation tool. Through this series of actions, students become progressively more confident in a single diagnosis. Once the student has submitted their final diagnosis, they are asked to justify their choice by sorting all the evidence as supporting, contradicting, or irrelevant to the final diagnosis. Afterwards, the student is asked to prioritize their final list of supporting evidence from the most important to the least important. Once the student has justified their reasoning in an open-response case summary, they receive individualized feedback on their solution based on an expert solution.

2.3   Measures

As learners interact with BioWorld, the system records learner-system interactions in log-files. There are three different types of performance metrics in the log-files generated by the BioWorld system: diagnostic efficacy (e.g., accuracy and percentage of matches with experts), efficiency (e.g., time taken to solve a case), and affect (e.g., confidence). Information saved in the log-file included the attempt identifier (participant and case ID), a timestamp, the BioWorld space (e.g., chart), the specific action taken (e.g., add test), and details in relation to the action (e.g., Thyroid Stimulating Hormone (TSH) Result: 0.2 mU/L).

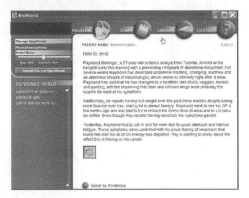

Fig. 1. The BioWorld interface

2.4   Study Procedure

This data was collected as part of an experiment that examined factors that influenced attention to feedback in BioWorld (Naismith, 2013). Participants were asked to complete a demographics questionnaire and an achievement motivation questionnaire (i.e., PALS; [13]). Participants then completed a training case, which allowed them to learn how to use the BioWorld system. Following the training case, participants solved 3 endocrinology cases in a 2-hour session with BioWorld. The three cases participants were asked to solve were: Amy (diabetes Type 1), Cynthia (pheochromocytoma), and Susan Taylor (hyperthyroidism). The order of the cases was counterbalanced to mitigate practice effects. After each case was completed, participants were asked to complete a retrospective outcome achievement emotions questionnaire (AEQ; [14]). After all three cases were finished participants completed a final questionnaire, which assessed their prior knowledge of endocrinology and the perceived difficulty of each case. It is our contention that cognitive errors are more likely to arise when solving a difficult case relative to an easy case. Therefore, for the purposes of this paper only the most difficult case, Cynthia, was analyzed. The anticipated accuracies for the three cases were Amy (94%), Cynthia (33%), and Susan Taylor (78%) [15].

3   Results

3.1   Research Question 1

With regard to the first research question, "Can diagnostic performance be predicted from premature closure?" premature closure was inferred from the time taken to solve the case and selecting the final diagnosis from one of the participant's initial three hypotheses. To answer this first question, a standard binary logistic regression was used to model the binary variable of diagnostic performance (i.e., correct diagnosis or incorrect diagnosis). The predictor variables in this analysis were the continuous variable for time taken to solve the case, and the binary variable for selecting the final diagnosis from one of the first three (yes or no). Based on a classification threshold that predicted probability of target group membership of .50, results of the logistic analysis indicate that the two predictor models did not provide a statistically significant prediction of diagnostic performance, χ^2 (2, $N = 30$) = 4.31, $p = .116$, Participants who selected one of their initial hypotheses as their final diagnosis were equally likely to choose an incorrect diagnosis compared to those who did not chose one of their initial hypotheses as their final diagnosis. The time to solve the case was also equal across groups.

Once possibility is that participants with sufficient prior knowledge obtained enough information from the patient case history alone to identify the correct diagnosis of pheochromocytoma as one of their initial 3 hypotheses. Selecting the final diagnosis from one of the first 3 initial hypotheses might not be indicative of premature closure, but instead reflect faulty knowledge. Specifically some participants lacked knowledge and were therefore not able to identify the correct diagnosis of pheochromocytoma as an initial hypothesis and thus took more time to submit a diagnosis. Thus selecting an incorrect diagnosis might be indicative of faulty knowledge rather than faulty synthesis. To address this alternative we answered the follow-up question, "Can diagnostic performance be predicted from faulty knowledge?" To answer this follow-up question, a standard binary logistic regression was used to model the binary variable of diagnostic performance (i.e., correct diagnosis or incorrect diagnosis). The predictor variables in this analysis were the continuous variable for time taken to solve the case, and the binary variable for selecting the correct diagnosis from one of the first three diagnoses (yes or no).   Based on a classification threshold that predicted probability of target group membership as .50, results of the logistic analysis indicate that the two-predictor model provided a statistically significant prediction of diagnostic performance, χ^2 (2, $N = 30$) = 17.49, $p < .001$.   The Nagelkerke pseudo R^2 indicated that the model accounted for approximately 59% of the total variance. Classification of diagnostic performance based on a classification cutoff value of .50 for predicting membership in the correct diagnosis group was high, with an overall prediction success rate of 83.3%, and correct prediction rates of 80% for participants who selected the correct diagnosis, with 86.7% for participants who selected the incorrect diagnosis. Table 1 presents the partial regression coefficients, the Wald test, odds ratio [Exp(B)], and statistical significance for each predictor. The Wald test indicated that selecting the correct diagnosis of pheochromocytoma from one of the first three hypotheses was the only statistically significant predictor of success. By selecting the correct diagnosis from one of the first three hypotheses, there is a 56.12% greater likelihood of choosing the correct final diagnosis after controlling for time taken to solve the case. Although selecting the correct diagnosis from one of the first three hypotheses was the only significant predictor, we retain the predictor of time taken to solve the case in the model because it was approaching significance at $p = .052$. With a larger sample it is possible that this predictor could become significant. Further analyses will need to be conducted to test this assumption.

Table 1. Results of the Binary Logistic Regression Conducted for Faulty Synthesis

Variable	B	Wald Test	Exp(B)	p
Correct Initial Hypothesis	4.027	8.960	56.119	.003
Time to Solve	.001	3.771	1.001	.052

3.2   Research Question 2

With regards to the second research question, "Do participants who are highly confident in their wrong diagnosis engage in more faulty data gathering via confirmation bias?" confidence was split into high and low groups using the median split (Median = 80), yielding a high confidence ($n = 16$, $M = 86.50$, $SD = 6.16$), and low confidence ($n = 14$, $M = 61.50$, $SD = 13.27$) groups. These groups were further divided by assessing diagnostic performance, which produced 4 different groups (see table 2).

An ANOVA was conducted with one categorical independent variable with four levels (i.e., WLC, WHC, RLC and RHC), and three continuous dependent variables (i.e., lab tests ordered, library searches, and consult requests). The statistical assumptions of normality and independence of observations were met. The results from the Levene's Test suggests that the assumption of equal variances was met for the lab tests ordered as well as the library searches, $F(3, 26) = .363$, $p = .781$ and $F(3, 26) = 2.22$, $p = .110$, respectively. This assumption was violated for consult requests $F(3, 26) = 5.748$, $p = .004$. However, the effect of inequality of variance can be mitigated when group sample sizes are equal [16]. Since the group sample sizes are roughly equal we have chosen to interpret the results with caution. The results from the ANOVA suggests that there is a significant difference in mean number of consult requests between groups, $F(3,26) = 3.332$, $p = .035$ (see table 3). Tukey post-hoc comparisons indicate that that the only difference in data gathering occur between the WHC group and the WLC group from mean consult requests, where participants in the WHC requested significantly fewer consults than participants in the WLC group ($M = .167$, $SD = .408$ and $M = 2.500$, $SD = 1.195$, respectively), $p = .035$. These results suggest that participants who were wrong with high confidence might exhibit less metacognitive awareness compared to participants who were wrong with low confidence. Consequently, participants who were wrong with high confidence might have engaged in faulty data gathering.

Table 2. Descriptive statistics for Diagnostic Performance and Confidence Groups

Group	n	Mean Confidence
Wrong High Confidence (WHC)	6	84
Wrong Low Confidence (WLC)	8	58
Right High Confidence (RHC)	10	88
Right Low Confidence (RLC)	6	67

Table 3. Results of the ANOVA Conducted for Faulty Data Gathering and Confidence

Variable	df	MS	F	p
Library Search	3	12.453	2.112	.123
Consult Request	3	6.244	3.332	.035
Lab Test	3	8.608	.225	.878

4   Discussion

The purpose of this study was to investigate the impact of cognitive errors on diagnostic reasoning in medical students. This was accomplished by answering two research questions: (1) Can diagnostic performance be predicted from premature closure? and (2) Do participants who are highly confident in their wrong diagnosis engage in more faulty data gathering via confirmation bias? With regards to the first research question, the primary finding suggests that faulty synthesis in the form of premature closure was not the reason medical students failed to provide a correct diagnosis. As a follow-up to this first research question we asked, "Can diagnostic performance be predicted from faulty knowledge?" Faulty knowledge was inferred from whether or not participants were able to identify the correct diagnosis from the patient case history alone. These results indicate that medical students were more likely to select the correct final diagnosis if they had selected it as one of their initial hypothesis immediately after reading the patient history. This suggests that some participants were able to obtain sufficient information from the patient history alone in order to identify the correct diagnosis as an initial hypothesis, while others were not.

With regards to the second research question, the primary finding was that medical students who were confident in their wrong diagnoses asked for significantly less consults than those who were not confident in their wrong diagnoses. These results suggest that participants in the wrong high confidence group might exhibit less metacognitive awareness and more dysregulation compared to participants in the wrong low confidence group. This supports the conjecture that to reduce cognitive errors metacognitive skills should be promoted. Further analyses are needed, however, to corroborate this conclusion. It is worth mentioning that these analyses only considered the mean number of the respective data gathering methods, not the specific content of the data gathered. It is still possible that participants who where highly confident in their wrong diagnosis engaged in faulty data gathering by way of confirmation bias by running laboratory tests or searching for information in the library that would confirm their hypothesis rather than searching for contradictory evidence. A more detailed analysis of the data gathered is needed to address this prospect. Such an analysis might reveal important patterns of behaviors that can better explain why medical students make diagnostic mistakes.

The occurrence of diagnostic errors is a concern for patient care and healthcare systems. Although cognitive errors contribute to making mistakes, cognitive errors are difficult to investigate in clinical settings. The majority of research in this area relies on retrospective judgments of these errors, which makes it difficult to identify the cause and mechanism of diagnostic mistakes. In this study we investigated the impact of cognitive errors and overconfidence on diagnostic performance in medical students by analyzing process data. The results suggest that diagnostic errors made by medical students are the result of faulty knowledge and faulty data gathering spurred by a lack of metacognitive awareness. This study supports the notion that to improve diagnostic performance medical education programs should promote the development of metacognitive skills.

Acknowledgements. The research presented in this paper has been supported a Master's Joseph-Armand Bombardier Canada Graduate Scholarship from the Social Science and Humanities Research Council (SSHRC) awarded to the first author. This research ahs also been supported by a SSHRC partnership grant, headed by Dr. Susanne Lajoie.

References

1. Elstein, A.S., Schwartz, A.: Clinical reasoning in medicine. In: Clinical Reasoning in the Health Professions, pp. 49–59. Butterworth-Heinemann, Woburn (1995)
2. Bartlett, E.E.: Physicians' cognitive errors and their liability consequences. Journal of Healthcare Risk Management **18**(4), 62–69 (1998)
3. Graber, M.L., Franklin, N., Gordon, R.: Diagnostic error in internal medicine. Archives of Internal Medicine **165**(13), 1493–1499 (2005)
4. Norman, G.R., Eva, K.W.: Diagnostic error and clinical reasoning. Medical Education **44**(1), 94–100 (2010)
5. Podbregar, M., Voga, G., Krivec, B., Skale, R., Parežnik, R., Gabršček, L.: Should we confirm our clinical diagnostic certainty by autopsies? Intensive Care Medicine **27**(11), 1750–1755 (2001)
6. Lajoie, S.: Developing professional expertise with a cognitive apprenticeship mode. In: Development of professional expertise, Cambridge, UK, pp. 61–83 (2009)
7. Berner, E.S., Graber, M.L.: Overconfidence as a cause of diagnostic error inmedicine. The American Journal of Medicine **121**(5), S2–S23 (2008)
8. Azevedo, R., Feyzi-Behnagh, R.: Dysregulated learning with advanced learning technologies. In: AAAI Fall Symposium: Cognitive and Metacognitive Educational Systems
9. Croskerry, P.: The importance of cognitive errors in diagnosis and strategies to minimize them. Academic Medicine **78**(8), 775–780 (2003)
10. Lajoie, S.P., Poitras, E.G., Doleck, T., Jarrell, A.: Modeling metacognitive activities in medical problem-solving with BioWorld. In: Metacognition: Fundaments, Applications, and Trends, pp. 323–343. Springer International Publishing (2015)
11. Lajoie, S., Naismith, L., Poitras, E., Hong, Y., Panesso-Cruz, I., Ranelluci, J., Wiseman, J.: Technology rich tools to support self-regulated learning and performance in medicine. In: Azevedo, R., Aleven, V. (eds.) International Handbook of Metacognition and Learning Technologies. Springer, Amsterdam (2013)
12. Naismith, L.: Examining motivational and emotional influences on medical students' attention to feedback in a technology-rich environment for learning clinical reasoning (Unpublished doctoral dissertation). McGill University, Canada (2013)
13. Midgley, C., Maehr, M.L., Hruda, L.Z., Anderman, E., Anderman, L., Freeman, K.E. et al.: Manual for the Patterns of Adaptive Learning Scales. University of Michigan (2000)
14. Pekrun, R., Goetz, T., Frenzel, A.C., Barchfeld, P., Perry, R.P.: Measuring emotions in students' learning and performance: The Achievement Emotions Questionnaire (AEQ). Contemporary Educational Psychology **36**, 36–48 (2011)
15. Gauthier, G., Lajoie, P.S., Naismith, L., Wiseman, J.: Using expert decision maps to promote reflection and self-assessment in medical case-based instruction. In: Proceedings of Workshop on the Assessment and Feedback in Ill-Defined Domains at ITS, Montréal, Canada (2008)
16. Howell, D.: 8th Edition of statistical methods for psychology. Wadsworth, Belmont (2013)

Studying Student Use of Self-Regulated Learning Tools in an Open-Ended Learning Environment

John S. Kinnebrew[✉], Brian C. Gauch, James R. Segedy,
and Gautam Biswas

Department of EECS and ISIS, Vanderbilt University,
Nashville, TN 37212, USA
{john.s.kinnebrew,brian.gauch,james.segedy,
gautam.biswas}@vanderbilt.edu

Abstract. This paper discusses a design-based research study that we conducted in a middle school science classroom to test the effectiveness of SimSelf, an open-ended learning environment for science learning. In particular, we evaluated two tools intended to help students develop and practice the important regulatory processes of planning and monitoring. Findings showed that students who used the supporting tools as intended demonstrated effective learning of the science topic. Conversely, students who did not use the tools effectively generally achieved minimal success at their learning tasks. Analysis of these results provides a framework for redesigning the environment and highlights areas for additional scaffolding and guidance.

Keywords: Open-ended learning environments · Self-regulated learning · Learning environment design

1 Introduction

Cognitive scientists have established that the ability to regulate one's own learning is critical for developing effective learning practices. Self-regulated learning (SRL) is an active theory of learning that describes how learners set goals, create plans to achieve their goals, and continually monitor their progress in completing the plan. A realization of inadequate performance may lead to revising plans and goals. SRL is a multi-faceted construct that involves emotional and behavioral control, management of one's learning environment and cognitive resources, perseverance in the face of difficulties, and social interactions to achieve effective learning [12]. *Open-ended computer-based learning environments* (OELEs; [4]) provide students with opportunities to develop and practice their SRL processes; they provide students with a learning task and a set of tools for exploring, hypothesizing, and building solutions to authentic and complex problems.

In this paper, we present our recent work in developing *SimSelf*, an OELE for learning SRL strategies in the context of science learning tasks. *SimSelf* challenges students to learn science by creating models of scientific processes, and our

© Springer International Publishing Switzerland 2015
C. Conati et al. (Eds.): AIED 2015, LNAI 9112, pp. 185–194, 2015.
DOI: 10.1007/978-3-319-19773-9_19

goals in developing it are to research techniques for supporting students' understanding of specific SRL processes. The discussion in this paper focuses specifically on two tools in *SimSelf*:(1) a *planning interface* that support students' development and practice of strategies for *making plans*; and (2) a *monitoring interface* for students to analyze their own cognitive, metacognitive, affective, and motivational processes [1].

The results from this study were mixed. The analysis showed that some students utilized the planning and self-monitoring tools in a manner consistent with our expectations,and these students tended to have higher pre-post test gains and science modeling task performance. However, others did not use the tools as intended and often had correspondingly lower learning and task performance. A deeper evaluation and interpretation of these results provides us with a framework for redesigning some of the tools and interfaces, as well as identifying areas for additional scaffolding and guidance in the next version of *SimSelf*.

2   OELEs that Support Self-Regulated Learning

Winne and Hadwin [10] have developed a conceptual framework called COPES (Conditions, Operations, Products, Evaluations and Standards) for modeling and analysis of SRL processes. They posit that learning occurs in four basic phases: (1) task definition, (2) goal-setting and planning, (3) use of studying tactics and methods, and (4) adaptations to metacognition. Winne and Hadwin further operationalize this SRL model by hypothesizing sets of information-processing operations that govern behaviors in each step. Thus, the model complements other more conceptual SRL models (e.g., [8]) by introducing an operational description of the processes underlying each phase of SRL.

A variety of computer-based learning environments have been developed that support the development of SRL processes. Winne and his colleagues developed *gStudy*, a system for assessing SRL processes as described by their COPES model [6]. Another example is the hypermedia environment called *MetaTutor*, which adapts the COPES model to detect, model, trace, and foster students' SRL about human body systems [1].

More recently, Chi and VanLehn [11]) have developed *Pyrenees*, a system that requires students to construct models using explicit strategies (*e.g.*, goal reduction for complex problem solving). In work with the *Betty's Brain* OELE [3,5], students learned science concepts by building causal models of science phenomena, such as interdependence and balance in ecological systems. Studies with this system have shown that teaching students open-ended problem solving strategies can lead to their constructing higher-quality causal models [9]. However, the use of better strategies often has not translated to better learning of domain content. Given the importance of SRL processes in developing independent learners and the fact that there is not much conclusive evidence of how best to teach SRL to middle school students in OELEs, we have developed a system called *SimSelf* that explicitly focuses on SRL instruction.

3   SimSelf

SimSelf is an OELE that presents students with a complex array of tasks united in a single context: creating accurate models of scientific systems and processes. Students demonstrate their understanding by creating concept maps of the *structure* and *behavior* of the science topic under study. Both structure and behavior maps represent the system as a set of entities connected by directed links. The structure map captures the connections (*e.g.*, the hypothalamus *sends signals to* skeletal muscles) and hierarchical relationships (*e.g.*, the hypothalamus is *a part of* the brain) among entities. The behavior map captures causal relationships among entities (*e.g.*, skeletal muscle contractions *increase* friction in the body), and they may either describe increase (+) or decrease (-) relationships [5].

SimSelf includes tools for acquiring information, applying that information to map building, and assessing the quality of constructed maps. Students can acquire domain knowledge by reading hypertext resources.As students read, they need to identify structural and behavioral relationships and use this learned information to build their maps. Learners can assess their maps by having *Sim-Self* automatically reason with the maps to complete *quizzes*. The software can then grade the generated answers and show how they were derived from the maps by highlighting the entities and links that were used to generate the answer. The system also includes a strategy guide that discusses the declarative, procedural, and conditional knowledge of important SRL strategies.

3.1   Planning and Monitoring Tools in SimSelf

To support students' SRL processes, *SimSelf* includes planning and monitoring tools that students may choose to use to help regulate their learning. Students can use the planning tool (Figure 1) to set a learning goal and then specify the steps they will take to achieve that goal. Students can add and delete activities and SRL processes to each step from lists on the right-hand side of the interface. For example, in Step 2 of the plan shown in Figure 1, the student has specified that she will read the science book page on skin contraction, evaluate the material, and check her learning as she constructs her structure map. Students can also mark steps as completed. Ideally, thoughtful planning and keeping track of those plans will help students monitor their progress more effectively, reflect on any difficulties they experience, and take action to overcome those difficulties.

The monitoring tool allows students to evaluate and record their use of various learning strategies and their cognitive, affective, and motivational states during learning. Students monitor by answering "yes or no" questions about themselves (or selecting a "not sure" option). Ideally, answering these questions will allow students to practice monitoring and make them more aware of their own internal states, an important step in effectively regulating their learning.

4   Experimental Study

We report an initial study of students' use of the *SimSelf* planning and monitoring tools and the extent to which their use of the tools was productive for

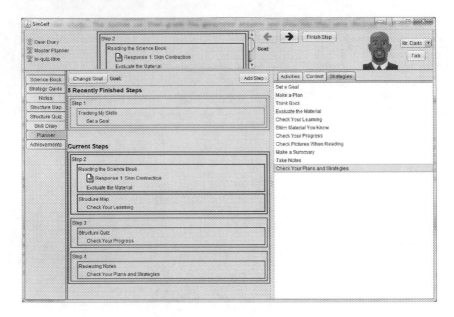

Fig. 1. The SimSelf planning interface

learning. To ensure that all students used the tools, we instructed them to: (1) use the planner at the beginning of each day to plan their approach; and (2) use the monitoring tool at the end of each day to reflect on their approach. Further, we told students that careful use of these tools throughout their work in *SimSelf* would facilitate their learning. We investigated the following questions:

1. Did students revise and/or update their plans regularly?
2. Did students execute the steps that they put in their plans?
3. Did students accurately monitor their own abilities, as reflected in their behaviors while using the system?
4. Did these behaviors relate to learning and task performance?

4.1 Participants, Topic Unit and Text Resources

Twenty-five 5th-grade students from a middle Tennessee classroom used *SimSelf* to learn about human thermoregulation when exposed to cold temperatures. The expert structure map contained 10 concepts, 9 hierarchical links, and 3 connection links covering skin and the nervous, muscular, and circulatory systems. The expert behavior map contained 10 concepts and 11 causal links, and students constructed this map in three parts: (1) cold detection (cold temperatures, heat loss, body temperature, cold detection, hypothalamus response); (2) vasoconstriction (blood vessel constriction, blood flow to the skin, heat loss); and (3) shivering (skeletal muscle contractions, friction in the body, heat in the body).

The thermoregulation resources were organized into two introductory pages discussing the nervous system and homeostasis, one page discussing the structure, behavior, and function method of understanding scientific systems[2], as well as the structure of the thermoregulatory system. These pages were followed by one page each discussing cold detection, skin contraction, vasoconstriction, and shivering. Additionally dictionary pages defined the main concepts. The text was 16 pages (2,682 words) with a Flesch–Kincaid reading grade level of 8.1.

4.2   Learning Assessments

Learning was assessed using a pre- and post-test design. Each test consisted of 7 causal reasoning questions and 10 science content questions. The causal reasoning questions presented students with an abstract causal map and asked students to reason with the map to answer questions like "If concept A increases, what would happen to concept B?" Students were awarded one point for each correct answer. Science content questions included 6 multiple choice questions and 4 short answer questions. The multiple choice questions, each with four choices, tested students' understanding of primary concepts and simple relations among them. One point was awarded for each correct answer. Short answer questions asked students to consider a given scenario (e.g., alcohol consumption) and explain its causal impact on thermoregulation. These questions were coded by identifying the causal relationships in learners' answers, which were scored by comparing them to the causal relationships in the expert map. One point was awarded for each causal relationship in the student's answer that was the same as or closely related to a relation specified in the expert map. Two coders independently scored five of the pre- and post-tests with over 85% inter-rater reliability, at which point one of the coders individually coded the remaining answers. The maximum combined score for all science questions was 17.

4.3   Log File Analysis

SimSelf automatically generates *event logs* that capture every time-stamped *action* taken by the student (*e.g.*, deleting a concept) and interface view that was displayed while the system was running. We used these log files to calculate measures of students' behaviors and task performance while using the system. The *map score* for a structure or behavior map is calculated as the number of correct links (*i.e.*, links that appear in the expert map) minus the number of incorrect links in the student's map. A student's *best map score* for a particular topic is the highest map score they attained while working on that topic[1]. Our behavior analyses focused on students' use of the planning and monitoring interfaces. We calculated the following measures:

1. *Planning Activities*: when and how often students set goals, changed their plan, and marked steps complete.

---

[1] We use best map scores because students sometimes delete their entire map.

2. *Plan Adherence*: the proportion of time students' spent performing activities that were specified in their plans.
3. *Content Evaluation Proficiency*: content evaluation is an SRL process in which learners evaluate the utility of information. During each day that learners used *SimSelf*, they were expected to model a particular aspect of thermoregulation. By tracking the resource pages students viewed, we determined whether they were viewing potentially *relevant* material. Content evaluation proficiency is the percentage of a student's reading time spent viewing potentially relevant material for their assigned goal.
4. *Content Evaluation Monitoring*: students' ability to assess their own content evaluation skills. When students accessed the monitoring tool, they were asked the question *"have I been reading things that are related to my current goal?"* A student's content evaluation monitoring score is the difference between the proportion of times they responded with "yes" and the proportion of time they spent reading relevant material. A score closer to 0 is interpreted as more accurate monitoring.

4.4   Procedure

The full study duration was 10 50-minute class periods. During the first two periods of the study, one author led classroom lessons introducing students to the modeling languages and presenting an overview of SRL. During the third period, students were introduced to *SimSelf* and its features, and they were allowed to practice on the system. During the fourth period, students completed the pretest.

During period 5 they worked on the thermoregulation structure map. During period 6, one author led a classroom lesson on thermoregulation. He explained how the body detects cold temperatures and how it responds by triggering shivering and vasoconstriction responses. Students then spent three class periods working on the three sections of the behavior map (as described previously). During periods 8 and 9, students started with the correct map from the previous period. During period 10, students completed the post-test.

During the classroom intervention, we observed that very few students completed the structure map on its allocated day. Therefore, if a student completed a behavior unit early, they were allowed to continue working on their structure map. Because students worked for different amounts of time on the structure map, the focus of the data analyses in this paper is on students' behaviors while building the thermoregulation behavior map.

5   Results

Table 1 summarizes students' pre- and post-test scores. Overall, students exhibited moderate gains on science content ($d = 1.02$), suggesting that the intervention helped them learn to recognize and reason with concepts and relations describing thermoregulation. Students did not show learning gains on causal

Table 1. Means (and standard deviations) of assessment test scores

Measure	Max.	Pretest	Posttest	t	p	Cohen's d
Causal reasoning	7	4.20 (1.65)	4.16 (1.67)	0.123	0.903	0.025
Science content	17	3.32 (1.26)	5.68 (2.96)	4.264	0.001	1.024

reasoning questions. This may be explained by the decision to administer the pre-test after the lesson on reasoning with structure and behavior maps.

To address our first research question, we created a heat map representation of students' planning activities over the course of their time in each unit (Figure 2). The results show that students primarily worked on their plans during the first 10–20% of their time on the system. Further analysis indicated that most planning activities after 20% of their time involved marking existing plan steps complete. In terms of our first research question, this suggests that students did keep track of their plans as they worked on *SimSelf* but did not revise them.

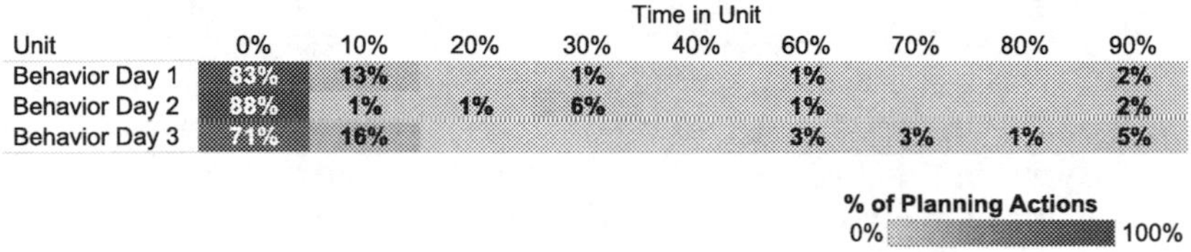

Time in Unit									
Unit	0%	10%	20%	30%	40%	60%	70%	80%	90%
Behavior Day 1	83%	13%		1%		1%			2%
Behavior Day 2	88%	1%	1%	6%		1%			2%
Behavior Day 3	71%	16%				3%	3%	1%	5%

% of Planning Actions
0% ▬▬▬▬▬▬▬ 100%

Fig. 2. Proportions of students' planning behaviors over time

Table 2 shows the means (and standard deviations) of the percentage of time students spent on activities listed in their plans (Planned Activities) and reading material specified in their plans (Planned Reading). Results show that students spent a majority of their time performing planned activities. Conversely, students spent only a small percentage of their reading time on planned reading. In terms of our second research question, one possible explanation for these behaviors is that students were better at planning high-level strategies (*e.g.*, iterating between reading and map building) than they were at planning specific details of their approaches (*e.g.*, the pages they would read).

Although students exhibited low proportions of planned reading, they may have been better at dynamically evaluating the material they were reading. Table 3 shows the means (and standard deviations) of students' content evaluation proficiency and monitoring scores. The results show that students spent an

Table 2. Proportion of time performing activities in their plans

	Day 1	Day 2	Day 3
Planned Activities	55.0% (30.5%)	66.7% (30.5%)	65.0% (30.2%)
Planned Reading	11.9% (27.3%)	9.3% (19.9%)	14.9% (25.0%)

overwhelming majority of their time ($> 89\%$) reading relevant pages on all three behavior map days. These numbers are higher than the percentage of pages in the resources that were relevant (row 3) on each of the three days, suggesting students' proficiency was better than chance.

Table 3. Content evaluation scores with means (and standard deviations) and the percentage of relevant pages by day for comparison

	Day 1	Day 2	Day 3
Proficiency	91.4% (15.1%)	89.8% (15.9%)	93.8% (12.3%)
Monitoring	7.5% (25.3%)	6.5% (36.7%)	11.8% (34.3%)
% Rel. Pages	73.3%	60.0%	73.3%

In terms of our third research question regarding students' ability to monitor their own content evaluation, the results show that students, on average, slightly underestimated their proficiency. Students' self-assessments of their content evaluation were, on average, 7.5%, 6.5%, and 11.8% less than their actual proficiency scores. This suggests that students were mostly accurate in their self-judgment abilities. If this pattern is indicative of their ability to monitor other aspects of their learning behaviors, it suggests that this population of 5th grade students were quite capable of self-assessing this aspect of their learning behavior.

Our final set of analyses investigated our fourth research question regarding whether the planning and monitoring assessments correlate with learning gains and normalized best map scores. We calculated bi-variate correlations between these measures and students' planning and content evaluation scores, each averaged over the three days. We found significant correlations between best map scores and: (1) average planned activity scores ($r = 0.472$, $p = 0.017$); and (2) average planned reading scores ($r = 0.434$, $p = 0.030$). However, the analysis failed to identify a relationship between map scores and content evaluation proficiency or monitoring. In other words, students who spent a larger proportion of their time engaging in planned activities and planned reading tended to construct more accurate behavior maps, but the same was not true of students who spent more time reading relevant material.

Moreover, students' science learning gains were also moderately (but not significantly) correlated with planned activity scores ($r = 0.340$, $p = 0.096$) and planned reading scores ($r = 0.329$, $p = 0.108$). However, no relationship was found between learning and content evaluation proficiency or monitoring. One possible explanation is that the more engaged students were more willing to exert the effort necessary to create a meaningful plan, stay with it, and carefully analyze their modeling performance. As a result, they achieved greater success and may have learned more of the material.

6   Discussion and Conclusions

The study showed mixed results: students used some aspects of the planning and monitoring interfaces productively, but they did not take advantage of other aspects that would have demonstrated higher SRL proficiency. Reflection on the results reported in the last section provides us with some useful lessons that will motivate the next iteration of SimSelf. Our first lesson pertains to the planning interface. Post-study interviews showed that some students were unsure of how to best use the planner. They were reluctant to mark plan steps complete because they expected to repeat these steps in the near future. As a result, we believe it will be more useful to move the focus from *exact plan steps* to *conditional knowledge* that underlies successful planning and re-planning. We are currently re-designing the planning interface so students can specify the conditions under which they expect to invoke specific SRL processes during their learning. In this interface, students will be responsible for specifying when, for example, it is appropriate to employ content evaluation. We believe that this will help students link generic SRL processes (which they seem to understand) to specific learning tasks (for which they currently do not show proficiency). It will also provide a better platform for feedback to help students operationalize SRL processes, contextualized by their current learning activity.

A second lesson relates to the apparent lack of a relationship between content evaluation proficiency and task performance or learning in this study. A reasonable expectation is that students who can identify relevant information would have higher learning gains and map scores in *SimSelf*, but our results did not support this connection. We realize that identifying important content is not, by itself, sufficient for effective understanding, which also requires the ability to interpret the content under study. In future work, we plan to adopt the approach of [9] and provide students with opportunities to practice related skills and strategies important for success in interpreting domain content in *SimSelf*.

The third lesson relates to the inability to identify a relationship between content evaluation monitoring and task performance or learning. This may be due to shortcomings in the monitoring tool. Monitoring during problem solving is valuable only when it can be used to identify and correct problems in one's current approach. However, the monitoring tool did not include supports that helped students revise their approaches when faced with challenging circumstances. In future work, we will augment the *SimSelf* monitoring interface and use pedagogical agents to suggest strategies for checking domain content understanding and causal model correctness.

In summary, we provided students with an OELE, including tools to support SRL approaches, but students needed additional support to use these tools effectively. In the next version of the system, we will focus on both the procedural and conditional knowledge necessary for effective planning through revised tools and additional support. Further, we will include additional scaffolds that help students understand how to adapt their current approach to become more effective learners and problem solvers. Several researchers have shown that students struggle to succeed in complex OELEs when support and scaffolding is not adaptive to students (*e.g.*, [4,7]). We are in the process of developing these adaptive supports, which, along with revised *SimSelf* tools, will bring us closer to our goal of helping middle school students develop effective SRL processes.

Acknowledgments. This work has been supported by the Institute of Education Sciences CASL Grant #R305A120186. We would also like to acknowledge the time and expertise contributed by our collaborators at North Carolina State University led by Prof. Roger Azevedo.

References

1. Azevedo, R., Johnson, A., Chauncey, A., Burkett, C.: Self-regulated learning with metatutor: advancing the science of learning with metacognitive tools. In: Khine, M., Saleh, I. (eds.) New Science of Learning, pp. 225–247. Springer (2010)
2. Goel, A., Rugaber, S., Vattam, S.: Structure, behavior & function of complex systems: The sbf modeling language. AI for Engineering Design, Analysis and Manufacturing **23**, 23–35 (2009)
3. Kinnebrew, J., Segedy, J., Biswas, G.: Analyzing the temporal evolution of students behaviors in open-ended learning environments. Metacognition and Learning, 1–29 (2014)
4. Land, S.: Cognitive requirements for learning with open-ended learning environments. Educational Technology Research and Development **48**(3), 61–78 (2000)
5. Leelawong, K., Biswas, G.: Designing learning by teaching agents: The Betty's Brain system. International Journal of Artificial Intelligence in Education **18**(3), 181–208 (2008)
6. Perry, N., Winne, P.: Learning from learning kits : gStudy traces of students self-regulated engagements with computerized content. Educational Psychology Review **18**(3), 211–228 (2006)
7. Roll, I., McLaren, B., Koedinger, K.: Improving students' help-seeking skills using metacognitive feedback in an intelligent tutoring system. Learning and Instruction **21**(2), 267–280 (2011)
8. Schraw, G., Crippen, K., Hartley, K.: Promoting self-regulation in science education: Metacognition as part of a broader perspective on learning. Research in Science Education **36**(1), 111–139 (2006)
9. Segedy, J.R., Biswas, G., Blackstock, E.F., Jenkins, A.: Guided skill practice as an adaptive scaffolding strategy in open-ended learning environments. In: Lane, H.C., Yacef, K., Mostow, J., Pavlik, P. (eds.) AIED 2013. LNCS (LNAI), vol. 7926, pp. 532–541. Springer, Heidelberg (2013)
10. Winne, P., Hadwin, A.: The weave of motivation and self-regulated learning. In: Schunk, D., Zimmerman, B. (eds.) Motivation and Self-Regulated Learning: Theory, Research, and Applications, pp. 297–314. Taylor & Francis, NY (2008)
11. Zhang, L., VanLehn, K., Girard, S., Burleson, W., Chavez-Echeagaray, M.E., Gonzalez-Sanchez, J., Hidalgo-Pontet, Y.: Evaluation of a meta-tutor for constructing models of dynamic systems. Computers & Education **75**, 196–217 (2014)
12. Zimmerman, B.: Self-regulating academic learning and achievement: The emergence of a social cognitive perspective. Educational Psychology Review **2**(2), 173–201 (1990)

Situated Pedagogical Authoring: Authoring Intelligent Tutors from a Student's Perspective

H. Chad Lane[1(✉)], Mark G. Core[2], Matthew J. Hays[2], Daniel Auerbach[2], and Milton Rosenberg[2]

[1] Department of Educational Psychology and Illinois Informatics Institute,
University of Illinois, Urbana-Champaign, IL, USA
hclane@illinois.edu
[2] Institute for Creative Technologies, University of Southern California,
Playa Vista, CA, USA
{core,hays,auerbach,rosenberg}@ict.usc.edu

Abstract. We describe the Situated Pedagogical Authoring (SitPed) system that seeks to allow non-technical authors to create ITS content for soft-skills training, such as counseling skills. SitPed is built on the assertion that authoring tools should use the learner's perspective to the greatest extent possible. SitPed provides tools for creating tasks lists, authoring assessment knowledge, and creating tutor messages. We present preliminary findings of a two-phase study comparing authoring in SitPed to an ablated version of the same system and a spreadsheet-based control. Findings suggest modest advantages for SitPed in terms of the quality of the authored content and student learning.

Keywords: Authoring tools · Intelligent tutoring systems · Virtual humans

1 Introduction

Despite decades of strong empirical evidence in their favor, the uptake of intelligent tutoring systems (ITSs) remains disappointing [1]. Although many factors have contributed to this lack of adoption [2], one widely agreed upon reason behind slow adoption and limited scalability of ITSs is that the engineering demands are simply too great. This is no surprise given that many attribute the effectiveness of ITSs to the use of rich knowledge representations [3, 4], which are inherently burdensome to build. Heavy reliance on software engineers has proven to be a significant hindrance for the widespread adoption of ITS technologies.

These challenges have led to decades of research aimed at reducing both the skills and time to build intelligent tutors. The resulting ITS authoring tools generally seek to enable creating, editing, revising, and configuring the content and interfaces of ITSs [5]. A significant challenge lies in the accurate capture of the domain and pedagogical expertise required by an ITS, and many authoring tools focus on eliciting this knowledge. In Murray's review of authoring tools [6], the top two goals identified are to decrease (1) the effort required to build an ITS (e.g., time, cost), and (2) the "skill threshold" for building ITSs. Systems addressing the first goal include those built for

© Springer International Publishing Switzerland 2015
C. Conati et al. (Eds.): AIED 2015, LNAI 9112, pp. 195–204, 2015.
DOI: 10.1007/978-3-319-19773-9_20

cognitive scientists and programmers, such as the cognitive modeling suite of tools in CTAT [7]. Murray's second goal, reducing the skill threshold of authors, is the focus of this paper. Systems in this category seek to leverage intuitively accessible tools that elicit the content and knowledge required by an ITS from non-technical users, such as instructors and subject-matter experts. Further, they share much in common with earlier efforts to address the knowledge elicitation problem [8], but with the additional burden of needing to address issues related to pedagogy.

A number of research efforts have directly sought to lower the skill threshold of ITS creation. For example, CTAT's second mode of authoring (distinct from the cognitive modeling components) allows authors to develop *example-tracing* tutors [9] that heavily leverage demonstration as a key knowledge elicitation technique. REDEEM, another extensive effort to reduce the technical expertise needed for building ITSs, provides intuitive interfaces and a well-defined workflow to produce adaptive, lightweight ITSs for the presentation and assessment of knowledge [10]. ASPIRE, also in the same category, asks users to design a basic domain ontology and solve problems while the system infers constraints for an ITS [11]. Evaluations of these tools typically focus on demonstrating efficiency [7] and completeness (to what degree do authored models align with hand-crafted models) [12]. Very little work has attempted to demonstrate the teaching efficacy of the ITSs that can be created, with REDEEM being a major exception [13]. The remaining sections of this paper summarize situated authoring (our approach), describe our authoring prototype that focuses on soft-skills training, and report initial results of an experiment intended to test the hypothesis that novice authors working in an environment that matches the learner's environment create higher quality and more effective tutoring content.

2   Situated Pedagogical Authoring

Like REDEEM, ASPIRE, and example-tracing tutors, the Situated Pedagogical Authoring system (SitPed) is designed as an easy-to-use authoring tool for eliciting ITS content from subject-matter experts. The current implementation focuses on problem-solving through conversation, such as how to address personal problems in the workplace or motivational interviewing for therapists and social workers. Our research builds on a substantial history of using virtual humans in support of learning [14], and specifically to act as role players that provide practice opportunities for soft skills [15]. In all previous cases, ITS technologies included in these systems were implemented by programmers based on expert interviews and cognitive task analyses.

SitPed was created to overcome this limitation by allowing non-technical authors to provide ITS content without programming. The aim is to place authors in an environment that is maximally similar to the one learners see, in part to constantly remind authors of the learner's experience, but also because it is the context in which their expertise is most beneficial. *We want authors to explicitly tell the system what learners should, and should not, be doing in a way that is familiar to them already.* For the purposes of this paper, therefore, we define "situated" authoring to be authoring that is completed in the same learning environment that learners will be using. Our primary hypothesis is that novice authors will create pedagogical content of higher quality when authoring is situated, and thus produce a more effective resulting product. We return to this hypothesis in section 3.

The implementation of SitPed described here is designed to support practice in the ELITE learning environment for leadership training [16]. Scenarios involve interacting with a virtual human via menus and according to an instructional model derived from a cognitive task analysis. Tutoring in this context involves the assessment of actions that are taken (i.e., how well they align with the prescriptions of the cognitive task analysis) and provision of guidance (i.e., hints and feedback). The ELITE team worked with the USC's Center for Innovation and Research on Veterans and Military Families to create a variation of the system designed for motivational interviewing, MILES, and we specifically used this content while developing and testing the system. In the rest of this section, we describe the current implementation of SitPed and discuss our approach to make authoring of this content more intuitive.

2.1   SitPed Workflow

SitPed includes several connected supporting tools and typically involves many iterations over scenario data. The primary activities, shown in figure 1, include 1) defining tasks that will be practiced, 2) connecting those tasks to scenario data to enable assessment, 3) authoring feedback messages that learners will see, and 4) adding support for post-practice reflection. In this paper, we focus on the provision of coaching during practice (i.e., 1-3). In addition, we assume that scenarios are created by scenario writers separately, leaving SitPed authors the tasks identified above. In the case of ELITE, a separate tool is used for the creation of scenarios,[1] and so tighter integration of the complete authoring process is something we will consider in future work. For the purposes of this paper and the study below, authors focus only on ITS content and use pre-defined scenario files.

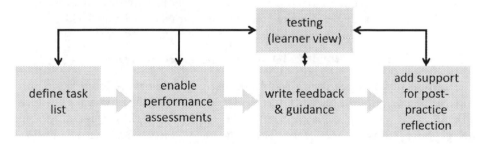

Fig. 1. The SitPed workflow

Testing one's work is critical in SitPed (as it is with all authoring systems) so the author can see the results of their work in context. The loops present in figure 1 show how an author might need to return to either edit or create tasks, adjust the assessment links, or update feedback content. The idea of being situated is most apparent when providing assessment knowledge and creating feedback in that the author must:

---

[1] http://www.chatmapper.com/

- specify paths through the problem space by simultaneously *solving* problems (either correctly or incorrectly) and indicating the relevant skills
- pause during problem solving to create hints and feedback messages associated with the current situation.

Since these activities take place in the same learning environment that learners use, SitPed falls roughly into the category of WYSIWYG authoring tools [6] because authors are constantly reminded of what the learner sees and does. With SitPed, demonstration is not simply a technique to hide technical details, but a way of organizing the tasks of authoring. It can be difficult for authors to visualize a learner's perspective when working in environments that are simply believed to be intuitive.

2.2   Defining Tasks

SitPed provides a simple tool to create simple, hierarchal task models, which define correct and incorrect behavior in scenarios (an example task list can be seen on the right of figure 2, which shows it being used in the assessment phase of authoring). Task lists in SitPed are roughly equivalent to multi-level numbered lists available in many word processors. Such tasks should be derived from a cognitive task analysis or some definitive resource, but we currently impose no such requirement (it is not an automated cognitive task analysis system).

The resulting list, which can be updated as needed throughout the workflow, acts as the functional glue holding the system together. It is not only a description of correct and incorrect behavior, but also a lightweight knowledge representation allowing the linking of instructional elements (e.g., a choice in a scenario) to behavior descriptions at other stages in the authoring workflow. Task lists form the basis for assessment and communication of that assessment to instructors and students. Higher levels of the hierarchy act as general categories while branches and leaves are more concrete, often corresponding to actions that can be taken in a scenario. Leaves of the hierarchy can even contain common misconceptions/mistakes associated with a task.

2.3   Assessment and Situated Linking of Tasks to Scenario Data

The current version of SitPed targets branching conversations. At each step in the conversation, learners are selecting utterances from a menu and the virtual role player consults a tree to lookup its response and the next set of menu items. This conversation tree simply contains the lines of the conversation as well as the associated animations corresponding to performance of the role player lines. In branching conversations, it is necessary for the author to play through all branches of the tree and link each possible learner choice to the skills and misconceptions of the domain. This process is illustrated in figure 2. Although the goal is to recreate the learner experience as much as possible, authors need to be able to see relevant context (e.g., the dialog history in the middle) and make annotations corresponding to the skills and common mistakes of the domain.

To avoid overwhelming novice authors, they are first presented with just dialogue choices and the character, but once they choose to annotate an utterance, a list of tasks is opened and they are allowed to indicate any links that are relevant. For example, if an utterance is an example of reflective listening, the author will click the "+" button next to reflective listening in the task list (see figure 2). This action updates the screen to show the task has been assigned, and this assignment will re-appear on the authoring screen any time this utterance is revisited. SitPed also provides a progress bar which tracks coverage of the problem space.

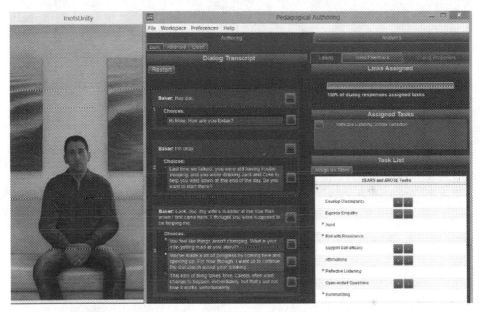

Fig. 2. SitPed authoring screen used for linking scenario content to tasks. The virtual role player is animated and speaks according to author choices in the center column (which advances as the interaction proceeds).

This exhaustive exploration of the possibilities is necessary because of the difficulty of automatically understanding the dialogue well enough to identify skills such as reflective listening. As an author works through a scenario, s/he will frequently restart the dialogue to explore new branches and establish links along all or most of the branches in the space. It is acceptable to not tag every action (essentially saying they are not associated directly with any task) and to link an action to multiple tasks. In task domains like counseling it is common to have actions that have both pros and cons – this can be captured by creating a positive link (e.g., clicking the "+" sign next to reflective listening) and creating a negative link (e.g., linking to a mistake such arguing with the client). SitPed displays a colored shape next to each utterance as tags are added: a red circle means "incorrect" (all links are negative), a green square means "correct" (all links are positive), and a yellow diamond means a "mixed" set of links.

2.4   Authoring Hints and Feedback

When an ITS gives a hint or explains why something is wrong, it is a critical moment in learning. In SitPed, it is simple to create either hints (that are delivered when a learner is stuck or unsure about what is best) or feedback (that explain why an action had a specific impact on the character). Authors can choose to author tutor messages simultaneously with assessment tagging, or do it separately in a second pass through the scenario. To do so, when an action is selected (i.e., an utterance is

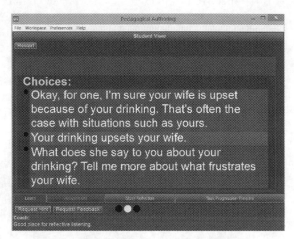

Fig. 3. SitPed testing screen

clicked in the center column of figure 2), the author can select the "Hints/Feedback" tab in the authoring environment and enter the text they want to be delivered. To see a message delivered, an author can use "testing" mode, which is described next.

2.5   Testing and Iterative Development

Although the main authoring screen is situated, it was still necessary to provide a special testing screen. One advantage of the testing screen is that all editing controls and displays can be removed. Furthermore, the testing screen can replicate the user interface that delivers the authored content. Figure 3 shows the current testing screen. The virtual human is also displayed but we omit this from figure 3 for space reasons. The choices for how to respond to the virtual human appear on the testing screen. The correct, incorrect and mixed color codes are shown to learners in a sideways traffic light display which currently shows a mixed assessment of the previous choice. The lights provide immediate flag feedback and come from the links authors have made to the task list (section 2.3). Hints and feedback are solicited and learners click the appropriate button to request guidance when it is available. In this case, the user has clicked "Request Hint" and we see the hint in the bottom left corner.

3   Preliminary Two-Phase Study

The hypothesis driving the design of SitPed was that an authoring environment that maximizes similarity to the actual learning environment will be more accessible to novice authors and support them in creating more pedagogically effective and higher quality ITS content. The study summarized in this section focuses on both properties of the authored content *and* on how well students learn from it. Thus, a two-phase study of SitPed was conducted in 2014 with subject-matter experts (phase 1, in the spring) and with college students (phase 2, in the fall) who had no experience with motivational interviewing (MI), our selected task domain.

3.1 Experimental Design and Procedure

In the first phase, a set of 11 domain experts from the USC School of Social Work with academic training and practical experience in MI were paid $50 to author ITS content for one scenario. They were split across three authoring conditions with the authoring interface acting as the lone independent variable:

1. **Full SitPed (N=4)**: the system as described in this paper.
2. **SitPed Lite (N=4)**: scaled-down version with hypertext-only (no graphics or sound, or supporting tools, like the progress bar)
3. **Spreadsheet (N=3)**: a specialized spreadsheet containing fields corresponding to data populated by SitPed, such as assessment links and tutor messages.

The Spreadsheet group was designed to intentionally be *non-situated* and those authors did not have the opportunity to test their resulting system at any time (i.e., they only filled in a spreadsheet and were given none of the SitPed tools). The spreadsheet was carefully created by an Excel expert (the third author) and designed to be as supportive as possible by restricting values in certain places, fixing the title rows, and so on. As a way to learn about why they were authoring, participants in phase 1 (experts) were asked to interact with a character from a different scenario and see tutoring in action. All participants were told that the data they were providing would be used for novice MI students at a later time. The same scenario data and task lists were given to all authors who were asked to link actions in the scenario to tasks and craft tutor messages (both hints and feedback). The predefined task list was a simplified version of the actual task list used in the MILES system, and contained 12 entries. The design of the three conditions is intended to capture three varying degrees of "situatedness", with a spreadsheet being entirely divorced from the learning environment and full SitPed being an almost full match. SitPed lite ablates many of the features of full SitPed and was designed to provide interactive authoring without many of the immersive features (animation, sound, etc.).

In the second phase, the data sets generated from each condition were used to create three separate tutoring systems, randomly using one of the data sets from each corresponding group. 71 college students from the University of Southern California participated in phase 2 of the study and were either compensated with course credits or paid. To measure knowledge, we used the Motivational Interviewing Knowledge and Attitudes Test (MIKAT) [17], which consists of 15 true/false questions followed by a selection task that gauges understanding of MI principles. Participants began by taking the MIKAT, watching a video about MI and how to use the testing screen of SitPed, and then interacted with the test scenario (from one of the three conditions) 3 times in a row. Participants then interacted with a new scenario without tutoring, to act as a performance-based post-test. Finally, participants took the MIKAT again and completed a post-test survey. A summary of the full experiment is shown in figure 4.

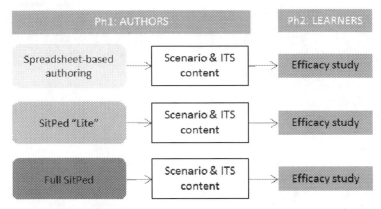

Fig. 4. SitPed two-phase experimental design

3.2   Phase 1 Results: Differences in Authored Content

Because of the low number of authors (a total of 11 spread across the 3 conditions), we report only the raw, descriptive data here and consider them as formative. In general, the 11 experts were observed to work diligently in the three hours allocated and revise their work frequently. Further, they were also told that completeness was not a requirement, but to focus on areas they believed would be the most difficult for students. So, for example, it was not necessary to create a hint for each and every choice point or link multiple tasks to every action.

First, some important differences in terms of the number of tutoring messages created (see the "count" columns in Table 1). Authors using the spreadsheet created, on average, 40.7 hints out of a maximum of 72 and 80 feedback messages out of a maximum of 113 in the given scenario while those in the two SitPed conditions created far fewer. These large differences may be due to the spreadsheet doing a better job of helping the author see the scope of the work in front of them – i.e., they are able to see two columns of a spreadsheet that they are being asked to fill. However, when we look at the length of the messages authored ("length" columns in Table 1, which show the character counts of the messages), the reverse pattern is seen. Authors in the SitPed conditions created longer messages (113, 68, 105, and 98 characters) than those in the Spreadsheet group.

Table 1. Differences in tutor messages authored and authored links between groups

Condition	Fbk count	Fbk length	Hint count	Hint length	1st links	2nd links
SitPed full	22.5	105	4.50	113	106	67.5
SitPed lite	6.25	98.0	11.8	68.0	98.3	59
Spreadsheet	80.0	42.0	40.7	17.0	111	37

Second, with respect to task links established, authors are being asked to identify tasks that are relevant to actions available at any given choice point. Table 1 (last two columns) show very few differences in this dimension, with the possible exception of creating second links, which imply that the author feels a particular action is related to more than one task.

3.3 Phase 2 Results: Impacts of SitPed on Student Learning

In phase 2, participants were randomly assigned to one of three groups. Due to technical problems and participant errors (some independently chose to work through scenarios more times than requested), we ended up with 18, 20, and 16 in the three conditions (SitPed, SitPed lite, and the spreadsheet); thus, we only used data from 54 participants.

The MIKAT provided two different measures of learning: responses to the true/false questions and score on the concept selection task. In terms of T/F responses, we found a main effect of condition between participants favoring SitPed over the spreadsheet group (mean gains of .135 to .054, F(2,52)=3.635, p=.033). No other significant differences exist between the other groups, although a main effect overall was found (F(1,52)=20.511, p<.001). On the concept selection task, no significant differences emerged between conditions,

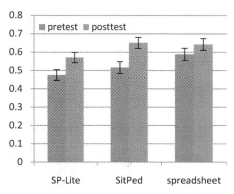

Fig. 5. MIKAT scores across three authoring conditions

although again an overall effect was found (F(1,52)=132.734, p<.001). Thus, the lower quantity of feedback and hint messages created in SitPed authoring did not hurt performance of learners. It may be the case that the SitPed condition had higher quality of links which drive the flag feedback seen by learners. Alternatively, messages in the spreadsheet condition may have actually hindered learning.

4 Conclusion

We have presented Situated Pedagogical Authoring (SitPed), an approach to authoring built on the assertion that authoring tools should use the same learning environment that students use, to the greatest extent possible. Leveraging proven techniques such as programming by demonstration, SitPed authors are able to define positive and negative learner behaviors and create tutor messages in the context of the same environment that students use. Our preliminary study shows modest advantages for SitPed in terms of the quality of authored content and learning gains from the resulting tutors. In future work, we hope to deepen the integration of scenario authoring with ITS authoring and better understand the qualitative differences between tutoring content created in SitPed versus that created in less immersive systems, such as a spreadsheet or other non-contextualized approach.

References

1. Nye, B.D.: ITS and the Digital Divide: Trends, Challenges, and Opportunities. In: Lane, H., Yacef, K., Mostow, J., Pavlik, P. (eds.) AIED 2013. LNCS, vol. 7926, pp. 503–511. Springer, Heidelberg (2013)
2. Nye, B.D.: Barriers to ITS Adoption: A Systematic Mapping Study. In: Trausan-Matu, S., Boyer, K.E., Crosby, M., Panourgia, K. (eds.) ITS 2014. LNCS, vol. 8474, pp. 583–590. Springer, Heidelberg (2014)
3. Mark, M.A., Greer, J.E.: The VCR Tutor: Effective Instruction for Device Operation. The Journal of the Learning Sciences **4**, 209–246 (1995)
4. Shute, V.J., Psotka, J.: Intelligent tutoring systems: Past, present, and future. In: Jonassen, D.H. (ed.) Handbook for research for educational communications and technology, pp. 570–599. Macmillan, New York, NY (1996)
5. Murray, T., Blessing, S., Ainsworth, S.: Authoring Tools for Advanced Technology Learning Environments. Kluwer Academic Publishers, Dordrecht (2003)
6. Murray, T.: An overview of intelligent tutoring system authoring tools: updated analysis of the state of the art. In: Murray, T., Blessing, S., Ainsworth, S. (eds.) Authoring Tools for Advanced Technology Learning Environments, pp. 491-544. Springer (2003)
7. Aleven, V., McLaren, B.M., Sewall, J., Koedinger, K.R.: The Cognitive Tutor Authoring Tools (CTAT): Preliminary Evaluation of Efficiency Gains. In: Ikeda, M., Ashley, K.D., Chan, Tak-Wai (eds.) ITS 2006. LNCS, vol. 4053, pp. 61–70. Springer, Heidelberg (2006)
8. Hoffman, R.R., Shadbolt, N.R., Burton, A.M., Klein, G.: Eliciting knowledge from experts: A methodological analysis. Organizational behavior and human decision processes **62**, 129–158 (1995)
9. Aleven, V., McLaren, B.M., Sewall, J., Koedinger, K.R.: A New Paradigm for Intelligent Tutoring Systems: Example-Tracing Tutors. International Journal of Artificial Intelligence in Education **19**, 105–154 (2009)
10. Ainsworth, S., Major, N., Grimshaw, S., Hays, M., Underwood, J., Williams, B.: REDEEM: simple intelligent tutoring systems from usable tools. In: Murray, T., Ainsworth, S., Blessing, S. (eds.) Authoring Tools for Advanced Technology Learning Environments, pp. 205-232 (2003)
11. Mitrovic, A., Martin, B., Suraweera, P., Zakharov, K., Milik, N., Holland, J., Mcguigan, N.: ASPIRE: An Authoring System and Deployment Environment for Constraint-Based Tutors. Int. J. Artif. Intell. Ed. **19**, 155–188 (2009)
12. Mitrovic, A., Martin, B., Suraweera, P., Zakharov, K., Milik, N., Holland, J., McGuigan, N.: ASPIRE: an authoring system and deployment environment for constraint-based tutors. International Journal of Artificial Intelligence in Education **19**, 155–188 (2009)
13. Ainsworth, S., Grimshaw, S.: Evaluating the REDEEM authoring tool: can teachers create effective learning environments? International Journal of Artificial Intelligence in Education **14**, 279–312 (2004)
14. Swartout, W., Artstein, R., Forbell, E., Foutz, S., Lane, H.C., Lange, B., Morie, J.F., Rizzo, A.S., Traum, D.: Virtual humans for learning. AI Magazine **34**, 13–30 (2013)
15. Kim, J.M., Hill, R.W., Durlach, P.J., Lane, H.C., Forbell, E., Core, M., Marsella, S.,
16. Pynadath, D.V., Hart, J.: BiLAT: A Game-based Environment for Practicing Negotiation in a Cultural Context. Int. Journal of Artificial Intelligence in Education **19**, 289–308 (2009)
17. Campbell, J.E., Hays, M.J., Core, M., Birch, M., Bosack, M., Clark, R.E.: Interpersonal and leadership skills: using virtual humans to teach new officers. In: Proc. of the 33rd Interservice/Industry Training, Simulation, and Education Conference, Orlando (2012)
18. Leffingwell, T.R.: Motivational Interviewing Knowledge and Attitudes Test (MIKAT) for evaluation of training outcomes. MINUET **13**, 10–11 (2006)

Two Modes Are Better Than One:
A Multimodal Assessment Framework
Integrating Student Writing and Drawing

Samuel Leeman-Munk(✉), Andy Smith, Bradford Mott, Eric Wiebe, and James Lester

North Carolina State University, Raleigh, NC 27695, USA
{spleeman,pmsmith4,bwmott,wiebe,lester}@ncsu.edu

Abstract. We are beginning to see the emergence of advanced automated assessment techniques that evaluate expressive student artifacts such as free-form written responses and sketches. These approaches have largely operated individually, each considering only a single mode. We hypothesize that there are synergies to be leveraged in multimodal assessments that can integrate multiple modalities of student responses to create a more complete and accurate picture of a student's knowledge. In this paper, we introduce a novel multimodal assessment framework that integrates two techniques for automatically analyzing student artifacts: a deep learning-based model for assessing student writing, and a topology-based model for assessing student drawing. An evaluation of the framework with elementary students' writing and drawing assessments demonstrate that 1) each of the framework's two modalities provides an independent and complementary measure of student science learning, and 2) together, the multimodal framework significantly outperforms either uni-modal approach individually, demonstrating the potential synergistic benefits of multimodal assessment.

Keywords: Formative assessment · Multimodal assessment · Student writing analysis · Student sketch analysis

1 Introduction

Recent years have seen a growing interest in real-time formative assessment. Recognizing that the more restrictive methods traditionally used in summative assessment, such as multiple choice questions, are limited in their ability to provide the analyses necessary for guiding real-time scaffolding and remediation for students, a broad base of research in science education has been investigating the role of formative assessment in instruction [1].

As a tool for formative assessment, short-text constructed response items reveal cognitive processes and states in students that are difficult to uncover in multiple-choice equivalents [2]. Even when it seems that items could be designed to address the same cognitive construct, success in devising multiple-choice and constructed-response items that behave with psychometric equivalence has proven to be challenging [3]. Because standards-based STEM education in the US explicitly promotes the

© Springer International Publishing Switzerland 2015
C. Conati et al. (Eds.): AIED 2015, LNAI 9112, pp. 205–215, 2015.
DOI: 10.1007/978-3-319-19773-9_21

development of writing skills for which constructed response items are ideally suited, the prospect of designing text analytics techniques for automatically assessing students' textual responses has become even more appealing and has spawned a growing body of research in the area [4].

In a parallel development, drawing is becoming recognized as central activity in science education, particularly in earlier grades. Van Meter and Garner posit that the benefits of student-generated drawing arise from students engaging in three key cognitive processes: selecting relevant information, organizing the information to build up an internal verbal model, and constructing an internal nonverbal representation to connect with the verbal representation [5]. A wide range of studies have shown that learning strategies focusing on student-generated drawing can produce effective learning outcomes, such as improving science text comprehension and student engagement [6].

The intelligent tutoring systems community has begun to investigate each of these modalities for assessment. Automated assessment methods for short answer text has been the focus of many studies, with techniques ranging from Latent Semantic Analysis to Soft Cardinality achieving varying degrees of success [4]. Though less common, sketch understanding systems have been used to analyze undergraduate student drawings in a variety of contexts, including clustering via an analogical generalization [7], and drawing-based simulations[8]. However, this prior work has focused on single modality assessment frameworks.

To investigate the potential of multimodal assessment, we explore two research questions. First, we investigated how accurately an individual modality (student writing assessment and student drawing assessment) can automatically assess student artifacts in relation to a gold standard human coding. We found that a convolutional neural network approach for analyzing writing and a topology-based approach for analyzing drawing closely mirror the assessments performed by human graders.

Second, we investigated how accurately a multimodal assessment framework that considers student artifacts from multiple modalities can automatically assess student artifacts. We found that not only does each modality individually predict student learning outcomes, as measured by a summative post-test, but the integrated multimodal framework outperforms either uni-modal assessment individually.

2   Data Collection and Coding

For the past four years our laboratory has been developing a digital science notebook for elementary school science education, LEONARDO (Figure 1) [9]. Designed to run on both conventional and tablet computing platforms, LEONARDO integrates intelligent tutoring systems technologies into a digital science notebook that enables students to graphically model science phenomena with a focus on the physical and earth sciences. LEONARDO is designed to be used in the classroom in conjunction with physical experiments and is aligned with the Next Generation Science Standards for elementary school science education.

LEONARDO's curriculum is organized around focus questions that encourage students to follow the scientific method. For each focus question, students explore natural phenomena through writing and drawing about underlying scientific principles. Writing exercises are in the form of short answer questions where the student reads a question and answers it in a sentence or two. Drawing exercises consist of students creating symbolic sketches of different concepts depending on the current topic. Given the challenges of machine recognition of freehand sketch, as well as concerns of excessive cognitive load for fourth graders working on such an unstructured task, LEONARDO supports symbolic drawing. While drawing, students choose from a variety of semantically grounded objects and can add, remove, rotate, and move the elements to produce the visual artifact.

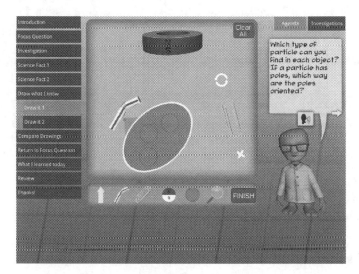

Fig. 1. Leonardo Digital Science Notebook

For the data analyzed in this study, student writing and drawing samples were collected from a learning activity in which students investigate what happens to magnetic particles in the presence of a magnetic field. Two writing samples for each student were evaluated. The first sample was taken at the beginning of the exercise in response to the prompt, "What happens to the particles when an object is turned into a temporary magnet?" The second written response was collected at the end of the exercise using the same prompt. During the exercise, two drawings were also collected. The first drawing prompt instructed students to draw what a paperclip and straw's particles look like when far from a magnet, and the second prompt asked what the particles would look like when close to the magnet.

To manually assess student learning, a rubric was designed to evaluate student responses in both written and graphic form. This rubric evaluated student responses against several criteria. Four of the criteria concerned the usage of core 'actors' from the magnetism investigation: paperclips, straws, magnifiers, and particles. Three dimensions were related to the accurate depiction of the particulate nature of permanent magnets, objects that could be magnetized (e.g., paper clips), and nonmagnetic objects (e.g., straws). Written responses were also scored on the dynamic and symbolic nature of the response. The dynamic dimension scored whether students referenced a change over time. The semiotic dimension indicated whether the nature of the written arguments was evaluated as iconic (i.e., only using words to represent concrete ideas, or symbolic, (i.e., using words representing abstract concepts).

Two raters coded the graphic and textual artifacts created by students in response to specific prompts in LEONARDO. Inter-rater reliability was calculated via Cohen's kappa (κ) and a protocol for drawing and writing coding using a 3-classroom training set before coding the entire corpus. Coders initially coded a portion of the training set and discussed differences in order to refine the coding process and ambiguities in the rubrics. Coders then independently coded drawings for each question from the three training classrooms and achieved an acceptable level of agreement ($\kappa = .88$) before coding the remainder of the corpus. The procedure was then repeated for the writing prompts, achieving a $\kappa = .76$, after which the remainder of the corpus was coded.

3   Methods

To explore the hypothesis that multimodal assessment offers the potential to more accurately assess student learning than conventional uni-modal assessment, we created a multimodal assessment framework that considers two modalities: 1) student writing, which is assessed with a convolutional neural network (a type of deep learning neural network) for short answer response analysis, and 2) student drawing, which is assessed with a topology-based drawing analysis model.

3.1   A Convolutional Neural Network for Short Answer Analysis

To analyze students' written responses, we used a convolutional neural network with max-pooling. A *convolutional neural network* (CNN) differs from a feed-forward network in that it can evaluate inputs of arbitrary length, which is useful in language processing where statements can be anywhere from one word to pages or chapters of text. We select it over a more conventional method such as latent semantic analysis because it takes word order into account and has proven to be effective in recent applications to other text analytics tasks, such as sentiment prediction and question type classification [10]. We also select this method because it automatically learns relevant features and constructs from the text itself, thus requiring no labor-intensive human engineering of features.

Analysis of a student short answer using our CNN is a four-step process: vectorization, convolution, max-pooling, and sending the output to a shallow feed-forward neural network. This process is illustrated in Figure 2. The first step, vectorization, consists of taking the input words and converting them into semantic vector representations. These representations are trained along with the model or via unsupervised techniques on large corpora. We used the word vectors available from GLoVe: 300 dimensions trained on 840 billion tokens in the Common Crawl corpus [11]. The second step, convolution, performs an affine transformation on, or *convolves*, sets of adjacent word vectors, defined by a window of a fixed size. For example, for the student answer "north and south poles," our system's convolution layer would take word vectors in groups of three, such as the vector representations of "north and south." In order to avoid words on the ends of the sentence being underrepresented, we add empty padding values on either side. These convolutions go to the max pooling layer. Max pooling selects the three hundred highest values (based on the length of the word vector). The convolution and max-pooling layers can have multiple copies with different weights, each of which is known as a feature map. Each of these copies generates three hundred values. Finally, the values from the max-pooling layer are concatenated and used as the input layer to a shallow feed-forward neural network. This network outputs a real-valued grade. For training, the objective function is the root mean squared error between human and machine score, which is backpropagated through the network. For more details on CNNs for sentence modeling, see Kalchbrenner et al. [10].

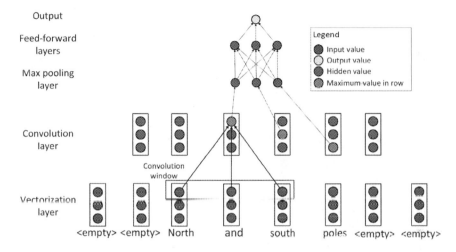

Fig. 2. A Convolutional Neural Network For Short Answer Analysis

We built the convolutional neural network for this task in Theano, a python-based deep learning library [12]. Because many students had written answers to the relevant questions but were missing data elsewhere, we used these students' answers for training. Our dummy values that padded the ends of each sentence were simply vectors with zeros in every dimension. Words that did not appear in the GLoVe vectors list we used are also represented with the same dummy value.

Hyperparameters were selected based on making a low-dimensional model with small root mean squared error (RMSE). Three is the smallest symmetric window size that still takes advantage of context. In a sweep over one through nine the best-performing number of feature maps was five. We use only one feed-forward hidden layer, and it is one hidden word in size, i.e., 300 values. Out of 50,100,150, and 200 as options for epochs, 50 performed best.

3.2   Topology-Based Drawing Assessment

Building on previous work on automatic assessment of symbolic drawings [9], we endeavored to emulate human assessment of drawing evaluation through automated analyses of the topological relations between objects in the drawing space. We first defined a set of possible relations between objects for this domain. Because both target drawings used the same set of elements (paperclip, arrow, straw, magnetic particle, inert particle, magnifying bubble, magnet), we were able to use the same set of relations for both drawing prompts. In this domain, the relevant relationships between elements were identified as near, far, and contains. Next, a mapping was created between the 2-dimensional arrangement of the particles and the semantic relations. This mapping was hand-authored by defining thresholds for distance between objects (using bounding boxes and rectangle-to-rectangle distance) and checking for intersections between objects' bounding boxes. Figure 3 shows an example student drawing and the corresponding topological network. For this question "far" was defined as closer than 100 pixels from the magnet, which is always present at a fixed location in the diagram. The "contains" relation is based on more than one 2D relation between objects.

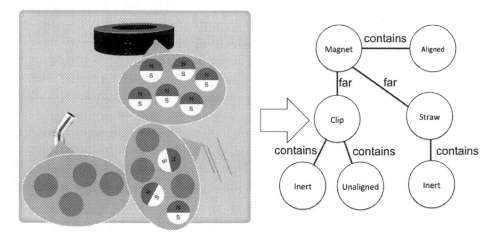

Fig. 3. Student Drawing Converted Into Semantic Network

Because particles could only be evaluated in relation to another object, the system assigns particles by first determining if it can assign a relationship between any magnifiers in the drawing and any straws, paper clips, or magnets. It does this by checking if each magnifier's magnification point intersects with any such objects. If a magnifier happens to intersect multiple objects, the particle is assigned to the object with the closest center. After assigning magnifiers, particles are assigned to the magnifier that they overlap, deciding shared overlaps based on closeness to the magnifier's center. Any remaining unassigned particles are then checked to see if they overlap with a straw, a paperclip or the magnet, as some students did not use the magnifier and instead placed particles directly on the objects. Particles assigned to the same parent object are split into two groups, inert and magnetic. The orientation of the magnetic particles is then checked to determine if the group is "aligned," signaling that all particles are rotated to the target rotation, or "unaligned", signaling that at least one particle's rotation does not match the target rotation for this group. After the final network is completed, it can be queried to generate scores based on the expert-defined rubric. For example in the network shown in Figure 3, points would be credited for the presence of a "far" edge between the magnet and paperclip, a "contains" edge between aligned particles and magnet, as well as the other connections relevant to the rubric described in Section 2.

4   Evaluation and Discussion

To evaluate how well the uni-modal assessment models' performance levels compare to the gold standard human scoring, machine-generated scores were compared to human scores. To measure the accuracy of the continuous scores generated for writing, root mean squared error (RMSE) was used. Although the rubric described earlier allowed for scores between zero and sixteen, no student achieved a score above nine. The deep learning model produced a RMSE of 1.23, or 13% when normalized by the observable range across the 190 student answers analyzed (95 students, 2 answers per student). A Pearson correlation between the human and machine writing scores was conducted with an r of .53 (p < .001), in range with scores from previous systems on a similar task [4]. Further analysis of our model's RMSE shows that is greatly impacted by a small number of outliers in the human grades with 5 answers out of 190 accounting for 22.7% of the total squared error.

For the drawings, our system was able to produce scores for each of the seven rubric criteria. Cohen's κ was calculated to measure agreement between machine and human scorings for each criteria of the two drawings with an average κ =.89 for the first drawing and an average κ = .85 for the second drawing. This result suggests that the drawing assessment model is capable of replicating human scoring with a high level of agreement.

The encouraging results also suggest directions for future work. For example, since the topology is generated from a list of elements placed in the drawing space, it makes no assumptions about occlusion. In several student drawings paperclips, particles, or other elements affecting the machine score were fully obscured from the image viewed by the human grader causing a mismatch in scoring.

The next question we investigated was whether machine-scored written and drawing artifacts are useful predictors of student conceptual knowledge. We first looked at the predictive power of drawing and writing separately and found them to be significant predictors, even when controlling for pre-test. We next built a model combing the predictors and found that, even when combined, both scores provide unique and complementary predictive value. These results are summarized in a series of multiple linear regression models shown in Table 1. For all models, the dependent variable predicted was the student performance on a summative multiple-choice post-test. The independent variable pre-test represents student performance on a 20-question multiple-choice assessment administered before students used LEONARDO. We include the pre-test score as a covariate in our analysis as a proxy for prior knowledge and to provide a more rigorous standard for our model to meet. Auto Writing Score and Auto

Drawing Score represent the average of the machine-generated scores for the two exercises of each modality.

By themselves, writing score and drawing score are both significant predictors of post-test performance, even when controlling for pre-test performance. Both models explain similar amounts of variance, with Drawing providing slightly more predictive value. Further supporting the value of combining writing and drawing is the almost 8% increase in variance explained by the third model containing averages of both scores as well as the pre-test score. Writing and Drawing Score are both significant predictors in this model, with analysis of the semi-partial R^2 values showing that while there is some common variance captured by the different factors, writing and drawing uniquely represent 8% and 11% respectively of the total variance captured by the model. These results suggest that the level of conceptual understanding in the student writings and drawings are complementary, and that there is additive value in assessment across multiple modalities.

A potential explanation for the cause of these encouraging results is the "cognitive complementarity" of the two modalities. Recognizing that writing and drawing exercises different cognitive processes, the science education community advocates the use of science notebooks in the elementary grades because they provide an effective tool for promoting learning through both writing and drawing [13]. Prior research has demonstrated that students' scientific knowledge is distributed across both of these sources [14], and not surprisingly, because both drawing and writing shape and reveal underlying student mental models [15], there is a growing recognition that science notebooks offer a potent source of data for formative assessment of students' scientific knowledge.

Table 1. Regression Models Using Machine Assigned Scores

Variable	B	t	sr^2	R^2	ΔR^2
Pre-Test Only				.270	.270
Pre-Test	.52	5.87***			
Pre-Test + Writing				.380	.110
Pre-Test	.439	5.20***	.182		
Auto Writing Score	.34	4.03***	.110		
Pre-Test + Drawing				.412	.032
Pre-Test	.37	4.30***	.118		
Auto Drawing Score	.405	4.71***	.141		
Full Model				.491	.079
Pre-Test	.317	3.87***	.084		
Auto Writing Score	.292	2.56***	.079		
Auto Drawing Score	.362	.426***	.112		

Note. N=95; *p<.05, **p<.01, ***p<.001

Table 2. Regression Model of Human Scores

Variable		Sig	sr^2	R^2
Model				**.451**
Pre-test	.356	.000	.109	
Human Writing Scores	.216	.010	.040	
Human Drawing Scores	.332	.000	.090	

One particularly curious result is that both of our automatic systems outperform their human equivalents in predicting post-test score, as seen by the predictive power of the human scores in Table 2. As one possible explanation on the writing side, it might in fact be an advantage rather than a disadvantage that our system dampens some of the high variance found in the human scores.

5   Conclusions and Future Work

Formative assessment is a crucial part of the instructional process, enabling both teachers and students to evaluate conceptual understanding and misconceptions. Similarly, automated assessment methods are emerging that can evaluate students' understanding across an increasingly wide range of modalities. These modalities are typically studied in isolation, with research often stopping at measuring the reliability and validity of a given assessment. However, there is great potential in better understanding how the different modalities work in consort. For example, automated writing and drawing assessment each provide meaningful insights into student science understanding. Together, writing and drawing assessment have the potential to provide a much more nuanced picture of student science comprehension than either alone.

To investigate the potential of assessment with multiple modalities, we have introduced an integrated multimodal assessment framework. The multimodal assessment framework has been studied in the context of science education with a student writing assessment model that uses a convolutional neural network approach and a student drawing assessment model that uses a topology-based approach for drawing analysis. An evaluation shows that 1) both methods are capable of assessing student work accurately compared to a human scoring, and that 2) the multimodal assessment framework utilizing both models is predictive of students' post-test performance, even when controlling for prior knowledge. These results suggest that multimodal assessment may be a valuable approach to utilizing the new generation of formative assessment approaches designed to evaluate students' responses formulated in more than a single mode.

In future work, it will be important to identify the families of modalities that offer the greatest potential synergistic benefits. We anticipate that some combinations of modalities may have overlap in their diagnostic power, while others will be exhibit great complementarity. Future data collections will focus on more closely coupling the drawing and writing tasks and encouraging explicit references between artifacts.

It will also be important to empirically investigate how multimodal assessment can be integrated into a real-time formative assessment system and used as the basis for generating personalized scaffolding.

Acknowledgments. The authors wish to thank our colleagues from the LEONARDO project for their contributions to the design, development, and classroom implementations of LEONARDO: Courtney Behrle, Mike Carter, Angela Shelton, and Robert Taylor. This material is based upon work supported by the National Science Foundation under Grant No. DRL-1020229. Any opinions, findings, and conclusions or recommendations expressed in this material are those of the authors and do not necessarily reflect the views of the National Science Foundation.

References

1. Abell, S., Lederman, N.: Handbook of Research on Science Education. Routledge, New York, NY (2007)
2. Nicol, D.: E-assessment by Design: Using Multiple-choice Tests to Good Effect. Journal of Further and Higher Education **31**, 53–64 (2007)
3. Kuechler, W., Simkin, M.: Why is Performance on Multiple-Choice Tests and Constructed-response Tests not More Closely Related? Theory and an Empirical Test. Decision Sciences Journal of Innovative Education **8**, 55–73 (2010)
4. Burrows, S., Gurevych, I., Stein, B.: The Eras and Trends of Automatic Short Answer Grading. International Journal of Artificial Intelligence in Education 60–117 (2014)
5. Van Meter, P., Garner, J.: The Promise and Practice of Learner-Generated Drawing: Literature Review and Synthesis. Educational Psychology Review **17**, 285–325 (2005)
6. Schmeck, A., Mayer, R.E., Opfermann, M., Pfeiffer, V., Leutner, D.: Drawing Pictures during Learning from Scientific Text: Testing the Generative Drawing Effect and the Prognostic Drawing Effect. Contemporary Educational Psychology **39**, 275–286 (2014)
7. Chang, M., Forbus, K.: Clustering hand-drawn sketches via analogical generalization. In: Proceedings of the Twenty-fifth Annual Conference on Innovative Applications of Artificial Intelligence, pp. 1507–1512. Bellevue, WA (2013)
8. Van Joolingen, W., Bollen, L., Leenaars, F.: Using Drawings in Knowledge Modeling and Simulation for Science Teaching. Advances in Intelligent Tutoring Systems pp. 249–264 (2010)
9. Smith, A., Wiebe, E., Mott, B., Lester, J.: SketchMiner: mining learner-generated science drawings with topological abstraction. In: Proceedings of the Seventh International Conference on Educational Data Mining, pp. 288–291. London, U.K. (2014)
10. Kalchbrenner, N., Grefenstette, E., Blunsom, P.: A convolutional neural network for modelling sentences. In: Proceedings of the Fifty-Second Annual Meeting of the Association for Computational Linguistics. pp. 655–665. Baltimore, MD (2014)
11. Pennington, J., Socher, R., Manning, C.D.: GloVe: global vectors for word representation. In: Proceedings of Empiricial Methods in Natural Language Processing. Doha, Quatar (2014)
12. Bastien, F., Lamblin, P., Pascanu, R., Bergstra, J., Goodfellow, I., Bergeron, A., Bouchard, N., Warde-Farley, D., Bengio, Y.: Theano: New Features and Speed Improvements. The Deep Learning and Unsupervised Feature Learning Workshop. pp. 1–10. Lake Tahoe, CA (2012)

13. Campbell, B., Fulton, L.: Science Notebooks: Writing About Inquiry. Heinemann, Portsmouth, NH (2003)
14. Minogue, J., Wiebe, E., Bedward, J., Carter, M.: The Intersection of Science Notebooks, Graphics, and Inquiry. Science and Children. **48**, 52–55 (2010)
15. Schnotz, W., Bannert, M.: Construction and Interference in Learning from Multiple Representation. Learning and Instruction. **13**, 141–156 (2003)

To Resolve or Not to Resolve?
That Is the Big Question About Confusion

Blair Lehman[1(✉)] and Art Graesser[2]

[1] Educational Testing Service, Princeton, NJ, USA
blehman@ets.org
[2] University of Memphis, Memphis, TN, USA
graesser@memphis.edu

Abstract. Positive relationships between confusion and learning have been found for the last decade. Most theoretical foundations for confusion hypothesize that it is not the mere occurrence of confusion, but rather the successful resolution that benefits learning. Empirical research has provided some support for this hypothesis, but investigations of the confusion resolution process are still sparse. The present work is a preliminary investigation of the confusion resolution process within two learning environments that experimentally induce confusion (false feedback, contradictory information). Findings showed that learners did benefit from confusion resolution compared to when confusion was unresolved, but it was not merely from increased effort. The nature of the confusion induction method also influenced the positive impact of confusion resolution on learning. Implications for intelligent tutoring systems are discussed.

Keywords: Confusion resolution · Cognitive effort · Learning · Intelligent tutoring systems

1 Introduction

Research over the last decade has shown that experiences of confusion can be beneficial for learning, particularly at deeper levels [1-8]. Intelligent tutoring systems (ITS) are even built to detect and respond to confusion in order to promote learning [9-12]. These findings are often explained by theories of learning that emphasize cognitive conflict (see [13] for a review), cognitive disequilibrium [14-16] and impasse-driven learning [17-18]. These theories propose that it is not the mere occurrence of confusion that leads to learning, but rather it is the effortful cognitive activities that are triggered by a desire to resolve confusion that benefit learning. It is important to note, however, that many of these learning opportunities are missed because learners either do not attend to their confusion or do not fully acknowledge there is a problem with their current mental model [19]. Both of these situations preclude confusion resolution from occurring and therefore are not predicted to benefit learning.

There can still be negative consequences for learning even when the learners (1) attend to their confusion and (2) attempt to resolve their confusion. Learners can be unsuccessful at their resolution efforts and enter what D'Mello and Graesser [20]

© Springer International Publishing Switzerland 2015
C. Conati et al. (Eds.): AIED 2015, LNAI 9112, pp. 216–225, 2015.
DOI: 10.1007/978-3-319-19773-9_22

have deemed the vicious cycle where persistent confusion turns into frustration and may ultimately transition to boredom. These findings suggest that although confusion can be beneficial for learning, there are many instances in which confusion could potentially have a detrimental effect. It is important then that ITSs not only monitor the occurrence of confusion but also learner attempts at confusion resolution.

Recent research by Baker and colleagues [21-23] and D'Mello and colleagues [2,20,24] have moved beyond the occurrence of confusion to investigate whether the hypothesized benefits of confusion resolution (compared to persistent confusion) actually occur during learning. D'Mello and colleagues found support for the proposed role of confusion by investigating the dynamics of confusion during interactions with AutoTutor, a mixed-initiative natural language ITS. Specifically, they found that transitions from confusion-to-confusion (persistent confusion; [24]), confusion-to-frustration, and confusion-to-engagement/flow (persistent versus resolved confusion, respectively; [20]) occurred at frequencies significantly greater than chance and that lower confusion persistence was related to greater learning [2].

In three studies Baker and colleagues investigated sequences of confusion (e.g., confused-confused, confused-confused-not confused) when learning alone [21] and with Cognitive Tutor, an ITS [22-23]. These studies revealed that non-persistent, but not necessarily resolved, confusion was generally positively correlated with learning. Persistent confusion, on the other hand, was either not related to [22] or negatively correlated with learning outcomes [21,23]. Overall these findings support cognitive conflict, cognitive disequilibrium, and impasse-driven theories of learning. However, the findings from Liu et al. [22] and Rodrigo et al. [23] open the door to the possibility that complete confusion resolution may not be necessary for learning to occur.

D'Mello and Graesser [4] conducted a more fine-grained investigation of the temporal dynamics of confusion in a study that experimentally induced confusion via system breakdowns. Participants were shown everyday devices (e.g., doorbell) in an illustrated text. The first time participants viewed the devices they were asked to try to understand how the device functioned. The second time they saw the device it was accompanied by a prompt that presented a breakdown (e.g., the doorbell does not ring) and asked participants to determine why the breakdown occurred (Breakdown). In the Control condition there was no mention of a breakdown but there was a prompt that instructed participants to focus on the component(s) of the devices that were the cause of the breakdowns in the Breakdown condition. D'Mello and Graesser found two patterns of confusion resolution from a second-by-second analysis of confusion intensity (on a 1-10 scale) over the two minutes participants viewed the devices. Participants were found to either have partially-resolved or unresolved confusion. Cases of partially-resolved confusion outperformed unresolved confusion in the Breakdown condition on a device comprehension task. These findings once again show that persistent or unresolved confusion may inhibit learning, but it may not be necessary to fully resolve confusion to benefit learning.

The present paper continues the investigation of confusion resolution during learning in two ways across two experiments. First, we investigated whether or not there was a learning benefit when confusion was resolved compared to when confusion was unresolved (Research Question #1). Similar to D'Mello and Graesser [4], we investigated confusion resolution within learning environments that experimentally induced confusion via false feedback (Experiment 1) and contradictory information

(Experiment 2) during conversations with animated pedagogical agents. The present work builds on previous research by providing learners with an aid for confusion resolution after confusion induction, a feature that was not present in the previously discussed research. We explored the amount of effort that learners invested in the confusion resolution task and how that effort impacts both confusion resolution (Research Question #2) and learning (Research Question #3).

2   Method

2.1   Confusion Induction Manipulation

In both experiments confusion induction manipulations were introduced during conversations that identified flaws in research case studies. For example, one case study discussed a new diet pill that miraculously made people lose weight without any change to diet or exercise, but the comparison group in the study was faulty.

Each experiment consisted of conditions that were meant to induce confusion (Experimental) and those that were not predicted to induce confusion (Control). For the present investigation we only consider those cases when learners were in the Experimental conditions (Experiment 1: *positive-negative*, *negative-positive*; Experiment 2: *true-false*, *false-true*, as elaborated below).

Experiment 1. Confusion was experimentally induced with a false feedback manipulation [8] during dialogues with the tutor agent. The tutor agent delivered feedback after the learner attempted to diagnose the flaw in a case study. There were two false feedback conditions. Learners who responded correctly received inaccurate, negative feedback in the *positive-negative* condition, whereas learners who responded incorrectly received inaccurate, positive feedback in the *negative-positive* condition.

Experiment 2. Confusion was experimentally induced with a contradictory information manipulation [5,7] via a disagreement between the tutor and student agents during a trialogue (three-party conversation) that discussed a case study (see Figure 1). Participants were asked to state whether they agreed with the tutor or student agent. There were two contradictory information conditions in which the agents disagreed. The tutor agent provided a correct opinion in the *true-false* condition, whereas the student agent provided the correct opinion in the *false-true* condition.

It should be noted that all misleading information was corrected and participants were fully debriefed at the end of both experiments.

2.2   Design

Both experiments had a within-subjects design. Each conversation in both experiments involved the discussion of a different research methods concept (Experiments 1 & 2: control group, experimenter bias, random assignment, replication; Experiment 2 only: construct validity, generalizability). Experiment 1 had four conditions: *positive-positive*, *positive-negative*, *negative-negative*, and *negative-positive*. Learners completed two conversations in which they received accurate feedback and two in which they received false feedback (4 total). It was not guaranteed that each learner would be in all four conditions due to the fact that condition assignment was dependent upon learner responses. Experiment 2 had three conditions: *true-true*, *true-false*, and *false-true*. Learners completed two conversations in each condition (6 total). In both studies, order of induction condition, order of topics, and assignment of topics to conditions were counterbalanced across learners with a Graeco-Latin Square.

2.3   Participants

Participants (called learners for the remainder of the paper) were undergraduate students from a mid-south university in the US who received course credit for participation in both studies. In Experiment 2, some learners did receive monetary payment ($20) for participation. In Experiment 1, there were 167 learners (116 females and 51 males), 60% of which were African-American, 2% were Asian, 35% were Caucasian, and 4% were Hispanic. In Experiment 2, there were 180 learners (112 females and 68 males), 53% of which were African-American, 2% were Asian, 35% were Caucasian, 4% were Hispanic, and 6% were other.

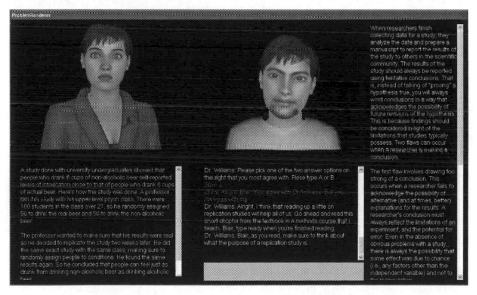

Fig. 1. Screenshot of Experiment 2 learning environment

2.4   Procedure

Transfer Tasks. Research methods knowledge was assessed with a flaw identification task that was administered after all conversations with the agents were completed. The flaw identification task consisted of a description of a previously unseen study and learners were asked to identify flaw(s) in the study by selecting as many items as they wanted from a list of eight research methods topics associated with potential flaws (e.g., a study lacked random assignment of participants to conditions). The list included topics that could potentially be flawed in a particular study (i.e., discussed in the conversations) as well as distractor topics. Learners also had the option of selecting that there was no flaw, even though each study contained at least one flaw.

In each experiment there were near and far transfer versions of the studies that were presented in the conversations. The near transfer studies differed from the studies in the conversations on surface features, whereas the far transfer studies differed on both surface and deep structure features. For Experiment 1, each topic discussed during the dialogues had one near and one far transfer study, resulting in eight transfer studies on the posttest. For Experiment 2, each topic discussed during the trialogues had one near transfer study and two topics were included in each far transfer study, resulting in a total of nine transfer studies in all (6 near transfer and 3 far transfer).

Conversations. In both experiments, learners engaged in a series of conversations on flawed case studies. These conversations consisted of a dialogue between the learner and a tutor agent (Experiment 1) or a trialogue between the learner, a tutor agent, and a student agent (Experiment 2).

Each conversation consisted of four phases in both experiments. In Phase 1, learners read the description of the case study to be discussed. In Phase 2, learners were presented with the confusion induction manipulation and gave their opinion about the scientific merits of the study via a forced-choice question. In Experiment 1, learners selected one of four forced-choice options and then received feedback from the tutor agent (e.g., *No, that's wrong.* or *Yes, that's the right answer.*). Induction condition was based on the alignment or misalignment between learner response quality and tutor feedback. In Experiment 2, the tutor and student agents presented their opinions about the study and then learners selected one of two forced-choice options (i.e., agree with tutor agent or student agent). Induction condition was based on the agreement or disagreement between the tutor and student agents.

At the end of Phase 2 learners made a confusion judgment after receiving the confusion induction manipulation. It is important to note that the confusion judgment was phrased "Would a classmate be confused?" The judgment was phrased in this manner to avoid learners' potentially biased responses due to a negative perception of being in a state of confusion [5]. In previous research, the confusion judgment responses in Experiment 1 were found to be significantly related to increased processing time after feedback [8]. Processing time was assessed by asking learners to indicate when they were ready to proceed with the conversation after receiving feedback.

In Phase 3, learners were presented with the confusion regulation task. In both experiments learners were given an explanatory text to facilitate confusion resolution. The texts were adapted from the electronic textbook in the *Operation ARA* ITS [25]. The texts contained an average of 364 words ($SD = 41.7$) and provided learners with more information about the concept being discussed. However, the text did not directly address the case study being evaluated. In Experiment 1 learners only read the text, whereas in Experiment 2 learners were also given the task to construct an argument with access to the text. The latter task involved learners constructing an argument that their diagnosis of the case study was correct and presenting it to the agent with which they disagreed. In Phase 4, learners made a second confusion judgment, with the same phrasing as the first confusion judgment.

3   Results and Discussion

The present analyses are organized around the three research questions previously discussed. We are interested in confusion resolution in the present research, so we considered only those cases in which learners were successfully confused by the induction. Resolved confusion was defined as being confused after the confusion induction but not confused after the confusion regulation task (Experiment 1: 115 cases; Experiment 2: 249 cases), whereas unresolved confusion was defined as being confused at both time points (Experiment 1: 50 cases; Experiment 2: 176 cases). Mixed-effects logistic regression models were constructed for each dependent measure.

3.1   Does Confusion Resolution Improve Learning?

We adopted a one-tailed test of significance because all theories would predict that conflict resolution would improve learning. Table 1 shows the proportional occurrence of correct flaw identifications for resolved and unresolved confusion cases. For Experiment 1, observations with resolved cases performed better on the far transfer task than those with unresolved cases ($\chi^2(1) = 3.23$, $p = .072$). For Experiment 2, we found the same pattern for both the near and far transfer tasks (Near: $\chi^2(1) = 3.25$, $p = .071$; Far: $\chi^2(1) = 2.72$, $p = .099$). These two findings suggest that there is a marginally significant learning benefit for confusion resolution compared to when confusion remains unresolved. This result is consistent with cognitive conflict [13], cognitive disequilibrium [14-16], and impasse-driven theories of learning [17-18]. They are also compatible with previous empirical findings [4,21-23], although the present findings support complete confusion resolution.

Table 1. Learning outcomes by confusion resolution

	Experiment 1		Experiment 2	
	Resolved	*Unresolved*	*Resolved*	*Unresolved*
Near Transfer	.482	.458	**.386**	.290
Far Transfer	**.345**	.208	**.386**	.301
Condition 1				
Near Transfer	.446	.429	.368	.270
Far Transfer	.270	.214	**.408**	.247
Condition 2				
Near Transfer	.556	.500	.403	.310
Far Transfer	**.500**	.200	.363	.356

Notes. Condition 1: Experiment 1 = *positive-negative*, Experiment 2 = *true-false*; Condition 2: Experiment 1 = *negative-positive*, Experiment 2 = *false-true*. Significant differences are bolded.

In each experiment there were two confusion induction conditions, which have previously been found to differ in their effectiveness of confusion induction [4,7-8]. Therefore we also investigated the resolution (resolved, unresolved) × induction condition interaction (see Table 1). The interaction term was significant for Experiment 1 ($\chi^2(3) = 7.73$, $p = .052$) and marginally significant for Experiment 2

($\chi^2(3) = 5.95$, $p = .100$) on the far transfer task. In Experiment 1, the benefit for successful confusion resolution was found for the *negative-positive* condition ($\chi^2(1) = 6.20$, $p = .013$), but there was no difference in the *positive-negative* condition ($p > .10$). Similarly, in Experiment 2 resolved confusion outperformed unresolved confusion only in the *true-false* condition ($\chi^2(1) = 6.02$, $p = .014$), with no difference in the *false-true* condition ($p > .10$). These findings are similar to prior research that suggests that the benefit of confusion resolution might not be as absolute as hypothesized by cognitive conflict, cognitive disequilibrium, and impasse-driven theories of learning.

3.2   Does Effort Matter for Confusion Resolution?

The previous findings are in line with theoretical perspectives on the role of confusion during learning; however, the prior analyses do not address the critical aspect of *effort*. In the present research we define regulation effort as the amount of time spent on the confusion regulation task in Phase 3 of each conversation. The more time spent on the regulation task was presumed to be indicative of more in-depth processing of the information in the explanatory text. Cases were separated into high and low regulation effort via a median split. To address this second research question we investigated whether or not there were differences in confusion resolution outcomes (resolved, unresolved) as a function of regulation effort (low, high). Table 2 shows the proportional occurrence of confusion regulation for low and high regulation effort cases.

Table 2. Confusion resolution and learning outcomes as a function of regulation effort

	Experiment 1		Experiment 2	
	Low Effort	*High Effort*	*Low Effort*	*High Effort*
Resolved Confusion	.648	.734	.531	.633
Near Transfer	.529	.433	.306	.380
Far Transfer	.250	.344	.337	.362
Resolved Cases				
Near Transfer	.545	.439	.356	.407
Far Transfer	.295	.379	.375	.393
Unresolved Cases				
Near Transfer	.500	.417	.250	.333
Far Transfer	.167	.250	.293	.310

In both experiments there were no significant differences in confusion resolution outcomes based on regulation effort (p's $> .10$). The regulation effort × induction condition interaction was also not significant for either experiment (p's $> .10$). These findings suggest that the *amount* of regulation effort does not impact confusion resolution outcome, at least as assessed in the present experiments.

3.3 Does Effort Moderate the Relationship Between Confusion Resolution and Learning?

The findings from the second research question did not show that regulation effort predicted confusion resolution outcome, but it is still possible that regulation effort directly affected learning. We therefore investigated the main effect of regulation effort on learning and the regulation effort (high, low) × resolution outcome (resolved, unresolved) interaction term (see Table 2). Neither the main effect of regulation effort nor the interaction term was significant for either task in Experiment 1 (p's > .10). However, a different pattern was found for Experiment 2.

In Experiment 2 the main effect for regulation effort was significant for the far transfer task ($\chi^2(1) = 10.4$, $p = .001$), but the interaction was not significant ($p > .10$). When learners spent more time on the regulation task, they performed better on the far transfer task than when less time was spent. For the near transfer task the regulation effort main effect was not significant ($p > .10$), but the regulation effort × resolution outcome interaction was significant ($\chi^2(3) = 8.03$, $p = .045$). Separate models were constructed for low and high regulation effort cases. The model was marginally significant for only the low regulation effort cases ($\chi^2(1) = 2.96$, $p = .085$), with confusion resolved cases outperforming confusion unresolved cases. Cognitive conflict, cognitive disequilibrium, and impasse-driven theories of learning would suggest that effortful cognitive activities would aid successful confusion resolution and ultimately benefit learning. However, the present results do not support this relationship. Overall, successful confusion resolution was found to benefit learning, but it does not appear that increased regulation effort is needed for learning to occur.

4   Conclusion

Learning inevitably involves challenges and moments of confusion. For ITSs to be effective they must not only monitor the occurrence of confusion, but also whether or not learners are able to successfully resolve their confusion. In other words, ITSs must know when to let learners struggle and work through their confusion on their own and when to intervene and facilitate confusion resolution. This has been proposed by cognitive conflict [13], cognitive disequilibrium [14-16], and impasse-driven theories of learning [17-18], as well as supported by empirical research [4,21-23]. Currently there are ITSs that adaptively respond to confusion in order to aid confusion resolution [9-10,12]. The present work explored the benefit of confusion resolution within learning environments that experimentally induced confusion. The present findings support the theoretical predictions that there are learning benefits when confusion is successfully resolved compared to persistent, unresolved confusion. It is interesting to note that this was the case across both experiments, even though different confusion induction and regulation methods were used. It was also the case, across both experiments, that the benefit of confusion resolution differed based on the nature of the confusion induction manipulation. This suggests that the source of confusion or to what the confusion is attributed should be taken into consideration when supporting learners.

Prior research has focused on the *outcome* of confusion resolution, but has largely ignored the *process* of confusion resolution. Understanding the process of confusion resolution will allow ITSs to more effectively determine when and how to intervene. The present work made a very preliminary investigation into this process by addressing the impact of effort during confusion resolution, as measured by the amount of time spent on the confusion regulation task. In general we found that more time spent on the confusion regulation task did not facilitate confusion resolution or learning, with one exception. However, the investigation of regulation effort in the present work was limited in two ways. First, we did not assess confusion intensity. It is likely that confusion at different intensity levels (e.g., 2 vs. 9 on a 1-10 scale) would require different amounts or types of effort for successful resolution. Second, we investigated only the *quantity* but not the *quality* of the confusion resolution effort. Although there is an assumption that more time spent on the regulation task is an indicator of deeper processing, we do not have evidence from the present experiments to confirm this assumption. For example, a learner may spend a long time reading because they have become more confused by new or challenging material, whereas another learner may quickly and strategically extract information that directly addresses their confusion without reading the entire text. The comparison of these two learners shows that quantity and quality do not always align in the confusion resolution process.

Future work will need to take a more in depth approach to understanding the process of confusion resolution. Specifically, we will need to monitor (1) confusion onset; (2) confusion intensity; (3) whether or not confusion resolution is attempted; (4) if attempted, the quantity and quality of the confusion resolution effort; and (5) if attempted, the outcome of the confusion resolution effort. Prior work has typically only addressed parts (1) and (5) of confusion resolution. By understanding how each part of the confusion process impacts both the confusion resolution outcome and learning, we can build ITSs that are more effective at promoting learning.

Acknowledgements. The research was supported by the National Science Foundation (0325428, 633918, 0834847, 0918409, 1108845) and the Institute of Education Sciences (R305A080594, R305G020018). Any opinions, findings, and conclusions or recommendations expressed in this material do not necessarily reflect the views of these funding sources.

References

1. Craig, S., Graesser, A., Sullins, J., Gholson, B.: Affect and learning: An exploratory look into the role of affect in learning. J. Educational Media **29**, 241–250 (2004)
2. D'Mello, S., Graesser, A.: The half-life of cognitive-affective states during complex learning. Cognition & Emotion **25**, 1299–1308 (2011)
3. D'Mello, S., Graesser, A.: Confusion. In: Pekrun, R., Linnenbrink-Garcia, L. (eds.) International handbook of emotions in education, pp. 289–310. Routledge, New York (2014)
4. D'Mello, S., Graesser, A.: Confusion and its dynamics during device comprehension with breakdown scenarios. Acta psychological **151**, 106–116 (2014)
5. D'Mello, S., Lehman, B., Pekrun, R., Graesser, A.: Confusion can be beneficial for learning. Learning & Instruction **29**, 153–170 (2014)

6. Graesser, A., D'Mello, S.: Emotions during the learning of difficult material. In: Ross, B. (ed.) Psychology of Learning and Motivation, vol. 57, pp. 183–226. Elsevier (2012)
7. Lehman, B., D'Mello, S., Graesser, A.: False feedback can improve learning when you're productively confused. (in preparation)
8. Lehman, B., D'Mello, S., Strain, A., Millis, C., Gross, M., Dobbins, A., Wallace, P., Millis, K., Graesser, A.: Inducing and tracking confusion with contradictions during complex learning. Int. J. Artificial Intelligence in Education **22**, 85–105 (2013)
9. D'Mello, S., Lehman, B., Graesser, A.: A motivationally supportive affect-sensitive AutoTutor. In: Calvo, R., D'Mello, S. (eds.) New Perspectives on Affect and Learning Technologies, pp. 113–126. Springer, New York (2011)
10. Forbes-Riley, K., Litman, D.: Benefits and challenges of real-time uncertainty detection and adaptation in a spoken dialogue computer tutor. Speech Communication **53**, 1115–1136 (2011)
11. Grafsgaard, Joseph F., Boyer, Kristy Elizabeth, Phillips, Robert, Lester, James C.: Modeling confusion: facial expression, task, and discourse in task-oriented tutorial dialogue. In: Biswas, Gautam, Bull, Susan, Kay, Judy, Mitrovic, Antonija (eds.) AIED 2011. LNCS, vol. 6738, pp. 98–105. Springer, Heidelberg (2011)
12. Woolf, B., Burleson, W., Arroyo, I., Dragon, T., Cooper, D., Picard, R.: Affect-aware tutors: Recognizing and responding to student affect. Int. J. Learning Technology **4**, 129–164 (2009)
13. Limón, M.: On the cognitive conflict as an instructional strategy for conceptual change: A critical appraisal. Learning & Instruction **11**, 357–380 (2001)
14. Festinger, L.: A theory of cognitive dissonance. Row Peterson, Evanston (1957)
15. Graesser, A., Lu, S., Olde, B., Cooper-Pye, E., Whitten, S.: Question asking and eye tracking during cognitive disequilibrium: Comprehending illustrated texts on devices when the devices breakdown. Memory & Cognition **33**, 1235–1247 (2005)
16. Piaget, J.: The origins of intelligence. International University Press, New York (1952)
17. Brown, J., VanLehn, K.: Repair theory: A generative theory of bugs in procedural skills. Cognitive Science **4**, 379–426 (1980)
18. VanLehn, K., Siler, S., Murray, C., Yamauchi, T., Baggett, W.: Why do only some events cause learning during human tutoring? Cognition & Instruction **21**, 209–249 (2003)
19. Chinn, C., Brewer, W.: The role of anomalous data in knowledge acquisition: A theoretical framework and implications for science education. Review of Educational Research **63**, 1–49 (1993)
20. D'Mello, S., Graesser, A.: Dynamics of affective states during complex learning. Learning & Instruction **22**, 145–157 (2012)
21. Lee, Diane Marie C., Rodrigo, MaMercedes T., Baker, Ryan SJd, Sugay, Jessica O., Coronel, Andrei: Exploring the relationship between novice programmer confusion and achievement. In: D'Mello, Sidney, Graesser, Arthur, Schuller, Björn, Martin, Jean-Claude (eds.) ACII 2011, Part I. LNCS, vol. 6974, pp. 175–184. Springer, Heidelberg (2011)
22. Liu, Z., Pataranutaporn, V., Ocumpaugh, J., Baker, R.: Sequences of frustration and confusion, and learning. In: D'Mello, S., Calvo, R., & Olney, A. (eds.) EDM 2013, pp. 114–120. International Educational Data Mining Society (2013)
23. Rodrigo, M., Baker, R., Nabos, J.: The relationships between sequences of affect states and learner achievements. In: Wong, S., Kong, S., Yu, F.-Y. (eds.) Computers in Education, pp. 56–60. Faculty of Educational Studies, Universiti Putra Malaysia, Serdang (2010)
24. D'Mello, S., Taylor, R., Graesser, A.: Monitoring affective trajectories during complex learning. In: McNamara, D., Trafton, J. (eds.) Cognitive Science Society 2007, pp. 203–208. Cognitive Science Society, Austin (2007)
25. Halpern, D., Millis, K., Graesser, A., Butler, H., Forsyth, C., Cai, Z.: Operation ARA: A computerized learning game that teaches critical thinking and scientific reasoning. Thinking Skills and Creativity **7**, 93–100 (2012)

Motivational Design in an Intelligent Tutoring System That Helps Students Make Good Task Selection Decisions

Yanjin Long$^{(\boxtimes)}$, Zachary Aman, and Vincent Aleven

Human Computer Interaction Institute, Carnegie Mellon University,
5000 Forbes Avenue, Pittsburgh, PA 15213, USA
{ylong,aleven}@cs.cmu.edu, zaman@cmu.edu

Abstract. Making effective problem selection decisions is an important yet challenging self-regulated learning (SRL) skill. Although efforts have been made to scaffold students' problem selection in intelligent tutoring systems (ITS), little work has tried to support students' learning of the transferable problem selection skill that can be applied when the scaffolding is not in effect. The current work uses a user-centered design approach to extend an ITS for equation solving, *Lynnette*, so the new designs may motivate and help students learn to apply a general, transferable rule for effective problem selection, namely, to select problem types that are not fully mastered ("Mastery Rule"). We conducted user research through classroom experimentation, interviews and storyboards. We found that the presence of an Open Learner Model significantly improves students' problem selection decisions, which has not been empirically established by prior work; also, lack of motivation, especially lack of a mastery-approach orientation, may cause difficulty in applying the Mastery Rule. Based on our user research, we designed prototypes of tutor features that aim to foster a mastery-approach orientation as well as transfer of the learned Mastery Rule when the scaffolding is faded. The work contributes to the research of supporting SRL in ITSs through a motivational design perspective, and lays foundation for future controlled experiments to evaluate the transfer of the problem selection skill in new tutor units where there is no scaffolding.

Keywords: Problem selection · Self-Regulated Learning · Mastery orientation · Motivations · User-centered design · Intelligent tutoring system · Open learner model

1 Introduction

Making problem selection decisions is an important self-regulated learning (SRL) process [17]. Strategic problem selection can lead to better learning outcomes as compared to randomly selected problems [13]. Although students generally prefer to have control over their own problem selection [7], studies have found that giving students control over which problems to solve often leads to worse learning outcomes than system-selected problems [3]. Therefore, researchers of intelligent tutoring systems (ITSs) have tried to design systems that have motivational advantages of student control while mitigating the downside of potentially poor problem selection decisions.

© Springer International Publishing Switzerland 2015
C. Conati et al. (Eds.): AIED 2015, LNAI 9112, pp. 226–236, 2015.
DOI: 10.1007/978-3-319-19773-9_23

For example, one ITS shares control over problem selection between students and the system, fostering student motivation through some student control while preventing the students from making decisions that are detrimental to learning [12]. Adaptive navigational support has also been designed and implemented in hypermedia learning environments to aid students in making effective problem selection decisions through visual cues [5]. However, the prior work has mainly focused on scaffolding making problem selection decisions during learning. Little work has investigated whether and how an ITS can be designed to help students learn the transferable skill of making problem selection decisions that can be applied when the scaffolding is not in effect.

The current work focuses on extending an ITS for equation solving, *Lynnette* [12], so that it can motivate and help students learn to apply an effective strategy for selecting problems in ITS, namely, to select problem types that are not fully mastered while avoiding problem types that are (we will refer to this as the "Mastery Rule"). The Mastery Rule is based on theories of mastery learning [11]. System-controlled problem selection in an ITS based on this rule has been shown to significantly enhance student learning [8]. As a first step towards teaching students problem selection skills, we keep the Mastery Rule simple by not taking into account the spacing effects [1]. Our goal is to help students become better at self-regulating problem selection in their own learning, so that they can actively apply the Mastery Rule later when there is no ITS support for problem selection.

Theories of SRL stipulate that effective self-regulation requires not only knowledge of metacognitive strategies, but also motivations that foster the active use of the strategies [17]. Scaffolding for SRL processes in ITSs often aims at helping students correctly apply the metacognitive strategies (e.g., [2], [4]). Very little research has tried to foster students' motivation for applying the metacognitive strategies in ITSs. One study promoted a teammates relationship between students and the tutor, which motivated the students to engage in more effective help-seeking behaviors [16]. However, it is still largely an open question how we can use motivational design in ITSs to help students *want* to use the metacognitive strategies.

We emphasize motivational design (design to foster motivations) in *Lynnette* to help students *want* to apply the Mastery Rule when they are given control over problem selection, in addition to designs that help them correctly apply the rule. We adopted a user-centered design approach to solve the design problem: How to motivate and help students learn to apply the transferable skill of making problem selection decisions based on the Mastery Rule. The user-centered design approach entails conducting user research to uncover user needs and help generate design ideas [10]. Thorough user research will help ground our designs in empirical findings about the users' knowledge, motivations and behaviors regarding selecting problems in ITSs.

Specifically, we combined user-centered design techniques including experimentation, interviews, and storyboards to study how students naturally select problems in the tutor, what knowledge they have for the Mastery Rule as well as their motivations for following the rule. Next, we built prototypes of tutor features that foster motivation and learning of the Mastery Rule based on results of our user research and grounded in motivation theories. We present and discuss results from our user research, as well as the final design prototypes.

2   Classroom Experimentation

As a first step in our user-centered design process, we conducted an exploratory class-room experiment to investigate how students naturally select problems in *Lynnette* with and without mastery information displayed by an Open Learner Model (OLM). OLM is a type of learning analytics that displays information about students' learning status (how much/how well they have learned for each type of problems) tracked and assessed by the system's student model, e.g., skill bars. Prior work highlights that an OLM has the potential to support students' problem selection [6], but no work has investigated whether and how the presence of an OLM might influence students' problem selection decisions.

Lynnette offers practice for five types of equations (categorized into five levels as shown in Figure 1), with increasing difficulty. *Lynnette* provides step-by-step feed-back on students' equation solving, as well as on-request hint messages. There were two conditions in the experiment. Both conditions needed to select problems from a problem selection screen by clicking one of the "Get One Problem" buttons. As shown in Figure 1, for the OLM condition, the problem selection screen showed the student's progress towards mastery for the five levels, calculated by Bayesian Knowledge Tracing. For the noOLM condition, no mastery information was dis-played on the problem selection screen – behind the scenes, the tutor still computed the mastery estimates so that they were available in the log data for later analysis. The levels were never locked and the students were able to keep selecting problems from a mastered level. Once the student selected a level, the tutor picked a problem from the chosen level and brought the student to the problem solving interface, which was the same for the two conditions.

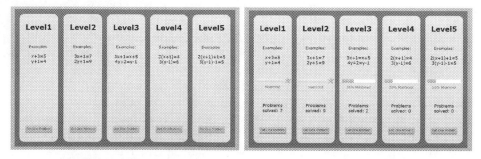

Fig. 1. Problem selection screen for the noOLM (left) and the OLM condition (right)

Twenty-five 7th and 8th grade students from 2 classes participated in the experi-ment. They were taught by 2 teachers at the same local public school. The students were randomly assigned within each class to one of the two conditions. There were 13 students in the OLM condition, and 12 in the noOLM condition. The students learned with the two versions of *Lynnette* for two 41-minute class periods on one school day. No instructions were given to the students with respect to how they should select problems in the tutor during the experiment. We analyzed the tutor log data to investigate what problems students selected to practice during the two class periods, especially whether the students selected problems from levels that had already been mastered, i.e., whether they violated the Mastery Rule.

On average, the OLM condition completed 21.08 (SD=7.65) problems, and the noOLM condition completed 28.75 (SD=14.32) problems. A 1-way ANOVA shows that the difference was not statistically significant. Table 1 shows the two conditions' average percentages (number of unmastered/mastered problems completed in a level/total number of problems completed) of problems completed in each level. (Note that under perfect application of the Mastery Rule, students practice unmastered problems only.) For both conditions, students selected most problems from level 1, 2, and 3. For the noOLM condition, on average, 34% of the problems completed by each student were from mastered levels, while only 8% of the problems were selected from the mastered levels for the OLM condition. A 1-way ANOVA shows that the difference of the percentages is statistically significant (F (1, 23)=7.207, p=.013, d=1.07).

Table 1. Means and SDs for percentages of problems completed in each level

	Unmastered Problems						Mastered Problems		
	L1	L2	L3	L4	L5	Total	L1	L2	Total
noOLM	.35(.26)	.12(.12)	.08(.08)	.04(.07)	.07(.09)	.66(.29)	.27(.27)	.06(.12)	.34(.29)
OLM	.27(.09)	.34(.12)	.26(.19)	.02(.04)	.03(.12)	.92(.17)	.06(.12)	.03(.05)	.08(.17)

The results of the classroom experiment shed light on how students select problems in an ITS that offers student-control over problem selection:

1) OLM helps students effectively select problems. Students in the OLM condition selected significantly fewer mastered problems as compared to the noOLM condition. (To recall, practicing mastered problems is considered to be redundant under the Mastery Rule.) On one hand, it is likely that the students have knowledge of the Mastery Rule, but are not capable of accurately assessing their mastery of the levels. The OLM aided the students by displaying their learning status, which in turn led to more effective problem selection. On the other hand, the OLM might have encouraged the students to work in new levels in order to fill all the mastery bars.

2) Students tend not to challenge themselves with new levels, and often fail to persevere in more difficult levels. We found some interesting patterns by examining the sequence of problems selected by individual students. For example, student H from the OLM condition kept alternating between level 1 and level 2 without trying any of the higher levels. Student M from the noOLM condition first tried to select one problem from each level, and then stayed in level 1 for the rest of the time. Student C from the noOLM condition selected one problem from level 1, 2, and 3 to start with, and then worked in level 1 for several problems even after reaching mastery, according to the system (though without mastery bars communicating that fact). In general, students often selected some problems from mastered lower levels after trying to solve a higher level problem, even with the presence of the OLM. Moreover, the classroom experiment only involved two class periods. It is possible that with longer practice time, the students in the OLM condition will more frequently violate the Mastery Rule when they encounter higher levels with more difficult problems.

3   Interviews and Storyboards

Our next step in the user-centered design process was to gather qualitative data to help explain and further investigate the quantitative results observed in the classroom experiment. Specifically, we conducted interviews and used storyboards to find out 1) how the OLM helps students make better problem selection decisions; 2) how much knowledge the students have about the concept of mastery and how to apply the Mastery Rule; and 3) what design features may motivate students to challenge themselves with unmastered problem types. 12 6th – 8th grade students participated in the study. The students participated either individually or with one or two friends/siblings. Each session took 45 – 60 minutes, starting with an interview followed by discussions on storyboards. All sessions were audio-recorded for later analysis. Two experimenters ran the sessions together, one serving as the interviewer/facilitator of the discussions, and one as the note-taker. None of the participants had used *Lynnette* before the study.

We designed interview questions that target students' understanding of mastery and the Mastery Rule, with and without the aid of the OLM. Specifically, the interviewer first introduced what *Lynnette* is, and brought up one of the problem selection screens (half of the participants saw the noOLM screen, and half saw the OLM one as both shown in Figure 1). The students were asked to select one level to start with and explain why they decided to pick that level. Next they solved one problem from the level they chose, and were brought back to the problem selection screen. Then they were again asked what level they wanted to select next and why, but were not asked to solve the problem again. For students who saw the OLM, they were also asked what had led to the change of the mastery bars.

James is working through level 3 in Lynnette and having some difficulty. He is tempted to go back to level 2, which he has already mastered.

However, James can see that if he picks 5 unmastered problems in a row, he will receive an achievement badge.

James decides to persevere on level 3 and at least work through 5 of the level 3 problems.

Fig. 2. A storyboard illustrates earning badges for persevering with a difficult level

We created 18 storyboards that reflect design ideas we brainstormed based on prior literature on supporting self-regulated learning. Storyboarding is an effective technique in user-centered design for quickly identifying user needs and generating feedback on design ideas [9].   Each storyboard contains one design idea, and consists of 3 to 4 frames, with explanatory text under each frame. The 18 storyboards reflect three main themes of design ideas of features in *Lynnette*: 1) Help students know when they have had enough practice (4 storyboards); 2) Help students learn the knowledge of the Mastery Rule (6 storyboards); and 3) Motivate the students to challenge themselves by selecting unmastered levels and persevere (8 storyboards). Figure 2 shows an example storyboard that illustrates the idea of using badges to motivate students to persevere in a new and difficult level. The students were given a copy of the story-boards, and then the interviewer read the storyboard aloud and led discussions with the students about their initial reaction to the idea and how they would react to the features if they were the student in the story.

The interviews and discussions with storyboards provide ample qualitative data:

1) The students do not understand the concept of mastery, and have misconceptions about the mastery bars in the OLM. In general, we found that mastery is a difficult concept for the students. When no OLM was present on the problem selection screen, a common answer to our question, "How many problems would you do for each level?" was, "I will do 5 problems in each level." On the other hand, when the OLM was present, almost all of the students perceived the mastery bars simply to mean how many problems they had completed in a level, instead of the degree to which they had mastered the skills to solve problems in that level.

2) It is not difficult to explicitly communicate the Mastery Rule to the students. Some of our participants were able to state the Mastery Rule when asked how they would select problems for themselves, such as "I know how to do level 1, so I will pick level 2." When we introduced the Mastery Rule in some of our storyboards, we also found that it was not difficult for students to understand and accept the rule. The Mastery Rule can be explicitly taught to the students.

3) Students have limited motivation with respect to why they should practice problems from unmastered new problem levels. Most of our participants admitted that they only would do what the teacher gives to them, and few mentioned they would learn new things in new levels. Also, math seems uninteresting to some of the students, and one of them said, "Sometimes I just feel lazy and just want to do easy problems." The lack of motivation may prevent the students from applying the Mastery Rule even if they are aware of the strategy.

We have also identified motivating design features for middle school students:

1) Mastery bars in the OLM. All of the participants expressed that they liked the mastery bars. The bars stimulate a desire for completion, and probably encouraged them to work on the new levels, as observed in the classroom experiment. However, as we found that the students had misconceptions about the meaning of the bars, it was clear that we needed to communicate the concept of mastery to them explicitly.

2) Rewards. The students liked all kinds of rewards, including badges, stars, achievements, and even positive messages from the tutor. One student commented, "Who wants to go out on a rainy cold night on Halloween if not for candies?" Therefore, well-designed rewards may encourage desirable problem selection behaviors.

4   Prototypes of Tutor Features That Foster Motivation and Learning of the Mastery Rule

We designed and created paper and HTML/Javascript prototypes of tutor features that foster motivation and learning of the Mastery Rule based on results gathered from our user research. There were two main goals of our design: 1) To support students' motivation of applying the Mastery Rule; and 2) To support the learning of the Mastery Rule. We also have the ultimate goal of enabling transfer of the learned rule when the scaffolding is not in effect, with the fostered motivation.

With respect to the goal of supporting motivation, we specifically focused on fostering a mastery-approach orientation. We found from our user research that the main obstacle for applying the Mastery Rule is lack of motivation to select new and challenging problems and to persevere when encountering difficulties, even with the presence of the OLM. Therefore, our designs need to help foster the motivation that will engender desirable problem selection behaviors. We decided to ground our design in motivation theories of achievement goals [15]. There are generally two types of achievement goals, mastery orientation and performance orientation [14]. While a performance orientation focuses on demonstration of competence, a mastery orientation emphasizes developing competence [15]. The orientations are further divided into approach and avoidance forms [15]. A mastery-approach orientation is generally associated with positive learning behaviors such as perseverance, willingness to take on challenges and desire to learn new things [14], which align with the desirable behaviors for applying the Mastery Rule. Research has also found that a mastery orientation can be fostered through interventions, and can last even after the interventions are faded [14]. Therefore, we designed tutor features that may foster a mastery-approach orientation. Meanwhile, given math is uninteresting to some of the students, we included some game elements (avatars, stars and badges) to make the tutor more fun.

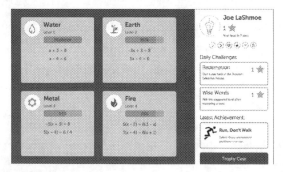

Fig. 3. The problem selection screen that also displays Daily Challenges and Achievements

Daily Challenges and Achievements. We designed Daily Challenges and Achievements to reward students for challenging themselves with new problem types and persevering when encountering difficulties, aiming to help them develop a mastery-approach orientation. For example, as shown in Figure 3, one Achievement students can earn is by selecting three unmastered problems in a row.

We also designed features aimed at helping students learn the Mastery Rule. Notably, all of these features also contribute to fostering a mastery-approach orientation.

The Tutorial. An interactive tutorial is presented to the students when they first log in to *Lynnette*. It explains to students that they are learning a separate skill of making problem selection decisions, in addition to learning to solve equations. We kept the mastery bars in the redesigned tutor, as our experiment suggests that *Lynnette*'s OLM can help students make significantly better problem selection decisions. However, we also found that explanations of the concept of mastery and the mastery bars needed to be presented to address students' misconceptions. Therefore, as shown in Figure 4, the tutorial explains the concept of mastery, the Mastery Rule, and the mastery bars. All of the explicit explanations and instructions from the tutorial emphasize the mastery-approach orientation. After going through the tutorial, the students start working with the tutor on the problem selection screen shown in Figure 3.

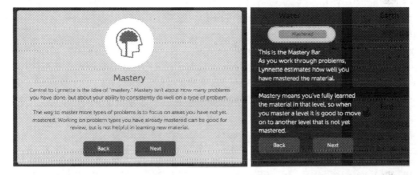

Fig. 4. Explicit explanations of mastery (left) and of the mastery bars (right) from the tutorial

Feedback Messages. We designed messages to serve as feedback on students' problem selection decisions. Figure 5 shows a message that a student could receive from his/her avatar after selecting several mastered problems. The message reminds the student of the ineffective problem selection decisions, and reinforces the mastery-approach orientation by saying, "Don't forget to work on mastering new materials."

Problem Selection Recap. We designed a problem selection recap screen to let students reflect on their problem selection history when they reach mastery for a level. The students are provided the levels they have selected before reaching mastery for that particular level (if they effectively apply the Mastery Rule, they should only have selected the current level or the levels above), and are asked to identify the mastered/unmastered levels they have selected. Students receive immediate feedback messages about whether they have correctly identified the mastered/unmastered levels, and the messages are also phrased to foster a mastery-approach orientation (as shown at the bottom of the left image in Figure 5).

Fig. 5. Problem selection recap screen (left) and feedback message (right) students receive after several ineffective problem selection decisions

We conducted user testing using the HTML/Javascript prototypes (not yet integrated with *Lynnette*) with 10 6th – 8th grade students. The sessions were conducted either individually or in groups of two, and ranged from 40 to 45 minutes. All sessions were audio-recorded. The user testing helped us improve the usability issues of the interface and provided preliminary feedback on the effectiveness of the design features. In general, the participants perceived the redesigned tutor interface as fun and engaging. One student said, "Yes, I will definitely use it." They also felt that the Daily Challenges, Achievements and feedback messages were motivating and helpful.

5   Conclusions and Future Work

The current paper uses a user-centered design approach to extend an ITS for equation solving, so that the new designs may motivate and help students learn to apply an effective problem selection strategy in a way that lasts, even when the scaffolding is no longer in effect. We started with a theoretically interesting question: How can an ITS help students learn to make good problem selection decisions? We conducted user research to identify user needs and help generate design ideas. Lastly, we designed prototypes of features in *Lynnette* that may foster the motivation and learning of the Mastery Rule based on results and insights gained from our user research. We also grounded our designs in motivation theories about mastery-approach orientation.

Our user research has produced interesting results that can inform future design of learner-controlled ITSs. We studied how an OLM influences students' problem selection decisions when students are free to select any problem they like. We found that an OLM can help the students effectively select problems, as the OLM condition selected significantly fewer mastered problems than the noOLM condition; this is one reason why ITSs should include an OLM when students have control over problem selection. Our experiment helps empirically establish the significant role of OLM in supporting problem selection in ITS, which has not been addressed by prior work. We also investigated what may have caused the difficulty in applying the Mastery Rule. It appears that lack of motivation, especially the lack of a mastery-approach orientation, may be a stronger factor than metacognitive knowledge of the rule.

Our work contributes to the research of supporting self-regulated learning in ITS. Our prototypes are designed to foster a mastery-approach orientation as well as transfer of metacognitive knowledge when the scaffolding is not in effect (although with the OLM, as it is a common feature in ITS). Not much work in ITSs has investigated motivational design to help students *want* to apply metacognitive strategies needed for effective self-regulation, and little prior work has supported the transfer of SRL skills in ITSs. Lastly, the current work lays the foundation for future controlled experiments. We will conduct experiments and measure if our designs can successfully foster the mastery-approach orientation, and whether the motivation and knowledge of the Mastery Rule can transfer to new tutor units when the scaffolding is removed.

Acknowledgement. We thank Ken Koedinger, Jesse Schell, Jodi Forlizzi and Tim Nokes-Malach for the comments and suggestions on the work. We thank Gail Kusbit and Jonathan Sewall for their kind help with the classroom experiment. We also thank the participating teachers and students. This work is funded by an NSF grant to the Pittsburgh Science of Learning Center (NSF Award SBE0354420).

References

1. Anderson, J.R.: Learning and Memory. Wiley, New York (1994)
2. Aleven, V., Roll, I., Koedinger, K.R.: Progress in assessment and tutoring of lifelong learning skills: an intelligent tutor agent that helps students become better help seekers. In: Adaptive Technologies for Training and Education, pp. 69–95 (2012)
3. Atkinson, R.C.: Optimizing the learning of a second-language vocabulary. Journal of Experimental Psychology **96**(1), 124–129 (1972)
4. Azevedo, R., Witherspoon, A., Chauncey, A., Burkett, C., Fike, A.: MetaTutor: a metacognitive tool for enhancing self-regulated learning. In: Proceedings of the AAAI Fall Symposium on Cognitive and Metacognitive Educational Systems, pp. 14–19 (2009)
5. Brusilovsky, P., Sosnovsky, S., Shcherbinina, O.: QuizGuide: increasing the educational value of individualized self-assessment quizzes with adaptive navigation support. In: Proceedings of World Conference on E-Learning, AACE, pp. 1806–1813 (2004)
6. Bull, S., Kay, J.: Metacognition and open learner models. In: Proceedings of Workshop on Metacognition and Self-Regulated Learning in Educational Technologies, pp. 7–20 (2008)
7. Clark, C.R., Mayer, E.R.: E-Learning and the science of instruction: proven guidelines for consumers and designers of multimedia learning. Jossey-Bass, San Francisco (2011)
8. Corbett, A.: Cognitive Mastery Learning in the ACT Programming Tutor. AAAI Technical Report SS-00-01 (2000)
9. Davidoff, S., Lee, M.K., Dey, A.K., Zimmerman, J.: Rapidly exploring application design through speed dating. In: Krumm, J., Abowd, G.D., Seneviratne, A., Strang, T. (eds.) UbiComp 2007. LNCS, vol. 4717, pp. 429–446. Springer, Heidelberg (2007)
10. Goodman, E., Kuniavsky, M., Moed, A.: Observing the User Experience, Second Edition: A Practitioner's Guide to User Research. Morgan Kaufman, Waltham (2012)
11. Kulik, C.C., Kulik, J.A., Bangert-Drowns, R.L.: Effectiveness of mastery learning programs: A meta-analysis. Review of Educational Research **60**, 265–299 (1990)

12. Long, Y., Aleven, V.: Gamification of joint student/system control over problem selection in a linear equation tutor. In: Trausan-Matu, S., Boyer, K.E., Crosby, M., Panourgia, K. (eds.) ITS 2014. LNCS, vol. 8474, pp. 378–387. Springer, Heidelberg (2014)
13. Metcalfe, J., Kornell, N.: A Region of proximal learning model of study time allocation. Journal of Memory and Language **52**(4), 463–477 (2005)
14. O'Keefe, P.A., Ben-Eliyahu, A., Linnenbrink-Garcia, L.: Shaping achievement goal orientations in a mastery-structured environment and concomitant changes in related contingencies of self-worth. Motivation and Emotion **37**, 50–64 (2013)
15. Schunk, D.H., Pintrich, P.R., Meece, J.L.: Motivation in education: Theory, research, and applications. Pearson/Merrill Prentice Hall, Upper Saddle River (2008)
16. Tai, M., Arroyo, I., Woolf, B.P.: Teammate Relationships Improve Help-Seeking Behavior in an Intelligent Tutoring System. In: Lane, H., Yacef, K., Mostow, J., Pavlik, P. (eds.) AIED 2013. LNCS, vol. 7926, pp. 239–248. Springer, Heidelberg (2013)
17. Zimmerman, B.J.: Self-regulation involves more than metacognition: A social cognitive perspective. Educational Psychologist **29**, 217–221 (1995)

SNS Messages Recommendation
for Learning Motivation

Sébastien Louvigné[✉], Yoshihiro Kato, Neil Rubens, and Maomi Ueno

Graduate School of Information Systems,
University of Electro-Communications, Tokyo, Japan
{louvigne,y-kato,rubens,ueno}@ai.is.uec.ac.jp

Abstract. Setting goals for learning enhances motivation and performance. This research shows that observing learning goals from peers on
social networks allows learners to specify new learning purposes and to
enhance the perception of their own expertise. This study consists of:
1) a model recommending goal-based messages from peers with diverse
textual contents (i.e. purpose) for a same goal (e.g. mastering English),
and 2) a Web-based implementation using an LDA (Latent Dirichlet
Allocation) model, known as a highly accurate text latent topic model.
The experiment was conducted by university students who expressed
and evaluated their goals before observing similar/diverse messages from
other peers. Results showed that observing the diversity of peers' learning
purposes is an important factor positively affecting intrinsic motivational
attributes such as goal specificity and confidence to achieve the goal.

Keywords: Learning motivation · Social networks · Recommendation ·
Latent Dirichlet Allocation

1 Introduction

Pedagogical goals and purposes for learning are strongly connected and represent
a prominent view of motivation [8, 20]. Learning goals are efficient when linked
with learner's needs and purposes because learners want to know the reasons
why learning is important for them [1, 14]. Educational institutions therefore
provide highly structured education with syllabus stating specific outcomes.

However learners as individuals have various conceptual perceptions and different purposes for learning. Students are then often unable to relate to the objectives stated by their formal education. This matter appears even more clearly in
informal and self-regulated learning environments where curricula may be absent
and where learners monitor their own actions, motivation, and goals [9, 19]. This
results in risks of conflict and discouragement that might harm learner's intrinsic
motivation. Learners need a resource of a larger variety of goals and purposes
from peers for better goal orientation and learning motivation.

Vygotsky claimed that individuals learn and build their knowledge in social
context, through external relations with others [23]. Other research works later

© Springer International Publishing Switzerland 2015
C. Conati et al. (Eds.): AIED 2015, LNAI 9112, pp. 237–246, 2015.
DOI: 10.1007/978-3-319-19773-9_24

developed approaches demonstrating that learners build knowledge by observing others [3], collaborating with others [22], and reflecting new knowledge on new situations [7]. The main interest of this research is therefore about whether the concept of learning from peers can be applied to learning motivation.

Social networks represent an essential and influential factor, including for learning [4]. However, peers also use social media to express and share their motivation. Figure 1 shows examples of Twitter users expressing some goals and purposes for learning.

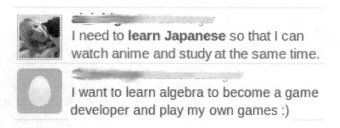

Fig. 1. Example of goal-based messages collected from the social media Twitter. This research consisted in the recommendation of similar/diverse goal-based messages for a same learning subject using LDA.

The purpose of this research consisted in determining how to use social networks in order to enhance motivation for learning, in particular by using the diversity of goal-based motivational messages from peers. Similarity in recommendation e-learning systems showed enhancements and reinforcements in learning performance and behavior (including motivation). However, the difficulty for many learners in following formal education's goals called for a larger and more diverse choice of purposes for learning to be recommended. The purpose of this study was therefore twofold:

1. Design a goal-based recommendation system to let learners observe messages from peers containing diverse purposes for learning a same subject (e.g. English),
2. Web-based implementation using an Latent Dirichlet Allocation (LDA) model in a social environment.

The highly accurate text latent topic model LDA assumes a latent structure based on several topics, also called themes, distributed probabilistically over document [6]. LDA therefore estimated the diversity of topics (i.e. purposes for learning) within a single dataset of goal-based messages from peers. The recommendation model offered then different learning purposes from peers expressed as Twitter messages.

This research viewed the observation and adoption of diverse learning purposes as an important factor to enhance learners' motivation and to positively impact their perception on their goal attributes. This study therefore aimed at (1) designing a model to recommend diverse learning purposes from peers and (2) evaluating the effect on learners' perception of their motivation and the attributes related to the initial goal: *importance, attainability, easiness, specificity, commitment, confidence, achievement, satisfaction,* and overall *motivation.*

2   Learning Goals

A general definition for *goal* can be a terminal point towards which actions or behaviors are directed. In learning, goal represents then an outcome that one intends to attain as a result of a cognitive process (e.g. mastering a language). Goals provide the direction to guide learners to act, the force to satisfy a need, to motivate behaviors [20].

2.1   Goal-Setting

Goal-setting focuses on the properties and attributes of learning goals (e.g. importance, difficulty, attainability). In other words goal attributes define the learning goal and give an estimation of how a learner can relate to a learning goal. In his excellent works [12,14] Locke summarized some goal setting research works and gave a list of different goal attributes. Bekele [5] also reviewed studies about satisfaction and motivation in Internet-Supported Learning Environments.

Fig. 2. Goal Attributes. This diagram summarizes the different goal attributes and how they can be connected to each other. It shows that each of these moderators can affect Performance and that Achievement and Fulfillment represent the final outcomes of a learning experience based on a goal.

Among all goal attributes, goal specificity gives a direction to learners and leads to higher performance than ambiguous tasks. Learners with more specific tasks can better control their performance on them. In addition goals both specific and difficult lead to higher performance because they generate higher commitment, in contrast with ambiguous goals (e.g. *"do your best"*). Self-efficacy refers to one's beliefs in the ability to control goals and has a wider influence on motivational moderators (e.g. confidence) and therefore performance [4].

Goal attributes are various and affect each other to lead eventually to achievement and fulfillment (or personal satisfaction). Figure 2 summarizes the connections between those goal attributes and their importance as motivational moderators in a learning experience.

2.2 Goal Orientation

Goal orientation has been in recent years an active research area in educational psychology and achievement motivation. It refers to the purposes and the ways to approach and engage in achievement tasks.

Learners have various goal orientations or purposes for learning, but there are also different types of goal orientations, often referred as mastery and performance goals [1]. The former focuses on mastering tasks according to self-set standards whereas the latter represents the demonstration of a skill based on external judgments [19].

This distinction, like others, is based on whether goals relate to intrapersonal or external aspects. Considering the high influence of self-set goals on intrinsic motivation [13], learners can adopt new purposes for engaging in a task in order to follow a more intrapersonal and therefore more efficient goal orientation.

The diversity of purposes for achieving a similar goal expressed by peers on social media appears as an important factor able to affect motivation for learning and the self-perception of one's goals.

3 Social Networks for Learning and Motivation

Vygotsky claimed that individuals build their consciousness through external relations with others [23]. Behaviors strongly related to needs are learned in social situations and mediation with other persons. Vygotsky's findings and the concept of learning from peers strongly influenced many research works in the past decades.

Several approaches demonstrated that knowledge and behaviors are acquired by observing [3] and collaborating with others [22]. Learners subsequently articulate, reflect their new knowledge, and explore new goals [7].

Eccles et al. extensively discussed theoretical perspectives and empirical works on motivation, and reviewed many social cognitive models [8]. Authors demonstrated the important impact of social settings on motivation and indicated the influence of emotions for future developments.

Therefore, social networks appear to operate naturally as behaviors recommenders [4] influencing learners behaviors, and therefore motivation and purposes for learning [1].

This high potential called for a new recommender model aiming at using the large and diverse amount of motivational contents from peers to influence learners' perceptions of their goals and purposes.

4 Goal-Based Recommendation System

Recommender Systems took a major part in the development of advanced technologies, based on the similarity of item contents, user profiles (Collaborative Filtering) or other information [11]. Previous implementations in education showed positive results in enhancing learning by recommending personalized contents to learners [18].

The main purpose of this research consisted in designing a goal-based recommendation model for learning motivation enhancement. This model aimed at recommending motivational contents from peers (i.e. goal-based Twitter messages containing learning purposes) using social settings. This study focused on the positive effect of observing diverse purposes for learning on learners' perceptions of their own goals.

This goal-based model therefore used LDA, known as a highly accurate text latent topic model, to determine different topics (i.e. learning purposes) within a same dataset of Twitter messages where users expressed why they learn a given subject (e.g. English).

4.1   Latent Dirichlet Allocation

Latent Dirichlet Allocation (LDA) is a probabilistic model for collections of discrete data such as text corpora [6]. Such model is useful when each document is a mixture of topics and when the words observed in the dataset communicate the meaning of the message as a latent structure [10].

There are different categories of goal-based messages (e.g. "traveling", "business", "manga") for a same subject of study (e.g. "Japanese"). This study used a model based on LDA considering that each document (i.e. Twitter message) contains several topics and that each word is attributable to one of these topics. This model determined several learning purposes as topics in a dataset of goal-based messages for a same learning subject, as done in a preliminary study [15].

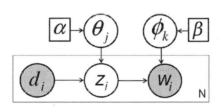

Fig. 3. Graphical model for LDA. Boxes denote the parameters α and β. Shaded and unshadded circles respectively denote observed and hidden variables. [2]

Figure 3 shows the graphical model for LDA used in this study where θ and ϕ respectively represent the estimated distribution of a topic Z for a document d and the distribution of a word W for a topic Z. α and β are the parameters of the Dirichlet prior on respectively the per-document topic distributions and the per-topic word distributions.

This study used the Collapsed Gibbs Sampling method [10] to construct a Monte Carlo Markov chain and to determine the full conditional distribution (1) and the Dirichlet distribution of words per topic (2):

$$P(z_i = j | z_{-i}, w) \propto \frac{n_{-i,j}^{(w_i)} + \beta}{n_{-i,j}^{(\cdot)} + W\beta}(n_{-i,j}^{(d_i)} + \alpha) \qquad (1)$$

$$\hat{\phi}_j^{(w)} = \frac{n_j^{(w)} + \beta}{n_j^{(\cdot)} + W\beta} \qquad (2)$$

in which W represents all words in all documents. w and z represent respectively the words and the topics. $n_{-i}^{(\cdot)}$ denotes a word count not including the current assignment of z_i.

4.2   Recommendation System Architecture

The LDA-based model aimed at recommending goal-based messages from peers expressing diverse purposes for learning a same subject. Figure 4 illustrates the different steps of the recommendation process as listed below:

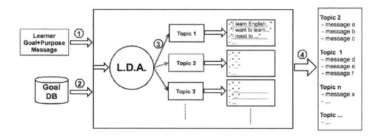

Fig. 4. Illustration of the goal-based messages recommendation process. The model recommends Twitter messages from diverse categories of learning purposes from peers for a same learning subject.

1. **Learner Input:** user's message expressing the reason(s) for engaging in learning a chosen subject,
2. **System Input:** existing dataset containing similar types of messages previously created by other users or collected from the social media Twitter,
3. **Topic distribution:** estimation of topics' probabilistic distribution from the input database, and estimation of the appartenance of user's input message,
4. **Output:** selection of messages from topics others than the one estimated to relate to user's input message.

The recommender model used user's written expression of learning purposes to list goal-based messages from other peers. It required an initial dataset of messages (16,000 Twitter messages) built in previous stages of this research [17,21].

The recommender process utilized the LDA-based model described in Sect. 4.1 during two different situations: offline and online. The former consisted in initially estimating the probabilistic distribution of words and documents (i.e. Twitter messages from the goal-based dataset) over topics corresponding to different learning purposes. In relation to these estimations, the recommender model determines the attribution of a user's goal-based message.

Results from the recommender model showed finally messages belonging to other topics than the one attributed to user's input goal-based message. Most recommender systems focus on similarity with contents or peers. This study considered however the diversity of motivational contents essential for recommendation. Results described in Sect. 5 compared learners' self-evaluation of their goal perception between users who were recommended similar or diverse goal-based messages.

5   Results and Evaluation

The goal-based recommender model was implemented into a Web application [16] in order to create a social environment. Learners could express their learning purposes in the form of a Twitter message and observe messages from other peers.

Undergraduate students in the Tokyo University of Electro-Communications participated in the experiment. Students were randomly assigned into two groups based on the recommendation way: 1) similar messages (attributed to the same topic), 2) diverse messages (attributed to other topics). In total, 77 students taking English classes expressed and evaluated their goals from November 2014 to January 2015.

5.1   Experiment Scenario

The experiment consisted into three specific tasks:

1. Creating and updating "Learning Goal Profile(s)",
2. Observing Twitter messages from peers.
3. Repeating the previous steps (starting with Observation)

Learners managed their learning goals by creating what was called "Goal Profile(s)". In addition to the subject of study (e.g. *"English"*), users were asked to express the reason(s) why they study this subject (e.g. *"I want to learn English so I can travel around the world"*) using a Twitter message format (within 140 characters).

This stage of the experiment also included learner's self-evaluation of the perception of their goals. This feature, essential for the analysis of observing goal-based messages from peers, consisted in rating goal attributes moderating learning performance and fulfillment as shown previously in Fig. 2. Therefore, for each goal profile created, users rated how they think about their goal achievement using the questionnaire shown in Fig. 5.

The recommender model listed then some Twitter messages from other peers based on (1) the messages created in the Goal Profile(s), and (2) the recommendation way (messages from similar/diverse topic(s)).

Fig. 5. List of questions in Goal Profile for learners' self-evaluation

Students were asked to repeat the tasks every week over the school semester in order to analyze of the recommendation system over a long-term period. From the second attempt, however, they first observed peers' messages based what they expressed the first time. After the observation step, students could re-express and re-evaluate their learning goals. This last part was an essential step to analyze the effect of both recommendation ways on learners' perceptions of their goals.

5.2   Evaluation of Learners' Perceptions

77 Japanese undergraduate students taking English classes expressed their goals for studying English. They also rated their perceptions on their goals based on the motivational attributes previously cited. Each attribute was rated from 0 to 100% (0=very low, 100=very high).

Results consisted in comparing both recommendation ways (similar/diverse messages). Table 1 shows in both cases the average ratings from users for each motivational attribute. Results are also summarized for three different times of the experiment: T_0: initially (before any observation of peers' messages); T_1: after the first observation; T_{final}: after the last observation.

"*Diff.*" column of Table 1 shows the change of ratings average from T_0 to T_n, or in other words from the initial evaluation (i.e. before any observation) to the last evaluation (i.e. after observing n times peers' messages).

The results from the evaluations showed that observing diverse goal-based messages from peers generally affected more positively learners' perceptions of their goals, especially for feelings of attainability, goal specificity and confidence for achievement.This utilization of messages from social media also showed an improvement of overall motivation for all users, although slightly superior when observing diverse messages.

Table 1. Self-evaluation: average results of learner's perceptions of their goals

Motivation Attributes	Similar messages				Diverse messages			
	T_0	T_1	T_{final}	Diff.	T_0	T_1	T_{final}	Diff.
Importance	89.23	86.15	86.15	−3.08	91.43	87.14	87.14	−4.29
Attainability	73.85	72.31	78.46	4.62	64.29	71.43	72.86	8.57
Easiness	44.62	42.31	45.38	0.77	44.29	47.14	45.71	1.43
Specificity	81.54	79.23	76.15	−5.38	67.14	77.14	78.57	11.43
Commitment	70.77	72.31	72.31	1.54	67.14	72.86	71.43	4.29
Confidence	66.15	61.54	63.08	−3.08	57.14	62.86	68.57	11.43
Achievement	66.15	66.92	66.92	0.77	62.86	62.86	65.71	2.86
Satisfaction	72.31	78.46	78.46	6.15	61.43	62.86	65.71	4.29
Overall Motivation	78.46	80.77	82.31	3.85	68.57	68.57	74.29	5.71

6   Conclusion

Setting goals that are intrinsically purposeful and meaningful for learners enhances learning motivation and performance. Contemporary social media offer a large variety of motivational contents from peers where they express their goals and purposes for learning. This research interest was based on the influence from peers from social networks on learning motivation. This study regarded the diversity of purposes for learning from peers as an important resource for intrinsic motivation enhancement.

This study consisted in a goal-based recommendation model utilizing social networks to present peers' Twitter messages. The model utilized LDA to estimate the diversity of topics (i.e. learning purposes) within a dataset of Twitter messages expressing the same goal (i.e. mastering a subject). The implementation of this model recommended peers' messages based on the similarity/diversity with learner's purpose.

A total of 77 university students expressed their goals and evaluated their perceptions of their overall motivation. The implemented system recommended similar or diverse Twitter messages to learners. Their self-evaluations showed the positive effect of observing diverse learning purposes from peers on motivation and especially on goal attributes, in particular confidence to achieve the goal, goal specificity and attainability.

References

1. Ames, C.: Classrooms: Goals, Structures, and Student Motivation. Journal of Educational Psychology **84**(3), 261–271 (1992)
2. Asuncion, A., Welling, M., Smyth, P., Teh, Y.W.: On smoothing and inference for topic models. In: Conference on Uncertainty in Artificial Intelligence, pp. 27–34. AUAI Press (2009)
3. Bandura, A.: Social Foundations of Thought and Action: A Social-Cognitive Theory. Prentice Hall, Englewood Cliffs (1986)
4. Bandura, A.: Social Cognitive Theory of Mass Communication. Media Psychology **3**, 265–299 (2001)

5. Bekele, T.A.: Motivation and Satisfaction in Internet-Supported Learning Environments: A Review. Educational Technology & Society **13**, 116–127 (2010)
6. Blei, D.M., Ng, A.Y., Jordan, M.I.: Latent Dirichlet Allocation. Journal of Machine Learning Research **3**, 993–1022 (2003)
7. Collins, A.: Cognitive apprenticeship. In: Sawyer, R.K. (ed.) The Cambridge Handbook of The Learning Sciences, pp. 47–60. Cambridge University Press (2006)
8. Eccles, J.S., Wigfield, A., Schiefele, U.: Motivation to succeed. In: Eisenberg, N. (ed.) Handbook of child psychology, 5th edn., pp. 1017–1095. Wiley, New York (1998)
9. Eraut, M.: Informal Learning in the Workplace. Studies in Continuing Education **26**(2), 247–273 (2004)
10. Griffiths, T.L., Steyvers, M.: Finding scientific topics. In: Proceedings of the National academy of Sciences of the United States of America 101, pp. 5228–5235 (2004)
11. Herlocker, J.L., Konstan, J.A., Terveen, L.G., Riedl, J.T.: Evaluating collaborative filtering recommender systems. ACM Transactions on Information Systems **22**(1), 5–53 (2004). http://portal.acm.org/citation.cfm?doid=963770.963772
12. Locke, E.A.: Motivation through conscious goal setting. Applied and Preventive Psychology **5**(2), 117–124 (1996)
13. Locke, E.A., Latham, G.P.: A theory of goal setting and task performance. Prentice Hall (1990)
14. Locke, E.A., Latham, G.P.: Building a practically useful theory of goal setting and task motivation: A 35-year odyssey. American Psychologist **57**(9), 705–717 (2002)
15. Louvigné, S., Kato, Y., Rubens, N., Ueno, M.: Goal-based messages Recommendation utilizing Latent Dirichlet Allocation. In: The 14th IEEE International Conference on Advanced Learning Technologies (ICALT), pp. 464–468 (2014)
16. Louvigné, S., Kato, Y., Rubens, N., Ueno, M.: Goal-based Recommendation System (2014). http://130.153.209.92/GBRSys/signin
17. Louvigné, S., Rubens, N., Anma, F., Okamoto, T.: Utilizing social media for goal setting based on observational learning. In: 2012 IEEE 12th International Conference on Advanced Learning Technologies (ICALT), pp. 736–737 (2012)
18. Manouselis, N., Drachsler, H., Verbert, K., Duval, E.: Recommender Systems for Learning. Springer Science & Business Media (2012)
19. Pintrich, P.R.: The role of goal orientation in self-regulated learning. In: Boekaerts, M., Pintrich, P.R., Zeidner, M. (eds.) Handbook of self-regulation, pp. 451–502. Academic Press, San Diego (2000)
20. Schunk, D.H., Meece, J.L., Pintrich, P.R.: Goals and goal orientations. In: Motivation in Education: Theory, Research, and Applications, pp. 170–209. Pearson Education, Inc. (2002)
21. Shi, J., Louvigné, S.: Goal-Setting and Meaning-Making in Mined Dataset of Tweets Using SFG Approach. Journal of Electrical Engineering **2**(1), 20–28 (2014)
22. Vygotsky, L.S.: Mind in Society: The Development of Higher Psychological Processes. Harvard University Press, Cambridge (1978)
23. Vygotsky, L.S.: Thought and Language. MIT Press, Cambridge (1986)

How Spacing and Variable Retrieval Practice Affect the Learning of Statistics Concepts

Jaclyn K. Maass[✉], Philip I. Pavlik Jr., and Henry Hua

Institute for Intelligent Systems and Department of Psychology,
University of Memphis, Memphis, TN, USA
{jkmaass,ppavlik,hhua}@memphis.edu

Abstract. This research investigated key factors in learning conceptual material about statistics, and tested the effect of variability during retrieval practice. The goal was to build a model of learning for schedule-based interventions. Participants ($n = 230$) completed multiple reading and test trials with fill in the blank sentences about basic statistics concepts. The experiment was a 2 (trial type: read or drill) × 3 (learning trial spacing: wide medium, or narrow) × 2 (fill-in term during learning: variable or constant) × 2 (fill-in term during posttest: variable or constant) within-subjects design. The model of the results captures the data with recent and long-term components to explain posttest transfer and the testing and spacing effects. These results, and data on the conceptual confusions amongst statistical terms, are discussed with respect to implications for future intelligent learning systems.

Keywords: Fill in the blank · Learner modeling · Testing effect · Spacing effect

1 Introduction

Over the history of spacing effect research, many experiments involved memorizing a set of items that were completely unfamiliar to the learners [e.g. 1, 2]. This procedure stems from an effort to avoid confounding the participant's familiarity with the topic with the effects of spaced practice, but the use of completely novel stimuli does not aptly simulate student learning in a classroom setting. Recently however, there has been a growth in the number of studies using more educationally relevant, ecologically valid, and complex material [e.g., 3]. Oftentimes, the spacing effect goes hand in hand with the testing effect (i.e., retrieval practice). Like the spacing effect, the testing effect is a fairly consistent phenomenon well replicated with different formats and domains, such as vocabulary [e.g., 4], paired-associates [e.g., 5], procedural knowledge [e.g., 6], and text materials [e.g., 7]. However, much of this type of research uses the same items for retrieval practice and posttest. The problem is that this provides a measure of memory for verbatim responses and does not offer a measure of deeper, integrated learning or transfer.

While many current intelligent tutoring systems focus on procedural knowledge [e.g., 8], certain domains require the prerequisite of a strong conceptual knowledge base. Therefore, we have chosen to focus our work on learning semantic knowledge.

© Springer International Publishing Switzerland 2015
C. Conati et al. (Eds.): AIED 2015, LNAI 9112, pp. 247–256, 2015.
DOI: 10.1007/978-3-319-19773-9_25

We aimed to use model-based discovery [9] to describe learning in this task in a way that will aid in the creation of an tutoring system which implements simple reactive artificial intelligence to optimally schedule the repetition of retrieval practice for conceptual knowledge. This paper focuses on three key features of such a model in this domain: spacing of practice, retrieval practice, and variable practice. The current experiment tested those factors using a free entry cloze (fill-in-the-blank) task with a collection of 18 sentences about statistics. This is the second experiment in a series of cloze item research aimed at building an intelligent tutoring system (ITS) focused on didactic, verbal and/or conceptual information. Unlike the previous study, the current experiment used related sentences to measure spacing effects in an educationally relevant domain, rather than with decontextualized trivia facts [10]. Participants completed 162 drill and reading trials with sentences about statistics concepts (e.g., definition of a sample, characteristics of a normal distribution, etc.). For this paper we developed a learner model that predicts performance given the prior accuracy, spacing, repetition, testing, and concept difficulty.

In addition to the above goals, we had four experimental hypotheses: 1) wider spacing will lead to worse performance during learning but better performance at posttest; 2) spacing effects will be larger for sentences in which participants fill in the same term during the learning trials; 3) testing trials will have more impact on learning than reading trials; and 4) testing with variation in the retrieval term will lead to more generalizable learning. Further, the free entry nature of the cloze task provided rich insight into students' confusions, which has direct implications for creating customized hint and/or error messages in the next stage of this research project.

2   Methods

2.1   Design

A brief overview of terminology specific to this experiment may be helpful. Each trial involved the presentation of a sentence either to be read by the participant (reading trials) or with a missing word to be filled in by the participant (drill trials). Retrieval term refers to which one of four key terms in each sentence can be left blank for a drill trial. Variability in retrieval term refers to having to fill in different retrieval terms across drill trials for a sentence. The two main portions of the experiment are referred to as the learning portion (consisting of six trials for each sentence), and the posttest portion (consisting of three drill trials for each sentence).

This study used a within-subject design with the following factors: 2 (trial type: read or drill) x 3 (learning trial sentence spacing: wide medium, or narrow) x 2 (learning trials retrieval term: variable or constant) x 2 (posttest trials retrieval term: variable or constant). While the design was fully factorial for the other factors, the assignment to reading or drill trial for each sentence during the learning portion was selected randomly, with a 50% chance of reading on Trials 1 and 4, and a 25% chance of reading for Trials 2, 3, 5, and 6. The posttest portion (Trials 7-9) contained only drill trials. If the retrieval term was constant during the learning or posttest portions, the participant would only see one of the four key terms left blank in the sentence, and this retrieval term would remain constant, e.g. always the 3rd of 4, for all trials. If the retrieval term was variable, any one of the four key terms could be left blank for the participant to fill in for each trial. For the learning portion, half of the sentences were randomly selected to have a constant retrieval term and half were selected to have variable retrieval terms. Retrieval term variability was manipulated for the learning portion and for the posttest portion, independently, meaning each of the nine sentences that had a constant retrieval term during learning was individually assigned as having variable or constant retrieval terms during posttest. Therefore, on average, 4.5 of the constant retrieval term sentences during learning were tested as variable at posttest and the other 4.5 continued as constant at posttest). Note that when the posttest retrieval term varied, it was randomly selected from only the other three fill in locations, excluding the "constant" location for that learner. Therefore, the constant learning to variable posttest had no repetition of responses (i.e., all transfer posttest drills). Conversely, the constant to constant condition only ever filled in one of the key terms (i.e., no transfer posttest drills). The other two conditions, variable to variable and variable to constant, would have had some posttest items they had seen before and some they had not (i.e., some transfer posttest drills). Of course by "transfer" we are not referring to completely novel sentences; rather, the retrieval term for that sentence would not have been previously retrieved during the learning drill trials. This type of "within-sentence" posttest transfer measure has been used by others [11].

Therefore, participants received some sentences in each of the four drill trial conditions: variable retrieval terms during learning and variable retrieval terms during posttest (variable-variable), variable retrieval terms during learning and a constant retrieval term for posttest (variable-constant), constant retrieval term for all learning trials and variable retrieval terms for posttest trials (constant-variable), and a constant retrieval term for all learning trials and constant retrieval term for posttest trials (constant-constant). Each sentence was also randomly placed in one of the three spacing conditions during practice, resulting in 12 possible retrieval practice conditions.

2.2   Participants

The experiment was delivered through the Amazon Mechanical Turk (MTurk) service, an online data collection platform. A total of 231 people participated, but one subject was excluded ($n = 230$) because they produced no correct responses. The requirements for participation were for the person to be at least 18 years of age, a native English speaker from the United States or Canada, and to be a reliable MTurk "worker." This last qualification was to ensure quality results. It requires participants to have previously completed at least 50 tasks (referred to as "Hits") on the website, with at least 95% of those tasks approved (i.e., the person had done adequately enough to not be refused payment). Although this sample is not restricted to formal students, studies have reported that MTurk participants appear to produce qualitatively and quantitatively similar results to university and other online participants [12]. MTurk users were paid $4 for approximately 45 minutes of participation.

2.3   Materials

The 18 sentences used for the experiment were developed from basic statistics content authored by the three authors of this study. The sentences were not designed to be explicitly related, but naturally resulted in the reuse of several key terms; for example, several sentences mention the concept of *standard deviation* with regards to various other concepts. For each sentence we chose four crucial words (or two-word phrases) to create four versions of each sentence in which each version has one word or phrase removed (i.e., left blank). For example, in the sentence, "Although samples are variable, they are intended to represent the population from which they come," the four selected key terms were *samples*, *variable*, *represent*, and *population*. Only one key term was left blank for any given trial (i.e., the participants never saw a sentence with two blanks, except to indicate the same word used twice).

2.4   Procedure

The experiment was delivered online, using the Fact and Concept Training (FaCT) system, which is designed to handle complex designs of this sort [13]. The sentences were delivered in the center of the screen for study trials and for drill trials. For drill trials, participants were told whether their answer was correct or incorrect; after an incorrect response, the correct response was displayed on the screen for a review period. Participants were given eight seconds to read each sentence both for reading trials and for the review period after incorrect drill trials. Reading trials never indicated which terms could be left blank during drill trials.

For the drill trials, participants had 12 seconds to begin to type their response for the missing word, otherwise the trial timed-out, was counted as an incorrect response, and the system continued to the review. However, as long as the participants were trying to answer (i.e., if they had started to type in the answer box), the system allowed the participants as long as they wanted to finish typing. For the review that occurred after an incorrect drill trial, the computer program showed the whole sentence again, but with no missing words (i.e., without indicating which word or phrase had just been blank) for eight seconds, identical to reading trials.

The experiment consisted of the informed consent, instructions, learning portion (consisting of the 18 sentences, presented six times each in a combination of drill and reading trials, each at different spacing intervals), a 5-minute distractor task (an N-back task, data for which was not available at the time of writing due to a parsing error), and a posttest (three drill trials for each sentence). The learning portion lasted an average of approximately 30 minutes, the distractor task (i.e., retention interval) was approx. five minutes, and the posttest lasted an average of approx. ten minutes.

3   Results and Discussion

In order to eventually build an "intelligent" program that can adapt and respond to an individual student's progress, we must first understand the underlying features affecting memory. To begin this process, we ran two repeated-measure ANOVAs to determine the changes in performance between the learning portion and posttest portion, based on 1) spacing of practice trials, and 2) variability during practice. The levels of the dependent measure, referred to as the trial variable, were proportion correct during the last learning trial (Trial 6) and proportion correct on the first posttest trial (Trial 7). The results of the first ANOVA indicated a presence of the spacing effect (i.e., a significant interaction between spacing and trial), $F(2, 458) = 29.28$, $p < .001$. Namely, during the last learning trial, performance was best for those sentences with narrow spacing, followed by medium spacing, with worst performance for the wide spacing (all spacing pairwise comparisons had $ps < .001$). However, these differences between spacing conditions disappeared at the first posttest trial (all $ps > .2$).

Similarly, the second repeated measures ANOVA, comparing change in performance from learning to posttest between sentences with variable retrieval terms during practice and sentences with a constant retrieval term during practice, showed a significant retrieval variability by trial interaction, $F(1, 230) = 138.11$, $p < .001$. During learning, participants scored higher on sentences that had a constant retrieval term than on those sentences with variable retrieval terms, pairwise comparison $p < .001$. However, this difference was no longer significant at posttest, pairwise $p = .44$. This shows a much steeper forgetting rate over the 5-minute retention interval for those with a constant retrieval term during practice. Our final preliminary analysis confirmed the presence of the testing effect through a simple logistic regression model (not shown) using only two parameters: count of prior reading trials for the sentence and count of prior drill trials for the sentence. This revealed drill trials to be about three times as effective as readings ($z = 7.531$, $p < .001$). In order to build a tutoring program, however, we will need more than these preliminary analyses can offer. Such a program will require a predictive model of student performance which would act as the main source of "intelligence" in optimally scheduling retrieval practice.

The process of developing a predictive model of student performance required an iterative, theory driven method known as model based discovery [9]. Specifically, we started by entering in factors we presumed, based on previous memory research thus far discussed, would be most influential in learning. Through a process of elimination, focused on parsimony and correspondence with prior theory, we were able to narrow down which factors had the greatest influence on learning. For example, we expected to see fast forgetting in addition to durable learning, as a function of spacing of practice, based on prior work with other verbal material [e.g., paired associates; 14]. Other features were implemented based on prior learner modeling. For instance, a distinction between the effects of incorrect and correct responses was based on Performance Factors Analysis [15], and a general track of all prior performance, which is similar to work with Bayesian knowledge tracing [16]. The final model is a logistic regression with the following parameters or factors: prior performance, term difficulty, recency, pure massing effect, spacing for drill trials, spacing for incorrect drill trials, and spacing for key terms. Table 1 contains the coefficients and z scores obtained for each factor, which is explained in more detail below. The z scores are a particularly useful measure to compare the coefficients and understand their relative importance in the model. For example, the most predictive features of the model, described in detail below, are recency ($z = 51.50$) and term difficulty ($z = -42.71$). The model fit with an

R^2 of .399 and a mean absolute probability deviation of .298 for the predictions of each of the 28,912 drill trial observations across the 230 learners. We also cross-validated the model using ten runs of 10-fold cross-validation. We observed an R^2 of .399 in the training and an R^2 of .357 in testing, which means we retained 89% of the fit when generalizing. It should be noted that the model was found using the entire dataset (rather than a portion); thus, the cross-validation might suffer some inflation. However, we did not further tune the model to optimize the cross-validation results. Additionally, we minimized the number of parameters relative to the number of conditions, to help protect against overfitting.

Table 1. Coefficients, standard errors, and z scores for each model parameter (all $ps < .001$)

Factor	Coefficient	SE	Z score
Intercept	-2.53	0.04	-61.95
Prior performance	0.92	0.02	40.56
Recency	8.78	0.17	51.50
Term difficulty	-1.48	0.03	-42.71
Pure massing	-0.15	0.03	-4.78
Spacing for drills	0.37	0.01	28.71
Spacing for incorrect trials	-0.35	0.01	-26.09
Spacing of terms	0.05	0.01	8.47

Prior performance is measured as the proportion[1] of previously correct trials which is transformed into a logit, ranging from, $-\infty$ to $+\infty$. This variable is seeded with a value equal to the overall grand mean to prevent the prior probability from ever actually taking an infinite value. The transformation to a logit serves to increase the predictive influence as prior learning nears 0 or 1. The high z value for this parameter indicates that transformed previous accuracy is one of the biggest predictors of future success. The recency coefficient in the model scales the influence of the most recent trial as a function of how many seconds ago that trial occurred according to the function 1/ sqrt (recency in seconds). This function was computed for both the most recent trial of any type (read or drill) and the most recent same response drill trial. These values were summed before being log transformed. This method essentially double counts the amount of learning for the specific recent drill trial compared to a recent reading trial. Otherwise, this method is equivalent to the base level activation computation in the ACT-R computational modeling system [17]. The term difficulty parameter is the average number of incorrect responses for that key term across all participants. This is averaged across the sample, with the expectation that the values for these terms will generalize to another sample in the future. Again, we use the logit of this proportion to transform the scale in a way that increases the influence of proportions near zero. The difficulty of the terms (i.e., their error rates) is a key component in this model and will be discussed in more detail below.

---

[1] To eliminate the possibility of calculating a logarithm of 0 (which would be undefined), all logarithmic transformations were calculated from the observed value plus 1.

The pure massing effect parameter accounts for the effect of having prior back to back drills of the same sentence with no spacing at all. This effect is computed by taking the log of the number of prior back-to-back same-response drills, multiplied by the log of the total number of back-to-back repetitions of the sentence (i.e., both drill and reading trials). The negative coefficient for this parameter captures the negative effect of fully massed practice and the increasingly negative effect as more back-to-back drills are added. While this coefficient had the least significance, it was necessary to model the crossover interactions seen in Figure 1.

One feature of this model is that the spacing is not categorical (e.g., narrow, medium, wide), but rather is a function of the mean average time between prior repetitions of the sentence. This means that the model can be used to make predictions for spacing as a function of time rather than as a nominal effect, which would be less useful for inferring pedagogical decisions from the model. The last three parameters account for different spacing effect interactions, and are calculated by taking the log of some count of prior practices times the log of mean average spacing. The first of these parameters uses the log of the count of all same-response drill trials (i.e., previous drill trials for the same sentence, with the same retrieval term), which was found to predict a strong positive gain that increases with wider spacing. The second uses the count of *incorrect* same-response drill trials; its negative coefficient indicates that incorrect drills reduce the prediction of future successes for the sentence, indicating that incorrect retrieval attempts do not add much benefit to learning. This parameter, along with the first prior performance parameter, allows the model to adapt to student responses on both a student and item level. This capability will be key to using the model in the adaptive learning system we plan for future work. Finally, the last spacing coefficient scales the added effect of the prior repetitions of a *specific retrieval term*. Since some key terms were repeated in multiple sentences, this parameter demonstrates that specific retrieval term practice transfers between different sentences. It also provides preliminary evidence, combined with the semantic errors discussed below, that participants treated this as a meaningful task rather than as rote memorization.

In addition to modeling learning, our experiment also aimed to investigate the effect of variability during retrieval practice. Specifically, we hypothesized that the varying of retrieval terms in a sentence would have an effect on posttest performance for key terms they had not retrieved during practice. Figure 1 (left) illustrates this result by showing the change in performance from Trial 6 (the last learning trial) to performance on Trial 7 (the first posttest trial). The decrease in performance is likely attributed to the 5-minute distractor task between the learning and posttest portions. Figure 1 (right) illustrates the model's fit to Trials 6 and 7. Although only Trials 6 and 7 are graphed, the model fit just as well for the other trials; a full graph could not be included due to space restrictions.

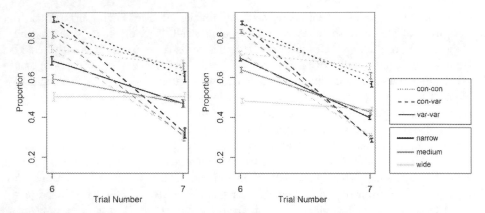

Fig. 1. Fig. 2. Actual performance by participants (left) and predicted performance by model (right) for the last learning trial (Trial 6) and first posttest trial (Trial 7). Line color indicates spacing level. Line style indicates retrieval term condition: constant during learning and constant during posttest (con-con), constant during learning and variable during posttest (con-var), and variable during learning and variable during posttest (var-var).

In Figure 1 (left), we see that participants performed best during learning when they were repeatedly tested on the same terms (con-con); in this condition, all posttest retrieval terms were the same as they had been tested on during learning, which explains why performance is the best for these sentences during both learning and posttest. Perhaps more interesting is the performance of the other groups on this figure. First we can see that when constant retrieval term practice switches to variable retrieval terms at posttest (which included no overlap between retrieval terms during learning and posttest; con-var), posttest performance is much worse than when retrieval terms were variable during learning and variable during posttest (var-var). In other words, variable practice resulted in better transfer to the varied retrieval terms at posttest. Note that the var-var lines in the figure include the var-con condition trials because the var-con was effectively equivalent for Trials 6 and 7. We also see a reduction in the spacing effect when there is less constancy, similar to other results showing reductions in spacing with variable learning [18].

The last component of this experiment we will discuss is the confusions witnessed in participants' incorrect responses. These confusions may have important implications for maximizing the potential of cloze practice. Figure 2 provides a partial graph of the most common confusions participants made between terms related to variance. The proportion of times a specific confusion was made is denoted on the links between terms. For example, participants fairly often (incorrectly) used the term *variance* in place of *standard error* (7.7% of the time), *density* (10.6% of the time), and *standard deviation* (6.9% of the time). This information about commonly confused terms will be indispensable for creating specific hint and error messages in an ITS.

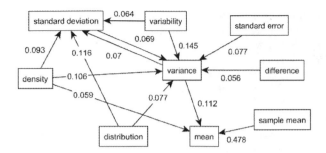

Fig. 2. The proportion of confusions participants made between terms. The figure is read as [correct answer] → [student response].

4   Conclusion

Our model captures many facets of learning conceptual material with retrieval practice and may be used within an adaptive learning system to optimally schedule retrieval practice. The model is able to accurately capture the effects of interest with relative parsimony through the integration of short term practice effects and long-term spacing effects to explain specific and general learning, while accounting for individual differences in performance. The results of this experiment replicate and extend results from an earlier study with trivia facts, showing similar short-term learning and spacing effects for variable posttest fill-ins [10]. The results also support the current experiment's hypotheses. Specifically, spacing effects were larger when the retrieval term was constant during learning; drill (i.e., test) trials had significantly more impact on learning than reading trials; and variation in retrieval terms during learning led to better performance on posttest trials with variable retrieval terms. Our hypothesis that wider spacing would lead to worse performance during learning but better performance at posttest, was also supported, although the difference at posttest was not significant. We attribute this to the relatively brief retention interval (5 minutes), since the spacing effect is usually more pronounced over time [17]. Lastly, the slower forgetting rate for sentences with variable retrieval terms during practice (rather than constant retrieval terms) may suggest more durable learning when practice is variable. However, this is a tentative conclusion. Future experiments will attempt to replicate these results with multiple retention intervals in an effort to get closer to our goal of developing an ITS to effectively schedule practice to maximize conceptual learning.

References

1. Carpenter, S.K., Pashler, H., Wixted, J.T., Vul, E.: The Effects of Tests on Learning and Forgetting. Memory & Cognition **36**, 438–448 (2008)
2. Ebbinghaus, H.: Memory: A Contribution to Experimental Psychology. Teachers College, Columbia University, New York (1913/1885)

3. Smith, M.A., Karpicke, J.D.: Retrieval Practice with Short-Answer, Multiple-Choice, and Hybrid Tests. Memory **22**, 748–802 (2014)
4. Karpicke, J.D., Roediger III, H.L.: The Critical Importance of Retrieval for Learning. Science **319**, 966–968 (2008)
5. Underwood, B.J., Ekstrand, B.R.: Effect of Distributed Practice on Paired-Associate Learning. Journal of Experimental Psychology **73**, 1–21 (1967)
6. Rohrer, D.: The Effects of Spacing and Mixing Practice Problems. Journal for Research in Mathematics Education **40**, 4–17 (2009)
7. Roediger III, H.L., Karpicke, J.D.: Test-Enhanced Learning: Taking Memory Tests Improves Long-Term Retention. Psychological Science **17**, 249–255 (2006)
8. Leelawong, K., Biswas, G.: Designing Learning by Teaching Agents: The Betty's Brain System. International Journal of Artificial Intelligence in Education **18**, 181–208 (2008)
9. Baker, R.S.J.D., Yacef, K.: The State of Educational Data Mining in 2009: A Review and Future Visions. Journal of Educational Data Mining **1**, 3–17 (2009)
10. Pavlik Jr., P.I., Geno, A.: Deconstructing Cloze Practice. Manuscript submitted for publication (2015)
11. McDaniel, M.A., Anderson, J.L., Derbish, M.H., Morrisette, N.: Testing the Testing Effect in the Classroom. European Journal of Cognitive Psychology **19**, 494–513 (2007)
12. Paolacci, G., Chandler, J., Ipeirotis, P.G.: Running Experiments on Amazon Mechanical Turk. Judgment and Decision making **5**, 411–419 (2010)
13. Pavlik Jr., P.I., Presson, N., Dozzi, G., Wu, S.-M., MacWhinney, B., Koedinger, K.R.: The FaCT (Fact and Concept Training) System: A New Tool Linking Cognitive Science with Educators. In: McNamara, D., Trafton, G. (eds.) Proceedings of the Twenty-Ninth Annual Conference of the Cognitive Science Society, pp. 1379–1384. Lawrence Erlbaum, Mahwah (2007)
14. Pavlik Jr., P.I.: The Microeconomics of Learning: Optimizing Paired-Associate Memory. Dissertation Abstracts International: Section B: The Sciences and Engineering **66**, 5704 (2005)
15. Pavlik Jr., P.I., Cen, H., Koedinger, K.R.: Performance Factors Analysis – a New Alternative to Knowledge Tracing. In: Dimitrova, V., Mizoguchi, R., Boulay, B.D., Graesser, A. (eds.) Proceedings of the 14th International Conference on Artificial Intelligence in Education, Brighton, England, pp. 531-538 (2009)
16. Corbett, A.T., Anderson, J.R.: Knowledge Tracing: Modeling the Acquisition of Procedural Knowledge. User Modeling and User-Adapted Interaction **4**, 253–278 (1995)
17. Pavlik Jr., P.I., Anderson, J.R.: Practice and Forgetting Effects on Vocabulary Memory: An Activation-Based Model of the Spacing Effect. Cognitive Science **29**, 559–586 (2005)
18. Appleton-Knapp, S.L., Bjork, R.A., Wickens, T.D.: Examining the Spacing Effect in Advertising: Encoding Variability, Retrieval Processes, and Their Interaction. Journal of Consumer Research **32**, 266–276 (2005)

Leveraging Multiple Views of Text for Automatic Question Generation

Karen Mazidi[(✉)] and Rodney D. Nielsen

HiLT Lab, University of North Texas, Denton, TX, USA
KarenMazidi@my.unt.edu, Rodney.Nielsen@unt.edu

Abstract. Automatic question generation can play a vital role in educational applications such as intelligent tutoring systems. Prior work in question generation relies primarily on one view of the sentence provided by a parser of a given type, such as phrase structure trees or predicate argument structure. In contrast, we explore using multiple views from different parsers to create a tree structure which represents items of interest for question generation. This approach resulted in a 17% reduction in the error rate compared with our prior work, which achieved a 44% reduction in the error rate compared to state-of-the-art question generation systems. Additionally, the work presented in this paper generates with greater question variety than our previous work, and creates 21% more semantically-oriented versus factoid questions.

Keywords: Question generation · Dependency parse · Semantic role labels

1 Introduction

The model of automatic question generation described in this work is a pattern-matching NLP task in which text, parsed or plain, is searched for patterns from which questions can be generated. Although research into automatic question generation dates back decades [21], a renewed interest was sparked by the development of dialogue-based intelligent tutors [19], and the subsequent question generation workshops and STEC.[1]

Recent years have seen a wide range of question generation approaches, brought about in part by the variety of NLP tools available to researchers. A look through the Proceedings of QG2010: The Third Workshop on Question Generation [3] demonstrates this variety of approaches based on different NLP tools. One popular approach involves using a parser to produce syntactic constituency trees and a set of syntactic transformations to create questions, as in Heilman and Smith [9] and Kalady et al. [12]. Minimal recursion semantics was used by Yao and Zhang [23], while semantic role labelers were used in both the Pal et al. [18] and Mannem et al. systems [14]. In addition, many of these

---

[1] http://www.questiongeneration.org/

© Springer International Publishing Switzerland 2015
C. Conati et al. (Eds.): AIED 2015, LNAI 9112, pp. 257–266, 2015.
DOI: 10.1007/978-3-319-19773-9_26

systems take advantage of other NLP tools and techniques to refine their systems such as named entity recognizers and gazeteers, anaphor resolution, dependency parses, chunking, pos taggers, and more. Looking beyond QG2010, examples of wide ranging approaches include Olney et al. [17], which generated questions from concept maps, and Curto et al. [6], which used lexico-syntactic patterns extracted from the web for generating question-answer pairs.

Identifying patterns in the output of parsing software is an important component of these diverse question generation approaches. The most commonly used approach creates PSG (phrase structure grammar) trees; in contrast, semantic role labelers identify the predicate-argument structure of sentences.

An additional parsing tool is a dependency parser, which identifies a set of typed relations between individual words in a sentence [7]. Nivre [16] observes that dependency relations provide a relatively direct encoding of the semantic relations between predicates and their arguments. The utility of dependency parses has led to their application in a wide variety of NLP tasks such as textual entailment [20], and information extraction [22]. Cheong and Shu [4] used dependency parses to extract causal relations from biological text in order to find analogies for biomimetic engineering, focusing on four dependency parse labels (xcomp, prepc_by, purpcl and csubj), combined with a set of heuristics. A dependency parse was used as an ancillary tool in two of the QG2010 systems [18], [14]. Afzal and Mitkov [1] used a dependency parse to aid in sentence simplification and transformation in creating multiple choice questions. However, to date no system has fully explored the set of dependency relations that can be sources for question generation. Vanderwende (2008) notes that QG systems should focus on generating important questions, not just grammatical ones, and the work in this paper demonstrates that dependency parse relations are fruitful sources of important content.

In most question generation systems, declarative sentences are transformed into questions in one of two ways: syntactic manipulation or templates. In a recent comparison of question generation approaches for educational applications[13], Le et al. observed that, in general, template based systems achieved better results than syntactic-transformation based systems, an observation that is in accord with results from our prior work. In this work, we present a template-based question generation system that is built on a dependency parse, paired with information from semantic role labels and discourse cues. Contributions of this work include:

- Novel use of dependency parses as a foundation for question generation
- Innovative use of multiple views of text: syntactic structure, predicate-argument structure, and discourse cues
- Development of a question generation tree structure in which major and minor branches represent items of interest for question generation
- Analysis and findings regarding specific dependency relations as sources for question generation

In medical imaging technology, the salt TlCl is used as a radiopharmaceutical because it acts like NaCl and follows the blood.

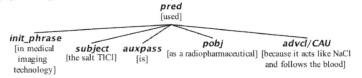

Fig. 1. Sample Lexical-Semantic Tree (QG tree)

2   System Overview

The question generator described here builds a lexical-semantic tree structure using the steps in Algorithm 1. First the dependencies from the Stanford dependency parser [7] are input. The collapsed form of dependencies was used, which collapses certain function words to yield direct dependencies between content words [7]. The QG Tree Construction algorithm then groups these dependencies into components and places them in the QG tree. Having the dependency parse as a foundation for the QG tree has advantages in its independence of word order, freeing the system from having to set up patterns for every possible arrangement of sentence constituents [11]. Next, the predicate-argument parse from the SENNA semantic role labeler [5] is input. For each sentence, select modifiers (ArgM) such as causal, temporal, and locative, are extracted from the predicate-argument parse and added to the QG tree. Figure 1 shows a sample input sentence and the QG tree created from its dependencies via Algorithm 1.

Algorithm 1. QG Tree Construction

---
for each sentence: **do**
    Input dependency parse
    Combine dependencies into components
    Add components to QG tree
    Input predicate-argument parse
    Add ArgMs to QG tree

The lexical-semantic tree (QG tree) identifies semantic and syntactic components by labels that are matched to patterns for question generation. The inclusion of ArgM labels from SENNA allows the generation of semantically oriented questions such as *how* and *why* questions.

The following questions were generated from the QG tree shown in Figure 2:

- How is the salt TlCl used in medical imaging technology?
- Why is the salt TlCl used as a radiopharmaceutical?

For question generation, each sentence is matched against a list of possible patterns from an external template file, and questions are generated whenever a pattern matches the sentence.

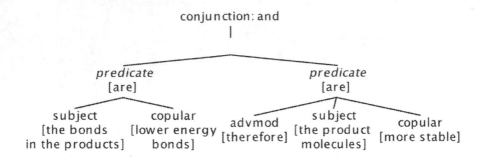

Fig. 2. Sentence with two independent clauses linked by a discourse connective

The question *Why is the salt TlCl used as a radiopharmaceutical?* is generated from the pattern: Why|aux||subject||pred||pobj|? Templates also indicate which QG Tree component is the answer to the question. In this case, the answer is the ArgM-causation text. The pattern above shows that questions are generated partly from text in the pattern, such as *Why*, and partly from text extracted from the QG tree. Symbols within pipe symbols, |x|, are replaced by source text, sometimes modified. The |aux| field, for example, is replaced by the auxiliary in the QG tree. Other templates use a |do| field, which is replaced by do, does or did, as appropriate. Each template has multiple fields. Category and label fields are used to identify which type and template generated a specific question. This is used for evaluation purposes. The sentence type field specifies which type(s) of sentences match this template. Sentence types can be regular, copular, passive, progressive or existential. The surface form field specifies the realization pattern that will be used to generate the final surface form of the question and the answer field indicates which QG Tree component is the answer for this question. Other optional fields provide a means to match constituents and words in the source text. If present, the system will check that required objects and conditions are present and excluded ones are not before generating.

In addition to requirements and exclusions specified within templates, there are system filters and condition checks which apply to all templates. For example, when the subject of a sentence contains no nouns, the resulting question will be vague and therefore the system does not generate a question.

2.1 Discourse Cues

Discourse cues and connectives can be good sources of question generation [2]. In addition to the discourse cues inherent in certain ArgM constituents, patterns look for the presence of specific verbs and words that serve as discourse cues or key words for given question types. The following sentence contains two examples: *If the atoms are pushed closer, the potential energy goes up because you are crowding the nuclei together.* The presence of words *if* and *because* leads to the generation of the following questions:

- What happens if the atoms are pushed closer together?
- Why does the potential energy go up if the atoms are pushed closer together?

Additionally, the system looks for specific discourse connectives that connect two independent clauses of a sentence joined by a conjunction as in the following source sentence:

The bonds in the products are lower energy bonds and therefore, the product molecules are more stable. Figure 2 shows the QG tree for this sentence. This structure enables generation of the following:

- Q: What can you conclude from the statement that the bonds in the products are lower energy bonds?
- A: the product molecules are more stable

2.2   Pros and Cons of Sentence Simplification

A common approach to handling complex sentences in prior work involves sentence simplification, which not only has the possibility of introducing errors into the pipeline, as observed by Heilman and Smith [9], but also can lead to the loss of important semantic information. Using a semantic role labeler as the sole source of input for a question generator provides similar benefits and risks as sentence simplification. A predicate-argument parse would be created for every verb. Given the sentence *The quantity theory of money also states that the growth in the money supply is the primary cause of inflation*, the following parse would be generated for the second predicate, *is*:

[A1 the growth in the money supply] is [A2 the primary cause of inflation]

This parse would lead to the generation of the question: *What is the primary cause of inflation?* which would take the cause of inflation out of the context of discussing a theory and places it on the level of fact. This is one limitation of an approach that relies only on the predicate-argument parse, and one of the motivating factors in creating the QG structure which keeps the sentence as one integral unit. From this same source sentence, the QG tree enabled the system to generate the question: *How would you characterize the quantity theory of money?* by utilizing the *ccomp* dependency relation encompassing the text: *that the growth in the money supply is the primary cause of inflation.*

2.3   Template Creation

The current system has around 50 templates. Templates were manually constructed to match features that might appear within the QG tree output by Algorithm 1. The most basic templates only utilize subject-verb-object information to create *what* and *who* questions. These SVO templates account for 12% of the templates. Another subsection of the templates employs discourse cues from

Table 1. Examples of Generated Questions

Example 1 source text: Because of their complex level of organization, eukaryotic cells can carry out many more functions than prokaryotic cells. **Question:** Why can eukaryotic cells carry out many more functions than prokaryotic cells?
Example 2 source text: Cytoplasm is made up of cytosol, a watery fluid that contains dissolved particles and organelles. **Question:** Describe the composition of cytoplasm.
Example 3 source text: Inflation is defined as an increase in the price level. **Question:** How is inflation defined?
Example 4 source text: Prokaryotic DNA usually forms a circular molecule and is found in the cell's cytoplasm along with ribosomes. **Question:** Where is prokaryotic DNA found?
Example 5 source text: Given a constant money supply, the velocity of money must increase to fund all these purchases. **Question:** Why must the velocity of money increase given a constant money supply?

the text. Templates that utilize ArgM modifiers account for 36% of templates and create questions of types *why, when, how, describe* and *consequence.* The largest group (43%) is the category which exploits various dependency relations such as *agent, xcomp, vmod,* to name just a few. Templates that utilize multiple types of features from the QG tree are categorized according to the most important components in the template. The following observations result from a recent evaluation of approximately 2700 questions produced from these templates. The DP and ArgM templates generate roughly in proportion to their frequency in the templates, whereas the SVO templates tend to over-generate. Together, the DP and ArgM templates account for almost 75% of the generated questions which is significant because these questions tend to go beyond the more factoid SVO questions.

The productivity of the system varies with different input texts but averages around 2 questions per input sentence. Future experiments with ranking systems will enable selection of the best questions from the pool of generated questions.

3   Question Types Produced by the System

Question forms created by the templates include: *why, how, where, what, when, who, list* and *describe* questions. Table 1 shows sample generated questions. Example 1 demonstrates the use of the ArgM-causation *because of their complex level of organization.* Example 2 matches the predicate-particle pattern *made up* to generate a *composition* question. Examples 3 and 4 show cases where a question can be generated from the QG tree but not from a predicate-argument approach alone, which requires two arguments [2]. By recognizing when prepositional phrases act as objects, the system is able to generate either *how* or *where* questions, depending upon the preposition. Example 5 utilizes the ArgM-purpose argument.

3.1   Fine-Grained Target Identification

The dependency parse, by virtue of the fact that it identifies relationships between individual words, can identify finer-grained targets for question generation than relying on syntactic constituents or semantic role labels alone. There are certain dependency relations that allow for very fine-grained questions, two of which are examined next.

The parataxis relation is between the main verb of a clause and another sentence element that is coordinate rather than subordinate, [8] as seen in this sentence: There are three types of muscle tissue: smooth muscle, skeletal muscle, and cardiac muscle. In this existential construction, the subject is *three types of muscle tissue*. The presence of the parataxis relation allows the generation of: Name the three types of muscle tissue.

The appositive relation also provides opportunities for questions as in the sentence: In 1767, Parliament passed the Townshend duties, a series of taxes on certain imported goods. The appositive relation makes it straightforward to ask the question: Describe the Townshend duties.

4   Evaluation

In prior work [15], we developed a question generator that used the predicate-argument parse view alone, and achieved a 44% reduction in the error rate compared to state-of-the-art systems. This earlier work, labeled Pred Arg in Table 2, is used as a baseline for the current work, labeled DP++ for dependency parse +ArgM +discourse cues. For source texts, we chose one Chemistry passage[2], which has 59 sentences representing one section of a textbook chapter, and one Economics passage[3], which has 42 sentences. All generated questions from each system were evaluated using Amazon's Mechanical Turk. Heilman and Smith [10] showed how satisfactory AMT evaluations can be achieved on this task by submitting work in small batches, and closely monitoring each batch. In this evaluation, each worker was presented a source sentence and a question generated from that sentence. Workers were asked to evaluate the quality of the question on a 1 - 3 scale, using the labels not acceptable, borderline acceptable, acceptable. Two workers evaluated each question. Workers were required to be native speakers of English and have acceptance rates of 95% or better. The inter-rater agreement between two sets of workers over all annotations was 74%, with a Pearson's correlation coefficient of 0.45, which indicates a strong positive relationship[4] and is statistically significant, $p < 0.001$.

---

[2] www.ck12.org

[3] www.sparknotes.com/economics/macro/money

[4] http://faculty.quinnipiac.edu/libarts/polsci/statistics.html

Table 2. Average Scores on 3-point Scale

	Pred Arg	DP++
Avg. Score	2.58	2.65
Reduction in Error Rate		17%

The DP++ system achieved a 17% reduction in the error rate (equation 1) relative to the prior question generator. In addition, the DP++ system has greater question variety than the predicate argument question generation system. No one question type has more than 5% of the output for the DP++ system, whereas three of the question types in the Pred Arg system account for 36% of the output. Further, the DP++ system generated 21% more questions with a semantic focus than did the Pred Arg system.

$$\frac{rating_{system2} - rating_{system1}}{maxPossibleRating - rating_{system1}} \times 100.0 \tag{1}$$

5   Error Analysis

The question generator has built-in processing to avoid generating some vague and problematic questions. For example, questions will not be generated if the subject contains no nouns (such as the subject *it*), or if the system detects a problem with the sentence structure, such as having no predicate. Analysis of questions that did not receive acceptable ratings showed that some were good questions, but involved uncommon technical terminology such as *velocity of money* that may have caused the workers to give them a low score. This leads to the observation that an ideal evaluation of automatically generated questions would be in the context of an authentic user study which is currently in the planning stages.

For the errors which are truly errors, 15% are attributable to parsing errors, while the rest indicate that further refinement of the templates is needed. These improvements include dealing with light verbs, and developing heuristics to decide whether or not to include adverbial modifiers. The most common parsing error observed was failure to discriminate between noun and verb forms of a word as in the sentence shown in Figure 3.

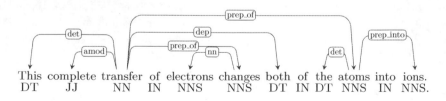

Fig. 3. Dependency Parse Error (*changes* as NNS)

6 Discussion

In this work we present a novel approach to automatic question generation which leverages multiple views of the text. There are many NLP tools that quickly and accurately parse sentences into different views, such as PSG trees, predicate argument structure, and dependency relations. There is no one view of a sentence that tells us everything we would like to know. This is one of the motivations for the current work which blends output from different parsers into a lexical-semantic QG tree structure that allows direct access to items of interest for question generation. This same structure could be useful for question understanding which is necessary in educational applications such as intelligent tutoring systems.

The results show that the dependency parse can provide a good foundation for question generation, particularly when combined with information from multiple sources. This initial version of the DP++ approach achieved a 17% reduction in the error rate compared with our previous work, which in turn achieved a 44% reduction in the error rate compared to prior state-of-the-art question generation systems. Further, the DP++ approach achieved greater question variety, and produced 21% more more questions with a semantic focus than our prior work which did not include information from the dependency parse.

Acknowledgments. This research was supported by the Institute of Education Sciences, U.S. Dept. of Ed., Grant R305A120808 to UNT. Opinions expressed are those of the authors.

References

1. Afzal, N., Mitkov, R.: Automatic generation of multiple choice questions using dependency-based semantic relations. Soft Computing **18**(7), 1269–1281 (2014). Springer
2. Agarwal, M., Shah, R., Mannem, P.: Automatic question generation using discourse cues. In: Proceedings of the 6th Workshop on Innovative Use of NLP for Building Educational Applications. Stroudsburg. PA, USA (2011)
3. Boyer, K., Piwek, P.: QG2010: The third workshop on question generation. In: International Conference on Intelligent Tutoring Systems. Carnegie Mellon University, Pittsburgh, PA (2010)
4. Cheong, H. and Shu, LH.: Automatic extraction of causally related functions from natural language text for biomimetic design. In: ASME 2012 International Design Engineering Technical Conferences and Computers and Information in Engineering Conference (2012)
5. Collobert, R., Weston, J., Bottou, L., Karlen, M., Kavukcuoglu, K., Kuksa, P.: Natural language processing (almost) from scratch. The Journal of Machine Learning Research **12** (2011)
6. Curto, S., Mendex, A., Coheur, L.: Question generation based on lexico-syntactic patterns learned from the web. Dialogue & Discourse **3**(2) (2012)
7. De Marneffe, M., MacCartney, B., Manning, C.: Generating typed dependency parses from phrase structure parses. In: Proceedings of LREC, vol. 6, (2006)

8. De Marneffe, M., Manning, C.: Stanford typed dependency manual (2008)
9. Heilman, M., Smith, N.: Good question! statistical ranking for question generation. In: Human Language Technologies: The 2010 Annual Conference of the North American Chapter of the Association for Computational Linguistics (2010)
10. Heilman, M., Smith, N.: Rating computer-generated questions with mechanical turk. In: Proceedings of the NAACL HLT 2010 Workshop on Creating Speech and Language Data with Amazon's Mechanical Turk (2010)
11. Jurafsky, D., Martin, J.: Speech and Language Processing, 2nd edn. Pearson (2009)
12. Kalady, S., Elikkottil, A., Das, R.: Automatic question generation using discourse cues. In: Proceedings of the 6th Workshop on Innovative Use of NLP for Building Educational Applications. Stroudsburg, PA, USA (2011)
13. Le, N., Kojiri, T., Pinkwart, N.: Automatic question generation for educational applications-the state of the art. Advanced Computational Methods for Knowledge Engineering 325–338 (2014)
14. Mannem, P., Prasad, R., Joshi, A.: Question generation from paragraphs at upenn: Qgstec system description. In: Proceedings of QG2010: The Third Workshop on Question Generation (2010)
15. Mazidi, K., Nielsen, R.D.: Linguistic considerations in automatic question generation. In: Proceedings of ACL, Baltimore, Maryland (2014)
16. Nivre, J.: Dependency grammar and dependency parsing. MSI report **5133**(1959), 1–32 (2005)
17. Olney, A., Graesser, A.C., Person, Nl: Question generation from concept maps. Dialogue & Discourse **3**(2), 75–99 (2012)
18. Pal, S., Mondal, T., Pakray, P., Das, D., Bandyopadhyay, S.: Qgstec system description-juqgg: A rule based approach. In: Proceedings of QG2010: The Third Workshop on Question Generation (2010)
19. Rus, Vasile, Cai, Zhiqiang, Graesser, Arthur C.: Experiments on generating questions about facts. In: Gelbukh, Alexander (ed.) CICLing 2007. LNCS, vol. 4394, pp. 444–455. Springer, Heidelberg (2007)
20. Rus, V., McCarthy, P.M., McNamara, D.S., Graesser, A.C.: A study of textual entailment. International Journal on Artificial Intelligence Tools **17**(04) (2008)
21. Wolfe, J.H.: Automatic question generation from text-an aid to independent study. ACM SIGCUE Outlook **10**(SI) (1976)
22. Wu, F., Weld, D.: Open information extraction using wikipedia. In: Proceedings of the 48th Annual Meeting of the Association for Computational Linguistics, pp. 118–127 (2010)
23. Yao, X., Zhang, Y.: Question generation with minimal recursion semantics. In: Proceedings of QG2010: The Third Workshop on Question Generation (2010)

Mind Wandering During Learning with an Intelligent Tutoring System

Caitlin Mills[1(✉)], Sidney D'Mello[1,2], Nigel Bosch[2], and Andrew M. Olney[3]

[1] Departments of Psychology, University of Notre Dame, Notre Dame, IN 46556, USA
{cmills4,sdmello}@nd.edu
[2] Department of Computer Science, University of Notre Dame, Notre Dame, IN 46556, USA
pbosch@nd.edu
[3] Institute for Intelligent Systems, University of Memphis, Memphis, TN 38152, USA
aolney@memphis.edu

Abstract. Mind wandering (zoning out) can be detrimental to learning outcomes in a host of educational activities, from reading to watching video lectures, yet it has received little attention in the field of intelligent tutoring systems (ITS). In the current study, participants self-reported mind wandering during a learning session with Guru, a dialogue-based ITS for biology. On average, participants interacted with Guru for 22 minutes and reported an average of 11.5 instances of mind wandering, or one instance every two minutes. The frequency of mind wandering was compared across five different phases of Guru (Common-Ground-Building Instruction, Intermittent Summary, Concept Map, Scaffolded Dialogue, and Cloze task), each requiring different learning strategies. The rate of mind wandering per minute was highest during the Common-Ground-Building Instruction and Scaffolded Dialogue phases of Guru. Importantly, there was significant negative correlation between mind wandering and learning, highlighting the need to address this phenomena during learning with ITSs.

Keywords: Mind wandering · Intelligent tutoring · Engagement · Attention

1 Introduction

Students do not always pay attention during learning. To make matters worse, it can be quite difficult to distinguish students who are concentrating intently from those who have completely zoned out [1]. Indeed, the phenomenon of zoning out might go particularly unnoticed in intelligent tutoring systems (ITS) and other advanced learning technologies that do not monitor lapses in attention. To date, many ITSs have focused on modeling a host of motivational and affective states, including types of engagement and disengagement (e.g., gaming the system, off-task behaviors) [2–5]. However, very little research has been done to uncover students' moment-to-moment level of attention, or lack thereof, a proposition we address in the current study.

Mind wandering is defined as an *involuntary* lapse in attention from task-related thoughts to internal task-unrelated thoughts [6]. Mind wandering is related to other "off-task" states, such as boredom, behavioral disengagement, and distractions

© Springer International Publishing Switzerland 2015
C. Conati et al. (Eds.): AIED 2015, LNAI 9112, pp. 267–276, 2015.
DOI: 10.1007/978-3-319-19773-9_27

[2, 7, 8], but is inherently distinct in that it is largely involuntary and that attention is directed towards internal self-generated thoughts that are unrelated to learning. Thus, mind wandering can be considered to be a form of attentional disengagement.

Emerging research suggests mind wandering occurs frequently during learning activities (see [9] for a review). For example, mind wandering occurs anywhere from 20-40% during reading and about 40% while viewing online lectures [1, 9, 10]. Mind wandering can also have negative consequences on learning [9, 10]. For example, information missed during episodes of mind wandering is not properly integrated into students' overall mental representations of a concept. Gaps in mental representations thus hinder the ability to make inferences and understand subsequent information that builds on earlier facts/concepts. For example, if a student is mind wandering when learning concepts such as, "folded chains of amino acids are proteins" or "enzymes are proteins" they might not be able to make the inference that "enzymes are folded chains of amino acids." To date, much of the research on mind wandering during learning has focused on non-interactive learning contexts, such as reading or lecture viewing. An open question pertains to the frequency of mind wandering when learning from more engaging technologies (ITSs, educational games) and whether mind wandering correlates with learning in these contexts? In this paper, we study mind wandering during interactions with an ITS.

In addition to studying overall rates of mind wandering, we are also interested in comparing mind wandering across the different types of ITS interactions. Some ITSs combine multiple teaching strategies, including modeling problems, scaffolding, quizzing, and so on. These strategies are inherently different from each other, involving different levels of overt student behavior. It is therefore possible that mind wandering will vary across the different types of activities in a single ITS. According to the Interactive-Constructive-Active-Passive (ICAP) hypothesis [11, 12], task types can be rank-ordered in terms of interactivity and effectiveness for learning (Interactive $\geq$ Constructive $\geq$ Active $\geq$ Passive). Whereas *passive* learning does not involve any overt behaviors (e.g., listening), *active* learning includes activities such as taking verbatim notes or reading. *Constructive* activities include summarizing, adding, and organizing ideas, while *interactive* activities include co-constructive learning situations that include dialogue.

An expansion of the ICAP hypotheses (called the ICAP-A or ICAP-Attention) predicts that mind wandering will follow the same pattern ($I \leq C \leq A \leq P$) based on the type of learning activity [13]. The ICAP-A hypothesis is based on theories of mind wandering that suggest that mind wandering occurs when the executive control system fails to suppress off-task thoughts when the appropriate level of goal construal (e.g., relevance) is not maintained [14]. Goal construal is more likely to be maintained during interactive and constructive learning activities (versus passive), thus facilitating attentional focus. In their review and re-analysis of the literature, student mind wandering indeed shifted as a function of the ICAP category [13]. This analysis included an array of learning activities, such as note-taking, video lectures, reading, and self-explanations [1, 15–18]. Although the ICAP-A hypothesis would posit that mind wandering might be deterred while using intelligent learning technologies, their analyses did not include any learning technologies, a proposition we consider in the current research. Using ICAP-A as our model, we investigate overall rates of mind wandering, as well as mind wandering rates during different ICAP activity types within a single ITS.

In addition to activity type, ICAP-A posits mind wandering is also influenced by top down influences. Therefore, it is possible that students' prior knowledge and topic interest might also affect attention during learning with an ITS [18, 19]. Low prior knowledge or low interest may be related to less concrete goal structures during learning, and likely more mind wandering since off-task thoughts have been linked to less concrete goals [14] However, it is also possible the increased level of interactivity afforded by an ITS will promote concrete goals, thus minimizing the importance of top down influences.

We attempt to address a gap in the literature by investigating mind wandering in the context of learning with an ITS for the first time. In the current study, students interacted with GuruTutor, a dialogue-based ITS that contains a broad range of ICAP task types at different phases of the system (discussed in detail below). Four research questions will be addressed based on student interactions with GuruTutor: (1) How often does mind wandering occur during learning? (2) How does mind wandering vary across different phases in the tutoring session that differ in interactivity? (3) How does mind wandering relate to learning in GuruTutor? (4) To what extent do trait level factors, such as interest and prior knowledge, relate to mind wandering?

2   Description of GuruTutor

Participants interacted with an ITS called GuruTutor in the current study. GuruTutor is modeled after expert-human tutors and is designed to teach students biology topics through collaborative conversations in natural language. In GuruTutor, an animated tutor agent engages the student in a natural-language conversation that references (with gestures) a multimedia workspace displaying and animating content that is relevant to the

Fig. 1. Example image from the *Common Ground Building* phase in GuruTutor

conversation (see Figure 1). GuruTutor analyzes student responses (which are typed into open dialog boxes) via natural language understanding techniques and maintains a student model used for tailoring the session to individual student's knowledge. For a more detailed description of GuruTutor, see [20, 21].

GuruTutor covers biology topics aligned with state curriculum standards, each taking 15 to 40 minutes to cover. Topics contain sets of interrelated concepts, e.g. *proteins help cells regulate functions*. GuruTutor attempts to get students to articulate each concept over a five phase session. GuruTutor begins with a brief preview making the topic concrete and relevant to the student before beginning the five phases. *Phase 1*: GuruTutor engages in a **Common-Ground-Building Instruction (CGB Instruction),** sometimes called collaborative lecture, where basic information and terminology is covered (this step is essential because biology involves considerable specialized terminology that needs to be discussed before more collaborative knowledge building activities can proceed). *Phase 2*: Students then generate natural-language **Intermittent Summaries (Summary)** of covered content, which are automatically analyzed to determine the concepts to target in the remainder of the session. *Phase 3*: For target concepts, students complete skeleton **Concept Maps** which are node-link structures that are automatically generated from concept text. *Phase 4*: Next students complete a **Scaffolded Dialogue**; GuruTutor uses a Prompt → Feedback → Verification Question → Feedback → Elaboration cycle to cover target concepts. A second Concept Mapping and Scaffolded Dialogue phase is initiated if students are having difficulty mastering particular concepts. *Phase 5*: A **Cloze** task requiring students to fill in an ideal summary by supplying key relations ends the tutorial session for a topic.

Importantly, GuruTutor is ideal for an investigation of mind wandering, as its five distinct phases vary in interactivity. In the context of GuruTutor, CGB Instruction is a combination of active and passive learning activity because it does not require constructive responses from the student other than responses to common ground questions (i.e., "do you understand") and forced-choice questions. Summary, Concept Map, and Cloze phases are all constructive activities, though perhaps not all equally constructive. For example, generating a summary is entirely constructive, whereas fill-in-blanks during the Cloze task are less constructive. Finally, Scaffolded Dialogue is only superficially interactive according to the requirements proposed by I-CAP. The tutor agent does not engage in co-construction by helping the student generate and revise answers, thus Scaffolded Dialogue is considered a combination of constructive, active, and passive (see [12] for an in-depth descriptions of the ICAP task types). The expected pattern of mind wandering in GuruTutor based on the ICAP-A hypothesis [13] is CGB Instruction > Scaffolded Dialogue > [Summary = Concept Map = Cloze Task].

3   Method

3.1   Participants and Design

Participants were 21 students from a Midwestern university in the U.S. Each participant received class credit for completing the study. The mean age was 20 years ($SD = 1$ year) and 85% were females. None of the participants were biology majors. Participants were randomly assigned to complete one of three biology topics in GuruTutor: biochemical catalysts, protein function, or carbohydrate function.

3.2   Materials and Procedure

Before interacting with GuruTutor, participants' interest in biology was measured with the following question: "How interested are you in learning about biology?" Participants responded by selecting a number on a 6-point scale between (1) *not at all interested* and (6) *very interested*.

Mind wandering was self-reported while students interacted with GuruTutor. Participants were given the following instructions regarding reporting mind wandering during GuruTutor: "Your primary task is to complete the learning session with Guru-Tutor in order to understand the biology topic." Participants were then explicitly instructed to report instances when they caught themselves mind wandering about anything unrelated to GuruTutor content. Thoughts generated from the content are not considered mind wandering. The following description of mind wandering, taken from previous studies [6, 22], was provided to the participants, "At some point during the tutoring session, you may realize that you have no idea what you just heard or saw. Not only were you not thinking about the topic, you were thinking about something else altogether." Participants indicated mind wandering by pressing a key labeled "ZONE OUT" on the keyboard. The instructions also emphasized that the participants should be as honest as possible when reporting mind wandering and that the results will have no influence on their performance or their progress in the study.

Participants completed a pretest in order to gauge prior knowledge on the assigned topic, followed by a self-paced learning session with GuruTutor, after which they answered a posttest. Pretest and posttest knowledge assessments were multiple choice tests consisting of at least 12 items, targeting shallow (factual knowledge) and deep knowledge (requiring inference). All questions were derived from either previously administered standardized tests or from the content of the CGB Instruction. Pre- and post-test questions were randomly selected by question type (shallow and deep) for each participant and the same question was never presented twice to the same student.

4   Results and Discussion

4.1   Overall Mind Wandering Rates

Mind wandering was reported a total of 363 times across the 21 participants while learning from GuruTutor. Analyses of mind wandering reports are limited to the five phases of GuruTutor where students are learning and do not include the time students spent on the pre and posttests. Two participants' volume of mind wandering reports as well as time spent in the learning session fell well outside the range of a normal distribution. The participants who reported 64 and 80 instances of mind wandering, greater than three standard deviations away from the mean, were removed from the analyses. Analyses proceeded with the remaining 19 participants who reported 219 instances of mind wandering.

On average, participants spent 22 minutes interacting with GuruTutor (not including the pre and posttests) and reported 11.5 ($SD = 8.60$) instances of mind wandering. We computed a mind wandering per minute (MW/Min) rate for each participant by dividing the total number of mind wandering reports by the number of minutes they interacted with GuruTutor. Participants reported mind wandering at a rate of .496 ($SD = .310$) reports per minute, or about one report every two minutes.

4.2   Mind Wandering Across Phases of GuruTutor

There were five phases of GuruTutor: lecture, summary, concept map, scaffolding, and cloze phase. A MW/Min rate was computed during each of the five phases for each participant. The CGB Instruction and Scaffolded Dialogue phases had the highest rates of mind wandering, while the cloze phase had the lowest (see Table 1 for descriptive statistics on mind wandering during each phase). In fact, over 90% of mind wandering reports occurred during the CGB Instruction and Scaffolded Dialogue phases combined.

A repeated measures ANOVA yielded significant differences in MW/Min rates based on phase, $F(4,68) = 7.67$, $p < .001$. The ANOVA included Phase was a within-subjects factor (5 levels) and biology topic was a between-subjects factor (3 levels) to address topic effects. There was no main effect of topic and no significant interaction between phase and topic so our discussion is limited to phase only.

Table 1. Means and standrad deviation (in parantheses) for mind wandering during each of the five phases in GuruTutor

	MW Per Minute	Avg. Prop. of MW Reports	Time Spent (Min)
CGB Instruction	.748 (.512)	.494 (.277)	7.31 (2.34)
Summary	.123 (.318)	.017 (.045)	1.87 (.782)
Concept Map	.202 (.322)	.059 (.088)	4.34 (1.67)
Scaffolded Dialogue	.670 (.498)	.422 (.278)	6.26 (2.98)
Cloze	.039 (.119)	.008 (.024)	2.53 (1.24)
Overall	.496 (.310)	-	22.3 (6.71)

Notes. Avg. Prop. = average propotion of participants' mind wandering reports during each phase;
MW = mind wandering

Pairwise comparisons were examined using a Bonferroni correction in order to account for multiple comparisons ($\alpha = .005$ or .05/10 since there were 10 comparisons). The pattern of results indicated that [Scaffolded Dialogue = CGB Instruction] > [Summary = Concept Map = Cloze]. This pattern partially confirmed predictions based on the ICAP-A hypothesis (predicted pattern: CGB Instruction > Scaffolded Dialogue > [Summary = Concept Map = Cloze Task]). Indeed, CBG Instruction, the most passive phase of GuruTutor, had significantly higher rates of mind wandering compared to each of the three constructive phases of GuruTutor (Concept Map, Cloze, Summary). The major inconsistency between the predicted pattern and observed results pertained to the rate of mind wandering during the Scaffolded Dialogue phase. Based on the ICAP-A hypothesis, Scaffolded Dialogue was predicted to have less mind wandering compared to CGB Instruction because of the constructive responses required by students and more evenly distributed dialogue turns between the tutor agent and student (6:1 dialogue turn ratio during the CBG and 3:1 during

Scaffolded Dialogue) [12, 21]. However, rates of mind wandering in Scaffolded Dialogue were statistically equivalent to the rates during CGB Instruction phase of GuruTutor. This was unexpected based on the contrast in constructive elements between Scaffolded Dialogue and CGB Instruction phases. However, despite differences in the phases, Scaffolded Dialogue and CGB Instruction phases had similar rates of mind wandering, which were individually higher than all other phases combined.

4.3   Relationship Between Mind Wandering and Learning

Participants' performance on the pretest and posttest were computed as the proportion of items answered correctly. A paired-samples t-test indicated that pretest ($M = .651$, $SD = .147$) and posttest scores ($M = .826$, $SD = .147$) were significantly different, $t(18) = 4.22$, $p < .001$, $d = 1.19$. Participants learned from interacting with GuruTutor, supporting findings from previous studies [21].

We correlated number of mind wandering reports with posttest scores. In order to account for prior knowledge and time, we computed partial correlations controlling for pretest performance and time spent in GuruTutor. Indeed, mind wandering was strongly and negatively related to learning, $r(15) = -.566$, $p = .018$. This finding replicates the negative relationship between mind wandering and performance across a range of learning activities [9, 10].

4.4   Individual Differences that Predict Mind Wandering

We also examined the relationship between mind wandering and two trait level factors: prior knowledge (pretest score) and interest. We correlated number of mind wandering reports with pretest score and participants' interest ratings taken before GuruTutor. Partial correlations were computed to control for time spent in GuruTutor. Although the correlations were not significant, mind wandering was correlated with both pretest ($r = -.233$, $p = .367$) as well as interest ($r = -.291$, $p = .257$) in the expected negative direction. It is also important to note that given this relatively small sample size, correlations with learning and trait level variables may be particularly sensitive to outliers and non-normal distributions. However, examinations of histograms and scatter plots alleviated these concerns.

5   General Discussion

Mind wandering is a ubiquitous phenomenon that is common during learning (e.g., during reading and online video lectures) and that is negatively related to learning outcomes [1, 9, 22, 23]. Given the paucity of research on mind wandering during interactive learning environments, the current study investigated mind wandering in the context of learning with an ITS for the first time.

Main Findings. In the present study, students reported mind wandering about once every two minutes while interacting with GuruTutor, a dialogue-based ITS modeled after expert human tutors [21]. This frequency of mind wandering, combined with the significant negative relationship with learning, highlights a concern for this phenomenon in the context of ITSs.

Results also suggest that mind wandering occurs at different rates depending on the type of learning activity (i.e. ICAP activity type). Based on the ICAP-A hypothesis, the following pattern was predicted for mind wandering in GuruTutor: CGB Instruction > Scaffolded Dialogue > [Summary = Concept Map = Cloze Task]. However, results indicated the Scaffolded Dialogue and CGB Instruction phases had similar rates of mind wandering, suggesting the constructive conversation in the Scaffolded Dialogue phase of GuruTutor did not deter mind wandering. One explanation for the deviation from the predicted pattern is that Scaffolded Dialogue and CGB Instruction were the longest phases in GuruTutor, and time on task has been correlated with mind wandering [24]. Additionally, participants were not exposed to Scaffolded Dialogue until about 9 minutes ($SD = 3$) into the session. The delayed onset in combination with the length of the phase ($M = 6$ min, $SD = 3$) may also have influenced participants' level of attention, as a previous study also found participants were more likely to report mind wandering during the second half of an online lecture [1].

Limitations. It is important to note the limitations of this study. For one, this was a lab study. Investigating mind wandering during learning with an ITS in more ecological settings, such as a classroom is an important next step. Second, this investigation was limited to a single ITS, so future work is needed to determine if mind wandering rates are comparable across ITSs. Another related limitation is that the order of phases in GuruTutor was constant across all participants. Therefore, differences in mind wandering based on phase should be interpreted with caution, due to issues such as carryover effects, time on task, and fatigue. Finally, analyses were limited to 19 participants, so replication with a larger sample is warranted.

Future Work. ITS research provides new ways of investigating levels of interactivity in relation to the ICAP/ICAP-A hypotheses, since we can precisely manipulate the qualities of the dialogue to bring it closer or further away from co-construction, while otherwise keeping it superficially interactive. For example, this could be done through modifications to GuruTutor through revising longer answers/summaries.

Additionally, future research may include other ways of measuring mind wandering. In the current study, mind wandering reports were collected using self-caught reports compared to responding to periodic thought probes during learning (e.g., Are you zoned out right now?). We chose the self-caught method of mind wandering for this initial investigation, as it is not limited by the placement of thought probes, thereby limiting the places and number of instances of mind wandering that can be recorded. However, this method only captures mind wandering reports that involved some level of metacognitive awareness. Thus future work should also investigate mind wandering in the context of learning with an ITS using other methods of to collect mind wandering reports, such as via thought-probes.

Future work should also consider behavioral/physiological indicators of mind wandering, via eye tracking or physiological measurements. Previous work has demonstrated success in predicting instances of mind wandering using eye tracking and peripheral physiology in the context of reading [25, 26]. Therefore, it is feasible that additional measures could aid in developing a more fine-grained models of mind wandering during learning with ITSs. Combining information about task factors (current phase) and trait-level factors (student interest) with physiological measures and eye tracking could be an initial step towards predicting when a learner begins to mind wander. Interventions may then be put into place to restore attentional focus to the learning task. This paper provides a foundation for this avenue of research by systematically studying mind wandering during learning with an ITS.

Acknowledgments. This research was supported by the National Science Foundation (NSF) (DRL 1235958) and Institute of Education Sciences (IES), U.S. Department of Education (DoE), through Grant R305A080594. Any opinions, findings and conclusions, or recommendations expressed in this paper are those of the authors and do not necessarily reflect the views of NSF, IES, or DoE.

References

1. Risko, E.F., Anderson, N., Sarwal, A., Engelhardt, M., Kingstone, A.: Everyday attention: variation in mind wandering and memory in a lecture. Applied Cognitive Psychology **26**, 234–242 (2012)
2. Baker, R.S.J.: Modeling and understanding students' off-task behavior in intelligent tutoring systems. In: Proceedings of the SIGCHI conference on Human factors in computing systems, pp. 1059–1068 (2007)
3. Calvo, R.A., D'Mello, S.: Affect detection: An interdisciplinary review of models, methods, and their applications. IEEE Transactions on Affective Computing **1**, 18–37 (2010)
4. Forbes-Riley, K., Litman, D.: When Does Disengagement Correlate with Performance in Spoken Dialog Computer Tutoring? International Journal of Artificial Intelligence in Education **22**, 39–58 (2013)
5. Baker, R.S.J., D'Mello, S.K., Rodrigo, M.M.T., Graesser, A.C.: Better to be frustrated than bored: The incidence, persistence, and impact of learners' cognitive–affective states during interactions with three different computer-based learning environments. International Journal of Human-Computer Studies **68**, 223–241 (2010)
6. Smallwood, J., Schooler, J.W.: The restless mind. Psychological bulletin **132**, 946 (2006)
7. Beck, J.E.: Using response times to model student disengagement. In: Proceedings of the ITS2004 Workshop on Social and Emotional Intelligence in Learning Environments, pp. 13–20 (2004)
8. Drummond, J., Litman, D.: In the zone: towards detecting student zoning out using supervised machine learning. In: Aleven, V., Kay, J., Mostow, J. (eds.) ITS 2010, Part II. LNCS, vol. 6095, pp. 306–308. Springer, Heidelberg (2010)
9. Smallwood, J., Fishman, D.J., Schooler, J.W.: Counting the cost of an absent mind: Mind wandering as an underrecognized influence on educational performance. Psychonomic Bulletin & Review. **14**, 230–236 (2007)
10. Szpunar, K.K., Moulton, S.T., Schacter, D.L.: Mind wandering and education: from the classroom to online learning. Frontiers in psychology **4** (2013)
11. Chi, M.: Active-constructive-interactive: A conceptual framework for differentiating learning activities. Topics in Cognitive Science **1**, 73–105 (2009)
12. Chi, M., Wylie, R.: The ICAP Framework: Linking Cognitive Engagement to Active Learning Outcomes. Educational Psychologist. **49**, 219–243 (2014)

13. Olney, A., D'Mello, S., Risko, E.F., Graesser, A.C.: Attention in educational contexts: the role of the learning task in guiding attention. In: Fawcett, J., Risko, E.F., Kingstone, A. (eds.) The Handbook of Attention. MI Press, Cambridge, MA, (in press)

14. Kane, M.J., Brown, L.H., McVay, J.C., Silvia, P.J., Myin-Germeys, I., Kwapil, T.R.: For whom the mind wanders, and when an experience-sampling study of working memory and executive control in daily life. Psychological science. **18**, 614–621 (2007)

15. Moss, J., Schunn, C.D., Schneider, W., McNamara, D.S.: The nature of mind wandering during reading varies with the cognitive control demands of the reading strategy. Brain research. **1539**, 48–60 (2013)

16. Sousa, T.L.V., Carriere, J.S., Smilek, D.: The way we encounter reading material influences how frequently we mind wander. Frontiers in psychology **4** (2013)

17. Young, M.S., Robinson, S., Alberts, P.: Students pay attention! Combating the vigilance decrement to improve learning during lectures. Active Learning in Higher Education. **10**, 41–55 (2009)

18. Lindquist, S.I., McLean, J.P.: Daydreaming and its correlates in an educational environment. Learning and Individual Differences. **21**, 158–167 (2011)

19. Grodsky, A., Giambra, L.M.: The consistency across vigilance and reading tasks of individual differences in the occurrence of task-unrelated and task-related images and thoughts. Imagination, Cognition and Personality. **10**, 39–52 (1990)

20. Olney, A., Person, N.K., Graesser, A.C.: Guru: designing a conversational expert intelligent tutoring system. Cross-Disciplinary Advances in Applied Natural Language Processing: Issues and Approaches, pp. 156–171 (2012)

21. Olney, A.M., D'Mello, S., Person, N., Cade, W., Hays, P., Williams, C., Lehman, B., Graesser, A.: Guru: a computer tutor that models expert human tutors. In: Cerri, S.A., Clancey, W.J., Papadourakis, G., Panourgia, K. (eds.) ITS 2012. LNCS, vol. 7315, pp. 256–261. Springer, Heidelberg (2012)

22. Feng, S., D'Mello, S., Graesser, A.C.: Mind wandering while reading easy and difficult texts. Psychonomic bulletin & review 1–7 (2013)

23. Smallwood, J.: Mind-wandering while reading: Attentional decoupling, mindless reading and the cascade model of inattention. Language and Linguistics Compass **5**, 63–77 (2011)

24. Thomson, D.R., Seli, P., Besner, D., Smilek, D.: On the link between mind wandering and task performance over time. Consciousness and cognition. **27**, 14–26 (2014)

25. Bixler, R., D'Mello, S.: Toward fully automated person-independent detection of mind wandering. In: Dimitrova, V., Kuflik, T., Chin, D., Ricci, F., Dolog, P., Houben, G.-J. (eds.) UMAP 2014. LNCS, vol. 8538, pp. 37–48. Springer, Heidelberg (2014)

26. Blanchard, N., Bixler, R., Joyce, T., D'Mello, S.: Automated physiological-based detection of mind wandering during learning. In: Trausan-Matu, S., Boyer, K.E., Crosby, M., Panourgia, K. (eds.) ITS 2014. LNCS, vol. 8474, pp. 55–60. Springer, Heidelberg (2014)

DeepStealth: Leveraging Deep Learning Models for Stealth Assessment in Game-Based Learning Environments

Wookhee Min[✉], Megan H. Frankosky, Bradford W. Mott, Jonathan P. Rowe,
Eric Wiebe, Kristy Elizabeth Boyer, and James C. Lester

Center for Educational Informatics, North Carolina State University, Raleigh, NC 27695, USA
{wmin,rmhardy,bwmott,jprowe,wiebe,keboyer,lester}@ncsu.edu

Abstract. A distinctive feature of intelligent game-based learning environments is their capacity for enabling stealth assessment. Stealth assessments gather information about student competencies in a manner that is invisible, and enable drawing valid inferences about student knowledge. We present a framework for stealth assessment that leverages *deep learning*, a family of machine learning methods that utilize deep artificial neural networks, to infer student competencies in a game-based learning environment for middle grade computational thinking, ENGAGE. Students' interaction data, collected during a classroom study with ENGAGE, as well as prior knowledge scores, are utilized to train deep networks for predicting students' post-test performance. Results indicate deep networks that are pre-trained using stacked denoising autoencoders achieve high predictive accuracy, significantly outperforming standard classification techniques such as support vector machines and naïve Bayes. The findings suggest that deep learning shows considerable promise for automatically inducing stealth assessment models for intelligent game-based learning environments.

Keywords: Game-based learning environments · Stealth assessment · Deep learning · Computational thinking · Educational games

1 Introduction

Recent years have witnessed growing interest in intelligent game-based learning environments, which simultaneously provide adaptive pedagogical functionalities delivered through intelligent tutoring systems and engaging learning experiences afforded by digital games [1–3]. A key benefit of game-based learning environments is their ability to embed problem-solving challenges within interactive virtual environments, which can enhance students' motivation [4] and facilitate learning through customized narratives and feedback [5, 6].

Stealth assessment is a pedagogical process, enabled by digital games, that involves real-time, invisible measurement of students' learning processes and outcomes. In game-based learning environments, stealth assessments have the potential to draw valid inferences about student competencies in an invisible and non-disruptive manner [6]. Stealth assessment is methodologically grounded in evidence-centered

© Springer International Publishing Switzerland 2015
C. Conati et al. (Eds.): AIED 2015, LNAI 9112, pp. 277–286, 2015.
DOI: 10.1007/978-3-319-19773-9_28

design, and models typically consist of three components: a competency model, an evidence model, and a task model [6, 7]. A *competency model* represents students' knowledge and skills, which are modeled probabilistically. An *evidence model* identifies how observations of students' learning behaviors reveal student competencies on different skills and knowledge. A *task model* characterizes the challenges with which students interact, thereby producing evidence to infer the student's competency levels. Stealth assessments offer the potential to dynamically identify gaps in student knowledge, enabling personalized learning while simultaneously preventing students from "gaming the system" [5, 8]. With stealth assessments in place, it is possible for game-based learning environments to effectively diagnose student competencies and thus adaptively scaffold skill development, remediate misconceptions, and discourage behaviors that are not conducive to learning.

A key challenge posed by current stealth assessment techniques is manually devising models that enable valid inferences about student knowledge and skills. To address this challenge, we propose DeepStealth, a stealth assessment framework that leverages *deep learning* to automatically induce predictive models of student competency based on student interaction data. Deep learning is a family of machine learning methods that utilize deep artificial neural networks to model hierarchical representations of data for prediction tasks [9]. An empirical evaluation conducted with the ENGAGE game-based learning environment for middle grade computational thinking demonstrates that DeepStealth significantly outperforms support vector machines and naïve Bayes models at predicting students' competency levels (post-test performance on knowledge) under 10-fold cross validation. The results suggest that the DeepStealth approach holds significant promise for competency modeling in stealth assessment.

2   Related Work

Intelligent game-based learning environments seek to increase learners' motivation through rich settings, engaging characters, and compelling plots, and they foster learning through tailored scaffolding and context-sensitive feedback. Narrative-centered learning environments have been found to deliver experiences in which learning and engagement are synergistic [5]. Recent work in game-based learning has been undertaken for a broad range of subject matters ranging from high school mathematics [10] to language learning [3].

Intelligent game-based learning environments can support many forms of knowledge assessment. Shute proposed Bayesian network-based competency models, utilizing them in the context of stealth assessment [6]. Quellmalz and colleagues proposed an approach using simulation-based assessment, which was found to effectively assess science learning and inquiry practices [11]. Factor analysis techniques, such as performance factor analysis and matrix/tensor factorization, have been investigated for student performance prediction for knowledge assessment and problem-solving assessment [12, 13]. Bayesian knowledge tracing has been widely explored to assess latent knowledge and skills in the context of cognitive modeling [14]. The approach presented here is the first to utilize deep learning techniques [9] to assess students' competency and performance levels within a technology-rich learning environment.

3   ENGAGE Game-Based Learning Environment

ENGAGE is an immersive game-based learning environment for middle school computer science education, built with the Unity game engine and FLARE user interface toolkit [15]. The curriculum underlying ENGAGE is based on the AP Computer Science Principles course [16] with learning objectives that are developmentally appropriate for U.S. middle school students (ages 11-13). The ENGAGE learning environment was designed to expose students to problems that encourage the development of computational thinking. Computational thinking is a problem-solving process that involves abstraction and algorithmic thinking, and leverages computational tools for data analysis, modeling, or simulations [17]. Additionally, the problem-solving activities within ENGAGE are designed to increase interest in computer science and provide a foundation for more advanced computer science work in high school.

In ENGAGE, students play the role of the protagonist who has been sent to a research facility to determine why all communication with the station has been lost. As students explore the research facility, they progress through each level, which consists of a series of interconnected rooms. Each room presents students with a set of computational challenges they solve by programming devices located in the room. Devices are programmed using a visual programming interface in which "blocks" that represent program elements are dragged and stacked together to create programs. Students interact with a cast of non-player characters who offer clues and relevant details via dialogue. The narrative is advanced through cinematics and learning is scaffolded by dialogue hints and animated vignettes.

The work presented in this paper focuses on students' problem-solving activities within ENGAGE's Digital World unit, which focuses on investigating how binary sequences are used to represent digital data. In one set of problem-solving activities, students must find the binary representation of a base-ten number to activate a lift device (Figure 1, left), which requires students to review an existing program for the lift device (Figure 1, right) to determine what base-ten number activates the lift, as well as to understand the concept of bits in binary numbers and the weight assigned to each bit. Students read the program using the visual programming interface, flip binary tiles on the lift device (the white squares at the top of the lift device in Figure 1, left) to change the binary sequence until it matches the base-ten number specified in

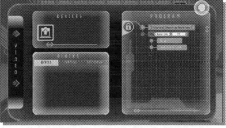

Fig. 1. (Left) A lift device with an existing program, and (Right) the programming interface displaying the lift's program

the program (Figure 1, right), and then stand on the lift device and execute its program, which allows them to jump to a previously inaccessible area of the room. Students are provided immediate feedback on the base-ten number interpretation of the binary sequence as they flip tiles on the lift device through a display above the binary sequence (e.g., 31 in Figure 1, left). In later parts of the level, the function that converts the binary sequence to a base-ten number is corrupted and students must correct the weights associated with each bit before executing the program.

During gameplay, students complete 16 problem-solving activities. Eleven activities involve matching binary sequences with base-ten numbers, and five activities involve correcting weights of bits. Four key features are logged from these problem-solving interactions. The features include the number of binary tile flips, the number of binary tile double flips (a binary tile flipped and then immediately flipped again), the number of times the device programs are executed, and the amount of time students spent in the programming interface. Since the tasks can be solved in a brute-force manner without understanding the binary representation of numbers or the programs that control the devices, it is important to be able to dynamically assess students' competency levels on binary representation.

In this work, we analyze the interaction data from 49 students (28 male, 21 female) from a teacher-led deployment of ENGAGE in two public middle school classrooms. Students interacted with ENGAGE over several weeks in their science class. Prior to beginning the unit, and immediately following the unit, students completed online pre- and post-test assessments measuring cognitive skills, computer science attitudes, and subject knowledge (e.g., binary representation). We investigated whether students achieved improvements in content knowledge from the Digital World, and a paired t-test comparing pre-test (M=0.42, SD=0.23) to post-test (M=0.63, SD=0.25) indicated that students' learning gains were statistically significant with a large effect size, $t(48) = 6.22, p < .001, d = .89$.

4   Feature Engineering: Problem-Solving Strategy Identification

In this section, we present a clustering analysis, which was conducted as a precursor to training deep learning models for stealth assessment. We anticipate that clustering on students' interaction data has the potential to identify distinct problem-solving strategies that students employed during ENGAGE's binary number learning activities. We hypothesize that clustering can serve as a form of automated feature engineering, producing strategy cluster features that enhance the predictive performance of the deep learning-based competency model. To perform the clustering analysis, we utilized expectation maximization (EM) [18] on the four features from the game interaction logs described in Section 3.

EM clustering was conducted on 49 students' interaction data with standardized features, where the number of clusters was automatically chosen to maximize the log-likelihood of the data based on 10-fold cross validation. We found three student clusters that reflected distinct differences in students' problem-solving strategies. We also conducted an after-clustering analysis to examine normalized learning gains of each individual cluster [19]. All significance tests were performed using the Wilcoxon signed-rank test.

Cluster 1 containing 31 students (63%) included the most efficient problem solvers. These students comprised the highest performing group, with averaged normalized learning gains of 0.40. This group had significantly lower number of flips and double flips, and low program reading time compared to the other two clusters (all with $p<.01$). These results indicate that this group easily acquired concept knowledge, understood program meaning, and as a result were able to solve the binary challenges in the most principled way among the three groups.

Students in Cluster 2, 12% (6 students), and Cluster 3, 24% (12 students), differed along one principal dimension. Cluster 2 had a significantly higher number of double flips than Cluster 3 ($p=0.01$) while conducting a similar number of single flips ($p=0.84$). This difference could indicate that Cluster 2 may have reevaluated the problem by leveraging a guess-and-check strategy. Cluster 3 did not use a double flip strategy indicating that they may have been randomly flipping tiles to solve the problem. Overall, the number of program executions did not differ between clusters, indicating that each group only differed in the way that they prepared a solution to the problem, and not in the number of times they submitted an answer to the problem. With respect to averaged normalized learning gains, students in Cluster 2 and Cluster 3 achieved 0.26 and 0.20, respectively.

This clustering analysis suggests that each group exhibited distinctive patterns of interaction while solving the computational challenges. Because problem-solving strategies are related to students' learning processes, as evidenced by observed differences in normalized learning gains across groups, it appears that it may be possible to utilize students' problem-solving strategy clusters as inputs to deep learning-based competency models to improve their predictive performance. Next, we describe an automated stealth assessment framework that uses the clustering results as input, and we evaluate their benefit.

5   Stealth Assessment Leveraging Deep Learning

In this section, we first describe how our work is framed in evidence-centered design to support stealth assessment from the three model perspectives.

- *Competency Model:* We assess students' competency levels on knowledge about binary representation. We run cross validation tests to evaluate the model's performance based on actual labels from students' post-test performance.
- *Evidence Model:* Students' knowledge about binary representation can be revealed through their interactions during gameplay. These interactions are characterized by the four features described in Section 3. Also, the three problem-solving strategies discussed in Section 4 as well as the students' pre-test scores on the knowledge assessment, cognitive skill, and computer science attitude are considered as evidence.

- *Task Model:* We use 16 problem-solving tasks that have an objective of either "finding binary representations" or "correcting weights" in ENGAGE. Students' interactions on these tasks produce evidence that informs competency models to assess students' knowledge about binary representation.

Prior to training a predictive model for inferring students' competency, each student's data is labeled with their post-test performance, based on a tertile split ('A', 'B', or 'C') with respect to post-test scores in knowledge assessments, and thus the prediction is cast as a three-class classification that predicts one's performance.

Three input feature sets are considered to evaluate the impact of the engineered feature, strategy, as evidence: 1) the raw feature set (RF) based on the four features logged from interactions in the game, 2) the strategy feature set (SF) based on the strategy captured from the clustering, and 3) the combined feature set (CF) leveraging both RF and SF, and are independently analyzed to measure impacts of the features. These feature sets also include external learning measures, such as pre-test scores on knowledge, cognitive skills, and computer science attitudes, which are accessible and promising as predictors when reasoning competencies during the game-based learning activities.

The current work on competency modeling employs deep learning (DL), which learns hierarchical representations through multi-layer abstraction of data, often in the context of artificial neural networks [9]. One specific type of DL leverages *pre-training* that initializes weights in deep neural architectures [9, 20] with the objective of minimizing the reconstruction error of the original input. The pre-training process has been shown to help find a region of parameter space that can reach a better local optimum in a non-convex optimization graph, without which training deep neural networks often becomes hard to optimize due to underfitting and vanishing/exploding gradient problems [9]. After pre-training, models can be fine-tuned with standard optimization methods such as stochastic gradient descents to perform classification or regression tasks. DL based techniques have proven very successful in achieving state-of-the-art performance on a wide range of machine learning tasks [9].

We utilize DL with a pre-training technique, stacked denoising autoencoders (SDAEs) [20], for competency modeling. We describe the SDAE technique, as well as autoencoders (AEs), a basic form of SDAEs. An autoencoder (AE) is a pre-training technique that features (1) encoding (f) that deterministically maps (W_1) an input vector (x) into a hidden representation $f(x)$ using a non-linear transformation characterized by an activation function, s (Equation 1) and (2) decoding (g) that maps (W_2) the hidden representation $f(x)$ back to $g(f(x))$, a reconstructed vector of the input vector (x), using s (Equation 2). The objective in AEs is on learning representations (W_1 and W_2) along with two bias terms (b_1 and b_2) by minimizing the reconstruction error between x and $g(f(x))$ through backpropagation methods (e.g., stochastic gradient descent) using an unsupervised criterion.

$$f(x) = s(W_1 x + b_1). \tag{1}$$

$$g(f(x)) = s(W_2 f(x) + b_2). \tag{2}$$

Stacked denoising autoencoders (SDAEs) extend AEs from two perspectives. First, deep neural networks can be pre-trained by stacking layers of AEs (stacked autoencoders). Second, SDAEs hypothesize that effective representations should be able to robustly recover corrupted inputs into the uncorrupted original inputs (denoising) [20]. The first objective can be achieved using layer-wise pre-training, which is a technique to pre-train the entire network using an iterative process, from the first to last layer. For example, once the first layer is pre-trained based on the reconstruction criterion, the output from the first layer is fed as the input to the next layer, and then the second layer can be pre-trained in the same manner. On the other hand, to achieve the latter objective, SDAE performs a corruption process by injecting noise (we set random neurons to 0) into the original input vector (x), as illustrated in Figure 2. In this method, the input vector x is partially corrupted into x' based on the corruption level that defines the probability of corrupting input neurons. Then, x' is deterministically mapped to $f(x')$ via an encoding process, and $f(x')$ is recovered to $g(f(x'))$ via a decoding process following standard AEs. A key difference in SDAE is that the objective function is to minimize the reconstruction error (L) between the uncorrupted input x and the decoded output based on the corrupted input, $g(f(x'))$, interpreted as denoising corrupted inputs. As a result, SDAEs provide benefits over AEs by effectively dealing with noisy input data utilizing denoising techniques and preventing weights from reaching a trivial solution (identity matrix) that could cause overfitting in prediction tasks [20]. As noted above, once pre-training of the entire network is completed, all the initialized weights from pre-training can be fine-tuned using a supervised criterion.

As in other machine learning techniques, selecting hyperparameters for DL and a corruption level (fraction of corrupted input neurons) for SDAE often must be empirically determined. In this work, on the one hand, we explore the model space using a grid search of some parameters such as the corruption level (0.02, 0.1, or 0.5), the number of hidden layers (3–5), and the input feature set (Raw, Strategy, or Combined). On the other hand, we have fixed the following parameters: the number of neurons per hidden layer (50), the gradient descent optimization method (stochastic gradient descent), the learning rate (0.1), the activation function (sigmoid), the loss criterion (mean square error), and the number of epochs for gradient descent learning (100). Input to DL is encoded with 70 neurons (64 raw features, 6 pre-test scores), 9 neurons (3 strategy features, 6 pre-test scores), or 73 neurons (64 raw features, 3 strategy features, 6 pre-test scores) based on the feature set that the model utilizes, RF, SF, and CF, respectively, while every model has 3 output neurons ('A', 'B', and 'C') for the predicted post-test performance.

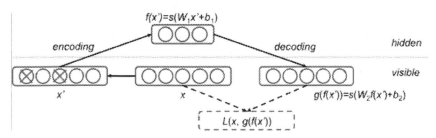

Fig. 2. Illustration of stacked denoising autoencoders; red crosses denote corruption [20]

6   Empirical Evaluation

We evaluate how accurate our predictive competency models are using 10-fold student-level cross validation. Similar to the method applied to SDAEs, we run a grid search for choosing support vector machines' (SVMs) hyperparameters, and the model that achieves the highest accuracy rate is selected according to cross validation results. This work examines two hyperparameters that are popularly explored for optimization: the penalty parameter (C) and gamma (γ) for SVMs with a radial basis function [21]. C is chosen from {1, 10, 100}, and γ is chosen from {0.005, 0.01, 0.1, 0.5, 1.0}. For naïve Bayes (NB) models, we use non-parametric kernel density estimation, since our training data does not necessarily follow a normal distribution.

Table 1. Averaged accuracy rates of the highest performing NB, SVM, and DL[1]

	NB	SVM	DL
Raw Feature Set (RF)	53.5%	56.5%	65.5%
Strategy Feature Set (SF)	51.0%	55.0%	55.0%
Combined Feature Set (CF)	53.5%	56.5%	**71.5%**

Model evaluation is performed along two dimensions. In the first evaluation, we train models based on the three machine learning techniques (NB, SVM, DL) along with all adjustable parameters and evaluate models' predictive performance using 10-fold cross validation. From the results, we choose the model that achieves the highest average accuracy rate per pair of machine learning approach and feature set (Table 1). In cross validations, all models use the same split of the training and validation set for pairwise comparisons. Overall, the highest performing DL model (the number of hidden layers: 3, corruption level: .02, combined feature set) achieves 71.5% accuracy rate, which significantly outperforms both the highest performing models from NB and SVM (C=1, γ=0.005) as well as the majority class baseline (36.7%).

For additional analyses, we run the Friedman test with a post hoc analysis with Wilcoxon signed-rank tests to compare high performing models. The Friedman test indicates there is a statistically significant difference in accuracy rates depending on the models, χ^2 (2)=6.93, p=.03. The Wilcoxon signed-rank post hoc tests indicate the DL model elicits statistically significant improvements in accuracy rates over the SVM model (Z=-2.06, p=.04) and the NB model (Z=-2.25, p=.02), but SVM vs. NB does not constitute a statistically significant difference.

In the second evaluation, by aggregating fold-based validation accuracies and conducting Wilcoxon tests, we measure the impact of each parameter used in DL, such as input feature set types, corruption levels, and the number of layers (Table 2). DL models that leverage CF utilizing both RF and SF obtain the highest average accuracy rate. The Wilcoxon signed-rank test indicates that there is not a statistically significant difference

---

[1] With respect to DL's runtime performance, a prediction takes 0.3 milliseconds on average for 3 hidden layer models on the test machine with a 2.7 GHz Intel Core i7 CPU and 8 GB RAM.

between CF-based models and RF-based models (Z=-1.69, p=.09). However, CF shows promise as a strong predictor set by achieving both the highest performance across models (Table 1) and the highest average performance across parameter settings (Table 2). This result demonstrates that the performance of DL can be further improved by taking advantage of human-engineered features, while SVMs and NBs seem to not easily benefit from the additional information in this evaluation.

Table 2. Parameter-wise SDAE model evaluation (left: feature set as the independent variable (IV), middle: corruption level as IV, right: number of layers as IV)

Feature Set	Accuracy Rate	Corruption Level	Accuracy Rate	Num. of Layers	Accuracy Rate
Raw (RF)	60.7%	0.02	57.8%	3	57.9%
Combined (CF)	**62.8%**	**0.1**	**58.2%**	4	56.4%
Strategy (SF)	49.5%	0.5	57.2%	**5**	**58.2%**

7   Conclusions and Future Work

This paper has introduced DeepStealth, a novel stealth assessment framework based on deep learning, which shows considerable promise for accurately assessing learners' competency levels. Using data from classroom studies with a game-based learning environment for middle grade computational thinking, we conducted an empirical evaluation that found that DeepStealth, which uses deep learning models with stacked denoising autoencoders, significantly outperforms baseline approaches, including naïve Bayes models and support vector machines, as well as the majority class baseline. Moreover, results suggest that the performance of deep learning in DeepStealth can be further improved when utilizing engineered features through deep learning's pre-training and fine-tuning process. In the future, it will be important to investigate how much the external learning measures (i.e., pre-test scores) contribute to the competency model's performance beyond game interaction logs, explore other deep learning techniques that can effectively deal with evidence with variant lengths, and examine parameter and hyperparameter optimization techniques for improved performance. Together, these techniques may be able to further improve deep learning-based approaches to stealth assessment.

Acknowledgments. This research was supported by the National Science Foundation under Grant CNS-1138497. Any opinions, findings, and conclusions expressed in this material are those of the authors and do not necessarily reflect the views of the National Science Foundation.

References

1. Lester, J., Ha, E., Lee, S., Mott, B., Rowe, J., Sabourin, J.: Serious games get smart: Intelligent game-based learning environments. AI Magazine **34**(4), 31–45 (2013)
2. Jackson, T., McNamara, D.: Motivation and Performance in a Game-based Intelligent Tutoring System. Journal of Educational Psychology **105**(4), 1036–1049 (2013)

3. Johnson, L.: Serious use of a serious game for language learning. International Journal of Artificial Intelligence in Education **20**(2), 175–195 (2010)
4. Garris, R., Ahlers, R., Driskell, E.: Games, motivation, and learning: a research and practice model. Simulation & Gaming **33**(4), 441–467 (2002)
5. Rowe, J., Shores, L., Mott, B., Lester, J.: Integrating learning, problem solving, and engagement in narrative-centered learning environments. International Journal of Artificial Intelligence in Education **21**(2), 115–133 (2011)
6. Shute, V.: Stealth assessment in computer-based games to support learning. Computer games and instruction **55**(2), 503–524 (2011)
7. Mislevy, R., Steinberg, L., Almond, R.: On the structure of educational assessment. Measurement: Interdisciplinary research and perspective **1**(1), 3–62 (2003)
8. Baker, R., Corbett, A., Koedinger, K., Wagner, A.: Off-task behavior in the cognitive tutor classroom: when students game the system. In: SIGCHI conference on Human factors in computing systems, pp. 383-390 (2004)
9. Bengio, Y.: Learning deep architectures for AI. Foundations and Trends in Machine Learning **2**(1), 1–127 (2009)
10. Kebritchi, M., Hirumi, A., Bai, H.: The effects of modern mathematics computer games on mathematics achievement and class motivation. Computers & Education **55**(2), 427–443 (2010)
11. Quellmalz, E., Timms, M., Silberglitt, M., Buckley, B.: Science assessments for all: Integrating science simulations into balanced state science assessment systems. Journal of Research in Science Teaching **49**(3), 363–393 (2012)
12. Sahebi, S., Huang, Y., Brusilovsky, P.: Predicting student performance in solving parameterized exercises. In: Trausan-Matu, S., Boyer, K.E., Crosby, M., Panourgia, K. (eds.) ITS 2014. LNCS, vol. 8474, pp. 496–503. Springer, Heidelberg (2014)
13. Min, W., Rowe, J.P., Mott, B.W., Lester, J.C.: Personalizing embedded assessment sequences in narrative-centered learning environments: a collaborative filtering approach. In: Lane, H., Yacef, K., Mostow, J., Pavlik, P. (eds.) AIED 2013. LNCS, vol. 7926, pp. 369–378. Springer, Heidelberg (2013)
14. Corbett, A., Anderson, J.: Knowledge tracing: Modeling the acquisition of procedural knowledge. User Modeling and User-Adapted Interaction **4**(4), 253–278 (1994)
15. Mott, B., Rowe, J., Min, W., Taylor, R., Lester, J.: FLARE: an open source toolkit for creating expressive user interfaces for serious games. In: the 9th International Conference on the Foundations of Digital Games (2014)
16. AP® Computer Science Principles Draft Curriculum Framework: 2014. http://www.csprinciples.org/. accessed: 2014-09-05
17. Barr, V., Stephenson, C.: Bringing Computational Thinking to K-12: What is Involved and What is the Role of the Computer Science Education Community? ACM Inroads **2**(1), 48–54 (2011)
18. Fraley, C., Raftery, A.: How many clusters? Which clustering method? Answers via model-based cluster analysis. The computer journal **41**(8), 578–588 (1998)
19. Marx, J., Cummings, K.: Normalized change. American Journal of Physics **75**(1), 87–91 (2007)
20. Vincent, P., Larochelle, H., Lajoie, I., Bengio, Y., Manzagol, P.: Stacked denoising autoencoders: Learning useful representations in a deep network with a local denoising criterion. The Journal of Machine Learning Research **11**, 3371–3408 (2010)
21. Keerthi, S., Lin, C.: Asymptotic behaviors of support vector machines with Gaussian kernel. Neural computation **15**(7), 1667–1689 (2003)

Learning Mental Models of Human Cognitive Processing by Creating Cognitive Models

Kazuhisa Miwa[1]([⊠]), Nana Kanzaki[2], Hitoshi Terai[1], Kazuaki Kojima[3], Ryuichi Nakaike[4], Junya Morita[1], and Hitomi Saito[5]

[1] Nagoya University, Nagoya 464-8601, Japan
miwa@is.nagoya-u.ac.jp
[2] College of Nagoya Women's University, Nagoya 467-8610, Japan
[3] Teikyo University, Utsunomiya 320-8551, Japan
[4] Kyoto University, Kyoto 606-8501, Japan
[5] Aichi University of Education, Kariya 448-8542, Japan

Abstract. We investigated how creating cognitive models enhances learners' construction of mental models on human cognitive information processing. Two class practices for undergraduates and graduates were performed, in which participants were required to construct a computational running model of solving subtraction problems and then develop a bug model that simulated students' arithmetic errors. Analyses showed that by creating cognitive models, participants learned to identify buggy procedures that produce systematic errors and predict expected erroneous answers by mentally simulating the mental model. The limitation is that this benefit of creating cognitive models was observed only in participants who successfully programmed a computational model.

Keywords: Cognitive models · Production system · Mental model

1 Introduction

Cognitive modeling has assumed a central role in investigating the human mind. The model-based approach is a primary methodology, in cooperation with the experimental approach, in cognitive science. Many cognitive scientists have used computational models as research tools for in-depth understanding of the human mind. The authors have examined functions of cognitive modeling as a learning tool, and proposed the learning by the creating cognitive models paradigm [7]. Fum et al. indicated three advantages of computational cognitive modeling: clarity and completeness, better exploration and evaluation, and serendipity and emergence [5]. We believe that these functions may provide students the opportunity to learn more about human cognitive information processing.

Rule-based modeling is a traditional framework that many cognitive scientists have approved. Several standard production system architectures have been developed, including the ACT-R [1] and Soar [11], as advanced technical tools for expert cognitive scientists. We have developed a web-based production system architecture for novice users, called "DoCoPro," based on the server and

© Springer International Publishing Switzerland 2015
C. Conati et al. (Eds.): AIED 2015, LNAI 9112, pp. 287–296, 2015.
DOI: 10.1007/978-3-319-19773-9_29

client model for educational use [9]. Learners can use DoCoPro by simply accessing the server through standard web browsers without any preparation, such as installing the architecture itself along with related software. Additionally, we have performed cognitive science class practices using DoCoPro.

Previous studies have confirmed that creating cognitive models improves learners' theory-based thinking. The semantic network theory [13] and the dual storage theory on the human memory system [8] were examined. The studies revealed that students more actively explained experimental data from the theoretical perspectives by creating cognitive models through simulating the experimental results.

A conceptual model as a theory predicts only abstract and qualitative experimental results. Therefore, it is impossible for a theory to correspond directly with data. Computational models that are embodied as computer programs predict specific experimental results and enable researchers to verify the theories that underlie the models based on a direct comparison of results of computer simulations and human experiments. This function as a mediator connecting a theory and data contributes to the improvement of students' theory-based thinking.

In this paper, we explore another benefit of learning by creating cognitive models. People tend to construct a mental model of an object they understand [14]. A mental model is a structural, behavioral, or functional analog representation of a real-world or imaginary situation, event, or process [10]. A mental model can be manipulated and draw expectations on target phenomenon; thus, allowing people to predict hypothesized situations by such mental simulations.

Thought experiments are believed to have played decisive roles in the discoveries of Einstein's theory of relativity and Maxwell's equations of electromagnetism[10]. These thought experiments are likely considered as qualitative mental simulations, implying that understandings based on mental models and expectations from mental simulations have been crucial in historic scientific discoveries. Additionally, the importance to support learners' mental model construction has been recognized in educational contexts.

In this paper, we investigate how creating cognitive models enhances learners' construction of mental models on human cognitive information processing. This topic is crucial in teacher education because instructors need to understand students' cognitive information processing. If they accurately identify students' cognitive status and find errors in their operation, they are able to properly repair their mental bugs. Our insight is that creating cognitive models may contribute to the construction of such mental models.

Subtraction problems are the task used in the current study. Procedural knowledge for such arithmetic problems has been confirmed as well-formalized rule-based knowledge representation. In many standard textbooks, rule-based models for solving subtraction problems are widely taken up as subjects for introducing the basics of production system modeling (e.g., [6] [1]). Undergraduates and graduates at the university education level can easily solve standard subtraction problems; however, they may experience difficulty describing the knowledge used in calculation because the knowledge is procedural and is automatically executed without conscious step-by-step operations. To construct mental models that can be manipulated in mental simulations, the knowledge should be explicitly externalized.

Brown and Burton (1978) assembled a list of typical bugs that elementary students are inclined to make and demonstrated that almost all miscalculation can be accounted for based on a single bug, or combinations of multiple bugs [3]. Similarly, in the current experiments, participants are required to identify students' bugs in their operation from their error cases. To do so, participants must construct mental models of students' cognitive information processing. To code rules for calculation, participants must segment and formalize operations in calculating arithmetic problems. We expect that, through the process, they will learn to construct more accurate mental models.

2 Cognitive Models

2.1 Cognitive Models for Subtraction Problems

Participants constructed cognitive models for solving subtraction problems through three steps. In the first step, participants programmed a basic model that solved problems without processing for borrowing a carry from the left column. Next they implemented an advance model that solved problems involving a column with an upper row digit smaller than the lower digit. To program the model, they needed to implement processing for borrowing a carry from the next left column with a top digit that was not zero. Finally, participants implemented a complete model that solved problems that involved a column with an upper row digit of zero. They needed to program complex processing for borrowing a carry from a removed column across zero columns.

To process a carry from the left column, the following rules were added to the basic model:

- IF a goal is LeftCarry THEN shift a focus to the left column, and set a goal to GetCarry.
- IF a goal is GetCarry, the top number at the focused column is not zero THEN subtract one from the top number, shift a focus to the right column, and set a goal to PutCarry.
- IF a goal is PutCarry, the focused column reached the column requiring the answer THEN add ten to the upper number of the focused column, and set a goal to FindDifference.

To construct the complete model that processed a column with an upper row digit of zero, the following rules were added:

- IF a goal is GetCarry, the top number at the focused column is zero THEN set a goal to LeftCarry.
- IF a goal is PutCarry, the focused column did not reach the column requiring the answer THEN add ten to the upper number of the focused column, and set a goal to GetCarry.

2.2 Bug Model

After implementing the complete model, a model with a bug in the rule set was introduced. The implemented bug was a typical error that is often made by students who begin to learn subtraction problems. When borrowing a carry from the left column with a top digit of zero, they replaced zero with nine at the column but did not continue borrowing from the next left column whose top number was not zero. See Figure 2(a) for confirming typical behaviors of the buggy model.

The bug was simulated by replacing the above rule with the following buggy procedure:

- IF a goal is GetCarry, the top number at the focused column is zero THEN replace zero at the focused column with nine, shift a focus to the right column, and set a goal to PutCarry.

3 Class Activities

3.1 Learning System

Figure 1 demonstrates an example of a screenshot of the user interface of the learning system. All information is displayed in a single window. The production rules displayed on the right side of the window can be directly manipulated (e.g., editing, inserting, deleting, and sorting) without a text editor. The contents of the working memory are displayed in the upper-center window and system messages appear in the lower-center window. Participants can understand the processing of the model through observing updates of the working memory by applying production rules to the working memory.

In the upper-left window, the focused columns are identified: the blue-colored column requires an answer, and the red-colored column is to be focused for borrowing a carry. In the lower-left window, the goal structure is presented; the red-colored circle is a current goal to be achieved. Participants simulated the process of solving a subtraction problem while confirming the goal transition and focused columns on this window.

3.2 Participants

We performed two class practices for evaluation. In the first practice, 20 undergraduate students from the Nagoya University's School of Informatics and Sciences participated as part of an introductory cognitive science class.

The second practice was performed after the analysis of the first class practice was completed replicating results of the first practice. As part of an advanced cognitive science class, the second practice comprised 16 graduates from the Graduate School of Information Science in Nagoya University.

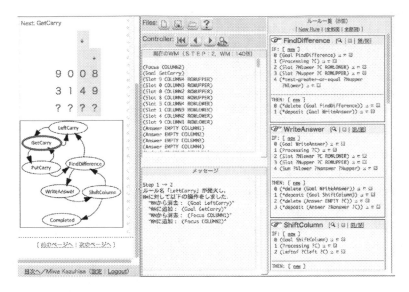

Fig. 1. An example screenshot of user interface of learning system

3.3 Class Overview

The following describes the participants' activities performed in the undergraduate class. The activities in the graduate class were almost the same as those in the undergraduate class. During the class introduction, the participants implemented a production system model that rearranged blocks on a table. Through the introduction, the participants learned the basics of production system programming and understood how to operate the system.

The first class included a 20-minute pre-test and was followed by the participants implementing the basic model to solve problems without borrowing from a column. The model consisted of four rules. A teacher lectured how to program rules by illustrating the coding for an example, which was the first rule. The participants coded the other three rules by themselves: two rules by filling in slots of templates given by the tutoring system and one rule by themselves without the system's supports. The students had their models solve a three-digit subtraction problem without borrowing and tested the model's behavior. The total learning time was 60 minutes.

In the second class, the participants implemented the advanced model to solve problems by borrowing a carry from the left column. First, the participants examined their mental operation for solving the advanced problem by monitoring their own thinking process of how to process a carry. In the initial stage, a constraint of problems, i.e., the top number at each column was not zero, was assured. The participants implemented four rules, three of which are illustrated in 2.1.

Finally, the participants added two rules, one of which is illustrated in 2.1, for constructing the complete model that solved any problem including those with

```
  9008     806303      9008     806303
 -3149    -182465     -3149    -182465
  5959     623938      3969     623748
    (a) isomorphic        (b) transfer
```

Fig. 2. Isomorphic and transfer problems in the identification task

a top digit of zero and tested the model's behavior by having the model solve an eight-digit subtraction problem. The total learning time was 90 minutes.

In the third class, the participants constructed the bug model to simulate the error illustrated in 2.2. The bug model was embodied by replacing one of the nine rules of the complete model with the buggy rule. A teacher provided the participants a hint for constructing the buggy model, such as the error can be simulated by replacing one of the rules of the complete model with a buggy rule. The total learning time was 40 minutes. A post-test was performed after the learning session.

3.4   Pre- and Post-tests

Two types of tasks were presented in the pre- and post-tests. In the identification task, the participants were required to infer erroneous procedures based on sample wrong answers and described those in the natural language. Two buggy procedures were identified: the identical bug as implemented in the learning phase (isomorphic problem), and a new bug that the participants did not learn (transfer problem). The error in the transfer problem was as follows: If the top digit of the focused column is zero, then reach a possible column to the left across zero columns from which a carry is borrowed and return back across zero columns to the current column at which the answer is required. Figure 2 demonstrates two examples in each of the isomorphic and transfer problems presented to the participants.

Descriptions by the participants were scored on a scale from zero to two points. A buggy rule that the participants identified as correct scored as two points. A buggy rule that was incorrect and which the participants tried to explain the wrong answers based on a unified rule scored as one point. If no rules or individual cases of the wrong answers were described, the point was scored as zero. The average score of two problems was used for evaluation.

The other task was the replication task, for which the participants were required to predict wrong answers drawn by each of the two buggy procedures identified in the identification task. Two problems were used: 708-139 and 900600803-123732349. The predicted answers were: 669 and 786968554 by the identical bug, and 479 and 587778364 by the new bug.

If a predicted answer is correct, the point is scored as one or if it is incorrect, the point is scored as zero. The sum of the scores of the two problems is used for evaluation.

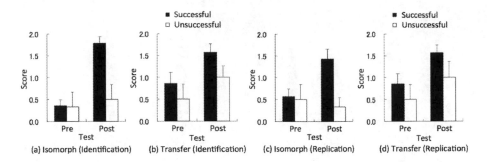

Fig. 3. Pre- and post-test scores of identification and replication tasks in undergraduate practice

In the graduate practice, only the identification task was performed for replicating the results in the undergraduate practice.

4   Results

In the undergraduate practice, we divided the participants into one group consisting the successful group, in which the participants successfully constructed the bug model in the learning phase and another group, the unsuccessful group, in which they did not. Fourteen participants comprised the successful group and six participants comprised the unsuccessful group.

4.1   Identification Task in Undergraduate Practice

The left side of Figure 3 demonstrates the results of the isomorphic and transfer problems in the identification task. In the isomorphic problem, a mixed 2 (test: pre and post, within) x 2 (participant: successful and unsuccessful, between) ANOVA indicated significant main effects of both the test and participant factor ($F(1, 18) = 18.75$, $p < .01$; $F(1, 18) = 6.99$, $p < .05$) and also revealed a significant interaction between the two factors ($F(1, 18) = 11.73$, $p < .01$). There was a significant simple main effect of the test factor of the successful participants ($F(1, 18) = 30.07$, $p < .01$) but not of the unsuccessful participants ($F < 1$, n.s.).

In the transfer problem, the same ANOVA revealed only a main effect of the test factor ($F(1, 18) = 6.07$, $p < .05$) but revealed neither a main effect of the participant factor ($F(1, 18) = 2.11$, n.s.) nor an interaction between the two factors ($F < 1$, n.s.).

4.2   Replication Task in Undergraduate Practice

The right side of Figure 3 demonstrates the results in the replication task. A mixed 2 (test: pre and post, within) x 2 (participant: successful and unsuccessful, between) ANOVA indicated a significant interaction between the two factors

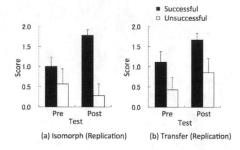

Fig. 4. Pre- and post-test scores of replication tasks in graduate practice

$(F(1, 18) = 5.45, p < .05)$. The main effect of the participant factor indicated marginal significance $(F(1, 18) = 4.14, \text{p} = 0.057)$, but the main effect of the test factor did not $(F(1, 18) = 2.48, \text{n.s.})$. There was a significant simple main effect of the test factor of the successful participants $(F(1, 18) = 7.64, p < .05)$ but not of the unsuccessful participants $(F < 1, \text{n.s.})$.

In the transfer problem, the same ANOVA revealed only a main effect of the test factor $(F(1, 18) = 10.76, p < .01)$ but revealed neither a main effect of the participant factor $(F(1, 18) = 1.87, \text{n.s.})$ nor an interaction between the two factors $(F < 1, \text{n.s.})$.

4.3   Replication Task in Graduate Practice

We performed the same analysis for the results in the graduate practice. In the graduate practice, nine participants comprised the successful group and seven participants comprised the unsuccessful group.

Figure 4 demonstrates the results. A mixed 2 (test: pre and post, within) x 2 (participant: successful and unsuccessful, between) ANOVA indicated a significant interaction between the two factors $(F(1, 14) = 6.94, p < .05)$. The main effect of the participant factor indicated significance $(F(1, 14) = 9.96, p < .01)$, but the main effect of the test factor did not $(F(1, 14) = 1.49, \text{n.s.})$. There was a significant simple main effect of the test factor of the successful participants $(F(1, 14) = 7.42, p < .05)$ but not of the unsuccessful participants $(F(1, 14) = 1.00, \text{n.s.})$.

In the transfer problem, the same ANOVA revealed significant main effects of both the test and participant factor $(F(1, 14) = 8.99, p < .01; F(1, 14) = 4.91, p < .05)$, but there was no significant interaction $(F < 1, \text{n.s.})$.

4.4   Summary of the Results

The two class practices revealed consistent results. In the isomorphic problems, the successful participants who completed constructing the bug model revealed learning effects in both the identification and replication tasks, but the unsuccessful participants did not. In the transfer problem, the main effect of the test factor reached significance, revealing learning gains through the model construction. There was no significant difference between the successful and unsuccessful participants.

5 Discussion and Conclusions

The computer simulation method is widely used in science education for enabling students to learn more by constructing sophisticated mental models [4] [12]. A few practices allow students to learn scientific issues by creating a running computer simulation model. For example, Borkulo confirmed that students who learned the global warming system by constructing a simulation model and observing simulations solved complex problems more accurately than those who learned through traditional text books [2]. In this paper, we expanded this method by including sciences of the human mind.

Overall results support the conclusion that students who successfully constructed a computational model for simulating the bug learned to understand procedural knowledge of arithmetic problems and performed mental simulations with such identified knowledge. We confirmed this effect in the transfer problem, meaning that such participants constructed adaptive mental models that can be applied to various arithmetic problems, generalizing a few specific learning cases. This result indicates that for successful participants who have abilities for constructing models, creating cognitive models contributes to sophisticated construction of mental models on human mental operations.

In contrast, the unsuccessful participants who could not construct a computational model for simulating the bug did not reveal consistent results. In the isomorphic problem, the unsuccessful participants did not gain learning effects but increased their score from the pre- to post-test similar to the successful participants in the transfer problem. Both bugs in the isomorphic and transfer problems can be simulated by replacing a single rule of the complete model with a buggy procedure, but performing mental simulations with a buggy procedure in the transfer problem might be easier than simulations in the isomorphic problem.

Various factors may determine the effects on mental model construction, such as complexity of bugs, difficulties of problems, and steps of simulations. In this paper, we confirmed only a specific case, leaving detailed examination to primary future work.

Why does creating cognitive models contribute to mental model construction? Understanding procedural knowledge relates to meta-cognitive activities. To characterize such activities, two dimensions are decisively important: monitoring either memory or processing and either ongoing or retrospective activities.

When constructing cognitive models for arithmetic tasks, participants have to understand what procedures underlie the solution processes of a specific task. They are expected to be led to focus on their own cognitive processing to understand such processes. Therefore, the meta-cognition that we intended to focus on in this manuscript is monitoring on-going cognitive processing. When creating cognitive models, learners are guided to monitor their thinking processes for formalizing knowledge based on the rule description framework to run on computers. Such formalization may elaborate their knowledge and promote mental model construction.

References

1. Anderson, J.R.: Rules of the Mind. Lawrence Erlbaum Associates Inc., Publishers (1993)
2. van Borkulo, S.P., van Joolingen, W.R., Savelsbergh, E.R., de Jong, T.: What can be learned from computer modeling? comparing expository and modeling approaches to teaching dynamic systems behavior. Journal of Science Education Technology **21**, 267–275 (2012)
3. Brown, J.S., Burton, R.R.: Diagnostic models for procedural bugs in basic mathematical skills. Cognitive Science **2**, 155–192 (1978)
4. De Jong, T., van Joolingen, W.R.: Scientific discovery learning with computer simulations of conceptual domains. Review of Educational Research **68**, 179–201 (1998)
5. Fum, D., Missier, F.D., Stocco, A.: The cognitive modeling of human behavior: Why a model is (sometimes) better than 10,000 words. Cognitive Systems Research **8**, 135–142 (2007)
6. Klahr, D., Langley, P., Neches, R.: Production System Models of Learning and Development. MIT Press (1987)
7. Miwa, K., Morita, J., Nakaike, R., Terai, H.: Learning through intermediate problems in creating cognitive models. Interactive Learning Environments **22**, 326–350 (2014)
8. Miwa, K., Morita, J., Terai, H., Kanzaki, N., Kojima, K., Nakaike, R., Saito, H.: Use of a cognitive simulator to enhance students' mental simulation activities. In: Trausan-Matu, S., Boyer, K.E., Crosby, M., Panourgia, K. (eds.) ITS 2014. LNCS, vol. 8474, pp. 398–403. Springer, Heidelberg (2014)
9. Nakaike, R., Miwa, K., J., M., Terai, H.: Development and evaluation of a web-based production system for learning anywhere. In: Proceedings of 17th International Conference on Computers in Education, pp. 127–131 (2009)
10. Nersessian, N.: Creating Scientific Concepts. MIT press (2008)
11. Newell, A.: Unified theories of cognition. Harbard University Press (1990)
12. Rutten, N., van Joolingen, W.R., van der Veen, J.T.: The learning effects of computer simulations in science education. Computers & Education **58**, 136–153 (2012)
13. Saito, H., Miwa, K., Kanzaki, N., Terai, H., Kojima, K., Nakaike, R., Morita, J.: Educational practice for interpretation of experimental data based on a theory. In: Proceedings of 21th International Conference on Computers in Education, pp. 234–239 (2013)
14. Vosniadou, S., Brewer, W.F.: Model based learning as a key research area for science education. International Journal of Science Education **18**, 123–183 (1994)

A Player Model for Adaptive Gamification in Learning Environments

Baptiste Monterrat[1,2] (✉), Michel Desmarais[3], Élise Lavoué[4], and Sébastien George[5]

[1] Woonoz company, 69009 Lyon, France
baptiste.monterrat@liris.cnrs.fr
[2] Université de Lyon, CNRS, INSA-Lyon, LIRIS, UMR 5205, 69621 Lyon, France
[3] Polytechnique Montréal, Montréal, Canada
michel.desmarais@polymtl.ca
[4] Magellan, IAE Lyon, Université Jean Moulin Lyon 3, Lyon, France
elise.lavoue@univ-lyon3.fr
[5] LUNAM Université, Université du Maine, EA 4023, LIUM 72085 Le Mans, France
sebastien.george@univ-lemans.fr

Abstract. Many learning environments are swiftly abandoned by the learners, even if they are effective. Gamification is as a recent game-based learning approach that can enhance the learners' motivation. However, individual expectations and preferences towards game-like features may be very different from one person to another. This paper presents a model to adapt gamification features according to a player profile of the learners. Two version of this model are evaluated within a gamified online learning environment. The first version comes from experts' judgment, and the second one is induced from empirical data. Our experiments confirm that the first version can be efficient to predict the player's preferences among the gamification features.

Keywords: Gamification · Adaptation · Web-based learning · Motivation · Player model

1   Introduction

Research in the field of game-based learning aims at making the learning activities more fun and more engaging for the users by proposing two main approaches: learning games and gamification. Learning games, often named "serious games", refer to the use of games for learning purposes [1]; gamification relies instead on game design elements embedded in a learning environment to foster student motivation [2]. Turning the learning environment into a serious game requires a complete redesign, which could be very expensive and time consuming. In this paper, we focus on gamification in order to integrate gaming features in already existing learning environments.

More specifically, we address the problem of motivation in a web-based learning environment within which the learner is guided by the system. In this type of environment, the absence of a human tutor often causes a lack of learner's interest.

© Springer International Publishing Switzerland 2015
C. Conati et al. (Eds.): AIED 2015, LNAI 9112, pp. 297–306, 2015.
DOI: 10.1007/978-3-319-19773-9_30

Our approach relies on gamification where we integrate game mechanics to existing learning environments, such as scoreboards, rewards, and other fun features. This approach is generally easier to realize than to turn the whole learning experience into a game.

The word "gamification" has been introduced in early 2010. This approach is used in various fields such as marketing, health, and crowdsourcing. In this work we are interested in the use of gamification in education [3]. Games have always been used for learning, but the arrival of the gamification perspective brought major changes in the way we study games for learning. Some even consider gamification as a new educational theory [4], alongside of behaviorism, cognitivism, constructivism and connectivism.

Gamification has been proven to be effective in numerous situations [5], but little is known about adaptivity for gamification. Most gamified systems integrate the game elements under a "one size fits all" approach, without means to adapt the learning process or the learning environment. Whereas it has long been recognised than individualised learning is much more efficient than classroom learning [6], we believe the same principles are at stake in gamification: one means of gamifying does not fit to all users.

The research question studied in this paper is the following: "How to adapt the game elements of a learning environment to learners according to their player types?" A review of gamification and player models for adaptation is presented is section 2. The model we propose for adaptive gamification is presented in section 3. Section 4 presents two experimental evaluations of various versions of the model. One model is based on human expertise, and the others rely on empirical data. Section 5 concludes on the validity of the experts based model.

2   Gamification and Player Profiles

In this section we first review common gamification elements, and then review various player profiles by which adaptation can be derived. Finally we study adaptation techniques and models that can help to relate the gamification elements with the player profiles factors.

2.1   Gamification Elements

Game elements are at the core of gamification and they can be categorized from the more abstract to the more concrete ones. Deterding *et al.* [2] propose five levels of abstraction. The game design methods come first, e.g. playtesting. Secondly come the game models like engagement loops and feedback loops. At the third level are the game design principles and heuristics, including setting clear goals and a variety of game styles. One of the most popular principle relies on the balance between challenge and player skills in order to reach the state of flow [7]. At the fourth level are the game mechanics such as the use of time constraints, points systems, and limited resources. Finally, those game mechanics are reified by interface elements. Among the most common game elements are the following:

- Points counter
- Badges (trophies symbolizing a task accomplishment)
- Leaderboards

Those elements rely on quantifying the user's activity in order to reward it. In this paper we place adaptation on the game mechanics level. We will refer to "game features" as a game mechanic emerging from one or more user interface elements. As an example, a game feature can be a points counter associated with some badges to reward a given score.

2.2   Player Typologies

Players generally have favorite types of games, and they feel engaged with some game mechanics but not all of them. Bartle's classification in four player types [8] is well known (*killer, achiever, explorer, socializer*), but it does not reflect diversity of player types that has been highlighted in several works more recently. For example, Yee [9] identifies three main motivational components (*achievement, social interaction and immersion*). A review of player types studies by Ferro *et al.* [10] distinguishes five player types (*dominant, objectivist, humanist, inquisitive* and *creative*). As they focus on personalized gamification (rather than games), they relate player types directly to game elements and mechanics. One of the most recent contributions in this area is the BrainHex gamer typology [11]. This classification includes seven player types based on insights from neurological findings: *seeker, survivor, daredevil, mastermind, conqueror, socializer* and *achiever*. Contrary to previous typologies, the BrainHex one is not related to a specific game genre like MMORPG. In addition, it is backed by an online survey that was taken by more than 60,000 players. For these reasons, we selected this classification as a player model for an adaptive gamification.

2.3   Adaptation of Games and Gamification

Adaptation in Games. A review of sixteen game adaptation techniques designed between 2002 and 2009 [12] focused on both entertainment games and serious games. A large majority of these techniques adjusts the difficulty level of the activity under various forms: they adapt the opponent's behavior, the game speed, the scenario or the feedback, mostly with the intent to prevent the game from being too difficult or too easy. The rest of the works studied in this review propose a generic adaptation of game parameters values according to player satisfaction, or adapt the learning part of the games rather than the gaming part.

Only one study addresses the difference in the game mechanics by proposing a scenario adapted to the personality of the players: the work of Natkin et al. [13]. The personality types are based on the Five-Factor Model (ibid.), and are used to select diverse quests for the players, like defeating other players or solving puzzles. Their system allows the use of various game dynamics for various players. We aim at applying a similar approach to existing learning environments by using game features instead of quests.

Models for Gamification. The adaptation of gamification is still in its infancy, but some models identify the concepts we can rely on. In order to adapt game features to players, we need to establish their links with the a player typology. Robinson and Bellotti [14] present one of the first taxonomies of gamification elements. They are classified in 6 categories, such as social elements and status information. Sailer [15] proposes a list of game elements and describes their links to various motivational concepts. These two contributions help understanding how the game features can influence player motivation, but do not show how to relate them to player profiles.

Zichermann and Cunningham [16] propose to use the MDA model (Mechanics, Dynamics, Aesthetics) developed by Hunicke *et al.* [17]. In this framework, mechanics refer to game elements in the user interface. Dynamics are at a higher level of abstraction, they refer to the interactions between the mechanics and the player. Finally, aesthetics describe the emotional response of the player to the experienced dynamics. This framework can help to relate game features to dynamics, and then to link the dynamics to the players who are receptive to those emotions. However, introducing more levels of abstraction between the game features and the player may multiply the risk of mistakes.

In this paper we propose a method to relate directly the game features to player types, without considering intermediate concepts.

3   Player Model for Adaptive Gamification

Our approach to the adaptive interface of the learning environment relies on two separate engines developed independently, one for the didactic content adaptation and the other for the gamification adaptation [18]. The didactic adaptation takes into account the learner's knowledge state, whereas the gamification adaptation takes into account a gamer profile based on the BrainHex classification. The didactic content engine chooses the items to present to the learner, whereas the gamification engine adapts the interface game features displayed on the interface. In this paper, we only focus on the gamification engine. The game features are implemented in such a way as to be toggled on or off independently of the didactic content engine and the general workflow.

3.1   Player Adaptation Model

In order to adapt the game features to the learner profile, we need a model to estimate the quality of fit of the game features to a player/student profile. We developed a model that estimates the preference for a feature by a weighted sum of personality traits, which bears similarities to existing learner models that predict student success based on a linear or boolean combination of skills [19].

Assume a matrix $\mathbf{B}$ of size $m \times k$ that represents the k traits of m users, and a matrix $\mathbf{A}$ of size $k \times n$ that represents the weights of the k for each of the n game features. Then, the product of these two matrices represents the expected preferences of the m users for the n game features: $\mathbf{R} = \mathbf{B}\,\mathbf{A}$.

	f1	f2	f3
u1	10	00	05
u2	00	06	12
u3	06	03	09
u4	-08	03	02

=

	C	S
u1	10	00
u2	00	12
u3	06	06
u4	-08	06

x

	f1	f2	f3
C	1	0	½
S	0	½	1

Fig. 1. An example of linear model **R = B A**. This example comprises 4 users (u1-u4), 3 game features (f1-f3) and a 2-factors player model: competition (C) and social (S).

An example of this simple linear model is given in Figure 1. The preferences of users *u1* to *u4* for features *f1* to *f3* are the product of the users' score over two traits, competitor (*C*) and socializer (*S*), and the weights of each trait for the three different features. For example, for *f3*, the C trait has a 0.5 weight and the S trait a weight of 1. Taking the scores of u4 on these respective traits yields the following result for f3: 0.5 x -8 + 1 x 6 = 2. Taking the vector of scores for u4 indicates that feature f1 is proscribed with a value of -8, whereas features f2 and f3 have a relatively close score of 2 and 3 respectively.

Figure 1 example contains only two traits. In this work, we use the BrainHex gamer profile, which contains 7 traits as explained in section 2.2. This model allows a player to be represented on this vector of traits with values in the range [-10, 20]. Therefore, the **B** matrix for our study has 7 columns and the negative values are values over the traits can result in negative values in matrix **R**, which are indicative of a feature misfit which can result in a negative motivational impact.

3.2 Estimating Matrix A

Whereas matrix **B** can be directly obtained from the answers to the BrainHex questionnaire over the 7 traits of the gamer profile, matrix **A** must be derived by some other means. Two such means are considered in this study:

Human Expert Derived (1). The BrainHex traits were designed within the space of gaming motivational factors. Therefore, it becomes relatively straightforward for an expert to intuitively estimate what motivational factors can be involved in some of the features, such as the *socializer* type who will strive for features that allows interaction with other users, or the *conqueror* who will prefer features that can provide a measure of progress towards some end.

Empirically derived from observed data (2). If a matrix **R** can be obtained either by some means to measure the preference of students for the features, or through observation or through direct questioning, and that the **B** matrix is provided by the BrainHex questionnaire, then the matrix **A** can be estimated by the least squares method through the following equation:

$$A = (B \, B^T)^{-1} B^T R \tag{1}$$

In our study, we asked the students to rate each feature. These ratings are an estimate for matrix **R**, with which the above equation is used to estimate matrix **A** in return.

Both approaches have their inherent advantages and caveats. The expert derived matrix is prone to subjective biases, but it is straightforward for experts to estimate it. The empirically derived matrix is more objective and potentially more accurate, but only under the condition that sufficient data is gathered. We conducted experiments to investigate these questions.

4   Implementation and Evaluation

We first conducted an experiment to investigate the effectiveness of the expert derived vs. the empirically derived A-matrices. In a later experiment, we chose the expert derived A-matrix to adapt game features and assess the quality of the adaptation it provides to the learners.

4.1   Learning Environnement and Games Features

Let us first describe in more details the learning environment within which the gamification adaptation takes place, named *Projet Voltaire*[1] and developed by Woonoz Inc. The environment is designed to learn and memorize the French grammar rules. As mentioned earlier, a content engine adapts the difficulty of the learning material by taking into account the history of success outcome of the learner. Combined to this content adaptation, five game features are also available.

All the game features implement different game mechanics. The first feature is a set of stars lighted by the players when a grammar rule is learnt. The second feature is a leader board that reports the number of consecutive correct answers and the first name of the students who are close to this score. The user can appreciate through this feature whether s/he is getting ahead or behind the neighbouring student on this board. The third feature provides users with a way to give tips to each other, in order to better understand the grammar rules. It aims at enhancing social interactions. The fourth feature represents a walker climbing a mountain. Some flags are placed on the way, they give the user an access to anecdotes about French spelling. The last feature is a timer that encourages the user to move quickly.

4.2   Experiment 1: Estimating Matrix A

Experiment Settings. 140 users participated to the first experiment. They had to answer a survey before using *Projet Voltaire* for three weeks. After this period, they had to answer a second survey. The first survey contained the BrainHex test[2], which provided us with the full BrainHex profile of the users: seven values in [-10, 20]. This data provided the **B** matrix. During the three weeks of use of *Projet Voltaire*, only two of the five game features were activated avoid overloading the interface. The two game features were randomly selected among the five available features. In the

---

[1] The *Projet Voltaire*, developed by Woonoz, is available on *projet-voltaire.fr*.
[2] The BrainHex test, developed by International Hobo, is available on *brainhex.com*.

second survey we asked the users if they felt the game features were a motivating factor. The answers were used to build the **R** matrix.

As each user only had two game features, their answers are not sufficient to complete the **R** matrix: there are three missing values on each line. In order to fill the blanks, we follow the recommendation of Ayers *at al.* [20] to obtain values with minimal information: the value between the mean of the column and the mean of the row. In the **R** matrix, the mean of the column indicates the global motivational effect of the game feature on all users. The mean of the row indicates whether the user tends to give high or low values. The ratings of the R matrix was thereafter used to calculate the empirical A-matrix.

Human Expert A-Matrix (1). Six experts[3] were asked to fill an A-matrix of weights for mapping BrainHex categories to game features. They first learnt the BrainHex classification. They then used *Projet Voltaire* for about one hour, interacting with all the five game features. Finally they had to provide a value to link each feature (5) to each player type (7), and thus build a 7 x 5 A-matrix. The values could be chosen among the following:

1. Very strong match: 1
2. Strong match: 0.75
3. Medium match: 0.5
4. Weak match: 0.25
5. No match: 0

To get a single A-matrix from the six experts, we took the median of the six judgements for each of the 35 values (see Table 1). The median is a way to get the value most experts will agree with, and it prevents the result from being influenced by an extreme value. The resulting A-matrix was used in the formula $\mathbf{R} = \mathbf{B} \, \mathbf{A}$ to obtain the $\hat{\mathbf{R}}_e$ predictions.

Table 1. Experts A-matrix. Columns: game features. Rows: BrainHex player types.

	Stars	Leader board	Tips	Walker	Timer
Seeker	0.5	0	0.75	0.88	0
Survivor	0.13	0.5	0	0	0.38
Daredevil	0.63	0.63	0	0.13	0.88
Mastermind	0.63	0.63	0.38	0.25	0.25
Conqueror	0.75	1	0.13	0.38	0.75
Socializer	0.13	0.13	1	0.25	0
Achiever	1	0.75	0.13	0.88	1

In order to confirm the validity of the $\hat{\mathbf{R}}_e$ matrix, we measured the experts' agreement with IntraClass Correlation (ICC) [21] and obtained a value of 0.43. This is

---

[3] The experts are academics specialised in serious games and gamification.

considered as a moderate value but high enough to confirm the agreement between experts.

Data derived A-matrix (2). A least square estimate of matrix **A** is obtained from equation (1) given the matrix of user ratings **R** and the **B** matrix that contains their BrainHex answers. Akin to the procedure for the expert A-matrix, formula $\mathbf{R} = \mathbf{B}\,\mathbf{A}$ yields the **R** predictions, this time using the least-square estimate $\hat{\mathbf{A}}_{\mathbf{d}}$. An eight fold cross-validation is used to avoid any bias in the predictions, where each fold's predictions of the test set in **R** are replaced by their expected values (column-row average) in the training set. We refer to the obtained prediction as $\hat{\mathbf{R}}_{\mathbf{d}}$.

Results and Discussion. The predictions $\hat{\mathbf{R}}_{\mathbf{e}}$ and $\hat{\mathbf{R}}_{\mathbf{d}}$ have been compared to the real values provided by the users (2/5 values of **R**) to be evaluated. If a prediction is correct, the high values of the predicted R will match to the high values of the real R, and the same goes for the low values. Accordingly we evaluated the predictions with a linear correlation between the predicted and real values. The correlation coefficient between the values of **R** and $\hat{\mathbf{R}}_{\mathbf{e}}$ is $r = 0.2207$. The correlation coefficient between the values of **R** and $\hat{\mathbf{R}}_{\mathbf{d}}$ is $r = 0.1822$.

Two factors led us to choose the experts derived A-matrix over the empirical data derived A-matrix. Firstly, the agreement among the six experts (ICC) provides some validity to the experts matrix. Secondly, the prediction of the experts has a better correlation with the answers provided by the users. Accordingly the experts A-matrix was selected for the second experiment.

4.3   Experiment 2 : Adaptation of Game Features

The second experiment consisted in using matrix **A** from the experts to adapt the game features based on the learners' BrainHex profile obtained from the questionnaire.

Experiment Settings. 280 users participated to this second experiment, after being divided into two groups. As in the experiment 1 they filled in the BrainHex survey, then got access to *Projet Voltaire* for three weeks, and answered a game feature assessment questionnaire. Before they started using *Projet Voltaire*, we used the Brain-Hex results (**B**) and the experts matrix (**A**) to predict the motivational impact of the five game features on each user ($\hat{\mathbf{R}}_{\mathbf{e}}$). The members of Group 1 were provided with the two game features that best matched their profile, and the members of Group 2 with the two features that worse matched their profile.

Results and Discussion. The second experiment revealed two interesting results regarding the choice of the A-matrix.

Firstly, the members of Group 1 with adapted features spent on average 2 hours and 38 minutes on *Projet Voltaire*, whereas the members of Group 2 with counter-adapted features spent on average 1 hour and 54 minutes on the environment. Thus members of Group 1 spent 39% more time on the learning environment. A Student-t test over this difference reveals a p-value of 0.0426, and confirms that the adaptation model relying on the experts matrix has indeed a positive impact on the learners engagement at $p<0.05$.

Secondly, the members of Group 1 and 2 gave similar values for the evaluation of their game features. To the item *"This feature is motivating for me"* (on a scale from 1 to 7), the mean value given by Group 1 is 4.58, whereas it is 4.55 for Group 2. This result shows that the users seem not aware of the impact of the adapted features on their engagement.

5   Conclusion and Perspectives

In this paper we presented an adaptation model to provide learners with game features that match to their player profile. It is based on a linear relation between game features and player types. The model is generic, but relies on an association matrix that is specific to the game features implemented in the learning environment. This matrix can rely on experts' judgment or empirical data. An experiment has proven the effectiveness of the experts-based matrix, as the members of the group with adapted features spent 39% more time on the learning environment than the members of the group with counter adapted features. The model based on empirical data could not be validated in this experiment for two reasons. First this type of model requires a large amount of users, which was not sufficient here. Then the model has to rely on a variable that is significantly impacted by the level of matching between the game features and the user, which seems not to be the case with the values provided consciously by the users.

At present, the adaptation is made possible thanks to the BrainHex test answered by the learners before using the learning environment. The next step of our work will be to update the model in real time according to the users' interactions. For example, if a user disables a game feature, then s/he's probably not responsive to its game mechanics.

Acknowledgements. We thank the ANRT and Woonoz for funding this research work. We also would like to thank Woonoz for the development of the experimental version of *Projet Voltaire* and for linking us to their users who accepted to participate in our experiments. We also thank the experts for their work on the A-matrix. Finally we thank International Hobo for providing us with the BrainHex test.

References

1. Prensky, M.: Digital game-based learning. McGraw-Hill, New York (2001)
2. Deterding, S., Dixon, D., Khaled, R., Nacke, L.: From game design elements to gamefulness: defining gamification. In: Proceedings of the 15th International Academic MindTrek Conference: Envisioning Future Media Environments, pp. 9–15 (2011)

3. Kapp, K.M.: The Gamification of Learning and Instruction: Game-based Methods and Strategies for Training and Education. John Wiley & Sons (2012)
4. Bíró, G.I.: Didactics 2.0: A Pedagogical Analysis of Gamification Theory from a Comparative Perspective with a Special View to the Components of Learning (2014)
5. Hamari, J., Koivisto, J., Sarsa, H.: Does gamification work?—a literature review of empirical studies on gamification. In: Proceedings of the 47th Hawaii International Conference on System Sciences (2014)
6. Bloom, B.S.: The 2 sigma problem: The search for methods of group instruction as effective as one-to-one tutoring. Educational Researcher, 4–16 (1984)
7. Csikszentmihalyi, M.: Finding flow: The psychology of engagement with everyday life. Basic Books (1998)
8. Bartle, R.: Richard A. Bartle: Players Who Suit MUDs (1996)
9. Yee, N.: Motivations for play in online games. CyberPsychology & Behavior 9(6), 772–775 (2006)
10. Ferro, L.S., Walz, S.P., Greuter, S.: Towards personalised, gamified systems: an investigation into game design, personality and player typologies. In: Proceedings of The 9th Australasian Conference on Interactive Entertainment: Matters of Life and Death, p. 7 (2013)
11. Nacke, L.E., Bateman, C., Mandryk, R.L.: BrainHex: A neurobiological gamer typology survey. Entertainment Computing 5(1), 55–62 (2014)
12. Hocine, N., Gouaïche, A., Di Loreto, I., Abrouk, L.: Techniques d´adaptation dans les jeux ludiques et sérieux. Revue d'intelligence Artificielle 25(2), 253–280 (2011)
13. Natkin, S., Yan, C., Jumpertz, S., Market, B.: Creating multiplayer ubiquitous fames using an adaptive narration model based on a user's model. In: Digital Games Research Association International Conference (2007)
14. Robinson, D., Bellotti, V.: A preliminary taxonomy of gamification elements for varying anticipated commitment. In Proc. ACM CHI 2013 Workshop on Designing Gamification: Creating Gameful and Playful Experiences (2013)
15. Sailer, M.: Psychological Perspectives on Motivation Through Gamification. Interaction Design and Architecture(s) Journal - IxD&A, 28–37 (2013)
16. Zichermann, G., Cunningham, C.: Gamification by Design: Implementing game mechanics in web and mobile apps. O'Reilly Media, Inc. (2011)
17. Hunicke, R., LeBlanc, M., Zubek, R.: MDA: a formal approach to game design and game research. In: Proceedings of the AAAI Workshop on Challenges in Game AI 04-04 (2004)
18. Monterrat, B., Lavoué, É., George, S.: Motivation for learning - adaptive gamification for web-based learning environments. In: 6th International Conference on Computer Supported Education, pp. 117–125 (2014)
19. Desmarais, M.C., Naceur, R.: A matrix factorization method for mapping items to skills and for enhancing expert-based Q-matrices. In: Lane, H., Yacef, K., Mostow, J., Pavlik, P. (eds.) AIED 2013. LNCS, vol. 7926, pp. 441–450. Springer, Heidelberg (2013)
20. Ayers, E., Nugent, R., Dean, N.: A Comparison of Student Skill Knowledge Estimates. International Working Group on Educational Data Mining (2009)
21. Shrout, P.E., Fleiss, J.L.: Intraclass correlations: uses in assessing rater reliability. Psychological Bulletin 86(2), 420 (1979)

Exploring the Impact of a Learning Dashboard on Student Affect

Kasia Muldner[1](✉), Michael Wixon[2], Dovan Rai[2], Winslow Burleson[3],
Beverly Woolf[4], and Ivon Arroyo[2]

[1] Institute of Cognitive Science, Carleton University, Ottawa, Canada
Kasia.muldner@carleton.ca
[2] Learning Sciences and Technologies, Worcester Polytechnic Institute, Worcester, USA
[3] School of Computer Science, University of Massachusetts, Amherst, MA, USA
[4] New York University College of Nursing, New York University, New York, NY, USA

Abstract. Research highlights that many students experience negative emotions during learning activities, and these can have a detrimental impact on behaviors and outcomes. Here, we investigate the impact of a particular kind of affective intervention, namely a learning dashboard, on two deactivating emotions: boredom and lack of excitement. The data comes from a study we conducted with over 200 middle school students interacting with an intelligent tutor that provided varying levels of support to encourage dashboard use. We analyze the data using a range of techniques to show that the learning dashboard is associated with reduced deactivating emotions, but that its utility also depends on the way its use is promoted and on students' gender.

Keywords: Affect · Learning dashboard · Intelligent tutoring system

1 Introduction

A key factor that influences students' academic success is their emotions and affective experiences while learning. For instance, positive affect has a facilitative effect on cognitive functioning in general [11], and on creative problem solving in particular [12, 15]. Even emotions traditionally viewed as negative can be beneficial, e.g., confusion is associated with learning under certain conditions [10]. In contrast, other emotions can hinder learning – for instance, boredom reduces task performance [16] and increases ineffective behaviors like gaming [7]. In general, given the pivotal role that affect plays, there is growing interest in developing educational technologies that recognize and respond to student affect. To date, however, the emphasis has been on the former, namely affect recognition through the construction of user models [8, 20]. Thus, little work exists exploring the impact of affective support.

Our research takes a step in this direction by analyzing the impact on affect of a particular kind of intervention, namely a *learning dashboard*. The dashboard graphically and textually presents individualized reports about student progress and performance, e.g., problems solved, utility of strategies used, knowledge gained (shown in Figure 1 and described in Section 2.1). Prior work has utilizing learning dashboards

© Springer International Publishing Switzerland 2015
C. Conati et al. (Eds.): AIED 2015, LNAI 9112, pp. 307–317, 2015.
DOI: 10.1007/978-3-319-19773-9_31

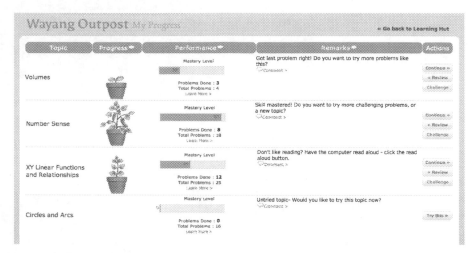

Fig. 1. The Student Progress Page (SPP) encourages students to reflect on their effort (plants, column 2) for each math topic, reflect about their mastery (bars, column 2) and recent behaviors (column 4), and make informed decisions about challenging themselves with harder problems (column 5)

for supporting cognitive or meta-cognitive behaviors. For instance, Arroyo et al. [3] integrated a basic progress chart into an intelligent tutor and found that students who had access to the chart had higher learning gains. On the meta-cognitive side, learning dashboards reifying student gaming behaviors (e.g., hint abuse) have been shown to discourage gaming [6, 19]. Since a learning dashboard shows an assessment of skills or behaviors, it is a step towards *open learner models* (OLM) [9]. Several studies have shown that OLM improved learning [13] and self reflection [18].

In contrast to the above-described research focusing on cognitive or meta-cognitive outcomes, a recent study analyzed the impact an affective agent Scooter, which appears angry when students game [14]. While overall, no effect was found on students' affect, Scooter's responses were limited to affective expressions, which may be insufficient to influence student affect.

Following Zimmerman & Moylan's [21] model of self-regulation, we hypothesize that a learning dashboard has the potential to reduce negative affect, since it can help students self regulate, e.g., feel less "lost" in the learning process, set goals, and reflect on progress towards those goals. Here, we focus on two *deactivating negative* emotions, lack of interest and excitement, because these can be especially detrimental to student learning [7]. Our target domain is middle-school mathematics, a

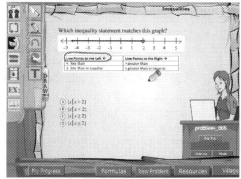

Fig. 2. MathSpring. A button (bottom left) allows students to access the Student Progress Page (SPP).

challenging topic for many students. By the time students reach high school, they report lack of interest and excitement in mathematics at an alarming rate [2].

2   The Tutor and Student Progress Page (SPP)

This research was conducted within an established intelligent mathematics tutor called MathSpring (formerly called Wayang) (see Figure 2) [1]. The tutor includes a student model that assesses individual students' knowledge and effort exerted, and adapts the choice of problem accordingly [4]; it also provides hints and explanations and worked-out examples. To expand the range of support offered, we have integrated into MathSpring a learning dashboard we call the *student progress page* (SPP).

As shown in Figure 1, the SPP lists the available domain topics as rows. Students click on a topic to view a list of problems available, along with details about their corresponding progress to encourage reflection about that topic, as follows:

- **Progress (Column 2):** The tutor shows its assessment of the student's problem-solving effort for problems in a given topic. The tutor makes this inference based on student behavior (e.g., help seeking behavior, incorrect answers, time spent reading problems and hints, quick guesses). To visualize progress, the tutor uses the metaphor of a potted plant that grows when effort is invested, bares fruit when the topic is mastered, or withers when the system detects lack of student effort.
- **Mastery (Column 3):** This is a probabilistic assessment of student knowledge for each topic (column 1) based on Bayesian knowledge tracing.
- **Feedback (Column 4):** The tutor provides customized feedback based on the student's overall performance and most recent behavior, e.g., *"That last problem was a hard one. Good work!"*; *"You got the last problem right! Do you want to try more problems like this?"*. The tutor also highlights instances when student behaviors are sub-optimal, e.g., *"You don't seem to have spent time reading the problems –did you know there is a 'read aloud' button?"*
- **Navigation (Column 5):** Students can choose different modes of navigation for subsequent problems (e.g., review prior problems, work on higher difficulty 'challenge' problems); tutor recommendations are provided (e.g., *"You have already mastered this topic. Maybe you should try 'challenge' problems or a new topic."*)

3   Experiment and Results

To evaluate the impact of the Student Progress Page on student affect, we conducted a study with grade seven students ($N = 209$). Students used MathSpring over three consecutive class sessions. On part of the first and last day, students filled in an pre- and post-affect survey, respectively, which included questions related to various types of affect, including interest and excitement, and so provided baseline data on affect.

To obtain information on affect as students were solving math problems, Math-Spring prompted students to self-report their affect every five minutes, or every eight problems, whichever came first, but only after a problem was completed to avoid interruption. The prompts were shown on a separate screen and asked students to report on a target emotion (interest or excitement) via a 1-5 point Likert scale (e.g., for interest, "*How interested are you feeling right now? Not at all interested* (1) ... *somewhat interested (3)* ... *extremely interested* (5);" an analogous question appeared for excitement). The software cycled through the two emotions and students typically self reported several times on each emotion.

The study used a between subjects design with four conditions that ranged in terms of degree of access to the SPP tool: (1) *no-button* ($N = 49$): the SPP button was not present in the MathSpring interface (the only way to access SPP was through a convoluted set of steps that students were not informed about), (2) *button* ($N = 53$): the SPP button was present and prominent but MathSpring did not encourage SPP use, (3) *prompt* ($N = 52$): MathSpring invited students to view the SPP immediately after they self-reported low interest or low excitement (< 3), but students could ignore this invitation, (4) *force* ($N = 55$): same as in *prompt* except that MathSpring took students to the SPP page and viewing it was not optional. Students within a given class were randomly assigned to one of the four conditions.

Prior to data analysis, as a manipulation check we verified that SPP access indeed increased across conditions, from *no-button* to *force*: $M = 1.3$, $M = 3.1$, $M = 6.0$, $M = 8.8$. We also confirmed that there were no differences between conditions in terms of baseline interest and excitement as measured by the pre-affect survey (*ns*).

3.1   Does the Student Progress Page Impact Student Affect?

To analyze the impact of SPP on affect, we obtained a mean value of self-reported *interest* and *excitement* for each student using the student's self-report data. For excitement, there was little difference between the middle two conditions ($M = 2.6$ for both), while the *force* and *no-button* conditions had the highest ($M = 2.8$) and lowest ($M = 2.5$) reported excitement, respectively. In contrast, for interest, the *force* condition had the lowest value ($M = 2.5$), and there was little difference between the remaining conditions ($M = 2.7$ for all three). Neither affective state produced a significant overall effect or follow-up pairwise comparisons as reported by an ANCOVA with the target emotion as the independent variable, the corresponding pre-affect survey emotion as the covariate baseline, and condition as the independent variable (*ns*).

Thus, overall we did not find an effect of the various SPP conditions. However, in our prior work, gender influenced students' reception of affective support [5]. To see if this was the case here, we conducted follow up exploratory analyses splitting across gender. Fig. 3 shows the mean affect for each gender and condition. We first checked that baseline affect (obtained from the pre-affect survey for each target emotion within a given gender) was not different across conditions; two marginal baseline differences between conditions emerged for male students for excitement, despite the random assignment: *prompt* vs. *force* ($p = .07$) and *prompt* vs. *button* ($p = .1$). Thus, to avoid confounding our results, these two comparisons were excluded from the analysis. We then carried an ANCOVA as for the overall analysis but within each gender.

For excitement, female students reported similar levels of excitement for the top three SPP-access conditions (*button, prompt, force*), and no effects were significant. In contrast, male students reported marginally lower excitement in the *no-button* condition vs. the *button* condition ($p = .07$), and the *no-button* condition vs. the *force* condition ($p = .06$).

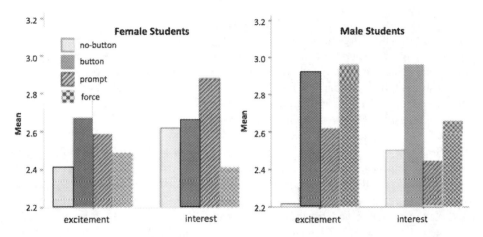

Fig. 3. Adjusted[1] mean excitement and interest for female students (left) and male students (right) ([1]adjustment is by the covariate in the ANCOVA corresponding to the baseline affect)

For interest, female students reported marginally lower interest in the *force* condition than in the *prompt* condition ($p = .06$). Male students, on the other hand, reported lower interest in the *prompt* condition than *button* condition ($p = .1$). To further explore this effect of prompting vs. forcing SPP usage between the male and female students, we conducted exploratory analysis by restricting the analysis to the *prompt* and *force* conditions. We first checked that there were no baseline differences between genders for *interest* and this was the case (*ns*). An ANCOVA with *gender* and *condition (prompt* vs. *force)* as the independent variables, *interest* as the dependent variable, and baseline *interest* as the covariate revealed a marginally significant interaction between gender and condition ($p = .09$). This interaction (see Fig. 3) indicates that female students reported higher interest when MathSpring prompts gave them the choice to use SPP rather than when it enforced SPP usage, while the opposite pattern existed for male students.

3.2   Is Student Progress Page Usage Associated with Positive Affect?

Another way to analyze the impact of SPP is to check for associations between its usage and affect, and in particular to evaluate if higher SPP usage is associated with less deactivating emotions (boredom, lack of excitement). However, this analysis is complicated by the fact that MathSpring encouraged SPP usage in two of the conditions (*prompt* and *force*) when low interest or low excitement was self reported. Thus, SPP usage could be correlated with *negative* emotions in these two groups. In contrast, in the other two conditions (*no-button* and *button*), students were not encouraged to view the SPP and so it was up to them to access the tool or not. To take these considerations into account, we checked for correlations between SPP usage and self-reported affect separately in each of these two groups.

For the *SPP not promoted* group (*no-button, button* conditions), interest was positively associated with SPP usage ($r = .24$, $p = .023$) – excitement also was positively associated with SPP but this did not reach significance ($r = .13$, $p = .26$). One explanation for these findings is that in the *SPP not promoted* conditions, students who had positive affect to begin with (high interest and excitement) used SPP more because they were more motivated, and so SPP usage did not impact affect per se. To check for this possibility we controlled for students' pre-existing affect as derived from the pre-affect survey by running partial correlations. We found that the results held, i.e., interest was still significantly associated with SPP usage ($r_p = .25$, $p = .036$) and the result for excitement did not change ($r_p = .14$, $p = .3$). Overall, these results suggest that SPP usage may have improved student affect, but given the correlational nature of this analysis these results should be interpreted with caution.

In contrast, for the *SPP promoted (prompt, force* conditions*)*, as predicted interest was negatively associated with SPP usage ($r = -.32$, $p < .01$); there was also a trend for excitement being negatively associated with SPP but this did not reach significance ($r = -.15$, $p = .16$). These results held after controlling for the pre-affective survey data ($r = -.31$, $p = .012$ for interest; excitement-SPP correlation negative and *ns*).

3.3   How do Conditions Impact Affective State Transitions?

While the above analysis uncovered interesting indications of SPP impact, it did not shed light on how students transitioned between affective states (e.g., if they got "stuck" in the negative deactivating states in some conditions). Addressing this question requires information on student affect more frequently than provided by the self-reports. Thus, we generated affect predictions using two user models built from the data, one for each target emotion. Note that we did not use the models during the study to obtain affective information because that would have required having the data from this target population prior to the study, in order to construct the models (or alternatively having a model that was proven to generalize to the present population, which we did not have).

Affect Models. The affect models generate a prediction of a given student's target affect (interest or excitement) after each problem the student solves. While the two models were created specifically for this analysis, the methodology for their construction comes from our prior work [20]. Here, the models were trained using 4-fold student level batch cross validation over the target data set. Each model employed a total of 10 features to predict students' self reports. The excitement model used 2 features based on student's interactions with MathSpring; the interest model used 3. The models' performance (excitement $R = 0.43$, *Kappa* = 0.18; interest $R = 0.46$, *Kappa* = 0.28) is comparable with existing sensor free affect detector results [8].

High-level and Specific Path Models. Using the affect model predictions, we followed the procedure in [3] and generated Markov Chain models for the two target emotions for each condition. These high level "path" models provide the probabilities of transitioning between levels of a given affective state (e.g., from neutral to excited) −we restricted this analysis to three levels for a given affective states (e.g., interest: *bored, neutral, interested*). Since the affect model outputs decimal values, we collapsed these so that values < 2.49 correspond to a negative affective state (*bored,*

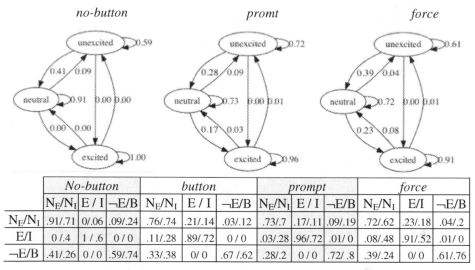

Fig. 4. Visual representation of the high-level path models for excitement in the *no-button*, *prompt* and *force* conditions from left to right, respectively (top) and transition probabilities for all the high level path models (for each condition and target emotion), shown in text form (bottom): N_E = Neutral given that the target emotion is excited; N_I = neutral given that the target emotion is interested; E = excited; I = interested; ¬E = unexcited; B = bored

unexcited), values between [2.5 and 3.49] indicate the *neutral* state and values > 3.5 correspond to a positive affective state (*interested, excited*). We then calculated the transition probabilities (e.g., the probability of a transition from bored (B) to interested (I) = (#transitions B➔I) / [(#transitions B➔I) + (#transitions B➔B) + (#transitions B➔Neutral)]. The transition probabilities and models are shown in Fig. 4.

The path models provide a high level view of how a student transitions between levels of an affective state. For instance, we can ascertain that for excitement, overall the probability of transitioning from neutral to excited is the highest in the *force* condition (Fig. 4). However, these models are difficult to interpret and compare between conditions. This can be addressed by computing the joint probability of a student's affect undergoing particular transitions (i.e., following an *affective path*). For instance, given the condition forcing SPP usage, what is the probability that a student starting in a neutral state ends up excited? The next analysis answers such questions.

Assuming that a student starts in a "neutral state" with a certain prior probability, we can estimate the joint posterior probability of a given affective path. To illustrate, starting in a neutral state at time t_0, two "positive" paths (i.e., ones that do not include a negative state) that take a student to an excited state: (P1) N➔E ➔E, or (P2) N➔ N ➔ E. The probability of path P1 is $P(S_{t2}=E \mid N➔E ➔E) = P(S_{t0}=N) * P(N➔E) * P(E➔E)$, where $P(S_{t0}=N)$ is the prior probability of the student being in a neutral state at time 0 (obtained from affective pre-survey baselines). In general:

$$P(S_{t2} = S2 \mid S0➔S1➔S2) = P(S_{t0}=S0) * P(S0➔S1) * P(S1➔S2) \qquad [\text{Eq 1.}]$$

The joint probability provides the probability of a given affective state after a specific path in the affect transition model. The individual transition probabilities (right-most two in Eq. 1) come from the high-level path models (Fig. 4). Here, we focus on (1) paths of length two, (2) assume the starting point is the neutral state, (3) and assume a *positive* path only includes neutral or positive states / a *negative* path only includes neutral or negative states (note, however, that our approach can be extended to any starting point and path length/types). To illustrate, Table 1 shows partial computations of the joint probability of a student following a certain affective path using Eq 1. In the case of the *no-button* condition, where there was very restricted access to the SPP, students were more likely to end up in unexcited state than excited at time t_2. Note these probabilities are very low (as the most likely affective state in paths of length 2 is "neutral", $P(St_2=N \mid St_0=N) \sim 0.3$ across conditions, which is reasonable as affect may not change drastically in short affective paths.

Table 2 aggregates and synthesizes the results of Table 1 for comparison across conditions. For excitement, Table 2 shows that the *no-button* condition fared worst compared to all other conditions. This suggests that in general, having the SPP present resulted in positive affective paths (ones that led to excitement). For interest, again the *no-button* condition was the least effective at promoting interest, compared to the other conditions. However, the other conditions were not highly effective in promoting the beneficial affective paths (ones that led to interest), except for the condition that left   it up to the student to choose when to see the progress page (i.e., *button*).

Table 1. Probabilities of a student ending up excited (E) vs. unexcited (U) at t_2 after a two affective transitions for the *no-button* condition, given the baseline $P(\mathbf{St_0=N}) = .418$

Type of Path		t_0	t_1	t_2	$P(St_0 \rightarrow St_1)$ / $P(St_1 \rightarrow St_2)$ / $P(St_2)$	$P(P1 \ or \ P2)$	Likelihood of Path
Positive (Leads to	P1	N	E	E	.001 / .999 / .0004	.001	
excited)	P2	N	N	E	.91 / .001 / .0004		Neg. Affect Path
							>
Negative (Leads	P1	N	U	U	.09 / .59 / .0222	.06	Pos. Affect Path
to unexcited)	P2	N	N	U	.91 / .09 / .0342		

Table 2. Probabilities of a student finishing in a (1) Positive Affect at t_2 for excited (EXC) or interested (INT); (2) Negative Affect for unexcited (Un-EXC) or bored (BOR). For excited, neutral at t_0 is $P(St_0 = N) = 0.418$; for interested, neutral at t_0 is $P(St0=N) = 0.503$.

	no button	*button*	*prompt*	*force*
(1) Positive Affect (Leads to EXC / INT)	.001 / .04	.14 / .10	.12 / .08	.16 / .10
(2) Negative Affect (Leads to Un-EXC/ BOR)	.06 / .18	.02 / .08	.06 / .14	.02 / .14
EXC: Which path is more likely?	NEG > POS	POS > NEG	POS > NEG	POS > NEG
INT: Which path is more likely?	NEG > POS	POS > NEG	NEG > POS	NEG > POS

4   Conclusion and Future Work

We explored the utility of a learning dashboard, called the Student Progress Page (SPP), as a form of metacognitive support to alleviate negative affective states (boredom and lack of excitement) and promote the positive affective counterparts. In general, we found that SPP usage was associated with more positive interest in conditions where MathSpring did not prompt for SPP usage. While the opposite pattern was found for the conditions that MathSpring did prompt SPP usage, this was expected given that the prompts were triggered by negative student affect. When considering all four conditions, however, overall we did not find significant differences in terms of affect. This was somewhat unexpected. On the one hand, students are not good at monitoring their own progress and this can negative affective consequences, so one might expect the conditions that encouraged or even forced SPP usage would improve affect more. On the other hand, however, some theories of motivation argue that having control over ones' activities increases intrinsic motivation, which is related to interest and possibly excitement [17]. When we broke the data down by gender, and considered only the top two SPP conditions (prompt and force), we did find indications of the latter possibility, albeit only for female students, who reported more positive affect (interest) when tailored prompts invited SPP usage than when SPP was enforced. However, the opposite pattern emerged for male students. Given the preliminary nature of this analysis, further research is needed to understand how to design affective interventions taking into account factors related to gender.

Thus far, we have been discussing our analysis related to *overall* affective differences. However, exploring more fine-grained implications of affective interventions is also paramount. This level of explanation was accomplished by analyzing how students transitioned between levels of affective states, such as from bored to excited, as well as how likely certain affective paths were in the four conditions. This analysis focused on affective paths of length two, and in this context, the SPP promoted positive changes towards excitement in students, but was less effective at promoting interest. One possibility for these results is that excitement is a short-term affective state, which would be captured by the short paths we confined our analysis to, while interest might take more time to develop, and so was not captured by the particular length of affective paths we focused on.

In general, our results highlight the utility of having a learning dashboard available but leave questions for how its use should be encouraged. One future work avenue will involve using talk aloud protocol during students interaction with MathSpring to gather more fine-grained data on students' reactions and affect. A second avenue will employ data mining techniques to further get at student behaviors directly before and after SPP usage and subsequent impact on affect.

References

1. Arroyo, I., Beal, C.R., Murray, T., Walles, R., Park Woolf, B.: Web-based intelligent multimedia tutoring for high stakes achievement tests. In: Lester, J.C., Vicari, R.M., Paraguaçu, F. (eds.) ITS 2004. LNCS, vol. 3220, pp. 468–477. Springer, Heidelberg (2004)
2. Arroyo, I., Burleson, W., Tai, M., Muldner, K., Woolf, B. Gender Differences In the Use and Benefit of Advanced Learning Technologies for Mathematics. Journal of Educational Psychology. (in press)
3. Arroyo, I., Ferguson, K., et al.: Repairing disengagement with non-invasive intervention. In: Proc. of Artificial Intelligence in Education, pp. 195–202 (2007)
4. Arroyo, I., Mehranian, H., Woolf, B.: Effort-based tutoring: an empirical approach to intelligent tutoring. In: Proc. of EDM, pp. 1–10 (2010)
5. Arroyo, I., Woolf, B.P., Cooper, D.G., Burleson, W., Muldner, K.: The impact of animated pedagogical agents on girls' and boys' emotions, attitudes, behaviors and learning. In: Proc. of ICALT, pp. 506–510 (2011)
6. Baker, R.S., Corbett, A.T., Koedinger, K.R., Evenson, S., Roll, I., Wagner, A.Z., Naim, M., Raspat, J., Baker, D.J., Beck, J.E.: Adapting to when students game an intelligent tutoring system. In: Ikeda, M., Ashley, K.D., Chan, T.-W. (eds.) ITS 2006. LNCS, vol. 4053, pp. 392–401. Springer, Heidelberg (2006)
7. Baker, R., D'Mello, S.K., Rodrigo, M.M.T., Graesser, A.C.: Better to Be Frustrated than Bored: The Incidence, Persistence, and Impact of Learners' Cognitive-Affective States during Interactions with Three Different Computer-Based Learning Environments. International Journal of Human-Computer Studies **68**(4), 223–241 (2010)
8. Baker, R.S.J.d., Gowda, S.M., Wixon, M., Kalka, J., Wagner, A.Z., Salvi, A., Aleven, V., Kusbit, G., Ocumpaugh, J., Rossi, L.: Sensor-free automated detection of affect in a cognitive tutor for algebra. In: Proc. of EDM, pp. 126–133 (2012)
9. Bull, S.: Preferred features of open learner models for university students. In: Cerri, S.A., Clancey, W.J., Papadourakis, G., Panourgia, K. (eds.) ITS 2012. LNCS, vol. 7315, pp. 411–421. Springer, Heidelberg (2012)
10. D'Mello, S.K., Lehman, B., Pekrun, R., Graesser, A.C.: Confusion Can be Beneficial For Learning. Learning & Instruction **29**(1), 153–170 (2014)
11. Hidi, S.: Interest and Its Contribution as a Mental Resource for Learning. Review of Educational Research **60**(4) (1990)
12. Isen, A.M., Daubman, K., Nowicki, G.: Positive affect facilitates creative problem solving. Journal of Personality and Social Psychology **52**, 1122–1131 (1987)
13. Long, Y., Aleven, V.: Supporting students' self-regulated learning with an open learner model in a linear equation tutor. In: Lane, H., Yacef, K., Mostow, J., Pavlik, P. (eds.) AIED 2013. LNCS, vol. 7926, pp. 219–228. Springer, Heidelberg (2013)
14. Pedro, R., et al.: The Effects of an Interactive Software Agent on Student Affective Dynamics while Using an Intelligent Tutoring System. IEEE transactions on affective co-anchormputing **3**(2), 224–236 (2012)
15. Pekrun, R., Elliot, A.J., Maier, M.A.: Achievement Goals and Achievement Emotions: Testing a Model of Their Joint Relations With Academic Performance. Journal of Educational Psychology **101**(1), 115–135 (2009)
16. Pekrun, R., Goetz, T., Daniels, L., Stupinsky, R., Perry, R.: Boredom in Achievement Settings: Exploring Control-Value Antecedents and Performance Outcomes of a Neglected Emotion. Journal of Educational Psychology **102**(3), 531–549 (2010)
17. Ryan, R., Deci, E.: Self-determination theory and the facilitation of intrinsic motivation, social development, and well-being. American psychologist **55**(1), 68–78 (2000)

18. Santos, J.L., Verbert, K., Govaerts, S., Duval, E.: Addressing learner issues with StepUp!: an evaluation. In: Proc. of Learning Analytics and Knowledge, pp. 14–22 (2013)
19. Walonoski, J.A., Heffernan, N.T.: Prevention of off-task gaming behavior in intelligent tutoring systems. In: Ikeda, M., Ashley, K.D., Chan, T.-W. (eds.) ITS 2006. LNCS, vol. 4053, pp. 722–724. Springer, Heidelberg (2006)
20. Wixon, M., Arroyo, I., Muldner, K., Burleson, W., Lozano, C., Woolf, B.: The opportunities and limitations of scaling up sensor-free affect detection. In: Proc. of Educational Data Mining, pp. 145–152 (2014)
21. Zimmerman, B.J., Moylan, A.R.: Self-regulation: where motivation and metacognition intersect. In: Handbook of Metacognition in Education (2009)

Cognitive Tutor Use in Chile: Understanding Classroom and Lab Culture

Amy Ogan[1(✉)], Evelyn Yarzebinski[1], Patricia Fernández[2], and Ignacio Casas[2]

[1] Human-Computer Interaction Institute, Carnegie Mellon University, Pittsburgh, USA
{aeo,eey2}@cs.cmu.edu
[2] School of Engineering, Pontificia Universidad Católica de Chile, Santiago, Chile
pifernac@uc.cl, icasas@ing.puc.cl

Abstract. As technological capabilities flourish around the world, intelligent tutoring systems are being deployed globally to provide learners with access to quality educational interventions. Such systems have been widely studied in in-vivo deployments in the Western world, allowing for the development of sophisticated models of behavior within the system that have been shown to accurately represent and support learning. Yet, these models have recently been shown not to reliably transfer across cultures. In this paper, we report on our quantitative field observations of student behaviors in two different schools (urban and rural) and two different learning contexts (ITS lab and the math classroom) in central Chile. We observed that students across schools exhibit different behaviors in the ITS lab vs the classroom, especially with respect to student interaction, movement, and on-task behavior, yet these students behave altogether differently from previously observed U.S. student populations. These results have implications for future modeling efforts of help-seeking and engagement in advanced learning technologies in new global contexts.

Keywords: Classroom observation · International deployment · Off-task behavior · Collaboration

1 Introduction

A worldwide increase in social connectivity through expanding Internet capabilities, the proliferation of computing technologies, and the growing sophistication of educational tools and systems has provided significant promise for educating a global society. As these technological capabilities flourish around the world, intelligent tutoring systems (ITS) are being deployed globally to provide learners with access to quality educational interventions. Such systems have been widely studied in *in-vivo* classroom deployments in the Western world, allowing for the development of sophisticated models of behavior within the system that have been shown to accurately represent and support students' cognitive and affective capabilities. Yet, as systems move worldwide, these models have recently been shown not to reliably transfer across cultures [1]. Given that culture has been shown to have a strong influence on the types of behaviors that affect learning processes and outcomes, such as help-seeking and motivation [2], it is important to

© Springer International Publishing Switzerland 2015
C. Conati et al. (Eds.): AIED 2015, LNAI 9112, pp. 318–327, 2015.
DOI: 10.1007/978-3-319-19773-9_32

understand how these learning behaviors affect system use in new cultures in order to both develop accurate models and best support students using these systems. While some of this effort can be conducted through the analysis of log data from student use of a system, there is enough evidence that management and organization, student behaviors, numbers of students and instructors, and other features of the classroom can be quite distinct, such that foundational analyses in the classroom are warranted (e.g., [3,4])

In this paper, we use quantitative field observations to investigate learner behaviors in two different school types (urban and rural) and two different learning contexts (ITS lab and the math classroom) in central Chile, and draw comparisons to prior data collected in the United States. We find that student behaviors across our two school types in Chile are remarkably similar. A significant proportion of student learning activities involved working together with another student, including taking control of other students' input devices and moving out of their own seat in order to do the work for or with them. These results are in strong contrast to prior reports of more individual work from the U.S., but even so, the observed ITS labs were less collaborative than the Chilean math classroom. These results have implications for future modeling efforts of learning, help-seeking and engagement in advanced learning technologies deployed in new contexts.

2   Background

Intelligent tutoring systems are predicated on their ability to analyze and understand student behavior. Once a system is developed, a typical process for creating new learner models of the type that underlie such systems often starts with collecting classroom data (cf. [5,6,7,8]). This data collection frequently involves human observers collecting such features as on- and off-task behaviors (or "gaming the system"), observations of student affect, or help-seeking behaviors.

Off-task behavior and interaction with other students have been deemed to be particularly important, as the amount of time students spend on task may be a significant indicator of learning. Researchers studying classrooms employing intelligent tutors report results with estimates of off-task behavior constituting 15% to 25% of instructional time. [5] found that in U.S. ITS classrooms, students were on-task and working alone on the computer an average of 78% of the time, and working on-task with other students 4% of the time. [6] found that 82% of students' time with a different system was spent on-task, with another 7% being on-task conversation with another student. [7] found that students were on-task on average 76% of the time, but did not explicitly code for working with another student.

Early qualitative work by Schofield from the 1990s [9] would indicate that these reports of student interaction were representative across time and place, as she found in a multi-year study that students were typically on-task, and that ITS systems were typically used individually, which teachers believed was the most appropriate paradigm for student learning from the technology. In fact, observed on-task frequencies with ITS appear to be a small increase from normal classroom behavior, which is one of the hypothesized benefits of AIED systems – that students are more engaged with the technology than with lecture-style classroom content, perhaps because they are receiving more individualized support. Prior research examining the frequency of off-task behavior in regular classrooms has estimated that students spend between 10% and 40% of their time off-task [10, 11].

Because ITS systems have been most frequently developed in the world's wealthiest countries [12], the vast majority of these ITS observation studies are conducted in the U.S., followed distantly by the UK, Canada, and two Asian countries (China and Taiwan) [13]. This means that most of this classroom data is collected from American middle and high school students, and most underlying models are developed in the United States based on this data. ITS systems, however, are gaining traction around the world. Some of these systems are simply translated from the original language and deployed in a new context. For example, REAP (REAder-specific Practice) was extended to Portuguese by researchers who created an equivalent vocabulary list and extended the ITS [14]. Others are "home-grown," that is, developed by researchers from a less represented context for learners from that context. In either case, they are likely to draw from the models developed and published on American students.

As this happens, evidence is beginning to accumulate that the models that underlie such systems are not always transferrable from one context to another. [1] investigated a model of help-seeking with data from a study conducted in the United States, the Philippines, and Costa Rica, and found that different help-seeking behaviors were present in each context and that none of the individual models, or a model using the combined data, could predict learning from the other contexts. This finding is supported by evidence from cognitive psychology and learning science that suggests that there are differences in how students across cultures think, act, and learn [2].

The necessary foundational work to understand this issue has not frequently been done for deployments in underrepresented cultures, however. A notable exception is work using the BROMP protocol to look at affect, which also captured on/off-task behavior and student collaboration. For instance, [15] ran a study in the Philippines with students using educational software. They found that 71% of the behavior observed was on-task and individual, while another 9% involved talking while on-task.

These numbers are similar to those reported in the United States. Our prior qualitative work in Latin America, however, would suggest that collaboration can be a key component of the classroom experience there and that there is reason to believe that student behaviors will differ while using ITS [1,3]. Alternatively, it may be that U.S-developed technologies, including the very paradigm of individualized learning represented in ITS, imposes particular behavior patterns that alter students' behavioral tendencies from their regular classroom.

We therefore conducted our current study to investigate some of these foundational issues in a Latin American context in which U.S.-developed AIED technologies are being deployed: Santiago, Chile. Chile represents an interesting case in that while it is not one of the world's top fifty economies, many barriers to educational technology deployment are lower: access to and proficiency with technology by students is high, while test scores are lower than OECD averages but higher than other countries in Latin America [4]. This allows for comparisons of cultures with similar technology and mathematics performance profiles. On the other hand, Chile along with the rest of

Latin America has shown many distinctions from the U.S. on international culture surveys [16]; e.g., a strong collectivist value system compared to extreme individualism in the United States is likely to result in more collaboration.

In this study, we therefore ask the following research questions:

RQ1: What are the frequencies of ITS-critical behaviors in Chilean classrooms?
RQ2: Do behaviors from the Chilean math classroom transfer to the ITS lab?
RQ4: How consistent are observed behaviors across contexts *within* Chile?
RQ3: How do observed behaviors compare to previously reported results from U.S. contexts?

3   Method

The work in this study was conducted in Chile in conjunction with a larger study that was investigating barriers and facilitators to success in deploying ITS in Chile [17]. This larger study included more than twenty-five schools, which were in various stages of deployment at the time of the current data collection. In this study, in order to obtain a comparison across contexts *within* Chile, we selected two sites that had been using the ITS for more than a year and which represented distinct populations: "City Subsidized" (CS), a government-subsidized private school in a major city, and "Rural State" (RS), a municipal school located an hour outside of the same city.

We observed students' behaviors in 10 math classroom sessions at these two sites as a baseline for understanding typical student behaviors, and 10 computer lab sessions while using the Cognitive Tutor Algebra that had been translated and localized into Spanish (see [17] for details). These sessions were divided across four class sections from $5^{th} - 7^{th}$ grade. We additionally observed and collected data at seven other sites, which is not reported here, in order to assess whether the schools we studied in-depth appeared to be atypical in some way.

Two observers conducted observations. The first observer took in-depth qualitative field notes, watching small groups of students for a few minutes each before moving to the next one. The second observer took quantitative observations, observing each member of the class with peripheral vision for ten seconds and recording as many behaviors as the student completed in that time frame, via a partial interval recording method (c.f. [18]). Observations in the class were assisted by a Java-based computer program to track student locations. The lab required more observer movement to access all of the students, and so observations were recorded on paper for later digitization into individual student transaction logs.

During recording, the observer noted the following about each student's behaviors. Codes were binary and not mutually exclusive; that is, an observation could be on-task while interacting with a friend and using their keyboard, etc:

- **On task** (relative to the whole-class activity)
- **Interaction with another student(s)** (talking, pointing to or looking at their screen, etc.)
- **Controlling another student's materials** (notebook, keyboard, mouse, ...)
- **In-seat** (the seat chosen at the beginning of class)

Although the BROMP protocol has collected similar behaviors, it has focused less on interactions between students such as pointing to a partner's screen, physically taking control of their materials, or leaving one's own seat to work across the room.

After recording observations for each student, the observer coded the teacher's behaviors and then started at the beginning of the class again, iterating through the students and teachers continuously until the class period finished. A second rater conducted quantitative observations at the same time during one of the days and found substantial agreement between the two raters.

4   Results

4.1   Site Context

Each school had a computer lab consisting of desktop machines running Windows, which were in heavy use by a variety of classes including mathematics and Spanish language. The lab at CS had a dedicated lab tech whose job was to oversee maintenance and care of the computers, and who occasionally stepped in during teacher absences. One of the math teachers we worked with at RS filled the role of lab tech when it was needed, outside of his regular duties. Both computer labs typically had enough computers to implement a 1-to-1 student to computer protocol. RS had occasional issues with providing consistent electricity that were not present at CS.

CS had class sizes ranging from 38-45, while RS had class sizes of 10-16 (while OECD puts average class size in Chile at 30 [4], in our observations at other schools, we noted that these numbers were typical of urban and rural schools respectively). The classes we were observing had had regularly-scheduled, weekly lab sessions using the Cognitive Tutor over the past year. We found that students were generally familiar with technology and had no issues operating the system.

The Cognitive Tutor, however, suffered from a number of connectivity issues (likely due to insufficient or inconsistent internet bandwidth) that required frequent reloading or longer than desirable wait times, particularly at CS.

4.2   Behavioral Results

Below, we address RQ1 by presenting data on the four main behaviors observed in our coding scheme. We answer RQ2 by comparing results on these behaviors across the math classroom and ITS lab contexts. RQ3 is addressed by comparing results across our two Chilean contexts, and finally when available we include data from prior studies in the U.S. as a point of comparison that helps to illuminate RQ4.

To assess student behaviors, we ran univariate analyses on the collected data (about 7000 recorded transactions in all). Since the number of observations achieved within a period differed across each class due to the varying activities and placements of students, we divided all of the transactions of each completed round (that is, all students were observed an equal number of times within a period) into quartiles post-hoc for a more parallel comparison across all periods, and use percentages of behaviors in each quartile as the unit of analysis. Only full rounds of observation were included for analysis; that is, if a class bell dismissed students in the middle of a round it was excluded. Students in each session were treated as a different set of learners since it was not possible to link observations across the sessions, given that students were not assigned seats and class sizes were large. Each observed behavior (listed below in their own sections) was the dependent variable in the model, while school and location were both fixed factors and an interaction term. Class section and quartile were covariates; although we hypothesized that quartile would affect some behaviors as off-task interactions increase at the end of class, we were less interested in these outcomes as main findings. We report the results of these models below:

On-task Behavior. We first investigated how frequently students were on-task (see Table 1). Amount of on-task behaviors depended on the school, with more on-task behavior in RS. The interaction of location and school was also significant, with the order of most on-task to least on-task as follows: RS lab, RS class, CS class, and CS lab. Of co-variates, Quartile was significant with more off-task behavior typically happening towards the end of class, as was Section, with some sections displaying more off-task behavior than others.

Table 1. Frequency of on-task behavior. $df = 74$ for each factor.

	Context	Means(SD)	F	p
Location	Chile class	0.68 (0.13)	2.27	0.14
	Chile lab	0.62 (0.20)		
	US class[‡]	0.60 – 0.90	n/a	n/a
	US lab[‡]	0.76 – 0.89		
School	Rural	0.82 (0.11)	4.67	< 0.05
	Urban	0.59 (0.15)		
Location* School			12.52	< 0.001
Quartile			10.45	< 0.01
Section			10.78	< 0.01

Note: [‡] Data was collected by [5,6,7,10]; shown here for comparative purposes only.

Qualitatively, we saw that the ability for students to self-direct the learning pace during lab periods sometimes led to more observed off-task behaviors (particularly in the CS lab). In the classes, however, teachers would sometimes direct the class pace at the board, which would gather all student attention to a single location. Since class sizes at CS were double to triple the size of those of RS, it was comparatively more difficult for the teacher to keep the students on-task.

Interacting with Other Students, on or Off-task. We next investigated how frequently students interacted with one another, whether on- or off-task. Only the location of observation had any impact on students' propensity to work, talk, or play together, with more interaction occurring in the classroom than the lab (see Table 2).

Table 2. (light grey) Frequency of on- and off-task student interaction; (white) Frequency of on-task student interaction. $df = 74$ for each factor.

	Context	Means(SD) on/off	F on/off	p on/off	Means (SD) on	F on	p on
Location	Chile class	0.47 (0.14)	55.06	<	0.30 (0.15)	53.98	< 0.001
	Chile lab	0.26 (0.08)		0.001	0.14 (0.07)		
	US lab[‡]	n/a	n/a	n/a	0.04 – 0.07	n/a	n/a
School	Rural	0.37 (0.16)	0.36	0.55	0.28 (0.15)	1.89	0.17
	Urban	0.36 (0.16)			0.20 (0.14)		
Location* **School**			0.17	0.69		1.75	0.19
Quartile			1.72	0.19		0.29	0.59
Section			3.43	0.07		2.57	0.11

Note: [‡] Data was collected by [5,6,7,10]; shown here for comparative purposes only.

This may be the result of spending more of their time in the lab at their individual computer – whether working on the tutor or not. The self-directed pace of learning in the lab may have reduced student interaction because they could take their time and understand the content without as much support, or because the internet provided many individual distractions. In the class, when off-task they would make small conversation clusters based on desk location. When on-task, they often checked with each other to repeat what the teacher had said or demonstrate a step in a particular problem.

We next investigated how much of this student interaction was productive and on-task (i.e., students were working together on something related to the math content). Once again, only location was a significant contributor to the model, with students interacting on-task more frequently in the classroom than in the lab (see Table 2).

We observed a great deal of helping behaviors between students in both class and lab locations. One student told us, "Sometimes I look to my side and see that my friend's in trouble so I ask: how are you doing? I'm good, so do you need help?" This attitude was prevalent despite features of the ITS encouraging them to do otherwise: "Anyway, we usually help each other, even though the colors (of the ITS feedback tool) drives us to compete, to go faster." In some cases in the lab, however, students were working together and collaborating in exemplary ways, except the computer screen was showing an off-task website instead of the ITS. In the classroom, particularly in CS, students frequently interacted with the student beside, behind, in front, or across the room from them in order to understand the material while the teacher moved forward with the lesson.

Controlling Other Students' Materials While On-task. We observed that students physically took control of other students' input devices or notebooks and entered answers for them. Location and the interaction of location and school were significant contributors to the model, in that students were more likely to be working on another students' computer at RS, while they were more likely to be using other students' math notebooks in class at CS (see Table 3).

Taken together with the previous analyses, this indicates that an appreciable amount of on-task student interactions involved this physical exchange (e.g., on average 5/28 on-task interactions at RS, or 18%). From our qualitative observations, we believe that these actions were rarely malicious or intended to distract. Rather, students shared answers with each other frequently and freely, whether or not they were requested to do so, which contributed towards an atmosphere of casual collaboration at a class-wide level. In the lab, one student might take another's keyboard or mouse, input or click on the right answer, and return the item. Occasionally students even forged a partnership with one another, where one student would control the mouse as another controlled the keyboard and they discussed. In the class, student interaction typically manifested itself in students taking notebooks or papers, writing the answer, and returning it.

Table 3. (light grey) Frequency of on-task control of a peer's materials; (white) Frequency of out of seat behavior. $df = 74$ for each factor.

	Context	Means (SD) control	F control	p control	Means (SD) seat	F seat	p seat
Location	Chile class	0.02 (0.03)	5.66	< 0.05	0.01 (0.01)	17.64	< 0.001
	Chile lab	0.03 (0.07)			0.04 (0.04)		
School	Rural	0.05 (0.09)	2.49	0.12	0.03 (0.04)	0.32	0.57
	Urban	0.01 (0.02)			0.02 (0.03)		
Location*			7.36	< 0.01		0.41	0.52
School							
Quartile			1.58	0.21		1.49	0.27
Section			0.01	0.91		2.00	0.16

Note: there is no known available observations of US classrooms or labs to compare

Out of Seat, on or Off Task. Finally, given the qualitative observation that students moved around the classroom to work, we looked at whether students spent most of the time in their own seat or moving about the classroom. Once again, the location was the only significant contributor to the model, with more out-of-seat behavior occurring in the lab (see Table 3).

Students tended to wander around the room much more in the lab than in the class, in part due to the seating density of the classroom. The more relaxed atmosphere in the lab, along with the previously mentioned casual collaboration between students, led them to check in with each other frequently. We also see that the percentages of out of seat behavior are much smaller in comparison to the percentages of interacting behavior, indicating that when students do interact with each other it is typically with their immediately adjacent neighbors. However, we believe the numbers on this analysis in particular are low, as students more frequently returned to their seats when observers approached their general area of the room than stopped talking.

5   Discussion and Conclusion

In this study, we have described the frequencies of common ITS-related behaviors in the math classroom and the ITS lab, in two sites in Chile, and then compared them to previously observed frequencies of behavior in the U.S.

We found that use of the ITS did change students' typical classroom behavior. Although students were equally on-task in the lab and the classroom, they were more likely to be interacting with other students in the classroom (almost 50% of class time!) and more likely to be interacting on-task with other students in the classroom, but more likely to be up and out of their seats in the lab. They were more likely to help another student in the lab by working on a peer's machine, even in many cases physically taking the mouse or keyboard from a struggling classmate to input the correct answer for them.

In contrast, we found few differences between our two Chilean sites. In many respects the two schools showed remarkable consistency despite their very different contexts (rural vs. urban, staff responsibilities, size, income level). The few differences observed might relate to class size, in that the smaller class size at RS enabled greater teacher interaction and oversight, including more immediate responses to students who exhibited behavior patterns that indicated confusion or uncertainty.

These results differ from previous observations of ITS labs which have reported higher on-task time than in the classroom, only occasionally measure interactions with classmates (and when they do, report much lower rates), and have not assessed the amount of time students leave their own computers to work elsewhere. These findings and the choice of analyses that underlie them are likely indicative of the expectations of researchers about typical classroom behavior (and the highly individualistic nature of American society [2]).

These expectations are drawn in part from literature on observations of American classrooms, as no ITS studies have reported their own quantitative observations of paired non-technology supported math classrooms in order to assess whether classroom behaviors transition to the lab.

In particular, we found that the lab environment significantly damped students' propensity to collaborate, even as the absolute numbers were substantially higher for interaction than in American classrooms, underscoring a need to understand not only the ITS lab but also the traditional educational environments of previously understudied contexts.

It is also clear that understanding the context has many implications for system design. In this particular case, high collaboration rates indicate that students are working together on systems that are designed for individual use – even when the machines are 1-to-1. As speculated on in [3], this may lead to the inaccurate student modeling found in [1]. And yet, designers may want to consider incorporating support for even more offline collaboration, as the individual nature of the computers shifts students' typical patterns. While automatic detectors of these behaviors would be an exciting next step for such systems, these foundational results remind us of a need to continue to understand our target population prior to system deployment.

Acknowledgments. We would like to thank all of our teachers for letting us into their classrooms, Pilar Naranjo and the PUC support team, as well as Steve Ritter, Susan Berman, and the Carnegie Learning team who supported this deployment remotely.

References

1. Ogan, A, Walker, E, Baker, R, Rodrigo, M.M.T., Soriano, I.C., Castro, M.J.: Towards Understanding How to Assess Help-Seeking Behavior Across Cultures. Int. J. of Artificial Intelligence in Ed. (in press)
2. Henrich, J., Heine, S.J., Norenzayan, A.: Most people are not WEIRD. Nature 466(7302), 29–29 (2010)
3. Ogan, A., Walker, E., Baker, R.S., Rebolledo Mendez, G., Jimenez Castro, M., Laurentino, T., de Carvalho, A.: Collaboration in cognitive tutor use in latin america: field study and design recommendations. In: Proc of the SIGCHI Conf. on Human Factors in Computing Systems, pp. 1381–1390 (2012)
4. OECD Education at a Glance, Table D2.2 (2012). http://dx.doi.org/10.1787/888932667995
5. Baker, R.S., Corbett, A.T., Koedinger, K.R., Wagner, A.Z.: Off-task behavior in the cognitive tutor classroom: when students game the system. In: Proc. of the SIGCHI Conference on Human Factors in Computing Systems, pp. 383–390 (2004)
6. Ocumpaugh, J., Baker, R.S., Gaudino, S., Labrum, M.J., Dezendorf, T.: Field observations of engagement in reasoning mind. In: Lane, H., Yacef, K., Mostow, J., Pavlik, P. (eds.) AIED 2013. LNCS, vol. 7926, pp. 624–627. Springer, Heidelberg (2013)
7. Dragon, T., Arroyo, I., Woolf, B.P., Burleson, W., el Kaliouby, R., Eydgahi, H.: Viewing student affect and learning through classroom observation and physical sensors. In: Woolf, B.P., Aïmeur, E., Nkambou, R., Lajoie, S. (eds.) ITS 2008. LNCS, vol. 5091, pp. 29–39. Springer, Heidelberg (2008)
8. de Vicente, A., Pain, H.: Informing the detection of the students' motivational state: an empirical study. In: Cerri, S.A., Gouardéres, G., Paraguaçu, F. (eds.) ITS 2002. LNCS, vol. 2363, pp. 933–943. Springer, Heidelberg (2002)
9. Schofield, J.W.: Computers and Classroom Culture. Cambridge University Press (1995)
10. Lee, S.W., Kelly, K.E., Nyre, J.E.: Preliminary report on the relation of students' on-task behavior with completion of school work. Psychological Reports 84, 267–272 (1999)
11. Karweit, N., Slavin, R.E.: Measurement and modeling choices in studies of time and learning. American Educational Research J. 18(2), 157–171 (1981)
12. Blanchard, E.G.: Socio-Cultural Imbalances in AIED Research: Investigations, Implications and Opportunities. Int. J. of Artificial Intelligence in Ed., 1–25 (2014)
13. Nye, B.: Intelligent Tutoring Systems by and for the Developing World: A Review of Trends and Approaches for Educational Technology in a Global Context.IJAIED. (in press)
14. Silva, A., Mamede, N., Ferreira, A., Baptista, J., Fernandes, J.: Towards a serious game for portuguese learning. In: Ma, M., Fradinho Oliveira, M., Madeiras Pereira, J. (eds.) SGDA 2011. LNCS, vol. 6944, pp. 83–94. Springer, Heidelberg (2011)
15. Rodrigo, M.M.T., Baker, R.S., Lagud, M.C., Lim, S.A.L., Macapanpan, A.F., Pascua, S.A.M.S., Santillano, J.Q., Sevilla, L.R.S., Sugay, J.O., Tep, S., Viehland, N.J.: Affect and usage choices in simulation problem solving environments. Frontiers in Artificial Intelligence and Applications. 158, 145 (2007)
16. Hofstede, G.: Dimensionalizing cultures: The Hofstede model in context. Online readings in psychology and culture 2(1), 8 (2011)
17. Casas, I., Imbrogno, J., Ochoa, S., Ogan, A.: Cultural factors in the implementation and use of an intelligent tutoring system in latin america. In: World Conf. on E-Learning in Corporate, Government, Healthcare, and Higher Ed., vol. 1, pp. 323–331 (2014)
18. Hintze, J.M., Volpe, R.J., Shapiro, E.S.: Best practices in the systematic direct observation of student behavior. Best practices in school psychology 4, 993–1006 (2002)

TARLAN: A Simulation Game to Improve Social Problem-Solving Skills of ADHD Children

Atefeh Ahmadi[1], Antonija Mitrovic[1(✉)], Badroddin Najmi[2], and Julia Rucklidge[3]

[1] Department of Computer Science and Software Engineering,
University of Canterbury, Christchurch, New Zealand
atefeh.ahmadi@pg.canterbury.ac.nz,
tanja.mitrovic@canterbury.ac.nz
[2] Psychology Clinic, Noor Specialized Hospital, University of Isfahan, Isfahan, Iran
najmi@bsrc.mui.ac.ir
[3] Department of Psychology, University of Canterbury, Christchurch, New Zealand
julia.rucklidge@canterbury.ac.nz

Abstract. Attention Deficit Hyperactivity Disorder (ADHD) is a developmental disorder which can impact different aspects of sufferers' lives, including their social skills. We present TARLAN, a game that teaches social problem-solving skills to ADHD children. TARLAN is a simulation game with 40 scenarios based on children's everyday experiences. We conducted a study to investigate how the social problem-solving skills of ADHD children are affected by interactions with TARLAN. Forty children with ADHD aged 8-12 were randomly allocated to two conditions: a computer-based intervention wherein children worked with TARLAN, and the control group with the standard psychological intervention. Another group of 20 children without ADHD but with inadequate social skills also worked with TARLAN. Results show that TARLAN significantly improved social problem-solving skill of the ADHD children compared to their peers who were in the psychological intervention. The game is also beneficial for chil-dren who have social skills deficit but who are not diagnosed with ADHD.

Keywords: Simulation games · ADHD · Social problem-solving skills

1   Introduction

ADHD is a developmental disorder composed of different difficulties with unknown etiology [1]. Inattention, hyperactivity and impulsivity are three main symptoms of ADHD [2-3]. Gaining social skills is difficult for ADHD children, as they lack the ability to analyze social situations, and fail to recognize different perspectives that an ordinary person may take away from a social situation. Therefore they do not take appropriate actions in specific situations [4]. As the result, they cannot realize right and wrong issues easily and repeat ineffective behaviors. The main drawback of poor social skills in ADHD children is peer rejection [5], which can result in low self-esteem, depression and anxiety. Also, if they do not learn these skills during child-hood, they may struggle with the same problems in their adult-

© Springer International Publishing Switzerland 2015
C. Conati et al. (Eds.): AIED 2015, LNAI 9112, pp. 328–337, 2015.
DOI: 10.1007/978-3-319-19773-9_33

hood. By learning social skills, they can improve peer relation, academic progress, taking responsibilities and self-esteem [6-7].

Application of computer games in educational contexts has been studied for more than two decades [8-10]. Designers of educational games have different points of view about the objective of the games. Some designers emphasize the importance of motivating and engaging the learner [10], while others focus more on including mean-ingful activities [11]. However, an intersection of these two approaches has been found as an effective way in designing educational games [12-13].

There is some research on games for ADHD children, for example for teaching basic maths skills [14] or attention training [1]. The STAR project [4] teaches social problem-solving skills to ADHD adolescents, based on the model consisting of four steps: Stop, Think, Act and Reflect. The user is presented with a social situation via a video, and needs to decide on the actions to take by using the four steps. A study con-ducted with 60 ADHD adolescents aged from 10 to 16 compared the performance of the attention-placebo (control) group to the group which interacted with STAR (in pairs), and a the-rapist-directed group. The STAR group performed significantly better on the post/test than the control group, and comparably to the therapist-led group. However, participants worked in pairs, and have not received any feedback from the system as it was not fully functional. Furthermore, the learning scenarios were not based on real-life situations the participants were familiar with.

We present TARLAN, an educational game that teaches social problem solving skills to 8-12 year old children with ADHD. We start by presenting the game and the model for teaching social problem solving, followed by a description of the study in Section 3. The results are presented in Section 4. Finally, we present the conclusions and directions of further work in Section 5.

2   TARLAN

We developed TARLAN (simulaTion gAme to impRove sociaL problem-solving skill of ADHD childreN), an educational game aimed at teaching 8-12 year-olds about social problem-solving skills. TARLAN is based on SOCCSS (Situa-tion-Options-Consequences-Choices-Strategies-Simulation) [15], which is a step-by-step approach for solving social problems. In the first step, the child needs to think about the prob-lem, and then in the second step to identify potential solution op-tions. The next step requires the child to think about the consequences of identified options, followed by choosing one of the options in step 4. In the fifth step, the child needs to develop a strategy for performing the selected solution option, and then in the last step to per-form the necessary actions. When designing TARLAN, we followed the principles of the cognitive theory of multimedia learning [16]. TARLAN was developed using Adobe Flash 3.

Goldsworthy et al. [4] argue that lack of inhibition is one of the difficulties ADHD children experience. ADHD children do not think about consequences before taking actions. In order to overcome this problem, they suggest teaching ADHD children about metacognitive strategies to increase goal-oriented actions and also inhibit prem-ature response, as well as equipping them with appropriate social skills.

TARLAN follows that approach: we developed animated scenarios wherein chil-dren can practise solving social problems step by step in order to gain social compe-tency. The scenarios are goal oriented, and children are expected to solve social prob-lems. Moreover, they also practice inhibition as they have to go through the process step by step and cannot skip any steps. Interaction with TARLAN starts with an ani-mated tutorial that teaches different steps of SOCCSS. After the tutorial, TARLAN presents an animated example in order to clarify the necessary steps.

Social skills can be categorized into four general groups of behaviours: self-related, environmental, task-related and interpersonal [18]. Starting from this classification, we selected five social skills for TARLAN: requesting help, resolving conflicts, offer-ing assistance, joining a group and making hard decisions. Those five skills are cho-sen so to cover each of the four categories identified in [18]. TARLAN provides 20 scenarios for children to practice in, presented in four different social contexts: school yard, store, classroom and a friend's house. The scenarios present social problems designed to be close to children's everyday experience.

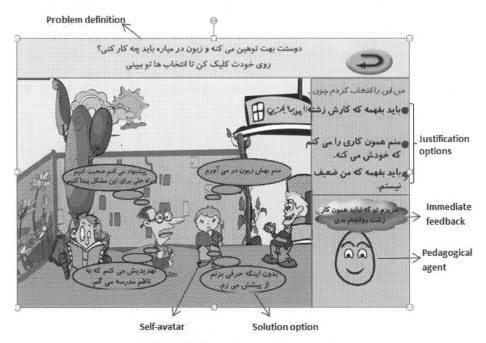

Fig. 1. Different elements of a scenario

The interaction is divided into three phases. In the first phase, TARLAN provides a lot scaffolding to support children's learning. Figure 1 presents a scenario[1] for resolv-ing conflicts in the schoolyard. The self-avatar for the user is presented as the boy in the pink shirt. The problem in this particular scenario is that a friend was rude, and the child needs to take an action. There are four solution options, presented in the thought bubbles: a) be rude to the friend; b) talk to the friend to find a resolution;

---

[1] Please note that TARLAN was developed for Iranian children.

c) threaten to tell the teacher and d) leave and not say anything. If the child selects option a), three justification options will be given: 1) My friends needs to know what he did was wrong; 2) I am doing the same thing my friend did; and 3) I want to show him that I am not weak. Since the selected solution option was wrong, any of those justification options are also wrong, and the system will present an explanation via the animated agent. In Figure 1, the agent is saying "My dear, your friend was rude to you, but you should not be rude to him." Then the child can go back and try another solution/justification option.

The pedagogical agent was designed to support the learning process. As a result, the child does not feel alone in the environment. The agent reads the problem text and guides children to ease their interaction with the system. The agent also demonstrates different emotions according to the child's chosen options (Figure 2).

Default	Sad	Worried	Happy

Fig. 2. Different emotions of the pedagogical agent

Compared to the first phase, the second phase is more demanding, as the system provides no justification options but only general feedback, and children have to come up with their own justification options. In this phase, the agent asks the child to click on wrong options to delete them. On each click, the agent is zoomed in and asks the child why the option is wrong (as in Figure 3). The child does not need to enter the justification option, but instead is encouraged to think about an ap-

Fig. 3. The agent is waiting for child's justification

propriate justification. The agent counts from 10 to 1 by showing a counter to give time to the child to think of a justification.

The third phase is conducted outside of the system. The child is given a worksheet with six sections, corresponding to the six steps of SOCCSS. The child is first asked to specify a recent problem he/she experienced, and to suggest some solution options. Then the child needs to choose one of the solution options and try it in real life. If he/she managed to solve the problem with the selected solution option, the recommendation is to that solution option in mind to solve possible similar problems in future and that is when the process ends. Otherwise, if the selected solution option was not helpful in solving the problem, the child has to check whether there are any untried solution options. If yes, the child should take the untried solution option and go through the process once more. If no, the child is recommended to think of another solution option.

3   Study

Sixty children aged 8 to 12 were recruited to participate in the study which was conducted in Iran. Forty participants were children diagnosed with ADHD and 20 were children without ADHD but diagnosed with social skills deficit. We allocated the children to two interventions: a computer-based intervention and a psychotherapist-directed intervention. The 20 children without ADHD were allocated to the computer-based intervention directly (NOADHD group), as we wanted to investigate whether TARLAN would be effective for this population. The remaining 40 children with ADHD were randomly assigned to the computer-based group (ADHD-Com group) and the psychotherapist-directed intervention (ADHD-Psy group). The latter was conducted by a clini-

cal psychologist in group sessions (50 minutes long), where ADHD children learned about social problem solving skills. The groups consisted of 3-5 children doing role-playing. The reason for having this condition was to have a control condition, which would allow us to compare TARLAN to the existing way of treating ADHD children.

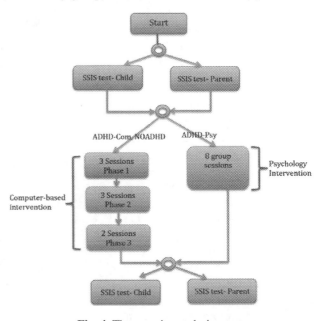

The study consisted of 8 sessions (two sessions per week). Children used TARLAN in individual, 20-30 minutes long sessions. As indicated in Figure 4, the study started by conducting

Fig. 4. The experiment design

pre-tests for both the chil-dren and their parent. SSIS (Social Skills Improvement System) Rating Scale [17], which measures social skills and problem behavior, was used as the pre/post-test. Children who were allocated to the computer-based intervention worked on the first phase of the system for 3 sessions, on the second phase for 3 sessions and on the third phase for 2 ses-sions. In the first two phases, the participants could solveas many problems as they wanted, including repeating problems. At the end of session 6, they were introduced to the requirements of the last phase. In session 7, the chil-dren discussed the problems they identified and their solutions with the experimenter. In the final session, they handed in the solution for the second problem they did on their own, but there was no discussion about the solution. At the end, we administered the post-test to the children and their parents.

4   Results and Discussion

We extracted four variables from SSIS (used as the pre/post-test): Social Skills of the student on the Child questionnaire (SSC), Social Skills of the student on the Parent questionnaire (SSP), Problem Behavior of the student on the Child questionnaire (PBC) and finally Problem Behavior of the student on the Parent questionnaire (PBP). Table 1 presents the SSIS scores of the three conditions.

Table 1. SSIS scores (*ns* denotes not significant)

	ADHD-Com	NOADHD	ADHD-Psy
SSC pre-test	86.25 (16.68)	92.55 (15.67)	80.45 (15.94)
SSC post-test	96.20 (10.29)	99.50 (11.61)	82.95 (12.96)
Improvement on SSC	t=3.16, p<0.01**	t=2.19, p<0.05**	ns
SSP pre-test	74.7 (19.70)	88.85 (16.64)	68.5 (13.01)
SSP post-test	78.7 (19.29)	96.3 (18.16)	74.4 (17.13)
Improvement on SSP	ns	t=2.38, p<0.05**	t=1.51, p=0.07*
PBC pre-test	115.1 (14.95)	100 (12.66)	117.8 (18.84)
PBC post-test	104.75 (11.74)	98.55 (14.08)	116.2 (20.39)
Improvement on PBC	t=4.42, p<0.001**	ns	ns
PBP pre-test	130.45 (12.39)	117.4 (16.66)	130.95 (23.49)
PBP post-test	128.85 (6.97)	105.9 (15.07)	129.2 (22.42)
Improvement on PBP	ns	t=3.99, p<0.001**	ns

The social skills and problem behaviours of students in the ADHD-Com group improved significantly between pre- and post-test based on the child questionnaire. After working with our system, the children without ADHD improved in all areas except PBC. On the other hand, the ADHD-Psy group marginally improved on SSC.

It is interesting to note the difference in children's and parents' scores. For instance, in the ADHD-Com group, children improved significantly on both social skills and problem behaviour based on the child questionnaire, but not in the parent questionnaire. Our intervention is therefore perceived as more beneficial by the children than by their parents. This may be because TARLAN is aimed at children: instead of looking at a social problem as a barrier, they start to see social problems as challenges to solve. As this change is internal to the child, parents may not able to notice the impact on their children in a short period of time. Another potential explanation of the different results on the child/parent scores might be the timing of the post-test, which was administered during the last session. As a result, the parents may not have had opportunities to see their children's improved problem-solving skills in action.

The parents' scores on their children's social skills improved marginally from pre-to post-test (SSP) for the ADHD-Psy group, but not for ADHD-Com. We believe the reason for this difference is that the parents of the children from these two groups had different experiences. The ADHD-Psy condition met in groups, and their parents were sitting together in the waiting area and talking. They could even see their children from where they were sitting, whereas in the other two conditions children worked with the system individually in a separate room. Their parents therefore had less ex-posure to other parents, and may have thought their child was playing with yet anoth-er computer game with no impact on the child's learning.

Although we expected the NOADHD children to score better on PBP compared to the ADHD children, a significant improvement on PBP scores between pre- and post-test shows that parents have noticed a big difference even in a short period of time, thus showing the effectiveness of TARLAN for this population of children.

We analysed SSIS scores using ANCOVA, with the pre-test score as a co-variate. Post hoc analysis was performed with the Bonferroni adjustment to obtain pairwise comparisons. There was a significant difference on SSC scores of the three groups (F(2,56)=8.102, p<0.005).The mean SSC score for the ADHD-Com group (M=96.26, SD=2.32) was significantly higher than the score of the ADHD-Psy group (M=84.98, SD=2.38), p=0.004. That means the ADHD-Com group improved significantly more on SSC than the ADHD-Psy group. Also, the mean score on SSC for NOADHD group (M=97.41, SD=2.38) was significantly higher than the ADHD-Psy group (M=84.98, SD=2.38), p=0.002. Comparisons between ADHD-Psy group and the NOADHD group are not of importance for our study, because in these two groups children were different (with and without ADHD) and the interventions were also different (computer-based intervention vs. group-based intervention).

Post-intervention SSP and PBC scores did not show any significant differences in between-groups comparison. However, we have found a significant difference on PBP post-test scores, F(2,56)=4.857, p<0.05. The mean PBP score for the NOADHD group (M=111.34, SD=3.85) was significantly lower than the ADHD-Com group (M=126.28, SD=3.73), p=0.025. That means NOADHD group improved significantly more on PBP than the ADHD-Com group. PBP measures problem behaviour, so the lower score represents a better result. Also, the mean score on PBP for NOADHD group was significantly lower than the ADHD-Psy group (M=126.33, SD=3.74), p=0.025. Therefore, problem behaviours of NOADHD children improved significant-ly more than the other two groups.

Table 2. Performance of children in phase 1

Item	ADHD-Com	NOADHD	p
Solved problems	9.18 (3.29)	11.48 (4.04)	p<0.05**, t=1.84
Abandoned problems	1.42 (0.58)	1.1 (0.68)	p=0.06*, t=1.57
Solution options per problem	1.85 (0.28)	1.62 (0.25)	p<0.01**, t=2.71
Correct solution options (%)	49.78 (10.15)	59.44 (9.56)	p<0.01**, t=3.09
Justification options per problem	2.81 (0.5)	2.26 (0.37)	p<0.001**, t=3.97
Correct justification options (%)	32.72 (7.18)	41.49 (8.61)	p<0.001**, t=3.50

We also extracted data about from participants' interactions with the system. Table 2 shows that the NOADHD group was more successful in Phase 1 overall. The NOADHD children solved significantly more problems in phase 1, and also had significantly higher percentages of correct solution and justification options, compared to the ADHD-Com group. Moreover, children with ADHD abandoned marginally significantly higher number of problems than children without ADHD. The ADHD-Com group selected significantly more solution/justification options per attempted problem than children without ADHD. These differences between the two groups may be due to attention deficits of the ADHD-Com children.

It is interesting to study those differences on a finer granularity level. Fig. 5 shows the number of solution/justification options in each session of Phase 1. In Session 1, there is a significant difference on the number of justification options ($t=2.84$, $p<0.01$) and a marginally significant difference on the number of solution options ($t=1.74$, $p=0.08$). However, by Session 3, there is no difference between the two groups, showing that interaction with TARLAN is beneficial for ADHD children.

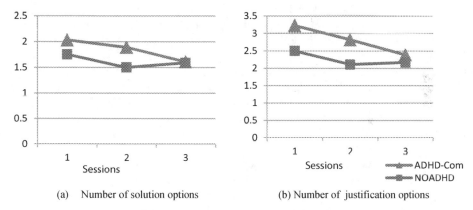

(a)   Number of solution options   (b) Number of justification options

Fig. 4. Performance of children in phase 1

Due to technical problems, we do not have all the data for Phase 2. The ADHD-Com group solved on average 11.85 problems in this phase (sd=3.04), while the NOADHD group solved 12.13 problems (sd=2.84). There is neither a significant dif-ference on the number of solved problems in Phase 2 overall, nor in individual ses-sions of this phase.

Phase 3 was paper-based, and the participants worked on two problems they iden-ti-fied themselves. Table 3 presents the success rates of both groups in this phase. A comparison between the two groups on the performance of the participants showed no significant differences.

Table 3. Percentage of solved problems in Phase 3

	ADHD-Com	NOADHD	p
Average	82.5%	90%	ns
Problem 1	70%	80%	ns
Problem 2	90%	100%	ns

We designed phase 3 of TARLAN with the purpose of simulating transfer. In phase 3, there were no prespecified problems, but children selected their own prob-lems. Analysing the data in phase 3 showed the children (with and without ADHD) could apply their knowledge about social problem-solving skills from TARLAN in solving their self-defined problems.

5   Conclusions

In this paper we presented TARLAN, a simulation game which teaches social-problem solving to ADHD children. Our game helps ADHD children to acquire social problem-solving skill by providing support for each step of the SOCCSS process. Children can practice in TARLAN without worrying about the consequences of mak-ing mistakes. The game teaches five social skills, presented to children in familiar contexts. Using TARLAN is cost-effective compared to common psychotherapist-directed treatments.

We conducted a study in which we compared TARLAN to the psychotherapist-directed intervention, with ADHD children. We also evaluated the effectiveness of TARLAN on children without ADHD but with social skills deficit. The results show that TARLAN improved social skills and problem behaviours of ADHD children more than their peers who were in the psychologist-led treatment. At the same time, TARLAN is effective with children without ADHD. Our study showed that although performance of the ADHD children was poor at the beginning of the study, they caught up with children without ADHD as a result of working with TARLAN. The results of phase 3, in which the children identified their own problems from real life, and solved them, show that TARLAN enables the ADHD children to transfer what they learned to real life. This is an important achievement, made possible by realistic problem-solving scenarios, which were designed to be close to the children's every-day life and culture.

At the moment, TARLAN is only available in Farsi, and converting it to English is one of our major future plans. Furthermore, our system provides one scenario for each pair of social skill and social context. Adding additional scenarios would provide more practice opportunities. Having additional scenarios would also support another future goal: to make TARLAN adaptive, so that it can provide practice opportunities tailored to the strengths and weaknesses of each individual child. In order to make the results of our study stronger, it would be desirable to use the SSIS assessment of teachers. The SSIS Rating Scale is a comprehensive tool containing different sub-variables for social skills and problem behavior. We have additional low-level data that can be analyzed to obtain insight into the participant's communication and coop-eration skills, among others. Instead of using the self-avatar, the scenarios can be designed from the view point of the user, so that the user can move virtually through the environment and interact with different people situated in scenarios.

While the results of this study revealed the effectiveness of simulation games in teaching social skills to ADHD children, many questions remain unanswered. For ex-ample, will we get similar results from teaching other social skills? Do simulation games have a similar positive impact on social skills of children with other disabili-ties, such as Asperger or autism? Can simulation games be used to teach other skills, such as problem solving in science, to the ADHD children?

Another possible extension of our research is to investigate the effectiveness of simu-lation games on ADHD adults with social skills deficit. Developing standard guidelines for designing educational software for ADHD children would be helpful in order to customize the software environments to meet the ADHD users' special re-quirements.

References

1. Parsons, T.D., Bowerly, T., Buckwalter, J.G., Rizzo, A.: A controlled clinical comparison of attention performance in children with ADHD in a virtual reality classroom compared to standard neuropsychological methods. Child Neuropsychology 13(4), 363–381 (2007)
2. Excoffier, E.: What is child attention deficit hyperactivity disorder? La Revue Du Praticien 56(4), 371–378 (2006)
3. Cho, B.H., Ku, J., Jang, D.P., Kim, S., Lee, Y.H., Kim, I.Y., Lee, J.H., Kim, S.I.: The effect of virtual reality cognitive training for attention enhancement. Cyberpsychology & Behavior: The Impact of the Internet, Multimedia and Virtual Reality on Behavior and Society 5(2), 129–137 (2002)
4. Goldsworthy, R., Sasha, B., Goldsworthy, E.: The STAR project: Enhancing adolescents' social understanding by video-based, multimedia scenarios. Special Education Technology 15(2), 13–26 (2000)
5. Modesto-Lowe, V., Danforth, J.S., Brooks, D.: ADHD: does parenting style matter? Clinical pediatrics 47(9), 865–872 (2008)
6. Brown, R.T., Perrin, J.M.: Measuring outcomes in attention-deficit/hyperactivity disorder. Journal of Pediatric Psychology 32(6), 627–630 (2007)
7. Hupp, S.D.A., Leblanc, M., Jewell, J., Warnes, E.: Social behavior and skills in children, New York (2009)
8. O'Neil, H., Perez, R.S.: Computer games and team and individual Learning, Oxford (2007)
9. Bonk C.J., Dennen, V.P.: Massive multiplayer online gaming: A research framework for military training and education. Technical report, Consortium Research Fellows Program (2005)
10. Zimmerman, E.: Gaming Literacy: Game design as a model for literacy in the twenty-First century. Revista Digital 4, 155–165 (2013)
11. VanEck, R.: Where do we go from here? Ten critical areas to guide future research in digital games-based learning. Conference on Game, Learning, and Society, Madison (2006)
12. Cannon-Bowers, J., Bowers, C.: Serious game design and development: technologies for training and learning. Hershey, PA (2010)
13. Shelton, B., Wiley, D.: The design and use of simulation computer games in education, Rotterdom (2007)
14. Baghaei, N., Casey, J., Harris, G.: COMAC☐: Educational games for children with ADD/ADHD. In: Proc. 10th Asia Pacific Conference on Computer Human Interaction, Matsue (2012)
15. Myles, B., Diane, A.: Understanding the hidden curriculum: An Essential Social Skill for Children and Youth with Asperger syndrome. Intervention in School and Clinic 36(5), 279–286 (2001)
16. Mayer, R.E.: Multimedia Learning, Cambridge (2001)
17. Gresham, F.M., Elliott, S.N.: SSIS Social Skills Improvement System, Bloomington (2008)
18. Merrel, K., Gimpel, G.: Social Skills of Children and Adolescents: Conceptualization, Assessment, Treatment. Erlbaum, New York (1998)

Blocking vs. Interleaving: Examining Single-Session Effects Within Middle School Math Homework

Korinn Ostrow[1(✉)], Neil Heffernan[1], Cristina Heffernan[1], and Zoe Peterson[2]

[1] Worcester Polytechnic Institute, 100 Institute Road, Worcester, MA 01609, USA
{ksostrow,nth,ch}@wpi.edu
[2] Carleton College, 1 North College Street, Northfield, MN 55057, USA
petersonz@carleton.edu

Abstract. The benefit of interleaving cognitive content has gained attention in recent years, specifically in mathematics education. The present study serves as a conceptual replication of previous work, documenting the interleaving effect within a middle school sample through brief homework assignments completed within ASSISTments, an adaptive tutoring platform. The results of a randomized controlled trial are presented, examining a practice session featuring interleaved or blocked content spanning three skills: Complementary and Supplementary Angles, Surface Area of a Pyramid, and Compound Probability without Replacement. A second homework session served as a delayed posttest. Tutor log files are analyzed to track student performance and to establish a metric of global mathematics skill for each student. Findings suggest that interleaving is beneficial in the context of adaptive tutoring systems when considering learning gains and average hint usage at posttest. These observations were especially relevant for low skill students.

Keywords: Interleaving · Blocking · Adaptive tutoring system · Mathematics education · Randomized controlled trial

1 Introduction

The benefit of interleaving cognitive content has gained attention in recent years. A simple intervention rooted in kinesthetic research pertaining to the acquisition of motor skills [18], interleaving has since evolved into a powerful tool for the modern classroom. Specifically, significant effects have been verified in the realm of mathematics education in classroom trials and through simulated studies [9, 17, 6, 19, 7]. Research within this realm has examined the interleaving effect by mixing or alternating the delivery of skill or problem content, such that similar problems are no longer 'blocked' or presented in uniform segments. The benefits observed when interleaving mathematics content are often credited to the discriminative-contrast hypothesis [1], which purports that the effect is rooted in a student's enhanced ability to pinpoint differences in problem content. As such, interleaving provides an obvious tool within a domain that relies largely on problem type identification and solution strategy choice [15].

© Springer International Publishing Switzerland 2015
C. Conati et al. (Eds.): AIED 2015, LNAI 9112, pp. 338–347, 2015.
DOI: 10.1007/978-3-319-19773-9_34

Despite this clarity, the details of interleaving remain somewhat obscure. It is heavily documented that interleaving is confounded by an inherent spacing effect [15], yet few researchers effectively isolate interleaving by examining a single session or controlling for the spacing of content [19]. Researchers have also added complexity to the issue, questioning which dimension of cognitive content (i.e., the skill, the task type, the representation, etc.) to interleave for optimal results [12, 13]. Further, despite continued reports of significant learning gains observed at posttest after interleaved practice, policymakers and educational designers fail to interleave mass-produced content, claiming that it is detrimental to the student's learning *experience* [16, 19, 5]. Essentially, the practice has earned a bad reputation for making the learning process more complex, or for adding what Bjork terms 'desirable difficulty' [2].

The present study serves as a conceptual replication of Rohrer & Taylor's work on shuffling mathematics practice problems [17]. While replications are rare in general [14], a recent analysis of leading education journals found that less than 0.13% of publications were replications [8]. However, repeated observations of significant educational findings, especially within different contexts, have the power to produce systemic change. While not a direct replication, we similarly aim to assess the interleaving effect within mathematics skills amidst a single practice session, considering delayed posttest measures as dependent metrics. More uniquely, we seek to document the effect using a brief homework assignment completed within ASSISTments, an online adaptive tutoring system. We also consider a global metric of mathematics skill for each student, in and attempt to gauge how the effect differs across skill level.

ASSISTments is fast growing platform offered as a free service of Worcester Polytechnic Institute and used for homework and classwork by over 50,000 students around the world [4]. The system offers teachers a library of prebuilt content, primarily with a focus on mathematics skills aligned to the Common Core State Standards, as well as the ability to build content to match their curriculum or course goals. Simultaneously, students benefit from correctness feedback and tutoring strategies within an adaptive environment that advances skill practice beyond that achieved through traditional classroom practices. ASSISTments also serves as shared scientific tool for education research [4]. Adaptive tutoring systems provide a natural learning environment from which to assess best practices, and yet, to our knowledge, little work has been done to examine interleaving within these settings. Thus, a randomized controlled trial was designed within ASSISTments to examine the subtleties of interleaving, as guided by the following research questions:

1. When controlling for student skill level, do learning gains (as measured by average posttest score) differ when practice session content is interleaved?
2. When controlling for student skill level, does interleaving practice session content lead students to interact differently with the system at posttest (as measured by average hint usage and average attempt count)?

It was hypothesized that interleaving skill content in the practice session would have a beneficial effect on student performance as measured at posttest, leading to increases in posttest score and reductions in the average number of hints and attempts used during posttest problems.

2   Methods

This study was conducted with five classes spanning three teachers at a suburban middle school in Massachusetts. All teachers and students within the sample population were familiar with ASSISTments, having used the system for classwork and homework throughout the school year. Researchers worked with a participating teacher to design problem content for two homework assignments (i.e., a practice session and a delayed posttest). In April 2014, the teacher isolated three mathematics skills that her students had learned earlier in the year to serve as review while allowing for the observation of relearning via hint usage. The skills covered were Complementary/Supplementary Angles (Skill A; originally covered in February/March 2014), Surface Area of a Pyramid (Skill B; originally covered in November/December 2013), and Probability of Compound Events without Replacement (Skill C; originally covered in January 2014). A problem exemplifying Skill B with all available hint feedback is provided in Figure 1; problems exemplifying Skills A and C can be accessed at Ostrow [11] for further reference.

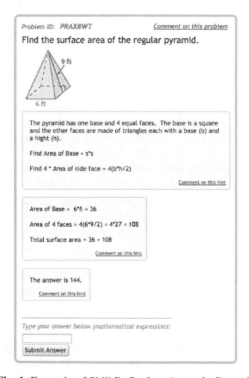

Fig. 1. Example of Skill B, Surface Area of a Pyramid

For the practice session, four problems were created for each skill, resulting in a single assignment with twelve problems. These problems were isomorphic in structure, but designed such that problem difficulty would increase with each practice opportunity. Hence, a student's first experience with Skill A was relatively easy, while her fourth experience with the skill was more challenging. One additional problem was created for each skill, matching the highest difficulty level presented during practice, to establish a separate, three-problem assignment that would serve as a delayed posttest. Practice and posttest sessions were both assigned as homework, establishing an authentic learning experience and reducing the potential for immediate assistance from and adult. Settings for homework completion were ultimately unknown and were likely differential across students.

Further, although straying from the conventions of a 'formal' posttest, permitting the use of hints and multiple attempts during the posttest assignment allowed researchers to investigate variables of student performance extending beyond average posttest score (i.e., an average of the student's accuracy on their first attempt at solving each problem).

3   Procedure

After the creation and release of content, five teachers assigned this study to an initial sample of 226 7th grade students. Students were randomly assigned to either the experimental condition, in which skill problems within the practice assignment were presented in an interleaved or mixed pattern, or to the control condition, in which skill problems within the practice assignment were presented using a blocked approach. Random assignment was accomplished using a pseudo-random number generator within the ASSISTments tutor, and occurred at the student level rather than the class level to control for potential teacher and class effects.

Regardless of condition, students received the same twelve problems during the practice session, with the only difference being presentation order. Problem delivery patterns for each group are depicted in Figure 2. Using this design, the effects of interleaving were not specifically isolated from the effects of spacing. For instance, students in the interleaved condition experienced problem A_4 at a later point in time than students in the blocked condition. However, the practice session was delivered as a single assignment in an attempt to minimize the effects of spacing [16, 3].

Regardless of condition, all students received a second homework assignment consisting of three problems in a static delivery pattern, serving as a delayed posttest. Participating teachers assigned this posttest anywhere from two to five days following the practice session. Details pertaining to the design of this study, including access to question content and the student experience can be found at Ostrow [11].

Blocked	$A_1, A_2, A_3, A_4, B_1, B_2, B_3, B_4, C_1, C_2, C_3, C_4$
Interleaved	$A_1, A_2, B_1, B_2, C_1, C_2, A_3, B_3, C_3, B_4, C_4, A_4$
Posttest	A_5, B_5, C_5

Fig. 2. Experimental Design: Skill Problem Delivery Across Groups

Tutor log files were retrieved from the ASSISTments database and problem level data, including correctness, hint usage, and attempt count was isolated for each student. Using previously logged data, it was also possible to calculate a global metric of mathematics skill for each student based on the average accuracy of all problems he or she had ever completed within the system. This measure was then discretized using a median split to bin students as generally 'high' or 'low' skill.

Within the initial sample of 226 students assigned the practice session, one participating teacher failed to assign the posttest, resulting in the removal of 68 students from final analysis. Of the remaining 158 students, three students failed to complete enough of the practice session to verify their condition based on logged data, and were therefore excluded from analysis. Additionally, nine low-skill students failed to start the posttest assignment. Further assessment of these nine students revealed that six had experienced the blocked condition during the practice session, while three had experienced the interleaved condition. Only five of these students completed the practice session, with four students failing to complete the blocked session and one student failing to complete the interleaved session. A two-tailed independent t-test was performed to compare the number of practice session problems completed by these students across groups, revealing that condition was not a significant factor in disparate completion rate, $t = 0.048$, $p = .963$. These nine students were therefore excluded from posttest analysis without introducing an obvious bias.

A Chi-squared test of independence of the remaining 146 students did not indicate a significant relationship between condition and student skill level, χ^2 (1, N = 146) = 0.195, $p > .05$. However, the distribution across conditions was not equivalent (Blocked, n = 60; Interleaved, n = 86) due to the pseudo-random number generator that conducted student level randomization. Given the successful use of this assignment method in previous research, the authors had no reason to believe that a selection effect had occurred or that this process was in any way biased (i.e., affected by specific student characteristics). Thus, the skewed distribution observed here was not regarded as a threat to validity. The log files discussed herein have been stripped of identifiers and are available at Ostrow [11] for further reference.

4   Results

To examine our first research question, an ANCOVA was performed to analyze average posttest score across conditions when controlling for student skill level. Within 146 students, after controlling for the effect of student skill level, the effect of condition on posttest score trended toward significance, $F(1,143) = 2.69$, $p = 0.103$, $\eta^2 = 0.02$, Hedge's $g = 0.22$. As a covariate, student skill level was significantly related to posttest score, $F(1, 143) = 29.308$, $p < .001$, $\eta^2 = 0.17$. Levene's test was not significant, $p > .05$, and thus error variance was assumed to be equal across conditions. A summary of the effects of condition on average posttest score is depicted in Table 1. Analysis of means revealed that students in the interleaved condition (M = 0.67, SD = 0.27, n = 86) outperformed those in the blocked condition (M = 0.61, SD = 0.27, n = 60).

Split file ANOVAs were conducted to further examine the effect of condition across student skill level. For low skill students, condition had a significant effect on average posttest score, $F(1, 62) = 5.59$, $p < .05$, $\eta^2 = 0.08$, Hedge's $g = 0.60$. Levene's test was significant, $F(1, 62) = 5.16$, $p < .05$ suggesting the assumption of equivalent variance has been violated. Analysis of means revealed that students in the interleaved condition (M = 0.58, SD = 0.29, n = 39) significantly out performed those in the blocked condition (M = 0.42, SD = 0.23, n = 25). Within high skill students, condition no longer had a significant effect on posttest score, $F(1, 80) = 0.01$, $p > .05$. Students in the interleaved condition (M = 0.74, SD = 0.23, n = 47) performed quite similarly to those in the blocked condition (M = 0.74, SD = 0.21, n = 35). Summaries of the effects of condition on average posttest score for both skill levels are presented in Table 2. Figure 3 depicts the interaction of condition and student skill level observed in average posttest score.

Table 1. ANCOVA of the Effects of Condition on Average Posttest Score

Source	df	SS	MS	F	p	η^2
Skill Level	1	1.80	1.80	29.21	.000	0.17
Condition	1	0.17	0.17	2.69	.103	0.02
Error	143	8.80	0.06			
Total	146	71.25				

Table 2. ANOVA of the Effects of Condition on Average Posttest Score by Skill Level

Source	df	SS	MS	F	p	η^2
Low Skill						
Condition	1	0.41	0.41	5.59	0.021	0.08
Error	62	4.51	0.07			
Total	64	22.19				
High Skill						
Condition	1	0.00	0.00	0.01	0.945	0.00
Error	80	4.06	0.05			
Total	82	49.06				

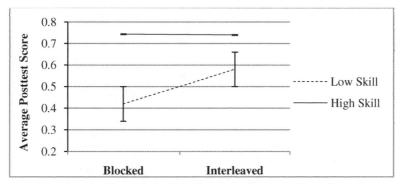

Note. Standard Error for high skill students is not visible at this scale.

Fig. 3. Means for Average Posttest Score Across Conditions and Student Skill Levels

To examine our second research question, a MANCOVA was used to analyze the dependent measures of average posttest hint usage and average posttest attempt count as a function of condition after controlling for student skill level. Pillai's Trace is reported throughout, as the assumption of equality of covariance matrices was violated and this parameter offers a more robust understanding of variance. Within 146 students, after controlling for the effect of student skill level, there was a significant main effect of condition, Pillai's Trace = 0.06, F (2, 142) = 4.81, p < 0.05. At the multivariate level, student skill level was significant as a covariate, Pillai's Trace = 0.36, F (2, 142) =

39.25, p < .001, explaining approximately 36% of the total variance. Tests of between subjects effects revealed that condition had a significant effect on average posttest hint usage, $F(1, 143) = 6.24$, $p < .05$, $\eta^2 = 0.03$, Hedge's $g = -0.29$. Students in the interleaved condition used significantly less hints on average (M = 0.33, SD = 0.57, n = 86) than those in the blocked condition (M = 0.50, SD = 0.64, n = 60). However, condition did not significantly affect average posttest attempt count, $F(1, 143) = 0.10$, $p > .05$, with those in the interleaved condition (M = 1.75, SD = 1.08, n = 86) and those in the blocked condition (M = 1.68, SD = 0.57, n = 60) using a similar amount of attempts. A summary of univariate results is presented in Table 3.

Split file analyses revealed that the effects of interleaving were more impressive when low skill students were considered in isolation. Within 64 low skill students, condition had a significant multivariate effect, Pillai's Trace = 0.12, $F(2, 61) = 4.20$, p < 0.05. Univariate analyses revealed that condition had a significant effect on posttest hint usage, $F(1, 62) = 5.38$, $p < .05$, $\eta^2 = 0.08$, Hedge's $g = -0.59$, with students in the interleaved condition using less hints on average (M = 0.64, SD = 0.70, n = 39) than those in the blocked condition (M = 1.04, SD = 0.62, n = 25). Condition did not significantly affect posttest attempts, $F(1, 62) = 0.08$, $p > .05$, with those in the interleaved condition (M = 2.12, SD = 1.42, n = 39) and those in the blocked condition (M = 2.04, SD = 0.58, n = 25) using a similar amount of attempts.

Within high skill students, condition no longer had a significant multivariate effect, Pillai's Trace = 0.02, $F(2, 79) = 0.84$, p > 0.05. Summaries of the effects of condition on the dependent variables for both skill levels are presented in Table 4. Figure 4 depicts the interaction of condition and student skill level observed in average posttest hint usage.

Table 3. Univariate Summaries of the Effects of Condition on Dependent Variables

Source	df	Ave. Posttest Hints					Ave. Posttest Attempts				
		SS	MS	F	p	η^2	SS	MS	F	p	η^2
Skill Level	1	18.24	18.24	79.06	.000	0.35	15.13	15.13	21.07	.000	0.13
Condition	1	1.44	1.44	6.24	.014	0.03	0.07	0.07	0.10	.749	0.00
Error	143	32.98	0.23				102.67	0.72			
Total	146	75.75					552.06				

Table 4. ANOVA of the Effects of Condition on Dependent Variables by Skill Level

Source	df	Ave. Posttest Hints					Ave. Posttest Attempts				
		SS	MS	F	p	η^2	SS	MS	F	p	η^2
Low Skill											
Condition	1	2.43	2.43	5.38	.024	0.08	0.10	0.10	0.08	.785	0.00
Error	62	27.93	0.45				84.32	1.36			
Total	64	71.00					363.94				
High Skill											
Condition	1	0.06	0.06	1.09	.299	0.01	0.01	0.01	0.03	.865	0.00
Error	80	4.01	0.05				18.31	0.23			
Total	82	4.75					188.13				

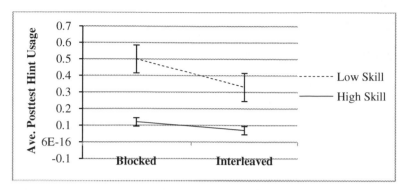

Fig. 4. Means for Average Posttest Hint Usage Across Conditions and Student Skill Levels

5   Discussion

The findings herein highlight the promising effects of interleaving skill content within brief mathematics homework assignments in the context of adaptive tutoring systems. Despite failing to achieve an effect size as large as that observed by Rohrer & Taylor [17] (Cohen's d = 1.34), we observed trends toward significance aligning with past work, serving as further evidence that interleaving skill content enhances learning gains as measured at a delayed posttest. This study also expanded upon interleaving literature to examine how these learning gains differ across student skill level. Further, the findings of the present study extended beyond binary measures of correctness to consider students' differential use of hints and attempts within an informal posttest setting. While this approach was somewhat novel, adaptive tutoring systems allow for the comparison of a variety of rich features within the learning experience that may provide deeper insight than accuracy alone. The observation of significantly different hint usage across conditions suggested that the consideration of feedback utilization, perhaps through a partial credit metric, may offer a more robust explanation for differential learning gains in future research.

The findings observed for low skill students were especially impressive and could prove groundbreaking for future design of adaptive tutoring content. Systems like ASSISTments already provide educational resources in a manner that has been shown to produce significantly greater learning gains than those found using traditional classroom practices [10]. This study suggests that learning outcomes can be further enhanced simply by adding support for a dynamic approach to content delivery through interleaving.

A major limitation of this study was the loss of a large portion of the original sample due to the failure of a participating teacher to assign the posttest to her students. It is possible that a larger sample would better reveal subtleties in the interaction between condition and student skill level. The sample distribution was also suboptimal, with random assignment resulting in more students in the interleaved condition than in the blocked condition. Further, analyses may have been weakened by the discretization of students as generally 'high' or 'low' skill. Departing from the use of a median split should be examined in future work.

Future iterations of this work should incorporate a pretest assignment and use novel skill content rather than skills intended for review. Future work should also examine variables pertaining to student performance within the *practice session* (i.e., average problem time, hint usage, and attempt count) to investigate Bjork's theory of desirable difficulties [2]. Additionally, future research should investigate more robust measures of learning, including extended retention rates following interleaved assignments and the effects on far transfer application.

6   Contribution

While many studies have examined the effect of interleaving, we offer a significant contribution to the field of artificial intelligence in education in that our work replicates the effect of interleaving within a brief homework assignment delivered using an adaptive tutoring system. Emphasized significance was observed for low skill students. Further, the use of homework assignments as both intervention and posttest resulted in the observation that rich features common to adaptive tutoring systems may allow researchers to pinpoint effects in variables other than correctness. The ease with which interleaving can be conducted within adaptive tutoring systems offers a low-cost, high-benefit approach to enhancing student learning outcomes.

Acknowledgments. We acknowledge funding from the NSF (1316736, 1252297, 1109483, 1031398, 0742503, 1440753), the U.S. Dept. of Ed. GAAN (P200A120238), ONR's "STEM Grand Challenges," and IES (R305A120125, R305C100024). Thanks to S.O. & L.P.B.O.

References

1. Birnbaum, M.S., Kornell, N., Bjork, E.L., Bjork, R.A.: Why interleaving enhances inductive learning: the roles of discrimination and retrieval. Mem Cogn **41**, 392–402 (2013)
2. Bjork, R.A.: Memory and metamemory considerations in the training of human beings. In: Metcalf, J., Shimamura, A.P. (eds.) Metacognition: Knowing about knowing, pp. 185–295. MIT Press, Cambridge, MA (1994)
3. Cepeda, N.J., Pashler, H., Vul, E., Wixted, J.T., Rohrer, D.: Distributed practice in verbal recall tasks: A review and quantitative synthesis. Psy Bulletin **132**, 354–380 (2006)
4. Heffernan, N., Heffernan, C.: The ASSISTments Ecosystem: Building a Platform that Brings Scientists and Teachers Together for Minimally Invasive Research on Human Learning and Teaching. Int. J. of AI. in Ed. **24**(4), 470–497 (2014)
5. Kornell, N., Bjork, R.A.: Learning concepts and categories: Is spacing the "enemy of induction"? Psychological Science **19**, 585–592 (2008)
6. LeBlanc, K., Simon, D.: Mixed practice enhances retention and JOL accuracy for mathematical skills. 49th Annual Meeting of the Psychonomic Society, Chicago, IL (2008)
7. Li, Nan, Cohen, William W., Koedinger, Kenneth R.: Problem order implications for learning transfer. In: Cerri, Stefano A., Clancey, William J., Papadourakis, Giorgos, Panourgia, Kitty (eds.) ITS 2012. LNCS, vol. 7315, pp. 185–194. Springer, Heidelberg (2012)

8. Makel, M.C., Plucker, J.A.: Facts Are More Important Than Novelty: Replication in the Education Sciences. Educational Researcher. AERA (2014)
9. Mayfield, K.H., Chase, P.N.: The effects of cumulative practice on mathematics problem solving. J. of Applied Behavior Analysis **35**, 105–123 (2002)
10. Mendicino, M., Razzaq, L., Heffernan, N.T.: Comparison of Traditional Homework with Computer Supported Homework. J. of Research on Tech in Ed. **41**(3), 331–358 (2009)
11. Ostrow, K.: Materials for Study on Blocking vs. Interleaving, January 13 2015. http://tiny.cc/AIED-2015-Interleaving
12. Rau, M.A., Aleven, A., Rummel, N.: Interleaved practice in multi-dimensional learning tasks: Which dimension should we interleave? Learning and Instr. **23**, 98–114 (2013)
13. Rau, M.A., Aleven, V., Rummel, N., Pacilio, L., Tunc-Pekkan, Z.: How to schedule multiple graphical representations? A classroom experiment with an intelligent tutoring system for fractions. In: The Future of Learning: Proceedings of the 10th ICLS (2012)
14. Roediger, H.L.: Psychology's woes and a partial cure: the value of replication. The Academic Observer, The Association for Psychological Science (2012). http://tiny.cc/RoedigerReplication
15. Rohrer, D.: Interleaving helps students distinguish among similar concepts. Educational Psychology Review **24**, 355–367 (2012)
16. Rohrer, D., Pashler, H.: Recent research on human learning challenges conventional instructional strategies. Educational Researcher **39**(5), 406–412 (2010)
17. Rohrer, D., Taylor, K.: The shuffling of mathematics practice problems boosts learning. Instructional Science **35**, 481–498 (2007)
18. Shea, J.B., Morgan, R.L.: Contextual interference effects on the acquisition, retention, and transfer of a motor skill. Journal of Experimental Psychology: Human Learning and Memory **5**(2), 179–187 (1979)
19. Taylor, K., Rohrer, D.: The effects of interleaved practice. Applied Cognitive Psychology **24**, 837–848 (2010)

Impact of Adaptive Educational System Behaviour on Student Motivation

Jan Papoušek[✉] and Radek Pelánek

Faculty of Informatics, Masaryk University Brno,
Brno, Czech Republic
{jan.papousek,xpelanek}@mail.muni.cz

Abstract. In this work we try to connect research on student modeling and student motivation, particularly on the relation between task difficulty and engagement. We perform experiments within widely used adaptive practice system for geography learning. The results document the impact of the choice of a question construction algorithm and target difficulty on student perception of question suitability and on their willingness to use the system. We also propose and evaluate a mechanism for a dynamic difficulty adjustment.

1 Introduction

The goal of adaptive educational systems is to make learning more effective and engaging by tailoring the behaviour of the system to a particular student. The adaptive behaviour is based on student models which estimate the knowledge of students (and potentially other characteristics like their affective state). While a lot of research has focused on development and evaluation of student models, relatively little attention has been devoted to the way the outputs of models are actually used in educational systems. The typical use of student models is for mastery learning, e.g. research studies [3,6,9] have evaluated the impact of used models and their thresholds on over-practice and under-practice.

The use of student models only for judging mastery is, however, only one possible way of making a system adaptive to behaviour of its users. Adaptive educational systems have the potential to make learning more engaging by keeping students in the concentrated flow state [4]. One of the conditions for the flow state is the balance between skills and difficulty of presented problems. The Inverted-U Hypothesis predicts that maximum engagement occurs with moderate challenge [10]. There is extensive research on this topic (e.g. [1]); the research is, however, based mainly on laboratory studies, the results of research are to a certain degree contradictory (see e.g. the discussion in [10]), and it is not clear how to apply the hypothesis in the development of a practical educational application.

In this work we connect the use of student models with the research on optimal level of challenge. We study the impact of adaptive behaviour of an educational system on student motivation in a widely used educational system for learning geographical facts.

© Springer International Publishing Switzerland 2015
C. Conati et al. (Eds.): AIED 2015, LNAI 9112, pp. 348–357, 2015.
DOI: 10.1007/978-3-319-19773-9_35

In the previous works the specification of the adaptive behaviour was based mainly on intuition of system developers and was not evaluated [8,11] or was evaluated using only comparison to a control group without any tuning of the difficulty [2]. The most similar research is by Lomas et al. [10] who evaluated the Inverted-U Hypothesis by testing many variants of an educational game (numberline estimation). They failed to find the U-shaped relation between difficulty and motivation. For their study the relation was monotone (simpler problems were more engaging). Explaining the result they state that maybe they "never made the game easy enough" [10]. Our experiments are similar, the main difference is that we use a more realistic educational application. Another similar research was done using Math Garden software [7]. The authors compared three conditions (target success rate 60%, 75%, 90%) and showed that the easiest condition led to the best learning (mediated by a number of solved problems).

For our work we use a widely used application [11] for learning geography. We have performed randomized online experiments (multivariate testing) to evaluate the impact of the adaptive behaviour on student motivation. The appropriate difficulty of questions is evaluated using proxy measure of student motivation (number of questions answered) and student self-reports (perception of question difficulty). The results show that the adaptive behaviour is advantageous and that the suitable portion of correct answers per user (success rate) is around 65% (with students who used the system in school preferring easier questions). We also propose a dynamic difficulty adjustment of the target success rate and we show that this mechanism improves the adaptive system behaviour and makes it more robust to misalignment of the parameter setting.

2   Question Construction

We start by describing a question construction module for adaptive practice of facts (e.g. vocabulary, geography, human anatomy). Different variants of this module are used for the below reported experiments. The process of question construction has two phases. In the first phase we select a target item, which the question is concerned with, and in the second phase we construct the question itself.

2.1   Selecting a Target Item

The selection of a target item needs to balance several criteria. The main focus of the current work is on appropriate difficulty – according to the flow theory (Inverted-U hypothesis), questions should be adequately hard to ask, since with easy questions students can get bored and with difficult questions students may be frustrated. Another criterion is that questions concerning the same item should not repeat in a close succession [5]. Finally, no item should be left out while practicing, i.e. even students with high knowledge should be asked at least once about each item (our experience suggests this is an intuitive expectation of students). We combine these criteria using the mechanism of scoring functions.

Each item is evaluated by a scoring function according to each criterion and the item with the highest weighted sum is used as a candidate to ask about.

The difficulty aspect is taken into account with the use of a student model. The actual system used for experiments [11] uses a combination of Elo rating system [13] and Performance factor analysis [12]. For the purposes of question construction the details of the used student model are not important – we use it as a black box which provides for each item estimated probability P_{est} that a particular student will answer correctly. The first scoring function depends on the distance between the estimated probability for the given item and the target success rate P_{target}. Assume that our goal is to ask a question in case of which the student has 75% chance of answering correctly. The distance from the probability for the difficult countries (nearly 0% chance of the correct answer) is higher than for easy ones (almost 100%), so it is necessary to normalize it. We use the following scoring function:

$$S_{prob}(P_{est}, P_{target}) = \begin{cases} \frac{P_{est}}{P_{target}} & \text{if } P_{target} \geq P_{est} \\ \frac{1-P_{est}}{1-P_{target}} & \text{if } P_{target} < P_{est} \end{cases}$$

The second scoring function penalizes items based on the time elapsed since the last question, because we do not want to repeat items in a short time interval when they are still in short term memory. We use the function $S_{time}(t) = -1/t$, where t is time in seconds. Using just the above mentioned attributes the system would ask questions for only a limited pool of items. To induce the system to ask questions about new items we introduce the third scoring function that uses the total number n of questions for the given item answered by the student: $S_{count}(n) = 1/\sqrt{1+n}$. The total score is given as a weighted sum of individual scores, the weights are currently set manually, reflecting experiences with the system: $W_{prob} = 1$, $W_{count} = 1$, $W_{time} = 12$.

2.2   Dynamic Adjustment of Target Difficulty

One of the key parameters whose role we experimentally evaluate is the target success rate P_{target}. In the context of computerized adaptive testing the optimal success rate is 50% – such choice leads to the most informative answers and to the best estimate of a student's skill. We are, however, primarily interested in student practice. In this context student motivation is crucial and 50% success rate does not seem very encouraging. The default success rate of our system is 75% (similarly to other applications, e.g. [8]), below we report experiments with different values of the target success rate.

To strengthen the adaptivity of system behaviour we propose an additional dynamic adjustment of target difficulty. With this mechanism the target probability is modified depending on student's recent performance (as a measure of recent performance we use the success rate on the last ten questions). Our system poses easier questions to less successful students and more difficult questions to more successful ones; a specific function for transformation of the target rate is depicted in Fig. 1. Note that by using this mechanism we also indirectly correct a potential estimation bias given by the used student model.

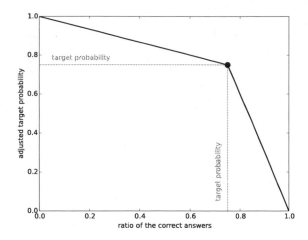

Fig. 1. Adjustment of the target probability of the correct answer

2.3   Choice of Options

Even though the difficulty of the item the system asks about is already taken into account by the first scoring function, it is possible that the predicted difficulty of the selected candidate does not match the target difficulty. Unfortunately, there is nothing to do in case of too easy items. In case of a more difficult candidate the system can use a multiple choice question to give the student a chance to guess the correct answer. With the probability of guessing P_{guess} the probability of answering correctly is $P_{guess} + (1 - P_{guess}) \cdot P_{est}$, where P_{est} is the estimated probability of the correct answer on an open question asking about the given item.

Our goal is to make the probability of the correct answer close to P_{target}. This can be achieved by making P_{guess} close to:

$$G = \frac{P_{target} - P_{est}}{1 - P_{est}}$$

For $G \leq 0$ we use an open question without options, otherwise we use a multiple choice question with n options, where n is the closest integer to $\frac{1}{G}$. For obvious reasons the minimal possible value of n can be 2, for practical reasons there is also an upper bound for n (more than 6 options would look cluttered). To ensure that the options are not easy to disregard, the algorithm takes into account what other items are most commonly mistaken with the given question candidate in open questions. For example, in case of our application, Cameroon is most often confused with Niger (38%), Nigeria (27%), Central African Republic (10%), the Republic of the Congo (9%), Gabon (6%), the Ivory Coast (5%), Uganda (3%), and Guinea (2%). This ratio determines the probability that a given item appears among options in the constructed multiple choice question.

3   Experimental Setting

For experiments we use an adaptive educational system `slepemapy.cz` – an application for learning geography [11]. Students[1] can choose a specific map (e.g. Africa, the United States) and a type of places (e.g. countries, regions, cities, rivers). The system offers adaptively selected questions to students who answer them using an interactive map. After a series of 10 questions the system provides feedback on student's progress. Students can also access a visualization of their knowledge using an open learner model. The application is currently used by hundreds of students per day, majority of students is from the Czech Republic and Slovakia since the interface was originally only in Czech. English and Spanish are currently also available.

3.1   Available Data

So far we have collected almost 6 million answers. For each answer we log all details about the question (target item, options), the student ID, the chosen answer, and also the timing information. We have no personal information about students, we only log their IP address. Part of the data is made public[2].

The system is available to anybody, free of charge. We have no control over the number of answered questions, the time when students practice, or whether they ever return to the system after one session of practice. Thus we assume that the data about students' usage of the system is a reasonable proxy for their motivation to learn using the system. There is one important exception – the system is also used in some schools directly during the class time, in this case the usage of the system may not be related to student motivation. Therefore, for most of the reported experiments, we did not consider these students (an exception is an analysis in Section 4.2). To detect the 'in-school usage' we currently use only a coarse method based on IP address (a group of at least 5 students who started using our system from the same IP address). The 'in-school' usage represents about 20% of the data.

The student model currently used in the application has been calibrated using data containing mainly countries [11]. There are few areas (e.g. Czech cities) where the quality of prediction is worse than the quality of predictions for countries. Since the algorithm for question construction uses predictions as its input, we suppose its behaviour is worse for this kind of areas. Therefore we filtered the data to contain information only about users who were answering solely questions concerning countries.

To perform experiments we used multivariate testing where we randomly divided students into several groups and assigned to each of these groups a different version of the algorithm for the question construction. For analysis we filtered out students using our system before the experiments started. We have

---

[1] Note that the system is publicly available and can be used by anybody, for terminological consistency we use the word 'student' to denote any user.

[2] https://github.com/adaptive-learning/data-public

also removed students having less than 10 answers, since in this case there are not enough opportunities for differences among the tested versions to emerge.

3.2   Metrics

For our experiments we need to measure effects of different variants of the adaptive algorithm on students. We have chosen two different ways to do so. Firstly, we collect students' subjective evaluation of the provided practice. Secondly, we look at the students' behaviour.

In the first case we ask students to evaluate the difficulty of questions. After 30, 70, 120, and 200 answers the system shows the dialog "What is the difficulty of asked questions?", students choose one of the following options: "Too Easy", "Appropriate", "Too Difficult". We look at the ratio of students choosing the given option for the first time and call this metric an *explicit feedback*. In the second case we measure the total number of answered questions. The distribution of number of answers across students is highly skewed, therefore we use the median as a summary statics. For testing statistical significance between distributions we use the t-test over logarithm of number of answers (logarithm transformation is used to reduce the skew).

The two metrics are related. When we divide the students according to their first evaluation, the median number of answers is 91 for group "Too Easy", 110 for group "Appropriate", and 97 for group "Too Difficult". The difference between the group "Appropriate" and both other groups is statistically significant. The observed median is much higher than the median in the following experiments because we include only users with at least one evaluation record.

4   Experiments

Performed experiments corespond to the main aspects of the question construction algorithm. Each experiment was run only for a certain time within the system, so for each of them we report the size of data set used in evaluation.

4.1   Impact of Question Construction Algorithm

The key question of our first experiment is: "Is the proposed algorithm better than a random construction of questions?". As we already mentioned, the mechanics behind the system for constructing questions for a student consists of two main parts. Firstly, the algorithm selects the target item (i.e. which country to ask about). Secondly, it chooses the number of options and options themselves. In the first experiment we evaluated the role of both of these parts. For each part we considered the proposed adaptive mechanism and a random choice. For this experiment we collected more than 30,000 answers.

Table 1. shows how the given versions of the algorithm differ according to the median of the number of answers per student in the given group. The results show that adaptivity brings improvement, and that it is necessary to make both parts

Table 1. Algorithm variants for the question construction used in the first experiment, for each variant we report the median of the the number of answers per student in the given group

Target item	Options	Answers
adaptive	adaptive	33.0
adaptive	random	20.0
random	adaptive	20.0
random	random	19.5

of the algorithm adaptive. The difference between completely adaptive version and other tested versions is in two cases statistically significant ($p < 0.01$). In the case of comparison with the the completely random algorithm the results are on the edge of statistical significance ($p = 0.06$) due to relatively small number of students (26) in the corresponding multivariate group. Unfortunately during this experiment we were not collecting the explicit feedback from students, so only the implicit one is available.

4.2   Impact of Difficulty

In the second experiment we study the question: "Does the difficulty of the questions matter?". The Inverted-U Hypothesis suggests that really easy and really hard questions should have negative impact on students' motivation. In this experiment we deployed several variants of the adaptive algorithm which differ only in the target probability of the correct answer. For this experiment we do not consider the mechanism for adjustment of the target probability (to simplify interpretation of the results).

The results of this experiment and their interpretation are not straightforward. With regard to the total number of answers we have not discovered any statistically significant trend. The biggest issue is probably the relation between the target probability parameter and the real success rate of students. The success rate is only partially influenced by the target rate, other factors include for example students choice of maps. Although the target probability is from the interval [50%, 95%], the average real success rate varies only from 65% to 90%. On several maps (e.g. countries in Europe, for which we have most data) there are not sufficiently difficult items to achieve 50% success rate (for most students).

On the other hand, the relation between achieved success rate and perceived difficulty of questions shows a clear U-shaped pattern[3] (Fig. 2.). The curve does not have a sharp peak, but there is a clear dynamics between the classes. With the increasing difficulty the growth of the number of "Too Easy" votes is compensated by the drop of "Too Difficult" votes. The peak of the "Appropriate"

---

[3] This analysis is less dependent on the calibration of student model, thus we take into account all answers, not only countries.

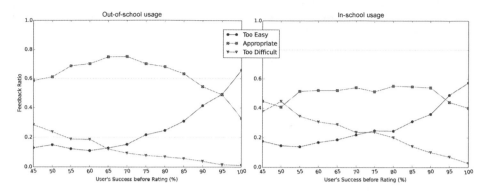

Fig. 2. Explicit feedback given by students according to their previous real success rate. The used data set consists of more than 1,700,000 answers and 12,000 feedback records.

answers as well as the equal votes for "Too Easy" and "Too Difficult" occur at the success rate 65%. This experiment thus suggests that the value 65% may be a suitable target rate for this kind of application.

Previous research [1] suggests that the optimal difficulty may differ depending on the type of motivation (internal, external), particularly that in school-related activities students prefer lower levels of challenge. To examine this hypothesis we compared results for out-of-school usage of the system with in-school usage. Fig. 2. shows that there is really a substantial difference. The in-school group prefers easier questions (the optimal difficulty is around 75%) and they are also generally less satisfied with the practice in the system. Note that we currently use only very simplified detector of in-school/out-of-school usage, therefore it is probable that the real difference is even higher.

Finally, Fig. 3. shows the relation between algorithm's target probability and obtained explicit feedback. As we already mentioned the target probability parameter influences the real student's success rate only partially, thus the relation is less pronounced than in the previous graph. The maximum satisfaction with the practice is reached when the target probability is 60%-65%, which corresponds to the 70% from the perspective of the real success rate.

4.3   Impact of Difficulty Adjustment

The last studied question concerns the difficulty adjustment and is: "Does the difficulty adjustment mechanism have an impact on the student's behaviour?" Although the average success rate is not affected by the adjustment (about 75% for both variants), student's experience is different. Median of the number of answers is 28 for enabled adjustment and 21 for disabled, the difference between the two variants is significant ($p = 0.02$).

As Fig. 3. shows, the main reason for the better effect is that the adjustment increases the robustness of the algorithm with respect to the target probability of

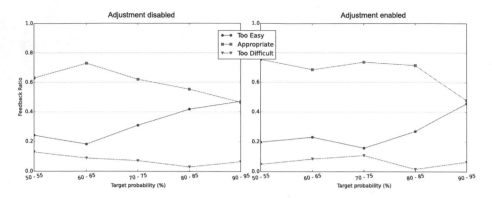

Fig. 3. Explicit feedback given by students according to the target probability used in the algorithm, depending on whether the dynamic adjustment of difficulty is disabled or enabled. The used data set for this experiment consists of 176,000 answers and 1,450 feedback records.

the correct answer. For this reason the choice of the target probability becomes less important. Regarding the explicit feedback, the ratio of "Appropriate" votes is 5% higher when the adjustment is turned on (68% vs. 63%).

5   Conclusions

We performed experiments with a widely used adaptive practice system to evaluate the impact of system behaviour on student motivation and perception of question difficulty. The results show that the adaptive algorithm for construction of questions which is based on a student modeling [11] has a positive impact on student willingness to use the system.

Based on student self-reported perception of difficulty of questions it seems that a good target success rate is around 65%. There is a difference between in-school and out-of-school usage of the system. Students using the system in schools prefer easier questions, which is in accordance with previous literature [1]. Nevertheless in the artificial intelligence in education community this aspect is worth attention, since it is usually not studied or taken into account.

For the actual behaviour of students (number of answered questions), however, we did not get significant trend with respect to the target rate (as predicted by Inverted-U Hypothesis). It seems that even for our relatively simple application for learning geography there are enough interacting factors (e.g. success rate, student skill, choice of maps) to obfuscate the relation between difficulty and motivation. Moreover, the used proxy for motivation – the number of answered questions – may be insufficient.

We also proposed a dynamic mechanism for adjustment of question difficulty. The results of experiments show that this mechanism is effective (improves students' willingness to use the system) and that it makes the behaviour of the system robust with respect to the choice of the target success rate. This mechanism can thus both simplify the development and improve the behaviour of new adaptive practice systems.

References

1. Abuhamdeh, S., Csikszentmihalyi, M.: The importance of challenge for the enjoyment of intrinsically motivated, goal-directed activities. Personality and Social Psychology Bulletin **38**(3), 317–330 (2012)
2. Barla, M., Bieliková, M., Bou Ezzeddinne, A., Kramár, T., Šimko, M., Vozár, O.: On the impact of adaptive test question selection for learning efficiency. Computers & Education **55**(2), 846–857 (2010)
3. Cen, H., Koedinger, K.R., Junker, B.: Is over practice necessary?-improving learning efficiency with the cognitive tutor through educational data mining. Frontiers in Artificial Intelligence and Applications **158**, 511–518 (2007)
4. Csikszentmihalyi, M.: Flow: The psychology of optimal experience. Harper Perennial (1991)
5. Delaney, P.F., Verkoeijen, P.P.J.L., Spirgel, A.: Spacing and testing effects: A deeply critical, lengthy, and at times discursive review of the literature. Psychology of learning and motivation **53**, 63–147 (2010)
6. Bosch, N., D'Mello, S., Mills, C.: What emotions do novices experience during their first computer programming learning session? In: Lane, H.C., Yacef, K., Mostow, J., Pavlik, P. (eds.) AIED 2013. LNCS, vol. 7926, pp. 11–20. Springer, Heidelberg (2013)
7. Jansen, B.R.J., Louwerse, J., Straatemeier, M., Van der Ven, S.H.G., Klinkenberg, S., Van der Maas, H.L.J.: The influence of experiencing success in math on math anxiety, perceived math competence, and math performance. Learning and Individual Differences **24**, 190–197 (2013)
8. Klinkenberg, S., Straatemeier, M., Van der Maas, H.L.J.: Computer adaptive practice of maths ability using a new item response model for on the fly ability and difficulty estimation. Computers & Education **57**(2), 1813–1824 (2011)
9. Lee, J.I., Brunskill, E.: The impact on individualizing student models on necessary practice opportunities. In: Educational Data Mining (EDM), pp. 118–125 (2012)
10. Lomas, D., Patel, K., Forlizzi, J.L., Koedinger, K.R.: Optimizing challenge in an educational game using large-scale design experiments. In: Proceedings of the SIGCHI Conference on Human Factors in Computing Systems, pp. 89–98. ACM (2013)
11. Papoušek, J., Pelánek, R., Stanislav, V.: Adaptive practice of facts in domains with varied prior knowledge. In: Educational Data Mining (EDM), pp. 6–13 (2014)
12. Pavlik, P.I., Cen, H., Koedinger, K.R.: Performance factors analysis-a new alternative to knowledge tracing. In: Proceedings of Artificial Intelligence in Education (AIED). Frontiers in Artificial Intelligence and Applications, vol. 200, pp. 531–538. IOS Press (2009)
13. Pelánek, R.: Time decay functions and elo system in student modeling. In: Educational Data Mining (EDM), pp. 21–27 (2014)

Understanding Student Success in Chemistry Using Gaze Tracking and Pupillometry

Joshua Peterson[1](✉), Zachary Pardos[1], Martina Rau[2], Anna Swigart[1],
Colin Gerber[1], and Jonathan McKinsey[1]

[1] University of California, Berkeley, California
{jpeterson,pardos}@berkeley.edu
[2] Department of Educational Psychology, University of Wisconsin, Madison, Wisconsin
marau@wisc.edu

Abstract. Eye tracking allows us to identify visual strategies through gaze behavior, which can help us understand how students process content. Furthermore, understanding which visual strategies are successful can help us improve educational materials that foster successful use of these visual strategies. Previous studies have demonstrated the predictive value of eye tracking for student performance. Chemistry is a highly visual domain, making it particularly appropriate to study visual strategies. Eye tracking also provides measures of pupil dilation that correlate with cognitive processes important to learning, but have not yet been assessed in any realistic learning environments. We examined the gaze behavior and pupil dilation of undergraduate students working with a specialized ITS for chemistry: Chem Tutor. Chem Tutor emphasizes visual learning by focusing specifically on graphical representations. We assessed the value of over 40 high-level gaze features along with measures of pupil diameter to predict student performance and learning gains across an entire chemistry problem set. We found that certain gaze features are strong predictors of performance, but less so of learning gains, while pupil diameter is marginally predictive of learning gains, but not performance. Further studies that assess pupil dilation with higher temporal precision will be necessary to draw conclusions about the limits of its predictive power.

Keywords: Eye tracking · Intelligent tutoring systems · Performance prediction · Chem tutor

1 Introduction

Eye tracking provides behavioral and physiological metrics that researchers can use to study a number of psychological and physiological processes. In the context of education, these metrics can reveal visual strategies and provide clues as to how students process content. Armed with such knowledge, instructional designers can build better content and interfaces for Massive Open Online Courses (MOOCs), Intelligent Tutoring Systems (ITS), and with the advent of affordable and wireless head-mounted trackers, perhaps even traditional classrooms. While eye tracking research applied to education has already begun to yield insights into students' behavior and internal

© Springer International Publishing Switzerland 2015
C. Conati et al. (Eds.): AIED 2015, LNAI 9112, pp. 358–366, 2015.
DOI: 10.1007/978-3-319-19773-9_36

states, we identify two important research questions that deserve considerable attention, namely, whether gaze behavior predicts performance and learning gains in a highly visual, STEM-related, domain-specialized ITS, and whether the recognized utility in measuring cognitive processes by tracking pupil diameter transfers to realistic learning contexts.

Current eye tracking technology provides information on blink rate, fixation, saccades and pupil diameter at high sampling rates [1]. Blink rate is a measure of how frequently eyelids are closed, then opened. Saccades are abrupt, rapid movements from one element to another. Fixation is the amount of time the eyes are focused on a given point on the screen, such as a letter within a word. Pupillometry is concerned with measurement of the pupillary diameter and its fluctuation over time in response to external stimuli or internal state changes.

Much of the current work in applying eye tracking to education has focused on what content students fixate on, for how long, and in what order or sequence. Some of this research has been aimed at distinguishing the gaze behavior of high-performing and low-performing students. For instance, when given a standardized multiple-choice science exam involving chemistry, biology and physics questions, participants who had more expertise in a specific subject area needed fewer eye fixations to process information in problem statement, image, and multiple choice zones and had fewer saccades between zones [2]. High-performing students also spend more time looking at relevant problem details and candidate solution choices than low-performing students [3]. Other studies have shown that gaze tracking data can be used to disambiguate problem-solving strategies in an algebra ITS [4], understand effects of adaptation on engagement in a programming ITS [5], and identify which factors affect attention in educational games [6].

A more recent study aimed at visual problem-solving sought to understand the differences in eye tracking patterns between high and low performers in three engineering-related computer games that required spatial ability, problem-solving skills, and a capacity to interpret visual imagery [7]. Successful players showed shorter first fixations after a stimulus presentation, which has been correlated with high attentional readiness [1]. High performers also used fewer clicks, more unique fixation points, and a longer duration on average for each eye fixation, which was speculated to be associated with engagement and cognitive processing prior to taking action. In contrast, low performers were characterized by longer first fixations after stimulus presentation, more mouse clicks, and shorter durations for each fixation point, which might suggest a trial-and-error approach. This constitutes the first attempt to our knowledge to apply eye tracking to a highly visual problem-solving domain that focuses entirely on skills that are important to core subjects like chemistry [8]. One pathway to expanding such an endeavor will require a closer look at several aspects of gaze behavior in learning environments aimed specifically at more direct instruction of the target field of study.

The role of pupillometry in the science of learning and education is far less explored than gaze behavior. However, there is reason to believe it may provide equal insight to the field. In cognitive psychology, pupillometry has been shown to indicate a number of cognitive processes in highly-controlled cognitive task paradigms. Notably, pupil size correlates with the difficulty of a task across a number of domains [9]. For example, pupils dilate while doing difficult versus easy multiplication problems, recalling complicated sentences [10], and performing difficult analogy tasks [11]. Pupil dilation also reliably increases with the number of digits to be remembered, reflecting short term memory load [9]. Lastly, pupil diameter has even been shown to fluctuate with attention and mental effort [12]. Pupillometry is a more accurate, less noisy measure of these processes than EEG and a cheaper, more practical alternative to imaging methods such as fMRI. Given the utility of pupillometry in indexing cognitive processes across a wide range of tasks, it is reasonable to assume that pupil dilation measurements may help predict student performance and learning gains. Further, our current understanding of cognitive load has led to improvements in instructional design and procedures that can improve learning [13]. Pupillometry may provide a new window into cognitive processes such as cognitive load during complex realistic learning scenarios, but only if the utility of which can be shown to be more externally valid. Current research on pupil dilation and learning is sparse and has yielded mixed results. In particular, researchers have failed to find a link between pupil dilation and certain factors such as reading difficulty [14] and self-explanation [15], although pupil dilation has been shown to increase with the difficulty of certain file management subtasks [16]. A great deal more work will be needed to understand the role that pupillometry might play in learning science.

Here, we ask whether a large number of gaze features along with pupil diameter can predict student performance and learning gains in learning concepts from chemistry in an intelligent tutoring system.

2   Methodology

2.1   Experimental Design and Data Collection

We obtained gaze and pupil diameter for 95 undergraduate students using a SMI RED 250 eye-tracker as they worked with an ITS for chemistry: Chem Tutor [17]. This data set was drawn from an experiment that investigated the effects of different types of support students were given for making connections between graphical representations (e.g. identifying multiple aspects of the same concept in each graphic) such as Lewis structures and ball-and-stick figures (please refer to [17] for information on these support types). Fig. 1 shows a truncated example of the student-problem level data. Students had to complete all problems that were part of the intervention of the experiment. Each problem contained a series of steps with unlimited attempts. Students could request hints from Chem Tutor for steps they struggled with. In addition, each student took a pretest and posttest to assess reproduction and transfer of representational skills and chemistry knowledge.

student	problem	errorRate_medianSplit	...	1stFixDur_GR
1	U1_I1	0	...	347
1	U1_I2	0	...	203
1	U1_I3	1	...	115
1	U2_I1	1	...	320
...	...	...	...	...

Fig. 1. Truncated example of data set

2.2 Feature Engineering

We constructed forty problem-level gaze features averaged over the time taken to complete each problem. From the raw eye tracking data, we created areas of interest (AOIs) from elements of the tutor that included graphic representations (GR), whitespace, titles, hints, the progress bar, and the interaction pane. We use "whitespace" here as a catch-all for any screen space that was not occupied by other AOIs. We computed *frequency of switching* between unique AOIs, a metric that has been associated with perceptual integration [18]. We also computed the *frequency of switching between GRs* as the number of times a fixation on one AOI was followed by one on another AOI. Next, we computed the *duration of fixation after the first inspection* of an AOI. A first inspection of an AOI is thought to indicate early processing of content [19]. The duration of fixations after the first inspection is thought to reflect intentional processing to integrate one source of information with another [19]. We then computed the *duration of second-inspection fixations* on each AOI as the sum of fixation durations that occurred after the first fixation on AOIs. In addition, we computed the *sum of total fixation durations* on each AOI. Beyond single-AOI fixation features, we also computed *fixation sequence features*. These features involve a specific ordering of fixation targets. For instance, a student may first focus on a graphic, then on the text of a hint, and finally back to the graphic again. The majority of them involve focus on GRs in reference to other information, computed as the counts of fixations on one AOI followed by fixation on either one other (2-point sequence), or two other AOIs (3-point sequence).

2.3 Analysis

To investigate which features were predictive of student performance and learning gains, we first identified a number of features that correlated with our two outcome measures. Our performance outcome variable was a metric termed first-incorrect rate (FIR) that is defined as the number of times a student gave an incorrect answer on first attempt of a question step normalized by the total number of steps for that question, which is standard practice in ITS research [20]. We used the number of first-attempt incorrect instead of the total number of incorrect attempts in order to capture performance on new steps (students could re-attempt steps until they were correct).

Our outcome variable representing a learning gains score (LGS) was defined as post-test minus pretest score for each student. To predict student performance and learning gains from multiple features, we used Gaussian logistic regression on a median split of each outcome variable. Finally, we evaluated the prediction accuracy of each model using four-fold cross validation.

3   Results

Several fixation features significantly predicted FIR (see Table 1), and were highest when the values for each feature and FIR were averaged over subjects. Correlations between FIR and all other features including pupil diameter were not significant. The majority of these features involved fixation on titles, the progress indicator, and the interaction pane. All associations were positive (e.g. longer fixation on titles accompanied higher error rates) with the exception of those involving the progress indicator and screen/interface whitespace. Fixation on titles seemed to have the strongest negative effect on error rate. This may be because lower performers tended to focus longer on the titles when they were confused about the topic. Features involving fixation on the progress indicator were consistently associated with smaller error rates, perhaps because learners who kept track of their progress to budget time or used progress as motivation perform better as a result.

Table 1. Correlations between FIR (first-incorrect rate) and selected fixation features

Feature	r	Feature Description
fixDur_Titles	0.80***	sum of fixation durations on titles
fixDur_Progress	-0.61**	sum of fixation durations on progress indicator
fixDur_Interaction	0.48*	sum of fixation durations on interaction pane
1stFixDur_Titles	0.81***	duration of first fixation on titles
1stFixDur_Interaction	0.60**	duration of first fixation on interaction pane
1stFixDur_Progress	-0.43*	duration of first fixation on progress indicator
1stFixDur_WhiteSpace	-0.50*	duration of first fixation on whitespace
2ndFixDur_Titles	0.80***	duration of second fixation on titles
2ndFixDur_Progress	-0.61**	duration of second fixation on progress indicator
2ndFixDur_Interaction	0.48*	duration of second fixation on interaction pane

* p < 0.05, ** p < 0.01, *** p <0.0001

In addition, Table 2 shows a number of fixation sequence features that correlate significantly with FIR. No significant correlations involved fixation on GRs alone, suggesting that successful learners spend more time interpreting graphics by relating them to other information. Looking between GRs or between GRs and hints was associated with higher error rates, while looking at GRs or hints in reference to the interaction pane was associated with lower error rates.

Table 2. Correlations between FIR (first-incorrect rate) and selected fixation sequence features

Feature	r	Feature Description
seq2_betweenGRs	-0.58*	2-point sequence between GR
seq2_GR-IP	0.54**	2-point sequence between GR and IP
seq2_IP-HT	0.47*	2-point sequence between IP and HT
seq3_betweenGRs	-0.60**	3-point sequence between GR
seq3_IP-GR-IP	0.61**	3-point sequence between IP, GR, and IP
seq3_GR-HT-GR	-0.49*	3-point sequence between GR, HT, and GR
seq3_HT-GR-HT	-0.47*	3-point sequence between HT, GR, and HT
seq3_GR-PI-GR	-0.44*	3-point sequence between GR, PI, and GR

$* \text{ p} < 0.05, ** \text{ p} < 0.01, *** \text{ p} < 0.0001$

GR = Graphical Representations, IP = Interaction Pane, HT = Hint Text, PI = Progress Indicator

3.1   Prediction and Model Evaluation

While pretest scores alone had some predictive value with respect to FIR, fixation features provided a much more accurate model. A model containing both sets of predictors outperformed either set by itself. Pupil diameter was the least effective predictor of FIR. Top coefficients for the gaze-only model were consistently made up of a subset of the sequence features, the highest of which involved either interaction pane, GRs, or both. Following the correlations, the fixation sequence between the interaction pane, a GR, and back to the interaction pane was frequently the highest coefficient. Moreover, nearly all top coefficients involved GRs only when in relation to other AOIs. In general, more complex sequence features (3-point) were not more predictive than simple sequence features (2-point). The most accurate model contained only a binary indicator of which problem was given, which was likely representing difficulty. This model was not improved by the addition of gaze or pretest features. LGS was best predicted by pretest features alone, but pupil diameter did predict 5% above the majority class by itself. Table 3 provides a summary of these results.

Table 3. Average prediction accuracy for logistic regression models predicting FIR and LGS

Model	Accuracy (FIR)	Accuracy (LGS)
Majority Class	51.6%*	50%
Pretest Scores	58%	68%
Gaze Features	63%	53%
Pupil Diameter	51%	55%
Pretest Scores, Gaze Features	66%	68%
Problem	72%	44%

* Median splits of the criterion were not perfectly symmetrically distributed (Majority Class = High Error Rate)

4   Limitations and Future Work

While both gaze behavior and pupil diameter were predictive and informative, neither comprised the best predictors for our outcome variables. However, we expect these metrics to be more useful when problem difficulty and pretest scores are held approximately constant. While our simple gaze features were enough to outperform pretest-based prediction accuracy, not all of our results are directly interpretable in ways that can inform instructional design. Of particular interest is the finding that successful students relate graphical representations to other information as opposed to reviewing them in isolation. This spontaneous behavior may indicate that those students are using available resources more productively. This finding aligns with research on learning with multiple representations, which indicates that students need to integrate information presented across different representations [21]. Additional work will be needed to identify why exactly some of these features are such powerful predictors. While pupil diameter was somewhat predictive of learning gains, as a first glimpse at the utility of pupillometry in the wild, it was generally a very poor predictor of performance in our analysis. It is possible that even controlled ITS sessions introduce too much noise for pupil measurements to be useful. More likely, since cognitive phenomena detectable through pupil dilation are typically observed on the order of a few seconds, our dataset, which only contained average pupil dilation per problem, may very well have lacked the granularity necessary to capture these variations. In the time it takes to solve an entire, multi-step problem, learners may go through several positive and negative states of arousal, affect, cognitive load, and attentional shifts. Due to current difficulties with accurate time synchronization of the ITS and eye-tracking hardware, the current data set does not accurately represent smaller time scales. In future work, we plan to work with more granular, synchronized data to address this limitation.

5   Conclusion

Several of our analyses indicate that eye fixation and fixation sequence features are good predictors of how we have chosen to quantify student performance. While pupil diameter lacked similar predictive power, we expect that future experiments with higher temporal precision at smaller scales still hold considerable promise. Once a satisfactory set of features and level of granularity is established, one can explore the reasons why such features are indicative of the many fascinating aspects of the learning process and implement changes to instructional design based on this knowledge. Our results provide further motivation to explore the usefulness of eye tracking in educational research.

References

1. Poole, A., Ball, L.J.: Eye Tracking in Human-Computer Interaction and Usability Research: Current Status and Future. Prospects. Chapter in Ghaoui, C. (Ed.) Encyclopedia of Human-Computer Interaction. Idea Group Inc, Pennsylvania (2005)
2. Tai, R.H., Loehr, J.F., Brigham, F.J.: An exploration of the use of eye-gaze tracking to study problem-solving on standardized science assessments. International journal of research & method in education. **29**, 185–208 (2006)
3. Tsai, M.-J., Hou, H.-T., Lai, M.-L., Liu, W.-Y., Yang, F.-Y.: Visual attention for solving multiple-choice science problem: An eye-tracking analysis. Computers & Education. **58**, 375–385 (2012)
4. Gluck, K.A., Anderson, J.R., Douglass, S.A.: Broader bandwidth in student modeling: what if ITS were "Eye" TS? In: Gauthier, G., Frasson, C., VanLehn, K. (eds.) Intelligent Tutoring Systems, pp. 504–513. Springer, Berlin Heidelberg (2000)
5. Loboda, T.D., Brusilovsky, P.: User-adaptive explanatory program visualization: evaluation and insights from eye movements. User Model User-Adap Inter. **20**, 191–226 (2010)
6. Conati, C., Jaques, N., Muir, M.: Understanding Attention to Adaptive Hints in Educational Games: An Eye-Tracking Study. Int J Artif Intell Educ. **23**, 136–161 (2013)
7. Gomes, J.S., Yassine, M., Worsley, M., Blikstein, P.: Analysing Engineering Expertise of High School Students Using Eye Tracking and Multimodal Learning Analytics
8. Wu, H.-K., Shah, P.: Exploring visuospatial thinking in chemistry learning. Sci. Ed. **88**, 465–492 (2004)
9. Beatty, J.: Task-evoked pupillary responses, processing load, and the structure of processing resources. Psychological bulletin. **91**, 276 (1982)
10. Zekveld, A.A., Festen, J.M., Kramer, S.E.: Task difficulty differentially affects two measures of processing load: The pupil response during sentence processing and delayed cued recall of the sentences. Journal of Speech, Language, and Hearing Research. **56**, 1156–1165 (2013)
11. Bornemann, B., Foth, M., Horn, J., Ries, J., Warmuth, E., Wartenburger, I., van der Meer, E.: Mathematical cognition: individual differences in resource allocation. ZDM **42**, 555–567 (2010)
12. Wierda, S.M., van Rijn, H., Taatgen, N.A., Martens, S.: Pupil dilation deconvolution reveals the dynamics of attention at high temporal resolution. Proceedings of the National Academy of Sciences **109**, 8456–8460 (2012)

13. Paas, F., Renkl, A., Sweller, J.: Cognitive load theory and instructional design: Recent developments. Educational psychologist **38**, 1–4 (2003)
14. Schultheis, H., Jameson, A.: Assessing cognitive load in adaptive hypermedia systems: physiological and behavioral methods. In: De Bra, P.M., Nejdl, W. (eds.) AH 2004. LNCS, vol. 3137, pp. 225–234. Springer, Heidelberg (2004)
15. Conati, C., Merten, C.: Eye-tracking for user modeling in exploratory learning environments: An empirical evaluation. Knowledge-Based Systems. **20**, 557–574 (2007)
16. Iqbal, S.T., Bailey, B.P.: Using eye gaze patterns to identify user tasks. The Grace Hopper Celebration of Women in Computing, pp. 5–10 (2004)
17. Rau, M.A., Michaelis, J.E., Fay, N.: Connection making between multiple graphical representations: A multi-methods approach for domain-specific grounding of an intelligent tutoring system for chemistry. Computers & Education **82**, 460–485 (2015)
18. Johnson, C.I., Mayer, R.E.: An eye movement analysis of the spatial contiguity effect in multimedia learning. Journal of Experimental Psychology: Applied **18**, 178 (2012)
19. Mason, L., Pluchino, P., Tornatora, M.C.: Effects of picture labeling on science text processing and learning: Evidence from eye movements. Reading Research Quarterly **48**, 199–214 (2013)
20. Koedinger, K.R., Baker, R.Sj., Cunningham, K., Skogsholm, A., Leber, B., Stamper, J.: A data repository for the EDM community: The PSLC DataShop. Handbook of educational data mining 43 (2010)
21. Ainsworth, S.: DeFT: A conceptual framework for considering learning with multiple representations. Learning and Instruction **16**, 183–198 (2006)

AttentiveLearner: Improving Mobile MOOC Learning via Implicit Heart Rate Tracking

Phuong Pham and Jingtao Wang[✉]

Computer Science and LRDC, University of Pittsburgh, Pittsburgh, PA, USA
{phuongpham,jingtaow}@cs.pitt.edu

Abstract. We present AttentiveLearner, an intelligent mobile learning system optimized for consuming lecture videos in both Massive Open Online Courses (MOOCs) and flipped classrooms. AttentiveLearner uses on-lens finger gestures as an intuitive control channel for video playback. More importantly, AttentiveLearner implicitly extracts learners' heart rates and infers their attention by analyzing learners' fingertip transparency changes during learning on today's unmodified smart phones. In a 24-participant study, we found heart rates extracted from noisy image frames via mobile cameras can be used to predict both learners' "mind wandering" events in MOOC sessions and their performance in follow-up quizzes. The prediction performance of AttentiveLearner (accuracy = 71.22%, kappa = 0.22) is comparable with existing research using dedicated sensors. AttentiveLearner has the potential to improve mobile learning by reducing the sensing equipment required by many state-of-the-art intelligent tutoring algorithms.

Keywords: Heart rate · Attention-aware interfaces · Mind Wandering · MOOC · Intelligent tutoring system · Affective computing · Zoning out · Mobile device

1   Introduction

With the rapid growth in recent years, Massive Open Online Courses (MOOCs) provide both opportunities and obstacles to learning at scale. On one hand, MOOCs allow learners to get access to diversified high quality learning materials at low cost, and "*to control where, what, how and with whom they learn*" [12]. As a result, there were around 16.8 million registered MOOC learners by the end of 2014 [1]. On the other hand, educators and researchers have raised concerns on the low completion rates (10% in [6], less than 7% in [15]), high in-session interruptions [7], and lack of interactions among students and instructors. In current MOOCs, pre-recorded lecture videos, split into 3 – 15 minutes pieces, is the dominant format for knowledge dissemination. In fact, major MOOC providers such as Coursera, edX, and Udacity, have released mobile apps to allow learners to consume video materials "on the move".

Unfortunately, MOOCs today face at least three major challenges. First, learners are more prone to "*mind wandering*" (MW, or zoning out) in non-classroom environments [16]. This is in part due to external distractions and the lack of *sustained motivation* when studying alone. The second problem is the current design of MOOCs is

© Springer International Publishing Switzerland 2015
C. Conati et al. (Eds.): AIED 2015, LNAI 9112, pp. 367–376, 2015.
DOI: 10.1007/978-3-319-19773-9_37

primarily *uni-directional*, i.e. from instructors to students. Although feedback forms and learner activity logs (e.g. log-in frequency, in-page dwell time, click-through rates) can be used to infer learning efficacy [11], such measurements are only *indirect measurement* of the cognitive states in learning. As a result, instructors have little information on how well lectures are received by the learners. Finally, there is little personalization of instruction. It is hard for the instructors in MOOCs to cater learning materials for individual learners' need and learning process. Different from traditional classrooms, the instructors can no longer rely on facial cues and in-class activities to discover learners who are struggling or MW.

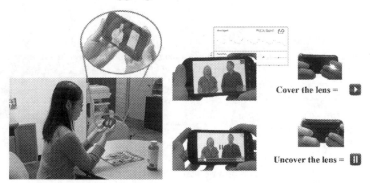

Fig. 1. AttentiveLearner uses the back camera as both a video play control channel in MOOC and an implicit heart rate sensing channel in learning

In response to these challenges, we propose AttentiveLearner (Fig. 1), an intelligent mobile learning system which supports attentive and bi-directional learning on *unmodified mobile phones*. AttentiveLearner uses on-lens finger gestures as an intuitive control mechanism for video playback (i.e. covering and holding the camera lens to play an instructional video, uncovering the lens to pause the video, Fig. 1 right). More importantly, AttentiveLearner *implicitly* extracts learners' heart rates and infers "zoning out" events by analyzing fingertip transparency changes captured by the built-in cameras. With MW information from learners, AttentiveLearner has the potential to enable adaptive tutoring features on today's mobile phones (e.g., alerting learners when zoning out, providing more relevant review exercises). AttentiveLearner can also help instructors to improve their syllabus and teaching style by providing an aggregated timeline view of learners' attention levels synchronized with the learning material.

Our main contributions are two folds. First, we discuss the design, implementation, and evaluation of AttentiveLearner. To our knowledge, AttentiveLearner is the first mobile MOOC learning system that infers learners' cognitive states during video watching via implicit heart rate tracking on today's unmodified mobile phones. Second, our 24-subject experiment shows AttentiveLearner can predict learners' MW states and their quiz performance in a user-independent fashion via heart rate signals implicitly captured from today's commodity mobile cameras. The accuracy and kappa of AttentiveLearner are comparable with existing technologies that rely on dedicated sensors.

2   Related Work

Various techniques have been explored to enrich both the output and feedback of MOOCs. For example, L.IVE by Monserrat et al [14] allows learners to comment, annotate, and complete assessment questions directly on top of MOOC videos. Kim et al [11] mined mouse-click logs on edX to infer drop-out patterns in MOOCs. In comparison, AttentiveLearner enables a new heart rate sensing channel directly correlated with learners' attention and cognitive states on mobile devices without hardware modification. AttentiveLearner can bring new opportunities to enrich large scale learning analytics and adaptive learning in MOOCs.

Existing research on using physiological signals to infer learners' cognitive states, affective states, and attention levels can be a promising direction complimentary to MOOCs. Researchers demonstrated the feasibility of using heart rates [20], galvanic skin response [3], facial expressions [3], mouse mounted with pressure sensor [20], and Electroencephalography (EEG) [18] to infer learners' attention and affective states. However, all of these approaches require dedicated sensors for signal collection. The cost, availability and portability of sensors may prevent the wide adoption of such technologies in large scale in the near future.

Mind Wandering (MW), or zoning out, is ubiquitous in both learning and everyday activities. In a large scale study involving 2240 adults, Killingsworth et al [10] discovered that MW occurred in 46.9% of the everyday random samples. Researchers have attempted to automatically detect MW in learning environments using various signals, such as pitch features in speech dialogues [4], eye fixation time and locations [1], skin conductance and skin temperature features [2]. In this paper, we show that it is possible to design an easy to learn and intuitive to use camera-based interface on today's mobile phones, to capture learner's heart rates and detect their MW states implicitly during MOOC learning without any hardware modification.

3   The Design of AttentiveLearner

The AttentiveLearner mobile client has four unique components when compared with today's MOOC mobile apps: 1) a tangible video control channel; 2) an implicit heart rate sensing module, 3) an on-screen AttentiveWidget visualizing real-time states of video control and heart rate sensing; and 4) an algorithm that infers learners' attention states (MW or not) from heart rate signals captured.

3.1   Tangible Video Control

In AttentiveLearner, the camera lens on the back of mobile phones is used as the "play" button for video/media control (Fig. 1 right). A learner uses his/her finger to cover and hold the camera lens to play an instructional video. Uncovering the lens will pause the video. We used the *Static LensGesture* detection algorithm in [21] to detect lens covering actions (sensitivity parameters can be adjusted to accommodate inadvertent finger jittery). The user independent detection algorithm can achieve an accuracy of 97.9% in different illumination conditions at the speed of 2.3ms per estimate [21]. Our benchmarking results and informal tests also show that the algorithm is accurate and responsive as a video control channel. Anecdotally, users reported that on-lens gesture based video control is easier to use than traditional on-screen touch widgets for two reasons: 1) the edge/bezel of the camera optical assembly can provide natural tactile feedback to users' index finger; 2) In landscape mode, which is common in video watching, users can play or pause the lecture video when holding a mobile phone with both hands (Fig. 1, left). To overcome inadvertent "finger jittery", we keep playing video for 4.5 seconds and then pause even if the lens is uncovered.

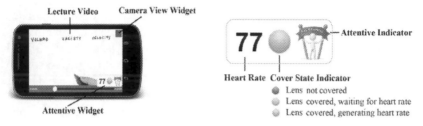

Fig. 2. The AttentiveWidget Interface

3.2   Implicit Heart Rate Sensing

In addition to video play back control, AttentiveLearner also captures learners' heart rates *implicitly* during learning by monitoring the fingertip transparency changes captured by the back camera. This technique is essentially commodity camera based Photoplethysmography (PPG) sensing. The underlining theory of PPG sensing is: in each cardiac cycle, the heart pumps blood to capillary vessels and changes the transparency of the corresponding human body parts, including the lens covering fingertip. These transparency changes correlate directly with heart beats and can be detected by the built-in camera lens when it is covered by the learner's fingertip. We used *LivePulse* [9], a heuristic based peak counting algorithm, to measure heart rates. The *LivePulse* algorithm is accurate (+/- 2 beat per minute when compared with a medical grade oximeter), robust, and can run efficiently in mobile device in real time.

3.3   AttentiveWidget

We designed an on-screen widget (Fig. 2) to visualize finger covering states, real time heart rates, and attention states (MW or not). The AttentiveWidget disappears if the system detects that the learner is in a no MW state for three minutes. The widget can be dragged and dropped around the screen or explicitly toggled by double tapping.

3.4   Mind Wandering Detection

By extracting learners' heart rates during MOOC learning on unmodified mobile phones in real time, we have the opportunity to infer important cognitive states such as stress levels, affective states, and attention states in learning. We focus on the detection of MW in this paper and plan to infer and incorporate other cognitive states in our learning system in the future. Although existing research exists that uses heart rate and heart rate variability signals to improve learning, AttentiveLearner is the first to achieve heart rate enhanced learning on unmodified mobile devices.

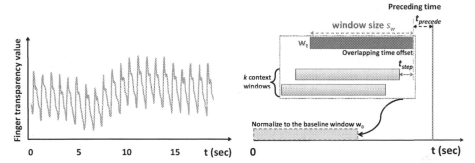

Fig. 3. Feature extraction in PPG signals (**left**: 20 seconds of PPG signal captured from mobile camera during video watching; **right**: using multiple moving windows for feature extraction)

We extracted two types of features, *heart rate features* and *lecture content features* for MW prediction. *Heart rate features* were extracted from multiple, overlapping *context windows* imposed on real time PPG readings (Fig. 3 left) before the time of prediction (Fig. 3 right). We extracted 12 dimensions of heart rate feature from each context window. The 12 dimension of features are: 1) AVNN (average heart rate); 2) SDNN (temporal standard deviations of heart beats); 3) pNN50 (percentage of adjacent heart beats with a difference longer than 50 ms); 4) rMSSD; 5) SDANN; 6) SDNNIDX; 7) SDNNIDX / rMSSD; 8) LF: low frequency (0.04 – 0.15 Hz); 9) HF: high frequency (0.15 – 0.4 Hz); 10) LF / HF; 11) totalPSD (total power spectral density); 12) MAD (median absolute deviation). The detailed definitions of features 2 to 7 can be found in [19], and the detailed definitions of features 8 to 12 are in [8], [19]. All of these features (except MAD) are based on heart rate variability features which are used by many researchers in heart rate signal related studies. We have tried multiple context window numbers, sizes, overlapping time, and preceding time offsets when training the classifier and we defer the details to the evaluation session.

We split lecture videos into equal-length, non-overlapping *content windows*. We extracted 7 dimensions of *lecture content features* from each *content window*. The 7 features are: 1) Lecture style (pure slide[1] or Khan-style[2]); 2) Duration of the current page; 3) Duration of the previous page; 4) Speech rate (words/min); 5) speech rate (words/min) of the previous page; 6) Cosine similarity between current and the previous page (Bag-of-words representation of the transcribed lecture text); 7) Cosine similarity previous two pages. A page is a slide (slide-style) or a small clip (Khan-style).

We applied feature rescaling and feature selection techniques to raw features above before training the classifiers. We report the detailed parameter selection and experimental results in the next section.

---

[1] Slide-style: slides are shown full screen and instructors' voice is played in background.
[2] Khan-style: instructors are facing front with handwriting notes as transparent overlays.

3.5   Implementation

AttentiveLearner was written in Java for Android 4.1. We used the LensGeture algorithm for lens-covering detection and LivePulse algorithm for extracting heart rates from fingertip transparency images. We used WEKA to train and optimize the classifiers. The final prediction algorithm (KNN) can run in real time on mobile devices.

4   Evaluation

4.1   Participants and Procedure

We have recruited 24 participants (5 females) between 22 and 31 years old (μ=25.2, σ=2.3) in our study. All the participants were graduate students in a local university. We use a within-subjects design and all the participants learned two MOOC lectures in the study. One was a 21-minute lecture on Hadoop (Khan-style) with 24 quiz questions; the other was a 23-minute lecture on R programming (slide-style) with 19 quiz questions. All subjects had little or no knowledge about the two topics used. The order of the two lectures was randomized. We used a Google Nexus Galaxy smartphone running Android 4.1 in the experiment.

We ran a tutorial session and collected a background questionnaire at the beginning of each session and then followed by presenting two MOOC lectures. Participants were required to complete corresponding quizzes after each lecture and there was a 5-minute break between lectures. Finally, the participants took an exit survey.

During learning, we used auditory probes [1,2] to figure out whether the participant was MW. After hearing an audio beep, the subjects report verbally "Yes" or "No" to indicate whether they were MW the moment before the probe. Auditory probes were triggered randomly at a 3 minute mean interval, and at the end of each page.

Table 1. Number of PPG sampling and frames/second of each subject

Signal	Average	SD	Max	Min
# of PPG samples	21,267.4	1,916.5	23,845	17,840
Sampling rate (fps)	16.1	0.5	16.6	14.7

In total, we collected 991 responses to auditory probes and 227 (22.9%) responses were MW. This ratio is similar to previous study (24.4%) in comprehensive reading [2]. The average accuracy of quiz questions was 78.3%. The average sampling rate 16.1 Hz (Table 1) was lower than the 30Hz normal camera frame rate, we attribute this to the extra CPU cycles used in video decoding and play back. Participants covered the lens of the camera 99.2% of the time during MOOC learning (min = 94.1%, max = 100%, σ = 1.4%).

4.2   Classifier Training

Five supervised machine learning algorithms were used in this study. The classifiers were K nearest neighbors (*KNN*), Gaussian mixture model (*GMM*), support vector machine with linear kernel (*SVM*), logistic regression with lasso regularization (*LogReg*), and local outlier factor (*LOF*). *LogReg* was trained by LibLinear and all other models were trained by WEKA. We also tested *SVM* with nonlinear kernels, but preliminary results showed their performances were worse than the linear kernel.

We used the leave-one-participant-out method to ensure that data from each participant was exclusive to either the training or testing set. As a result, all the results reported were user-independent.

Feature selection was performed to remove correlated features and those did not have sufficient discrimination power. This technique can restrict the model complexity and ensure sufficient speed when running on mobile devices.

We tried to use different parameter combinations for both feature extraction and classifiers. The optimal combination was the one giving the best average Kappa over all subjects. To be specific, we have tried 3 different context window numbers (1, 3, 5) × 4 context window widths (30s, 60s, 90s, 120s) × 4 context window overlaps (5s, 10s, 30s, 60s) × 3 preceding time values (1s, 2s, 5s) × model specific parameters. The model specific parameters are: *KNN* (number of nearest neighbors: 1, 3, 5), *GMM* (number of clusters: 2), *SVM* (feature weight for the MW class: 1, 3, 5), *LogReg* (feature weights for the MW class: 3, 5, 10), and *LOF* (number of neighbors: 7, 10, 20).

In summary, we extract $7 + 12 (k + 1)$ dimensions of features where k is the number of context windows. We used information gain based feature selection to select the top 5 features to train classifiers.

5   Results and Discussions

Table 2 shows the MW prediction performance, i.e. predicting whether a participant was MW at a moment or not. The KNN classifier (K=5) led to the best overall accuracy (71.22%) and kappa (0.22). This performance is comparable with existing systems that rely on acoustic-prosodic features by Drummond and Litman [4] (learner dependent model, accuracy = 64.3%), eye gaze fixation features by Bixler and D'Mello [1] (learner independent model, accuracy=72%, kappa =0.28), and skin conductance and skin temperature features by Blanchard et al. [2] (learner dependent model, kappa=0.22). It is worth noting that our performance was achieved on today's mobile phones *without any hardware modifications*.

We also explored the feasibility of predicting learners' question-answering performance, i.e. determining whether a participant will make an error in the follow-up quiz based on heart rate signals when the topic was first mentioned in the lecture video (Table 3). The GMM classifier achieved the best kappa (0.22) with an accuracy of 65.14%. Although such accuracy can be considered to be moderate at best, it can be used to provide adaptive reviewing exercises to encourage learners practice on topics they didn't pay enough attention to during learning [18]. E.g., when using the LogReg model (highest recall = 74.69% in Table 3), AttentiveLearner can recommend learners to review around 58.59% of the lesson (rather than the whole lecture) in order to cover all topics learners may make mistakes. In other words, AttentiveLearner has the potential to save around 41.41% of reviewing time when compared with a full review.

Table 2. Mind Wandering detection performance. Standard deviation in parenthesis.

Model	Precision	Recall	Accuracy	Kappa
LOF	30.06 (24.8)	23.45 (21.1)	70.51 (18.6)	0.08 (0.18)
GMM	33.51 (13.4)	**65.00 (21.7)**	60.15 (12.9)	0.18 (0.15)
KNN	**40.00 (24.3)**	40.99 (22.0)	**71.22 (10.8)**	**0.22 (0.22)**
LogReg	28.80 (15.3)	42.18 (13.4)	64.08 (09.4)	0.11 (0.13)
SVM	29.55 (12.9)	47.14 (18.6)	62.73 (09.5)	0.12 (0.13)

Table 3. Quiz error prediction performance. Standard deviation in parenthesis.

Model	Precision	Recall	Accuracy	Kappa
LOF	37.25 (29.1)	20.77 (16.6)	66.02 (14.0)	0.07 (0.2)
GMM	44.35 (20.2)	52.88 (22.3)	65.14 (10.0)	**0.22 (0.16)**
KNN	**44.80 (31.0)**	32.80 (18.3)	**68.13 (9.6)**	0.17 (0.13)
LogReg	36.47 (18.3)	**74.69 (16.0)**	55.05 (14.6)	0.17 (0.16)
SVM	37.06 (18.7)	74.32 (18.7)	54.79 (16.7)	0.16 (0.17)

Fig. 4 shows aggregated MW histogram of 24 subjects over two lectures. We have normalized cross-bin MW events to avoid biases. For example, if a learner has 2 MW events at the 6th and the 20th minute respectively. Each MW event will contribute ½ counts for each moment in the histogram. In the Hadoop lecture, the MW events peaked at around the 6th minute when discussing several open question. The second peak was around the 14th minute when the instructor was teaching the 2nd longest page (3.2 min) in this lecture. The three most frequent MW moments in R programming (the 6th, 13th-16th and 20th minute) were the three longest pages of the lecture, discussing Input (2.4 min), Matrices (2.7 min) and Factors (4.6 min) respectively.

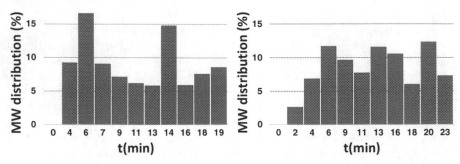

Fig. 4. MW histogram of the Hadoop lecture (left) and the R lecture (right)

6   Conclusions and Future Work

We presented AttentiveLearner, an intelligent mobile learning system optimized for consuming lecture videos in Massive Open Online Courses (MOOCs) on today's smartphones without any hardware modifications. In a 24-participant study, we found that AttentiveLearner can extract heart rates reliably from noisy image frames captured by mobile cameras and that it can be used to predict both learners' "mind wandering" events in MOOC sessions and their performance in follow-up quizzes.

Given the scale and scope of the current study, our current efforts should be treated as a "proof-of-concept" towards follow-up research work in the future. First of all, we plan to increase both the number of participants and the number of learning sessions in the follow-up studies. Second, the prediction performance reported here was based on offline benchmarking rather than live measurement. Third, we plan to use the prediction model to provide intelligent learning interventions on mobile devices. We plan to focus on features that can tolerate reasonable levels of false predictions, such as adaptive reviewing, non-intrusive MW alerting, etc. Fourth, we also plan to explore instructor side visualization interfaces. We hope that an instructor side interface could answer questions like a) Did most students keep up when I was teaching concept X? b) Did my joke "wake up" the students? or c) Were students bored by the end of the lecture? Considering that only PPG compatible live body parts such as fingers can be used to operate AttentiveLearner, AttentiveLeaner may take "virtual attendance" for instructors, addressing in part one of the major concerns in flipping a course.

Acknowledgements. We thank Andrew Head, Chris Schunn, Chris Thomas, Wenchen Wang, Zhijie Wang and Xiang Xiao for the help and support. We also thank anonymous reviewers for the constructive feedback.

References

1. Bixler, R., D'Mello, S.: Toward fully automated person-independent detection of mind wandering. In: Dimitrova, V., Kuflik, T., Chin, D., Ricci, F., Dolog, P., Houben, G.-J. (eds.) UMAP 2014. LNCS, vol. 8538, pp. 37–48. Springer, Heidelberg (2014)
2. Blanchard, N., Bixler, R., Joyce, T., D'Mello, S.: Automated physiological-based detection of mind wandering during learning. In: Trausan-Matu, S., Boyer, K.E., Crosby, M., Panourgia, K. (eds.) ITS 2014. LNCS, vol. 8474, pp. 55–60. Springer, Heidelberg (2014)
3. Calvo, R.A., D'Mello, S.: Affect detection: an interdisciplinary review of models, methods, and their applications. In: IEEE Transactions on Affective Computing, vol 1, pp 18–37. IEEE Press, New York (2010)
4. Drummond, J., Litman, D.: In the zone: towards detecting student zoning out using supervised machine learning. In: Aleven, V., Kay, J., Mostow, J. (eds.) ITS 2010, Part II. LNCS, vol. 6095, pp. 306–308. Springer, Heidelberg (2010)
5. Fisher, D.: Warming up to MOOCs. http://chronicle.com/blogs/profhacker/warming-up-to-moocs/44022
6. Fowler, G.A.: An Early Report Card on Massive Open Online Courses. The Wall Street Journal (2013)

7. Guo, P.J., Kim, J., Rubin, R.: How video production affects student engagement: an empirical study of MOOC videos. In: Proceedings of the First ACM Conference on Learning@ Scale Conference, pp. 41–50. ACM, New York (2014)

8. Haapalainen, E., Kim, S., Forlizzi, F.J., Dey, K.A.: Psycho-physiological measures for assessing cognitive load. In: Proceedings of the 12th ACM International Conference on Ubiquitous Computing, pp. 301–310. ACM, New York (2010)

9. Han, T., Xiao, X., Shi, L., Canny, J., Wang, J.: Balancing accuracy and fun: designing engaging camera based mobile games for implicit heart rate monitoring. In: CHI 2015 Human Factors in Computing Systems. ACM, New York (2015)

10. Killingsworth, M.A., Gilbert, D.T.: A Wandering Mind is an Unhappy Mind. Science **330**(6006), 932 (2010)

11. Kim, J., Guo, P.J., Seaton, D.T., Mitros, P., Gajos, K.Z., Miller, R.C.: Understanding in-video dropouts and interaction peaks in online lecture videos. In: Proceedings of the First ACM Conference on Learning@ Scale Conference, pp. 31–40. ACM, New York (2014)

12. Kop, R., Fournier, H.: New Dimensions to Self-Directed Learning in an Open Networked Learning Environment. International Journal of Self-Directed Learning **7**(2), 2–20 (2011)

13. Malik, M., Bigger, J.T., Camm, A.J., Kleiger, R.E., Malliani, A., Moss, A.J., Schwartz, P.J.: Heart rate variability: standards of measurement, physiological interpretation, and clinical use. European heart journal **17**(3), 354–381 (1996)

14. Monserrat, T., Zhao, S., Li, Y., Cao, X.: L.IVE: an integrated interactive video-based learning environment. In: Proceedings of the 32nd Annual ACM Conference on Human Factors in Computing Systems, pp. 3399–3402. ACM, New York (2014)

15. Parr, C.: Not Staying the Course, Times Higher Education (2013)

16. Risko, E., Buchanan, D., Medimorec, S., Kingstone, A.: Everyday attention: Mind wandering and computer use during lectures. Computers & Education **68**, 275–283 (2013)

17. Smallwood, J., Schooler, J.W.: The restless mind. Psychological Bulletin **132**(6), 946–958 (2006)

18. Szafir, D., Mutlu, B.: Artful: adaptive review technology for flipped learning. In: Proceedings of the SIGCHI Conference on Human Factors in Computing Systems, pp. 1001–1010. ACM, New York (2013)

19. Task Force of the European Society of Cardiology, & Task Force of the European Society of Cardiology: Heart rate variability: standards of measurement, physiological interpretation and clinical use. Circulation **93**(5), 1043–1065 (1996)

20. Woolf, B., Burleson, W., Arroyo, I., Dragon, T., Cooper, D., Picard, R.: Affect-aware tutors recognising and responding to student affect. International Journal of Learning Technology **4**(3), 129–164 (2009)

21. Xiao, X., Han, T., Wang, J.: LensGesture: augmenting mobile interactions with back-of-device finger gestures. In: Proceedings of the 15th ACM on International Conference on Multimodal Interaction, pp. 287–294. ACM, New York (2013)

Distractor Quality Evaluation in Multiple Choice Questions

Van-Minh Pho[1,2]([✉]), Anne-Laure Ligozat[1,3], and Brigitte Grau[1,3]

[1] LIMSI-CNRS, Orsay, France
prenom.nom@limsi.fr
[2] Université Paris-Sud, Orsay, France
[3] ENSIIE, Evry, France

Abstract. Multiple choice questions represent a widely used evaluation mode; yet writing items that properly evaluate student learning is a complex task. Guidelines were developed for manual item creation, but automatic item quality evaluation would constitute a helpful tool for teachers.

In this paper, we present a method for evaluating distractor (i.e. incorrect option) quality that combines syntactic and semantic homogeneity criteria, based on Natural Language Processing methods. We perform an evaluation of this method on a large MCQ corpus and show that the combination of several measures enables us to validate distractors.

Keywords: Multiple choice questions · Natural language processing · Automatic quality evaluation · Production of educational material

1 Introduction

Multiple Choice Questions (MCQs) are widely used in many educational and evaluation contexts since their assessment can be automated and they have proven to be relevant and objective indicators of the learner skills [5]. Yet, writing multiple choice items is costly, and the quality of MCQ is crucial in order to ensure that learners will perform according to their skills. Guidelines have been developed [1] to help create quality MCQs. However, actual MCQs can present flaws because educators may not have formal instruction for writing MCQs [16]. An automatic evaluation of MCQs quality could thus help educators.

A MCQ is composed of two parts (cf. example below): the *stem* and the *options* (or *choices*), which include both the answer (correct option), and one or several *distractors* (incorrect options).

Stem: What country is Kimchi from?
Answer: Korea
Distractors: Japan, China, Mongolia

Selecting distractors is a difficult task when creating a MCQ: the quality of a MCQ relies heavily on the quality of these options [15].

© Springer International Publishing Switzerland 2015
C. Conati et al. (Eds.): AIED 2015, LNAI 9112, pp. 377–386, 2015.
DOI: 10.1007/978-3-319-19773-9_38

The objective of this paper is the automatic evaluation of the quality of options according to writing rules. In particular, the rule *"Keep choices homogeneous in content and grammatical structure"* leads us to propose a definition of syntactic and semantic homogeneity. Homogeneous in content means that options must share semantic features, but are, nonetheless, sufficiently different to be plausible answers but not possible answers.

We propose to evaluate homogeneity by comparing each distractor to the answer and by computing criteria based on syntactic parsing and the use of different semantic resources to cover numerous semantic relationships that are combined in a machine learning model. We focused our work on short options, expressed by chunks (lowest-level phrases) and named entities. Previous research on automatic distractor selection had more restrictions on the type of options [6, 11], or was dedicated to a specific domain [6]. To our knowledge, it is the first attempt to evaluate automatically the semantic quality of MCQ distractors. We will show that our method outperforms state-of-the-art methods.

2   Evaluating the Homogeneity of Options

In order to help teachers create well-formed MCQs, guidelines were developed. One of the most popular set of guidelines was written by [5]. It is composed of 43 rules grouped in categories related to MCQ content, MCQ formatting, MCQ style, stem writing and option writing.

Concerning option writing, the most important ones for quality evaluation are the following: *"Keep choices homogeneous in content and grammatical structure"* and *"Keep choices independent; choices should not be overlapping"*.

Grammatical homogeneity can be verified on the syntactic representation of the options provided by a natural language (NL) parser. In the example of Section 1, all options are noun chunks. Semantic characterization of options can be based on different NL tools, each able to provide different semantic properties according to the resources they are based on.

To evaluate the quality of distractors, we compare them to the answer, both on syntactic and semantic features. We do not want to learn a decision that would state on distractor homogeneity or not because homogeneity is more a question of degree than a binary decision. Thus, we formulate homogeneity evaluation as a ranking problem: the most homogeneous distractors should be classified in the first ranks. The candidates to rank, except for distractors, are selected according to syntactic homogeneity criteria, which proved to be a valid selection criteria in the corpus study of [12].

3   Semantic Homogeneity

Semantic homogeneity states that options share common semantic characteristics. In the example of Section 1, all options are Asian countries.

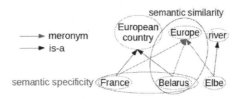

Fig. 1. Semantic characterization of pairs of nodes

We will define several notions close to semantic homogeneity by considering a knowledge organization in the form of a hierarchical graph (Figure 1) carrying typed concepts referred by the terms of the options and semantic relations.

The definition of *semantic relatedness* by [13] is the following: "Semantic relatedness indicates how much two concepts are semantically distant in a network or taxonomy by using all relations between them (i.e. hyponymic/hypernymic [1], antonymic [2], meronymic [3] and any kind of functional relations including is-made-of, is-an-attribute-of, etc.)". Thus, semantic relatedness holds between two concepts when there exists a path between them, and the degree of relatedness is dependent on the path length and the types of relations. In Figure 1, all concepts are semantically related.

We define *semantic similarity* as a particular case of semantic relatedness: two terms are similar if they share the same meaning (i.e. synonyms) or a partial meaning, i.e. the concepts to which they refer are linked by a purely ascending or descending chain of is-a or meronymy relations, as "Belarus" and "Europe" in Figure 1.

We define *semantic specificity* as a particular case of semantic relatedness between two concepts that share a common ancestor, as "France" and "Belarus" in Figure 1.

We define *semantic homogeneity* as a particular case of semantic relatedness: it considers all relations between compared concepts. Moreover, semantic homogeneity excludes the notion of semantic similarity: two options cannot be similar. Finally, a better homogeneity is reached if semantic specificity is respected.

To estimate semantic homogeneity between a distractor and the answer, we compute several semantic relatedness scores. These measures are based on different criteria: measures based on hierarchical semantic representations of concepts, and data driven measures based on contextual relatedness, i.e. the principle stating that terms with similar contexts in a corpus are likely to be semantically related. Hierarchical representations allow us to take into account explicit semantic relations to compare two concepts. However, the resources (DBpedia, WordNet) corresponding to these representations are often limited in their coverage

---

[1] Two concepts of which the first has a more specific/general sense than the second.

[2] Two concepts of which their senses are opposite.

[3] Two concepts of which the first is a part or a member of the second.

(proportion of options present in the resources). Measures based on contextual relatedness have a broader coverage, but the nature of semantic relations is unknown.

In the following sections, we present each of these measures.

3.1   Identity of Named Entity Types

A named entity (NE) is an particular expression referred by a semantic class called NE type. Two options annotated with the same NE type are semantically specific, if they do not refer to a same concept. In order to measure their specificity, we consider 3 large categories: *location*, *organization* and *person*. For such types, NE recognizer are based on surface criteria and gazetteers and do not require a semantic knowledge base.

To compare the NE type of two terms, we use the following measure:

$$same\_NE\_type(t_1, t_2) = \begin{cases} 1 \text{ if } NE(t_1) = NE(t_2) \wedge t_1 \text{ is a NE} \wedge t_2 \text{ is a NE} \\ 0 \text{ else} \end{cases}$$

(1)

where t_1 and t_2 are two terms and $NE(t)$ is the NE type of the term t.

3.2   Similarity of Semantic Types Provided by Dbpedia

In addition to comparing general NE types, we compare semantic types at a more fine-grained and hierarchical level, which allow us to verify more precisely semantic specificity. However, while NE types can be recognized independently of a resource, specific types have to be recognized for concepts belonging to a hierarchical taxonomy. We chose DBpedia [4], a hierarchical resource built from Wikipedia articles. DBpedia entities are associated with semantic types which represent classes of the DBpedia ontology, organized in a taxonomy [5].

To compute semantic homogeneity between two terms t_1 and t_2 based on their DBpedia type and position in the taxonomy, we use Wu and Palmer's measure [17], $wup(t_1, t_2)$, which is based on is based on the shortest path between two concepts weighted by their depth in the taxonomy.

$$wup(t_1, t_2) = \frac{2 \times depth(lcs)}{depth(type(t_1)) + depth(type(t_2))}$$

(2)

where $type(t)$ is the DBpedia type of the term t, $depth(u)$ is the depth of a type u in the taxonomy and $lcs(type(t_1), type(t_2))$ is the least common subsumer (in terms of path length in the taxonomy) between $type(t_1)$ and $type(t_2)$. Thus, two deep concepts with a common parent get a higher score than two less deep concepts with a common parent.

---

[4] http://dbpedia.org/About
[5] http://mappings.dbpedia.org/server/ontology/classes/

3.3   Relatedness Measures Based on WordNet

To measure semantic homogeneity for all kinds of options and in particular non NE ones, we use measures defined on WordNet [6], a lexical network that clusters synonym words in *synsets* linked by semantic relations. To each synset is associated a gloss, i.e. a definition in NL. WordNet also contains named entities for a few kinds of entities (large cities, countries, continents...). We use the four measures selected by [11]: the extended gloss overlap measure based on textual similarity between the glosses of two concepts; Leacock and Chodorow's measure based on the shortest path between concepts; and Jiang and Conrath's and Lin's measures, both based on *information content* [14]. Terms can have multiple senses, so they can be associated with multiple synsets. To compute semantic relatedness between two terms, we compute the measures on all pairs of synsets associated with the terms and we keep the maximal score.

3.4   Comparison of Links of Wikipedia Articles

We also considered measures based on contextual relatedness. A possible contextual representation of a term is the sets of incoming and outgoing links associated with a page in Wikipedia. We consider pages whose title corresponds to an option. The incoming and outgoing "manually created" links represent associated concepts. The tool Wikipedia Miner [10] computes a score learned on these links from Wikipedia dumps.

3.5   Explicit Semantic Analysis

Another contextual representation of terms is their distribution through documents in a corpus. Two terms having close distributions in the same documents are likely to be semantically related. In order to compare the distributions of a candidate and the answer, we computed a measure based on Explicit Semantic Analysis (ESA) [4]. ESA is based on a vector representation of texts in which the dimensions are the weights of the text in each document belonging to a corpus. A word is represented by a vector containing weights on its frequency in each document and a text is represented by the centroid of the weighted vectors representing each word of the text. The relatedness score of two texts is the cosine of the vectors representing these texts. In our case, the document corpus is Wikipedia. To compute the measure based on ESA, we use the tool ESAlib [7].

4   Evaluation of Distractor Quality

In order to evaluate the quality of distractors, we merge existing distractors with non-distractors (terms which have not been manually selected to be distractors for the MCQ). Our purpose is to learn an assessment model able to

---

[6] http://wordnet.princeton.edu/
[7] http://ticcky.github.io/esalib/

rank distractors above non-distractors, as they should be more homogeneous to the answer than the non-distractors. None of the proposed measures directly estimates semantic similarity but we made the hypothesis that a high score of semantic relatedness can represent semantic similarity, which should be learned by our model. MCQs that we process are associated with a document from which stems have been conceived. Non-distractors are selected in this document according to syntactic homogeneity. A first step involves annotation of the options and the non-distractors.

4.1   Document and Options Annotation

To extract non-distractors and compute the different measures, candidates and answers have to be annotated by syntactic and semantic information, which is better realized if these text excerpts are analyzed in the reference document. Thus, we perform four annotations of the document, in the following order:

1. syntactic parsing with the Stanford Parser [7];
2. NE annotation with the Stanford Named Entity Recognition tool [3];
3. specific type annotation, to find entities which are related to a DBpedia entity (and, by extension, a Wikipedia article), with DBpedia Spotlight [2]. This tool associates DBpedia entities with corresponding entities of the document and disambiguates these entities if required. However, some terms (chunks and/or NEs) are not annotated by DBpedia Spotlight. We associate these terms with all DBpedia entities whose title corresponds to them, so without disambiguation;
4. WordNet concept annotation, aiming at associating terms with a WordNet concept. This annotation is performed on chunks and/or NEs, i.e. single or multiword expressions, as following:
   – if the expression appears in WordNet, the expression is associated with its corresponding concept;
   – if the expression does not appear in WordNet and is not a NE, the expression is associated with the concept corresponding to its syntactic head (for instance, the expression "the little cat" is associated with the WordNet concept "cat").

Annotations of the options are extracted from their occurrences in the document. If an option does not appear in the document, its annotations are performed similarly to the document.

4.2   Non-distractor Extraction and Annotation

Since MCQs are related to a reference document, non-distractors are extracted from this document. All non-distractors are syntactically homogeneous to the answer. If the answer is a NE, the non-distractors are the NEs of the reference document, as [12] showed that distractors generally have the same NE type as the answer. Nevertheless, in order to take metonymy into account, we keep all

Table 1. Characteristics of the corpora

corpus	set	# q.	# opt.	# opt./q.	% allMCQ	purpose
	qa4mre	56	252	4.5		machine reading
mcqNE	englishEval	47	150	3.2		language evaluation
	total	103	402	3.9	14	
	qa4mre	51	239	4.7		machine reading
mcqNonNE	englishEval	100	342	3.8		language evaluation
	total	151	581	3.8	20	

non-distractors with a NE type, regardless of the type. If the answer is a chunk
and not a NE, the non-distractors are the chunks of the reference document with
the same syntactic type as the answer. The chunks are selected from the parse
tree of the document sentences, with Tregex [9], a tool that selects nodes in parse
trees from patterns. We associate non-distractors with their NE type, DBpedia
entity and WordNet concept annotated in the document. A last filtering consists
of removing non-distractors similar to an option, in order to avoid overlaps: two
elements are considered similar if they are associated with the same DBpedia
entity or if they refer to the same synset in WordNet.

4.3   Semantic Ranking

Ranking of the candidates (distractors and non-distractors) according to the different criteria of semantic homogeneity is performed by the tool SVMRank [8], an
automatic ranker based on a SVM model, that compares couples of distractors-
non-distractors of a same MCQ and learns the weights of the criteria such as for
each couple of distractor-non-distractor (d, nd), $svm(d) > svm(nd)$.

5   Experiments

5.1   Data Sets

In order to evaluate our method, we use an English corpus of MCQs (corpus
allMCQ, 735 MCQs) extracted from different sources: machine reading system
tests provided by QA4MRE [9] (set qa4mre) and several websites of English language learning (set englishEval). We assume that these MCQs tend to be well-
written. From this corpus, we established two sub-corpora: the first is composed
of MCQs which answers are NEs (corpus mcqNE, 14 % of allMCQ), and the
second is composed of MCQs which answers are chunks and not NE (corpus
mcqNonNE, 20 % of allMCQ).

The questions that we process (chunks and NEs) compose more than one
third of the original corpus which shows that these types of questions are frequently asked in tests. Learning was performed separately on each sub-corpus.

---

[8] http://www.cs.cornell.edu/people/tj/svm_light/svm_rank.html
[9] http://www.celct.it/newsReader.php?id_news=74

Table 2. Results of semantic relatedness methods

	mcqNE			mcqNonNE		
	R	P	F	R	P	F
NE similarity	0.83	0.26	0.40			
DBpedia type similarity	0.70	0.34	0.46	0.94	0.14	0.24
Extended gloss overlap	0.67	0.25	0.36	0.37	0.23	0.28
Leacock & Chodorow	0.73	0.27	0.39	0.42	0.22	0.29
Jiang & Conrath	0.83	0.23	0.36	0.40	0.18	0.25
Lin	0.84	0.23	0.36	0.40	0.18	0.25
Wikipedia link similarity	0.41	0.32	0.36	0.76	0.22	0.34
ESA	0.40	0.34	0.37	0.35	0.24	0.28
Combination	0.48	**0.46**	**0.47**	0.39	**0.36**	**0.37**

5.2   Evaluation Methodology

We consider that distractors are semantically closer to the answer than non-distractors and should thus have a higher rank. In order to evaluate candidate ranking, we compute the average precision (Equation (3)) and recall (Equation (4)), as well as the f-measure (Equation (5)).

$$AP = \frac{\sum_i^{nbQ} P_{i,nbD}}{nbQ} \quad (3) \qquad AR = \frac{\sum_i^{nbQ} R_{i,nbD}}{nbQ} \quad (4)$$

$$F = 2 \times \frac{AP \times AR}{AP + AR} \quad (5)$$

where nbQ is the number of MCQs in the corpus, nbD the number of distractors of the evaluated MCQ, and $P_{i,nbD}$ and $R_{i,nbD}$ are the precision (Equation (6)) and recall (Equation (7)) of MCQ i.

$$P_{i,nbD} = \frac{\#D \text{ of rank} \leq nbD}{\#C \text{ of rank} \leq nbD} \quad (6) \qquad R_{i,nbD} = \frac{\#D \text{ of rank} \leq nbD}{nbD} \quad (7)$$

where D means distractors and C means candidates.

Precision and recall are computed for each semantic relatedness measure, as well as for the ranking model. We evaluate the ranking by 7-fold cross-validation.

5.3   Results

Table 2 shows that the ranking model gives higher balance between recall and precision than individual measures, regardless of the corpus. In particular it gives a higher precision than other measures and better results than WordNet-based measures, used by [11].

Some measures give a higher recall than the ranking model. We distinguish two cases: the first concerns (NE and specific) type-based measures which are more efficient for filtering candidates than selecting distractors. The second case concerns measures whose resource coverage is low (WordNet in mcqNE and Wikipedia in mcqNonNE).

The results are overall lower in the mcqNonNE corpus. The main reason is that non NE candidates and answers are associated with less semantic information than NE, particularly on semantic types.

In the corpus mcqNE, most cases where non-distractors are better ranked than distractors are due to the fact that distractors and answers are not typed by a very specific (DBpedia) type. The remaining non-distractors are relevant enough to be distractors or are similar to the answer, so cannot be distractors.

The majority of non-distractors of the corpus mcqNonNE which are better ranked than distractors are clearly non-distractors but some measures (particularly WordNet-based) consider that these non-distractors are more semantically related than distractors. Among the remaining non-distractors, some of them are not semantically related to the answers in the current context (reference document) or they are relevant enough to replace distractors.

6   Related Work

Automatic distractor selection is usually based on similarity measures between the candidates and the answer and is evaluated by learners or teachers.

Existing work on automatic distractor selection is based either on hierarchical domain-specific resources (WordNet, UMLS) [6,11] and/or document corpora [8,11]. From these resources, candidates are selected according to common syntactic and semantic characteristics with the answer: common syntactic type [6,8,11], common semantic classes [6,11] or terms sharing the same head as the answer [11]. Then, distractors are selected from candidates according to different measures: context-based [6,8] or a strategy based on these first measures, WordNet-based and phonetic-based measures [11]. Evaluation of distractors is performed by learners (through psychometric tests) [8,11] or judgment of domain experts [6], but none of this work evaluated distractors on a reference corpus. Moreover, related work is dedicated to a specific domain (linguistics, medicine, preposition learning), whereas our work is not specific to a domain. Related work is also limited by the syntactic types of answers (words, noun chunks) whereas our work covers all kinds of chunks (noun and verb phrases) and NEs.

7   Conclusion

In this paper, we proposed a method to automatically evaluate the quality of distractors according to criteria relative to syntactic and semantic homogeneity. Results outperform the state-of-the-art methods for automatic distractor selection, and are better on NE than other kinds of chunks. Measures based on hierarchical semantic resources allow us to filter candidates according to properties like types and semantic relations. Measures based on contextual relatedness allow us to refine distractor recognition.

These criteria are relevant but are not sufficient to automatically recognize distractors: considering other information like stems and the context of the options, we would recognize distractors more precisely. Moreover, in future work, we will adapt our approach to all kinds of answers (phrases, clauses and sentences). We will also evaluate distractor quality *a posteriori*, from scores obtained by learners answering to MCQs.

References

1. Burton, S.J., Sudweeks, R.R., Merrill, P.F., Wood, B.: How to prepare better multiple-choice test items: Guidelines for university faculty (1991)
2. Daiber, J., Jakob, M., Hokamp, C., Mendes, P.N.: Improving efficiency and accuracy in multilingual entity extraction. Proceedings of SEMANTICS, 121–124 (2013)
3. Finkel, J.R., Grenager, T., Manning, C.: Incorporating non-local information into information extraction systems by gibbs sampling. Proceedings of the 43rd Annual Meeting on ACL, 363–370 (2005)
4. Gabrilovich, E., Markovitch, S.: Computing Semantic Relatedness Using Wikipedia-based Explicit Semantic Analysis. IJCAI **7**, 1606–1611 (2007)
5. Haladyna, T.M., Downing, S.M., Rodriguez, M.C.: A review of multiple-choice item-writing guidelines for classroom assessment. Applied measurement in education **15**(3), 309–333 (2002)
6. Karamanis, N., Ha, L.A., Mitkov, R.: Generating multiple-choice test items from medical text: A pilot study. Proceedings of NLG, 111–113 (2006)
7. Klein, D., Manning, C.D.: Accurate unlexicalized parsing. Proceedings of ACL **1**, 423–430 (2003)
8. Lee, J., Seneff, S.: Automatic generation of cloze items for prepositions. INTERSPEECH, 2173–2176 (2007)
9. Levy, R., Andrew, G.: Tregex and Tsurgeon: tools for querying and manipulating tree data structures. Proceedings of LREC, 2231–2234 (2006)
10. Milne, D., Witten, I.H.: An open-source toolkit for mining Wikipedia. Artificial Intelligence **194**, 222–239 (2013)
11. Mitkov, R., Ha, L.A., Varga, A., Rello, L.: Semantic similarity of distractors in multiple-choice tests: extrinsic evaluation. Proceedings of the EACL Workshop GEMS, 49–56 (2009)
12. Pho, V.-M., André, T., Ligozat, A.-L., Grau, B., Illouz, G., François, T.: Multiple Choice Question Corpus Analysis for Distractor Characterization. Proceedings of LREC, 4284–4291 (2014)
13. Ponzetto, S.P., Strube, M.: Knowledge derived from wikipedia for computing semantic relatedness. JAIR **30**, 131–212 (2007)
14. Resnik, P.: Using information content to evaluate semantic similarity in a taxonomy. arXiv preprint cmp-lg/9511007 (1995)
15. Rodriguez, M.C.: Three options are optimal for multiple-choice items: A meta-analysis of 80 years of research. Educational Measurement: Issues and Practice **24**(2), 3–13 (2005)
16. Tarrant, M., Ware, J.: Impact of item-writing flaws in multiple-choice questions on student achievement in high-stakes nursing assessments. Medical Education **42**(2), 198–206 (2008)
17. Wu, Z., Palmer, M.: Verbs semantics and lexical selection. Proceedings of ACL, 133–138 (1994)

Interpreting Freeform Equation Solving

Anna N. Rafferty[1]([⊠]) and Thomas L. Griffiths[2]

[1] Computer Science Department, Carleton College, Northfield, MN 55057, USA
arafferty@carleton.edu
[2] Department of Psychology, University of California, Berkeley, CA 94720, USA
tom_griffiths@berkeley.edu

Abstract. Learners' step-by-step solutions can offer insight into their misunderstandings. Because of the difficulty of automatically interpreting freeform solutions, educational technologies often structure problem solving into particular patterns. Hypothesizing that structured interfaces may frustrate some learners, we conducted an experiment comparing two interfaces for solving equations: one requires users to enter steps in an efficient sequence and insists each step be mathematically correct before the user can continue, and the other allows users to enter any steps they would like. We find that practicing equation solving in either interface was associated with improved scores on a multiple choice assessment, but that users who had the freedom to make mistakes were more satisfied with the interface. In order to make inferences from these more freeform data, we develop a Bayesian inverse planning algorithm for diagnosing algebra understanding that interprets individual equation solving steps and places no restrictions on the ordering or correctness of steps. This algorithms draws inferences and exhibits similar confidence based on data from either interface. Our work shows that inverse planning can interpret freeform problem solving, and suggests the need to further investigate how structured interfaces affect learners' motivation and engagement.

1 Introduction

Observing students' solutions to problems can provide valuable insights into their understanding. The approach that a student takes may reveal gaps in her knowledge, or the way she executes a particular step may demonstrate a misunderstanding or misconception. Often, educational technologies structure problem solutions in order to provide targeted, step-by-step feedback to learners [8]. This structuring may include requiring students to get each individual step of a problem correct before continuing, to complete steps in a fixed order, or to indicate what action they are taking to go from one step to another.

While this structuring of students' problem solving may assist in making automated inferences about students' understanding and step-by-step feedback could be beneficial for student learning, it could be frustrating to some learners. Entering individual actions may be time consuming, making practice less efficient, and could be infeasible for some beginning learners. Rigid structuring of

© Springer International Publishing Switzerland 2015
C. Conati et al. (Eds.): AIED 2015, LNAI 9112, pp. 387–397, 2015.
DOI: 10.1007/978-3-319-19773-9_39

the ordering of steps or their correctness may lead some users to disengage and give up more easily, potentially outweighing the benefits of immediate feedback.

We explore the tension between providing structure to push learners towards correctness and limiting frustration through an experiment comparing user satisfaction and improvement in problem solving across two interfaces. Our experiment focuses on equation solving both because algebra is a core topic in curricula, and because interfaces for this domain could allow very freeform solving. We find users are more satisfied with the freeform interface, and we thus explore how to automatically diagnose understanding based on data from this interface. In the Bayesian inverse planning algorithm we develop, we use the patterns of equation transformations, both correct and incorrect, to compute student ability parameters for distinct skills. We find that the model's inferences are equally confident when interpreting data from either interface. We end by discussing implications and highlighting future directions as well as limitations of this work.

2   Interfaces for Algebra Tutors

A number of systems with a variety of interfaces exist to help students practice multistep problem solving. Because we focus on linear equation solving, we concentrate here on systems for algebra. Some systems ask students to enter only a final answer (e.g., ALEKS [6]), preventing feedback on individual steps. In ASSISTments [15], questions are often structured to ask students first for their final answer, and then, if the student answers incorrectly, scaffolding is provided to structure the problem and divide it into smaller parts, each of which must be answered correctly before the student can continue. Cognitive Tutor Algebra [8] typically structures problem solving into individual steps which students must complete correctly before continuing, and feedback is targeted at these individual steps. This tutor improves students' algebra skills and standardized test scores [8]. Previous work comparing the typical interface to a handwriting interface for this tutor, which only provided feedback on students' final answers, found that while step-by-step feedback was more beneficial for learning [1], students preferred the handwritten interface [2]. Beyond the efficiency of handwriting, students may also have appreciated being able to show their work without constraints on step correctness. These studies point to a divide in students' preferences for particular interfaces, which may affect motivation and engagement, with learning outcomes. Research on novice programmers has found fewer differences in outcomes between learners who received step-by-step feedback versus less intrusive feedback, although students who received less intrusive feedback tended to take longer to complete the same number of exercises [5].

3   Satisfaction with a Freeform vs. Structured Interface

Given the prevalence of step-by-step feedback in existing tutors and previous work demonstrating a potential preference for more freeform responses, we conducted an experiment to explore how the interface which people used to solve

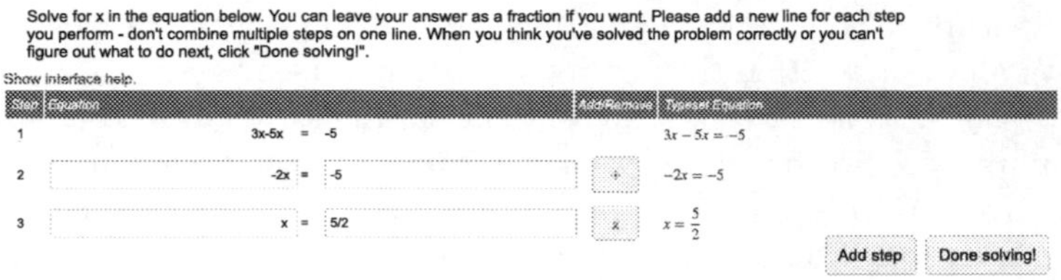

Fig. 1. Screenshot of the step-by-step problem solving interface on the website. The first line in the interface shows the problem the user must solve, and the user adds lines to show her problem solving steps.

algebraic equations affected their satisfaction with the system and their learning outcomes. We focused on adult problem solvers who had some algebra experience, but may not have used their skills recently. The structured interface could be helpful to these participants by giving them more specific feedback while solving equations, but might also be frustrating due to limiting their ability to demonstrate what they do know, as these learners are not complete novices but are in need of remediation. We hypothesize that this frustration will lead these participants to give up more quickly and be less satisfied with the system.

3.1 Methods

Participants. 40 participants in the USA were recruited from Amazon's Mechanical Turk (AMT) and compensated $3 for session 1, $5 for session 2, and $7 for session 3. Participants had experience with algebra, either in a secondary or postsecondary class, and had not completed college math classes beyond algebra.

Stimuli. Participants completed a multiple choice assessment, solved algebra problems on a website, and responded to surveys about their mathematics background and the usability of the website. The multiple choice assessment was based on College Board ACCUPLACER® tests used for math placement in many postsecondary institutions[11]; questions were adapted from sample questions from the College Board[4]. The assessment included 12 elementary algebra questions (the same length as the Elementary Algebra ACCUPLACER), and 16 college math questions (shortened from 20 questions in the College Math ACCUPLACER). Instructions informed participants that if they did not know how to solve the problem, they could leave the question blank.

On the algebra website we developed, participants are shown the equation to solve, and with each problem step, they add a line to show their work (Figure 1). In the *corrected* interface, the current step is checked via a symbolic algebra system [9] when the add step button is clicked. If the step is mathematically incorrect, combines multiple steps, or is not the best next action, then a dialog tells the participant to correct the step before continuing. The dialog distinguishes among syntactic, mathematical, and action choice errors. Allowed action choices are calculated by comparing the user's actions to all possible legal actions. We allow any action that is close to optimal (see Section 5 for details).

In the *freeform* interface, the system checks for syntactic errors when the user submits the entire set of steps for a problem. Rows with syntactic errors are highlighted. After submitting the problem and either correcting syntactic errors or moving forward without correction, any steps with mathematical errors are highlighted and the user is given the opportunity to look at her problem solving. This occurs to provide similar amounts of feedback to participants in both conditions. The user chooses when to move on to the next problem.

In the usability survey, all participants completed ten questions on a 5-point Likert-scale, with participants in the *corrected* condition completing two additional questions. The initial ten questions were adapted from existing usability surveys, such as [10], and focused on perceived learning as well as satisfaction with features of the website. The *corrected*-only questions focused on feelings about having to get each step correct before continuing and whether they found this feedback helpful. The survey also contained three open-ended questions.

Procedure. Participants completed three sessions, separated by at least one day. The first session included the multiple choice assessment followed by the mathematical background survey. In the second session, participants were randomly assigned to one of two conditions and solved 20 problems on the algebra website. The website included a short tutorial about how to use the interface. This tutorial was identical across conditions except for explanations of differing features. In the final session, participants completed the same assessment as in session one, and then responded to the usability survey.

3.2   Results

Overall, performance improved from pretest to posttest. A repeated measures ANOVA with factors for condition and pre- versus post-test showed a small but significant improvement ($F(1, 79) = 14.5$, $p < .001$; mean 11.3 correct on pretest to 12.8 correct at posttest, Cohen's $d = .27$); no interaction between condition and time of test was found ($F(1, 79) = 0.66$, $p = .42$). Given the short nature of the intervention and the far transfer nature of some questions on the assessment assessment, we would not necessarily expect a large improvement. As shown in Figure 2a-b, participants in both conditions attempted similar numbers of problems and gave comparable numbers of correct answers on the website. However, participants in the *corrected* condition entered fewer answers, likely due to being unable to give a correct next step. Note that participants in the *corrected* condition could give an answer without the intervening steps, but they would be warned that they had not entered the correct next step. We counted these cases as having given an answer (and as correct if the answer was correct).

The low scores on the assessment and the website demonstrate that AMT participants were not already proficient with algebra and have gaps in their knowledge and misunderstandings. Comments from participants suggested that their scores were not due to lack of effort but due to the difficulty of the task:

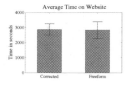 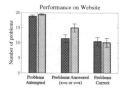 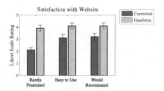

Fig. 2. (a) Time spent on website by condition. Error bars show one standard error. (b) Performance on website by condition. "Attempted" problems are those where the user entered at least one step; correct indicates the final answer was mathematically correct. (c) Website usability ratings.

"humbling" and "very hard" were common sentiments. Given the need for mathematical skills across a range of careers, developing systems that meet the needs of adult learners and testing effectiveness for these learners is an important goal.

Satisfaction with the website varied between conditions. As shown in Figure 2c, participants in the *freeform* tended to be less frustrated ($t(38) = 5.3$, $p < .001$) and thought that the website was easier to use ($t(38) = 2.6$, $p < .05$). They also more strongly agreed that they would recommend the site to others ($t(38) = 2.4$, $p < .05$). Responses to other questions, including ability to understand the interface and finding feedback helpful, trended towards more satisfaction with the *freeform* interface but were similar across conditions.

4   Inverse Planning

Given that the *freeform* interface is less frustrating, we would like to use data from this interface to infer understanding. However, most existing models require that highly structured data and these models do not use the pattern of action *choices* to draw conclusions about misunderstandings. We thus developed a Bayesian inverse planning algorithm to model equation solving, enabling us to make specific inferences based on data from either interface.

Inverse planning is a type of inverse reinforcement learning in which an agent's observed actions are used to make inferences about its goals and understanding of the world. Previous applications to cognition have focused on inferring people's goals based on their action choices [3] and recognizing people's beliefs about how their actions affect their environment [14]. Here, we focus on using inverse planning to diagnose (mis)-understandings, where we assume we have some space of hypotheses θ representing all possible understandings. This diagnosis is computed as a posterior distribution over θ given observed problem solutions $d_1, \ldots, d_N$: $p(\theta|d_1, \ldots, d_N) \propto p(\theta) \prod_{i=1}^{N} p(d_i|\theta)$, where each term $p(d_i|\theta)$ is the likelihood of the observed data for a single problem.

To calculate the likelihood for a problem, we must model how people choose actions and how their transitions from one problem solving step to another are affected by their understanding. We model these choices and transitions using a Markov decision process (MDP). MDPs are decision-theoretic models for action planning that are commonly used when multiple, non-deterministic actions must be taken over time. Formally, MDPs are defined by a tuple $\langle S, A, T, R, \gamma \rangle$. At each time step t, the process is in some state $s \in S$. The agent chooses an action $a \in A$, and with probability $p(s'|a, s)$, specified by the transition model $T(s, a, s')$, the state transitions to next state s'. The reward model $R(s, a, s')$ encodes the incentives. To calculate the likelihood of an observed solution, we use the Markov assumption that given the present, future states are independent of past states:

$$p(s_{1:M}|\theta) = p(s_1|\theta) \prod_{i=1}^{M-1} p(s_{i+1}|\theta, s_i) \propto \prod_{i=1}^{M-1} \sum_{a \in A} p(s_{i+1}|\theta, s_i, a)p(a|\theta, s_i), \quad (1)$$

where the final state s_M is reached by taking a **stop** action. We sum over actions due to the fact that in our data, only steps, not actions, are observed. The term $p(s_{i+1}|\theta, s_i, a)$ can be calculated if we assume that the person's understanding θ maps to a particular MDP: it is the transition model reflecting the person's pattern of moving from one step to another. The term $p(a|\theta, s)$ is the policy for this MDP and is expanded on in the next section as a function of the long term expected value of taking an action a in a state s, known as the Q-value:

$$Q(s, a) = \sum_{s'} p(s'|\theta, s, a)(R(s, a, s') + \gamma \sum_{a' \in A} p(a'|\theta, s')Q(s', a')), \quad (2)$$

where γ reflects the relative weight of immediate versus future rewards. The policy and Q-values can be computed simultaneously through value iteration [17].

5   Modeling Equation Solving

To diagnose understanding from observations of solutions to linear equations, we developed a Bayesian inverse planning algorithm specifically for this domain, building on preliminary previous work [13]. We define the states, actions, and hypotheses for linear equation solving, and then address a technical challenge not present in previous applications of inverse planning to cognition: the state and action spaces for modeling linear equation solving are infinite.

Each equation is mapped to a state, and actions correspond to the way a person changes the equation when solving. The state is represented as the set of terms on each side of the equation, ignoring their ordering. We consider six general types of actions, corresponding to possible equation transformations:

1. **move**: Move a specific term from one side of the equation to another.
2. **divide**: Divide both sides by the coefficient of a specific term.
3. **multiply**: Multiply both sides by a specific constant.
4. **combine**: Combine two specific terms on the same side of the equation.
5. **distribute**: Multiply out a specific complex term like $3(x + 6)$ to get $3x + 18$ or transforming $-3(x + 6)$ to $-(3x + 18)$.
6. **stop**: Stop solving the current problem.

The first five actions represent typical equation solving behavior; below, we describe how errors in these actions are modeled. The final action is taken by a student who believes she has finished solving the problem or is giving up.

The reward model includes a positive reward for choosing **stop** in a state $x = c$ or $c = x$, where x is the variable and c is a constant, and a negative reward for choosing **stop** in any other state. A small negative reward is also incurred for each action: using fewer steps is preferable to using more steps.

5.1   Defining the Hypothesis Space

We define the hypothesis state θ as a vector representing six different student ability parameters. Four parameters are related to specific actions and are based on mal-rules from prior work [12,16]. The *sign error* parameter refers to moving a term to the other side without changing the sign ($2x + 3 = 6 \rightarrow 2x = 6 + 3$). The *reciprocal error* parameter refers to multiplying rather than dividing by a coefficient ($5x = 1 \rightarrow x = 5$). The *distributive error* parameter refers to multiplying only the first term in parentheses by a value ($4(x + 3) \rightarrow 4x + 3$). Each parameter is a value in $[0, 1]$ that reflects the probability of producing the error for the relevant action. These first three dimensions of θ thus govern the transition model of an MDP. Representing erroneous rules as probabilities allows us to account for prior data showing inconsistent application of mal-rules [12]. The fourth action parameter indicates whether only like terms may be combined (only constants or only variables). This is implemented by including versions of the *combine terms* action for non-like terms only if this parameter is zero.

Two additional parameters affect each action choice and transformation. The *arithmetic error* parameter is the probability of making an arithmetic error in each operation in a transformation. Like the first three dimensions of θ, this parameter affects transition probabilities. It allows us to distinguish between misunderstandings about the rules of algebra and difficulties with arithmetic. The final parameter relates to solving efficiency. Following prior work modeling human action planning [3,14], we assume a noisily optimal Boltzmann policy $p(a|s) \propto \exp(\theta_\beta Q(s, a))$, where θ_β controls the noisiness of the policy. Larger θ_β indicates more probability on the actions with highest expected value. Inferring θ_β allows us to detect how efficiently an individual is choosing actions.

5.2   Computing the Diagnosis

The diagnosis of understanding is expressed as a posterior distribution over θ. Because θ is continuous, we approximate the posterior using Metropolis Hastings [7]. We place a Beta(1, 3) prior on the four probability parameters in θ, favoring values closer to normative algebra solving. The prior was not tuned.

Metropolis Hastings calculates the likelihood of the data using sampled values of θ. To calculate the transition model and policy for a specific θ, we must compute the Q-values for the corresponding MDP. We approximate the solution because the state and action spaces are infinite. First, we discretize the actions by creating generic versions of each action that indicate what types of terms

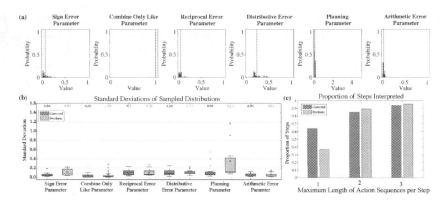

Fig. 3. (a) Diagnosis from a participant who used the *corrected* interface. (b) Distribution of the standard deviations of the sampled distributions, by condition. (c) Proportion of steps where inverse planning found at least one valid action sequence.

(constant, variable, or complex) are acted on but ignore the coefficients. To discretize the state space, we aggregate states into a finite set of possibilities, and then solve $Q(s, a)$ using the aggregated states and discretized actions, such that all equations mapping to the same state have the same Q-values [17].[1]

6   Modeling Human Problem Solving Data

We applied Bayesian inverse planning to diagnose the understanding of each participant in our experiment. Figure 3a shows a graph of the posterior distributions for a single participant in the *corrected* condition. The somewhat low planning parameter is likely due to the fact that the participant gave up on several problems without reaching an answer. The participant had difficulty with problems involving the distributive property, reflected by the high estimated value for the distributive error parameter. The relatively large spread of the posterior for this parameter suggests that the algorithm has low confidence in an exact value. Since inverse planning computes the diagnosis as a distribution, we can easily see the confidence of the algorithm in particular parameter values.

We explored whether the algorithm's diagnoses were as confident based on the *freeform* data as from the *corrected* data. While interpreting *freeform* data is a natural fit for this algorithm, these data are also likely to exhibit ambiguity. Since this interface does not force particular action choices and allows mathematical errors, there may be cases where more than one action or error could account for a step, and people may combine actions.

To measure how confident the diagnoses were for different conditions, we calculated the standard deviation of the sampled values for each participant. As

---

[1] Q-values are also used to find optimal actions in the *corrected* interface. Assuming no errors and letting $\theta_\beta = 5$, we calculate a close to optimal policy. Actions were accepted if they had probability within $\epsilon = 0.05$ of the highest probability.

shown in Figure 3b, the distribution of these standard deviations are generally similar across conditions except for the planning parameter: for most parameters, the lack of constraints in the *freeform* interface did not decrease confidence. For the planning parameter, we believe the difference in confidence is due to participants in the *corrected* condition giving up more frequently. This lead to lower inferred planning parameters on average. Since variance in sampled values tends to increase with the parameter's magnitude, we would expect that this difference in values would result in less absolute confidence for this parameter in the *freeform* condition. This difference also highlights the fact that one might want to separate choices about when to stop solving from suboptimal choices among other actions, which could be incorporated via a two part choice function.

Another measure of the algorithm's performance is its ability to interpret steps as actions in the model. Figure 3c shows the proportion of two-step sequences for which at least one action had non-zero probability; this includes all attempts at steps, including steps that participants entered in the *corrected* condition that were incorrect or the wrong action. When each step transition must be interpreted as a single action, many more steps in the *corrected* condition can be interpreted than in the *freeform* condition. We hypothesized that participants may combine multiple actions in a single step; this could be due to a mismatch between our definition of an individual step and participants beliefs about what defines a step. To address this, we extended the algorithm to sum over sequences of actions rather than only single actions in Equation 1; this may increase noise, as there is more ambiguity, but allows for broader coverage. We only sum over sequences of actions in cases where no single action has non-zero probability. As Figure 2c shows, this results in similar coverage across conditions.

7 Discussion

Our results demonstrate that Bayesian inverse planning can interpret equation solving regardless of which interface is used. However, people who used the *freeform* interface were less frustrated and more able to reach solutions. Several participants commented that they wanted to solve problems "their way"; the *freeform* interface comes much closer than the *corrected* interface to realizing this goal, and inverse planning provides a powerful tool for understanding actions with minimal structuring. While it may be beneficial to eventually guide learners towards more efficient actions, forcing this sequence immediately, especially for those with partial understanding, could be frustrating.

Our results have several limitations. AMT participants may have different motivations than typical algebra students. However, we believe these participants still provide valuable evidence about the usability of the interfaces and have varying algebra skills, similar to other adult learners. Comments from several participants indicated they wanted to learn more algebra or appreciated practicing old skills, suggesting some interest in the topic. An additional limitation is our choice of interfaces. Specifically, some tutoring systems are less constrained than our *corrected* interface, requiring only that steps be mathematically correct but not that they be in a normative order. Our constraint on order represents minimal ambiguity for inverse planning, providing a best case scenario for the algorithm to which we can compare, and the fact that we allowed slightly suboptimal actions means that some action choice was still permitted.

This work demonstrates that inverse planning can interpret equation solving data, providing a way to allow more freeform solutions without sacrificing automated knowledge tracking. In the future, we plan to more closely examine the accuracy of inverse planning for knowledge diagnosis; this study provides some evidence of its effectiveness, but a more thorough investigation is needed. Additionally, we plan to explore the use of inverse planning for customizing feedback, and to compare the effectiveness of the immediate and specific *corrected* interface feedback to holistic, conceptual feedback. Investigation of a blend of structured and freeform interfaces may also suggest ways to maintain engagement and motivation while still guiding learners towards normative solving. While many questions remain, the technical innovations of inverse planning provide a foundation for addressing these issues.

Acknowledgements. This work was funded by NSF grant number DRL-1420732 to Thomas L. Griffiths.

References

1. Anthony, L.: Developing handwriting-based Intelligent Tutors to enhance mathematics learning. Ph.D. thesis, Carnegie Mellon University (2008)
2. Anthony, L., Yang, J., Koedinger, K.R.: Evaluation of multimodal input for entering mathematical equations on the computer. In: CHI 2005 Extended Abstracts on Human Factors in Computing Systems, pp. 1184–1187. ACM (2005)
3. Baker, C.L., Saxe, R.R., Tenenbaum, J.B.: Action understanding as inverse planning. Cognition **113**(3), 329–349 (2009)
4. Board, C.: Accuplacer® sample questions for students. https://accuplacer.collegeboard.org/students (Accessed 15 October 2014)
5. Corbett, A.T., Anderson, J.R.: The effect of feedback control on learning to program with the lisp tutor. In: Proceedings of the Twelfth Annual Conference of the Cognitive Science Society, pp. 796–803 (1990)
6. Falmagne, J.C., Doignon, J.P.: Learning spaces. Springer (2011)
7. Gilks, W., Richardson, S., Spiegelhalter, D.J. (eds.): Markov Chain Monte Carlo in Practice. Chapman and Hall, Suffolk (1996)
8. Koedinger, K.R., Anderson, J., Hadley, W., Mark, M.: Intelligent tutoring goes to school in the big city. International Journal of Artificial Intelligence in Education **8**, 30–43 (1997)
9. Kramer, A.: Symja library - Java symbolic math system (2010–2014). https://bitbucket.org/axelclk/symja_android_library/wiki/Home
10. Lund, A.: Measuring usability with the USE questionnaire. STC Usability SIG Newsletter **8**(2) (2001)
11. Mattern, K.D., Packman, S.: Predictive validity of ACCUPLACER scores for course placement: A meta-analysis. Tech. Rep. 2009–2, College Board, New York, NY, December 2009
12. Payne, S., Squibb, H.: Algebra mal-rules and cognitive accounts of error. Cognitive Science **14**(3), 445–481 (1990)

13. Rafferty, A.N., Griffiths, T.L.: Diagnosing algebra understanding via Bayesian inverse planning. In: Proceedings of the 7th International Conference on Educational Data Mining, pp. 351–352 (2014)
14. Rafferty, A.N., LaMar, M.M., Griffiths, T.L.: Inferring learners' knowledge from their actions. Cognitive Science (in press)
15. Razzaq, L.M., Heffernan, N., Feng, M., Pardos, Z.: Developing fine-grained transfer models in the Assistment system. Journal of Technology, Instruction, Cognition, and Learning 5(3), 289–304 (2007)
16. Sleeman, D.: An attempt to understand students' understanding of basic algebra. Cognitive Science 8(4), 387–412 (1984)
17. Sutton, R.S., Barto, A.G.: Reinforcement learning. MIT Press (1998)

ITS Support for Conceptual and Perceptual Connection Making Between Multiple Graphical Representations

Martina A. Rau[⊠] and Sally P.W. Wu

Department of Educational Psychology, University of Wisconsin – Madison, Madison, USA
{marau,pwwu}@wisc.edu

Abstract. Connection making between representations is crucial to learning in STEM domains, but it is a difficult task for students. Prior research shows that supporting connection making enhances students' learning of domain knowledge. Most prior research has focused on supporting one type of connection-making process: *conceptual* reasoning about connections between representations. Yet, recent research suggests that a second type of connection-making process plays a role in students' learning: *perceptual* translation between representations. We hypothesized that combining support for both conceptual and perceptual connection-making processes leads to higher learning gains on a domain-knowledge test. We tested this hypothesis in a lab experiment with 117 undergraduate students using an intelligent tutoring system for chemistry. Results show that the combination of conceptual and perceptual connection-making supports leads to higher learning outcomes. This finding suggests that the effectiveness of educational technologies can be enhanced if they combine support for conceptual and perceptual connection-making processes.

Keywords: Multiple representations · Connection making · Conceptual and perceptual processes · Intelligent tutoring systems · Chemistry

1 Introduction

Instructional materials in STEM domains typically use multiple graphical representations to make abstract concepts accessible to students [1, 2]. For example, when learning about atomic structure, students typically encounter the representations shown in Fig. 1: Lewis structures show only valence electrons, Bohr models show all electrons in atomic shells, energy diagrams depict electrons in orbitals by energy level, and orbital diagrams show the spatial arrangement of non-empty orbitals. Each of these representations emphasizes different aspects of domain-relevant concepts. Through connection making, students integrate the information each representation depicts about domain-relevant concepts into a coherent mental model [3]. However, making connections between representations is difficult. Students often do not make connections spontaneously [3], including chemistry students at the graduate level [4]. Difficulties in making connections are a major obstacle to students' success in STEM [5].

© Springer International Publishing Switzerland 2015
C. Conati et al. (Eds.): AIED 2015, LNAI 9112, pp. 398–407, 2015.
DOI: 10.1007/978-3-319-19773-9_40

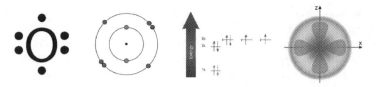

Fig. 1. Graphical representations of oxygen: Lewis, Bohr, energy diagram, orbital diagram

Prior research shows that educational technologies can considerably enhance students' learning of domain knowledge if they support students in making connections between representations [6-8]. Most prior research on connection making has focused on supporting only one type of connection-making learning process; namely, *conceptual connection-making processes* [6, 7]. Conceptual support targets explicit connection-making processes by helping students reason about how different representations show the same concepts and how the information shown about the given concept differs between representations [3]. Recent research draws attention to a second type of connection-making process; namely, *perceptual connection-making processes* [8]. Research on perceptual connection-making support builds on research on expertise, which shows that experts can quickly and effortlessly translate between representations by "just seeing" connections between representations, without cognitive effort [8].This highly practiced fluency in connection making comes from exposure to large numbers of examples and does not require explicit instruction. Such perceptual fluency frees cognitive headroom that experts can invest in higher-order thinking. Building on this research on expertise, research on perceptual connection-making support proposes that exposing students to numerous translation tasks while providing feedback on their performance might enhance their learning of domain knowledge. Thus, perceptual support targets implicit connection-making processes. It helps students become acute in paying attention to relevant perceptual features and use them to efficiently translate between representations. Perceptual support has been shown to enhance students' learning of domain knowledge [8]. Cognitive theories of learning propose that both conceptual and perceptual connection making plays a role in robust learning [9].

However, little research has investigated whether instruction is most effective if it provides support for both conceptual connection-making processes and perceptual connection-making processes, or whether support for only one type of connection-making processes is sufficient. To the best of our knowledge, an experiment on elementary-school fractions learning was the first to show that both conceptual and perceptual processes play a role in connection making [10]: An intelligent tutoring system (ITS) that combined conceptual and perceptual support led to higher learning gains than versions of the ITS with either type of connection-making support alone. Yet, it remains an open question whether this finding holds as a general principle. Do conceptual and perceptual connection-making processes play a role in domains, student populations, and educational settings other than elementary-school fractions?

This question is of particular relevance to ITSs. If both conceptual and perceptual processes play a role in student learning, ITSs that combine both types of support will be most effective. Moreover, knowing which connection-making processes we need to support is a prerequisite to developing adaptive connection-making support. Case studies show that adapting instruction to students' skills in using representations enhances their learning outcomes [11]. Thus, ITSs may be most effective if they adapt connection-making support to a student's ongoing acquisition of conceptual and perceptual connection-making skills. Since connection making is key to success in many STEM domains, this research may yield more effective ITSs at a broad scale.

We conducted a lab experiment to investigate the effects of conceptual and perceptual connection-making support on undergraduate chemistry learning. We hypothesized that combining conceptual and perceptual support is most effective. Further, we explored whether the effectiveness of conceptual and perceptual support interacts with mental rotation ability, because spatial skills are a significant predictor of learning outcomes in STEM fields that rely on the use of graphical representations [12].

2   Methods

2.1   Chem Tutor: An ITS for Undergraduate Chemistry

We conducted the experiment in the context of an ITS for undergraduate chemistry: Chem Tutor [13]. Chem Tutor is a type of ITS called example-tracing tutors [14]. Example-tracing tutors do not use a cognitive model that is based on production rules but rely on generalized examples of correct and incorrect solutions. The design of Chem Tutor is based on user-centered studies [13]. Chem Tutor supports chemistry learning by helping students make connections between graphical representations.

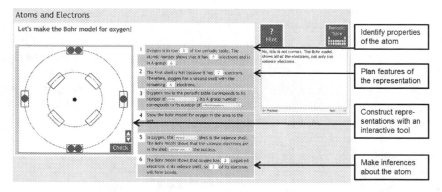

Fig. 2. Example of an individual-representation problem

Individual-Representation Problems. Before students can make connections between representations, they have to understand each individual representation [3]. To this end, Chem Tutor provides problems in which students reason about one representation at a time (Fig. 2). First, they reflect on properties of the atom. Second, they plan how to construct the given representation. Third, they use an interactive tool to construct the representation. They receive error-specific feedback on their interactions, and they have to construct a correct representation before they can continue. Fourth, students are prompted to use the representation to make inferences about the atom.

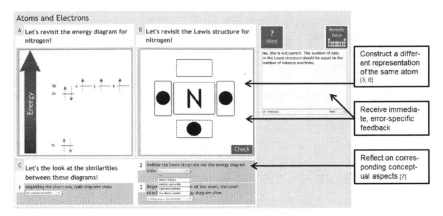

Fig. 3. Example of a conceptual connection-making problem

Conceptual Connection-Making Problems. In addition, Chem Tutor provides problems designed to help students conceptually make sense of how different representations provide corresponding and complementary information about chemistry concepts (see Fig. 3). First, students receive a representation of an atom and are asked to use an interactive tool to construct a different representation of the same atom. Second, students are prompted to reflect on which concepts are depicted in both representations (e.g., both show the valence electrons) or on what information is shown in one representation but not in the other (e.g., the energy diagram shows orbitals, but the Lewis structure does not). The design of the conceptual problems is based on prior research on conceptual connection-making support [6, 7].

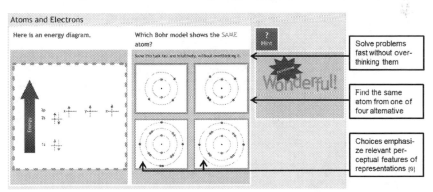

Fig. 4. Example of a perceptual connection-making problem

Perceptual Connection-Making Problems. Finally, Chem Tutor provides problems designed to help students become perceptually fluent in translating between representations (see Fig. 4). In these problems, students are presented with one representation and have to select one out of four representations that shows the same atom. The four alternative representations are chosen so that they emphasize features that students should learn to pay attention to (e.g., an incorrect representation might show the same number of shells as the correct representation but a different number of valence electrons). The different choice options provide variations of irrelevant features of the representations and contrast perceptual features that provide relevant information (e.g., geometry, location of the local charges). Chem Tutor prompts students to solve these problems fast, without overthinking them, in order to encourage perceptual rather than conceptual strategies. Each problem is short (i.e., it involves only one step). Students receive a dozen of these problems in a row, and they receive only correctness feedback. Thus, the perceptual problems are designed to help students become faster and more efficient at extracting relevant information from graphical representations based on repeated experience with a large variety of problems. The design of the perceptual problems is based on prior research on perceptual connection making [8].

2.2   Test Instruments

We assessed students' chemistry knowledge three times: before they started working with Chem Tutor, after they completed half of the tutor problems, and after they completed all tutor problems. We used three isomorphic test forms that asked structurally identical questions but used different problems (e.g., with different atoms). The order in which students received the test forms was counterbalanced. The tests assessed reproduction and transfer of the chemistry content covered in Chem Tutor. Reproduction items used a format similar to the Chem Tutor problems. Transfer items asked students to apply the knowledge Chem Tutor covered in ways they had not been asked to do in the Chem Tutor problems. The tests included items with and without representations. Further, we used the Vandenberg & Kuse test to assess mental rotation ability [15]. Students completed this test prior to the chemistry pretest.

2.3   Participants

117 undergraduate students participated in the experiment. Students were recruited with posters and by advertising in introductory chemistry courses. 79% of the students were currently enrolled in general chemistry for non-science majors, 13.4% were enrolled in general chemistry for science majors, 2.5% were enrolled in advanced general chemistry, and 5% were not currently enrolled in a chemistry course.

2.4   Experimental Design

Students worked with versions of Chem Tutor designed specifically for this experiment. We used a 2 (conceptual support) x 2 (perceptual support) design to investigate the effects of connection-making support on students' learning of chemistry. The conceptual-support factor had two levels: students either received conceptual connection-making problems or not. The perceptual-support factor also had two levels: students received perceptual connection-making problems or not. Thus, students were randomly assigned to one of four conditions: Students in the no-conceptual / no-perceptual condition worked only on individual-representation problems. Students in the conceptual / no-perceptual condition worked on individual-representation problems and on conceptual connection-making problems. Students in the no-conceptual / perceptual condition worked on individual-representation problems and on perceptual connection-making problems. Students in the conceptual / perceptual condition worked on individual-representation problems, conceptual connection-making problems, and perceptual connection-making problems.

We adjusted the number of problems in each condition so that the number of steps was equal across conditions. For example, students in the control condition worked on more individual-representation problems than students in the other conditions, and students in the conceptual / no-perceptual condition worked on more conceptual problems than students in the conceptual / perceptual condition. Equating the number of steps (rather than the number of problems) was necessary because the problems had different number of steps (e.g., each perceptual problem has only one step). This adjustment yielded interventions that took about the same time for all conditions.

The sequence of individual-representation problems, conceptual and perceptual connection-making problems was organized as follows. For each pair of representations, students first received individual-representation problems (e.g., one Lewis structure problem, and one Bohr model problem). Next, if they were in one of the conceptual conditions, they received conceptual connection-making problems for this pair of representations. Then, if they were in one of the perceptual conditions, they received perceptual connection-making problems for this pair of representations. This sequence proved to be more effective than other sequences in prior research [16].

2.5   Procedure

The experiment took place in the laboratory and involved two sessions of 90 minutes each, no more than three days apart. In session 1, students completed the mental rotation test and the chemistry pretest. They then received an introduction into using Chem Tutor. Next, they worked on half of the tutor problems, using the version of Chem Tutor that corresponded to their condition. At the end of session 1, students took the intermediate chemistry posttest. In session 2, students worked through the remainder of the tutor problems and then took the final chemistry posttest.

3   Results

Table 1 shows means and standard deviations of students' performance on the tests. To report effect sizes, we use p. η^2. An effect size p. η^2 of .01 corresponds to a small, .06 to a medium, and .14 to a large effect. Differences between conditions at pretest were not significant, $F(3,114) = 1.01, p = .39$.

3.1   Learning Gains

First, we investigated whether working with Chem Tutor led to learning gains. We used a repeated measures ANOVA with test-time (pretest, intermediate test, final posttest) as the repeated, within-subjects factor and scores on the chemistry tests as the dependent measure. The main effect of test-time was significant, $F(2,232) = 37.31, p < .01$, p. $\eta^2 = .24$. The interaction of test-time with mental rotation ability was not significant; thus students improved regardless of their mental rotation ability.

Table 1. Means and standard deviations (in parentheses) for tests by condition and test time

Condition	Mental rotation ability	Chemistry knowledge		
		Pretest	*Intermediate test*	*Final posttest*
No-conceptual / no-perceptual	.58 (.24)	.49 (.20)	.60 (.23)	.62 (.19)
Conceptual / no-perceptual	.63 (.18)	.47 (.21)	.55 (.23)	.6 (.18)
No-conceptual / perceptual	.53 (.23)	.38 (.22)	.52 (.19)	.55 (.17)
Conceptual / perceptual	.55 (.20)	.42 (.20)	.58 (.19)	.61 (.20)

3.2   Effects of Conceptual and Perceptual Connection-Making Support

Next, we investigated the hypothesis that conceptual and perceptual connection-making support leads to better learning of chemistry knowledge. We used a repeated measures ANCOVA with test-time (intermediate test, final posttest) as the repeated, within-subjects factor, conceptual support and perceptual support as between-subjects factors, mental rotation ability and scores on the chemistry knowledge pretest as covariates, and scores on the chemistry test as the dependent measure.

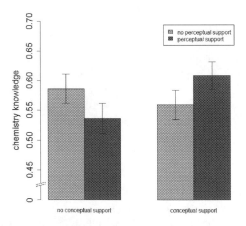

Fig. 5. Effects of conceptual and perceptual support on the chemistry knowledge posttest

The main effect of conceptual support was not significant, $F(1,109) = 1.39$, $p > .10$. There was a positive main effect of perceptual support, $F(1,109) = 6.28$, $p < .05$, p. $\eta^2 = .06$. The interaction of conceptual and perceptual support was significant, $F(1,109) = 4.05$, $p < .05$, p. $\eta^2 = .04$, such that perceptual support was effective only if provided in combination with conceptual support (see Fig. 5). To verify the accuracy of this interpretation, we used post-hoc comparisons. Students who did not receive conceptual support had significantly lower learning outcomes if they received perceptual support than without perceptual support, $F(1,110) = 9.34$, $p < .01$, p. $\eta^2 = .08$. Students who received conceptual support had significantly higher learning outcomes if they received perceptual support than without perceptual support, $F(1,110) = 9.34$, $p < .01$, p. $\eta^2 =.08$. Finally, there was a marginally significant advantage of the conceptual / perceptual condition over the no-conceptual / no-perceptual condition, $F(1,110) = 2.69$, $p = .10$, p. $\eta^2 =.05$. In sum, the results indicate that the combination of conceptual and perceptual connection-making support is most effective.

Finally, to investigate whether the effectiveness of conceptual and perceptual support depends on students' mental rotation ability, we used the same ANCOVA model to examine interactions of mental rotation ability with conceptual support and with perceptual support. The interaction was not significant for conceptual support ($F < 1$), but it was significant for perceptual support, $F(1,109) = 7.15$, $p < .01$, p. $\eta^2 =.06$, such that perceptual support was more effective for students with high mental rotation ability than for students with low mental rotation ability.

4   Discussion

We had hypothesized that combining conceptual and perceptual support for connection making would enhance students' learning gains in chemistry. Our results support this hypothesis: we found that combining conceptual and perceptual support leads to the highest learning gains on a domain-knowledge test. This finding is in line with cognitive theories that suggest that both processes play a role in robust learning [9]. Our finding extends prior research on connection making that has focused only on conceptual support [6, 7] or only on perceptual support [8]. Finally, it extends prior research that found an advantage of combining conceptual and perceptual support in an ITS for fractions learning [10]. We show that this effect generalizes to a different domain, student population, and setting, suggesting that it is indeed a robust effect.

To our surprise, we found that perceptual support was only effective in combination with conceptual support: providing only perceptual support resulted in lower learning gains than providing no connection-making support at all. This finding extends previous research on perceptual support for connection making by showing that the effectiveness of perceptual support depends on whether students also receive conceptual support. To the best of our knowledge, participants in prior research on perceptual support were typically not novices [8]. As part of prior instruction, they may have acquired conceptual understanding of connections. Thus, it is possible that the effectiveness of perceptual support in these studies depended on students' prior conceptual learning. Also to our surprise, the advantage of the conceptual / perceptual condition over the control condition was only marginally significant. It is possible that a longer intervention might have yielded stronger effects. In particular, the amount of practice students need to become perceptually fluent has been found to vary across individuals [3]. Thus, adaptive perceptual support might yield stronger effects.

Furthermore, we found that the effectiveness of perceptual support depends on students' mental rotation ability. Students with high mental rotation ability benefited more from perceptual connection-making support than students with low mental rotation ability. Since perceptual problems ask students to map perceptual features that are not always spatially aligned across representations, students might have to mentally rotate representations when solving perceptual problems. Therefore, students with low mental rotation abilities may particularly struggle with perceptual connection-making problems. Future research should investigate how to tailor perceptual support to the needs of students with low mental rotation ability. Our findings suggest that students with low mental rotation ability might benefit more from perceptual support that provides assistance in mentally rotating representations or that uses examples in which perceptual features are spatially aligned.

One limitation of the experiment is that it was conducted in a lab setting. Chem Tutor is designed to be used as a homework system within undergraduate chemistry courses. In future research, we will investigate whether we find the same effects when students use Chem Tutor in a homework setting. A further limitation is that the majority of participants were non-science majors. These students are likely to have a lower interest in learning chemistry and lower prior knowledge about the domain than science majors. In future research, we will investigate whether our findings generalize to a broader population of undergraduate students.

To conclude, our findings suggest that ITSs should incorporate instructional support for both conceptual and perceptual processes involved in connection making. The fact that a study on undergraduate chemistry learning found the same effect as prior research on elementary-school fractions learning suggests that this effect is robust across domains, student populations, and educational settings. Our findings also have implications for the design of adaptive connection-making support. Case studies suggest that such adaptive support for representational skills can significantly enhance students' learning in STEM [11]. Our findings suggest that a cognitive model that selects appropriate connection-making problems for an individual student at any time during the intervention should reflect conceptual and perceptual skills in making connections. Thus, connection-making support might be most effective if it adapts in real time to students' acquisition of conceptual and perceptual skills. Given that the ability to make connections between representations is critical to students' learning success in many STEM domains, this research has the potential to impact a broad range of educational technologies.

Acknowledgements. The UW-Madison Graduate School and the Wisconsin Center for Education Research supported this research. We thank John Moore for his advice. We thank Teri Larson, Ned Sibert, Stephen Block, Amanda Evenstone, and Jocelyn Kuhn for their help in recruiting students. We thank Greyson Bahr, Youn Ku Choi, Natalie Fay, Ashley Hong, Will Keesler, Amber Kim, Ashley Lee, Marguerite Lee, Aditi Renganathan, Jamie Schuberth, Mike Schwanke, Peter Van Sandt, and Philip Zimring for their help in conducting the experiment.

References

1. Kozma, R., Russell, J.: Students becoming chemists: Developing representationl competence. In: Gilbert, J. (ed.) Visualization in science education, pp. 121–145. Springer, Dordrecht (2005)
2. Arcavi, A.: The Role of Visual Representations in the Learning of Mathematics. Educational Studies in Mathematics **52**, 215–241 (2003)

3. Ainsworth, S.: DeFT: A conceptual framework for considering learning with multiple representations. Learning and Instruction **16**, 183–198 (2006)
4. Strickland, A.M., Kraft, A., Bhattacharyya, G.: What happens when representations fail to represent? Graduate students' mental models of organic chemistry diagrams. Chemistry Education Research and Practice **11**, 293–301 (2010)
5. Cheng, M., Gilbert, J.K.: Towards a better utilization of diagrams in research into the use of representative levels in chemical education. In: Gilbert, J.K., Treagust, D.F. (eds.) Multiple Representations in Chemical Education, pp. 191–208. Springer, Berlin / Heidelberg (2009)
6. Bodemer, D., Faust, U.: External and mental referencing of multiple representations. Computers in Human Behavior **22**, 27–42 (2006)
7. van der Meij, J., de Jong, T.: Supporting students' learning with multiple representations in a dynamic simulation-based learning environment. Learning and Instruction **16**, 199–212 (2006)
8. Kellman, P.J., Massey, C.M.: Perceptual Learning, cognition, and expertise. The Psychology of Learning and Motivation **558**, 117–165 (2013)
9. Koedinger, K.R., Corbett, A.T., Perfetti, C.: The Knowledge-Learning-Instruction Framework: Bridging the Science-Practice Chasm to Enhance Robust Student Learning. Cognitive Science **36**, 757–798 (2012)
10. Rau, Martina A., Aleven, Vincent, Rummel, Nikol, Rohrbach, Stacie: Sense making alone doesn't do it: fluency matters too! ITS support for robust learning with multiple representations. In: Cerri, Stefano A., Clancey, William J., Papadourakis, Giorgos, Panourgia, Kitty (eds.) ITS 2012. LNCS, vol. 7315, pp. 174–184. Springer, Heidelberg (2012)
11. Davidowitz, B., Chittleborough, G.: Linking the macroscopic and sub-microscopic levels: diagrams. In: Gilbert, J.K., Treagust, D.F. (eds.) Multiple Representations in Chemical Education, pp. 169–191. Springer, Dordrecht (2009)
12. Stieff, M.: Mental rotation and diagrammatic reasoning in science. Learning and Instruction **17**, 219–234 (2007)
13. Rau, M.A., Michaelis, J.E., Fay, N.: Connection making between multiple graphical representations: A multi-methods approach for domain-specific grounding of an intelligent tutoring system for chemistry. Computers and Education **82** (2015)
14. Aleven, V., McLaren, B.M., Sewall, J., Koedinger, K.R.: A new paradigm for intelligent tutoring systems: Example-tracing tutors. International Journal of Artificial Intelligence in Education **19**, 105–154 (2009)
15. Peters, M., Laeng, B., Latham, K., Jackson, M., Zaiyouna, R., Richardson, C.: A Redrawn Vandenberg & Kuse Mental Rotations Test: Different Versions and Factors that affect Performance. Brain and Cognition **28**, 39–58 (1995)
16. Rau, M.A., Aleven, V., Rummel, N.: Sequencing sense-making and fluency-building support for connection making between multiple graphical representations. In: Polman, J.L., et al. (eds.) Proceedings of ICLS 2014, vol. 2, pp. 977–981. International Society of the Learning Sciences, Boulder (2014)

Discovering Individual and Collaborative Problem-Solving Modes with Hidden Markov Models

Fernando J. Rodríguez[✉] and Kristy Elizabeth Boyer

Department of Computer Science, North Carolina State University,
Raleigh, NC 27695, USA
{fjrodri3,keboyer}@ncsu.edu

Abstract. Supporting students during learning tasks is the main goal of intelligent tutoring systems, and the most effective systems can adapt to students based on a model of their current state of knowledge or their problem-solving actions. Most tutoring systems focus on individual students, but there is growing interest in supporting student pairs. However, modeling student pairs involves considerations that may differ from individual students. This paper reports on hidden Markov models (HMMs) of student interactions within a visual programming environment. We compare HMMs for individual students to those of student pairs and examine the different approaches the students take. The resulting models suggest that there are some important differences across both conditions. There is potential for using these models to predict problem-solving modes and support adaptive tutoring for collaboration in problem-solving domains.

Keywords: Collaboration · Hidden markov models · Pair programming · Visual programming

1 Introduction

Intelligent tutoring systems (ITSs) support student learning by adapting problem difficulty [1], providing personalized hints [2, 3], or giving feedback on the learner's progress [4]. However, ITSs' ability to support problem solving have traditionally been limited when the problem is a creative or open-ended learning task because such problems have many possible correct solutions [4, 5]. While some lines of research are actively investigating complex domains whose problems do not have formulaic solutions [6], much work is needed in order to seamlessly support users in solving open-ended problems. Nonetheless, this type of learning task support is an essential step in supporting human learning with computers, as solving open-ended problems is a central component of many real-life endeavors.

In addition to the limitation of most tutoring systems to well-defined tasks, the vast majority of adaptive learning environments focus on supporting individual users. However, collaborative problem solving is not only mandated within curricular standards for a variety of disciplines, it arises organically both inside and outside classroom settings [7]. When people solve problems collaboratively, their approaches and strategies differ from individual problem solving [8], and developing an understanding of those differences is crucial for adaptively supporting collaborative problem solving.

© Springer International Publishing Switzerland 2015
C. Conati et al. (Eds.): AIED 2015, LNAI 9112, pp. 408–418, 2015.
DOI: 10.1007/978-3-319-19773-9_41

This paper represents a step toward automatically supporting collaborative pairs in a complex problem-solving domain. We examine paired problem solving as it arises when solving computer science problems, within structured collaboration referred to as pair programming [9]. We present an exploratory study of the differences in problem-solving approaches between individual students and student pairs. Based upon detailed interaction logs of the problem-solving collaboration, we built hidden Markov models of the interaction sequences for both individual students and collaborative student pairs. While not predictive of learning gains, the models highlight that many of the problem-solving modes are shared across both groups; however, each exhibits a different mode that may have emerged as a result of working individually or with a partner. These findings point the way toward building adaptive support for paired problem solving.

2   Related Work

Many ITSs build a representation of the student's progress, which allows the system to adapt to that specific student's needs and provide appropriate scaffolding [10]. Aspects of a student's problem-solving process that have been utilized to create student models within ITSs range from low-level actions, such as textual edits [3], to combinations of several features of an action, such as the action type, involved components, and final outcome [11]. The research community has taken an interaction-based perspective, attempting to model learners based on their interactions within an ITS's interface. In particular, models of problem-solving strategies have been utilized to inform the design of adaptive systems [1] by building hidden Markov models of students' problem-solving strategies within an ITS for middle school algebra [12] and concept mapping within a teachable agent for middle school science [13]. The present work builds upon this prior research by focusing on computer science as the learning domain and on comparing individual students to students working in pairs.

The vast majority of ITSs have historically focused on individual students. Although this is still the norm, recent years have shown an increased interest in adapting ITSs to support student pairs and groups in general. In computer science, pair programming is an effective paradigm for supporting learning [9, 14–16]. Even at the elementary school level, student pairs collaborating through an ITS achieved similar learning gains to individual students and were able to do so having completed fewer problems within the tutor [8]. System logs and audio recordings have been used to detect when students are collaborating, as well as the intensity of the collaboration [17]. A framework for detecting common patterns of collaboration based on students' speech and interactions within a touch-based tabletop system has also been proposed [18]. The work presented in this paper contributes to this field of research by presenting models that can be used to compare individual students and student pairs completing a problem-solving task.

3   Study

In this study, students implemented a simple game using a visual programming language, and their collaborative or individual problem-solving actions were recorded.

Students were recruited from the second course on computer programming at North Carolina State University. These students had prior experience with programming in Java, but were pre-screened to ensure that none had interacted with visual programming languages before. A total of 30 students participated in the study: 14 worked individually and 16 were assigned to the paired condition, for a total of 8 student pairs. Students were paired based upon their schedules and then through random selection for mutual availability. Participants' ages varied between 18 and 28 ($\mu=21$), with one participant of age 40. Two of the 30 participants were female, commensurate with the population of computer science undergraduate students at the university; one female student was randomly paired with a male student and the other was in the individual students condition. In exchange for participating in the study, students received credit for a homework assignment in their programming course. The programming task was to implement the win conditions for a game of "Rock-Paper-Scissors." Fig. 1 shows a partially implemented student program and its output.

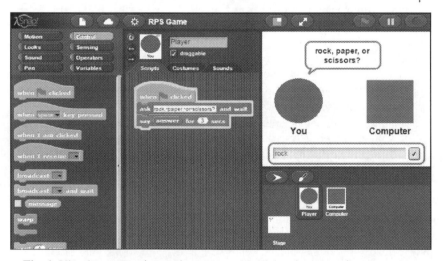

Fig. 1. Visual programming environment and partial rock-paper-scissors program

Students were first given a brief tutorial of the *Snap!* programming language in which program structures are represented by *blocks*, which can be *grabbed*, *dropped*, and *snapped* together to create programs [19]. The students were allowed to ask questions of the research coordinator during and after the initial tutorial, but not during the programming task. Students were provided with two paper artifacts: a scaffolding document for building the program, and a Snap! block reference sheet that included the blocks required to complete the task and where to locate them within the interface. Students working in pairs followed the pair programming paradigm, sharing one computer and performing one of two roles at any given moment during the task: the *driver* used the computer and created the program, and the *navigator* read the scaffolding document and provided instructions to the driver. They switched roles three times (at moments indicated within the scaffolding document), giving each student the opportunity to take on both roles twice during the task. Individual students completed the task in an average of 37 minutes ($n_{individuals}$=14; min=23 minutes; max=60 minutes; σ=10.5 minutes), while student pairs tended to complete the task slightly faster, on average 34 minutes (n_{pairs}=8; min=23 minutes; max=42 minutes; σ=6.3 minutes). This difference was not statistically significant (Mann-Whitney U test: p=0.73).

Students were given an individual multiple-choice pre-test before the Snap! tutorial and an identical post-test following the task. There were no significant differences in pre-test scores between the individual and collaborative students ($\mu_{individuals}$=0.78; μ_{pairs}=0.81). Overall, students achieved a statistically significant increase in test score over the course of the study (μ_{pre}=0.79; μ_{post}=0.86; one-tailed t-test p=0.02). Disaggregating by condition, there was a significant increase in test score for the individual students (μ_{pre}=0.78; μ_{post}=0.89; one-tailed t-test p=0.01), but this was not the case for the student pairs (μ_{pre}=0.81; μ_{post}=0.83; one-tailed t-test p=0.29).

4   Modeling Interaction Sequences

Having collected the full sequential interaction traces, we proceeded to model the event sequences. The underlying notion is that problem-solving sequences comprise visible actions that reflect problem-solving modes. We use hidden Markov models (HMMs) to model the problem-solving sequences [20]. These represent stochastic processes through states and transitions. At any given moment, the HMM is in one of its hidden states. Each state emits an observation after each event, and these observations can be directly measured and used to predict which state the model is currently in (see Fig. 2). One model was built for each condition of the study: one for individual students and another for student pairs. We interpret the hidden states to represent the "modes" that the students employ during their programming task. (Note that since HMMs model unobservable constructs, the theoretical constructs that they represent are subject to interpretation.) The observations correspond to the event sequences stored in the database of problem-solving logs from the study. Each observation in this model has three dimensions:

- *Event type*: These represent semantically meaningful events within the interface.
  - CREATE: a block was added onto the scripting area
  - DELETE: a block was removed from the scripting area
  - SNAP: two blocks in the scripting area were connected
  - UNSNAP: two blocks in the scripting area were separated
  - MOVE: a block was dragged and dropped within the scripting area
  - PARAM: a block's parameter was set or changed
  - CATEGORY: the current block category was switched
  - RUN: the current program was run

- *Edit distance from final solution*: The textual representation of the session's current program was compared to the final session program (note that each student and student pair completed the task), and edit distance (number of character changes that need to be made to a string to match another string) was calculated. The observation consisted of determining if the student was getting <u>closer</u> or <u>farther</u> from the final solution or remained the <u>same edit distance</u> away from the solution after the event.
- *Elapsed time since previous event*: These were classified as either being <u>under 30 seconds</u> (QUICK) or <u>over 30 seconds</u> (DELAY). This threshold was empirically determined by measuring the elapsed time when the students were either reading the instructions or consulting with their partner.

Table 1. Observation symbols

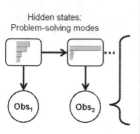

Hidden states:
Problem-solving modes

Obs₁   Obs₂

Fig. 2. Sequential HMM diagram

Event	Dist.	Time	Obs. symbols
CREATE	CLOSE	≤ 30s	CREATE_CLOSE_QUICK
DELETE	FAR	(QUICK)	CREATE_CLOSE_DELAY
MOVE	SAME	> 30s	CREATE_FAR_QUICK
SNAP		(DELAY)	...
UNSNAP			DELETE_CLOSE_QUICK
PARAM			...
CATEGORY			CATEGORY_QUICK
RUN			CATEGORY_DELAY
			RUN_QUICK
			RUN_DELAY

With eight event types, two elapsed time tags, and three edit distance tags, there were 48 possible observations from the combinations of these dimensions (see Table 1 for examples). Removing the events that did not occur in the dataset, there were a total of 36 observation symbols. Overall, the individual students carried out an average of 199 task actions to complete the problem-solving task ($n_{individuals}$=14; min=104 events; max=323 events; σ=63.1 events); the student pairs carried out an average of 181 task actions (n_{pairs}=8; min=130 events; max=258 events; σ=41.6 events). The difference between means was not statistically significant (Mann-Whitney U test; p=0.36), and the higher standard deviation for individuals could be attributed to both the differences in programming skills and the lack of a partner to help direct the activity. The events were classified into a set of defined observation symbols based on the elapsed time since the previous event and the edit distance of the current solution from the final session solution, as described in Table 1.

To determine the number of states for the HMMs, leave-one-session-out cross-validation was used. Models were trained using all but one of the problem-solving sessions, and the log-likelihood was calculated for the probability that the remaining session could be generated from the trained model; this was repeated for each session in a given condition (14 times for the individual students, 8 for the student pairs). The same process was repeated for each possible number of states from 3 to 20 (roughly half the number of the observation symbols), and the average log-likelihood for each number of states was stored. The Bayesian Information Criterion (BIC) was calculated for each number of states and averaged between the two conditions; the lowest average BIC corresponded to the 4-state models. Thus, 4-state HMMs were built for each condition by retraining the models with all sessions for each condition.

5   Results

The HMMs for both conditions are presented in Fig. 3. State transition arrows are thicker for higher probabilities and dotted for lower probabilities. Only the observation probabilities greater than 0.05 are shown in the figure. We named the states based on qualitative interpretation of the observation frequencies. The descriptions for the individual student HMM state interpretations are as follows:

- Block search: frequent category switches
- Program testing and refining: running the program and making changes that take the program closer to its final solution
- Program creation: creating new blocks and snapping them to the existing code, moving closer to the final solution
- Program tweaking: snapping blocks with varying effects to the edit distance, moving blocks and editing parameters without affecting the edit distance to the final solution

The descriptions for the student pair HMM states are as follows:

- Block search: frequent category switches with high frequency of snapping blocks and moving closer to the final solution
- Program testing and refining: running the program and making changes that take the program closer to its final solution
- Program planning: high frequency of category switching with blocks being created and moved within the scripting area to get closer to the final solution
- Program building: moving blocks within the scripting area, snapping them together, and taking them apart (unsnapping) with varying effects to proximity to the final solution

6   Discussion

Through the use of the Viterbi algorithm, in combination with the HMMs and observation sequences, we determined the most likely sequence of hidden states that the individuals and pairs went through during the task. Table 2 shows summary statistics on the percentage of time that individuals spent on each state. In general, most of their time was spent in program tweaking, followed by block search as the second most frequent. As mentioned earlier, category switching was the most common event, which would justify the high frequency of the block search state. The program tweaking state does not appear to be productive at first, but students may have engaged in off-task behaviors due to being stuck, leading them closer to the solution [21].

Table 2 also shows the summary statistics for the state frequencies of student pairs. Pairs tended to spend more time in the program building state, followed closely by the block search state; these states have high frequency of getting closer to the final solution. The pairs also demonstrated a program planning state, which may be where the collaborative aspect of the task is most prominent.

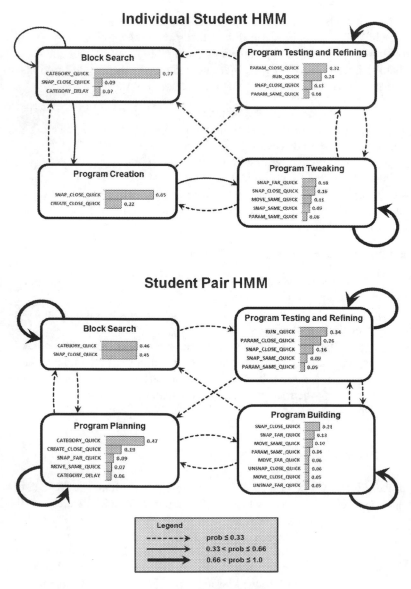

Fig. 3. Student HMMs

Table 2. State frequency summary

Ind. state	μ	σ	Min	Max	Pair state	μ	σ	Min	Max
Search	0.27	0.07	0.17	0.44	Search	0.27	0.08	0.12	0.37
Test/Refine	0.20	0.05	0.12	0.28	Test/Refine	0.24	0.07	0.08	0.33
Tweaking	0.37	0.11	0.11	0.53	Planning	0.20	0.06	0.15	0.35
Creation	0.16	0.03	0.12	0.21	Building	0.29	0.08	0.12	0.37

State Composition. Both models exhibited *block search* and *program testing and refining* states. *Search* was characterized by high probability of category switching within 30 seconds of prior events. For individual students, however, there was also a small probability of category switching after longer than 30 seconds from the previous event, perhaps in part because individual students did not have a partner assisting in their search. Additionally, although both conditions featured snapping events that brought the program closer to the final solution, the probability was higher for student pairs. The *test/refine* state featured high probability of program run events, as well as parameter editing and block snapping. This could indicate that students tested their programs, found errors, and fixed parameters or block order. One event was present in the pair condition that was not present in the individual: parameter editing with no change in distance to final solution. This may be due to partners having conflicting ideas for correcting errors, trying multiple values before finding the correct one.

Individuals exhibited two additional states: *program tweaking* and *program creation*. *Tweaking* consisted of quick block snapping with varying effects on distance to the final solution, as well as block movement and parameter editing with no effect on distance to the final solution. This interpretation was chosen due to the opposing nature of the snapping events: snapping blocks and moving both closer and farther from the final solution. This seems contradictory at first, but may indicate that students were putting together their programs and modifying the block layout to make corrections. *Creation* included block creation and snapping, both bringing the program closer to the final solution. Students spent the least amount of time on average in this state, and the self-transition probability was nearly zero. This suggests that the state serves more as a transition, connecting block search, program tweaking, and testing and refinement.

The pairs also had two additional states: *program planning* and *program building*. *Planning* featured category switching, similar to the search state, but also included events for block creation, movement, and snapping, all with varying effects on distance to the final solution. When a block is created but not snapped, it is placed in the scripting area; similarly, movement involves grabbing and dropping a block within the area. This suggests that the students may be rearranging the blocks' layout to help visualize a proposed solution. *Building* included a large number of prominent observations: snapping, unsnapping, and moving blocks, and editing parameters, all with varying effects on distance to the final solution. This appears to serve a similar purpose to the tweaking state for individuals.

An additional difference between the individual and pair HMMs involves the state transition probabilities: pairs had higher self-transition probabilities than the individuals for common states (*Search*: pair=0.76, ind.=0.49; *Test*: pair=0.76, ind.=0.67) and in general. This could indicate that pairs persisted with a single problem-solving mode longer than the individuals. Interesting to consider is the difference between the individuals' *tweaking* state and the pairs' *planning* state. Both appear to be states in which students explore solution alternatives, but individuals appear to be more willing to snap blocks when modifying their program, while pairs preferred to move blocks within the scripting area; this could be a key difference between the conditions.

7   Conclusion

During problem solving, adaptive systems can provide a customized learning experience that is likely very different for individuals and pairs. This paper has presented work toward understanding the different problem-solving modes that individuals and pairs utilize. The results show that student pairs appear to persist in a mode more often than individual students. Depending on a task's learning goals, it may be useful to help students persist in a particular problem-solving mode, which could be achieved through the use of scaffolding, for example.

Moving forward, an ITS could use information about an individual's or a pair's current problem-solving mode to provide adaptive support. For example, if the system hypothesizes that students are spending too long in a state of *program tweaking*, it could prompt them to move into a *planning* state with tailored feedback. Additionally, by updating the HMMs with new interaction sequences that include intelligent support, a system could continuously adapt to new modes that may emerge. These types of models can serve as the basis for the next generation of ITSs that support collaborative problem solving, and the methodology could potentially be generalized to support other problem-solving domains.

Acknowledgements. Thanks to the members of the LearnDialogue Group and the Center for Educational Informatics at NCSU for their helpful input. Thanks to Alexandria Vail, Xiaolong Li, and Allison Martínez-Arocho for their contributions. This material is based upon work supported by the National Science Foundation through a graduate research fellowship and IIS-1409639. Any opinions, findings, and conclusions or recommendations expressed in this material are those of the authors and do not necessarily reflect the views of the National Science Foundation.

References

1. Guin, N., Lefevre, M.: From a customizable ITS to an adaptive ITS. In: Lane, H., Yacef, K., Mostow, J., Pavlik, P. (eds.) AIED 2013. LNCS, vol. 7926, pp. 141–150. Springer, Heidelberg (2013)
2. Stamper, J.C., Eagle, M., Barnes, T., Croy, M.: Experimental Evaluation of Automatic Hint Generation for a Logic Tutor. IJAIED **22**(1), 3–17 (2013)

3. Lazar, T., Bratko, I.: Data-driven program synthesis for hint generation in programming tutors. In: Trausan-Matu, S., Boyer, K.E., Crosby, M., Panourgia, K. (eds.) ITS 2014. LNCS, vol. 8474, pp. 306–311. Springer, Heidelberg (2014)
4. Kazi, H., Haddawy, P., Suebnukarn, S.: Leveraging a domain ontology to increase the quality of feedback in an intelligent tutoring system. In: Aleven, V., Kay, J., Mostow, J. (eds.) ITS 2010, Part I. LNCS, vol. 6094, pp. 75–84. Springer, Heidelberg (2010)
5. Walker, E., Walker, S., Rummel, N., Koedinger, K.R.: Using problem-solving context to assess help quality in computer-mediated peer tutoring. In: Aleven, V., Kay, J., Mostow, J. (eds.) ITS 2010, Part I. LNCS, vol. 6094, pp. 145–155. Springer, Heidelberg (2010)
6. Ogan, A., Walker, E., Aleven, V., Jones, C.: Toward supporting collaborative discussion in an Ill-Defined domain. In: Woolf, B.P., Aïmeur, E., Nkambou, R., Lajoie, S. (eds.) ITS 2008. LNCS, vol. 5091, pp. 825–827. Springer, Heidelberg (2008)
7. Ogan, A., Walker, E., Baker, R.S.J.d., Rebolledo-Mendez, G., Jimenez Castro, M., Laurentino, T., de Carvalho, A.: Collaboration in cognitive tutor use in latin america: field study and design recommendations. In: Proceedings of the SIGCHI Conference on Human Factors in Computing Systems, pp. 1381–1390 (2012)
8. Olsen, J.K., Belenky, D.M., Aleven, V., Rummel, N.: Using an intelligent tutoring system to support collaborative as well as individual learning. In: Trausan-Matu, S., Boyer, K.E., Crosby, M., Panourgia, K. (eds.) ITS 2014. LNCS, vol. 8474, pp. 134–143. Springer, Heidelberg (2014)
9. Williams, L., Wiebe, E., Yang, K., Ferzli, M., Miller, C.: In Support of Pair Programming in the Introductory Computer Science Course. Comput. Sci. Educ. **12**(10), 197–212 (2002)
10. Koedinger, K.R., Stamper, J.C., McLaughlin, E.A., Nixon, T.: Using data-driven discovery of better student models to improve student learning. In: Lane, H., Yacef, K., Mostow, J., Pavlik, P. (eds.) AIED 2013. LNCS, vol. 7926, pp. 421–430. Springer, Heidelberg (2013)
11. Kardan, S., Roll, I., Conati, C.: The usefulness of log based clustering in a complex simulation environment. In: Trausan-Matu, S., Boyer, K.E., Crosby, M., Panourgia, K. (eds.) ITS 2014. LNCS, vol. 8474, pp. 168–177. Springer, Heidelberg (2014)
12. Tenison, C., MacLellan, C.J.: Modeling strategy use in an intelligent tutoring system: implications for strategic flexibility. In: Trausan-Matu, S., Boyer, K.E., Crosby, M., Panourgia, K. (eds.) ITS 2014. LNCS, vol. 8474, pp. 466–475. Springer, Heidelberg (2014)
13. Jeong, H., Gupta, A., Roscoe, R., Wagster, J., Biswas, G., Schwartz, D.L.: Using hidden markov models to characterize student behaviors in learning-by-teaching environments. In: Woolf, B.P., Aïmeur, E., Nkambou, R., Lajoie, S. (eds.) ITS 2008. LNCS, vol. 5091, pp. 614–625. Springer, Heidelberg (2008)
14. McDowell, C., Werner, L., Bullock, H., Fernald, J.: The effects of pair-programming on performance in an introductory programming course. In: Proceedings of the 33rd ACM Technical Symposium on Computer Science Education (SIGCSE 2002), pp. 38–42 (2002)
15. Braught, G., MacCormick, J., Wahls, T.: The benefits of pairing by ability. In: Proceedings of the 41st ACM Technical Symposium on Computer Science Education (SIGCSE 2010), pp. 249–253 (2010)
16. Thomas, L., Ratcliffe, M., Robertson, A.: Code warriors and code-a-phobes: a study in attitude and pair programming. In: Proceedings of the 34rd ACM Technical Symposium on Computer Science Education (SIGCSE 2003), pp. 363–367 (2003)
17. Martinez, R., Wallace, J.R., Kay, J., Yacef, K.: Modelling and identifying collaborative situations in a collocated multi-display groupware setting. In: Biswas, G., Bull, S., Kay, J., Mitrovic, A. (eds.) AIED 2011. LNCS, vol. 6738, pp. 196–204. Springer, Heidelberg (2011)

18. Martinez-Maldonado, R., Kay, J., Yacef, K.: An automatic approach for mining patterns of collaboration around an interactive tabletop. In: Lane, H., Yacef, K., Mostow, J., Pavlik, P. (eds.) AIED 2013. LNCS, vol. 7926, pp. 101–110. Springer, Heidelberg (2013)
19. Harvey, B., Mönig, J.: Bringing "No Ceiling" to scratch: can one language serve kids and computer scientists? In: Constructionism, pp. 1–10 (2010)
20. Rabiner, L.R., Juang, B.H.: An Introduction to Hidden Markov Models. IEEE ASSP Mag. **3**, 4–16 (1986)
21. Sabourin, J., Rowe, J.P., Mott, B.W., Lester, J.C.: When off-task is on-task: the affective role of off-task behavior in narrative-centered learning environments. In: Biswas, G., Bull, S., Kay, J., Mitrovic, A. (eds.) AIED 2011. LNCS, vol. 6738, pp. 534–536. Springer, Heidelberg (2011)

Improving Student Problem Solving in Narrative-Centered Learning Environments: A Modular Reinforcement Learning Framework

Jonathan P. Rowe$^{(\boxtimes)}$ and James C. Lester

Center for Educational Informatics, North Carolina State University, Raleigh, NC 27695, USA
{jprowe,lester}@ncsu.edu

Abstract. Narrative-centered learning environments comprise a class of game-based learning environments that embed problem solving in interactive stories. A key challenge posed by narrative-centered learning is dynamically tailoring story events to enhance student learning. In this paper, we investigate the impact of a data-driven tutorial planner on students' learning processes in a narrative-centered learning environment, CRYSTAL ISLAND. We induce the tutorial planner by employing *modular reinforcement learning*, a multi-goal extension of classical reinforcement learning. To train the planner, we collected a corpus from 453 middle school students who used CRYSTAL ISLAND in their classrooms. Afterward, we investigated the induced planner's impact in a follow-up experiment with another 75 students. The study revealed that the induced planner improved students' problem-solving processes—including hypothesis testing and information gathering behaviors—compared to a control condition, suggesting that modular reinforcement learning is an effective approach for tutorial planning in narrative-centered learning environments.

Keywords: Narrative-centered learning environments · Tutorial planning · Modular reinforcement learning · Game-based learning

1 Introduction

Over the past decade, the education research community has shown growing interest in digital games, largely inspired by a key question: how can we motivate and engage students in learning? A promising class of games is narrative-centered learning environments, which integrate the motivational qualities of stories, along with the adaptive pedagogy of intelligent tutoring systems, to foster student engagement in learning and problem solving. When students use narrative-centered learning environments, they become active participants in ongoing narratives whose outcomes are shaped by students' learning behaviors. As a result of recent advances in game engines and authoring tools, there are now a range of narrative-centered learning environments under investigation across different domains, including language learning [1], anti-bullying education [2], biosafety training [3], and science inquiry [4].

A key benefit of narrative-centered learning environments is their capacity to discreetly support students' learning processes by integrating pedagogical and narrative elements. This form of scaffolding depends upon the presentation of events that fulfill

© Springer International Publishing Switzerland 2015
C. Conati et al. (Eds.): AIED 2015, LNAI 9112, pp. 419–428, 2015.
DOI: 10.1007/978-3-319-19773-9_42

dual roles: advancing problem-centric storylines, and providing tutorial support such as feedback or hints. Yet, despite a substantial research base on the cognitive principles of student learning [5], there is limited research on how to effectively design narrative-centered learning environments. If designed or deployed ineffectively, narrative-centered learning environments risk the introduction of seductive details, which can be harmful for learning [6]. Moreover, a one-size-fits-all approach to the design of narrative-centered learning environments has important limitations, due to the role of students' individual differences in learning.

To address these challenges, we conceptualize adaptive scaffolding in narrative-centered learning environments as an instance of tutorial planning. We seek to devise computational models for generating, sequencing, and personalizing story events in a narrative-centered learning environment, with the explicit aim of enhancing student learning and engagement. To solve this problem, we employ a data-driven framework for inducing *narrative-centered tutorial planners* that leverages modular reinforcement learning. This formulation is made possible by the observation that tutorial planning in narrative-centered learning environments can be decomposed in terms of multiple independent sub-problems, each focused on a particular class of scaffolding events. Our framework is inspired by work on reinforcement learning methods for tutorial dialogue management [7], adapting and extending these techniques to meet the requirements of narrative-centered learning.

To evaluate our framework, we present results from an experiment investigating the impact of an induced tutorial planner integrated with the CRYSTAL ISLAND narrative-centered learning environment. Empirical findings indicate that the induced planner improves students' problem-solving behaviors, including hypothesis-testing and information-gathering processes, compared to a control condition. The results suggest that our modular reinforcement-learning framework is a promising method for devising data-driven tutorial planners that scaffold learning effectively in narrative-centered learning environments.

2   Tutorial Planning with Modular Reinforcement Learning

We formalize tutorial planning as a modular reinforcement learning problem. Modular reinforcement learning is a multi-goal extension of classical single-agent reinforcement learning [8,9]. In reinforcement learning, an agent learns a policy for selecting actions in an uncertain environment, guided by delayed rewards, in order to accomplish a goal [10]. The agent utilizes an environment-based reward signal in order to learn a policy, denoted π, which maps observed states to actions and maximizes total accumulated reward. Agents in reinforcement learning problems are typically modeled with Markov decision processes (MDPs).

Modular reinforcement learning tasks are formally defined in terms of N concurrent MDPs, $M = \{M_i\}_1^N$, where each $M_i = (S_i, A_i, P_i, R_i)$, corresponding to a sub-problem in the composite reinforcement learning task. Each agent M_i has its own state sub-space S_i, action set A_i, probabilistic state transition model P_i, and reward model R_i. The solution to a modular reinforcement learning problem is a set of N policies, $\pi^* = \{\pi_i^*\}_1^N$, where π_i is the optimal policy for the constituent MDP M_i. Any circumstance where two policies π_i and π_j with $i{\neq}j$ recommend different actions in the same state requires the application of an arbitration procedure.

Tutorial planning in narrative-centered learning environments is naturally represented as a modular reinforcement learning problem: *state* consists of the learner's state and history as well as the learning environment's; *actions* represent the pedagogical decisions the planner can perform; a *probabilistic state transition model* encodes how learners, and the learning environment, respond to the planner's tutorial decisions; and a *reward model* encapsulates measures of students' learning outcomes, which the tutorial planner seeks to optimize. The solution to a modular reinforcement-learning problem is a set of *policies*, or mappings between states and tutorial actions, that govern how the tutorial planner scaffolds students' learning. If two policies conflict, externally defined arbitration procedures specify which policy prevails.

By decomposing tutorial planning into multiple sub-problems, we can reduce the complexity of reinforcement learning by reframing the task in terms of several smaller, concurrent Markov decision processes. To perform this decomposition, we employ the concept of an *adaptable event sequence* (AES), an abstraction for a series of one or more scaffolding-related events that, once triggered, can unfold in several different ways within the learning environment [11]. To illustrate the concept of an AES, consider an example of an event sequence that occurs when a player asks a non-player character (NPC) about her backstory. The NPC could respond in one of several ways: 1) providing a detailed explanation and a hint about how her backstory information is useful, 2) providing an explanation but no hint, 3) responding suspiciously and revealing only a few details, or 4) not responding at all. Each of these four responses is an alternate manifestation of the *NPC Backstory* event sequence. Each option is coherent within the storyline, can be interchanged with any other, and provides a distinct level of problem-solving support. We refer to the event sequence as *adaptable*, or in other words, it is an adaptable event sequence (ΛES).

AESs can encode a broad range of scaffolding types. For example, an AES could specify the location of an important object, or determine what level of hint to provide to a student, or select whether to prompt a student to self-explain their problem-solving strategy or not. Further, multiple AESs can be interleaved. AESs encode distinct threads of story events, each potentially involving multiple decision points spanning an entire story. For this reason, AESs are sequential and operate concurrently. Each AES is modeled separately as a MDP, and tutorial decisions about scaffolding are determined through modular reinforcement learning.

Leveraging the concept of an AES, narrative-centered tutorial planning can be cast as a collection of sequential decision-making problems about scaffolding student learning within a narrative-centered learning environment. Modular reinforcement learning is applied as follows. Each AES is modeled as a distinct Markov decision process, M_i. For each AES, every occurrence of the event sequence corresponds to a decision point for M_i. The set of possible scaffolding options for the AES is modeled by an action set, A_i. A particular state representation, S_i, is tailored to the AES using manual or automatic feature selection techniques. Rewards, R_i, can be calculated from formative or summative assessments of student learning, such as a post-test. A state transition model P_i encodes the probability of transitioning between two specific states during successive decision points for the AES. To estimate the values of these parameters, we can collect training data from students by deploying a tutorial planner that selects actions randomly, in effect sampling the space of tutorial policies and rewards [7]. Leveraging this mapping between AESs and MDPs, and a training corpus of random tutorial decision data, we can employ model-based reinforcement learning techniques to induce policies for tutorial planning. Specifically, we utilize dynamic programming methods (e.g., value iteration) to compute solution policies for each MDP using estimates of the state transition model and reward model inferred from the training corpus [7,10]. In cases where two policies conflict, we utilize *greatest mass arbitration*, a domain-independent arbitration procedure that selects the action with the largest Q-value calculated during policy induction [8,9]. In combination, this formulation provides a method for formulating narrative-centered tutorial planning as an instance of modular reinforcement learning.

3   Corpus Collection

To investigate our modular reinforcement learning framework for tutorial planning, we used CRYSTAL ISLAND, a narrative-centered learning environment for middle school microbiology (Figure 1). The version of CRYSTAL ISLAND used in this study was built on Valve Software's Source™ engine. The environment features a science mystery in which students investigate the identity and source of an infectious disease that is pla-

guing a research team on a remote island. Students adopt the role of a medical detective who must save the research team from the outbreak. Over the past decade, CRYSTAL ISLAND has been the subject of extensive empirical investigation, and has been found to provide substantial learning and motivational benefits [12].

To investigate narrative-centered tutorial planning in CRYSTAL ISLAND, we developed a modified version of the system that includes 13 AESs. We selected 13 AESs in order to incorporate a broad range of scaffolding ca-

Fig. 1. Crystal ISLAND narrative-centered learning environment

pabilities. Space limitations preclude a detailed description of every AES, but they included decisions about whether to provide hints and prompts during the mystery (e.g., prompt the student to record her findings in a diagnosis worksheet, prompt the student to self-explain her problem-solving strategy); whether to administer embedded assessments of content knowledge; which disease and transmission source caused the outbreak; how much detail should NPCs provide about their symptoms; what level of feedback should be provided on students' proposed diagnoses; and manipulations to the number of hypotheses that students can test in the virtual laboratory. For additional details, a more comprehensive discussion of the AESs is available in [13].

To illustrate how AESs unfolded within CRYSTAL ISLAND, consider the following scenario. When a student begins the narrative, the *Mystery's Solution* AES occurs behind the scenes, selecting one of 6 possible solutions to the mystery. The tutorial planner selects *salmonellosis* as the mystery disease and *contaminated milk* as the disease's transmission source. This AES decision is invisible to the student, but the selection dictates which symptoms and medical history are reported by the sick characters. As the student explores the camp, she initiates a conversation with a sick scientist named Teresa. The student asks Teresa about her symptoms, triggering a decision point for the *Details of Teresa's Symptoms* AES. This AES controls how much information Teresa provides in her response. The tutorial planner has Teresa provide minimal information, leading Teresa to groan and explain that she has a fever. If the student chooses to ask Teresa about her symptoms again later, the planner may choose a different response to help the student narrow on a diagnosis. Next, a decision point for the *Record Findings Reminder* AES is triggered, because the student has just received useful information for diagnosing the illness. The tutorial planner chooses whether to hint to the student that she should take a note about the symptom information. The narrative continues in this manner, driven by the student's actions, and periodically triggering scaffolding events that shape how the experience unfolds.

After modifying CRYSTAL ISLAND to incorporate AESs, we conducted a pair of classroom studies to collect training data for inducing a tutorial planner. The first study involved 300 students from a North Carolina middle school, and the second study involved 153 students from another middle school. All students used the same version of CRYSTAL Island, followed the same study procedure, and used the game individually. One week prior to using CRYSTAL ISLAND, students completed a pretest, which collected data on students' demographics, game-playing experience, and microbiology content knowledge. The microbiology content test consisted of 19 multiple-choice questions, and was created iteratively by the research team and a group of eighth-grade science teachers. During the studies, students interacted with CRYSTAL ISLAND until they solved the mystery, or 55 minutes elapsed, whichever occurred first. Immediately afterward, students completed a post-test, which included the same content knowledge assessment as the pre-test, as well as several self-report measures of engagement. Both the pre- and post-tests lasted no more than 30 minutes.

While using CRYSTAL ISLAND, students unknowingly encountered AESs several times. At each AES decision point, the environment selected a scaffolding-related event according to a uniform random policy. By logging these tutorial planning decisions, as well as students' responses, the environment broadly sampled the space of policies for controlling adaptable event sequences. The data from both studies were combined into a single corpus consisting of two parts: students' interaction logs, and students' pre- and post-test results. After removing incomplete or inconsistent records, there were 402 participants remaining. The resulting data consisted of 315,407 events. In addition to student actions, there were 10,057 instances of AESs in the corpus, which corresponded to approximately 25 tutorial planning decisions per student.

4   Implemented Planner

Using the corpus, we induced a policy for each MDP to control CRYSTAL ISLAND's scaffolding features, with the exception of one AES for which we had insufficient training data (off-task behavior discouragement). All of the MDPs shared the same state representation, which consisted of 8 binary features drawn from three categories: narrative features, individual difference features, and problem-solving features. We limited the state representation to 8 binary features to mitigate potential data sparsity issues. The first four features were narrative-focused. Each feature was associated with a salient plot point from CRYSTAL ISLAND's narrative and indicated whether the plot point had been completed thus far. The next two features were based on students' individual differences. The first feature was computed from a median split on students' microbiology pre-test scores, and the second feature was computed from a median split on students' self-report data about how often they played video games. The final two state features were computed from students' observed problem-solving behaviors. Specifically, we computed running median splits on the frequency of students' lab-testing and book-reading behaviors within CRYSTAL ISLAND.

The action sets for the 12 MDPs corresponded to the scaffolding options for the associated AESs. The action sets' cardinalities ranged from binary to 6-way decisions. If the entire planning task were modeled as a single MDP, it would require encoding approximately 1,644,000 parameters to populate the entire state transition model (256 states × 25 distinct actions × 257 states, including the terminal state), although not all state transitions were possible.[1]

Each MDP shared the same reward function, which was based on students' normalized learning gains (NLG). NLG is the normalized difference between participants' pre- and post-study knowledge test scores. To determine reward values in the corpus, NLG was first calculated for each participant, and then a median split was performed. Students who had a NLG that was greater than or equal to the median were awarded +100 points at the conclusions of their episodes. Participants with a NLG that was less than the median were awarded -100 points.

To induce the tutorial policies, we used *value iteration* [10]. The 12 MDPs, one for each AES in CRYSTAL ISLAND, were implemented with a reinforcement-learning library written in Python by the first author. Policies were induced using a discount rate of 0.9. The discount rate parameter governs how rewards are attributed to planner actions during reinforcement learning. Our previous work has found that discount rate has a limited effect on the policies induced for CRYSTAL ISLAND [11].

5   Evaluation Experiment

After inducing tutorial planning policies for each adaptable event sequence, we evaluated the tutorial planner's impact on students' learning experiences in the run-time CRYSTAL ISLAND learning environment. This required incorporating the induced

---

[1] Several AESs included an action choice of *do nothing*. We count all of these *do nothing* choices as a single action, yielding a total of 25 distinct actions across the 12 AESs.

tutorial planning policies into CRYSTAL ISLAND by replacing the exploratory tutorial policies from the corpus collection studies with the newly induced policies.

To evaluate CRYSTAL ISLAND's induced tutorial planner, we conducted a follow-up controlled experiment with middle school students comparing the induced policies to a control condition. Participants were drawn from a different school than the corpus collection studies. A total of 75 eighth-grade students participated. Among these students, 14 were removed due to incomplete or inconsistent data.

The study had two conditions: an Induced Planner condition and a Control Planner condition. Students in both conditions played CRYSTAL ISLAND, but the conditions differed in terms of the tutorial planning policies employed by the narrative-centered learning environment. The Induced Planner followed policies obtained by inducing solution policies for each Markov decision process associated with an AES in CRYSTAL ISLAND, with conflicts resolved via greatest mass arbitration [9]. The Control Planner employed a uniform random policy, where tutorial decisions were selected randomly whenever the planner encountered a decision point. This was the same policy used by the exploratory planner during the corpus collection studies.

Students were randomly assigned to the two conditions when they entered the experiment room. Among students with complete data, 33 were randomly assigned to the Induced Planner condition, and 28 were assigned to the Control Planner condition. Students played until they solved the mystery or the interaction time expired, whichever occurred first. The study procedure, pre-test, and post-test were otherwise identical to the corpus collection studies.

6   Results

Analyses of students' learning gains found students achieved significant improvements in microbiology content knowledge in both experimental conditions. In the Induced Planner condition, students significantly improved their content test scores by 1.6 questions on average from pre-test ($M = 7.8$, $SD = 2.2$) to post-test ($M = 9.4$, $SD = 3.6$), $t(32) = 2.67$, p < .02. In the Control Planner condition, students also achieved significant improvements in content test score from pre-test ($M = 7.2$, $SD = 2.5$) to post-test ($M = 9.5$, $SD = 3.4$), $t(27) = 4.09$, $p < .001$, a gain of 2.3 questions on average. A comparison between the two conditions' average post-test scores did not find evidence of a significant condition effect on microbiology content learning. Similarly, no condition effects were observed on students' normalized learning gains or self-reported engagement. In hindsight, the lack of a condition effect on learning is unsurprising. A majority of the AESs provided scaffolding for students' inquiry behaviors, rather than microbiology content exposure, which was the focus of the pre- and post-tests. Students in both conditions had the same access to the game's microbiology content. Additionally, we had anticipated a potential *test effect* from the *Knowledge Quiz* AES, which controlled decisions about whether to administer embedded assessments in CRYSTAL ISLAND, and would be hypothesized to yield increased learning gains [5]. However, the Induced Planner tended to not deliver the assessments, surprisingly, making it unlikely to find such an effect.

Next, we investigated students' problem-solving processes in CRYSTAL ISLAND. In particular, we sought evidence of deliberate problem solving, in contrast to strategies

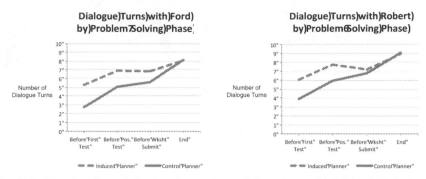

Fig. 2. Students' dialogue behaviors by problem-solving phase, which include 1) before running the first lab test, 2) before running a positive lab test, 3) before first submitting the diagnosis worksheet, and 4) before solving the science mystery

that involve extensive guessing or non-purposeful behavior. To perform this investigation, we calculated several metrics that had previously yielded insights about problem solving in CRYSTAL ISLAND, including measures of hypothesis testing efficiency [14] and early information gathering behavior [15].

We first analyzed students' hypothesis testing behaviors. In CRYSTAL ISLAND, students test hypotheses about potential sources of the outbreak in the camp's virtual laboratory. A two-tailed t-test indicated that students in the Induced Planner condition ($M = 13.7$, $SD = 10.9$) conducted marginally fewer tests than students in the Control Planner condition ($M = 19.5$, $SD = 14.4$), $t(59) = 1.80$, $p < .08$. Additionally, the Induced Planner group ran significantly fewer tests ($M = 4.7$, $SD = 7.7$) after identifying the transmission source than students in the Control Planner group ($M = 11.0$, $SD = 12.6$), $t(59) = 2.39$, $p < .03$. These findings suggest that students in the Induced Planner condition tested their hypotheses more efficiently.

Next, we examined student behaviors during the early stages of problem solving by investigating how students collected background information on the microbiology curriculum prior to forming, testing, and reporting their hypotheses. First, we investigated students' conversations with virtual characters (Figure 2). In terms of total number of conversations, as well as total number of dialogue turns, no significant differences between conditions were observed. However, there were significant condition effects on student dialogue behavior with specific virtual characters. Students in the Induced Planner condition engaged in significantly more dialogue turns with Ford, the camp's virus specialist, prior to running a laboratory test, $t(59) = -2.31$, $p < .03$. Conversely, Induced Planner students engaged in significantly fewer dialogue turns with Ford after running their first test, $t(59) = 2.25$, $p < .03$.

Similar patterns were observed for students' conversational behaviors with Robert, the camp's bacteria specialist. Students in the Induced Planner condition engaged in more dialogue turns with Robert prior to running a laboratory test, $t(59) = -1.71$, $p = .09$. Students in the Induced Planner condition also engaged in fewer dialogue turns with Robert after running their first laboratory test, $t(59) = 2.21$, $p < .04$. In a related finding, the Induced Planner students engaged in significantly more dialogue turns with the camp nurse Kim—a character who provides general background on pathogens, mutagens, and carcinogens—prior to first submitting their diagnosis worksheet, $t(59) = -2.19$, $p < .04$. These patterns are consistent with strategic information gathering in CRYSTAL ISLAND. The findings suggest that students in the Induced Planner condition collected more background information about microbiology prior to testing their hypotheses in the laboratory, which is a desirable problem-solving approach, whereas students in the Control condition gathered background information afterward, which is consistent with an ad hoc approach.

As a further investigation of students' information gathering strategies, we examined poster-viewing behaviors between experimental conditions. In these analyses, we only considered instances lasting longer than one second in duration. Similar to the character dialogue findings, no significant differences in total poster viewing metrics were observed. However, in an examination of the camp's six disease-focused posters, two-tailed t-tests indicated that students in the Induced Planner condition spent significantly more time reading the Salmonellosis poster prior to submitting their diagnosis worksheet than students in the Control Planner condition, $t(59) = -2.18$, $p < .04$. Similarly, students in the Induced Planner condition viewed the Anthrax poster more times prior to submitting their diagnosis worksheet, $t(59) = -1.67$, $p = .1$. Students in the Induced Planner condition viewed the Botulism poster more times prior to successfully testing the transmission source in the laboratory, $t(59) = -1.73$, $p < .09$. And students in the Induced Planner condition viewed the Ebola poster more times prior to submitting their diagnosis worksheet, $t(59) = -1.96$, $p = .05$. No analogous condition effects were observed for the Influenza or Smallpox posters.

These findings suggest that students in the Induced Planner condition examined disease-specific posters more frequently before testing hypothesized diagnoses, particularly for posters about bacterial diseases. The findings raise questions about whether similar patterns were observed for students reading virtual books, which provide similar information for diagnosing the illness. However, an investigation of virtual book-reading behaviors failed to find evidence of significant condition effects. Furthermore, significant condition effects were not observed for students' diagnosis worksheet behaviors, another key problem-solving feature in CRYSTAL ISLAND.

7 Conclusions and Future Work

We have found that a narrative-centered tutorial planner, induced using modular reinforcement learning, significantly improves students' problem-solving processes in the CRYSTAL ISLAND learning environment. We trained the tutorial planner directly upon a corpus of data from students who used CRYSTAL ISLAND in their science classrooms, producing data-driven tutorial planning models capable of adaptive scaffolding. We evaluated the planner's impact in a controlled experiment conducted with 75 middle school students. Results indicated that students in the Induced Planner condition demonstrated greater efficiency at hypothesis testing, as well as greater evidence of strategic information gathering, during their investigations. These findings provide evidence that narrative-centered tutorial planners, induced using modular reinforcement learning, can have positive effects on students' problem solving behaviors. Building on these findings, in future work it will be important to investigate the impacts of alternate MDP state representations on induced tutorial planning policies. In addition, it will be informative to investigate the framework's generalizability by applying it to different types of learning environments.

Acknowledgments. This material is based upon work supported by the National Science Foundation under grants IIS-1344803, REC-0632450, IIS-0812291, and DRL-0822200. Any opinions, findings, and conclusions or recommendations expressed in this material are those of the author(s) and do not necessarily reflect the views of the National Science Foundation.

References

1. Johnson, W.L.: Serious Use of a Serious Game for Language Learning. International Journal of Artificial Intelligence in Education **20**(2), 175–195 (2010)
2. Vannini, N., Enz, S., Sapouna, M., Wolke, D., Watson, S., Woods, S., Dautenhahn, K., Hall, L., Paiva, A., Andre, E., Aylett, R., Schneider, W.: "FearNot!": A Computer-Based Anti-Bullying-Programme Designed to Foster Peer Intervention. European Journal of Psychology of Education **26**(1), 21–44 (2011)
3. Alvarez, N., Sanchez-Ruiz, A., Cavazza, M., Shigematsu, M., Prendinger, H.: Narrative Balance Management in an Intelligent Biosafety Training Application for Improving User Performance. Intl Journal of Artificial Intelligence in Education **25**(1), 35–59 (2015)
4. Nelson, B.C., Kim, Y., Foshee, C., Slack, K.: Visual Signaling in Virtual World-Based Assessments: The SAVE Science Project. Information Sciences **264**, 32–40 (2014)
5. Graesser, A., Halpern, D., Hakel, M.: 25 Principles of Learning. Task Force on Lifelong Learning at Work and at Home, Washington, DC (2008)
6. Adams, D.M., Mayer, R.E., MacNamara, A., Koenig, A., Wainess, R.: Narrative Games for Learning: Testing the Discovery and Narrative Hypotheses. Journal of Educational Psychology **104**(1), 235–249 (2012)
7. Chi, M., Vanlehn, K., Litman, D., Jordan, P.: Empirically Evaluating the Application of Reinforcement Learning to the Induction of Effective and Adaptive Pedagogical Strategies. User Modeling and User-Adapted Interaction **21**, 137–180 (2011)
8. Bhat, S., Isbell, C. L., Mateas, M.: On the difficulty of modular reinforcement learning for real-world partial programming. In: Proceedings of the 21st National Conference on Artificial Intelligence, pp. 318–323. AAAI Press, Menlo Park (2006)
9. Karlsson, J.: Learning to Solve Multiple Goals. Ph.D. diss., Dept. of Comp. Sci., University of Rochester (1997)
10. Sutton, R., Barto, A.: Reinforcement Learning: An Introduction. MIT Press, Cambridge (1998)
11. Rowe, J., Mott, B., Lester, J.: Optimizing player experience in interactive narrative planning: a modular reinforcement learning approach. In: Proceedings of the 10th AAAI Conference on Artificial Intelligence and Interactive Digital Entertainment, pp. 160–166. AAAI Press, Menlo Park (2014)
12. Lester, J., Ha, E., Lee, S., Mott, B., Rowe, J., Sabourin, J.: Serious Games Get Smart: Intelligent Game-Based Learning Environments. AI Magazine **34**(4), 31–45 (2013)
13. Rowe, J.: Narrative-Centered Tutorial Planning with Concurrent Markov Decision Processes. Ph.D. diss., Dept. of Comp. Sci., North Carolina State University (2013)
14. Spires, H., Rowe, J., Mott, B., Lester, J.: Problem Solving and Game-Based Learning: Effects of Middle Grade Students' Hypothesis Testing Strategies on Science Learning Outcomes. Journal of Educational Computing Research **44**(4), 453–472 (2011)
15. Sabourin, J., Rowe, J., Mott, B.W., Lester, J.C.: Exploring inquiry-based problem-solving strategies in game-based learning environments. In: Cerri, S.A., Clancey, W.J., Papadourakis, G., Panourgia, K. (eds.) ITS 2012. LNCS, vol. 7315, pp. 470–475. Springer, Heidelberg (2012)

Filtering of Spontaneous and Low Intensity Emotions in Educational Contexts

Sergio Salmeron-Majadas[1](✉), Miguel Arevalillo-Herráez[2], Olga C. Santos[1],
Mar Saneiro[1], Raúl Cabestrero[3], Pilar Quirós[3], David Arnau[4], and Jesus G. Boticario[1]

[1] aDeNu Research Group, Artificial Intelligence Dept. Computer Science School,
UNED, Calle Juan del Rosal 16, Madrid 28040, Spain
`{sergio.salmeron,ocsantos,marsaneiro,jgb}@dia.uned.es`
`http://adenu.ia.uned.es`
[2] Departament d'Informàtica, Universitat de València,
Avda de la Universidad s/n 46100, Bujassot, Valencia, Spain
`miguel.arevalillo@uv.es`
[3] Basic Psychology Dept, UNED, Calle Juan del Rosal 10, Madrid 28040, Spain
`{rcabestrero,pquiros}@psi.uned.es`
[4] Departament de Didàctica de la Matemàtica, Universitat de València,
Avda Tarongers 4 46022, Valencia, Spain
`david.arnau@uv.es`

Abstract. Affect detection is a challenging problem, even more in educational contexts, where emotions are spontaneous and usually subtle. In this paper, we propose a two-stage detection approach based on an initial binary discretization followed by a specific emotion prediction stage. The binary classification method uses several distinct sources of information to detect and filter relevant time slots from an affective point of view. An accuracy close to 75% at detecting whether the learner has felt an educationally relevant emotion on 20 second time slots has been obtained. These slots can then be further analyzed by a second classifier, to determine the specific user emotion.

Keywords: Affective computing · Educational scenarios · Emotion detection · Multi-modal · Data mining · Machine learning

1 Introduction

Affective computing is being considered as a way to improve learning [1]. However, findings reported in the literature (and discussed in the next section) show that detecting emotions in educational scenarios is still a challenging research task as there are still many open issue regarding data collection, pre-processing and labelling.

In the MAMIPEC and MARES projects we have made an attempt to provide some light into these open issues. As a first step, we carried out a large scale experiment in the Science Week held in Madrid in 2012 [2]. 75 participants were asked to perform several mathematical exercises while emotional information was gathered from different input sources, including a written emotional report. These data were used to

© Springer International Publishing Switzerland 2015
C. Conati et al. (Eds.): AIED 2015, LNAI 9112, pp. 429–438, 2015.
DOI: 10.1007/978-3-319-19773-9_43

report on the benefits of using a combined analysis of interactions (keyboard and mouse), facial movements, physiological signals, sentiment analysis and personality traits. In [3], we applied machine learning techniques in an incremental way, considering a subset of the collected input sources. Findings suggested that the combination of keystroke analysis with text mining improved detection results. A different analysis that aimed at detecting emotions by using low intrusive mechanisms has been reported in [4], by exclusively considering keyboard and mouse interactions. Again, the combination of both sources of information yielded better detection rates.

Assuming a multi-modal detection approach, a follow up objective of our research is to be able to detect emotions in real educational settings. Besides major difficulties related to the particularities of educational contexts (i.e., emotions are spontaneous and usually subtle), this is a computationally challenging problem from a classification perspective, because of the high dimensionality of the input data. Additional constraints are imposed by the need to provide affective responses in a reasonable time. In this paper, we propose a two-step detection approach. At the first stage, we use a two-class classifier to identify relevant time slots. These slots are then further analyzed at a second classification stage. We focus on the first step, proposing a classification approach for filtering spontaneous and subtle emotions in educational contexts. Although we have also made preliminary attempts to deal with the second stage, they are only outlined in this paper.

The proposal lies on an experimental work carried out by using an Intelligent Tutoring System (ITS) that focuses on teaching the resolution of story problems in an arithmetic way [5]. To account for the personality and physiological influence of the individual at expressing emotions [6], exhaustive data from two students was collected by using a similar set-up as in the Science Week held in Madrid in 2012.

The rest of the paper is structured as follows. First, we review the state of the art on emotions detection, focusing on the application of the different data sources here presented and their use in educational contexts. Next we describe the method proposed and the results obtained. After that, we discuss on the applicability of the approach in the forthcoming technological scenarios and outline some conclusions.

2   State of the Art

Emotion detection has usually been faced from different viewpoints. From physiology, signals related to autonomic nervous system responses have been widely used due to the significant effect of emotional stimuli on their activity [7], such as changes in heart rate, blood pressure, etc. Some works have been done using physiological signals to predict emotions in a diversity of learning contexts, e.g. skin conductance in a web-based ITS [8], skin conductance and temperature to detect mind wandering during learning [9], and the combination of electroencephalography, skin conductance and blood volume pressure [10] measured while dealing with different educational environments. Although these signals have widely been used in many contexts [11], it is hard to detect different emotions from them, needing more information, such as context information [12], to give sense to their fluctuations.

The analysis of facial expressions to detect emotional aspects has also been addressed in the literature. A comprehensive review was carried out in [2], showing that different approaches can be used by observers to detect expressions (based on facial expressions, types and frequency of movements, etc.) and different procedures can be used depending on the focus of analysis (e.g., to locate facial regions to extract characteristic points in specifics facial movements). Most of the reviewed models are based on the Facial Action Coding System (FACS) [13], that inspired other coding systems used to tag databases of recordings of human emotional experiences, mainly from actors [14]. Although these systems have provided some positive results at classifying archetypal facial expressions, they also have important limitations. First, some facial action units may not appear in meaningful facial expressions. Second, they do not consider information about the cognitive process associated with the expressions [15], and this is especially relevant in educational scenarios. In addition, there are still limitations in the detection of emotions through facial expressions. In particular, many studies have used static images, which do not represent the natural spontaneous expressions for the corresponding emotional state showed in real interaction contexts (and specially, the low intensity that characterize emotions in educational scenarios). To ensure ecological validity, it is essential to study the occurrence and nature of affect displays in situ, as they occur [16]. Moreover, they should be simultaneously analyzed along with other variables such as the cognitive process (memory, attention, etc.) developed by the user and the contextual information available.

Recently, some multimodal approaches that combine different data source types have been proposed. These aim to improve emotion detection accuracy rates, and offer affective adaptation in a wider range of circumstances, including educational scenarios [17]. For example, a framework based on image and audio processing for emotion recognition in e-learning environments has been presented in [18]; and in [19], video signals have been combined with keystroke analysis.

However, most common approaches address the detection problem as a one-step process, using standard classification methods to yield an emotional label for the user. In this paper, we outline the benefits of using a pre-filtering phase to distinguish between affect-relevant and not relevant time intervals across a learning process.

3   Method and Results

3.1   Data Gathering

Data collection was done by running an experiment in a Mathematical class of 14-year old students, whose parents agreed to sign an informed monitoring consent. Students were asked to solve (creating the variables needed to build the problem solution from the known quantities at each step of the problem) a series of 6 mathematical story problems adapted to their age and knowledge, using a modified version of the ITS presented in [20]. This ITS was modified to capture emotional data (through self-reporting) at several stages:

- At the beginning of the experiment, and before solving the first problem, the student had to fill the *Attributional Achievement Motivation Scale* [21] to gather what are the causes and motivations of the participants' general academic achievement.
- After completing each problem, the student had to report on her affective state (valence and activation) by using the *Self-Assessment Manikin (SAM)* scale [22].
- At the end of the series, the student wrote a *descriptive self-report* detailing aspects related to her affective state during problem solving that she considered relevant.
- Once the experiment finished, the participant was invited to *visualize the experiment recording* with a psychologist who had followed the experiment remotely, performing a retrospective think aloud on those points where the psychologist detected affective variations.

During the session, and other than the self-reports, exhaustive data from two students (one male and one female) were gathered by using the following input sources:

- **Physiological data:** heart rate, breath volume, skin conductance and temperature captured at a frequency of 10 Hz with a J&J Engineering I-330-C2 system in a single comma-separated (.csv) file, each row representing 100ms of the experiment (the finest granularity of all the logs recorded). A 3-minute baseline recording was taken for each user at the beginning and at the end of the experiment session.
- **Interaction data** (e.g., problem being solve, hint requests, correct and incorrect user actions, etc.) of events reported by the ITS were stored in a .csv file.
- **Video data** (webcam video and a desktop recording) stored in a single file generated by Camtasia Studio that contains a synchronized recording of both data flows. To focus on the emotional analysis without cumbersome video processing, webcam videos were analyzed by a human expert as described in subsection 3.2.

To allow for the corresponding synchronization, the first column of all files corresponds to the timestamp of the event collected.

3.2   Pre-processing

Video data were processed by a psycho-educational expert trained on emotion detection. She applied the methodology proposed in a previous research [2] to detect the facial expressions and body movements associated with emotions elicited while solving the ITS problems. For this, the expert simultaneously analyzed the webcam video (with participants' face) and the corresponding desktop recording (with the learning tasks carried out). The annotation process followed a mixed (judgment and sign based) approach and used predefined tags defined in a previous research, enriched by adding the "movement duration" feature to consider the length of each movement.

In order to identify a temporal window for the analysis of the physiological variables that could allow to detect oscillations in affective states (taking into account the need of a common window for all the signals –heart rate, breath, skin conductance and temperature– and avoiding oscillations due to physiological noise), a recursive analysis was performed with different time windows (1 minute, 30 seconds, 20 seconds). First of all, each physiological signal was studied separately from raw data (sampling rate of 100 milliseconds). The initial baseline was disregarded, because, i) some signals such as temperature and skin conductance did not reach stabilization until almost 10 minutes after the beginning of the recording and, ii) much of this phase is revealing reactions to the experimental situation. Therefore, we ended up using the final baseline as a baseline indicator of no reaction, in particular, the last 20 second time window before the end of the baseline.

With the previous scope in mind, we proceeded to average raw data into the afore-mentioned temporal windows, to identify (looking for significant differences between the final baseline and the task using ANOVA and its corresponding post hoc compari-sons) which of them could reveal a better compromise between a sufficient level of results granularity and significant discrimination capacity of the signal changes trig-gered by the performance on the ongoing task. Temporal windows of 1 minute and 30 seconds were discarded due to the excessive smoothing of the signal that could be masking the small oscillations that tend to appear in such low intensity emotional reac-tions. Finally, the analysis ended up revealing significant changes from the final base-line for the 20 second window that could be linked to the different phases of the learning task. Similarly, other authors have used this same temporal window to identify the pres-ence of affective reactions in learning situations, reporting that it is even possible to detect several subjectively emotional states within this time window [23].

After determining the temporal window, we proceeded to truncate raw physiologi-cal data into 20 second bins (200 values each) for each signal and every problem (initial and final seconds of each problem were disregarded to make sure that each window had 200 values). With these data, an ANOVA was conducted for each of the temporal windows of the problem and the last temporal window included in the final baseline, indicating which temporal windows (per subject and signal) were signifi-cantly different from the final baseline (p <0.001). These were labeled as "activated".

As a result, rows were grouped in 20 s time slots, and a new feature vector per time slot was created with the following contents: i) a sequential identifier for the time slot; ii) the four features described in the previous paragraph, indicating if the values of each physiological signal during that time slot has suffered significant variations re-garding the student baseline (binary: 0= no; 1= yes); iii) the sum of the previous four features to show how many signals suffered variations; iv) the number of incorrect operations during the time slot, v) the number of hints requested in the time slot; vi) from the movements recorded, a feature for each part of the body with the fraction of time that that part of the body has been involved in a movement, and vii) from the movements recorded, a feature for each type of movement indicating the fraction of the time slot that that movement has been detected. Values assigned to these attributes, in the range [0, 1], rely on the movements reported by the expert.

This grouping operation yielded a total of 246 registries, each with 31 features.

3.3   Data Labelling

Emotions labelling is one of the most controversial and critical issues in emotion detection as the way it is done may limit future processing. Two main approaches are usually considered: i) a categorical approach, assuming the existence of a limited set of emotions [24], being open issues the number of simultaneous emotions to choose or how to represent their intensity, and ii) the dimensional approach, that represents different dimensions of the emotions, such as the "Circumplex Model of Affect" [25] that hypothesizes that the emotional space could be defined in terms of two orthogonal dimensions (arousal and valence). W3C EmotionML [26] supports both.

In our research, we are also using both of them. On the one hand, after each problem, participants were asked to report on their affective state regarding the dimensions of valence and arousal using the SAM. On the other hand, emotions tagged by the expert follow the categorical approach. Here, emotions were coded when watching the recorded videos. Then, the coded emotions are compared with the emotion aloud process carried out with the participants just after the experiment. This emotion aloud was recorded with each participant visualizing the recordings with her face and desktop and being asked to spontaneously comment aloud how she felt during the experiment. She was also asked by the expert when she detected some movement or expression of relevance uncommented by the participant. With this information, the expert assigned relevant time-stamped educationally emotional labels when appropriate to each recording. Labels followed the EmotionML specification and explicitly include emotions that could appear in a learning context such as anxiety, confused, concentrated, frustrated, happy, shame or surprise, as well as none (absence of emotion).

3.4   Classification Approach

The data gathered, labelled and pre-processed has been used in a typical classification setup. To filter spontaneous and low intensity emotions in educational contexts as corresponds to the first proposed stage aimed to detect relevant emotionally time slots, each registry was labelled with a binary value. Using the emotional labeling performed by the expert, 1 is used if an emotion is present in the time slot, and 0 otherwise. This labelling allows us to adopt a binary classification setting to predict relevant time slots from an affective perspective (i.e., those where some emotion is detected). SAM labelling was not used in this analysis as it was obtained at the end of each problem, thus would not make much sense to assign its value to all the 20 second registries reported per problem (problem resolution average length was 6 minutes).

To generate the model, we have used the C4.5 algorithm [27]. We have tried other algorithms such as Naïve Bayes and used Bagging [27] but we did not obtain a significant variation in the results. We have also tried a number of dimensionality reduction methods such as Backward Feature Elimination (BFE) [28] and Principal Component Analysis (PCA) [27], but they did not improve the results obtained either. The accuracy of the model produced has been assessed by using a leave-one-out cross validation on the labelled data. 74.8% (Kappa: 0.49) of registries were correctly predicted, with physiological (temperature, heart rate and conductance) and behavioral (head and mouth movements) in the top 3 levels of the prediction tree generated.

Preliminary experiments to predict the specific emotion of each registry using this two-stage method yielded an accuracy rate of 62.6% (Kappa: 0.31). In contrast, emotion predictions from the initial dataset (without previously filtering registries with no emotional content) showed an accuracy below 60% (Kappa: 0.31). Besides the slight improvement in the accuracy, this two-stage approach provides benefits in terms of reducing the computational requirements when large amount of data are to be processed, as their number is reduced with the first-stage filtering.

4   Discussion

Emotion detection in educational scenarios has many open issues. While in this paper we have focused on improving the detection approach using a two-stage classification process, we have also identified other issues that are to be considered to improve our approach and overcome some current limitations. First of all, and regarding data gathering, advances towards less intrusive ways to collect the data need to be pursued. In particular, wearable devices offer new ways of collecting physiological data in a less intrusive way [29], and research in the field of fabrics has allowed the creation of clothes that can register physiological variables [30]. Other open issues in collecting physiological signals on educational context are i) the existence of diverse factors that are not directly linked to emotional reactions but may affect physiological signals e.g.the mental workload or participant's personality traits; and ii) the usually low intensity of the emotions observed in this context.

Regarding the pre-processing of the physiological signals, overlapping time slots (instead of 20 s slices) may add some valuable information about the previous context of the current time slot to model and predict the affective state generated during the current time slot. In turn, the processing of recorded videos could take advantage of the head and hand tracking capabilities of Microsoft Kinect [31].

We have contributed with methodological aspects to data labelling in order to a) deal with some difficulties at detecting short duration emotions (using a new parameter to represent the duration of the user movements) and b) increase the reliability of the detection and labelling process (establishing a double labelling where emotions are tagged both by participants and more than one expert, and then compared). Other problems dealt with during the experimentation were related to the annotation effort required to register the beginning and end of the user movements in an accurate way, and also to the difficulty of comparing affective labels gathered with different scales. We shall also remark on the potential benefits of collecting and using the SAM scores. These have not been used in this work because the time slots used in the experiments are much smaller than the ones represented by the SAM scores, which are only requested at the end of each problem. Using the SAM labeling at the end of each problem requires to carry out more experiments, collecting enough data to generate both i) a large dataset of data grouped by problem (each problem is a case in the dataset) ii) more instances of each emotion looking for generating a more balanced distribution of class labels (while "anxiety" was the 57.9% of the emotions labeled, "happy", "shame" and "surprise" were the 1.7% each one) in order to improve the stage 2 of the proposed approach. Further experiments including additional users would also be required to evaluate the generalization error and scalability of the approach.

Our future research aims to consider the user's individualities. This implies to analyze data for each user independently, to yield a personal affective learner model. Some very preliminary studies carried out in our work suggest that significant improvements can be achieved by producing an individual model, rather than a global one which turns valid for all users. In addition, the registries generated could alternatively be analyzed by grouping the raw data by math problem i.e. with each registry summarizing the emotional state of the participant while solving the problem. This would yield an emotional model for each problem that could be used to yield conclusive results on specific problem characteristics that lead to specific affective states.

5   Conclusions

In order to advance some of the open issues in emotions detection in educational contexts we have proposed a two-step detection approach that combines 2 classifiers. The first one aims to determine whether a time slot is relevant from an emotional perspective, and it is able to filter spontaneous subtle emotions by using several data sources. The second classifier is only triggered when a positive prediction occurs (the less frequent case) to infer the concrete emotion, considerably reducing computational needs. In addition, this second classifier has the ability to correct false positives predicted during the first stage, by considering a "neutral" label in the emotional model.

Results from this research will be used to build a new affect-aware version of the ITS, that provides emotional and formative feedback. This will be done by replacing the current help-on-demand mechanism by a rule-based system. This system will use interaction data to both provide automatic recommendations and adapt the content of help messages, according to the user's affective state. The emotional support to be provided by the emotional formative feedback will be defined with the TORMES methodology [32] in terms of content (selecting and specifying the information provided within feedback), scheduling and timing (e.g., delayed vs. immediate feedback, feedback on work in progress vs. on complete work), sequencing (e.g., from general to specific) and presentation (e.g., multi-sensorial feedback delivery). This methodology will help investigating what kind of feedback is effective, when it should be provided, whether there are individual differences in seeking and using feedback, and its effect, for instance, on current and next problem performance, transfer, retention, future learning, motivation, affect, achievement orientation and so on.

Acknowledgements. This work has been partly supported by the Spanish Ministry of Economy and Competitiveness through projects TIN2011-29221-C03-01 (MAMIPEC), TIN2011-29221-C03-02 (MARES) and a FPI grant BES-2012-054522.

References

1. Picard, R.W., Papert, S., Bender, W., Blumberg, B., Breazeal, C., Cavallo, D., Machover, T., Resnick, M., Roy, D., Strohecker, C.: Affective learning—a manifesto. BT Technol. J. **22**, 253–269 (2004)
2. Saneiro, M., Santos, O.C., Salmeron-Majadas, S., Boticario, J.G.: Towards Emotion Detection in Educational Scenarios from Facial Expressions and Body Movements through Multimodal Approaches. Sci. World J. **2014**, e484873 (2014)
3. Santos, O.C., Salmeron-Majadas, S., Boticario, J.G.: Emotions Detection from Math Exercises by Combining Several Data Sources. In: Lane, H., Yacef, K., Mostow, J., Pavlik, P. (eds.) AIED 2013. LNCS, vol. 7926, pp. 742–745. Springer, Heidelberg (2013)
4. Salmeron-Majadas, S., Santos, O.C., Boticario, J.G.: An Evaluation of Mouse and Keyboard Interaction Indicators towards Non-intrusive and Low Cost Affective Modeling in an Educational Context. Procedia Comput. Sci. 35, 691–700 (2014)
5. Arevalillo-Herráez, M., Arnau, D., Marco-Giménez, L.: Domain-specific knowledge representation and inference engine for an intelligent tutoring system. Knowl.-Based Syst. **49**, 97–105 (2013)
6. Ayesh, A., Arevalillo-Herraez, M., Ferri, F.J.: Cognitive reasoning and inferences through psychologically based personalised modelling of emotions using associative classifiers. 2014 IEEE 13th International Conference on Cognitive Informatics Cognitive Computing (ICCI*CC). pp. 67–72 (2014).
7. Andreassi, J.L.: Psychophysiology: Human behavior and physiological response, 4th edn. Lawrence Erlbaum Associates Publishers, Mahwah (2000)
8. D'Mello, S.K.: Emotional rollercoasters: day differences in affect incidence during learning. In: The Twenty-Seventh International Flairs Conference (2014)
9. Blanchard, N., Bixler, R., Joyce, T., D'Mello, S.: Automated Physiological-Based Detection of Mind Wandering during Learning. In: Trausan-Matu, S., Boyer, K.E., Crosby, M., Panourgia, K. (eds.) ITS 2014. LNCS, vol. 8474, pp. 55–60. Springer, Heidelberg (2014)
10. Jraidi, I., nc, Chaouachi, M., Frasson, C.: A Hierarchical Probabilistic Framework for Recognizing Learners' Interaction Experience Trends and Emotions. Adv. Hum.-Comput. Interact. 2014, e632630 (2014)
11. Novak, D., Mihelj, M., Munih, M.: A survey of methods for data fusion and system adaptation using autonomic nervous system responses in physiological computing. Interact. Comput. **24**, 154–172 (2012)
12. Aldao, A.: The Future of Emotion Regulation Research Capturing Context. Perspect. Psychol. Sci. **8**, 155–172 (2013)
13. Ekman, P., Friesen, W.V.: Manual for the Facial Action Coding System. Consulting Psychologists Press, Palo Alto, Calif, USA
14. Szwoch, M.: FEEDB: A multimodal database of facial expressions and emotions. In: 2013 The 6th International Conference on Human System Interaction (HSI), pp. 524–531 (2013)
15. Ioannou, S.V., Raouzaiou, A.T., Tzouvaras, V.A., Mailis, T.P., Karpouzis, K.C., Kollias, S.D.: Emotion recognition through facial expression analysis based on a neurofuzzy network. Neural Netw. **18**, 423–435 (2005)
16. Afzal, S., Robinson, P.: Designing for Automatic Affect Inference in Learning Environments. Educ. Technol. Soc. **14**, 21–34 (2011)
17. D'Mello, S., Graesser, A.: AutoTutor and Affective Autotutor: Learning by Talking with Cognitively and Emotionally Intelligent Computers That Talk Back. ACM Trans Interact Intell Syst. **2**, 23:1–23:39 (2013)

18. Bahreini, K., Nadolski, R., Westera, W.: Towards multimodal emotion recognition in e-learning environments. Interact. Learn. Environ. 0, 1–16 (2014)
19. Felipe, D.A.M., Gutierrez, K.I.N., Quiros, E.C.M., Vea, L.A.: Towards the Development of Intelligent Agent for Novice C/C++ Programmers through Affective Analysis of Event Logs. Proc. Int. MultiConference Eng. Comput. Sci. 1 (2012)
20. Arnau, D., Arevalillo-Herráez, M., Puig, L., González-Calero, J.A.: Fundamentals of the design and the operation of an intelligent tutoring system for the learning of the arithmetical and algebraic way of solving word problems. Comput. Educ. 63, 119–130 (2013)
21. Más, M.A.M., Alonso, Á.V.: Validación de una Escala de Motivación de Logro. Psicothema 10, 333–351 (1998)
22. Bradley, M.M., Lang, P.J.: Measuring emotion: the self-assessment manikin and the semantic differential. J. Behav. Ther. Exp. Psychiatry. 25, 49–59 (1994)
23. Porayska-Pomsta, K., Mavrikis, M., Mello, S., Conati, C., Pomsta, K.: Knowledge elicitation methods for affect modelling in education. Int. J. Artif. Intell. Educ. 22, 107–140 (2013)
24. D'Mello, S.K., Dowell, N., Graesser, A.: Unimodal and Multimodal Human Perception of Naturalistic Non-Basic Affective Statesduring Human-Computer Interactions. IEEE Trans. Affect. Comput. 4, 452–465 (2013)
25. Russell, J.A.: A circumplex model of affect. J. Pers. Soc. Psychol. 39, 1161–1178 (1980)
26. Schröder, M., Baggia, P., Burkhardt, F., Pelachaud, C., Peter, C., Zovato, E.: EmotionML – An Upcoming Standard for Representing Emotions and Related States. In: D'Mello, S., Graesser, A., Schuller, B., Martin, J.-C. (eds.) ACII 2011, Part I. LNCS, vol. 6974, pp. 316–325. Springer, Heidelberg (2011)
27. Witten, I.H., Frank, E.: Data Mining: Practical Machine Learning Tools and Techniques, Second Edition. Morgan Kaufmann (2005)
28. Guyon, I., Elisseeff, A.: An Introduction to Variable and Feature Selection. J Mach Learn Res. 3, 1157–1182 (2003)
29. Mukhopadhyay, S.C.: Wearable Sensors for Human Activity Monitoring: A Review. IEEE Sens. J. 15, 1321–1330 (2015)
30. Koo, H.R., Lee, Y.-J., Gi, S., Khang, S., Lee, J.H., Lee, J.-H., Lim, M.-G., Park, H.-J., Lee, J.-W.: The Effect of Textile-Based Inductive Coil Sensor Positions for Heart Rate Monitoring. J. Med. Syst. 38, 1–12 (2014)
31. Suau, X., Ruiz-Hidalgo, J., Casas, J.R.: Real-Time Head and Hand Tracking Based on 2.5D Data. IEEE Trans. Multimed. 14, 575–585 (2012)
32. Santos, O.C., Boticario, J.G.: Practical guidelines for designing and evaluating educationally oriented recommendations. Comput. Educ. 81, 354–374 (2015)

Contextual Recommendation of Educational Contents

Nidhi Saraswat[(⊠)], Hiranmay Ghosh, Mohit Agrawal, and Uma Narayanan

TCS Research, New Delhi, India
{nidhi.saraswat,hiranmay.ghosh,uma.narayanan}@tcs.com,
mohitleoagrawal@gmail.com

Abstract. This paper proposes a recommendation engine for educational contents in the organizational context of a user. The novelty in this paper lies in creating a context model for a user incorporating the role and the tasks assigned to him, and its application to recommendation problem. The recommendations are made on the basis of the estimated gap that exists between an employee's current knowledge level and the skill-set required in his job-context. A probabilistic reasoning framework is used for recommendations, to account for the inexact specifications of user competencies and requirements of the job context.

1 Introduction

Education in a corporate environment is driven by the need to improve the performance level of an employee in his current job-context and to realize his professional aspirations. However, the quest for knowledge often gets compromised in a busy corporate schedule. While ample educational contents may exist on the corporate network and on the Internet, they generally remain under-utilized. A prime reason for such under-utilization is that the busy schedule of an employee seldom permits him to research the content-library and to discover the approriate contents. We propose a contextual content recommendation engine to address this problem. The goal of the proposed system is proactive recommendation of educational contents in specific job-context of an employee.

There has been significant interest in educational content recommendation in the recent past. The e-learning repository is modeled as a network in [12], where a user is recommended a resource based on his learning history and group behavior on network traversal. Past browsing pattern of a learner is used for user modeling in [11] and recommendation is based on association mining. These systems primarily represent content-based filtering approach with some rule based techniques being used in [12]. Recommendation is based on user model in terms of his interests and preferences in [3], which considers resource popularity as an additional input for recommendation. A rule based engine is presented in [2], where recommendation rules bridge the current state of user knowledge and learning objects from multiple repositories. A hybrid recommendation engine using collaborative, content-based and rule based filtering techniques has been

© Springer International Publishing Switzerland 2015
C. Conati et al. (Eds.): AIED 2015, LNAI 9112, pp. 439–448, 2015.
DOI: 10.1007/978-3-319-19773-9_44

proposed in [14]. The recommendation systems reviewed so far are primarily designed for academic environment, where the user model is based on his academic goals, preferences and past learning history. Past reading behavior of the user is the guiding factor for recommendations in most of these approaches, which cannot cope up with dynamic contextual needs of a learner in a corporate environment.

Our prime contribution in this paper is to model the job-context of a person and a reasoning model for contextual recommendation engine for educational contents. Our method essentially represents an uncertain rule-based recommendation engine, where the recommendation set is a function of the user profile and the job-context. The system can integrate contents from multiple educational repositories as well as informal knowledge resources on the Internet. A probabilistic reasoning model is deployed to produce robust recommendations despite inaccurate specification of context parameters and inexact knowledge about how they influence selection of the contents.

The rest of the paper is organized as follows. Section 2 provides an overview of the proposed system with a motivating example. Section 3 presents the findings of a survey that justifies the need for a recommendation system within an organizational context. Data model and the algorithm for recommendation in the proposed system are described in sections 4 and 5 respectively. Section 6 presents the implementation of a research prototype and the experimental results. We conclude the paper with a summary of our findings and the scope of future work in section 7.

2   Overview

User profile, job context and learning content characteristics form three major inputs in our recommendation system. The recommendation rules connects these three components. Primary attributes of user profile comprise his background (current knowledge state) and role that defines his long-term aspirations. A user profile may include many additional attributes, such as his preferences over different types of contents and his reading habits. The job context relates to the allocated tasks that are characterized by required proficiency level in different knowledge domains. Time available to accomplish a task is also an important parameter. Environmental contexts may comprise, time of the day, the state of the user (in-office, travelling, etc.), his device and network connectivity and many such factors. The contents are characterized by several attributes, like content type (video or e-book, etc.), topics covered, depth of contents and estimated learning time.

As a motivating example, consider a new learner to a research lab, exploring suitable model for an 'object recognition' problem based on 'deep neural networks'(DNN). She needs to report her progress to a research council on periodic basis. This job-definition requires that the researcher acquires in-depth knowledge of 'DNN' and basic familiarity with an editing tool, such as 'Latex' . Assuming that the user has some familiarity with 'DNN', but is altogether naive with

'Latex', the recommendation engine should provide her with some short tutorial on the type-setting tool and some in-depth learning material on 'DNN', for example an e-book or a web-course. In our recommendation engine, the suitability of each of the available learning resources is determined with respect to parameters, such as user background, role and tasks in hand. The suitability values for a learning resource are then combined to compute its overall suitability score, which is used to rank the recommendations. Further, we introduce diversity in the recommended list in order to balance the recommendations on different topics that user may need.

3   Learning Needs in an Organization

A survey in an IT organization yielded the information that there are two main motivators for learning. (a) *Intrinsic motivation* that results from inherent curiosity to understand and discover. Intellectual provocation from colleagues and superiors often stimulates the quest for knowledge. It results in more confidence and self-respect on the part of employee. The learning led by intrinsic motivation can follow either an informal or a formal method. *(b) Extrinsic motivation* that results from an urge to establish credibility in the organization and professional circles. In longer term, it is generally viewed as a strength or a weapon towards career growth and opportunities. Learning led by extrinsic motivation is always in a structured form and often associated with certification. It is often linked with rewards and recognition in the organization.

The survey also reveals three distinct time-frames for learning. (a) *Immediate:* requirements that need to be fulfilled within 24 to 48 hours. They generally pertain to *how to*, e.g. how to implement a particular logic, how to use a particular tool, and so on. They empower an employee to attend to his immediate job function. They are generally answered from informal resources on the intranet and the Internet, such as technical blogs and short tutorials. (b) *Short-term:* this type of knowledge requirement involves deep knowledge about some specific topic and need to be acquired within a time-frame of 2 to 6 weeks. Examples include algorithms that can achieve some specific results, e.g. machine learning algorithms for clustering. Learning use of complex tools, such as *Latex* or *OpenCV* also falls into this category. They form about 10-15% of total requirements. The sources of such knowledge can be tutorials, short courses, and survey papers available on the formal internal knowledge repository and web-sites hosted by reputed institutes. (c) *Long-term:* these requirements need to be fulfilled, typically within 3 to 6 months, though flexibility exists. They involve acquiring domain expertise in specific domains, e.g. big data, computer vision or mobility. The sources of such knowledge are generally web based courses, e-books and such other resources available in the organizational resource pool or in public domain.

Immediate knowledge requirements dominate the overall learning landscape in an organizational setting, though it has been reported that personal satisfaction level on receiving such knowledge is low and there is little retention. Time taken to go through several possible sources is perceived to be a challenge. For short-term learning requirements, learners generally rely on the available search tools on the intranet or the Internet; sometimes, expert help is solicited. Long-term learning is generally guided by individual motivation and pro-activeness and the contents are often selected through peer or supervisor recommendation. It is generally found to be aligned to the job requirements of an employee. The survey identifies learning contexts in an organization and justifies a strong need for a recommendation system for learning contents. Further, the survey identifies the preferred nature and source of learning contents for the different learning contexts in the organization.

4   Data Model

Table 1 depicts the data model used in the proposed recommendation system. A brief explanation follows. A basic building block for the data models is ⟨topic, proficiency⟩ tuple. It indicates proficiency value in a certain topic. In our research prototype, the topics have been chosen from an established classification system [4] in Information Technology domain with some customization. We model the proficiency for the different topics on a six-point scale. The topic-proficiency tuples have different semantics in different contexts. For example, it describes the proficiency level of a user in various topics in user profile. On the other hand, it indicates the proficiency requirement in a topic in context of a task or a role model.

User profile in e-learning context generally comprises user competencies and his learning goals. Obtaining reliable information in either of the two aspects is a difficult job. There are two sources of such information: (a) Self-declared: as declared by the learner, e.g. in a bio-data or his personal web-site, and (b) Assessed: as obtained from a formal evaluation and recorded in some Learning Management System (LMS). While results of formal assessment may be more reliable, they are generally less granular. We have mostly used the information as declared by the learner towards their competencies. The information has been subjectively validated with the records available in the LMS. For the learning goals, we have combined inputs from his role definition in the organization and his self-declared aspirations.

Context is one of the most difficult aspect to understand and model. In general, context can include many facets including the user persona, the environment where it is situated and many such factors [1]. For the current paper, we have considered two major aspects of context based on the organizational needs: (a) the role assigned to an employee and (b) tasks assigned to user. At any given point of time, an employee is assigned a role that broadly defines the activities he is expected to perform. Each role requires certain competencies or skill-sets that an employee needs to acquire to perform his duties and for his career growth. Thus, the role of an employee sets a long-term context for his learning. Generally, there are a number of predefined roles in an organization. An employee is generally assigned one or more tasks at any given point of time. Each task

Table 1. Data Model used in the Recommendation Engine

A. Topic-Proficiency tuple	
Topic	One or more set of topics from [4]
Proficiency	One of {0:Naïve , 1:Basic knowledge, 2:Novice, 3:Intermediate, 4:Advanced, 5:Expert}
B. User Profile Model	
User-ID	Unique Identifier for a user
User Name	Given name of the user
Competencies	An array of ⟨topic, proficiency⟩ tuples
C. Role Model	
Role-ID	Unique identifier for a given role
Skill requirement	An array of ⟨topic, proficiency⟩ tuples
D. Task Model	
Task ID	Unique Identifier
Task Description	Description of the task assigned
Topic-Proficiency	An array of ⟨topic, proficiency⟩ tuples
E. Task-Time tuple	
Task ID	See above
Time	One of {0:Immediate, 1:Short, 2: Long}
F. Allocation	
User-ID	See above
User Role	One of Role-ids
User Tasks	An array of ⟨task-ID, time⟩ tuples
G. Content Modelling	
General/Identifier	Unique identifier of Learning Object.
General/Title	Name of Learning Object.
General/Author	Author of Learning Object.
General/Description	Description about Learning Object.
General/Keyword	Topics selected from a set of topics [4].
Educational/Difficulty Level	One of {0:Very Easy, 1: Easy, 2: Medium, 3: Difficult, 4: Very Difficult}
Educational/Learning Resource Type	One of {0:Category-1 (E-book, Web Course, etc.),1:Category-2 (Primer, Tutorials, Slides, etc.), 2:Category-3 (Reference Doc)}
Educational/Typical Learning Time	One of {0:Very Low ($\leq \frac{1}{2}$ day), 1:Low ($\frac{1}{2}$ - 2 days), 2:Medium (2 - 15 days), 3:High (15 - 45 days), 4:Very High ($\geq$ 45 days)}
Technical/Location	URL of Learning Object.

requires some skill-set and needs to be completed with a finite deadline. We classify the time-frame in three categories in accordance with the findings of the survey. We assume that the set of tasks are repetitive and a task database exists in the organization. However, this is not a restrictive assumption because new task definitions can always be added to the database. Other context information, such as reading preferences of the user, time of the day, etc. can also be defined be easily incorporated in our reasoning framework.

As discovered in the survey, the employees use learning contents from many different sources. In order to integrate the variety of resources, a recommendation system needs to use some common metadata. The virtual library of contents can be built through a collaborative effort of subject experts and reference librarians and the metadata for the learning contents can be created either manually or in an automated way [7]. IEEE LOM [6] provides a comprehensive set of metadata fields for describing educational contents. Several application profiles are available for use of this standard in specific application scenario. We have defined an application profile over a subset of LOM attributes.

5   Recommendation Algorithm

Our recommendation engine is motivated by the generic and conceptual framework for enterprise contextual intelligence proposed in [9]. Different attributes pertaining to users, contents and context in a learning environment cannot be strictly quantified. Moreover, the contextual utilities of different attributes of the contents are *inexactly* known and can sometimes be conflicting. A probabilistic reasoning model is necessary for achieving robust results combining these possibly conflicting requirements with inaccurately specified parameters. We use a mixed mode of reasoning, where we determine the utility of a learning content from different perspectives independently using causal reasoning mode of Bayesian network and combine the results with sigmoid probability distribution functions [5].

Figure 1 depicts the reasoning model used in the proposed recommendation system. A task is characterized by an array of ⟨*topic, proficiency*⟩ tuples. Additionally, a task needs to be completed in a finite time. Thus, the *utility of a Learning Object with respect to a task* has two components: (a) *Content Utility:* It is determined by the overlap of the topics present in the content and those required by the task, as ascertained by Jaccard Coefficient [10]. An assessment of the content if it can elevate a user to the desired proficiency level with respect to these topics is yet another consideration. The achievement of proficiency is a function of learner's current proficiency and the nature of the learning object. (b) *Time Utility:* Each task needs to be completed within a finite time. Thus the time utility of a learning object is determined by an estimate of whether it can be consumed in the desired time-frame. Figure 1(a) depicts determination of *task utility* of a LO, combining Content Utility and Time Utility. Note that, in general, a user is allocated with more than one task. The utility of a LO with respect to each task is independently determined using the Bayesian network discussed above. The results are combined at a later stage.

Like a task, a role is characterized by an array of ⟨*topic, proficiency*⟩ tuples. However, there is no time-frame associated with it. We interpret it as that the proficiencies relating to a role can be acquired in a longer term. Thus, the computation for *utility of a LO with respect to the user's role* is similar to estimating content utility as described above. Figure 1(b) depicts determination of *role utility* of a LO.

A user should be recommended learning contents, which suits his current background. It should neither be too difficult nor too elementary for him. Thus, the *utility of a learning content with respect to user background* is determined by user's current background in the subject and the learning object's nature and difficulty level. Figure 1(c) depicts determination of *user utility* of a LO.

In all the three cases, the root nodes of the Bayesian networks (shown towards the left), are initialized to certain states based on the observed values of some user, task and LO attributes. This leads to a belief propagation in the network. The posterior probability of the target variable (shown towards the right) represents the belief in the utility value of the LO from the respective perspective.

Figure 1(d) depicts the method for combining the results of the earlier stages using sigmoid probability distribution functions to produce an overall contextual utility of a LO. The task utility values for the various tasks assigned to a user are combined to determine an overall task utility value, which is then combined with role utility and user utility to determine the overall contextual utility. The contextual utility for each of the LO is determined with this reasoning model, which is subsequently used for ranking the LO's.

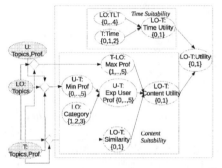

(a) Determining content utility in *task* context.

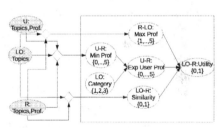

(b) Determining content utility in *role* context.

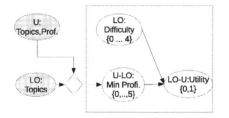

(c) Determining content utility in *user* context.

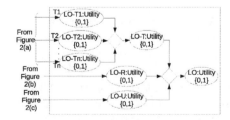

(d) Combining utility values in different contexts.

Fig. 1. Reasoning model for Content Recommendation

5.1   Diversity

The ranking algorithm described in the previous sections runs the risk of producing too many similar contents on top of the list, thereby over-recommending for certain proficiencies while depriving others. This is particularly true, if the LO collection is quite large and contains many similar and competing contents, e.g. a number of textbooks by different authors to learn a programming language. We need to re-rank the LOs' to bring in some diversity in the recommendations.

Increasing diversity implies redefining utility value of the items in such a way that the utility value of an item decreases if there are similar items preceding it in the ranked recommendation list. We have used a method to combine utility and diversity scores to re-rank the items based on the combined score [13]. The similarity measure between two LO has been based on a subset of LOM metadata.

6   Experimental Validation and Results

We have implemented a research prototype for use by the members of a research lab in an IT organization, with a collection of about 100 Learning Objects that are generally considered useful by the researchers. These contents are diverse and belong to various sources, e.g. web-based courses offered by Coursera and edX, e-books and video tutorials from lynda.com, books24x7, etc. as well as freely available tutorials and articles from reputed sources on the web. We created a database with the metadata (see section 4) about the selected Learning Objects. While the database of contents may be arbitrarily large, only a small fraction of contents is relevant to any given topic. In order to optimize the recommendation process, the LOs that have at least one common keyword with respect to the contextual (tasks and role) topics are subjected to the reasoning algorithm described in section 5. This optimization not only improves the real-time performance of the system, but also improves the quality of results. The user and the task profiles are imported from corporate databases. The probability tables in the Bayesian networks and parameters of the sigmoid functions have been chosen based on some heuristics.

We have experimentally validated the recommendation engine based on observations with 10 employees of the research lab, 6 men and 4 women. The employees were between 22 and 26 years of age and held bachelors or masters degree in engineering sciences. Each of the users was asked to select a set of LOs from a given set of collection (without ranking), which he considered useful *in context of* his role and his tasks in hand. This data constituted the ground-truth against which the recommendation results were compared. The user profile and current task description for each of the users were created based on the inputs from these subjects and the results of recommendation were observed. We also created a set of recommendation for each of the cases with simple topic match (ranking based on Jaccard's coefficient) between user's requirements and topics of each LO, to benchmark the performance of *contextual* recommendation.

We constructed the average interpolated precision-recall graph [8] for each of the recommendation sets for a user as follows: Let U_i represents the set of LO's that user i considers contextually useful and let R_i represent the recommended set. The recall and precision of recommendation for user i are computed as $\mathcal{R}_i = \frac{|U_i \cap R_i|}{|U_i|}$ and $\mathcal{P}_i = \frac{|U_i \cap R_i|}{|R_i|}$ respectively. Repeating the experiment over k users, we obtain k tuples $\{\langle \mathcal{R}_1, \mathcal{P}_1 \rangle \ldots \langle \mathcal{R}_k, \mathcal{P}_k \rangle\}$. We interpolate these recall and precision values to obtain the average interpolated precision-recall graph.

The solid line in figure 2 shows the precision-recall graph for the contextual recommendation set and the dotted line shows that for the recommendations obtained with topic match only. The performance of the contextual recommendation is found to be significantly superior than the topic-only recommendation. In absolute terms, we have

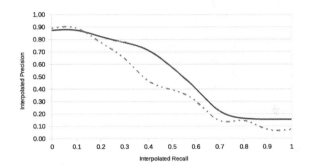

Fig. 2. Average interpolated Precision-Recall Graph for proposed recommendation engine

obtained an average precision in the range $70 - 80\%$ for $20 - 40\%$ recall, a result that is sufficient for putting the system to practical use.

7   Conclusion and Future Work

In this paper, we have presented a probabilistic framework for the recommendation of Educational Contents in context of specific user needs in a corporate environment. We have created a research prototype and tested it with users in an industrial lab. The novelty of our work lies in probabilistic reasoning with the given users' proficiencies, requirements of tasks in hand and the skill requirements for the users' current role in assessing the relevance of accessible Learning Objects. In practice, the recommendation engine will be situated in a corporate learning environment, which will provide opportunity to include additional features. For example, formal assessment of the learners will lead to periodic revision in his skill-profile. A user's reading history will provide inputs for his preferences for the types of Learning Objects (video-lectures or e-books, etc.). The actual usage of the contents in specific contexts will lead to assessment of their *contextual* utility (quality). In our framework, it is possible to easily extend our recommendation framework to integrate these additional inputs, which are likely to improve the quality of recommendations.

References

1. Dey, A.K.: Understanding and using context. Personal Ubiquitous Comput. 5(1), 4–7 (2001). http://dx.doi.org/10.1007/s007790170019
2. Gil-Gonzalez, A.B., Garcia-Penalvo, F.: Multiagent system for learning objects retrieval with context attributes. Int. J. Comput. Appl. Technol. 33(4), 320–326 (2008). http://dx.doi.org/10.1504/IJCAT.2008.022428
3. Gotardo, R.A., Teixeira, C.A.C., Zorzo, S.D.: Ip2 model - content recommendation in web-based educational systems using user's interests and preferences and resources' popularity. In: Proceedings of the 2008 32nd Annual IEEE International Computer Software and Applications Conference, COMPSAC 2008, pp. 460–463. IEEE Computer Society, Washington, DC (2008). http://dx.doi.org/10.1109/COMPSAC.2008.198
4. Computer science-subject classification system (mathematics and computer science library) (2010). http://www.ma.huji.ac.il/library/classcab.htm
5. Koller, D., Friedman, N.: Partially Directed Models, p. 179 (2009)
6. Learning Technology Standards Committee of the IEEE: Draft standard for learning technology - learning object metadata. Tech. rep., IEEE Standards Department, New York (July 2002). http://ltsc.ieee.org/wg12/files/LOM_1484_12_1_v1_Final_Draft.pdf
7. Motelet, O., Baloian, N.: Hybrid system for generating learning object metadata. In: Proceedings of the Sixth IEEE International Conference on Advanced Learning Technologies, ICALT 2006, pp. 563–567. IEEE Computer Society, Washington, DC (2006). http://dl.acm.org/citation.cfm?id=1156068.1156362
8. Appendix A. Common evaluation measures. In: Proceedings of the Twenty-Second Text Retrieval Conference, TREC 2013. NIST (2013). http://trec.nist.gov/pubs/trec22/trec2013.html
9. Shroff, G., Dey, L., Ghosh, H.: Enterprise contextual intelligence. In: Proceedings of 2014 IEEE/WIC/ACM International Joint Conferences on Intelligence (WI) and Intelligent Agent Technologies (IAT), vol. 2 (2014)
10. Niwattanakul, S., Jatsada Singthongchai, E.N., Wanapu, S.: Using of jaccard coefficient for keywords similarity (2013)
11. Wang, F.H.: Content recommendation based on education-contextualized browsing events for web-based personalized learning. Educational Technology & Society 11(4), 94–112 (2008). http://dblp.uni-trier.de/db/journals/ets/ets11.html#Wang08
12. Wang, X., Yuan, F., Qi, L.: Recommendation in education portal by relation based importance ranking. In: Li, F., Zhao, J., Shih, T.K., Lau, R., Li, Q., McLeod, D. (eds.) ICWL 2008. LNCS, vol. 5145, pp. 39–48. Springer, Heidelberg (2008). http://dx.doi.org/10.1007/978-3-540-85033-5_5
13. Yang, K., Wang, M., Hua, X., Zhang, H.: Tag-based social image search: Toward relevant and diverse results. In: Social Media Modeling and Computing, pp. 25–45 (2011). http://dx.doi.org/10.1007/978-0-85729-436-4_2
14. Zhuhadar, L., Nasraoui, O., Wyatt, R., Romero, E.: Multi-model ontology-based hybrid recommender system in e-learning domain. In: Proceedings of the 2009 IEEE/WIC/ACM International Joint Conference on Web Intelligence and Intelligent Agent Technology, WI-IAT 2009, vol. 3, pp. 91–95. IEEE Computer Society, Washington, DC (2009). http://dx.doi.org/10.1109/WI-IAT.2009.238

Coherence Over Time: Understanding Day-to-Day Changes in Students' Open-Ended Problem Solving Behaviors

James R. Segedy[✉], John S. Kinnebrew, and Gautam Biswas

Institute of Software Integrated Systems, Department of Electrical Engineering and Computer Science, Vanderbilt University, 1025 16th Avenue South, Nashville, TN 37212, USA
{james.segedy,john.s.kinnebrew,gautam.biswas}@vanderbilt.edu

Abstract. Understanding students' self-regulated learning (SRL) behaviors in open-ended learning environments (OELEs) is an on-going area of research. Whereas OELEs facilitate use of SRL processes, measuring them reliably is difficult. In this paper, we employ *coherence analysis*, a recently-developed approach to analyzing students' problem solving behaviors in OELEs, to study how student behaviors change over time as they use an OELE called *Betty's Brain*. Results show interesting patterns in students' day-to-day transitions, and these results can be used to better understand the individual student's characteristics and the challenges they face when learning in OELEs.

Keywords: Open-ended learning environments · Coherence analysis · Self-regulated learning · Temporal analysis

1 Introduction

Open-ended computer-based learning environments (OELEs) [1-2] are learner-centered; they present students with a challenging problem-solving task, information resources, and tools for completing the task. Students must use the resources and tools to construct and verify problem solutions, and in this process learn about the problem domain and develop their general problem-solving abilities. In OELEs, students have to distribute their time and effort between exploring and organizing their knowledge, creating and testing hypotheses, and using their learned knowledge to create solutions. Since there are no prescribed solution steps, students may have to discover the solution process over several hours. For example, learners may be given the following:

Use the provided simulation software to investigate which properties relate to the distance that a ball will travel when rolled down a ramp, and then use what you learn to design a wheelchair ramp for a community center.

Whereas OELEs support a constructivist approach to learning, they also place significant cognitive demands on learners. To solve the overall problem, students must simultaneously wrestle with their emerging understanding of a complex topic, develop

© Springer International Publishing Switzerland 2015
C. Conati et al. (Eds.): AIED 2015, LNAI 9112, pp. 449–458, 2015.
DOI: 10.1007/978-3-319-19773-9_45

and utilize skills to support their learning, and employ *self-regulated learning* (SRL) processes to manage the open-ended nature of the task. SRL is a theory of learning that describes how learners actively set goals, create plans for achieving those goals, continually monitor their progress, and revise their plans when necessary to continue to make progress [3]. As such, OELEs can *prepare students for future learning* [4] by developing their ability to independently investigate and develop solutions for complex open-ended problems.

This strong connection between self-regulation and OELEs make these environments ideal for studying SRL, an important research topic in the educational technology research community (*e.g.*, [5]). The open-ended nature of the environment forces students to make choices about how to proceed, and these choices reveal information about students' understanding of: (i) the problem domain; (ii) the problem-solving task; and (iii) strategies for solving the problem. By studying these choices, we can gain a better understanding of how students regulate their learning and how best to design scaffolds to support students who struggle to succeed.

In this paper, we employ *coherence analysis* (CA) [6] to study students' problem-solving behaviors. CA analyzes learner behaviors in terms of their demonstrated ability to seek out, interpret, and apply information encountered while working in the OELE. By characterizing behaviors in this manner, CA provides insight into students' problem-solving strategies as well as the extent to which they understand the nuances of the learning and problem solving tasks they are currently completing. We extend our previous work by applying coherence analysis to study how students' behaviors change over time as they use an OELE called *Betty's Brain* [7]. Results show interesting patterns in students' day-to-day behavior transitions, and these results provide insight into how students regulate their learning over an extended period of time.

2   Background

A comprehensive approach to measuring students' self-regulation in real time is difficult; it requires detecting aspects of goal setting, planning, monitoring, and reflection from the actions students take in the learning environment. In OELEs, this involves assessing learners' skill proficiencies, interpreting their actions in terms of goals and learning strategies, and evaluating their success in accomplishing their tasks. The open-ended nature of OELEs further exacerbates the measurement problem: since OELEs are learner-centered, they typically do not restrict the approaches that learners take to solving their problems. Thus, interpreting and assessing students' learning behaviors is inherently complex; they may pursue, modify, and abandon any of a large number of approaches they adopt for completing their tasks.

Despite this complexity, researchers have developed several approaches to measuring aspects of self-regulation in OELEs. For example, several OELEs measure SRL by developing a predictive data-driven model for diagnosing constructs related to SRL in real time. In some OELEs, such as Crystal Island [8] and EcoMUVE [9], models have been created by first employing human coding to label students' log data with aspects of SRL and then using that labeled data to construct predictive models.

For example, Sabourin et al. [8] asked students to author "status updates" at regular intervals while using Crystal Island. These updates were later coded according to whether or not they included evaluations of the student's progress toward a goal, and this coded data was used to build a predictive model of good vs. poor self-regulation.

In other OELEs, researchers have developed theory-driven models of SRL and embedded those models into learning environments. For example, Snow, Jackson, & McNamara [10] measured the order and stability of students' behavior patterns as they used iSTART-ME, a science learning environment for helping students improve their science comprehension. In their model, lower levels of Shannon Entropy were interpreted as indicative of ordered and self-regulated behaviors.

Coherence analysis (CA) is also a theory-driven technique for modeling learning behaviors in OELEs. CA focuses on students' ability to seek, interpret, apply, and verify information within the OELE. In doing so, CA models aspects of students' problem-solving skills and metacognitive abilities. The approach is designed to be general, and should allow researchers to study the coherence aspect of SRL in multiple learning environments. A more in-depth presentation of coherence analysis appears in Section 4.1 and in [6].

3   Betty's Brain

Betty's Brain [6-7] presents the task of teaching a virtual agent, Betty, about a science phenomenon (e.g., climate change) by constructing a causal map that represents that phenomenon as a set of entities connected by directed links representing causal relationships. Once taught, Betty can use the map to answer causal questions. The goal for students is to construct a causal map that matches an expert model of the domain.

In *Betty's Brain*, students acquire domain knowledge by reading resources that include descriptions of scientific processes (*e.g.*, shivering) and information pertaining to each concept that appears in the expert map (*e.g.*, friction). As students read, they need to identify causal relations such as "*skeletal muscle contractions create friction in the body.*" Students can then apply this information by adding the entities to the map and creating a causal link between them (which "teaches" the information to Betty). Learners are provided with the list of concepts, and link definitions may be either increase (+) or decrease (-).

Learners can assess their causal map by asking Betty to answer questions and explain her answers. To answer questions, Betty applies qualitative reasoning to the causal map (*e.g.*, *the question said that the hypothalamus response increases. This causes skin contraction to increase. The increase in skin contraction causes...*) [7]. After Betty answers a question, learners can ask Mr. Davis, another pedagogical agent that serves as the student's mentor, to evaluate her answer. If Betty's answer and explanation match the expert model (*i.e.*, in answering the question, both maps utilize the same causal links), then Betty's answer is correct.

Learners can also have Betty take *quizzes* (by answering sets of questions). Quiz questions are selected dynamically by comparing Betty's current causal map to the expert map such that a portion of the chosen questions, in proportion to the completeness of the current map, will be answered correctly by Betty. The rest of her quiz answers will be incorrect or incomplete, helping the student identify areas for correction or further exploration. When Betty answers a question correctly, students know that the links she used to answer that question are correct. Otherwise, they know that at least one of the links she used to answer the question is incorrect. Students may keep track of correct links by annotating them as such.

4   Classroom Study

The data presented in this paper comes from a study of students using *Betty's Brain* over a period of approximately six weeks covering two instructional units: climate change and thermoregulation. This paper focuses on the second unit only. Additional details of this study can be found in [6].

Ninety-nine 6th grade students from four middle Tennessee science classrooms participated in the study. However, one student was excused from the study due to an unrelated injury. Students used *Betty's Brain* to learn about human thermoregulation when exposed to cold temperatures. The expert map contained 13 concepts and 15 links representing cold detection and three bodily responses to cold: goose bumps, vasoconstriction, and shivering. The resources were organized into 15 pages (1,974 words) with a Flesch-Kincaid reading grade level of 9.0.

Betty's Brain generates event logs that capture every action taken by the student, Betty, and Mr. Davis. Actions correspond to atomic expressions of intent (*e.g.*, adding a causal link). In addition, the logs contain information on every view that was displayed while the system was running. A view captures the information visible to a user during a specific time interval. To analyze these logs, we first divided students' data into per-day sequences of actions and views, resulting in 395 student-days. We then removed all particularly short (< 30 minutes) and long (> 60 minutes) student-days to control for outliers, reducing the dataset to 332 student-days. For each student-day, we calculated a measure of task performance as the change in map score during the day. The *map score* at any point in time is calculated as the number of correct links (*i.e.*, links that appear in the expert map) minus the number of incorrect links in the student's map.

4.1   Learning Behavior Analysis

To analyze learners' behaviors in *Betty's Brain*, we employed our coherence analysis (CA) approach [6] that combines information from sequences of student actions to produce measures of *action coherence*. CA interprets student behaviors in terms of the information they encounter in the system and whether or not this information is utilized during subsequent actions. When students come into contact with information that can help them improve their current map, they have *generated potential* that should *motivate future actions*. The assumption is that if students can recognize relevant information in the resources and quiz results, then they should act on that information. Otherwise, CA assumes that they did not recognize or understand its relevance. This may stem from incomplete or incorrect understandings of the science topic, the learning task, and/or strategies for completing the learning task. Additionally, when students edit their map when they have not encountered information that could motivate the edit, CA assumes that they are guessing[1].

More formally, two ordered actions are *action coherent* if the second action is based on information generated by the first action. In this case, the first action *provides support* for the second action, and the second action is *supported* by the first action. Note that these two actions need not be consecutive. CA assumes that learners with higher levels of coherence possess stronger understandings of the problem-solving task and strategies for solving the problem. In studying students' coherence in *Betty's Brain*, we have focused on three primary action coherence relations: (1) accessing a resource page that discusses two concepts *provides support* for adding, removing, or editing a causal link that connects those concepts, *regardless* of whether or not these edits improve the causal map; (2) viewing assessment information (usually quiz results) that proves that a causal link is correct *provides support* for annotating that link as being correct; and (3) viewing assessment information (usually quiz results) that proves that a causal link is incorrect *provides support* for deleting it.

Student behaviors were described by the following CA-derived metrics, which are explained in more detail in [6]: (i) *edit frequency*, the number of causal link edits / annotations made by the student per minute; (ii) *unsupported edit percentage*, the percentage of unsupported causal link edits / annotations not supported by previous views within a five-minute window; (iii) *information viewing percentage*, the percentage of time the student spent viewing resources and quiz results; (iv) *potential generation percentage*, the percentage of the information viewing time spent viewing information that could support causal map edits that would improve the map score; (v) *used potential percentage*, the percentage of potential generation time associated with views that both occur within a five minute window of and also support an ensuing causal map edit; and (vi) *disengaged percentage*, the proportion of time students spent *not measurably engaged* with the system. *Disengaged time* is defined as the sum of all periods of time, at least five minutes long, during which the student neither viewed a source of information for at least 30 seconds nor edited the map. We have previously used these measures to study overall characteristics of students' problem-solving approaches in *Betty's Brain* [6]. In this paper, we extend our work to study how student behaviors (assessed by the coherence metrics) change on a day-by-day basis. We hypothesize that students' problem-solving approaches will fluctuate as they use the system, and that the nature of these fluctuations provides insight into how to develop adaptive supports for individual student learning.

To test these hypotheses, we characterize common behavior profiles exhibited during the student-days with an unsupervised machine learning approach. Specifically, we clustered student-days with a complete-link hierarchical clustering algorithm [11], where each student-day was described by the CA metrics. Euclidean distance between students' normalized CA metrics was used as the measure of dissimilarity among

---

[1] Students may be applying their prior knowledge, but the assumption is that they are novices to the domain and should verify their prior knowledge during learning.

pairs of students. After characterizing student-days by these clusters, we reconstituted them into the specific sequence of days exhibited by each student. Using these day sequences, we calculated the number of transitions observed between each possible student-day characterization. In order to identify especially common and uncommon transitions in students' day-to-day problem solving behaviors, we compared the observed frequency of each possible transition to the expected frequency from a baseline independent random model of transitions. This random model assumes that the characterization of any student-day is independent from all others. Specifically, in this model the probability of any student-day being characterized as a specific cluster is the a priori probability of that cluster (approximated by the observed cluster frequency out of all student-days) without respect to previous (or future) days for the student. This allows us to identify the more important transitions characterizing day-to-day behavior by their deviation from the random model, analogous to the analysis of associations in other domains using the *lift* measure [12].

5   Results

The clustering analysis revealed four high level clusters among the 332 student-days, three of which split into two more specific clusters. Table 1 shows the CA metrics for all clusters. Cluster 1 student-days ($n = 52$) may be characterized as students who were strategic experimenters but struggling readers. On these days, students edited their maps often, but most of these edits were unsupported. They spent 1/3 of their time viewing information, but a majority of this time (67.6%) generated no potential. This cluster contained three student-days (Cluster 1-2) that corresponded to complete disengagement from the task. These students rarely viewed information, never generated any potential, and spent an average of 37.5% of their time in a disengaged state.

Cluster 2 student-days ($n = 119$) are characterized by engaged, effective, and strategic behaviors. Students on these days performed several supported map edits. They spent 1/3 of their time viewing sources of information, and most of this time generated potential (77.5%) that was later used (83.5%). These students were rarely disengaged from the task. Cluster 3 student-days ($n = 74$) may be characterized as researchers and careful editors. Students on these days spent large proportions of their time (46.4%) viewing sources of information but did not edit their maps very often. The edits these students made were usually supported (76.2%) and most of the information they viewed was useful for improving their causal maps (potential generation percentage = 64.2%). However, they often did not take advantage of this information (used potential percentage = 47.7%). A subset of these student-days (Cluster 3-1, $n = 39$) may be better characterized as inconsistently engaged students who spent less time viewing information but generated and used proportionally more potential compared to the rest of the student-days in Cluster 3 (*i.e.*, Cluster 3-2). Additionally, these student-days showed much higher levels of disengagement (25.3%).

Cluster 4 student-days ($n = 83$) are characterized by confusion and disengagement. Students on these days performed high proportions of unsupported edits (80.3%), used little of the potential they generated (28.7%), and spent a large proportion of their time disengaged (16.3%). Cluster 4-1 student-days ($n = 65$) are more characteristic of confused students, as students on these days were rarely disengaged from learning (7.3%), and Cluster 4-2 student-days ($n = 18$) are more characteristic of disengaged students.

Table 1. Means (and standard deviations) of CA-derived metrics by cluster

Cluster	Edit Freq.	Unsup. Edit %	Info. View %	Potential Gen. %	Used Potential %	Disengaged %
1. Strategic Experimenters / Struggling Readers ($n = 52$)	0.58 (0.29)	65.5% (20.4%)	35.6% (15.7%)	32.4% (15.4%)	78.9% (14.5%)	8.8% (11.7%)
1-1. Strategic Experimenters / Struggling Readers ($n = 49$)	0.60 (0.28)	64.2% (19.5%)	37.5% (14.0%)	34.3% (13.6%)	78.9% (14.5%)	7.0% (9.5%)
1-2. Disengaged ($n = 3$)	0.34 (0.25)	100.0% (0.0%)	4.4% (2.0%)	0.0% (0.0%)	-----	37.5% (4.9%)
2. Engaged, Effective, Strategic ($n = 119$)	0.86 (0.44)	45.3% (22.6%)	35.3% (13.7%)	77.5% (14.5%)	83.5% (12.3%)	4.2% (9.5%)
3. Researchers / Careful Editors ($n = 74$)	0.27 (0.19)	23.8% (21.3%)	46.4% (17.4%)	64.2% (17.5%)	47.7% (24.9%)	14.6% (14.4%)
3-1. Inconsistently Engaged ($n = 39$)	0.28 (0.18)	25.7% (21.0%)	34.9% (8.7%)	68.2% (17.2%)	57.3% (21.8%)	25.3% (11.0%)
3-2. Researchers / Careful Editors ($n = 35$)	0.25 (0.20)	21.6% (21.4%)	59.3% (15.5%)	59.7% (16.8%)	36.9% (23.7%)	2.6% (5.7%)
4. Confused / Disengaged ($n = 83$)	0.41 (0.30)	80.3% (15.9%)	34.4% (16.8%)	58.5% (23.3%)	28.7% (21.9%)	16.3% (20.1%)
4-1. Confused ($n = 65$)	0.45 (0.30)	78.8% (15.4%)	38.6% (15.7%)	58.6% (22.6%)	31.4% (21.8%)	7.3% (9.6%)
4-2. Disengaged ($n = 18$)	0.26 (0.22)	86.6% (16.0%)	19.1% (10.1%)	57.8% (25.6%)	18.4% (18.9%)	48.5% (14.1%)

Table 2 shows the change in map scores by cluster. In general, there are wide variations within each cluster, indicating that student-days within clusters resulted in varying levels of success. However, the days characterized as engaged, effective, and strategic resulted in much larger changes in map scores when compared to all other clusters. Because previous research has shown that map scores in *Betty's Brain* usually follow a non-normal distribution, we tested for differences in map score changes among the clusters using a Kruskal-Wallis H test. The test identified a statistically significant difference in map scores between the clusters ($\chi^2 = 40.15$, $p < 0.001$). Follow-up Mann-Whitney tests between the groups showed that cluster 2 student-days resulted in significantly higher changes in map scores when compared to all other clusters except for cluster 1-2. No other significant differences were found between the remaining clusters. These results show that when students exhibited higher levels of coherence, they also made more progress in teaching Betty the correct map. It is important to remember that coherent behaviors are not always correct behaviors: an incorrect causal map edit is still coherent if it is supported by previous reading.

Table 2. Means (and standard deviations) of map scores by cluster

Cluster	1-1	1-2	2	3-1	3-2	4-1	4-2
Map Score Change	-0.57 (5.71)	-1.00 (5.57)	2.92 (4.73)	-0.13 (4.02)	-0.03 (2.91)	-0.63 (4.33)	-0.67 (3.34)

To understand how students' behaviors changed over time, we analyzed their day-to-day transitions by grouping student-days into sequences of days performed by individual students. These sequences show how students' problem-solving behaviors changed on a day-to-day basis. Table 3 shows the frequency of all day-to-day transitions made by students with the ratio (in brackets) of the observed frequency of that transition to the frequency expected from a baseline random transition model[2]. For example, the table shows that there were 14 instances of a student moving from cluster 1-1 to cluster 2, which is roughly the frequency predicted by the random transition model (a ratio of 1.1 : 1). Further, transitions to the same cluster are italicized and the five highest and five lowest transition ratios across different clusters (with respect to the random transition model) are shown in bold.

The results of this analysis show several interesting trends. First, transitions to the same cluster were more common than expected from a random transition model for all clusters. This suggests there is some stability to these characterizations of student activities that can persist from day to day. In particular, students characterized as engaged, effective, & strategic (cluster 2) were likely to exhibit similar behaviors the next day (45 out of 78, 150% vs. random) but were relatively less likely (with respect to the random transition model) to become confused (10 of 78, 60% vs. random) or any other characterization except inconsistently engaged (10 of 78, 100% vs. random). Further, all other clusters are less likely to transition to engaged, effective, & strategic, except the strategic experimenters / struggling readers (cluster 1-1).

At the opposite end of the spectrum, students who are characterized as confused or disengaged (clusters 4-1 and 4-2) were likely to remain confused or disengaged during the next day (22 of 55) and much less likely to become engaged, effective, and strategic (11 of 55, 50% vs. random from the confused cluster). Further, over one third of the days in which students were characterized as researchers / careful editors (cluster 3-2) were followed with a transition to the confused cluster (12 of 31, 250% vs. random) and also relatively more likely to transition to inconsistently engaged (6 of 31, 210% vs. random). These students were also the least likely to transition into the engaged, effective, and strategic cluster (4 of 31, 40% vs. random). This illustrates a behavior profile *at risk* for confusion and disengagement. Perhaps by properly scaffolding students exhibiting this behavior, we can prevent them from becoming con-

---

[2] Rare transitions that only occurred for 2 or fewer students are marked [NA] in Table 3.

fused or disengaging from the task. An important caveat of this analysis is the small number of instances of many transitions in Table 3. Additional data will be needed to further support these observations.

Table 3. Frequency of day-by-day cluster transitions [and ratio with respect to random]

Cluster	1-1	1-2	2	3-1	3-2	4-1	4-2
1-1. Strat. Experim. / Struggling Readers	8 [1.6]	0 [NA]	14 [1.1]	2 [NA]	6 [1.6]	7 [1.0]	4 [2.1]
2. Engaged, Effective, Strategic	7 [0.6]	0 [NA]	45 [1.5]	10 [1.0]	5 [0.6]	10 [0.6]	1 [NA]
3-1. Inconsistently Engaged	3 [0.7]	0 [NA]	7 [0.7]	6 [1.8]	3 [1.0]	2 [NA]	3 [2.0]
3-2. Researchers / Careful Editors	2 [NA]	0 [NA]	4 [0.4]	6 [2.1]	6 [2.3]	12 [2.5]	1 [NA]
4-1. Confused	8 [1.2]	0 [NA]	9 [0.5]	5 [0.9]	5 [1.0]	10 [1.1]	4 [1.6]
4-2. Disengaged	0 [NA]	3 [NA]	2 [NA]	1 [NA]	0 [NA]	5 [2.0]	3 [NA]

6   Discussion and Conclusions

In this paper, we presented an analysis of students' day-to-day problem solving approaches in *Betty's Brain* [7] using coherence analysis [6]. The results showed that, taken all together, students' day-to-day problem solving behaviors varied considerably, but in well-defined ways (when compared against random). By understanding these shifts, we may be able to identify opportunities to scaffold students in order to prevent them from transitioning into confusion and disengagement.

For example, the cluster transition analysis showed that students were more likely than expected to transition from researcher/careful editor behaviors to both confused and inconsistently engaged behaviors. This suggests a need to scaffold students who begin to exhibit the researcher/careful editor behavior profile for a sufficiently long period of time. Recognizing these behavior profiles based on problem solving activities will help us design better scaffolds that can be delivered at opportune moments to avoid extended confusion, disengagement, and frustration.

Our recent findings in [6] show the promise of coherence analysis by demonstrating possible links between coherent behavior, prior ability, learning, and success in *Betty's Brain* [6]. The findings in this paper further demonstrate the value of coherence analysis in *Betty's Brain*, but the approach is designed to be general; it should apply to OELEs beyond this one. Overall, these analyses help us understand nuances of how students approach open-ended problem solving. In Table 3, for example, we see 10 instances of students who transitioned from engaged, effective, and strategic one day to confused the next day. Similarly, there were 9 instances of students transitioning from confused one day to engaged, effective, and strategic the next day. The causes of these transitions and their relation to research on how students respond to confusion (*e.g.* [13]) needs further study. We hope this will lead to better understanding of SRL processes and how they can be developed in novice learners through proper scaffolding and support.

Acknowledgements. This work has been supported by Institute of Educational Sciences CASL Grant #R305A120186 and the National Science Foundation's IIS Award #0904387

References

1. Land, S., Hannafin, M., Oliver, K.: Student-centered learning environments: Foundations, assumptions and design. In: Jonassen, D., Land, S. (eds.) Theoretical Foundations of Learning Environments, pp. 3–25. Routledge, New York (2012)
2. Segedy, J.R., Biswas, G., Sulcer, B.: A model-based behavior analysis approach for open-ended environments. The Journal of Educational Technology & Society **17**(1), 272–282 (2014)
3. Zimmerman, B., Schunk, D. (eds.): Handbook of Self-Regulation of Learning and Performance. Routledge, New York (2011)
4. Bransford, J., Schwartz, D.: Rethinking transfer: A simple proposal with multiple implications. Review of Research in Education **24**(1), 61–101 (1999)
5. Winters, F., Greene, J., Costich, C.: Self-regulation of learning within computer-based learning environments: A critical synthesis. Educational Psychology Review **20**(4), 429–444 (2008)
6. Segedy, J.R., Kinnebrew, J.S., Biswas, G.: Using coherence analysis to characterize self-regulated learning behaviours in open-ended learning environments. Journal of Learning Analytics (in press)
7. Leelawong, K., Biswas, G.: Designing learning by teaching agents: The Betty's Brain system. International Journal of Artificial Intelligence in Education **18**(3), 181–208 (2008)
8. Sabourin, J., Shores, L., Mott, B., Lester, J.: Understanding and predicting student self-regulated learning strategies in game-based environments. International Journal of Artificial Intelligence in Education **23**, 94–114 (2013)
9. Baker, R.S., Ocumpaugh, J., Gowda, S.M., Kamarainen, A.M., Metcalf, S.J.: Extending log-based affect detection to a multi-user virtual environment for science. In: Dimitrova, V., Kuflik, T., Chin, D., Ricci, F., Dolog, P., Houben, G.-J. (eds.) UMAP 2014. LNCS, vol. 8538, pp. 290–300. Springer, Heidelberg (2014)
10. Snow, E.L., Jackson, G.T., McNamara, D.S.: Emergent behaviors in computer-based learning environments: Computational signals of catching up. Computers in Human Behavior **41**, 62–70 (2014)
11. Jain, A., Dubes, R.: Algorithms for clustering data. Prentice Hall, Upper Saddle River (1988)
12. Brin, S., Motwani, R., Ullman, J.D., Tsur, S.: Dynamic itemset counting and implication rules for market basket data. In: Proceedings of the ACM SIGMOD International Conference on Management of Data, vol. 26(2), pp. 255–264 (1997)
13. Lehman, B., D'Mello, S., Graesser, A.: Confusion and complex learning during interactions with computer learning environments. The Internet and Higher Education **15**(3), 184–194 (2013)

From Learning Companions to Testing Companions

Experience with a Teachable Agent Motivates Students' Performance on Summative Tests

Björn Sjödén[✉] and Agneta Gulz

Lund University Cognitive Science, Lund, Sweden
{Bjorn.Sjoden,Agneta.Gulz}@lucs.lu.se

Abstract. In three quasi-experimental studies, we investigated the effects of placing a Teachable Agent (TA) from a math game in a digital summative test. We hypothesized that the TA would affect test performance, even without actual "teachability", by social influence on the test situation. In Study 1 (N=47), students did a pretest, played the math game for seven weeks, and did a posttest either with or without the TA. In Study 2 (N=62), students did not play the game but were introduced to a TA directly in the posttest. In Study 3 (N=165), the game included a social chat with the TA, and the posttest offered a choice of more difficult questions. Results showed significant effects of the TA on choice and performance on conceptual math problems, though not on overall test scores. We conclude that experience with a TA can influence performance beyond interaction and informative feedback.

Keywords: Learning-by-teaching · Teachable agents · TA · Assessment · Summative test · Social influence · Test performance

1 Introduction

Education is transformed as more educational technologies are used in schools. The present research grew from the concern that, despite the fact that digital learning environments, such as educational games and ITS have produced engaging and innovative ways of learning and teaching, students are still burdened by the constraints of traditional testing situations. We argue that there are motivational elements from educational software that can similarly benefit traditional school tests, albeit in a digital format. Specifically, we expand upon a previous study [1] with two conceptual replication studies focusing on the social influence of a Teachable Agent (TA).

A theoretical starting point is the role of educational technology for formative versus summative assessments in school. Formative assessments, such as diagnostic tests or quizzes during class, monitor students' understanding and feed back in the instructional process. Summative assessments evaluate students' learning gains at the end of an instructional unit, commonly in school tests or end exams. As such, formative and summative assessments complement each other for informing educational practice.

© Springer International Publishing Switzerland 2015
C. Conati et al. (Eds.): AIED 2015, LNAI 9112, pp. 459–469, 2015.
DOI: 10.1007/978-3-319-19773-9_46

AI-governed systems with automated feedback and individual adaptation can offer effective support for students' formative learning process – not to mention making learning more fun. However, interaction and feedback are almost by definition excluded from traditional summative tests, where a main point is to demonstrate what one learned without any communication and external influence.

Arguably, test situations are deprived of social interaction not to be tough on students per se, but because one must maintain control and regulation of the test environment in order to provide clear measures of individual performance. Although student might benefit from each other's "moral support", they are for practical reasons not allowed to interact during tests, due to the uncontrollable and unwarranted input this might entail. In effect, test situations often suffer from negative influences such as test anxiety, need for self-confirmation, stress, competition and other social factors known to affect test performance [2]. As evidenced by research on "math anxiety", mathematics particularly might be subject to such negative influence [3, 4].

The point to be pursued here is that the constraints of traditional test situations stem from the difficulties of separating social engagement from unwarranted cognitive content. Such limitations can be overcome in a digital environment by separating cognitive and social influence in a way that is not possible in non-digital settings. A virtual agent, for instance, can be both socially engaging and supportive without the unpredictability of a human agent, while conveying only and exactly the kind of information that the designers intend.

In the present work, we investigate how young students' engagement and responsibility developed in relation to a TA in a math learning game might be reestablished when the TA character is added to a digital, summative math test, without any kind of informative feedback. This represents an attempt to isolate the socio-motivational influence that the TA may carry simply by its presence from one situation (learning) to another (testing). Our main hypothesis was that students perform better on a test where their TA is present compared to a test where there is no TA, and that this might depend on students' social relationship with their TA.

2   Cognitive and Social Effects of Teachable Agents

Previous research has addressed cognitive learning gains versus effects on social engagement and motivation of TA's. In short, a TA is a computer agent that is taught by a student, where AI techniques guide the agent's behavior based on what it is taught. The TA provides so-called recursive (student-to-teacher) feedback through its behavior, using a learning-by-teaching approach that has proved effective in both digital and non-digital settings [5]. As discussed by Ogan et al [6], researchers have proposed both cognitive and social mechanisms as to the effectiveness of TA systems. It is then useful to distinguish between the TA as a social character – its looks, the things it says, and the types of interaction that make students relate to it socially – and the underlying AI which directs the TA's information processing and "teachability".

In cognitive terms, researchers have explained the educational efficiency of TA by factors such as higher demands on cognitive organization, the schemas and self-explanation needed for teaching, and that the TA offers a familiar teacher/student metaphor that help students frame their interactions [6, 7, 8, 9]. A detailed example is provided by Chin et al [9] who showed that students who worked with a TA system partly adopted their TA's reasoning patterns, which made them better prepared to learn new material even without support of the software.

In contrast, socio-motivational adaptation may account for students' preferences for working with a TA to other educational material (e.g. non-TA systems or a book) as well as why they make more efforts and spend more time learning with a TA than when alone. For example, a TA may increase students' feelings of responsibility for the learning tasks while at the same time remove the potential social backlash of wrong-doings to a human peer. As to oneself, the TA can serve as an "ego-protective buffer" to feelings of failure and inferior ability [8].

The educational math game used in the present research has been extensively studied in classroom settings over the past ten years [10]. It was an explicit goal of the game developers to add a TA for both cognitive gains (improved learning) and affective or motivational gains (higher engagement and challenge-seeking). Another aim was that the TA should facilitate transfer of the learning content to domains outside the game itself. Evidence to this effect has been provided both by positive correlations between extended game-playing and increased scores on math tests [10], and by learning gains of game-playing groups compared to regular math instruction [11, 12].

A pilot study [1] represented the first step to assessing the effect of the TA on test performance beyond the gaming environment. The results were suggestive of differential effects for low- and high-performers, but came partly from post hoc-analysis and a limited sample size to draw any strong conclusions. Since then, the game has been developed in order to provide extended opportunities for social interaction with the TA, including an in-game chat module for social conversation with the TA between game sessions [13, 14]. Here, we report a reanalysis and two additional studies in order to clarify some of the factors underlying the effect of a TA on test performance.

3   Overview of the Present Studies

The three substudies followed the same general outline and were all conducted in authentic classroom settings as part of math class, at different schools in southern Sweden. The sessions were supervised by the researchers or assistants for formal instructions and technical assistance. Besides initial instructions (including explaining the TA as a "digital pupil" for the students to teach), the math game was designed to be self-explanatory. Otherwise, we kept interventions to a minimum and encouraged the students to "practice on your own". Importantly, we did not help the students, and took care that students did not help each other, with the test questions.

Participants. All participants were Swedish 4th-graders (9-10-year-olds). The teachers had all expressed interest in having their classes participating but they had no previous experience with the particular math game. Typically, the teacher was teaching half the class while the other half played the game (or performed the tests).

Instruments. The studies employed the same web-based math game for training basic arithmetic [10]. The game has a board-game-like design, using digital "playing cards" with colored squares representing numbers. The game is designed for two players but the players can be either human or artificial (a TA or a neutral computer). The interface was graphically updated in connection with developing the social features and conversational module of the TA [13]. Figure 1 shows screenshots from the two versions of the game. There were three game modes of TA engagement: (1) "Show"-mode, in which the TA learns from how the student plays and from posing occasional questions about events in the game (e.g. why a particular card was chosen); (2) "Try"-mode, in which the TA selects a card, which the student can either accept or deny; (3) "Play"-mode, in which the TA automatically plays a round against another player and leaves the student to observe how well it performs. For further details about the game and its conceptual model, we refer to previous accounts [1, 10].

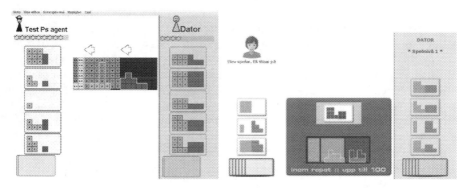

Fig. 1. Screenshots from gameplay in the original version of the math game (left, Study 1) and the revised version (right, Study 3). The TA is depicted on the upper left corner of each.

A digital pretest and posttest was designed for each study, with slightly different designs but with identical question content. There were 41 items (score range 0-41), all targeting base-10 transformations, except one control question on multiplication. Most items were multiple-choice of the type "Circle the sums that end with 00" (e.g. 236+364). Six questions were of a problem-solving type with a free response format that targeted deeper conceptual understanding. For example, one set of questions introduced "Nature money" with assigned base-10 values (e.g. "A stone costs 100 monies and a leaf costs 10 monies; how many leaves do you get for two stones?"). There were only superficial differences between the pre- and posttest items (e.g. substituting "13+37" for "27+13") so as to permit direct comparisons while preventing effects of remembering past answers.

The posttest appeared in two versions, one "TA version" and one "standard version". The two versions were identical in question content, but the TA version added the graphical image of the TA from the math game. The TA was placed in the margin of the test form with a written presentation (e.g. "Hi, it's me – your agent – can you help me answering this questionnaire? I learn from you."). The standard version contained corresponding but impersonal statements (e.g. "Please answer this questionnaire"). To create an impression of being "teachable", the TA was shown responding to similar items following some test questions (e.g. by a simple, animated gif or a still picture of the TA with a speech bubble "I think these sums end with 00"). The TA never gave any corrective feedback and always mirrored the student's performance (e.g. if the student answered wrong, the TA answered a similar question wrong).

Design and methodology. All three studies were quasi-experimental, meaning that they employed experimental and control groups (here: TA vs standard conditions) in real classrooms but with limited control over surrounding variables, such as student groups, teachers, computer equipment, scheduling, logistics and several other factors. Whereas these limitations might affect the internal validity, the ecological validity was high, resembling what educational interventions are like in actual practice, with real students performing curriculum-relevant tasks [cf. 15]. Our approach to maintain methodological rigor can be summarized in three points: (1) Where random or matched assignment to experimental conditions was not practically feasible, we aimed to control statistically for crucial effects; (2) We aimed to balance out the effects of hypothetically non-crucial differences by increasing the sample size and repeated studies while keeping systematic experimental manipulations; (3) We added qualitative measures, including observations and notes of students' spontaneous interactions during the study, as a way of informing the interpretations of quantitative results.

Procedure. The studies followed the same general procedure. First, the students performed the digital pretest on their school computers. Second, there was an educational intervention: students played the math game for an extended period of time (Study 1 and 3) or followed one week of regular class (Study 2). Third, students were subject to the experimental manipulation, by performing either the TA version or standard version of the posttest. Test versions were randomly assigned on the level of class- or group size rather than individuals; this was due to logistic reasons and in order to keep coherent test conditions when testing whole groups together (though on individual computers). As a result, the sample size differed slightly between the TA and standard test conditions. Test scores were independently graded and cross-checked by two researchers. Specific details of each study follow below.

3.1 Study 1

Aims and design. This was the very first study of using a TA from a math game in a digital math test. Here, we add to the original account of this study [1] by presenting a post hoc analysis of the results so as to clarify its relationship to the subsequent studies and the possible co-dependence of other factors for students' test performance.

Method. 49 students played the math game in school in 30-minute sessions, once per week for seven weeks. Of these, 43 students completed the pretest and were divided into two matched groups based upon a median split of their pretest scores. The TA or standard versions were randomly assigned to one half of each group.

Results. A *t*-test comparison of the overall posttest scores for the TA version ($M=30.0$) and the standard version ($M=26.5$) did not yield significance on the $p<.05$ level ($p=.12$). When plotting the data in relation to pretest scores, it appeared as if the 25% low-performers (n=12) on the pretest improved dramatically on the posttest with the TA (from pretest $M=16.5$ to posttest $M=25.5$ with the TA, compared to $M=15.0$ on the standard version). The 25% high-performers (n=13) seemed unaffected by the TA (scoring $M=34$ on either posttest), thus indicating an interaction effect of previous performance and posttest version. As we returned to the data for the present research, we wanted to clarify the results for the whole sample (N=43). We conducted a post hoc-analysis of co-variance (ANCOVA) using students' pretest scores as a co-variate, posttest version as the main factor, and posttest score as the dependent variable. There was a significant main effect of posttest version which the previous t-test failed to reveal; $F(1,39)=12,548, p=.001$. However, the results must be interpreted with respect to the significant interaction with the co-variate, which indicated that the effect of the TA in the posttest depended on students' pretest performance; $F(1,39)=9.129, p=.004$.

Conclusions. It is important to understand the significant interaction within the experimental design [16].[1] Notably, the TA/standard manipulation was not introduced until the posttest, why the manipulation itself could not have interfered with the covariate. Also, there was no initial difference in pretest scores between the posttest groups ($M=25.5$ and $M=25.6$ for the TA and standard groups respectively; $SD=7.0$ in both). We interpret the results with respect to later findings that the math game seems to particularly benefit math low-achievers [10] and that low-performers in general may be more dependent on a supportive social context for school performance [17, 18]. Importantly, the results suggest that we cannot account for any overall main effect of TA presence without also considering previous performance. In effect, the post hoc-analysis enabled us to formulate more specific hypotheses for follow-up studies.

3.2   Study 2

Aims and design. One question was whether any effects of the TA depended on students' experience with the TA from its original context (the math game) or whether a similar effect would be achieved by TA presence in the posttest only. In order to test for the effect of immediate influence (compared to established experience in Study 1), we designed a posttest which first introduced the TA as a "digital pupil", whom students should "teach" by answering the test questions. Besides an introductory screen and some practice items for the TA, the posttest was the same as in Study 1.

Method. Three new 4th grade classes participated (N=62), following the same procedure as in Study 1, except that students followed regular math class for one week instead of playing the math game. Students with the TA version of the posttest (n=31) were instructed to "show their TA how to answer" and those with the standard version were only instructed to "answer the questions". Time constraints did not allow an eight-week period between test occasions but since we were only interested in the effect of TA presence (rather than educational interventions), we deemed that the time between tests was not of decisive importance. Following Study 1, we conducted an ANCOVA for analyzing the posttest results, using pretest scores as the co-variate and including the interaction term with posttest version (TA or standard) in the model.

Results. Overall posttest scores hardly differed between test versions ($M=30.5$ for the TA version; $M=30.2$ for the standard version). The ANCOVA excluded one participant who had not done the pretest. The only significant effect was of the pretest ($F(1,57)=49.33; p<.001$), indicating that students who performed well on the pretest also performed well on the posttest, irrespective of the presence of the TA.

---

[1]   For enlightening discussions on this topic, we recommend the related postings on the website The Analysis Factor (www.theanalysisfactor.com); search for "ANCOVA".

Conclusion. We could not rule out that any potential effect depended on students' experience with the TA over an extended period of time, or that a testing effect took precedence over any possible TA effect due to the relatively short time between test occasions. That is, the experimental variable (TA presence) might have been too weak or unspecific in terms of social influence. Another explanation would be that students could not relate to the TA because they did not understand the concept or that it did not make sense to them in the posttest. This explanation is however contradicted by the relatively high test scores (out of max 41) as well as observations indicating that students spontaneously accepted the TA and managed to teach it throughout the test. A third explanation would be that the first findings were artificial, due to coincidences with a small sample. We set out to address these concerns in a follow-up study.

3.3   Study 3

Aims and design. Study 3 was designed so as to deal with the inconclusive results from Study 1 and 2 by testing more specific hypotheses on a larger sample. This included taking into account research findings by other researchers since the first studies (a time period of four years). In particular, a recent study based on the results of 283 students reported that it was only in the category of conceptual math problems that the game had statistically significant effects on test performance [10]. Still, the effect concerned the game as a whole (compared to a control class) and did not differentiate between social and cognitive influence of the TA. We therefore wanted to study specific effects of the TA on the subset of the six conceptual problems (scoring 0-6) in the test. As a refined measure, we added an active choice of continuing with or skipping conceptual problems in both versions of the posttest. The rationale was to distinguish between the motivational effects of the TA to make extra efforts in the test, and the cognitive effects of the TA on performance in terms of higher scores. In a parallel development, the math game was extended with a TA social chat module [13, 14], allowing for more elaborated social engagement with the TA, prior to taking the posttest. In sum, our hypotheses were that an established social relationship would yield stronger effects of the TA in the test, particularly on conceptual understanding, and that low-performers would benefit more than high-performers.

Method. Nine 4th-grade classes (N=165) participated. The social chat-extended game made game sessions slightly longer than before, 30-40 min, otherwise following the procedure in Study 1. The chat module was activated for one minute between game rounds (i.e. off-task). By random assignment, the TA expressed more or less positive attitudes in the chat (referred to as being "positive/negative"), thus providing some variation even with identical input from students. (The chat data are subject to future studies.) The TA was given new, more life-like visual looks (Fig. 1, right) and a gender-neutral name (Eli or Lo). On the posttest (but not the pretest), approximately half-way through the questionnaire and after the student had encountered two conceptual problems, he/she was asked whether to continue with similar but more challenging questions. In the TA version, this choice was presented with the TA asking "Would you like to teach me some more difficult problems?" adding that "This could earn Lo more points". In the standard version, the question was put more directly to the student, "Would you like to continue with some more difficult questions?" adding

"This could earn you more points". If clicking "Continue", the student was given four more conceptual problems. If clicking "Skip", the student skipped these four problems and continued with the remaining items in the questionnaire. Finally, having completed all math questions, students were asked to assess their own performance and rate their effort in the test on a scale from 1 (very small) to 9 (very big).

Results. 143 students completed both the pretest and posttest (n=64 in the standard version and n=79 in TA version, due to variations in class size). Again, we conducted an ANCOVA for assessing the effect of the TA on posttest scores, but this time on the subset of six conceptual problems with pretest scores on the corresponding subset as the co-variate. We also included the interaction term of posttest version * subset pretest score. The results showed a significant main effect of the TA version; $F(1,139)=8,572$; $p=.004$. There was no interaction effect ($p=.833$), indicating that the effect of the TA did not depend on prior performance. Having controlled for pretest scores, the estimated marginal mean scores were 1.88 ($SE=.16$) with the TA compared to 1.06 ($SE=.17$) in the standard version. The corresponding effect size, in terms of Cohen's adjusted d, was .60.

Because students' choice of pursuing these conceptual problems was a not previously studied variable, we wanted to explore the effect of the TA in relation to several other factors. We therefore conducted a logistic regression analysis with choice (Continue or Skip) as the dependent variable. As predictor variables, we included subset pretest scores (0-6), the type of TA in the chat (positive or negative), students' self-rated effort in the posttest (1-9), and the posttest version (TA or standard). Only pretest score and posttest version significantly predicted students' choice ($p=.003$ and $p=.014$ respectively). The odds ratio of posttest version was 2.652, meaning that the likelihood for a student to continue with the challenging questions was more than 165% higher with a TA in the test form, than when there was no TA present.

Finally, as to the overall scores, students scored higher on the TA version ($M=24.9$; $SD=7.4$) than the standard version ($M=22.7$; $SD=5.8$). This difference was not significant when controlling for pretest scores. The interaction term approached but did not reach significance ($p=.078$). Thus, the results did not support the findings of Study 1.

Conclusion. A closer analysis revealed more specific effects of the TA than indicated in the first studies. Although the overall test scores showed differences in the predicted direction, presence of the TA seemed only to have significant effects on conceptual math problems. An explanation might be that these items were of a problem-solving type that particularly benefitted from students' efforts to reflect and their motivation to spend time on the task. Notably, whereas students' self-rated effort did not reliably predict their own choice of undertaking this challenge, presence of the TA did reliably predict their choice, even beyond the effect of previous performance.

4   Discussion

The present research stemmed from the idea that there are more causes to sub-optimal performance on traditional school tests than lack of knowledge. A digital environment can regulate contextual factors affecting a test situation and thereby influence how students apply their cognitive resources on the task at hand. Virtual characters, such as TA, represent unprecedented means for construing social engaging situations through technology without the unpredictability of human-to-human interactions. In sum, we showed that students could effectively relate to a TA even when it was removed from its original learning context and put in a completely different environment (Study 1 & 2). In addition, the results indicated that a prolonged interaction with the TA might be necessary for it to have any substantial effects on motivation and performance, and that the effects would be greater on the kinds of tasks that typically benefit from increased efforts and sustained problem-focus (Study 3).

The results still leave open the possibility that low-performers and high-performers were both motivated by the TA but for different reasons; low-performers might be more susceptible to social support and an "ego-protective buffer" for making the test less threatening, and high-performers might be particularly triggered by achievement motivation and responsibility for improving their TA, as reflected in their higher test scores. In either case, the TA is used as a means for preparation for future tasks. As such, Chin and colleagues referred to TA as an effective means for "PFL", Preparation for Future Learning [9]. This may be compared to the reverse situation of the present study, in which everything but the TA was removed from the original context, using the TA as a means for "PFT", Preparation for Future Testing.

In other words, even when there was no explicit feedback to learn from, students seemed to respond to the TA as a contextual "bridge" between otherwise detached situations of practice and performance on related tasks. The results indicate that this bridge may hold stronger for certain tasks than for others, hypothetically depending on the extent to which task performance is affected by affective and motivational factors. For example, conceptual problems require more in-depth and creative thinking, which is subject to more situational influence than do tasks of recognition and automatized knowledge [19], such as identifying which sums end in "000" or whether one sum is larger than another. In fact, the conceptual problems accounted for less than 15% (6/41) of the math items in the posttest, which might explain why there was no overall effect of TA influence on test scores.

We chose to maintain the complete math test for contextual reasons and to facilitate comparisons of students' performance across the three studies. Also, this test was ecologically valid in the sense that the set of questions were representative of a regular math test in school for the age group. It remains a question whether students' choice to continue with more conceptual problems were also motivated by a perceived contrast to the previous, possibly less engaging tasks in the test. Future research could clarify to what extent the effect of the TA is dependent on the whole context of test questions and whether the effect we obtained here would replicate, or be even stronger, in a math test that focused exclusively on conceptual problems.

In conclusion, the present research illustrates the value of conducting conceptual replication studies in order to both validate and differentiate previously obtained findings. This appears particularly important in a field where technical development and the limited control over factors in actual educational settings continuously change the conditions for experimental research. We suggest that future research further address how TA's can contribute to decrease negative emotions experienced particularly by some students in math and make test situations more positively engaging, respectively.

First, the concept of a TA is interesting in relation to one's "math self-concept" [4] since the TA represents some "mediated self" to performing math tasks. Do math anxious students experience less test anxiety with the TA? Can the TA compensate for lack of social support from others, peers or teachers? Second, if the TA reframes the test situation, how can it be effectively incorporated for increasing students' efforts and engagement in different tasks? Subjectively, does the TA make students feel they require less – or make more – efforts for performance? Ideally, students are as engaged in showing what they learned on a test as in a positive learning experience.

We hold as a further goal for educational technology to bridge the contextual gap between learning and testing so as to increase students' efforts, improve their performance and enrich their overall educational experience.

References

1. Sjödén, B., Tärning, B., Pareto, L., Gulz, A.: Transferring teaching to testing – an unexplored aspect of teachable agents. In: Biswas, G., Bull, S., Kay, J., Mitrovic, A. (eds.) AIED 2011. LNCS, vol. 6738, pp. 337–344. Springer, Heidelberg (2011)
2. Zeidner, M.: Test anxiety: The state of the art. Springer, Heidelberg (1998)
3. Richardson, F.C., Suinn, R.M.: The Mathematics Anxiety Rating Scale. Journal of Counseling Psychology **19**, 551–554 (1972)
4. Jameson, M.: Contextual Factors Related to Math Anxiety in Second-Grade Children. The Journal of Experimental Education **82**(4), 518–536 (2014)
5. Okita, S.Y., Schwartz, D.L.: Learning by teaching human pupils and teachable agents: the importance of recursive feedback. Journal of the Learning Sciences **22**, 375–412 (2013)
6. Ogan, A., Finkelstein, S., Mayfield, E., D'Adamo, C., Matsuda, N., Cassell, J.: Oh dear stacy!: social interaction, elaboration, and learning with teachable agents. In: Proc. of the SIGCHI Conference on Human Factors in Computing Systems, pp. 39–48. ACM (2012)
7. Biswas, G., Leelawong, K., Schwartz, D., Vye, N., TAG-V.: Learning by teaching: a new agent paradigm for educational software. In: Applied AI, vol. 19, pp. 363–392 (2005)
8. Chase, C., Chin, D., Oppezzo, M., Schwartz, D.: Teachable agents and the protégé effect: Increasing the effort towards learning. J. of Sci. Edu. and Tech. **18**, 334–352 (2009)
9. Chin, D.B., Dohmen, I.M., Cheng, B.H., Oppezzo, M.A., Chase, C.C., Schwartz, D.L.: Preparing students for future learning with teachable agents. Educational Technology Research and Development **58**(6), 649–669 (2010)
10. Pareto, L.: A Teachable Agent Game Engaging Primary School Children to Learn Arithmetic Concepts and Reasoning. Int. J. of AI in Education **24**, 251–283 (2014)
11. Pareto, L., Schwartz, D.L., Svensson, L.: Learning by guiding a teachable agent to play an educational game. In: Proc. AIED 2009, pp. 662–664 (2009)
12. Pareto, L., Haake, M., Lindström, P., Sjödén, B., Gulz, A.: A teachable agent based game affording collaboration and competition – evaluating math comprehension and motivation. Educational Technology Research and Development **60**(5), 723–751 (2012)
13. Gulz, A., Haake, M., Silvervarg, A., Sjödén, B., Veletsianos, G.: Building a social conversational pedagogical agent – design challenges and methodological approaches. In: Perez-Marin, D., Pascual-Nieto, I. (eds.) Conversational Agents and Natural Language Interaction: Techniques and Effective Practices, pp. 128–155. IGI Global, Hershey (2011)
14. Gulz, A., Haake, M., Silvervarg, A.: Extending a teachable agent with a social conversation module – effects on student experiences and learning. In: Biswas, G., Bull, S., Kay, J., Mitrovic, A. (eds.) AIED 2011. LNCS, vol. 6738, pp. 106–114. Springer, Heidelberg (2011)

15. Ross, S.M., Morrison, G.R., Lowther, D.L.: Educational technology research past and present: Balancing rigor and relevance to impact school learning. Contemporary Educational Technology **1**(1), 17–35 (2010)
16. Keppel, G.: Design and analysis. Prentice-Hall, Englewood Cliffs (1991)
17. Dweck, C.S.: Self-theories: Their role in motivation, personality, and development. Psychology Press, Philadelphia (2000)
18. Wentzel, K.R.: Social-Motivational Processes and Interpersonal Relationships: Implications for Understanding Motivation at School. J. of Educational Psych. **91**(1), 76–97 (1999)
19. Ohlsson, S.: Deep learning: How the mind overrides experience. Cambridge University Press, New York (2011)

Negotiation-Driven Learning

Raja M. Suleman$^{(\boxtimes)}$, Riichiro Mizoguchi, and Mitsuru Ikeda

School of Knowledge Science, Japan Advanced Institute
of Science and Technology, Nomi, Ishikawa, Japan
{Suleman,Mizo,ikeda}@jaist.ac.jp
http://www.jaist.ac.jp

Abstract. Negotiation mechanisms used in the current implementations of Open Learner Models are mostly position-based and provide minimal support for learners to understand why their beliefs contradict with that of the system. In this paper, we propose the paradigm of Negotiation-Driven Learning with the aim to enhance the role of negotiations in open learner models with special emphasis on affect, behavior and metacognitive abilities of the learners.

Keywords: Intelligent tutoring systems · Open learner models · Negotiation · Metacognition · Affect · Learner behavior · Interest-Based negotiation

1 Introduction

The paradigm of Open Learner Models (OLM) was introduced in Intelligent Tutoring Systems in order to involve the learner in the overall learning experience [1, 11]. OLMs provide learners with the opportunity to view and edit their Learner Models (LM). This is done in order to provide transparency and increase learner's trust in the system. Allowing the learner to edit their LM resulted in scenarios where the learner's belief about their own knowledge is different from that of the system. Such events trigger an interrupt where the system tries to negotiate the changes made by the learner in an effort to remove the difference of beliefs. The aim of this negotiation is to increase the accuracy of the system's LM [2, 12].

The underlying principle of negotiation in current OLMs is to *"test"* whether the learner can justify the change they made to their LM. The system deploys a direct questioning strategy to test the learner's knowledge and the results are used to update the LM accordingly. Although this strategy of OLMs has shown to produce significant learning gains, the negotiations in OLM follow a very Position-Based Negotiation (PBN) [3] approach, since the dialogues primarily focus on the *"positions"* held by the learner. This strategy of negotiation is often challenging because as the negotiations advance, the negotiating parties become more and more committed to their positions and without any information about why a certain position is held by the learner, any agreement that is reached produces unsatisfactory results.

© Springer International Publishing Switzerland 2015
C. Conati et al. (Eds.): AIED 2015, LNAI 9112, pp. 470–479, 2015.
DOI: 10.1007/978-3-319-19773-9_47

In OLM implementations, the affective and behavioral states of a learner are mostly ignored. A vast body of research shows that expert human-tutors are successful as they try to engage students according to these states, which provides a sense of empathy and encourages learner involvement [5]. The negotiations in OLM are confined into the scope of *"testing"* with little cues about the learner's states, which results in a disengaging partial negotiation.

Although improving the metacognitive abilities of the learner has always been a key role of OLMs [13], the current OLMs rarely scaffold the metacognitive processes. Since the system is actively involved in testing the learner about their knowledge, how they are reflecting or evaluating themselves is mostly left on the part of the learner. The system does not explicitly involve the learner into a discussion that can motivate them to practice these skills more actively.

A conflict may occur because the learner may be confused about their knowledge, or simply have a misconception which leads them to change their LM. The system challenges the change made by the learner and requires them to justify himself. This creates an interesting prospect to involve the learner into a discussion about their belief and what led them to believe so. Humans become stronger advocates of their beliefs once they are challenged and are intrinsically motivated to defend their beliefs [10]. This provides an excellent opportunity to involve an intrinsically motivated learner in a deep learning dialogue which not only tests their knowledge but also encourages them to reflect upon their own thinking. In order to capture this opportunity and make use of the context, we propose a paradigm of Negotiation-Driven Learning (NDL).

Learning is maximized by proactive participation of learners; we believe that such a context is ideal to engage a learner in a dialogue that explicitly targets the metacognitive skills of the learner and provides them the scaffolding to utilize and enhance these skills. Research on the effects of using learner's affective and behavioral states to shape negotiations has shown a positive impact on the overall learning gains [6]. However this has been missing in the context of OLMs. In contrast to the current implementations of OLMs which undermine the negotiation by using it as a testing tool, in NDL we aim to exploit the utility created by the occurrence of a conflict by engaging a learner according to their affective and behavioral states. The rest of the paper is organized as the follows; Section 2 introduces the paradigm of Negotiation-Driven Learning. Section 3 discusses the design of dialogues in NDL. Section 4 illustrates the approach with a case study and Section 5 concludes the paper.

2   Negotiation-Driven Learning

This paper proposes a learning paradigm of Negotiation-Driven Learning which aims at *"enhancing"* the role of negotiations in OLMs to facilitate constructive learning. When a learner is involved in a learning exercise, they are not only learning something new, but they are also implicitly involved in learning how to learn. More often than not they are more inclined towards executing well-practiced strategies rather than monitoring themselves. NDL aims at encouraging learners to use these metacognitive skills more actively and effectively.

NDL acts as a component of the ITS which is triggered when a conflict between the beliefs of the system and the learner occur. During its interaction with the learner the system tries to understand why the learner holds a certain belief (cause of the conflict) and tries to help them understand why it might not be true. The system uses the information about the learner's affective and behavioral states to engage them more actively. An NDL dialogue session is concluded when the learner is able to defend their claim, or shows an understanding of their incorrect belief by accepting the system's justification/proposal. The system's LM is updated with the outcome of the dialogue and the ITS resumes the normal course of tutoring.

2.1   Generating Dialogues in NDL

Unlike most OLM implementations, NDL allows learners to interact with the system in an open environment. In order to accomplish this, the system follows the negotiation protocol proposed in [7] to allow the learner to provide justification of their change. The justification provided by the learner is challenged by the system if it contains an incorrect idea. The system then initiates a reasoning process which is used to understand the motivation behind the change made by the learner. The system and the learner have equal rights to accept or reject a justification provided by the other party; therefore the system needs to be capable of deploying an alternative strategy in case a learner rejects its proposal/justification.

2.2   Facilitating Metacognitive Skills

Facilitating metacognitive skills has been the core of recent research on ITSs and OLMs. It has been shown that learners who are good at using their metacognitive skills perform better than those who are unable to use such skills actively. NDL emphasizes the importance of actively using and enhancing these skills during an interaction between the learner and the system. Fig. 1 shows the dialogue session after a few dialogue moves encompassing domain-specific reasoning. Once the learner is able to answer the domain specific questions to an acceptable standard, the system requires them to summarize their answers and reflect upon how they were able to improve them.

The dialogue session in Fig. 1 highlights how NDL is different from the current implementations of OLMs. At the end of a dialogue session, the system explicitly encourages the learners for self-assessment. This is the time when the learner feels confident about their knowledge and is able to use this understanding to cognize where he was wrong. Engaging the learner to reflect upon the task and evaluate their final answers with respect to their initial answers encourages self-reflection.

2.3   Identifying Learner's States

All ITSs aim to engage learners to maximize learning; however a learner's engagement highly depends upon the affective and behavioral state they are in [4].

T: Great! Now can you summarize your answers in one paragraph?

S: A Stack is a Data Structure that uses the First In Last Out scheme. It allows us to put an element on the top of the stack by using the Push function. We can only remove the Top element of the stack by using the Pop function. When an element is popped it reduces the size of the stack, so it has one less element.

T: Good job! Do you see the difference between the flow of logic in your initial answer and the last answer?

S: Yes! My first answer was not complete. I think I missed out some important details. The last answer looks much more complete and I think it covers the important points about a stack. I think it is a proper definition of a stack.

T: Why do you think you were not able to come up with a complete answer the first time?

S: I thought that was a complete answer. But now I realize that it wasn't. I think I was not sure about the requirements of your question. But as you asked me further questions, I realized that I had only given a partial answer. I knew what stacks are, but I was not able to synchronize the details. When you asked me to summarize my answer, I realized that I had known all the details about a stack, but I was not able to combine them into a complete answer.

Fig. 1. Envisioned NDL dialogue

If a learner is in some sub-optimal state, the system needs to diagnose such states in order to help a learner move into an optimal state that is more conducive to learning. When a learner is in an optimal state of learning, they are more focused and learn better. Hence the system needs to ensure that such a state is maintained. There is an abundance of literature on modeling affect, metacognition and behaviors with varied conflicting views. However it is agreed that an exact estimation of such states is not required in practice as the main focus of an ITS is to improve the cognitive state of a learner, and the knowledge about these states support the system in its reasoning process [6]. The outcome of an interaction between a learner and the system highly depends upon the affective & behavioral state a learner is in. It is to say that the process of learning requires the learner to be interested, motivated and confident to engage in a productive discussion with the system. Table 1 shows a list of Affective & Behavioral states that are used in NDL in order to model the affective state of the learner. These states have been selected from previous research on the subject [4,6]. These are not the only states that affect the learner and the selection of these states may be argued but as pointed out earlier, these states have been shown to provide a good approximation of the learner [4]. The precision of modeling these states is not of principal importance, but an approximation of these states can allow the system to engage the learner more actively.

2.4   System Architecture

As discussed earlier, the use of a PBN like approach in OLMs confines the scope of negotiations. As an alternative to PBN, we propose the use of Interest-Based Negotiations (IBN) [3] in NDL. IBN aims at exploring underlying interests of the parties rather than their negotiating positions and considers negotiating

Table 1. Affective & Behavioral States of learner in NDL

Affective States

Confusion	Poor comprehension of material, attempts to resolve erroneous belief
Frustration	Difficulty with the material and an inability to fully grasp the material
Engagement	Emotional involvement or commitment

Behavioral States

POSITIVE STATES	NEGATIVE STATES
Confident	Unconfident
Motivated	Demotivated
Interested	Uninterested

parties as allies working together for mutual gain. Since in NDL, we are not only concerned with testing a learner but also helping them understand how they learn. For this the system needs to be able to understand the underlying goals/beliefs of the learner. Therefore IBN is more suited in such a scenario. In order to realize the envisioned interactions in NDL we extend the computational model proposed in [8] on the automation of IBN. Our system consists of the following functional components:

– *State Engine*: handles all the state related tasks. It generates the State Model (SM) for the learner by translating learner inputs to the corresponding affective, behavioral and metacognitive states. The SE updates all these state in real-time with each transaction. It also stores previously held states of the learner to understand learner progression.
– *Reasoning Engine*: uses the information from the SM in conjunction with the LM in order to select the next system move with the maximum utility. It consists of a *Context_Analyzer* submodule which uses the information from the SE and the DE in order to articulate the current context.
– *Dialogue Engine*: this is the core module for providing a Natural Language interface to the learner. NDL does not require a complete NLP understanding as we are interested in the concept-level cognition of the learner's input. To accomplish this, the DE consists of submodules which include; i) *Concept_Classifier*: uses a minimum-distance matcher to return a list of concept identifiers that most closely match the learner input. ii) *Normalizer*: manages stemming and spell checking for the learner input. iii) *History_Manager*: stores information about the concepts used by the system and the concepts expressed by the learner. This information is passed to the RE, which uses it to classify the current context. iv) *Sentence_Generator*: uses the concepts identified along with the current context to generate a list of possible utterances of the system. These possibilities are matched with the library of template phrases and the best matching phrase is selected to generate sentences automatically.

– *Plan Base*: holds the different negotiation moves available to the system according to the current context. The information regarding the consequences of using a move in a specific context and state are used to update a move's adequacy to that context in the PB.

3   Designing Dialogues for NDL

Realizing an interaction such as the one shown in the Fig. 1 requires that the system not only understands the learner's characteristics but is also able to comprehend their answers to provide a proper response. In order to understand the typical learner response to system stimuli and their relationship to the current context, a Wizard-of-Oz (WoZ) experiment was conducted. The WoZ approach has been shown to be valuable for collecting data in scenarios which require complex interactions between the users and the systems [9]. Since in the WoZ experiments, users are under the impression that they are interacting with a system, many application-specific characteristics of a textual dialogue can be elicited.

3.1   Experimental Setup

The study was conducted with the students of Bahria University, Islamabad, Pakistan. A total of 45 students from semester of the Software Engineering course participated in the experiment. All participants had completed the compulsory courses of computer programming (C++, OOP, and Data Structures) as a course requirement. The participants were given a short introduction to ITSs and an initial survey was conducted to understand their expectations from such a system. The participants were provided with a web interface to interact with the system. All interactions between the system and the participants were logged and the interaction transcripts were stored for future analysis. Once the participants had completed their sessions with the system, another survey was conducted to get their feedback about the system and the interaction possibilities it provided.

3.2   Results

The interaction logs and the conversation transcripts form the WoZ experiment were transcribed and analyzed in order to understand the kind of dialogues the participants engaged in with the system. In the 45 conversations between the student's and the wizard there were a total of 195 negotiation fragments. The number of user initiated conversations was 80. The mean interaction time was 27.4 minutes. Off-topic discussions or small talk constituted 13.4% of all conversations. 45.6% of the conversations were related to domain-specific discussions while the remaining 41% conversations constituted the inputs used to approximate learner characteristics. These inputs were analyzed to generate a list of possible markers in the input that identified the learner's current state.

To ensure transparency in selecting the specified states, learners were also requested to mark their inputs from a list of given states periodically. Analysis of these choices showed that the states identified in NDL were used majority of the time by the learner to define their current situation.

Inputs Related to Affective. The inputs provided by the learners were transcribed to corresponding possible affective and behavioral state. Learner responses were translated to correspond to specific category of affective state. Table 2 shows a list of learner inputs and their corresponding affective state.

Table 2. User inputs and corresponding affective states

User Input	Affective State classified
I don't understand	Confusion
No, I still don't understand	Confusion, Frustration
I don't know	Confusion, Frustration
I don't need your help	Frustration
What is this?	Confusion
How?	Confusion
I can't do this	Frustration
Wow, I did it!	Engagement
Yes, I think I got it	Engagement
I know it	Engagement

Inputs Related to Behavioral States. User inputs were also used to identify the approximate behavioral state of the learner. As with the affective states, an approximation of the behavioral states were considered to be sufficient for the purpose of this study. Table 3 shows a list of learner inputs and corresponding behavioral states.

Table 3. User inputs and corresponding behavioral states

User Input	Behavioral State
Yes I know	Confident
Ok, Yes, Yeah sure, sure, Yeah (context dependent)	Motivated, Confident
I want to discuss this	Motivated, Interested
No (context dependent)	Uninterested
I'm not sure	Unconfident
I don't think so.,	Unconfident
I don't want to...	Uninterested
I can't do this	Demotivated
I want to solve this	Motivated
Can you help me?	Interested
Let's talk about something else	Uninterested
Not now	Uninterested

4   Case Study

The data collected in the WoZ experiment helped us in indentifying the different state-transitions that are likely to occur during a dialogue session in NDL. Using the states identified in our experiment and their relations with learner inputs we envision the following generalized dialogue in NDL. The example describes how the system classifies a learner utterance and uses this information to generate a corresponding feedback. Consider an arbitrary time t where the system has the following parameters, State Model (SM){Affective State (AS), Behavioral State (BS) and Metacognitive State (MS)} in the working memory (WM):

$$WM(ASprevious\{..\}, BSprevious\{..\}, MSprevious\{..\}) \tag{1}$$

The system identifies a conflict and interrupts the current interaction with the following question:

```
T: You just updated your belief in your knowledge about Stacks
to "high". I am afraid I do not agree with your assessment. What
made you change your belief?
```

The learner responds with the following:

```
S: I just completed the section on Stacks. I know what stacks
are now!
```
This statement is interpreted by the system as follows:

– The learner has confidence in their belief about their knowledge. (**Confident**)

The SE updates the WM as:

$$WM(ASprevious\{..\}, BScurrent\{Confident\}, MSprevious\{..\}) \tag{2}$$

The RE infers that the learner is confident; hence provides them with an overview of their performance in order for them to understand why their claim might be wrong.

```
T: That's good! But you did not perform well in your test on
Stacks! You answered 05 questions and got 02 answers correct.
```

A confident learner would take this opportunity to justify why they could not do well. The learner responds:

```
S: Yes I know that! I don't understand why I couldn't get more
correct answers. I completed the whole topic!
```

This statement provides the following information:

1. The student is aware of his performance in the past test. This shows they have **evaluated** how they have performed the task. (**Evaluation**)
2. The student doesn't **understand why** they couldn't perform better.(**Confusion**)
3. The student showed effort to complete the whole topic. (**Motivation**)

The WM is updated as follows:

$$WM(AScurrent\{Confusion\}, BScurrent\{Confident + Motivated\}, \\ MScurrent\{Evaluation\}) \tag{3}$$

The system infers that this is a *positive* situation since the student is motivated and has shown his ability to deploy metacognitive skill.As this is a positive situation where the student is confused, the next move t+1 by the system provide feedback that encourages the student to go over the topic again in order to clarify any misunderstandings. Hence the move t+1 is:

```
T: Maybe you need to revise what you have just learned. Do you
want to discuss the topic with me? We can try to improve your
understanding of the topic.
S: Yeah, I would like to do that.
```

When the learner accepts the systems advice to revise the topic shows that they are interested in discussing the topic. Hence the WM would be as follows:

$$WM(AScurrent\{Confusion\}, BScurrent\{Confident + Motivated + Interested\}, \\ MScurrent\{Evaluation\})$$

$$\tag{4}$$

This creates an "ideal" situation where the learner attributes are all positive while their affective state is that of confusion. The RE selects the "comprehension gauging questions" to help the learner understand their knowledge gaps. The system provides the necessary scaffolding to the learner to help them remove any misconception of incorrect knowledge.

Once the learner is able to answer the system's questions, the system engages them in explicit metacognitive tasks. The learner is asked to summarize their discussion with the system and reflect upon how they were able to improve their answers. This is done entirely to promote self-reflection in learners and to encourage them to evaluate themselves at the end of each interaction.

5   Conclusion

OLMs have deployed different strategies of negotiation to improve the accuracy of the learners LM. Most of these implementations follow a PBN approach that restricts the role of negotiation as a means of testing the learners knowledge. In this paper we proposed a paradigm of Negotiation-Driven Learning which follows the notion that learning is maximized by learner participation by exploiting good opportunities provided by negotiation in OLM contexts. While OLMs confine the scope of negotiation, NDL builds on this by approximating the different affective & behavioral states of a learner, to generate engaging dialogues that explicitly target the learners metacognitive skills.

We specified the system architecture and provided an overview of the modules responsible for handling different aspects of the interactions. Providing a NL interface to learners can ease the communication process but adds to the overall complexity. NDL does not require a complete NL understanding therefore to keep this complexity to a minimum; we used the minimum-distance classifier which has been widely used for pattern recognition because it is simple and fast as compared to other complex classifiers. Automatic sentence generation was made possible by merging the template phrases with the concepts and context of the current interaction. We conducted a case study to illustrate the feasibility of how the NDL system will be able to generate the envisioned dialogue. We are currently acquiring rules for handling the envisioned dialogues by analyzing the logs generated by WoZ experiment.

References

1. Bull, S., Vatrapu, R.: Negotiated learner models for today. In: ICCE (2012)
2. Bull, S., Pain, H.: Did I say what I think I said, and do you agree with me?: inspecting and questioning the student model. In: Greer, J. (ed.) AIED 1995, pp. 501–508. AACE, Charlottesville (1995)
3. Fisher, R., Ury, W.: Getting to Yes: Negotiating Agreement without giving in. Penguin books, New York (1983)
4. Lehman, B., Matthews, M., D'Mello, S., Person, N.: What are you feeling? investigating student affective states during expert human tutoring sessions. In: Woolf, B.P., Aïmeur, E., Nkambou, R., Lajoie, S. (eds.) ITS 2008. LNCS, vol. 5091, pp. 50–59. Springer, Heidelberg (2008)
5. Lepper, M.R., et al.: Motivational techniques of expert human tutors: lessons for the design of computer-based tutors. In: Computers as cognitive tools, pp. 75–105 (1993)
6. Du Boulay, B., et al.: Towards systems that care: a conceptual framework based on motivation, metacognition and affect. International Journal of Artificial Intelligence in Education 20(3), 197–229 (2010)
7. Miao, Y.: An intelligent tutoring system using interest based negotiation. In: Control, Automation, Robotics and Vision, ICARCV (2008)
8. Tao, X., Miao, Y., Shen, Z., Miao, C.Y., Yelland, N.: Interest based negotiation automation. In: Huang, D.-S., Li, K., Irwin, G.W. (eds.) ICIC 2006. LNCS (LNBI), vol. 4115, pp. 211–222. Springer, Heidelberg (2006)
9. Dählback, N., Jönsson, A., Ahrenberg, L.: Wizard of Oz studies - why and how. In: International Workshop on Intelligent User Interfaces 1993, pp. 193–200. ACM (1993)
10. Gal, D., Rucker, D.D.: When in doubt, shout! Paradoxical influences of Doubt on Proselytizing. Psychological Science 21(11), 1701–1707 (2010)
11. Dimitrova, V.: STyLE-OLM: Interactive open learner modelling. International Journal of Artificial Intelligence in Education 13, 35–78 (2003)
12. Kerly, A., Ellis, R., Bull, S.: CALMsystem: A Conversational Agent for Learner Modelling. Knowledge-Based Systems 21(3), 238–246 (2008)
13. Bull, S., Kay, J.: Open learner models as drivers for metacognitive processes. In: International Handbook of Metacognition and Learning Technologies, pp. 349–365. Springer, New York(2013)

From Heterogeneous Multisource Traces
to Perceptual-Gestural Sequences:
The PeTra Treatment Approach

Ben-Manson Toussaint[1,2] (✉), Vanda Luengo[1], Francis Jambon[1], and Jérôme Tonetti[3]

[1] Université Grenoble Alpes, 38406, St-Martin D'Hères, France
{ben-manson.toussaint,vanda.luengo,francis.jambon}@imag.fr
[2] Ecole Supérieure D'Infotronique D'Haïti, Port-Au-Prince, Haïti
[3] Département Orthopédie-Traumatologie, CHU de Grenoble, La Tronche, France
j.tonetti@chu-grenoble.fr

Abstract. This paper presents PeTra, a framework proposed for representing and treating multi-source heterogeneous traces from simulated learning environments. We tested our proposition on traces from TELEOS, a simulation-based ITS dedicated to percutaneous orthopedic surgery. This ITS captures learners interactions from three different and independent sources. The conducted experiment demonstrated that the sequences generated by PeTra fostered efficiently: 1) the learning analytics task of evaluating the influence of visual perceptions on learners' errors; 2) the extraction of interesting association rules potentially reusable for tutoring services production. However, its genericity has not been tested and it will need to be evaluated at a larger scale.

Keywords: Intelligent Tutoring Systems · Knowledge modeling · Perceptual-gestural knowledge · Educational data mining · Heterogeneous traces

1 Introduction

Perceptions refer to the use of senses to gather information from the environment either passively or not. Perceptual knowledge for its part refer to knowledge that is actively expressed through the use of a sense. For example, in a learning context, visual perceptions can state knowledge when specific locations are gazed and potentially in a certain order. That is the case, for instance, when a surgeon examines the position of the surgical tools relatively to specific points of the anatomical environment of the patient. The points that are checked up, missed or ignored state the level of mastery of knowledge related to the execution of a surgical procedure. We designate by the term "gesture" the motor abilities used to solve a problem, possibly through the manipulation of a tool. From this angle, gestural knowledge points out specific skills involving mastery of spatial and motion parameters such as speed, force, positioning (inclination, orientation, etc.). The execution of a one-handed backhand in tennis or the insertion of a surgical tool based on an oblique transpedicular trajectory are examples of gestural knowledge-related skills. Perceptual-gestural knowledge are multimodal knowledge that involves a combination of actions and/or gestures along with perceptions used as controls for de-

© Springer International Publishing Switzerland 2015
C. Conati et al. (Eds.): AIED 2015, LNAI 9112, pp. 480–491, 2015.
DOI: 10.1007/978-3-319-19773-9_48

ciding on actions execution or validation [8]. The term "actions" here specifies punctual elements of the whole activity that do not require any specific perceptual or gestural knowledge (e.g.: turning on headlights in car driving or triggering an X-Ray in percutaneous surgery). However, in the literature, ITSs dedicated to domains involving this type of knowledge often discard the analysis of its perceptual part. Such knowledge is often tacit and empirical and, thus, hard to capture and model. In fact, capturing perceptual-gestural knowledge in a learning environment requires the use of complementary sensing devices such as eye-trackers for visual perceptions, haptic devices for the touch or computer vision technology to detect postures, facial expressions, etc. The multiplicity of sources generate heterogeneous traces. To provide tutoring services based on these traces, one of the main challenges is to foster their transformation into sequences that reflect consistently the perceptual-gestural aspect of involved knowledge.

The framework PeTra (PErceptual-gestural TRAces treatment), presented in this paper is a proposition to addressing this challenge. Our case study is TELEOS (Technology Enhanced Learning Environment for Orthopaedic Surgery), a simulation-based Intelligent Tutoring System dedicated to percutaneous orthopedic surgery. Knowledge involved in this domain is perceptual-gestural [1, 8]. In fact, practicing this type of surgery requires mastery of coordination of visual analyzes of X-rays, theoretical knowledge on the human anatomy and interpretation of resistance felt on the tools at different points of progression. Specifically, visual analyzes require the perfect coordination of the anatomical environment with their imaging representation, that is, a mental coordination combining 2D images (X-Rays) and 3D objects (patient's body, surgical tools, etc.).

The evaluations conducted on the validity of our proposition are twofold. We tested first the possibility to analyze learners' performance through their behavior related to perceptual analyses from the proposed representation of generated perceptual-gestural sequences. Secondly, we evaluated the possibility to extract from the set of generated sequences interesting perceptual-gestural association rules based on domain experts' belief. The rest of the paper is organized as follows. The 2nd section presents related works on capturing and analyzing perceptions in Intelligent Tutoring Systems; the 3rd section describes the methodology for capturing actions, perceptions and gestures in our case study; the 4th section presents the transformation process of raw traces into perceptual-gestural sequences; the 5th section describes the rules extraction process from the set of transformed sequences; the 6th section presents our evaluation and findings; finally, the 7th section presents our conclusion and perspectives.

2   Related Works

The literature reports many prominent works on Intelligent Tutoring Systems dedicated to domains where perceptual-gestural knowledge is involved. We can mention ITSs that have been proposed for training helicopters [10] and planes [11] piloting as well as car driving [15, 16]. As one of the most recent related researches, we can also cite CanadarmTutor that was designed to train astronauts of the International Space Station for handling an articulated robotic arm [4]. However, the emphasis is generally carried in these works on actions and gestures and not on the perceptions accompanying these latter. In CanadarmTutor, the manipulation of the robotic arm from one configuration to another is guided by cameras through the operation scenes. Visual perceptions that are likely in play for this guidance would be worth further analysis. Other works has been conducted on the analysis of perceptions in learning contexts. For example, visual perceptions are captured and analyzed to deduce learners' cognitive abilities [13] or their metacognitive skills in exploratory learning [2]. Some researchers would rather use collected perceptual information for measuring the learners' mental workload or cognitive effort [7], or for inferring their behavior in the learning process [3, 9]. In other studies, sensing devices are used for capturing postures, facial expressions and body language as emotional signals [12]. For our part, we believe that perceptions denote knowledge states along with actions they are related to and, therefore, should be analyzed from an epistemic point of view. They can bring more precision to generated pedagogical feedback as experts strongly underline the importance of verifying specific anatomic points on the X-Rays to support decision or validation of surgical gesture [1]. The aim is to point out the benefits from studying perceptual-gestural knowledge up on its original multimodal characteristics. To realize this, we need first to foster the consistent representation of perceptions-related behaviors and actions/gestures into perceptual-gestural sequences.

3   Recording Perceptual-Gestural Traces: TELEOS Case Study

The simulation interface of TELEOS is composed of sections that represent the main artefacts of a percutaneous operating room. Namely, as illustrated in Fig. 1.a, it includes a 3D model section where the patient's model is displayed; the current and previous X-rays sections and the settings panel that embeds three settings subsections: the fluoroscope settings panel; the cutaneous marks panel and the trocar manipulation panel. The "fluoroscope" is the unit used to generate X-rays throughout the operation; the "trocar" is the surgical tool used to define the trajectory through which the cement injection tool will be inserted until the targeted vertebra; the cutaneous marks are basically lines drawn by the surgeon on the patient's skin to spot the insertion point of the surgical tools. These sections represent the areas of interest (AOI) of the interface, i.e., areas that are recorded throughout the simulation session when they are fixed by the user. The AOIs associated to the X-rays embed the points of interest of the targeted vertebra, i.e., specific parts of the vertebra that should be analyzed on X-rays to support decisions on surgical actions and gestures. These points of interest have been determined by expert surgeons for each modelled clinical case and integrated as annotations to the patients' models. As shown in Fig 1.b, the learners' visual perceptions, including fixed areas and points of interest, are recorded by a scanpath analyzer [6].

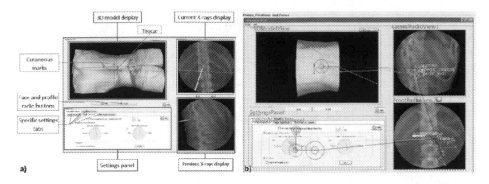

Fig. 1. a) TELEOS simulation interface. b) Visual path traced by the scanpath analyzer

For capturing surgical gestures involved in vertebroplasty procedures, an haptic arm has been configured to render the bones and body resistance through the insertion trajectory [8]. The surgical gestures consist of different types of prehension of the trocar, the force applied for its manipulation and the consequent speed of its progression, as well as its incline, orientation and direction of insertion. The main insertion stages considered for vertebroplasty are skin contact, bone contact, pedicle entry, crossing of the vertebral body until the point of validation of the trocar trajectory.

Finally, punctual actions are captured from the simulation software interface. This is for example the tracing of a cutaneous mark. They are punctual as opposed to the continuity of a visual path or the spatial and temporal dynamism of a gesture. They are therefore recorded only at the moment of their execution as opposed to the continuous recording of information from the complementary sensing devices that are sent on a milliseconds basis: (100 milliseconds for the haptic arm and 200 milliseconds for the eye-tracker). Furthermore, traces from the three sources are recorded independently. They are heterogeneous in their content types and format, and their time granularities. Traces from the simulator are alphanumeric as well as traces from the eye-tracker. On the contrary, those from the haptic arm are numeric. Likewise, their lengths are also different: traces from the simulator contain up to 54 items (e.g.: the name of the executed action, the coordinates (x, y, z) of the position of the fluoroscope in front and lateral configurations; the position of the trocar; the coordinates (x, y) of the position of current and previous triggered vertebrae, etc.); those from the haptic arm include 14 items (e.g.: orientation and inclination of the trocar based on the coordinates of its handle and tips; the speed and force applied on the trocar represented as vectors in the plan (x, y, z); finally, those from the eye-tracker include 7 items (e.g.: the coordinates (x, y) of the fixations, the name of the areas and points of interest gazed, the duration of the fixations, etc.).

Hence, each knowledge element involved in the process is captured into three different and separate modalities. From this point, the challenge is to link those latter on a basis that reflect properly all aspects of each involved knowledge element into one sequence.

4 The Treatment Process with PeTra

The PeTra framework is composed of several single-function software that we call "operators". As illustrated in Fig. 2, the operators are structured as a process. This structure has been chosen to keep the framework flexible and scalable. In fact, some operators can be moved or discarded based on treatment needs. It is as well possible to integrate new operators at any level of the process. The operators are divided into 5 phases of treatments, namely, multi-source traces preparation, multi-source traces transformation, perceptual-gestural sequences analysis, perceptual-gestural knowledge extraction and post-processing.

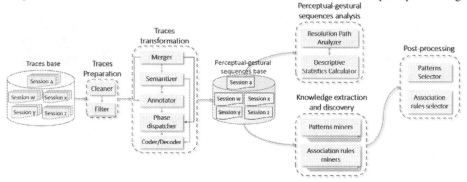

Fig. 2. Overview of the framework PeTra

The preparation operators are applied to clean traces from known formatting errors and to discard if needed parameters that are not pertinent for the treatment. The transformation phase embeds the operators that generate perceptual-gestural sequences from the multisource traces. One can follow the process from the merger to the coder/decoder via the semantization operator and the annotator. However, the semantization operator can be skipped if necessary. Likewise, the semantization operation can be applied equally well before or after the annotation operation. We describe further the main operators used in this study.

4.1 Transforming the Multisource Traces

The Merger. The merger is used to link automatically action to the perceptions that support their execution. The result expected is a set of sequences that render the perceptual-gestural aspect of each interaction. This operation is realized in two steps. First, traces from the different sources are joined in one set and then ordered sequentially. Depending on the domain or didactic interest, perceptions linked to an action can precede or follow this latter. In other words, this link is either descending (perceptions to action) or ascending (perceptions from action). In the second step, the operator checks the chosen configuration and merge the parameters of the related perceptions and action into one sequence. In our case study, an action from the simulator is associated to several sequences from the eye-tracker and the haptic arm. The link between actions and perceptions is descending.

The Semantization Operator. This operator is used for the automatic transposition of changes in the coordinates of the simulation tools into semantic states. These changes are the consequence of executed actions and gestures. This semantic information can translate a discrete manipulation (e.g. *"the fluoroscope has a caudal incline"*) or a continuous one (e.g. *"the trocar is quickly inclined on the sagittal axis"*). The semantic denominations used for our case study are based on the standard anatomical terms of location. To transpose discrete manipulations of the surgical tools, the operator considers the current and previous position coordinates of each tool. For continuous manipulations, it considers the continuum of sequences from the first that reports a position change to the last that reports a homogeneous evolution of this change (e.g.: a change on the same axis and the same direction through several sequences). The last known states of the tools are reported from sequence-to-sequence for keeping track of the current simulation state, i.e., the positions of all the tools, in each perceptual-gestural sequence.

The Annotator. This operator is used to automatically enrich sequences with expert assessments. In TELEOS, elements of knowledge that are put into play by learners are diagnosed by a Bayesian network based on their suitability to a set of expert-defined controls [10]. These controls are elements of knowledge formulated by expert surgeons and integrated in the knowledge model of the simulator. We refer to the assessment items returned by the Bayesian Network based on these controls as "situational variables". Table 1 shows an example of control and situation variable as well as the actions they are associated to and steps of the simulation in which execution of these actions can be observed.

Table 1. An example of control and situation variable.

Action	Phase	Control	Situation Variable
Check the position of the trocar on a lateral radio	Insertion	At the cutaneous entrance spot, the trocar must be tipped towards the pedicle.	Orientation of the trocar at the cutaneous entrance spot.

The Phase Dispatcher. The phase dispatcher executes the automatic classification of sequences within phases when the resolution of exercises provided in the learning environment is realized through different phases. To determine the phase to which an action belongs, the operator takes as input either the predefined lists of actions for each phase or the list of characteristics that define each phase. At this stage of the treatment process, we have a representation of the perceptual-gestural sequences from which we can proceed to more advanced treatment like learning analytics and data mining tasks.

4.2   Analyzing Generated Perceptual-Gestural Sequences

The Resolution Path Analyzer. The resolution path analyzer helps in the analysis of exercises whose resolution is a progression of phases' validation. The operator records each phase validation as well as backward steps due to validation errors. It also records both regular or corrective actions and gestures executed at each point of the resolution path along with associated perceptions. In our case study, two types of visual perceptions are distinguished. 1) Visual perceptions used to verify and/or validate executed actions. They are carried out on the current state of the simulation after the execution of an action and on specific points of interest returned by the X-rays. 2) Visual perceptions used to decide on the next action to execute. They are carried on the tools commands. The simulation of a vertebroplasty is performed in three phases: fluoroscope position setting, cutaneous marks tracing, and trocar insertion. However, the ITS does not constrain the evolution of the simulations in one direction: the interns can freely jump from one phase to any other. But the frequency of backward steps reflects the level of mastery of knowledge.

The Miner and Rules Selector. The miner embeds several algorithms proposed in the literature for mining frequent sequential patterns and association rules. For this study, we are interested in extracting sequential rules from the set of generated perceptual-gestural of sequences. The algorithm used is a modified version of CMRules [5, 14]. This topic is not discussed in the paper, however, in a few words, we modified this algorithm as to consider information sequences phase when computing the support of sequences items. The rules selector is an operator used to filter the mining results as to select and/or exclude patterns and rules based on user-specified characteristics. For example, one can be interested in selecting only rules including actions from a specific tool and certain types of perceptions, as well as, excluding specific types of actions or both. In our case study, we are interested in rules reporting perceptions, states of the tools, expert evaluation and at least one punctual actions or one gesture. Fig. 3 gives an example of extracted rule.

{The fluoroscope is positioned for front X-rays with a cranial incline}; {the learner positions the cutaneous marks slider on the patient's body}; {the learner takes a front X-ray}; {the learner visualizes the position of the spinous of the targeted vertebra on the X-ray} ⇒ {the transverse cutaneous mark is correct}; {the left cutaneous mark is correct}

Fig. 3. An example of selected rule

5   Evaluations and Findings

The traces used for this experiment were recorded from 9 simulation sessions of vertebroplasty performed by 5 interns and 1 expert surgeon of the University Hospital of Grenoble. The proposed simulation exercises consisted of treating a fracture of the 11th and/or the 12th thoracic vertebra. Each session lasts around one hour. The interns have never used the simulator before but have already assisted to at least one vertebroplasty operation in real life. We integrated an expert in the group as to define a reference scope for the performance of a simulated vertebroplasty. Table 2 presents the characteristics of collected and treated data.

Table 2. Collected and treated data characteristics

Profiles	Session	Treated vertebra	#Raw Traces	#Annotated p.-g. seq.	#Fixations	#SV incorrectes	#Validation errors	#Correction sequences
Intern	S01	11ᵗʰ T	2702	113	2033	750	9	11
Intern	S02	11ᵗʰ T	1636	37	885	178	4	4
Intern	S03	12ᵗʰ T	118	33	690	208	3	5
Intern	S04	11ᵗʰ T	5107	128	2482	644	10	39
	S05	12ᵗʰ T	1677	41	858	174	6	10
Expert	S06	11ᵗʰ T	3432	59	1452	249	4	31
	S07	12ᵗʰ T	1828	47	1040	239	5	9
Intern	S08	11ᵗʰ T	5068	117	2514	644	20	36
	S09	12ᵗʰ T	1496	41	869	193	4	22

Our aim is to demonstrate that the proposed representation of perceptual-gestural sequences generated with the framework PcTra fosters key learning analytics and knowledge extraction results involving perceptions along with gestures and actions to which they are associated. To achieve this, we first evaluate the influence of the visual perceptions on learners' errors over operation simulations; secondly, we evaluate the interestingness of perceptual-gestural association rules extracted from the set of generated sequences and the significance of visual perceptions in this estimate. Further, to test our assumption on the pertinence of representing state of the simulation in the sequences, we also evaluate the significance of reported states of the tools in the estimate of rules interestingness. The evaluation of selected perceptual-gestural rules interestingness has been completed by 5 surgeons specialized in percutaneous surgery at the University Hospital of Grenoble.

5.1   Analyzing Influence of Visual Perceptions on Learners' Performance

We are interested in the analysis of the number of validation errors, the number of corrective actions and gestures applied on these errors and, the number and type of visual perceptions associated to these corrective actions and gestures for each session. The graph of Fig. 4.a summarizes the distribution of visual perceptions, incorrect situational variables and validation errors for each session. Pearson index indicates strong negative correlation (-0.62) between visual perceptions and incorrect situational variables. On the other hand, correlation between visual perceptions taken as a whole and validation errors is rather moderate (-0.31). However, strong negative correlation is noticed between visual perceptions of verification type and validation errors (-0.53).

In fact, the session with the highest rate of perceptions (24.6) reports 19% fewer incorrect situational variables than the others, in average. The same link can be observed between visual analysis and validation errors for all the sessions, except for S08. This can be explained by the fact that the subject performed few corrective actions and visual analysis to support these actions. In fact, in the graph b of Fig. 4, we can notice that this session has one of the lowest averages of corrective sequences (1.7) along with the lowest average of visual perceptions (15.5) associated to these sequences. As a comparison, session S02 reported the lowest average of corrective actions (1.0. See Fig. 4.b) but numerous visual analyzes (20.5) for supporting validation decisions and consequently limiting the number of errors (4. See Fig. 4.a). Moreover, it can be seen in Fig. 4.c that few visual analysis in S08 are of verification type (7.7 against 13.8 of decision perceptions). S09 was performed by the same intern. Conversely, less validation errors and fewer incorrect situational variables were observed even with approximately the same rate of visual perceptions. This is the consequence of the reversal of the amount of visual perceptions and the execution of more corrective actions (See Fig. 4.b).

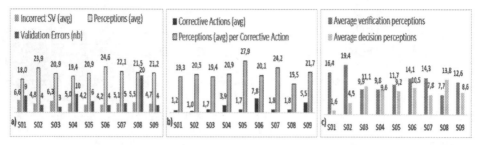

Fig. 4. a) Histogram of average incorrect situational variables, average visual perceptions and number of validation errors per session. b) Histogram of corrective actions and average associated visual perceptions per session. c) Histogram of average verification perceptions and average decision perceptions.

5.2   Evaluating the Extracted Perceptual-Gestural Association Rules

Association rules that are interesting from experts' point of view possibly include rules that are not frequent in the dataset, i.e., rules of relatively low support and confidence. For this reason, we set these parameters as low enough to yield extraction of infrequent rules and high enough to avoid irrelevant ones. This selection process has been performed empirically. On this basis, a minimum support of 0.3 and a minimum confidence of 0.7 have been selected. A total of 188 803 rules were mined with these support and confidence. The rules selector then identified 3 895 out of those based on the constraint that each rule should contain actions and/or gestures, visual perceptions, states of the simulation tools and situational variables in either its *if*-clause or its *then*-clause. We randomly pulled out 20 rules to be evaluated by 5 experts in vertebroplasty. 4 of these experts are teaching surgeons. They were asked to estimate from their belief the educational interestingness of each rule in a Likert scale ranging from 1 to 5, 1 being *very low* and 5, *very high*. Besides this overall evaluation, we asked them to provide as well their rating for 1) the reusability of the rules in a teaching context; 2) the novelty of the rules; 3) the pertinence of the reported visual perceptions and 4) the pertinence of the reported states of the tools.

The rating of the rules reusability in a teaching context aimed at evaluating the prospective exploitation of the rules as partial elements of knowledge that can be integrated to the ITS as to produce key tutoring services like providing live guidance based together on actions/gestures and perceptions. The estimate of their novelty was for determining if the uncovered rules bring significant novel insights on learners' performance, i.e., hard or impossible to catch in real life teaching context in the operating room. Finally, the rating of the pertinence of visual perceptions and states of the tools aimed at measuring the importance of the presence of these latter along with actions and gestures in the simulation sequences. To measure the level of agreement among experts surgeon we computed the Jaccard distance of their answers. The Jaccard distance is a statistic metric to compute dissimilarity between sample sets. The Jaccard distance between two sample sets X and Y is given by the function $J_\delta(X,Y)$ such that $J_\delta(X,Y)=1-J(X,Y)$ where $J(X,Y)$ is the Jaccard index. $J(X,Y)$ is the size of the intersection of X and Y divided by the size of their union. Formally, $J(X,Y)=|X\cap Y|/|X\cup Y|$. Consequently, $J_\delta(X,Y)=(|X\cup Y|-|X\cap Y|)/|X\cup Y|$. The Jaccard distance can be inferred as the percentage of disagreement after excluding joint negative pairs between the sample sets, i.e., in our case, the scores provided by experts taken two-by-two for each rule.

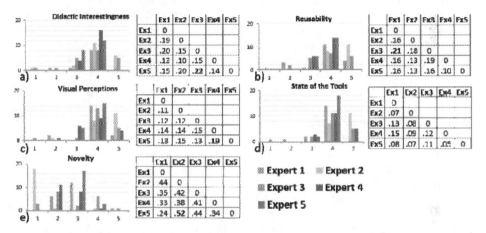

Fig. 5. Histograms of the distribution of the rules scores by each expert and the corresponding Jaccard distance matrix of their ratings two-by-two for the 5 evaluated variables. *(Ex1... Ex5 = Expert 1 ... Expert 5).*

The overall average of the scores for the didactic interestingness of the rules is 3.8 out of 5. The weakest average rating is 3.0 for one rule; the average ratings for the 19 other rules range from 3.2 to 4.4, including 12 with an average score greater than or equal to the overall score of 3.8. This reveals that the selected rules are likely of somewhat high or very high didactic interestingness in average from the experts' point of view. The Jaccard distance computed upon the experts' ratings of this variable denotes a good level of agreement among them. In fact, the largest distance observed is of 21% between the expert 3 and expert 5. Fig. 5 shows the histograms for the distribution of the rules on the Likert scale by each expert and the corresponding Jaccard distance matrix among experts' ratings two-by-two for the 5 studied variables.

The same tendency can be observed for the ratings assigned to the reusability of the rules, the pertinence of reported visual perceptions and reported states of the tools. The assigned scores report either high or very high rating for most of the rules for these variables along with little disagreement among the experts. Conversely, the assigned scores for novelty, range from moderate to very low for most of the rules. The agreement among the experts for this variable is also moderate since the reported distance between ratings goes up to 52% among the expert 2 and expert 5 (See Fig. 5.e).

6   Conclusion and Future Works

We presented in this paper the framework PeTra implemented for addressing the challenge of processing multi-source heterogeneous traces from ITSs dedicated to domains involving perceptual-gestural knowledge. The aim is to consistently connect perceptions to actions and gestures they support as to foster the consideration of all aspects of involved knowledge. We demonstrated the efficiency of our proposition for processing traces recorded on TELEOS, a simulation-based Intelligent Tutoring System (ITS) dedicated to percutaneous orthopedic surgery. We showed that the proposed representation and treatment of traces recorded from three sources in the learning environment (the simulation interface, an eye-tracker and a haptic arm) further the analysis of the influence of visual perceptions upon interns' performance in simulation sessions of vertebroplasty. We also demonstrated the possibility to mining didactically interesting perceptual-gestural association rules from the set of sequences generated by the framework. The interestingness of the rules were evaluated by 5 expert surgeons who also rated as high the reusability of the rules in a teaching context as well as the pertinence of reported visual perceptions and states of the simulation tools. Jaccard distance measure of their ratings showed significant agreement among them. Conversely, the novelty of the rules was rated as moderate at best but with relatively low agreement between the experts.

However, the study is of rather small scale. We plan to go further by confronting the quality of traces treatment performed by our framework to the evaluation of a larger panel of experts with use of more diverse inter-rater reliability and agreement measures. We also consider extending our analyses to the measure of the effective gain from taking into account perceptual aspect of multimodal knowledge compared to treatment that discard either facet of this type of knowledge. As next step on improving the framework, we want to increase the efficiency of the rules selection operator based on main characteristics shared by the top-rated rules. Furthermore, the next evaluation planned will be conducted on the genericity of the framework. An experiment is presently underway for testing its operators on traces from a flight simulator.

Acknowledgements. This work has been partially supported by the LabEx PERSYVAL-Lab (ANR-11-LABX-0025-01). The authors would like to thank Elena Elias for her participation to the data collection organization and Nadine Mandran for her assistance for the data analysis process. They would also like to thank Dr. M. Boudissa, Dr. L. Bouyou-Garnier, Dr. G. Kershbaumer and Dr. S. Ruatti for their kind participation in this study.

References

1. Ceaux, E., Vadcard, L., Dubois, M., Luengo, V.: Designing a learning environment in percutaneous surgery: models of knowledge, gesture and learning situations. Paper Presented at the EARLI Symposium Simulation-Based Learning: Analyzing and Fostering Complex Skills in the Context of Medical Education, Amsterdam (2009)

2. Conati, C., Merten, C.: Eye-tracking for user modeling in exploratory learning environments: An empirical evaluation. Knowl.-Based Syst. **20**(6), 557–574 (2007)
3. D'Mello, S., Olney, A., Williams, C., Hays, P.: Gaze tutor: A gaze-reactive intelligent tutoring system. Int. J. Hum.-Comput. Stud. **70**(15), 377–398 (2012)
4. Fournier-Viger, P., Nkambou, R., Mayers, A., Nguifo, E.M., Faghihi, U.: An hybrid expert model to support tutoring services in robotic arm manipulations. In: Batyrshin, I., Sidorov, G. (eds.) MICAI 2011, Part I. LNCS(LNAI), vol. 7094, pp. 478–489. Springer, Heidelberg (2011)
5. Fournier-Viger, P., Faghihi, U., Nkambou, R., Nguifo, E.M.: CMRules: Mining sequential rules common to several sequences. Journal Know.-Based Syst. **25**(1), 63–76 (2012)
6. Jambon, F., Luengo, V.: Analyse oculométrique avec zones d'intérêt dynamiques : application aux environnements d'apprentissage sur simulateur. In: Actes de la Conférence Ergo'IHM sur les Nouvelles Interactions, Créativité et Usages, Biarritz France (2012)
7. Lach, P.: Intelligent Tutoring Systems Measuring Student's Effort During Assessment. In: Za\"ıane, O.R., Zilles, S. (eds.) Canadian AI 2013. LNCS, vol. 7884, pp. 346–351. Springer, Heidelberg (2013)
8. Luengo, V., Larcher, A., Tonetti, J.: Design and implementation of a visual and haptic simulator in a platform for a TEL system in percutaneous orthopedic surgery. In: Medecine Meets Virtual Reality 18. (eds.) Westwood J.D., Vestwood, S.W., pp. 324–328 (2011)
9. Mathews, M., Mitrovic, A., Lin, B., Holland, J., Churcher, N.: Do your eyes give it away? using eye tracking data to understand students' attitudes towards open student model representations. In: Cerri, S.A., Clancey, W.J., Papadourakis, G., Panourgia, K. (eds.) ITS 2012. LNCS, vol. 7315, pp. 422 427. Springer, Heidelberg (2012)
10. Mulgund, S.S., Asdigha, M., Zacharias, G.L., Ma, C., Krishnakumar, K., Dohme, J.A., Al, R.: Intelligent tutoring system for simulator-based helicopter flight training. In: Flight Simulation Technologies Conference. American Institute of Aeronautics and Astronautics, Baltimore (1995)
11. Remolina, E., Ramachandran, S., Fu, D., Stottler, R., Howse, W.R.: Intelligent simulation-based tutor for flight training. In: Interservice/Industry Training, Simulation, and Education Conference, pp. 1–13 (2004)
12. Ríos, H.V., Solís, A.L., Aguirre, E., Guerrero, L., Peña, J., Santamaría, A.: Facial expression recognition and modeling for virtual intelligent tutoring systems. In: Cairó, O., Sucar, L.E., Cantu, F.J. (eds.) MICAI 2000. LNCS(LNAI), vol. 1793, pp. 115–126. Springer, Heidelberg (2000)
13. Steichen, B., Carenini, G., Conati, C.: User-adaptive information visualization: using eye gaze data to infer visualization tasks and user cognitive abilities. In: Proceedings of the 2013 Int. Conf. on Intelligent User Interfaces, pp. 317–328. ACM, New York (2013)
14. Toussaint, B.-M., Luengo, V.: Mining surgery phase-related sequential rules from vertebroplasty simulations traces. In: Holmes, J.H., Bellazzi, R., Sacchi, L., Peek, N. (eds.) AIME 2015. LNCS, vol. 9105, pp. 32–41. Springer, Heidelberg (2015)
15. Weevers, I., Kuipers, J., Brugman, A.O., Zwiers, J., van Dijk, E.M.A.G., Nijholt, A.: The virtual driving instructor creating awareness in a multi-agent system. In: Xiang, Y., Chaib-Draa, B. (eds.) AI 2003. LNCS, vol. 2671, pp. 596–602. Springer, Heidelberg (2003)
16. de Winter, J.C.F., de Groot, S., Dankelman, J., Wieringa, P.A., van Paassen, M.M., Mulder, M.: Advancing simulation-based driver training: lessons learned and future perspectives. In: Proceedings of the 10th International Conference on Human Computer Interaction with Mobile Devices and Services, pp. 459–464. ACM, New York (2008)

Probability Based Scaffolding System with Fading

Maomi Ueno[✉] and Yoshimitsu Miyasawa

University of Electro-Communications, Tokyo, Japan
ueno@ai.is.uec.ac.jp

Abstract. We propose a scaffolding system that provides adaptive hints using a probabilistic model, i.e., item response theory (IRT). First, we propose an IRT for dynamic assessment, whereby learners are tested under dynamic conditions of providing a series of graded hints. We then propose a scaffolding system that presents adaptive hints to a learner according to the estimated ability of IRT from the learner response data. The system provides hints so that the learner's correct response probability is 0.5. It decreases the number of hints (amount of support) automatically as a fading function according to the learner's growth capability. We conducted some experiments with students. The results demonstrate that the proposed system is effective.

Keywords: Learning science · Constructivism · Scaffolding · Dynamic assessment · Cognitive apprenticeship · Item response theory

1 Introduction

The leading metaphor of human learning has recently been transferred from instructionism to social constructivism [1],[2] in an education society. Vygotsky [1] introduced the Zone of Proximal Development (ZPD) with problem solving, by which a learner cannot solve difficulties alone, but can with an expert's help, thereby promoting learner development. Bruner (1978), like Vygotsky, emphasized the social nature of learning, reporting that other people should help a child develop skills through the process of "scaffolding" [3]. He defined scaffolding as steps taken to reduce the degrees of freedom in carrying out some task so that children can concentrate on difficult skills. The term "scaffolding" first appeared in the literature when Wood et al. described how tutors interacted with preschoolers to help them solve a block reconstruction problem [4]. Scaffolding situations were those in which learners obtained assistance or support to perform tasks beyond their own reach if pursued independently when unassisted. Stone (1998) emphasized the dynamic characteristics of the scaffolding process, which is dependent on cycles of assessment and adaptive support [5].

Brown and Ferrara [6] and Collins et al. [7] worked on a new method of assessment, called "dynamic assessment," by which a cascading sequence of hints was provided to enable dynamic assessment of how much support learners needed

© Springer International Publishing Switzerland 2015
C. Conati et al. (Eds.): AIED 2015, LNAI 9112, pp. 492–503, 2015.
DOI: 10.1007/978-3-319-19773-9_49

to complete various benchmark tasks. Subsequently, scaffolding was incorporated in cognitive apprenticeship theory [8] and has played important roles in several learning theories. Collins et al. [8] introduced "fading" to scaffolding, meaning that once learners accomplish a target skill, the teacher reduces (or fades) learner participation, providing only limited hints, refinements, and feedback to learners, who practice successive approximation of smooth executions of the whole skill. Pea (1993) claimed that scaffolding with fading is an intrinsic component that enabled what he called "distributed intelligence" [9].

Recently, a great deal of interest has arisen in the use of software tools to scaffold learners in complex tasks (e.g., [10]–[16]). However, these studies have been degraded in their usefulness because of three main problems.

1. No previous study has defined what common abilities in all tasks should be developed by scaffolding or dynamic methods of assessment.
2. Previous systems have been unable to predict learner performance with scaffolding based on their estimated abilities.
3. No previous study has used a reasonable strategy of how to scaffold learners. The strategies must provide appropriate support to increase learners' abilities.

Pea (2004) pointed out that many software features in the current scaffolding systems did not have a fading function [17]. The scaffolding system would necessarily derive the fading function if we were able to solve the three problems in the previous studies. The first problem is how to clarify the abilities developed by scaffolding. It is difficult to define the abilities directly because scaffolding does not directly transfer knowledge to learners but instead develops common abilities through solving tasks. However, in the test theory area, the representation of common abilities for all of tasks is known to be a latent variable model in item response theory (IRT) [18]. The probability of a correct response to a test item is modeled in IRT as a mathematical function of an individual latent ability that represents the common ability for all tasks. Our main idea is using this IRT to provide optimal help for scaffolding learners. We first propose an IRT model for dynamic assessment, by which learners are tested when dynamic conditions of providing a series of graded hints and estimate the model parameters from the obtained data. Next, we describe a scaffolding system that predicts the learner's performance with hints based on his/her estimated ability and presents adaptive hints to him/her. The system provides hints so that the learner's correct probability is 0.5. We assume an optimal correct response probability of 0.5 for scaffolding that can increase learners' abilities when the difficulty of tasks is slightly beyond the learners' abilities.

As a result, it automatically decreases the number of hints as a fading function, according to the learner's increasing ability. We conducted some actual experiments to demonstrate the effectiveness of the proposed scaffolding system by changing the predictive correct response probability. Results reveal that the adaptive hint function is the most effective in learning when we determine 0.5 to be the correct response probability. Therefore, over-assistance and lack of help hinder rather than support a learner's development.

2   Item Response Theory for Dynamic Assessment

2.1   Dynamic Assessment

The scaffolding process requires dynamic assessment to predict learner performance after a teacher's help is presented to them, as explained previously. Collins et al. compared the performance of children's responses to IQ test items under two conditions [8]. The first was "static assessment," which involved children trying to solve problems under conventional test conditions where they did not receive any help or guidance. The same children were also tested on the same items under dynamic conditions of providing a series of graded hints. The results demonstrated that dynamic assessment provided a stronger basis for predicting learning outcomes than static measures did. The most important result was that the greatest learning gain tended to be achieved by children who only needed minimal levels of guidance. The magnitude of the 'gap' between assisted and unassisted performance indicated by the amount of help needed was therefore prognostic of individual differences in learning outcomes. Assessing how much help a learner needed to succeed provided more decisive information about readiness for learning than determining how often they failed on the same, untutored tasks. Consequently, dynamic assessment integrated the assessment of learners' prior knowledge with the task of helping them to learn [12].

The problem with previous studies was that the number of hints needed was not a reliable measure of dynamic assessment because it strongly depended on the task difficulty. In addition, earlier studies did not clarify which ability should be developed by scaffolding or how to estimate it. In the next subsection, we propose an IRT model for dynamic assessment to resolve these problems.

2.2   Data from Dynamic Assessment System

We developed a dynamic assessment system to obtain learners' response data from tasks using a series of graded hints to apply IRT to dynamic assessment data.

We consider a series of graded hints $\{k\}$, $(k = 1, 2, \ldots, K-1)$ for task j. For that series, $k = 0$ when the task is presented without hints. First, the dynamic assessment system in a computer presents task j without hints to learner i.

If the learner responds incorrectly, then the system presents hint $k = 1$, or else the system stores the learner's response and presents the next task, $j + 1$. If the learner responds incorrectly to task j with hint $k = 1$, then the system presents hint $k = 2$; alternatively, the system stores the learner's response and presents the next task, $j + 2$. Consequently, the system presents hints from $k = 1$ to $k = K - 1$ until the learner answers correctly. This procedure is repeated until $j = n$. Taking this procedure for N learners, we obtain dynamic assessment data

$$X = \{x_{ijk}\}, (i = 1, \cdots, N, j = 1, \cdots, n, k = 0, \cdots K), \qquad (1)$$

where

$$x_{ijk} = \begin{cases} 1 : \text{learner } i \text{ answers correctly to task } j \text{ when hint } k \text{ is presented} \\ 0 : \text{else other,} \end{cases}$$

and x_{ijK} indicates the response data when learner i cannot answer correctly with hint $K - 1$.

2.3   Item Response Theory for Dynamic Assessment

Item response theory [18], which is a recent test theory based on mathematical models, is widely being used in areas such as human-resource assessments, entrance exams, and certification tests with the widespread use of computer testing. It has three main benefits:

1. The learners' responses to different items can be assessed on the same scale.
2. It predicts the individual probability of correct answers from past response data.

We propose application of item response theory to data X obtained in dynamic assessment, where the problems with traditional dynamic assessment methods are solvable as a result of these three benefits. The probability, $p(u_j = k|\theta_i)$, that learner i will respond correctly task j after the k-th hint is assumed by the following graded response model [19]

$$p(u_j = k|\theta_i) = \frac{1}{1 + exp(\ a_j\theta_i + b_{j(k-1)})} - \frac{1}{1 + exp(-a_j\theta_i + b_{j_k})}, \quad (2)$$

where a_j stands for a discrimination parameter expressing the discriminatory power for learners' abilities of task j, b_{jk} is a difficulty parameter expressing the degree of difficulty of task j after the k-th hint is presented, and θ_i is an ability parameter expressing the ability of learner i. In addition, $p(x_j = 0|\theta_i) = 1$ and

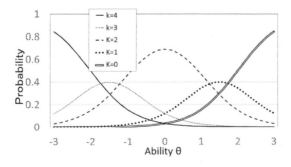

Fig. 1. Graded response model for hints

$p(x_j = K|\theta_i) = 0$. Here, we simply assume a unidimensional ability variable. Figure 1 depicts an example of item response function (2) for a task with four hints. The horizontal axis plots learners' abilities. The vertical axis plots the probability, $p(u_j = k|\theta_i)$, that learner i will correctly answer task j after k-th hint is presented.

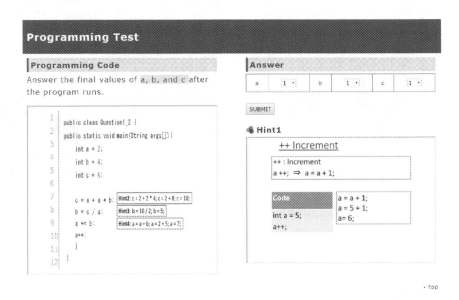

Fig. 2. Example of adaptive hints

2.4 Dynamic Assessment for Programming Trace Problems

We applied the proposed IRT to assess computer programming trace problems dynamically. We used the tasks to find the final numerical value of the target variable in the programs. We used seven tasks with four hints. The first hint presented required prior knowledge to solve the task, followed by successive hints with visualized trace results from the top of the program one after another.

We obtained response data X from 156 examinees using the dynamic assessment system. The examinees were first-year technical college students who had begun to study programming.

2.5 Estimated Parameters

We estimated the parameters of the graded response model in Eq. (2) using data X obtained in the previous section. We used the Newton–Raphson method to maximize the Bayesian posterior with a convergence criterion of 0.001. Table 1 presents the correct answer rates (CAR) for the tasks without hints, and shows the estimated parameters of a_j and b_{jk} for each task and associated hints.

Almost all tasks were slightly difficult from the CAR because all correct answer rates were less than 0.51. It is apparent from a_j that tasks 3–7 greatly discriminated learners' abilities but tasks 1 and 2 had poor discrimination. The estimated parameters, b_{jk}, for each hint were ordered according to the order in which the hints were presented because the hints were presented cumulatively. In the table, NA means that no learners answered correctly when a hint was presented. Therefore, there were only three available hints in task 7.

Table 1. Estimated parameters for each task and associated hints

	CAR	a_j	b_{j4}	b_{j3}	b_{j2}	b_{j1}	b_{j0}
Task 1	0.27	0.79	-2.59	-1.05	-0.54	0.23	0.99
Task 2	0.07	0.45	-1.62	-0.16	0.65	1.13	2.54
Task 3	0.26	2.03	-0.79	-0.25	0.33	0.77	1.06
Task 4	0.13	1.08	-1.04	-0.66	0.68	1.10	1.94
Task 5	0.37	1.02	-1.34	-0.52	-0.25	0.13	0.54
Task 6	0.37	1.15	-0.99	-0.66	-0.35	-0.20	0.52
Task 7	0.51	1.09	NA	-0.76	-0.57	-0.28	-0.04

We then compared the reliabilities of the ability estimators with the numbers of hints that were used in previous studies [8] of dynamic assessment. We calculated the correlation coefficients between the estimated abilities using data for tasks 1–4 and those using data for tasks 4–7. The results revealed a high correlation coefficient value of 0.862. We similarly calculated correlation coefficients between the average number of hints needed for tasks 1–4 and those for tasks 4–7. We obtained a comparatively low value of 0.662. The main reason the number of necessary hints was less reliable is that the variance of the numbers of used hints tended to be small because only a few hints were needed for learners; then the magnitude of estimation error tended to be large. In contrast, the proposed estimated ability for dynamic assessment was a more reliable measure by minimizing the effects of heterogeneous or aberrant responses that might have affected poor accuracy in the estimates. Consequently, the proposed method improves the reliability of dynamic assessment.

3   Probability Based Scaffolding System with Fading

Our main interest in this study was to clarify the mechanism for effective scaffolding. The main difficulty with scaffolding is that over-assistance or lack of help interrupts effective learning. The problem is how to optimize the magnitude of help using dynamic assessment. Here, we introduce a method of presenting adaptive hints to control learners' predictive correct response probabilities in tasks. Here, we assume that some optimal correct response probability to increase learners' abilities that is achieved by scaffolding when the difficulty of tasks is slightly beyond the learners' abilities. The most important problem is to ascertain how great the optimal correct response probability is. We assume that the optimal probability is 0.5 in this study because this is the borderline level of help to enable the learners to solve the task.

According to this idea, we developed a scaffolding system to solve the programming trace problem. Fig. 2 depicts an example of the system by which all of four hints are presented. First, the system presents the first task without hints. In Fig. 2, the task is presented on the left of screen. If a learner answers correctly, then the system estimates the learner ability using the learner response data; then the system presents the next task. Here, the initial value of θ_i is zero, which is the average of θ_i. If the learner answers incorrectly, then the system searches the hint, with which the learner predictive correct answer probability is nearest to 0.5 from the hints' database. The learner's predictive correct answer probability, $p(u_j = k|\theta_i)$, is estimated using the learner's estimated ability θ_i and hint parameters a_j, b_{jk} stored in the database. Then, the system presents the selected hint to the learner. On the right of screen in Fig. 2, Hint 1 is presented to explain "increment :++" in the program. The system re-estimates the learner's ability and presents the optimal hint from the remaining hints in the database if the learner answers the task incorrectly with the hint. This procedure is repeated until the learner answers correctly or until there are no remaining hints in the database. On the left of screen in Fig. 2, Hint 2, Hint 3, and Hint 4 are presented sequentially. The system presents the next task if the learner answers correctly.

This algorithm was inspired by adaptive testing that presented optimal items for measuring learners' abilities.

4   Evaluation Experiment

This section explains how we evaluated the proposed scaffolding system using actual data. The participants in these experiments were 93 first-year university students of the faculty of engineering who had begun to study programming.

4.1   Method

The participants were divided into six groups (A–F) for different experiments.

A) The system presented hints so that the learner's predictive correct answer probability was close to 0.8.
B) The system presented hints so that the learner's predictive correct answer probability was close to 0.65.
C) The system presented hints so that the learner's predictive correct answer probability was close to 0.5 (proposed method).
D) The system presented no hints. (the learner's predictive correct answer probability was 0.1–0.5). The system presented the correct answer if the learner answered incorrectly once.
E) The system presents the graded hints sequentially in the same way as the method explained in section 2.2. The system presents the next hint if the learner answers incorrectly. This procedure was repeated until the learner answered correctly.

F) The system presents the correct answer, and provides an explanation for this if the learner answers incorrectly once. The explanation included the contents for all the hints.

We developed these six versions of the system. The experiments were conducted according to five steps:

1. The examinees took a pre-test to assess their prior knowledge using the system. The pre-test consisted of programming trace problems asking for the final values of variables after the program began working. The examinees had to solve the problems without hints by themselves.
2. The system presented basic knowledge related to programming trace problems to the examinees after the pre-test had taken place.
3. The system started the scaffolding module corresponding to each group (A-F) after previous learning had taken place.
4. The examinees took a post-test after learning with the scaffolding system. The post-test consisted of new problems combined with the previously learned programming grammars. The examinees had to solve the problems by themselves without hints.
5. After a week, the examinees took a memory holding test that consisted of similar items to those in the post-test.

4.2   Results

Evaluation of Basic Functions. This section explains our evaluation of the basic functions of the proposed system. We first tested and confirmed that the system presented adaptive hints so that the learners' correct answer rates were close to 0.5. Figure 3 depicts the average correct answer rates over all examinees for tasks when hints were presented. The error bar shows the standard error. Figure 3 also indicates that the system controlled learners' correct answer probabilities are around 0.5 by presenting adaptive hints to various levels of learners. This evidence of control demonstrates that the function of adaptive hints functioned precisely because the correct answer rates without hints were between 0.1 and 0.37 except for task 7. The average correct answer rate tended to be higher than 0.6 for task 7, whose correct answer rate was beyond 0.5. We tested and confirmed that the system increased the learners' abilities. Figure 4 depicts the average estimated abilities for tasks when learning with the system. The average ability increases monotonically from 0.1 in the figure when learners proceed with learning until task 6; it converges to around 0.4. This result demonstrates the effectiveness of the proposed system for learner development.

We subsequently confirmed the fading function of the system. Figure 5 depicts the transition in the average number of hints presented to learners in the system. The number of presented hints does not decrease monotonically because the characteristics of hints differ for tasks. However, the average number of presented hints decreases dynamically after learning task 4. The system gradually decreases the amount of help according to increases in learner's ability. This is the fading function that is expected to enhance learners' autonomous learning and their self-reliance in solving tasks.

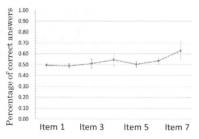

Fig. 3. Average correct answer rate

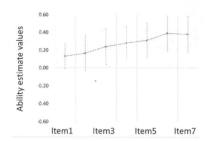

Fig. 4. Transition in estimated abilities

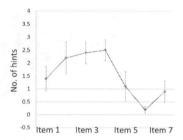

Fig. 5. Average number of presented hints

Evaluation of Scaffolding. This section presents a comparison of the performance of pre-test and post-test examinees groups from A to F that were used to evaluate the proposed system. The test results are presented in Table 2, which lists the number of examinees allocated to each group, the average score obtained from pre-tests, the average score from post-tests, the average score from memory-holding tests, and the average learning time using the system. The values in parentheses in the table represent standard errors. The χ^2 test with a significance level of 5% indicates that the results from the pre-test are equivalent to those of the other groups. Therefore, no differences were found in the groups before the experiment. In addition, the average pre-test scores were extremely low because the examinees were beginners at programming.

We assessed differences between groups using one-way analysis of variance (ANOVA) in the results from post-tests; then we used the Tukey–Kramer method for the detected differences. The proposed scaffolding method outperformed the others, from Table 2, with a significance level of 5% despite the short average learning times. Conversely, Group F, which provided the answers and their explanations, exhibited the worst performance, although the explanation included the content for all hints. This method provided less opportunity for learners for deep consideration of problems because the average learning time was the shortest. In contrast, group D, with no hints, provided the second-best performance. The average learning time for group D was longer than that for group F. Presenting answers only after learners' incorrect answers might induce deep thinking from this to solve problems. Moreover, this result suggests that over-instruction is ineffective for attaining learner development.

The system presented herein hints in groups A and B so that learners' predictive correct answer probability was near 0.8 for the former and 0.65 for the latter. In these cases, the system tended to present more help (content of hints) than that for group C. The average scores for groups A and B were less than that of group D, although the averages of learning times for groups A and B were longer than those for the others. This result shows that setting correct answer probabilities by scaffolding strongly affects learning effectiveness. We conducted a conventional dynamic assessment procedure for group E. The average score for group E was almost identical to those for groups A and B from the results. Actually, the effectiveness of the conventional method was the same as that of the other methods with slight over-assistance. The proposed method, group C, provided the best average score in the results for the memory holding test. In contrast, the average score for group F was the worst. The average scores for the other groups were almost identical. These results indicate that the proposed scaffolding method with a correct answer probability of 0.5 was superior.

We also administered two questionnaires to the examinees: 1) Did you think that you achieved the correct answers to the tasks by yourself? and 2) Did you have confidence in solving similar tasks by yourself? The examinees answered them by responding on a five-point Likert scale:
1. Strongly disagree, 2. Weakly disagree, 3. I am not sure, 4. Weakly agree, and 5. Strongly agree.

The results, presented in Table 3, indicate that the proposed method has the best scores. Therefore, the proposed method enabled learners to think that they could solve tasks independently.

Table 2. Results from pre- and post-tests (Tukey–Kramer method and significant difference from group C: *5 %, **1%)

Group	A	B	C	D	E	F
No. of subjects	14	16	18	15	12	18
Pre-test score	1.14 (1.59)	1.69 (2.44)	1.78 (2.44)	1.33 (1.89)	2.17 (1.40)	2.72 (2.23)
Post-test score	35.4** (2.94)	34.8** (2.13)	40.0 (3.15)	36.5* (2.22)	34.8** (2.44)	30.9** (4.92)
Memory holding test	20.8 (2.73)	20.8 (2.27)	23.0 (2.18)	20.6 (1.81)	20.8 (1.81)	18.3 (5.41)
Learning time (min)	69 (26)	78 (28)	71 (22)	67 (15)	72 (24)	64 (24)

Table 3. Results from questionnaires (Tukey–Kramer method and significant difference: *5%)

Group	A	B	C	D	E	F
Questionnaire 1	2.57 (0.979)	2.16 (0.601)	3.00*(0.882)	2.06(0.680)	2.31(0.583)	2.00*(0.577)
Questionnaire 2	3.79 (0.340)	3.81 (0.674)	4.05 (0.726)	3.87 (0.705)	3.75 (1.01)	3.67 (1.00)

5   Conclusions

This article proposed a scaffolding system that provided adaptive hints using a probabilistic model, i.e., item response theory (IRT). We first proposed IRT for dynamic assessment in which learners were tested under dynamic conditions of providing a series of graded hints. We then explained a scaffolding system we had developed that presented adaptive hints using the estimated ability using IRT from learner's response data. The system provided hints so that learner's correct response probability was 0.5. We conducted some experiments with the students and obtained four results: 1) The scaffolding system enhanced learner development to increase the learner ability. 2) The system achieved scaffolding with fading. 3) Neither over-instruction nor lack of instruction was effective for learner development. 4) Scaffolding so that learners' correct answers were 0.5 provided superior results for learner development.

We have three plans for future work: A) We intend to increase the number of hints because the proposed system will become more effective as the number of hints increases. B) We intend to expand IRT to one with multidimensional abilities or to Bayesian network because the unidimensional ability model has limitations that are too strict for actual scaffolding processes. C) We did not consider unique features in which the estimated ability was dynamically increased in the system design. Discarding response data from earlier presented tasks might improve the accuracy of estimating a learner's current ability.

References

1. Vygotsky, L.S.: Thought and language, Cambridge. MIT Press, MA (1962)
2. Vygotsky, L.S.: Mind in society, Cambridge. MIT Press, MA (1978)
3. Bruner, J.S.: The role of dialogue in language acquisition. In: Sinclair, A., Jarvelle, R.J., Levelt, W.J.M. (eds.) The Child's Concept of Language. Springer, New York (1978)
4. Wood, D.J., Bruner, J.S., Ross, G.: The role of tutoring in problem solving. Journal of Child Psychiatry and Psychology 17(2), 89–100 (1976)
5. Stone, C.A.: The metaphor of scaffolding: Its utility for the field of learning disabilities. Journal of Learning Disabilities 31, 344–364 (1998)
6. Brown, A., Ferrara, R.: Diagnosing zones of proximal development. In: Wertsch, J. (ed.) Culture, Communication, and Cognition: Vygotskian Perspectives, pp. 273–305. Cambridge University Press, Cambridge (1985)
7. Campione, J.C.: Assisted assessment: A taxonomy of approaches and an outline of strengths and weaknesses. Journal of Learning Disabilities 22, 151–165 (1989)
8. Collins, A., Brown, J.S., Newman, S.E.: Cognitive apprenticeship: Teaching the craft of reading, writing and mathematics (Technical Report No. 403). Center for the Study of Reading, University of Illinois, BBN Laboratories, Cambridge, January 1987
9. Pea, R.D.: Practices of distributed intelligence and designs for education. In: Salomon, G. (ed.) Distributed Cognitions, pp. 47–87. Lawrence Erlbaum Associates Inc., Hillsdale (1993)

10. Bell, P., Davis, E.A.: Designing mildred: scaffolding students' reflection and argu-
    mentation using a cognitive software guide. In: Fishman, B., O'Connor-Diveelbiss,
    S.F. (eds.) International Conference of Learning Sciences, pp. 142–149. Lawrence
    Erlbaum Associates, Mahwah (2000)
11. Davis, E.A., Linn, M.C.: Scaffolding students' knowledge integration: Prompts for
    reflection in KIE. International Journal of Science Education **22**, 819–837 (2000)
12. Wood, D.: Scaffolding contingent tutoring and computer-supported learning. Inter-
    national Journal of Artificial Intelligence in Education **12**, 280–292 (2001)
13. Reiser, B.J.: Scaffolding Complex Learning: The mechanisms of structuring and
    problematizing student work. The Journal of Learning Science **13**(3), 273–304
    (2004)
14. Tabak, I.: Synergy: A complement to emerging patterns of distributed scaffolding.
    The Journal of the Learning Science **13**(3), 305–335 (2004)
15. Quintana, C., Reiser, B.J., Davis, E.A., Krajcik, J., Fretz, E., Duncan, R.G.,
    Kyza, E.: A scaffolding design framework for software to support science inquiry.
    The Journal of the Learning Science **13**(3), 337–386 (2004)
16. Rittle-Johnson, B., Koedinger, K.R.: Designing knowledge scaffolds to support
    mathematical problem solving. Cognition and Instruction **23**(3), 313–349 (2005)
17. Pea, R.: The social and technological dimensions of scaffolding and related theo-
    retical concepts for learning, education, and human activity. The Journal of the
    Learning Science **13**(3), 423–451 (2004)
18. Lord, F.M.: Applications of item response theory to practical testing problems.
    Lawrence Erlbaum Associates, Inc., Mahwah (1980)
19. Samejima, F.: Estimation of latent ability using a response pattern of graded scores,
    Psychometric Monograph (17) (1969)

Understanding Students' Use of Code-Switching in a Learning by Teaching Technology

Evelyn Yarzebinski[1](✉), Amy Ogan[1], Ma. Mercedes T. Rodrigo[2], and Noboru Matsuda[1]

[1] Human-Computer Interaction Institute, Carnegie Mellon University, Pittsburgh, USA
{eey2,aeo,noboru.matsuda}@cs.cmu.edu
[2] Department of Information Systems and Computer Science,
Ateneo de Manila University, Quezon City, Philippines
mrodrigo@ateneo.edu

Abstract. Personalized learning systems have shown significant learning gains when used in formal classroom teaching. Systems that use pedagogical agents for teaching have become popular, but typically their design does not account for multilingual classrooms. We investigated one such system in classrooms in the Philippines to see if and how students used code-switching when providing explanations of algebra problem solving. We found significant amounts of code-switching and explored cognitive and social factors such as explanation quality and affective valence that serve as evidence for code-switching motivations and effects. These results uncover complex social and cognitive interactions that occur during learning interactions with a virtual peer, and call for more affordances to support multilingual students.

Keywords: Teachable agents · Personalized learning systems · Self-explanations · Code-switching

1 Introduction

Personalized learning systems (PLS) [1] are an important part of 21st century classrooms, as they provide teachers with technology-based curricula that have been demonstrated to show significant learning gains across many domains. Used in conjunction with traditional classroom instruction, these systems give students the opportunity to receive individualized feedback, hints, and more as they practice solving problems. Many of these systems incorporate natural language technologies in an effort to bring them ever closer to the gold standard of expert human tutoring [2,3].

Such advanced or intelligent educational technology is still overwhelmingly designed by and for a western, Caucasian, English-speaking audience [4]. Even in American classrooms, however, the concept of a majority demographic in schools continues to lessen. While educators can expect that some students enter the classroom as monolingual native English speakers, more students enter the classroom as members of two or more cultures, as native speakers of multiple English dialects, and even as native speakers of other languages.

© Springer International Publishing Switzerland 2015
C. Conati et al. (Eds.): AIED 2015, LNAI 9112, pp. 504–513, 2015.
DOI: 10.1007/978-3-319-19773-9_50

While we know that multilingual students perform better when they are able to choose which of their languages to use in a learning situation [5], monolingual PLSs may not have the affordances and capabilities to support students in this way. Some existing intelligent educational technologies have been designed to cater to some of these excluded audiences [6,7], but the majority do not consider that their design choices make the inclusion of students who do not fit normative values difficult. This is especially important because as PLSs are deployed more extensively and even exported to other countries, they take with them their design principles – and limitations.

One illustrative example of these types of multilingual classrooms is the Philippines, in which students speak at least one of over 150 regional languages at home in addition to the common language, Filipino [8]. Since the Philippines is a multilingual country but retains English as a language of instruction, it provides an interesting testbed for the cross-cultural investigation of PLSs, as language translation is not a strict requirement for deployment. In fact, in a systematic review of AIED and ITS papers over the last four years, [9] found that the Philippines was one of the highest producers of ITS research outside of the World Bank's list of high-income nations.

With English often as the sole language of instruction on frequently deployed PLSs [9], students in these contexts may need to choose between their native language of cognition and their language of interaction with a given PLS. Previous research in written tasks involving one's second language has shown that bilingual students chose to use their mother tongue double to triple the amount of time over their second language when performing a math reasoning task, regardless of whether that task had high or low cognitive demands [10]. Despite this evidence from even simple written tasks, PLSs have not typically been designed to address these concerns, even as they become more widely deployed on a global scale. In fact, little prior research has investigated student language use in such systems. It is not known what language students choose to use in a PLS or why. However, this information is a critical component for designers of systems that allow for natural language input, and may even impact those that simply provide content in English.

In this paper, we report on an investigation into the cognitive and social underpinnings of students' interactions with a specific PLS deployed in the Philippines, particularly what language they chose to use and how they positioned themselves towards the pedagogical agent used in the system. We found that students did indeed switch between the language of instruction and their home language, with low prior knowledge students using less English. Student ability was additionally a factor in the affective quality of their language use. We report on these findings below, which together suggest that students may be code-switching to avoid face-threatening situations or to express their frustration with the system – findings that have implications for the design of systems that will be deployed in multi-language contexts.

2   Background and Related Work

The educational technology we deployed in this investigation is SimStudent [11], a machine-learning based system that employs the concept of learning by teaching. In this system, students use an equation-solving interface to "teach" algebra to Stacy, who is an onscreen pedagogical agent introduced to the students as a peer learner. Students decide what problem Stacy should solve and then, after typing it in the interface, lead her through the process step by step, confirming or rejecting her problem steps, or providing the next step if she has no idea what to do next. Stacy asks a number of contextually-relevant questions in order to elicit deeper thinking from the student, such as questions like: "Why did you choose $3x+5 = 9x-2$ for the problem?" and "How did you know to divide 3?". The student's goal is to tutor Stacy well enough to pass all 4 sections of a quiz given by the system. This system has previously been successfully used in studies in U.S. classrooms [11].

We believe that SimStudent is a representative PLS for study in multilingual classrooms because it allows for natural language input in the form of self-explanation (SE) and always responds with an "Okay!," regardless of the language of input or its content (students, however, may believe that the system more deeply parses their input). A system which focuses on learning with a pedagogical agent also creates an interesting potential for deeper social issues to arise in students' language use, since such systems are intended to simulate human interaction in such a way that students feel they are engaging with a virtual "person" they might care about [12, 13]. Previous research with SimStudent indicates that students do indeed treat Stacy as a social being, using language with the agent that is very similar to that of human friends [14, 15]. SimStudent has also been evaluated previously in the Philippines [16], although students' use of multiple languages was not explicitly studied.

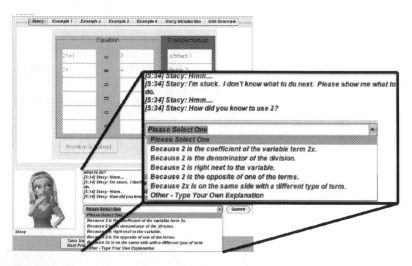

Fig. 1. The SE version of the SimStudent interface with an inset of the feedback module

Alternating between languages within a sentence or conversation is known as code-switching, a common phenomenon that occurs in speakers of multiple dialects or languages as they navigate their multiple linguistic representations of the world around them. Though there is debate in the linguistics field about code-switching vs. code-mixing (as highlighted in [17]), we use the term 'code-switching' (CS) for these analyses. There are many ways one can define instances of CS; we operationalize it here to mean the use of at least one word of Filipino in a SE intended for an English-only system. We use the term CS to indicate students are choosing to switch from using the expected input language (English) to a language they were told that Stacy did not understand (Filipino).

In general, there are many complex reasons why someone might choose to use CS. Ritchie & Bhatia [17] discuss four broad motivations: social and interpersonal dynamics, compartmentalizing particular language use only for certain topics (e.g., if words for particular math concepts are not known in one language), indicating additional pragmatic meaning like emphasis or vagueness, and social acceptability of using a particular language in a given context. To further expand on the social dynamics described by [17], CS can also function as a broad label to include people part of an 'in-group' or exclude an 'out-group', based on whether a particular person can understand what is being said [18].

This subtle, but powerful way to demonstrate inclusion and exclusion has the ability to cause friction within groups, especially in situations with speakers of a diverse number of languages. CS in the Philippines is an especially tricky matter. More than 150 languages are spoken around the country, and classroom language policy in the Philippines has historically been the subject of much debate between educational researchers and government leadership. Despite President Arroyo declaring in 2003 that from as young as Grade 3 the medium of instruction for mathematics would be English only, research in Philippines classrooms (as in other multilingual classrooms) has indicated that gains in mathematic problem solving are greater when teaching a student in her native language - whether that language is English or Filipino - than in her second language [19]. A new policy was enacted beginning with the 2012-2013 school year mandating mother-tongue based instruction in grades K-3, but starting in Grade 4, English and Filipino would both be used as mediums of class instruction, with English mandated for math classes [20]. Our dataset was collected prior to this new policy. Based on the language situation in the Philippines, the structure of our technology, and prior literature, we believe there are several viable explanations for why some students may choose to use CS when providing SEs to SimStudent:

Cognitive Explanations.
1. *Cognitive load reduction* [18]: students may use Filipino to express math concepts that they are unable to express as well in English.
2. *Knowledge activation* [18]: students may employ CS when using particular math concepts if they were learned in a specific language.

Social Explanations.
3. *Rapport building* [18]: if students believe that the system understands their home language, they may use it to build feelings of solidarity or teamwork.
4. *Face threat reduction* [18]: students may answer in a language they believe the system cannot understand, to reduce feelings of shame or inadequacy about being wrong or uncertain in front of a partner.
5. *Frustration with own knowledge* [21]: use of affective language is more strongly linked to one's native rather than second language, so students may use their native tongue to express negativity if they do not feel self-efficacious about their tutoring.
6. *Frustration with partner* [18]: students may blame the system for errors and exclude the agent from the conversation by using their native language.

Alternate explanations posed in the literature for CS, like 'an attempt to be globally-minded,' are unlikely to apply given that the direction of CS in this student population is from the more global, English, to the less common, Filipino. In this paper, we investigate which of the six explanations above have merit.

3   Research Questions

To better understand which explanations have merit, we ask the following research questions regarding students' interactions with Stacy, formulated around factors contained in each of the hypotheses:

RQ1) To what extent do students use CS in a natural language-based PLS?
RQ2) Does a student's prior knowledge affect the likelihood of CS?
RQ3) What content are students expressing via CS?
    a) Is student CS associated with math content?
    b) Is student CS associated with negative affect?

4   Methodology

The data we use to examine these questions was collected as part of a study run as a class-level randomized study in five classrooms in Manila, Philippines during students' normally scheduled algebra classes. Students were assigned to one of two versions of SimStudent: (1) the Baseline condition, in which students tutor Stacy or (2) the Self Explanation (SE) condition, which additionally prompted the student to provide a SE after some specific actions, such as the student entering a new problem, indicating that one of Stacy's suggested next steps was not correct, or providing the next step if Stacy has trouble. The Baseline condition only allowed students to help Stacy with numerical responses, while in the SE condition students could either choose a SE from a pre-populated menu or elect instead to type in their own SE in a text box. Since we were investigating cognitive and social implications of students' interactions with Stacy, we focused only on the students in the SE condition (who were able to type SEs in natural language). All of the pre-populated menu SEs were only in English, as seen in Fig 1.

Prior to tutoring, students were given a pretest consisting of 5 sections that tested declarative and conceptual knowledge. In this analysis we focus on the conceptual knowledge, because SEs are strongly linked to conceptual learning [22]. After a 3 day intervention, students received an isomorphic posttest [11]. Overall, 131 students took the pretest, posttest, and used SimStudent: 52 Baseline condition students and 78 Self-Explanation condition students. We focus on these 78 students below.

We coded each SE (N = 1810) for the binary categories of CS (Yes or No) and Valence (Non-negative or Negative), and a 6-level category of Quality (labels marking level of mathematic relevance). CS was labeled as Yes for input that included at least one word in Filipino. A Negative label was given to input that e.g., showed frustration or anger or used caps lock (shouting). To decide Quality, 3 coders used a manual that specified whether SEs contained particular content, specifically, (a) a conceptual link; (b) a procedural link; (c) contextually-related, but without having conceptual or procedural links; (d) expression of uncertainty; or (e) a nonsense response or one that was completely unrelated to math. The coding schemes for Valence and Quality are described in full in [16]. Cohen's Kappa was computed for these three code categories: κ(CS)=98.9%, κ(Valence)=68.1%, and κ(Quality)=82.5%. A label of Source noted whether an SE was a pre-existing menu item or was typed in by the student. Source was automatically derived; there is no reported coding scheme or reliability. Some results from this Philippines study were previously published in [16], but the CS data has not been investigated.

5   Results

Below, we describe results from the three research questions which we analyzed using paired t-tests or independent samples t-tests, as appropriate.

RQ1 – To what extent do students use CS in a natural language-based PLS? We first investigated whether students used CS in SimStudent. It is important to note that when students asked if Stacy understood Filipino, the native Filipino experimenters recommended that they provide English SEs to Stacy. Per student, the mean number of SEs prompted by the system was 22.9 (SD = 16.0), of which students elected to provide an average of 15.2 (SD = 12.6) SEs in natural language. Seventy-four of the seventy-eight students (94.9%) typed at least one SE in natural language, while four students used only menu SEs. Of the seventy-four who used natural language, we found that a full 26% provided at least one CS SE; that is, SEs that included at least one word in Filipino. On average, these students who did employ CS produced 2.25 (SD = 1.5) CS SEs.

RQ2 – Does a student's prior knowledge affect the likelihood of CS? We investigated which types of students might be more likely to demonstrate CS behaviors. One such factor suggested by our six hypotheses was student ability. We thus performed a pretest median split to differentiate between high prior knowledge (PK) students and low PK students. This enables us to compare successful and struggling students and the different types and amounts of SEs they gave. The median split occurred at a pretest score of 34%, with 39 students both above and below the split.

We compared the conceptual learning gains (defined as (posttest-pretest)/(1-pre)) of these groups to ensure that they were indeed different from each other. Students in the low PK group did have a significantly higher conceptual normalized gain than students in the high PK group: low PK students showed significant conceptual pretest-posttest improvement, but high PK students did not (see Table 1). Given that between-group differences in conceptual learning existed, we could then continue to look at whether they used language differently.

Table 1. Test scores

Measure	Group	Mean (SD)	t	Cohen's d	df
Conceptual	High PK	-0.05 (0.34)	1.97*	0.50	62[a]
Normalized	Low PK	0.08 (0.20)			
Gain					
Number of	High PK	0.54 (1.27)	0.27	0.06	76
CS SEs	Low PK	0.62 (1.21)			
Number of	High PK	18.10	-2.61*	-0.60	76
English-only	Low PK	(11.32)			
SEs		11.08			
		(12.43)			

Note: a = Levene's Test was significant; DF were adjusted.   * = p < 0.05

Within the low and high PK groups, there was a statistically equivalent number of students who used CS, at 28% and 23% respectively. While similar *proportions* of both groups used CS, we found different *rates* of language use; while students in the low PK group (M=0.62) wrote a statistically equivalent amount of CS SEs as high PK students (M=0.54), low PK students wrote significantly fewer SEs exclusively in English (M=11.08) than high PK students (M=18.10) (see Table 1).

RQ3: What content are students expressing via CS? Is student CS associated with math content or non-math content? Is student CS associated with negative affect? Given the lower frequency of English use by low PK students, we investigated what students expressed when they used CS. When considering the mathematical relevance of students' SEs, half (49%) of all CS SEs were classified as being completely unrelated to any mathematical content (Quality code (e)), compared to 38% of all English SEs. For example, students brushed Stacy off without helping:

Stacy: *"What will doing the problem b-2=5 help me learn?"*
S2-(H): *"basta sumagot ka na lang"* [it doesn't matter, just give an answer]

Another third (31.9%) of CS SEs stated that they didn't know the answer to Stacy's question (Quality code (d)), as opposed to only 2.7% of English SEs. Of the remaining CS SEs (19%), the best example of providing part of a valid, mathematical SE (Quality code (a), (b), or (c)) came from a high PK student:

Stacy: *"What will doing divide 1 accomplish?"*
S1-(H): *"kasi nga parehas silang 9 that what i do is to divide it from both side"*
        [because they are both 9]

We next considered the valence of SEs students provided, as many motivations for CS involve affective behavior. Across all students and all natural language explanations, the mean number of negative SEs was 12.9 (12.0), while the mean number of non-negative SEs was 10.2 (8.8). We then investigated the relative valence of CS SEs, including only students who code-switched (N=20). We found that indeed students provided significantly more negative CS SEs than non-negative (See Table 2).

Comparing by ability, while the low PK group (M=11.31) gave a statistically indistinguishable amount of negative SEs from the high PK group (M=14.51), they gave fewer non-negative SEs (M=7.13) than the high PK group (M=13.36) (See Table 2). For example, S3 – low PK - first provides a seemingly innocuous SE in English, but starts using Filipino in order to insult Stacy:

Stacy: *"Why did you choose this problem?"*
S3-(L): *"because I should teach you first in a easy way. tanga"* [stupid]

while other students stuck completely to Filipino for their insults:

S4-(H): *"wag ka ngang pakialamera masyado ka kcng epal e kaya ang daming nagkakamali"* [stop being nosy. you're such a (expletive), that's why people are making mistakes]

Table 2. Self Explanation Counts

	Groups	Mean (SD)	t	Cohen's d	df
Number of Negative SEs	High PK Low PK	14.51 (13.90) 11.31 (9.7)	-1.18	-0.27	76
Number of Non-Neg. SEs	High PK Low PK	13.36 (8.55) 7.13 (8.03)	-3.32***	-0.76	76
Number of CS SEs	Positive SEs Negative SEs	0.10 (0.45) 2.15 (1.42)	-6.10***	-2.80	19

Note: ***= p < 0.001

We did not compare the relative rates of negative vs. non-negative explanations in low PK students, as the numbers were too low to be meaningful.

6   Discussion and Conclusion

We found that language use is indeed a factor to pay attention to in PLS deployments, as students did code switch while using an English-only system in a classroom with English as the language of instruction. Over a quarter of students provided one or more SEs in Filipino. While identical numbers of high and low PK students chose to employ CS, low PK students wrote fewer SEs in English than high PK students, at first glance suggesting that a cognitive factor may underlie the CS effect. However, CS SEs in general contained less math-related content than English SEs (with 81% containing no math content or coded as "I don't know"), suggesting that students were not simply reducing cognitive load or activating prior knowledge in a language they were more comfortable with. Instead, students frequently used Filipino to make a statement of uncertainty (whether real or feigned) – which they very rarely did in English – or chat off-topic. These two findings point towards explanations that include social features.

Given that students were told that Stacy did not speak Filipino and that they should use English with her, our results likely do not indicate that students were working to *build rapport* with the agent. CS SEs also had a more negative valence overall than SEs in English. Although prior work indicates that learners can build rapport with an agent through teasing and impoliteness to learning benefit [15], an informal look at the exact student SEs in our study argues against this interpretation: e.g., despite being told to use English with Stacy, one student called her out in Filipino for not understanding a previous SE in Filipino:

S5-(H): *"the meaning of that is 'let's go'. ang gago ka "* [you're stupid]

Negative valence may indicate students saw Stacy as part of an out-group, with the fact that Stacy appears Caucasian and speaks English reinforcing her status as a cultural "other."

Of the remaining proposed explanations in Section 2, we see some evidence for *face threat reduction*, as admissions of uncertainty occurred mainly in Filipino; *frustration with their own knowledge*, as more negative SEs occurred in Filipino; and *frustration with their partner*, as many negative insults directed at the system and its math abilities (despite being learned directly from the student tutor!) were in Filipino.

None of these explanations are purely social – they all interact with student knowledge, self-efficacy, and meta-cognition. This is particularly salient when combined with the finding from this same dataset that negativity was significantly associated with lower achievement [16]. While our future work will include a wider student sample and deeper analyses of language phenomena, even these first results indicate that systems may well benefit from detecting alternate language use as a signal to trigger an intervention at early stages, even if the language cannot be parsed or understood. Such interventions could provide cognitive support, addressing students who may be lost or frustrated, but more sophisticated systems might equally address social concerns that can augment cognitive support in a more human-like, effective way.

Multilingual classrooms can be difficult places to effectively implement language policy even without technology. Here we have discussed the investigation of a personalized learning system with students who may speak a different language at home than the language of school. In a first look at code-switching in a PLS, we saw that students indeed made use of multiple languages to express themselves when interacting with a virtual agent, with evidence pointing towards underlying social rather than simply cognitive factors. The complex and critical nature of these results calls for further study and deeper consideration of learning system designs that not only support learners' cognitive needs, but social concerns as well.

Acknowledgements. This work was supported in part by NSF Grant 1252440 and the Pittsburgh Science of Learning Center, funded by NSF Award SBE-0836012. We thank Regina Ira Antonette M. Geli, Aaron Ong, and Gabriel Jose G. Vitug for helping interpret the data, Rex Bringula, Roselle S. Basa, and Cecilio dela Cruz for data collection and logistical support; Kevin Soo and Joel Chan for their advice; and Gierad Laput for translations.

References

1. Schneider-Hufschmidt, M., Malinowski, U., Kuhme, T.: Adaptive user interfaces: Principles and practice. Elsevier Science Inc. (1993)
2. Biswas, G., Jeong, H., Kinnebrew, J.S., Sulcer, B., Roscoe, R.D.: Measuring Self-Regulated Learning Skills through Social Interactions in a teachable Agent Environment. Research and Practice in Technology Enhanced Learning **5**(2), 123–152 (2010)

3. Ritter, S., Anderson, J.R., Koedinger, K.R., Corbett, A.: Cognitive Tutor: Applied research in mathematics education. Psychonomic bulletin & review **14**(2), 249–255 (2007)
4. Henderson, L.: Theorizing multiple cultures instructional design model for e-learning and e-teaching. Globalized e-learning cultural challenges, pp. 130–153 (2007)
5. Webb, L., Webb, P.: Introducing discussion into multilingual mathematics classrooms: An issue of code switching? Pythagoras: Teaching and learning mathematics in multilingual classrooms **67**(10), 26–32 (2008)
6. Pinkard, N.: Rappin' Reader and Say Say Oh Playmate: Using children's childhood songs as literacy scaffolds in computer-based learning environments. Journal of Educational Computing Research **25**, 17–34 (2001)
7. Gilbert, J.E., Arbuthnot, K., Hood, S., Grant, M.M., West, M.L., McMillian, Y., Eugene, W.: Teaching algebra using culturally relevant virtual instructors. International Journal of Virtual Reality **7**, 21–30 (2008)
8. Martin, I.P.: Diffusion and directions: English language policy in the Philippines. English in southeast Asia: features, policy and language in use, pp. 189–205 (2012)
9. Nye, B.: Intelligent Tutoring Systems by and for the Developing World: A Review of Trends and Approaches for Educational Technology in a Global Context. International Journal of Artificial Intelligence in Education. (in press)
10. Qi, D.S.: An inquiry into language-switching in second language composing processes. Canadian Modern Language Review **54**(3), 413–435 (1998)
11. Matsuda, N., Yarzebinski, E., Keiser, V., Raizada, R., William, W.C., Stylianides, G.J., Koedinger, K.R.: Cognitive anatomy of tutor learning: Lessons learned with SimStudent. Journal of Educational Psychology **105**(4), 1152–1163 (2013)
12. Chase, C.C., Chin, D.B., Oppezzo, M.A., Schwartz, D.L.: Teachable agents and the protégé effect: Increasing the effort towards learning. Journal of Science Education and Technology **18**(4), 334–352 (2009)
13. Lester, J.C., Converse, S.A., Kahler, S.E., Barlow, S.T., Stone, B.A., Bhogal, R.S.: The persona effect: affective impact of animated pedagogical agents. In: Proceedings of the SIGCHI Conference on Human factors in computing systems, pp. 359–366 (1997)
14. Ogan, A., Finkelstein, S., Mayfield, E., D'Adamo, C., Matsuda, N., Cassell, J.: Oh dear stacy!: social interaction, elaboration, and learning with teachable agents. In: Proceedings of the SIGCHI Conference on Human Factors in Computing Systems, pp. 39–48 (2012)
15. Ogan, A., Finkelstein, S., Walker, E., Carlson, R., Cassell, J.: Rudeness and rapport: insults and learning gains in peer tutoring. In: Cerri, S.A., Clancey, W.J., Papadourakis, G., Panourgia, K. (eds.) ITS 2012. LNCS, vol. 7315, pp. 11–21. Springer, Heidelberg (2012)
16. Rodrigo, M.M.T., Geli, R., Ong, A., Vitug, G., Bringula, R., Basa, R., Dela Cruz, C., Matsuda, N.: Exploring the Implications of Tutor Negativity Towards a Synthetic Agent in a Learning-by-Teaching Environment. Philippine Computing Journal **8**, 15–20 (2013)
17. Ritchie, W.C., Bhatia, T.: Social and Psychological Factors in Language Mixing. Handbook of Bilingualism and Multilingualism (2012)
18. Sert, O.: The Functions of Code-Switching in ELT Classrooms. Online TESL Journal **11**(8) (2005)
19. Bernardo, A.B.I.: Language and mathematical problem solving among bilinguals. Journal of Psychology **136**(3), 283–297 (2002)
20. Philippines Dept. of Ed. http://ceap.org.ph/upload/download/201210/1714521500_1.pdf
21. Pavlenko, A.: Emotion and emotion-laden words in the bilingual lexicon. Bilingualism: Language and cognition **11**(2), 147–164 (2008)
22. Chi, M.T.H.: Self-explaining expository texts: The dual process of generating inferences and repairing mental models. Advances in Instructional Psychology **5**, 161–238 (2000)

Posters

Improving Learning Maps Using an Adaptive Testing System: PLACEments

Seth Akonor Adjei[✉] and Neil T. Heffernan

Worcester Polytechnic Institute, 100 Institute Road, Worcester, MA 01609, USA
{saadjei,nth}@wpi.edu

Abstract. Several efforts have been put forth in finding algorithms for identifying optimal learning maps for a given cognitive domain. In (Adjei, et. al. 2014), we proposed a greedy search algorithm for searching data fitting models with equally accurate predictive power as the original skill graph, but with fewer nodes/skills in the graph. In this paper we present PLACEments, an adaptive testing system, and report on how it can be used to determine the strength of the prerequisite skill relationships in a given skill graph. We also present preliminary results that show that different learning maps need to be designed for students with different knowledge levels.

Keywords: Learning maps · Skill graphs · Adaptive testing

1 Introduction

Learning maps have been designed to represent what students should know for many domains. Many of these are hand-designed by experts. Several methods have been proposed to refine many of these learning maps. Cen, Koedinger, and Junker (2006) described a process for analyzing multi-dimensional skill maps whereby successive adjustments to a map were analyzed to determine the arrangement of nodes and connections that best fit available data. Desmarais, et al. (2007) presented a framework for identifying structures from students' data and calls these structures Partial Order Knowledge Structures (POKS). While these approaches have their strengths and weaknesses, none of the approaches present a method to determine the strength of the relationships in a prerequisite skill graph. In our quest to find the best methods for improving the predictive and representative powers of learning maps, we observe that one possible method of improving skill graphs is to determine the strength of the links in the graph and to propose changes to the graph based on those strengths. Could we use empirical studies to determine the strength of the relationships between skills in learning maps and hence to determine whether these links belong in the graph? To be specific, we want to determine the strength of prerequisite skill relationships between skills and determine which of the relationships to remove or maintain in a skill graph.

This paper presents an adaptive testing system that traverses a prerequisite skill graph based on a student's performance. We present a brief description of how the

© Springer International Publishing Switzerland 2015
C. Conati et al. (Eds.): AIED 2015, LNAI 9112, pp. 517–520, 2015.
DOI: 10.1007/978-3-319-19773-9_51

system works, the design of the study, our method and the results we found. The paper concludes with a discussion of the findings.

1.1 PLACEments, an Adaptive Testing Systems

PLACEments is a computer aided adaptive testing system which was implemented in ASSISTments, an intelligent tutoring system for middle and high school students. (Razzaq, et. al., 2009) PLACEments presents items to students based on how well they perform on an initial set of questions chosen based on a predefined prerequisite skill graph. Although we currently use a prerequisite skill graph developed based on the Massachusetts Common Core State Standards for Mathematics (2010), the system is designed such that it can use any prerequisite skill graph from which tests can be drawn. The initial set of problems is chosen from the initial set of skills chosen by the assigner of the test. Each skill has one problem chosen from the item pool. When students get an item for a skill incorrect, implying that the student does not have that cognitive skill, the test is expanded by including the problems from the prerequisite skills of the initial skill the student has answered incorrectly. The test bank increases until the grade boundaries chosen at test creation are reached. For a given student, the test terminates when all the skills in the initial set of skills have been tested, and the student gets all the items for that skill correct. If the student is unable to answer any of the initial problems correctly, the test terminates when there are no prerequisite skills remaining to be tested.

2   Methodology

To answer our research question, we ran a study in which the navigation of a skill graph in a series of PLACEments tests is modified for a random sample of students. Figure 1 demonstrates the modifications made to PLACEments in order to answer this question. For those randomly chosen students, a random initial skill (skill 'A' in figure 1) is selected and the students get to answer questions from the prerequisite skills ('B' and 'C') of the chosen skill if they get the initial skill correct.

Fig. 1. Sample navigation of the graph for this study

It is hoped that if a higher percentage of the students in the study answer the prerequisite skills of a given skill correctly, this would suggest a strong relationship between the skills, and hence maintain the link in the graph. On the other hand, if the percentage is below a predetermined threshold, it would suggest that that prerequisite link in the graph would either require further scrutiny or must be removed.

The dataset includes a prerequisite skill graph developed by a Mathematics domain expert. This graph contains skills from the Common Core Standards (2010) spanning grades K-9. The graph, which is used in PLACEments, has a total of 495 prerequisite skill relationships. See http://www.corestandards.org/Math/ for a complete listing and a detailed description of the standards. The data set represented 60 of the 495 prerequisite relationships in the skill graph.

The dataset additionally includes 1272 student responses from PLACEments. Each row in the dataset represents a student's response to a placements test item. That dataset also includes a matrix of item to skill tagging. The responses were from 601 distinct students whose grades ranged between 6 and 12.

3   Results and Analysis

As of the time of reporting this study, data had been collected on 60 of the 495 relationships/prerequisite skill links. Of these 60 skill links, 35 had at least 10 responses. (See table 1 for the complete list of 35 links) We limited the number of responses per relationship to 10 in order to achieve some generalization of the results. The graph in figure 2 shows that three of the relationships had link strength of 0, since none of the students had answered the prerequisite questions correctly even though they knew the post-requisite skills. Two of the links were of the maximum strength (i.e. 1). A larger proportion of the links examined so far has strengths ranging between 0 and 1. As many as 24 of the links have a significantly low link strength as the figure shows.

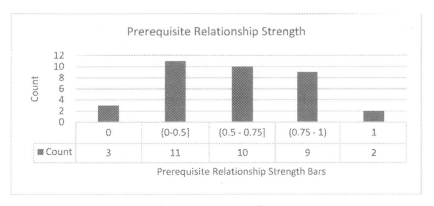

Fig. 2. Prerequisite Link Strength

As the chart in fig. 2 indicates, we can make general statements about the relationships. For three of the relationships, none of the students knew the prerequisite skills even though they performed well on the post-requisite skill. Similarly two of the links can be believed since all the students who knew the post-requisite skills also knew the pre-requisite, suggesting that the link belongs in the graph. There was a larger number of the links for which strengths were inconclusive. Of particular interest are the skill links with strength below 0.5. Those strength values show that a big percentage of students did not know the prerequisite skill even though they all got the post-requisite skills correct. These low numbers suggest that the prerequisite relationship between the skills need to be looked at extensively, and may warrant a removal from the skill graph. It may be safe to assume that the skills with a link strength above 0.5 may be valid and the reason for which the strength is not 1 may be because the items used in the test have high slip rates. However this assertion needs further studies to ascertain.

We did further analysis of the results and found that some of the links were stronger and/or weaker for students with different knowledge levels. Space limitations prevent us from presenting all of that data in this paper, however we can state that the results of this further analysis show that we learning map designers may need to build different maps for student with different knowledge levels.

4   Contribution and Future Work

This paper proposes an intuitive but novel method for improving prerequisite skill graphs. The freely available adaptive testing system, PLACEments, can be used to collect and analyze student performance data on the items tagged by the skills in a skill graph in order to determine the appropriateness of some of the skill links in a given prerequisite skill graph. The Artificial Intelligence Community can take a good look at this process and augment the search for better fitting models with this new technique.

We have also shown that students of different knowledge levels learn differently and as such there should be a different representation of the skills their learning trajectory in a given domain. Our results suggest that curriculum designers may want to think about the needs of these different knowledge levels in the design of curricula.

In future studies we intend to vary the number of problems used to determine a student's mastery of a skill in PLACEments and determine how those changes will affect the search. Additionally more student data will help to strengthen the findings from the study.

References

1. Adjei, S.A., Selent, D., Heffernan, N.T., Broadus, A, Kingston, N.: Refining learning maps with data fitting gtechniques: searching for better fitting learning maps. In: Stamper, J., Pardos, Z., Mavrikis, M., McLaren, B.M. (eds.) Proceedings of the 7th International Conference on Educational Data Mining, pp. 413–414 (2014)
2. Cen, H., Koedinger, K.R., Junker, B.: Learning factors analysis – a general method for cognitive model evaluation and improvement. In: Ikeda, M., Ashley, K.D., Chan, T.-W. (eds.) ITS 2006. LNCS, vol. 4053, pp. 164–175. Springer, Heidelberg (2006)
3. Common Core State Standards: National Governors Association Center for Best Practices, Council of Chief State School Officers, Washington D.C. (2010)
4. Razzaq, L., Feng, M., Nuzzo-Jones, G., Heffernan, N.T., Koedinger, K.R., et al.: The assistment project: blending assessment and assisting. In: Proceedings of the 12th Artificial Intelligence In Education, pp. 555–562. IOS Press, Amsterdam (2005)

Domain Module Building From Textbooks: Integrating Automatic Exercise Generation

Itziar Aldabe, Mikel Larrañaga[✉], Montse Maritxalar,
Ana Arruarte, and Jon A. Elorriaga

University of the Basque Country, UPV/EHU,
Manuel Lardizabal pasealekua, 20018 Donostia-San Sebastián, Spain
{itziar.aldabe,mikel.larranaga,montse.maritxalar,
a.arruarte,jon.elorriaga}@ehu.eus

Abstract. *DOM-Sortze* is a framework for the semiautomatic generation of *Domain Modules* from textbooks. It identifies not only topics and relationships between topics but also Learning Objects (e.g., definitions, examples, problem-statements) included in an electronic document. *ArikIturri* is a NLP-based system designed to automatically generate test-based exercises from corpora. To enrich the Learning Object Repository of *DOM-Sortze* with new test-based exercises, both systems have been integrated. The experiment conducted to verify the validity of the proposal is described throughout the paper.

Keywords: Domain module · Automatic exercise generation · Natural language processing · Learning objects

1 Introduction

The *Domain Module* is considered the core of any Technology Supported Learning System (TSLS) as it represents the knowledge about the subject matter to be studied by the learner [3]. In the approach presented throughout this paper, the *Domain Module* of a TSLS is described by means of an Educational Ontology, named Learning Domain Ontology (LDO), and a set of Learning Objects (LOs) [4]. The LDO contains the main domain topics and the pedagogical relationships among them. Pedagogical relationships can be structural –*isA* and *partOf*– or sequential –*prerequisite* and *next*–. LOs refer to meaningful fragments of the document related to one or more topics of the LDO with a particular educational purpose, annotated with descriptive metadata and stored in a Learning Object Repository (LOR) to facilitate their reuse during future learning sessions.

DOM-Sortze [4] was developed to generate the *Domain Module* in a semiautomatic way from electronic textbooks. While *DOM-Sortze* generates LOs directly from the text of electronic textbooks, other systems generate new exercises from text corpora; they create new exercises not explicitly represented in the input texts. This is the case of *ArikIturri* [2] a system that automatically generates test questions from corpora. In ArikIturri teachers can, for instance, decide the topic or phenomenon to work on, choose the examples (sentences or texts) from which to create the tests, and customize the tests in other appropriate ways.

© Springer International Publishing Switzerland 2015
C. Conati et al. (Eds.): AIED 2015, LNAI 9112, pp. 521–524, 2015.
DOI: 10.1007/978-3-319-19773-9_52

Integrating *ArikIturri* with *DOM-Sortze* would result in a system not only capable of building the *Domain Module* by extracting the contents (i.e. domain topics and LOs) explicitly represented in the textbooks but also generating new LOs that are new exercises, not explicitly represented in such textbooks. The main aim of this paper is to analyse the validity of the proposed integration and to test the quality of the new generated exercises. *DOM-Sortze* and *ArikIturri* share two characteristics: both were initially developed for the Basque language and later enhanced to support new languages, and both allow human supervision. The Basque language was chosen to carry out the experiment presented throughout the paper.

2   Integrating DOM-Sortze and ArikIturri

DOM-Sortze can extract existing LOs from the textbooks. However, it is not able to generate new LOs not explicitly represented in them, for example, new exercises. *ArikIturri*, however, was developed to generate new exercises from text corpora, which are not explicitly represented in the text.

The integration of both, *DOM-Sortze* and *ArikIturri*, would result in a system capable of building a *Domain Module* that entails the LDO and an enriched set of LOs: those identified by *DOM-Sortze* plus those generated by *ArikIturri*. Concretely, the present work is focused on the generation of Multiple-Choice Questions (MCQs). In [1], *ArikIturri* generated the MCQs for manually selected target terms, i.e., human experts were responsible for selecting the target terms to be assessed. These terms were the seeds given to *ArikIturri* to generate the MCQs. In contrast, in this work the generation process is based on seeds automatically identified: the domain topics of the created LDO are the target terms of the MCQs and the LOs are the input texts to generate the MCQs.

The integration follows a three-step process:

1. Creation of the LDO represented in an specific textbook (LDO gathering) and extraction of the set of LOs represented in the textbook (LOs gathering). This step is widely explained in [4].
2. Selection of LOs and MCQ target terms. To proceed with the generation of MCQ-based exercises, the LOs referred to the topics represented in the LDO are selected first. Then, to generate MCQs from an LO, the topic to be learnt is stated in two steps: (a) Extract the keywords from the LO metadata, and (b) Check the list of its keywords, only keeping those keywords related to the LDO and that explicitely appear in the text of the selected LO. Figure 1 shows two real examples of automatically selected target terms, LOs and the generated MCQs. The system selects two different type of target terms: single word and multiword target terms. In this particular example, both target terms are paired with the same LO so that the resulting MCQs have the same source input. For the sake of better understanding, the examples are presented in English.
3. Generation of MCQ-based LOs. To fulfil this task, *ArikIturri* uses the topics and LOs selected in the previous step as the input of the exercise generation

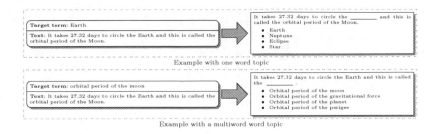

Fig. 1. Examples of two LO and target terms and the generated MCQs

process. All MCQs have a stem (the question part), a set of options that include the target term (the correct option) and distractors (the incorrect options). The stem is the LO containing a blank and the correct answer to the stem is the term of the question. In previous works, Arikiturri was applied with single word nouns and verbs. In contrast, in the present work, the MCQ target terms can be single words or multiword concepts. Thus, the generation of the distractors has been extended to multiword target terms. In all the cases, the target terms are nouns because the topics of the LDOs are nouns. Based on the part-of-speech of the target terms and their semantic features, different heuristics are applied (a more detailed explanation of the methods can be found in [1]). In the case of multiwords, the distractors are obtained for the head following the same strategy as for single word target terms.

3   Experiment

The experiment has been carried out with two textbooks on Nature Sciences written in Basque used in the *Nature Science subject* in the first course of secondary education. *Textbook1, Airea eta ura: gure altxorrak* (*Air and water: our treasures*), has 33 pages and 7,890 words whilst *textbook2, Izarrei begira* (*Look at the stars*) has 30 pages and 8,495 words.

DOM-Sortze extracted 29 LOs from *textbook1* and 88 from *textbook2*. The LOs extracted from *textbook1* covered up 37 domain topics whilst the LOs gathered from *textbook2* referred to 73 domain topics. So, in total, and to generate MCQs, 112 and 365 *LO - domain topic* pairs were obtained respectively.

Two aspects have been assessed to evaluate the integration of *DOM-Sortze* and *ArikIturri*. On the one hand, the authors have measured how the process improved the availability of MCQ-based LOs for each domain topic. On the other hand, the quality of the new generated MCQ-based LOs has also been evaluated.

Regarding the availability of MCQ-based LOs for each topic, the following was measured: (1) the percentage of domain topics for which exercise-based LOs were available in the LOR when using *DOM-Sortze*, (2) the percentage of domain topics for which exercise-based LOs were available in the LOR after using the combined approach, (3) the percentage of domain topics for which there were not exercise-based LOs before but exercise-based LOs were available after the integration process. For *textbook1*, *DOM-Sortze* was able to extract exercise-based LOs for 51.56% of the domain topics. *ArikIturri* generated new MCQ-based LOs for 45.31% of the domain topics. Moreover, 7.81% of the domain topics that had not any available exercise-based LO were provided with MCQ-based LOs after having integrated *ArikIturri*. For *textbook2*, *DOM-Sortze* was able to extract exercise-based LOs for 55.06% of the domain topics. *ArikIturri* generated new MCQ LOs for 49.44% of the domain topics. Moreover, 12.36% of the domain topics that had not any available exercise-based LO were provided with MCQ LOs after the integration of *ArikIturri*.

Regarding the number of the new MCQ-based exercises, a total of 84 and 174 MCQs were created by *ArikIturri* for *textbook1* and *textbook2* respectively. More concretely, MCQs were succesfully generated from 75% of the given LO-domain topic pairs for *textbook1* and 47.67% for *textbook2*. The LOs and domain topics used to generate the MCQs do not require any manual evaluation as their validity is presupposed. A sample of the MCQs was evaluated by one human judge. For each MCQ, the expert evaluated the first six distractor candidates. The human judge had different options: to accept the distractor, to discard it if the distractor could be a valid answer or to mark it as inappropriate if the distractor was too obvious. In total, 168 distractors in *textbook1* and 221 distractors in *textbook2* were evaluated.

In the case of *textbook1*, 58.93% were valid distractors, 18.45% were discarded and 22.61% were marked as inappropriate. For *textbook2*, 71.49% were marked as valid, 8.14% were rejected and 20.36% were considered inappropriate. Thus, the MCQs generated from *textbook2* obtain more valid distractors and the number of inappropriate distractors is similar in both cases.

The evaluation results confirm that the integration of both systems is a promising research line which obtains interesting results. Future work will be done in multiword target terms and generation of new types of LOs.

Acknowledgments. This work is supported by the Basque Government (IT722-13, IE12-333), the Spanish Ministry of Education (TIN2012-38584-C06-02) and the European Commision (FP7-ICT-2011-8-316404).

References

1. Aldabe, I., Maritxalar, M.: Semantic similarity measures for the generation of science tests in basque. IEEE Transactions on Learning Technologies **7**(4), 375–387 (2014)
2. Aldabe, I., de Lacalle, M.L., Maritxalar, M., Martinez, E., Uria, L.: ArikIturri: an automatic question generator based on corpora and NLP techniques. In: Ikeda, M., Ashley, K.D., Chan, T.-W. (eds.) ITS 2006. LNCS, vol. 4053, pp. 584–594. Springer, Heidelberg (2006)
3. Anderson, J.R.: The expert module. In: Polson, M.C., Richardson, J.J. (eds.) Foundations of Intelligent Tutoring Systems, pp. 21–54. Lawrence Erlbaum Associates Inc, Hillsdale (1988)
4. Larrañaga, M., Conde, A., Calvo, I., Elorriaga, J.A., Arruarte, A.: Automatic Generation of the Domain Module from Electronic Textbooks. Method & Validation. IEEE Transactions on Knowledge and Data Engineering **26**(1) (2014)

The Beginning of a Beautiful Friendship?
Intelligent Tutoring Systems and MOOCs

Vincent Aleven[1(✉)], Jonathan Sewall[1], Octav Popescu[1], Franceska Xhakaj[2],
Dhruv Chand[3], Ryan Baker[4], Yuan Wang[4], George Siemens[5],
Carolyn Rosé[1,6], and Dragan Gasevic[7]

[1] Human-Computer Interaction Institute, Carnegie Mellon University, Pittsburgh, United States
{aleven,sewall,cprose}@cs.cmu.edu, octav@cmu.edu
[2] Computer Science Department, Lafayette College, Easton, United States
xhakajf@gmail.com
[3] Department of Mechanical Engineering, National Institute of Technology Karnataka,
Mangaluru, India
dhruvchand@live.com
[4] Teacher's College, Columbia University, New York, United States
ryanshaunbaker@gmail.com, elle.wang@columbia.edu
[5] LINK Lab, The University of Texas at Arlington, Arlington, United States
gsiemens@gmail.com
[6] Language Technologies Institute, Carnegie Mellon University, Pittsburgh, United States
[7] Schools of Education and Informatics, University of Edinburgh, Edinburgh, United Kingdom
dgasevic@acm.org

Abstract. A key challenge in ITS research and development is to support tutoring at scale, for example by embedding tutors in MOOCs. An obstacle to at-scale deployment is that ITS architectures tend to be complex, not easily deployed in browsers without significant server-side processing, and not easily embedded in a learning management system (LMS). We present a case study in which a widely used ITS authoring tool suite, CTAT/TutorShop, was modified so that tutors can be embedded in MOOCs. Specifically, the inner loop (the example-tracing tutor engine) was moved to the client by reimplementing it in JavaScript, and the tutors were made compatible with the LTI e-learning standard. The feasibility of this general approach to ITS/MOOC integration was demonstrated with simple tutors in an edX MOOC "Data Analytics and Learning."

1 Introduction

MOOCs and online courses are by now very widespread and popular [7]. At their best, they succeed at offering open and free opportunities to complete courses offered by some of the best universities in the world and at creating large-scale social participation, Although they are perhaps best known for the use of video lectures, they also support learning by doing, offering either simple activities with automated feedback (e.g., multiple choice questions to test your understanding) or complex activities with peer help, peer discussion, and peer grading. Although these solutions have been quite

© Springer International Publishing Switzerland 2015
C. Conati et al. (Eds.): AIED 2015, LNAI 9112, pp. 525–528, 2015.
DOI: 10.1007/978-3-319-19773-9_53

successful at scale, they have their drawbacks. A single question with feedback on the final answer is a minimal way of scaffolding an elaborate reasoning process [8][9]. Peer discussion and feedback are not always timely; peers may not know the right answer or may disagree, and many learners may be reluctant to post questions and concerns to a large audience [2]. MOOCs sometimes have limited capabilities to support individual learning [4] or personalizing instruction.

Intelligent tutoring systems (ITSs) address some of these limitations. Their effectiveness in helping students learn has been well-documented [5][9]. They provide step-by-step guidance during (moderately) complex problem solving. They can track learners' skill growth and select problems on an individual basis. They can adaptively respond to student strategies and errors. On the other hand, MOOCs support learning in ways that ITSs do not, for example with video lectures, discussions forums, and so forth. Hence, we propose integrating ITS-style learning-by-doing into MOOCs.

To achieve this integration, we see two main challenges: ITSs tend to be technologically complex and not always compatible with browser technology, at least without substantial server-side processing. Also, ITSs are often not interoperable with existing MOOC platforms or other learning management systems. In the current paper, we address these challenges. We present a case study in which a widely used set of ITS authoring tools, the Cognitive Tutor Authoring Tools [1] (CTAT, http://ctat.pact.cs. cmu.edu) was extended so that tutors built with these tools can run in browsers in a way that is compatible with e-learning platforms. We demonstrated the technical feasibility of this approach in an edX MOOC during the Fall of 2014.

2   CTAT/TutorShop and Example-Tracing Tutors

CTAT supports the authoring, without programming, of example-tracing tutors, a type of tutoring system that provides step-by-step guidance in complex problem-solving activities [1]. Example-tracing tutors have been widely used in ITS research and development projects and have been shown to support student learning in a range of domains. CTAT is integrated with TutorShop, a module that provides course management and learning content management services for CTAT-built ITSs. .

For the discussion that follows, it is important to explain how key tutoring functionality is separated and distributed in the CTAT/TutorShop architecture. In this architecture, the tutor interface, the tutor's inner loop functionality, and its outer loop are all strictly separate. By the inner loop, VanLehn [9] means the tutor's within-problem guidance. In CTAT/TutorShop's architecture, the tutor engine (which implements the example-tracing algorithm) takes care of the inner loop. Prior to the changes described in this paper, it ran on the server and was implemented in Java. TutorShop takes care of the outer loop; it personalizes the selection of problems based on a student model [3]. This student model is computed in the inner loop and communicated to the outer loop at the end of each problem, where it is stored between sessions. The tutor interface is separated from the tutor back-end. This is referred to as the tool-tutor separation, with a well-specified API [6]. The interface is launched from the Tutor-Shop at the start of each problem, but after that communicates only with the inner loop (the example tracer) until the student finishes the problem, when the interface updates TutorShop with the revised student model and requests the next problem.

3   Technical Integration and Pilot Test

Given the factored architecture described above, our approach to tutor/MOOC integration involved two key technical changes. First, we moved the inner loop (the example-tracing tutor engine) to the client, to reduce client-server traffic and server load; we did so by reimplementing it in JavaScript. The second change was to make the TutorShop LTI-compliant so that tutors embedded in the host MOOC platform (here, edX) could be launched from the TutorShop and communicate with both the edX course management facilities and the TutorShop (e.g., for storing the student model and other analytics). We implemented the Leaning Tools Interoperability (http://www.imsglobal.org/lti/) tool provider interface in the TutorShop. The availability of Ruby packages for OAuth and LTI greatly simplified our task.

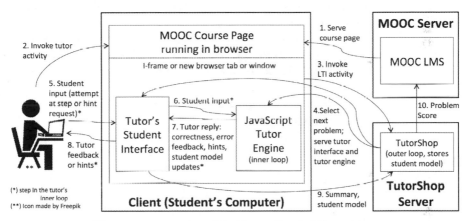

Fig. 1. Overview of the CTAT/TutorShop/edX integration

Figure 1 summarizes the data flow in a MOOC with CTAT/TutorShop as an LTI tool. After the student (1) sees a course page and (2) invokes the tutor activity, the page (3) invokes TutorShop's tool provider URL; TutorShop (4) replies by downloading HTML with the student interface and the JavaScript tutor engine into the page's iframe. Thereafter, whenever the student (5) attempts a step in the problem, the user interface (6) passes the action to the JavaScript tutor engine, which (7) replies with correctness feedback, possibly an error feedback message, and student model updates; the UI (8) displays the feedback, and steps 5-8 repeat until the student has finished the problem. At that point, the UI (9) sends a performance summary with revised student model to TutorShop, and TutorShop (10) updates the LTI score. TutorShop chooses the next problem (adaptively, based on the student model) and returns to (4).

To test the technical integration of CTAT/TutorShop and edX, we tried out simple CTAT tutors in the edX Data Analytics and Learning MOOC. Specifically, CTAT tutors were included in 2 of the 8 weeks as part of the weekly activities/assignments Since this was the first attempt to incorporate CTAT tutors in MOOC assignments, the tutor activities were not required for students seeking to receive a course certificate. Students' performance on these two activities did not influence their final grades. As a result, only a small number of learners completed the tutor activities.

4   Discussion and Conclusion

Our pilot study demonstrates the feasibility of the MOOC/ITS integration between edX and CTAT/TutorShop. Although the pilot study involved a very simple tutor, the integration makes it possible to embed any CTAT tutor in an LTI-compliant MOOC or online course platform. To the best of our knowledge, it was the first technical demonstration of embedding an ITS in a MOOC, an important first step towards tutoring at scale. Testing with very large numbers of participants remains for future work. This technology integration may benefit other ITSs or ITS authoring tools, as some of the same steps might apply. Key is the separation of tutor interface, inner loop, and outer loop, so interface and inner loop can run on the client, while the outer loop is its own server-based web application. MOOC/ITS integration is attractive from a practical and from a research perspective. Tutors could enhance MOOCs by supporting some forms of learning by doing with detailed feedback and adaptive problem selection. The integration may enable MOOC researchers to address research questions about how learning by doing might best supplement other forms of learning in MOOCs and may open up opportunities for ITS researchers to do research at scale.

Acknowledgments. The work reported in this paper was supported by grants DRL-1418378 and SBE-0836012 and funding from Google.

References

1. Aleven, V., McLaren, B.M., Sewall, J., Koedinger, K.R.: A new paradigm for intelligent tutoring systems: Example-Tracing tutors. International Journal of Artificial Intelligence in Education **19**, 105–154 (2009)
2. Baxter, J.A., Haycock, J.: Roles and student identities in online large course forums: Implications for practice. The International Review of Research in Open and Distance Learning **15** (2014)
3. Corbett, A., McLaughlin, M., Scarpinatto, K.C.: Modeling student knowledge: Cognitive tutors in high school and college. User Modeling and User-Adapted Interaction **10**, 81–108 (2000)
4. Mackness, J., Mak, S., Williams, R.: The ideals and reality of participating in a MOOC. In: Dirckinck-Holmfeld, L., Hodgson, V., Jones, C., De Laat, M., McConnell, D., Ryberg, T. (eds.) Proceedings of the 7th International Conference on Networked Learning 2010, pp. 266–275. University of Lancaster, Lancaster (2010)
5. Pane J.F., Griffin B.A., McCaffrey D.F., Karam R.: Effectiveness of cognitive tutor algebra I at scale. Educational Evaluation and Policy Analysis :0162373713507480 (2013)
6. Ritter, S., Koedinger, K.R.: An architecture for plug-in tutor agents. International Journal of Artificial Intelligence in Education **7**, 315–347 (1996)
7. Siemens, G.: Massive Open Online Courses: Innovation in education? Open Educational Resources: Innovation, Research and Practice **5** (2013)
8. VanLehn, K.: The relative effectiveness of human tutoring, intelligent tutoring systems, and other tutoring systems. Educational Psychologist **46**, 197–221 (2011)
9. VanLehn, K.: The behavior of tutoring systems. International Journal of Artificial Intelligence in Education **16**, 227–265 (2006)

Predicting Misalignment Between Teachers' and Students' Essay Scores Using Natural Language Processing Tools

Laura K. Allen[1]([⊠]), Scott A. Crossley[2], and Danielle S. McNamara[1]

[1] Learning Sciences Institute, Arizona State University, Tempe, AZ 85287, USA
laurakallen@asu.edu, dsmcnamra1@gmail.com
[2] Department of Applied Linguistics/ESL, Georgia State University,
34 Peachtree St. Suite 1200, One Park Tower Building, Atlanta, GA 30303, USA
scrossley@gsu.edu

Abstract. We investigated linguistic factors that relate to misalignment between students' and teachers' ratings of essay quality. Students (n = 126) wrote essays and rated the quality of their work. Teachers then provided their own ratings of the essays. Results revealed that students who were less accurate in their self-assessments produced essays that were more causal, contained less meaningful words, and had less argument overlap between sentences.

Keywords: Cohesion · Intelligent tutoring systems · Natural language processing · Corpus linguistics · Computational linguistics · Writing pedagogy

1   Introduction

One factor that is important for students' writing proficiency is their ability to monitor their own performance [1]. Importantly, the accuracy of this monitoring is a key component to successfully navigating any learning task. When students are aware of how well they are performing, they can more carefully select their learning goals and behaviors, which consequently leads to better performance and retention [2].

Previous studies have reported that students' ratings of their own essay performance are largely divergent from the ratings provided by their teachers or other expert raters [1; 3]. This indicates that there may be a "breakdown" in the link between students' understanding of their own performance and more objective criteria for quality writing. Varner and colleagues (2013) referred to these differences as *evaluative misalignment* [3]. They suggested that students may struggle to produce high-quality texts because their criteria for quality rating are not in line with those of their teachers. As a result, they may produce essays that do not meet the standards set by their teachers and not understand why they receive the scores that they do.

The current study investigated the linguistic factors that relate to the degree of misalignment between students' and teachers' ratings of essay quality. We first examine whether there are specific linguistic features of students' essays that predict the magnitude of their misalignment from the teachers. We then conduct correlations to determine whether and how these indices relate to students' and teachers' essay ratings.

© Springer International Publishing Switzerland 2015
C. Conati et al. (Eds.): AIED 2015, LNAI 9112, pp. 529–532, 2015.
DOI: 10.1007/978-3-319-19773-9_54

2   Methodology

The participants were high school students (n=126) enrolled in tenth-grade English courses. They wrote 25-minute essays as practice for the writing portion of the SAT and were asked to rate the quality of their essays on a scale from 1-6. Additionally, teachers rated the essays from 1-6. Linguistic features of the essays were calculated to identify misalignment between the teachers' and the students' essay scores and to assess relations between the essay scores and these linguistic features.

2.1   Student and Teacher Essay Ratings

Students assigned their essays an average score of 4.04 (SD=0.81), whereas teachers displayed an average rating of 3.67 (SD=1.01). Thus, students tended to overestimate their essay ratings; $t(125)$=3.86, $p<.001$, Cohen's d=.40. Further, the student and teacher ratings were only moderately correlated (r=.26, $p<.01$). These results suggest a possible misalignment between students' and teachers' criteria for writing quality.

2.2   Selected Linguistic Features

To examine the linguistic features that were predictive of misalignment, we used three natural language processing tools: Coh-Metrix [4], TAALES [5], and TAACO [6]. We selected linguistic features that fell into four categories: Text length indices, syntactic complexity indices, lexical sophistication indices, and cohesion indices. We refer the reader to 4, 5, and 6 for additional information. We removed all selected indices from the analysis that lacked normal distributions.

2.3   Statistical Analysis

For each student, a misalignment score was calculated by using the absolute value of the difference between the student's self-assessment and the teacher's essay rating. The scores were placed into three categories: *aligned* (i.e., the student and teacher assigned the same grade), *misaligned by 1* (i.e., difference of 1 between scores), or *misaligned by 2 or greater* (i.e., differences in score 2 or greater).

3   Results

3.1   Group Prediction

A MANOVA was conducted using the linguistic indices as the dependent variables and the misalignment groups as the independent variables. Sixteen variables related to lexical sophistication and cohesion demonstrated significant differences between the groups while not demonstrating multi-collinearity with each other.

A stepwise discriminant function analysis (DFA) retained three of these variables related to lexical sophistication and cohesion as significant predictors of whether essay scores were aligned, misaligned by 1, or misaligned by 2 or greater. These variables were *causal verbs*, *word meaningfulness*, and *part of speech overlap between adjacent sentences*. Results demonstrate that the DFA using these three indices correctly allocated 69 of the 126 texts in the total set, χ^2 (*df*=1, n=126) = 25.022 $p < .001$, for an accuracy of 54.8%. The reported Cohen's Kappa was .310, indicating a fair agreement. For the leave-one-out cross-validation (LOOCV), the discriminant analysis also allocated 66 of the 126 texts for an accuracy of 52.4%. The accuracy of these DFA analyses did not vary for low- and high-quality essays. For essays that were rated between 1-3 by the teachers, the model accuracy was 54.7% and for essays that were rated between 4-6, the model accuracy was 54.8%.

3.2   Correlations with Student and Teacher Scores

Correlations were conducted between the selected indices from the DFA and the essay scores assigned by the students and by the teachers. Neither students' nor teachers' scores correlated strongly with indices related to text length, syntactic complexity, or lexical sophistication. However, a number of the cohesion indices demonstrated small effects. For the student scores, four indices demonstrated at least a small (but not significant) effect: *adjacent overlap three sentences content words*, *adjacent overlap one sentence POS tags*, *adjacent overlap two sentences nouns*, and *adjacent overlap two sentences all words*. This analysis revealed that student scores were negatively related to all three of these indices, except for *adjacent overlap two sentences nouns*. For the teacher scores, four indices demonstrated at least a small effect size (only one index was significant): *adjacent overlap one sentence lemma*, *causal verbs*, *adjacent overlap two sentences all words*, and *LSA paragraph to paragraph standard deviation*. This analysis revealed that the teachers' scores were also related to both local and global cohesion indices, albeit different indices than the students' scores.

4   Discussion

The results of our DFA analyses revealed that student and teacher misalignments were, indeed, systematically related to specific linguistic features in the essays written by the students. Students with misalignments produced essays that were more causal, contained less meaningful words, and had less argument overlap between sentences. In other words, these students produced more narrative texts (i.e., causal texts) that contained more difficult words, and less local cohesion. These results may suggest that the students and teachers in this study varied in their sensitivity to certain linguistic properties, which may have driven them to assign different ratings to the essays.

The correlational results indicated that differences in the students' and teachers' essay scores were most apparent at the cohesion levels. These results potentially suggest that the teachers were more aware of the nuances related to essay cohesion, whereas the students may have simply perceived all cohesion indices to be similarly (i.e., negatively) associated with quality. More importantly, however, the results of the correlation analyses revealed that the linguistic indices that were predictive of student-teacher misalignment were different than the linguistic indices that predict essay quality (from both the student and teacher perspective). Previous research studies have shown that linguistic features of students' essays are related to student and teacher ratings of essay quality [7]. However, in the current study, these variables were not the same variables that were predictive of misalignment. This suggests that the properties of essays that may contribute to perceptions of essay quality are different than those that lead students to make inaccurate assessments of their own performance.

Overall, the results from this study suggest that students' difficulties with monitoring performance may stem, at least in part, from their misunderstandings of the criteria for quality writing. Additionally, they suggest that natural language processing tools can provide more fine-grained information related to these differences.

Acknowledgments. This research was supported in part by the Institute for Education Sciences (IES R305A080589 and IES R305G20018-02). Ideas expressed in this material are those of the authors and do not necessarily reflect the views of the IES.

References

1. Varner, L.K., Roscoe, R.D., McNamara, D.S.: Evaluative Misalignment of 10th-Grade Student and Teacher Criteria for Essay Quality: An Automated Textual Analysis. Journal of Writing Research **5**, 35–59 (2013)
2. Dunlosky, J., Ariel, R.: Self-Regulated Learning and the Allocation of Study Time. In: Ross, B. (Ed.) Psychology of Learning and Motivation, pp. 103–140 (2011)
3. Kos, R., Maslowski, C.: Second Graders' Perceptions of What is Important in Writing. The Elementary School Journal **101**, 567–585 (2001)
4. McNamara, D.S., Graesser, A.C., McCarthy, P.M., Cai, Z.: Automated Evaluation of Text and Discourse with Coh-Metrix. Cambridge University Press, Cambridge (2014)
5. Kyle, K., Crossley, S.A.: Automatically Assessing Lexical Sophistication: Indices, Tools, Findings, and Application. TESOL Quarterly (in press)
6. Crossley, S.A., Kyle, K., McNamara, D.S.: Automatic Assessment of Local and Global Cohesion: Implications for Text Comprehension, Coherence, and Quality. Discourse Processes (under review)
7. McNamara, D.S., Crossley, S.A., Roscoe, R.D., Allen, L.K., Dai, J.: Natural Language Processing in a Writing Strategy Tutoring System: Hierarchical Classification Approach to Automated Essay Scoring. Assessing Writing **23**, 35–59 (2015)

Am I Wrong or Am I Right? Gains in Monitoring Accuracy in an Intelligent Tutoring System for Writing

Laura K. Allen[1(✉)], Scott A. Crossley[2], Erica L. Snow[1], Matthew E. Jacovina[1], Cecile Perret[1], and Danielle S. McNamara[1]

[1] Learning Sciences Institute, Arizona State University, Tempe, AZ 85287, USA
{LauraKAllen,Erica.L.Snow,Matthew.Jacovina,
CPerret,DSMcnama}@asu.edu
[2] Department of Applied Linguistics/ESL, Georgia State University,
25 Park Place, Atlanta, GA 30303, USA
scrossley@gsu.edu

Abstract. We investigated whether students increased their self-assessment accuracy and essay scores over the course of an intervention with a writing strategy intelligent tutoring system, W-Pal. Results indicate that students were able to learn from W-Pal, and that the combination of strategy instruction, game-based practice, and holistic essay-based practice led to equivalent gains in self-assessment accuracy compared to heavier doses of deliberate writing practice (offering twice the amount of system feedback).

Keywords: Tutoring · Intelligent tutoring systems · Self-assessment · Metacognition · Writing · Automated writing evaluation

1 Introduction

Computer-based writing instruction provides students with feedback on their essays in the absence of a teacher. Research on these instructional systems has largely focused on evaluating the accuracy of the automated scores [1-2], as well as whether students increase the quality of their essays after receiving feedback [3]. Few studies, however, have investigated the impact of these systems on students' ability to monitor their own performance. This is a significant exclusion, because *monitoring accuracy* is important for durable, long-term learning [4]. Unfortunately, students struggle with this skill, indicated by the fact that they are often largely inaccurate in their self-assessments of academic performance [5].

The Writing Pal (W-Pal) is an intelligent tutoring system (ITS) designed to improve the writing proficiency of students through explicit strategy instruction, deliberate practice, and automated feedback [6-7]. Within W-Pal, students are provided with strategy instruction and practice in the context of eight instructional modules, which contain lesson videos and mini-games. Additionally, W-Pal contains an essay-writing component where students can practice holistic essay writing. This feature contains a word processor where students can generate essays and receive automated summative

© Springer International Publishing Switzerland 2015
C. Conati et al. (Eds.): AIED 2015, LNAI 9112, pp. 533–536, 2015.
DOI: 10.1007/978-3-319-19773-9_55

and formative feedback. Previous studies point to the effectiveness of W-Pal, as training has been linked to gains in essay scores and strategy knowledge over time [7-8].

The purpose of this study is to investigate the efficacy of W-Pal to improve the monitoring accuracy of its student users. Our research questions are outlined below:

1) Prior to writing strategy training, do students provide accurate assessments of their own writing?
2) Does the alignment between the students' self-assessments and the ratings provided by the W-Pal tutor increase over the training sessions?
3) Does the student-system alignment vary according to the type of training that students receive?

2   Method

High school students (n = 87) attended a 10-session study and were randomly assigned to one of two conditions: *W-Pal condition* (n=42) or *Essay condition* (n=45). *Sessions 1 and 2* were devoted to the pretest and posttest, respectively. *Sessions 2-9* were reserved for training. Students in both the W-Pal and Essay conditions began each session by writing and revising one 25-minute essay. Once this draft was complete, they rated their essay, received W-Pal feedback, and were given 10 minutes to revise the essay. Students in the Essay condition then repeated this process (wrote a second essay, self-assessed, received feedback, and revised this essay). Students in the W-Pal condition completed one instructional module (lesson videos and mini-games)

3   Results

W-Pal essay ratings (possible range=1-6) were calculated using the *W-Pal algorithm* (see 2 for details). This score aligns well with expert and teacher ratings of essays [2]. Additionally, students' self-assessments (possible range=1-6) were collected. A *misalignment score* was calculated for each student by taking the absolute value of the difference between the student's self-assessment and the W-Pal essay rating.

3.1   Initial Essay Attempt

On Session 2, all students wrote and self-assessed an essay before receiving feedback. Because students received no training prior to producing this essay, its quality and the self-assessments served as baseline measures of students' abilities. On average, W-Pal assigned these essays a score of 2.35 (SD=0.91), whereas students provided an average self-assessment of 3.75 (SD=0.89). Thus, in relation to W-Pal, students tended to overestimate their essay ratings; $t(84)$=11.36, p<.001. Additionally, the W-Pal and student ratings were not significantly correlated (r=.20, p=.069). The absence of a significant correlation and the differences in the average ratings are indicative of a weakness in students' monitoring accuracy.

3.2   Alignment During Training

Three repeated-measures ANOVAs were calculated to investigate whether essay scores, self-assessments, and misalignment scores changed across training sessions. Additionally, 8 t-tests were conducted to determine whether misalignment persisted for all sessions. We hypothesized that W-Pal training would lead to an increase in essay scores, but a decrease in self-assessment (to account for overestimation early in training) and misalignment scores

The results support our hypotheses. There was a significant linear effect of essay, self-assessment, and misalignment scores across sessions. Essay scores increased, $F(1,78)=6.31$, $p=.01$, whereas self-assessment $[F(1,81)=28.11$, $p<.001]$ and misalignment scores $[F(1,78)=6.49$, $p=.01]$ decreased, suggesting that training promoted better alignment between self-assessments and system scores. Results of the t-tests, however, indicated that there were significant differences between scores across all sessions ($p<.001$). Therefore, students' monitoring accuracy still had room for improvement. An important note is that students did not simply perceive their performance to be decreasing across time.   A repeated-measures ANOVA on students' responses to a daily survey indicated that students' *perceived writing improvement* increased across the sessions, $F(1,74)=23.57$, $p<.001$.

3.3   Alignment by Training Condition

Our final research question concerned the influence of condition on students' alignment with W-Pal. A mixed-design ANOVA on misalignment scores (session as within-subjects factor; condition as between-subjects factor) indicated that, although there was a significant linear effect of session $[F(1,78)=6.49$, $p=.01]$, there was no significant effect of condition ($F<1$), nor interaction between condition and session ($F<1$).

4   Discussion

Results of this study indicate that students were able to learn from W-Pal, and that the combination of strategy instruction, game-based practice, and essay-writing practice led to equivalent gains in self-assessment accuracy compared to heavier doses of deliberate writing practice (offering twice the amount of feedback). Our interpretation is that students' exposure to writing strategies helped them to increase the accuracy of their performance monitoring. Prior to receiving training, students in this study were largely inaccurate in their self-assessments of essay quality. However, over the course of 8 training sessions, students in both conditions were able to significantly increase the accuracy of these assessments. This interpretation is additionally supported by the similarities found between the training conditions. We suggest that the strategy instruction and game-based practice in the W-Pal condition provided students with a deep understanding of the system feedback, which helped them to understand when they were (and were not) meeting the requirements of the writing task. As a result, these students were able to align their self-assessments with the assessments provided by the tutor at the same rate as their peers, despite engaging in fewer self-assessments and being exposed to a significantly smaller number of feedback messages.

These results are important because they indicate that computer-based writing instruction can promote better monitoring accuracy amongst students, which is an important element of transfer learning. In particular, this study suggests that students may not simply be relying on the tutor to provide them with assessments of their own performance. Rather, they seem to be internalizing the information in the feedback and using this to adjust their metacognition over time. Previous research indicates that students' self-assessments are typically inaccurate – therefore, this work has important educational implications, as it suggests that these self-assessments can be enhanced through training with a writing-based tutoring system.

Acknowledgments. The research reported here was supported by the Institute of Education Sciences, U.S. Department of Education, through Grant R305A080589 to Arizona State University. The opinions expressed are those of the authors and do not represent views of the Institute or the U.S. Department of Education.

References

1. Attali, Y., Burstein, J.: Automated Essay Scoring with E-rater V.2. Journal of Technology, Learning, and Assessment **4**(3) (2006)
2. McNamara, D.S., Crossley, S.A., Roscoe, R.D., Allen, L.K., Dai, J.: Natural Language Processing in a Writing Strategy Tutoring System: Hierarchical Classification Approach to Automated Essay Scoring. Assessing Writing **23**, 35–59 (2015)
3. Roscoe, R.D., Snow, E.L., Allen, L.K., McNamara, D.S.: Automated Detection of Essay Revising Patterns: Application for Intelligent Feedback in a Writing Tutor. Technology, Instruction, Cognition, and Learning (in press)
4. Dunlosky, J., Hertzog, C., Kennedy, M., Thiede, K.: The Self-Monitoring Approach for Effective Learning. Cognitive Technology **10**, 4–11 (2005)
5. Varner, L.K., Roscoe, R.D., McNamara, D.S.: Evaluative Misalignment of 10th-Grade Student and Teacher Criteria for Essay Quality: An Automated Textual Analysis. Journal of Writing Research **5**, 35–59 (2013)
6. Roscoe, R., Allen, L., Weston, J., Crossley, S., McNamara, D.: The Writing Pal intelligent tutoring system: Usability testing and development. Computers and Composition **34**, 39–59 (2014)
7. Allen, L.K., Crossley, S.A., Snow, E.L., McNamara, D.S.: Game-Based Writing Strategy Tutoring for Second Language Learners: Game Enjoyment as a Key to Engagement. Language Learning and Technology **18**, 124–150 (2014)
8. Crossley, S.A., Varner, L.K., Roscoe, R.D., McNamara, D.S.: Using automated indices of cohesion to evaluate an intelligent tutoring system and an automated writing evaluation system. In: Lane, H., Yacef, K., Mostow, J., Pavlik, P. (eds.) AIED 2013. LNCS, vol. 7926, pp. 269–278. Springer, Heidelberg (2013)

Predicting Students' Emotions Using Machine Learning Techniques

Nabeela Altrabsheh[(✉)], Mihaela Cocea, and Sanaz Fallahkhair

School of Computing, University of Portsmouth,
Lion Terrace, Portsmouth, UK
{nabeela.altrabsheh,mihaela.cocea,sanaz.fallahkhair}@port.ac.uk

Abstract. Detecting students' real-time emotions has numerous benefits, such as helping lecturers understand their students' learning behaviour and to address problems like confusion and boredom, which undermine students' engagement. One way to detect students' emotions is through their feedback about a lecture. Detecting students' emotions from their feedback, however, is both demanding and time-consuming. For this purpose, we looked at several models that could be used for detecting emotions from students' feedback by training seven different machine learning techniques using real students' feedback. The models with a single emotion performed better than those with multiple emotions. Overall, the best three models were obtained with the CNB classifier for three emotions: amused, bored and excitement.

1 Introduction

Emotions play an important role in the learning process, and, thus, their detection can improve our understanding of the role they play [2]. For example, positive emotions can increase students' interest in learning, increase engagement in the classroom and motivate students [2], and happy students are generally more motivated to accomplish their goals.

Research on the prediction of specific emotions from text is in its early days, with very few studies reported in this area [1], end even fewer with focus on education [6]. Moreover, from these approaches, only some use machine learning in their approach for emotion prediction from text, e.g. [1,6].

In this paper we focus on the prediction with machine learning of emotions relevant for learning from students' textual feedback in a classroom context, which to the best of our knowledge, has not yet been investigated. To establish which emotions are relevant for learning, research evidence is used from previous studies. To investigate the prediction of the identified emotions from text, we experimented with several preprocessing and machine learning techniques.

There are four main steps to create prediction models from text with machine learning: preprocessing the data, selecting the features, applying the machine learning techniques and evaluating the results. *Preprocessing* is the process of cleaning the data from unwanted elements and has been applied in specific emotion prediction, e.g. removal of stop words and stemming [4]. *Feature selection*

© Springer International Publishing Switzerland 2015
C. Conati et al. (Eds.): AIED 2015, LNAI 9112, pp. 537–540, 2015.
DOI: 10.1007/978-3-319-19773-9_56

allows a more accurate analysis of the sentiments and detailed summarization of the results. The most common feature is unigrams which is found in many research works, e.g. [4]. A variety of *machine learning techniques* have been used for polarity and emotions prediction from text. In our experiments we used classifiers previously shown to work well [4,6]: Naive Bayes (NB), Multinomial Naive Bayes (MNB), Complement Naive Bayes (CNB), Support Vector Machines (SVM), Maximum Entropy (ME), Sequential Minimal Optimization (SMO), and Random Forest (RF). The models are *evaluated* using accuracy, precision, recall, F-score, Area under curve (AUC), kappa statistic and error rate.

Previous research on emotions related to learning indicates a variety of emotions. Some studies grouped similar emotions, which may be beneficial as using too many emotions is difficult to classify and may cause conflicts [5]. This, however, could be misleading for the real emotion, such as in the case of grouping disgust with boredom or frustration with sadness [7].

We chose the following emotions in our research due to their importance in learning and their common use in previous research [5,7]: Amused, Anxiety, Appreciation, Awkward, Bored, Confusion, Disappointed, Embarrassed, Engagement, Enthusiasm, Excitement, Frustration, Happy, Motivated, Proud, Relief, Satisfaction, Shame, and Uninterested.

2   Emotion Prediction from Students' Feedback

The data was collected from lectures taught in English in Jordanian universities. The students submitted feedback, opinions, and feelings about the lecture through Twitter. For each tweet, they were asked to choose one emotion from a set of emotions provided (the 19 emotions from the previous section).

The total amount of data collected was 1522 tweets with the corresponding emotion label, one tweet from each student. Some of the emotions appeared more frequently than others.The most frequent emotions were: Bored (336), Amused (216), Frustration (213), Excitement (178), Enthusiasm (176), Anxiety (130), Confusion (73), and Engagement (67).

We experimented with all the emotions combined and then subtracted, in turn, the emotion with the lowest number of data. In total, we experimented with 15 models: all emotions (8 classes); 7 emotions (All except engagement) +other (8 classes); 6 emotions (7 emotions except confused) + other (7 classes); 5 emotions (6 emotions except anxiety) + other (6 classes); 4 emotions (5 emotions except enthusiasm) + other (5 classes); 3 emotions (4 emotions except excitement) + other (4 classes); 2 Emotions (Amused, Bored) + other (3 classes); and each emotion + other (2 classes).

We experimented with two levels of preprocessing: (a) high preprocessing, which includes: tokenization, covert text to lower case, remove punctuation, remove numbers, remove stop words, remove hashtags, remove URLs, remove retweets, remove user mentions in tweets, and remove Twitter special characters; (b) low processing, which includes: tokenization, covert text to lower case, and remove stop words. The high preprocessing was only used for all the emotions combined model, i.e. the 8 classes model. Due to the low results observed for this model, only low preprocessing was used for the other models.

All the models were tested using 10-fold cross-validation; the accuracy, error rate and kappa statistics were used to assess the overall performance of the classifiers, while precision, recall, F-score and Area under curve (AUC) were used to assess the ability of the classifier to correctly identify the specific emotions. For the multi-class models, the metrics for the emotion classes were averaged. The best results for each model are represented in Table 1. These were chosen based on the highest precision, recall, F-score, and AUC.

Table 1. Best models

	Method	Accuracy	Error	Precision	Recall	F-score	kappa	AUC
ALL Preprocessed	ME	0.28	0.72	0.28	0.27	0.25	0.14	0.64
ALL W/O Preprocessing	ME	0.31	0.69	0.30	0.31	0.27	0.17	0.67
7 Emotions+ other	MNB	0.26	0.75	0.26	0.24	0.24	0.14	0.62
6 Emotions+ other	MNB	0.27	0.73	0.27	0.26	0.27	0.14	0.62
5 Emotions+ other	MNB	0.28	0.72	0.28	0.30	0.29	0.14	0.63
4 Emotions+ other	MNB	0.33	0.67	0.30	0.37	0.33	0.16	0.65
3 Emotions + other	ME	0.43	0.57	0.32	0.33	0.30	0.18	0.62
2 Emotions+ other	*CNB*	*0.53*	*0.47*	*0.35*	*0.48*	*0.41*	*0.23*	*0.63*
Amused+ other	**CNB**	**0.65**	**0.35**	**0.23**	**0.56**	**0.33**	**0.14**	**0.61**
Anxiety+ other	CNB	0.66	0.34	0.12	0.40	0.18	0.05	0.54
Bored+ other	**CNB**	**0.66**	**0.34**	**0.38**	**0.63**	**0.47**	**0.24**	**0.65**
Confused+ other	CNB	0.65	0.35	0.06	0.39	0.11	0.02	0.53
Engagement+ other	CNB	0.64	0.36	0.04	0.27	0.07	0.02	0.47
Enthusiasm + other	CNB	0.62	0.38	0.15	0.41	0.22	0.04	0.53
Excitement+ other	**CNB**	**0.67**	**0.33**	**0.21**	**0.60**	**0.32**	**0.16**	**0.64**
Frustration+ other	CNB	0.68	0.32	0.24	0.48	0.48	0.14	0.6

The results indicate that in terms of accuracy the models with a single emotion performed better than the multi emotion models. Accuracy alone, however, does not indicate how well a classifier can predict specific emotions. The precision, recall, and F-score for the emotion classes indicate how well the models perform in terms of detecting emotion. Since precision, recall, and F-score for the emotion class(es) are relatively low, the accuracy is due to the correct identification of the other class (which is also the majority class in most cases).

AUC is the probability that a classifier will rank a randomly chosen positive instance higher than a randomly chosen negative one. It is usually used in machine learning to test how well the models perform, however, it can be noisy as a classification measure [3]. Our AUC results are all relatively low, indicating that our models are not very good at identifying specific emotions. Similarly, the kappa statistic for all model are low, indicating that the models perform better than chance, but only to a limited level. This statistic is comparable across models, regardless of their number of classes, thus indicating that the "2 emotions + other" model is performing better than some of the 2-class models.

When looking at the machine learning techniques that lead to the best identification of emotions (i.e. the recall for the emotion class), Multinomial Naive

Bayes (MNB) and Maximum Entropy (ME) led to the best results for the multi-emotion models. However for the single emotion models, Complement Naive Bayes (CNB) performs best, leading to the highest recall for all eight models.

The results indicate that some emotions can be more easily detected than others. When looking at the overall picture and the balance of the evaluation metrics considered, three 2-class models (in bold) and a 3-class model (in italics) stand out in Table 1. The models are: Amused + other, Bored + other, Excitement + other and Amused + Bored + other.

3   Conclusions and Future Work

In this paper, we investigated different models to detect specific emotion from students' real-time feedback. We found that the most frequent learning emotions in students' feedback were: Amused, Anxiety, Bored, Confusion, Engagement, Enthusiasm, Excitement, and Frustration.

We found that some emotions are more easily detectable than others, i.e. Amused, Anxiety and Bored; however, all models were relatively low in performance. The detection of emotion from text is a difficult process due to the different interpretations of words, as well as the limited data availability; hence further investigation is needed to improve the models.

Future work includes experimenting with other n-grams such as bigrams and trigrams, using learning-related emotion lexicons, and investigating the relation between learning emotions and sentiment polarity.

References

1. Danisman, T., Alpkocak, A.: Feeler: Emotion classification of text using vector space model. Convention Communication, Interaction and Social Intelligence **1**, 53–59 (2008)
2. D'Mello, S., Jackson, T., Craig, S., Morgan, B., Chipman, P., White, H., Person, N., Kort, B., el Kaliouby, R., Picard, R., et al.: Autotutor detects and responds to learners affective and cognitive states. In: Workshop on Emotional and Cognitive Issues at the International Conference on Intelligent Tutoring Systems (2008)
3. Hanczar, B., Hua, J., Sima, C., Weinstein, J., Bittner, M., Dougherty, E.R.: Small-sample precision of roc-related estimates. Bioinformatics **26**(6), 822–830 (2010)
4. Kaur, J., Saini, J.R.: Emotion detection and sentiment analysis in text corpus: a differential study with informal and formal writing styles. International Journal of Computer Applications **101**(9), 1–9 (2014)
5. Kort, B., Reilly, R., Picard, R.W.: An affective model of interplay between emotions and learning: Reengineering educational pedagogy-building a learning companion. In: Advanced Learning Technologies, pp. 43–436. IEEE Computer Society (2001)
6. Tian, F., Gao, P., Li, L., Zhang, W., Liang, H., Qian, Y., Zhao, R.: Recognizing and regulating e-learners emotions based on interactive chinese texts in e-learning systems. Knowledge-Based Systems **55**, 148–164 (2014)
7. Tian, F., Zheng, Q., Zheng, D.: Mining patterns of e-learner emotion communication in turn level of chinese interactive texts: Experiments and findings. In: Computer Supported Cooperative Work in Design (CSCWD), pp. 664–670. IEEE (2010)

Using Artificial Neural Networks to Identify Learning Styles

Jason Bernard[1(✉)], Ting-Wen Chang[2], Elvira Popescu[3], and Sabine Graf[1]

[1] Athabasca University, Athabasca, Canada
`c.j.bernard@ieee.org`, `sabineg@athabascau.ca`
[2] Beijing Normal University, Beijing, China
`tingwenchang@bnu.edu.cn`
[3] University of Craiova, Craiova, Romania
`popescu_elvira@software.ucv.ro`

Abstract. Adaptive learning systems may be used to provide personalized content to students based on their learning styles which can improve students' performance and satisfaction, or reduce the time to learn. Although typically questionnaires exist to identify students' learning styles, there are several disadvantages when using such questionnaires. In order to overcome these disadvantages, research has been conducted on automatic approaches to identify learning styles. However, this line of research is still in an early stage and the accuracy levels of current approaches leave room for improvement before they can be effectively used in adaptive systems. In this paper, we introduce an approach which uses artificial neural networks to identify students' learning styles. The approach has been evaluated with data from 75 students and found to outperform current state of the art approaches. By increasing the accuracy level of learning style identification, more accurate advice can be provided to students, either by adaptive systems or by teachers who are informed about students' learning styles, leading to benefits for students such as higher performance, greater learning satisfaction and less time required to learn.

Keywords: Artificial neural network · Felder-silverman learning style model · Identification of learning styles

1   Introduction

Adaptive mechanisms may be used to personalize content to students based on different characteristics such as their learning styles, knowledge level, cognitive traits, and others. Although there is some controversy on the use of learning styles, especially in technology enhanced learning several benefits were found when adapting courses to learning styles of students [e.g., 1,2]. However, identifying learning styles in a reliable and non-intrusive way is still an open issue. In order to avoid disadvantages of

---

The authors acknowledge the support of Alberta Innovates Technology Futures, NSERC, and Athabasca University.

C. Conati et al. (Eds.): AIED 2015, LNAI 9112, pp. 541–544, 2015.
DOI: 10.1007/978-3-319-19773-9_57

questionnaires such as additional time that students need to spend and the influence of factors such as lack of motivation to fill out the questionnaire, over the past few years, research has been conducted on automatic approaches where the behavior of students is analyzed to identify their learning styles automatically. Such approaches use either an artificial/computational intelligence technique [e.g., 3,4,5] or are based on rules retrieved from literature [e.g., 6,7]. Current approaches achieve results that are typically lower than 80% of precision, with most results being around 70% or even lower.

In this paper, we introduce LSID-ANN, a novel approach using artificial neural networks to identify students' learning styles based on the Felder-Silverman learning style model (FSLSM) [8]. While there exist many learning style models, we selected the FSLSM due to several advantages of this model, such as describing learning styles in much detail and using scales to represent the strength of learning style preferences instead of learner types. To do so, FSLSM uses four dimensions (active/reflective (A/R), sensing/intuitive (S/I), visual/verbal (V/V) and sequential/global (S/G)), where a learner has a preference on each of these four dimensions. Furthermore, FSLSM is one of the most often used learning style models in technology enhanced learning and considered as one of the best models to use in adaptive systems [9,10]. Besides focuses on achieving highly accurate results, LSID-ANN also aims at providing a solution that is generalizable, so that it can be used in different learning systems.

The remainder of the paper is structured as follows: Section 2 provides a brief overview on how the artificial neural networks are built. Section 3 describes the evaluation of LSID-ANN and Section 4 concludes the paper.

2   Building ANNs to Identify Learning Styles

LSID-ANN uses four artificial neural networks (each for one of the four learning style dimensions) with a 3-layer perceptron configuration.

As a first step to build an ANN, the input values of the ANN have to be determined, which are behavior patterns in the case of LSID-ANN. As our approach aims at being applicable in different learning systems, it was important to use generic behavior patterns. Graf et al. [6] have investigated the use of generic behavior patterns and used such patterns in their automatic learning style identification approach, achieving one of the highest precision results in literature so far. Thus, for LSID-ANN, we used the same behavior patterns.

Next, we need to determine how to assess the output of the ANN. To calculate the back propagation error, the output of the ANN is compared to the learning style as identified by the Index of Learning Styles (ILS) questionnaire [11], a questionnaire that has been proven to be valid and reliable to identify learning styles based on the FSLSM [12]. The difference between the result from the ANN and the result from the ILS questionnaire is used as back propagation error.

The parameters of the ANN were optimized through experimentation using suggested values/ranges from literature. As a result, the number of hidden nodes was set to 1 for A/R, 5 for S/I, 8 for V/V and 2 for S/G. The learning rate was set to 0.08 for A/R, 0.06 for S/I, 0.08 for V/V and 0.07 for S/G. The momentum was set to 0.1 for A/R, 0.09 for S/I, 0.06 for V/V and 0.01 for S/G. The training mode was set to individual mode for all four learning style dimensions. Furthermore, two techniques for reducing overfitting were investigated and used. Stratification is improving results for A/R, S/I and V/V and therefore is used for these dimensions. Weight decay is used for all dimensions with a weight decay of 0.05 for A/R, 0.05 for S/I, 0.01 for V/V and 0.1 for S/G. These settings were again determined through experimentation.

Parameter optimization, overfitting reduction analysis and obtaining final results were done using 10 fold cross validation to ensure generalization of our results to independent datasets.

3   Evaluation

To evaluate LSID-ANN, data from 127 computer science undergraduate students were collected, including their behavior data in a university course and their results on the ILS questionnaire. Only students who spent more than 5 minutes on filling out the ILS questionnaire, submitted more than half of the assignments, and attended the final exam were considered for this study, leading to a dataset of 75 students.

Two performance metrics are used to demonstrate the performance of LSID-ANN. The first metric is SIM, a metric commonly used for measuring the performance of learning style identification in literature [4-6]. SIM divides the learning style values into high, low and balanced regions and returns 1 when the actual (LS_{actual}) and identified ($LS_{identified}$) learning style values are in the same region, 0.5 when they are in adjacent regions, and 0 when they are in opposite regions. SIM values are calculated for each student and then an average SIM value is built to measure the overall precision.

SIM has a drawback of reduced accuracy due to classifying results when the actual and/or identified learning style values are near the region edges. With neural networks, the exact difference between LS_{actual} and $LS_{identified}$ can be measured, leading to a more accurate performance metric, which we call ACC. ACC is calculated for each student, and an average ACC is built to measure the overall precision.

As can be seen from Table 1, LSID-ANN and DeLeS [6] are the two approaches that achieved the best results using SIM, with LSID-ANN outperforming other approaches in the A/R and S/G dimensions and DeLeS outperforming other approaches in the other two dimensions. Since the SIM metrics is not as accurate as ACC and DeLeS is the leading approach using SIM, raw results from DeLeS were obtained to calculate ACC for DeLeS. As can be seen in Table 2, using ACC, LSID-ANN outperforms DeLeS clearly in V/V and S/G, achieves little higher results in A/R and achieves the same results in S/I.

Table 1. Comparison of SIM results

	A/R	S/I	V/V	S/G
LSID-ANN	**0.802**	0.741	0.727	**0.825**
DeLeS [6]	0.793	**0.773**	**0.767**	0.733
Bayesian [4]	0.580	0.770	-	0.630
NBTree [5]	0.700	0.733	0.533	0.733

Table 2. Comparison of ACC results

	A/R	S/I	V/V	S/G
LSID-ANN	**0.802**	**0.790**	**0.840**	**0.797**
DeLeS [6]	0.799	**0.790**	0.788	0.702

4   Conclusions

This paper introduced LSID-ANN, an artificial neural network approach for identifying students' learning styles based on the Felder-Silverman learning style model [8]. LSID-ANN was evaluated with real data from 75 students, showing that it outperforms the leading approach, DeLeS, in three out of four dimensions of the FSLSM and achieved the same results for the fourth dimension. By identifying students' learning styles with higher accuracy, adaptive learning systems can use this learning style information to provide more accurate personalization. Furthermore, teachers can use this learning style information to provide more accurate advice to their students.

In future work, we plan to investigate other artificial intelligence / computational intelligence approaches as well as hybrid approaches for learning style identification.

References

1. Popescu, E.: Adaptation provisioning with respect to learning styles in a Web-based educational system: an experimental study. Journal of Computer Assisted Learning 26(4), 243–257 (2010)
2. Graf, S., Chung, H.-L., Liu, T.-C., Kinshuk: Investigations about the effects and effectiveness of adaptivity for students with different learning styles. In: Proceedings of the International Conference on Advanced Learning Technologies, Latvia, pp. 415–419. IEEE, July 2009
3. Dorça, F.A., Lima, L.V., Fernandes, M.A., Lopes, C.R.: Comparing strategies for modeling students learning styles through reinforcement learning in adaptive and intelligent educational systems: An experimental analysis. Expert Systems with Applications 40(6), 2092–2101 (2013)
4. García, P., Amandi, A., Schiaffino, S., Campo, M.: Evaluating Bayesian networks' precision for detecting students' learning styles. Computers & Education 49(3), 794–808 (2007)
5. Özpolat, E., Akar, G.B.: Automatic detection of learning styles for an e-learning system. Computers & Education 53(2), 355–367 (2009)
6. Graf, S., Kinshuk, Liu T.-C.: Supporting teachers in identifying students' learning styles in learning management systems: An automatic student modelling approach. Educational Technology & Society 12(4), 3–14 (2009)
7. Latham, A., Crockett, K., McLean, D., Edmonds, B.: A conversational intelligent tutoring system to automatically predict learning styles. Computers & Education 59(1), 95–109 (2012)
8. Felder, R.M., Silverman, L.K.: Learning and teaching styles in engineering education. Engineering Education 78(7), 674–681 (1988)
9. Kuljis, J., Liu, F.: A comparison of learning style theories on the suitability for eLearning. In: Proceedings of the International Conference on Web Technologies, Applications, and Services. pp. 191–197, July 2005
10. Carver Jr, C.A., Howard, R.A., Lane, W.D.: Addressing different learning styles through course hypermedia. IEEE Transactions on Education 42(1), 33–38 (1999)
11. Felder, R.M., Solomon, B.A.: Index of learning styles. North Carolina State University (1997). http://www.engr.ncsu.edu/learningstyles/ilsweb.html. (accessed 1 September 2014)
12. Felder, R., Spurlin, J.: Applications, reliability and validity of the index of learning styles. International Journal of Engineering Education 21(1), 103–112 (2005)

Measuring Argumentation Skills
with Game-Based Assessments:
Evidence for Incremental Validity and Learning

Maria Bertling[1(✉)], G. Tanner Jackson[1], Andreas Oranje[1], and V. Elizabeth Owen[2]

[1] Educational Testing Service, Princeton, NJ, USA
{mbertling,gtjackson,aoranje}@ets.org
[2] GlassLab Games, Redwood City, CA, USA
liz.owen@glasslabgames.org

Abstract. Cognitive scientists and assessment developers have long been concerned with creating comprehensive, authentic measures–especially which elicit evidence of proficiency on one or more constructs under conditions of focus and engagement of test takers reflecting their true performance level. This challenge is particularly arduous for complex constructs, including 21st century skills, that can be highly contextualized and involve the interplay of multiple skills. The current work describes the recent development and evaluation of a game-based assessment on argumentation skills, called Mars Generation One (MGO). Our results show that the in-game process data can substantially improve the measurement of argumentation compared to non-interactive multiple-choice tests. Lastly, students' show high levels of engagement and improve their argumentation skills during gameplay.

Keywords: Game-based assessment · ECgD · Argumentation

1 Introduction

There are many indicators that large assessment systems (e.g., PARCC) are increasingly interested in and poised to adopt cognitively-based assessments [1], entailing assessing and reporting on the cognitive processes involved in solving and reasoning about a problem [2]. An important driver is a gradual shift in focus for curriculum and assessment standards from declarative knowledge to the interplay of practices and contexts (e.g., NGSS) and an increased interest in more complex 21st century skills.

The advances in technology and the way people interact with it opens up the possibility to create safe, interactive, and engaging learning and assessment environments to simulate and manipulate otherwise time-, space-, or cost-prohibitive objects and interactions. It also opens up the possibility to record those interactions more directly and continuously as a basis for making inferences about performance. The development of scenario-based tasks and educational simulations are important developments in this direction. *Game-based assessment* (GBA) is another, taking particular advantage of the interactivity and engagement games are built around.

© Springer International Publishing Switzerland 2015
C. Conati et al. (Eds.): AIED 2015, LNAI 9112, pp. 545–549, 2015.
DOI: 10.1007/978-3-319-19773-9_58

Ubiquitously produced and consumed, games have matured considerably as a paradigm for defining, designing, and interacting with systems [3]. GBA is progressing beyond just promises [e.g., 4], emerging as an empirically supported and reasoned approach to learning and assessment [5] based on engaging and compelling experiences. The learning that is so vital for assessment is aligned with the fundamental learning involved in productive gameplay [6]. Particularly, leveraging the development guidelines of *Evidence Centered Game Design* [ECgD, 7] provides educators and researchers with the necessary arguments and principled design practices to produce quality assessment games.

Mars Generation One: Argubot Academy is an original game developed through the collaboration of GlassLab and ETS. Mars Generation One (MGO) teaches and assesses students' argumentation skills through an RPG-adventure-based educational game for the iPad. The design and development of MGO is founded upon the "Reasons and Evidence" section of the argumentation learning progression developed at ETS [8] and leverages the Toulmin [9] argumentation framework. This framework touches on a range of standards, including 21st Century Skills, Next Generation Science Standards (evidence-based argumentation), and Common Core State Standards (ELA persuasive writing and logical reasoning). An analysis of the learning progression was used to identify the sub-skills necessary for successful argumentation within the game environment (called "skill milestones"). The skill milestones were developed as individual actions that map onto the latent argumentation construct and delineate potential dependencies and prerequisites for performance. For example, at a relatively basic level, students must first be able to identify if evidence is related to a specific claim (within an argument) before they can evaluate its strength.

The skill milestones were subsequently selected and implemented within MGO as different game mechanics (i.e., explore, equip, battle) involving aspects of argument identification, organization, and evaluation. Figure 1 portrays an example visual mapping between selected game actions and skill milestone variables.

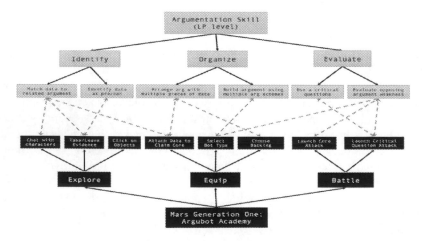

Fig. 1. Example mapping between game mechanics and argumentation skills

The current study investigates the validity of the MGO game. We analyze MGO's predictive validity for a criterion measure and provide empirical evidence for students' engagement with the game and learning during gameplay. We aim to address several research questions: (1) can in-game process data improve the measurement of argumentation skills over and beyond scores from a classical, non-interactive argumentation survey measure; (2) does gameplay improve students' argumentation skills; and (3) do test takers experience gameplay itself as engaging?

1.1   The Current Study

The current data was collected as part of a larger pilot study in fall 2014. Approximately 950 middle school students took part in the study. Due to classroom constraints, the study was designed such that only a subset of students played the game and completed the full battery of measures.

In the beginning students completed a 10-item multiple-choice pre-test, followed by the extensive gameplay itself. This MGO gameplay extended through 5 days of class, after which students completed a 10-item self-report engagement survey [Student Opinion Survey (SOS), 10]. Then, students answered another set of 10 multiple-choice items as the post-test. The two alternative forms of argumentation measure that were used as a pre-post test included a three overlapping common items and several different item types (e.g. interactive "matching" item types). Finally, a subset of student (N=181) completed an 8-item scenario-based measure that is part of the "Cognitively Based Assessment of, for, and as Learning" (CBAL^{TM}) assessment research initiative.

After the data collection was completed, key telemetry actions from the gameplay were linked to the relevant skill milestones. For instance, variables reflective of student's proficiency with identifying relevant data to a particular claim (Strong Cores) or variables related to student's ability to evaluate and critique opponent's claims (e.g., Core Attacks and Critical Question attacks variables) were built. Due to space constraints we do not describe the process and detailed rationale for these variables.

2   Results

A series of stepwise multiple linear regression analyses were applied to investigate whether in-game process data can improve the measurement of argumentation skills beyond scores from a classic non-interactive argumentation measure. The first step in the regression model predicted performance on the CBAL criterion task based only on the multiple-choice pre-test argumentation measure. The initial model indicated that around 15 percent of the CBAL task variation could be explained based on the pre-test (R=.389, R^2=.152, $p<.001$). Adding in-game actions as predictors to the model (steps 2-4) led to doubling the predictive power of the model resulting in a value of R^2=.299 and a multiple correlation of R=.547 (ΔR^2=.147, p<.001). The order of inclusion of in-game variables into the model was based upon the sequence of appearance of these variables within the gameplay. Further investigation of partial correlations for the predictor variables confirmed the importance of in-game actions for predicting argumentation skills over and beyond the performance on the traditional pre-test measure. The regression coefficients indicate that in-game actions related to higher level skills (e.g., Core Attack Not Supporting) account for larger proportions of explained variance on the learning progression than actions related to lower level skills (e.g., Strong Cores; Core Attack Not Supporting: $\beta = .324$, $p<.001$, versus Strong Cores: $\beta = .068$, $p>.05$).

Analyses were also conducted to compare performance between the pre-test and post-test argumentation measure. These analyses were applied to the complete dataset from all students who completed MGO and the pre- and post-test argumentation measures (N=589). Results showed clear mean differences in test-scores with students' performing significantly higher on the post-test ($t(588)=10.779$, $p<.001$, Cohen's $d=0.44$). This finding indicates that students' overall argumentation skills improve following the gameplay.

Finally, we analyzed students' responses to the engagement survey to discern whether students were engaged during gameplay, and tested whether student scores on the two sub-scales, effort and importance, were higher than previously published scale midpoint responses [11]. Results confirmed strong engagement of students during MGO gameplay, and one-sample t-tests comparing average scores on both sub-scales to the scale midpoints showed that scores on both sub-scales significantly exceeded moderate levels of effort and importance ($t(434)_{Effort}=21.089$, $p<.001$, $t(434)_{Importance}=11.432$, $p<.001$).

3   Discussion

This paper described the recent development and evaluation for a game-based assessment aimed at providing sufficient evidence for the hard-to-measure argumentation construct. The game represents an example of emerging Evidence Centered Game Design (ECgD) efforts that substantially change not only how cognitive scientists and assessment designers think about assessments, but also how K-12 assessments "look and feel". The results suggest that a well-designed formative assessment game is appealing to both players and educators and provides robust evidence of proficiency on the targeted domain.

Additionally, in-game actions substantially improved prediction of argumentation skills (as evidenced by doubling R Square in a multiple regression). These findings extend previous research by demonstrating both feasibility of tackling hard-to-measure constructs and 21st century skills within game-based assessments as well as some improvements in criterion validity. We showed examples of evidence fragments for a latent construct that were derived from in-game process data and how better measures can be constructed if process data is used in scoring models. As such, the study presented here marks an important milestone in the transition to more valid and engaging assessments of complex 21st century constructs that involve the interplay of multiple skills.

Large-scale testing programs and audit assessments are currently facing wide-ranging changes as part of a transition towards technology-based interactive tasks involving complex skills. With this in mind, our study aims to improve how we measure what students know and can do and bear the potential of building enhanced accountability metrics for policymakers and educators.

References

1. Bennett, R.E.: Cognitively Based Assessment of, for, and as Learning (CBAL): A Preliminary Theory of Action for Summative and Formative Assessment. Measurement: Interdisciplinary Research & Perspectives 8(2–3), 70–91 (2010)
2. Leighton, J.P., Gierl, M.J.: The learning sciences in educational assessment: The role of cognitive models. Cambridge University Press (2011)
3. Salen, K., Zimmerman, E.: Rules of Play: Game Design Fundamentals. The MIT Press, Cambridge (2003)
4. Klopfer, E., Osterweil, S., Salen, K.: Moving Learning Games Forward: Obstacles, Opportunities & Openness (2009). http://education.mit.edu/papers/MovingLearningGames Forward_EdArcade.pdf. (retrieved July 14 2012)
5. Mislevy, R.J., Oranje, A., Bauer, M., von Davier, A., Gao, J., Corrigan, S., Hoffman, E., DiCerbo, K., John, M.: Psychometric Considerations for Game Based Assessment. Institute of Play, New York (2014)
6. Mislevy, R.J., Behrens, J.T., DiCerbo, K.E., Frezzo, D.C., West, P.: Three things game designers need to know about assessment. In: Ifenthaler, D., Eseryel, D., Ge, X. (eds.) Assessment in Game-Based Learning: Foundations, Innovations, and Perspectives, pp. 59–81. Springer, New York (2012)
7. Hoffman, E., John, M., Makany, T.: How Do Game Design Frameworks Align With Learning and Assessment Design Frameworks? Paper presented at the annual meeting for the National Council for Measurement in Education, Philadelphia, PA (2014)
8. Song, Y., Deane, P., Graf, E.A., van Rijn, P.: Using argumentation learning progressions to support teaching and assessments of English language arts. R&D Connections, no. 22 (2013). http://www.ets.org/Media/Research/pdf/RD_Connections_22.pdf
9. Toulmin, S.E.: The Uses of Argument. Cambridge University Press, Cambridge (1958)
10. Sundre, D.L., Moore, D.L.: The Student Opinion Scale: A measure of examinee motivation. Assessment Update 14, 8–9 (2002)
11. DeMars, C.E., Bashkov, B.M., Socha, A.B.: The role of gender in test-taking motivation under low-stakes conditions. Research and Practice in Assessment 8, 69–82 (2003)

Student Performance Prediction
Using Collaborative Filtering Methods

Hana Bydžovská[✉]

CSU and KD Lab Faculty of Informatics, Masaryk University, Brno, Czech Republic
bydzovska@fi.muni.cz

Abstract. This paper shows how to utilize collaborative filtering methods for student performance prediction. These methods are often used in recommender systems. The basic idea of such systems is to utilize the similarity of users based on their ratings of the items in the system. We have decided to employ these techniques in the educational environment to predict student performance. We calculate the similarity of students utilizing their study results, represented by the grades of their previously passed courses. As a real-world example we show results of the performance prediction of students who attended courses at Masaryk University. We describe the data, processing phase, evaluation, and finally the results proving the success of this approach.

Keywords: Student performance · Prediction · Collaborative filtering methods · Recommender system

1   Introduction

Student modeling is a crucial task in educational environment. We utilize collaborative filtering (CF) methods [5] to predict students' performance. CF is a common technique for generating personalized recommendation. The main idea of collaborative recommendation approaches is to exploit information about the past behavior of users for predicting the behavior of the current user of the system.

We are interested in predicting whether students will succeed or fail in a course that they want to enroll in at the beginning of a term. This means that we have no information about students' knowledge, skills or enthusiasm for a particular course. In this paper, we report on a possibility to estimate student performance in a particular course based only on knowledge of student's previously passed courses.

We utilize different CF methods to estimate the final prediction. We compare the results with the results of our previous approach when we utilized classification algorithms implemented in Weka [7] on study-related and social behavior data about students [1, 2]. The reliable prediction might help teachers to identify weak students in order to help them to pass the course or to achieve better grades. We can also recommend passable voluntary courses to the students and warn them about difficult mandatory courses that they have to pass.

© Springer International Publishing Switzerland 2015
C. Conati et al. (Eds.): AIED 2015, LNAI 9112, pp. 550–553, 2015.
DOI: 10.1007/978-3-319-19773-9_59

2   Experiment

Our hypothesis is that students' knowledge can be characterized by courses that students passed during their studies. Based on this information we can select students with similar interests and knowledge and predict if a particular student has sufficient skills needed for a particular course.

For our purposes, students can be represented with a set of grades of their passed courses and we can obtain these grades from the information system. Textual grades can be transformed into real numbers as follows: A (excellent) → 1, B (very good) → 1.5, C (good) → 2, D (satisfactory) → 2.5, E (sufficient) → 3, F (failed) → 4, - (waived) → 4. The last two represent student's failure; the others represent a full completion. As we have already mentioned, we need to estimate if a student is at the risk. The exact grade prediction is very difficult and thus we aim for less powerful prediction that can still be sufficient. We defined three tasks that differ in granularity of a prediction class: the prediction of the exact grade, the prediction of good grade (A, B) → 1 / bad grade (C, D, E) → 2 / failure (F, -) → 4, and the prediction of success (A,B,C,D,E) / failure (F, -).

In order to confirm our hypothesis, we selected 62 courses offered to the students in the years 2010 – 2013 at Masaryk University. Students without a history in the system were omitted from the experiment. The extracted data set comprised of 3,423 students and their 42,635 grades. Our aim was to predict the grades of students enrolled in the investigated courses in the year 2012 based on the results of similar students enrolled in the same courses in the years 2010 and 2011. Then we selected the most suitable method with its settings and validated it on students' data from 2013.

2.1   Data Processing

For each student s enrolled in a course c in the year 2012, we can construct a similarity matrix with a set of students (S') enrolled in the course c in the year 2010 or 2011. For each student $s' \in S'$ we can compute a similarity to the student s based on the courses that they passed (b_n). An example of such a matrix can be seen in Table 1. Values marked as X means, that the student did not attend the course. Values $1 - 4$ define the students' obtained grades. The symbol $?$ represents the predicted grade of the investigated student s enrolled in the course c.

Table 1. Example of a similarity matrix and computation of used similarity methods

Students/Courses	b_1	b_2	b_3	c	MAE	COS	JC	HM
s	1	X	3	?				
s'_1	2.5	X	X	2	1.5	0.93	1/2	0.65
s'_2	2	2.5	2	3	1	0.89	2/3	0.76
s'_3	X	3	2	1.5	1	0.83	1/3	0.47

For the purpose of computing the similarity between students, the following four methods were employed. *Mean absolute error (MAE)* and *cosine similarity (COS)* measure the similarity of grades of students' shared courses. *Jaccard's coefficient (JC)* defines the ratio of shared and different courses. Since we supposed that student knowledge can be represented using the knowledge about their passed courses, it was very important to calculate the overlap of students' courses. We supposed that the similarity of grades as well as the overlap of courses is crucial for the prediction. Therefore we also calculated the *harmonic mean (HM) of cosine similarity and Jaccard's coefficient.*

Now we need to select an appropriate neighborhood consisting of the most similar students to the investigated student. We selected several methods to compute the suitable neighborhood:

- Top x, where x = 1; 25; 35; 50; (an analysis [4] indicates that a neighborhood of 20 to 50 neighbors is optimal in general).
- More similar than a threshold y; y was selected to cover the whole interval (avg(sim), max(sim)] with respect to the similarity function: MAE: 0.5; 0.3; 0.1; COS: 0.96; 0.98; 0.99; JC: 0.4; 0.6; 0.8; HM: 0.5; 0.7; 0.9.
- We also utilized the idea of a baseline user [6] and selected only those students into the neighborhood that were more similar to the investigated one than the investigated one to the baseline user.

When the neighborhood was defined, we could make a prediction. We used different calculations to estimate the grades from the grades of students in the neighborhood: mean value, median, value of the majority class. We also utilized significance weighting [3], and lowering the importance of students with only few co-ratings [4].

3   Results

We compared the predicted grades with the real grades of students enrolled in the courses offered in the year 2012. Using all the mentioned settings, we have retrieved more than 70 results per the course and the task. We selected the most suitable method in average for each task. Then we calculated the success rate for the data from the year 2013. The results were compared to the baseline (a prediction into the majority class) and also to the results on the same data set obtained by our previous approach [1, 2] using classification algorithms (CA) on study-related and social behavior data about students. We computed the accuracy and also MAE because there was a significant difference when we predicted the grade 1 or 2.5 and the student obtained 3. In Table 2, we introduce the comparison of the results of the approaches.

The results indicate that the both approaches reached almost similar results even if they analyzed different data obtained from the information system. Therefore, we consider the CF results to be very satisfactory. The advantage of the CF approach is that all information systems store the data about students' grades unlike the data about student social behavior. Therefore, this approach can be generally employed in all systems. On the other hand, we did not have a prediction for all students because we were not able to find sufficiently similar students for all investigated ones (the coverage was about 78%).

Table 2. Comparison of the results of the approaches

	Grade	Good/bad/failure	Success/failure
	MAE	MAE	Accuracy
Baseline	0.88	0.80	66.71%
CA	0.84	0.61	78.72%
CF	0.69	0.65	77.69%

4   Conclusion and Future Work

In this paper, we used CF methods for student modeling. Our experiment reveals that CF approach is a suitable technique for student performance prediction. The data set comprised of 62 courses with 3,423 students and their 42,635 grades. We confirmed our hypothesis, that students can be sufficiently characterized only by their previously passed courses that cover their knowledge of the field of their study. We processed the data about students' grades stored in the information system and we were able to estimate students' interests, enthusiasm and prerequisites for passing enrolled courses at the beginning of each term. For each investigated student, we search for students enrolled in the same courses in the last years that are the most similar to the investigated one. Based on their study results, we predict the student performance. This approach is not suitable if we have no information about the history of a particular student. It was not the goal of this approach, however, we intend to investigate it in the future.

Reference

1. Bydžovská H., Popelínský L.: Weak student identification: how technology can help. In: Proceedings of the 13th European Conference on e-Learning, pp. 89–97 (2014)
2. Bydžovská H., Popelínský L.: The influence of social data on student success prediction. In: Proceedings of the 18th International Database Engineering & Applications Symposium, pp. 374–375 (2014)
3. Herlocker, J.L., Konstan, J.A., Borchers, A., Riedl, J.: An algorithmic framework for performing collaborative filtering. In: Proceedings of the 22nd Annual International ACM SIGIR Conference, pp. 230–237 (1999)
4. Herlocker, J.L., Konstan, J.A., Riedl, J.: Explaining collaborative filtering recommendations. In: Proceedings of the ACM Conference on Computer Supported Cooperative Work, pp. 241–250 (2000)
5. Jannach, D., Zanker, M., Felfernig, A., Friedrich, G.: Recommender Systems: An Introduction. Cambridge University Press (2010)
6. Matuszyk, P., Spiliopoulou, M.: Hoeffding-CF: neighbourhood-based recommendations on reliably similar users. In: Dimitrova, V., Kuflik, T., Chin, D., Ricci, F., Dolog, P., Houben, G.-J. (eds.) UMAP 2014. LNCS, vol. 8538, pp. 146–157. Springer, Heidelberg (2014)
7. Witten, I., Frank, E., Hall, M.: Data Mining: Practical Machine Learning Tools and Techniques, 3rd edn. Morgan Kaufmann Publishers (2011)

Steps Towards the Gamification of Collaborative Learning Scenarios Supported by Ontologies

Geiser Chalco Challco[1]([⊠]), Riichiro Mizoguchi[2],
Ig Ibert Bittencourt[3], and Seiji Isotani[1]

[1] University of São Paulo, ICMC, São Carlos, SP, Brazil
geiser@usp.br, sisotani@icmc.usp.br
[2] Japan Institute of Science and Technology, Ishikawa, Japan
mizo@jaist.ac.jp
[3] Federal University of Alagoas, Maceio, AL, Brazil
ig.ibert@gmail.com

Abstract. The Computer-Support Collaborative Learning (CSCL) script is an effective approach to support meaningful interactions and better learning. Unfortunately, in some situations, scripted collaboration demotivates students, which makes more difficult its use over time. To deal with this problem, we propose the use of gamification to positively change learners' motivation and engagement. Nevertheless, the adequate application of gamification is a complex task that requires deeper knowledge about game design and their impact on collaborative learning (CL). Thus, we develop an ontology called OntoGaCLeS to provide a formal systematization of the knowledge about gamification and its correct application. In this paper, we focus in the formalization of concepts relate to gamification as persuasive technology.

Keywords: Ontology · Gamification · Collaborative learning

1 Introduction

Despite of the success of design scripts in CSCL, there are situations in which these scripts may cause demotivation. Sometimes, a learner may neglect his personal behavior to get the task completed as the script requests it and, other times, the lack of choice over the sequence of activities may increase the sense of obligation [7]. The demotivation can negatively influence the learner's attitudes and behaviors, degrade classroom group dynamics, and result in negative learning outcomes [3]. Thus, in recent last years, the researches and practitioners at looking a gamification to motivate and engage students in the entire instructional process of a CL scenario. However, gamification can fail, primarily due to poor design [12], because its effects are greatly dependent of contexts in which this technology is applied [5].

In this sense, instead of offering game rewards to perform certain behaviors, our goal is the building of CL scenarios, which make learners decide to do the activities of CSCL scripts using game elements. Thus, we must see gamification as a persuasive technology that influences the learners' activities and how this technology can change

© Springer International Publishing Switzerland 2015
C. Conati et al. (Eds.): AIED 2015, LNAI 9112, pp. 554–557, 2015.
DOI: 10.1007/978-3-319-19773-9_60

the learners' behavior using these scripts. In this paper, we focus on the formalization of the concepts related to gamification as persuasive technology into the ontology **OntoGaCLeS** - *Ontology to Gamify Collaborative Learning Scenarios*. This formalization has been developed using the Hozo Ontology editor [8], and it is available at http://labcaed.no-ip.info:8003/ontogacles. In the Section 2, we present the ontological structure to represent gamified CL scenarios, and we present the conclusion and future steps in our research in the Section 3.

2   Gamifying Collaborative Learning Scenarios

In previous papers [1, 2], we defined semantic structures in which a gamified CL scenario (see Figure 1) was formalized through the concepts: **I-mot goal** as the individual motivational goal of person in focus (*I*); **Y<=I-mot goal** as the motivational strategy that enhances the learning strategy (*Y<=I-goal*); **I-player role** as the player role of person (*I*); and **You-player role** as the player roles of person (*You*). In the new formalization, as showed in the Figure 1, we included the concept of **W(A)-gameplay** to represent the *rational arrangement of gameplays*, where each gameplay defines the

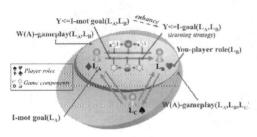

Fig. 1. Concepts and terms defined in gamified CL scenarios

specific manner in which a player (in this case, a learner) interacts with the game components (i.e. point system, badges system, and quests system) [9].

Figure 2 (a) shows the ontological structure to represent gamified CL scenarios. In this structure, the *W(A)-gameplay* as *CL gameplay* contains *CL Game dynamics* playing the role of "*how to play*" to define the CL scenario as game. In this sense, the game dynamic is the run-time behavior of game mechanics acting on player inputs over time [6], and the game mechanics are methods invoked by agents, designed for interaction with the game state [10]. Therefore, the *CL game dynamic* is a sequence of *gamified influential I_L events* that play the role of necessary and complementary interactions. Each *gamified influential I_L event* contents a *gamified instructional event* and a *gamified learning event* to describe how these events have been gamifying using gamification as persuasive technology. It means to use gamification to influence and change the intended learning behavior of CSCL script. This behavior is defined as actions in the instructional/learning events.

According to Fogg's Behavior Model [4], for a behavior to occur, the motivation, ability and trigger must converge at the same moment reaching the activation threshold. In this sense, the appropriate trigger at the right moment tells and prompts the person to carry out the target behavior in a predictable behavior. Thus, in a gamified CL scenario, as showed in Figure 2 (b), the game components are triggers in which the actions done by these components persuade the learners' actions defined in instructional/learning events. The ontological structure to represent this persuasion in a gamified instructional (or learning) event is a *game event* defined as a *trigger event*, where the *game component* plays the *trigger role*, and the *game actions* are related by the relationship "*persuade*" with the actions done by instructors/learners.

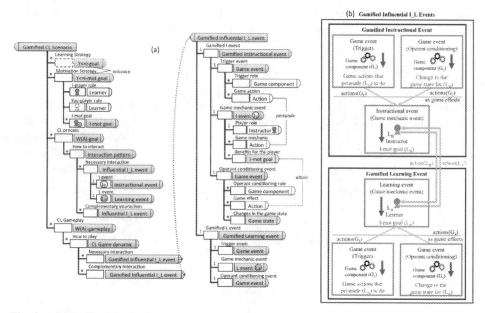

Fig. 2. (a) Ontological structure used to represent gamified CL scenarios. (b) Representation of actions/interactions as gamified influential I_L events.

According to Skinner's reinforcement theory [11], a human behavior is learned using operant conditioning as consequences that modify the tendency to repeat a behavior. In a gamified CL scenario, as showed in Figure 2 (b), the game components can be operant conditioning in which the actions done by these components define game effects that follow actions done by students (playing the instructor/learner roles). The ontological structure to represent this fact in a *gamified instructional* (or *learning*) *event* is a *game event* defined as an operant conditioning event that is showed in Figure 2 (a), where the *game component* plays the *operant conditioning role*, and the actions done by these components are *game effects* that produce changes in the game state. These actions as *game effects* are related by the relationship "*attain*" with the *individual motivational goals* defined in the instructional/learning events. Finally, the *instructional/learning events* are *game mechanics events* in a gamified instructional (or learning) event, where the *actions* of students play the role of *game mechanics*.

3   Conclusions and Future Research

In this paper, we extended our ontology to gamify CL scenarios through the formalization of concepts related to gamification as persuasive technology. These new concepts, such as *gamified influential I_L event*, game dynamic and gameplay were included in the new version of our ontological structure to represent gamified CL scenarios. This structure will allow us to define personalized game dynamics that persuade learners to do the intended learning behavior defined in CSCL scripts. We believe that the results of this work are the first steps forward to create sistems that will provide assistance and recommendation for the development of more engaging and motivating CL scenarios. Our next steps will consider how to formalize strategies of persuasion in our ontology. Furthermore, for future works, we will work in the modeling and application of flow theory, player's journey, and fun design in CL scenarios.

Acknowledgements: We thank CNPq and CAPES for supporting this research.

References

1. Challco, G.C., Moreira, D., Mizoguchi, R., Isotani, S.: Towards an ontology for gamifying collaborative learning scenarios. In: Trausan-Matu, S., Boyer, K.E., Crosby, M., Panourgia, K. (eds.) ITS 2014. LNCS, vol. 8474, pp. 404–409. Springer, Heidelberg (2014)
2. Challco, G.C., Moreira, D.A., Mizoguchi, R., Isotani, S.: An ontology engineering approach to gamify collaborative learning scenarios. In: Baloian, N., Burstein, F., Ogata, H., Santoro, F., Zurita, G. (eds.) CRIWG 2014. LNCS, vol. 8658, pp. 185–198. Springer, Heidelberg (2014)
3. Falout, J., Elwood, J., Hood, M.: Demotivation: Affective states and learning outcomes. System **37**(3), 403–417 (2009)
4. Fogg, B.: A behavior model for persuasive design. In: Proceedings of the 4th International Conference on Persuasive Technology, Persuasive 2009, pp. 40:1–40:7. ACM, New York (2009)
5. Hamari, J., Koivisto, J., Sarsa, H.: Does gamification work? - A literature review of empirical studies on gamification. In: 47th Hawaii International Conference on System Sciences (HICSS), pp. 3025–3034. IEEE (2014)
6. Hunicke, R., LeBlanc, M., Zubek, R.: MDA: a formal approach to game design and game research. In: Proceedings of the AAAI Workshop on Challenges in Game AI. AAAI Press, San Jose (2004)
7. Isotani, S., Inaba, A., Ikeda, M., Mizoguchi, R.: An ontology engineering approach to the realization of theory-driven group formation. International Journal of Computer-Supported Collaborative Learning **4**(4), 445–478 (2009)
8. Kozaki, K., Kitamura, Y., Ikeda, M., Mizoguchi, R.: Hozo: an environment for building/using ontologies based on a fundamental consideration of "role" and "relationship". In: Gómez-Pérez, A., Benjamins, V. (eds.) EKAW 2002. LNCS (LNAI), vol. 2473, pp. 213–218. Springer, Heidelberg (2002)
9. Mäyrä, F., Ermi, L.: Fundamental components of the gameplay experience: analysing immersion. In: Proceedings of DiGRA 2005: Changing Views-Worlds in Play (2005)
10. Sicart, M.: Defining game mechanics. Game Studies **8**(2), 1–14 (2008)
11. Staddon, J.E.R., Cerutti, D.T.: Operant conditioning. Annual Review of Psychology **54**(1), 115–144 (2003)
12. Webb, E.N.: Gamification: when it works, when it doesn't. In: Marcus, A. (ed.) DUXU 2013, Part II. LNCS, vol. 8013, pp. 608–614. Springer, Heidelberg (2013)

Towards the Development of the Invention Coach: A Naturalistic Study of Teacher Guidance for an Exploratory Learning Task

Catherine C. Chase[1], Jenna Marks[1(✉)], Deena Bernett[1],
Melissa Bradley[1], and Vincent Aleven[2]

[1] Teachers College, Columbia University, New York, USA
{chase,jnm2146,dlb2175,mb3754}@tc.columbia.edu
[2] Human-Computer Interaction Institute, Carnegie Mellon University, Pittsburgh, USA
aleven@cs.cmu.edu

Abstract. We describe a study of naturalistic teacher guidance for an exploratory learning activity called Invention. Our study illustrates a specific pedagogical style, whereby the teacher offers little feedback and few explanations, but largely poses questions, to help students identify and remedy their own errors. These findings have informed the design of a computerized Invention Coach and may apply more broadly to other exploratory learning environments.

Keywords: Exploratory learning environments · Intelligent learning environments · Human tutoring · Exploratory learning · Intelligent tutors

1 Introduction

Invention is an exploratory task that invites students to engage with deep, conceptual ideas by analyzing a set of data. Students are asked to invent an expression of an underlying structure that runs throughout a set of contrasting cases. Cases are examples of scientific phenomena with predesigned contrasts that highlight key features, providing students with clues to the abstract, underlying concepts. After exploring the cases and inventing their own structures, students are told the canonical principles, through traditional expositions (lecture, reading).

In several studies, Invention has been more effective than traditional instruction at enhancing transfer and deep learning in science and math domains, with adolescents and adults [1, 2, 3, 4]. But in most studies, students need subtle guidance from a teacher to engage in productive invention. Therefore, in a move towards scaling up, we are developing a computer-based Invention Coach that will provide adaptive guidance as students engage in Invention.

The literature on human tutoring offers many insights into the process of guiding individual learning through typical activities such as reading and problem-solving [5, 6, 7, 8]. However, far less is known about how to tutor exploratory tasks [9]. Therefore, before building our computer-based Invention Coach, we undertook a study of human guidance in the context of exploratory problem solving with Invention, to identify productive types of teacher guidance.

© Springer International Publishing Switzerland 2015
C. Conati et al. (Eds.): AIED 2015, LNAI 9112, pp. 558–561, 2015.
DOI: 10.1007/978-3-319-19773-9_61

2   A Study of Naturalistic Teacher Guidance of Invention

2.1   Methods

Participants and Materials. Three experienced science teachers coached the Invention tasks. Student participants were 18 seventh and eighth graders in an afterschool program for low-income, urban youth. Students completed two paper-based Invention activities, guided one-on-one by a teacher: Crowded Clowns (focusing on density, $d=m/v$) and Car Fastness (focusing on speed, $s=d/t$), shown in Figure 1. Though students did not know it, they were inventing the formulas for density and speed. Common to both tasks is the deep structure of ratio, which was the target learning we hoped students would transfer to other physical science equations (e.g. pressure=force/area). In the Crowded Clowns task, students were asked to invent a numerical "index" to describe how crowded the clowns are in each set of buses. The buses are carefully designed contrasting cases that highlight critical features of "crowdedness" (e.g. # of objects, space).

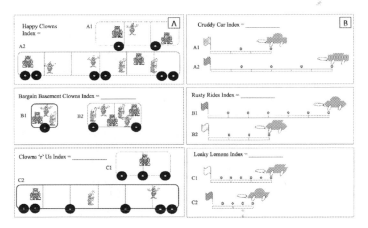

Fig. 1. Invention tasks, adapted from Schwartz et al., 2011. A.) Crowded Clowns B.) Car Fastness.

Procedure. On the first day of the study, students took a 15-minute pretest. 1-21 days later, depending on scheduling, they completed the coaching/posttest session. During each session, students spent 30 minutes on the Invention tasks with guidance from a teacher. Teachers then gave a brief lecture using a provided PowerPoint presentation, to explain the deep structure of ratio. Then, students completed a 20-minute posttest.

Measures. Sessions were videotaped and dialogue was transcribed. To identify types of guidance, we coded teacher dialogue at the statement level for both structure and strategy. Structure codes reveal the structure of teachers' speech (e.g. questions, explanations), while strategy codes represent specific teacher tactics. Assessments included a pretest and posttest of conceptual and transfer items. All data were coded by two experimenters and agreement was satisfactory (kappas ranged from .70 to .82).

2.2   Results

Students learned and transferred from the coached Invention tasks. On conceptual problems, students scored .6 times higher on the posttest. On the transfer test, students scored 2.5 times higher at post. A repeated measures ANOVA confirmed that pre and posttest scores differed significantly, $F(1, 17) = 13.95, p < .01$. This suggests our teachers were effective at enhancing conceptual knowledge and transfer to novel domains. Thus, their coaching is a good model for the design of our Invention Coach.

Most of the teacher talk was structured as question asking (58%). Teachers gave explanations far less frequently (23%). This differs markedly from the guidance given by tutors during standard types of tasks. For instance, in a study of tutored reading by Chi et al., 53% of the tutor talk consisted of explanations while only 15% consisted of questions or other scaffolds (similar results have been found for tutored problem-solving) [5], [7]. Explicit correctness feedback made up only 7% of the strategies teachers used, whereas in the Chi et al. work, roughly twice as much of the tutor dialogue (15%) consisted of feedback [5]. The exploration-focused Invention activity may have led teachers to do more question-asking with less direct explaining and feedback.

To determine which kinds of teacher guidance and student characteristics were related to transfer outcomes, we carried out three sets of stepwise regression analyses. Scores on posttest transfer items were regressed on individual student characteristics, structure types, and strategy types. To control for individual differences in prior knowledge, scores on the pre-transfer test were first entered into the equation before additional variables were added in a stepwise fashion. Several likely predictors such as prior achievement in school, performance on the Invention tasks, specific teacher, and total amounts of student and teacher talk were not associated with transfer.

The only significant predictor of transfer was the frequency of teacher explanations. Teacher explanations were inversely related to transfer, such that every additional explanation given by a teacher was associated with a .6 standard deviation drop in transfer scores, $\beta = -.60, t(15) = 2.90, p = .01$. Teacher explanations accounted for 36% of the variance in transfer scores, $R^2 = .36, F(1, 15) = 8.44, p = .01$. In fact, high scorers on the transfer test received almost half the number of explanations that low scorers received, though they received an equal number of prompts and other scaffolds. Our interpretation of this result is that teacher explanations cut short students' exploration, resulting in less transfer [3]. One might surmise that teachers gave more explanations to students who were having more difficulty with the material; however the frequency of explanations is not related to performance on the Invention task.

3   Discussion and Conclusion

Teacher guidance of Invention is very different from teacher guidance of standard activities. Teachers coaching Invention activities posed more questions, gave fewer explanations, and gave less direct feedback than human tutors who coach problem-solving or reading. We also found that more teacher explanations were associated with lower transfer performance. This aligns with Invention theory, where explicit instructions given before students have had the opportunity to adequately explore cuts short their opportunity to learn [10], [3]. Overall, these findings illustrate a style of guidance where the teacher leads students to diagnose and remedy their own errors through questioning rather than giving didactic explanations of what students should see and do.

We are now building the computer-based Invention Coach[1], applying the pedagogical style employed by teachers in our study. Consequently, our brand of guidance is far more student-centered than that of standard ITSs. Rather than giving students direct feedback, our system will help students to realize their own mistakes. Rather than provide didactic explanations, our system will engage students in an extended interactive dialogue to enable them to construct their own explanations.

This work contributes more broadly to work on Invention, ILEs, and exploratory learning environments. To the best of our knowledge, the work presented here is the first study of naturalistic teacher guidance within the Invention paradigm. Additionally, our work offers insight into possible strategies and styles of guidance that could be broadly applicable in exploratory, computer-based learning environments and tasks.

References

1. Schwartz, D.L., Martin, T.: Inventing to Prepare for Future Learning: The Hidden Efficiency of Encouraging Original Student Production in Statistics Instruction. Cognition and Instruction **22**(2), 129–184 (2004)
2. Schwartz, D.L., Bransford, J.D.: A Time for Telling. Cognition and Instruction **16**(4), 475–522 (1998)
3. Schwartz, D.L., Chase, C.C., Oppezzo, M.A., Chin, D.B.: Practicing Versus Inventing with Contrasting Cases: The Effects of Telling First on Learning and Transfer. Journal of Educational Psychology **103**(4), 759 (2011)
4. Shemwell, J.T., Chase, C.C., Schwartz, D.L.: Seeking the General Explanation: A Test of Inductive Activities for Learning and Transfer. Journal of Research in Science Teaching **52**(1), 58–83 (2015)
5. Chi, M.T., Siler, S.A., Jeong, H., Yamauchi, T., Hausmann, R.G.: Learning from Human Tutoring. Cognitive Science **25**(4), 471–533 (2001)
6. Graesser, A.C., Person, N.K., Magliano, J.P.: Collaborative Dialogue Patterns in Naturalistic One-to-one Tutoring. Applied Cognitive Psychology **9**(6), 495–522 (1995)
7. McArthur, D., Stasz, C., Zmuidzinas, M.: Tutoring Techniques in Algebra. Cognition and Instruction **7**(3), 197–244 (1990)
8. VanLehn, K., Siler, S., Murray, C., Yamauchi, T., Baggett, W.B.: Why Do Only Some Events Cause Learning During Human Tutoring? Cognition and Instruction **21**(3), 209–249 (2003)
9. Collins, A., Stevens, A.L.: Goals and Strategies of Inquiry Teachers. Advances in instructional psychology **2**, 65–119 (1982)
10. Kapur, M.: Productive Failure. Cognition and Instruction **26**(3), 379–424 (2008)

---

[1] The design of the Invention Coach is described in Chase, C.C., Marks, J., Bernett, D., & Aleven, V. (2015). The design of an exploratory learning environment to support Invention. Workshop Proceedings of the 17th International Conference on Artificial Intelligence in Education.

Adaptive Representation of Digital Resources Search Results in Personal Learning Environment

Daouda Sawadogo[✉], Cyrille Suire, Ronan Champagnat, and Pascal Estraillier

L3i Laboratory, University of La Rochelle, La Rochelle, France
{daouda.sawadogo,cyrille.suire,ronan.champagnat,
pascal.estraillier}@univ-lr.fr
http://l3i.univ-lr.fr

Abstract. The massive explosion of digital resources available in the user's personal environment creates many issues. Users aim to select among a mass of heterogeneous digital resources, the best one to use in the activity. Traditionally, this process is time consuming and requires a lot of effort for the user to optimize selecting parameters. That often makes unexploitable digital resources available in repositories or digital libraries. In this paper, we proposed an approach that allows a user to have new ways of interpreting the resource search results. We proposed a method for adaptive visual representation of these results based on the context of use and the user profile. This approach use an adaptive tf-idf scoring and adaptive visual representation to allow relevant digital resources selection. This study was conducted as part of the design of a personal environment for consolidated digital resource management called PRISE (PeRsonal Interactive research Smart Environment).

Keywords: Visual representation · Relevance · Digital resources · User profile · Personal learning environment

1 Introduction

The production of digital resources (DR) and content for learning and education is reaching a new level [1]. These resources are the results of individual or collective efforts, academic or from private initiatives. Their large quantity makes more complex their discovery and the use for users. Moreover, their quality varies substantially, often reflecting the different levels of investment committed to their development. The abundance and variety of digital resources call for a reflection on the tools that support their discovery and relevant exploitation for learning. Indexing systems and search engines now allow us to finely customize search algorithms taking into account the user profile and its context of use. Clustering techniques allow to highlight the themes of search and group results maintaining, for some of them, the diversity of viewpoints [2]. However, digital resources for education provide metadata that is difficult to exploit by these techniques. The main question that arises is : how to contextualize search results according

© Springer International Publishing Switzerland 2015
C. Conati et al. (Eds.): AIED 2015, LNAI 9112, pp. 562–565, 2015.
DOI: 10.1007/978-3-319-19773-9_62

to user's profile and user's needs to offer him a better interpretation of these results?

In this study, we use a model of digital resources based on LOM and all its metadata. We have created a LOM application profile for research [3]. We have also worked on methods of resource adaptation to user's characteristics [4]. In parallel, there are approaches exploiting metadata for visualization. In order to promote the use of contextualized digital resources and allow a better understanding of each resource shown in the search results, it seems relevant to be interested in the graphic representation of these results [5,6] [7]. This may indeed allow the user to enjoy and interpret data indirectly related to resources which, if they are presented precisely, may make sense [8]. This article focuses on the use of digital resources and practices of users whose analysis is critical to the design and quality of IT environments for human learning. The contribution of this research study is twofold : First, we use digital resource model with user's profile and user's needs to generate relevance search results and Second, we propose adaptive visual representation based on trace-based system to enhance user search results interpretation and to facilitate digital resource selection.

2   PRISE Methods

2.1   Digital Resource, User Profile and Trace-Based System

Metadata is information that describes a digital resource. Each resource in our system is modeled using the IEEE-LOM application profile metadata. Our method uses this resource modeling and trace-based system which stores the traces of digital resources execution to generate results of relevant resources based on the user's profile.

The user model is a representation of information about an individual user that is essential for an adaptive system to provide the adaptation effect [9]. Indeed, the user's profile provides the system with the required information to assist the user in resource selection process. Adaptive representation is data-driven and continually takes data from users and adapts their visual representation to change and improve over time for each user.

In PRISE system we proposed a trace-based system, which collects the user's actions in situation-based scenario and then analyses them to provide a better completion of their visual representation. The purpose of trace-based management system is to identify the trace elements necessary to propose a relevant user profile and system for the automatic update of user?s search results and visual representation. These traces were collected from the interaction of the user with the digital resource. The user?s traces were used by carrying out three steps consecutively (Afference, Inference, Efference).

2.2   Relevance Computing and Visual Representation

Our goal in this paper is to provide a visual and adaptive representations of digital resource search results indexed in the user's learning environment or in any other repository or library. This visual representation might be adaptive and controllable [5,7]. Adaptive because it takes into account the context of the user's activity, its profile and its usage need. Controllable because the user can customize the settings of the visual representation. The purpose of this representation is to allow the user to select efficiently the relevant digital resource that is best to achieve a situation-based [10] objective. Based on our adaptive digital resources engine [4], we use the adaptive logic to present visually the resource search results. We proceed in four steps:

1. The user expresses his need through a request for information;
2. The user can control the criterion he wants to optimize;
3. The system generates a list of results using adaptive *TF-IDF scoring* [11];
4. The system offers several models of visual representations of the results provided by the indexing engine. To adapt this representation, the system use the contextual information of the resource and those of the user. It first analyzes the defined contexts (defined by the creator of the resource) and the real context (after analyzing traces of use [10]). Then, these results are related to the context of use, computed according to the user profile.

In addition of adapting the results and resources, this approach has the advantage of adapting their visual representations (list, chart, diagram etc.). However, it assumes a full traceability of the system, especially during the execution of each situation. These traces are used to reflect the user's experience to improve the system performance, relevance of the results and quality of adaptation.

3   Discussion and Related Work

During our work, we found that similar approach exist, in [7], the authors have shown the interest of control interfaces in recommender systems. The results of this study clearly showed that the means of control and representation available to users improved their engagement in the system and therefore the quality of recommendations. The main difference to our approach can be found in the levers operated to allow adaptation. [7] and [12] scale the results depending on preferences and criteria explicitly selected by the user. Our system operates user profile and contextual metadata from the history of use of resources themselves. The adaptation of search results was also seen in terms of the organization of search results. The authors in [2] have clearly shown that the current trend of search engines to gather relevant information in a single cluster could be negative. They explain that this does not present the various aspects of his request to the user and restricts his perception to a unique viewpoint. The authors propose a dissemination of search results based on the analysis of the search query for a better consideration of the request. Our approach is slightly different because it is built on the analysis of user contexts and resource history. However, our goals are similar. Adaptive representation must be an instrument in favor of the diversity of viewpoints and for a better interpretation of the query results by users.

4   Conclusion and Future Work

In this article, we propose an approach allowing users to have a greater freedom of interpretation of search results. This visual and adaptive representation correlates contextual user data with those of the resource. This correlation facilitates an informed choice and decreases the black box effect stem from relevance calculation. Moreover, it promotes better use of digital resources by taking into account their history, built on the experience of previous users.

This approach requires the setting up of a system-wide adaptive processing chain in the learning environment. This processing chain must contextualize the user profile, manage the use of digital resources and adapt the visual representation of search results. We plan to include visual representations that take advantage of the observation of the sequence of digital resources in an educational situation. This future work will allow us to precise our aim to offer user better means of interpretation.

References

1. Gao, X.: Towards the next generation intelligent BPM – in the era of big data. In: Daniel, F., Wang, J., Weber, B. (eds.) BPM 2013. LNCS, vol. 8094, pp. 4–9. Springer, Heidelberg (2013)
2. Lamprier, S., Amghar, T., Levrat, B., Saubion, F.: Organize information seeking results. Clustering, distribution of information and easy access. Document numérique 13(1), 9–39, April 2010
3. Sawadogo, D., Champagnat, R., Estraillier, P.: PRISE : adaptive environment for consolidated management of digital resources. In: UMAP Workshops (2014)
4. Sawadogo, D., Champagnat, R., Estraillier, P.:Adaptive digital resource modelling for interactive system. In: International Conference on Control, Decision and Information Technologies (CoDIT), pp. 663–668. IEEE (2014)
5. Ahn, J.W., Brusilovsky, P.: Adaptive visualization of search results: Bringing user models to visual analytics. Information Visualization 8(3), 167–179 (2009)
6. Ahn, J.W., Brusilovsky, P.: What You See Is What You Search : Adaptive Visual Search Framework for the Web, pp. 1049–1050 (2010)
7. Parra, D., Brusilovsky, P., Trattner, C.: See what you want to see: visual user-driven approach for hybrid recommendation. In: Proceedings of the 19th International Conference on Intelligent User Interfaces, pp. 235–240 (2014)
8. Drucker, J.: Graphesis : visual forms of knowledge production (2014)
9. Brusilovsky, P., Millán, E.: User models for adaptive hypermedia and adaptive educational systems. In: Brusilovsky, P., Kobsa, A., Nejdl, W. (eds.) Adaptive Web 2007. LNCS, vol. 4321, pp. 3–53. Springer, Heidelberg (2007)
10. Ho, H.N., Rabah, M., Nowakowski, S., Estraillier, P.: A trace-based decision making in interactive application: case of tamagotchi systems. In: International Conference on Control, Decision and Information Technologies (CoDIT), pp. 123–127. IEEE (2014)
11. Wu, H.C., Luk, R.W.P., Wong, K.F., Kwok, K.L.: Interpreting TF-IDF term weights as making relevance decisions. ACM Transactions on Information Systems 26(3), 1–37 (2008)
12. Verbert, K., Parra, D., Brusilovsky, P., Duval, E.: Visualizing recommendations to support exploration, transparency and controllability. In: Proceedings of the 2013 International Conference on Intelligent User Interfaces, pp. 351–362. ACM (2013)

Towards Investigating Performance Differences in Clinical Reasoning in a Technology Rich Learning Environment

Tenzin Doleck[1], Amanda Jarrell[1(✉)], Eric Poitras[2], and Susanne Lajoie[1]

[1] Department of Educational and Counselling Psychology, McGill University,
Montreal, QC, Canada
{tenzin.doleck,amanda.jarrell}@mail.mcgill.ca,
susanne.lajoie@mcgill.ca
[2] Department of Educational Psychology, University of Utah, Salt Lake City, UT, USA
eric.poitras@utah.edu

Abstract. Technology Rich Learning Environments (TREs) are increasingly used to support scholastic activities. BioWorld is an example of a TRE designed to support the metacognitive activities of learners tasked with solving virtual patient cases. The present paper aims to examine the performance differences of novice physicians in diagnosing cases in BioWorld. We present an empirically guided line of research concerning the performance differences: (1) across three endocrinology cases, (2) between genders, (3) between goal orientations, and (4) in diagnosis correctness.

Keywords: Technology rich learning environments · Clinical reasoning · Performance differences · Learner outcomes

1 Introduction

It is widely acknowledged that clinical reasoning, a process "that uses formal and informal thinking strategies to gather and analyse patient information, evaluate the significance of this information and weigh alternative actions" [1], is a crucial skill for medical students [2, 3]. However, current teaching and learning approaches have been found to be inadequate in developing the necessary clinical reasoning skills [4]. Thus, there is a need for affording learners opportunities to learn, practice, and improve their clinical reasoning skills. The educational technology literature is rife with studies documenting the efficacy of Technology Rich Learning Environments (TREs) in spawning positive learning outcomes in varied learning contexts [e.g. 5, 6, 7]. Thus, it is worthwhile to consider such learning systems to support and enrich learners. The present research concerns investigations of learner outcomes in a medical TRE designed to support learners in developing expertise in clinical reasoning. This paper lays the foundation for an empirically guided line of research concerning the performance differences: (1) across three endocrinology cases, (2) between genders, (3) between goal orientations, and (4) in diagnosis correctness.

© Springer International Publishing Switzerland 2015
C. Conati et al. (Eds.): AIED 2015, LNAI 9112, pp. 566–569, 2015.
DOI: 10.1007/978-3-319-19773-9_63

Examining performance differences in clinical reasoning can have implications for both instructional design and learner outcomes. In this paper, we outline the general methods, provide details about the data and data analysis, and present preliminary results for the first study, i.e., performance differences across the three patient cases of varying difficulty levels.

2   Methods

2.1   Participants and Study Procedure

Participants were recruited through advertisements (on classified website) and newsletter (via email). A total of 30 medical undergraduate students from a large Northeastern Canadian University volunteered to participate. The convenience sample comprised of 11 men and 19 women, with an average age of 23 ($SD = 2.60$). Participants were compensated $20 at the completion of a 2-hour study session.

Data for this project was collected as part of work that examined factors that influenced attention to feedback in BioWorld [8]. Initially, participants completed a training case, which provided an opportunity to familiarize with the BioWorld system. Upon completion of the training case, participants solved 3 endocrinology cases. The three endocrinology cases (*correct diagnosis for each case indicated in brackets*) participants were asked to solve were: Amy (*diabetes Type 1*), Cynthia (*pheochromocytoma*), and Susan Taylor (*hyperthyroidism*). The order of the cases was counterbalanced to mitigate practice effects. The difficulty levels of the cases were ascertained through a previous study [9]: the anticipated accuracies for the three cases were Amy (94%), Cynthia (33%), and Susan Taylor (78%).

2.2   Learning Environment: BioWorld

BioWorld [10, 11] is a technology rich learning environment (TRE) that supports learners in practicing clinical reasoning skills. BioWorld consists of four main spaces (Problem, Chart, Library, and Consult). The 'Problem' space provides the patients' case history. In solving the patient case, the learner reviews the patient summary and formulates a differential diagnosis (with the help of the Hypothesis Manager Tool), along with updating their level of confidence in relation to the most likely diagnosis (via the Belief Meter). In the Chart space, learners can review patient's vital signs and order lab-tests to confirm or disconfirm specific diagnosis. The Library and Consult serve as help-seeking tools. The final step in problem solving involves submitting a final diagnosis, sorting and prioritizing evidence, and writing a patient case summary.

2.3   Measures: Log-Files

The BioWorld system logs learner-system interactions in log-files. There are three different types of performance metrics in the system logs: *diagnostic efficacy* (e.g., percentage of matches with experts), *efficiency* (e.g., time taken to solve a case), and *affect* (e.g., confidence). The specific information logged include: the *attempt identifier* (participant and case ID), a *timestamp*, the BioWorld *space* (e.g., chart), the specific *action taken* (e.g., add test), and *details in relation to the action* (e.g., Thyroid Stimulating Hormone (TSH) Result: 0.2 mU/L).

3   Data Analysis

3.1   Data Cleaning

A box plot analysis was conducted for each of the performance variables in order to identify potential outliers in the dataset; this analysis identified few outliers. To preserve the sample size, these extreme values were replaced using the next most extreme value within their corresponding case.

3.2   Performance Metrics

Performance metrics that characterize diagnostic accuracy and efficiency were extracted from the system logs. Within this study, we operationalize *Accuracy* by the number of evidence matches with the expert solution and define *Efficiency* by the total time taken to solve the case and the number of laboratory tests ordered.

3.3   Preliminary Results

We present preliminary results for performance differences across the three endocrinology cases of varying difficulty levels. A MANOVA analysis was conducted with the three indices of performance as dependent variables (i.e., number of lab tests ordered, number of correct matches with the expert solution, and time taken to solve the case) and the case with three levels as the independent variable. The results from the MANOVA suggest that there is a significant difference in the pattern of means between cases across participant performance indices, $F(6, 168) = 9.474$, $p < .001$, $\eta^2 = .25$. For comprehending the nature of these differences, a series of ANOVA post-hoc comparisons were conducted which revealed that there was a significant difference in number of matches with the expert solution between cases, $F(2, 86) = 18.39$, $p < .001$, $\eta^2 = .30$ and in how many lab tests were ordered, $F(2, 86) = 10.39$, $p < .001$, $\eta^2 = .20$. However, there were no significant differences in elapsed time across cases, $F(2, 86) = 4.18$, $p = .019$, $\eta^2 = .089$. To understand how the cases differed, Tukey HSD post-hoc comparisons were conducted; the results suggest that participants had significantly more matches with the expert solution for the Amy and Susan Taylor cases in comparison to the Cynthia case ($M = 6.39$ $SE = .35$, $M = 7.09$ $SE = .35$ and $M = 4.26$ $SD = .35$, respectively). The results also indicate that participants ordered significantly more lab tests for the Cynthia case in comparison to the Amy and Susan Taylor cases ($M = 13.77$ $SD = .95$, $M = 9.67$ $SD = .95$ and $M = 7.83$ $SD = .95$, respectively).

4   Concluding Remarks

In this paper, we have discussed ongoing research on empirically investigating the performance differences in clinical reasoning in a TRE for medical education. We presented the preliminary results obtained for our first research question: "Are there performance differences in the manner in which novices solve cases with varying levels of complexity?" Our next step is to complete the series of analyses to investigate performance differences (1) between genders, (2) between goal orientations, and (3) in diagnosis correctness.

References

1. Simmons, B.: Clinical reasoning: concept analysis. Journal of Advanced Nursing **66**(5), 1151–1158 (2010)
2. Delany, C., Golding, C.: Teaching clinical reasoning by making thinking visible: an action research project with allied health clinical educators. BMC Medical Education **14**(1), 20 (2014)
3. Norman, G.: Research in clinical reasoning: Past history and current trends. Medical Education **39**(4), 418–427 (2005)
4. Levett-Jones, T., Hoffman, K., Dempsey, J., Jeong, S., Noble, D., Norton, C., Roche, J., Hickey, N.: The 'five rights' of clinical reasoning: An educational model to enhance nursing students' ability to identify and manage clinically 'at risk' patients. Nurse Education Today **30**(6), 515–520 (2010)
5. Beal, C.R., Walles, R., Arroyo, I., Woolf, B.P.: On-line tutoring for math achievement testing: A controlled evaluation. Journal of Interactive Online Learning **6**(1), 43–55 (2007)
6. Matsuda, N., Yarzebinski, E., Keiser, V., Raizada, R., William, W.C., Stylianides, G.J., Koedinger, K.R.: Cognitive anatomy of tutor learning: Lessons learned with SimStudent. Journal of Educational Psychology **105**(4), 1152–1163 (2013)
7. Vanlehn, K., Lynch, C., Schulze, K., Shapiro, J.A., Shelby, R., Taylor, L., Treacy, D., Weinstein, A., Wintersgill, M.: The Andes physics tutoring system: Lessons learned. International Journal of Artificial Intelligence in Education **15**, 147–204 (2005)
8. Naismith, L.: Examining motivational and emotional influences on medical students' attention to feedback in a technology-rich environment for learning clinical reasoning (Unpublished doctoral dissertation). McGill University, Canada (2013)
9. Gauthier, G., Lajoie, P.S., Naismith, L., Wiseman, J.: Using expert decision maps to promote reflection and self-assessment in medical case-based instruction. In: Proceedings of Workshop on the Assessment & Feedback in Ill-Defined Domains at ITS, Montréal, Canada (2008)
10. Lajoie, S.P.: Developing professional expertise with a cognitive apprenticeship model: examples from avionics and medicine. In: Ericsson, K.A. (ed.) Development of Professional Expertise: Toward Measurement of Expert Performance and Design of Optimal Learning Environments, pp. 61–83. Cambridge University Press (2009)
11. Lajoie, S.P., Poitras, E.G., Doleck, T., Jarrell, A.: modeling metacognitive activities in medical problem-solving with bioworld. In: Peña-Ayala, A. (ed.) Metacognition: Fundamentals, Applications, and Trends, pp. 323–343. Springer (2015)

Emotional, Epistemic, and Neutral Feedback in AutoTutor Trialogues to Improve Reading Comprehension

Shi Feng[✉], Janay Stewart, Danielle Clewley, and Arthur C. Graesser

Institute for Intelligent Systems, University of Memphis, Memphis, TN, USA
{sfeng,jstwart7,dnclwley,a-graesser}@memphis.edu

Abstract. We manipulated three types of short feedback (emotional, epistemic, and neutral) in an intelligent tutoring system designed to help struggling adult readers improve reading comprehension strategies. Although participants self-reported a preference for emotional feedback, there were no differences in individual motivation or usefulness ratings between emotional and epistemic feedback. Analysis from coded facial emotions indicated that participants tended to be more sensitive to epistemic feedback than emotional feedback.

Keywords: Feedback · Intelligent tutoring systems · Emotions · Agents

1 Introduction

Feedback has been widely shown to be an important facilitator of learning and performance [1]. Recently, an ITS, called AutoTutor-CSAL (Center for the Study of Adult Literacy [2]), has been developed that has a teacher agent (Cristina) and a student agent (Jordan) trialogue system to assist struggling adult readers. Feedback is implemented in this system as an important feature to enhance learning gains and motivation.

In the current framework, feedback is usually a short general emotive feedback response to immediate performance [3], such as "_name_, you were right! Great effort!" The learner also receives an explanation (called "answer") for the correct answer afterwards. These short feedback speech acts are designed to mimic feedback given by human tutors, which would increase the learner's engagement [4]. One open research question is whether giving short emotive feedback that emphasizes positive or negative emotions benefits both the learner's engagement and performance, compared with an epistemic feedback which simply informs whether any given item is correct or incorrect, or a neutral feedback that simply acknowledges the learner's input.

The aim of the present research is to investigate whether different types of short feedback would affect learners' engagement and performance in a usability study with college students interacting with AutoTutor CSAL. Specifically, we examined whether short emotional feedback, commonly utilized in lessons in AutoTutor CSAL, would improve or engage learners' performance better than short epistemic or neutral feedback. If emotional feedback motivates learners in a learning environment, then there should be an increase in response time, since in the context of reading, it was

© Springer International Publishing Switzerland 2015
C. Conati et al. (Eds.): AIED 2015, LNAI 9112, pp. 570–573, 2015.
DOI: 10.1007/978-3-319-19773-9_64

previously found that time spent on reading has a strong relationship with motivation [5], higher performance, and a better learner experience using the system. Furthermore, we analyzed the participants' facial emotions while interacting with AutoTutor CSAL. Past research has found six emotions that frequently occur during learning. Those emotions are: confusion, boredom, frustration, flow, delight, and surprise [6]. Students vary in experiencing these emotions during learning. By tracking participants' moment-to-moment affective states, we can get a better sense of their user-experience when they encounter different types of feedback after participants answer comprehension questions.

2   Method

Participants were 63 college undergraduates from the University of Memphis Subject Pool who participated in this study for course credit. The experiment used a within-subjects design with three text and three feedback conditions: short emotive feedback ("_user_, you were correct. Good job!"/ "unfortunately, _user_, you did not get it correct this time"), short epistemic feedback ("_user_, you were correct"/ "_user_, you were incorrect"), and short neutral feedback ("ok"). The learning materials consisted of a lesson from AutoTutor CSAL designed to teach learners how to comprehend narrative texts using the reading strategy called summarization. The college participants read all three texts of easy, medium and difficult levels. After reading each text, participants were presented with comprehension questions tailored to a specific portion of the text. Order of feedback condition, and order of texts were counterbalanced across participants with a Graeco-Latin Square. Participants' facial expressions were recorded. After each interaction with each text, they were asked to fill out a questionnaire to rate their impressions and experiences using the system on a 1 to 5 Likert Scale.

3   Results and Discussion

There was no significant difference between the average correct responses on a comprehension question item ($M = .86$, $SD = .34$). We found that there was a significant main effect of response time between the three texts conditions ($F(2, 180)=5.35$, $p <.01$). The interaction was significant ($F(4,180) = 3.77$, $p = .003$). Only the medium difficulty level text ("*The Legend of the Evening Star*") showed a significant mean difference of response time between the three feedback conditions ($F(2, 690) = 5.123$, $p = .006$). According to a Tukey Post Hoc test, while reading the medium difficulty level text, participants spent significantly longer time answering the comprehension questions when they received emotional feedback. This suggests that they may be more motivated when they received emotional feedback while answering questions from the medium text.

We were particularly interested in the participants' change of affective state when they received the first positive feedback versus the first negative feedback statement within each feedback condition. Each participant was rated on a 1 to 6 signal detect scale segregating absence (1-3) and present of emotion (4-6) for each of the six emotions. The rating of confidence for each side of the segregation varies so that the low number signifies the lowest confidence in ratings. Cronbach's Alpha for continuous scale showed high inter-rater reliability of .86 on the items between thee raters. Overall, participants are significantly more likely to be frustrated when they received the first negative feedback statement regardless of feedback condition (emotional: $t(41) = 2.11, p = .044$; epistemic: $t(36) = 3.16, p = .002$; neutral: $t(43) = 2.13, p = .039$). They were more likely to be confused when they received the first negative emotional feedback ($t(41) = 2.04, p = .047$). They were more engaged (in flow state) when they received the first positive epistemic feedback ($t(36 = 2.93, p = .008$), and more bored and surprised when they received the first negative epistemic feedback (boredom: $t(36) = 2.61, p = .014$; surprise: $t(36) = -2.61, p = .014$). Participants in general are most sensitive to epistemic feedback in terms of affective state change (Table 1).

Table 1. Mean ratings of learning emotions for the first positive and first negative feedback as a function of feedback conditions

	Emotional Feedback		Epistemic Feedback		Neutral Feedback	
	Pos. Feed	Neg. Feed	Pos. Feed	Neg. Feed	Pos. Feed	Neg. Feed
Boredom	2.95 (1.20)	3.67 (1.23)	2.43 (.80)*	3.20 (.98)*	2.75 (1.21)	3.11 (1.14)
Flow	4.35 (.87)	3.95 (.99)	4.81 (.51)**	4.22 (.70)**	4.67 (.89)	4.19 (.97)
Frustration	1.38 (.41)*	1.85 (.95)*	1.43 (.54)**	2.16 (.82)**	1.25 (.46)*	1.63 (.70)*
Confusion	1.35 (.53)*	1.77 (.80)*	1.62 (.74)	1.94 (.66)	1.33 (.46)	1.61 (.54)
Delight	1.14 (.36)	1.09 (.23)	1.32 (.63)	1.24 (.54)	1.11 (.29)	1.03 (.09)
Surprise	1.16 (.66)	1.38 (.74)	1.12 (.22)*	1.50 (.56)*	1.16 (.54)	1.28 (.59)

Notes: *significant mean difference between positive and negative feedback with respect to alpha = .05; **significant at alpha = .01; SD in parenthesis.

Sixty-six percent of the participants reported that they liked the emotional feedback the best. Four mixed-effect linear modeling approach was adopted to analyze the four impression ratings of usefulness, naturalness, confidence boosting, and motivation. All four models were significant (usefulness: $\eta^2 = 0.04$, $F(2, 204) = 12.06, p < .001$; naturalness: $\eta^2 = 0.01$, $F(2, 203) = 4.59, p = .011$; confidence boosting: $\eta^2 = 0.03$, $F(2, 204) = 6.60, p = .002$; motivation: $\eta^2 = 0.05$, $F(2, 203) = 12.10, p < .001$). Tukey Post Hoc tests showed that emotional and epistemic did not significantly differ in these ratings, but both were rated higher than neutral.

4   General Discussion

Although participants reported preferring emotional feedback over epistemic or neutral feedback, they overall rated epistemic feedback to be just as useful and motivating as emotional feedback. Therefore it is not clear that giving emotional short feedback has benefits over epistemic in terms of engaging the learner in our ITS with

AutoTutor agents. Our results suggest that the effect of giving emotional feedback may vary with the content and nature of the materials. Our participants spent the majority of their time in the affective state of flow or engagement, which is in accordance to previous findings [7], but our research also revealed that participants' facial emotion tended to be the most sensitive to the epistemic feedback. For example, the positive emotion of delight was generally rated higher when participants received epistemic feedback than neutral or emotional, although our methods of determining delight may overlap with frustration to some degree [8]. Similarly, the emotion of surprise, which usually occurs when a learner receives a negative feedback [9], also seems to occur more frequently when participants receive epistemic feedback. One explanation is that the nature of the task was overall a bit too easy for the college population. The short emotional feedback had little benefit perhaps because it appeared patronizing or ineffectual, whereas an epistemic feedback is more motivating by virtue of its being succinct and clear. Nevertheless, the question remains whether struggling adult readers will show a different profile of responses to feedback.

Acknowledgments. This research was supported by the Institute of Education Sciences (IES) (R305C120001).

References

1. Shute, V.J.: Focus on Formative Feedback. Review of Educational Research. **78**(1), 153–189 (2008)
2. Graesser, A.C., Baer, W., Feng, S., Walker, B., Clewley, D., Hayes, D.P.: Emotions in Adaptive Computer Technologies for Adults Improving Reading. In: Tettegah, S., Ferdig, R. (eds.) Emotions and Technology: Communication of Feeling For, With, and Through Digital Media, pp. 1–35. Elsevier, San Diego (2014)
3. Cai, Z., Feng, S., Baer, W., Graesser, A.C.: Instructional strategies in trialoguebased intelligent tutoring systems. In: Goldberg, B., Graesser, A.C., Hu, X., Sottilare, R. (eds.) Design Recommendations for Intelligent Tutoring Systems, vol. 2, pp. 225–235. U.S. Army Research Laboratory, Orlando (2014)
4. Price, M., Handley, K., Millar, J., O'Donovan, B.: Feedback: All that Effort, but What is the Effect? Assessment & Evaluation in Higher Education **35**(3), 277–289 (2010)
5. Person, N.K., Kreuz, R.J., Zwaan, R., Graesser, A.C.: Pragmatics and Pedagogy: Conversational Rules and Politeness Strategies May Inhibit Effective Tutoring. Cognition and Instruction **13**, 161–188 (1995)
6. Guthrie, J.T., Wigfield, A., Metsala, J.L., Cox, K.E.: Motivational and Cognitive Predictors of Text Comprehension and Reading Amount. Scientific Studies of Reading **3**, 231–256 (1999)
7. D'Mello, S.K.: A Selective Meta-analysis on the Relative Incidence of Discrete Affective States During Learning with Technology. Journal of Educational Psychology **105**, 1082–1099 (2013)
8. Hoque, M.E., McDuff, D.J., Picard, R.W.: Exploring Temporal Patterns in Classifying Frustrated and Delighted Smiles. Affective Computer **3**, 323–334 (2012)
9. D'Mello, S.K., Graesser, A.C.: AutoTutor and Affective AutoTutor: Learning by Talking with Cognitively and Emotionally Intelligent Computers that Talk Back. ACM Transactions on Interactive Intelligent Systems **2**(4), 1–38 (2012)

Comparison of Expert Tutors Through Syntactic Analysis of Transcripts

Reva Freedman[✉] and Douglas Krieghbaum

Northern Illinois University, Dekalb, IL, USA
rfreedman@niu.edu, dkrieghbaum@aol.com

Abstract. In this paper we show that the C4.5 machine learning algorithm, applied to a number of syntactic features in transcripts, can be used to accurately differentiate between two expert human tutors. Although these tutors had taught together for years and explicitly discussed their tutoring style with one other, an analysis based on frequency of parts of speech and higher-level syntactic constructs was able to easily separate their productions.

Keywords: Transcript analysis · Intelligent tutoring systems · Author identification

1 Introduction

As a preliminary study for future work on the effect of tutoring style on students, we decided to see if we could use selected syntactic features to identify individual tutors in our corpus. In this paper we will study student dialogues with two expert human tutors. Although the tutors seemed to have superficially similar styles – they had worked together for years and explicitly discussed their tutoring style with one another – we will show that we can differentiate them quite accurately through the use of syntactic features.

Interactivity and deep learning are two features often mentioned with regard to the effectiveness of teaching [1, 2]. Although we cannot measure these features directly, we can look at related syntactic features such as the frequency of questions asked and the frequency of domain words.

In this paper we will attempt to answer the following research questions:
1) Can syntactic features be used for author identification?
2) If so, which linguistic features contribute most strongly to author identification?

2 Background

While researchers have attempted to do author identification using features varying from trigram frequency to lexical semantics, features based on the vocabulary of the writer have been the most commonly used [3]. We are particularly interested in using syntactic phenomena. In addition to parts of speech and phrase and clause structure,

© Springer International Publishing Switzerland 2015
C. Conati et al. (Eds.): AIED 2015, LNAI 9112, pp. 574–577, 2015.
DOI: 10.1007/978-3-319-19773-9_65

we have also experimented with frequency of questions, the use of domain words, turn statistics, and the results of readability tests. We examined several markers of text sophistication, including average sentence length, height of the syntax tree, frequency of subordinate clauses and vocabulary size.

There are a few other authors who have begun to use syntactic features in author identification. In AIED the most prominent is Coh-Metrix [4], which uses parts of speech and word frequency statistics, among others, to measure cohesion. Connectives and logical operators are two of its most important categories.

3 Methodology

The data was derived from a corpus collected by the Circsim-Tutor project [5]. This project built a language-based intelligent tutoring system for first-year medical students to learn about reflex control of blood pressure. This project was one of the first attempts to characterize human tutoring language and behavior and adapt it for computer use. Joel Michael and Allen Rovick, faculty members in the Department of Physiology of Rush Medical College in Chicago, served as expert tutors.

The transcripts were collected using an instant-messaging application. The database contains dialogues between the two professors and over thirty students. Dr. Michael was the tutor in 23 transcripts, using a total of 29,844 words, while Dr. Rovick was the tutor in 17 transcripts, using a total of 20,819 words.

We used the Stanford Parser [6] to tag parts of speech and create a parse tree for each sentence. Spelling correction, expanding contractions, removing unnecessary punctuation, and writing out the names of variables used in equations reduced the frequency of erroneous parses and also reduced the unique word count from about 3000 words to 2645. Fig. 1 shows an example of dialogue before cleaning.

> T: Why did you predict that IS and TPR were both 0?
> S: IS does not change b/c there is no change in the symp innerv
>   on the heart w/ the change in the pacemaker.
> T: TPR does not change b/c of the same reason.
> T: Another way of saying this is that both IS and TPR are
>   determined by the reflex and the reflex wont happen until RR.

Fig. 1. Snippet from a Circsim-Tutor transcript

The Stanford Parser uses Penn Treebank tags [7]. We combined subtypes of parts of speech, e.g., the six types of verb forms identified by the Penn Treebank.

We calculated about 100 features per transcript. The main categories of features used were:

1.   POS and constituent counts – the major parts of speech and phrases headed by them (e.g., NP for nouns)

2.   Sentence complexity measures: average words per sentence, sentence tree height and frequency of subordinate clauses. The Stanford parser generates an SBAR whenever a subordinating conjunction such as *that* is used.

3.   *Domain word usage.* We obtained a list of biology specific domain words from Project Medical Words (http://medicalwords.sourceforge.net).

4.   *Unique words.* Unique words for each individual.

5.   *Questions:* Frequency of question use.

6.   *Turn statistics.* Average number of sentences per turn and words per turn.

7.   *Readability formulas.* The results of three calculated readability formulas.

Since sentences and dialogues had different lengths, we normalized the numeric features in two different ways, per sentence and per 100 words. For each input feature we also added a shadow element $\log_2 n$ to reduce the influence of larger values. The numeric results shown use a median split.

We used WEKA 3 [8] for our experiments. WEKA's J48 is an implementation of the decision tree algorithm C4.5 developed by Quinlan [9]. For clustering we used Simple K-Means, WEKA's version of K-means.

4   Results and Discussion

Table 1 shows the results of the top scoring runs. The input features used are shown along with accuracy and the kappa statistic. All experiments used 10-fold cross-validation. In this table, "%" means per 100 words and "/S" means per sentence.

Table 1. Accuracy of Tutor Identification

Input Features	Accuracy	Kappa
AdvP/S, Questions/S	87.5%	0.74
NP %, ConjP %, VP %, V %, Adj %, Pronouns %	85.0%	0.69
NP %, VP %, V %, ConjP %	82.5%	0.65
Questions/S, Adverbs/S, Pronouns/S, $\log_2$ Interjections	80.0%	0.59
SBARs/S, Questions/S, Adj/S, $\log_2$ Interjections	80.0%	0.58
Questions/S, Verbs/S, AdjP/S, Pronouns/S, $\log_2$ Interjections, PrepP/S	77.5%	0.53

We note that the highest-scoring runs relied mostly on the frequency of parts of speech and the phrases which they headed. Although frequency of questions and in-terjections were also relevant, the frequency of subordinate clauses (SBARs) occurred only once, and some features, such as sentence length, vocabulary size, turn statistics and the use of domain words, did not occur at all in the highest-scoring runs. Thus future research on the relevance of these different categories of features is required.

As a visual aid, Fig. 2 shows the result of using the K-means algorithm to identify the tutor using two features frequently chosen by J48, noun phrases per 100 words and prepositions per 100 words. The x's signify Dr. Michael and the circles indicate Dr. Rovick.

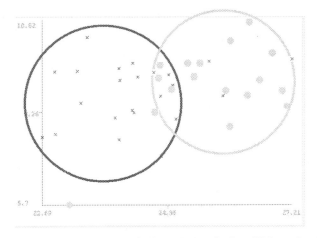

Fig. 2. Output of K-means: X-axis: NP/100 words; y-axis: Prep/100 words; shape: tutors

Acknowledgements. We thank Martha Evens of Illinois Institute of Technology and Joel Michael and the late Allen Rovick of Rush Medical College for the transcripts.

References

1. Chi, M.: Active-constructive-interactive: A Conceptual Framework for Differentiating Learning Activities. Topics in Cognitive Science **1**, 73–105 (2009)
2. Graesser, A., McNamara, D., VanLehn, K.: Scaffolding Deep Comprehension Strategies through Point & Query, AutoTutor, and iSTART. Educational Psychologist **40**, 225–234 (2005)
3. Stamatatos, E.: A Survey of Modern Authorship Attribution Methods. Journal of the American Society for Information Science and Technology **60**(3), 538–556 (2009)
4. Graesser, A., McNamara, D., Louwerse, M., Cai, Z.: Coh-Metrix: Analysis of Text on Cohesion and Language. Behavior Research Methods, Instruments and Computers **36**, 193–202 (2004)
5. Evens, M., Michael, J.: One-on-One Tutoring by Humans and Computers. Erlbaum, Mahwah (2006)
6. Klein, D., Manning, C.: Accurate unlexicalized parsing. In: Proceedings of the 41st Meeting of the Association for Computational Linguistics, pp. 423-430 (2003)
7. Santorini, B. Part-of-Speech Tagging Guidelines for the Penn Treebank Project. University of Pennsylvania, Natural Language Processing Project. Technical Report MS–CIS-90-47 LINC LAB 178 (1995)
8. Hall, M., Frank, E., Holmes, G., Pfahringer, B., Reutemann, P., Witten, I.: The WEKA Data Mining Software: An Update. SIGKDD Explorations **11**(1), 10–19 (2009)
9. Quinlan, J.: C4.5: Programs for Machine Learning. Morgan Kaufmann, San Mateo (1992)

Exploring Through Simulation an Instructional Planner for Dynamic Open-Ended Learning Environments

Stephanie Frost$^{(\boxtimes)}$ and Gord McCalla

ARIES Lab, Department of Computer Science,
University of Saskatchewan, Saskatoon, Canada
stephanie.frost@usask.ca,
mccalla@cs.usask.ca

Abstract. Modern online courses can be characterized as *dynamic open-ended* learning environments (DOELEs). For instructional planning to work in DOELEs, an approach is needed that does not rely on data structures such as prerequisite graphs that would need to be continually rewired as the LOs change. A promising approach is collaborative filtering based on learning sequences (CFLS) using the ecological approach (EA) architecture. We developed a CFLS planner that compares a given learner's most recent path of LOs (of length b) to other learners to create a neighbourhood of similar learners. The future paths (of length f) of these neighbours are checked and the most successful path ahead is recommended to the target learner, who then follows that path for a certain length (called s). An experiment with simulated learners was used to explore what are the best values of b, f and s. Results showed that the CFLS planner should avoid sending a learner any further ahead (s) than they have been matched in the past (b), a prediction that can be applied to the real world.

Keywords: Instructional planning · Collaborative filtering · Dynamic open-ended learning environments · Simulated learning environments · Simulated learners · Ecological approach

1 Introduction

Online courses need to be able to personalize their interactions with their many learners not only to help each learner overcome particular impasses but also to provide a path through the learning objects (LOs) that is appropriate to that particular individual. This is the role of *instructional planning* (IP), one of the core AIED sub-disciplines. IP is particularly needed in open-ended learning environments (OELEs), where learners choose their own goals, because it has been shown that sometimes learners require an outside push to move forward [4]. An added challenge is what we call a *dynamic open-ended* learning environment (DOELE), where both the learners and LOs are constantly changing. Learners

© Springer International Publishing Switzerland 2015
C. Conati et al. (Eds.): AIED 2015, LNAI 9112, pp. 578–581, 2015.
DOI: 10.1007/978-3-319-19773-9_66

come and go, and material can be added or deleted over time, in response to changes in the course or the material, or to learner demand. For IP to be possible in DOELEs, an approach is needed where centralized course structures would not need to be continually revamped (by instructional designers, say) as learners and LOs change.

We wish to explore how IP can be done in a DOELE. We model a DOELE in the ecological approach (EA) architecture [5]. In the EA there is no overall course design. Instead, courses are conceived as collections of learning objects each of which captures usage data as learners interact with it. Over time this usage data accumulates and can be used for many pedagogical purposes, including IP [1]. Drawing inspiration from work like [2], we propose a new IP algorithm based on collaborative filtering of learning sequences (CFLS). For a given learner our planner finds other learners who have traversed a similar sequence of learning objects with similar outcomes (i.e. similar paths). Then it suggests paths to the learner that were successful for these similar learners going forward. Two questions that arise: how far back to look in finding similar paths, and how far forward to plan before replacing. As in [1] we explore these questions through simulation.

2   Experiment Setup

The simulation is low-fidelity, using very simple abstractions of learners and LOs, as in our earlier work [3]. Each of the 40 LOs has a difficulty level and possible prerequisite relationships with other LOs. Each simulated learner has an attribute, *aptitude-of-learner*, a number between $(0,1)$ representing a learner's basic capability for the subject and allows learners to be divided into groups: low ($\leq .3$), medium ($.4 - .7$) and high aptitude ($\geq .8$).

A number called *P[learned]* is used to represent the learning that occurred when a learner visits a LO, or the probability that the learner learned the LO. P[learned] is generated by an *evaluation function*, a weighted sum: 20% of the learner's score on a LO is attributed to *aptitude-of-learner*, 50% attributed to whether the learner has mastered all of the prerequisite LOs, 20% attributed to whether the learner had seen that LO previously, and 10% attributed to the difficulty level of the LO.

The simulated learners move through the course by interacting with the LOs, one after another. In the EA architecture, everything that is known about a learner at the time of an interaction with a LO (in this case, including P[learned]) is captured and associated with that LO. The order of the LOs visited is determined by a planner such as the CFLS planner. To allow for the comparison of different planning approaches without advantaging one approach, each simulated learner halts after its 140th LO regardless of the type of planner being used.

The CFLS planner works as follows. For a given target learner the CFLS planner looks backward at the b most recent learning objects traversed. Then, it finds other learners who have traversed the same b learning objects with similar P[learned] values. These are learners in the target learner's "neighbourhood".

The planner then looks forward at the f next LOs traversed by each neighbour and picks the highest value path, where value is defined as the average P[learned] achieved on those f LOs ahead. This path is then recommended to the learner, who must follow it for at least s (for "sticky") LOs before replanning occurs. Of course, s is always less than f. In our research we explored various values of b and f to find which leads to the best results (we set $f = s$ for this experiment). "Best" is defined as the average P[learned] on the LOs that are the leafs of the prerequisite graph (interpreted as the ultimate target concepts, or the final exam).

Table 1. Baseline results for each group of simulated learners (high, medium and low aptitude) when visiting LOs randomly and following a simple prerequisite planner

Planning Type / Aptitude	low	medium	high
Random	N=21	N=26	N=18
Average Score on Final Exam (P[learned])	0.107	0.160	0.235
Simple Prerequisite Planner (SPP)	N=21	N=26	N=18
Average Score on Final Exam (P[learned])	0.619	0.639	0.714

Before running our CFLS planner, we first simulated a simple prerequisite planner (SPP) in order to create a baseline for comparison with the CFLS planner and to initialize the case base with a population of simulated learners. As Table 1 shows, the SPP works much better than a random planner. Our simulation experiment was aimed at seeing if, with appropriate choices of b and f, the CFLS planner could work as well or better than the SPP.

3   Results

We ran the CFLS planner 25 different times with all pairings of the values of b and s ranging from 1 to 5. Each of the 25 simulation runs was initialized with the same synthetic dataset, the baseline interactions created by the SPP. Then a population of 65 learners with the same distribution of aptitudes as the baseline was used to test the CFLS planner. The heat map in Fig. 1 shows the measurements for each of the 25 simulations, for each aptitude group, with the highest relative scores coloured red, mid-range scores coloured white, and the lowest scores coloured blue. In general, simulated learners achieved higher scores when following the CFLS planner than when given LOs randomly. The CFLS planner even exceeded the SPP in many cases. A success triangle is visible in the lower left of each aptitude group. The success triangles can be interpreted to mean that if a path is going to be recommended, never send the learner any further ahead (s) than you have matched them in the past (b). For example if a learner's neighbourhood was created using their $b = 2$ most recent LOs, then never make the learner follow in a neighbour's steps further than $s = 2$ LOs. One reason for the eventual drop at high values of b is that no neighbour could be found and a random match is used instead.

LOW					MEDIUM					HIGH				
b=1 s=1	b=2 s=1	b=3 s=1	b=4 s=1	b=5 s=1	b=1 s=1	b=2 s=1	b=3 s=1	b=4 s=1	b=5 s=1	b=1 s=1	b=2 s=1	b=3 s=1	b=4 s=1	b=5 s=1
0.6587	0.1036	0.1314	0.1283	0.146	0.6894	0.1851	0.2105	0.2099	0.2425	0.7641	0.2514	0.2805	0.2866	0.2702
b=1 s=2	b=2 s=2	b=3 s=2	b=4 s=2	b=5 s=2	b=1 s=2	b=2 s=2	b=3 s=2	b=4 s=2	b=5 s=2	b=1 s=2	b=2 s=2	b=3 s=2	b=4 s=2	b=5 s=2
0.5178	0.4387	0.1398	0.1248	0.1363	0.7004	0.698	0.2058	0.22	0.1972	0.77	0.7694	0.2673	0.2738	0.2748
b=1 s=3	b=2 s=3	b=3 s=3	b=4 s=3	b=5 s=3	b=1 s=3	b=2 s=3	b=3 s=3	b=4 s=3	b=5 s=3	b=1 s=3	b=2 s=3	b=3 s=3	b=4 s=3	b=5 s=3
0.4051	0.266	0.2256	0.1586	0.132	0.6942	0.6761	0.6715	0.1944	0.2152	0.7653	0.7638	0.7727	0.3019	0.3097
b=1 s=4	b=2 s=4	b=3 s=4	b=4 s=4	b=5 s=4	b=1 s=4	b=2 s=4	b=3 s=4	b=4 s=4	b=5 s=4	b=1 s=4	b=2 s=4	b=3 s=4	b=4 s=4	b=5 s=4
0.4138	0.2984	0.3016	0.2755	0.176	0.6931	0.6867	0.6874	0.6856	0.2292	0.768	0.7697	0.7633	0.7697	0.3431
b=1 s=5	b=2 s=5	b=3 s=5	b=4 s=5	b=5 s=5	b=1 s=5	b=2 s=5	b=3 s=5	b=4 s=5	b=5 s=5	b=1 s=5	b=2 s=5	b=3 s=5	b=4 s=5	b=5 s=5
0.357	0.2884	0.2859	0.2679	0.2249	0.6912	0.6884	0.6924	0.6965	0.6899	0.7601	0.7612	0.7591	0.7644	0.7636

Fig. 1. Average Score on Final Exam (P[learned]) by aptitude group

4   Analysis and Conclusion

Through simulation, we have shown that a CFLS planner can be "launched" from an environment that has been conditioned with interaction data from another planner, such as an SPP, and operate successfully using only learner usage data kept by the EA and not needing centralized metadata such as a prerequisite graph. This is one of the key requirements for DOELEs. Like biological evolution, the EA is harsh in that it observes how learners succeed or fail as various paths are tried. Successful paths for particular types of learners, regardless of whether they follow standard prerequisites, is the only criterion of success. While this experiment was not a true test of a DOELE because new learners and LOs were not inserted, this can be readily explored in future work. New additions could be matched randomly a few times in order to build enough data in the EA, and then automatically incorporated into neighbourhood matches or into future plans.

Acknowledgments. We would like to thank the Natural Sciences and Engineering Research Council of Canada for funding some aspects of this research.

References

1. Champaign, J.: Peer-Based Intelligent Tutoring Systems: A Corpus-Oriented Approach. Ph.D. Thesis, University of Waterloo, Waterloo, Canada (2012)
2. Elorriaga, J., Fernández-Castro, I.: Using Case-Based Reasoning in Instructional Planning: Towards a Hybrid Self-improving Instructional Planner. International Journal of Artificial Intelligence in Education 11(4), 416–449 (2000)
3. Erickson, G., Frost, S., Bateman, S., McCalla, G.: Using the ecological approach to create simulations of learning environments. In: Lane, H.C., Yacef, K., Mostow, J., Pavlik, P. (eds.) AIED 2013. LNCS, vol. 7926, pp. 411–420. Springer, Heidelberg (2013)
4. Land, S.: Cognitive Requirements for Learning with Open-Ended Learning Environments. Educational Technology Research and Development 48(3), 61–78 (2000)
5. McCalla, G.: The Ecological Approach to the Design of e-Learning Environments: Purpose-based Capture and Use of Information about Learners. Journal of Interactive Media in Education (2004). http://jime.open.ac.uk/jime/article/view/2004-7-mccalla

Modeling Self-Efficacy Across Age Groups with Automatically Tracked Facial Expression

Joseph F. Grafsgaard[1](✉), Seung Y. Lee[2], Bradford W. Mott[1],
Kristy Elizabeth Boyer[1], and James C. Lester[1]

[1] North Carolina State University, Raleigh, NC, USA
{jfgrafsg,bwmott,keboyer,lester}@ncsu.edu
[2] SAS Institute, Cary, NC, USA
seungyong.lee@sas.com

Abstract. Affect plays a central role in learning. Students' facial expressions are key indicators of affective states and recent work has increasingly used automated facial expression tracking technologies as a method of affect detection. However, there has not been an investigation of facial expressions compared across age groups. The present study collected facial expressions of college and middle school students in the CRYSTAL ISLAND game-based learning environment. Facial expressions were tracked using the Computer Expression Recognition Toolbox and models of self-efficacy for each age group highlighted differences in facial expressions. Age-specific findings such as these will inform the development of enriched affect models for broadening populations of learners using affect-sensitive learning environments.

Keywords: Affect · Facial expression recognition · Nonverbal behavior · Self-efficacy · Game-based learning environments

1 Introduction

Affect plays an important role in learning. While learning, students transition through a wide range of cognitive-affective states, such as *confusion*, *boredom*, *engagement*, and *frustration* [1]. These states may signal—or promote—effective learning while also interacting with broader constructs, such as motivation and self-efficacy. With a growing recognition of the importance of affect, new learning theories have begun to incorporate affective states into models of learning [2, 3].

Despite the significant body of work in facial expression tracking of learning-centered affect [4], there has not been an investigation that compared facial expressions across age groups. The present study provides the first examination of facial expression tracking of middle school and college students in an identical task: solving a science mystery with the aid of a human tutor in a game-based learning environment, CRYSTAL ISLAND, during a series of Wizard of Oz studies. Facial expressions were tracked using the Computer Expression Recognition Toolbox (CERT) and models of self-efficacy constructed for each age group highlighted differences in facial expressions, with only mouth dimpling appearing across models. These results

© Springer International Publishing Switzerland 2015
C. Conati et al. (Eds.): AIED 2015, LNAI 9112, pp. 582–585, 2015.
DOI: 10.1007/978-3-319-19773-9_67

suggest that there are key differences in facial expression between middle school and college students. Further analyses in this vein will contribute to the development of future learning environments, as affect detector functionalities will likely need to be tailored to specific age groups.

2   CRYSTAL ISLAND Wizard of Oz Studies

The CRYSTAL ISLAND game-based learning environment provides an effective "laboratory" for studying affect because students are engaged in deep learning while exploring an immersive virtual environment, experiencing cognitive-affective states related to challenge and enjoyment during the learning task. CRYSTAL ISLAND Wizard of Oz studies were conducted in order to build an automated director agent built on human narrative interventions [5]. The human "wizard" controlled narrative progress by guiding the student through reading information, testing objects in the environment, and developing a diagnosis to solve the mystery.

A middle school study was conducted with 32 students, including surveys and identical multiple-choice pretest/posttest on microbiology and the scientific method. The surveys consisted of demographics, the Big Five personality inventory (not analyzed here), a presence questionnaire, and self-efficacy for self-regulated learning [6]. An initial pilot study was also conducted with 38 college students to test the CRYSTAL ISLAND Wizard of Oz interface and protocol. Only the self-efficacy survey was administered during that pilot study. Webcam video, audio, and data logs were collected during both studies. Consent for image publication was not received, therefore no participants are shown in this paper.

3   Modeling Self-Efficacy Across Age Groups

Students' motivation and self-efficacy impact learning [2, 3]. In our prior research, we found that self-efficacy was associated with distinct nonverbal behaviors over the course of a tutoring session [7]. In the present study, models of self-efficacy were constructed for middle school and college students. Each model was built using relative frequencies of facial expression features provided by the Computer Expression Recognition Toolbox [8].

The models were constructed with the JMP statistical software. Features were standardized and model averaging was used to identify the top forty features based on the absolute value of a ratio between coefficient estimate and standard error. Then, stepwise forward linear regression was run with leave-one-student-out cross-validation. After a feature was selected at each step, all other features from the same CERT output channel were excluded in order to prevent over-fitting to a single output channel (e.g., selecting AU2 would then exclude further AU2). Bayesian Information Criterion (BIC) was used to select models that balanced model complexity with performance. The model of self-efficacy for middle school students is shown in Figure 1 and the model of self-efficacy for college students is shown in Figure 2.

Self-Efficacy =	p
0.66 * AU2 (*mean-center, threshold=0.05*)	<0.001
0.46 * AU12 Left (*z-score, threshold=0.5*)	<0.001
-0.26 * Fear Brow (*mean-center, threshold=0.45*)	0.057
-0.22 * AU14 Right (*mean-center, threshold=0.45*)	0.096
0.01 (intercept)	1
Leave-One-Student-Out Cross-Validated R^2 = 0.670	

Fig. 1. Model of self-efficacy for middle school students (N=31)

Self-Efficacy =	p
0.56 * AU4 (*orig., threshold=0*)	<0.001
0.39 * Contempt (*orig., threshold=0.1*)	0.041
0.31 * AU14 (*orig., threshold=0*)	0.074
0 (intercept)	1
Leave-One-Student-Out Cross-Validated R^2 = 0.434	

Fig. 2. Model of self-efficacy for college students (N=31)

4   Discussion

Models of self-efficacy constructed for each age group showed key differences in facial expressions. AU2 was most associated with self-efficacy for middle school students, with no analogous feature for college students. Similarly, AU4 was most associated with self-efficacy for college students, but did not appear in the model for middle school students. The "fear brow" facial expression was associated with lower self-efficacy in middle school students and has been previously correlated with anxiety [9]. Lower face features played a role in both models, with lip corner pulling (AU12) associated with middle school students and mouth dimpling (AU14) appearing in the model for college students. The prototypical contempt facial expression involves unilateral mouth dimpling (AU14 on either the right or left side). Contrary to the "basic" emotion interpretation, AU14 facial movement may be related to mental effort during learning, as evidenced in our prior research [10]. Thus, the model of self-efficacy for college students may be related to moments of mental effort (evidenced by AU4 and AU14) that did not result in negative affect, such as *frustration*. In contrast, middle school students with high self-efficacy may have smiled more, as evidenced by AU12. Collectively, these models provide empirical evidence of facial expression differences associated with self-efficacy across middle school and college students.

5   Conclusion

Recognizing and responding to affect during learning is a central requirement of affect-sensitive learning environments. Recent theories of learning incorporate affect as a vital component of student success and a growing body of research has aimed to recognize learning-centered affect using facial expression tracking. The present study provided first evidence of differences in middle school and college students' facial expressions during an identical task. Models of self-efficacy constructed for each age group incorporated different features, with only mouth dimpling appearing across models. These results provide insight into how facial expressions related to learning phenomena differ across age groups.

Acknowledgements. This work is supported in part by the North Carolina State University Department of Computer Science along with the National Science Foundation through Grant IIS-1409639. Any opinions, findings, conclusions, or recommendations expressed in this report are those of the participants, and do not necessarily represent the official views, opinions, or policy of the National Science Foundation.

References

1. Sabourin, J.L., Lester, J.C.: Affect and Engagement in Game-Based Learning Environments. IEEE Transactions on Affective Computing **5**, 45–56 (2014)
2. Pekrun, R.: The Control-Value Theory of Achievement Emotions: Assumptions, Corollaries, and Implications for Educational Research and Practice. Educational Psychology Review **18**, 315–341 (2006)
3. D'Mello, S.K., Lehman, B., Pekrun, R., Graesser, A.C.: Confusion Can Be Beneficial for Learning. Learning & Instruction **29**, 153–170 (2014)
4. D'Mello, S.K., Calvo, R.A.: Significant Accomplishments, New Challenges, and New Perspectives. In: Calvo, R.A., D'Mello, S.K. (eds.) New Perspectives on Affect and Learning Technologies, pp. 255–271. Springer, New York (2011)
5. Lee, S.Y., Rowe, J.P., Mott, B.W., Lester, J.C.: A Supervised Learning Framework for Modeling Director Agent Strategies in Educational Interactive Narrative. IEEE Transactions on Computational Intelligence and AI in Games. **6**, 203–215 (2014)
6. Bandura, A.: Guide for Constructing Self-Efficacy Scales. In: Pajares, F., Urdan, T. (eds.) Self-Efficacy Beliefs of Adolescents, pp. 307–337. Information Age Publishing, Greenwich, CT (2006)
7. Grafsgaard, J.F., Wiggins, J.B., Boyer, K.E., Wiebe, E.N., Lester, J.C.: Embodied affect in tutorial dialogue: student gesture and posture. In: Lane, H., Yacef, K., Mostow, J., Pavlik, P. (eds.) AIED 2013. LNCS, vol. 7926, pp. 1–10. Springer, Heidelberg (2013)
8. Littlewort, G., Whitehill, J., Wu, T., Fasel, I., Frank, M., Movellan, J.R., Bartlett, M.S.: The Computer Expression Recognition Toolbox (CERT). In: Proceedings of the IEEE International Conference on Automatic Face and Gesture Recognition, pp. 298–305 (2011)
9. Harrigan, J.A., O'Connell, D.M.: How Do You Look When Feeling Anxious? Facial Displays of Anxiety. Personality and Individual Differences. **21**, 205–212 (1996)
10. Grafsgaard, J.F., Wiggins, J.B., Vail, A.K., Boyer, K.E., Wiebe, E.N., Lester, J.C.: The Additive Value of Multimodal Features for Predicting Engagement, Frustration, and Learning during Tutoring. In: Proceedings of the 16th International Conference on Multimodal Interaction, pp. 42–49 (2014)

Adapting Feedback Types According to Students' Affective States

Beate Grawemeyer[1]([✉]), Manolis Mavrikis[2], Wayne Holmes[2],
and Sergio Gutierrez-Santos[1]

[1] London Knowledge Lab, Birkbeck,
University of London, London, UK
{beate,sergut}@dcs.bbk.ac.uk
[2] London Knowledge Lab, Institute of Education,
University College London, London, UK
{m.mavrikis,w.holmes}@ioe.ac.uk

Abstract. Affective states play a significant role in students' learning behaviour. Positive affective states can enhance learning, while negative ones can inhibit it. This paper describes the development of an affective state reasoner that is able to adapt the feedback type according to students' affective states in order to evoke positive affective states and as such improve their learning experience. The reasoner relies on a dynamic Bayesian network trained with data gathered in a series of ecologically valid Wizard-of-Oz studies, where the effect of feedback on students' affective states was investigated.

1 Introduction

This paper reports on the development of an affect state reasoner, which is able to tailor different feedback types according to student's affective state during their interaction with a learning environment.

Affective states interact with and influence the learning process [1,2] and therefore detecting student's affective states and helping them regulate their affect is important. Most of the related work in the field focusses on detecting emotions in different input stimuli, ranging from spoken dialogue (e.g. [3]) to keyboard and mouse interactions [4]. Only a limited amount of research has been undertaken into how those detected emotions can be used in a tutoring system to enhance the learning experience. One example is Conati et al. [5], who developed a pedagogical agent that is able to provide support according to the emotional state of the student and their personal goal. Another example is Shen et al. [6] who tailor the learning material according to a student's affective state. D'Mello et al. [7] use the student's affective state to respond via a conversation.

In this work, we report on the development of an affective state reasoner, which aims to change negative into positive affective states by adapting the feedback type. It is a dynamic Bayesian network trained with data from Wizard-of-Oz studies (WoZ) where the effect of different feedback types on students' affective states was investigated (*c.f.* [8]).

© Springer International Publishing Switzerland 2015
C. Conati et al. (Eds.): AIED 2015, LNAI 9112, pp. 586–590, 2015.
DOI: 10.1007/978-3-319-19773-9_68

2   The iTalk2Learn Platform

iTalk2Learn is a learning platform for children aged between 8-12 years old who are learning fractions. It includes an exploratory environment called Fractions Lab. The platform is being designed to detect children's speech in real time which, together with their interactions, are analyzed in order to provide adaptive support.

2.1   Intelligent Support

Figure 1 provides an overview of the different layers of support in the platform. Similar to [9] it consists of three main layers: the analysis or evidence detection layer, the reasoning layer, and the feedback generation layer. In the evidence detection layer, the student's interactions with the platform are identified. It includes the affective state detector, where the student's affective state is detected via their speech and their interaction with the learning environment.

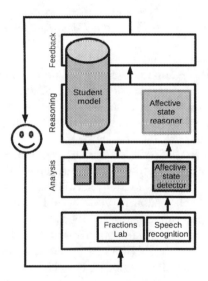

Fig. 1. Components of the intelligent support

Based on the evidence detection component, the reasoning layer decides if and what feedback should be provided. This layer includes a student model and the affective state reasoner. The student model includes the affective state of the student as well as information about actions that the student preformed, such as whether they followed the advice that was provided by the feedback. The affective state reasoner uses the information from the student model to decide what type of feedback should be provided as described below.

The feedback generation layer receives the output from the reasoning layer and with further information from the student model decides how the feedback should be presented; for example high- or low-interruptive feedback.

2.2 Affective State Reasoner

The aim of the affective state reasoner (see the orange box in Figure 1) is to tailor the feedback according to the affective state of the student, in order to evoke a positive affective state and thus enhance their learning experience. We focus on a subset of affective states identified by Pekrun [10]: flow, surprise, frustration, and boredom. We also add confusion, which has been identified elsewhere as an important affective state during learning for tutor support [11].

The affective state reasoner is a dynamic Bayesian network, based on data gathered in ecologically-valid WoZ studies [8] which investigated the impact of different feedback types on the affective state of students. The feedback types include problem solving support, reflective prompts, talk aloud and talk maths prompts, task sequence feedback, and affect boosts. The data from those studied showed that, to be effective, different student affective states require different feedback types. For example, when a student is confused, affect boosts or guidance feedback are more effective than others at enhancing the student's affective state. Figure 2 shows the dynamic Bayesian network of the affective state reasoner. We trained the network with the data from the WoZ studies annotated by three researchers. For the annotations we used the Baker-Rodrigo Observation Method Protocol (BROMP) and the HART mobile app that facilitates coding in the classroom [12]. Kappa based on the the annotation was .56, p<.001. We also annotated the affective states after the WoZ studies using screen and voice recordings. This was then compared against the field annotations. Kappa between the consolidated annotation and the HART data was .71, p<.05.

For the trained dynamic Bayesian network we employed a 10-fold cross-validation that shows encouraging results so far (accuracy=82.35%; Kappa=0.58; recall true=0.69). The affective state reasoner receives the affective state of the student (based on speech and interaction) as well as information about previous feedback followed. For each feedback type the enhanced affective state is predicted. This is used to determine which feedback type will be the most effective at enhancing the affective state. After appropriate feedback has been provided to the student, the CPT of the network is updated according to the student's affective state (and whether the previous feedback was followed) after feedback was delivered. In this way, the affective state reasoner is able to accommodate individual differences.

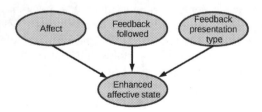

Fig. 2. Dynamic Bayesian network of the affective state reasoner

3   Conclusion and Future Work

We have developed an affective state reasoner, which is able to tailor different types of feedback according to the affective state of the student, in order to enhance their affective state. The affective state reasoner is a dynamic Bayesian network trained with data from WoZ studies, which investigated the effect of feedback on affective states. The results of the trained network are encouraging. The next stage in our research is to test the model with a new set of data, collected from future studies.

Acknowledgments. This research has been funded by the EU in FP7 in the iTalk2-Learn project (318051).

References

1. Baker, R.S.J.D., DMello, S.K., Rodrigo, M.T., Graesser, A.C.: Better to be frustrated than bored: The incidence, persistence, and impact of learners cognitive-affective states during interactions with three different computer-based learning environments. Int. J. Hum.-Comput. Stud. **68**(4), 223–241 (2010)
2. DMello, S.K., Lehman, B., Pekrun, R., Graesser, A.C.: Confusion can be beneficial for learning. Learning & Instruction **29**(1), 153–170 (2014)
3. Vogt, T., André, E.: Comparing feature sets for acted and spontaneous speech in view of automatic emotion recognition. In: Multimedia and Expo (ICME 2005), pp. 474–477 (2005)
4. Salmeron-Majadas, S., Santos, O., Boticario, J.: Exploring indicators from keyboard and mouse interactions to predict the user affective state. In: EDM 2014 (2014)
5. Conati, C., MacLaren, H.: Empirically building and evaluating a probabilistic model of user affect. User Modeling and User-Adapted Interaction (2009)
6. Shen, L., Wang, M., Shen, R.: Affective e-learning: Using emotional data to improve learning in pervasive learning environment. Educational Technology & Society **12**(2), 176–189 (2009)
7. DMello, S., Craig, S., Gholson, B., Franklin, S., Picard, R., Graesser, A.: Integrating affect sensors in an intelligent tutoring system. In: Affective Interactions: The Computer in the Affective Loop Workshop at 2005 International Conference on Intelligent User Interfaces, pp. 7–13 (2005)
8. Grawemeyer, B., Mavrikis, M., Holmes, W., Hansen, A., Loibl, K., Gutiérrez-Santos, S.: Affect Matters: Exploring the Impact of Feedback during Mathematical Tasks in an Exploratory Environment. In Proc. AIED 2015 (2015)
9. Gutiérrez-Santos, S., Mavrikis, M., Magoulas, G.: A separation of concerns for engineering intelligent support for exploratory learning environments. Journal of Research and Practice in Information Technology **44**(3), 347–360 (2012)
10. Pekrun, R.: The control-value theory of achievement emotions: Assumptions, corollaries, and implications for educational research and practice. J. Edu. Psych. Rev. pp. 315–341 (2006)

11. Porayska-Pomsta, K., Mavrikis, M., Pain, H.: Diagnosing and acting on student affect: the tutors perspective. UMUAI **18**(1), 125–173 (2008)
12. Ocumpaugh, J., Baker, R.S.J.D., Rodrigo, M.M.T.: Baker-Rodrigo Observation Method Protocol (BROMP) 1.0. Training Manual version 1.0. Tech. rep., New York, NY: EdLab. Manila, Philippines: Ateneo Laboratory for the Learning Sciences (2012)

Can Young People with Autism Spectrum Disorder Benefit from an Open Learner Model?

Beate Grawemeyer[1]([⊠]), Hilary Johnson[2], and Mark Brosnan[3]

[1] London Knowledge Lab, Birkbeck, University of London, London WC1E 7HX, UK
beate@dcs.bbk.ac.uk

[2] Department of Computer Science, University of Bath, Bath BA2 7AY, UK
h.johnson@bath.ac.uk

[3] Department of Psychology, University of Bath, Bath BA2 7AY, UK
m.j.brosnan@bath.ac.uk

Abstract. This paper describes the evaluation of Maths Island Tutor - an intelligent tutoring system for children with autism spectrum disorder (ASD). The tutor includes an open learner model (OLM). In order to benefit from this feature, the learner needs to be able to process metacognitive attributes, which can be impaired in ASD. In order to address the needs of this specific population, young people with ASD were involved in the design of the software for their use, including the OLM. A preliminary study evaluating the system demonstrated that young people with ASD did initiate access to their OLM, could correctly reproduce details from their OLM, and could also highlight the location of (study-intended) errors within their OLMs giving rise to suggestions about their abilities to remember and potentially meta-cognitively reflect on their learning.

1 Introduction

The research aim was to develop and assess the utility of educational tutoring software for mathematics, especially designed for the needs of young people with ASD. The mathematics tutor includes an open learner model (OLM) that could encourage self-reflection to enhance learning outcomes. The research sought to extend the benefits of OLMs to young people with ASD by involving them in the design of the OLM through a process of participatory design. OLMs are an external representation of a learner model. They can demonstrate to students their own learning trajectories in order that they are made aware of which learning strategies they had adopted and which were or were not successful. The aim of OLMs is to support metacognitive processes, for instance in reflecting on the use of different learning strategies with the intention of enhancing performance [1]. Different types of external representation have been applied in OLMs. They range from simple textual descriptions [2], to complex representations, such as conceptual graphs [3], and tree structures [4,5].

All of the research outlined above has been based on the general population. ASD is associated with a weakness in metacognition including self-reflection [6]. Consequently, the research sought to assess if this was the case with the OLM, given the young people's involvement in the OLM design.

C. Conati et al. (Eds.): AIED 2015, LNAI 9112, pp. 591–594, 2015.
DOI: 10.1007/978-3-319-19773-9_69

2   Maths Island Tutor

Maths Island Tutor is a system for teaching multiplication, which is part of the 'number' subject from the UK National Curriculum for Mathematics. It includes an OLM. For the development of the OLM young people with ASD were involved in the design process.

A map was chosen by the participants as a basic idea for the representation of the OLM. Maps were preferred above other representations by young people with and without ASD [7]. Figure 1 shows an example of the OLM which was developed with the young people with ASD in the participatory sessions. Each mathematical concept is represented as an island. The flags on each island 'fill up' with colour as the student answers questions correctly and include a symbol which appears when the topic has been concluded. The position of the user on their learning route is represented by a car that moves along from topic to topic.

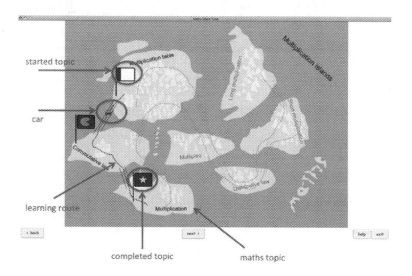

Fig. 1. Example of the OLM

The OLM can be accessed by the student at any time by clicking on a button. Additionally, the OLM will be displayed automatically at the beginning of a new mathematical concept, and also after completing the mathematical concept.

3   Evaluation

We were specifically interested in identifying whether young people with ASD are able to benefit from an OLM and whether it encourages self-reflection. Participants were 24 school children with a clinical diagnosis of ASD (19 male and 5 females), with a mean age of 13.6 years (s.d.=1.3). Although these schoolchildren had an IQ within the normal range, they were underperforming in mathematics. The control group chosen therefore were typically developing (TD) children who were studying the same course material in class. There were 28 TD school children, 10 males and 18 females, with a mean age of 10.5 years (s.d.=0.5).

To investigate the young peoples awareness and understanding of the information provided by the OLM, a decision was made to include both accurate but crucially also inaccurate information (i.e. errors) in the OLM. We therefore conducted three 20-minute sessions, where in two sessions the OLM was altered in a way that would give insight into its effectiveness as a tool for self-reflection: **session 1** - OLM with no error; **session 2** - OLM with an error - participants were not informed that the OLM included an error; **session 3** - OLM with an error - participants were informed that the OLM included an error. After sessions 2 and 3 participants were provided with a screen printout of an empty OLM representation for the purpose of self-reporting. They were requested to indicate which mathematical concept they had learned by ticking the flags on the relevant mathematics islands and circling the flag that included any error.

3.1   Results

The TD group completed roughly double the number of mathematical concepts as the ASD group in all 3 sessions. This also means that the TD group was provided with the OLM automatically more often after a mathematical concept was completed. However, there was no differences between the groups in how often they self-initiated the OLM (through the button).

There were no significant differences in the proportion of flags (mathematical concept learned) correctly identified as being present in sessions 2 or 3 by the TD and ASD groups (0.71 vs 0.59 $(t(50)=1.06$, ns; 0.77 vs. 0.73 $(t(50)=0.33$, ns). A pairwise t-test also showed no significant difference in the proportion of correctly identified flags *between* Session 2 and 3 for both TD and ASD groups $(t(27)=1.16$, ns; $t(23)=1.61$, ns; respectively).

More of the TD group than the ASD group identified the presence of an error in both Sessions 2 and 3 (0.93 vs 0.71: $t(35.07)=2.06$, p<.05; 0.89 vs 0.46: $t(44.48)=3.33$, p<.01) suggesting either they were good at noticing errors or were guessing an error had occurred. However, of those who had identified the presence of an error, those with ASD were significantly more likely to accurately locate the error than the TD group, significantly so in Session 3 (.38 vs .53 $(t(41)=.92$, ns ; .33 vs .73 $(t(33)=2.27$, p<.05).

4   Discussion and Conclusion

There were no differences between the groups in correctly identifying flags after sessions 2 and 3. This implies either that young people with ASD can benefit from an OLM despite the ASD weakness in metacognition, or that they were very accurate in remembering the state of their OLM. This needs to be investigated further along with the potential implications for self-reflection of accurately remembering details of their OLM as this may relate to growing awareness as part of the processes necessary for successful self-reflection.

At some level, it is not surprising that more of the TD group identified an error than the ASD group, as ASD is associated with a weakness in metacognition. There are several possible explanations for this result: i) asking the TD group if there was an error might prime them to say Yes; ii) guessing might be more likely in the TD population; and iii) children with ASD might be less likely to believe the computer could be inaccurate and to literally believe all computer outputs. Interestingly, of those who had accurately identified the presence of an error, those with ASD were significantly more likely to accurately locate the error than the TD group, particularly in the last session (session 3) where participants were advised at the beginning to watch out for an error. This corresponds with the ASD trait of attention to detail [8].

The results crucially indicate where further research is necessary to eliminate any other interpretations of the results relating to guessing, enhanced memory and so on. Further studies and analyses specifically investigating whether benefits to learning occur as a result of accessing the OLM are being undertaken.

Acknowledgments. The authors gratefully acknowledge Brislington Enterprise College (BEC) in Bristol (especially the ASD unit). The support of the Engineering and Physical Sciences Research Council (EPSRC, EP/G031975/1) is also gratefully acknowledged.

References

1. Bull, S., Kay, J.: Open learner models as drivers for metacognitive processes. In: International Handbook of Metacognition and Learning Technologies, pp. 349–365. Springer, New York (2013)
2. Bull, S., Pain, H.: Did I say what I think I said, and do you agree with me? Inspecting and Questioning the Student Model. Proc. AIED **1995**, 501–508 (1995)
3. Dimitrova, V.: StyLE-OLM: Interactive Open Learner Modelling. J. Artificial Intelligence in Education **13**(1), 35–78 (2003)
4. Kay, J.: Learner Know Thyself: Student Models to Give Learner Control and Responsibility. Computers in Education, 17–24 (1997)
5. Brusilovsky, P., Hsiao, I.-H., Folajimi, Y.: QuizMap: open social student modeling and adaptive navigation support with TreeMaps. In: Kloos, C.D., Gillet, D., Crespo García, R.M., Wild, F., Wolpers, M. (eds.) EC-TEL 2011. LNCS, vol. 6964, pp. 71–82. Springer, Heidelberg (2011)
6. Carruthers, P.: How we know our own minds: the relationship between mindreading and metacognition. Behav. Brain Sci. **32**(2), 138–182 (2009)
7. Grawemeyer, B., Johnson, H., Brosnan, M., Ashwin, E., Benton, L.: The impact of Autism Spectrum Disorder on the Categorisation of External Representations. Proc. CogSci **2011**, 2202–2207 (2011)
8. Shah A, Frith U.: An islet of ability in autism: a research note. J. Child Psychol Psychiatry (1983)

Affect Matters: Exploring the Impact of Feedback During Mathematical Tasks in an Exploratory Environment

Beate Grawemeyer[1]([✉]), Manolis Mavrikis[2], Wayne Holmes[2], Alice Hansen[2],
Katharina Loibl[3], and Sergio Gutiérrez-Santos[1]

[1] London Knowledge Lab, Birkbeck, University of London, London, UK
{beate,sergut}@dcs.bbk.ac.uk
[2] London Knowledge Lab, Institute of Education,
University College London, London, UK
{m.mavrikis,w.holmes,a.hansen}@ioe.ac.uk
[3] Institute of Educational Research,
Ruhr-Universität Bochum, Bochum, Germany
katharina.loibl@rub.de

Abstract. We describe a Wizard-of-Oz study that investigates the impact of different types of feedback on students' affective states. Our results indicate the importance of matching carefully the affective state with appropriate feedback in order to help students transition into more positive states. For example when students were confused affect boosts and specific instruction seem to be effective in helping students to be in flow again. We discuss this and other effective ways to and implications for the development of our system and the field in general.

1 Introduction

It is well understood that affect interacts with and influences the learning process [1,2]. While positive affective states such as surprise, satisfaction or curiosity contribute towards constructive learning, negative ones including frustration challenge learning. The learning process is indeed full of transitions between positive and negative affective states and regulating those is important.

In related work, students' affective states have been used to tailor motivational feedback and learning material in order to enhance the learning experience. For example, Santos et al. [3] show that affect as well as motivation and self-efficacy impact the effectiveness of motivational feedback and recommendations. Additionally, Woolf et al. [4] developed an affective pedagogical agent which is able to mirror a student's affective state. Another example is Conati & MacLaren [5], who developed a pedagogical agent to provide support according to the affective state of the student and their personal goal. Also, Shen et al. [6] recommend learning material to the student based on their affective state. D'Mello et al. [7] developed a system that is able to respond to students via a conversation that takes into account the affective state of the student.

© Springer International Publishing Switzerland 2015
C. Conati et al. (Eds.): AIED 2015, LNAI 9112, pp. 595–599, 2015.
DOI: 10.1007/978-3-319-19773-9_70

In this paper, we investigate the impact of different types of feedback on students' affective state and how and whether they can help students regulate their affect and thus improve learning.

2 The Wizard-of-Oz Study

One of our research aims is to develop intelligent support that enhances the learning experience by taking into account the student's affective state. We were interested in identifying how different feedback types modify affective states. We focus on a subset of affective states identified by Pekrun [8]: flow/enjoyment, surprise, frustration, and boredom. We also add confusion, which has been identified elsewhere as an important affective state during learning [9].

In total, 26 Year-5 (9 to 10-year old) students took part in a Wizard-of-Oz study where students undertook tasks in an exploratory learning environment for fractions (Fractions Lab). Each session lasted on average 20 minutes. More information about the set up of the study can be found in Mavrikis et al. [10].

Wizards followed a script with pre-specified messages to send feedback to the students through the learning platform and deliberately limited their communication capacity in order to simulate the actual system.The different types of feedback that were provided from the wizards to the students as follows:

- AFFECT - affect boosts ('You're working really hard! Well done!")
- INSTRUCTION - instructive task-dependent feedback ('Use the comparison box to compare your fractions')
- OTHER PROBLEM SOLVING - task-dependent feedback ('To add two fractions together, they first need to have the same denominator')
- TALK ALOUD - talking aloud ('Remember to talk aloud, what are you thinking?')
- REFLECTION - reflecting on task performance and learning ('Why did you change the denominator?')
- TALK MATHEMATICS - using particular domain specific mathematics vocabulary ('Can you explain that again using the terms denominator or numerator?')
- TASK SEQUENCE - moving to the next taskt ('Well Done. When you are ready, click 'next' for the next task')

We explored these particular types of feedback because the literature suggests they support students in their learning and because they fit our context [10].

From the Wizard-of-Oz study we recorded the students' screen display and their voices. From this data, we annotated affective states (e.g. screen interaction and what the students said) before and after feedback was provided.

3 Results

In total 396 messages were sent to 26 students. The video data in combination with the sound files were analysed independently by three researchers who categorised the affective states of students before and after the feedback messages were provided. Additionally, we used the Baker-Rodrigo Observation Method Protocol (BROMP) and the HART mobile app that facilitates coding of affective states in the classroom [11]. Kappa between the researchers' annotations and the HART data was .71, p<.05.

The affective states that occurred *before* the feedback was provided were confusion in 181 cases, flow in 169 cases, frustration in 34 cases, boredom in 9 cases, and surprise in 3 cases. The affective states that occurred *after* the feedback was sent were flow in 250 cases, confusion in 131 cases, frustration in 10 cases, boredom in 3 cases, and surprise in 2 cases.

In order to investigate whether there was an effect of the feedback on the learning experience, we looked at whether a student's affective state was enhanced (e.g. changed from frustration to confusion or flow) or was worsened (e.g. changed from flow to frustration or confusion). As the data is categorical [12], we apply chi-square tests to investigate statistical significant differences.

When students were in **flow**, there was no significant difference between the feedback types on whether the affective state stayed in the same flow state ($X^2(6, N=169) = 4.31$, p>.05) or worsened ($X^2(6, N=169) = 4.89$, p>.05).

When students were **confused**, there was a significant effect of the feedback type on whether students' affective state was enhanced into a flow state ($X^2(6, N=181) = 13.65$, p<.05). The most effective feedback types were affect boosts with 68% of the cases, followed by guidance feedback with 67%, and task sequence prompts with 63%. Reflective prompts resulted in a flow state in 48% of the cases, talk aloud prompts 38%, and problem solving support with 34%. Talk math prompts were the least effective with only 25% of the cases. There was no significant association between the feedback type and whether the affective state worsened ($X^2(6, N=181) = 4.65$, p>.05).

There was not sufficient data available when students were **frustrated**, nor when they were **bored**, or **surprised** to run a statistical test across the different affective states and feedback types.

4   Discussion and Conclusion

Our results confirm related research on the role of feedback in enhancing students' affective states, and allow us to tease apart the impact of the various feedback types on the students' affective state.

When students were in flow there was no significant difference between the feedback types on whether or not the affective state stayed the same or worsened. This suggests that, when students are in flow, challenging feedback can be provided without negative implications.

However, when students were confused there was a difference between the feedback types on whether the affective state was enhanced, stayed the same or worsened. The feedback types that most effectively moved the student out of a confusion state were affect boosts, instruction, and task sequence. When they were struggling to overcome problems, affect boosts appeared to encourage some students to redouble their efforts without the need for task specific support.

We can hypothesise that this enabled students to self-regulate their affect and move forward. As expected, instructive feedback appears to have given the students the next steps that they needed, whereas other problem solving was less successful. Other problem solving feedback seems to have led students to be more confused because of the increased cognitive load to understand the hint or the question provided. While talk aloud and talk math, encouraged students to vocalize what they are trying to achieve, they appear not to have helped the students address their confusions. Instead, when they were confused, students appeared to have welcomed a new task.

Our next steps using the data collected is to train an intelligent system that is able to tailor the type of feedback according to the affective state of the student in order to enhance the learning experience and investigate in more detail the impact of feedback and affect in students' learning.

Acknowledgments. This research has been funded by the EU under the FP7 iTalk2Learn project (318051). For more information http://www.italk2learn.eu.

References

1. DMello, S.K., Lehman, B., Pekrun, R., Graesser, A.C.: Confusion can be beneficial for learning. Learning & Instruction **29**(1), 153–170 (2014)
2. Baker, R.S.J.D., DMello, S.K., Rodrigo, M.T., Graesser, A.C.: Better to be frustrated than bored: The incidence, persistence, and impact of learners cognitive-affective states during interactions with three different computer-based learning environments. Int. J. Hum.-Comput. Stud. **68**(4), 223–241 (2010)
3. Santos, O., Saneiro, M., Salmeron-Majadas, S., J.G., B.: A methodological approach to elicit affective educational recommendataions. In: IEEE 14th International Conference on Advanced Learning Technologies (2014)
4. Woolf, B., Burleson, W., Arroyo, I., Dragon, T., Cooper, D., Picard, R.: Affect-aware tutors: recognising and responding to student affect. Int. J. Learning Technology **4**(3–4), 129–164 (2009)
5. Conati, C., MacLaren, H.: Empirically building and evaluating a probabilistic model of user affect. User Modeling and User-Adapted Interaction (2009)
6. Shen, L., Wang, M., Shen, R.: Affective e-learning: Using emotional data to improve learning in pervasive learning environment. Educational Technology & Society **12**(2), 176–189 (2009)
7. DMello, S., Craig, S., Gholson, B., Franklin, S., Picard, R., Graesser, A.: Integrating affect sensors in an intelligent tutoring system. In: Affective Interactions: The Computer in the Affective Loop Workshop at 2005 International Conference on Intelligent User Interfaces, pp. 7–13 (2005)
8. Pekrun, R.: The control-value theory of achievement emotions: Assumptions, corollaries, and implications for educational research and practice. J. Edu. Psych. Rev., 315–341 (2006)
9. Porayska-Pomsta, K., Mavrikis, M., Pain, H.: Diagnosing and acting on student affect: the tutors perspective. UMUAI **18**(1), 125–173 (2008)

10. Mavrikis, M., Grawemeyer, B., Hansen, A., Gutiérrez-Santos, S.: Exploring the potential of speech recognition to support problem solving and reflection. EC- TEL **2014**, 263–276 (2014)
11. Ocumpaugh, J., Baker, R.S.J.d., Rodrigo, M.M.T.: Baker-Rodrigo Observation Method Protocol (BROMP) 1.0. Training Manual version 1.0. Tech. rep., New York, NY: EdLab. Manila, Philippines: Ateneo Laboratory for the Learning Sciences (2012)
12. Rosenthal, R., Rosnow, R.: Essentials of Behavioral Research: Methods and data analysis. McGraw Hill, 3rd edn. (2008)

How Do Learners Behave in Help-Seeking When Given a Choice?

Sebastian Gross$^{(\boxtimes)}$ and Niels Pinkwart

Humboldt-Universität zu Berlin, Berlin, Germany
{sebastian.gross,niels.pinkwart}@hu-berlin.de

Abstract. We describe the results of a study that investigated learners'
help-seeking behavior using two feedback options implemented in an ITS
for Java programming. The 25 students had the choice between asking for
feedback on errors in their programs and feedback on possible next steps
in the solution process. We hypothesized that learners' choices would
depend on correctness of their programs and their progress in problem-
solving. Surprisingly, this hypothesis was not confirmed.

Keywords: Intelligent tutoring system · Help-seeking · Feedback choice

1   Introduction

Many ITS systems favor a feedback on demand model, as this supports self-
regulated learning better than feedback on the initiative of the system and avoids
risks of undesired interference when feedback messages disturb learners' cognitive
processes. Yet, if feedback is presented upon request, the help-seeking behavior
of the learner plays an important role for the success of the learning technology.
Previous research has investigated aspects of learners' help-seeking attitudes,
including detection of misuse [2] and instructing learners to improve their help-
seeking behavior [1].

An under-investigated question in this area is how learners would behave
when given a choice between two or more help options: are the learners' choices
in line with what the feedback options are intended to be used for? We previously [4] proposed a novel approach for providing feedback in ITSs by employing
example-based learning. Research on worked examples that provide an expert's
solution on how to solve a given problem has proven to be effective in various
learning domains such as mathematics [5] or programming education [3]. In our
approach, prototype-based classification of dissimilarity data is used to identify
an appropriate example from a data set consisting of successful and unsuccessful learners' solution attempts and sample solutions (or parts thereof) created
by experts. This selected element of the data set (called counterpart) is then
used to provide feedback to a learner by presenting the learner's current solution attempt, contrasting it with the selected element of the data set, and asking
her to compare the two. In previous work [4], we implemented the approach in
an ITS for Java programming and tested it with students of an introductory

© Springer International Publishing Switzerland 2015
C. Conati et al. (Eds.): AIED 2015, LNAI 9112, pp. 600–603, 2015.
DOI: 10.1007/978-3-319-19773-9_71

programming course, comparing four strategies (randomly chosen by the ITS) for selecting an appropriate example from a data set. The results supported the hypothesis that using a data set consisting of expert solution steps is superior to using complete sample solutions only and to using learner solution attempts only. The previous study also suggested that two feedback strategies seem to be most promising: selecting the most similar sample solution part in the data set, or selecting the next step of this most similar solution. However, it remained unclear *when* (depending on learners' progress) the most similar sample solution step or its next step should be provided as feedback to help learners fix mistakes or proceed in problem-solving. This is the question investigated in this paper.

2   Study Description

In order to answer the question stated above, we modified our ITS for Java programming in such a way that the feedback strategy is not randomly chosen by the system anymore. Instead, we allowed learners to choose between two feedback options. In both options, learners' current programs were analyzed and compared to the data set consisting of sample solution parts created by experts. The difference between the feedback options was that in feedback option 1 (marked with *"I don't know where the error in my program is."*), the most similar sample solution step in the data set was selected as counterpart. In feedback option 2 (marked with *"I don't know how to continue with my program."*), the next step of the most similar sample solution part was selected as counterpart. Based on the counterpart, the system then provided feedback to learners. In accompanying text, the system clearly informed learners about the difference between the two options, suggesting that option 1 would likely be more appropriate if students did not know how to fix an error in their program (since the feedback shows a similar but correct part of a sample solution), and option 2 would be preferable if students did not know how to proceed (since the feedback shows a more advanced part of a sample solution).

With this study design, we wanted to investigate the help-seeking behavior of students in this example based feedback provision scenario: do students select the feedback option that is (probably) more helpful for them? Specifically, our hypotheses were that:

H1 if their current program is erroneous, learners would ask for the most similar sample solution step, and

H2 if their current program is correct (but not necessarily complete), learners would ask for the next step of the most similar sample solution step

To evaluate the hypotheses, we conducted a field study in which the ITS was used in the context of an introductory programming course at Humboldt-Universität zu Berlin. The system was shown to the students in class, and the content available in the system (exercises, sample solution steps etc.) matched the course content. Students had the opportunity to use the system over a period of 10 weeks from anywhere they wanted at anytime. Participation was completely voluntary and possible with a self-chosen login.

3   Results

For 39 programming tasks, 25 students requested feedback 340 times. They chose
option 1 in 187 cases and option 2 in 153 cases. We asked an experienced Java
tutor to assess each student program as to whether (i) the program is syntactically correct, and (ii) the program is on target with respect to the given problem.
For the latter criterion, we measured the interrater reliability by having a 10%
random sample assessed by a second experienced Java tutor, resulting in an
acceptable Cohen's kappa of $\kappa = .58$. We also asked the human tutor to identify misuse of the feedback options where students requested multiple feedbacks
within a few minutes without (substantially) changing their programs. Overall the expert identified 116 cases of such misuse. As stated in Section 2, we

Table 1. Program states and chosen feedback options. Numbers in parentheses include
the feedback requests classified as misuse. Choices that we expected to be chosen by a
learner (depending on her program's state) are shaded in gray.

	Feedback option 1 (show similar sample)		Feedback option 2 (show next step)		Total
syntax error but program on target	32 (52)	55% (52%)	15 (24)	52% (46%)	47 (76)
syntax error and program not on target	38 (44)		35 (46)		73 (90)
syntax correct and program on target	48 (75)	45% (48%)	21 (28)	48% (54%)	69 (103)
syntax correct but program not on target	9 (16)		26 (55)		35 (71)
Total	127 (187)		97 (153)		224 (340)

expected that feedback option 1 would mainly be chosen by students whose programs are erroneous (i.e., have syntax errors or are not on target) while option
2 would mainly be chosen by students who got stuck in problem-solving (but
their programs are syntactically correct and on target). Table 1 summarizes the
observed student behavior, numbers in parentheses include the feedback requests
classified as misuse. When feedback option 1 was chosen, only 55% (52%) of the
programs were syntactically erroneous, while only 48% (54%) of the programs
were syntactically correct when feedback option 2 was chosen. It is obvious that
this data does not support the hypotheses. If we consider whether a student's
program was on target as an indicator of correctness, the data even shows a picture completely contrary to our expectations: if feedback option 1 was chosen,
the correct student's program was on target in 63% (68%) of the cases, whereas
this was true only in 37% (34%) of the cases if feedback option 2 was chosen. This
difference is statistically significant ($\chi^2 = 14.75$ (38.85), $df = 1, p < .001$). While
Table 1 contains all feedback requests regardless of individual student behavior,
we were also interested in individual student characteristics: were there some
students with help-seeking behavior as hypothesized and others who behaved
differently, or did all students exhibit a more or less homogeneous help-seeking
attitude? We therefore examined how often a student chose feedback option 1

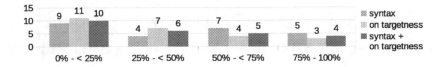

Fig. 1. Percentages of how often students chose feedback options as hypothesized

when her program was syntactically erroneous or not on target, and how often a student chose feedback option 2 when her program was syntactically correct and on target. Figure 1 shows the results, grouped into four ranges where each range indicates in how many cases a learner behaved as hypothesized in Section 2. The diagram illustrates that learners' help-seeking behavior cannot be distinctly divided into "predicted" and "unpredicted" but the number of learners is almost evenly distributed in the four ranges. This implies that indeed for some learners our hypotheses hold, but not for others.

4   Conclusion and Future Work

We investigated learners' help seeking behavior when given a choice, hypothesizing that learners' choice would depend on the correctness of their programs. Yet, the hypotheses were not confirmed in the study - to the contrary: when considering on-targetness, learners' choices were largely in contrast with our prediction. There are some possible explanations for this: (1) learners may be fully aware of what kind of help they actually need, but the underlying factors of this reasoning do not correlate with our predictions, (2) the hypotheses indeed hold but learners are not aware of what kind of help they actually need (i.e., they do not know if they have a problem to fix or not before they can make the next step), and they probably need help-seeking assistance, or (3) the hypotheses hold only for some learners (as suggested by Figure 1) and we need to determine the factors that account for this. In future work, we plan to address these issues by conducting a qualitative analysis of students' programs before and after requesting feedback.

References

1. Aleven, V., Mclaren, B., Roll, I., Koedinger, K.: Toward meta-cognitive tutoring: A model of help seeking with a cognitive tutor. IJAIED **16**(2), 101–128 (2006)
2. Baker, R.S., Corbett, A.T., Koedinger, K.R.: Detecting student misuse of intelligent tutoring systems. In: Lester, J.C., Vicari, R.M., Paraguaçu, F. (eds.) ITS 2004. LNCS, vol. 3220, pp. 531–540. Springer, Heidelberg (2004)
3. Brusilovsky, P., Yudelson, M.: From webex to navex: Interactive access to annotated program examples. Proceedings of the IEEE **96**(6), 990–999 (2008)
4. Gross, S., Mokbel, B., Hammer, B., Pinkwart, N.: How to select an example? a comparison of selection strategies in example-based learning. In: Trausan-Matu, S., Boyer, K.E., Crosby, M., Panourgia, K. (eds.) ITS 2014. LNCS, vol. 8474, pp. 340–347. Springer, Heidelberg (2014)
5. Renkl, A.: Learning mathematics from worked-out examples: Analyzing and fostering self-explanations. Europ. Journ. of Psych. of Education **14**(4), 477–488 (1999)

Modeling Children's Pedestrian Safety Skills in an Intelligent Virtual Reality Learning Environment

Yecheng Gu[✉], Sergey Sosnovsky, and Carsten Ullrich

German Research Center for Artificial Intelligence (DFKI), Stuhlsatzenhausweg 3,
Saarbrücken 66123, Germany
{yecheng.gu,sergey.sosnovsky,carsten.ullrich}@dfki.de

Abstract. This work presents an intelligent virtual reality environment for training child traffic safety. Key pedestrian skills are discussed. The overall system design is described together with a set of implemented practical exercises. An evaluation study shows that the approach is well accepted and that children struggle with the same skills in the virtual environment as in the real world.

1 Introduction

Children are endangered traffic participants. They are hard to see, fragile, have limited perceptual-motor abilities and lack both knowledge and experience in traffic situations [1]. Existing traffic education programs focus on theoretical aspects and needs to be supplemented with individualized practical street side training [2]. However, such training is hard to provide in the real world due to safety reasons and dependence on environmental conditions. One promising alternative is to employ Virtual Reality (VR) technologies and conduct training in safe and controllable virtual environments. In fact, a number of previous studies have investigated the use of VR as a tool for practical child pedestrian training. Thomsen et al. showed in a study that children aged 7-11 were able to better their skill of finding appropriate gaps in traffic to cross a road through VR training [3]. Further, Schwebel et al. were able to show that children exhibit consistent road crossing behavior in VR and in the real world [4]. However, these systems were very limited in terms of tutoring capabilities and diversity of training scenarios. At the same time, the combination of Intelligent Tutoring Systems (ITS) with VR training has shown to be successful in other domains [5]. In this work, we build on the early success in the field by implementing SafeChild – a VR-based training environment with ITS capabilities for the domain of child pedestrian safety.

2 Pedestrian Safety Skills

Children need to learn a number of behavior rules and master corresponding skills in order to become safe pedestrians. These skills differ greatly in their cognitive demand and some are especially difficult for young children as many studies show. This includes the detection of non-obvious threats [6], paying selective attention to those parts of traffic that affects safety while ignoring others [7] and observing the traffic situation from a global perspective [8]. We have conducted a cognitive analysis of this domain informed

© Springer International Publishing Switzerland 2015
C. Conati et al. (Eds.): AIED 2015, LNAI 9112, pp. 604–607, 2015.
DOI: 10.1007/978-3-319-19773-9_72

by the existing literature on pedestrian traffics safety [9] and in consultation with traffics safety experts. As a result, we have identified two groups of skills. The basic skills, which are less demanding cognitively and should be easier for children to apply and master, include: crossing in designated areas; crossing at green light; keeping distance to roads unless trying to cross; stopping at a curb; looking both sides for incoming traffic; crossing straight without stopping (unless an emergency is detected). The advanced skills involve more complex decision making and planning procedures and maintaining the awareness of other traffic participants. They include: making sure that cars are stopping; observing traffic while crossing; recognizing dangerous cars; selecting appropriate gap to cross; recognizing shortcomings of a crossing place; anticipating traffic light change; finding a suitable place to cross; plan route through multiple crossings. We anticipate that children in a VR environment will have fewer problems with basic skills, but will struggle with the advanced skills that pose difficulty in real-word traffic education. For the SafeChild platform, this means that its instructional component should especially support acquisition of advanced skills.

3   Exercises in SafeChild

The SafeChild system provides a freely explorable virtual city environment with simulated traffic. The standard interface is based on a single monitor as display and a keyboard as input device. Other interfaces with higher degree of immersion are supported and panned for future research. In order to train the skills described in Chapter 2, a preliminary set of ten road-crossing exercises have been designed. Each exercise requires a set of skills to cross the road under different conditions (ranging from five to ten skills per exercise depending on the difficulty) and to reach the goal safely. The set of exercises consists of three tasks related to using traffic light; three exercises related to using zebra crossing, three exercises related to unregulated crossings and one combination exercise. For traffic light and zebra crossing, the learner starts once directly in front of the designated crossing area; once, within a small distance, but with the traffic light / zebra crossing still in sight; and once, further away, where a turn in the virtual city environment is required to find the designated place to cross. In all cases, the final goal is directly visible and the learner is supposed to utilize the available regulated crossing to reach it. For the unregulated crossings tasks, the user starts once on a sidewalk next to a straight road without obstacles; once, with a parking truck as an obstacle; and once, close to a road curve obstructing the field of vision. The task is to recognize shortcomings of the crossing place if they are present and cross the road safely. In the final exercise the learner can plan own route to the goal and is given the opportunity to either cross the road once with an unregulated crossing or to cross twice using traffic light and zebra crossing; the expected behavior is to prefer the combination of traffic light and zebra crossing over the unregulated crossing. Fig. 1, shows a screenshot from a "traffic light" exercise, with the yellow arrow designating the goal. It also shows two feedback screens for reaching the goal and failing it (if hit by a car). Finally, it shows the help screen explaining key-binding controls for navigating in the environment.

The system logs all interactions in real-time to generate lossless replays of learner performances and assist in detecting if a skill has been applied correctly or not. It is important to mention that a leaner might fail one or more skill, but still reach the goal. The system does not restrict such behavior and does not yet generate formative feedback reflecting it.

Fig. 1. Road Crossing Tasks in SafeChild

4   Pilot Evaluation

We have conducted a pilot study with ten children aged 6-9 solving road crossing tasks in a Web-version of SafeChild. The main goals of the study were to elicit a general attitude that children would have toward training pedestrian safety in a game-like VR environment; observe typical patterns of their interaction with SafeChild, and get initial understanding of how they apply various pedestrian safety skills in VR settings. A pre-questionnaire collected children's demographics and experience with traffic education and computer games. The main session consisted of a familiarization task and the ten exercises described in chapter 3. A post-questionnaire at the end asked for children's feedback on the exercises and the city environment. Overall, it took about 20 minutes for children to finish the experiment. The entire study was conducted over Internet using the browser-based version of SafeChild. All interactions and answers to questionnaires were logged at a central web-server. Parents were asked to supervise and monitor the performance of their children, but not help with the traffic exercises.

Children liked SafeChild in general, thought it was realistic and believed they could improve their traffic skills with it. However, they provided mixed opinions about the difficulty of exercises and the ease of control. This confirms the overall potential of the approach and indicates possible value of adaptive support. It also shows the need for control refinement. The log analysis shows that children made only a few errors when applying basic skills, and when they did, they were able to correct them during the next exercise. However, rarely they were able to correctly apply all the advanced skills, and when they had a problem, the current simplistic feedback of SafeChild did not help them correct it at the next attempt. This observation is consistent with the literature on application of advanced and basic pedestrian safety skills in the real world and hints toward implementing an instructional support component of the SafeChild system especially targeting advanced skills.

5   Conclusion

The results of the conducted pilot study indicate that the general approach of SafeChild has been well received and that the system is capable to reproduce the real-world problems of child pedestrians. This forms a solid basis for future research toward assisting children in acquiring theses skills. This includes not only the development of an ITS that can model these skills automatically [10] but also research on the use of different VR interfaces [11] that could facilitate the transfer of skills acquired in a VR environment to the real world situations.

Acknowledgments. This research was conducted within the SafeChild project funded by BMBF (grant 01IS12050) under the Software Campus program.

References

1. Whitebread, D., Neilson, K.: The contribution of visual search strategies to the development of pedestrian skills by 4-11 year-old children. British Journal of Educational Psychology **70**(4), 539–557 (2000)
2. Schwebel, D.C., Davis, A.L., O'Neal, E.E.: Child Pedestrian Injury A Review of Behavioral Risks and Preventive Strategies. American Journal of Lifestyle Medicine **6**(4), 292–302 (2012)
3. Thomson, J.A., Tolmie, A.K., Foot, H.C., Whelan, K.M., Sarvary, P., Morrison, S.: Influence of virtual reality training on the roadside crossing judgments of child pedestrians. Journal of Experimental Psychology: Applied **11**, 175–186 (2005)
4. Schwebel, D.C., Gaines, J., Severson, J.: Validation of virtual reality as a tool to understand and prevent child pedestrian injury. Accident Analysis & Prevention **40**(4), 1394–1400 (2008)
5. Lane, H.C., Hays, M.J., Core, M., Gomboc, D., Forbell, E., Auerbach, D., Rosenberg, M.: Coaching intercultural communication in a serious game. In: Proceedings of the 16th International Conference on Computers in Education, pp. 35–42 (2008)
6. Ampofo-Boateng, K., Thomson, J.A.: Children's perception of safety and danger on the road. British Journal of Psychology **82**, 487–505 (1991)
7. Hill, R., Lewis, V., Dunbar, G.: Young children's concepts of danger. British Journal of Developmental Psychology **18**, 103–120 (2000)
8. Underwood, J., Dillon, G., Farnsworth, B., Twiner, A.: Reading the road: the influence of age and sex on child pedestrians' perceptions of road risk. British Journal of Psychology **98**, 93–110 (2007)
9. Van der Molen, H.H., Rothengatter, J.A., Vinjé, M.P.: Blueprint of an analysis of the pedestrian's task—I: Method of analysis†. Accident Analysis & Prevention **13**(3), 175–191 (1981)
10. Gu, Y., Sosnovsky, S.: Recognition of student intentions in a virtual reality training environment. In: Proceedings of the Companion Publication of the 19th International Conference on Intelligent User Interfaces, pp. 69–72 (2014)
11. Orlosky, J., Weber, M., Gu, Y., Sonntag, D., Sosnovsky, S.: An interactive pedestrian environment simulator for cognitive monitoring and evaluation. In: Proceedings of the 20th International Conference on Intelligent User Interfaces Companion, pp. 57–60 (2015)

Measuring Misconceptions Through Item Response Theory

Eduardo Guzmán[✉] and Ricardo Conejo

Dpto. Lenguajes y Ciencias de la Computación, E.T.S.I. Informática,
Universidad de Málaga, Bulevar Louis Pasteur, 25. Campus de Teatinos, 29071 Málaga, Spain
{guzman,conejo}@lcc.uma.es

Abstract. In this paper we propose an assessment model to measure both student knowledge and misconceptions through testing. For this purpose we use a well-founded psychometric theory, i.e. the Item Response Theory (IRT). Our proposal is an extension of our previous work in this field and permits, in the same test, the data-driven evaluation of knowledge and several misconceptions, thereby more efficiently using the evidence provided by the students, while solving a test, to enrich student perturbation models.

Keywords: Misconceptions · Assessment · Student modeling · Item Response Theory

1 Introduction

A tutoring system uses the information stored in a student model to tailor the way it interacts with a student [1]. A precise student model should contain not only information about learning (overlay modeling), but also data about errors made by the learners and the misconceptions they may have (i.e. perturbation models [2]). *Misconceptions refer to ideas that learners have incorporated into their cognitive.*

Testing is perhaps the most extended strategy for assessment. Among the underlying techniques for computing a student's state of learning, the *Item Response Theory* (IRT) is the most widely used when accurate and invariant diagnostic measures are required. In IRT [3] diagnostics are made in terms of the evidence provided by the students through their performance in a set of *items* (e.g. test questions). IRT is based on two principles: a) The student's performance in a test can be explained by means of a single trait (generally, in educational domains, the knowledge level), which can be measured as an unknown numerical value. b) The performance of a student with an estimated trait level answering an item i can be probabilistically predicted and modeled by means of a function called *Item Characteristic Curve* (ICC). It expresses the probability that a student with certain trait level θ has to answer the item correctly. The greater the student's trait level, the higher the probability of them answering the item correctly.

However IRT determines the student's score by identifying his/her location along a single proficiency continuum and therefore does not provide sufficient data to

© Springer International Publishing Switzerland 2015
C. Conati et al. (Eds.): AIED 2015, LNAI 9112, pp. 608–611, 2015.
DOI: 10.1007/978-3-319-19773-9_73

enhance instruction and learning [4]. In this paper we present a model based on the hypothesis of that certain incorrect choices of test questions can be used to infer students' misconceptions. Accordingly, after a testing session, the student model could be updated not only with information about his/her knowledge, but also with data about his/her state of misconception. This proposal is also an extension of our student knowledge diagnosis model [5] currently implemented in, Siette (www.siette.org), our web-based system for automatic assessment [6].

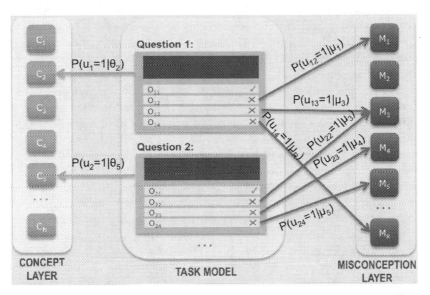

Fig. 1. Relationship between tasks (questions), concepts and misconceptions

2   A Model for Assessing Misconceptions Through IRT

Our model is framed under the *Evidence-Centered Design* (ECD) proposal, i.e. a guideline for designing, producing and delivering educational assessments [7]. In accordance with that idea, our proposal is composed of the following three submodels: (1) *Student model*, is formed by a *concept layer*, consisting of the set of domain concepts $C_1,...,C_N$, and a *misconception layer* consisting of a set of misconceptions $M_1,...,M_R$. The set of concepts and misconceptions are measured through probability distributions, which relate the student's level in the concept or misconception, and the probability of having it. (2) *Task model*, which consists of the elements through which evidence of knowledge can be captured. It is formed, therefore, by assessment activities (e.g. exercises, problems or test questions). (3) *Evidence model*: It is the connection between the two previous models. It is used thus to transform the raw observations about the student's performance into updates in his/her student model. This process can be carried out thanks to the underlying relationship of tasks with concepts and with misconceptions (see Fig. 1). The transformation is done according to the response model, explained below.

Incorrect responses to items can provide evidence of this misconception. Let us consider, for instance, the algebra domain in which a student is solving questions in a test about fractions. If the student in question does not know how to add fractions correctly, he/she may think, for example, that the fraction resulting from adding two fractions has a numerator equal to the sum of the numerators, and that the denominator is also the addition of the denominators. If, in a test there are several questions involving the adding up of two fractions, and these questions have an option where this addition is calculated wrongly in the way that the student misunderstands, and therefore this will be the response chosen. Fig. 1 summarizes this hypothesis, graphically. In the figure, the task model has been simplified to a set of two questions with four choices. Each question Q_i is linked to one concept C_j modeling the fact that that item can be used to assess C_j. In the figure, Q_1 assesses C_2 and Q_2 assesses C_5. Regarding the relationship between questions and misconceptions, Q_i could be related to more than one misconception. For instance, Q_1 can provide evidence about M_1, M_3 and M_R. In the figure, if a student holds M_3, when posed Q_2, she will tend to select choice o_{22}.

In our proposal, relationships between questions and concepts and between questions and misconceptions is modeled by characteristic curves. The first relationship is the classical one used in IRT and is represented by the ICCs. For example, ICC $P(u_i=1|\theta_2)$ relates the performance of students in Q_1 with their knowledge in C_2. However, we add a new type of characteristic curve, the *Misconception Characteristic Curve* (MCC), $P(o_{ij}=1|\mu_k)$ which models the probability of selecting the *i-th* choice of the *j-th* item, that is, $o_{ij}=1$, given the student level μ_k in misconception M_k. This data-driven curve can be modeled with the same functions as the ICCs, since it is also an increasing monotone function (the greater the misconception level, the higher the probability of selecting that item choice).

Our assessment or diagnostic algorithm is an extension of our previous work summarized in [5]. Let us assume a student is taking a test. The assessment procedure will consist of the following steps:

1. For each concept C_i involved in the test, an equiprobable probability distribution $P(\theta_i)$ will be initialized. Analogously, for each misconception M_i involved in the test another equiprobable probability distribution, $P(\mu_i)$, will be also initialized.
2. Each time the student answers a question Q_i choosing the j-th choice c_{ij}:
   2.1. If Q_i assesses C_k, the probability distribution $P(\theta_k)$ will be updated with the ICC, $P(u_i=1|\theta_k)$, if the answer is correct. Otherwise, the opposite curve to ICC, i.e. $1-P(u_i=1|\theta_k)$, will be used to update $P(\theta_k)$:

$$P(\theta_k) = P(u_i=1|\theta_k)^{u_i}(1-P(u_i=1|\theta_k))^{(1-u_i)}P(\theta_k) \qquad (1)$$

   2.2. If Q_i is related to one or more misconceptions, for each one of them, its probability distribution will be updated. Let M_r be one of these misconceptions. The probability distribution $P(\mu_r)$ will be updated with the MCC, $P(o_{ij}=1|\mu_r)$, if this misconception is linked with choice o_{ij}. Otherwise the opposite curve to MCC, $1-P(o_{ij}=1|\mu_r)$, will be used:

$$P(\mu_k) = P(o_{ij} = 1|\mu_k)^{o_{ij}} (1 - P(o_{ij} = 1|\mu_k))^{(1-o_{ij})} P(\mu_k) \qquad (2)$$

3. Step 2 will be repeated for each question posed to the student.

The process of assessment will give, as a result, a set of concept or misconception probability distributions. The student's level in that concept or misconception can be computed directly from its probability distribution. The Bayesian MAP or EAP estimators can be used to infer this value.

3 Conclusions

This paper has presented a new approach for assessing misconceptions through testing. Historically, tests have been used to measure knowledge. However, with our model, assessment information provided by a test can be optimized by including estimates about certain misconceptions. Estimates about knowledge and misconceptions inferred by our model are invariant and independent of the test thanks to the underlying IRT-based model we use. The main shortcoming of our proposal is related to the test elicitation. The construction of tests with incorrect choices targeting misconceptions is a time consuming task and requires certain experience and an extra effort from tutors. However we think that this model in combination with the inference technique described in [9] could leverage this process. The synergy between both techniques could be useful to produce accurate student models. Moreover, we would like to mention that this proposal will be integrated into Siette in the near future.

Acknowledgements: This work is part of DEDALO project which has been financed by the Andalusian Regional Government (P09-TIC-5105).

References

1. Millán, E., Loboda, T., Pérez-de-la-Cruz, J.L.: Bayesian networks for student model engineering. Computers & Education **55**(4), 1663–1683 (2010)
2. Brown, J.S., Burton, R.R.: Diagnostic models for procedural bugs in basic mathematics skills. Cognitive Science **2**, 155–192 (1978)
3. Hambleton, R.K., Swaminathan, H., Rogers, H.J.: Fundamentals of Item Response Theory. Sage, Newbury (1991)
4. de la Torre, J., Minchen, N.: Cognitively diagnostic assessments and the cognitive diagnosis model framework. Psicología Educativa **20**(2), 89–97 (2014)
5. Guzmán, E., Conejo, R., Pérez-de-la-Cruz, J.L.: Adaptive Testing for Hierarchical Student Models. User Modeling and User-Adapted Interaction **17**, 119–157 (2007)
6. Conejo, R., Guzmán, E., Millán, E., Trella, M., Pérez-De-La-Cruz, J.L., Ríos, A.: SIETTE: A web-based tool for adaptive testing. IJAIED **14**(1), 29–61 (2004)
7. Mislevy, R.J., Almond, R.G., Lukas, J.F.: A Brief Introduction to Evidence-Centered Design, CSE Report 632, National Center for Research on Evaluation, Standards and Student Testing (CRESST), May 2004
8. Guzmán, E., Conejo, R., Gálvez, J.: A data-driven technique for misconception elicitation. In: De Bra, P., Kobsa, A., Chin, D. (eds.) UMAP 2010. LNCS, vol. 6075, pp. 243–254. Springer, Heidelberg (2010)

No Child Behind nor Singled Out? – Adaptive Instruction Combined with Inclusive Pedagogy in Early Math Software

Magnus Haake, Layla Husain, Erik Anderberg, and Agneta Gulz[✉]

Lund University Cognitive Science, Lund University, Lund, Sweden
{magnus.haake,erik.anderberg,agneta.gulz}@lucs.lu.se,
l.husain.05@gmail.com

Abstract. We describe a unique play-&-learn game for early math, designed to provide adaptive instruction with respect to support and challenge as well as to cater for an inclusive pedagogy where no child, whether far behind or far ahead, is exposed as being "different".

Keywords: Educational software · Adaptive instruction · Inclusive pedagogy · Early math · Preschool

1 Why Adaptive Instruction Combined with Inclusive Pedagogy in an Early Math Intervention?

1.1 Why Early Math Intervention at all – and Why via Adaptive Instruction?

It is well established that there are large individual differences among children at the onset of formal education in skills and competences with respect to early numeracy [1,2]. In addition, a child that lags behind at this point in time is likely to continue to stay behind all through school [3]. Longitudinal studies have also shown that early numeracy is the strongest single predictor for subsequent school achievement in general [3,4].

However, the majority of children who lag behind in early math do not have any developmental disorder, but their low performance rather stems from external factors like low SES and low exposure and training at home and at kindergarten [1], [5].

A fair amount of studies demonstrate interventions that stimulate and enhance early numerical skills and competences of young children [6,7,8], but these successful interventions are rarely (or never) implemented on a large scale. Here, digital interventions are potentially promising. They do not require preschool teachers to be particularly knowledgeable and interested in early math and they can be implemented with reasonable time investment by teachers (overwhelmed by the everyday activities) [9] – as children often can explore educational software with little instruction.

An even more essential property of digitally based interventions is the possibility of dynamic individual adaptation of challenges and support that follow each child's particular progress. As pointed out, there are large individual differences

© Springer International Publishing Switzerland 2015
C. Conati et al. (Eds.): AIED 2015, LNAI 9112, pp. 612–615, 2015.
DOI: 10.1007/978-3-319-19773-9_74

in early numeracy by the end of preschool and children have different profiles of relative strengths and weaknesses. This applies to both middle- and low-performers; and also high-performers have need of adequate challenges and support. Thus, "one-size-fits-all" interventions will not do – we need interventions using adaptive instruction.

1.2   Why also Add *Inclusion* to Early Math Interventions?

What has been said this far is neither novel, nor controversial – but what about *inclusion*? We will argue that educational software based interventions for early math can and should cater for an *inclusive pedagogy* in the following sense: At the same time as *individual differences between learners are responded to*, the marginalization that can occur *when students are treated differently* should be counteracted [10]. In other words, one should make sure that all children in a group – with differing abilities, strengths, and weaknesses – can participate in a given activity without being exposed as being ahead or lagging behind their peers. The challenge is to *actually* treat children differently depending on their particular need for support and challenge – but not make the differential treatments visible.

A main argument for inclusiveness in this sense is to avoid early establishments of low self-efficacy in math. Even though the developmental path of self-efficacy in preschoolers is not well explored, already by the age of 7 or 8 many children have low self-efficacy in – and may even fear – mathematics [11]. Given that the large variability in early math skills at this young age mainly originates from environmental and contextual differences, it is particularly unfortunate with unwarranted labels on a child – self-labelling or not – as being unsmart, slow, bad in math, etc. Likewise, it can also be stigmatizing to be singled out as being particularly ahead receiving special treatment. To put it simple, being exposed as different can be detrimental for learners – both those who struggle and those who excel.

Some common approaches for individualizing do not cater for inclusion in our sense. One is when different tasks as selected by a teacher for different students. Not only can children feel exposed; teachers' expectations on children implicitly come forth and children presented with low expectations risk to align with these expectations [12]. Another is when all tasks and material are freely available for all children to choose from – but the drawback with this is that young learners are not necessarily capable of choosing appropriately challenging material. For example, some prefer to remain in their comfort zone, whereas others take on tasks far too difficult.

Next we will describe how our educational game, Magical Garden, has been designed in order to combine adaptive instruction while catering for inclusiveness.

2   Magical Garden – Early Math Software Catering for Adaptive Instruction Combined with Inclusion

Magical Garden (hence MG) is developed by the Educational Technology Group (ETG) at Lund and Linköping Universities with the collaboration of AAA-lab, Stanford University. The game makes use of teachable agents acting as friends [13,14], and is designed to improve *number sense* basing on work by Griffin, Case, and Siegler [6]. The goal is to offer meaningful tasks in this domain with respect to challenges and support for all 4- to 6-year-olds in a preschool group (including the most and least advanced) *and* cater for an inclusive pedagogy. The challenge is to *actually* treat children differently depending on their particular need, but not make the differential treatments visible. To our knowledge, MG is the only educational software that combines adaptive instruction with an explicit catering for inclusion.

At its core, MG is currently composed of a set of 60 *pedagogical scenarios* defined by: *method* (counting, stepwise counting or proto-addition/subtraction, addition, subtraction), *range* (1-4, 1-9), and *representation* (fingers, objects, dots, strikes, dices, numbers, mixed, transitions). The scenarios are ordered according to difficulty and each scenario is repeated in three subsequent modes: child learns and practices on her own, child teaches her friend how to play, and child supervises and helps her friend who attempts to play. The same pedagogical scenario can be presented in one of several *mini-games* featuring different contexts, for example a nearsighted bumble bee needing help to find the right flower with nectar or a passionate treasure hunter who needs help to reach the right cave in a cliff by attaching balloons to his basket.

The inclusive pedagogy is built around the explicit narrative of MG, which is for the child to help her friend collect water drops for the garden to flourish by solving different tasks. The inclusive strategy is based on: (i) the main reward system of collecting water drops, which is the same all through MG with no additional reward systems at higher levels; (ii) all completed tasks give the same amount of water drops independent of difficulty; (iii) the plants in the garden are randomly generated – thus the gardens will look different and not allow straightforward comparisons on "how far one has got"; and (iv) the different mini-games are randomly distributed over the 60 pedagogical scenarios making typical "game level" comparisons difficult. Thus, the only visible differences require knowledge of basic math, why an educator, but not the children themselves, can recognize differences in advancement between children.

These are deliberate design decisions and although competition can be used in education to inspire and motivate children, we argue that competition should be downplayed in the area of mathematics for this young age group. Possibilities to compare individual performance may have undesired consequences like early establishment of low self-efficacy in math – considering that the differences primarily originate from differences in exposure and training.

A proof of concept of whether the software works as intended does, however, not reside in design intentions as such but in children's actual use of it, their learning experiences, and their teachers' views. In the following comes a brief summary of the results from a recent study involving 28 children, 4- to 6-years-old, who were using MG during one month, 2-3 times a weak (all game data logged), with researchers first having an introduction session and then returning at a later occasion to observe children play and to talk about their experience with the children and their teachers.

Notably (but not surprisingly) children spontaneously found many ways to compare what happens on their respective screens, but none of these comparisons mapped to actual progress in MG. Furthermore all children seemed to experience progress when they entered (as they all did, even if at different paces) a novel stage. However, while the inclusive strategy to not expose children at the ends of the "early math skill" spectrum as deviating did meet our expectations, all children were not adequately stimulated and challenged – in particular for high-performing children, more challenging tasks need to be added.

Some readers may still hold that MG, by not inviting comparisons of early math competence, misses out on competition as an important source of motivation. We still argue that the costs in the delicate domain of early math are larger than the gains. Our stance is to instead work hard on other motivational features of the game.

References

1. Jordan, N., Kaplan, D., Ramineni, C., Locuniak, M.: Early Math Matters: Kindergarten Number Competence and Later Mathematics Outcomes. Dev. Psychol. **45**, 850–867 (2009)
2. Aunio, P., Hautamäki, J., Sajaniemi, N., Van Luit, J.: Early Numeracy in Low Performing Young Children. Br. Educ. Res. J. **35**, 25–46 (2009)
3. Missall, K., Mercer, S., Martínez, R., Casebeer, D.: Concurrent and Predictive Patterns and Trends in Performance on Early Numeracy Curriculum-Based Measures in Kindergarten and First Grade. Assess. Eff. Interv. **37**, 95–106 (2012)
4. Duncan, G., Dowsett, C., Claessens, A., Magnuson, K., Huston, A., Klebanov, P., et al.: School Readiness and Later Achievement. Dev. Psychol. **43**, 1428–1446 (2007)
5. Mononen, R., Aunio, P., Koponen, T., Aro, M.: A Review of Early Numeracy Interventions for Children at Risk in Mathematics. INT-JECSE **6**, 25–54 (2014)
6. Griffin, S., Case, R., Siegler, R.: Rightstart: providing the central conceptual prerequisites for first formal learning of arithmetic to students at risk for school failure. In: McGilly, K. (ed.) Classroom Lessons: Integrating Cognitive Theory and Classroom Practice, pp. 24–49. MIT Press, Cambridge (1994)
7. Jordan, N., Glutting, J., Dyson, N., Hassinger-Das, B., Irwin, C.: Building Kindergartners' Number Sense: A Randomized Controlled Study. J. Educ. Psychol. **104**(3), 647–660 (2012)
8. Ramani, G., Siegler, R.: Promoting Broad and Stable Improvements in Low-income Children's Numerical Knowledge through Playing Number Board Games. Child. Dev. **79**(2), 375–394 (2008)
9. Bullough, R., Hall-Kenyon, K., MacKay, K., Marshall, E.: Head Start and the Intensification of Teaching in Early Childhood Education. Teaching and Teacher Education **37**, 55–63 (2014)
10. Florian, L., Black-Hawkins, K.: Exploring Inclusive Pedagogy. Br. Educ. Res. J. **37**(5), 813–828 (2011)
11. McLeod, D.: Research on affect in mathematics education: a reconceptualization. In: Grouws, D. (ed.) Handbook of Research on Mathematics Learning and Teaching, pp. 575–596. Macmillan, New York (1992)
12. Rattan, A., Good, C., Dweck, C.: It's Ok – Not Everyone Can Be Good at Math. J. Exp. Soc. Psychol. **48**, 731–737 (2012)
13. Husain, L., Haake, M., Gulz, A.: Early Math Software – Rationales and Requirements (2014) (submitted)
14. Axelsson, A., Anderberg, E., Haake, M.: Can preschoolers profit from a teachable agent based play-&-learn game in mathematics? In: Lane, H., Yacef, K., Mostow, J., Pavlik, P. (eds.) AIED 2013. LNCS, vol. 7926, pp. 289–298. Springer, Heidelberg (2013)

An Integrated Emotion-Aware Framework for Intelligent Tutoring Systems

Jason M. Harley[1,2(✉)], Susanne P. Lajoie[2], Claude Frasson[1], and Nathan C. Hall[2]

[1] Computer Science and Operations Research, Université de Montréal, Montréal, QC, Canada
jason.harley@umontreal.ca
[2] Educational and Counselling Psychology, McGill University, Montréal, QC, Canada

Abstract. This conceptual paper integrates empirical studies and existing conceptual work describing emotion regulation strategies deployed in intelligent tutoring systems and advances an integrated framework for the development and evaluation of emotion-aware systems.

Keywords: Emotions · Affect · Emotion regulation · Emotion-aware systems · Intelligent tutoring systems

1 An Integrated Emotion-Aware Framework

D'Mello and Graesser [1] provide a good starting dichotomy of emotion-aware systems by differentiating proactive from reactive system features. *Proactive* features represent components that induce or impede emotional states whereas *reactive features* are those that respond to states in real-time (typically negative states). The present framework elaborates upon these two types of features by mapping out their different components, dependencies, and interrelationships in order to capture and structure the rich and creative variety of ways ITS can support positive emotions.

1.1 Proactive Features

Proactive features can be classified as either user-adaptive or non-adaptive, where *adaptive* refers to whether the ITS uses information it has collected about the user to make changes to any part of its interaction with the student. The left-hand side of Figure 1 summarizes user-adaptive and non-adaptive proactive features.

User-Adaptive Features. These features include making changes to the learning material (e.g., human circulatory system, algebra), conditions (e.g., time available), and assessments (e.g., quizzes), or the nature of ITS interactions with the learner (e.g., through a pedagogical agent; PA). These adaptive features can be better understood in the context of the information that drives them: *student models*. Student models are generated from data collected before the learning session that determines a student profile by identifying unique student characteristics or combinations of. Individual differences can include gender, psychological traits (e.g., personality traits), and prior knowledge of relevant content or skills that comprise an ITS' learning objectives [2]. This information can be used to adapt ITSs to learners even before a learning session,

© Springer International Publishing Switzerland 2015
C. Conati et al. (Eds.): AIED 2015, LNAI 9112, pp. 616–619, 2015.
DOI: 10.1007/978-3-319-19773-9_75

for example, by matching PA gender to learner gender and adapting instructional strategies to psychological traits.

Non-Adaptive Features. However, not all proactive features require adaptation to individual learners to effectively foster positive emotions. Non-adaptive features are characteristics strategically built into the design of an ITS with this goal in mind. These features focus on eliciting learners' engagement through features such as narrative (e.g., story-telling) and gamification. They can also support student autonomy (e.g., choice) by providing opportunities for learners to explore ITS content and features through hypermedia, rich 3D worlds, and customization. A recent review revealed that ITSs that used game-like features and afforded choice tended to elicit a greater proportion of positive emotions from students than those that did not [3].

1.2 Reactive Features

Although reactive features are adaptive in nature, the type of information they are programmed to respond to, as well as the nature of the response, can vary tremendously. At the broadest level, these features can be divided into two groups: *direct system prompts* and *CALM features* that refer to conditions, assessments, and learning material. The right-hand side of Figure 1 summaries the relationship between reactive features and the information they reply upon.

Dynamic User Models. The data that drives the reactive features stems from *dynamic user models* that include information collected on an ongoing basis about students' *psychological states* and *learning trajectories*. *Psychological state* information includes learners' concurrent state emotions (how they are feeling at the moment) and their attention to and engagement with the ITS. Collecting data at multiple intervals is critical because of potential changes in learners' emotions as a session progresses. Similarly, ITS student models can and should make use of formative assessments of students' evolving understanding (or lack thereof) as the session progresses and adapt accordingly. We refer to this data as information on students' *learning trajectory*.

CALM Reactive Features. These reactive features refer to non-prompt-based strategies for adapting ITSs to a learner's evolving psychological state and performance. They include adapting system conditions, assessments, and learning material. *Conditions* refer to the interaction parameters of an ITS, such as the degree of autonomy provided to students by the system (e.g., meaningful choice) and the availability of tools, such as embedded note-taking features. *Assessments* can be adapted to help up-regulate students' emotions in at least two ways. First, their administration can be altered to allow students more time to interact with content before being evaluated, or receive quizzes more regularly to maintain a more engaging learning pace and mitigate boredom. Assessments can also be made easier or more difficult to align with students' zone of proximal development (appropriately challenging items selected) and minimize feelings of frustration and hopelessness [4]. *Learning material* refers to the content or skills that an ITS is intended to facilitate (e.g., human biology, algebra). The difficulty of learning material can be adjusted by switching modules to more basic or advanced material or giving the learner an opportunity to take a break.

Direct System-Delivered Prompts. Most empirical work to date has examined the utility of system prompts provided to students through dialogue boxes or speech (using a text-to-speech engine), typically from an animated pedagogical agent [1,3,4,5]. Direct system-delivered prompts can target emotions either directly or indirectly depending on whether the aim is to change learners' *behavior* regarding their interaction with the system, or how the learner is *thinking*. We would classify a prompt recommending that a student return to task (e.g., off-task behavior) as a behavioral prompt because it is designed to change a student's emotional state by having them change their behavior. Most metacognitive and self-regulatory prompts are also behavioral at their core because of their explicit focus on scaffolding learners to engage in more effective learning behaviors. These effective learning behaviors help students regulate their emotions by targeting negative learning outcomes and situations that can elicit negative emotions. Such prompts may prevent negative situations from occurring, address the underlying problem, and/or influence appraisals of control.

The most popular and widely recognized emotional regulation strategies are those associated with cognitive change, and reappraisal in particular [4,5,6]. As such, prompts that target specific appraisals, such as learners' value of a task, self-efficacy, or locus of causality (i.e., control) are, in fact, more directly targeting how a learner *thinks (cognition)* as opposed to *feels (emotion)* about a task. Most of the motivational and emotion regulatory prompts tend to be targeting these processes, but are often referred to by different names (reactive empathy, general encouragement; [7]). Learners' emotions may also be regulated through social information such as *parallel empathy* which may be instilled through messages that direct learners' attention to the (alleged) feelings of a pedagogical agent who may also find an activity *boring* or *frustrating*. The underlying mechanism at work here is an appeal to the learner that their emotions are valid, but we would assert that the learner may positively modify one of their other appraisals as a result (e.g., self-efficacy or locus of causality).

Deployment of Direct System-Delivered Prompts. As with formative assessments and the administration of behavioral prompts, the frequency and timing of their administration are important considerations. The efficacy of direct system-delivered prompts thus depends, in part, on the source of the emotion information to which the system is programmed to react to. If the prompts are triggered in response to self-reported emotions, they then can only occur as often as the emotions are reported. If, however, the system is using continuous (online) data that is analyzed and processed in real time, more specific prompting decisions must be made such as: How often is too often to prompt students? Given these and other questions, there is one overarching guideline that can be safely heeded: Do no harm. More specifically, prompts need not be delivered if a learner is detected to be in a positive state.

1.3   Integrating Proactive and Reactive Features

Another important consideration in the deployment of prompts and other emotion-aware features is their combination. While some ITSs use more than one type of message in the prompts provided, no published work to date actively incorporates and evaluates the effectiveness of combinations of different proactive and reactive features (summarized in Figure 1). Given the preceding discussion, it is possible that this lack of knowledge may be addressed by integrating information about specific learners into user models. In this manner, it becomes possible to adapt system parameters before a learning session begins by augmenting the ITSs architecture with information concerning proactive features that, if administered, could positively affect engagement, positive emotions, and learning outcomes. Next, student models could be dynamically updated during the learning session with information on students' psychological states obtained from concurrent self-report measures of emotion or online methods such as physiological sensors or automatic facial expression recognition software. Reactive features such as system prompts, learning material, assessments, conditions (i.e., interaction parameters) can be adapted accordingly.

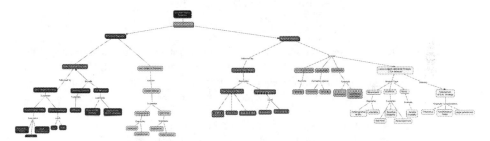

Fig. 1. Integrated Emotion-aware Frame Feature Map

Acknowledgements. The research presented in this paper has been supported by a postdoctoral fellowship from the Fonds Québécois de recherche – Société et culture (FQRSC) awarded to the first author.

References

1. D'Mello, S.K., Graesser, A.C.: Feeling, thinking, and computing with affect-aware learning technologies. In: Calvo, R.A., D'Mello, S.K., Gratch, J., Kappas, A. (eds.) Handbook of Affective Computing, pp. 419–434. Oxford University Press (2015)
2. Harley, J.M., Carter, C.K., Papaionnou, N., Bouchet, F., Landis, R.S., Azevedo, R., Karabachian, L.: Examining the predictive relationship between personality and emotion traits and learners' agent-directed emotions. Artificial Intelligence in Education (in press)
3. Harley, J.M., Azevedo, R.: Toward a feature-driven understanding of students' emotions during interactions with agent-based learning environments: A selective review. Int. Journal of Games and Computer Mediated Simulation 6(3), 17–34 (2014)
4. Arroyo, I., Muldner, K., Burleson, W., Woolf, B.: Adaptive interventions to address students' negative activating and deactivating emotions during learning activities. Design Recom. Ad. ITS, pp. 79–92 (2014). U.S. Army Research Lab.
5. D'Mello, S.K., Blanchard, N., Baker, R., Ocumpaugh, J., Brawner, K.: I feel your pain: A selective review of affect-sensitive inst. strateg. Design Recommendations for Adaptive Intell. Tutoring, pp. 35–48 (2014). U.S. Army Research Lab.
6. Gross, J.J.: Emotion regulation. Emotion 13, 359–365 (2013)
7. McQuiggan, S.W., Robison, J.L., Lester, J.C.: Affective transitions in narrative-centered learning environments. Ed. Tech. & Science 13, 40–53 (2010)

Purpose and Level of Feedback in an Exploratory Learning Environment for Fractions

Wayne Holmes[1(✉)], Manolis Mavrikis[1], Alice Hansen[1], and Beate Grawemeyer[2]

[1] London Knowledge Lab, UCL Institute of Education,
University College London, London, UK
{w.holmes,m.mavrikis,a.hansen}@ioe.ac.uk
[2] London Knowledge Lab, Birkbeck, University of London, London, UK
beate@dcs.bbk.ac.uk

Abstract. This paper reports on our progress on a systematic approach to operationalizing support in Fractions Lab – an exploratory learning environment for learning fractions in primary education. In particular, we focus on the question of what feedback to provide and consider in detail the implementation of feedback according to two dimensions: the purpose of the feedback, depending on the task-specific needs of the student, and the level of feedback, depending on the cognitive needs of the student. We present early findings from our design-based research that includes Wizard-of-Oz studies of the intelligent feedback system and student perception questionnaires.

1 Introduction

It is well known that for discovery or exploratory learning to be most effective, students usually require some form of support – such as scaffolding, elicited explanations or feedback [1]. Feedback in particular is thought to be especially important. However, while feedback has been extensively researched over decades (*cf.* [2], [3]), further work is needed for it to be incorporated successfully in exploratory learning environments (ELEs) [4]. For example, as suggested by Carenini *et al.* [5], any systematic approach to operationalizing feedback in an ELE needs to address the 'when', 'what', and 'how' questions: when should the feedback be provided, what should it contain, and how should it be presented? Here, we report on our approach to personalized task-dependent feedback, which has been developed iteratively as part of a design-based research study [6] of an ELE for 9-11 year old students learning fractions. First, we describe the ELE in question, Fractions Lab; then, we consider related work and the operationalization of feedback in two dimensions: its purpose and level. We conclude by presenting some early findings emerging from our research.

2 Fractions Lab

Fractions Lab is an ELE that is hosted in a speech-enabled platform, iTalk2learn (which has been co-funded by the EU in FP7, Project #318051). It provides students in primary education with opportunities to visualize fractions, to learn about fractions equivalence, and to engage in fractions addition and subtraction operations. Users can

© Springer International Publishing Switzerland 2015
C. Conati et al. (Eds.): AIED 2015, LNAI 9112, pp. 620–623, 2015.
DOI: 10.1007/978-3-319-19773-9_76

select one of four representations (number lines, liquid measures, geometrical shapes, and sets), which they can explore and manipulate as they choose (change, compare, add or subtract) in response to given tasks (e.g., "Make a fraction that equals 3/4 and has 12 as denominator."). From its inception, Fractions Lab (and the iTalk2Learn platform that hosts it) was designed to incorporate intelligent feedback. In its current iteration, the system delivers feedback in response to the student's affective state and to other general interactions [7] and feedback specific to the task that the student is undertaking within Fractions Lab (known as task-dependent support or TDS). TDS, which is the focus of this paper, aims to enhance the student's learning of fractions by responding flexibly to their changing needs, as evidenced by their response to tasks, and by helping them to learn from their errors. Drawing on the literature and the outcomes of our Wizard-of-Oz studies [8], feedback rules (to regulate the 'what' and 'when' of TDS in Fractions Lab) have been operationalized according to two dimensions: the purpose of the feedback, depending on the task-specific needs of the student, and the level of feedback, depending on the cognitive needs of the student.

2.1   Purpose of Feedback

Drawing on the ELE literature (*cf.* [4]), the feedback literature (especially [2] and [3]) and outcomes from our Wizard-of-Oz studies [8], six feedback purposes have been identified (see Table 1), each of which is triggered by a particular student response (the 'when' of TDS). Together, these purposes reflect the recursive and iterative problem solving processes involved in exploratory tasks. They are Polya, instruction (next step), instruction (problem solving), instruction (opportunity), affirmation, and reflection. The first purpose relates to Polya's Steps 1 and 2 [9]: understanding the problem, formulating goals and devising a plan. Others suggest a next step, support problem solving by addressing misconceptions, or suggest an opportunity for higher-level work. The final purposes are affirmation, which draws on the work of Dweck and colleagues [10], and reflection [11].

2.2   Level of Feedback

The second dimension of feedback to be operationalized in Fractions Lab extends the feedback literature mentioned earlier (see Table 2). It is novel in comprising four levels designed to address different levels of cognitive need. As noted above, a particular student response in Fractions Lab triggers some feedback. Thereafter, if the same student response is repeated, the next level of feedback is triggered. The four levels of feedback are: Socratic, guidance, didactic-conceptual and didactic-procedural. The first level, Socratic, draws on the dialogic approach to teaching [12], which emphasizes the benefits of open questioning to encourage students to think about and verbalize possible solutions. The second level, guidance, reminds students of key domain-specific rules and the system's affordances. The third level, didactic-conceptual, specifies a possible next step in terms of the fractions concept currently being explored. The fourth level, didactic-procedural, specifies the next step that needs to be undertaken in order to move forward. This rarely-delivered final procedural feedback operates as a backstop, ensuring that the student is not left floundering.

Table 1. Purpose of feedback (including *Level 2* feedback examples, see Table 2)

FEEDBACK	TRIGGER	PURPOSE	EXAMPLE
Polya's Steps 1 and 2	After receiving new task, student hesitates for [4] seconds.	To promote understanding of the problem, formulating goals and devising a plan.	*"Read the task again, and explain how you are going to tackle it."*
Instruction (next step)	On successfully completing a useful step (1).	To suggest a next-step towards the core goal.	*"You can use the arrow buttons to change the fraction."*
Instruction (problem solving)	On making a procedural error.	To support problem solving, addressing any identified misconceptions.	**"The denominator is the bottom part of the fraction.*"**
Instruction (opportunity)	On successfully completing a useful step (2).	To suggest an opportunity for higher-level work	*"You could now use the partition tool to make an equivalent fraction."*
Affirmation	On completing a task (1).	To acknowledge success and promote self-efficacy.	*"The way that you worked that out was excellent. Well done."*
Reflection	On completing a task (2).	To encourage metacognition.	*"Please explain why you made the denominator 12."*

Table 2. Level of feedback (including *Instruction (problem solving)* feedback examples, see Table 1)

LEVEL	FEEDBACK	PURPOSE	EXAMPLE
1	Socratic	To encourage students to verbalize possible solutions.	*"Have you changed the numerator or denominator?"*
2	Guidance	To remind students of key domain specific rules or of the system's affordances.	**"The denominator is the bottom part of the fraction.*"**
3	Didactic conceptual	To specify a next step, in terms of the concept currently being explored.	*"Check that the denominator in your fraction is correct."*
4	Didactic procedural	To specify a next step in procedural terms.	*"Check that the denominator, the bottom part of your fraction, is 12."*

*NB This is a single piece of feedback as it appears in each of the two dimensions.

3   Design-Based Research and Formative Evaluation

We are undertaking an iterative design-based approach [6] to the study of TDS. To date, 51 students have taken part in a series of ecologically-valid formative Wizard-of-Oz studies conducted in a classroom equipped with computers [8]. One computer was set up to allow a human facilitator (the wizard) to listen to the student's thinking-aloud, to view their interaction and to send messages that are shown and read aloud by the system. Initially, the wizard deliberately limited their communication capacity in order to simulate an actual system. In subsequent studies, based on earlier results, the system automatically generated the TDS.

We have encouraging findings. For example, in our latest study, which involved ten students (9-10 years old), the system provided a total of 74 TDS messages, after which, in 85% of cases, the students were observed to modify their behavior as a human tutor might have hoped. Grouping the reflective prompts (34) against all the other feedback messages (40) reveals no significant difference with respect to whether students reacted (t(72)=-.68, p>.05), suggesting that students were open both to traditional problem-solving support and to less traditional reflective feedback. In addition, our studies have highlighted the importance of 'how' TDS is delivered. Analysis of questionnaire responses showed that there were, for example, significant correlations between the questions "How much did the feedback get in your way?" and "Was the feedback useful?" (r=.44 p<.05). Thus a key outcome of our studies is a hypothesis that we are beginning to develop: if students are to find the system and its feedback helpful and are to feel positive following their experience, we must find ways to make the mode of feedback delivery appropriate to the student's needs – interruptive when it is important that the feedback is viewed, and non-interruptive when it might otherwise interfere with the student's attention and enjoyment [7]. Fractions Lab and its TDS (and the full iTalk2Learn system) are currently being summatively evaluated.

References

1. Alfieri, L., Brooks, P.J., Aldrich, N.J., Tenenbaum, H.R.: Does Discovery-Based Instruction Enhance Learning? J. Educ. Psychol. **103**(1), 1 (2011)
2. Hattie, J., Timperley, H.: The Power of Feedback. Rev. Educ. Res. **77**(1), 81–112 (2007)
3. Shute, V.J.: Focus on Formative Feedback. Rev. Educ. Res. **78**, 153–189 (2008)
4. Reiser, B.J., Copen, W.A., Ranney, M., Hamid, A., Kimberg, D.Y.: Cognitive and Motivational Consequences of Tutoring and Discovery Learning. DTIC Document (1998)
5. Carenini, G., Conati, C., Hoque, E., Steichen, B., Toker, D., Enns, J.: Highlighting interventions and user differences: informing adaptive information visualization support. In: Proceedings of the 32nd Annual ACM Conference on Human Factors in Computing Systems, pp. 1835–1844 (2014)
6. Design-Based Research Collective: Design-Based Research: An Emerging Paradigm for Educational Inquiry. Educ. Res. **32**(1), 5–8 (2003)
7. Grawemeyer, B., Holmes, W., Gutierrez-Santos, S., Hansen, A., Mavrikis, M., Loibl, K.: Light-bulb moment? towards adaptive presentation of feedback based on students' affective state. In: Proceedings of 20th ACM conference of Intelligent User Interfaces (2015)
8. Mavrikis, M., Grawemeyer, B., Hansen, A., Gutierrez-Santos, S.: Exploring the potential of speech recognition to support problem solving and reflection. In: de Freitas, S., Rensing, C., Ley, T., Muñoz-Merino, P.J. (eds.) EC-TEL 2014. LNCS, vol. 8719, pp. 263–276. Springer, Heidelberg (2014)
9. Polya, G.: How to Solve it: A New Aspect of Mathematical Method. Princeton University Press (1945)
10. Dweck, C.S.: Self-theories: Their role in motivation, personality, and development. Psychology Press, Philadelphia (2000)
11. Boyd, E.M., Fales, A.W.: Reflective Learning Key to Learning from Experience. J. Humanist. Psychol. **23**(2), 99–117 (1983)
12. Alexander, R.: Dialogic teaching essentials. National Institute of Education, Singapore (2010)

Off the Beaten Path: The Impact of Adaptive Content Sequencing on Student Navigation in an Open Social Student Modeling Interface

Roya Hosseini[1]([✉]), I-Han Hsiao[2], Julio Guerra[3], and Peter Brusilovsky[3]

[1] Intelligent Systems Program, University of Pittsburgh, Pittsburgh, PA, USA
roh38@pitt.edu
[2] School of Computing, Informatics and Decision Systems Engineering,
Arizona State University, Tempe, AZ, USA
[3] School of Information Sciences, University of Pittsburgh, Pittsburgh, PA, USA

Abstract. One of the original goals of intelligent educational systems is to guide every student to the most appropriate educational content. Exploring both knowledge-based and social guidance approaches in past work, we learned that each of these approaches has weak sides. In this paper we follow the idea of combining social guidance with more traditional knowledge-based guidance to support more optimal content navigation. We proposed a greedy sequencing approach that maximizes student's level of knowledge and tested it in a classroom. Results indicated that this approach positively impacts students' navigation.

Keywords: Personalized guidance · Open social student modeling · Adaptive navigation support · E-learning · Java programming

1 Introduction

One of the original goals of intelligent educational systems was to guide every student to the most appropriate educational content. A range of knowledge-based guidance technologies were reported [1,6]. In our recent research we discovered and evaluated a new approach to guide students to the "right" content based on the ideas of open social student modeling (OSSM) [4]. The idea of OSSM is to enhance its cognitive aspects with social aspects by allowing students to explore each other models or cumulative model of the class [2]. Although past studies have shown that OSSM increases student engagement, they also revealed that OSSM approach makes students more conservative in their work with content, which decreases the 'personalization' power of 'social' guidance [4].

This paper explores an idea of combining social guidance with more traditional knowledge-based guidance in a hope to support more optimal content navigation. We introduce a greedy sequencing approach for selecting learning activities that could maximize student's level of knowledge and demonstrate how this approach could be implemented in the context of OSSM. The results of a classroom study confirm the value of sequencing approach in promoting the non-sequential navigation pattern.

© Springer International Publishing Switzerland 2015
C. Conati et al. (Eds.): AIED 2015, LNAI 9112, pp. 624–628, 2015.
DOI: 10.1007/978-3-319-19773-9_77

2   Greedy Sequencing in the Context of OSSM

To compensate the conforming nature of OSSM on student navigation, we developed a sequencing approach that we call greedy sequencing (GS). The goal of GS is to guide student in the space of learning materials by proactively recommending student activities that could *maximize* the chance to gain new knowledge while avoiding content that is too complex to comprehend. GS utilizes information about concepts associated with content, more specifically, prerequisite and outcome concepts for each activity. Prerequisite concepts should be mastered before working with the activity while outcome concepts are being learned in the process of working with the activity. All concepts were extracted from contents using our parser [3].

The GS algorithm ranks activities by balancing the knowledge level of the student in the prerequisite concepts and the knowledge that can be gained from the outcome concepts. The rank of an activity (R) is computed using (1):

$$R = \frac{n_p P + n_o O}{n_p + n_o} \quad (1) \quad P = \frac{\sum_i^{n_p} k_i w_i}{\sum_i^{n_p} w_i} \quad (2) \quad O = \frac{\sum_i^{n_o} (1 - k_i) w_i}{\sum_i^{n_o} w_i} \quad (3)$$

where n_p and n_o are the number of prerequisite and outcome concepts in the activity, respectively; P represents the ratio of known prerequisites and is the weighted average of student's knowledge in the prerequisite concepts of the activity (equation 2); O represents the ratio of unknown outcomes and is the amount not learned in each of the outcome concepts (equation 3). In these two equations k_i is the knowledge level of the student in the concept i, has the minimum value of 0 and asymtotically reasches 1. The w_i is the smoothed weight of the concept obtained by performing *log* function on TF-IDF values of the concepts. The rank R of an activity is in the interval $[0, 1]$ with 1 representing the highest rank.

In our study, the GS guidance was implemented inside Mastery Grids, an open social student model interface to access online course materials [5]. Figure 1 shows Mastery Grids. The system organizes a course in topics, displayed as columns of the grid. The first row shows topic-by-topic knowledge progress of the current student by using green colors, the darker the higher the progress. The third row shows the aggregated progress of the rest of the students of the class in shades of orange. The second row presents a differential color comparing the student and the class. For example, in Figure 1 the student has a higher progress than the class in most of the topics where the cells in the second row are green, but the class is more advanced in two of the topics (13th and 20th column) where the cells in the second row are orange. The student has same progress as the class in four topics with light gray color (11th, 15th, 18th, and 19th column). By clicking in cells, the student can access the content inside the topic. For example, in Figure 1, the student has clicked the topic *Classes* and the system displays cells to access questions and examples related with this topic. Additionally, by clicking the button "Load the rest of learners", an anonymized ranked list of individual student models is shown in a grid form.

In the current study, we implemented GS on the top of Mastery Grids using red stars to show top – 3 recommended items and their containing topics. The size of the star represents the rank of the recommendation. The resulting interface combined the social guidance of OSSM with personal guidance of GS.

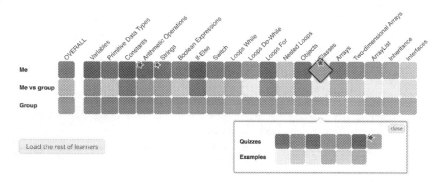

Fig. 1. The presentation of recommendations in the context of Mastery Grids' OSSM interface, a cell with a star symbol represents a recommended topic or activity

3   Navigational Pattern Analysis

To explore the effect of GS on students' navigation and performance, we performed a classroom study in an undergraduate programming course offered by the Computer Science Engineering program in Arizona State University during Fall 2014. System usage was non-mandatory. To investigate how students navigate with and without the presence of the sequencing, we split the study into two parts. Part 1, from Aug. 21 to Sep. 25, used Mastery Grids system with no sequencing. In part 2, from Sep. 26 to Oct. 21, sequencing was enabled.

While OSSM interface demonstrated good ability to move the students timely along the common path through the topic sequence, the goal of the GS algorithm was to help the students in breaking out from the common path when it is personally beneficial: not staying too long on already sufficiently mastered topics, while also making sure that knowledge from the past topics are mastered.

To see to what extent the GS encouraged non-sequential navigation, we first classified students' moves from current to next activity into four groups: (1) Within-Topic: moving between activities in the same topic; (2) Next-Topic: moving from an activity in a topic to the activity in the next topic; (3) Jump-Forward: jumping to an activity in a topic two or more steps further; (4) Jump-Backward: jumping to an activity in an earlier topic. Then, we calculated the probability of topic-based patterns across different parts in the study. Figure 2 shows the heatmap frequency table of four navigation patterns in the three contexts: part 1 and part 2 separating student navigation to *not-recommended* (part 2-N) and *recommended* activities (part 2-R). The value in each cell is the frequency of the

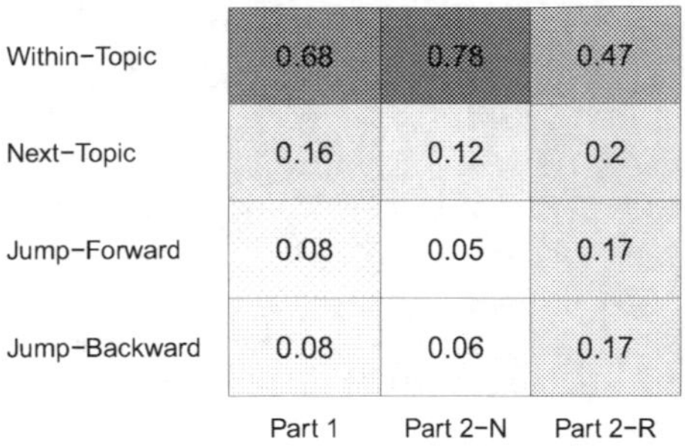

	Part 1	Part 2-N	Part 2-R
Within–Topic	0.68	0.78	0.47
Next–Topic	0.16	0.12	0.2
Jump–Forward	0.08	0.05	0.17
Jump–Backward	0.08	0.06	0.17

Fig. 2. Relative frequencies of four topic-based navigational patterns during the study

corresponding pattern in each context with light blue for lower probability and dark blue for higher probability.

According to this figure, when students make navigation decision without sequencing (Part 1) or ignore it (Part 2-N), they mostly follow sequential pattern working Within-Topic before moving to the Next-Topic. This shows that students tend to attempt most of the activities in the topic before moving to the next one even if it is not the best strategy for their knowledge. The OSSM does hint the students when to move, but its guidance is quite conservative since it is defined by the class as a whole. On the other hand, when students follow GS recommendations, their "groupthink" of staying on the current topic shortens considerably. They move to the next topic faster and remarkably expand their non-sequential navigation (Jump-Forward and Jump-Backward). This is a good evidence that GS encouraged the non-sequential navigation, guiding weaker students to not-mastered materials in previous lectures and advancing stronger to master materials in future lectures. For future work, we plan to investigate the impact of GS recommendations on students' learning.

References

1. Brecht, B., McCalla, G., Greer, J., Jones, M.: Planning the content of instruction. In: Proceedings of 4-th International Conference on AI and Education, Amsterdam, pp. 24–26 (1989)
2. Bull, S., Britland, M.: Group interaction prompted by a simple assessed open learner model that can be optionally released to peers. In: Proceedings of Workshop on Personalisation in E-Learning Environments at Individual and Group Level (PING), User Modeling, vol. 2007 (2007)
3. Hosseini, R., Brusilovsky, P.: Javaparser: A fine-grain concept indexing tool for java problems. In: The First Workshop on AI-supported Education for Computer Science (AIEDCS 2013), pp. 60–63 (2013)

4. Hsiao, I.H., Bakalov, F., Brusilovsky, P., König-Ries, B.: Progressor: social navigation support through open social student modeling. New Review of Hypermedia and Multimedia **19**(2), 112–131 (2013)
5. Loboda, T.D., Guerra, J., Hosseini, R., Brusilovsky, P.: Mastery Grids: An Open Source Social Educational Progress Visualization. In: de Freitas, S., Rensing, C., Ley, T., Muñoz-Merino, P.J. (eds.) EC-TEL 2014. LNCS, vol. 8719, pp. 235–248. Springer, Heidelberg (2014)
6. Vassileva, J., Deters, R.: Dynamic courseware generation on the www. British Journal of Educational Technology **29**(1), 5–14 (1998)

Alleviating the Negative Effect of Up and Downvoting on Help Seeking in MOOC Discussion Forums

Iris Howley[⊠], Gaurav Tomar, Diyi Yang, Oliver Ferschke,
and Carolyn Penstein Rosé

Carnegie Mellon University, 5000 Forbes Ave., Pittsburgh, PA, USA
{ihowley,gtomar,diyiy,ferschke,cprose}@cs.cmu.edu

Abstract. Through the lens of Expectancy Value Theory, we examine the effect of help giver badges, information about helper expertise, and up- and downvoting on help seeking in a MOOC discussion forum. Results show that badges alleviated the negative impact on help seeking introduced by up- and downvoting.

Keywords: Help seeking · MOOCs · Reputation systems · Discussion forums

1 Introduction

Recent years have seen the rapidly rising popularity of Massive Open Online Courses (MOOC), and with the growing number of MOOCs there is also a growing demand for supporting students' learning in a scalable manner. In particular, students use discussion forums to have their questions answered by classmates and instructors, but often those questions end up buried underneath other students' posts. Our Quick Helper uses a social recommendation algorithm to connect help seeking students with peers who could help them. However, many factors influence whether learners seek help, and requesting help from a peer increases the salience of some of these factors.

Leveraging artificial intelligence methods to acquire data from MOOC hosting sites, we can determine a variety of features that would influence a help seeker's expectations and values of the help source that would affect whether or not she seeks help. Of particular interest is (1) the helper's propensity to give help (i.e., the expectation that help will be offered), (2) the helper's expertise (i.e., the accuracy or quality of the help), and (3) whether the helper evaluates the question being asked (i.e., costs of being judged by a social other). Our corresponding research hypotheses are:

1. Emphasizing a potential helper's propensity to give help increases the likelihood of the student seeking help from more recommended peers.
2. Emphasizing a potential helper's ability to provide quality help will increase the number of helpers invited to a public forum thread.
3. Presenting a potential helper as an evaluator of the question being asked increases the cost of the help, resulting in fewer helpers being selected by the help-seeker.
4. Knowing the selected usernames of potential helpers may interfere with the hypotheses derived from Expectancy Value Theory.

© Springer International Publishing Switzerland 2015
C. Conati et al. (Eds.): AIED 2015, LNAI 9112, pp. 629–632, 2015.
DOI: 10.1007/978-3-319-19773-9_78

2   Related Work

The large scale of MOOCs introduces several issues related to help seeking, learning, and social networking that are relevant to our research questions. Forums are a common means of developing communication and community within MOOCs, but they often lose participation due to poor thread management and an overwhelming number of discussion forum threads [5]. When these forums fail to properly sustain a sense of community, high rates of student dropout often follow. To address this issue, we developed a social recommendation algorithm based on our work in Yang et al. (2014) for automatically identifying appropriate helpers to answer student queries, but were then confronted with how to present these potential helpers. For this we build on the work of reputation systems. Coetzee et al (2014) determined that the usage of reputation systems in a MOOC increases the response time and number of responses to discussion threads. In this instance, voting and other reputation system features lead to improved student engagement, but there are additional outcomes that affect student learning and participation that were not specifically explored in this paper. Our experiment looks explicitly at how voting affects help seeking.

Makara & Karabenick (2013) adapted a model of Expectancy Value Theory specifically for help seeking in which expectations of the help source are based upon the belief that the source will make help available or accessible [3]. Values for the help source consist of whether the help provided will be of an appropriate quality and accuracy. In this model, expectations and values of the source interact to impact the likelihood of students asking for help and actually using the help that is provided. We incorporate costs of seeking help into the value of the help. There are certain public and private costs to seeking help [4] that can reduce the perceived value of the help. There is often implicit evaluation from others from asking a question in a public forum, but this evaluation becomes explicit with the popular usage of up and down voting in which readers upvote contributions they believe to be more worthwhile, interesting, etc. Students may place varying values and perceive varying costs on help originating from their potential helpers that influence how they obtain help from both.

3   Study Design and Methodology

Students in a learning analytics course hosted on the edX[1] platform had the option to post their questions directly to the course discussion forums, or to click our "Quick Helper" button. Using the Quick Helper would still post the question to the public discussion forum, but would also privately invite selected peers to the thread. We integrated our Quick Helper in the edX platform via a novel method that allowed us to maintain our own codebase without deploying any code to the edX servers. When our QuickHelper Javascript button was clicked, it called the edX discussion forum client. Using jquery's ajaxComplete API, we watched for these calls and then triggered our own external Quick Helper client. Then our context-aware matrix factorization model

---

[1] https://www.edx.org/

would predict students' preferences for answering a given question by taking into account features from students, questions, and student connections as described in [5]. Because the recommender system requires information about the students in order to provide appropriate matches, we used a "TA Version" of Quick Helper for the initial two weeks of the course. This solves the cold start problem by recommending TAs as helpers until enough data has been gathered about the other users.

Our experiment investigates student help seeking decisions in a MOOC through the lens of Expectancy Value Theory. Students are given the option to select up to three potential helpers as their question is posted to the course discussion board, and it is through the presentation of these potential helpers that we apply our expectancy value lens. Our three main experimental dimensions consist of components of the expectancy value theory: an expectancy emphasis, a value emphasis, and a cost emphasis. To investigate how these expectations, value, and costs influence help seeking in MOOCs, we performed a 2 (expectancy) X 2 (value) X 2 (cost) X 2 (username) factorial experiment in the context of MOOC discussion forums. Our experiment manipulates how potential helpers are presented to the help-seeking student. Number of helpers selected is the main help seeking outcome we are investigating.

In order to emphasize the expectation that a helper will provide help, we used a Help Giver badge system. The number of stars on the help giver badge is determined by ranking the three potential helpers. We based these badges on the visual appearance of the OLDS MOOC badges [2], but our Help Giver badges were only displayed within our Quick Helper system and not rewarded to students external display

We emphasized the value of the help source by providing insight into the helper's knowledge. The student could then evaluate the potential helpers' ability to provide accurate help. The sentence displayed was "This student has been participating in the course for <#> weeks and the matching of his/her knowledge and the topic of your query is <#>%." The numbers were provided by the social recommendation algorithm. If not assigned to the value emphasis condition, students were shown one of four less value-evident sentences about their potential helper similar to the following sentence: "This colleague is involved in the course."

We emphasized a potential cost of seeking help through asking the selected helpers to evaluate whether the student's question was good. We did this through a common upvote/downvote interactional archetype. Knowing that one's post will explicitly be evaluated by any selected helpers should increase public threats to self-esteem, thereby producing an emphasis on the costs of selecting helpers.

4   Results

Throughout the duration of the learning analytics MOOC, approximately 20,000 individuals were enrolled, although after the initial three weeks no more than 2,493 students were active in a given week. 285 MOOC students posted a total of 671 threads to the discussion forum throughout the entire course and 96 of these students used the Quick Helper at least once. Due to initial set up complications, our dataset included only 161 of the Quick Helper instances by 66 users, selecting a mean of 0.79 helpers. Participants were randomly assigned to 2^4 conditions. Prior to our analysis we removed instances that were not relevant to our hypotheses about help seeking.

An ANOVA analysis revealed a trend between our up/downvoting manipulation and number of helpers selected, $F(1, 148) = 2.05$, p=0.16, but no effect of badges. There was a significant interaction between expectancy emphasis (badges) and cost emphasis, $F(3,143) = 3.81$, $p = 0.05$ with a post-hoc analysis revealing that voting only appears to have an effect when no badges are present. Fewer helpers are selected in the up/downvoting condition, but this effect is eliminated when Help Giver badges are shown. There was also a marginal effect of the value emphasis condition on number of helpers selected, $F(1,150) = 3.42$, $p < 0.07$. A Student's t post-hoc analysis revealed that students in the value emphasis condition selected marginally more helpers to be invited to their help request thread.

5   Conclusion

Future work involves a deeper analysis of student help seeking in our MOOC, including a more generalized evaluation of help seeking in the discussion. We are also investigating how our operationalizations of expectancy, value, and cost are linked to their theoretical foundations through a self-report survey in a follow-up study.

Our model of Expectancy Value Theory of help seeking is partly supported by our results in a MOOC which suggest important effects that should be considered in order to place MOOC designers in a better position to design course infrastructure that support important interactions such as help exchange. Being provided with information about the value of a helper's knowledge and knowing one's forum post will be upvoted/downvoted in the absence of help giver badges both have an impact on the number of helpers the students select to help them. Courseware designers must think critically about the features they implement in their online courses, and how they might interact to influence student behaviors including help seeking. Design implications of our results include providing insight into helper expertise and pairing help giver badges with the usage of up and downvoting.

References

1. Coetzee, D., Fox, A., Hearst, M.A., Hartmann, B.: Should your MOOC forum use a reputation system? In: Proceedings of the 17th ACM Conference on Computer Supported Cooperative Work & Social Computing 1176–1187. ACM (2014)
2. Cross, S.: Evaluation of the OLDS MOOC curriculum design course: participant perspectives, expectations and experiences (2013)
3. Makara, K.A., Karabenick, S.A.: Characterizing sources of academic help in the age of expanding educational technology: A new conceptual framework. Advances in Help-seeking Research and Applications: The Role of Emerging Technologies (2013)
4. Wolters, C.A., Pintrich, P.R., Karabenick, S.A.: Assessing academic self-regulated learning. In: What Do Children Need to Flourish? Springer US, pp. 251–270 (2005)
5. Yang, D., Piergallini, M., Howley, I., Rose, C.: Forum thread recommendation for massive open online courses. In: Proc. of 7th Intl Conf. on Educational Data Mining (2014)

Challenges of Using Observational Data to Determine the Importance of Example Usage

Yun Huang[1]([⊠]), José P. González-Brenes[2], and Peter Brusilovsky[1]

[1] Intelligent Systems Program, University of Pittsburgh, Pittsburgh, PA, USA
{yuh43,peterb}@pitt.edu
[2] Pearson Research and Innovation Network, Philadelphia, PA, USA
jose.gonzalez-brenes@pearson.com

Abstract. Educational interventions are often evaluated with randomized control trials, which can be very expensive to conduct. One of the promises of "Big Data" in education is to use non-experimental data to discover insights. We focus on studying the impact of example usage in a Java programming tutoring system using observational data. For this, we compare different formulations of a recently proposed generalized Knowledge Tracing framework called FAST. We discover that different formulations can have the same predictive performance; yet their coefficients may have opposite signs, which may lead researchers to contradictory conclusions. We discuss implications of using fully data-driven approaches to study non-experimental data.

Keywords: Student modeling · Example usage · Knowledge Tracing

1 Introduction

Tutoring systems offer different educational content to help students. For example, programming tutoring systems store a variety of program examples and present it to students in the learning process [1]. Prior work has studied the impact of examples on learners using randomized control trials [8,10]. In this paper we study issues of evaluating example usage using observational data. The motivation of using non-experimental data is to enable cheaper experimentation.

Our work differs from previous work [2,9,11] in that we focus on example usage and not general hints. More importantly, our work suggests a reconciliation of seemingly conflicting results in the literature. While some researchers [2,9] find that hints affect positively learning, others [11] find the opposite.

2 Approach

We focus on the effect of examples in student performance. Student performance is often modeled with the Knowledge Tracing algorithm [3]. Knowledge Tracing has four parameters: the probability of the student knowing the skill before

© Springer International Publishing Switzerland 2015
C. Conati et al. (Eds.): AIED 2015, LNAI 9112, pp. 633–637, 2015.
DOI: 10.1007/978-3-319-19773-9_79

Table 1. Different FAST parameterizations. Each square represents a parameter.

Model	Init	Learn	Guess	Slip	How to handle example features E_t?
Knowledge Tracing	▨	▨	▨	▨	can't handle features
InitScaff	i_1 i_2	▨	▨	▨	init = logistic($i_1 + i_2 \cdot E_t$)
LearnScaff	▨	l_1 l_2	▨	▨	learn = logistic($l_1 + l_2 \cdot E_t$)
EmitScaff	▨	▨	g_1 g_2	s_1 s_2	guess = logistic($g_1 + g_2 \cdot E_t$)
					slip = logistic($s_1 + s_2 \cdot E_t$)

practice (*init*), the learning rate (*learn*), the probability of *guessing* and *slipping*. The guess and slip probabilities are often called *emission* probabilities.

We consider different combinations of parameterizations on how example usage affects student performance. Prior work has only parameterized learning parameters [9], or all four parameters [2]. We also consider fitting parameters per skill [2], or per student [9]. Fitting student-specific parameters allows to control for student differences that can be possible confounders [2]. Prior work [5] has focused on the predictive performance of different parameterizations; we believe we are the first to examine the fitted parameters.

For our analysis we use a student modeling toolkit called FAST [4], which enables features in Knowledge Tracing easily and efficiently. We define a binary feature E_t that gets activated on time t when a student requests an example immediately before t^{th} practice. We use FAST's coefficients on the feature E to measure the impact of example usage. For simplicity we report the inverse of the slip probability (1−slip) so that the positive coefficients indicate higher probability of correct. Table 1 describes the different parameterizations we consider.

3   Experimental Setup

Our data was collected from an online Java programming tutoring system that offers code examples and problems [6]. In each question, students are asked to predict the output of the provided Java program. In each code example students can interactively explore line-by-line explanations. There are 43,696 question attempts and 62,494 example line clicks from 328 students on 124 questions, 110 examples, and 14 topics in total.

For skill-specific models, we randomly selected 80% students for each skill to train and test on the rest. For student-specific models, we train one model per student using the first half of observations and predict the latter. For all models, we do 20 random restarts and pick the one with the maximum log likelihood on train set to avoid local optimum. We evaluated models using Area Under the Curve and report mean (across skills or students) and overall AUC. We computed the 95% confidence interval with bootstrap across skills or students for the mean AUC and the feature coefficients.

Knowledge Tracing has mean AUC 0.62(±0.03) and overall AUC 0.68 for skill-specific models, and mean AUC 0.54(±0.02) and overall AUC 0.65 for student-specific models. FAST with example features all have statistically the same mean and overall AUC as the corresponding Knowledge Tracing baseline by paired t-tests (α=0.05). Do these different model formulations show the same impact of example usage? We proceed with our investigation.

4   Empirical Results

Figure 1 and 2 report the relative effect of example usage for skill and student specific models, respectively. We report the difference between using an example or not for the different parameterizations of Table 1. For example, for guessing:

$$\Delta \operatorname{guess} = \operatorname{logistic}(g_1 + g_2 \cdot \mathbf{1}) - \operatorname{logistic}(g_1 + g_2 \cdot \mathbf{0})$$

On average, EmitScaff model suggests that an example activity has a negative association with performance, while LearnScaff model suggests a positive association with learning. For example, for skill *Objects*, viewing an example decreases the probability of succeeding suggested by EmitScaff model, but increases the learn probability suggested by LearnScaff model.

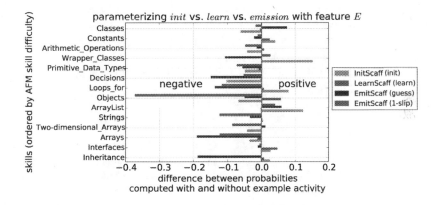

Fig. 1. Skill-specific comparison

On average skill-specific and student-specific models both suggest that an example activity has a negative association with performance. However, they differ in that student-specific models suggest a negative association with init probability and a stronger positive association with learn probability. We need to further study the implications of these two formulations.

Previous studies have reported both positive [2,9] and negative [11] effects on the usage of examples. To reconcile the conflicting results in the literature and in our analysis, we hypothesize that two processes may co-exist: students may learn from examples which can increase performance or knowledge, yet a lower ability student may be more likely to request an example. Future work may study this hypothesis.

parameterizing *init* vs. *learn* vs. *emission* with feature E

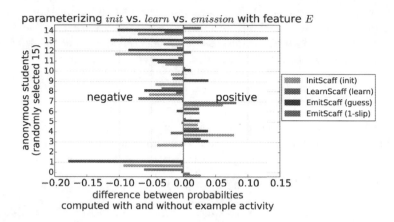

Fig. 2. Student-specific comparison

5   Contributions and Conclusions

We report an example of using different model formations fitted using observational data. We discover that equally predictive models may lead to conflicting conclusions. The implications of our study is that the common practice of simply reporting coefficients for a single formulation may not be appropriate. In follow up work [7] we extend this work and study more closely the parameters learned from observational data.

References

1. Atkinson, R.K., Derry, S.J., Renkl, A., Wortham, D.: Learning from examples: Instructional principles from the worked examples research. Review of Educational Research **70**(2), 181–214 (2000)
2. Beck, J.E., Chang, K., Mostow, J., Corbett, A.T.: Does Help Help? Introducing the Bayesian Evaluation and Assessment Methodology. In: Woolf, B.P., Aïmeur, E., Nkambou, R., Lajoie, S. (eds.) ITS 2008. LNCS, vol. 5091, pp. 383–394. Springer, Heidelberg (2008)
3. Corbett, A., Anderson, J.: Knowledge tracing: Modeling the acquisition of procedural knowledge. User Modeling and User-Adapted Interaction (1995)
4. González-Brenes, J., Huang, Y., Brusilovsky, P.: General features in knowledge tracing: Applications to multiple subskills, temporal item response theory, and expert knowledge. In: Educational Data Mining (2014)
5. Gu, J., Wang, Y., Heffernan, N.T.: Personalizing Knowledge Tracing: Should We Individualize Slip, Guess, Prior or Learn Rate? In: Trausan-Matu, S., Boyer, K.E., Crosby, M., Panourgia, K. (eds.) ITS 2014. LNCS, vol. 8474, pp. 647–648. Springer, Heidelberg (2014)
6. Hsiao, I.-H., Sosnovsky, S., Brusilovsky, P.: Guiding students to the right questions: adaptive navigation support in an e-learning system for java programming. Journal of Computer Assisted Learning **26**(4), 270–283 (2010)

7. Huang, Y., González-Brenes, J., Kumar, R., Brusilovsky, P.: A framework for multifaceted evaluation of student models. In: Educational Data Mining (2015)
8. Najar, A.S., Mitrovic, A., McLaren, B.M.: Adaptive Support versus Alternating Worked Examples and Tutored Problems: Which Leads to Better Learning? In: Dimitrova, V., Kuflik, T., Chin, D., Ricci, F., Dolog, P., Houben, G.-J. (eds.) UMAP 2014. LNCS, vol. 8538, pp. 171–182. Springer, Heidelberg (2014)
9. Sao Pedro, M., Baker, R., Gobert, J.: Incorporating scaffolding and tutor context into bayesian knowledge tracing to predict inquiry skill acquisition. In: Educational Data Mining, Memphis, TN, pp. 185–192 (2013)
10. Schwonke, R., Wittwer, J., Aleven, V., Salden, R., Krieg, C., Renkl, A.: Can tutored problem solving benefit from faded worked-out examples. Proceedings of EuroCogSci **7**, 59–64 (2007)
11. Velasquez, N.F., Goldin, I., Martin, T., Maughan, J.: Learning aid use patterns and their impact on exam performance in online developmental mathematics (2014)

Clique Algorithm to Minimize Item Exposure for Uniform Test Forms Assembly

Takatoshi Ishii[1]([✉]) and Maomi Ueno[2]

[1] Tokyo Metropolitan University, Tokyo, Japan
t_ishii@tmu.ac.jp
[2] University of Electro-Communications, Tokyo, Japan
ueno@ai.is.uec.ac.jp

Abstract. Educational assessments occasionally require "uniform test forms" (or parallel test forms), in which each test form consists of a different set of items, but the forms are equivalent (i.e., equivalent quality based on test information function of item response theory). However, the construction of uniforms tests often suffers bias of item exposure frequency. Ideally, the item exposure frequency should have a uniform and low distribution. For this purpose, we propose a clique algorithm for uniform test forms assembly with low item exposure. We formalize this test assembly as a searching the clique that has minimum item exposure in the maximum cliques. As the results, the proposed method utilizes the item pool more efficiently than traditional methods do. We demonstrate the effectiveness of the proposed method using simulated and actual data.

Keywords: Uniform tests assembly · Item exposure control · Clique problem

1 Introduction

ISO/IEC 23988:2007 provides global standards on the use of IT to deliver assessments. For high-stakes test, this standard is recommending to use "uniform test forms", in which each test form consists of a different set of items, but the forms are equivalent (i.e., equivalent quality based on test information function of item response theory). In practical use, the test administrator is required to assemble as many tests as possible for saving test security. To increase the number of assembled test, some test assembly methods allow that any two tests in uniform tests can include common items less than user allowed as test constraint (and this situation is called overlapping condition). However, these methods on overlapping condition do not control how many times each item used in assembled uniform test forms. Accordingly, item use count of each item is not equivalent (e.g., one item is included in 15% tests but another item is included in only less than 1% tests). This exposure deviation of items is called item exposure problem [6]. This problem decreases reliability of items and tests. Ideally, the item exposure of each item should have a uniform, and be as low as possible.

© Springer International Publishing Switzerland 2015
C. Conati et al. (Eds.): AIED 2015, LNAI 9112, pp. 638–641, 2015.
DOI: 10.1007/978-3-319-19773-9_80

To reduce this problem, we propose a clique algorithm for the uniform test forms assembly with low item exposure. We formalize the test assembly as searching the clique that has minimum item exposure in maximum cliques. As the results, the proposed method assembles uniform tests with less item exposure, and more number of uniform tests than the traditional methods [2–5] do. Thus, the proposed method utilizes the item pool more efficiently than traditional methods do. Finally, we demonstrate the effectiveness of the proposed method using simulated and actual data.

2 Clique Problem for Uniform Test Assembly with Low Item Exposure

2.1 Clique Problem for Uniform Test Assembly with Low Item Exposure

To assemble the uniform test assembly with low item exposure, we formalized test assembly as a clique problem. The first, we define the uniform tests. We employ the definition of "uniform test forms" that is the same as traditional methods (e.g., [2–4]). Accordingly, the uniform test forms is a clique in the following graph:

$$V = \left\{ \begin{array}{l} s : s \in S, \text{"Feasible test form"}, s \text{ satisfies all test constraints} \\ \text{excepting the overlapping constraint from a given item pool} \end{array} \right\}$$

$$E = \left\{ \begin{array}{l} \{s',s''\} : \text{The pair of } s' \text{ and } s'' \text{ has fewer common (overlapping) items} \\ \text{than the allowed number in the overlapping constraint} \end{array} \right\}.$$

The next, we define item exposure. The exposure Ex_i of item i in uniform tests U is formalized as follows:

$$Ex_i = \sum_{r=1}^{|U|} x_{i,r}, \tag{1}$$

where, $x_{i,r} = 1$ denotes that i-th item is selected into r-th test form, and $x_{i,r} = 0$ denotes otherwise. Then, we define item exposure Ex_U of uniform test forms U as follows:

$$Ex_U = \max(Ex_1, \cdots, Ex_r, \cdots, Ex_{|U|}). \tag{2}$$

Thus, the item exposure Ex_U of uniform tests U is the maximum exposure of items Ex_i in the uniform tests U. Accordingly, the minimizing the item exposure Ex_U is Min-Max for exposure of items Ex_i. Therefore, the minimizing the item exposure Ex_U minimizes the worst exposure of item in the uniform tests U.

The last, we define the uniform test assembly with low item exposure. We formalize this uniform test assembly as the following clique problem:

$$\text{minimize} \frac{Ex_C}{|C|} \tag{3}$$

$$\text{subject to} \forall v, \forall w \in C, \{v,w\} \in E \tag{4}$$

The eq:4 restrict C as clique. Increasing $|C|$ decreases term of $\frac{Ex_C}{|C|}$ in eq:3. And decreases Ex_C decreases term of $\frac{Ex_C}{|C|}$. Thus, the eq:3 optimize the number of tests $|C|$ and the item exposure Ex_C, simultaneously and indirectly. We call the term $\frac{Ex_C}{|C|}$ as "item exposure rate".

2.2 Algorithm for Uniform Test Assembly with Low Item Exposure

We propose an approximate algorithm for uniform test assembly with low item exposure. This algorithm consists of the four steps.

Algorithm for Uniform Test Assembly with Low Item Exposure

Step 1: (initialize)
Step 1 sets Clique C as assembled uniform test forms by our previous work [2], and clique set $C_{candidate}$ as empty ($C_{candidate} = \phi$).

Step 2: (Add step)
Step 2 assembles feasible test, and adds it to the current searching clique C. To assemble feasible test, Step 2 solves following optimization problem:

$$\text{maximize} \sum_{i=1}^{n} \lambda_i x_i \tag{5}$$

$$\text{subject to} \sum_{i=1}^{n} x_{i,r} x_i \leq \text{(overlapping constraint)} \tag{6}$$

$$(r = 1 \cdots |C|)$$

where $x_i = 1$ denotes that i-th item is selected into the assembling test form, and $x_i = 0$ denotes otherwise. All other test constraints (e.g., the information amount based on Item Responce Theory, average of answering time, and so on) are included in the constraints. Therein, coordinates $\lambda_1, \lambda_2, \ldots, \lambda_n$ denote random variables distributed uniformly on $[0, 1]$. $\lambda_i (0 \leq i \leq n)$ are resampled each problem is solved. (This formulation is generation of [1] to assemble to assemble uniform tests on overlapping condition.) While this problem has solution, Step 2 repeatedly solves this test assembling problem using LP solver (e.g., ILOG CPLEX). And Step 2 adds the solution of this problem to the current uniform test forms: clique C. If the current clique C is changed, Step 2 adds the current clique C to clique set $C_{candidate}$.

Step 3: (Delete Step)
Step 3 deletes tests from the current clique C for reduce item exposure Ex_C. The deleted test includes the item i with maximum exposure $Ex_i = Ex_C$. By repeating deletion of test, Step 3 reduces the current clique size to 90% of it self. If the current clique is changed, Step 3 adds the current clique to clique set $C_{candidate}$. If the computation time is less than given time, then jump to Step 2

Step 4: (Output)
Step 4 finds out the clique that has minimum item exposure rate $\frac{Ex_C}{|C|}$ from clique set $C_{candidate}$, and outputs it.

---

3   Experiments and Results

To demonstrate the performances of the proposed method, we compared the number of assembled test forms and the item exposure with proposed method and the traditional methods ("BST" : [5], "GA" : [4], "BA" : [3], and "RndMCP" : [2]). For this comparison, we used ILOG CPLEX 11.0 for solving the liner programming in [5] and the proposed method.

We used an actual item pool that was used for the Synthetic Personality Inventory (SPI) examination, which is a popular aptitude test in Japan. In addition, we used three simulated item pools with total numbers of items $I = 500, 1000$, and 2000. The parameters of items in the simulated item pools were set to have similar specification to the actual items. We set the test constraints as (1) the test includes 25 items, and (2) the numbers of allowed overlapping items are $0, 5$ and 10.

Table 1. The Number of Assembled Test Forms and Item Exposure

Pool Size	OC	BST $|C|$	BST Ex_C	BST $\frac{EX_C}{|C|}$	GA $|C|$	GA Ex_C	GA $\frac{EX_C}{|C|}$	BA $|C|$	BA Ex_C	BA $\frac{EX_C}{|C|}$	RndMCP $|C|$	RndMCP Ex_C	RndMCP $\frac{EX_C}{|C|}$	Proposal $|C|$	Proposal Ex_C	Proposal $\frac{EX_C}{|C|}$
500	0	12	1	8.3%	3	1	33.3%	5	1	20.0%	10	1	10.0%	17	1	5.9%
	5	20	6	30.0%	23	5	21.7%	96	16	16.7%	4380	362	8.3%	10736	823	7.7%
	10	20	12	60.0%	21	7	33.3%	107	15	14.0%	99983	12995	13.0%	100975	13141	13.0%
1000	0	21	1	4.8%	4	2	50.0%	6	2	33.3%	17	1	5.9%	33	1	3.0%
	5	40	14	35.0%	17	5	29.4%	104	11	10.6%	46305	3399	7.3%	48055	3504	7.3%
	10	40	21	52.5%	19	4	21.1%	105	14	13.3%	100000	8705	8.7%	101000	8630	8.5%
2000	0	53	1	1.9%	8	1	12.5%	12	1	8.3%	32	1	3.1%	70	1	1.4%
	5	80	27	33.8%	22	4	18.2%	104	6	5.8%	96876	3935	4.1%	97826	3829	3.9%
	10	80	43	53.8%	23	4	17.4%	103	7	6.8%	100000	4013	4.0%	100975	4014	4.0%
978 (actual)	0	24	1	4.2%	9	1	11.1%	9	1	11.1%	16	1	6.3%	31	1	3.2%
	5	39	10	25.6%	283	23	8.1%	371	23	6.2%	40814	2177	5.3%	44105	2163	4.9%
	10	39	13	33.3%	286	22	7.7%	381	24	6.3%	100000	5598	5.6%	101000	5274	5.2%

Table 1 shows the number of test forms $|C|$, the item exposure Ex_C, and the item exposure rate $\frac{EX_C}{|C|}$, for the proposed method and traditional methods.

In any case, proposed method assembled more number of test forms $|C|$, lower item exposure Ex_C, and lower item exposure rate $\frac{EX_C}{|C|}$ than traditional methods[2–5] did.

4 Conclusion

We proposed a uniform test assembly method to maximize the number of uniform test forms, and to minimize the item exposure. To archive this, the proposed method minimizes the item exposure rate = (item exposure)/(the number of tests).

To demonstrate the performance of proposed method, we conducted an experiment using simulated and actual data. The result was summarized that the proposed method assembled a greater number of uniform test forms with lower item exposure rate than the traditional methods did. Future work will include (1) revealing the feature of our method such as how long time cost and how much space cost does the proposed method requires and etc, and (2) assessing this method in various situations.

References

1. Belov, D.I.: Uniform test assembly. Psychometrika **73**(1), 21–38 (2008)
2. Ishii, T., Songmuang, P., Ueno, M.: Maximum clique algorithm and its approximation for uniform test form assembly. IEEE Transactions on Learning Technologies **7**(1), 83–95 (2014)
3. Songmuang, P., Ueno, M.: Bees algorithm for construction of multiple test forms in e-testing. IEEE Transactions on Learning Technologies **4**, 209–221 (2011)
4. Sun, K.T., Chen, Y.J., Tsai, S.Y., Cheng, C.F.: Creating irt-based parallel test forms using the genetic algorithm method. Applied Measurement in Education **2**(21), 141–161 (2008)
5. van der Linden, W.J.: Liner Models for Optimal Test Design. Springer (2005)
6. Wainer, H.: Educational Testing Service: CATS: Whither and Whence. Educational Testing Service (2000)

Game Features and Individual Differences: Interactive Effects on Motivation and Performance

Matthew E. Jacovina[1(✉)], Erica L. Snow[1], G. Tanner Jackson[2],
and Danielle S. McNamara[1]

[1] Learning Sciences Institute, Arizona State University, Tempe, AZ 85287, USA
{Matthew.Jacovina,Erica.L.Snow,Danielle.McNamara}@asu.edu
[2] Cognitive Science, Educational Testing Service, Princeton, NJ 08541, USA
gtjackson@ets.org

Abstract. To optimize the benefits of game-based practice within Intelligent Tutoring Systems (ITSs), researchers examine how game features influence students' motivation and performance. The current study examined the influence of game features and individual differences (reading ability and learning intentions) on motivation and performance. Participants ($n = 58$) viewed lesson videos in iSTART-2, an ITS designed to improve reading comprehension skills, and practiced with either a game-like activity or a minimally game-like activity. No main effects of game environment were observed. However, there was an interaction between game environment and pretest learning intentions in predicting students' self-reported effort. The correlation between learning intentions and self-reported effort was not significant for students who practiced with the more game-like activity, whereas it was for students who practiced in the less game-like activity. We discuss the implications for this interaction and how it might drive future research.

Keywords: Game-based learning · Intelligent Tutoring Systems · Motivation

1 Introduction

Intelligent Tutoring Systems (ITSs) have been successfully implemented across a variety of domains [1]. However, these systems often provide repetitive and prolonged practice, which can result in disengagement and boredom [2]. One approach to enhance motivation is through the inclusion of games and game-like features [3]. Games aim to leverage students' enjoyment to foster interest and engagement in a system, leading to an increased motivation to persist in practice, though there have been mixed findings about the link between games and motivation [4]. To best make use of educational games, researchers seek to understand how different game features function for different domains and contexts [3], and how students' individual characteristics influence the impact of game features [5, 6]. Toward achieving these goals, we investigated the effects of game features on motivation and performance. Subsequently, we examined how motivation and performance are influenced by the interaction between key individual differences and game features.

© Springer International Publishing Switzerland 2015
C. Conati et al. (Eds.): AIED 2015, LNAI 9112, pp. 642–645, 2015.
DOI: 10.1007/978-3-319-19773-9_81

2   Current Study and Results

The context of the current study is the Interactive Strategy Training for Active Reading and Thinking-2 (iSTART-2) system. iSTART-2 is a game-based ITS designed to enhance comprehension abilities through self-explanation strategy lessons and strategy practice games [7]. Previous work has compared game-based versions of iSTART to non-game based versions and found that over time, students (including those with lower reading abilities) equally benefitted from the game-based version and the non-game based version [6]. However, the game-based version yielded higher enjoyment and motivation [7]. Because these studies included an array of games and game types, however, it is difficult to pinpoint the effects of particular features.

With this study, we aim to disentangle the relative benefits (or costs) of game features by including two between-subjects conditions corresponding to an activity that is minimally game-like (Strategy Identification) and an activity that includes game features (Strategy Match). Each activity involved the same cognitive task that requires students to read a scientific passage and select which iSTART-2 strategies were used to generate example self-explanations. Strategy Identification only provided accuracy feedback. Strategy Match also included points and levels. Points were rewarded for correct answers, with point bonuses for selecting correct answers consecutively; students advanced through levels as their point total increased. We make comparisons between students who practiced with these activities to help answer our research questions: How does posttest motivation and performance differ as a function of game environment? Do game features affect the relationship between individual differences (reading ability and learning intentions) and students' motivation and performance?

Participants were 58 high school students and recent high school graduates who were paid to complete this 3-hour study. They were randomly assigned to practice with either Strategy Identification (n=29) or Strategy Match (n=29). One student was removed due to a computer error. All students completed a pretest that included measures of reading ability (Gates-MacGinitie Reading Test, 4th ed.), motivation [8], and self-explanation ability [7]. Next, students watched self-explanation lesson videos, and then spent 45 minutes practicing with either Strategy Identification or Strategy Match. Last, students completed a posttest which was similar to the pretest. Performance on pretest and posttest self-explanations was quantified by calculating a score from 0 to 3 on each self-explanation using an automated scoring algorithm [9].

Motivation and Performance. Between-participants ANCOVAs were used to test differences across the two game environments (Strategy Identification and Strategy Match) in three posttest motivation dimensions: reported effort, performance assessment, and emotional state. The covariates included pretest motivation dimensions to account for any pretest differences that emerged despite random assignment. No main effects of game environment were significant ($Fs < 2$, $ps > .10$). A between-participants ANCOVA was used to investigate the effect of game environment on posttest self-explanation quality, with pretest quality serving as the covariate. There was no main effect of game environment ($F < 1$, $p > .10$). Scores on the self-explanations at posttest were, however, lower than at pretest for participants in both the Strategy Identification and Strategy Match conditions. A repeated-measures, mixed ANOVA with test (pretest, posttest) as a within-participants factor and game environment as a between-participants factor showed that posttest scores were significantly lower than pretest scores [$F(1, 55) = 28.42, p < .001, \eta_p^2 = .34$]. This finding may be attributable to fatigue and the limited time practicing in the system.

Interactions with Individual Differences. To explore the question of how game environment moderates the relationship between individual differences and students' motivation and performance, we conducted hierarchical multiple regression analyses, which allowed us to determine if a model including an interaction term was significantly more predictive than a model without.

We first conducted a hierarchical multiple regression with *posttest reported effort* as the dependent variable. Model 1 included *reading ability* and game environment as predictors (for all regressions, Strategy Identification was dummy coded as 0 and Strategy Match as 1), and was not significantly predictive [$F(2, 54) = 0.96, R^2 = .034, p = .390$]. Model 2 added the interaction term between reading ability and game environment and was also not significant [$F(3, 53) = 0.67, R^2 = .037, p = .573$]. We conducted a second hierarchical multiple regression with posttest reported effort as the dependent variable. Model 1 included *learning intentions* and game environment as predictors and was significantly predictive of reported effort [$F(2, 54) = 11.08, R^2 = .291, p < .001$]. Students with higher learning intention scores reported exerting more effort during their interactions with iSTART-2. Model 2 added the interaction term between learning intentions and game environment, and was significantly more predictive [$F(1, 53) = 4.99, \Delta R^2 = .061, p = .030$]. To examine this effect, we calculated the correlations between learning intentions and posttest self-reported effort. This correlation was stronger for students who practiced with Strategy Identification ($r = .72, p < .001$) than with Strategy Match ($r = .30, p = .108$). For Strategy Identification (the less game-like activity) students, this means that if they began the study intending to work hard to learn from the task, at posttest they often did report working hard; or if they began the study without the intention to devote much effort to the task, at posttest they tended to report a lack of effort. By comparison, Strategy Match (the more game-like activity) students showed a weaker relationship: students' initial intention to learn did not strongly determine how much effort they later reported exerting.

We conducted similar hierarchical regressions predicting *posttest self-explanation* quality (including pretest self-explanation ability as a predictor to account for pretest differences). However, in the first hierarchical regression, adding the *reading ability* by game environment interaction term only marginally increased the predictive strength of the model [$F(1, 52) = 2.99, \Delta R^2 = .032, p = .090$]. And in the second hierarchical regression, adding the *learning intentions* by game environment interaction term did not increase the predictive strength of the model [$F(1, 52) = 0.73, \Delta R^2 = .010, p = .397$]. Thus, game environment did not significantly moderate the relationship between individual differences and performance.

3   Conclusions

This study compared students' motivation and performance after interacting with iSTART-2 using one of two game environments: Strategy Identification, which was minimally game-like, and Strategy Match, which rewarded students with points that advanced them through levels. No differences emerged in comparing motivational measures and performance across conditions. However, evidence emerged that the game environment moderated the relationship between learning intentions and reported effort. Thus, for students who practiced with the less game-like activity, there was a strong relationship between pretest learning intentions and posttest reported effort. However, for students who practiced with the more game-like activity, there was no relationship. The inclusion of game features thus resulted in students deviating from their initial learning intentions (which could be good or bad, depending on their intentions). Note that this project cannot suggest *why* the game features in Strategy Match caused normally strong relationships between self-reported pre-task and post-task motivational measures to break down. Future work focusing on the complex set of relationships between individual differences and game features can help endow ITSs with the ability to target game features to specific groups of students.

Acknowledgments. This research was supported in part by the Institute for Educational Sciences (IES R305A130124). Any opinions, findings, and conclusions or recommendations expressed are those of the authors and do not necessarily reflect the views of the IES.

References

1. Steenbergen-Hu, S., Cooper, H.: A meta-analysis of the effectiveness of intelligent tutoring systems on college students' academic learning. Journal of Educational Psychology **106**, 331–347 (2014)
2. D'Mello, S., Olney, A., Williams, C., Hays, P.: Gaze tutor: A gaze-reactive intelligent tutoring system. International Journal of Human-Computer Studies **70**, 377–398 (2012)
3. McNamara, D.S., Jackson, G.T., Graesser, A.C.: Intelligent tutoring and games (ITaG). In: Baek, Y.K. (ed.) Gaming for Classroom-Based Learning: Digital Roleplaying as a Motivator of Study. IGI Global, Hershey (2010)
4. Wouters, P., van Nimwegen, C., van Oostendorp, H., van der Spek, E.D.: A meta-analysis of the cognitive and motivational effects of serious games. Journal of Educational Psychology **105**, 249–265 (2013)
5. Gros, B.: Digital games in education: The design of games-based learning environments. Journal of Research on Technology in Education **40**, 23–38 (2007)
6. Jackson, G.T.: Varner (Allen), L.K., Boonthum-Denecke, C., McNamara, D.S.: The Impact of individual differences on learning with an educational game and a traditional ITS. International Journal of Learning Technology **8**, 315–336 (2013)
7. Jackson, G.T., McNamara, D.S.: Motivation and performance in a game-based intelligent tutoring system. Journal of Educational Psychology **105**, 1036–1049 (2013)
8. Boekaerts, M.: The on-line motivation questionnaire: A self-report instrument to assess students' context sensitivity. New Directions in Measures and Methods **12**, 77–120 (2002)
9. Jackson, G.T., Guess, R.H., McNamara, D.S.: Assessing cognitively complex strategy use in an untrained domain. Topics in Cognitive Science **2**, 127–137 (2010)

Gamification of Online Learning

Jincheul Jang, Jason J.Y. Park, and Mun Y. Yi[✉]

Department of Knowledge Service Engineering, KAIST, Daejeon, South Korea
{jcjang,j.park89,munyi}@kaist.ac.kr

Abstract. The gamification of online learning has been a subject of interest lately. This study attempts to explore two things in particular, the effects of gamification on learning and the moderating effects of user characteristics. The results demonstrate that the gamification elements contribute to higher learning outcomes while two user characteristics, agreeableness and pre-training motivation, are important moderators of the links between the gamification elements and learning outcomes. The study findings indicate that a gamified system in consideration of user characteristics is an effective means to improving the efficacy of the e-learning environment.

Keywords: Gamification · Engagement · Personalized learning

1 Introduction

Online education has become widely available and popular as more providers, such as leading universities, are launching online courses and educational services. However, it is still a big challenge to maintain the learner's motivation high even when the quality of online education is high. One possible solution is 'gamification,' which refers to 'the use of game design elements in non-game contexts' [2,4]. Gamification can be used to motivate and elevate the user's engagement with systems. Social media platforms (e.g. Foursquare) and many mobile applications (e.g., Nike+) implement gamification for raising and maintaining motivation of the user.

In this study, we designed a gamified e-learning environment to evaluate and observe the effects of gamification on student learning. Some recent studies [3] have shown the potential of using gaming elements for enhancing learning outcomes, but there is little attention on evaluating various dimensions of the user's reactions to gamification elements. The various dimensions can contribute to the understanding of users and ultimately help design a personalized gamification environment where gamification elements can be carefully controlled to fit the users' characteristics. Toward this goal, this study uses a mix of traditional game elements and time pressure in order to create a gamified environment. Gamification elements are carefully chosen from a list of game elements [4] while time pressure is chosen and treated separately because of its popularity in game environments and potential strength in altering human behavior [1]. The evaluation of the learning outcomes and user reactions from utilizing the proposed game environment should provide solid grounds to observe and understand the effects and user reactions to gamification elements and their interaction with users' personal characteristics.

C. Conati et al. (Eds.): AIED 2015, LNAI 9112, pp. 646–649, 2015.
DOI: 10.1007/978-3-319-19773-9_82

2   Test System Design

Our gamified system was designed to learn how to use the software Adobe Photoshop. The popularity of Photoshop made it a highly desirable skillset and the difficulty level was suited for university students. The developed system was envisioned to educate students to learn the image editing tools and procedures in Photoshop while providing important insights into student accomplishments and insights.

The system consisted of multiple sessions, each of which was focused on learning one specific tool. Each session in turn consisted of a series of segments. Each segment was divided into two components: a tutorial and a quiz. The tutorial component provided learning material and the quiz component tested the user on that learning material provided in the tutorial. Game elements applied to this system included: experience points and levels, a growing avatar that changed its form according to the level of the user, point system that accumulated points for correctly answering quizzes, hearts that provided challenge to learning materials by expelling the user from the session if they exceeded an incorrect limit for the quiz in a session, and finally time pressure on the quizzes to challenge the user as well.

3   Experiment

3.1   Participants

114 volunteers (74 male and 40 female) served as the experimental participants. They were either undergraduate or graduate students, who voluntarily participated in the experiment. The ages of participants ranged from 17 to 30, with the mean age of 21.13. Pre and post experiment comprehension was measured through a set of test that evaluated the learning achieved through the experiment. Also a pre-test survey of user characteristics including big five personality traits, pre-training motivation, Photoshop experience and demographic factors, was conducted while post-test survey for user engagement, Photoshop self-efficacy, and satisfaction were collected.

3.2   Experimental Settings

To examine the effects of proposed gamification in online education, we set two different training conditions with one control group.

Control Group. The aim of control group was to compare the performance of this group to treatment groups. The system did not include any of the game elements used. The participants in this group only had learning contents and quizzes. A simple feedback regarding the correctness of the answer was provided during a quiz.

Gamification Group. The system was added with game elements, levels, point, life points, avatars and imaged feedbacks. Solving quizzes in the learning session affected the user's level, point, and growth of avatar. There were three 'hearts' in each session that represented the number of chances to solve the quizzes. If the participants lost all of 'hearts', they would have to try the session again. If the answer was right, points were given. If the answer was wrong, a 'heart' was erased.

Gamification with Time Pressure (GTP) Group. In this treatment, a time limitation was added to the quiz session. The remaining time was displayed on the screen and alerts, the screen flashing red, were given for the last 5 seconds. If the answer were not given within the time limitation, it was considered an incorrect attempt.

4   Results

The descriptive statistics and analysis of variance (ANOVA) results of the experiment are shown in Table 1. The post comprehension test (F= 4.35, p < .05), average time taken for each quiz (F = 11.90, p < .001), the number of completed quiz (F = 27.68, p < .001) showed significant differences between the three treatment groups. Specifically, the gamification group demonstrated the highest score in post-comprehension, and the control group achieved the lowest score. Both environments with gamification produced higher learning outcomes relative to the control group. Interestingly, the time pressure group produced a higher level of comprehension than the control group while using much less time. Fisher's least significant difference (LSD) test revealed that the two treatment groups performed significantly better for post comprehension test and number of completed quiz than the control group. Likewise, the LSD test on average time showed that users in the time pressure group used significantly shorter time than the other groups.

Table 1. Descriptive Statistics and results of ANOVA (* p<.05, *** p<.001)

Group	N	Post-Comp	AvgTime	CompleteQuiz
Control	41	11.85 (2.14)	9.19 (1.52)	75.61 (10.03)
Gamification	40	13.03 (1.87)	8.76 (1.98)	94.58 (15.59)
GTP	33	12.91 (1.79)	7.46 (0.85)	98.67 (17.60)
F score		4.35*	11.90***	27.68***

Among the many user characteristics, two dimensions demonstrated strong influence to the post-comprehension of users. As shown in Table 2, analysis of covariance (ANCOVA) shows that agreeableness and pre-training motivation serve as important moderators of the gamification effects on post-comprehension. Users with low agreeableness (the ability to relate to a system) in the non-gamification conditions show lower learning while users with low agreeableness in the gamification conditions show higher learning, indicating that the gamification conditions were more conducive to learning for users with low agreeableness. It seems that those gamification elements effectively attracted those users with low agreeableness and those elements improved their comprehension of the material, relative to those similar low agreeableness users in the non-gamification condition. The results also show that time pressure heavily affects users with high motivation, but its effect is not so potent for users with low motivation (F=3.53, p=0.06). These study results provide useful insights for designing future systems with gamified elements tailored for different individuals.

Table 2. Descriptive statistics between gamification, time pressure and user characteristics

Treatment	Agreeableness	Post-comp (N)	Treatment	Motivation	Post-comp (N)
No gamification	High	12.20 (20)	No time pressure	High	12.26 (43)
	Low	11.52 (21)		Low	12.63 (38)
Gamification	High	12.48 (33)	Time pressure	High	13.38 (16)
	Low	13.38 (40)		Low	12.47 (17)

5   Conclusion

The observed results from the study show that the game elements, such as points, levels, avatars, and time pressure can improve the overall effectiveness of an online learning system. The results also show that depending on the user characteristics, different game elements can alter learning outcomes. We believe that such discovery is a positive step towards providing an online learning system that enhances learners' motivation with personalized game features. A future study should attempt to evaluate more detailed relationships between individual game elements and personal characteristics.

References

1. Zur, B.: H., Breznitz, S.J.: The effect of time pressure on risky choice behavior. Acta Psychologica **47**(2), 89–104 (1981)
2. Deterding, S., Khaled, R., Nacke, L., Dixon, D.: Gamification: toward a definition. In: CHI 2011, pp. 12–15 (2011)
3. Rai, D.: Modes and mechanisms of game-like interventions in computer tutors. In: Lane, H., Yacef, K., Mostow, J., Pavlik, P. (eds.) AIED 2013. LNCS, vol. 7926, pp. 924–927. Springer, Heidelberg (2013)
4. Zicbermann, G., Cunningham, C.: Gamification by Design: Implementing Game Mechanics in Web and Mobile Apps. O'Reilly (2011)

Examining the Relationship Between Performance Feedback and Emotions in Diagnostic Reasoning: Toward a Predictive Framework for Emotional Support

Amanda Jarrell[1(✉)], Jason M. Harley[1,2], Susanne Lajoie[1], and Laura Naismith[3]

[1] Department of Educational and Counselling Psychology, McGill University,
Montreal, Canada
amanda.jarrell@mail.mcgill.ca
[2] Computer Science and Operations Research, Université de Montréal, Montreal, Canada
[3] Toronto Western Hospital, University Health Network, Toronto, Canada

Abstract. The purpose of this research is to understand achievement emotions resulting from performance feedback in a medical education context where 30 first and second year medical students learned to diagnose virtual patients in an intelligent tutoring system (ITS), BioWorld. We found that students could be organized into groups using cluster analyses based on the emotions they reported after receiving performance feedback: a positive emotion cluster, negative emotion cluster, and low overall emotion cluster. Medical students in the positive achievement emotion cluster had the highest performance on the diagnostic reasoning cases; those in the negative achievement emotion cluster had the lowest performance; and students categorized as belonging to the low overall achievement emotion cluster had mean performance levels that fell between the two. From the results we propose critical performance thresholds that can be used to predict emotions following performance feedback.

Keywords: Emotions · Affect · Intelligent tutoring systems

1 Introduction: Success, Failure and Emotions

Failure and success generate emotional responses that have a strong impact on future learning, educational decisions, and even health [1]. Given that emotional responses influence motivation and behaviors following successes and failures, it is critical to understand achievement emotions. Achievement emotions are affective arousal tied to achievement activities or outcomes [1]. We focus on retrospective outcome achievement emotions. These emotions arise when learners reflect back on the outcome of an achievement task, and include feelings of pride, anger, shame, joy, and relief [1, 2]. Retrospective outcome emotions are important because they contribute to the formation of future appraisals, which can influence prospective and concurrent state emotions (e.g., anxiety) as well as motivation-related learning behaviors (e.g., drop-out) [1]. Supporting emotional resilience is especially important in educational contexts that train students for high-stakes, real-life situations, such as medical education [3].

© Springer International Publishing Switzerland 2015
C. Conati et al. (Eds.): AIED 2015, LNAI 9112, pp. 650–653, 2015.
DOI: 10.1007/978-3-319-19773-9_83

The purpose of this research is to understand achievement emotions resulting from performance feedback, as medical students learn to diagnose virtual patients in an intelligent tutoring system (ITS), BioWorld [4]. In this study we answered two research questions: (1) Do retrospective outcome emotions cluster in a meaningful way? And (2) is there a significant performance difference between emotion cluster groups?

2   Methods

Participants. This study consisted of 30 first and second year medical students from a North American university. The sample consisted of 11 men and 19 women, with an average age of 23 ($SD = 2.60$). The data analyzed in this paper were collected as part of a larger study in BioWorld [5].

BioWorld. BioWorld is an ITS that scaffolds students as they learn medical problem solving. Each case begins with a patient history where medical students gather evidence and based on this evidence propose initial hypotheses. Medical students obtain further evidence by ordering laboratory tests that confirm or disconfirm a particular hypothesis, search for information using the online library, and request help using the consultation tool. After the final diagnosis is submitted, they receive individualized feedback on their solution based on an aggregated expert solution.

Academic Achievement Emotions (AEQ). The emotion questionnaire used in this study was adapted from the Achievement Emotion Questionnaire (Retrospective) (AEQ; [6]) to measure emotions experienced after receiving performance feedback (i.e. pride, joy, relief, anger and shame).

Performance. Performance in BioWorld was measured by examining the accuracy of students' diagnoses. Accuracy was operationalized in this study based on the percentage of evidence matches with the expert solution.

Procedure. Participants were asked to solve three cases of varying levels of difficulty: easy, moderate and difficult. The order of the cases was counterbalanced to mitigate practice effects. Feedback on performance was provided to the learner at the end of each case. After finishing each case, learners completed the AEQ.

3   Results

3.1   Emotion Clusters

The results from the 3-cluster k-means cluster analyses portrayed a robust pattern of emotion clusters. For each analysis, participants in cluster 1 appear to experience low overall affect; cases in cluster 2 appear to experience high negative affect; and cases in cluster 3 appear to experience high positive affect. The final cluster centers and the number of cases in each cluster are shown in Table 1.

Table 1. Final cluster z-score means on the retrospective outcome emotion varibles

Analysis	Variable	Cluster 1 Low Affect	Cluster 2 Negative Affect	Cluster 3 Positive Affect
		$n = 17$	$n = 4$	$n = 9$
	Shame	-.46	**1.56**	-.61
	Anger	-.36	**1.95**	-.58
Easy	Joy	-.49	-.02	**1.85**
	Pride	.02	-.54	**1.60**
	Relief	-.54	.39	**1.37**
		$n = 13$	$n = 7$	$n = 10$
	Shame	-.68	**1.26**	-.03
	Anger	-.60	**1.49**	-.14
Moderate	Joy	-.71	.20	.61
	Pride	-.49	-.25	.72
	Relief	-.83	.58	.46
		$n = 17$	$n = 8$	$n = 5$
	Shame	-.28	**1.52**	-.14
	Anger	-.45	**1.43**	-.31
Difficult	Joy	-.86	.23	**1.24**
	Pride	-.74	-.60	**1.10**
	Relief	-.60	.33	.10
		$n = 47$	$n = 22$	$n = 21$
	Shame	-.42	**1.24**	-.35
	Anger	-.54	**1.47**	-.33
All cases	Joy	-.67	.19	**1.30**
	Pride	-.39	-.39	**1.27**
	Relief	-.69	.45	**1.08**

Note: Clusters were interpreted by the z-scores. Z-scores above |1| were interpreted as high (bolded) and scores approaching zero were interpreted as low [7].

3.2   Emotion Clusters and Performance

Four ANOVAs were conducted to determine if significant differences existed between emotion clusters and performance for the: (1) moderate, (2) difficult and (3) easy cases as well as (4) across all cases. The results of the ANOVAs revealed a significant difference in performance between emotion clusters for all analyses except for the moderate case (see Table 2).

Table 2. Results of the ANOVAs Conducted for Emotion Clusters and Performance

Analysis	df	MS	F	p	η^2
Moderate	2	82.24	.56	.580	.04
Difficult	2	1857.73	7.10	.003*	.35
Easy	2	988.11	4.16	.027*	.24
All Cases	2	2374.23	6.08	.003*	.12

The descriptive statistics suggest that participants in the positive affect cluster had the highest performance; those in the negative affect cluster had the lowest performance; and participants in the low overall affect cluster had mean performance that fell between the two (Table 3). Tukey LSD post-hoc comparisons were conducted for all significant ANOVAs. These results revealed that several of the emotion clusters differed significantly on performance (Table 3).

Table 3. Tukey Post-hoc Comparisons Conducted for Emotion Clusters and Performance

Analysis	Cluster	Performance		Comparisons			p
		M	SE				
	Cluster 1: Low Affect	41.07	3.37	Low.	>	Neg.	N.A.
Moderate	Cluster 2: Negative Affect	35.14	4.60	Neg.	<	Pos.	N.A.
	Cluster 3: Positive Affect	38.20	3.85	Pos.	<	Low	N.A.
	Cluster 1: Low Affect	48.94	17.34	Low.	>	Neg.	.838
Difficult	Cluster 2: Negative Affect	45.00	16.13	Neg.	<	Pos.	.005*
	Cluster 3: Positive Affect	77.20	10.40	Pos.	>	Low.	.005*
	Cluster 1: Low Affect	73.53	3.74	Low.	>	Neg.	.028*
Easy	Cluster 2: Negative Affect	50.00	7.70	Neg.	<	Pos.	.035*
	Cluster 3: Positive Affect	74.44	5.14	Pos.	>	Low.	.989
	Cluster 1: Low Affect	54.53	2.88	Low.	>	Neg.	.073
All cases	Cluster 2: Negative Affect	43.18	4.21	Neg.	<	Pos.	.002*
	Cluster 3: Positive Affect	64.14	4.31	Pos.	>	Low.	.159

4   Conclusion and Future Directions

We interpret these results to suggest that two critical performance thresholds that must be met for a participant to experience negative, positive or low affect (i.e. a low performance threshold and a high performance threshold). If a participant's performance falls (1) below the low performance threshold, then the participant will experience negative affect, (2) above the high performance threshold, then the participant will experience positive affect and (3) above the low performance threshold but below high performance threshold, then the participant will experience low overall affect. Future research could apply these thresholds to predict emotional responses without needing to ask students how they feel. This would allow ITSs to swiftly and appropriately debrief students to prevent the formation of harmful future appraisals and down-regulate the experience of negative emotions following poor performance and failure.

Acknowledgements. This research has been supported by SSHRC and FQRSC.

References

1. Pekrun, R., Perry P.P.: Control-value theory of achievement emotions. In: International Handbook of Emotions in Education, pp. 120–141. Routledge, New York (2014)
2. Pekrun, R.: The control-value theory of achievement emotions. Educational Psychology Review **18**(4), 315–341 (2006)
3. Artino Jr, A.R., Holmboe, E.S., Durning, S.J.: Can achievement emotions be used to better understand motivation, learning, and performance in medical education? Medical Teacher **34**(3), 240–244 (2012)
4. Lajoie, S.: Developing professional expertise with a cognitive apprenticeship mode. In: Development of Professional Expertise, Cambridge, UK, pp. 61–83 (2009)
5. Naismith, L.M.: Examining motivational and emotional influences on medical students' attention to feedback in a TRE for learning clinical reasoning. McGill University (2013)
6. Pekrun, R., Goetz, T., Frenzel, A.C., Barchfeld, P., Perry, R.P.: Measuring emotions in students' learning and performance. Contemporary Ed. Psychology **36**, 36–48 (2011)
7. Meyers, L., Gamst, G., Guarino, A.: Applied Multivariate Research: Design and Interpretation. SAGE, Thousand Oaks (2013)

Learning, Moment-by-Moment and Over the Long Term

Yang Jiang[1(✉)], Ryan S. Baker[1], Luc Paquette[1], Maria San Pedro[1],
and Neil T. Heffernan[2]

[1] Teachers College, Columbia University, New York, NY, USA
{yj2211,paquette,mzs2106}@tc.columbia.edu,
baker2@exchange.tc.columbia.edu
[2] Worcester Polytechnic Institute, Worcester, MA, USA
nth@wpi.edu

Abstract. The development of moment-by-moment learning graphs (MBMLGs), which plot predictions about the probability that a student learned a skill at a specific time, has already helped to improve our understanding of how student performance during the learning process relates to robust learning [1]. In this study, we extend this work to study year-end learning outcomes and to account for differences in learning on original questions and within knowledge-construction scaffolds. We discuss which quantitative features of moment-by-moment learning in these two contexts are predictive of the longer-term outcomes, and conclude with potential implications for instruction.

Keywords: Moment-by-moment learning · Scaffolding · Intelligent tutoring system · Educational data mining

1   Introduction

Recent advancements in educational data mining have allowed researchers to infer the probability that a student learned a skill at a specific time during learning [2]. With these estimates, it becomes possible to construct visual graphs of individual students' learning over time (moment-by-moment learning graphs, or MBMLGs). Different visual patterns of MBMLGs obtained from student usage of a tutor are associated with differences in student learning outcomes [3]. However, this type of visual analysis requires a human analyst. In more recent work, Hershkovitz and colleagues [1] distilled quantitative features from MBMLGs, in order to predict robust learning. In current study, we extend this work to analyze whether the features can predict a longer-term outcome, standardized exam performance. Another question addressed in this paper is whether learning in different contexts impacts these patterns, in particular whether there is a difference between original questions and scaffolding questions.

To research these questions, we replicate the quantitative features of MBMLGs that were successful at predicting robust learning outcomes with reasonable precision [1] and extend this prior work by distinguishing between original questions and scaffolding questions. We then analyze how these features of students' MBML correlate to student performance on the Massachusetts Comprehensive Assessment System (MCAS), a high-stakes standardized test given at the end of the year. We compute the

© Springer International Publishing Switzerland 2015
C. Conati et al. (Eds.): AIED 2015, LNAI 9112, pp. 654–657, 2015.
DOI: 10.1007/978-3-319-19773-9_84

correlations to outcomes for each of the features, specifically comparing the differences in correlations for original questions versus scaffolding questions.

2   Moment by Moment Learning Graph Features

We study the questions within the context of ASSISTments [4], a web-based tutoring system for middle school mathematics. ASSISTments data were used to investigate the correspondence between the fine-grained quantitative attributes of the MBMLGs and student math performance on the MCAS. This was done in two stages.

First, MBMLGs were constructed using a machine-learned model of MBML, using data from 7,647 middle school students from four school districts who used ASSISTments throughout an entire school year (2004-2005 to 2008-2009). Overall, students completed a total of 2,281,808 actions (i.e., submitting an answer or requesting help) across a range of 19,991 problems within the system. Next, a discovery with models approach was used to explore the relationship between MBML and MCAS scores among a subset of 613 students in one urban district for whom MCAS scores were available. Students used ASSISTments in the classroom as preparation for the MCAS test for two hours, twice a week, throughout the 2004-2005 school year, completing a total of 97,245 actions (56,343 on original questions and 40,902 on scaffolding questions) targeting a broad range of mathematical skills.

The construction of MBMLGs is a three-step process, described in detail in [2]. First, each problem step in the data is labeled with the probability $P(J)$ that the student learned that skill on that particular attempt, using data from the student's future performance. Second, a machine-learned model that predicts $P(J)$ is built from a broad set of features, using data only from the student's past and present performance. Last, we integrate across predictions to construct a MBMLG for each student/skill.

Once MBMLGs were created, a feature set (see Table 1) was distilled from the quantitative characteristics of each graph. In order to account for differences between original and scaffolding questions, we computed the MBMLG features separately for the original questions (denoted o) and scaffolding questions (denoted s). For each student, MBMLG features (except *sumByLen* and *areaByLen*) were computed separately for each skill, and averaged across all skills.

Table 1. List of all the features distilled from the MBMLGs.

avgMBML: Average moment-by-moment learning value in a given graph.
sumMBML: Sum of moment-by-moment learning values in a given graph.
graphLen: Number of steps in a MBMLG (number of problems received).
area: Area under the MBMLG.
peak: Height of the largest peak in the MBMLG.
2ndPeak: Height of the 2nd-largest peak in the MBMLG.
3rdPeak: Height of the 3rd-largest peak in the MBMLG.
peakIndex: First index of the largest peak in the MBMLG (Index = 1 equals the first step involving the skill).
2ndPeakIndex: First index of the 2nd-largest peak in the MBMLG.
2PeakDist: Distance between the largest and the 2nd-largest peaks.
2PeakAdjDist: 2PeakDist, divided by graphLen.
2PeakDecr: Decrease [%] of magnitude from largest to 2nd-largest peak.
2PeakDist-adjDecr: 2PeakDecr divided by 2PeakDist.
3PeakDecr: Decrease [%] of magnitude from largest to 3rd-largest peak.
3PeakDist-adjDecr: 3PeakDecr divided by 3PeakDist.
sumByLen: Avg. sumMBML across skills for student divided by avg. graphLen for that student.
areaByLen: Avg. area for student across skills divided by average graphLen for that student.

3   The Relationships Between Individual Features of the MBMLGs and Long-Term Learning Outcomes

In this section, we explore the relationships between individual features of the MBMLGs (defined in Section 2) and student math scores on MCAS, using correlation mining and significance tests with post-hoc controls (Storey's q-value method [5]), and whether the features based on original or scaffolding questions better predicted the MCAS, using statistical tests of the difference between two correlation coefficients for correlated samples with post-hoc controls.

Table 2. Correlation of MBMLG features to MCAS scores. ρ_{OM} and ρ_{SM} denote the Spearman correlation between MCAS scores and MBMLG features for *original* and *scaffolding* questions, respectively. Correlations that are sig. after controlling for false discovery ($q<0.05$) are marked by *.

Feature	ρ_{OM}	q_{OM}	ρ_{SM}	q_{SM}	t	q
avgMBML	-0.180	<0.001*	-0.046	0.080	-3.559	<0.001*
sumMBML	0.086	0.012*	-0.219	<0.001*	7.793	<0.001*
graphLen	0.275	<0.001*	-0.103	0.004*	9.632	<0.001*
area	0.130	<0.001*	-0.218	<0.001*	8.829	<0.001*
peak	0.031	0.136	0.082	0.015*	-1.273	0.070
2ndPeak	-0.216	<0.001*	-0.188	<0.001*	-0.652	0.152
3rdPeak	-0.283	<0.001*	-0.263	<0.001*	-0.435	0.188
peakIndex	0.112	0.002*	-0.216	<0.001*	7.775	<0.001*
2ndPeakIndex	0.140	<0.001*	-0.090	0.011*	4.543	<0.001*
2PeaksDist	0.145	<0.001*	-0.124	0.001*	5.379	<0.001*
2PeakAdjDist	-0.227	<0.001*	-0.037	0.113	-3.548	<0.001*
2PeakDecr	0.325	<0.001*	0.480	<0.001*	-3.875	<0.001*
2PeakDist-adjDecr	0.307	<0.001*	0.465	<0.001*	-3.804	<0.001*
3PeakDecr	0.323	<0.001*	0.477	<0.001*	-3.630	<0.001*
3PeakDist-adjDecr	0.150	<0.001*	0.381	<0.001*	-4.443	<0.001*
sumByLen	-0.300	<0.001*	-0.147	<0.001*	-4.150	<0.001*
areaByLen	-0.081	0.015*	-0.276	<0.001*	4.476	<0.001*

Table 2 shows the Spearman's correlations ρ between individual features and MCAS scores, and their post-hoc controlled statistical significance q. The strongest correlations involved differences between the largest peak values during scaffolding, including *2PeakDecr (s)*, the decrease [%] in magnitude from the largest to 2nd-largest peak on scaffolding questions ($\rho_{SM}(585) = 0.480$, $q < 0.001$); and *3PeakDecr (s)*, the decrease [%] in magnitude from the largest to 3rd-largest peak on scaffolding questions ($\rho_{SM}(546) = 0.477$, $q < 0.001$). Larger differences between these values indicate "spikier" graphs where considerable learning occurs in eureka learning moment(s) [1]. A weaker version of the same pattern was found for original questions.

MCAS scores were positively correlated with *peakIndex (o)*, the index of the largest peak in the Original MBMLG ($\rho_{OM}(612) = 0.112$, $q = 0.002$), but negatively correlated with *peakIndex (s)*, the index of the largest peak in the Scaffolding MBMLG ($\rho_{SM}(612) = -0.216$, $q < 0.001$). Most likely, this difference (which was significant, $t(609) = 7.775$, $q < 0.001$) demonstrates the contribution that the ASSISTments scaffolding system makes to learning. If students had their highest learning late in the learning process involving original questions (possibly due to scaffolding beforehand), they did better on the exam. But for scaffolding questions, earlier moments of high learning were associated with higher MCAS scores.

Other results also confirmed the importance of the learning context. Answering more original questions in ASSISTments (*graphLen*) was associated with higher test performance ($\rho_{OM}(612) = 0.275$, $q < 0.001$). In contrast, more problem steps on scaffolding questions corresponded to poorer learning outcomes ($\rho_{SM}(612) = -0.103$, $q = 0.004$). This difference ($t(609) = 9.632$, $q < 0.001$) likely reflects the fact that students receive more scaffolding if they are performing poorly. Similarly, area under the Original MBMLG (*area (o)*) was positively correlated with the MCAS while area under the Scaffolding MBMLG (*area (s)*) was negatively associated with the MCAS, the difference between the correlations ($t(609) = 8.829$, $q < 0.001$) was significant.

4   Conclusion

This paper explores the relationships between quantitative features of MBMLGs and students' performance on an end-of-year exam, comparing features based on performance during original questions and scaffolded tutoring. This separation allows us to discover significant temporal effects on student learning; students who demonstrate high learning early in their interactions with ASSISTments through scaffolding are most likely to perform well on the state exam. This finding suggests that the scaffolding in ASSISTments may be useful beyond simply producing better performance on the current skill. In general, the MBMLG appears to be able to shed light on fine-grained aspects of the learning process that are associated with important outcomes; figuring out the best uses of this method is an area for further research.

Acknowledgments. We acknowledge funding for ASSISTments from the NSF (1316736, 1252297, 1109483, 1031398, 0742503, 1440753), the U.S. Dept. of Ed. GAANN (P200A120238), ONR's "STEM Grand Challenges," and IES (R305A120125, R305C100024).

References

1. Hershkovitz, A., Baker, R.S.J.D., Gowda, S.M., Corbett, A.T.: Predicting future learning better using quantitative analysis of moment-by-moment learning. In: Proceedings of the 6th International Conference on Educational Data Mining, pp. 74–81 (2013)
2. Baker, R.S.J.D., Goldstein, A.B., Heffernan, N.T.: Detecting Learning Moment-by-Moment. IJAIED **21**(1–2), 5–25 (2011)
3. Baker, R.S.J.D., Hershkovitz, A., Rossi, L.M., Goldstein, A.B., Gowda, S.M.: Predicting Robust Learning with the Visual Form of the Moment-by-Moment Learning Curve. Journal of the Learning Sciences **22**(4), 639–666 (2013)
4. Razzaq, L., et al.: Blending assessment and instructional assistance. In: Nedjah, N., de Macedo Mourelle, L., Borges, M.N., Almeida, N.N. (eds.) Intelligent Educational Machines, pp. 23–49. Springer, Heidelberg (2007)
5. Storey, J.D., Taylor, J.E., Siegmund, D.: Strong Control, Conservative Point Estimation, and Simultaneous Conservative Consistency of False Discovery Rates: A Unified Approach. Journal of the Royal Statistical Society, Series B **66**, 187–205 (2004)

When Is It Helpful to Restate Student Responses Within a Tutorial Dialogue System?

Pamela Jordan[(⊠)], Patricia Albacete, and Sandra Katz

Learning Research and Development Center,
University of Pittsburgh, Pittsburgh, PA 15260, USA
pjordan@pitt.edu

Abstract. Tutorial dialogue systems often simulate tactics used by experienced human tutors such as restating students' dialogue input. We investigated whether the amount of tutor restatement that supports student inference interacts with students' incoming knowledge level in predicting how much students learn from a system. We found that students with lower incoming knowledge benefit more from an increased level of these types of restatement while students with higher incoming knowledge benefit more from a decreased level of such restatements.

Keywords: Tutorial dialogue · Restatement · Inference · Prior knowledge

1 Introduction

A tutor restating part of a student's dialogue contribution can serve many purposes and at the surface level can range from exact repetitions to semantic reformulations [6]. Some of the purposes for restatement that are found in human tutoring are acknowledging the correct parts of a student's response [3,4], marking (i.e., focusing on part of a response) and modeling a better answer [2,4]. Because restatements of correct responses have been shown to correlate with learning [4], this opens the possibility that restatements could cause learning by strengthening correct knowledge. While restatements of various types have been incorporated into a number of tutorial dialogue systems (e.g. Circsim-Tutor [5], AutoTutor [9], Beetle II [4]), restatement has not been tested in isolation from other tactics to determine whether it has any causal connection to learning.

Here, we explore a different type of restatement that has the purpose of showing consequence [6]–that is, making an inference explicit. We test two alternative hypotheses about this type of restatement: 1) that it will equally benefit all students and 2) that its effect varies according to students' incoming knowledge. If it strengthens learning of correct knowledge, then it should benefit all students equally. However, we expect students with lower incoming knowledge to benefit more from an increased level of consequence restatement while higher incoming knowledge students would benefit more from a decreased level of such restatements. Our expectation is motivated by prior research which found that

C. Conati et al. (Eds.): AIED 2015, LNAI 9112, pp. 658–661, 2015.
DOI: 10.1007/978-3-319-19773-9_85

unpacking the inferences in text supports comprehension among low-knowledge readers, while less cohesive (higher inference-inducing) text is better for high-knowledge readers [8]. Reduced cognitive load is a proposed alternative explanation for the "reverse cohesion effect", particularly for high-knowledge readers when reading a less coherent text. Cognitive load increases when they have to reconcile their existing schema about the topic discussed in the text with the background material provided in a "highly coherent" text [7].

2   Methods

Participants. The study was conducted in high school physics classes at three schools in the Pittsburgh PA area with 168 students participating. Students were randomly assigned to one of two conditions: high restatement (N= 88; 30 females, 58 males) and low restatement (N= 80; 27 females, 53 males).

Materials. We used an existing version of the Rimac natural-language tutoring system to conduct our experiment. A brief description of the system can be found in [1]. It engages students in post-problem solving reflection dialogues on the concepts involved in solving quantitative problems. Rimac's content was developed in consultation with high school physics teachers. For this experiment we used its dynamics content which covers three problems with two reflection questions per problem, and a 21 item pretest and isomorphic post-test which included nine multiple-choice problems and 12 open-response problems.

To create the high restatement system, three dialogue authors added consequence inference restatements of student responses when it would result in either: 1) an explicit concluding statement at the end of a sub-dialogue that draws upon the student's responses during the sub-dialogue or 2) an explicit if-then statement that draws the "if" or "then" part from the student's immediately preceding response. An example of the latter context for consequence inference restatements is shown below for the high restatement condition:

> T: While the arrow is flying is anything touching or in contact with it?
> S: No [there is nothing touching the arrow during its flight]
> T: I agree. Hence since **there is nothing touching the arrow during its flight** there is no contact force applied to it.

To create the low restatement version authors identified all restatements involving inference and either deleted or replaced the restatement with a pronoun, taking care not to disturb the coherency of the dialogue. The low restatement version of the above example is identical to the high restatement version, except for the second tutor turn, which would read: "I agree. Hence there is no contact force applied to it."

Procedure. On the first day, the teacher gave the pretest in class and assigned the three dynamics problems, referred to in the Materials section, for homework. During the next one to two class days (depending on whether classes were approximately 45 min. or 80 min. long), students used Rimac in class. For each homework problem, students watched a video "walkthrough" of a sample solution and then engaged in the problem's reflective dialogues. The videos focused on procedural/problem-solving knowledge, while the dialogues focused on conceptual knowledge. Finally, at the next class meeting, teachers gave the post-test, which was isomorphic to the pretest.

3   Results

Learning Performance. To determine whether interaction with the tutoring system, regardless of condition, promoted learning, we compared gains from pretest to post-test using paired samples t-tests. When students in each condition were considered separately, we found a statistically significant difference for all problems together (H: $t(87)=3.56$, $p<.01$; L: $t(79)=4.49$, $p<.01$), multiple-choice problems (H: $t(87)=2.73$, $p<.01$; L: $t(79)=2.39$, $p<.02$), and open-response problems (H: $t(87)=3.13$, $p<.01$; L: $t(79)=4.8$, $p<.01$), where H=high restatement, L=low restatement. These results suggest that students in both conditions learned from both versions of the system.

High Restatement vs. Low Restatement. To test whether students who used the high restatement version of the system performed differently from students who used the low restatement version, we compared students' gains from pretest to post-test using independent samples t-tests. We found no significant differences between conditions for any subset of problems even when controlling for pretest (there were no differences for mean time on task). This suggests that this type of restatement does not support learning by strengthening correct knowledge. If it did, then we would expect to see a difference between conditions for learners of all prior knowledge levels.

Prior knowledge-treatment interaction. To investigate whether there was a prior knowledge treatment interaction, we performed a multiple regression analysis using condition, prior-knowledge (as measured by pretest) and condition * prior-knowledge (interaction) as explanatory variables, and gain as the dependent variable. When all problems were considered together, we found a significant interaction between condition and prior knowledge in their effect on gains ($t=-2.126$, $p=0.04$). Likewise, we found a significant interaction when we considered only gains on open-response problems ($t=-2.689$, $p=0.01$). However, for multiple-choice problems we did not find a significant interaction.

Graphing gain vs. prior knowledge for all problems suggested that students with pretest scores that are 35 % correct or less benefit more from the high restatement version of the system. However students with pretest scores above 35 % correct benefit more from the low restatement version. Graphing gain vs. prior knowledge for open-response problems suggested that students with pretest scores of 23 % or less on open-response items benefit more from higher restatement and students with pretest scores greater than 23 % benefit more from lower restatement. Consistent with the results reported in [8], both findings offer evidence to support our hypothesis that lower knowledge students benefit more from high restatement in inferential contexts while higher knowledge students benefit more from low restatement.

4   Conclusions and Future Work

We found that students learned from the tutoring system, across conditions, as measured by normalized gain scores. There was no difference between conditions, which suggests that this type of restatement may not cause learning by strengthening correct knowledge. However, we did find a prior knowledge treatment interaction which supported our hypothesis that lower knowledge students would benefit more from a high restatement system while higher knowledge students would benefit more from a low restatement system. Thus system designers may need to be judicious in their use of restatement as it may dampen learning if there is a mismatch to students' prior knowledge levels.

In future research, we plan to determine if the benefits of the high and low restatement versions of Rimac can be used advantageously in a system that adapts to students' knowledge levels and to formulate and test additional hypotheses for other types of restatement (e.g., that have other purposes).

Acknowledgments. We thank Stefani Allegretti, Michael Lipschultz, Diane Litman, Dennis Lusetich, Svetlana Romanova, and Scott Silliman for their contributions. This research was supported by the Institute of Education Sciences, U.S. Department of Education, through Grant R305A130441 to the University of Pittsburgh. The opinions expressed are those of the authors and do not necessarily represent the views of the Institute or the U.S. Department of Education.

References

1. Albacete, P., Jordan, P., Katz, S.: Is a dialogue-based tutoring system that emulates helpful co-constructed relations during human tutoring effective? In: 17th International Conference on Artificial Intelligence in Education AIED (2015)
2. Becker, L., Ward, W., Vuuren, S.V., Palmer, M.: Discuss: a dialogue move taxonomy layered over semantic representations. In: The 9th International Conference on Computational Semantics IWCS 2011 Oxford, England, January 2011
3. Chi, M.T.H., Roy, M.: How adaptive is an expert human tutor? In: Aleven, V., Kay, J., Mostow, J. (eds.) ITS 2010, Part I. LNCS, vol. 6094, pp. 401–412. Springer, Heidelberg (2010)
4. Dzikovska, M., Campbell, G., Callaway, C., Steinhauser, N., Farrow, E., Moore, J., Butler, L., Matheson, C.: Diagnosing natural language answers to support adaptive tutoring. In: International FLAIRS Conference (2008)
5. Freedman, R.: Using a reactive planner as the basis for a dialogue agent. In: International FLAIRS Conference (2000)
6. Hyland, K.: Applying a gloss: Exemplifying and reformulating in academic discourse. Applied Linguistics **28**(2), 266–285 (2007)
7. Kalyuga, S., Ayres, P.: The expertise reversal effect. Educational Psychology **38**, 23–31 (2003)
8. McNamara, D., Kintsch, E., Songer, N., Kintsch, W.: Are good texts always better? text coherence, background knowledge, and levels of understanding in learning from text. Cognition and Instruction **14**, 1–43 (1996)
9. Person, N., Graesser, A., Kreuz, R., Pomeroy, V.: Simulating human tutor dialog moves in autotutor. International Journal of Artificial Intelligence in Education **12**, 23–39 (2003)

Quality of LOD Based Semantically Generated Questions

Corentin Jouault[1(✉)], Kazuhisa Seta[1,2], and Yuki Hayashi[2]

[1] Graduate School of Science, Osaka Prefecture University, Osaka, Japan
jouault.corentin@gmail.com
[2] College of Sustainable System Sciences, Osaka Prefecture University, Osaka, Japan

Abstract. This research aims to automatically generate questions to support history learning. The questions are generated semantically with natural language patterns using Linked Open Data (LOD). The generated questions are designed to reinforce history learning by supporting acquisition of new information and encouraging learners to think about their knowledge. In this paper, we describe an evaluation assessing the capability of the system to generate questions of a quality high enough to support learning. The evaluation had two main results: first, the questions generated by the system cover 87% of the questions generated by humans. Second, we confirmed that the system can generate questions that enhance history thinking of the same quality as human generated questions.

Keywords: Question generation · Linked open data · Semantic open learning space · Inquiry based learning · Self-directed learning · History learning

1   Introduction

Questions from the teacher are an important and integral part of the learning to deepen learners' understanding [8]. More specifically, in the history domain, asking questions to learners encourages them to form an opinion and reinforce their understanding [5]. Learners also naturally ask questions to themselves during their learning. However, they cannot always generate good questions by themselves [7].

Because the quality of the learning is dependent on the quality of the questions [3], asking good questions is important for performing satisfying learning. Learners are required to generate good questions to perform good quality of learning. This is one of the difficulties of learners performing their learning by themselves.

Our approach to solve this problem is to support learners with automatically generate meaningful questions depending on the contents of the documents studied by each learner. Our question generation method adopts a semantic approach that uses the LOD and ontologies to create content-dependent questions. Our function is part of a novel learning environment [6] that aims to provide meaningful support in history learning about any historical topic.

In this paper, we aim to clarify whether the quality of the questions generated by the system is sufficient to support history learning. The issues of the question generation and the learning support system embedding it are described in detail in [6].

© Springer International Publishing Switzerland 2015
C. Conati et al. (Eds.): AIED 2015, LNAI 9112, pp. 662–665, 2015.
DOI: 10.1007/978-3-319-19773-9_86

2   Overview of Question Generation Using Ontology

To generate meaningful and reliable questions, the system uses the combined information from two LOD sources, DBpedia [1] and Freebase [2]. To combine the information, the system uses its own history domain ontology to recognize equivalent types from Freebase and DBpedia.

The system also requires an understanding of a meaningful question's structure to generate meaningful history domain questions. To understand the structure and function of a question, we refer to Graesser's taxonomy [4] to build an ontology for the history domain. This taxonomy describes domain-independent question types that are meaningful to support learning.

Each definition of the question concept class in the History Dependent Question Ontology (HDQ Ontology) specifies the relation among the concept (relation) classes specified in the history domain ontology and the natural language patterns (NLP). Each NLP specifies a template of a natural language question for each question concept class and is used to generate the natural language text of the question.

Currently, the HDQ ontology defines 28 history domain questions. Based on the definition, two kinds of questions are generated:

- **R&C based Question:** Relation and Concept based Question. These questions require a concept instance with a relation instance. The answer to this type of question is identified based on a triple described explicitly e.g. *"Where did the Battle of Verdun take place?"* or *"Who commanded the German East Asia Squadron?"*
- **C based Question:** Concept based question. These questions require only a concept instance. These questions ask even about information not explicitly described e.g. *"How did the fights of the Battle of Verdun change the course of World War I (WWI)?"* or *"How would WWI have been different without Wilhelm II, German Emperor?"*

3   Evaluation

3.1   Method

For this evaluation, we evaluated the quality of the questions in supporting history learning compared to human generated questions. We asked a history professor to compare the quality of questions according to his own criteria. More detailed information about the evaluation is as follows.

- **Topic: WWI.** The current version of the system can generate history domain questions for any topic. For this evaluation, the topic is set to WWI.
- **Source of human generated questions: SparkNotes** [9], a popular website, whose main target users are junior high-school and high-school students. The questions for our experimental study were taken from the multiple choice quiz and essay questions.
- **Evaluator: A history professor in a university** with over 20 years of history teaching experience.

3.2   Results

Quality of the R&C based questions
Table 1 shows the number of couples for each mark. The evaluator described the criteria used for attributing grades during the evaluation as follows.
1. Both questions require different knowledge to be answered.
2. Both questions focus on different parts of the target relation instance, but they require the same knowledge to be answered, e.g. "Who won the Battle of the Falkland Islands?" (Human) and "What was the result of the Battle of the Falkland Islands?" (System).
3. Both questions assess the same knowledge from different viewpoints (they require the same knowledge to be answered), e.g. "Who assumed power in Germany and led negotiations with the Allies after Wilhelm II lost power?" (Human) and "Who succeeded Wilhelm II, German Emperor?" (System).
4. Both questions have the same meaning.

The evaluator judged that couples marked 2, 3, and 4 require the same knowledge for junior and high school students to be answered. In total, under the conditions of the system, 87% of the manually generated questions could be covered by the system.

As a result, the question generation function has potential to generate useful questions to construct learners' basic knowledge.

Quality of the C based questions
Table 2 shows the number of questions for each category. The result shows that, even if the system cannot generate questions of the highest quality (C5), it can generate questions of the same quality as the manually generated ones in weighted average.

The criteria defined by the evaluator were:
1. Questions asking facts or yes/no questions.
2. Questions asking causal relations.
3. Others (more complex than C2 but does not require integrated knowledge).
4. Questions requiring integrated knowledge of the topic.
5. Questions requiring a deep historical or political thinking.

The system only uses information specific to one topic, i.e., using one of the key concepts defined in SparkNotes, to generate a question in this experiment. Although it

Table 1. Shallow Questions Evaluation Results

Mark	1	2	3	4	Total
Number of couples	5 (13%)	15 (39%)	14 (37%)	4 (11%)	38

Table 2. Deep Questions Evaluation Results

	C1	C2	C3	C4	C5	W. Avg.
Human (n=20)	1	5	8	3	3	3.1
System (n=30)	1	1	19	9	0	3.2

depends on the templates that were used by the system, the majority of the questions
are of reasonable quality (C3 or C4).

As a result, the question generation function has potential to generate useful questions to reinforce learners' deep understanding of historical topics.

4   Concluding Remarks

In this paper, we overviewed a method for generating questions automatically by
using LOD. The history domain ontology makes it possible to use the concept (relation) instances from two semantic resources (DBpedia and Freebase), thus creating a
combined source with more reliable information used for the questions generation.
The history dependent question ontology makes possible to generate content dependent questions using domain dependent but content independent question concept
classes.

The evaluation showed that the system could generate good quality questions by
using the current LOD. The questions generated by the system can cover the majority
of the questions generated by humans. In addition, the questions enhancing history
thinking generated by the system and by human were of the same average quality.
By considering the system can generate much more questions not appearing on
SparkNotes and its adaptability, the results described in this paper seems quite meaningful in the situation of individual learners' support.

References

1. Bizer, C., Lehmann, J., Kobilarov, G., Auer, S., Becker, C., Cyganiak, R., Hellmann, S.:
   DBpedia-A crystallization point for the Web of Data. Web Semantics: Science, Services
   and Agents on the World Wide Web 7(3), 154–165 (2009)
2. Bollacker, K., Evans, C., Paritosh, P., Sturge, T., Taylor, J.: Freebase: a collaboratively created graph database for structuring human knowledge. In: Proceedings of the 2008 ACM
   SIGMOD International Conference on Management of Data, pp. 1247-1250 (2008)
3. Bransford, J.D., Brown, A., Cocking, R.: How people learn: Mind, brain, experience, and
   school. National Research Council, Washington (1999)
4. Graesser, A., Ozuru, Y., Sullins, J.: What is a good question?. In: Bringing Reading Research To Life. Guilford Press (2010)
5. Husbands, C.: What is history teaching?: Language, ideas and meaning in learning about the
   past. Open University Press, Berkshire (1996)
6. Jouault, C., Seta, K.: Adaptive self–directed learning support by question generation in a
   semantic open learning space. International Journal of Knowledge and Web Intelligence
   4(4), 349–363 (2013)
7. Otero, J.: Question generation and anomaly detection in texts. In: Hacker, D.J., Dunlosky,
   J., Graesser, A. C. (Eds.). Handbook of Metacognition in Education, pp. 47-59. Routledge
   (2009)
8. Roth, W.M.: Teacher questioning in an open-inquiry learning environment: Interactions of
   context, content, and student responses. Journal of Research in Science Teaching 33(7),
   709–736 (1996)
9. SparkNotes Editors: SparkNote on World War I (1914–1919). SparkNotes LLC. (2005).
   http://www.sparknotes.com/history/european/ww1/ (accessed December 12, 2014)

New Opportunities with Open Learner Models and Visual Learning Analytics

Judy Kay[1] and Susan Bull[2(✉)]

[1] School of Information Technologies, University of Sydney, Sydney, Australia
`judy.kay@sydney.edu.au`
[2] Electronic, Electrical and Systems Engineering, University of Birmingham, Birmingham, UK
`s.bull@bham.ac.uk`

Abstract. This paper compares approaches to visualising data for users in educational settings, contrasting visual learning analytics and open learner models. We consider the roots of each, and identify how each field can learn from experiences and approaches of the other, thereby benefiting both.

Keywords: Open learner model · OLM · Visual learning analytics · VLA

1 Introduction

Open learner models (OLM) can be understood as learner models that allow a user, usually the learner, to view the internal system's learner model data in a human-understandable form. This allows learners to either act on the information in some way, possibly with system guidance, to further their learning; and/or to reflect on it before following up with appropriate learning activities leading to the desired learning outcomes. Open learner models typically aim to allow learners greater control over their learning, as they can use the learner model data as information upon which to base decisions about their learning [12]. Instead of seeing the system's underlying rules, numerical values, logical or conceptual structures, etc., about their knowledge and skills, the human-understandable nature of the open learner model may be graphical, and so more readily understood. Learner models constructed in a variety of ways have been opened to users, for example: Bayesian networks [22]; concept maps [18]; constraint-based models [17]. As an illustration of the variety of ways in which learner models may be opened to users, we show the following three visualisations (of eight) from the Next-TELL OLM [1],[10], also used in the LEA's Box (learning analytics toolbox) OLM (http://www.leas-box.eu), in Figure 1. The reason for this particular choice for Figure 1 is to highlight that each visualisation is generated from the same underlying learner model, thus indicating that visualisations are not necessarily tied to particular learner modelling techniques. OLMs have been identified as an important sub-topic in learner modelling [7], and have also demonstrated significant learning benefits [14],[16],[17].

With the rapid emergence of big data in numerous fields, substantial interest has also grown in this area in education. Learning analytics, a relatively new field, includes the visualisation of learning-related data to help users interpret the vast amounts of data now available [15],[19]. The approach has some similarities to

© Springer International Publishing Switzerland 2015
C. Conati et al. (Eds.): AIED 2015, LNAI 9112, pp. 666–669, 2015.
DOI: 10.1007/978-3-319-19773-9_87

OLMs, and learning analytics dashboards are being developed to support user inter-pretation of the data [21].

However, while visual learning analytics (VLA) approaches have received substantial attention, their focus is very often on issues such as performance level, activity completion, navigation to information, or other behaviour-focussed statistics. We highlight three of the key differences between VLA and OLM in the next section.

Fig. 1. skill meter, concept map and overview-zoom-filter treemap visualisations from the Next-TELL and LEA's Box OLMs

2   Open Learner Models and Visual Learning Analytics

There are three important differences between the state-of-the-art in VLA and OLM:

1. VLA tends to take a more statistical approach, presenting the corresponding out-comes (such as number of pages viewed, or performance), for the user to then interpret; but OLM already presents processed data to the user, from the learner model (so they can see their competencies; or extent of coverage of material, perhaps in the form of a strategy used to try to gain understanding).
2. VLA are usually targeted at teachers or other stakeholders such as school or educational leaders, although the importance of learning visualisations to support learning is now growing (e.g. [8]). In contrast, OLMs have typically been developed primarily for learners, to help them reflect on, and take decisions about their learning, though there is also a history of OLMs shown to other stakeholders such as teachers [10], individual peers [4] or groups [20].
3. As stated above, VLA grew from growing recognition of the potential value of existing learning data, if it is made easier to interpret, if people are to be able to use it. In contrast, OLMs originated in intelligent tutoring systems, where the learner model was designed so that the system could adapt the interaction to suit the individual learner's needs. Opening the learner model enabled it to become a first class learning resource in its own right [2],[13]. Although OLMs began long before big data was so prevalent, they are now also looking towards big data, and approaches suitable for today's online learning contexts, for example: do-main-independent reusable services for other systems [6],[13], or taken in from multiple external systems, for visualisation of the combined evidence from these various sources, to the user [5], are being developed.

Thus, OLMs could be viewed as a specific kind of learning analytics, in that the visu-alisation is of the learner model rather than activities undertaken, performance, beha-viour, etc. However, with a few exceptions [3],[8],[9],[11], there has been relatively little reference to learning analytics visualisations together with OLM.

3   Conclusions

Both visual learning analytics and open learner models aim to make data available to help users to interpret aspects of students' learning. A core difference, however, is that in open learner models, inferences relating to learning have already been made during the learner modelling process. An approach similar to this, even if not part of an adaptive system, may be useful to those working on learning analytics visualisations. A teacher may benefit from seeing (graphical) data that they do not need to further interpret to make it immediately useful to support their decision-making. Achieving the above, VLA could also become more commonplace in environments for students. The potential for learning analytics to facilitate metacognition has already been recognised. This was a foundation aim of OLMs [2], and so VLA for metacognition may be further enhanced by approaches already explored in OLM systems. While there are some exceptions, we have also identified the different target users in VLA and OLM research. Both fields may benefit from greater consideration of the utility of the approaches to other user types - all stakeholders have some kind of interest in learning data. Finally, OLM research could benefit substantially by the attention given to making big data understandable, found in VLA research, as classrooms are increasing bringing large amounts of data about learners as well as data that may reasonably contribute to learner models that is sourced away from the formal learning setting. This latter situation is perhaps where experiences from VLA have much to offer OLM research in Artificial Intelligence in Education: we can look forward to using techniques from learning analytics to contribute to learner modelling processes with increased data, combined with the more learning-focused visualisations of OLMs, and providing OLM visualisations for a greater range of stakeholders.

Acknowledgement. The second author's research on OLM and VLA is supported by the European Commission (EC) under the Information Society Technology priority FP7 for R&D, contract 619762 LEA's Box. This document does not represent the opinion of the EC and the EC is not responsible for any use that might be made of its contents.

References

1. Bull, S., Johnson, M., Masci, D., Biel, C.: Integrating and visualising diagnostic information for the benefit of learning. In: Reimann, P., Bull, S., Kickmeier-Rust, M., Vatrapu, R., Wasson, B. (eds.) Measuring and Visualizing Learning in the Information-Rich Classroom, Routledge/Taylor and Francis (in press)
2. Bull, S., Kay, J.: Open learner models. In: Nkambou, R., Bordeau, J., Mizoguchi, R. (eds.) Advances in Intelligent Tutoring Systems. Studies in Computational Intelligence, vol. 308, pp. 301–322. Springer, Heidelberg (2010)
3. Bull, S., Kickmeier-Rust, M., Vatrapu, R.K., Johnson, M.D., Hammermueller, K., Byrne, W., Hernandez-Munoz, L., Giorgini, F., Meissl-Egghart, G.: Learning, Learning Analytics, Activity Visualisation and Open Learner Model: Confusing? In: Hernández-Leo, D., Ley, T., Klamma, R., Harrer, A. (eds.) EC-TEL 2013. LNCS, vol. 8095, pp. 532–535. Springer, Heidelberg (2013)
4. Bull, S., Mabbott, A., Abu Issa, A.: UMPTEEN: Named and Anonymous Learner Model Access for Instructors and Peers. International Journal of Artificial Intelligence in Education **17**(3), 227–253 (2007)

5. Bull, S, Wasson, B., Kickmeier-Rust, M., Johnson, M.D., Moe, E., Hansen, C., Meissl-Egghart, G., Hammermueller, K.: Assessing english as a second language: from classroom data to a competence-based open learner model. In: Biswas, G. et al. (eds.) International Conference on Computers in Education, APSCE (2012)
6. Conejo, R., Trella, M., Cruces, I., Garcia, R.: INGRID: A Web Service Tool for Hierarchical Open Learner Model Visualization. In: Ardissono, L., Kuflik, T. (eds.) Advances in User Modeling. LNCS, vol. 7138, pp. 406–409. Springer, Heidelberg (2012)
7. Demarais, M.C., Baker, R.S.J.D.: A Review of Recent Advances in Learner and Skill Modeling in Intelligent Environments. UMUAI **22**, 9–38 (2012)
8. Durall, E., Gros, B.: Learning analytics as a metacognitive tool. In: Proceedings of 6th International Conference on Computer Supported Education (CSEDU), 380-384 (2014)
9. Ferguson, R.: Learning Analytics: Drivers, Developments and Challenges. International Journal of Technology Enhanced Learning **4**(5/6), 304–317 (2012)
10. Johnson, M.D., Cierniak, G., Hansen, C., Bull, S., Wasson, B., Biel, C., Debus, K.: Teacher approaches to adopting a competency based open learner model. In: Wong, L.-H. et al. (eds), International Conference on Computers in Education. APSCE (2013)
11. Kalz, M.: Lifelong Learning and its Support with new Technologies. In: Smelser, N.J., Baltes, P.B. (eds.) International Encyclopedia of the Social and Behavioral Sciences. Pergamon, Oxford (2014). http://dspace.ou.nl/handle/1820/5321
12. Kay, J.: Learner know thyself: student models to give learner control and responsibility. In: International Conference on Computers in Education, AACE, pp. 17–24 (1997)
13. Kay, J., Kummerfeld, B.: Creating Personalized Systems that People can Scrutinize and Control: Drivers, principles and experience. ACM Transactions on Interactive Intelligent Systems (TiiS) **2**(4), 24 (2012)
14. Kerly, A., Bull, S.: Children's Interactions with Inspectable and Negotiated Learner Models. In: Woolf, B.P., A\"ımeur, E., Nkambou, R., Lajoie, S. (eds.) ITS 2008. LNCS, vol. 5091, pp. 132–141. Springer, Heidelberg (2008)
15. Klerkx, J., Verbert, K., Duval, E.: Enhancing Learning with Visualization Techniques. In: Spector, J.M., Merrill, M.D., Elen, J., Bishop, M.J. (eds.) Handbook of Research on Educational Communications and Technology, pp. 791–807. Springer, New York (2014)
16. Long, Y., Aleven, V.: Supporting Students' Self-Regulated Learning with an Open Learner Model in a Linear Equation Tutor. In: Lane, H., Yacef, K., Mostow, J., Pavlik, P. (eds.) AIED 2013. LNCS, vol. 7926, pp. 219–228. Springer, Heidelberg (2013)
17. Mitrovic, A., Martin, B.: Evaluating the Effect of Open Student Models on Self-Assessment. International Journal of Artificial Intelligence in Education **17**(2), 121–144 (2007)
18. Perez-Marin, D., Alfonseca, E., Rodriguez, P., Pascual-Neito, I.: A Study on the Possibility of Automatically Estimating the Confidence Value of Students' Knowledge in Generated Conceptual Models. Journal of Computers **2**(5), 17–26 (2007)
19. Tervakari, A.M., Silius, K., Koro, J., Paukkeri, J., Pirttilä, O.: Usefulness of information visualizations based on educational data. In: IEEE Global Engineering Education Conference (EDUCON), pp. 142–151. IEEE (2014)
20. Upton, K., Kay, J.: Narcissus: Group and Individual Models to Support Small Group Work. In: Houben, G.-J., McCalla, G., Pianesi, F., Zancanaro, M. (eds.) User Modeling, Adaptation and Personalization. Lecture Notes in Computer Science, vol. 5535, pp. 54–65. Springer, Heidelberg (2009)
21. Verbert, K., Duval, E., Klerkx, J., Govaerts, S., Santos, J.L.: Learning Analytics Dashboard Applications. American Behavioral Scientist **57**(10), 1500–1509 (2013)
22. Zapata-Rivera, J.D., Greer, J.E.: Interacting with Inspectable Bayesian Models. International Journal of Artificial Intelligence in Education **14**, 127–163 (2004)

The Relationship Between Working Memory Capacity and Students' Behaviour in a Teachable Agent-Based Software

Lisa Palmqvist[2], Camilla Kirkegaard[1], Annika Silvervarg[1(✉)],
Magnus Haake[3], and Agneta Gulz[1]

[1] Department of Computer Science, Linköping University, Linköping, Sweden
{camilla.kirkegaard,annika.silvervarg,agneta.gulz}@liu.se
[2] Department of Behavioural Sciences and Learning, Linköping University, Linköping, Sweden
lisa.palmqvist@liu.se
[3] Cognitive Science, Lund University, Lund, Sweden
magnus.haake@lucs.lu.se

Abstract. The current study investigated if and how students' behaviour when using a teachable agent-based educational software were related to their working memory capacity. Thirty Swedish students aged 11–12, participated in the study. Results showed that differences in behaviour such as time spent on an off-task activity, time spent on interactive dialogues, and the number of tests that students let their TA take, were associated with differences in working memory capacity.

Keywords: Teachable agent · Working memory capacity

1 Introduction

The pedagogy of learning-by-teaching and its' digital implementation in the form of Teachable Agent-based software has been recognized as a powerful learning method. For example, Chase et al. [1] found that low-achieving students who used an educational software including a Teachable Agent (TA) performed on par with high-achieving students who used the same educational software without a TA. Educational software in general have been suggested to provide ways of off-loading working memory during difficult tasks, which will benefit low-achievers the most [2].

It has been shown that working memory capacity (WMC) is an even more powerful predictor of academic success than IQ [3]. When developing frameworks for future pedagogy, it is important to investigate how all children can benefit, including children with lower academic success and children with low WMC. The aim of the current study was to investigate if and how students' behavior in a TA-based educational software differed with respect to their working memory capacity.

2 Study

The Guardian of Time (Fig. 1) is a TA-based software in which the student takes on a teacher role and the task of teaching a time elf (i.e. the teachable agent) about

© Springer International Publishing Switzerland 2015
C. Conati et al. (Eds.): AIED 2015, LNAI 9112, pp. 670–673, 2015.
DOI: 10.1007/978-3-319-19773-9_88

history [4]. The software includes a variety of activities: i) collecting information via dialogues with historic persons and via reading about objects and artefacts, ii) learning activities where the student either shows the TA how to do or works together with the TA to, for example, construct a timeline with historical facts, iii) test-taking by the TA, and iv) an off-task activity in the form of an Othello game. Thus, the software is rich in alternatives the student can choose from.

Fig. 1. The Teachable Agent

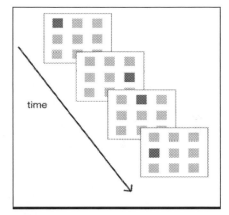

Fig. 2. Schematic illustration of the WMC-test

2.1   Method

19 female and 11 male 11-12-year olds from two classes in a Swedish school participated in the study. All participating students included in the analysis had a valid consent form signed by their caregiver. In Session 1 the students merely received the instruction to explore the software environment, in Session 2 the instructions were more precise and the students were encouraged to first collect information, thereafter do the teaching activity, and then to aim at having their TA reach a high test score. The students' actions and choices were logged by the software. They are presented in Table 1.

During the first session a visual, non-lingual visuo-spatial WMC-test (Fig. 2) based on [5] measured the children's WMC before they started using the educational software. The WMC-test consisted of a pattern of blinking squares that the student should observe and thereafter repeat, starting with a sequence of length two and then of increasing length. The highest level completed was used as a measurement of the students WMC (mLv in Table 1).

To investigate potential relations between the WMC measurements and students' behavior in terms of chosen activities while using the educational software, a multiple linear regression analysis was performed, to see which behaviors predicted the results of the working memory capacity test. A linear regression analysis was also performed to investigate if working memory capacity could predict how well the student taught their TA in terms of number of correct facts, i.e. an indirect measure of how much the students themselves had learnt.

2.2　Results

Means and standard deviations of the variables used are shown in Table 1.

Table 1. Definition of variables

Variable	Description	M	SD
mLv	Maximum level achieved in the WMC	6.13	0.94
noRoom	The total number of visited historical settings by the student	22.37	9.73
noTeach	The total number of teaching activities engaged in by the student	7.47	4.12
noTest	The total number of test engaged by the student	5.90	5.38
noOthello	Number of rounds of Othello initiated by the student	10.53	5.23
avgRoom	The average time spent in each historical setting	43.65	16.06
avgDialogue	Average time spent on each dialogue with the different characters	16.89	7.00
avgOthello	Average time spent playing one round of Othello	61.95	21.32

A model to predict mLv was chosen with backward model selection using AIC with the variables avgOthello, avgDialogue, and noTest as predictors (mLv ~ avgOthello + avgDialogue + noTest). A multiple linear regression analysis suggested a significant model ($F(3,26) = 4.823$, $p = .008$) that accounted for approximately 36% of the variance of mLv ($R^2 = .358$, $R^2_{adj} = .283$). Beta values, standard error, and standardized Beta for all individual models and variables are presented in Table 2.

Table 2. Beta values, standard error, and standardized Beta for the model mLv ~ avgOthello + avgDialogue + and noTest

	B	SE B	β
Constant	3.649	0.682	
noTest**	0.092	0.031	.529
avgDialogue*	0.054	0.023	.404
avgOthello*	0.017	0.007	.376

Note. The dependent variable was mLv; $R^2 = .358$ for Step 5 ($p = .008$); $*p<.05$, $**p<.01$

mLv was then used in a linear regression analysis as predictor of coFa (the number of correct facts taught by the student to the TA). The model was not statistically significant ($F(2,28) = 2.709$, $p = .111$) and accounted only for approximately 9% of the variance of coFa ($R^2 = .088$, $R^2_{adj} = .056$). Thus, coFa was not predicted by the WMC-test.

3　Conclusions and Discussion

This study investigated if and how students' behavior using a TA-based educational software related to their working memory capacity. The results suggests that differences in the following kinds of behavior were associated with differences in working memory capacity: the average time spent on the off-task activity per round, the average time spent on interactive dialogues, and the number of tests that the student let their TA take.

The significant variables seem to reflect some sort of level of ambition, or thoroughness in the use of the software; overall, children who scored low on the WMC-test spent less time per activity. Students with a low WMC capacity may have difficulty in sustaining attention and the results may consequently reflect differences in the ability to keep focus. Limitations in WMC have been shown to correlate with several executive functions including short attention span [6]. Being able to keep focus for a longer time will in turn will help the student to be more resolute when trying to achieve the goals set in the software. In order for the player to succeed in the game Othello, the player needs to plan and remember future moves in relation to old ones, which in turn requires a high WMC and a large attention span. Children with short attention span will also have a hard time reading long instructions or dialogues in an educational software.

Concerning whether differences in WMC could be associated with differences in how well the students taught the TA, there was a positive but not significant correlation between WMC and total number of correct facts (p=.55). The correlation is, however, close to being significant, which could mean that a study including more participants that use the software for a longer time, might yield a weaker correlation, or the correlation might become stronger depending on what behavior is crucial for successfully teaching the TA.

This study involved students from a regular school class, where few or none are likely to have a WMC so weak that it would be considered a disability. If there is a critical point for when WMC starts to effect performance, a regression model will fail in detecting it. We suggest that future studies identify children with particularly low WMC and compare with children with typical WMC regarding behavior and learning outcomes. Otherwise children with difficulties might stay unnoticed.

The results address the importance of keeping in mind a broad range of children with differing cognitive abilities and profiles when developing novel educational software. Software benefiting all children from will be a powerful tool in schools throughout the world.

References

1. Chase, C.C., Chin, D.B., Oppezzo, M.A., Schwartz, D.L.: Teachable agents and the protégé effect: Increasing the effort towards learning. Journal of Science Education and Technology **18**(4), 334–352 (2009)
2. Azevedo, R., Feyzi-Behnagh, R.: Dysregulated learning with advanced learning technologies. In: AAAI Fall Symposium: Cognitive and Metacognitive Educational Systems (2010)
3. Alloway, T.P., Alloway, R.G.: Investigating the predictive roles of working memory and IQ in academic attainment. Journal of experimental child psychology **106**(1), 20–29 (2010)
4. Kirkegaard, C., Gulz, A., Silvervarg, A.: Introducing a challenging teachable agent. In: Zaphiris, P., Ioannou, A. (eds.) LCT 2014, Part I. LNCS, vol. 8523, pp. 53–62. Springer, Heidelberg (2014)
5. Westerberg, H., Hirvikoski, T., Forssberg, H., Klingberg, T.: Visuo-spatial working memory span: A sensitive measure of cognitive deficits in children with ADHD. Child Neuropsychology **10**(3), 155–161 (2004)
6. Martinussen, R., Hayden, J., Hogg-Johnson, S., Tannock, R.: A meta-analysis of working memory impairments in children with attention-deficit/hyperactivity disorder. Journal of the American Academy of Child & Adolescent Psychiatry **44**(4), 377–384 (2005)

Lesson Discovery Support Based on Generalization of Historical Events

Tomoko Kojiri[1(✉)], Yusuke Nogami[2], and Kazuhisa Seta[2]

[1] Faculty of Engineering Science, Kansai University, Suita, Japan
kojiri@kansai-u.ac.jp
[2] Graduate School of Science, Osaka Prefecture University, 3-3-35 Yamate-Cho,
Suita, Osaka 564-8680, Japan

Abstract. Historical events include lessons of good and bad behaviors of human beings that can be readily applied to the modern world. To discover these lessons, one must generalize the basic attributes of multiple historical events, so that one can perceive the underlying patterns that commonly occur. This paper proposes a novel scheme for uncovering the typical patterns that emerge from multiple historical events by generalizing historical characters. We then construct a learning system that supports the generalization and discovery of common patterns based on the proposed scheme.

Keywords: Historical thinking · Generalization support · Comparative learning

1 Introduction

Learning history often involves rote learning: memorizing historical events, cultures, and so on. Especially, current history education focuses too much on memorization of facts. Although rote learning demands the least amount of effort to learn the basic knowledge required, it hinders the development of critical skills [1]. In addition, it is said that rote learning makes students think of history as being boring. On the other hand, historical thinking learns lessons from past historical events and applies them to the modern world is regarded as the very essence of historical learning [2]. This paper proposes a novel approach to grow historical thinking that helps us understand the nature of history and discover of valuable lessons.

Various researches aimed at making students aware that similar events occur throughout history [3, 4]. However, that none of these researches support or give methods for exploring lessons from historical events. In order to extract lessons, historical events should be observed from viewpoints of situation or attribute changes of historical figures who are involved in these events.

Lessons shall here refer to general expressions of good or bad outcomes with respect to some specific act or intent. In order to gain lessons from historical events, one must determine whether the events were good or bad based on generalized situational changes caused by the events. We develop a system that realizes this process and provides the meta-learning needed to acquire historical lessons.

© Springer International Publishing Switzerland 2015
C. Conati et al. (Eds.): AIED 2015, LNAI 9112, pp. 674–677, 2015.
DOI: 10.1007/978-3-319-19773-9_89

2   Learning Historical Lessons

Lessons are the often observed patterns of outcomes with respect to some specific act or intent. In order to grasp such lessons, the historical events must first be generalized, then apprehended as typical patterns. Here we propose the following four-step process for accomplish this.

    1. **Understand historical events:** The goal here is basic understanding of the events and facts surrounding the historical episodes.

    2. **Generalize historical events:** The role of key figures involved in the event and their attributes are generalized.

    3. **Extract common features of historical events:** Common patterns in generalized historical events are found by comparing their attribute changes.

    4. **Derive historical lessons:** More generalized lessons are understood and learned from common patterns extracted in Step 3.

    As an actual example, let us consider the Tokusei Edict issued by the Kamakura Bakufu in 1297 and the Kien Edict by the Edo Bakufu in 1789. A comparison of the generalization patterns in Figures 1 and 2 reveals a close similarity. While the Kamakura samurai and Edo retainers had different positions in society, both became indebted and saddled with onerous loans from moneylenders. One obvious lesson to be learned from these two events is that having one's debts arbitrarily canceled by executive fiat can make it exceedingly difficult to borrow money henceforth, and this can have a devastating effect on the quality of subsequent life.

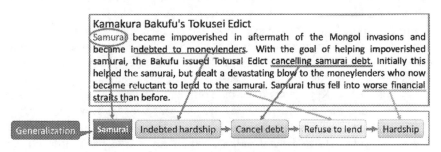

Fig. 1. Generalization of effects of Kamakura Bakufu's Tokusei Edict on samurai

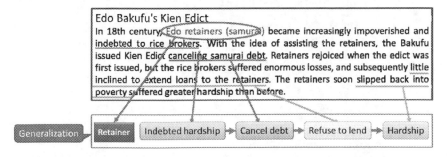

Fig. 2. Generalization of effects of Edo Bakufu's Kien Edict on samurai

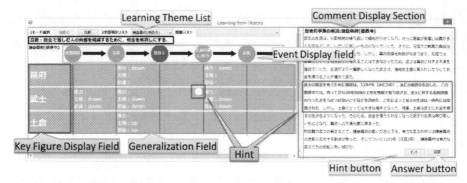

Fig. 3. Generalization Learning Screen – Attributes -

3 Lessons Discovery Support System

Generalization of historical events is fraught with difficulties. First, in order to derive lessons from two or more historical events, the generalization levels of the events must be roughly aligned. If events are not generalized at the same level, it is impossible to discover common patterns between the events. Moreover, in order to identify common patterns between different historical events, one must not only align the generalized attributes of the events, but also devise a scheme that facilitates side-by-side comparison of the generalized events. We developed a lessons learning support system with features that effectively solve these various problems.

The first support feature of the system assists in generalizing the attributes of the key figures. Since historical lessons are derived from changes in situations of figures, generalized points are confined to attribute changes that affect the events. The generalization support feature makes this task easier by offering candidates of attribute. Figure 3 is a screenshot. Key events from the comment text are described in the Event Display Field, and key historical figures are described in the Key Figure Display Field. As students read through the comment text, they click on events they think might cause changes in the Generalization Field and the places where they think key figures might associate. Then, the Situation Change Registration Screen shown in Figure 4 appears, where students can input attribute changes by selecting among the options presented in the Attribute Situation Change List.

The second support feature is a comparative learning support tool. To assist comparative learning between two historical events, a feature that displays two equivalent generalized patterns is provided. Figure 5 is a

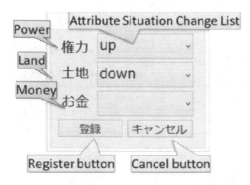

Fig. 4. Situation Change Registration Screen

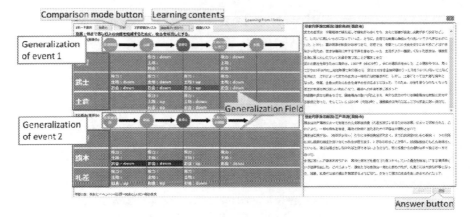

Fig. 5. Comparative Learning Screen

screenshot. By selecting an item from Learning Theme List, two events are presented at the same time. The student selects the same places in the both passages from the Generalization Field.

The third support feature assists in generalizing the key figure. Generalization of figure is supported by presenting candidates of different views of figures. The fourth support feature is helps for discovering historical lessons. This fourth support feature describes generalized common patterns in simple sentences as a story.

4   Conclusions

In this paper, we proposed a novel approach for learning history by discovering historical lessons through generalization and identifying common patterns. Building on these insights, we developed a system that supports this new learning approach.

The current system is designed in such a way that attributes and the generalized historical figure candidates are prepared in the system in advance. There are various levels of generalization, and determining the level of generalization is clearly an important capability. As future work, the system is improved by giving students the ability freely set their own attribute candidates and use those candidates to generalize the historical events.

References

1. Sivell, J.N.: Habitual Memorisation by Literature Students–A Help as Well as a Hindrance. English Language Teaching Journal **35**(1), 51–54 (1980)
2. Sokoloff, K.L., et al.: History Lessons: Institutions, Factors Endowments, and Paths of Development in the New World. The Journal of Economic Perspectives **14**(3), 217–232 (2000)
3. Ikejiri, T., et al.: Designing and evaluating a card game to support high school students in applying their knowledge of world history to solve modern political issues. In: Proc. of International Conference of Media Education (2012). http://icome.bnu.edu.cn/content/full-papaer
4. Horiguchi, T., et al: A learning environment for knowledge-constructing in history. In: Proc. of 6th International Conference on Human-Computer Interaction, pp.833-838 (1995)

Predicting Student Performance from Multiple Data Sources

Irena Koprinska[✉], Joshua Stretton, and Kalina Yacef

School of Information Technologies, University of Sydney, Sydney, Australia
{irena.koprinska,joshua.stretton,kalina.yacef}@sydney.edu.au

Abstract. The goal of this study is to (i) understand the characteristics of high-, average- and low-level performing students in a first year computer programming course, and (ii) investigate whether their performance can be predicted accurately and early enough in the semester for timely intervention. We triangulate data from three sources: submission steps and outcomes in an automatic marking system that provides instant feedback, assessment marks during the semester and student engagement with the discussion forum Piazza. We define and extract attributes characterizing student activity and performance, and discuss the distinct characteristics of the three groups. Using these attributes we built a compact decision tree classifier that is able to predict the exam mark with an accuracy of 72.69% at the end of the semester and 66.52% in the middle of the semester. We discuss the most important predictors and how such analysis can be used to improve teaching and learning.

Keywords: Computer science education · Student performance prediction

1   Introduction

Novel technology-enhanced teaching tools provide effective solutions to support computer programming courses, and also collect a lot of data about the students. In this paper we describe how the analysis of such multiple data sources, combined with student assessment marks, can give insights into student learning.

The context of our study is a first year programming course with 224 students, where different tools were used to support learning: (i) PASTA: an automatic marking and feedback system that allows students to submit their code online, checks their solution against a set of pre-specified tests and provides immediate formative feedback; students can then correct their mistakes and resubmit the solution until the code is correct; (ii) Piazza (www.piazza.com), a mix of discussion board and wiki allowing students to ask and answer questions, and post notes, all under teachers' guidance.

The data captured from these two systems, along with the assessment marks, provides different useful perspectives on student learning: progression in code writing and diagnostics (PASTA), interaction and engagement (Piazza) and student performance (assessment results).

© Springer International Publishing Switzerland 2015
C. Conati et al. (Eds.): AIED 2015, LNAI 9112, pp. 678–681, 2015.
DOI: 10.1007/978-3-319-19773-9_90

We extend previous work on predicting student performance, e.g. [1], by triangulating data from the three sources above to answer the following questions: 1) What are the characteristics of the high-, average- and low-level performing students? 2) How accurately can we predict the exam grade? What attributes are the best predictors? and 3) Can we predict the exam grade early enough for timely intervention?

2   Data

We define three groups of students based on their exam performance: High-level - HDD (High Distinction and Distinction) – exam mark of [75, 100], average-level - CRP (Credit and Pass) – exam mark of [50, 74] and low-level - F (Failing) – exam mark below 50. The number of students was: 64 in HDD, 83 in CRP and 77 in F.

The assessment during the semester consisted of five components: weekly homeworks (10%), two programming tasks and an assignment submitted via PASTA (2% in week 3, 6% in week 6 and 16% in week 12) and a practical test (16% in week 7) involving writing computer programs in front of the computer. The exam (50%) was paper-based, conducted at the end of the semester and required writing code for solving problems. We chose the exam mark as the performance index to predict, as the exam is the major and most comprehensive assessment component, conducted under strict conditions which minimizes cheating. The exam mark is highly correlated with the final course mark (r=0.937).

Table 1 shows the 22 attributes we extracted from the three data sources.

Table 1. Defined attributes to characterise student performance and activity

1. Assessment marks
homework_mark, task1_mark, task2_mark, prac_quiz_mark, assignment_mark – mark (%) awarded for each assessment component.
2. PASTA activity – submission history
Starting and finishing times for assessments
tasks_start, tasks_finish – the average number of days before the due date the student will start and finish the two tasks; *assignment_start, assignment_finish* – the average number of days before the due date the student will start and finish the assignment; *early_task, early_assignment* - 1 if the student starts the tasks/assignment earlier than the average student; 0 otherwise.
Multiple assignment submissions – improvement and consistency
assignment_only_improvement - 1 if the student's marks for compiling assignment submissions never decrease; 0 otherwise; *asignment_consistency* - goodness of fit (R^2) over each of the student's compiling submissions; range: [1,1], close to 1/-1 - linear increase/decrease in marks over time, close to 0 - random distribution of marks over submissions; *assignment_improvement* - slope of the trendline of the student's assignment marks over each compiling submission, a larger number indicates rapid improvement; *assignment_first_mark* - mark awarded for the student's first submission for the assignment.
3. Piazza activity – views, questions and answers
piazza_views, piazza_questions, piazza_answers - number of posts viewed, questions asked and questions answered by the student on Piazza; *piazza_activity* – calculated as: (*piazza_views* + 10*(*piazza_questions* + *piazza_answers*) + 5*(*piazza_posts* - *piazza_answers*)) / *total_posts,* where *piazza_posts* is the total number of student contributions (asking or answering a question, or posting a comment), and *total_posts* is the total number of question threads on Piazza; *piazza_active_viewer, piazza_active_questioner, piazza_active_answerer* - 1 if the student has an average or higher number of Piazza posts viewed, questions asked and questions answered; 0 otherwise.

3   Results

What are the Characteristics of High-, Average- and Low-level Students? We computed the mean values for each attribute and group, and conducted tests for statistical significance of the differences between these mean values. The results (not shown due to space limitation) lead to the following student characteristics:

- High-level students start and finish their assignments early. They tend to start an assignment strongly, and make consistent and significant improvement to their marks with successive attempts. They engage in peer to peer discussions by asking questions and reading the information provided to other students.
- Average-level students start an assessment early if the assessment is not worth a large amount of marks. They start an assignment at a fairly low level, and then make small improvements over time, occasionally decreasing their marks, until they are content that they have done enough to reach the average level. They engage in peer to peer discussions in the same way as the high-level students.
- Low-level students start an assessment task with very little time before the due date (on average only 2 days). They start an assignment at a low level; however they tend to make large improvements to their marks as they progress, even if not consistently with each attempt. They do not engage in discussion board activity.

How Accurately can we Predict the Exam Grade? To investigate how accurately we can predict the exam grade using the extracted attributes, and which of these attributes are the best predictors, we employed a Decision Tree (DT) classifier. DTs are popular for educational data mining as the generated rules provide an explanation about the decision, can be easily understood and applied by teachers and students. Although DTs have an inbuilt mechanism for attribute selection, their performance can benefit from prior attribute subset selection. Starting with the full set of 22 attributes from Table 1, we used several methods for attribute subset selection in the data mining tool Weka (automatic such as wrapper and also manual) before generating the DT.

The best DT achieved 72.69% accuracy and is shown in Table 2 (left). It consists of 13 rules using only 7 attributes from all data sources: from the assessment marks: *prac_quiz_mark*, *assignment_mark* and *homework_mark*, from Piazza: *piazza_active_viewer* and *piazza_views*, and from PASTA: *early_assignment* and *assignment_consistency*. Most of these attributes were also identified as important for discriminating the three groups in the data analysis above. An accuracy of 72.69% is considerably higher than the baseline accuracy of 37.05% (always predicting the majority class CRP, 83/224) and also reasonably high to be used in practical applications.

Can we Predict Accurately the Exam Grade Before the End of the Semester? We also investigated how accurately we can predict the exam grade in the middle of the semester, for the purpose of timely intervention. We chose the end of week 7, which is approximately the middle of the 13-week semester, and by which time the students have completed the two tasks and the practical test but not the assignment. We did not have the data from Piazza for this point of time. The best DT achieved 66.52% accuracy, which is very promising, and is shown in Table 2 (right). It consists of 10 rules using only 4 of the attributes – 2 assessment marks (*prac_quiz_mark* and *task1_mark*) and 2 activity attributes from PASTA (*early_task* and *tasks_finish*).

Table 2. Predicting exam grade – DT and accuracy using 10-fold cross validation

Predicting exam grade (HDD, CRP or F)	
At the end of the semester	**Half-way in semester (week 7)**
prac_quiz_mark <= 81.88	prac_quiz_mark <= 81.88
| prac_quiz_mark <= 54.38	| prac_quiz_mark <= 54.38: F
| | assignment_mark <= 97.5: F	| prac_quiz_mark > 54.38
| | assignment_mark > 97.5	| | task1_mark <= 80.31: F
| | | assignment_mark <= 98.75: CRP	| | task1_mark > 80.31
| | | assignment_mark > 98.75: F	| | | early_task <= 0
| prac_quiz_mark > 54.38	| | | | prac_quiz_mark <= 79.69
| | piazza_active_viewer <= 0	| | | | | tasks_finish <= 0: F
| | | homework_mark <= 31: CRP	| | | | | tasks_finish > 0: CRP
| | | homework_mark > 31: F	| | | | prac_quiz_mark > 79.69: F
| | piazza_active_viewer > 0	| | | early_task > 0
| | | assignment_mark <= 35.38: F	| | | | prac_quiz_mark <= 65.31
| | | assignment_mark > 35.38: CRP	| | | | | prac_quiz_mark <= 60.31: CRP
prac_quiz_mark > 81.88	| | | | | prac_quiz_mark > 60.31: F
| prac_quiz_mark <= 94.06	| | | | prac_quiz_mark > 65.31: CRP
| | early_assignment <= 0: CRP	prac_quiz_mark > 81.88
| | early_assignment > 0	| prac_quiz_mark <= 94.06: CRP
| | | assignment_consistency <= 0.79: CRP	| prac_quiz_mark > 94.06: HDD
| | | assignment_consistency > 0.79: HDD	**Accuracy: 66.52%**
| | prac_quiz_mark > 94.06	
| | | assignment_mark <= 86.56	
| | | | piazza_views <= 48: CRP	
| | | | piazza_views > 48: HDD	
| | | assignment_mark > 86.56: HDD	
Accuracy: 72.69%	

4   Conclusion

We triangulated data from three sources, offering different perspectives on student learning: automatic marking system, discussion forum and assessment data. We defined useful attributes that capture the distinctive characteristics of high-, average- and low-level performing students and used them to build a compact DT classifier that predicts the final exam grade with accuracy of 72.69% at the end of the semester and 66.52% mid-semester. It can be used to provide regular formative feedback to students during the semester if their current results and behavior are likely to be associated with high-, average- or low-level performance, where the problems are, and what remedial actions could be taken. This includes identifying both students who are at risk of failing and students who are not achieving their goals. Students and teachers can also be made aware of the characteristics of the three groups, which will encourage better learning and teaching.

Acknowledgement. This work was supported by the Human Centered Technology Cluster.

References

1. Romero, C., Ventura, S., Espejo, P.G., Hervas, C.: Data mining algorithms to classify students. In: Int. Conference on Educational Data Mining (EDM), pp. 8–17 (2008)

Automated Generation of Self-Explanation Questions in Worked Examples in a Model-Based Tutor

Amruth N. Kumar[✉]

Ramapo College of New Jersey, Mahwah, USA
amruth@ramapo.edu

Abstract. A framework is proposed for automated generation of self-explanation questions in worked examples. In the framework, in addition to the questions, the correct answer, distracters and feedback are also automatically generated. The framework is based on model-based generation of worked examples, and is domain-dependent rather than problem-specific.

Keywords: Self-explanation · Worked example · Model-based tutor

We have been developing and evaluating software tutors for program comprehension, called problets (problets.org), for over a decade. These tutors cover all the programming language topics (16 in all) typically included in an introductory programming course, and can be used for C++, Java or C#. The tutors engage students in problem-solving activity – they present a complete, but short program to the student and ask the student to debug, predict the output of, or identify the state of the variables in the program. After the student has submitted the answer, if the answer is incorrect, they present the same problem as a worked example, complete with step-by-step explanation of the program that justifies the correct answer. Prior evaluations have shown that students learn from this step-by-step explanation [1]. In order to improve the effectiveness of the worked examples and ensure that all the students closely trace the worked examples, we incorporated self-explanation prompts into them in anticipative reasoning style [4].

In prior studies of the use of self-explanation prompts in **anticipative reasoning** style, self-explanation questions were hand-coded for each problem, as were the correct answers to the questions and possible feedback presented to the learner. In a tutor that includes a handful of problems, this is a viable strategy. However, in our software tutors on programming, hand-coding self-explanation questions, answers and feedback for the 2868 problems contained in the 16 tutors was impractical. So, we explored automatic generation of self-explanation questions in worked examples.

We use model-based reasoning to build our software tutors [2], the advantages being that the domain model automatically generates correct answer to each problem, as well as steps in its worked example. Suppose the domain model of `if-else` statement generates the following generic explanation as a step in the worked example:

© Springer International Publishing Switzerland 2015
C. Conati et al. (Eds.): AIED 2015, LNAI 9112, pp. 682–685, 2015.
DOI: 10.1007/978-3-319-19773-9_91

*In the condition of the if-else statement, **<variable>** is compared to be **<relational-operator>** than **<value>**. The condition evaluates to **<result>**, so the **<clause>** is executed on line **<line number>**.*

If a program contains the following `if-else` statement:

```
if( count > 0 ) { ... } else { ... }
```

the generic explanation generated by the `if-else` statement model is customized with program-specific details as follows:

*In the condition of the if-else statement, **count** is compared to be **greater** than **0**. The condition evaluates to **true**, so the **if-clause** is executed on line **32**.*

The customization segments in the explanation include the name of the variable **count**, the comparison operator **greater**, the comparison value **0**, the value to which the condition evaluates, viz., **true**, and the line number of the if-clause, viz., **32**. *All these segments of customization are candidates for self-explanation*, e.g., the student can be asked to identify the variable compared in the condition of the `if-else` statement, the value to which it is compared, the result of the comparison, and/or the line number of the code segment executed after the evaluation of the condition.

These self-explanation questions can be categorized into two groups:

Syntactic questions that can be answered by reading the code, e.g., the variable or value compared in the condition of the `if-else` statement;

Semantic questions that require the student to understand and mentally execute the code before answering, e.g., the result of evaluating the condition of the `if-else` statement, and whether if-clause or else-clause is executed as a result.

All the segments where each line of explanation must be customized are clearly identified in the domain model. A tutor can be configured to automatically generate a self-explanation question at every customization segment of every line of explanation. However, this would result in too many self-explanation questions, e.g., the single line of explanation in the above example contains six self-explanation questions, and the overall explanation of even simple programs could contain tens of lines of such explanation. So, automatically generating a self-explanation question at every customization segment would result in too many self-explanation questions per problem, possibly overwhelming the student.

One approach for **filtering questions** is for a pedagogic expert to identify the specific segments in each line of explanation that would make the best candidates for self-explanation questions. Some heuristics used by the pedagogic expert are:

Semantic self-explanation questions are better than syntactic self-explanation questions because they induce the student to mentally execute the program using his/her mental model of the program.

Self-explanation questions with more answering options are preferable to those with limited answering options - the more the options, the less the likelihood that the student can arrive at the correct answer by guessing alone. For example, there are only two choices for the value to which the condition of the `if-else` statement can evaluate – true and false. On the other hand, there are an infinite number of choices for the result of evaluating an arithmetic expression.

Repetitive events are less preferable to one-off events, e.g., the line that is executed first after the condition of a loop evaluates to true is a potentially repetitive question, whereas the line that is executed after it evaluates to false is a one-off question. Asking the student to answer the former question for every iteration of a loop is not productive – the student is unlikely to benefit from answering it for the iterations of the loop after the first one.

In this work, a pedagogic expert with two decades of experience teaching introductory programming picked the segments of explanation that were candidates for self-explanation. These candidates were picked once for each domain component, and *not* for each problem. The domain model was modified to annotate these customization segments with *ask* tags, e.g., the domain model of `if-else` statement was modified to generate the following annotated explanation:

In the condition of the if-else statement, <variable> is compared to be <relational-operator> than <value>. The condition evaluates to <ask><result></ask>, so the <clause> is executed on line <ask><line number></ask>.

When presenting the worked example for a problem, each *ask* tag is presented as a self-explanation **question**, with a drop-down box of options from which the learner is asked to select the correct answer. Since the customized value of the segment enclosed by the *ask* tag is resolved by the problem model, the **correct answer** to each self-explanation question is known to the tutor. Based on the correct answer, the problem model automatically generates **distracters** for each self-explanation question as follows:

For program objects such as variable names, the problem model uses names of other variables in the program as distracters;

For literal values such as literal constants and line numbers (e.g., 32), the problem model generates distracters that randomly straddle the correct answer (e.g., 31, 33, 34, and 35).

Finally, the tutor randomly orders the distracters and the correct answer before presenting them as options in the drop-down box of the self-explanation question.

The problem model automatically generates **feedback** provided to a learner when the learner selects an incorrect option for a self-explanation question. A generic version of the feedback is:

For numerical answers (such as line numbers, literal constants in the program), the student is told whether the correct answer is higher or lower.

For symbolic answers (such as variable names), the student is told that the answer is incorrect.

This feedback is adequate to prompt the student to try again. It is generic, i.e., not specific to the self-explanation question being presented. Since the problem model is also the executable expert module, the problem model can also automatically generate more context-sensitive feedback based on the correct answer, e.g.:

For numerical answers (such as values of variables), the student is asked to review specified line(s) of code and try again, e.g., "Consult line 23 for the value last assigned to the variable and try again".

For symbolic answers (such as variable names), the student is told why the selected answer is incorrect, e.g., the selected variable is not in scope, or the
program does not contain any function with the selected name.

Both the generic and context-sensitive versions of feedback can be generated automatically by the problem model and do not have to be hand-coded by the author of
the problem.

The complete explanation of a typical program may involve 30-200 lines. Even
with the pedagogic expert picking the customization segments that are the most suitable candidates for self-explanation, a typical program might produce tens of
self-explanation questions per program/problem. In order to keep the number of self-
explanation questions reasonable, an additional configuration parameter is built into
the tutor that specifies the maximum number of self-explanation questions allowed
per problem, e.g., 3. So, after generating the worked example of a program, the tutor
picks the first three candidates, and turns them into self-explanation questions embedded in the worked example. If fewer than three candidates are available for a program,
all the candidates are turned into self-explanation questions.

All the steps in the generation of self-explanation questions: identification of candidates for self-explanation, creation of distracters for each question, selection of self-
explanation questions presented to the student, and the feedback presented when the
student selects an incorrect option for a self-explanation question – are resolved by
the domain model (of which, the problem model is a customized copy) for all the
problems. They do not have to be hand-coded individually for each problem. Therefore the entire process of generating self-explanation questions embedded in worked
examples is domain-specific, not problem-specific, and is in keeping with the benefits
of using model-based reasoning to build software tutors.

As a proof-of-concept, a model-based tutor on selection (`if-else`) statements
and another on `switch` statements were extended to automatically generate self-
explanation questions using the framework described above, and evaluated [3].

Acknowledgments. Partial support for this work was provided by the National Science Foundation under grants DUE-0817187 and DUE-1432190.

References

1. Kumar, A.N.: Explanation of step-by-step execution as feedback for problems on program
   analysis, and its generation in model-based problem-solving tutors. Technology, Instruction,
   Cognition and Learning (TICL) Journal **4**(1) 2006
2. Kumar, A.N.: Model-based reasoning for domain modeling in a web-based intelligent tutoring system to help students learn to debug C++ programs. In: Cerri, S.A., Gouardéres, G.,
   Paraguaçu, F. (eds.) ITS 2002. LNCS, vol. 2363, pp. 792–801. Springer, Heidelberg (2002)
3. Kumar, A.N.: An evaluation of self-explanation in a programming tutor. In: Trausan-Matu,
   S., Boyer, K.E., Crosby, M., Panourgia, K. (eds.) ITS 2014. LNCS, vol. 8474, pp. 248–253.
   Springer, Heidelberg (2014)
4. Renkl, A.: Learning from worked-out examples: A study on individual differences.
   Cognitive Science **21**, 1–29 (1997)

First Evaluation of the Physics Instantiation of a Problem-Solving-Based Online Learning Platform

Rohit Kumar[1]([✉]), Gregory K.W.K. Chung[2], Ayesha Madni[2], and Bruce Roberts[1]

[1] Raytheon BBN Technologies, Cambridge, MA, USA
{rkumar,broberts}@bbn.com
[2] National Center for Research on Evaluation, Standards, and Student Testing (CRESST),
University of California, Los Angeles (UCLA), Los Angeles, CA, USA
greg@ucla.edu, madni@cse.ucla.edu

Abstract. Problem solving is a commonly used learning activity around which a large number of state-of-the-art Intelligent Tutoring Systems are developed and evaluated. In this paper, we present our problem-solving-based online learning platform and discuss a preliminary laboratory trial of this platform. While the platform itself is domain independent, for this evaluation, it was instantiated with a collection of problems from the unit of Electricity and Magnetism taught in high-school-level physics. Results indicate pedagogical effectiveness of problem solving in the Physics instance of the platform, with 41% of participants exceeding the stringent reliable change index.

Keywords: Problem solving · Online learning platform · Evaluation

1 Introduction

Problem solving, as a learning activity, involves presenting the learner with one or more problems that exercise knowledge of the domain's concepts by requiring students to recall and apply those concepts to correctly solve the problems. Besides use of problem solving to provide practice opportunities, a student's ability to correctly solve a problem is used as an assessment of the student's knowledge and problem-solving skills. The wide use of problem solving as the underlying learning activity in several Intelligent Tutoring Systems [1][2][3] is motivated not only by its applicability to numerous learning domains but also because of the ability to observe the learner's progress through structured problems and provide them with real-time feedback. A number of automated tutoring approaches such as example-tracing [4], model-tracing [1], and constraint-based tutoring [5] rely on this ability.

At BBN, we are developing a state-of-the-art domain-independent online learning platform for building, delivering, and performing problem-solving learning activities over the web. The next section describes the functionality of this platform to support

This research was funded by the US Office of Naval Research (ONR) contract N00014-12-C-0535.

C. Conati et al. (Eds.): AIED 2015, LNAI 9112, pp. 686–689, 2015.
DOI: 10.1007/978-3-319-19773-9_92

three user roles: learners, educators, and content developers (authors). In Section 3, we describe the first user study and data collection conducted using a physics instantiation of this platform. Quantitative observations from this data are reported.

2   BBN Learning Platform

The BBN learning platform, referred to as *Learnform* in this paper, is an extensible platform that comprises a number of applications to support three user roles. The content development workbench that is part of *Learnform* comprises three domain-independent applications. The *Author* application can be used to create new problems using a WYSIWYG editor. Templatization of problems and steps supported in this application reduces authoring effort by allowing reuse. The *Model* application uses a programming-by-demonstration approach to facilitate the development of example-tracing tutor (ETT) models [4]. Integration of our recent work [6] on developing algorithms for automatically inducing ETT models by collating multiple behavior demonstrations allows rapid development of robust tutors. The *Administrate* application provides content management functionality to the authors.

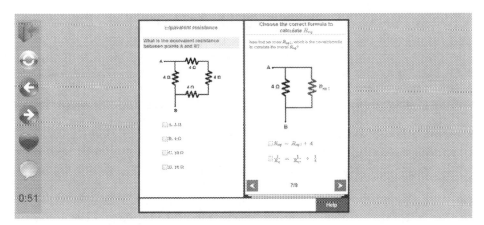

Fig. 1. Physics instance of the BBN Online Learning Platform

Teachers can use the *Assignment Builder* tool to create customized assignments by choosing from the problems available in the curriculum. Customized assignments can be shared between teachers who are using the same instance of *Learnform* (e.g., teachers within the same school system or following a common standard). Teachers can also view detailed reports of their students using the reporting interface. Reports include various knowledge, behavior, and engagement metrics and can be generated per student or for the entire class. Knowledge metrics present model-based assessment of a student's proficiency with various concepts and skills. We use a state-of-the-art implementation of feature-based knowledge tracing [7] for student modeling. Behavior metrics quantify students' use of the system in terms of help requests, correct/incorrect answers, etc. Engagement metrics report patterns of use by students such as amount of time spent per week.

The learning environment is used by students to access and work on their assignments. Students can also explore the curriculum of the learning domain to access additional problems for practice. Learners can solve a given problem without tutor assistance or can click on the *help* button in which case a decomposition of the problem into a sequence of solution steps is presented. Learners' work through the problems and steps are tracked by ETT models to provide feedback and scaffolded hints. Besides being accessible to authenticated learners, the learning environment can be integrated with third-party course websites in standalone mode, i.e., no authentication is required if teachers want to allow students to solve problems for practice without tracking their performance. We have also found this feature to be useful for conducting user studies.

In our current work, we have deployed a physics instance of *Learnform* that covers topics in Electricity and Magnetism (E&M). Figure 1 shows a screenshot of a Physics problem rendered within the problem solving interface of *Learnform*. Two teachers, working part-time over four months, authored a total of 114 problems across six units of E&M. In the user study described next, we used 10 of these problems from the *Electric Circuits* unit.

3   Preliminary User Study and Data Collection

Forty participants (28 males, 12 females) from a university in Southern California participated in a preliminary user study of the physics instance of *Learnform*. Participation was contingent on taking a class that covered DC circuit analysis and passing a three-item screener. Six participants reported electrical engineering as their major. Participants were first introduced to the study then administered the following tasks: background questionnaire, prior knowledge measure, knowledge probe task, pretest, 10 problems solved within *Learnform*, and a posttest. All tasks except the paper-based pretest and posttest were administered online and were completed within two hours.

Our analysis focuses on the last three tasks of this procedure. Participants were given two circuits with the same topology. One circuit had only variables and the other circuit had values assigned to resistors and battery. Participants were asked 11 conceptual questions for the circuit with variables and asked 10 computational questions for the circuit with values. The conceptual and computational items were administered immediately before and after problem solving using *Learnform* and counterbalanced. The pretest and posttest items were combined to form a single pretest measure (21 items, $\alpha = .92$) and posttest measure (21 items, $\alpha = .92$), respectively.

A paired-samples t test was conducted to compare participants' posttest scores to their pretest scores. A significant difference was found between the pretest ($M = .54$, $SD = .29$) and posttest ($M = .64$, $SD = .28$), $t(31) = 4.01$, $p < .001$, with an effect size of $d = 0.35$. Cohen's d is the standardized difference between group means. Participants' scores improved about 19%. This effect was consistent among the conceptual and computational items of the tests as well. A reliable change index [8] was computed and 13 participants (out of 32 participants with complete data) showed gains beyond the measurement error ($p < .05$). Thus, *Learnform* appears to have helped a substantial number of participants improve their knowledge of circuit analysis concepts.

We also examined whether participants' knowledge was related to their behavior in *Learnform*. One of the behavioral metrics captured from the trace logs is *#SolutionAttempts (#SA)* ($M = 17.9$, $SD = 8.2$) which measures the total number of times participants attempted to complete a problem over all 10 problems. Higher *#SA* is characteristic of students who make more mistakes while attempting to solve a problem likely to be indicative of students starting out at a lower knowledge level. To verify this, we formed two groups by splitting the sample into top and bottom halves of the pretest distribution. An independent-samples t test was conducted to compare *#SA* between the high and low knowledge groups. There was a significant difference between the groups, with the high knowledge group ($M = 14.1$, $SD = 5.1$) making fewer solution attempts than the low knowledge group ($M = 22.2$, $SD = 10.1$), $t(31) = 2.89$, $p = .007$, $d = 1.02$.

4   Next Steps

The preliminary laboratory study presented here indicates significant improvement in learning. We will be conducting a user trial in a high-school classroom in Southern California with over 50 students in April 2015. We are also making the online learning platform available to high schools in Massachusetts. Based on responses received from teachers so far, we expect to use this system in five classrooms this spring.

References

1. Koedinger, K.R., Anderson, J.R., Hadley, W.H., Mark, M.A.: Intelligent tutoring goes to school in the big city. Intl. Journal of Artificial Intelligence in Education **8**, 30–43 (1997)
2. Razzaq, L., Feng, M., Nuzzo-Jones, G., Heffernan, N.T., Koedinger, K.R., Junker, B., Ritter, S., Knight, A., Mercado, E., Turner, T.E., Upalekar, R., Walonoski, J.A., Macasek, M.A., Aniszczyk, C., Choksey, S., Livak, T., Rasmussen, K.: The assistment project: blending assessment and assisting. In: Intl. Conf. on Artificial Intelligence in Education (2005)
3. VanLehn, K., Lynch, C., Schulze, K., Shapiro, J.A., Shelby, R., Taylor, L., Treacy, D., Weinstein, A., Wintersgill, M.: The Andes physics tutoring system: Lessons learned. Intl. Journal of Artificial Intelligence in Education **15**(3), 147–204 (2005)
4. Aleven, V., McLaren, B.M., Sewall, J., Koedinger, K.R.: A new paradigm for intelligent tutoring systems: Example-tracing tutors. Intl. Journal of Artificial Intelligence in Education **19**(2), 105–154 (2009)
5. Ohlsson, S.: Constraint-based Student Modeling. In Student Modeling: The Key to Individualized Knowledge-based Instruction. Springer, pp. 167–189 (1994)
6. Kumar, R., Roy, M., Roberts, R.B., Makhoul, J.I.: Towards automatically building tutor models. In: Intl. Conf. on Intelligent Tutoring Systems (2014)
7. González-Brenes, J.P., Huang, Y., Brusilovsky, P.: General features in knowledge tracing: applications to multiple subskills, temporal item response theory, and expert knowledge. In: Intl. Conf. on Educational Data Mining (EDM 2014), London, England (2014)
8. Jacobson, N.S., Truax, P.: Clinical significance: a statistical approach to defining meaningful change in psychotherapy research. Journal of Consulting and Clinical Psychology **59**(1), 12–19 (1991)

FARMA-ALG: An Application for Error Mediation in Computer Programming Skill Acquisition

Alexander Robert Kutzke$^{(\boxtimes)}$ and Alexandre I. Direne

Department of Informatics, Federal University of Paraná, Curitiba, Brazil
{alexander,alexd}@inf.ufpr.br

Abstract. The central problem of using students' errors as a fundamental part of teaching and learning computer programming is presented in a critical manner. The literature review points out that previous research works have not accounted for the dynamic nature of mediation in educational interactions of the referred domain. To fill such a gap, an application named FARMA-ALG is introduced. The application aims to promote error mediation in teaching and learning computer programming, with effective teacher participation. The application details and preliminary tests are shown, highlighting relevant progress to error mediation.

1 Introduction

Research in computer programming education promotes frequent discussions in the literature. Although the programming activity is one of the basis for computer science courses, it is often pointed out by students as one of the most difficult disciplines, showing high dropout rates [6].

This complex scenario requires hard work from both teachers and students on the process of teaching and learning. During this process, the student faces difficulties that potentially generate errors (incorrect or imprecise answers to exercises). It is essential to overcome the common negative view of the error as a sign of a student's lack of skill. However, it is necessary to make the error an integral part of the teaching and learning process. In other words, it seems that mediating the error is a productive educational task.

According to the cultural-historical psychology [7], when dealing with the complexity of an activity such as computer programming, students need to form *scientific concepts* [7]. Only this type of concepts will become psychological instruments which are complex structures that reorganize the reasoning process to be reflexive. As opposed to spontaneous concepts, developed through an empirical learning or an immediate analysis of knowledge, scientific concepts depend on a proper mediation to develop into problem solving skills. In this sense, if there is no mediated concept assimilation in its advanced and correct form, errors are expected to become part of the process of scientific concept formation.

© Springer International Publishing Switzerland 2015
C. Conati et al. (Eds.): AIED 2015, LNAI 9112, pp. 690–693, 2015.
DOI: 10.1007/978-3-319-19773-9_93

In this context, the manipulation, i.e., the visualization and the analysis of relations among errors can be a powerful tool for a teacher's mediation tasks. An instrument for this manipulation can facilitate the teacher's reflection on the set of his/her students' errors to lower the burden of routine work. It can also approximate the teacher to the students' process of skill acquisition and to the concrete manifestations of their errors.

This paper presents concepts and a implemented tools to promote error mediation. The remainder of the text presents a brief overview of current work in the literature related to the use of error in computer programming education. It also describes the main features to the FARMA-ALG prototype software tool and its preliminary application in university-level classes.

2   Related Work

In general, few are the studies dedicated to forming dealing with error records in the teaching and learning processes. Some of them are in the field of Educational Data Mining (EDM) [5]. The most common analyses involve students' error rates or the use of student monitoring tools. However, the study of error records is still a secondary issue in EDM research [5]. In the same way, Intelligent Tutoring Systems (ITSs) often deal with students' errors. Normally, this is done through three processes: diagnosis [2], remediation [1] and error classification [4].

Few studies provide teacher support in students' error analysis. They usually feature automatic processes and statistical analysis without any teacher participation. Such a stance hinders a deeper study of error causes. Another negative fact of past research is the absence of any analysis of relations among different error logs. Thus, if one intends to make productive use of error records, it is possible to perform group and personalized error handling through the study of error connections and similarities.

3   Farma-Alg

FARMA-ALG is a web-based implementation of the framework presented in [3], which proposes a study on the existing similarity relations among different programming problem solutions. From the main objectives set by the framework, FARMA-ALG implements four features to support the teacher in authoring courseware and monitoring students' progress, as follows: (1) search for answer records; (2) timeline view; (3) solution graph manipulation; (4) automatic recommendation of answer records.

Based on the student error relations obtained automatically by the system and the ones defined by the teacher, the system generates a similarity graph of problem solutions. In this graph, the vertices represent answer records and the edges connect similar answers. The weight of each edge represents the degree of similarity between two responses. From the similarity graph, the main framework's data structure is formed. With it, it is possible to make assumptions and generalizations about the set of stored answers.

When submitting a response (source codes in C, Pascal or Ruby), the student's attempt is checked against input and output pairs, or test cases, previously defined by the teacher. The use of test cases is similar to the concept used in software for programming competitions. For each test case, the answer results are stored. If the result is considered incorrect, the student receives in return comments and hints, informed by the teacher or generated by the system. For each attempt sent by a student to solve a problem, the system compares the student's code execution output with all other stored answers to determine its similarity relations. The similarity between two answers, or the similarity function, is based on the weighted mean of several factors, including the following: (1) degree of similarity between each test case output and the expected output; (2) degree of similarity among the different test case outputs; (3) degree of similarity among the various answers' source code.

A search by keywords and meta-data is available to both teacher and students. Examples of search keys are the name of the student, classroom, time interval to solve a problem and problem statement text. Hence, it is possible to recover, in an easy way, specific data for the sake of error mediation.

Another type of visualization available in FARMA-ALG is the timeline view. This view makes it possible for teachers and students to access the answers on a timeline scale representation. That is, this data visualization respects the chronological order of students' attempts to solve problems. Thus, there are grounds for an contextualized analysis of the student's concept formation.

Through a third form of visualization, the graphical view of the similarity graph, FARMA-ALG users are able to view and to manipulate answer records in a fast manner. It is possible to observe and interact with stored answer records, and their relations, and access their specific data. Besides the answer visualization, the graph allows the manipulation of responses and their relations. The manipulation of answer records is characterized by answer classification and graph edge insertion and removal. The action of classification is an attribute of one or more *tags* to an answer record.

From the manipulation actions performed by the teacher, the system collects information to make generalizations about answer classification. Such generalizations refer to the task of automatic tagging similar answers. Thus, assuming that the teacher has classified an answer with tag A, the application scans all similar records and informs the degree of certainty with which it would identify such answers with the same tag. The tagging process occurs with all answers within the connected component, propagating the teacher's classification throughout the evolving dataset. For each generalization made by the system, the teacher can, if desired, confirm or deny it. The generalization process described above is defined as the process of *tag propagation* over the similarity graph. The tag propagation algorithm is defined in detail in [3].

Through similarity graph analysis, FARMA-ALG is also able to automatically recommend the analysis of potentially relevant answer records. In other words, the application is able to automatically find answer records and exercises that may be of high pedagogical relevance for a specific group of students.

The definition of which answers and exercises are relevant to a group of students consists of three steps: (1) groups of students with high similarity degree among their responses are found through the creation of a similarity graph of students, derived from the similarity graph of answers; (2) for each group, a set of exercises are defined as having, supposedly, greater relevance (an exercise is said to be relevant for a group of students if the mean similarity among the group's answers to that exercise is greater than a certain threshold); (3) among the group's answers to the considered relevant exercises, the most representative ones, i.e., those with the highest mean similarity among other responses are selected.

So far, three sessions of preliminary tests were conducted as an empirical study. The use of the system during testing and further analysis indicated a significant gain in the students' responses mediation and its effectiveness. The automatic recommendation, in most cases, indicated groups of students with real similarities on their errors. Besides the similarity graph analysis allowed error patterns detection for both an individual student and for groups of students.

4 Conclusion

The FARMA-ALG application was presented, introducing a new way to view and manipulate answer records. This application implements the framework presented in [3] and aims to promote and facilitate the error mediation when teaching and learning computer programming. Results of three preliminary empirical studies indicated a reasonable impact towards favoring error mediation through the application features.

Further experiments are planned to verify the learning effectiveness of the mediation process provided by the system and to confirm the preliminary results obtained so far.

References

1. Ainsworth, S.: Deft: A conceptual framework for considering learning with multiple representations. Learning and Instruction **16**(3), 183–198 (2006)
2. Johnson, W., Soloway, E.: Proust: Knowledge-based program understanding. IEEE Transactions on SE-Software Engineering **11**(3), 267–275 (1985)
3. Kutzke, A.R., Direne, A.I.: Mediação do erro na educação: um arcabouço de sistema para a instrumentalização de professores e alunos. In: Anais do Simpósio Brasileiro de Informática na Educação, vol. 25 (2014)
4. Leite, M.D., Pimentel, A.R., Oliveira, F.D.: Um estudo sobre classificação de erros: uma proposta aplicada a objetos de aprendizagem. In: Anais do Simpósio Brasileiro de Informática na Educação, vol. 1 (2011)
5. Peña-Ayala, A.: Educational data mining: A survey and a data mining-based analysis of recent works. Expert Systems with Applications **41**(4, Part 1), 1432–1462 (2014)
6. Robins, A., Rountree, J., Rountree, N.: Learning and teaching programming: A review and discussion. Computer Science Education **13**(2), 137–172 (2003)
7. Vygotsky, L.S.: Thought and language. MIT press (2012)

The Role of Peer Agent's Learning Competency in Trialogue-Based Reading Intelligent Systems

Haiying Li[✉], Qinyu Cheng, Qiong Yu, and Arthur C. Graesser

University of Memphis, Memphis, USA
{li5,qcheng,qyu1,graesser}@memphis.edu

Abstract. This paper investigates how the peer agent's learning competency affects English learners' reading, engagement, system self-efficacy, and attitudes toward the peer agent in a trialogue-based intelligent tutoring system (ITS). Participants learned a summarizing reading strategy in the compare-contrast text structure in the ITS. Results detected the significant main effect of the peer agent's learning competency on learners' performance and on engagement.

Keywords: Learning competency · Summarizing · Engagement · Self-efficacy

1 Introduction

Learning companion agents or peer agents have been included in the intelligent tutoring systems (ITSs) to facilitate learning [1,2]. The peer agent may provide correct or incorrect information, encourage or motivate the human learner, and collaborate or compete with the learner [3]. Previous work has shown the adoption of the peer agent impacts students' learning outcomes and system-self efficacy in one-on-one (i.e., peer agent and student) learning systems with limited pre-defined dialogue options [1,2]. However, relatively little work has investigated the effects of the peer agent's learning competency in trialogue-based learning systems.

Vygotsky's [4] zone of proximal development (ZPD) confirms the benefits of cooperative learning with peers. When compared to independent learning, students in peer learning appear to adopt more effective learning strategies by learning proactively in their thinking, questioning, and knowledge sharing [5]. A peer's learning competency can be broadly classified into high, middle and low [1,2]. A high-competency peer may tutor other students by providing feedback, hints and correct information, or by providing a model of the learning process [1,3]. When student peers have similar expertise and competency level, each student takes turns to model their learning and provide their perception of the content [5]. However, when there is a mismatch of competency and expertise between the student and the peer agent, the low-competency peer can enhance the student's self-efficacy beliefs and increase the student's self-esteem, confidence, and sense of responsibility [2].

Kim et al.'s study focused on a novice instructional design course in a one-on-one system. Whether their findings will hold true for other populations, academic skills, or in one-on-two trialogue-based learning systems is still unclear. The present study attempts to replicate these findings with the English as Foreign Language (EFL) learners as the population, the summarizing strategy as the target academic skill, and a

© Springer International Publishing Switzerland 2015
C. Conati et al. (Eds.): AIED 2015, LNAI 9112, pp. 694–697, 2015.
DOI: 10.1007/978-3-319-19773-9_94

trialogue-based intelligent system as the learning setting. We designed two conversational computer agents in the ITS, a teacher agent and a peer agent, and investigated four research questions: (1) Does the high-competency peer agent improve the EFL learners' reading performance and (2) enhance the EFL learners' positive attitude toward the peer agent? (3) Does the low-competency peer agent enhance the EFL learners' engagement and (4) the EFL learners' system self-efficacy?

2   Method

Participants consisted of 47 Chinese EFL learners (68% female; Age: M=37, SD=8.80), who have studied English for at least 8 years. Each participant was randomly assigned into one of the three conditions: low-competency, 20% of Jordan's answers were correct (n=18); middle-competency, 50% correct (n=15); and high-competency, 80% (n=14) based on gender. Actually, more participants would like to participate in the study, but later they rejected because of the requirement for their social security number for being paid. This resulted in an uneven distribution in the conditions. Participants first took the pre-survey (30 minutes), then interacted with the agents (20 minutes), and finally completed the post-survey (10 minutes). The pre-survey consisted of basic demographics questions, self-efficacy survey questions [6] (see Table 1), and the Gates MacGinitie reading test [7]. Participants were paid $15 for this one-hour experiment.

Participants learned a summarizing strategy in a compare-and-contrast text structure. The strategy involves the detection of the signal words that signify similarities and differences between two things/persons, and the identification of the good summary. The summarizing strategy lesson also prompts learners to provide a justification of good summaries. The mastery of these skills was evaluated by analyzing the quality of the learners' responses to the related reading comprehension questions. The reading comprehension questions were primarily multiple-choice questions with three options per question. Only one open-ended question was asked, which prompted participants to provide a justification for a good summary. All of answers were automatically evaluated by the system. To assess the open-ended response, the semantic match between a learner's verbal input and the expectations were evaluated by Regular-Expressions and latent semantic analysis. See Li, Shubeck and Graesser [4] for more details about the automatic scoring and rubrics.

The self-reported engagement after this reading was accepted as the engagement score, with 6-point scale from 1 (not at all engaged) to 6 (very engaged). The post-survey consisted of questions that gauged the students' system self-efficacy and attitudes toward the peer agent (see Table 1) with the same scale as prior self-efficacy.

3   Results and Discussion

Prior and post system self-efficacy and attitude toward the peer agent used in the Principal Components Analysis (PCA) to extract one component, respectively, named as prior self-efficacy, system self-efficacy, and attitude (see Table 1).

The prior self-efficacy component explained 62.93% of the total variance, and its regression score was performed on a One-way ANCOVA. Results showed there was no difference in participants' prior self-efficacy, $F(2,44)=.194$, $p>.05$, $M=1.53$, $SD=.504$. The regression score of prior self-efficacy was used as a covariate along with pretest reading score in the analyses. The system self-efficacy component explained 84.78% variance, and the attitude component, 71.24%. Both regression scores were used as dependent variables along with reading score and engagement score.

Table 1. PCA for Prior Self-efficacy, System Self-efficacy and Attitude toward Peer Agent

Items in Prior Self-efficacy	Loadings	Communalities
If I can't do a job the first time, I keep trying until I can.	.838	.703
Failure just makes me try harder.	.837	.701
When I have something unpleasant to do, I stick to it until I finish it.	.755	.570
When I make plans, I am certain I can make them work.	.737	.543
Eigenvalue	2.520	
Items in System Self-efficacy	Loadings	Communalities
The agents are helpful in learning reading strategies.	.964	0.929
This system could help me improve my reading comprehension.	.963	.927
The strategies could help me improve my reading.	.903	.815
A conversational discussion is a more valid assessment.	.849	.720
Eigenvalue	3.391	
Items in Attitude Toward Peer Agent	Loadings	Communalities
I enjoy reading with Jordan.	.870	0.756
I like Jordan very much.	.841	0.707
I like Jordan's reading to be better than me.	.821	0.674
Eigenvalue	2.137	

The ANCOVA on reading scores detected a significant main effect with the control of prior self-efficacy, $F(2,38)=3.47$, $p<.05$, $R^2=.241$. Results revealed marginal significant differences between low ($M=8.25$, $SD=1.406$) and high ($M=8.58$, $SD=1.436$), $F(1,38)=4.63$, $p=.076$, and low and middle ($M=8.30$, $SD=1.436$) conditions, $F(1, 38)=5.452$, $p=.075$. These findings suggest EFL learners who worked with both high- and middle-competency peer agents achieved higher reading performance than those with the low-competency agent in the trialogue-based ITS. These findings also suggest that the high-competency agent facilitates learning not only the novice knowledge on the instructional design [2], but also the reading strategies.

The ANCOVA revealed a marginal significant main effect on engagement with the control of prior reading score, $F(2,38)=2.540$, $p=.092$, $R^2=.182$. A marginal significant difference existed between low ($M=4.86$, $SD=1.150$) and high ($M=4.69$, $SD=1.351$) groups, $F(1,38)=4.96$, $p=.096$. These findings suggest learners who work with the low-competency agent tend to be more engaged in learning than those with the high-competency agent [2]. The majority of participants achieved extremely low pretest scores and consequently may have perceived their reading abilities as "low". This perception may have influenced reported self-efficacy beliefs before the intervention. When low-achievers work with the low-competency peer agent, they may find another person is worse than themselves. With this in mind, their confidence may increase, which would improve their overall engagement with the system. However, when low-achievers work with a high-competency agent, they may not experience the increase in confidence, which may lead to their lower engagement reports.

Results did not show any significant effects of competency on system self-efficacy and attitude toward the peer agent. Our study failed to support the assertion that learners who work with the low-competency agent achieve higher self-efficacy [2]. However, a trend was found that learners who worked with the low-competency peer agent reported higher system self-efficacy ($M=.09$, $SD=1.110$), followed by the middle- ($M=.03$, $SD=.681$) and high competency groups ($M=-.15$, $SD=1.179$). Similarly, our findings failed to support the claim that learners who work with high-competency agents have a higher positive attitude towards the peer agent [3]. However, another trend was found that learners who worked with the high-competency peer agent ($M=.29$, $SD=1.053$) reported they liked the system more than those in the middle ($M=-.06$, $SD=.734$) and low competency groups ($M=-.17$, $SD=1.145$). The insignificance effects may be caused either by the small sample size or by the influence of other individual differences, such as the experience of using educational techniques.

In conclusion, peer agents in educational intelligent systems do help to improve learning outcomes and enhance student engagement [1,2]. Specifically, the peer agent with the high or middle competency facilitates learners to achieve higher academic performance, whereas the low-competency agent enhances the learners' engagement. These findings are confirmed both by college students in learning the domain-specific academic skills [2], and by EFL learners in learning language reading skills. As both high- and low-competency agents benefit learners from different perspectives, the peer agent's competency in the educational ITS should be adaptively designed with the consideration of the trade-off of learning outcomes and engagement.

Acknowledgements. The research was supported by the Institute of Education Sciences (R305A080594, R305G020018, R305C120001, R305A130030).

References

1. Hietala, P., Niemirepo, T.: The Competence of Learning Companion Agents. International Journal of Artificial Intelligence in Education **9**, 178–192 (1998)
2. Kim, Y., Baylor, A.L.: PALS Groups: Pedagogical Agents as Learning Companions: The Role of Agent Competency and Type of Interaction. Educational Technology Research and Development **54**, 223–243 (2006)
3. Li, H., Shubeck, K., Graesser, A.C.: Using technology in language assessment. In: Tsagari, D., Banerjee, J. (eds.) Contemporary Second Language Assessment (in press)
4. Vygotsky, L.S., Cole, M., John-Steiner, V., Scribner, S., Souberman, E.: Mind in Society. Harvard University Press, Cambridge (1978)
5. Falchikov, N.: What is peer tutoring? In: Falchikov, N. (ed.) Learning Together: Peer Tutoring in Higher Education, pp. 7–66. RoutledgeFalmer, New York (2001)
6. Pintrich, P.R., De Groot, E.V.: Motivational and Self-regulated Learning Components of Classroom Academic Performance. Journal of Educational Psychology **82**, 33–40 (1990)
7. MacGinitie, W., MacGinitie, R.: Gates MacGinitie Reading Tests. Riverside, Chicago (1989)

Teaching a Complex Process:
Insertion in Red Black Trees

C.W. Liew$^{(\boxtimes)}$ and F. Xhakaj

Department of Computer Science, Lafayette College, Easton, PA 18042, USA
{liewc,xhakajf}@lafayette.edu

Abstract. Red black trees (and all balanced trees) are an important concept in computer science with many applications. This paper describes a new approach using an example tracing tutor and our experince in using it to teach insertion in red black trees.

Keywords: Computer science · Data structures · Learning process

1 Introduction

Data structures are part of the programming fundamentals and core topics in a computer science curriculum [1]. An example of a data structure with complex algorithms is the red black tree and other balanced tree structures. Learning the red black tree algorithms can be quite challenging and difficult for the students for many reasons. Many approaches to teaching red black trees have been tried [3–5] but our students still have quite a bit of difficulty with the concepts. We have designed a new approach using an example tracing tutor (RedBlackTree Tutor) that allows us to break down the algorithm into small steps explicitly and capture the students decisions while trying to construct a red black tree using a top-down insertion algorithm. This paper describes the tutoring system and our experience in using it to teach insertion in red black trees.

2 Red Black Trees

A red black tree is a self balancing binary search tree data structure, that has the following properties [5]:

1. The nodes of the tree are colored either red or black.
2. The root of the tree is always black.
3. A red node cannot have any red children.
4. Every path from the root to a null link contains the same number of black nodes.

A red black tree must display all of the properties listed above. In addition, every operation performed on a red black tree such as insertion or deletion,

C. Conati et al. (Eds.): AIED 2015, LNAI 9112, pp. 698–701, 2015.
DOI: 10.1007/978-3-319-19773-9_95

should preserve these properties resulting in a changed, but still correct red black tree. The top-down insertion algorithm described in [5] starts at the root of the tree and in a single iterative pass, modifies the tree by applying one or more of the insertion rules described below and eventually adds a new item to the tree. Just as with a binary search tree, the insertion algorithm starts at the root and traverses down to the leaf by comparing the value at the current node with the value to be inserted and selects the next node accordingly (left child if larger, otherwise right child). When a leaf is reached, a new node with the new value is inserted as a child of the node. The difference between the binary search tree and red black tree algorithms is that the red black tree algorithm can apply transformations on the tree at every iteration modifying the connections of the tree but not the values.

The insertion rules are: *color flip*, *single rotation*, *double rotation*, *simple insertion*, and *color root black*. The first rule (color flip) is to minimize the transformations arising from inserting a new leaf node that is colored red. The second (single rotation) and third rules (double rotation) are used to correct any violations (two red nodes in sequence) that arise from either applying rule 1 or by inserting a new node (simple insertion). The rule *color root black* is applied at the end of every insertion operation to ensure that the root of the tree is always black. The rules together ensure that only a single traversal from the root of the tree to a leaf is required to insert a new node and still maintain the red black tree properties.

Whether a rule is applicable at the current node is determined by the color and structural relationships of other nodes in relation to the current node. For example, for a color flip (rule 1) to be applicable the current node (X) must be black and its two children (C1,C2) must be red.

Insertion in red black trees is an example of a complex problem solving process. At every step of the process (each iteration in the algorithm) there are multiple choices and each choice has pre-conditions and they are affected by the decisions made in the previous step. At each iteration, a student must (1) select the current node, (2) identify the context - parent, sibling, grandparent, children and their colors, (3) select the applicable rule, and (4) apply the selected rule. Past approaches to teaching red black trees (or other balanced trees such as the AVL tree) [3–5] and the associated algorithms have treated the decisions at each iteration as a single compound decision. In addition, they have assumed (without data) that the students had difficulty in applying the rules and have focused on the mechanics of applying the rules, specifically the single and double rotation rules.

2.1   A New Approach

In contrast to previous approaches, our approach breaks down the decision point at each iteration into the following steps:

1. *identification of the current node* and its context (color, sibling, children, parent and grandparent) when iteratively traversing the tree and applying the rules,

2. *selection of the rule* to be applied at the current node, and
3. *application of the rule* correctly.

This approach explicitly separates out the identification of the current node and selection of the applicable rule from the the application of the rule itself.

3   The RedBlackTree Tutor

We implemented our approach both in the classroom (lecture) and in laboratory exercises. This section describes how the students use the laboratory exercises. The laboratory exercises were provided through an example tracing tutor (Red-BlackTree Tutor) that we developed using the Cognitive Tutor Authoring Tools (CTAT) [2].

The RedBlackTree Tutor imposes ordering restrictions on the problem solving path of the student. The first restriction requires the student to provide the correct answer for the current step before moving to the next step. The second restriction is imposed within a particular step, and requires students to answer the two questions at the top, namely identify the current node and select a rule, before going on to applying the rule. The tutor will not allow the student to work on the application of the rule before completing the identification questions correctly. The order restrictions make the students follow the granularity approach, while separating (1) steps from each other, and (2) the identification and selection parts of the problem from the application part.

We developed exercises to provide practice for the use of our approach to applying the five rules of top-down insertion, namely color flip, single rotation, double rotation, simple insertion and color the root black. The exercises varied in the context for the selection of each rule. For example, we created exercises where students could apply the color flip rule with the current node being (1) the root of the tree, (2) the left child of the root, and finally (3) the right child of the root. Similarly, we designed exercises for the other rules of top-down insertion.

4   Experiment Design

We evaluated the approach on the students in our data structures class during the fall semester of 2014. Students are introduced to red black trees during week 8, after they have covered binary trees and binary search trees.

This is the first balanced tree data structure that they will have seen. There were sixteen students in the class, mostly computer science and computer engineering majors and all the students participated in the study. We only analyzed the results for 12 of the students because 4 students had worked and practiced on additional problems on their own in the period between steps 2 and 3 of the evaluation process described below. Their results were discarded from the overall evaluation because we could not disambiguate between the effects of using the RedBlackTree Tutor and the work that they did on their own. The evaluation process followed the following steps (1) one week of lecture to cover red black trees including the granularity approach, (2) in the following week, a pre-test of 25 mins followed by, (3) a 1 hr session with the RedBlackTree Tutor, and (4) two days later, a 25 min post-test.

The pre-test and post-test were graded based on the correctness of each part of each step. We broke down each step in the exercises into 3 parts - identification of the current node, selection of the applicable rule, application of the rule - and graded the answers accordingly. We analyzed the scores of the students in (1) identifying the current node at a particular step, (2) selecting the rule, and (3) applying the rule, between the pre-test and post-test. The pre-test data shows that the students had the most difficulty (scoring 10.5 out of 25) in identifying the current node at each iteration even after a week of lectures that included examples and group work on practice problems. They had the least difficulty (score of 16.2 out of 25) in applying the selected rules. If these data are a true indication of student work, they would explain why the past approaches that focused on rule application were unsuccessful. The scores improved from pre-test to post-test from (1) 10.5 to 18.83 for node identification, (2) 14.17 to 21.92 for rule selection, and (3) 16.2 to 20.3 for rule application. Thus the scores for node identification increased by 79.33%, rule selection increased by 54.7% and rule application improved by 25.73%. The average score in the pre-test was 40.8 (out of 75) and it improved to 61.1 in the post-test.

5 Conclusion

This paper has described our approach for teaching red-black trees and its implementation in a tutoring system. The system has been evaluated in a class of 16 students (that is the size of the class in our college) and the results indicate that the approach can help improve the students performance.

References

1. ACM/IEEE-CS Joint Task Force on Computing Curricula. ACM/IEEE Computing Curricula 2001 Final Report (2001). http://www.acm.org/sigcse/cc2001
2. Aleven, V., McLaren, B.M., Sewall, J., Koedinger, K.R.: A new paradigm for intelligent tutoring systems: Example-tracing tutors. International Journal of Artificial Intelligence in Education **19**(2), 105–154 (2009)
3. Galles, D.: Data structure visualizations. http://www.cs.usfca.edu/galles/visualization
4. Ha, S.: VisuAlgo. http://www.comp.nus.edu.sg/stevenha/visualization
5. Weiss, M.A.: Data Structures & Problem Solving Using Java, 3rd ed. Pearson Education Inc. (2011)

Learner-Adaptive Pedagogical Model in SIAL, an Open-Ended Intelligent Tutoring System for First Order Logic

Jose A. Maestro-Prieto and Arancha Simon-Hurtado[✉]

Dpto. de Informática, Escuela Técnica Superior de Ingeniería Informática,
University of Valladolid, Campus Miguel Delibes,
Paseo de Belén, 15, 47011 Valladolid, Spain
{jose,arancha}@infor.uva.es

Abstract. SIAL is an Intelligent Tutoring System (ITS) for learning Computational Logic. It teaches classical refutation by resolution concepts using Robinson's Binary Resolution Rule. Furthermore, SIAL can be considered a Model-Based System, as its Domain Model is an Automated Theorem Prover (ATP) for First Order Logic (FOL). This allows SIAL to accept several solutions to the proposed exercise, all of which are correct, providing a kind of open-ended feature to the ITS. The Domain Model is in charge of carrying out the error diagnosis, identifying, in many cases, the misunderstandings. The focus of this paper is to describe the Pedagogical Model of SIAL that takes advantage of the error diagnosis capabilities of the Domain Model to offer a learner-adaptive tutorial action, according to the user cognitive profile.

Keywords: Intelligent tutoring system · Pedagogical model · Student model · First order logic · Artificial intelligence

1 Introduction

Teaching logic is a core part of several studies (maths, philosophy, engineering, computer science, ...). Hence, several tools have been developed to help with the learning and practising exercises of different kinds of logic, but mostly classical approaches to logic, for example [3,6,7]. In the special case of Computer Science, there exists a specific and particular kind of logic that is of interest: computational logic. It is particularly interesting that this deals with the automation of a reasoning process: automatic theorem proving. To the best of our knowledge, there are only a few tools dealing with this topic, such as [1,4,5].

There are several ways to construct an ITS. The most classical architecture proposes splitting the ITS into several modules which include interface, domain, pedagogical and student models. The domain module represents the domain to be taught. It can be implemented using different approaches, such as: cognitive tutors, Example-Tracing Tutors, Constraint-Based Models, and others. Some kinds of domain can be represented using Model-Based Reasoning approaches, as in [2]. However, new tutoring capabilities, such as dealing with open-ended solutions, are too complex to include in general architectures for ITSs.

C. Conati et al. (Eds.): AIED 2015, LNAI 9112, pp. 702–705, 2015.
DOI: 10.1007/978-3-319-19773-9_96

The SIAL architecture has been described in [4]. SIAL can be considered a Model-Based System, as its Domain Model is an ATP for FOL. This allows SIAL to accept several solutions to the proposed exercise, all of which are correct, providing a kind of open-ended feature to the ITS. SIAL always detects the mistakes made and, in many cases, can diagnose them. This is taken advantage of for developing a learner-adaptive pedagogical model in SIAL, capable of selecting the appropiate tutorial action for each student according to his/her learning profile.

Most of the systems referred to above allow the learner to receive an immediate, minimal feedback about the correctness of the action carried out. Some of them, such as Logic-ITA [7] or IDEAS [3], can provide on demand help, specific information about the mistake found, and hints about the next action the learner should take. Although it is not common in these tools, [7] includes a kind of assessment of the mastering of the knowledge to be learned: the learner should solve correctly a number of exercises or avoid making some kind of mistakes in order to progress in the tutorial. This paper presents the Pedagogical Model in SIAL.

2   Pedagogical Model in SIAL

This ITS is organised in 12 sub-topics or levels ranging from the simplest skills to the most complex ones. They include converting well-formed formulae (wff) to clause form, predicate unification, binary resolution, resolution refutation, factoring rule, and other rules and strategies for solving problems using FOL.

In SIAL, the pedagogical module is associated, inextricably, with the tutorial action proposed. Two types of tutorial action have been considered in SIAL: (i) to send a message to the learner, and (ii) to show him/her the next selected exercise.

The selection of the next exercise is guided by the Knowledge Base for the Tutorial Action (KBTA). It is possible to select an obligatory exercise or a reinforcement one. The minimum curriculum that a student will develop is contained in the obligatory exercises of each level. It is based on the instructor's experience in teaching this subject, as he/she knows what concepts the student has to learn and what kind of exercises facilitate their practise and comprehension. Once all obligatory exercises have been overcome successfully, a student would be in a good position to go onto the next level. SIAL implements a simple approach to assess the mastering of the concepts being taught in each level of the ITS, which is very close to the one proposed in [7], although the kind of logic, the model of interaction with the user, the domain model and the tutorial action in [7] are different to the ones chosen for SIAL.

A part of the adaptation ability of the Intelligent Tutor SIAL resides in the possibility of selecting some exercises depending on the answers provided by the student as he/she solves them. In SIAL, the set of reinforcement exercises makes it possible to adapt the exercises to the student. Its aim is to allow the student to train, in a more precise way, in one or more skills associated to a concept.

The information that SIAL takes into account to select the next tutorial action consists of the exercise currently proposed, the exercises previously completed, and the errors made while the student solved both current and previous exercises. Using this information, SIAL will choose the most appropriate tutorial action, which, in the experiment carried out, mainly consists of the selection or not of a reinforcement exercise, and in the extraction of the most suitable from those available, according to the errors made.

3   Designing the Knowledge Base for the Tutorial Action

The design of the KBTA in SIAL is intrinsically associated to:

- the design of the data base of the obligatory and reinforcement exercises
- the errors detected and identified by the Domain Model, which are codified by internal error codes in order to be used in the rules.

The exercises for each level have been designed taking into account our experience as teachers of the Introduction to the Artificial Intelligence course, acquired over many years in contact with many students. An incremental design, from lowest to highest difficulty, has been accomplished.

Both the exercises and the errors have associated identifiers, which are used in the rule premises of the knowledge base to give the most appropriate tutorial action, according to the student profile. The KBTA has been implemented as an expert system in CLIPS, by constructing abstraction and association rules designed using the CommonKADS methodology, and constitutes an independent module. The teacher can very easily control the exercise flow so it can be adapted to each learner profile in the best way, modifying the rules whenever he/she considers necessary, without having to compile the ITS again.

4   Experimental Results

Forty students used SIAL in the *Introduction to Artificial Intelligence* course with the Data Base of Exercises and KBTA built as indicated above. A satisfaction survey was filled in by 19 of them who finished the course.

The question related to the set of exercises says: Do you think that the set of exercises proposed is useful for understanding the concepts of FOL shown in the classroom? The possible four answers and the results were the following: (a) They do not help - 0, (b) They help a little bit - 2, (c) They are helpful - 9 and (d) They are very helpful - 8. So most of the students (17/19) think that the set of exercises is helpful or very helpful.

A log with the work of the students using SIAL was collected and analysed. Taking into account this analysis, the teacher can tune the minimum number of reinforcement exercises that he/she should propose, in such a way that the percentage of reinforcement exercise series that are finished with errors in the last exercise of each series is lower each time. Besides, from the most commonly registered errors, the teacher can identify the worst understood concepts and emphasise them in the theoretical classes or revise some studied in other courses.

5   Conclusions

An ITS including open-ended feature and learner-adaptive capabilities has been presented. This ITS is designed for teaching computational logic. In order to fulfill its goal, the ITS relies on a Model-Based Diagnosis approach.

The ability to deal with different solutions and identify the relevant errors while the learner solves the exercises is managed by the pedagogical model offering a learner-adaptive tutorial action, according to the user cognitive profile. The selection of the next exercise is guided by the KBTA. The ITS chooses the next reinforcement exercise, based on the information the student model contains, until the specific skill being taught has been mastered by the learner.

The pedagogical model has been implemented using a separate, high level, expert systems shell, so that understanding its content and changing it can be done easily.

A great percentage of the students surveyed stated that the set of exercises presented is useful or very useful for understanding the concepts of obtaining the clause form, the unification algorithm, the resolution rule and the resolution refutation.

Acknowledgments. This work has been partially supported by Intelligent Systems Group (GSI) at the University of Valladolid (Spain). Thanks also to A. F. Hynds B.A. Dip. TEFL for revising the English grammar, and to Dr. Alejandra Martinez-Mones for her useful suggestions.

References

1. Chronopoulos, T., Perikos, I., Hatzilygeroudis, I.: An example-tracing tutor for teaching NL to FOL conversion. In: Papadopoulos, H., Andreou, A.S., Bramer, M. (eds.) AIAI 2010. IFIP AICT, vol. 339, pp. 170–178. Springer, Heidelberg (2010)
2. de Koning, K., Breuker, J., Wielinga, B., Bredeweg, B.: Model-based reasoning about learner behaviour. Artificial Intelligence **117**(2), 173–229 (2000)
3. Lodder, J., Jeuring, J., Passier, H.: An interactive tool for manipulating logical formulae. Tech. Rep. UU-CS-2006-040, DSpace at Utrecht University(Netherlands) (2006).
4. Maestro, J.A., Simón, M.A., López, M., Martínez, A., Alonso, C.J.: A proposal of diagnosis for an ITS for computational logic. In: Conejo, R., Urretavizcaya, M., Pérez-de-la-Cruz, J.-L. (eds.) CAEPIA/TTIA 2003. LNCS (LNAI), vol. 3040, pp. 86–95. Springer, Heidelberg (2004)
5. Maestro-Prieto, J.A., Simon-Hurtado, M.A.: SLI: a tool for easing the understanding of automated proof construction. ACM Inroads **4**(2), 53–56 (2013)
6. Wildenberg, A., Scharff, C.: Oliver: an online inference and verification system. In: 32nd Annual Frontiers in Education (FIE 2002), vol. 2, pp. S1F22–26 (2002)
7. Yacef, K.: Making large class teaching more adaptive with the logic-ITA. In: Proceedings of the Sixth Conference on Australasian Computing Education, vol. 30, pp. 343–347. ACE 2004, Darlinghurst, Australia (2004)

Predictive Knowledge Modeling in Collaborative Inquiry Learning Scenarios

Sven Manske[✉], Tobias Hecking, and H. Ulrich Hoppe

University Duisburg-Essen, Duisburg, Germany
{manske,hecking,hoppe}@collide.info

Abstract. The ongoing EU project Go-Lab provides a generalized interface and tool set to enable and structure learning activities with online laboratories. In this context, we have studied collaborative inquiry learning activities using various tools in blended learning scenarios. Former research indicates that the composition of heterogeneous vs. homogeneous groups in terms of student competencies or skills has an effect on the learning gain. This has been investigated using a theory-driven approach for predictive modeling based on Markov logic with data from a recent classroom study.

Keywords: Predictive modeling · Inquiry learning · Collaborative learning

1   Introduction and Background

In the tradition of computer-supported inquiry learning, the European project Go-Lab aims to engage learners through student-centered teaching methods and to foster their interest in science [1]. The students dive into the roles of scientists to follow an inquiry-based learning approach aligned to an experiment with online labs in a blended learning scenario. This incorporates presence learning with an online learning environment, namely the Go-Lab portal. It serves as a general infrastructure and access point to a variety of online labs and offers a variety of scaffolds and guidance mechanisms to support the inquiry process.

1.1   Group Learning and Orchestration in Blended Learning Scenarios

The general Go-Lab infrastructure uses instructions in a minimal way and externalizes the student-centered approaches to the classroom. As a consequence, Go-Lab supports neither an explicit and direct way for student collaboration nor classroom orchestration on the part of teachers. While collaborative online tools, especially in the context of online experimentation, are not generally available, blended learning scenarios offer the opportunity to induce offline collaboration in the classroom. This demands the teacher to set up group learning scenarios and take care of the class-room and group orchestration [2]. There are indications from several systematic studies that heterogeneity of knowledge is beneficial for group performance [3], requiring a certain baseline of background knowledge [4]. In our own prior work we had also seen

© Springer International Publishing Switzerland 2015
C. Conati et al. (Eds.): AIED 2015, LNAI 9112, pp. 706–709, 2015.
DOI: 10.1007/978-3-319-19773-9_97

positive effects of diversity on the performance of learning groups [5,6]. Now we used data from a former experiment to build predictive models for students' learning gain based on Markov logic. A special challenge in classroom settings is that a relatively large set of independent features is used for predictions based on a limited amount of data.

1.2 Predictive Modeling with Markov Logic Programs

Markov Logic Programs (MLPs) combine first-order logic and probabilistic graphical models [7]. An MLP comprises a set of ground atoms and a set of first-order logic rules. The Markov theory allows for calculating the probability of a certain grounding of the variables. Thus, it is possible to infer the "most likely world" given evidence in terms of ground atoms. In contrast to pure logical programming where the violation of a rule by a certain grounding of the atoms results makes this world impossible in Markov logic the world just becomes less likely. Another property of Markov logic programs is that the importance of a rule is reflected by a weight between $-\infty$ and $+\infty$ which can also be learned according to the data. This allows for expressing theories in a formal logical language and learning weights according to the true facts. We call this top down theory building process "theory-driven predictive modeling".

2 Approach

In Go-Lab inquiry learning scenarios students create artifacts using a variety of different tools and scaffolds. The ensuing digital traces can be used to capture the learning process and to providing the system with a detailed view on the learner. To support the learners and possibly teachers in interpreting these basic data, we build predictive models based on features we extracted from the produced artefacts.

Fig. 1 shows the abstraction of the underlying conceptual model. The model of an inquiry learning scenario consists of different phases which represent different learning activities. In each phase, a learner uses a specific set of tools to support the inquiry process. Scaffolds are added to the learning environment during the authoring process and the setup is dependent on the given scenario.

The third layer consists of agents to extract features from the persisted artefacts. This feature extraction leads to a decomposition of students' skills. In our scenario, we used three categories of scores to be extracted: Motivational scores based on questionnaires, text writing scores based on wiki artefacts, and concept map measures assessing scores relative to an expert model. These features are persisted in the SQLSpaces server, which acts as a middleware. It uses an architectural approach that is based on a multi-agent system with a distributed shared memory [8], thus integrating Go-Lab data and external services, e.g. for the retrieval of models and artefacts, or for analytics services. All results are available for connected processing agents, e.g. for building predictors. The framework described was used to collect student-generated artifacts in our previous study [6] on group experimentation in classroom scenarios. Students were supposed to learn in an online inquiry learning scenario on building an osmotic power plant. While the former study focused on the group composition, the collected data has further been used in this work to continue our research. We apply a theory-driven approach to model and explain hypotheses about the effects of group work, particular the impact of heterogeneity to knowledge gain. The model is validated through the data from a classroom experiment.

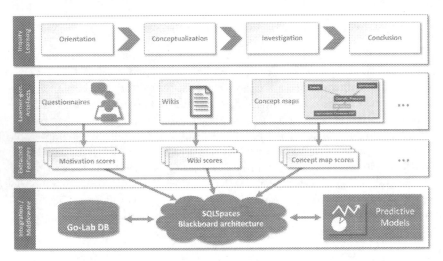

Fig. 1. Conceptual architecture aligned to a heterogeneous inquiry learning scenario in Go-Lab

3   Results and Interpretation

Our MLP model contains five different predicates that encode the students prior and post knowledge. In particular, *KnowsBefore(Stud, Item)* and *KnowsAfter(Stud, Item)* encode the student´s knowledge before and after the group work. A knowledge item corresponds to a question in the pre- and post- experiment knowledge test. *Group(Stud, G)* is used to encode to which group each student belongs and *IsHeterogeneous(G)* and *IsHomogeneous(G)* indicate the characteristic of the group G. All predicates except *KnowsAfter* are closed. This means that the full evidence is given in advance. KnowsAfter is a query predicate and will be inferred.

∞	KnowsBefore(Stud, Item) => KnowsAfter(Stud, Item). //Hard rule
3.38	Group(Stud1, G), Group(Stud2, G), IsHomogeneous(G), KnowsAfter(Stud1, Item) => KnowsAfter(Stud2, Item)
4.30	Group(Stud1, G), Group(Stud2, G), IsHeterogeneous(Item), KnowsAfter(Stud1, Item) => KnowsAfter(Stud2, Item)
-6.01	¬ KnowsBefore(Stud1, G) => KnowsAfter(Stud1, G)

Fig. 2. Group knowledge sharing model encoded as MLP

A model is created based on the theory that students in (heterogeneous) learning groups have a similar knowledge state after the group work phase. This is reflected by the second and third rule of the MLP in Fig 2. The first rule is a hard rule and all possible groundings of the atoms have to fulfil this rule. The last rule is not intended to contribute to the predictions, but is added for the sake of validation. The rules are weighted according to their coherence with the true facts. For weight learning and inference the Tuffy Markov logic engine [9] was used.

The weights assigned to the rules in the MLP of Fig. 2 correspond to the outcome of this process. The weights indicate the relative importance of the rules. The more groundings of the open atom *KnowsAfter* (prediction) violate a rule the lower becomes the rule`s weight. This implies further evidence for our hypothesis that heterogeneous groups are superior to homogeneous groups regarding the learning outcome. The high negative weight of the last rule indicates that the naive prediction that student learn with the scenario anyway is by far not as good as the predictions that incorporate the group information.

In conclusion, the application of predictive modeling in the context of collaborative inquiry learning has the potential to generate new insights on how intelligent group formation can influence individual knowledge gain. Since theory driven predictive modeling allows the incorporation of the analyst's knowledge and hypotheses in addition to the data, it can be considered as a useful alternative when underlying dataset is too limited to build a valid data-driven model. To bring the teacher back in control, in future work we will provide mechanisms for teachers or tutors to interactively intervene in this process and to manipulate parameters of the learning process and environment based on the models.

References

1. de Jong, T., Sotiriou, S., Gillet, D.: Innovations in STEM education: the Go-Lab federation of online labs. Smart Learning Environments **1**(1), 1–16 (2014)
2. Roschelle, J., Dimitriadis, Y., Hoppe, U.: Classroom Orchestration: Synthesis. Computers & Education **69**, 523–526 (2013)
3. Webb, N., Nemer, K., Zuniga, S.: Short circuits or superconductors? Effects of group composition on high-achieving students' science assessment performance. American Educational Research Journal **39**(4), 943–989 (2002)
4. Gijlers, H., De Jong, T.: The relation between prior knowledge and students' collaborative discovery learning processes. Journal of research in science teaching **42**(3), 264–282 (2005)
5. Chounta, I.-A., Giemza, A., Hoppe, H.U.: Multilevel analysis of collaborative activities based on a mobile learning scenario for real classrooms. In: Yuizono, T., Zurita, G., Baloian, N., Inoue, T., Ogata, H. (eds.) CollabTech 2014. CCIS, vol. 460, pp. 127–142. Springer, Heidelberg (2014)
6. Manske, S., Hecking, T., Chounta, I.-A., Werneburg, S., Hoppe, H.: Using Differences to Make a Difference: A Study on Heterogeneity of Learning Groups (2015)
7. Richardson, M., Domingos, P.: Markov logic networks. Mach. Learn. **62**, 107–136 (2006)
8. Weinbrenner, S.: SQLSpaces: a platform for flexible language heterogeneous multi-agent systems. Ph.D. dissertation (2012)
9. Niu, F., Ré, C., Doan, A., Shavlik, J.: Tuffy: Scaling up statistical inference in markov logic networks using an rdbms. Proceedings of the VLDB Endowment **4**(6), 373–384 (2011)

Worked Examples are More Efficient for Learning than High-Assistance Instructional Software

Bruce M. McLaren[1]([⊠]), Tamara van Gog[2], Craig Ganoe[1], David Yaron[1], and Michael Karabinos[1]

[1] Carnegie Mellon University, Pittsburgh, PA, USA
bmclaren@cs.cmu.edu, ganoe@acm.org, yaron@cmu.edu,
mk7@andrew.cmu.edu
[2] Erasmus University Rotterdam, Rotterdam, The Netherlands
vangog@fsw.eur.nl

Abstract. The 'assistance dilemma', an important issue in the Learning Sciences, is concerned with how much guidance or assistance should be provided to help students learn. A recent study comparing three high-assistance approaches (worked examples, tutored problems, and erroneous examples) and one low-assistance (conventional problems) approach, in a multi-session classroom experiment, showed equal learning outcomes, with worked examples being much more efficient. To rule out that the surprising lack of differences in learning outcomes was due to too much feedback across the conditions, the present follow-up experiment was conducted, in which feedback was curtailed. Yet the results in the new experiment were the same: there were no differences in learning outcomes, but worked examples were much more efficient. These two experiments suggest that there are efficiency benefits of worked example study. Yet, questions remain. For instance, why didn't high instructional assistance benefit learning outcomes and would these results hold up in other domains?

Keywords: Assistance dilemma · Classroom studies · Empirical studies · Worked examples · Erroneous examples · Tutored problems to solve · Problem solving

1 Introduction

An important question for the Learning Sciences to answer is how much guidance or assistance should be provided in order to help students learn, i.e., the 'assistance dilemma' [1]. In a recent experiment [2], the effectiveness and efficiency of three high-assistance instructional formats (which differ in the amount of student activity required) was compared to low-assistance problems to solve, which students have to attempt to solve largely on their own:

- *worked examples*, which present students with a fully worked-out problem solution to study;
- *tutored problems*, which provide step-by-step feedback and hints, either when an error is made or on demand; and
- *erroneous examples*, which are worked examples with errors in one or more of the problem-solving steps that students have to find and fix.

© Springer International Publishing Switzerland 2015
C. Conati et al. (Eds.): AIED 2015, LNAI 9112, pp. 710–713, 2015.
DOI: 10.1007/978-3-319-19773-9_98

It was found that worked example study resulted in a large efficiency benefit compared to all other conditions. Equal learning outcomes were attained in 50-65% less time and with less self-reported effort invested in the study phase [2]. That the more passive high-assistance format was most efficient is interesting in light of the assistance dilemma. However, it was remarkable that none of the high-assistance instructional formats improved learning outcomes compared to problem solving. Possibly, the feedback received in all of the conditions, including problem solving, in the form of a worked example if they made mistakes, could explain the lack of effect.

To find out whether worked example feedback contributed to the equal performance across conditions, a second study was conducted, reported here. Instead of receiving a correct worked example as feedback, students in all conditions would instead see highlighting of their correct steps in green, and their incorrect steps in red. Thus, the second study, like the earlier one, also directly compared the four instructional conditions, but under different (and lesser) feedback circumstances.

2   Method

Participants and Design. Participants were 116 tenth and eleventh grade students from two high schools in the U.S. ($M_{age} = 16.45$, $SD = 0.76$; 48 male; 15 of an original 131 participants were excluded for not fully completing all phases). Participants were randomly assigned to one of the four instructional conditions: (1) Worked Examples (*WE*), (2) Erroneous Examples (*ErrEx*), (3) Tutored Problems to Solve (*TPS*;), or (4) Problems to Solve (*PS*).

Materials and Procedure. We used the same web-based stoichiometry-learning environment as [2]. Stoichiometry is a subdomain of chemistry in which basic mathematics (i.e., multiplication of ratios) is applied to chemical quantities such as mass and solution concentration. The experiment was conducted at students' schools as replacement for their regular science class. In total, the study took 6 class periods to complete. Students received a login for the web-based environment and could work at their own pace on the materials they encountered in the learning phase.

They first completed a demographic questionnaire, followed by the pretest, consisting of four stoichiometry problems to solve (isomorphic to the Intervention Problems, described below) and four conceptual knowledge questions (max. score: 101 points). Subsequently, each condition watched an introductory video explaining how to interact with the web-based user interface. They then watched instructional videos introducing new stoichiometry concepts and procedures (the same in all conditions), after which students were presented with a total of 10 intervention problems, in an instructional format specific to their condition (explained below). The problems were grouped in five isomorphic pairs (e.g., WE-1 and WE-2 are an isomorphic pair, WE-3 and WE-4 are an isomorphic pair, etc.) and each pair was followed by an isomorphic embedded test problem (max. total score: 122 points). After each intervention item, students indicated how much mental effort they invested in studying/completing it, on a 9-point rating scale [3]. The complexity of the stoichiometry problems gradually increased, with each pair of intervention problems being preceded by instructional videos explaining new concepts and procedures. When they had finished with the intervention phase, however, they could not immediately progress to the posttest; this test took place on the sixth and final period for all students and was isomorphic to the pretest (max. score: 101 points). Performance was automatically scored, along with time on task and student self-reports of effort.

The worked examples *(WE)* consisted of problem statements and screen-recorded videos of the solution to the problem being entered, step-by-step, into the interface used in all four conditions. The videos had duration of between 30 and 70 seconds, and did not include any narration or explanation of why steps were taken; students only saw the steps being completed. When the video finished, students had to indicate the "reason" for each step by selecting this from a drop-down menu. After entering reasons, they could click the "Done" button and correct/incorrect feedback appeared (in the form of green highlighting for correct steps, red highlighting for incorrect steps). The Erroneous Examples *(ErrEx)*, consisted of screen-recorded videos of 30 to 70 seconds, except the items contained 1 to 4 errors that students were instructed to find and fix. They had to correct at least one step before they could click the 'Done' button, at which point correct/incorrect feedback appeared. The tutored problems *(TPS)* consisted of a problem statement and fields to fill in and students had to attempt to solve the problem themselves, but with assistance received in the form of on-demand hints and error feedback. There were up to 5 levels of hints per step, with the bottom-out hint being both a message giving the answer to that step and a worked example of the problem solved to that point, shown below the interface. Because the tutored problems always ended in a correct final problem state, students received no further feedback. The problems to solve *(PS)* consisted of a problem statement and fields to fill in by students themselves, without any assistance. They had to fill out at least one step before they could click the 'Done' button. When they clicked the 'Done' button, correct/incorrect feedback appeared. In all conditions, students could review their work – including correct/incorrect feedback – for as long as they wanted before selecting a "Next" button and proceeding to the next item.

3   Results

Data are presented in Table 1 and were analyzed with ANOVA. Analysis of the pretest scores confirmed that there were no significant differences among conditions in prior knowledge, $F(3,112) < 1$, $p = .500$. Test performance did not differ significantly among conditions, either on the embedded test problems, $F(3,112) = 1.031$, $p = .382$, or on the posttest, $F(3,112) < 1$, $p = .883$.

There was a significant difference among conditions in the average mental effort invested in the intervention problems, $F(3,112) = 9.709$, $p < .001$; Bonferroni post-hoc tests showed that WE < TPS ($p < .001$) and PS ($p = .002$); ErrEx < TPS ($p = .003$); no other differences were significant. Regarding time spent on the intervention problems, significant differences among conditions were found $F(3,112) = 72.93$, $p < .001$. Bonferroni post-hoc tests showed: WE < than all others, all $p < .001$; ErrEx < than TPS and PS, both $p < .001$; TPS > than PS, $p = .014$.

Table 1. Performance, mental effort, and time on task per condition. **Sig diffs indicated by ***

	WE (n = 29)	ErrEx (n = 28)	TPS (n = 27)	PS (n = 32)
Pre-test (0-101)	48.69 (17.62)	47.46 (20.27)	41.85 (16.77)	45.25 (16.26)
Embedded test (0-122)	92.21 (25.03)	79.79 (33.29)	85.30 (30.94)	80.69 (31.08)
Effort intervention (1-9)	**4.88 (1.44)***	5.31 (1.71)	6.70 (1.25)	6.27 (1.31)
Time intervention (min.)	**20.87 (5.50)***	40.48 (11.27)	67.11 (18.91)	56.82 (11.79)
Post-test (0-101)	68.21 (18.21)	65.68 (23.08)	67.78 (19.98)	69.88 (19.17)

4   Discussion and Conclusions

This study replicated the findings of [2], so across the two experiments, evidence was found for enormous efficiency benefits of worked example study, both in terms of effort and time investment, compared to all other conditions (except for effort on the erroneous examples in the present experiment).

The high-assistance instructional formats did not result in better learning outcomes than problem solving. We can only speculate about potential causes. One possibility is that the instructional videos on stoichiometry that were interspersed throughout the intervention in all conditions, and which sometimes included an example of how to apply a concept during problem solving, provided sufficient support for students in the problem-solving condition to benefit from practice, although that was slower and more effortful.

These surprising, and now replicated, results are worthy of further study, especially given that the interspersed conceptual videos, providing both theoretical and proce-dural explanations, are much closer to real educational practice and therefore give more ecologically valid information about the impact of various instructional formats on learning processes and outcomes.

This study, conducted in a classroom context, finds a clear time-efficiency advantage to worked examples. This result is a valuable finding for educational prac-tice, although one that should be verified in additional domains, with different materials.

Acknowledgements. The National Science Foundation funded this research, Award No. SBE-0836012 ("Pittsburgh Science of Learning Center").

References

1. Koedinger, K.R., Aleven, V.: Exploring the assistance dilemma in experiments with cogni-tive tutors. Educational Psychology Review **19**, 239–264 (2007)
2. McLaren, B.M., van Gog, T., Ganoe, C., Yaron, D., Karabinos, M.: Exploring the assistance dilemma: comparing instructional support in examples and problems. In: Trausan-Matu, S., Boyer, K.E., Crosby, M., Panourgia, K. (eds.) ITS 2014. LNCS, vol. 8474, pp. 354–361. Springer, Heidelberg (2014)
3. Paas, F.: Training strategies for attaining transfer of problem-solving skill in statistics: A cognitive load approach. Journal of Educational Psychology **84**, 429–434 (1992)

Domain Model for Adaptive Blended Courses on Basic Programming

Mikel Larrañaga and Ainhoa Álvarez[✉]

Department of Languages and Computer Systems,
University of the Basque Country UPV/EHU, Vitoria-Gasteiz, Basque Country
{mikel.larranaga,ainhoa.alvarez}@ehu.eus

Abstract. *Basic Programming* is a mandatory course that covers the fundamentals of programming in Computer Engineering degrees. During the last years, the authors have experimented different approaches to improve the course. For example, they have included Lego Mindstorms robots and visual programming environments in their lectures. However, the heterogeneity of the students in the course significantly affects the course development. To overcome this problem, the next step entails the adoption of adaptive learning systems in the frame of Blended Learning (B-Learning). In this context, the OWLish generic architecture has been defined. This paper centers on the adaptation of the Domain Model of OWLish to meet the requirements of programming courses.

Keywords: Programming tutor · Blended learning · Domain model

1 Technology Supported Learning Systems for Programming

There exist several kinds of Technology Supported Learning Systems, such as Learning Management Systems, Intelligent Tutoring Systems (ITSs), Collaborative Learning Systems or Adaptive and Intelligent Web-based Educational Systems. A positive relationship between such kinds of systems and student engagement and learning outcomes has been observed [1, 2], also in B-Learning scenarios [3].

Despite the existence of diverse tools to support both teaching and learning programming [4], most of them are oriented to the evaluation of implemented programs. Therefore, they are usually centered in the learning of a specific programming language such as C, Java or Lisp. However, this is not the real situation for many Programming courses. Although learning the syntax of a programming language is important, program design skills are essential. Furthermore, many teachers use several programming languages what should be taken into account during the same semester.

In the B-Learning frame, the authors' research group has developed OWLish [5], a conceptual architecture defined to meet the requirements of B-Learning environments. It integrates the components of the classic ITSs to provide adaptive behavior, with some other components to allow authoring processes, teacher management, and student control. It has been implemented as a dynamic system composed of a multi-agent structure called MAgAdI, which has been satisfactorily evaluated at the UPV/EHU [6]. However, its Domain Model (DM) does not allow representing all the characteristics of Programming courses. This paper presents the adaptation of the DM

© Springer International Publishing Switzerland 2015
C. Conati et al. (Eds.): AIED 2015, LNAI 9112, pp. 714–717, 2015.
DOI: 10.1007/978-3-319-19773-9_99

carried out to fulfill those needs. In this work, the DM relies in an ontology-based representation with two parts: terminology or TBox and instances or ABox [7].

2   Structure Ontology (TBox)

The DM represents the knowledge that must be mastered by students during their learning process in two levels: 1) the topics along with their relationships, and 2) the instructional resources (either presentation or evaluation resources) to be used.

The topic classification is based on the "Component Display Theory", which distinguishes four knowledge types: Facts, Concepts, Procedures and Principles [8]. The didactic Presentation and Evaluation resource attributes are based on LOM [9].

Every topic is described by an identifier and a description along with its pedagogical relationships (see Fig. 1). The composition (*hasComp*) structural relationship allows structuring the domain content, whereas the prerequisite (*hasPre*) sequential relationship restricts the order in which the topics can be covered.

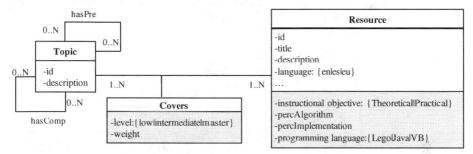

Fig. 1. TBox or Structure Ontology (new attributes are highlighted)

Topic mastering can be supported by different learning resources, and a resource might be related to various topics. This information is represented using the *covers* relationship (see Fig. 1). This relationship describes, for each resource, the topics it covers. In addition, the extent to which each topic is covered at (*Low*, *Intermediate* or *Master*) along with the *weight* of each topic on the resource is also represented.

In order to cope with the teaching requirements of Programming courses, the main changes have been introduced in the Resources class. Programming Courses aim at acquiring both program-design skills and implementation skills [10]. Two attributes indicate the learning goals the resource tackles: algorithm design (*perctAlgorithm*) or implementation (*perctImplementation*). The values assigned to those attributes indicate the extent each learning goal is tackled at on the didactic resource.

Bloom's taxonomy [11] classifies the different instructional objectives that educators might set for students. The taxonomy includes six levels related to the skills in the cognitive domain: *Knowledge, Comprehension, Application, Analysis, Synthesis,* and *Evaluation*. These categories are ordered from simple to complex and from concrete to abstract. In the *Basic Programming* course, teachers have identified that the resources can be oriented either to acquire *theoretical* (*Knowledge* and *Comprehension* objectives) or *practical* knowledge (*Application* objective). This is represented by the *InstructionalObjective* attribute.

3   Ontology for the Basic Programming Course (ABox)

The *Basic Programming* Ontology has been built upon the structure ontology i.e, it contains TBox-compliant statements describing the course contents. To define the ABox (instantiation of topics and existing relationships), the 5-step methodology defined in [12] was applied. In the first step, Glossary development, the essential objects and topics of the domain are selected and verbalized. Next, in the laddering step, the identified elements are structured defining taxonomies, parthood relationships, etc. Then, the obtained high-level elements are broken up into a set of more detailed elements (disintegration). Finally, they are hierarchically structured (categorization) and the visual structure is updated (refinement).

The glossary developed included, besides the topics students have to learn to master the *Basic Programming* course, topics related to the robots (i.e. *Sensor* or *Servomotor*), the application domain chosen for the design related learning sessions. Those topics were included as they are essential to properly describe some of the didactic resources developed for the course. Therefore, the ontology can be divided into two differentiated ontologies (see Fig 2): Learning Domain Ontology (LDO) and Application Domain Ontology (ADO_Robot).

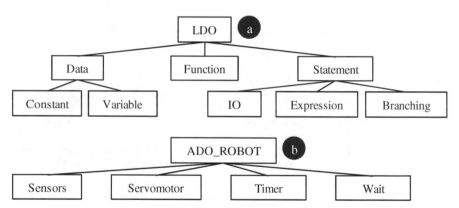

Fig. 2. Excerpt of the Learning (a) and Application Domain (b) ontologies

4   Evaluation

The main objective of the evaluation was the verification of the proposed Domain ontology, i.e., determining whether it is compatible or not with the course material (does the course material fit into the defined ontology?). Additionally, the evaluation also aimed at determining if such an ontology-based framework might help teachers to organize and design learning sessions.

To fulfill those goals, *ProgBle*, an implementation of OWLish for Programming Courses has been developed on top of a PostgreSQL database. Its Domain Model has been built on the Structure Ontology (TBox) and populated with the topics and relationships identified in the LDO and ADO_Robot ontologies. This experiment confirmed that the defined ontologies adequately support the definition of the course material. Moreover, the obtained didactic repository was satisfactorily used by teachers to help generating worksheets for lab sessions.

Given the satisfactory results, two main new work lines have been identified: The first one entails the improvement of the Student Model defined in OWLish to reflect the modifications introduced in the DM. The second one aims at the improvement of the recommendation techniques used in OWLish for adaptive problem selection so that it can also help teachers defining adaptive learning sessions.

Acknowledgements. This work has been supported by the Basque Government (IT722-13), the Gipuzkoa Council (FA-208/2014-B) and the University of the Basque Country (PIF/HBP 6819).

References

1. Chen, P.-S.D., Lambert, A.D., Guidry, K.R.: Engaging online learners: The impact of Web-based learning technology on college student engagement. Comput. Educ. **54**, 1222–1232 (2010)
2. Sabourin, J.L., Lester, J.C.: Affect and Engagement in Game-Based Learning Environments. IEEE Trans. Affect. Comput. **5**, 45–56 (2014)
3. López-Pérez, M.V., Pérez-López, M.C., Rodríguez-Ariza, L.: Blended learning in higher education: Students' perceptions and their relation to outcomes. Comput. Educ. **56**, 818–826 (2011)
4. Gómez-Albarrán, M.: The Teaching and Learning of Programming: A Survey of Supporting Software Tools. Comput. J. **48**, 130–144 (2005)
5. Álvarez, A., Martín, M., Fernández-Castro, I., Urretavizcaya, M.: Supporting Blended-Learning: tool requirements and solutions with OWLish. Interact. Learn. Environ. (in press)
6. Álvarez, A., Martín, M., Fernández-Castro, I., Urretavizcaya, M.: Blending traditional teaching methods with learning environments: Experience, cyclical evaluation process and impact with MAgAdI. Comput. Educ. **68**, 129–140 (2013)
7. Nkambou, R.: Modeling the domain: an introduction to the expert module. In: Nkambou, R., Bourdeau, J., Mizoguchi, R. (eds.) Advances in Intelligent Tutoring Systems, pp. 15–32. Springer, Heidelberg (2010)
8. Merril, M.D.: Component Display Theory. Instructional-Design Theories and Models: an overview of their current status, pp. 279–333. Lawrence Erlbaum Associates, Inc. (1983)
9. LTSC: 1484.12.1-2002 IEEE Standard for Learning Object Metadata (2002). http://standards.ieee.org/findstds/standard/1484.12.1-2002.html
10. Zhang, J.: An adaptive model customized for programming learning in e-learning. In: Int. Conf. on Computer Science and Information Technology (ICCSIT), pp. 443–447 (2010)
11. Anderson, L.W., Krathwohl, D.R.: A taxonomy for learning, teaching, and assessing: a revision of Bloom's taxonomy of educational objectives. Longman, New York (2001)
12. Gavrilova, T., Farzan, R., Brusilovsky, P.: One practical algorithm of creating teaching ontologies. Network- Based Education (NBE), pp. 29–37 (2005)

Learning Bayesian Networks for Student Modeling

Eva Millán[✉], Guiomar Jiménez, María-Victoria Belmonte,
and José-Luis Pérez-de-la-Cruz

ETSI Informática, University of Málaga, Campus de Teatinos 29080, Málaga, Spain
eva@lcc.uma.es

Abstract. In the last decade, there has been a growing interest in using Bayesian Networks (BN) in the student modelling problem. In order to develop a Bayesian Student Model (BSM), it is necessary to define the structure (nodes and links) and the parameters. Usually the structure can be elicited with the help of human experts (teachers), but the difficulty of the problem of parameter specification is widely recognized in this and other domains. In the work presented here we have performed a set of experiments to compare the performance of two Bayesian Student Models, whose parameters have been specified by experts and learnt from data respectively. Results show that both models are able to provide reasonable estimations for knowledge variables in the student model.

Keywords: Student modelling · Machine learning · Bayesian networks

1   Introduction

In the field of student modelling, Bayesian Networks (in what follows, BNs) have been proposed to represent and compute student's features, and their use is now well established: in the last decade, a number of Bayesian Student Models (BSMs) have been developed in a number of educational applications [1].

In order to define a BSM for a given field or task it is necessary to define both its structure (a graph) and a set of numerical parameters. While the structure can be easy to elicit, numerical parameters can become very difficult to estimate by teachers or human experts. A natural alternative is then to learn the parameters from a set of experimental data by means of machine learning techniques. In fact, such techniques have already been successfully used in the context of the student modelling problem [2]. However, will the diagnosed based on such learnt BSMs be more (or less) accurate than the diagnosis based on BSMs developed by human experts?.

To our knowledge, this problem has not been discussed before. In an interesting review of student modelling approaches in the last decade [1] it is shown that machine learning techniques have been used for different aspects of the student model, but "no adaptive and/or personalized tutoring system has used a compound student model which brings together an overlay model with machine learning algorithms or Bayesian networks".

© Springer International Publishing Switzerland 2015
C. Conati et al. (Eds.): AIED 2015, LNAI 9112, pp. 718–721, 2015.
DOI: 10.1007/978-3-319-19773-9_100

In a former work [3], a BSM for first-degree equations was defined and its diagnosis capabilities were evaluated with a set of 152 real students. The results showed that the BSM was able to provide accurate diagnosis at the various levels of granularity. In what follows we will call this model the *expert BSM*, to account for the fact that it relies entirely on expert (human) judgment. In the work presented in this paper, we have now used the data obtained in the former evaluation with the 152 real students to learn the parameters of the BSM. To this end, the structure of the expert BSM had to be simplified, because otherwise it would have been impossible to learn such a big number of parameters (110) with so little data (152 students). We have learned the parameters for four different structures and evaluated the diagnostic capabilities of the four *Learnt BSMs*. The results of this new study indicate that, even with such a little set of data, it is possible to learn the parameters and obtain reasonable estimations of student´s knowledge. However, the diagnosis is less accurate than in the case of the expert BSMs.

2   Materials and Methods

2.1   Previous Work: The Expert Bayesian Student Model

In order to understand the present study, we need to briefly present the settings and results of the previous study [3]. The expert BSM used included:

Knowledge variables (those labelled as C): that represent student's knowledge (1= the student knows, 0= the student does not know).
Evidence variables (those labelled as Q): these variables represent student's answers to questions that were posed to the students in the exam (1=correct answer, 0= wrong answer). For example, an actual question administered was:

$$Q_5: \text{Solve } 2 + x = 3.$$

Relations among variables are of two kinds: *aggregation* and *causal*. Real answers from 152 students from two different schools were input to and processed by the expert BSM, which then computed the probability of the knowledge variables. Independently of this BN computation, a team of three teachers independently graded each exam, providing an estimation for each knowledge variable. The inter-rater agreement was good enough, so the average of such values was used as a reliable measure of the hidden variables (the student's state of knowledge for each concept).

To evaluate the performance of this model, the two measures were compared. The validation method used in this study was the one proposed by Bland and Altman for clinical measurements of continuous variables: Bland–Altman plots and confidence intervals [4]. In this paper, only the confidence intervals will be shown (due to space limitations)[1].

---

[1] A complete version of this paper showing the Bayesian Network structures and Bland Altman plots is available upon request to the first author eva@lcc.uma.es

2.2   Methodology for Learning the Parameters

In order to be able to learn the parameters, the structure of expert BSM was simplified by removing the aggregation relationships. This simplification was taken because the structure of the expert BSM implied the learning of a great number of parameters (110), while the number of observations was relatively small (152 students). Four different structures were tested: a) *structure 1* (lower level of granularity): 8 elementary knowledge variables and their causal arcs; b) *structure 2* (higher level of granularity): global knowledge node and causal arcs to all question nodes; c) *structure 3* (intermediate level of granularity): intermediate knowledge nodes (C_i) and causal arcs from C_i to every question node that depends on C_i or on any of its children; and d) *structure 4* (intermediate level of granularity): similar to structure 3, but choosing a different set of four intermediate knowledge variables.

The parameters were learned by applying the EM algorithm [5]. The number of parameters to be learned for each of the 4 structures was 77, 39, 43 and 52, respectively.

3   Results

In each experiment i (i =1,2,3,4), the same structure i has been used for the two BSMs The first BSM uses the parameters of the original study (expert-BSM), while the second BSM uses the parameters estimated by the EM algorithm (learnt-BSM). The student´s answers have been used as input for both BSMs (expert and learnt), and the posterior probabilities of knowing each concept computed. These probabilities have been then compared to the average score given by teachers. Table 1 shows the results of this comparison: for every student and every knowledge variable, the difference between "real" (i.e. average estimation by teachers) and estimated variables has been calculated. Table 1 shows the mean (μ), standard deviation σ, 0.05 confidence interval (CI) and size of the confidence interval (s) of such differences:

Table 1. Results for the Expert BSMs vs Learnt BSMs

	Expert BSMs				Learnt BSMs			
Experiment	μ	σ	CI	s	μ	σ	CI	s
1	0.01	0.18	(0.003, 0.017)	0.014	-0.05	0.54	(-0.084, 0.023)	0.107
2	0.03	0.07	(0.020, 0.040)	0.020	-0.04	0.3	(-0.086, 0.009)	0.095
3	0.03	0.17	(0.010, 0.050)	0.040	-0.25	0.34	(-0.286, -0.224)	0.062
4	0.01	0.18	(-0.003, 0.026)	0.029	0.04	0.34	(0.016, 0.070)	0.054

Further information was also obtained by analyzing Bland-Altman plots. In experiment 1, the Bland-Altman plots showed that the bigger deviations occur in intermediate values (those whose probability of being known is 0.5, which are usually the more difficult to diagnose). In experiment 2, Bland-Altman plots did not show a clear pattern: deviations were big for some intermediate and for some extreme values. In experiments 3 and 4, Bland-Altman plots showed an unexpected result. The learnt

BSMs were systematically underestimating variables "poorly known" (values below 0.5) and overestimating variables "well known" (values over 0.5). In experiment 3, as sσ<0, underestimating is more intense that overestimating. In experiment 4, $\sigma \sim 0$, so underestimating and overestimating seem to be of similar strength. This performance is surprising, but not necessarily undesirable. The learnt BSMs are "magnifying" something that is implicit in the student's answers.

4   Conclusions and Future Work

In this paper we have presented the results of a set of experiments designed to evaluate the performance of several learnt Bayesian Student Models. Best performance was obtained for the model with just one hidden (or knowledge) variable, but reasonably good results were also obtained in other cases. In the case of the structures representing the intermediate levels of the granularity hierarchy, it seems that the learnt BSMs tend to polarize the results when compared to a more uniform estimation provided by the expert BSM. None of the four learnt models exhibited better performance than the human-adjusted models. Probably this result is due to the limitations inherent to this study. The first limitation is the size of the training set (152 cases) compared to the number of parameters to be learnt (ranging from 39 to 77 depending on the experiment). Another limitation is that the real state of knowledge of the student is unknown; therefore we are trying to infer variables that are intrinsically hidden.

All in one, we think that results presented here can be considered as a first encouraging step towards the use of machine learning techniques in overlay student models, which is still an open problem. With larger datasets (as planned in our future work), it seems reasonable to assume that the results would be much better.

Acknowledgments. First author would like to thank Dr. Rose Luckin and London Knowledge Lab for providing a rich research environment in which this work was partially elaborated.

References

1. Chrysafiadi, K., Virvou, M.: Student modelling approaches: A literature review for the last decade. Expert Systems with Applications **40**(11), 4715–4722 (2013)
2. Arroyo, I., Woolf, B.P.: Inferring learning and attitudes from a bayesian network of log file data. In: Proceedings of AIED 2005, pp. 33–40 (2005)
3. Millán, E., Descalco, L., Castillo, G., Oliveira, P., Diogo, S.: Using Bayesian networks to improve knowledge assessment. Computers and Education **60**(1), 436–447 (2013)
4. Hamilton, C., Stamey, J.: Using Bland-Altman to assess agreement between two medical devices – don't forget the confidence intervals. Journal Clinical Monitoring and Computing, 331–333 (2007)
5. Dempster, A.P., Laird, N.M., Rubin, A.D.: Maximum Likelihood from Incomplete Data via the EM Algorithm. Journal of the Royal Statistical Society Series B **39**(1), 1–38 (1977)

Tutorial Dialogue Modes in a Large Corpus of Online Tutoring Transcripts

Donald M. Morrison[1][(✉)], Benjamin Nye[1], Vasile Rus[1], Sarah Snyder[2],
Jennifer Boller[2], and Kenneth Miller[2]

[1] Institute for Intelligent Systems, University of Memphis, Memphis, Tennessee, USA
dmmrrson@memphis.edu
[2] Tutor.com, New York, USA

Abstract. Building on previous work in this area, we provide a description and justification for a new way of identifying modes and mode switches in tutorial dialogues, part of a coding scheme involving 16 modes and 125 distinct dialogue acts. We also present preliminary results from an analysis of 1,438 human-annotated transcripts, consisting of more than 90,000 turns. Among other findings, this analysis shows subtle differences in the "mode architecture" of successful vs. less successful sessions, as judged by expert tutors.

Keywords: Human tutorial dialogue · Dialogue mode · Data mining · Hybrid tutoring systems

1 Introduction

The notion of a "tutorial dialogue mode," introduced by Cade [1] and later taken up by Boyer's group at the University of North Carolina [2,3] is an important contribution to the analysis of tutorial dialogue. By acknowledging the presence of hidden, higher-level dialogue states, dialogue mode theory allows researchers to characterize the ways in which sequences of individual dialogue acts relate to each other, and to these hidden states. It also connects purely linguistic constructs, such as dialogue acts, to pedagogical constructs such as tactics, strategies, and metastrategies [4]. Within this framework, an individual dialogue act is understood as a tactic, modes are associated with strategies, and the choices a tutor makes in switching from one mode to another reflect a metastrategy.

2 Methodology

This research is part of a larger data mining project aimed at extracting useful knowledge from a corpus of more than 244,000 transcripts of online tutoring sessions in Algebra and Physics supplied by Tutor.com, a provider of online tutorial services for children and young adults [5]. The data used for the analysis reported here was based on a representative sample of 1,438 transcripts pulled at random from the full corpus,

© Springer International Publishing Switzerland 2015
C. Conati et al. (Eds.): AIED 2015, LNAI 9112, pp. 722–725, 2015.
DOI: 10.1007/978-3-319-19773-9_101

and annotated by a panel of 19 subject matter experts (SMEs) selected from a pool of some 2,800 Tutor.com tutors using a rigorous screening process.

We developed a mode taxonomy that built on the (a) Cade and (b) Boyer taxonomies, but was extended to include additional modes that we identified from (c) a survey of Tutor.com tutors, (d) a content analysis of Tutor.com literature, (e) and, in one case (Metacognition), a suggestion by a member of an external advisory panel. The resulting taxonomy (shown below with sources [a,b,c,d,e]) defines 16 dialogue modes:

Assessment [c]	Modeling [a,c]	Scaffolding [a,b,c]
Fading [a,c]	Opening [a,c]	Sensemaking [c]
Metacognition [e]	Problem Identification [a,c]	Session Summary [c]
Method Identification [c]	Process Negotiation [c]	Telling [a,b,c]
Method Roadmap [c]	Rapport Building [c]	Wrap Up/Closing [a,c]
Off Topic [a,b]		

The full taxonomy for dialogue acts and modes was iteratively refined over of two months, and working in close collaboration with the SMEs, an accompanying coding manual was also written, with coding guidelines and numerous examples.

3   Findings: Distribution of Dialogue Modes by Session Success

In addition to tagging dialogue acts and mode switches, annotators were asked to score each session on two dimensions—Educational Soundness (ES) and Evidence of Learning (EL2)—using a 5-point Likert scale. The first is a term that is used by Tutor.com professional staff to describe sessions that are conducted in such a way as to ensure that not only do students get the correct solution to a problem, but they are also given an opportunity to understand underling concepts. The second, EL2, was intended as a judgment as to whether the student actually had acquired new understanding, regardless of how the session was conducted. Figure 1 presents contrasting profiles of modes in sessions that were judged to be high on both ES and EL2 (the more "successful" sessions) and those that were low on both scores. The height of the box represents the average amount of time devoted to that mode, while the vertical position roughly represents the average position of dialogue acts devoted to that mode within a session, from 0.0 (the beginning of a session), to 1.0, the end.

Note the following:

1. While Scaffolding is the dominant mode in both successful and less successful sessions, it is even more dominant in the more successful sessions.
2. More Scaffolding and Fading occur in more successful sessions, while less time is devoted to Modeling, Telling, and Problem ID. In other words, in the more successful sessions, students are doing more of the work.
3. In the more successful sessions, Modeling tends to occur, on average, earlier than Scaffolding, whereas in the less successful ones, the average position is more toward the middle, sometimes due to repeated periods of Modeling.

4. Although the amount of time devoted to "early" Rapport Building segments is roughly the same for both categories, tutors and students in more successful sessions devote more time to Rapport Building at the close of a session.

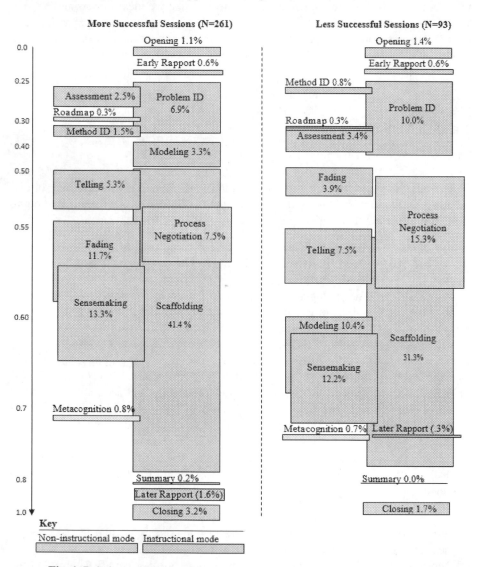

Fig. 1. Relative position and time devoted to different modes by session success

4   Discussion

The identification of dialogue modes is a useful tool in the analysis of tutorial dialogue transcripts. By linking individual dialogue acts to higher-level states, we were able to identify patterns in our data that reflect the tactics, strategies, and metastrategies that expert tutors use to help students learn. The results should be particularly interesting given the size and nature of the corpus (1,438 transcripts of sessions conducted by professional tutors), and the fact that the annotations were completed by a select group of expert tutors, who were also involved in developing the coding scheme itself.

Acknowledgements. The research described here is supported by Tutor.com, an IAC company, under a contract with the U.S. Department of Defense Advanced Distributed Learning Initiative (W911QY-14-C-0019). We also acknowledge the contributions of our subject matter experts and transcript annotators: Arlene L., Chad B., Christina R., Damian N., Daniel S., Gabriel L., Jeffrey W., Jeremy B., Joshua R., Katelynne S., Kristin M., Lindsay F., Lisa G. Y., Neil L., Nicole D., Promise C., Ryan S., Steven G., Stuart J., and Taha T. Without their careful attention to detail, thoughtful advice, and hard work, this important research would not have been possible.

References

1. Cade, W.L., Copeland, J.L., Person, N.K., D'Mello, S.K.: Dialogue modes in expert tutoring. In: Woolf, B.P., Aïmeur, E., Nkambou, R., Lajoie, S. (eds.) ITS 2008. LNCS, vol. 5091, pp. 470–479. Springer, Heidelberg (2008)
2. Boyer, K.E., Ha, E., Wallis, M.D., Phillips, R., Vouk, M.A., Lester, J.C.: Discovering tutorial dialogue strategies with hidden Markov models. In: AIED, pp. 141–148, July 2009
3. Boyer, K.E., Phillips, R., Ingram, A., Ha, E.Y., Wallis, M., Vouk, M., Lester, J.: Investigating the relationship between dialogue structure and tutoring effectiveness: A Hidden Markov Modeling approach. International Journal of Artificial Intelligence in Education **21**(1), 65–81 (2011)
4. Morrison, D.M., Rus, V.: Moves, tactics, strategies, and metastrategies: defining the nature of human pedagogical interaction. In: Sottilare, R., Hu, X., Graesser, A., Goldberg, B. (eds.) Design Recommendations for Adaptive Intelligent Tutoring Systems: Adaptive Instructional Strategies, vol. II. Army Research Laboratory (2014)
5. Morrison, D.M., Nye, B., Samei, B., Datla, V.V., Kelly, C., Rus, V.: Building an intelligent PAL from the Tutor. com session database-phase 1: data mining. In: Proceedings of the 7th International Conference on Educational Data Mining, pp. 335–336, July 2014

Data-Driven Worked Examples Improve Retention and Completion in a Logic Tutor

Behrooz Mostafavi[(⊠)], Guojing Zhou, Collin Lynch, Min Chi,
and Tiffany Barnes

Department of Computer Science, North Carolina State University,
Raleigh, North Carolina 27695, US
{bzmostaf,gzhou3,cflynch,mchi,tmbarnes}@ncsu.edu

Abstract. Research shows that expert-crafted worked examples can have a positive effect on student performance. To investigate the potential for data-driven worked examples to achieve similar results, we generated worked examples for the Deep Thought logic tutor, and conducted an experiment to assess their impact on performance. Students who received data-driven worked examples were much more likely to complete the tutor, and completed the tutor in less time. This study demonstrates that worked examples, automatically generated from student data, can be used to improve student learning in tutoring systems.

Keywords: Worked examples · Data-driven · Problem-solving

1 Introduction and Related Work

In this paper we describe our study on the impact of data-driven worked examples in Deep Thought (DT). DT is a data-driven tutoring system for propositional logic that provides automatic verification of student proofs, and provides high-or-low proficiency problem sets at level intervals based on a student's performance [2].

Many intelligent tutors use pedagogical decision processes where the system is responsible for selecting the next action to take [4]. Pedagogical strategies are system-level policies that are used to decide what action to take when multiple options are available. We focus on one such decision: worked examples vs. problem-solving. When a student begins a new problem, the system can decide whether to ask them to complete it (*problem solving*); or provide them with a completed solution for review (*worked example*).

While numerous laboratory studies have shown the benefits of combining worked examples with problem solving [1], it is not always clear how they should be combined or how often each should be given. In a recent survey of the literature Najar et al. concluded that the research is still inconclusive on when worked examples should be given, how they should be scaffolded, and how they should be designed [3]. Consequently, most existing systems choose problem solving [5].

We investigated the impact of incorporating data-driven worked examples on student performance in DT. While worked examples involved in prior research

© Springer International Publishing Switzerland 2015
C. Conati et al. (Eds.): AIED 2015, LNAI 9112, pp. 726–729, 2015.
DOI: 10.1007/978-3-319-19773-9_102

were either hand created by domain experts or using expert solutions generated from expert systems, the worked examples in this study were extracted from prior student data. We hypothesize that the addition of data-driven worked examples will reduce the number of students who drop out of the tutor before completing all problems. We also hypothesize that the ordering of worked examples versus problem solving can have an impact on completion time and dropout. This is the first literature to investigate whether data-driven worked examples can be used to improve student performance.

2 Methods

DT was designed to add worked examples to the existing problem set. We derived a worked example for each problem in the DT student data corpus by selecting the shortest student solution that contained all of the logic rules that the particular problem was constructed to illustrate. Annotations for worked example steps were procedurally generated. In a worked example, students view sequential steps, one-by-one, until the complete solution has been constructed on the screen using data from our corpus. Students can move backward and forward between steps, using arrow keys, as needed.

Worked examples were assigned randomly on a per-problem basis. When students began a problem the system would decide whether to give a worked example or require them to work it themselves. This policy was balanced to ensure that the students worked at least one problem per level. An additional problem was added to the end of each level, which mirrored the rules and problem solving strategies as the other problems in the respective levels. This problem provides a built-in post-test on each level of the tutor, for comparison of performance of the same problem set with and without worked examples.

DT with data-driven worked examples was tested to determine its effect on tutor completion, student dropout, and how the order of worked examples affects student performance. DT was used as a mandatory homework assignment by students in two computer science discrete mathematics courses (WE group, $n = 261$). This data was compared to data collected from the previous version of DT with no worked examples for tutor completion and dropout comparison (NoWE group, $n = 47$).

3 Results and Discussion

Our first hypothesis is that data-driven worked examples would increase students' completion rate. Table 1 shows the number of problems solved, worked examples received, and total time spent in tutor for the WE and NoWE groups. Students in both groups solved the same number of problems in the tutor on average with no significant difference between them ($p = 0.327, power = 1$). However, the WE group spent 27% less time in tutor on average than the NoWE, even with the added worked examples. This was marginally significant ($p = 0.063$).

Table 1. The number of problems solved, number of worked examples received, and total tutor time for the WE and NoWE groups

Group	# Solved Problems			# Worked Examples			Total Tutor Time (mins)		
	Mean	*Median*	*StDev*	*Mean*	*Median*	*StDev*	*Mean*	*Median*	*StDev*
WE	14.12	13	5.09	7.53	8	1.35	224.4	97.7	346.5
NoWE	13.08	13	4.94	–	–	–	307.2	244.4	263.4

We used percent completion as a measure of overall success for each group of students. Percent completion is a measure of *how far* students progress through the tutor, on average. Table 2(a) shows the average percentage of tutor completion by group. Student dropout is defined as the termination of tutor activity at any point in the tutor prior to completing all of the assigned problems. It is a measure of *how many* students are using the system at any point in time. Table 2(b) summarizes the number of students who completed and dropped out of the tutor across both groups. Table 2(c) compares the retention trends for the WE and NoWE groups at the end of each level. From these figures, it is evident that the worked examples are dramatically improving retention and tutor completion.

Our results show that students using Deep Thought with worked examples completed more of the assigned problems and were less likely to drop out. We found a statistically significant difference between the groups in terms of percent completion (one-way ANOVA: $F(2, 308) = 6.38$, $p = 0.014$). The average percentage of tutor completion was significantly greater for the WE group than for NoWE (94% vs. 79.8%), an improvement of 14.2%. Thus adding worked examples to Deep Thought enabled students to complete more of the tutor. Additionally, the WE group was significantly more likely than the NoWE group to finish the tutor, as shown in Table 2(c). A much smaller percentage of the WE group dropped out of the tutor (9.6%) compared to the NoWE group (44.7%). Moreover the WE students who dropped out did so at a later point than the dropouts in the NoWE group. This indicates that the addition of worked examples increases the chances that students will be able to finish the tutor, and increases the percentage of problems they will complete.

Table 2. (a) Percentage of tutor completion by group. A * indicates significance. (b) Student completion of the tutor by group. Dropped indicates that the student did not complete Deep Thought. (c) Percentage of students remaining in tutor at the end of each level by group.

(a)	Mean	StDev	(b)	Completed	Dropped	Total
WE	94.02*	21.07	**WE**	236 *(90.4%)*	25 *(9.6%)*	261
NoWE	79.79	29.88	**NoWE**	26 *(55.3%)*	21 *(44.7%)*	47
			Total	262	46	308

(c)	Level 1	Level 2	Level 3	Level 4	Level 5	Level 6
WE	96.2	95.0	93.9	92.7	92.3	90.4
NoWE	93.6	87.2	87.2	78.7	72.3	55.3

Our second hypothesis is that the ordering of worked examples and problem solving will affect student performance. We used the additional end-of-level post-test problems in DT3 to study the effect of the ordering of worked examples and problem solving practice in each level. We classified problem instances into two groups, *WE–PS* (where students viewed worked examples and then solved problems before the level's post-test problem) and *PS–WE* (where students solved problems, then viewed a worked example before the level's post-test problem). Our initial results show no significant differences between the *WE–PS* and *PS–WE* groups for step count and elapsed time. However, in levels 3 and 4 of DT, students in the low-proficiency track took significantly longer on each step in the post-test problem in both levels 3 and 4 if they saw worked examples before attempting to solve problems in these levels. These results indicate that there may be a disadvantage for low proficiency students to see efficiently-worked examples chosen from our corpus, however, further analysis is required. Therefore, our hypothesis that the ordering of worked examples versus problem solving would impact student performance was not confirmed.

4   Conclusions and Future Work

This study investigated the impact of data-driven worked examples on student performance in the Deep Thought logic proof tutor. Our results show that students who received with worked examples completed more of the required problems and were less likely to drop out of the tutor than those who only engaged in problem solving . Our results indicate that worked examples are very beneficial in Deep Thought. Our overall analyses do not show significant effects due to ordering of worked examples and problem solving across the tutor levels, however we found a difference in time per solution step in the ordering of practice problem types in levels 3 and 4 of the tutor, warranting further investigation. In future work, we plan to further investigate the impact of worked examples, and to apply machine learning to derive individualized pedagogical policies to select worked examples when it would be most beneficial for particular students.

References

1. Atkinson, R.K., Derry, S.J., Renkl, A., Wortham, D.: Learning from examples: Instructional principles from the worked examples research. Review of educational research **70**(2), 181–214 (2000)
2. Mostafavi, B., Eagle, M., Barnes, T.: Towards data-driven mastery learning. In: Proc. Learning, Analytics, and Knowledge (LAK 2015) (to appear, 2015)
3. Najar, A., Mitrovic, A.: Should we use examples in intelligent tutors? In: Proc. Computers in Education, pp. 5–7 (2012)
4. VanLehn, K.: The Behavior of Tutoring Systems. International Journal of Artificial Intelligence in Education **16**(2), 227–265 (2006)
5. Vanlehn, K., et al.: The Andes physics tutoring system: Lessons learned. International Journal of Artificial Intelligence in Education **15**(3), 147–204 (2005)

Improving Engagement in an E-Learning Environment

Kevin Mulqueeny[1(✉)], Leigh A. Mingle[1], Victor Kostyuk[1],
Ryan S. Baker[2], and Jaclyn Ocumpaugh[3]

[1] Reasoning Mind, Houston, TX, USA
Kevin.Mulqueeny@reasoningmind.org
[2] Teachers College, Columbia University, New York, NY, USA
[3] Worcester Polytechnic Institute, Worcester, MA, USA

Abstract. Student engagement indicators, such as behavior and affective states, are known to impact learning. This study uses an established quantitative field observation method to evaluate engagement during students' use of a new version of an online learning system (Reasoning Mind's Genie 3). Improvements to Genie 3's design intended to increase engagement include: using virtual small-group tutoring environment, separating text and speech, and using indicators to focus students' attention. In this study, Genie 3 classrooms outperformed a traditional classroom on key indicators of engagement, including time on-task, engaged concentration, and boredom. These results have important implications for further improvements to Reasoning Mind, for the design of other online learning systems, and for general pedagogical practices.

Keywords: Blended learning · Time-On-Task · Engaged concentration

1   Introduction

Several prior studies have found a relationship between student learning and their affective state when using the system. Findings suggest that confusion and engaged concentration (or "flow") are positively associated with learning, while boredom leads to poor learning outcomes [1–3].   One blended learning program that has successfully increased engagement in elementary school mathematics is Reasoning Mind (RM).

Observations of RM's Genie 2 platform estimated that RM students experienced engaged concentration 71% of the time and boredom only 10% [4]. RM works with expert teachers to automate as many instructional experiences as possible [5]. Students study on computers during class time, freeing teachers to conduct targeted interventions.

The latest RM platform, Genie 3, further refines earlier attempts to incorporate instructional design principles known to increase engagement in online instruction [6]. Reasoning Mind uses several principals to increase engagement: *Personalization* – simulating a small tutoring session, using conversational speech; *Multimedia* – lessons combine text, speech, and graphics; *Contiguity and Coherence* – illustrations are aligned to examples and unessential text is minimized; *Modality* – narrative, auditory instruction is prioritized over text; and *Segmenting* – lessons are segmented into

© Springer International Publishing Switzerland 2015
C. Conati et al. (Eds.): AIED 2015, LNAI 9112, pp. 730–733, 2015.
DOI: 10.1007/978-3-319-19773-9_103

manageable parts. The current study replicates observational methods used to study engagement with the Genie 2 platform [4].

2 Engagement in Genie 3 Compared to Traditional Instruction

We used the Baker-Rodrigo-Ocumpaugh Monitoring Protocol, or BROMP [7], to measure student engagement in two groups: one using the Genie 3 platform and one receiving traditional, teacher-driven classroom instruction.

2.1 Method

Design. Two BROMP coders [cf. 7] recorded student behavior and affect in a pre-determined order. Behavior codes included *On Task–Independent*, *On Task–Conversation*, *On Task–Pull Out*, and *Off Task*. Affective states included *Engaged Concentration, Boredom, Frustration, Confusion*, and *Delight*.

Participants. We observed twelve sixth-grade classrooms in a majority Latino, urban Texas school district. In the fall, 118 students used the Genie 3 curriculum and 95 students received traditional classroom instruction. In the spring 109 students used RM and 132 used the traditional curriculum.

2.2 Results

We used an arcsine transformation to normalize the distribution of proportional data [9]. An ANOVA showed a significant difference in the average proportions of all behavior categories between the Genie 3 and traditional groups (Figure 1). Genie 3 students spent more time in on task – independent ($p < 0.001$), more time in on task – pull out ($p < 0.001$), less time in on-task – conversation ($p < 0.001$), and less time off-task ($p < 0.001$).

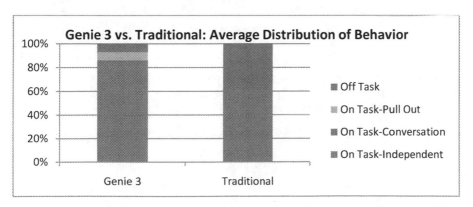

Fig. 1. Behavior distribution

Similarly, we used an arcsine transformation for affective categories. The two groups differed significantly in all affective states except frustration (Figure 2). Genie 3 students showed higher levels of engaged concentration ($p < 0.001$), less boredom ($p < 0.001$), less confusion ($p < 0.001$) and less delight ($p < 0.01$) than students in the traditional classroom. There was not a significant difference in frustration between conditions ($p = 0.054$).

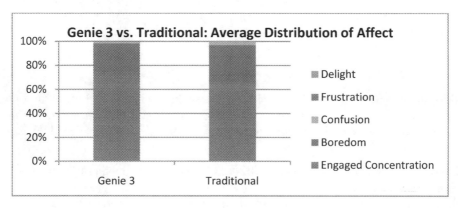

Fig. 2. Affect distribution

3   Discussion

This study demonstrated that blended learning can offer impressive student engagement rates compared to traditional instruction. Students showed much higher levels of engaged concentration in Genie 3, and they were much less bored. This is likely due to the individualized nature of blended learning, in addition to the various e-learning principles embodied by the program. When each student is going at his or her own pace through a lesson, students have fewer opportunities to disengage.

One notable weakness of the Genie 3 system is a marked decrease in on-task conversation, meaning that the students were spending less time learning cooperatively. This is likely due to the use of headphones to provide audio content. This limits the possibility of peer interaction during lessons.

Students were not randomly assigned to groups and there were no baseline measures, so future studies are needed to uncover which e-learning principles, as embodied by RM, have an impact on student engagement.

References

1. de Baker, R.S.J., D'Mello, S.K., Rodrigo, M.M.T., Graesser, A.C.: Better to be frustrated than bored: The incidence, persistence, and impact of learners' cognitive-affective states during interactions with three different computer-based learning environments. International Journal of Human-Computer Studies **68**(4), 223–241 (2010)

2. Craig, S.D., Graesser, A.C., Sullins, J., Gholson, B.: Affect and learning: An exploratory look into the role of affect in learning with AutoTutor. Journal of Educational Media **29**(3), 241–250 (2004)
3. D'Mello, S., Graesser, A.: Dynamics of affective states during complex learning. Learning and Instruction **22**(2), 145–157 (2012)
4. Ocumpaugh, J., de Baker, R.S.J., Gaudino, S., Labrum, M.J., Dezendorf, T.: Field observations of engagement in reasoning mind. In: Lane, H., Yacef, K., Mostow, J., Pavlik, P. (eds.) AIED 2013. LNCS, vol. 7926, pp. 624–627. Springer, Heidelberg (2013)
5. Khachatryan, G.A., Romashov, A.V., Khachatryan, A.R., Gaudino, S.J., Khachatryan, J.M., Guarian, K.R., Yufa, N.V.: Reasoning Mind Genie 2: An intelligent tutoring system as a vehicle for international transfer of instructional methods in mathematics. International Journal of Artificial Intelligence in Education **24**(3), 333–382 (2014)
6. Clark, R.C., Mayer, R.E.: E-Learning and the Science of Instruction: Proven Guidelines for Consumers and Designers of Multimedia Learning, 3rd edn. Pfeiffer, San Francisco (2011)
7. Ocumpaugh, J., de Baker, R.S.J., Rodrigo, M.M.T.: Baker-Rodrigo Observation Method Protocol (BROMP) 1.0 Training Manual version 1.0. Technical Report. New York, NY: EdLab. Manila, Philippines: Ateneo Laboratory for the Learning Sciences (2012). http://www.columbia.edu/~rsb2162/BROMP%20QFO%20Training%20Manual%201.0.pdf
8. Miller, W.L., Baker, R.S., Labrum, M.J., Petsche, K., Wagner, A.Z.: Automated detection of proactive remediation by teachers in Reasoning Mind classrooms. Manuscript in preparation (2014)
9. McDonald, J.H.: Handbook of Biological Statistics. Sparky House, Baltimore (2014)

Using Eye Tracking to Identify Learner Differences in Example Processing

Amir Shareghi Najar, Antonija Mitrovic[✉], and Kourosh Neshatian

Department of Computer Science and Software Engineering,
University of Canterbury, Christchurch, New Zealand
{amir.shareghinajar,tanja.mitrovic,
kourosh.neshatian}@canterbury.ac.nz

Abstract. In this paper, we focus on how students with different levels of knowledge study worked examples. In order to comprehend SQL examples, the learner needs to understand the database which is used as the context. We analysed eye movements collected from a quasi experiment, and found a significant difference in the amount of attention students paid to database schemas.

Keywords: Worked examples · Eye tracking · Learner differences

1 Introduction

Numerous studies have shown that learning from worked examples is beneficial for novices in comparison to unsupported problem solving, e.g. [1,2]. A worked example (WE) consists of the solution and additional explanations, thus providing knowledge that the learner might lack. Worked examples allow the learner to focus on important concepts, thus greatly reducing the cognitive load [1]. Recently researchers have started comparing learning from examples to Tutored Problem Solving (TPS) in ITSs [3,4], showing that learning from WE reduces learning time. Some studies have found no difference in the amount of learnt knowledge [5] between those two modes of learning. Our previous study [6] showed that learning from alternating WEs with problems is superior to learning from TPS or WE only, when the sequence of problems/examples is fixed. In a later study, we compared a fixed sequence of WE and TPS to an adaptive strategy which decided whether to present an example or a problem based on the student's performance [7]. The adaptive strategy was superior to the fixed alternating sequence.

In order to further improve our adaptive strategy, we decided to investigate whether there are meaningful differences in example processing between students with different levels of SQL knowledge. In this paper, we report on a study in which we collected eye gaze data, which provides fine-grained information about how learners study worked examples. Section 2 presents the version of SQL-Tutor used in the study, the experimental design and the results of the study. We also present conclusions and the directions of future work.

© Springer International Publishing Switzerland 2015
C. Conati et al. (Eds.): AIED 2015, LNAI 9112, pp. 734–737, 2015.
DOI: 10.1007/978-3-319-19773-9_104

2   Study

The study focused on the worked-example mode [6] of SQL-Tutor (Figure 1), which presents a worked example at the top, followed by an explanation, and a database schema. Once a student finishes studying the example, the system presents a self-explanation prompt (top right pane in Figure 1). We defined three Areas Of Interest (AOIs), corresponding to worked examples (W), explanations (E) and the database schema (D). The participants were 22 volunteers from a database course at the University of Canterbury, who also participated in our previous study [7]. The participants studied six WEs given in the fixed order, in individual, one-hour long sessions. Eye gaze data was collected using the Tobii TX300 eye tracker. We have not administered pre/post-tests, as they would take 20-30 minutes and therefore leave very short time for learning. Instead, we used the pre/post test results from the previous study [7], held one week before the start of the current study.

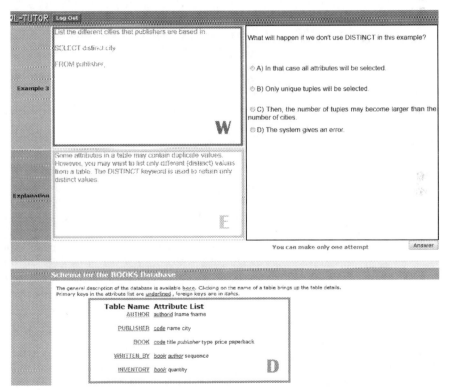

Fig. 1. A screenshot of the WE mode of SQL-Tutor, with the three AOIs marked W, E and D

We wanted to compare eye-gaze data for weak learners (WL) and advanced learners (AL). It was not appropriate to determine the two groups solely on the basis of the pre/post test scores from the previous study. Instead, we used the K-Medoids algorithm [8] using pre- and post-test scores from the previous study, and the P-SE scores and learning time from the current study. We labelled the two resulting clusters WL and AL (Table 1). The average scores of WL on the pre-test, post-test and P-SE prompts are lower than the average for the whole group (the *Total* column), and they also spent less time studying examples. There are significant differences between the two groups on the pre-test, post-test and P-SE scores.

Table 1. Statistics about the two clusters (standard deviations provided in brackets)

	Total (22)	WL (12)	AL (10)	p
Pre-test (%)	40 (13)	33 (11)	48 (11)	<0.01
Post-test (%)	70 (16)	63 (16)	79 (12)	0.02
P-SE (%)	83 (13)	76 (11)	92 (9)	<0.01
Time (min)	21.5 (9)	20 (8.6)	23 (9.8)	0.44

We divided recordings into segments corresponding to individual examples, and removed segments with low recording quality (from 3 participants). Additionally, one participant studied examples only after receiving P-SE prompts, and therefore we eliminated this participant's data. The results reported are produced by analysing the data for the remaining 18 participants. For each AOI, we extracted the average individual fixation duration (s), total fixation duration (s), fixation count, average duration of visits to a particular AOI, total visit duration (s), and visit count. The Mann-Whitney U test identified significant differences between the two groups only for D_{AOI}, but not for the other two AOIs. The advanced learners fixated on D_{AOI} more than weak learners. Moreover, total visit duration shows that AL spent significantly longer time studying database schema than WL.

We then identified eye-gaze patterns, showing a student's attention on an AOI or eye gaze movements from one AOI to another, over a short time period (~1.5s). We identified four types of patterns: reading (labelled by the AOI which the student examined, e.g. W); mixed reading (when a student reads one area and glances shortly at another area, e.g. EdE), transferring (when the student's eye gaze moves from one area to another, e.g. WE) and scanning, labelled S (normally appearing at the beginning of the session, when a student sees the interface for the first time or when they are searching for information). Table 2 reports the percentages of participants who used various patterns, and also the average pattern frequencies per group. The Mann-Whitney U test revealed no significant difference between the total number of patterns used by WL and AL. The AL group used the D and ED patterns significantly and marginally significantly more often than WL (p = 0.03 and p = 0.08 respectively). The D pattern was used by 90% of advanced students compared to only 25% of WL. The ED pattern was not used by WL at all, while half of AL have used it.

From our teaching experience, a good understanding of a database schema is critical in order to understand WEs and solve problems. Overall, the results reveal that the advanced students paid more attention to the database schema than the weak learners. The gaze plots also showed that AL and WL students studied examples differently.

The results suggest that the ITS could provide hints to weak learners, to examine the database schema. One of the limitations of our study is the small sample size. It would be interesting to observe how patterns change as students become more knowledgeable. Furthermore, it is possible to use the student's eye-gaze behaviour in order to provide additional support; e.g. if the student fixates on a part of the example for a long time, the system could provide additional explanations. Eye-gaze data may be further combined with the student model to provide adaptive examples.

Table 2. Pattern statistics

	Students using patterns		Average pattern frequency		
	AL (10)	WL (8)	AL (10)	WL (8)	p
All patterns			18.60 (5.19)	18.75 (5.26)	0.97
W	100%	100%	4.8 (2.2)	5.25 (1.39)	0.83
E	90%	100%	2.2 (1.32)	2.375 (1.19)	0.83
D	90%	25%	1.1 (0.57)	0.375 (0.74)	0.03*
WeW	40%	63%	1.2 (1.81)	0.625 (0.52)	0.90
WdW	50%	25%	1.4 (1.84)	0.25 (0.46)	0.24
EwE	60%	75%	1.2 (1.32)	2.125 (2.1)	0.41
EdE	20%	38%	0.3 (0.67)	0.5 (0.76)	0.57
WE	90%)0	100%	3.5 (2.01)	4.625 (1.69)	0.24
WD	40%	25%	0.4 (0.52)	0.25 (0.46)	0.63
EW	50%	50%	0.7 (0.82)	0.875 (1.13)	0.90
ED	50%	0%	0.5 (0.53)	0	0.08**
DW	30%	0%	0.3 (0.48)	0	0.32
DE	0%	25%	0	0.25 (0.46)	0.41
S	70%	100%	1 (0.94)	1.25 (0.46)	0.41

References

1. Sweller, J., Ayres, P., Kalyuga, S.: Cognitive load theory. Springer (2011)
2. Atkinson, R.K., Derry, S.J., Renkl, A., Wortham, D.: Learning from examples: instructional principles from the worked examples research. Review of Educational Research **70**, 181–214 (2000)
3. Koedinger, K., Aleven, V.: Exploring the assistance dilemma in experiments with cognitive tutors. Educational Psychology Review **19**, 239–264 (2007)
4. Schwonke, R., Renkl, A., Krieg, C., Wittwer, J., Aleven, V., Salden, R.: The worked-example effect: Not an artefact of lousy control conditions. Computers in Human Behavior **25**, 258–266 (2009)
5. McLaren, B.M., Isotani, S.: When is it best to learn with all worked examples? In: Biswas, G., Bull, S., Kay, J., Mitrovic, A. (eds.) AIED 2011. LNCS, vol. 6738, pp. 222–229. Springer, Heidelberg (2011)
6. Shareghi Najar, A., Mitrovic, A.: Examples and tutored problems: how can self-explanation make a difference to learning? In: Lane, H., Yacef, K., Mostow, J., Pavlik, P. (eds.) AIED 2013. LNCS, vol. 7926, pp. 339–348. Springer, Heidelberg (2013)
7. Najar, A.S., Mitrovic, A., McLaren, B.M.: Adaptive support versus alternating worked examples and tutored problems: which leads to better learning? In: Dimitrova, V., Kuflik, T., Chin, D., Ricci, F., Dolog, P., Houben, G.-J. (eds.) UMAP 2014. LNCS, vol. 8538, pp. 171–182. Springer, Heidelberg (2014)
8. Kaufman, L., Rousseeuw, P.: Clustering by means of medoids. In: Dodge, Y. (ed.) Statistical Data Analysis Based on the L1-Norm and Related Methods, pp. 405–416. North-Holland, Amsterdam (1987)

The Design Rationale of Logic-Muse, an ITS for Logical Reasoning in Multiple Contexts

Roger Nkambou[1](✉), Clauvice Kenfack[1,2], Serge Robert[1], and Janie Brisson[1]

[1] Université du Québec à Montréal, Montreal, Canada
nkambou.roger@uqam.ca
[2] University of Yaoundé, Yaounde, Cameroun

Abstract. This paper describes the design and implementation of Logic-Muse, an Intelligent Tutoring System (ITS) that helps learners develop reasoning skills on various contents. The study was conducted jointly with the active participation of logicians and reasoning psychologists. Logic-Muse's current version was internally validated. It is focused on propositional logic and supports learners reasoning in a wide range of situations.

Keywords: Reasoning skills · Cognitive diagnosis · ITS

1 Introduction

Many experiments in cognitive science have shown that systematic errors are common in human logical reasoning (Evans et al. 1993). A number of questions are raised when looking for solutions to improve human skills in this domain: What are the phenomena involved in learning logical reasoning skills? Does modeling allow to elicit them? What are the strategies to foster the development of reasoning skills? What are the characteristics of an ITS to support this learning?

Answers cannot be brought to these questions without an appropriate elicitation and understanding of the knowledge behind logical reasoning and errors made by humans. An active involvement of stakeholder experts is required including ITS experts, logicians, psychologists of reasoning, and educational professionals in logic.

The goal is to study the fundamentals of learning logical reasoning skills, to understand the difficulties in such learning and to build an ITS that can detect, diagnose and correct reasoning errors in various situations.

2 Logical Reasoning and ITS: Theoretical Background

Motivations: Logical reasoning plays an important role in our reasoning mechanisms. As a cognitive machine struggling to survive, humans tend to make systematic errors in their logical reasoning. Learning to think logically is to learn the valid laws and procedures of logical reasoning inseparably.

© Springer International Publishing Switzerland 2015
C. Conati et al. (Eds.): AIED 2015, LNAI 9112, pp. 738–742, 2015.
DOI: 10.1007/978-3-319-19773-9_105

Need of Technological Support: Although many ITSs have been developed since the early 70s, few dealt with logic as a learning domain (Lesta & Yacef 2002, Barnes & Stamper 2010, Tchetagni et al. 2007). Existing systems are limited in terms of strong semantic grounding in explicit reasoning knowledge structures or lack of metacognitive support in reasoning skills learning. Some eLearning tools for logic also exist but fail to explicitly encode the reasoning knowledge.

Multiple Standpoints on Reasoning Learning: It is worth noting that none of the systems previously mentioned uses the standpoint of dual processes, nor our correctionist theory of learning. In fact, the theoretical standpoint used in the development of Logic-Muse is correctionist in the sense that learning to reason is learning to correct creative inferences, so that our capacity for the prediction of events improves (Robert, 2009). Integrating an explicit catalog of reasoning errors in Logic-Muse and developing effective services to detect and address errors patterns in learner reasoning is our way to support this standpoint. Moreover, dual processes of inference (Stanovich 2011) is another standpoint of Logic-Muse from which, to learn logic and to become logically more competent is to recognize type 1 processes (spontaneous) and their fallacies, to learn how to inhibit them and to learn the type 2 processes that should be used instead. This standpoint is implemented in Logic-Muse through its capability to demarcate type 1 from type 2 processes.

3   Participatory Design and Implementation of Logic-Muse

Specifying Propositional Logic Semantics and Procedural Memories. The participatory design of each component of the expert module was carefully carried out in the team. First, we studied the propositional logic domain and came up with a thorough specification of all concepts related to it, which led to a formal ontology model. The ontology was then validated in another round with the logician experts.

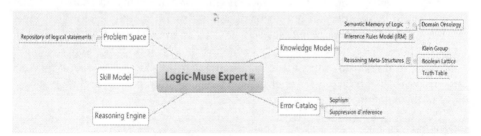

Fig. 1. Logic-Muse Expert Component

Multiple Reasoning Situations. Reasoning is not an absolute process. Many studies have shown that reasoners give different conclusions for formally identical inferences that only differ in premise content. For example, drawing the *modus ponendo ponens* (*MPP*) inference rule– to conclude "Q is true" from the premises "If P then Q, P is true"- in a given situation doesn't mean that it will be drawn in another. Our experts identified three main classes of reasoning situations, given the nature of the content:

Concrete, Contrary-to-fact and Abstract. Each class was refined into two sub-classes (e.g. *Concrete with Few Alternatives* (CFA); *Concrete with Many Alternatives* (CMA), *Formal, Abstract*). Therefore, one can clearly be evaluated as skilled on MPP in a CFA content but fails to be in CMA. This claim is supported by the results of many studies carried out by our team members (Brisson et al, 2014).

This reasoning content categorization not only provides a framework for classifying reasoning skills, but also a way to organized reasoning learning activities (or items). Because we focused on three reasoning mode (disjunction, implication and incompatibility) each having four inference rules, Logic-Muse for the propositional logic is made of 3x4x6 (72) reasoning skills. This includes 36 valid inferences rules (making the Inference Rule Model) as depicted in figure 1, and 36 invalid inferences (the error catalog). Our experts defined two types of reasoning errors: fallacies and suppressions of valid inferences. Fallacies are clear logical reasoning errors in which the reasoner fails to recognise the uncertainty of a conclusion. For example, the affirmation of the consequent inference – to conclude "P is true" from the premises "If P then Q, Q is true" is a fallacious one, while the logical answer is to be uncertain about this conclusion. Suppressions of valid inferences occur when the reasoner is incorrectly uncertain about a logical conclusion.

The Learner Model. The learner model has several dimensions including an episodic memory which keeps track of all the exercises performed by the learner. The cognitive model basically represents the state of the learner's knowledge. It is a Bayesian network where influence relationships between nodes (reasoning skills) as well as prior probabilities are provided by the experts. Some nodes are directly connected to the reasoning activities (items) while others refer to reasoning errors. The model can be opened on many perspectives (e.g. Mastered level of reasoning skills, etc.).

Tutoring Feedback. Together with the experts, we specified the tutor interventions when errors are detected and the way the tutor will help to correct it. For instance, in a simple syllogism problem in causal concrete situation with many alternatives (CMA content), if the learner decides not to conclude, the system should check if this is because he or she didn't considered other possible alternatives of the subject mentioned in the premises. Then, the tutor can ask for the reason of that inference suppression. If it appears that it is clearly due to that fact, the tutor will tackle the learner by making him/her aware about the existence of other alternatives that can hold. Here is an example of intervention rule (see its execution in figure 2):

```
IF ReasoningSituation is CMA
And Reasoning problem is Simple Syllogism
And the Inference type is the Affirming the Consequent fallacy
And the Learner Abstain
  Prompt the learner on the reasons of his abstain
  IF the reason is not link to the existence of possible alternative,
      It is a fallacy; Prompt the learner and Suggest the alternatives
```

The experts described such an intervention rule for each possible error in respect to the situation in which the reasoning is carrying out. Furthermore, one of our goals was to set up some metacognitive support to the learner. We carefully examine logical meta-structures (e.g. Boolean lattice) and analyse how they could be used to provide visual feedback to the learner so that she/he can reflect on her/his reasoning errors.

The Learning Environment. Logic-Muse tutoring system provides four levels of learning activity to the learner organized into four groups of learning services (figure 2): 1) Domain exploration service using the domain ontology; 2) General exercises on basic logic concepts including well-formed formulas (wff) checking, truth table building, etc. 3) Reasoning procedural learning service (e.g. syllogism and polysyllogism problem solving), which includes an automatic problem generator; some questions allow a limited answering time of just a few seconds, so that the spontaneous character of type 1 answers will be more easily determined while others invite the participants to briefly describe the procedure used to answer, so that it can help for the interpretation of the results and can reveal procedural differences between type 1 and type 2 answers; 4) Metacognitive support through logical meta-structure visualization.

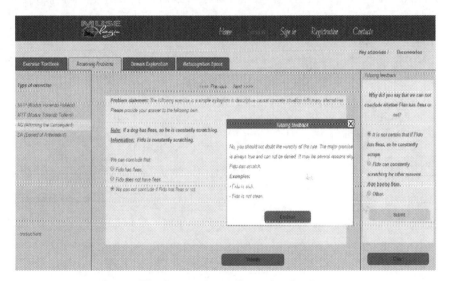

Fig. 2. Logic-Muse Reasoning Service

4   Conclusion

The Logic-Muse development is a multidisciplinary initiative which enabled us to enroll in a perspective of participatory design that has led to a set of valid components of logical reasoning implemented within an ITS. This paper was intended to share this unique experience with the reader. We presented the process undertaken to define and explained the reference components used in Logic-Muse. The system has been implemented for propositional logic with a fully functional and valid (internal) Expert module (which demonstrates all valid reasoning skills and detects and explains reasoning errors) plus a Tutor that integrates a reasoning problem generator in various contexts. The next step is the external evaluation of this first version of Logic-Muse in a logic course offered to first year students at the University of Quebec at Montreal.

Acknowledgement. We'd like to thank all Logic-Muse team members (J. Bourdeau, P. Kissok, A. Tato, M. Bélanger, A. Cloutier, J-B. Plouhinec, H. Markovits & M. Sainte-Marie) for their contributions.

References

1. Barnes, T., Stamper, J.: Automatic Hint Generation for Logic Proof Tutoring Using Historical Data. Educational Technology & Society **13**(1), 3–12 (2010)
2. Brisson, J., de Chantal, P.-L., Lortie-Forgues, H., Markovits, H.: Thinking & Reasoning (2014): Belief bias is stronger when reasoning is more difficult. Thinking & Reasoning (2014)
3. Evans, J.S.B.T., Newstead, S.E., Byrne, R.M.J.: Human Reasoning. Psychology Press (1993)
4. Stanovich, K.E.: Rationality and the reflexive mind. Oxford University Press, Oxford (2011)
5. Lesta, L., Yacef, K.: An intelligent teaching assistant system for logic. In: Cerri, S.A., Gouardéres, G., Paraguaçu, F. (eds.) ITS 2002. LNCS, vol. 2363, pp. 421–431. Springer, Heidelberg (2002)
6. Robert, S.: Logique de la découverte et naturalisation de la connaissance: L'épistémologie historique d'Imre Lakatos. Presses de l'Université Laval, Québec (2009)
7. Tchetagni, J., Nkambou, R., Bourdeau, J.: Explicit Reflection in Prolog-Tutor. International Journal on Artificial Intelligence in Education **17**(2), 169–217 (2007)

Evaluating the Effectiveness of Integrating Natural Language Tutoring into an Existing Adaptive Learning System

Benjamin D. Nye[✉], Alistair Windsor, Phillip Pavlik, Andrew Olney,
Mustafa Hajeer, Arthur C. Graesser, and Xiangen Hu

Institute for Intelligent Systems, University of Memphis,
Memphis, TN 38152, USA
benjamin.nye@gmail.com

Abstract. This paper reports initial results of an evaluation for an ITS that follows service-oriented principles to integrate natural language tutoring into an existing adaptive learning system for mathematics. Self-explanation tutoring dialogs were used to talk students through step-by-step worked solutions to Algebra problems. These worked solutions presented an isomorphic problem to a preceding Algebra problem that the student could not solve in an adaptive learning system. Due to crossover issues between conditions, experimental versus control condition assignment did not show significant differences in learning gains. However, strong dose-dependent learning gains were observed that could not be otherwise explained by either initial mastery or time-on-task.

Keywords: Intelligent Tutoring Systems · Natural language tutoring · Mathematics education · Worked examples · Isomorphic examples

1   Overview

Future intelligent tutoring systems (ITS) will need to integrate with other learning systems, particularly other intelligent systems. The **S**hareable **K**nowledge **O**bjects as **P**ortable **I**ntelligent **T**utors (SKOPE-IT) system was designed to integrate natural language tutoring dialogs into an existing learning environments. In this study, we combined the AutoTutor Conversation Engine [Nye et al., 2014] with the ALEKS (Assessment and Learning in Knowledge Spaces) commercial mathematics system [Falmagne et al., 2013]. AutoTutor and ALEKS have complementary strengths: AutoTutor focuses mainly on help during a problem (micro-adaptivity) and ALEKS focuses on macro-adaptivity, such as problem selection. Based on Knowledge Space Theory, students in ALEKS can only attempt a problem after mastering all of its prerequisites. Conversely, the AutoTutor Conversation Engine (ACE) directs conversations with one or more conversational agents. While ACE can be integrated with macro-adaptive models, each tutoring dialog adapts to the student's free-text input and other session events.

© Springer International Publishing Switzerland 2015
C. Conati et al. (Eds.): AIED 2015, LNAI 9112, pp. 743–747, 2015.
DOI: 10.1007/978-3-319-19773-9_106

When integrating these systems, the goal was to combine worked examples [Schwonke et al., 2009], self-explanation [Aleven et al., 2004], and impasse-driven learning [VanLehn et al., 2003]. The integration point between AutoTutor and ALEKS was the "Explain" page for ALEKS items. The ALEKS Explain page presents a worked solution to the specific problem that a learner could not solve. The SKOPE-IT system integrated AutoTutor dialogs by presenting a tutoring-enhanced worked solution for an isomorphic problem, with a series of small dialogs covering key principles. After each dialog finishes, more HTML for the worked example (including any images) is dynamically rendered until the next step-specific dialog is delivered. Figure 1 shows the first dialog of a tutored example, with most of the solution still hidden.

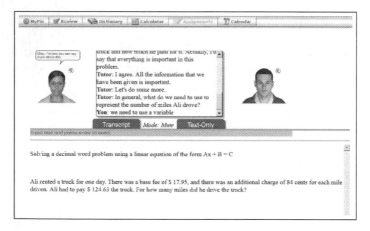

Fig. 1. Integration of a Tutored Worked Solution into ALEKS

2   Study Methodology and Population

50 ALEKS worked solutions drawn from items aligned to the Common Core were enhanced using AutoTutor dialogs. For each worked solution, 5 to 12 brief dialogs were authored (407 dialogs in total). Dialogs focused on Algebra concepts, such as representation mapping, systems of equations, or units of measurement. Two types of dialogs were authored: trialogs (75% of dialogs) and vicarious tutoring (25% of dialogs). In trialogs, the human student answered a conceptual question, with feedback and support from the tutor and peer student agents. In vicarious tutoring, the peer student agent modeled an explanation with the tutor.

Three sections of a mid-south college algebra class participated (112 students), which was a class for students with the lowest math placement scores. SKOPE-IT randomly assigned each student to an experimental condition with tutoring-enhanced items or to a control where ALEKS presented its usual non-interactive solutions. Unfortunately, due to a glitch in authentication, the control condition was presented with tutoring for 3 weeks out of the 12-week course, making the control condition a lower-dose treatment. The following analyses are based on the ALEKS course and AutoTutor interactions. ALEKS data included course mastery levels from adaptive assessments and time spent in ALEKS. ALEKS assessments determined course grades, so students were presumably motivated. The SKOPE-IT system collected dialog interaction data of the student with the AutoTutor system (e.g., # of inputs, # of hints given).

3   Results

Results from ALEKS assessment scores are presented in Table 1, with standard deviations in parentheses. Due to random chance, the experimental condition contained less subjects at both the start $(N_{E,0})$ and end $(N_{E,f})$ of the study. The experimental subjects slightly outperformed the control (+3.3 points learning gain), but this difference was not statistically significant (Cohen's d=0.2, p=0.45). Attrition rates for both conditions were high (and are generally high for that course), but were not significantly different.

Table 1. Assessment Outcomes by Assigned Condition

Condition	Initial Score $(N_0=103)$	Final Score $(N_f=76)$	Learning Gain $(N_f=76)$	Effect Size $(N_f=76)$
Experimental $(N_{E,0}=42, N_{E,f}=28)$	20.5 (5.5)	52.6 (18.9)	31.7 (19.4)	d=2.3
Control $(N_{C0}=61, N_{C,f}=48)$	23.2 (7.3)	51.8 (17.1)	28.4 (15.5)	d=2.1

The dosage of AutoTutor interactions was a confound for comparing conditions. Since students took different paths through the ALEKS adaptive system, they encountered different numbers of tutoring dialogs ($\mu=24$ and $\sigma=27$ among students with at least one dialog). Since each example had an average of 8 dialogs, students who received dialogs saw only about 3 worked examples out of 50. Also, due to crossover issues, the "experimental" subjects only averaged four more dialogs than the "control" subjects.

To look at dose-dependent effects, a linear regression was used to model the learning gain as a function of the logarithm of the time spent in ALEKS and logarithm of the number of AutoTutor dialogs interacted with (Table 2). Logarithmic transforms were applied because diminishing learning efficiency was observed for a subset of students who overdosed on the combined system (7 students spent 80+ hours in ALEKS, $\sigma=1.5$ above the mean). The regression improved the model fit ($R^2=0.54$) when compared to a model with only time spent studying ($R^2=0.49$). Dialog dosage was significant even after accounting for time on task (including time on dialogs). Including a term for dialogs that the learner encountered but ignored (e.g., returned to problem solving instead) did not improve the model fit (t=-0.32, p=0.75).

Table 2. Learning by Time and Tutoring Dialogs (R^2=0.54, R^2_{cv}=0.54)

Factor (N=76)	Coefficient	P-value
Log_{10}(# Hours in ALEKS)	43.0	<0.001 (t=6.6)
Log_{10}(# AutoTutor Dialogs Interacted With)	8.0	0.009 (t=2.7)
Intercept	-41.1	<0.001 (t=-4.2)

4   Discussion and Conclusions

Due to insufficient differences in dosage, the main conditions showed no significant differences in learning gains. With that said, the dosage of tutoring dialogs was strongly associated with learning gains. Moreover, no other explanatory factor was found that captured this difference. Student prior knowledge did not correlate with dialog interaction (Pearon's R=-0.03). Also, dialogs were only associated with learning when the learner interacted with them, making it unlikely that higher-achieving students simply encountered more dialogs. Finally, regressions found that AutoTutor dialogs predicted learning even after accounting for all time studying in the combined system. However, the available data cannot fully eliminate the possibility that students prone to interact with dialogs also learned faster due to some mutual cause. A follow-up study that controls for dialog time-on-task would be needed to address this question.

A second issue was that some learners reported that they did not understand the relevance of isomorphic examples. These comments expressed that explaining concepts on a similar problem does not show them "how to get the correct answer" for their earlier problem. This implies that these students may perceive that reaching the answer to the current problem is equivalent to learning. Prior research found that self-explanation can improve deep understanding, such as identifying when a problem cannot be solved [Aleven et al., 2004]. Unfortunately, even though self-explanation can improve learning efficiency [Aleven et al., 2004], students may believe the opposite because they do not complete as many problems, which may be their internal barometer for learning. Such students may need interventions to convey the role of self-explanation and dialog in learning. Tutoring such metacognition may be a key future direction.

Acknowledgments. This work was supported by the Office of Naval Research Grant N00014-12-C-0643. All views expressed are those of the authors alone.

References

Aleven, V., Ogan, A., Popescu, O., Torrey, C., Koedinger, K.R.: Evaluating the effectiveness of a tutorial dialogue system for self-explanation. In: Lester, J.C., Vicari, R.M., Paraguaçu, F. (eds.) ITS 2004. LNCS, vol. 3220, pp. 443–454. Springer, Heidelberg (2004)

Falmagne, J.C., Albert, D., Doble, C., Eppstein, D., Hu, X. (eds.): Knowledge Spaces. Springer, Berlin (2013)

Nye, B.D., Graesser, A.C., Hu, X., Cai, Z.: AutoTutor in the cloud: A service-oriented paradigm for an interoperable natural-language its. Journal of Advanced Distributed Learning Technology **2**(6), 35–48 (2014)

Schwonke, R., Renkl, A., Krieg, C., Wittwer, J., Aleven, V., Salden, R.: The worked-example effect: Not an artefact of lousy control conditions. Computers in Human Behavior **25**(2, SI), 258–266 (2009)

VanLehn, K., Siler, S., Murray, C., Yamauchi, T., Baggett, W.B.: Why do only some events cause learning during human tutoring? Cognition and Instruction **21**(3), 209–249 (2003)

Adapting Collaboration Dialogue in Response to Intelligent Tutoring System Feedback

Jennifer K. Olsen[1(✉)], Vincent Aleven[1], and Nikol Rummel[1,2]

[1] Human Computer Interaction Institute, Carnegie Mellon University, Pittsburgh, PA, USA
{jkolsen,aleven}@cs.cmu.edu, nikol.rummel@rub.de
[2] Institute of Educational Research, Ruhr-Universität Bochum, Bochum, Germany

Abstract. To be able to provide better support for collaborative learning in Intelligent Tutoring Systems, it is important to understand how collaboration patterns change. Prior work has looked at the interdependencies between utterances and the change of dialogue over time, but it has not addressed how dialogue changes during a lesson, an analysis that allows us to investigate the adaptivity of student strategies as students gain domain knowledge. We address this question by analyzing the shift in types of collaborative talk occurring within a single session and in particular how they relate to errors for 26 4th and 5th grade dyads working on a fractions tutor. We found that, over time, the frequency of interactive talk and errors both decrease in dyads working together on conceptual problems. Although interactive talk is often held as a gold standard in collaboration, as students become more proficient, it may not be as important.

Keywords: Problem solving · Collaborative learning · Intelligent tutoring system

1 Introduction

As students work together on collaborative problem solving, their behaviors may change over time. To understand how to best support learning with the use of technology, it is important to take this change into account so that the system can accurately adapt to the change in behaviors. This paper addresses changes in behavior that may be seen over a short period of time, namely, changes within a single collaborative learning session, which are often ignored by using an aggregate score for process data measures collected over an entire session. We focus our analysis on students' dialogue and how this is related to behavior in an Intelligent Tutoring System (ITS) designed to support collaborative learning.

Past work with Computer Supported Collaborative Learning has focused on changes over time based on interdependencies within the dialogue [1], [4], [7] and how communication changes permanently over long periods of time [3], [6]. However, neither of these perspectives takes into account how behaviors and strategies may change temporarily within a single lesson as students learn, which may show how

© Springer International Publishing Switzerland 2015
C. Conati et al. (Eds.): AIED 2015, LNAI 9112, pp. 748–751, 2015.
DOI: 10.1007/978-3-319-19773-9_107

language is being used as a tool for learning rather than showing the learning of collaboration strategies. For our study, we analyzed collaborative dialogue within a single lesson. Within an ITS, we often use a decrease in error rate as an indication of learning. As students make fewer errors, they may feel less of a need to discuss the answer and have less interactive talk. By using errors, we are able to investigate how students adapt their use of interactive talk as needed to help them through impasses. We analyzed how interactive talk changed between the first and second half of the session and how these changes were correlated to changes in error rates.

2   Methods

We analyzed data from a study in a school in which 26 4th and 5th grade dyads, paired within a grade (i.e., 13 4th and 13 5th grade dyads), engaged in a problem-solving activity geared towards either conceptual or procedural knowledge of fractions using a collaborative ITS [5]. The problem sets offered standard ITS support (immediate feedback and hints) as well as embedded collaboration scripts supported through three different collaboration features: assigned roles, individual information, and cognitive group awareness. Each student had their own view of the collaborative ITS while they were synchronously working on a problem and communicated through Skype (audio only). Each dyad worked with the tutor for 45 minutes in a pull-out design.

We coded the collaborative dialogue using a rating scheme with four major rating categories: interactive dialogue, constructive dialogue, constructive monologue, and other. For our analysis, we focused on the interactive dialogue category, in which students engage in actions such as co-construction and sequential construction, because it aligns with ICAP's joint dialogue pattern and is held as the gold standard for collaboration [2]. Our rating scheme was developed to look at groups of utterances associated with subgoals (i.e., a group of steps that all are for the same goal within a problem) to account for the interactions between students. An inter-rater reliability analysis was performed to determine consistency between two raters (Kappa= 0.72).

In our analysis, we used two different error counts. The first was the total number of errors made on a subgoal by either student in the dyad. The second error count was the number of steps within the given subgoal that contained errors. For all variables the change was calculated by subtracting the first half value from the second half value. Since each dyad completed a different number of subgoals, from 25 to 143, the first and second halves of the session were calculated by dividing the total number of subgoals completed in half. All variables used in analysis were calculated in proportion to the number of subgoals that were completed.

3   Results

Because the procedural and conceptual tutor problems were fundamentally different with regard to the types of knowledge that were being learned, each of these conditions was treated separately. To test our hypothesis that the percent of subgoals where interactive talk occurs will change from the first to the second half of the session, we conducted two paired t-tests, one for the procedural condition and one for the conceptual condition. For the procedural condition, there was no significant difference in the amount of interactive talk between the first ($M = 0.24$, $SD = 0.18$) and second half of the session ($M = 0.21$, $SD = 0.19$), $t(12) = 1.23$, $p = 0.24$. For the conceptual condition, there was a significant decrease in the amount of interactive talk between the first ($M = 0.32$, $SD = 0.20$) and second half of the session ($M = 0.19$, $SD = 0.12$), $t(12) = 3.50$, $p < 0.01$. There was also a significant increase in the amount of other talk between the first and second half of the session, $t(12) = -2.75$, $p < 0.05$.

To better understand how the change in interactive talk may be related to students' problem-solving behaviors with the ITS, we analyzed how our two error measures differed between the first and second half of the session. We used a paired t-test to compare the two time points. In the procedural condition, there was no significant difference in the total number of errors made between the first ($M = 1.27$, $SD = 0.63$) and second half of the session ($M = 1.44$, $SD = 1.02$), $t(12) = -0.87$, $p = 0.40$, and there was no significant difference between the number of steps where errors occurred ($M = 0.60$, $SD = 0.24$, $M = 0.53$, $SD = 0.26$), $t(12) = 1.48$, $p = 0.17$. In the conceptual condition, there was a significant decrease in the total number of errors that were made between the first ($M = 3.46$, $SD = 2.84$) and the second half ($M = 1.69$, $SD = 0.96$), $t(12) = 2.36$, $p < 0.05$ and there was also a significant decrease in the number of steps where an error occurred ($M = 0.72$, $SD = 0.15$; $M = 0.58$, $SD = 0.17$), $t(12) = 2.45$, $p < 0.05$. Thus, in the conceptual condition, we see a decrease from the first to the second half in both interactive talk and problem-solving errors.

To better understand this relationship, we computed two Pearson's correlations. Outliers were removed based on being more than 3 standard deviations away from the mean. First, we analyzed the relationship between the change in interactive talk and the change in the number of steps with errors. There was a strong positive correlation between the change in interactive talk and the change in the steps with errors, $r(10) = 0.59$, $p < 0.05$. Thus, both interactive talk and the number of incorrect steps decreased over time and these decreases were strongly associated with each other. The second relationship that we analyzed was the correlation between the change in interactive talk and the change in total errors. There was a negative correlation between the change in interactive talk and the change in total errors with marginal statistical significance, $r(10) = -0.53$, $p = 0.07$. This result indicates that dyads with a greater decrease of interactive talk from the first to second half of the session had less of a decrease in the total errors made.

4   Discussion and Conclusion

Through our analysis we found that in the conceptual condition, students who had a greater decrease in the amount of interactive talk tended to have a smaller decrease in the number of errors that they made, but students who tended to have a greater decrease in the amount of interactive talk tended to have a greater decrease in the number of steps where errors occurred. These results indicate that interactive talk may not be necessary for students to correctly solve a problem, which is supported by the positive correlation of decreased interactive talk and decreased steps with errors, but instead interactive talk may be a tool students can use when struggling. Interactive talk may not be so critical for correct problem-solving performance once students become more proficient, but it is helpful when students make errors. The negative correlation with the total errors would suggest other behaviors are occurring when students make multiple errors on the same step and where an area for future work. We did not find these same patterns for the procedural condition indicating that there may be different productive learning behaviors for procedural knowledge. The different results may indicate that for procedural knowledge there is less of a need for the deep understanding that is associated with interactive talk to overcome errors.

To be able to provide better support for learning through collaborative ITSs, it is important to understand how the collaboration may change as students work together. Although interactive talk is often held as the gold standard in collaboration [2], our results suggest that interactive talk may not be necessary for the entire duration of a collaborative session, but only when errors occur. It would follow that a decrease in interactive talk over time is not necessarily an indication that the quality of the collaboration is deteriorating. Rather, it may signal that the interactive talk is invoked in an adaptive manner, specifically to deal with impasses. By analyzing the change in collaborative dialogue over the course of a lesson, we were able to clarify how interactive talk and in-tutor learning relate to each other. By analyzing shorter time intervals than halves for future work, we may be able to build upon our findings presented in this paper and discern smaller patterns that may be present in the process data.

Acknowledgments. We thank the CTAT team, Daniel Belenky, and Amos Glenn, for their help. This work was supported by Graduate Training Grant # R305B090023 and by Award # R305A120734 both from the US Department of Education (IES).

References

1. Chen, G., Chiu, M.M., Wang, Z.: Social metacognition and the creation of correct, new ideas: A statistical discourse analysis of online mathematics discussions. Computers in Human Behavior **28**(3), 868–880 (2012)
2. Chi, M.T.H.: Active-constructive-interactive: a conceptual framework for differentiating learning activities. Topics in Cognitive Science **1**, 73–105 (2009)
3. Mercer, N.: The seeds of time: Why classroom dialogue needs a temporal analysis. The Journal of the Learning Sciences **17**(1), 33–59 (2008)
4. Molenaar, I., Chiu, M.M.: Dissecting sequences of regulation and cognition: statistical discourse analysis of primary school children's collaborative learning. Metacognition and learning, 1–24 (2014)
5. Olsen, J.K., Belenky, D.M., Aleven, V., Rummel, N.: Using an intelligent tutoring system to support collaborative as well as individual learning. In: Trausan-Matu, S., Boyer, K.E., Crosby, M., Panourgia, K. (eds.) ITS 2014. LNCS, vol. 8474, pp. 134–143. Springer, Heidelberg (2014)
6. Reimann, P.: Time is precious: Variable-and event-centred approaches to process analysis in CSCL research. International Journal of Computer-Supported Collaborative Learning **4**(3), 239–257 (2009)
7. Wise, A.F., Chiu, M.M.: Analyzing temporal patterns of knowledge construction in a role-based online discussion. International Journal of Computer-Supported Collaborative Learning **6**(3), 445–470 (2011)

The Role of Student Choice Within Adaptive Tutoring

Korinn S. Ostrow[✉] and Neil T. Heffernan

Worcester Polytechnic Institute, 100 Institute Road, Worcester, MA 01609, USA
{ksostrow,nth}@wpi.edu

Abstract. While adaptive tutoring systems have improved classroom education through individualization, few platforms offer students preference in regard to their education. In the present study, a randomized controlled trial is used to investigate the effects of student choice within ASSISTments. A problem set featuring either text feedback or matched content video feedback was assigned to a sample of 82 middle school students. Those who were able to choose their feedback medium at the start of the assignment outperformed those who were randomly assigned a medium. Results suggest that even if feedback is not ultimately observed, students average significantly higher assignment scores after voicing a choice. Findings offer evidence for enhancing intrinsic motivation through the provision of choice within adaptive tutoring systems.

Keywords: Choice · Adaptive tutoring · Feedback medium · Learning outcomes

1   Introduction

Although the perception of autonomy has been proven as an intrinsically motivating factor for learning [7, 2, 6, 3], student preference is rarely employed in education. Perhaps traditional classroom practices have failed to capitalize on student choice due to limitations in materials or resources. However, adaptive tutoring systems offer unique opportunities for students to invest in their learning experience. These platforms are becoming a staple for the modern classroom, serving to individualize the learning experience while providing students with more powerful feedback and teachers with more powerful assessment. One of these systems, ASSISTments, is fast growing platform used for homework and classwork by over 50,000 students around the world.

The present study was influenced by Cordova & Lepper's landmark study that unveiled the beneficial effects of choice within educational computer activities [1]. Coupled with findings from previous work surrounding feedback mediums within ASSISTments [5], the present study examines 1) how learning outcomes are affected if students are able to choose the feedback medium they will experience within a mathematics assignment, 2) whether a particular feedback medium is more popular or more effective, and 3) if an interaction exists between choice and feedback medium as measured by a variety of performance outcomes.

2   Methods

A randomized controlled trial was designed using problem content aligned to the fifth grade Common Core State Standard of Multiplying Simple Fractions. Two

C. Conati et al. (Eds.): AIED 2015, LNAI 9112, pp. 752–755, 2015.
DOI: 10.1007/978-3-319-19773-9_108

isomorphic problem sets were created within ASSISTments: a set of 40 problems, each containing three hints presented as text feedback, and an isomorphic set of 40 problems, each containing three hints presented as short (15-30 second) video snippets. For each problem, regardless of feedback medium, the first two hints served as a static worked example and its solution. The third and final hint for each problem walked students through the solution to the original problem. All problem content and feedback is available at Ostrow [4] for further reference. These problem sets were then embedded in a complex experimental design within ASSISTments, establishing a solitary assignment with multiple conditions. At the beginning of the assignment each student was randomly assigned to either the Choice (experimental) or No Choice (control) conditions. Those assigned to the control were immediately reassigned to either video or text feedback. Students who were assigned to the experimental condition were asked to choose the type of feedback they wished to receive while working on their assignment. The student experience is available at Ostrow [4] for reference.

3   Procedure

The study problem set was made openly accessible to all teachers for assignment to their students, allowing for natural and unbiased data collection. Log files were accumulated approximately one month after the release of the experiment. A total of 82 students from 4 classes spanning 2 middle schools in suburban Massachusetts had been assigned the problem set. All students within the sample were familiar with the ASSISTments platform. Of the 82 students originally assigned this problem set, 78 completed the assignment, following the distribution depicted in Figure 1. As shown, regardless of condition, the majority of students did not actually request hint feedback during the assignment. Thus, the results presented herein are primarily intended to guide future work.

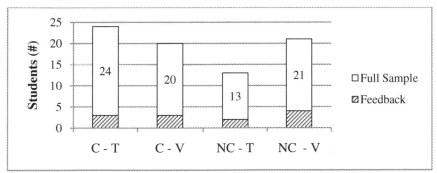

Note. Condition labeled as C (Choice, n = 44) and NC (No Choice, n = 34), Feedback Medium labeled as T (Text, n = 37) and V (Video, n = 41).

Fig. 1. Distribution of Students Experiencing Feedback Within Full Sample

4   Results

It was hypothesized that students would excel when provided choice, and that those receiving video feedback would outperform those receiving text feedback.

A MANOVA was conducted to examine the interaction between condition and feed-back medium across a number of dependent variables measuring student performance within the assignment. Within the 78 students who completed the assignment, there was no significant interaction effect, Pillai's Trace = 0.110, $F(6, 69) = 1.416$, p = 0.221. Further, although there was no significant main effect of condition, Pillai's Trace = 0.077, $F(6, 69) = 0.962$, p = 0.457, Table 1 reveals that students who made a preference about their feedback medium had significantly higher correctness on aver-age than those in the control condition, $p < .05$, $\eta^2 = 0.05$. Further, students who were given choice were more likely to master their assignment than those in the control condition, trending toward significance $p < .10$, $\eta^2 = 0.04$, they used fewer hints and attempts, and spent longer working on each problem. While these findings were not significantly reliable, they support further investigation of choice within adaptive tutoring contexts. Feedback medium was less relevant to performance than hypothe-sized; no significant differences were observed within any of the dependent variables.

Table 1. Means, SDs, & Univariate Results for Main Effect of Condition (Intent-To-Treat)

Variable	n	Choice	n	No Choice	F (1,74)	p	η^2	R^2
Ave. Correctness	44	0.95 (0.10)	34	0.87 (0.25)	4.03	.048	0.05	0.05
Ave. Hints	45	0.23 (0.68)	36	0.35 (1.15)	0.61	.436	0.01	0.02
Ave. Attempts	45	3.48 (1.19)	36	3.76 (1.74)	0.89	.348	0.01	0.02
Mastery	45	1.00 (0.00)	36	0.94 (0.24)	2.83	.097	0.04	0.04
Ave. Time (sec)	44	44.94 (45.76)	34	40.29 (34.52)	0.55	.461	0.01	0.04
Med. Time (sec)	44	36.45 (42.24)	34	27.00 (16.33)	1.90	.172	0.02	0.09

Note. Averages represent average student performance across all problems experienced in the assignment.

Across the full sample, only 12 students actually requested hint feedback (14.6%). A MANOVA of treated students lacked enough power to suggest a significant inte-raction effect, Pillai's Trace = 0.724, $F(6, 3) = 1.31$, p = 0.445. The main effect of feedback medium trended toward significance, Pillai's Trace = 0.889, $F(6, 3) = 4.02$, p = 0.141, with students requesting more hints (M = 2.80, SD = 2.05) and using more attempts (M = 6.20, SD = 2.17) when receiving text than when receiving video (M = 1.14, SD = 0.90; M = 4.86, SD = 2.91). Further, although there was no main effect for condition, Pillai's Trace = 0.641, $F(6, 3) = 0.89$, p = 0.588, the means and univariate results presented in Table 2 suggest that students showed consistently better performance when they were able to choose their feedback medium.

Table 2. Means, SDs, & Univariate Results for Main Effect of Condition (Treated)

Variable	Choice, n=6	No Choice, n=6	F (1, 8)	p	η^2	R^2
Ave. Correctness	0.74 (0.02)	0.66 (0.35)	0.23	.647	0.03	0.04
Ave. Hints	1.67 (1.03)	2.00 (2.19)	0.57	.472	0.05	0.33
Ave. Attempts	5.83 (1.72)	5.00 (3.41)	0.02	.895	0.00	0.30
Mastery	1.00 (0.00)	0.83 (0.41)	0.47	.512	0.05	0.18
Ave. Time (sec)	24.72 (10.14)	59.26 (37.92)	3.99	.081	0.33	0.34
Med. Time (sec)	14.52 (5.93)	35.30 (23.86)	3.49	.099	0.30	0.31

5   Discussion and Contribution

This study served as an initial foray into implementing student choice within ASSISTments, an adaptive tutoring platform that was previously unable to individualize learning via student preference. Results suggested that students who were able to invest in their learning experience outperformed those who were not asked their preference. Those provided choice averaged higher correctness on the assignment while using fewer hints and attempts. Further, choice significantly impacted performance, even when the outcome of choosing was not ultimately experienced. Aside from small sample size, this study was also somewhat limited in that the experimental design utilized feedback that was only provided upon the student's request. As such, proper analysis of main effects would require a much larger treated sample. The results of this study inspired infrastructure changes within the ASSISTments platform that will allow for future research in this area. Similar hypotheses can now be examined using ASSISTments on larger samples and within additional content domains. Findings offer evidence in support of allowing student autonomy within adaptive education.

Acknowledgments. We acknowledge funding from the NSF (1316736, 1252297, 1109483, 1031398, 0742503, 1440753), the U.S. Dept. of Ed. GAAN (P200A120238), ONR's "STEM Grand Challenges," and IES (R305A120125, R305C100024). <3 to S.O. & L.P.B.O.

References

1. Cordova, D.I., Lepper, M.R.: Intrinsic Motivation and the Process of Learning: Beneficial Effects of Contextualization, Personalization, and Choice. Journal of Educational Psychology **88**(4), 715–730 (1996)
2. Frenzel, A.C., Pekrun, R., Goetz, T.: Girls and mathematics – a "hopeless" issue? A control-value approach to gender differences in emotions towards mathematics. European Journal of Psychology of Education **22**(4), 497–514 (2007)
3. Murayama, K., Pekrun, R., Lichtenfeld, S., vom Hofe, R.: Predicting Long-Term Growth in Students' Mathematics Achievement: The Unique Contributions of Motivation and Cognitive Strategies. Child Development **84**(4), 1475–1490 (2013)
4. Ostrow, K.: Materials for Study on Student Choice within Adaptive Tutoring (2015). http://tiny.cc/AIED-2015-Choice. (retrieved 14 January 15)
5. Ostrow, K.S., Heffernan, N.T.: Testing the multimedia principled in the real world: a comparison of video vs. text feedback in authentic middle school math assignments. In: Stamper, J., Pardos, Z., Mavrikis, M., McLaren, B.M. (eds.) Proceedings of the 7th International Conference on Educational Data Mining, pp. 296–299 (2014)
6. Patall, E.A., Cooper, H., Robinson, J.C.: The Effects of Choice on Intrinsic Motivation and Related Outcomes: A Meta-Analysis of Research Findings. Psychology Bulletin. **134**(2), 270–300 (2008)
7. Pekrun, R.: The Control-Value Theory of Achievement Emotions: Assumptions, Corollaries, and Implications for Educational Research and Practice. Educational Psychology Review **18**(4), 315–341 (2006)

Identifying Affective Trajectories in Relation to Learning Gains During the Interaction with a Tutoring System

Gustavo Padrón-Rivera[✉] and Genaro Rebolledo-Mendez

Facultad de Estadística e Informática, University of Veracruz, Xalapa, Mexico
zS12020111@estudiantes.uv.mx, grebolledo@uv.mx

Abstract. This paper presents the identification of sequences of affective states and its consequential impact to learning in an intelligent tutor for Mathematics at secondary level. These trajectories are represented as time series obtained by DAE 1.0 a software capable of detecting and labeling points in human faces in relation to affective states. Data was collected from students (N=44) in one secondary school, in a semirural town in Veracruz, Mexico. The students were asked to interact with the tutoring system for 40 minutes and were photographed by DAE 1.0 at a pace of 1 picture each 5 seconds. Based on a dataset consisting of 480 pictures per student, we employed the SAX algorithm to make the data discrete and facilitate the interpretation of the time series. The results of classifying the data using ID3 showed an accuracy of 62.85% in identification of affective trajectories related to higher learning gains. Future studies will seek to test this algorithm on a different data set with the aim of predicting performance towards personalizing affective interventions in the tutoring system.

Keywords: Affective states · Learning · Intelligent tutor system · Time series · SAX · ID3

1 Introduction

This work aims at applying classification algorithms using decision trees to discern affective trajectories in relation to learning gains in a tutoring system for Mathematics. It is known affective states are usually present in the use of educational technologies [1]; the research question guiding this investigation revolves around the identification of one or more sequences that are related to the acquisition of knowledge as assessed by learning gains. To throw some light onto this issue, we applied decision trees to analyze sequential decisions based on the use of outcomes and associated probabilities. The recognition of emotional states is particularly important for learning Mathematics with educational technology as it is likely accompanied by emotional reactions on the part of students.

2 State of the Art

Automated detection of facial expressions has many potential applications for example detection of pain [2], depression [3] and helping people with autism [4]. Ekman's

© Springer International Publishing Switzerland 2015
C. Conati et al. (Eds.): AIED 2015, LNAI 9112, pp. 756–759, 2015.
DOI: 10.1007/978-3-319-19773-9_109

Facial Action Coding System (FACS) can be applied for identification of affective states based on muscle movements. The FACS catalog contains 46 action units (AUs) corresponding to each independent movement of the 44 facial muscles [5]. Combinations of AU create hundreds of facial expressions [6]. In one study set to analyze affective states using Ekman's framework, the authors identified action units that are linked to affective states [7]. In the same study, the level of agreement among independent observers was calculated using Cohen's Kappa [8] resulting in a significant (>= 0.6) level of agreement among observers. In order to process information from still pictures and reduce it to components expressed on action units, a detector of the AU identified as relevant in learning environments [7] was developed. We employed Principal Component Analysis (PCA) to detect features on the faces captured on still images. The software is named DAE 1.0 and runs on Windows operating system and Matlab R2011b with *OpenCV* libraries, specifically *mexOpenCV* [9]. The software capabilities include: 1) detection of human faces within a picture, 2) application of PCA to obtain the characteristics of the image and 3) comparison against sample images using the Euclidean distance as metric and 4) the result is a list of AU per image, see Fig. 1.

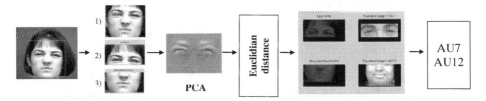

Fig. 1. Detecting action units (AU) in a human face using the software DAE 1.0

3   Methodology

To throw light onto our research question, we set up one experiment among a population of students (N=128) at a secondary school in Coatepec, Veracruz, Mexico. There were four participating groups of 32 students each, with students from both sexes and an average age of 14 years. The experiment was divided into 4 days. On day 1, the participants were lectured on the topic of scatterplots, which is also the topic of the tutoring system. Immediately after the presentation, the students did a *pre-test* asking them to solve scatterplots exercises. On days 2 and 3, the students were asked to use *"Scooter, the tutor"* [10], which aims to reinforce the topic of scatterplots. Finally on day 4, the students solved the *post-test*. All the activities were held during the class' schedule. Since we only had 11 webcams to capture students' faces at interaction time, we randomly selected 44 students to interact with Scooter the tutor while they were being photographed every 5 seconds for 40 minutes. Consent was asked for to the students' legal tutors and to the head teacher before carrying out of this experiment. We detected action units (AUs) for each of the 480 students' images stored on a database. Blurry or poor quality images were excluded. The final database consisted of 35 students, 9 students were discarded because they did not finish the 4 days of the experiment. Learning gains for the students in the sample were calculated with the following formula: learning gain = (post-test – pre-test) / (1 – pre-test). Action units can be divided into two categories with respect to their location in the human face: forehead-eyes (AU1, AU2, AU7, AU14, AU43, AU64) and mouth-chin (AU12, AU25, AU26). We manually looked for the combinations of action units and found there are 18 possible combinations. The information was reorganized to express the sequences of actions in terms of the 18 possible combinations obtaining a new data set. The final dataset was used as input for the SAX (Symbolic Aggregate Approximation) algorithm [11] for the discretization of the original time series into symbolic string. SAX reduces a time series of length n in another represented by a string with length w, where $w < n$. SAX takes an integer value a that determines the length of alphabet, where $a > 2$. We did this to reduce the data set consisting of 16800 pictures to facilitate the interpretation of the time series, getting a time series of 480 elements into a new time series of 5 elements. The dataset has 35 test examples: 20 paths associated to learning gains and 15 paths not associated to learning gains. We put the dataset into ARFF (Attribute-Relation File Format). The learning gain value was discretized using the following criteria: if the learning gain was greater than or equal to 0.6 then the path is considered *good* otherwise it is considered *bad*. Therefore, each example is a time series like "d,f,g,g,d,yes", "f,e,f,g,d,no", etc. This series was the input for a classification algorithm, ID3 (Induction Decision Trees) with 10 cross validation.

4   Results

We first report the results from the identification of affective trajectories using Weka machine learning software with ID3 algorithm with 10-fold cross-validation: correctly classified instances: 22 = **62.8571%**; incorrectly classified instances: 13 = **37.1429%.**

Although these results are preliminary, they show a possibility for the identification of affective trajectories and its association to learning gains. Because it is desirable that technology reacts to emotional states, newer versions of *Scooter the Tutor* could help student in case they need extra help at an affective level. We noticed that there are several trajectories for this population in the secondary school in Coatepec, Mexico. Therefore, in order to achieve generalization it was necessary to do new experiments with other population of students with the same tutoring system in Coatepec, Veracruz. This time the group has 47 students from both sexes and an average age of 13 years; we just analyzed 22 students. The results show that the classification accuracy is almost the same to the previous experiments: 68.1818%. For future work the tutoring system will employ AED_1.0 software in order to recognize affective states in real time using webcams and try to modify their activities based on calculating the probability of students going on certain affective trajectories. A beneficial aspect of the technology reported on this paper is its unobtrusiveness, as the students were not influenced by the presence of observers or teacher during the use of the system. The addition of affective recognition based on facial expressions could pave the way to the study of the interaction between affective and cognitive traits in students during the employment of tutoring systems and with learning technology in general.

Acknowledgements. The authors of this paper acknowledge the financial support of the CONACYT. We thank the teachers and students at the "Escuela Secundaria General Ignacio de la Llave" in Coatepec, Veracruz, Mexico for their help with the experiments. We also thank Prof. Ryan Baker for allowing us to experiment with "Scooter the Tutor".

References

1. Craig, S., Sullins, J., Gholson, B.: Affect and learning: an exploratory look into the role of affect in learning with AutoTutor. Journal of Educational Media **29**, 241–250 (2004)
2. Ashraf, S., Cohn, J., Chen, T., Ambadar, Z., Prkachin, K., Solomon, P., Theobald, B.: The painful face: pain expression recognition using active appearance models In: Proceedings of the 9th International Conference on Multimodal Interfaces, pp. 9–14 (2007)
3. Cohn, J., Matthews, I., Yang, Y., Nguyen, M., Padilla, M., Zhou, F., De la Torre, F.: Detecting depression from facial actions and vocal prosody. In: 3rd International Conference on Affective Computing and Intelligent Interaction and Workshops ACII 2009, pp. 1–7. IEEE (2009)
4. Kaliouby, R.: Real-time inference of complex mental states from facial expressions and head gestures. In: Real-Time Vision For Human-Computer Interaction, pp. 181–200 (2005)
5. Ekman, P.: Facial Expressions of Emotion: an Old Controversy and New Findings. Philosophical Transactions of the Royal Society, London **B335**, 63–69 (1992)
6. Ekman, P.: Facial Action Coding System. Consulting Psychologists Press (1977)
7. D'Mello, S., McDaniel, B., King, B., Chipman, P., Tapp, K., Graesser, A.: Facial Features for Affective State Detection in Learning Environments (2006)
8. Cohen, J.: A coefficient of agreement for nominal scales. Educational and Psychological Measuremen. Educational and Psychological Measurement, **XX** (1960)
9. Bradski, G.: Learning OpenCV. Computer vision with openCV Library. O'Reilly Media (2008)
10. Baker, R.S., Corbett, A.T., Koedinger, K.R., Wagner, A.Z.: Off-task behavior in the cognitive tutor classroom: when students "Game The System". In: Proceedings of ACM CHI 2004: Computer-Human Interaction, pp. 383–390 (2004)
11. Rechy-Ramírez, F.: Discretización de series de tiempo usando programación evolutiva con función multiobojetivo. MSc Thesis. University of Veracruz (2010)

A Predictive Model of Learning Gains for a Video and Exercise Intensive Learning Environment

José A. Ruipérez-Valiente[1,2]([✉]), Pedro J. Muñoz-Merino[1], and Carlos Delgado Kloos[1]

[1] Universidad Carlos III de Madrid, Avenida Universidad 30, 28911 Leganés, Madrid, Spain
{jruipere,pedmume,cdk}@it.uc3m.es
[2] IMDEA Networks Institute, Av. del Mar Mediterráneo 22, 28918 Leganés, Madrid, Spain

Abstract. This work approaches the prediction of learning gains in an environment with intensive use of exercises and videos, specifically using the Khan Academy platform. We propose a linear regression model which can explain 57.4% of the learning gains variability, with the use of four variables obtained from the low level data generated by the students. We found that two of these variables are related to exercises (the proficient exercises and the average number of attempts in exercises), and one is related to both videos and exercises (the total time spent in both) related to exercises, whereas only one is related to videos.

Keywords: Educational data mining · Prediction · Learning analytics

1 Introduction

There is a natural wish to be able to predict a future outcome. Prediction on education field has been extensively research over the years. The targeted objectives in education are diverse, for example to be able to predict the score of a future test [1, 2]. The increased use of Massive Open Online Courses (MOOCs) over the last few years provides of a perfect scenario to apply prediction techniques with large amounts of data. The high number of enrollments in these courses makes impossible to monitor each student separately, as an example the work by Brinton *et al.* [3] analyzes data from more than 100.000 students taking MOOCs in Coursera platform; therefore it is necessary the implementation of artificial intelligence tools to support and improve the learning process.

This work aims at proposing a predictive model of learning gains by using some variables which have been obtained through an experience using MOOC technology, specifically the Khan Academy platform. However the access was restricted to a predefined number of students in what is so called Small Private Online Courses (SPOCs). In this approach we have selected low level variables as predictors, which can be retrieved in a straightforward way from the learning environment. We can find other works which use similar variables such as *avg_attempts* or *total_minutes* to predict students' test scores [1, 2]. In addition, other studies use different variables such as Pardos and Baker [4] where the predictor variables represent affective states.

© Springer International Publishing Switzerland 2015
C. Conati et al. (Eds.): AIED 2015, LNAI 9112, pp. 760–763, 2015.
DOI: 10.1007/978-3-319-19773-9_110

2   Description of the Experience

The experience is framed in the 0-courses taken by freshmen students at Universidad Carlos III de Madrid (UC3M). A personalized Khan Academy instance with exercises and videos developed by the instructors of UC3M was provided. In this experience, the main educational resources were exercises and videos. For these experiences we have also enabled our learning analytics tool ALAS-KA [5], which implements many of the parameters that we use in this prediction model.

This research has been conducted in the chemistry and physics courses of 2014. Courses were composed of 51 exercises and 24 videos for chemistry, and 33 for both exercises and videos for physics. We have designed a pre-test and post-test from a pool of questions of equal hardness for both physics and chemistry. We define a student learning gain by obtaining the difference between post-test minus pre-test (LG = post − pre). We obtained only a total amount of valid samples of 44 students in physics and 25 in chemistry which were incorporated into the prediction model.

We have selected and retrieved a set of low level variables which are related to the learning process. The variables that we have considered are the *pre_test_score*, the *pre_test_time*, *correct_exercises* (percentage of correct exercises that the student tried to solve), *exercises_solved_once* (percentage of different exercises that were solved at least once), *proficient_exercises* (percentage of exercises in which the student has acquired a proficiency level), *avg_hints* (average number of hints in exercises), *avg_attempts* (average number of attempts in exercises), *avg_video_progress* (average progress by the student in all videos of the course), *videos_completed* (percentage of videos completed by the student), *total_time* (total time spent in both videos and exercises by the student), *exercise_time* and *video_time*.

3   Prediction Model and Discussion

After an exploratory analysis with our data and a review of the state of the art, we proceed to make the selection of variables and performed the linear regression analysis. We selected a hierarchical method with two entry steps and a total of four independent variables (introducing two of them in each step). The ANOVA test proved that both models are better than the baseline prediction of the learning gain; the F-value of the first model ($F = 30.5$, $p = 0.000$) is a bit higher than the second one ($F = 21.6$, $p = 0.000$) due to the insertion of more predictors.

We can check the model summary in table 1. The first model (with just two variables) has an R^2 of 0.481, while the second model (with four variables) rises to 0.574 after adding up the two new variables. Therefore, our second model is able to account a 57.4 % of the variation in the learning gains. In addition, the standard error of prediction is 15.1 points. Table 2 shows the report for the coefficients of the predictor variables in the two models; we can take a look at the standardized coefficients to have a feeling about the importance of each predictor in the model. In addition, equation 1 shows the prediction model formula. Next, we make an analysis of the different predictor variables:

LG = 25.489 - 0.604 * pre_test_score + 6.112 * avg_attempts + 0.017 * total_time + 0.084 * proficient_exercises   (1)

- *pre_test_score*: this is the most important predictor in the model. The negative sign implies that the higher is the initial knowledge of students, the lower is going to be the increment in their knowledge. For every point in the pre-test, the predicted learning gain decreases 0.604 points.
- *avg_attempts*: the average number of attempts in exercises was also found to be an important predictor, whereas others like the average number of hints or time in exercises were not as important. For every unit that the average number of attempts increases, the predicted learning gain increases 4.093 points.
- *total_time*: the total time spent in videos and exercises (in minutes) is the second most important predictor of the model. For every additional minute, the predicted learning gain increases 0.017 points. This relationship makes sense, because if the student spends more time doing learning activities, it is more probable that the student learns more.
- *proficient_exercises*: the percentage of proficient exercises is the least important variable of the model, which might be quite surprising as it is related to how much progress the student did on exercises on the platform. However we should also take into account that it was the last variable entered in the model and that the total time spent in the platform might imply a better performance.

We have only used four independent variables, which is a prudent number considering the number of cases of our data sample. Three of the selected variables are related to exercises (*avg_attempts*, *total_time* and *proficient_exercises*) while one is related to videos (*total_time*). An important aspect is that measures related only to video progress (*avg_video_progress* and *videos_completed*) were not found as important as the ones related to exercises. However, we should state that progress in videos was also a useful predictor, but progressing on exercises variables had a more powerful impact in the model. It is also noteworthy to say that there are only three cases with a standardized residual above ±2, and none of them is over ±2.7, which means that there are not outliers. Thus the model is well fitted. The number of cases in the data sample was too small to make a cross-validation. However, we can argue that all the assumptions (linearity, independence of variables and errors, homoscedasticity, multicollinearity, normally distributed errors) from the regression model were fulfilled, thus the model should generalize properly in experiences under a similar context and variables.

One of the issues from these results is that, while the pre-test variable was the most important predictor of the model, sometimes it is not feasible to have the initial knowledge of the students (via pre-test or from a different source). A future research question is if these results can be extrapolated to different platforms such as Open edX with different indicators and types of exercises. As part of future work, we would like to use new variables which provide higher level information such as student behaviors, students' efficiency or by the combination of different powerful predictors.

Table 1. Model summary of the linear regression model

Model	R	R Square	Std. Error of the Prediction
1	0.693	0.481	16.42
2	0.758	0.574	15.1

Table 2. Coefficients of the regression model

Model	Independent Variable	Un-std. Coeff.		Std. Coeff.
		B	Std. Error	Beta
1	Constant	38.556	7.88	
	pre_test_score	- 0.601	0.84	- 0.655
	avg_attempts	4.093	3.149	0.119
2	Constant	25.489	8.071	
	pre_test_score	- 0.604	0.08	- 0.658
	avg_attempts	6.112	3.134	0.177
	total_time	0.017	0.011	0.202
	proficient_exercises	0.084	0.084	0.134

Acknowledgements. This work has been supported by the "eMadrid" project (Regional Government of Madrid) under grant S2013/ICE-2715 and the EEE project (Spanish Ministry of Science and Innovation, "Plan Nacional de I+D+I) under grant TIN2011-28308-C03-01

References

1. Feng, M., Heffernan, N.T., Koedinger, K.R.: Predicting state test scores better with intelligent tutoring systems: developing metrics to measure assistance required. In: Ikeda, M., Ashley, K.D., Chan, T.-W. (eds.) ITS 2006. LNCS, vol. 4053, pp. 31–40. Springer, Heidelberg (2006)
2. Feng, M., Beck, J., Heffernan, N., Koedinger, K.: Can an intelligent tutoring system predict math proficiency as well as a standarized test? In: Baker and Beck (eds.) Proceedings of the 1st International Conference on Educational Data Mining, Montreal, pp. 107–116 (2008)
3. Brinton, C., Chiang, M., Jain, S., Lam, H., Liu, Z., Wong, F.: Learning about social learning in MOOCs: From statistical analysis to generative model. IEEE Transactions on Learning Technologies. 7(4), 346–359 (2014)
4. Pardos, Z., Baker, R.S.: Affective States and State Tests: Investigating How Affect and Engagement during the School Year Predict End-of-Year Learning Outcomes. J. Learn. Anal. 1, 107–128 (2014)
5. Ruipérez-Valiente, J.A., Muñoz-Merino, P.J., Leony, D., Delgado Kloos, C.: ALAS-KA: A learning analytics extension for better understanding the learning process in the Khan Academy platform. Journal of. Computers in Human Behavior. 47, 139–148 (2015)

Integrating Learning Progressions in Unsupervised After-School Online Intelligent Tutoring

Vasile Rus[✉], Arthur Graesser, Nobal Niraula, and Rajendra Banjade

Departments of Computer Science and Psychology, Institute for Intelligent Systems,
The University of Memphis, Memphis, USA
vrus@memphis.edu

Abstract. We present the design of a novel conversational intelligent tutoring system, called DeepTutor. DeepTutor is based on cognitive theories of learning, the framework of Learning Progressions proposed by the science education research community, and deep natural language and dialogue processing techniques and principles. The focus of the paper is on the role of Learning Progressions on the design of DeepTutor. Furthermore, we emphasize the role of Learning Progressions in guiding macro-adaptivity in conversational ITSs. We conducted a large-scale, after-school experiment with hundreds of high-school students using DeepTutor. Importantly, these students interacted with the system totally unsupervised, i.e. without any supervision from an instructor or experimenter. Our work so far validates the Learning Progressions theory.

1 Introduction

We present in this paper the design of the conversational intelligent tutoring system DeepTutor (www.deeptutor.org). DeepTutor is based on cognitive theories of learning, the framework of Learning Progressions (LPs; [1]), and deep natural language and dialogue processing techniques. In this paper, we focus on the role of Learning Progressions (LPs) on the design of DeepTutor.

The framework of LPs was developed by the science education research community as a way forward in science education. LPs are "descriptions of the successively more sophisticated ways of thinking about a topic that can follow one another as children learn about and investigate a topic over a broad span of time" [1]. That is, LPs capture the natural sequence of mental models and mental model shifts students go through while mastering a topic. Overall, the LPs framework provides a promising means to organize and align content, instruction, and assessment strategies in order to give students the opportunity to develop a deep and integrated understanding of science ideas.

LPs are critical components in handling core tasks in DeepTutor: modeling the task domain, tracking students' knowledge states, and the feedback mechanism. Advances in these core tutoring tasks enable a highly-adaptive ITS. DeepTutor was built around an LP which we developed and empirically validated using data collected from observing a cohort of high-school students in traditional instruction. This empirical

© Springer International Publishing Switzerland 2015
C. Conati et al. (Eds.): AIED 2015, LNAI 9112, pp. 764–767, 2015.
DOI: 10.1007/978-3-319-19773-9_111

LP became the central component in DeepTutor affecting the system's adaptivity at all levels (macro- and micro-adaptivity). We focus on this paper on the role of LPs to drive macro-adaptivity in ITSs.

We conducted a real-world experiment with high-school students using the LP-driven DeepTutor in an informal learning context: after-school, unsupervised, fully-online tutoring. The goal of the experiment was to show that LP-driven macro-adaptation (the selection of instructional tasks during a tutoring session) is critical for tutoring effectiveness. More specifically, we compared a fully-adaptive system, DeepTutor, which offers both macro-adaptivity (instructional tasks are selected appropriately for each student based on her level in the LP/level of mastery) and micro-adaptivity (once working on a task, students are offered help as needed based on their individual performance on that task) to a micro-adaptive-only system. The fully-adaptive (DeepTutor) and micro-adaptive-only systems, respectively, were further compared to a condition in which students were just reading worked-out solutions to problems. Due to space limits we focus here only on describing the role of LPs in the design and drawing some conclusions.

The role of macro-adaptivity in conversational ITSs has been less emphasized by the literature to the best of our knowledge. It should be noted that the role of macro-adaptation was noted early on [2]. Attempts to handle macro-adaptivity have been made but their exact impact on learning gains has not been pursued [3]. Our approach to macro-adaption is based on the LP theory proposed by the science education research community, which is different from the knowledge spaces theory in ALEKS. The only systematic study on the role of macro-adaptation in conversational ITSs that also offer micro-adaptivity was reported recently [3]. However, their experiment was with college students and macro-adaptation was guided by an Item Response Theory (IRT) based approach as opposed to LPs.

It should be noted that ITSs that emphasize micro-adaptivity have been shown to induce very good learning gains in students. These systems do offer a one-size-fits-all type of macro-adaptivity in the sense that researchers through a careful cognitive analysis selected tasks for the target population as a whole. That is, all students will be assigned the same set of tasks regardless of their knowledge state. Furthermore, results reported by these systems are from experiments conducted in the lab while in our case, the experiment is "in the wild", outside of a controlled environment. Students accessed our system after-school from home, library, or other places. They interacted with our system totally unsupervised by any instructor or experimenter. Our prototype and large-scale experiment is a solid proof that conversational intelligent tutoring is possible 24/7 at this moment in time.

We targeted the domain of conceptual Physics at high-school level in our initial system development. However, the design has been developed with scalability requirements in mind (cross-topic and cross-domain) such that it could be extended to new topics and new domains, e.g., biology.

2   Overview of the Intelligent Tutoring System Deeptutor

Our system is a dialogue-based intelligent tutoring system (ITS; [9]) that helps students master science topics through conceptual problem-solving. Besides the fact that conceptual reasoning fits well with a dialogue-based form of interaction, another important reason for targeting conceptual aspects of science topics is the fact that conceptual reasoning is more challenging. Furthermore, conversational ITSs have the potential of giving students the opportunity to learn the language of scientists, an important goal in science literacy. A student at a more shallow understanding of a science topic uses more informal language as opposed to more scientific accounts. Accordingly, students who use more informal language are at lower levels in a Learning Progressions (LPs) while students who talk more scientifically are at higher levels in an LP. The link between students' language characteristic and the LPs is beyond the scope of this paper.

When interacting with the DeepTutor, students are challenged to solve qualitative Physics problems. Students read a problem and then must provide an answer in the form of a short essay. Their solutions are automatically evaluated using natural language assessment methods and if necessary, e.g. the student provides an incorrect or incomplete solution, a scaffolding dialogue follows. The goal of the dialogue is to coach students in finding the solution by themselves based on constructivist theories of learning, self-explanation, and Socratic principles of instruction. For instance, the system helps students articulate the missing steps in their solutions through hints in the form of questions. Furthermore, our intelligent tutor corrects immediately any misconceptions students articulate. Feedback is provided as well (positive feedback – "Great job."; negative feedback – "This is incorrect."; neutral feedback - "Ok."). It is beyond the scope of this paper to offer all the details of DeepTutor. It should be noted that all the tutorial strategies that are part of the scaffolding tutorial dialogue while a student works on a problem enable micro-adaptivity (within-task adaptivity). We focus here on the LPs and their role in guiding macro-adaptivity in DeepTutor, which is another reason why we do not further elaborate on the within-task strategies.

3   Better Learner and Domain Modeling Using Learning Progressions

A key novel aspect of DeepTutor is the development of better learner and domain models through the integration of Learning Progressions (LPs). An advantage of LP-based learner and domain models is the focus on organizing the domain knowledge from a learner's perspective as opposed to an experts' perspective. That is, LPs encode successful paths towards mastery as discovered by observing students who mastered a target topic. This is in contrast to learning paths suggested by experts which may or may not lead to learners achieving mastery. Based on the LP theory, we conjectured that using LPs to guide macro-adaptivity in ITSs would lead to qualitative and tutoring effectiveness advantages.

An important argument for using LPs to increase adaptivity in ITSs is the fact that they were developed as part of an effort by the assessment in education community to increase adaptivity of traditional instruction. "Assessment for learning" has been a focus in this community for more than a decade ([5]). This effort led to the emergence of the framework of LPs.

4 Conclusions

We investigated in this paper the role of using LPs to drive the design of advanced ITSs that offer increased levels of adaptation to individual learners. The focus of the work presented here was on the role of LPs on the macro-adaption capabilities of these ITSs. While there is much work to be done to fully understand the role of LPs on the behavior and effectiveness of ITSs, there are some important implications of our work presented here. First of all, we conclude that the integration of LPs within traditional conversational ITSs leads to qualitative improvements and better learning as proven by the results of our experiment.

Second, the positive results obtained by the fully-adaptive system indicates that macro-adaptation plays a more important role on the effectiveness of ITSs than previously understood. This is the case because selecting the instructional tasks is an upstream decision during tutoring which, if suboptimal, negatively impacts downstream components, e.g. within-task adaptation. That is, if a task is incorrectly selected, e.g. a too easy task for an advanced learner, even if the micro-adaptation module is optimal there will be limited learning gains.

Third, the positive result for the LP-driven ITSs is a form of validation of the LP theory. That is, we empirically validated the developed LP through a massive online experiment with DeepTutor.

Acknowledgments. This research was supported in part by Institute for Education Sciences under awards R305A100875. Any opinions, findings or recommendations expressed in this material are solely the authors'.

References

1. Corcoran, T., Mosher, F.A., Rogat, A.: Learning progressions in science: An evidence based approach to reform. Consortium for Policy Research in Education Report #RR-63. Consortium for Policy Research in Education, Philadelphia (2009)
2. Brusilovsky, P.: A framework for intelligent knowledge sequencing and task sequencing. In: Frasson, C., McCalla, G.I., Gauthier, G. (eds.) ITS 1992. LNCS, vol. 608, pp. 499–506. Springer, Heidelberg (1992)
3. Rus, V., Stefanescu, D., Baggett, W., Niraula, N., Franceschetti, D., Graesser, A.C.: Macro-adaptation in conversational intelligent tutoring matters. In: Trausan-Matu, S., Boyer, K.E., Crosby, M., Panourgia, K. (eds.) ITS 2014. LNCS, vol. 8474, pp. 242–247. Springer, Heidelberg (2014)
4. Rus, V., D'Mello, S., Hu, X., Graesser, A.C.: Recent Advances in Conversational Intelligent Tutoring Systems. AI Magazine **34**(3), 42–54 (2013)
5. National Research Council. Systems for state science assessment. (Wilson, M.R., Bertenthal, M.W. (eds.)). National Academy Press, Washington (2005)

When More Intelligent Tutoring in the Form of Buggy Messages Does Not Help

Douglas Selent[(✉)] and Neil Heffernan

Worcester Polytechnic Institute, Worcester, MA, USA
{dselent,nth}@wpi.edu

Abstract. This paper reports on the null results from two large scale randomized controlled trials that were run in the ASSISTments online tutoring system. Both studies attempted to use reactive buggy messages to help students learn; one in the form of short 20–30 second videos and another in the form of large color-coded text. Bug messages were supplied for common wrong answers for one-step equation problems in both studies. Despite the large amount of prior research done on error analysis, both interventions using the predicted common wrong answers were unsuccessful at helping students.

Keywords: Buggy message · Randomized controlled trial · Video feedback

1   Introduction

A "buggy message" provides a unique and specific to the incorrect answer entered by the student. The notion of "bugs" was first introduced by Brown and Burton in 1978 and the early 1980's with their series of "BUGGY" programs [1]. The main goal of BUGGY was to show teachers that incorrect answers supplied by the student are not random and are a result of systematic errors and misconceptions. An extension of the BUGGY program called DEBUGGY and IDEBUGGY (an online interactive version of DEBUGGY) attempted to match the incorrect answer to a set of previously defined bug rules [3].

Brown and VanLehn continued this work using repair theory to explain why students make some errors but not others and the cause of the errors [2]. After running some empirical studies VanLehn found that errors were not stable and students did not consistently make the same mistake twice [8].

Sleeman also created a program to discover bugs. Sleeman ran an experiment on a group of 24 14-year-old students on algebra problem using the Leeds Modeling System (LMS) bug database to establish classes for the different types of errors [6]. Further analysis was done on the types of errors students made in attempt to explain bug-migration (inconsistent student errors). Sleeman proposed the mechanism of Mis-generalization (incorrectly inferring rules) to explain bug migration and why LMS originally missed several bugs [7].

Throughout the 80's and 90's there was a large amount of work focused on student modeling. This work includes student modeling based on the incorrect answers and

© Springer International Publishing Switzerland 2015
C. Conati et al. (Eds.): AIED 2015, LNAI 9112, pp. 768–771, 2015.
DOI: 10.1007/978-3-319-19773-9_112

automatically discovering the incorrect processes that generated the incorrect answers. Sison summarizes several machine learning programs that attempt automatically construct student models [5].

The two studies in this paper follow up on the randomized controlled trial run by Selent and Heffernan, who tried to help students with buggy messages [4]. Since it was believed that their initial experiment failed due to poor tutoring content, two additional randomized controlled trials were run with focus on improving the tutoring content. One experiment used buggy messages in the form of short 20-30 second videos. Combining both buggy messages with short videos has not been done before and is a novel form of tutoring. Another experiment provides buggy messages with large color-coded text providing both context to the problem and the reason why the answer is incorrect. The hypothesis is that the answer-specific help would help students more than on-demand help. This paper reports on the null results of the two randomized controlled trials run in the ASSISTments online tutoring system.

2   Experiment Design

2.1   Study 1 (Text Buggy Messages)

A skill builder problem set was created for problems on solving one-step equations with integers, which is typically taught in seventh grade for students of ages 12-13. The control group received problems where students had the option to click on a hint button. A student could click on the hint button up to three times. The first hint contained a similar example problem, showing all the steps to reach the solution. The second and third hint contained steps to solve the current problem each time the hint button was clicked, until the last hint revealed the answer to the problem. This currently is the best form of help for this problem set in the ASSISTments system, and therefore, was used as the problem set for the control group. The experiment group received the same problems as the control group with the addition of buggy text messages that appeared as soon as a student submitted an incorrect answer. These buggy messages showed the steps of the problem the student did correctly and the step that the student performed incorrectly as well as providing the correct rules the student needed to fix their mistake. If a student entered an incorrect answer that was not predicted, a generic message was shown to the student to notify the student that he/she had answered the problem incorrectly. This experiment design compares a strong control group, where students have a set of hints that walk through an example problem, to an experiment group that adds buggy messages to the current problems.

2.2   Study 2 (Video Buggy Messages)

Similar to the first study, a skill builder problem set was created for problems on solving one step equations with integers. The control group received problems where students had the option to click on a hint button which gave the answer. This is the standard form of help in ASSISTments, therefore was used as the control. The experiment group received problems that did not have the option to click on a hint button, but received help in the form of video buggy messages. Students received a short 20-30 second video when they entered a predicted incorrect answer. This video explained what process the student used to arrive at their incorrect answer and how to start on the correct solution path. The videos were created by Andrew Burnett, a former middle school teacher, where Andrew explained the problem using a white board. The videos did not give the solution to the student. This experiment design compares a weak control group, where students only had the option to see the answer, to an experiment group that had proactive help in the form of video buggy messages hints but did not have on-demand hints.

3   Analysis

Students who answered three problems correctly in a row and completed the problem set without any tutoring were removed. Since these students did not receive any tutoring, they did not experience the conditions of the experiment. A χ^2 test was used to ensure the number of students was not significantly different between the two groups for the initial condition assignment for study 1, χ^2 (1, n=490) = 2.359, p>0.05, and study 2, χ^2 (1, n=1379) = 0.059, p>0.05. A χ^2 test was also used to ensure the number of students that were removed was not significantly different between the two groups for study 1, χ^2 (1, n=268) = 1.493, p>0.05, and study 2, χ^2 (1, n=730) = 0.005, p>0.05. After removing these students a total of 222 (control = 104, experiment = 118) students remained for the first study and a total of 649 (control = 328, experiment = 321) students remained for the second study.

The following statistics were used to measure the helpfulness of the tutoring.

1. The number of students that finish the problem set
2. Number of problems it takes a student to complete the problem set
3. Correctness on the next problem following a student's first incorrect response
4. Attempts on the next problem following a student's first incorrect response
5. Hints on the next problem following a student's first incorrect response

The completion percentage for study 1 was 64% for the control group and 68% for the experiment group and the completion percent for study 2 was 88% for the control group and 86% for the experiment group. A χ^2 showed that there were no significant differences in completion rates between the control group and the experiment group for study 1, χ^2 (1, n=147) = 1.15, p>0.05 and study 2, χ^2 (1, n=564) = 0.348, p>0.05.

A two-tailed t-test showed that there were no significance differences for the number of problems it took students to complete the problem set in study 1 (μ_1 = 6.0, μ_1 = 5.8, n_1 = 67, n_2 = 80, p = 0.69) and study 2 (μ_1 = 7.3, μ_1 = 6.9, n_1 = 289, n_2 = 275, p = 0.30). A MANOVA was done using SPSS to see if there was a significant different between the control and experiment conditions on the next question after a student's first incorrect response. For the first study a MANOVA was run with condition as the only factor and correctness, attempts, and hints as dependent measures. The results show no main effect with Wilks' λ = 0.98, $F(3, 143)$ = 0.989, and p = 0.4. For the second study the same analysis was done, except hint use was excluded as a measure since the experiment group did not have the option to ask for hints. The results show no main effect with Wilks' $\lambda = 0.991$, $F(2, 561) = 2.674$, and $p = 0.07$.

4   Conclusions and Future Work

In this paper two studies were run in the ASSISTments tutoring system using tutoring with different types of buggy messages. Although both studies resulted in a null result, we choose to report on them for the following reasons. Despite the large amount of research done on error analysis, there were few interventions done using buggy messages and none done at the scale in this paper. We show that neither color-coded text messages nor short videos were effective. It is future work to focus less on how or why a student arrived at a specific wrong answer and focus other methods of tutoring to communicate better to the students.

Acknowledgement. We acknowledge funding for ASSISTments from the NSF (1316736, 1252297, 1109483, 1031398, 0742503, 1440753), the U.S. Dept. of Ed. GAANN (P200A120238), ONR's "STEM Grand Challenges," and IES (R305A120125, R305C100024).

References

1. Brown, J.S., Burton, R.R.: Diagnostic Models for Procedural Bugs in Basic Mathematical Skills*. Cognitive science **2**(2), 155–192 (1978)
2. Brown, J.S., VanLehn, K.: Repair theory: A generative theory of bugs in procedural skills. Cognitive science **4**(4), 379–426 (1980)
3. Burton, R.B.: DEBUGGY: diagnosis of errors in basic mathematical skills. In: Sherman, D., Brown, J.S. (eds.) Intelligent tutoring systems. Academic Press, London (1981)
4. Selent, D., Heffernan, N.: Reducing student hint use by creating buggy messages from machine learned incorrect processes. In: Trausan-Matu, S., Boyer, K.E., Crosby, M., Panourgia, K. (eds.) ITS 2014. LNCS, vol. 8474, pp. 674–675. Springer, Heidelberg (2014)
5. Sison, R., Shimura, M.: Student modeling and machine learning. International Journal of Artificial Intelligence in Education (IJAIED) **9**, 128–158 (1998)
6. Sleeman, D.: Basic algebra revisited: a study with 14-year-olds. International Journal of Man-Machine Studies **22**(2), 127–149 (1985)
7. Sleeman, D.: Mis-generalisation: an explanation of observed mal-rules. In: Proceedings of the Sixth Annual Conference of the Cognitive Science Society, pp. 51–56 (1984)
8. Van Lehn, K.: Bugs are not enough: Empirical studies of bugs, impasses and repairs in procedural skills. The Journal of Mathematical Behavior (1982)
9. https://sites.google.com/site/assistmentsdata/projects/selent2015

Supporting Students' Interactions
over Case Studies

Mayya Sharipova[✉] and Gordon McCalla

ARIES Lab, Department of Computer Science,
University of Saskatchewan, Saskatoon, Canada
{m.sharipova,gordon.mccalla}@usask.ca

Abstract. Having students analyze case studies is one of the common tutoring strategies for ill-defined domains. This paper presents a system, Umka, that supports learners as they form arguments about case studies in a professional ethics class. The system creates visualizations of the differences between students' case positions, and suggests to students certain peers to interact with who might help to provide deeper and broader insight. The system has been run in several iterations. Experiments with the latest version confirm the benefits of the approach in stimulating productive interactions among students, and causing students to reconsider and broaden their initial positions on a case study.

Keywords: Ill-defined domain of ethics · Case studies · Collaboration

1 Introduction

Analysis of case studies has been identified as one of the common tutoring strategies for many ill-defined domains including professional ethics. One of the most effective ways to organize the analysis of case studies is through peer discussions and interactions.

The social constructivist perspective on learning dictates that individuals create their own new understandings through meaningful social interactions with others. Particularly, peer interactions with sociocognitive conflicts lead to higher levels of reasoning and learning [6]. Similarly, Kohlberg argued that it is the cognitive conflict and exposure to the next higher moral reasoning stage that moves students up in their moral development [4]. Nucci also highlighted conflict as a characteristic of effective moral discussions [5].

While several tutoring systems have been developed to support students' ethical analysis of case studies (e.g. PETE [1], AEINS [3]), organizing and stimulating students' interactions was not a central focus of these systems.

We have developed several versions of a computer-based learning environment called Umka where students analyse case studies for professional ethics education [7]. In Umka students first analyze a case study individually: they propose a resolution for a case study, provide arguments for and against a particular resolution, and supply a conclusion justifying their choice of the resolution based on the provided arguments. After that the students collaborate on the case study:

© Springer International Publishing Switzerland 2015
C. Conati et al. (Eds.): AIED 2015, LNAI 9112, pp. 772–775, 2015.
DOI: 10.1007/978-3-319-19773-9_113

they access analyses of each other, rate and comment on each other's reasoning, and modify their own analyses based on received comments, and viewed analyses of others.

2   Supporting Students' Interactions in Umka

This paper focuses on the latest version of Umka, which supports students' interactions in the analysis of case studies through visualization of students' positions and explicit suggestions to consider certain helpful positions of others.

The visualization represents a student's position as a circle (Figure 1):

1. The size of the circle is determined by the number of different arguments the student has considered for a case study.
2. The darkness is determined by the average rating that the student's peers gave for the student's arguments and comments.
3. The distance between circles of different students reflects the differences between their arguments.
4. The color of the student's circle reflects the resolution that the student has chosen for the case study. Thus, circles of the same color represent students' positions with the same chosen resolution for an analyzed case study.

Umka also supports students' interactions by explicitly suggesting to students certain "helpful" peers to interact with. For a given student, these helpful peers will be peers who have the highest combination of the following factors: a) different case study resolutions from the student's resolution; b) the highest difference between their and the student's arguments; c) the highest ratings of their reasoning as assessed by others.

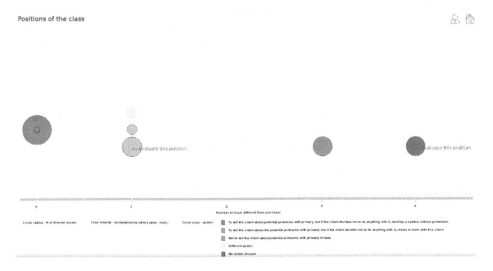

Fig. 1. Visualization of students' positions

Both Umka's suggestions and its visualization are based on modeling differences between student positions. To calculate differences between students' arguments we used a variation of Latent Semantic Analysis, a method called Weighted Textual Matrix Factorization (WTMF) [2]. WTMF was specifically designed for calculating similarity between short pieces of text, such as short students' arguments in Umka. For our experiments (Section 3), WTMF yielded precision of 0.7-0.8 when compared to human-based evaluation.

3   Experiments and Results

We expected that Umka's support in the form of visualization and suggestions would stimulate students' reflection and interaction with others, causing them to expand their initial positions with new ideas. Hence, our hypotheses were:

Hypotheses: Umka's visualization and suggestions foster productive interactions among students. Students with these support types, in comparison with students without these support types:

1. view more "helpful" analyses of their peers
2. give more comments to the analyses of their peers
3. spend more time in analyses of other students
4. (as the result of these interactions) introduce more changes to their own analyses during collaboration.

To test the effectiveness of the proposed support types, we conducted two experiments: 1) SIAST experiment with 44 technical school students, and 2) UofT experiment with 37 university students. Each of the SIAST and UofT groups was randomly broken into two sub-groups: a treatment group who used the Umka system with the visualization and suggestions, and a control group who used Umka without these features having only an interface where students could enter their arguments, and see and comment on arguments of others.

Table 1. Comparison of the SIAST and UofT treatment and control groups (statistically significant results are displayed with an asterisk)

N	Metric	SIAST Control	SIAST Treatment	UofT Control	UofT Treatment
1	Proportion of helpful positions of peers viewed from the total # of viewed peers' positions	66%	68%	37%*	75%*
2	Aver. # of comments given to their peers	1.3*	4.7*	2.9	3.2
3	Aver. time spent studying analyses of other students (in secs)	593	809	1211	2470
4	Aver. # of changes introduced to analyses during collaboration	3.5	4	1.75	2.15

Table 1 demonstrates experimental results — the comparison between the SIAST and UofT control and treatment groups according to the different metrics shown. As can be seen from this table, the treatment groups outperformed the control groups for all hypotheses, and in all types of productive interactions. However, we could achieve statistically significant differences only for hypothesis 1 in the UofT experiment (the Mann-Whitney test: p-value = 7.996e-06), and for hypothesis 2 in the SIAST experiment (the Mann-Whitney test: p=0.00834). Nevertheless, the fact that the trends from the SIAST experiment were replicated in the UofT experiment as well, could serve as an additional demonstration that these effects are actually occurring and not due to chance.

4   Conclusion

In this paper we have offered a way for organizing and supporting peer interactions based on sociocognitive conflicts. We have presented a learning environment, Umka, that through visualization and suggestions supports students' interactions as they analyze ethical case studies. The result was an increase in students' productive interactions. We believe that the techniques of the visualization and suggestions proposed in this paper could be generalized beyond ethics domain, for other ill-defined domains as well that need to support students' interactions over case studies. For more on the Umka project see [7].

Acknowledgments. The authors wish to thank the Natural Sciences and Engineering Research Council of Canada for their funding of this research project.

References

1. Goldin, I., Ashley, K., Pinkus, R.: Introducing PETE:computer support for teaching ethics. In: Proceedings of the 8th International Conference on Artificial Intelligence and Law, pp. 94–98. ACM (2001)
2. Guo, W., Diab, M.: Modeling sentences in the latent space. In: Proceedings of the 50th Annual Meeting of the Association for Computational Linguistics, pp. 864–872. Association for Computational Linguistics (2012)
3. Hodhod, R., Kudenko, D., Cairns, P.: AEINS: Adaptive educational interactive narrative system to teach ethics. In: Proceedings of the AIED 2009 Workshop on Intelligent Educational Games, p. 79 (2009)
4. Kohlberg, L.: Resolving, moral conflicts within the just community. In: Moral dilemmas: philosophical and psychological issues in the development of moral reasoning. Transaction Publishers (1985)
5. Nucci, L.: Synthesis of research on moral development. Educational Leadership **44**(5), 86–92 (1987)
6. Palincsar, A.: Social constructivist perspectives on teaching and learning. Annual Review of Psychology **49**, 345–375 (1998)
7. Sharipova, M.: Supporting students in the analysis of case studies for professional ethics education. Ph.D. thesis, University of Saskatchewan (2015)

A Framework for Automated Generation of Questions Based on First-Order Logic

Rahul Singhal$^{(\boxtimes)}$, Martin Henz, and Shubham Goyal

School of Computing, National University of Singapore (NUS),
Singapore, Singapore
{rahulsinghal,henz,shubham}@comp.nus.edu.sg

Abstract. In this work, questions are tasks posed to students to help them understand a subject, or to help educators assess their level of competency in it. Automated question generation is important today as content providers in education try to scale their efforts. In particular, MOOCs need a continuous supply of new questions in order to offer educational content to thousands of students, and to provide a fair assessment process. In this paper we establish first-order logic as a suitable formal tool to describe question scenarios, questions and answers. We apply this approach to the domain of mechanics (physics) in high school education.

Keywords: First order logic · Automated deduction · Pattern matching · Formal domains · Axiomatic approach · Constraint handling rules (CHR)

1 Introduction and Related Work

Developing assessment material is laborious. Teachers spend countless hours scavenging textbooks and developing original exercises for practice worksheets, homework problems, remedial material and exams. To prevent cheating, many teachers write several versions of each test, multiplying the work required for creating problems. Various standardized tests such as GRE, SAT and GMAT regularly require new questions.

This demand has become more acute with the rising popularity of massive open online courses (MOOCs), in which tens of thousands of students may be enrolled in a course. This massive scale poses a significant technical challenge: creating a large and diverse set of problems of varying difficulty, preventing cheating, and providing new practice problems to students. Hence, there is a need of a software that can quickly generate a large number of questions.

The best developed tutoring systems—JGEX Gao and Lin [2004], Geogebra Geogebra [2013] and Cinderella Cinderella [2013] for geometry, Active-Math Melis and Siekmann [2004] for algebra, and Andes Vanlehn et al. [2005] for physics—do not yet generate questions automatically. A question generation methodology for high school algebra is proposed in Singh et al. [2012], which generates questions similar to a given one, based on a combination of synthesizing

© Springer International Publishing Switzerland 2015
C. Conati et al. (Eds.): AIED 2015, LNAI 9112, pp. 776–780, 2015.
DOI: 10.1007/978-3-319-19773-9_114

Steps	Before	After
Initialization		$(\mathcal{E}_1, \mathsf{T}, \mathsf{T})$ where $\mathcal{E}_1$ is the formula in Figure 1b
Extension	$(\mathcal{E}_1, \mathsf{T}, \mathsf{T})$ where $\mathcal{E}_1$ is the formula in Figure 1b	$(\mathcal{E}_1, \acute{\mathcal{I}}, \mathsf{T})$, $\acute{\mathcal{I}} = equal(T_1, T_2)$ is fact of equal forces on rope added as an implicit fact
Enrichment	$(\mathcal{E}_1, \acute{\mathcal{I}}, \mathsf{T})$	$(\mathcal{E}_1 \wedge \acute{\mathcal{E}}, \acute{\mathcal{I}}, \mathsf{T})$, Instantiating masses of blocks and added to scenario $\acute{\mathcal{E}} = mass\_block(B_1, M_1), mass\_block(B_2, M_2)$
Commitment	$(\mathcal{E}_1 \wedge \acute{\mathcal{E}}, \acute{\mathcal{I}} \wedge \mathcal{H}, \mathsf{T})$, $\mathcal{H} = acc\_block$ $(B_1, (M_2 - M_1)/$ $(M_2 + M_1) * G)$ added as implicit fact	$(\mathcal{E}_1 \wedge \acute{\mathcal{E}}, \acute{\mathcal{I}}, \mathcal{H})$ A question generated from $\mathcal{H}$ is finding the acceleration of block B_1 given the masses of B_1 and B_2 as M_1 and M_2 respectively.

(c)

connected (B_1, R_1),
connected (B_2, R_2),
connected (P, R_1),
connected (P, R_2),
connected (R_1, R_2),
stationary_pulley (P),
acc_block (B_1, A_1),
acc_block (B_2, A_2),
massles_pulley (P),
block (B_1), block (B_2),
rope (R_1), rope (R_2),

(b)

(a)

Fig. 1. (a) pictorial representation of the generated/predefined scenario along with the user input; (b) logical representation of the scenario in the framework; (c) an instance of Question-setting $\mathcal{C}$

and numerical techniques. The generated questions in this approach resemble the given question syntactically and the approach does not consider solution generation.

Alvin et al. [2014] propose an algorithm for generating geometry proof questions for a high school curriculum. The problem generation approach firstly generates a hypergraph that represents all possible proofs over a given pair of user-provided figures and axioms. Later, it systematically enumerates all possible goal sets to find interesting problems. The approach is semi-automated as the user needs to provide a figure to generate questions. Furthermore, Singhal et al. [2014] propose a framework for automated generation of high school geometry questions. However, the scope is limited to the geometry domain.

In this paper, we address the problem of automatically generating new questions and solutions to the satisfaction of a user, based on a specified topic in a given, formally described domain. The proposed framework generates a *scenario* from the user-specified input and then repeatedly adds automatically deduced or generated consistent information, until a question is generated that satisfies the user's requirements. We argue that first-order logic is an adequate formalism to describe domains, scenarios and questions, and use high-school mechanics to demonstrate the resulting question generation framework.

2   Domain

A *domain* consists of objects, relationships between the objects and the rules that govern their arrangement. We represent a domain by a first-order structure where we describe each object type by a unary predicate and the relevant relationships between objects by non-unary predicates.

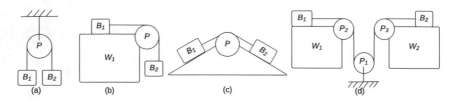

Fig. 2. (a) an existing figure scenario; (b) generated by from (a) by adding a fixed wedge; (c) generated from (a) by adding an inclined wedge; (d) generated from (a) by adding multiple wedges, pulleys and blocks

The properties of a domain are given by a set of axioms, which are first-order formulas. We illustrate these concepts using mechanics domains.

We represent various domain-objects such as pulleys, ropes and blocks by unary predicates such as *pulley*, *rope* and *block*, and their relationships by non-unary predicates. For example, the first order formula *connected*(P, R) expresses the fact that the pulley P and the rope R are connected. For representing quantitative relationships we use real numbers as arguments. For example, *force_block*($B, 10$) describes the fact that the force acting on the block B is 10 units. Figure 1b shows a partial list of first-order formulas for representing the mechanics domain. We describe the domain rules via axioms.

SWI-Prolog (Version 7.1.2) Schrijvers and Demoen [2004] is used for implementation of predicates. The axioms are represented using Constraint Handling Rules (CHR) Frühwirth and Raiser [2011]. In our implementation, we use the CHR library provided by K.U.Leuven, on top of SWI-Prolog. Mechanics domain requires solving of linear equations, for which we use the SWI-Prolog library CLPR.

3   Scenarios

Questions are typically situated in a *scenario*—an arrangement of domain objects that then gives rise to a problem to be solved by the student. We present scenarios by formulas $\exists \bar{X}\ \mathcal{F}(\bar{X})$, where $\mathcal{F}(\bar{X})$ is a formula whose free variables are in $\bar{X}$. We generate a scenario from the domain rules for adding, removing and modifying the objects and their arrangements.

In mechanics, Figure 2a shows a scenario generated from the domain rules for adding pulleys, blocks, ropes and wedges. Figure 1b represents a partial list of facts and their conjunction forms the scenario as shown in Figure 2a. Figure 2b, c, d and e show the generation of various new scenarios from Figure 2a with the application of domain rules.

4   Question Generation Framework

Let us assume a given scenario $\exists \bar{X}\ \mathcal{F}(\bar{X})$. A *question* based on this scenario is a more specific formula $\exists \bar{X}\ (\mathcal{F}(\bar{X}) \wedge \mathcal{G}(\bar{X}))$, where $\mathcal{G}(\bar{X})$ is the additional information that the question asks for and that the student needs to provide in an answer. For example, Figure 1c shows a generated fact $\mathcal{H}$ which can be converted to a quantitative question such as finding the acceleration of block B_1.

We propose a framework for producing a state sequence to generate questions where each state is a *question-setting* $\mathcal{C}$, which can be described as: $\mathcal{C} = (\mathcal{E}, \mathcal{I}, \mathcal{H})$, where $\mathcal{E}$ represents explicit facts to be made known to the student, $\mathcal{I}$ represents implicit facts to be hidden from the student and $\mathcal{H}$ represents facts that might constitute a solution to a generated question, of course also to be hidden from the student. In terms of first-order logic, a question-setting $\mathcal{C}$ can be described as a formula, as shown in Equation 1, which is the conjunction of its components $\mathcal{E}, \mathcal{I}$, and $\mathcal{H}$.

$$C = \exists \bar{X}((\mathcal{E}(\bar{X}) \wedge \mathcal{I}(\bar{X}) \wedge \mathcal{H}(\bar{X})) \tag{1}$$

Note that $\mathcal{I}$ and $\mathcal{H}$ may be $\top$. Each component of the state changes along the process of question generation. We discuss the steps used in question generation assisted with an example in mechanics as shown in Figure 1.

Initialization: $(\mathcal{E}_0, \top, \top)$, refers to the scenario generation from the user given topic. $\mathcal{E}_0$ is a scenario representing a set of generated explicit facts. For example, the first row of Figure 1c explains the state transformation in mechanics where we generate a scenario (see Figure 1a) from the user-given topic— pulleys, ropes and blocks. We assume $\mathcal{E}_0$ is sound.

Extension: $(\mathcal{E}, \mathcal{I}, \top) \Rightarrow (\mathcal{E}, \mathcal{I} \wedge \mathcal{I}', \top)$, refers to the generation of new facts from the predefined domain axioms and explicit facts. For example, the second row of Figure 1c shows an example of generation of a new implicit fact $\mathcal{I}'$. The fact $equal(T_1, T_2)$ implies that the forces acting on the blocks by the rope in the scenario are equal. Our framework generates this fact through application of an axiom that deals with the forces acting on a block by ropes. In first-order logic, this step is represented as $\forall \bar{X}(\mathcal{E}(\bar{X}) \wedge \mathcal{I}(\bar{X}) \rightarrow \mathcal{I}'(\bar{X}))$

Enrichment: $(\mathcal{E}, \mathcal{I}, \top) \Rightarrow (\mathcal{E} \wedge \mathcal{E}', \mathcal{I}, \top)$, generates new facts $\mathcal{E}'$ and adds them to the existing scenario. The third row of Figure 1c shows an example of an explicit fact $\mathcal{E}'$. The formula $mass\_block(B_1, M_1)$ assigns the mass of block B_1 to M_1. We add these facts to the list of explicit facts resulting in a specific scenario. In first-order logic, this step is represented as
$\exists \bar{X}(\mathcal{E}(\bar{X}) \wedge \mathcal{I}(\bar{X})) \rightarrow \exists \bar{X}(\mathcal{E}(\bar{X}) \wedge \mathcal{I}(\bar{X}) \wedge \mathcal{E}'(\bar{X}))$

Commitment: $(\mathcal{E}, \mathcal{I} \wedge \mathcal{H}, \top) \Rightarrow (\mathcal{E}, \mathcal{I}, \mathcal{H})$, refers to the generation of fact $\mathcal{H}$ which represents the answer of a question. For example, the last row of Figure 1c shows the fact $acc\_block(B_1, (M_1 - M_2) * G/(M_1 + M_2))$ that can be converted to answer of the question of finding the accelerations of blocks B_1 and B_2 given their masses as M_1 and M_2, respectively.

We call a question sound if it is internally consistent and has a solution generated from the domain axioms. We propose the following theorem regarding our framework.

Theorem 1. *Any algorithm that starts with an initialization step and generates a sequence of extension, enrichment and commitment steps generates sound questions.*

Each step is either generating implicit facts with the help of domain axioms, adding explicit facts with the help of a function or adding a question fact. The theorem is proven by induction on the number of steps required to generate a question. The initial question setting is sound and each step constitutes a sound transformation in first-order logic.

5 Future Work

In this paper, we have described a framework for generating questions, based on first-order logic, and demonstrated it using the domain of physics. In future work, we will use the framework across domains and explore its strengths and weaknesses for generating questions, and evaluates its use in practise. For this, we are planning to involve high school teachers to compare computer and human-generated questions.

References

Cinderella geometry tool (January 2013). http://www.cinderella.de/tiki-index.php

Geogebra geometry tool (January 2013). http://www.geogebra.org

Alvin, C., Gulwani, S., Majumdar, R., Mukhopadhyay, S.: Synthesis of geometry proof problems. In: Proceedings of the 28th AAAI Conference on Artificial Intelligence, pp. 245–252 (2014)

Frühwirth, T., Raiser, F. (eds.): Constraint Handling Rules: Compilation, Execution, and Analysis. Books On Demand (2011)

Gao, X.-S., Lin, Q.: MMP/geometer – a software package for automated geometric reasoning. In: Winkler, F. (ed.) ADG 2002. LNCS (LNAI), vol. 2930, pp. 44–66. Springer, Heidelberg (2004)

Melis, E., Siekmann, J.H.: ACTIVEMATH: an intelligent tutoring system for mathematics. In: Rutkowski, L., Siekmann, J.H., Tadeusiewicz, R., Zadeh, L.A. (eds.) ICAISC 2004. LNCS (LNAI), vol. 3070, pp. 91–101. Springer, Heidelberg (2004)

Schrijvers, T., Demoen, B.: The K. U. Leuven CHR system-implementation and application. In: First Workshop on Constraint Handling Rules-Selected Contributions, pp. 1–5 (2004)

Singh, R., Gulwani, S., Rajamani, S.: Automatically generating algebra problems. In: Brodley, C.E., Stone, P. (eds.) Proceedings of the 26th AAAI Conference on Artificial Intelligence, pp. 1620–1627 (2012)

Singhal, R., Henz, M., McGee, K.: Automated generation of geometry questions for high school mathematics. In: Proceeedings of the Sixth International Conference on Computer Supported Education, Barcelona, Spain (2014)

Vanlehn, K., Lynch, C., Schulze, K., Shapiro, J.A., Shelby, R.H., Taylor, L., Treacy, D.J., Weinstein, A., Wintersgill, M.C.: The Andes physics tutoring system-five years of evaluations. In: Proceedings of the Artificial Intelligence in Education Conference, pp. 678–685 (2005)

Fine-Grained Analyses of Interpersonal Processes and Their Effect on Learning

Tanmay Sinha[✉] and Justine Cassell

ArticuLab, Carnegie Mellon University, Pittsburgh, PA 15213, USA
tanmays@andrew.cmu.edu, justine@cs.cmu.edu

Abstract. Better conversational alignment can lead to shared understanding, changed beliefs, and increased rapport. We investigate the relationship in peer tutoring of convergence, interpersonal rapport, and student learning. We develop an approach for computational modeling of convergence by accounting for the horizontal richness and time-based dependencies that arise in non-stationary and noisy longitudinal interaction streams. Our results, which illustrate that rapport as well as convergence are significantly correlated with learning gains, provide guidelines for development of peer tutoring agents that can increase learning gains through subtle changes to improve tutor-tutee alignment.

1 Introduction

Accommodation [5], where participants in a conversation adapt (tendency to become similar over time) or differentiate (tendency to exaggerate their differences) their behaviors with time, has been shown to have powerful effects on collaboration quality [6], learning gain and task success [4], by the virtue of decreasing misunderstandings, attaining goals faster, building rapport and affiliation. In this work, we examine the nature of accommodation in dyadic peer tutoring conversations over time as a part of our research program on the social infrastructure of learning, with an eye towards implementing more effective intelligent peer tutoring systems. Following studies of joint action [9] that challenge the traditional assumption in cognitive psychology that higher-level cognitive processes can best be understood by investigating individual minds in isolation, in the current work the dyad is the unit of analysis. To fully understand what leads conversational partners to converge (adapt) or diverge (differentiate) in their behaviors over time, we therefore study the dynamics of interaction at a fine (30 second interaction segment) level of granularity to operationalize a metric for convergence, in contrast to prior work that has utilized coarse-grained division of the interaction into two or three sub-sessions to investigate effects of aggregated behavioral measures on longitudinal changes in accommodation. Moreover, the approach to accommodation in prior collaborative learning literature [7] has focused on joint construction activities that move the group towards problem solving goals and hence lead to members exhibiting knowledge convergence. Here we add an interactional perspective to the methodological toolkit for examining the effect of accommodation on learning.

© Springer International Publishing Switzerland 2015
C. Conati et al. (Eds.): AIED 2015, LNAI 9112, pp. 781–785, 2015.
DOI: 10.1007/978-3-319-19773-9_115

Study Context: We collected reciprocal peer tutoring data for 12 dyads of American English-speaking high school students (6 of whom were already friends), who tutored one another on procedural and conceptual aspects of an algebra topic, for 5 hourly sessions over as many weeks. Each session comprised two tutoring sessions (with role reversal between the tutor and tutee) sandwiched between three short social sessions. For the purpose of the current study, we selected a fairly balanced convenience sample of 9 dyadic conversational sessions (in terms of a)#friend versus #stranger dyads, b)session#).

2   Methodology

2.1   Operationalizing Features

Motivated by prior work [5] that has included speech rate, overlap (simultaneous speech frequency), laughing and smiling behaviors, we compute the following automatically harvestable features for each speaker for every consecutive 30 second segment from our peer tutoring conversations that have been transcribed and segmented into syntactic clauses: a)# words spoken, b)message density, which is the #independent clauses uttered, divided by the time difference between the first and last utterance, c)content density, which is the #characters spoken divided by the #independent clauses uttered, d)#overlaps, and e)#laughter expressions.

2.2   Operationalizing Convergence

We a)compute the difference in raw behavioral feature values for partner i and partner j engaged in the dyadic conversation for every 30 second slice (call this differenced series y), b)formulate the autoregressive model as $\Delta y_t = \alpha + \beta t + \gamma y_{t-1} + \delta_1 \Delta y_{t-1} + ... + \delta_{p-1} \Delta y_{t-p+1} + \varepsilon_t$, where α (constant term) is the drift or change of the average value of the stochastic process, βt is the deterministic time trend and p is the lag length (which is quantified as 3, similar to the prior influence computation), c)test the presence of unit-root in this time series framework using the Augmented Dickey Fuller (ADF) test at 1% LOS, following proposition 5 [2]. Intuitively, if the ADF test statistic is significant, we reject the null hypothesis that the differenced behavioral time series has a unit root and accept the alternative hypothesis that the variable was generated by a stationary process, which is an evidence for convergence (speakers become more similar to each other over the course of the entire conversation). Alternately, if ADF test statistic is not significant, we accept the null hypothesis of the presence of a unit root, in turn indicating that the process (change) is not stationary and the definition of convergence is violated. Thus, by moving beyond traditional Pearson correlation approaches between time and the absolute difference between a speaker and partner's behavioral feature value at an adjacent turn, we prevent ourselves from making falsifying assumptions about behavioral independence in the dyadic interaction. Finally, to construct a composite score for Convergence strength, we firstly scale the ADF test statistic for Convergence (call this x) along each feature dimension, between 0 and 1 using the formula $(x - minimum(x))/(maximum(x) - minimum(x))$, with an intuition to provide transparency and comparability. Secondly, in weighting across features, different feature dimensions are equally weighted (averaged).

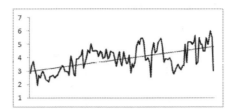

Fig. 1. Trend of increasing rapport for all dyadic sessions averaged over each 30 sec time slice. X axis: time on 30 second scale. Y axis: thin slice rapport rating (1-7).

2.3   Outcome Measures

Learning Gains: Normalized learning gain for each individual in the dyad was computed using the formula: (Post-assessment - Pre-assessment)/(100% - Pre-assessment), while the composite learning gain for a dyad was calculated using the average of the individual learning gains. For the 9 dyadic sessions used in the current analysis, a paired t-test reveals trend towards significant difference in the pre-test and post-test scores (t = -1.8439, df = 17, p-value = 0.0827+)

Thin Slice Rapport: We employ "thin-slice" [1] judgments of interpersonal rapport for our work, where two annotators rate every 30 second video segment of the peer tutoring sessions using an 7 point likert scale, with the segments presented to the annotators in random order. We also employed an eye-tracker to assess which aspects of behavior contributed to the annotator judgments (Oertel et al., in preparation). The consensual accuracy of thin-slice judgments (composite ratings), computed using average measures for intra class correlations (ICC), is greater than 0.7 for all the sessions used in our study.

3   Results and Discussion

We compute Pearson correlation to find relationships between our joint constructs and the outcome measures described above, while testing significance of the correlation via two tailed t-test. Results reveal that higher convergence strength is positively associated with higher average learning gains for the dyadic sessions in our study (r=0.658, p-value=0.05), substantiating convergence as having a positive effect on learning. This leads us to believe that a virtual peer tutor that both mimics its human partner and evokes mimicry may be a more effective learning partner.

If students are to critique the ideas of their peers, offer tentative ideas and interpret others' critiques as valuable, they need to trust each other and feel a sense of warmth and belonging before they will engage willfully in collaboration and treat peer learning as a valuable experience. [8] emphasize that the social phenomenon of rapport builds up over time. Such long term assessment of rapport [3] has already been shown to have enhanced math performance. Figure 1 shows a linearly increasing trend for the average value of thin-slice rapport, for each 30 second slice of our hourly dyadic interaction data. It is thus legitimate to hypothesize that the deepening rapport in later sub-sessions might be more connected to greater learning. Therefore, to assess the relationship between perceived rapport (thin slice annotation) and learning gains, we divide each dyadic session into 5 equal sub-sessions ($\approx$ 10.2 minutes each) and compute Pearson correlation for the averaged perceived ratings for each sub-session. Indeed, our results reveal that perceived rapport for only the fourth sub-session from the start ($\approx$ 30th-40th minute) exhibits a trending positive correlation with learning gains ($r=0.64$, p-value=0.06). This roughly corresponds to the time where the reciprocal tutoring is approaching an end in the session (the 5th segment is a final social session).

4   Conclusion

These results give us a roadmap for integrating convergence into our dialog-based reciprocal peer tutoring virtual agent, in such a way as to detect cues of decreasing alignment between the tutor and student in real time, strategically scaffold instruction by regulating the tutee's problem solving pace and adjusting the balance between message density and content density, improve tutor-tutee alignment by entraining on overlapping behavior to signal acknowledgment or understanding of what the tutee says, and predict learning outcomes based on current level of convergence in the tutor-tutee interaction, so as to provide early scaffolding as opposed to delayed scaffolding at the end of the entire interaction. While some prior literature has suggested a cognitive explanation for the impact of convergence on learning, such that it indexes greater shared understanding, and hence leads to improved learning, other literature suggests that greater similarity is an index of increased interpersonal rapport which, in turn, leads to greater willingness to examine misconceptions, and hence to improved learning. Disambiguating these mechanisms remains a topic for future work.

References

1. Ambady, N., Rosenthal, R.: Thin slices of expressive behavior as predictors of interpersonal consequences: A meta-analysis. Psychological Bulletin (1992)
2. Bernard, A., Durlauf, S.: Interpreting tests of the convergence hypothesis. Journal of Econometrics **71**, 161–173 (1996)

3. Cassell, J., Gill, A.J., Tepper, P.A.: Coordination in conversation and rapport. In: Proceedings of the Workshop on Embodied Language Processing, pp. 41–50. Association for Computational Linguistics (June 2007)
4. Friedberg, H., Litman, D.J., Paletz, S.B.: Lexical entrainment and success in student engineering groups. In: SLT, pp. 404–409 (2012)
5. Giles, H., Coupland, N., Coupland, J.: Accommodation theory: communication, context, and consequence, pp. 1–68. Developments in Applied Sociolinguistics, Contexts of Accommodation (1991)
6. Schneider, B., Pea, R.: The Effect of Mutual Gaze Perception on Students' Verbal Coordination. In: Proceedings of the 7th International Conference on Educational Data Mining (EDM 2014), pp. 138–144 (2014)
7. Teasley, S.D., Fischer, F., Weinberger, A., Stegmann, K., Dillenbourg, P., Kapur, M., Chi, M.: Cognitive convergence in collaborative learning. Proceedings of the ISLS **3**, 360–367 (2008)
8. Zhao, Ran, Papangelis, Alexandros, Cassell, Justine: Towards a Dyadic Computational Model of Rapport Management for Human-Virtual Agent Interaction. In: Bickmore, Timothy, Marsella, Stacy, Sidner, Candace (eds.) IVA 2014. LNCS, vol. 8637, pp. 514–527. Springer, Heidelberg (2014)
9. Sebanz, N., Bekkering, H., Knoblich, G.: Joint action: bodies and minds moving together. Trends in cognitive sciences **10**(2), 70–76 (2006)

Promoting Metacognitive Awareness within a Game-Based Intelligent Tutoring System

Erica L. Snow[1](✉), Danielle S. McNamara[1], Matthew E. Jacovina[1], Laura K. Allen[1], Amy M. Johnson[1], Cecile A. Perret[1], Jianmin Dai[1], G. Tanner Jackson[2], Aaron D. Likens[1], Devin G. Russell[1], and Jennifer L. Weston[1]

[1] Department of Psychology, Arizona State University, Tempe, AZ 85287, USA
{Erica.L.Snow,Danielle.McNamara,Matthew.Jacovina,
LauraKAllen,amjohn43,Cecile.Perret,Jianmin.Dai,
Aaron.Likens,Devin.Russell,Jennifer.Weston}@asu.edu
[2] Educational Testing Service, Princeton, NJ 08541, USA
gtjackson@ets.org

Abstract. Metacognitive awareness has been shown to be a critical skill for academic success. However, students often struggle to regulate this ability during learning tasks. The current study investigates how features designed to promote metacognitive awareness can be built into the game-based intelligent tutoring system (ITS) iSTART-2. College students (n=28) interacted with iSTART-2 for one hour, completing lesson videos and practice activities. If students' performance fell below a minimum threshold during game-based practice, they received a pop-up that alerted them of their poor performance and were subsequently transitioned to a remedial activity. Results revealed that students' scores in the system improved after they were transitioned (even when they did not complete the remedial activity). This suggests that the pop-up feature in iSTART-2 may indirectly promote metacognitive awareness, thus leading to increased performance. These results provide insight into the potential benefits of real-time feedback designed to promote metacognitive awareness within a game-based learning environment.

Keywords: Artificial intelligence · Metacognition · Educational technology design · Game-based learning

1 Introduction

In everyday life, we are exposed to a large amount of information about our surrounding environment. This information can be delivered in a variety of forms including television, radio, internet, and social media outlets. The abundance of this information can be overwhelming and often requires us to reflect upon our understanding of the contexts, facts, and prior knowledge of the subject matter. This ability to reflect upon what we do know and what we do not know is often referred to as metacognition [1]. In recent years, many researchers have attempted to identify effective techniques to stimulate and support metacognition during learning tasks [2]. In the current study, we test a new feedback and remediation feature designed to provide metacognitive support within the Interactive Strategy Training for Active Reading and Thinking-2 (iSTART-2).

© Springer International Publishing Switzerland 2015
C. Conati et al. (Eds.): AIED 2015, LNAI 9112, pp. 786–789, 2015.
DOI: 10.1007/978-3-319-19773-9_116

1.1 iSTART-2

iSTART-2 is a game-based intelligent tutoring system (ITS) designed to provide high school students with instruction on reading comprehension strategies, specifically focusing on science texts [3]. These strategies are presented during the training phase of iSTART-2 through a series of lesson videos presented by a pedagogical agent. After students complete the training phase of iSTART-2, they are transitioned to the practice phase. During the practice phase of iSTART-2, students are able to access a suite of practice games, customize the appearance of the interface, and monitor their recent performance through achievement screens [3, 4, 5]. Relevant to the current study, students can play generative practice games (Map Conquest, Showdown, and Coached Practice), where they read a text and then are prompted to generate their own self-explanation of the text.

1.2 Current Study

In this study, we test a new system feature designed to indirectly enhance metacognition within iSTART-2. This feature explicitly informs students when their performance is low (promoting metacognitive awareness) and subsequently transitions them to a remedial activity (i.e., Coached Practice), where they can receive more nuanced and direct strategy instruction. This *transition* feature is embedded within the practice games of iSTART-2 (Map Conquest and Showdown) and calculates students' average self-explanation score after each game play. This score is then compared to an experimenter-set threshold, and if this threshold is not met, students are presented with a pop-up message. The message alerts students that they scored below the threshold and that they will be transitioned to Coached Practice where they receive feedback on how to improve their performance. After closing the pop-up message, students are automatically sent to Coached Practice. This *transition feature* provides indirect support for metacognitive monitoring of reading comprehension by presenting students with information on their performance that promotes self-reflection. It is hypothesized that after students are aware of inadequate self-explanation performance, they will be more likely to reflect on and consider how they can improve the quality of their subsequent self-explanations.

2 Method

2.1 Participants

The current work included 28 college students from a large university campus in the Southwest United States who participated for course credit. These students were, on average, 19.6 years of age (range 18 to 24), and the majority were college freshmen. Of the 28 students, 50% were male, 41% were Caucasian, 41% were Asian, 6% were Hispanic, and 12% reported other ethnicities.

2.2   Procedure

The study included one 3-hour session, which consisted of a pretest, strategy training, game-based practice within iSTART-2, and a posttest. At pretest, students were asked to answer a battery of questions that included their prior science knowledge and motivation toward the learning task. During training, students watched iSTART lesson videos, designed to provide direct instruction on the self-explanation strategies. After completing the lesson videos, students were transitioned into Coached Practice where they completed one round of generative practice that provided them with formative feedback on their generated self-explanations. After students completed coached practice, they were transferred into a game-based practice menu embedded within iSTART-2. During this time, students were free to interact with the practice system, which included Map Conquest and Showdown (but not Coached Practice). Students spent approximately 1 hour within the game-based interface. Students' average self-explanation scores were calculated for each game play within the system. If students' average self-explanation score fell below a 2.0 for one game play, they received a message and were transitioned to Coached Practice. It is important to note that students could choose to close out of Coached Practice and return to the game-based practice menu; thus, the message simply served as a *recommendation* that students engage with Coached Practice. After students completed the game-based practice portion of the experiment (approximately 1 hour), they were transferred to the posttest, where they completed measures similar to those in the pretest.

2.3   Measures

2.3.1   *In-game strategy performance.* Students' generated self-explanation quality was assessed while they engaged with Map Conquest and Showdown. The iSTART algorithm scored the self-explanations on a scale from 0 to 3. This algorithm uses Latent Semantic Analysis (LSA; [6]) and word-based measures to assess self-explanation quality. Using this algorithm, students received an average game self-explanation strategy score for each generative practice activity (i.e., Showdown, Map Conquest, and Coached Practice) that they completed.

3   Results

3.1   In- System Performance

To examine the effects of the transition function on self-explanation quality, a repeated measures analysis was conducted. In this analysis, we examined how students' self-explanation scores changed from the game in which they scored below a 2.0 and the game directly after the transition.

Of the 28 students, 22 were transitioned at least once. Of these 22, 16 completed a game following the transition and were included in this analysis. Students' average self-explanation score prior to being transitioned was 0.96 (SD=0.70), whereas the average score after students completed or closed out of the remedial Coached Practice was 1.99 (SD=0.69), demonstrating a significant increase in self explanation scores

($F(1, 15)=17.15$, $p<.001$). Although this analysis has a small sample size (n=16), it achieves a high effect size (partial $\eta2 =.533$) and a high observed power of 0.97.

4   Conclusions and Implications

Metacognitive skills are crucial for academic success. However, students' vary in their ability to effectively control and regulate this behavior [7]. Recently, researchers have attempted to identify and develop more effective techniques that are designed to enhance metacognition during computer-based learning. The current study serves as a functional and empirical test of one such feature designed to indirectly promote meta-cognitive awareness and metacognitive control during self-explanation practice. The results presented here reveal positive results associated with the transition feature. Specifically, when students were alerted to their poor performance and transitioned to the remedial practice environment, their subsequent performance was significantly better. While this is by no means the end of the development of the transition feature, the results presented here are promising for the further development of this functionality. Overall, these findings afford researchers and developers the opportunity to better understand how students' metacognitive awareness can be prompted and promoted within game-based learning environments.

Acknowledgments. This research was supported in part by the Institute for Educational Sciences (IES R305A130124) and National Science Foundation (NSF REC0241144; IIS-0735682). Any opinions, findings, and conclusions or recommendations expressed in this material are those of the authors and do not necessarily reflect the views of the IES or NSF.

References

1. Flavell, J.H.: Metacognition and cognitive monitoring: A new area of cognitive–developmental inquiry. American Psychologist **34**(10), 906 (1979)
2. Bannert, M., Hildebrand, M., Mengelkamp, C.: Effects of a metacognitive support device in learning environments. Computers in Human Behavior **25**(4), 829–835 (2009)
3. Snow, E.L., Allen, L.K., Jacovina, M.E., McNamara, D.S.: Does agency matter?: Exploring the impact of controlled behaviors within a game-based environment. Computers & Education **26**, 378–392 (2014)
4. Snow, E.L., Jackson, G.T., McNamara, D.S.: Emergent behaviors in computer-based learning environments: Computational signals of catching up. Computers in Human Behavior **41**, 62–70 (2014)
5. Snow, E.L., Jacovina, M.E., Allen, L.K., Dai, J., McNamara, D.S.: Entropy: A stealth assessment of agency in learning environments. In Stamper, J., Pardos, Z., Mavrikis, M., McLaren, B.M. (eds.) Proceedings of the 7th International Conference on Educational Data Mining, London, UK, pp. 241–244 (2014)
6. Landauer, T., McNamara, D.S., Dennis, S., Kintsch, W.: Handbook of Latent Semantic Analysis. Erlbaum, Mahwah (2007)
7. Pintrich, P.R.: The role of metacognitive knowledge in learning, teaching, and ASSESSING. Theory into Practice **41**(4), 219–225 (2002)

Student Performance Estimation Based on Topic Models Considering a Range of Lessons

Shaymaa E. Sorour[1,2(✉)], Kazumasa Goda[3], and Tsunenori Mine[2]

[1] Kafr Elsheik University, Kafr Elsheikh 33516, Egypt
shaymaasorour@gmail.com
[2] Kyushu University, Motooka, Fukuoka 819-0395, Japan
[3] Kyushu Institute of Information Science, Dazaifu, Fukuoka 818-0117, Japan

Abstract. This paper proposes a prediction framework for student performance based on comment data mining. Given the comments containing multiple topics, we seek to discover the topics that help to predict final student grades as their performance. To this end, the paper proposes methods that analyze students' comments by two topic models: Probabilistic Latent Semantic Analysis (PLSA), and Latent Dirichlet Allocation (LDA). The methods employ Support Vector Machine (SVM) to generate prediction models of final student grades. In addition, Considering the student grades predicted in a range of lessons can deal with prediction error occurred in each lesson, and achieve further improvement of the student grade prediction.

Keywords: Prediction model · Topic models · Comments data mining

1 Introduction

Classroom assessment yields important data for teachers regarding students' learning, which leads to further development and improvement of teachers' instruction and revision of curriculum content to better serve the students' needs, enabling them to learn efficiently and effectively [4]. Thus, classroom assessment is an important method for developing the quality of students, detecting their difficulties with the courses early, and helping them to improve their performance. The current study proposes new methods to search on and estimate the unknown value of student performance through predicting their final grades by using comment data mining methods. Analyzing free-style comments written by students have some benefits for student assessment, such as understanding students behaviors, attitudes and situations, reflecting their activities and difficulties of learning in each lesson.

Goda et al.[2] proposed the PCN method to estimate learning situations from comments freely written by students. The PCN method classifies the student comments into three items P, C, and N. Item P indicates the learning activity before the class time. Item C shows the understanding and achievements of class subjects during the class time, and item N tells the learning activity plan until

© Springer International Publishing Switzerland 2015
C. Conati et al. (Eds.): AIED 2015, LNAI 9112, pp. 790–793, 2015.
DOI: 10.1007/978-3-319-19773-9_117

the next class. To understand student behavior more deeply and to enhance individualized feedback to them, this paper presents a study that applies text mining techniques not only to predict student grade in each lesson, but also to consider the predicted results with a range of lessons. We employ PLSA and LDA models to grasp student learning attitudes and situations. For our purposes, PLSA/LDA create some aspects of words known as "topics"; a topic is a probability distribution over a collection of words and is a formal statistical relationship between groups of observed and latent (unknown) random variables that specify a probabilistic procedure to generate the topics [6]. In this paper, we generate prediction models based on SVM technique and compare the prediction results of the two models. The experiments were conducted using C-comment data collected in each lesson from two classes, where the data for one class as training and for the other as test data. Although students learned the same subject in the two classes, there are differences between the comments. Each class data has its own characteristics. Also, the difficulty of the subject in the lesson affects student attitudes to expressing their behavior and sometimes does not give students leeway to write comments. Therefore this is a challenging problem.

2   Overview of the Prediction Methods

1. **Comment Data Collection**: Comment data were collected from 123 students in two classes: (Class A = 60 students) and (Class B = 63 students), who took introductory of information processing course consisting of 15 lessons (weeks). The main subject from lessons 1 to 6 is computer literacy, giving information on how to use some IT tools. Computer literacy education is compulsory throughout senior high schools in Japan, with only a few differences in the details of course contents. From lesson 7 students learn the basics of programming. The main subject in those lessons is introductory C programming. It is a new subject and not required until they enter the university [2].

2. **The PLSA and LDA models**: We employ two models: PLSA[3] and LDA[1], which are used in statistical natural language processing to discover categories and topics from documents. The both models use the 'bag of words' model, where positional relationships between features are ignored. To use PLSA/LDA models, we seek a vocabulary of words which will help to predict final student grades. In our research, we compare the two models to know which model highly affects to predict final student grades. We choose four grades (S, A, B, and C) instead of the mark itself as a student result. The assessment to a student was done by considering the average mark of the student's reports assigned three times, and the attendance rate.

3   Results and Discussion

We evaluated the prediction performance of our proposed models by 2-fold cross validation. We constructed a model from comment data in one class. Then, as a test, we applied the model to the comment data in the other class. The procedure was repeated in each lesson and the results were averaged. We run evaluation experiments by evaluating the prediction performance in four values: TP (True Positive), TN (True Negative), FP (False Positive) and FN (False Negative) and calculating the F-measure and the accuracy in each lesson.

Prediction of Student Grade: Fig. 1 displays the average overall prediction accuracy and F-measure results obtained using the SVM technique. Our methods achieved an average 60.30% and 66.34% prediction accuracy, 64.74% and 68.73% prediction F-measure using the PLSA and the LDA models, respectively. We can see that the overall accuracy and F-measure results from lessons 1 to 6 were higher than those from lessons 7 to 15; this means that the difficulty of the subject from lesson 7 affected student ability of accurately describing their experience in their comments.

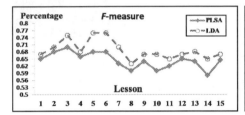 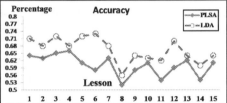

Fig. 1. Average accuracy and F-measure from lessons 1 to 15

By comparing our results with Sorour et al. [5], our methods outperformed their methods, they employed Latent Semantic Analysis (LSA) technique and two types of machine learning techniques: Artificial Neural Network (ANN) and SVM to predict final student grades. Their methods achieved an average 52.95% and 56.65% prediction accuracy, 49.95% and 51.05% prediction F-measure using the ANN and the SVM models, respectively.

The Predicted results with a range of lessons: The aim of this section is to understand each student more deeply and to grasp the characteristics of a range of lessons. We focus on the change of the prediction results of each student in each lesson. We separated our prediction results into 5 windows as shown in Fig.2. The majority vote was used to determine the predicted grade of each student in each range of lessons. For example, in a range window of L(1-3) we assume the predicted grades of a student were: S, A and S from lessons 1 to 3, respectively. The majority vote returns S in this window. We used the same way in each window and calculated the correct prediction (TP) rate from lessons 1 to 15, using the PLSA and LDA models. In the current experiment, we regarded the grade of students who didn't submit their comments as grade C, because their behaviors can be regarded as the worst ones. The prediction results increased about 3% compared to ignoring these comments, especially in the range L(1-9). In addition, if the results returned by the majority vote include the actual grade, we judge the case true. In our experiment, the majority

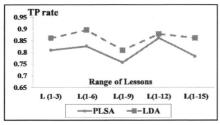 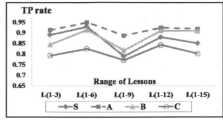

(a) Overall rate of correctly predicted results (TP) for each student.

(b) Correctly predicted rate (TP) of student grade.

Fig. 2. The average overall TP rate for 5 windows from lessons 1 to 15

vote always returned one or two grades. As shown in Fig.2(a) the LDA model outperformed the PLSA model in predicting each student grade. The overall correct prediction result (TP) were 78.3% and 86.0% by using the PLSA and the LDA models, respectively. The highest prediction results were achieved in lessons L(1-6). In addition, the lowest prediction results were in L(1-9). We can assume that the dropping of TP rate from lesson 7 due to the nature of the comments; students started coding and the comments included additional noise, i.e. programming/technical content. On the other hand, students wrote their learning situations precisely during lessons 1 to 6, about Computer Literacy. Fig.2(b) displays the TP rate of student grades with the LDA model from lessons 1 to 15. The graph shows that TP rate gradually decreased in the range L(1-9). TP rates of grades: A, B and S were higher than that of grade C.

Acknowledgments. This work was partially supported by JSPS KAKENHI Grant Numbers 25350311 and 26540183.

References

1. Blei, D.M., Ng, A.Y., Jordan, M.I.: Latent dirichlet allocation. Journal of Machine Learning Research **3**, 993–1022 (2003)
2. Goda, K., Mine, T.: Analysis of Students' Learning Activities through Quantifying Time-Series Comments. In: König, A., Dengel, A., Hinkelmann, K., Kise, K., Howlett, R.J., Jain, L.C. (eds.) KES 2011, Part II. LNCS, vol. 6882, pp. 154–164. Springer, Heidelberg (2011)
3. Hofmann, T.: Unsupervised learning by probabilistic latent semantic analysis. Machine Learning **42**, 177–196 (2001)
4. Qualters, D.M.: Using classroom assessment data to improve student learning. Center for Effective University Teaching & GE Master Teacher's Team, Northeatern University (2001)
5. Sorour, S.E., Mine, T., Goda, K., Hirokawa, S.: Comment data mining for student grade prediction considering differences in data for two classes. International Journal of Computer & Information Science **15**(2), 12–25 (2014)
6. Steyvers, T.L.G.M.: Finding scientific topics. Proceedings of the National Academy of Sciences **101**, 5228–5235 (2004)

Towards a Model of How Learners Process Feedback

Michael Timms[✉], Sacha DeVelle, Ursula Schwantner, and Dulce Lay

Australian Council for Educational Research, Camberwell, Australia
mike.timms@acer.edu.au

Abstract. It is well known that learners using intelligent learning environments (ILEs) make different use of the feedback provided by the ILE, exhibiting different patterns of behavior. The field of educational neuroscience offers the opportunity to study how learners process the feedback they receive in an ILE. Based on a literature review of what is known about the processing of feedback from cognitive psychology and neuroscience perspective, a model of how learners process feedback in ILEs is presented. The model represents how learners notice, process, and understand feedback. We are in the process of conducting a study to test the model. Preliminary evidence indicates that the model may be valid, but that further study must be conducted using other techniques such as eyetracking and EEG to fully validate the model.

Keywords: Feedback · Hints · Neuroscience

1 Introduction

Over the last 20 years or so the field of Artificial Intelligence in Education has developed approaches to providing feedback to learners using computer based intelligent learning environments (ILEs), and current systems are able to provide assistance to a range of learners. Designers of ILEs often spend considerable effort ensuring that the delivery of the feedback is carefully timed to occur at the point when a) the student needs it most and b) that it provides the necessary help to move learners forward in the task. An objective for the feedback system is to keep students in what Vygotsky [1] calls the Zone of Proximal Development, that area in which the challenge presented in the learning material is slightly in advance of the learner's current ability, but they are able to successfully tackle the task with some assistance. To date, the field has focused on modeling the learner's need for feedback. Typical systems deliver feedback to learners in the same mode each time often 'flagging' an error with red outline or bolded text, and providing hints through text boxes in a sequence that progresses from low amounts of help to "bottom-out hints" that provide full information on what to do next. What has not been studied in detail is how students notice, decode and act upon feedback. We report on results from a study that tested a model of how learners process feedback. The model draws upon a literature review from AIED, cognitive psychology, neuroscience and psycholinguistics. As a preliminary test of the model we investigated how students reacted to feedback in an established ILE, *Crystal Island: The Lost Investigation* (developed at North Carolina State University).

© Springer International Publishing Switzerland 2015
C. Conati et al. (Eds.): AIED 2015, LNAI 9112, pp. 794–799, 2015.
DOI: 10.1007/978-3-319-19773-9_118

2   What Is Known About Learners' Processing of Feedback

There exists a substantial body of research that addresses the relationship between feedback and learning (see Moray [2] for a historical review of the literature) over the last 60 years. As AIED has advanced as a field within that timespan, the quantity of research addressing different aspects of feedback (e.g. timing, help support, and ability level) within diverse classroom and laboratory settings has increased too. The emergence of computer-based learning (and theoretical discussions for feedback) has placed an emphasis on computational models of self-regulated [3,4] and reflective [5] learning. Self-regulated learning (SRL) describes a cognitive operation that involves an internal monitoring process. Learners are aware of their own knowledge, motivational aspirations and ways of thinking [4]. Recognising the need for help is a metacognitive skill that requires students to monitor their own progress and understanding [6]. However, there is research to suggest that higher ability learners do better within computer-mediated environments that allow for more learner control, compared to lower ability students that do not [7]. Secondly, those students with higher ability have shown to be better at using help after errors, compared to their lower ability peers [8]. Importantly, feedback operates as a catalyst for self-regulated activities. Mason & Bruning [9] reviewed the literature on feedback and computer based instruction (CBI) and then developed a theoretical framework that included student achievement levels, task level, timing of feedback, prior knowledge and type of feedback. Based on that work the authors showed that students with low achievement levels perform better on both simple and complex tasks when feedback is immediate. However, students with high achievement levels perform better with delayed feedback, particularly on complex tasks.

To briefly summarise, the research just presented suggests that successful use of help functions, task complexity and timing of feedback are all mediated by student ability. More specifically, higher ability students perform better on more complex tasks with delayed feedback. Lower ability students perform better with immediate feedback on simple tasks. It seems that higher ability students also do better with learner-centred help options.

While prior ability in the topic of study is important to how learners process feedback, it is not the only determining factor. Shute's [10] more recent review on formative feedback identifies key features that most effectively promote learning (e.g., feedback type, timing, ability level, goal orientation). Formative feedback is defined as the communication of information to a learner, with the intention of modifying their behaviour to improve the learning process [10]. The outcome of her review, however, shows an inconsistency in findings across studies. Shute suggests that such findings are due to Individual Differences (ID) among learners reflected in motivational expectations (intrinsic motivation, metacognitive skills or even academic achievement). She argues for an area of future research that focuses on the affective (emotional) components in feedback using cognitive theory [11].[1] The study we

---

[1] This is not a new argument; Vygotsky [1] also highlighted the lack of integration between intellect and the motivational and emotional (affective) aspects of thinking.

undertook attempts to model how the individual differences among learners might play out in how they notice, decode and act upon feedback.

Neuroscience research has shown that error detection, and response to errors, seem to play a central role in learning. When a learner takes an action but the reaction by the learning environment is not what he or she expected, there is a cognitive dissonance that is referred to as *salience* in neuroscience. Salience refers to the degree that an item stands out from its surroundings or neighbors, and it is this salience that stimulates the striatum. The striatum is activated by stimuli associated with reward, but also by unexpected events and cues associated with such events. The larger the gap between what the learner expected to happen and what actually happened, the greater the salience and the larger the activation of the striatum. There is neural evidence to suggest that learning from immediate feedback is carried out in the striatum area of the brain, and related dopaminergic inputs [12].

Brain imaging studies have investigated the impact of feedback on learning for the role of errors, delayed feedback, and the developmental trajectory of negative feedback. Brain studies using fMRI (combined with behavioural data) have predominated. Comparisons across different populations (healthy versus impaired) have also contributed to overall findings. Interestingly, much of the work discussed here has focused on probabilistic learning tasks within tightly controlled experimental laboratory conditions. To date there appears to be very little (if any) experimental research examining neural responses to student learning using ILE's, or within the messier realm of the classroom. There also appears to be a lack of eye tracking and EEG data to supplement feedback and learning studies to date.

3   A Model of Learner Processing of Feedback in Intelligent Learning Environments

From our review on learners' processing of feedback in ILE's, and corresponding neuroscientific studies, we created a model that we hypothesize captures how learners receive and react to feedback delivered by typical ILEs, as shown in Figure 1.

The process represented in the model begins at the top left with the circle labeled *Learner makes an error*. In this step an error is made following the actions of the learner. An "error" could be a mistake such as entering the wrong value in a math problem or choosing an incorrect option, or it could be that the learner is deviating from what the ILE judges as an optimal path for learning. After making an error, a decision point in the model is reached labeled *Learner detects error?* If the learner detects his/her own error they can then correct it unaided by the ILE's assistance system (*Learner corrects error*) and therefore learn from their own internal monitoring system. This will still constitute what we call a *learning event*. The model hypothesizes that this single learning event is not a guarantee that permanent learning has occurred, but rather the event that can contribute to long-term learning. It is an accumulation of such learning events that reinforces neural pathways that eventually may be encoded as more permanent knowledge or skills.

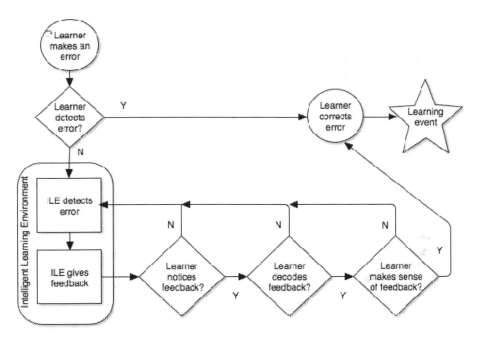

Fig. 1. Model of how learners process feedback in intelligent learning environments

The ILE is, of course, tracking the learner's progress and if the learner does not detect that he/she has made an error (*Learner detects an error?* = N) we can trace a path down the left side of the model to see a successful implementation from the ILE's help system. When the learner makes an error, but does not detect it, the error then the ILE will detect the error (*ILE detects "error"*) and give feedback to the learner (*ILE gives feedback*). Typical feedback upon initial error detection is "flagging", usually by highlighting or outlining the error in red. At this point, for the feedback to have any effect, the learner must notice it (*Learner attends to feedback?*). Assuming that the learner has noticed the feedback he/she must decode the feedback (*Student decodes feedback?*). By decoding we mean extracting the message from the medium. For example beyond flagging of errors, typical ILEs use written text in pop-up boxes to deliver hints. Decoding of a written hint would be the act of reading it. After the learner has decoded the feedback message from the medium, the next step is to make sense of it within the context of the learning task (*Student makes sense of feedback?*). In other words, the student must work out what the message means and determine what to do next. Assuming that the learner can do this, then he/she can correct the error (*Learner corrects error*) and then a learning event has taken place (*Learning event*).

Because of individual differences (ID) among learners, there are three decision points in the model, where the feedback delivered by the ILE may fail to achieve the intended effect. At the first point (*Learner notices feedback*), if the learner does not notice that feedback has been given he/she may just carry on regardless. The usual result of this event is that the learner remains in the feedback loop without reaching a learning event end point. This may involve the ILE increasing the level of help (e.g. providing a next level hint). The second way in which the learner may remain in the feedback loop is at the *Student decodes feedback?* point. Because of ID in their reading skills, some learners may find it hard to decode the message from the medium in which the feedback is delivered.   Thirdly, feedback may not reach a successful learning event when the learner notices to the feedback and decodes it, but cannot make sense of it in the context of the task. This may be due to low working memory capacity, that does not allow them to hold information and solve how to move to the next step in the task. Again, they would remain in the feedback loop.

The model posits that two learners may make the same kind of error and receive the same initial feedback from the ILE, but due to ID, they may process (or not) the feedback in different ways. We, therefore, hypothesise that there will be discernible differences among learners in how they process feedback. To investiage this further we are conducting a study to test the model, as described below.

4   Empirical Study

To test the model, we are studying how learners processed feedback in *Crystal Island: The Lost Investigation,* an ILE developed at North Carolina State University. In *Crystal Island* students have to identify the type of illness affecting a research community on an isolated island and track its source.

The research questions being addressed are (1) How do students notice, decode and make sense of the various types of feedback provided in the two typical ILE's? and (2) What differences are there among learners, at different stages in their learning of a topic, in how they use and react to the various types of feedback?

Our initial investigations in a pilot study indicated that there appear to be a variety of patterns to how students notices, decoded and made sense of feedback. This is consistent with other studies in AIED of feedback usage behaviors. At this point we are unable to validate the model of how learners process feedback because the data collected do not have sufficient sequence of actions that the learners took after receiving feedback and the design of the sequence of feedback in *Crystal Island*. Our plan is to work with the developers of *Crystal Island* to modify it so that it provides more feedback episodes and flags errors before providing the learner with a hint. We also plan to make the hints sequence have three levels that gradually provide greater amounts of help before receiving a bottom-out hint. In the long term, we plan to design an eye-tracking study but, due to the requirements of the equipment, we do not think that we can obtain a sufficient number of feedback sequences per student (we need at least 30) within the *Crytstal Island* ILE and may have to design a smaller system that maximizes the amount of feedback received by the learners.

References

1. Vygotsky, L.S.: Mind in society: The development of higher psychological processes. Harvard University Press, Cambridge (1978)
2. Mory, E.H.: Feedback Research Revisited. In: Jonassen, D.H. (ed.) Handbook of Research on Educational Communications and Technology, pp. 745–783. Lawrence Erlbaum Associates Publishers, Mahwah (2004)
3. Fischer, P., Mandl, H.: Knowledge acquisition by computerised audiovisual feedback. European Journal of Psychology of Education 3(2), 217–233 (1988)
4. Butler, D.L., Winne, P.H.: Feedback and Self-Regulated Learning: A Theoretical Synthesis. Review of Educational Research 65(3), 245 –281 (1995); Carey, S.: Cognitive science and science education. American Psychologist 41(10) 1123–1130 (1986)
5. Collins, A., Brown, J.S.: The computer as a tool for learning through reflection. In: Mandl, H., Lesgold, A. (eds.) Learning
6. Aleven, V., Koedinger, K.R.: Limitations of Student Control: Do Students Know When They Need Help? In: Gauthier, G., VanLehn, K., Frasson, C. (eds.) ITS 2000. LNCS, vol. 1839, pp. 292–303. Springer, Heidelberg (2000)
7. Recker, M., Pirolli, P.: Student strategies for learning programming from a computational environment. In: Frasson, C., Gauthier, G., McCalla, G.I. (eds.) Proceedings of the International Conference on Intelligent Tutoring Systems. LNCS, vol. 608, pp. 382–394. Springer, Heidelberg (1992)
8. Wood, H., Wood, D.: Help seeking, learning and contingent tutoring. Computers & Education 33(2), 153–169 (1999)
9. Mason, B., Bruning, R.: Providing feedback in computer-based instruction: What the research tells us (2001) (retrieved February 15, 2001)
10. Shute, V.: Focus on formative feedback. Review of Educational Research 78(1), 153–189 (2008)
11. Picard, R., Papert, S., Bender, W., Blumberg, B., et al.: Affective learning—a manifesto. BT Technology Journal 22(4), 253–269 (2004)
12. Pessiglione, M., Seymour, B., Flandin, G., Dolan, R.J., Frith, C.D.: Dopamine-dependent prediction errors underpin reward-seeking behaviour in humans. Nature 442(7106), 1042–1045 (2006). doi:10.1038/nature05051

Item Response Model with Lower Order Parameters for Peer Assessment

Masaki Uto[1](✉) and Maomi Ueno[2]

[1] Nagaoka University of Technology, Niigata, Japan
uto@oberon.nagaokaut.ac.jp
[2] University of Electro-Communications, Tokyo, Japan
ueno@ai.is.uec.ac.jp

Abstract. Peer assessment has become popular in recent years. However, in peer assessment, a problem remains that reliability depends on the rater characteristics. For this reason, some item response models that incorporate rater parameters have been proposed. However, in previous models, the parameter estimation accuracy decreases as the number of raters increases because the number of rater parameters increases drastically. To solve that problem, this article presents a proposal of a new item response model for peer assessment that incorporates rater parameters to maintain as few rater parameters as possible.

Keywords: Peer assessment · Rater characteristics · Reliability · Item response theory · Hierarchical Bayes model

1 Introduction

As an assessment method based on a constructivist approach, peer assessment, which is mutual assessment among learners, has become popular in recent years [4]. Peer assessment presents many important benefits [3,4]. Therefore, peer assessment has been adopted into various learning processes.

This article specifically examines the benefit of peer assessment to improve the reliability of assessment for learners' performance, such as essay writing. Although the assessment of learners' performance has become important, it is difficult for a single teacher to assess them when the number of learners increases [3]. Peer assessment enables realization of reliable assessment without burdening a teacher when the number of raters is sufficiently large [4]. However, it is difficult to increase the number of raters for each learner because one rater can only assess a few performances [3]. Therefore, the main issue of this article is to improve the reliability of peer assessment for sparse data.

In this article, the reliability is defined as *stability of learners' ability estimation.* The reliability reveals a higher value if the ability of learners are obtainable with few errors when the performance tasks or raters are changed.

The reliability of peer assessment is known to depend on rater characteristics [4]. Therefore, the reliability is expected to be increased if the ability of learners is estimated considering the following rater characteristics [5]. 1) *Severity:*

C. Conati et al. (Eds.): AIED 2015, LNAI 9112, pp. 800–803, 2015.
DOI: 10.1007/978-3-319-19773-9_119

Because each rater has a different rating severity. 2) *Consistency*: Because a rater might not always be consistent in applying the same assessment criteria.

For this reason, some item response models which incorporate the rater characteristic parameters have been proposed [1,2,4,5]. However, in previous models, the number of rater parameters increases extremely as the number of raters increases because the models include high dimensional rater parameters. The accuracy of parameter estimation is known to be reduced when the number of parameters increases because the data size per parameter decreases. If the accuracy of parameter estimation is reduced, the reliability is necessarily reduced.

To solve the problem, this article presents a proposal of a new item response model for peer assessment. The model incorporates rater's consistency and severity parameters to maintain as few rater parameters as possible. The model presents the following advantages. 1) The model has fewer rater parameters than previous models. Therefore, the model can provide higher parameter estimation accuracy when the number of raters increases. 2) The model can improve the reliability because it can estimate the learner's ability parameter with higher accuracy and can consider the rater's consistency and severity characteristics.

This article also proposes a parameter estimation method using a hierarchical Bayes model for the proposed model. In addition, this article demonstrates the effectiveness of the proposed model through actual data experiments.

2   Proposed Model

This article assumes that peer assessment data consist of categories $k \in \{1..., K\}$ given by each rater $r \in \{1, \cdots, R\}$ to each work of learner $j \in \{1, \cdots, J\}$ for each assignment $i \in \{1, \cdots, I\}$. This article proposes an item response model for the data by extending the graded response model. The model gives the probability that rater r responds in category k to learner j's assignment i as follows.

$$P_{ijrk} = P^*_{ijrk-1} - P^*_{ijrk}, \quad \begin{cases} P^*_{ijrk} = [1 + \exp(-\alpha_i \alpha_r (\theta_j - b_{ik} - \varepsilon_r))]^{-1}, \\ P^*_{ijr0} = 1, \quad P^*_{ijrK} = 0. \end{cases}$$

Therein, θ_j is the ability of learner j, α_i is a discriminant parameter of assignment i, α_r reflects the consistency of rater r, b_{ik} denotes the difficulty in obtaining the score k for assignment i ($b_{i1} < \cdots < b_{iK-1}$), and ε_r represents the severity of rater r. For model identification, $\alpha_{r=1} = 1$, $\varepsilon_1 = 0$ and $\Pi_r \alpha_r = 1$ are assumed.

The unique feature of the proposed model is that each rater has only one consistency and severity parameter. If higher dimensional rater parameters are used, such as that described by Ueno et al. [4] and Patz et al. [1], then the number of rater parameters increases rapidly concomitantly with the increasing number of raters. In the proposed model, the number of rater parameters increases slowly as the number of raters increases. Therefore, the proposed model is expected to improve the parameter estimation accuracy because the estimation accuracy generally increases when the number of parameters decreases.

Another feature of the proposed model is introducing the rater consistency parameter. The models of Patz et al. [1] and Ueno et al. [4] use no consistency parameters. However, the reliability is known to be increased if the ability of learners is estimated considering the rater consistency [5]. The parameter α_r used in the proposed model can optimally represent the rater consistency [5].

In summary, the proposed model is expected to improve the reliability of peer assessment because the ability of learners can be estimated with higher accuracy and can be considered with the rater's consistency and severity characteristics.

To estimate the parameters in item response models, the Bayes estimation has generally been used. However, the accuracy of the Bayes estimation depends on parameters, called *hyperparameters*, which are arbitrarily determined by an analyst. Therefore, this article employs a parameter estimation method using a hierarchical Bayes model (HBM) for the proposed model. This method can estimate the hyperparameters from given data.

3   Model Comparison Using Information Criteria

This section presents model comparisons using information criteria to confirm whether the proposed model is suitable for actual peer assessment data.

The actual data were gathered using the following procedures. 1) 20 learners' reports for 5 assignments were collected from an e-learning course offered by one author. 2) The reports were evaluated by 20 other raters who had attended the same e-learning course. The raters rated them using 5 categories.

Using the actual data, the BIC and DIC were calculated for the proposed model, the models of Patz et al. [1], Usami [5], and Ueno et al. [4], and the hierarchical rater model (HRM) [2]. In those information criteria, the BIC asymptotically selects the true model; the DIC selects the model to minimize the prediction error on future data. The model which maximizes the criteria is regarded as the optimal model. Here, the criteria were calculated with fixed hyperparameters. Only for the proposed model, the criteria were also calculated using HBM.

Table 1 presents results. Comparing the results of each model with the fixed hyperparameters, both information criteria selected the proposed model as the optimal model. It means that the proposed model was estimated as the best approximation of the true model and the best predictor of future data. Additionally, the proposed model with HBM further improved the performances.

4   Reliability Evaluation

This section evaluates the reliability of peer assessment using the actual data.

The procedure is as follows: 1) For the proposed model, the model of Patz, Usami, and Ueno, and HRM, the rater and assignment parameters were estimated using the actual data. Here, the hyperparameters were fixed. Only for the proposed model, the estimation using HBM was also conducted. 2) A subset of raters and assignments which consists of 10 raters and 3 assignments was created. Then, the data corresponding to the subset was created from the actual data. Given the data and the estimated rater/assignment parameters, the learners' abilities were estimated. 3) For 100 different subsets of raters and assignments,

Table 1. Scores of Information Criteria

	BIC	DIC
Proposed (HBM)	-1503.37	-2525.93
Proposed	-1508.27	-2531.50
Patz et al.	-1694.58	-2573.47
Usami	-1593.63	-2572.51
Ueno et al.	-1614.76	-2537.65
HRM	-2397.28	-3409.92

Table 2. The reliability evaluation result

Proposed (HBM)	.845 (.065)
Proposed	.831 (.066)
Patz et al.	.789 (.076)
Usami	.816 (.070)
Ueno et al.	.805 (.075)
HRM	.663 (.117)

* Shaded(Underlined) texts represent the maximum(second largest) values.

the procedure 2 was conducted. Then, the Pearson's correlations among all the pairs of the estimated ability vectors were calculated. Finally, Tukey's multiple comparison test was conducted to compare the mean of the correlations.

From the definition of the reliability, a model which reveals higher correlation values can be regarded as reliable. Table 2 presents the mean and standard deviation of the correlations. The results can be summarized as follows: 1) Given the fixed hyperparameters, the proposed model revealed significantly higher reliability than the other models. 2) The proposed model with HBM demonstrated the highest reliability in all models.

5   Conclusion

This article proposed a new item response model which incorporates the rater's consistency and severity parameters to maintain as few rater parameters as possible. The actual data experiments demonstrated that: 1) the proposed model was the most suitable for the actual data; 2) the model improved the reliability; and 3) the parameter estimation using HBM further improved those performances.

References

1. Patz, R.J., Junker, B.W.: Applications and extensions of mcmc in irt: Multiple item types, missing data, and rated responses. Journal of Educational and Behavioral Statistics **24**, 342–366 (1999)
2. Patz, R.J., Junker, B.W., Johnson, M.S.: The hierarchical rater model for rated test items and its application to large-scale educational assessment data. Journal of Educational and Behavioral Statistics **27**(4), 341–366 (1999)
3. Piech, C., Huang, J., Chen, Z., Do, C., Ng, A., Koller, D.: Tuned models of peer assessment in MOOCs. In: Proceedings of Sixth International Conference of MIT's Learning International Networks Consortium (2013)
4. Ueno, M., Okamoto, T.: Item response theory for peer assessment. In: Eighth IEEE International Conference on Advanced Learning Technologies. ICALT 2008, pp. 554–558 (2008)
5. Usami, S.: A polytomous item response model that simultaneously considers bias factors of raters and examinees: Estimation through a markov chain monte carlo algorithm. The Japanese Journal of Educational Psychology **58**(2), 163–175 (2010)

Selection Task and Computer-Based Feedback to Improve the Searching Process in Task-Oriented Reading Situations

María-Ángeles Serrano[✉], Eduardo Vidal-Abarca, Ignacio Máñez,
and Carmen Candel

ERI-Lectura, Universitat de Valencia, Valencia, Spain
{m.angeles.serrano,eduardo.vidal-abarca,
ignacio.manez,carmen.candel}@uv.es

Abstract. Adaptive feedback has showed to be effective to enhance strategic reading behaviors and performance in task-oriented reading situations, but it is difficult to be implemented in classroom environments. Computer-based systems allow overcoming these challenges. We conducted an experiment in which secondary-school students read two texts, answered comprehension questions and selected relevant text information while receiving automatic feedback about selection accuracy and performance. Two experimental conditions were designed to assess the effects of feedback and selection attempts. Then, students perform a transfer task without any of these elements. We found that one-attempt and two-attempt groups outperformed the control group on the training phase and improved their searching process in the transfer phase, although two-attempt group showed a more effective searching process. In addition, both experimental groups were more aware about the effective strategies. This study emphasizes the potential of computer-based systems to teach specific task-oriented readings skill.

Keywords: Self-regulation strategies · Selecting text information · Automatic feedback · Task-oriented reading

1 Introduction

In educational contexts feedback is regarded as a critical element to optimize learning processes [1,2]. However, personalized and adaptive feedback could be challenging to implement in a classroom environment.

In the case of reading comprehension instruction, teachers usually ask students to answer comprehension questions having the text available and provide them with general feedback, such as information on correct response [2,3,4]. Teachers may also provide feedback on task processing and strategies for information search, such as making appropriate decisions about when to refer back to the text and, what text information is relevant for the question [5]. Previous research has shown the importance of these strategies and making decision processes since they play an important role to success in these kinds of task-oriented reading situations [6]. In addition, recent literature in

© Springer International Publishing Switzerland 2015
C. Conati et al. (Eds.): AIED 2015, LNAI 9112, pp. 804–807, 2015.
DOI: 10.1007/978-3-319-19773-9_120

feedback about self-regulation processes claims that, feedback that guides students' "when" and "what" to search decisions improve students' strategic search decisions and comprehension performance [7]. However, feedback at this process level require adaptive and individual feedback addressing specific features of the student's performance in relation to the task [1], which is quite difficult to be implemented by a single teacher in a classroom environment. In response to this challenge, computer-based systems offer the possibility to trace accurately learners' activity and generate timely adaptive feedback [8].

In this line, [9] developed such a system, based on the software Read&Answer [6] which recorded all the students' actions and provided them with automatic adaptive feedback when selecting textual information and answering comprehension questions from an available text. The authors conducted an experiment in which students were presented with a text and questions. In one of the experimental conditions, they asked students to select relevant text information while an automatic system provided them with elaborate feedback on Knowledge of Response (KR), Knowledge of Correct Answer (KCR) on selection accuracy and specific tailored hints on task-specific strategies (KH). In the other experimental condition, students were not asked to select and were provided with elaborate feedback on Knowledge of Response (KR), Knowledge of Correct Answer (KCR) on response as well as specific tailored hints on task-specific strategies (KH). Results showed that students in the first condition improved performance and transfer of strategies into a new task oriented reading situation. At this stage, if one selection attempt allows students to learn and apply reading strategies into new reading scenarios, it would be interesting to explore to which extend encouraging students to perform a two-selection-attempt approach would increase student's performance since students get two loops of feedback on their own selection instead of only one. Another interesting point could be analyzing to what extent students are aware of the strategies they learn.

2   Objectives

The main goals are the following. First, to test the effectiveness of a two-selection-attempt procedure instead of one-selection-attempt, implemented by [9], on both, performance and strategic behavior. Second, to examine whether or not elaborate feedback on KR, KCR and KH might increase not only implicit (procedural), but also awareness of (declarative) strategic knowledge.

3   Methodology

One hundred and forty-four 7th and 8th graders took part in the study and were randomly distributed into three groups according to conditions: placebo, one-selection-attempt and two-selection-attempts. The study consisted in a training and transfer phase where students read two texts and responded to twenty multiple-choice questions. For this study, we compared two different experimental procedures for the training phase. In both procedures students received elaborate feedback on Knowledge of Response (KR), Knowledge of Correct Answer (KCR) on selection accuracy of textual information relevant to answer to a given question, and specific tailored hints on task-specific strategies (KH). The two-selection-attempts condition provided the same feedback but this one included a second attempt to select information.

The critical question is to what extent both procedures induce a significant change in the students strategies when feedback is not present (i.e., transfer phase). We focused on the students' strategic when and what decisions in order to assess this effect in the transfer phase.

A questionnaire about the strategies acquired during training phase was administered during the transfer phase.

4   Results and Conclusions

A one-way between-subjects ANOVA revealed a significant effect on performance in the training phase, $F(2,140)= 21.91$, $p=.00,\eta2p=.24$. Follow-up pairwise comparisons showed that two-selection-attempts condition outperformed both, one-selection-attempt and control condition, as well as one-selection-attempt feedback group scored better than the control one. It indicates that getting the chance to improve the quality of the information selected using adaptive feedback enhances deep processing, so that students increase their performance score.

Regarding the transfer phase, a one-way between-subjects ANOVA revealed a significant effect on performance, $F(2,140)=4.221$, $p=.02$, $\eta2p=.06$. Follow-up pairwise comparisons showed that one-selection-attempt condition outperformed control; meanwhile two-selection-attempts outperformed marginally control group. Interestingly, there were no differences between the two experimental groups.

Similar results were found on the search decisions before answering, $F(2,140)=6.557$, $p=.00$, $\eta2p=.08$. Follow-up pairwise comparisons showed that one-selection-attempt and two-selection-attempts conditions referred back to the text more often than the control group, meanwhile there were no differences between them.

We also found significant differences on finding out relevant information for the question, $F(2,140)=4.606$, $p=.01,\eta2p=.06$. When participants made the decision to refer back to the text, pairwise comparisons revealed that two-selection-attempts' participants found out relevant textual information more often than the control condition. No significant differences were found between one and two-selection attempts groups. More concretely, a one-way between-subjects ANOVA showed a significant effect on the last relevant information searched before answering the question, $F(2,140)=4.64$, $p=.01$, $\eta2p=.062$. Follow-up comparisons showed that only two-selection-attempts condition decided to stop searching more frequently when the last textual information read was relevant for the question. It indicates a development of self-regulatory in the search process, which may mean that learning to focus on relevant textual information improves the effectivity of searching the text.

Thus, a second attempt for a new selection improved performance in training and transfer tasks and helped students to recognize relevant information in a transfer task compared to students who perform only one attempt.

In addition, the questionnaire about strategies applied on the transfer phase reveals differences through conditions, $F(2,138)=5.760$, $p<.00$, $\eta2p=.08$. Both, one and two-selection-attempts conditions outperformed control group, showing that they not only increased procedural skills, but also were more aware about the effective strategies in task-oriented reading situations.

In conclusion, this study shows how computer-based instruction can be used to teach specific task-oriented readings skills, as well as to study the effect of different features of adaptive teaching. This study emphasizes the potential of computer-based instruction, since it allows providing automatic and adaptive feedback in a higher controlled setting than human tutors can provide.

Acknowledgements. Research supported by the project EDU2011-27091, granted by the Spanish Minister of Science and Innovation, and the project Prometeo/2013/081, granted by the Valencian Regional Government.

References

1. Narciss, S., Huth, K.: Fostering Achievement and Motivation with Bug-Related Tutoring Feedback in a Computer-Based Training for Written Subtraction. Learn. Instr. **16**(4), 310–322 (2006)
2. Hattie, J.A., Gan, M.: Instruction based on feedback. In: Mayer, R., Alexander, P. (eds.) Handbook of Research on Learning and Instruction, pp. 249–271. Routledge, New York (2011)
3. Shute, V.J.: Focus on Formative Feedback. Rev. Educ. Res **78**(1), 153–189 (2008)
4. Ness, M.: Explicit Reading Comprehension Instruction in Elementary Classrooms: Teacher Use of Reading Comprehension Strategies. J. Res. Child. Educ. **25**(1), 98–117 (2011)
5. Vidal-Abarca, E., Mañá, A., Gil, L.: Individual Differences for Self-regulating Task-Oriented Reading Activities. J. Educ. Psychol. **102**(4), 817–826 (2010)
6. Vidal-Abarca, E., Martínez, T., Salmerón, L., Cerdán, R., Gilabert, R., Gil, L., Mañá, A., Llorens, A., Ferris, R.: Recording On-line Processes in Task-Oriented Reading with Read&Answer. Behav. Res. Methods. **43**, 179–192 (2011)
7. Llorens, A.C., Cerdán, R., Vidal-Abarca, E.: Adaptive Formative Feedback to Improve Strategic Search Decisions in Task-Oriented Reading. J. Comput. Assist. Lear. **30**(3), 233–251 (2014)
8. Mason, B.J., Bruning, R.: Providing Feedback in Computer-Based Instruction: What the Research Tells Us (2001). Ret. Febr., 15 (2007)
9. Llorens, A.C., Vidal-Abarca, E., Cerdán, R.: Formative Feedback to Promote Transfer of Self-regulation Strategies in Task-Oriented Reading. J. Comput. Assist. Lear. (submitted)

Personalized Expert Skeleton Scaffolding in Concept Map Construction

Shang Wang[1](✉), Erin Walker[1], Rishabh Chaudhry[1], and Ruth Wylie[2]

[1] Computing, Informatics, and Decision Systems Engineering,
Arizona State University, Tempe AZ, USA
{swang158,Erin.A.Walker,rchaudh2}@asu.edu
[2] Mary Lou Fulton Teachers College, Arizona State University, Tempe AZ, USA
Ruth.Wylie@asu.edu

Abstract. Concept maps have been widely used in educational contexts to facilitate meaningful learning. Recent research has examined how concept mapping tools assist students in summarizing, relating, and organizing concepts. Our goal is to explore how personalized scaffolding can be applied to concept map construction. We provide personalized scaffolding in the form of an adaptive expert skeleton map based on student prior knowledge. We conducted a study comparing the adaptive map to a fixed map and to unscaffolded concept mapping. In an exploratory analysis, we examine the possible impacts of adaptive scaffolding on student learning processes.

Keywords: Concept maps · Expert skeleton maps · Adaptive scaffolding

1 Introduction

Adaptive scaffolding, the process of leveraging student characteristics and behaviors to provide students with personalized assistance, has been shown to lead to greater learning over fixed, non-personalized scaffolding [1]. Our goal is to examine how adaptive scaffolding can be applied to concept mapping activities. A concept map is a type of graphic organizer that uses labeled nodes to denote concepts and links to denote relationships among concepts. Learning takes place as students assimilate new concepts into existing propositional frameworks held by the learner [4]. Previous research has investigated how scaffolding tools can be used to reduce the time, effort, and cognitive load for constructing concept maps [2, 3]. In this previous research, an "expert skeleton map", which is a map previously prepared by an expert with some areas left blank for students to fill in, is often given to students as a guide.

Prior knowledge is a critical element in concept mapping, as knowledge construction occurs when students actively seek to integrate new knowledge with their prior knowledge [4]. Understanding learner's prior knowledge and providing relevant guidance could be a critical factor for scaffolding concept mapping [5]. Our work explores the potential effects of an adaptive expert skeleton scaffold that contains concepts and relationships for which the student has demonstrated prior knowledge. Filling in unknown or to-be-learned knowledge in the map is left as an exercise for the student.

© Springer International Publishing Switzerland 2015
C. Conati et al. (Eds.): AIED 2015, LNAI 9112, pp. 808–811, 2015.
DOI: 10.1007/978-3-319-19773-9_121

By presenting students with a map that already contains their prior knowledge, we hypothesize that students will both spend more time on unknown concepts and be better supported in connecting new knowledge to prior knowledge, thus improving learning.

2   Study Method

To investigate how different types of scaffolding affect learning, we had three conditions: adaptive scaffolding, fixed scaffolding and unscaffolded. In the adaptive scaffolding condition, the expert skeleton map was personalized to include concepts that students had already acquired. Students in the fixed scaffolding condition also received an expert skeleton map. However, instead of aligning the map to the student prior knowledge, students in this condition received one of the personalized maps from the adaptive scaffolding condition. In this way, the two conditions were yoked and we were able to control for content across conditions. Finally, in the unscaffolded condition, students constructed a map from scratch. In all three conditions, students were given a list of "suggested concepts", which included all the concepts in the original expert map, but not currently in the students' concept map. The system used for concept mapping was the Cmap tool, developed by Florida Institution of Human & Machine Cognition, which provides easy concept map construction and modification.

We conducted a study with 38 non-biology major students (22 undergraduate students and 16 graduate students). First, students were given a 10-minute online pretest to assess prior knowledge on plant reproduction. Next, students were given the chapter in an e-book format, and had 10 minutes to read. Students then received a 4-minute tutorial about what concept maps are and how to use the Cmap tool to construct one. Then, they were asked to construct a simple concept map from an example text. After the tutorial and practice, students were randomly assigned to conditions and received either an adaptive map, a fixed map, or a blank (no-scaffolding) map and were given 20 minutes to construct or complete the map based on the template. Finally, a posttest (counterbalanced with the pretest) was given.

To create the adaptive expert skeleton map, we first created an expert map to represent the concepts from the chapter. In order to determine which concepts to remove from the map, we mapped each question on the pretests to a portion of the expert map. This allowed us to modify the expert skeleton map based on students' pretests scores. For example, if a student incorrectly answers question 4 in Figure 1, the correct concept ("flower") is removed from the map and left for the student to complete.

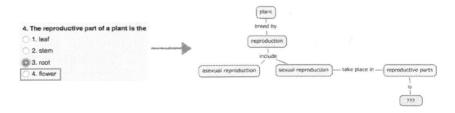

Fig. 1. Modifying the expert skeleton map based on a question testing the concept "flower"

3   Study Results

Our first step was to investigate the hypothesis that adaptive scaffolding is better than both fixed scaffolding and unscaffolded concept mapping. We conducted a two-way repeated-measures ANOVA with condition as a between-subjects variable and test-time as a within-subjects variable. Table 1a shows the mean and standard deviation of the overall scores on the 9 key ideas evaluated. Students got 1 point when they got a concept correct and 0 points when they got it wrong. All conditions had significant pre to post learning ($F[1,35]=39.60$, $p < 0.001$, $\eta^2 = 0.531$), but there were no significant differences between conditions ($F[2,35] = 1.16$, $p = 0.33$).

Table 1. (a) Test results between groups (b) Gains and number of concepts for each activity

	Pretest		Posttest			Gain per Student		# Concepts per Student	
	M	SD	M	SD		M	SD	M	SD
Adaptive	3.21	1.31	4.64	2.13	Exist close	0.59	1.18	1.59	0.51
Fixed	2.67	1.07	5.17	2.04	Exist far	-0.15	1.08	2.04	0.92
					Added	1.50	1.58	4.57	1.30
Unscaf-folded	3.00	1.60	5.50	2.02	Not added	0.25	0.64	1.75	0.79

As there was no significant difference between conditions, we were interested in exploring further how student interaction with the map influenced learning. We coded the 9 key ideas in the expert map as being: (1) added to the map by the student, (2) already existing in the expert skeleton maps, or (3) not added. For the already existing concepts in the expert map, we further categorized the concepts that were adjacent to the newly added concepts as "exist close" and the ones which were more than one hop away as "exist far". For each type of concept, we computed the learning gain for each user by subtracting pretest score from posttest score. As only students in the adaptive and fixed conditions experienced all types of concepts, we only analyzed results from this subset. Means and standard deviations of leaning gains and number of concepts in each interaction type are presented in Table 1b. It is not meaningful to make a statistical comparison between the types of interaction due to challenges with our data set (a small number of key ideas, each key idea maps to different numbers of concepts in the expert skeleton map, and it is likely that gain was influenced by level of prior knowledge for each type). However, looking at the means, it appears that adding concepts to the map was the most beneficial, followed by interacting with close existing concepts. "Exist far" concepts, which were not adjacent to concepts added, were not learned effectively. We see this exploratory analysis as a foundation for future work.

4   Discussion and Conclusions

We conducted a study where we compared adaptive scaffolding to fixed scaffolding and no scaffolding in concept map construction. While all students learned from the concept mapping activity, we found no significant differences between conditions. Exploratory results suggest that students may learn from concepts that are added to the map compared to ones that were not added, and, for the provided concepts in the template, students may benefit more from ones that are close to the interacted region.

There are several limitations in the data collection in this study that indicate caution in interpreting the results. The number of graduate students and undergraduates were not balanced throughout the conditions. Another potential problem was that the expert skeleton maps we gave to students might have been too large. While we assessed students on 9 key ideas, these ideas spanned more than 70 nodes in our expert map. The complexity of the given template might have imposed high cognitive load on students, reducing the benefits of the expert skeleton maps.

However, the tentative learning difference in the existing concepts that are close or far from the area of the map where students interacted is worth investigating. While adding concepts to the template, students may benefit most from relating existing concepts directly with the new knowledge that is being added, as they did for the close concepts. Students did not interact with the far concepts directly, and thus may not have fully mastered those concepts at posttest. Expert skeleton maps should be designed in a way where the provided concepts and structures lead to more interactions with newly added concepts. In our future research, we plan to make improvements to the study design and carry out further experiments to test the effect of adaptive expert skeleton scaffolding.

Acknowledgments. This research was funded by NSF CISE-IIS-1451431 EAGER: Towards Knowledge Curation and Community Building within a Postdigital Textbook.

References

1. Aleven, V.A.W.M.M., Koedinger, K.R.: An effective metacognitive strategy: Learning by doing and explaining with a computer-based Cognitive Tutor. Cognitive science **26**(2), 147–179 (2002)
2. Luchini, K., et al.: Scaffolding in the small: designing educational supports for concept mapping on handheld computers. In: CHI 2002 Extended Abstracts on Human Factors in Computing Systems. ACM (2002)
3. Chang, Kuo-En, Sung, Y.-T., Chen, S.F.: Learning through computer-based concept mapping with scaffolding aid. Journal of Computer Assisted Learning **17**(1), 21–33 (2001)
4. Novak, J.D., Cañas, A.J.: The theory underlying concept maps and how to construct them. Florida Institute for Human and Machine Cognition 1 (2006)
5. Amadieu, F., et al.: Effects of prior knowledge and concept-map structure on disorientation, cognitive load, and learning. Learning and Instruction **19**(5), 376–386 (2009)

Using Eye Gaze Data to Explore Student Interactions with Tutorial Dialogues in a Substep-Based Tutor

Amali Weerasinghe[1], Myse Elmadani[2], and Antonija Mitrovic[2(✉)]

[1] School of Computer Science, University of Adelaide, Adelaide, SA, Australia
amali.weerasinghe@adelaide.edu.au
[2] Intelligent Computer Tutoring Group, University of Canterbury, Christchurch, New Zealand
tanja.mitrovic@canterbury.ac.nz

Abstract. We used eye gaze data to investigate student interactions with tutorial dialogues in EER-Tutor. The results show that tutorial dialogues are effective as they enable students to correct their mistakes. However, some students do not take advantage of opportunities to reflect on what they have learnt. We identify several possible improvements to EER-Tutor, as well as future directions of work on using eye-tracking for on-line adaptation.

Keywords: Eye gaze data analysis · Substep-based tutor · Tutorial dialogues

1   Introduction

Studies of human one-on-one tutoring suggest that student's behaviour is a stronger predictor of learning gain than tutor's behaviour [1]. Therefore, it is beneficial to understand how students interact with ITSs. We are interested in understanding the effectiveness of tutorial dialogues in EER-Tutor. Dialogue-based ITSs represent sub-step tutoring, and are characterized with an even finer level of interaction granularity compared to step-based ITSs [2]. Step-based ITSs provide feedback on each step the student performed. In contrast, in sub-step tutoring the system engages the student in a tutorial dialogue about the step performed, which provides additional information about the student's intentions and allows the ITS to provide more effective instruction. Many studies have shown the benefits of tutorial dialogues in ITSs, e.g. [3-4].

In previous work, we enhanced EER-Tutor [5], a constraint-based tutor that teaches conceptual database modeling, with tutorial dialogues which help students reflect on their errors and learn relevant domain concepts [6,7]. In this paper, we focus on student behaviour following tutorial dialogues. For example, do students follow advice given in dialogues about how to correct errors? Do students reflect on their solution beyond specific advice provided in dialogues? We analyzed student-system interaction videos and eye-tracking data, and identified common change patterns. We present the design of our study, the findings and discussion in the next Section.

© Springer International Publishing Switzerland 2015
C. Conati et al. (Eds.): AIED 2015, LNAI 9112, pp. 812–815, 2015.
DOI: 10.1007/978-3-319-19773-9_122

2   Study and Discussion of Findings

The participants were 27 students enrolled in a database course at the University of Canterbury. During the session (50 minutes long), the students worked on three problems of increasing difficulty. We used the Tobii TX300 eye tracker, which allows unobtrusive eye-tracking. One student was excluded because no eye-tracking data was collected. The system log records only information about pedagogically significant actions and records information about each submission, rather than every single action performed. Therefore, it is not possible to perform the deep analysis of students' behaviours without eye gaze data. Figure 1 presents a screenshot of EER-Tutor, showing the problem statement at the top, the toolbox containing the EER components, the drawing area on the left, and the feedback area on the right. When the student's solution contains errors, s/he is presented with a tutorial dialogue selected adaptively. The problem statement, toolbar and drawing area are disabled but visible for the duration of the dialogue and the error is highlighted in red in the diagram.

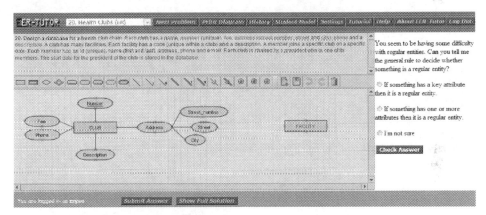

Fig. 1. EER-Tutor interface

We identified 349 segments, each starting when a dialogue finishes and ending when the student next submits their solution to the same problem, the session ends or the student switches to another problem. There were 11 segments in problem 1, 118 segments in problem 2 and 120 segments in the last problem. Generally, the results show that tutorial dialogues are effective: in 91.4% of segments, the students corrected errors discussed in dialogues. We identified eight interaction patterns:

- *fix*: the student corrects the error discussed in the tutorial;
- *attempt*: the student addresses the error but incorrectly;
- *wrong*: the student tries to fix the error by addressing the wrong issue;
- *check*: the student inspects his/her solution or rearranges diagram components;
- *similar*: the student corrects a similar error;
- *related*: the student makes related changes;
- *other*: the student continues working on other parts of the solution;
- *problem*: the student looks at the problem statement.

In Problem 1, there were seven segments during which the student switched to a different problem. We analyzed the remaining fragments, and described students' behaviours in terms of the change patterns (Table 1). The most frequent behaviour is *fix* (46.7%), when the student corrects the mistake discussed in the dialogue and submits the solution immediately. Out of 163 segments containing this behaviour, the next solution was correct in 24 cases (14.7%). Therefore, most students only perform the change discussed in dialogues, and do not think further about their solution. Depending on the previous submission, the student should do one or more of the following actions: make related changes (the *related* pattern); correct similar errors (*similar*); do more work if the solution is not already complete (*other*); check the solution for completeness and correctness (*check*) or check that the solution covers all requirements (*problem*). The second most frequent behaviour is *fix – check* (18.3%), which consists of fixing the mistake, and then checking the solution before asking feedback. The *check* pattern appears in 30% of segments, showing better metacognitive skills, as the students have assessed their solutions.

Table 1. Interaction sequences

Sequence	Segments / Distinct Students			
	Problem 1	Problem 2	Problem 3	Total
fix	52 / 19	55 / 19	56 / 11	163
fix - check	17 / 9	23 / 15	24 / 10	64
fix - other – check	1 / 1	3 / 3	11 / 7	15
fix – other	6 / 5	1 / 1	7 / 4	14
fix – related	2 / 2	5 / 5	5 / 4	12
attempt	6 / 4	4 / 4	2 / 1	12
fix – similar	6 / 5	5 / 3		11
fix - similar – check	1 / 1	2 / 2	3 / 3	6
fix - related – check		4 / 4	2 / 2	6
wrong	5 / 4			5
attempt - other		4 / 2	1 / 1	5
attempt - check		3 / 2	2 / 2	5
fix – problem	1 / 1	1 / 1	3 / 2	5
fix - related - other – check	1 / 1	2 / 2	2 / 2	5
fix - related – other	3 / 3		1 / 1	4
fix - related - similar – check		2 / 2		2
attempt - other – check		1 / 1		1
attempt - problem	1 / 1			1
attempt - similar		1 / 1		1
fix - related – similar		1 / 1		1
fix - similar – other	1 / 1			1
fix - wrong - other	1 / 1			1
fix - check – problem			1 / 1	1
related - similar – other		1 / 1		1

If the student learnt from the dialogue, s/he should also be able to fix similar errors. There is evidence of this: 23 segments include the *similar* pattern. Sometimes fixing the solution involved making related changes to other parts of the solution. The *related* pattern appears in 31 segments, showing that some students understand the need to make additional changes. However, the students recognized the need to perform related changes in only 58% of situations when they were required. There are 31 segments (8.8%) in which the students failed to correct mistakes, which show that students did not understand the tutorial dialogues they received. In 17 of those segments (4.8%), there was only one change pattern (*attempt* or *wrong*), while in others students performed additional actions after trying to correct the mistake.

We had expected students to reflect on their correct solutions, but only 18% of students looked at their solution to problem 1. This has improved in subsequent problems: all five students who completed problem 3 exhibited this behaviour. If the system can identify the lack of reflection, it can prompt the student to do so. Additionally, if the student repeats the same behaviour while failing to reflect, it may be beneficial to emphasize the importance of reflection.

We identified some improvements that can be made to EER-Tutor on the basis of observed student behaviours. Some segments show that the participants had difficulty understanding certain problems and tutorial dialogues, requiring modifications to the wording of those dialogues/problems.

Acknowledgments. We thank Angus Pope for helping with data analyses, as well as ICTG members for their support.

References

1. Chi, M.T.H., Siler, S.A., Jeong, H., Yamauchi, T., Hausmann, R.G.: Learning from Human Tutoring. Cognitive Science. **25**(4), 471–533 (2001)
2. VanLehn, K.: The Relative Effectiveness of Human Tutoring, Intelligent Tutoring Systems, and Other Tutoring Systems. Educational Psychologist **46**(4), 197–221 (2011)
3. Evans, M., Michael, J.: One-on-one Tutoring by Humans and Computers. Lawrence Erlbaum Associates (2006)
4. Graesser, A.C., Franceschetti, D.R., Gholson, B., Craig, S.D.: Learning Newtonian physics with conversational agents and interactive simulation. In: Stein, N.L., Raudenbush, S. (eds.) Developmental Cognitive Science goes to School, pp. 157–172. Routledge, New York (2011)
5. Zakharov, K., Mitrovic, A., Ohlsson, S.: Feedback micro-engineering in EER-Tutor. In: Proc. 12th Int. Conf. Artificial Intelligence in Education, pp. 718–725 (2005)
6. Weerasinghe, A., Mitrovic, A., Thomson, D., Mogin, P., Martin, B.: Evaluating a general model of adaptive tutorial dialogues. In: Biswas, G., Bull, S., Kay, J., Mitrovic, A. (eds.) AIED 2011. LNCS, vol. 6738, pp. 394–402. Springer, Heidelberg (2011)
7. Weerasinghe, A., Mitrovic, A., Shareghi Najar, A., Holland, J.: The effect of interaction granularity on learning with a data normalization tutor. In: Lane, H., Yacef, K., Mostow, J., Pavlik, P. (eds.) AIED 2013. LNCS, vol. 7926, pp. 463–472. Springer, Heidelberg (2013)

UML-IT: An ITS to Teach Multiple Modelling Tasks

Amali Weerasinghe[✉] and Bernard Evans

School of Computer Science, University of Adelaide, Adelaide, SA, Australia
{amali.weerasinghe,bernard.evans}@adelaide.edu.au

Abstract. Modelling software systems using Unified Modelling Language (UML) is a core skill expected from a software engineer. This involves modelling a software system using multiple diagrams. Students find it very difficult to develop this skill due to the open-ended nature of this task: the final outcome is defined in abstract terms but there is no well-defined procedure to achieve the outcome. Students also find it difficult to understand the different modelling conventions used to represent multiple perspectives of a particular system and the consistencies need to be maintained between these diagrams. We believe an ITS that teaches these multiple modelling tasks will be able to support learners to develop the skill of UML modeling efficiently and effectively.

Keywords: UML-modelling · Open-ended task · Multiple modeling tasks

1 Introduction

Modelling software systems using Unified Modelling Language (UML) is a core skill expected from a software engineer [4]. Thus UML modelling is a core topic in a majority of undergraduate computer science programmes. UML consists of multiple graphical notations, which capture different aspects of a software system including static structures, component behaviours and component interactions. These graphical notations enable software engineers to capture multiple perspectives of a single system. Students find it very difficult to develop this skill due to a number of reasons: (i) modelling is an open-ended task: the final outcome is defined in abstract terms but there is no well-defined procedure to achieve the outcome; (ii) the need to be familiar with multiple graphical notations; (iii) the need to understand and model the system from multiple perspectives and (iv) the need to maintain consistencies between these graphical notations. Thus, an ITS that can provide a customised learning environment that teaches UML modeling will assist novices to learn these multiple modeling tasks efficiently and effectively.

There have been several research attempts to develop automated tools to support the learning of UML modeling. However, the focus of the majority of attempts have been to ease the teachers' workload in assessing UML models and providing feedback to students [3,5]. Limited learning support was provided through feedback, but there was no customised support using an adaptive learning environment. However, COLLECT-UML provides customised learning support to learn system modeling via class diagrams [1]. Even though it has shown to significantly improve the performance of the

© Springer International Publishing Switzerland 2015
C. Conati et al. (Eds.): AIED 2015, LNAI 9112, pp. 816–819, 2015.
DOI: 10.1007/978-3-319-19773-9_123

students who learnt with COLLECT-UML, its focus is limited to teaching class diagrams. Hence it is not possible for COLLECT-UML to teach students the need to maintain consistencies between different types of diagrams. The overall goal of this research is to develop UML-IT, an ITS that support the learning of different types of UML diagrams including Class diagrams, Sequence diagrams, Activity diagrams and State diagrams.

2   UML-IT

The modelling process starts with a Use Case diagram, which enables to specify the boundary of the system being modelled. The boundary is represented as a square. Outside the boundary, we specify other systems, organizations or people that either provide information to the software system or consume information from the system. These other systems are known as Actors. Inside the boundary we model a set of Use Cases, which is a high-level view of the system requirements. Upon completion of the Use case diagram, the class diagram is developed. This provides the structure of the system by showing the classes, their attributes, methods and the relationships among classes. After the Class diagram, a Sequence diagram is created for each Use Case. A Sequence diagram represents the sequence of messages exchanged between the Classes that are needed to carry out the functionality of the Use Case. While Class diagrams represent a static view of the system, Sequence diagrams provide a dynamic view of the system. Even though there are many other types of diagrams available in UML, we will limit our discussion to these three types of diagrams (Use case diagrams, Class diagrams and Sequence diagrams) to stay within the scope of the paper.

UML-IT also supports the same modelling sequence. It provides the students with a correct Use Case diagram and will ask students to develop the Class diagram. After completing the Class diagram, students will be asked to develop the Sequence diagram for each of the use cases. Then the student will be asked to focus on other diagrams including Activity and State. Currently UML-IT focuses only on supporting the development of Class diagrams and Sequence diagrams. Figure 1 shows the interface of UML-IT, showing the problem statement at the top left corner, and the feedback area on the right. This figure shows a student attempting to create a sequence diagram (right-side of the screen) after completing the class diagram (left-side of the screen). A toolbox containing the required components for each diagram is available above the drawing area. As the required components for a diagram depends on the diagram, components of the toolbox will change accordingly. The student can select which diagram he/she wants on each side by using the drop-down menu (the first item in the tool box). The second component in the Sequence diagram toolbox specifies the Use Case for which the Sequence diagram being drawn. Students have the freedom both with the order in which they choose to model the components and their positions in the drawing area. The constraint-base of UML-IT is modelled as a set of constraints [2]. Upon a student's request, the constraint-base, the problem statement and the pre-specified correct solution will be used to diagnose the errors. A feedback message is associated with each constraint and the corresponding message for each violated constraint (a constraint violation identifies a mistake in the student solution) will be displayed in the feedback pane.

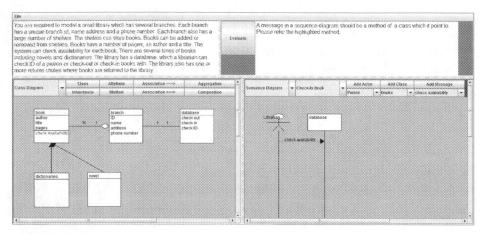

Fig. 1. UML-IT interface

3   Problem and Solution Representation

Each problem statement is tagged to identify which word/phrase has been selected during the modelling process. For instance, the first sentence of the problem statement in Fig.1 has a tag C1 for branch. The tag C1 is used to indicate that Branch should be modeled as a class. This approach is similar to that of constraint-based tutors [2].

Each problem has a set of solution types including a Class diagram and a Sequence diagram. We need an abstract model that captures the characteristics of all these different types of solutions as well as the consistencies between these diagrams. Figure 2 presents this model. The abstract model captures the characteristics of these different types of diagrams. An item (denoted by UItem in Figure 2) can be a construct such as a Use Case, an Actor or a Class. An item can also be a property (denoted by UProperty in Figure 2) or a link (denoted by ULink). A property can be a method or an attribute. A link is used to represent different kinds of relationships such as inheritance, aggregation and composition. Dotted lines indicate the items that are not included to avoid the diagram being cluttered. The diagram model (Figure 2) enables the system to visually generate a particular type of diagram without having to store each solution as an image. This is useful when a student requests the final solution for a particular diagram. A Class represented in a Class diagram (denoted by CDClass) contains attributes and methods. When the same class is represented in a Sequence diagram (denoted by SDClass), it is modelled without attributes and methods. This is because the focus of the Sequence diagrams is the messages that are passed between Classes.

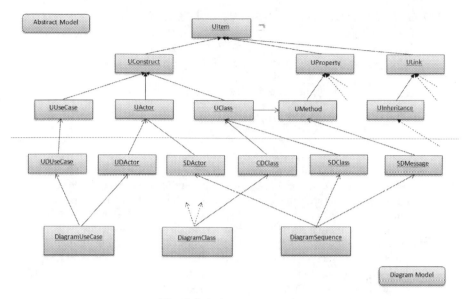

Fig. 2. Solution representation

4 Future Work

The next step is to test the constraint-base for its ability to identify all the errors in a student solution. Then we plan to evaluate the effectiveness of UML-IT through a study involving authentic users enrolled in an introductory software engineering course at The University of Adelaide.

References

1. Baghaei, N., Mitrovic, A.: From modelling domain knowledge to metacognitive skills: extending a constraint-based tutoring system to support collaboration. In: Conati, C., McCoy, K., Paliouras, G. (eds.) UM 2007. LNCS (LNAI), vol. 4511, pp. 217–227. Springer, Heidelberg (2007)
2. Mitrovic, A.: Fifteen years of Constraint-Based Tutors: What we have achieved and where we are going. User Modeling and User-Adapted Interaction 22(1–2), 39–72 (2012)
3. Outair, A., Lyhyaoui, A., Tanana, M.: Towards a semi automatic assessment of UML diagrams by graph transformation. In: Proc. of the International Conference on Multimedia Computing and Systems, pp. 668–673 (2014)
4. Sommerville, I.: Software Engineering, 9th edn. Pearson (2011)
5. Striewe, M., Goedicke, M.: Automated Checks on UML Diagrams. In: Proc. of the 16th Annual Joint Conference on Innovation and Technology in Computer Science Education, pp. 38–42 (2011)

Virtual Teams in Massive Open Online Courses

Miaomiao Wen[(✉)], Diyi Yang, and Carolyn Penstein Rosé

Language Technology Institute,
Carnegie Mellon University, Pittsburgh, USA
{mwen,diyiy,cprose}@cs.cmu.edu

Abstract. Previous work on MOOCs highlights both that the current MOOCs fail to provide the kind of social environment that is desired and that social interaction and exchange of support is important for slowing down attrition over time. However, little is known about how to support virtual teams in a MOOC context. In this paper, we demonstrate what factors distinguish successful and nonsuccessful virtual teams in NovoEd MOOCs, where team collaboration is an integral part of the course design. In particular, we find team leaders play a central role in determining team performance. We discuss implications for continued work towards intelligent support for team leaders in MOOCs.

Keywords: MOOC · Team based learning · Leadership behaviors

1 Introduction

Learning is a social act. Research suggests that Massive Open Online Course (MOOC) students prefer to study in groups, and that social facilitation within the study groups may render the learning of difficult concepts a pleasing experience[6]. Yet for most students, their experience with a MOOC is watching videos and taking quizzes. Around ten percent of the students participate in the discussion. This experience is more interactive than reading a textbook, but far less engaging than working with one's peers to create a shared understanding of knowledge.

NovoEd[1] began as a solution to promote social learning in a MOOC context. NovoEd's technology encourages active and peer learning through team based exercises, calibrated peer evaluation and feedback and visible student work[4]. The team-based MOOCs in NovoEd report a higher completion rate than traditional MOOCs[2]. Nevertheless, not all teams are successful. In our NovoEd MOOCs, more than half of the teams fail to submit the final team project. Prior work in CSCL also highlights the fact that vitual teams require support to function smoothly[7].

Despite the substantial amount of research on groups, there is comparatively less consistent evidence for which group processes promote good group

---

[1] https://novoed.com/

[2] https://gigaom.com/2013/04/15/novoed-another-stanford-mooc-startup-opens-small-group-learning-services-to-public/

© Springer International Publishing Switzerland 2015
C. Conati et al. (Eds.): AIED 2015, LNAI 9112, pp. 820–824, 2015.
DOI: 10.1007/978-3-319-19773-9_124

outcomes[3]. To support team based learning in MOOCs, we first identify the critical group activities and processes that distinguish successful and nonsuccessful teams. We find that the leader's behaviors are more predictive of team performance than activity count of a whole team. This study is an important step toward assessing the feasibility of using unobtrusive behavior as indicators of performance among real-world project teams.

2   NovoEd Virtual Teams

Our NovoEd dataset consists of two NovoEd MOOCs: elementary and secondary Constructive Classroom Conversations. They were offered simultaneously in 2014. The statistics are shown in Table 1.

Table 1. Statistics of two NovoEd MOOCs

NovoEd	#Registerd Students	#Students successfully joined a group	# Teams	# Course Weeks
Elementary	2,817	262	101	12
Secondary	1,924	161	76	12

2.1   The Nature of NovoEd Teams

Students in a NovoEd MOOC have to create or join a team in the beginning of the course. The student who creates the team will be the team leader. The homepage of a NovoEd team displays the stream of blog posts, events, files and other content shared with the group as well as the active members. Students can also communicate through private messages. The leader can select classmates based on their profiles and send them invitation messages to join the team. The invitation message contains a link to join the group. Subsequently, new members may request to join and receive approval from the team leader. Only a team leader can add a member to the team. Also, groups can only be deleted by its team leader.

Throughout the course, team work is a central part of the learning experience. In our two NovoEd courses, small tasks ("Housekeeping tasks") such as "introduce yourself to the team" are assigned(but will not be graded) early on in the course. Instructors encourage students to collaborate with team members on non-collaborative assignments as well. Individual performance in a group is peer rated so as to encourage participation and contribution. Collaborations among students are centered on the final team project, which accounts for 20% of the final score. The team project is to design a lesson plan collaboratively.

2.2   Latent Variable Modeling

In our NovoEd courses, slightly less than half of the teams successfully submit the final team project, but even within that set there is interesting variation on success according to the teacher assigned grade. Teams who failed to turn in the project received a 0, whereas the others received either 20 or 40. We refer to this score as the **Team Score**.

In order to understand the relative importance of factors contributing to Team Score as a success measure, we constructed a structural equation model. We included two latent factors we referred to as Team Activity and Leadership Behaviors that we hypothesize are predictive of team performance.

Team Activity. In this section, we describe the variables that account for variation in level of activity across teams. **MemberCnt** is the number of members in the team. Group size is an important predictor of virtual group success[5]. **Delete** is 1 if the team leader deleted the team. **BlogCnt** is the number of team blogs that are posted. **BlogCommentCnt** is the number of team blog comments that are made. **MessageCnt** is the number of messages that are sent among the team.

Leadership Behaviors. Leaders are important for the smooth functioning of teams but their effect on team performance is less well understood[2]. We identified three types of leadership behaviors by examining the messages sent by team leaders to the team members. Definitions and example messages are shown in Table 2. 30 team leader messages are randomly sampled and then coded separately by two experts. Inter-rater reliability was Kappa = .76, indicating substantial inter-rater reliability. Then one of the experts coded all the 855 leader messages in the two NovoEd MOOCs into these three types of leadership behaviors.

Thus we design three variables to characterize team leader's behaviors. **Team Building** is the number of Team Building messages sent by the team leader. Team Building behavior is critical for NovoEd teams since only the team leader can add new members to the team. **Initiating Structure** is the number of Initiating Structure messages sent by the team leader. Initiating Structure includes typical task-oriented leadership behaviors. Previous research has demonstrated that in comparison to relation-oriented or passive leader behavior, task-oriented leader behavior is more predictive of task performance[1]. In MOOC virtual teams, usually the team leader needs to break the ice by introducing him/herself and kicking off social conversation when the team is initially formed. When an assignment deadline is coming up, the team leader needs to remind the team

Table 2. Three different types of leadership behavior of virtual team leaders

Type	Behaviors	Example Team Leader Message
Team Building	Invite or accept users to join the group	*Lauren, We would love to have you. Jill and I are both ESL specialists in Boston.*
Initiating Structure	Initiate a task or assign subtask to a team member	*Housekeeping Task #3 is optional but below are the questions I can summarize and submit for our team.*
Collaboration	Collaborate with teammates	*I figured out how to use the Google Docs. Let's use it to share our lesson plans.*

Fig. 1. Structural equation model with maximum likelihood estimates (standardized). All links represent significant relationships at the $p<0.001$ level.

members to start working towards meeting that. We refer to these initiation behaviors as Initiating Structure. **Collaboration** is the number of Collaboration messages sent by the team leader. Different from previous research where the team leader mainly focuses on managing the team, we observe the leaders in these virtual teams taking on important subtasks in the team project, which is reflected in this Collaboration behavior.

Results. Above we described two latent factors we hypothesize are important in distinguishing successful and unsuccessful teams along with sets of associated observed variables. In this section, we validate the influence of each latent factor on team performance using a generalized Structural Equation Model(SEM) in Stata. Experiments are conducted on all the 177 NovoEd MOOC teams.

Fig. 1 shows the influence of each observed variable on its corresponding latent variable, and in turn the latent variable on team performance. The weights on each directed edge represent the standard estimated parameter for measuring the influence. Based on Fig. 1, Leadership Behaviors contribute more to team performance, with a standard estimated parameter of 0.58. Among the three leadership behaviors, Team Building is the strongest predictor of team performance. Since team building messages significantly correlate with the total number of members in the team($r = 0.62$), consistent with prior work[5], a team leader who recruits a larger group can increase the group's chances of success. We see also that the three leadership behaviors are more predictable than the crude activity counts, such as leader's team blog count. Team Activity is a less strong predictor of team performance. This is partly due to the fact that some successful teams communicate through Skype or Google Hangout and thus have smaller levels of activity in the NovoEd site, which renders that measure noisy.

3   Discussion and Future Work

Design of intelligent support for virtual teams in MOOCs could benefit from greater understanding of the reasons why some groups work well together while others do not. In our analysis, we identified two main factors that are predictive of virtual team performance: Team Activity and Leadership Behaviors. In particular, the team leader plays a critical role in distinguishing successful and nonsuccessful teams. In future work, we will work on building awareness tools to support team leader performance through guided reflection using predicative models with the identified factors.

Acknowledgments. This research was supported in part by NSF grants SBE-0836012 and IIS-1320064 and funding from Google.

References

1. DeRue, D.S., Nahrgang, J.D., Wellman, N., Humphrey, S.E.: Trait and behavioral theories of leadership: An integration and meta-analytic test of their relative validity. Personnel Psychology **64**(1), 7–52 (2011)
2. Ehrlich, K., Cataldo, M.: The communication patterns of technical leaders: impact on product development team performance. In: Proceedings of the 17th ACM conference on Computer Supported Cooperative Work & Social Computing, pp. 733–744. ACM (2014)
3. Isotani, S., Inaba, A., Ikeda, M., Mizoguchi, R.: An ontology engineering approach to the realization of theory-driven group formation. International Journal of Computer-Supported Collaborative Learning **4**(4), 445–478 (2009)
4. Kim, P.: Massive Open Online Courses: The MOOC Revolution. Routledge (2014)
5. Kraut, R.E., Fiore, A.T.: The role of founders in building online groups. In: Proceedings of the 17th ACM conference on Computer Supported Cooperative Work & Social Computing, pp. 722–732. ACM (2014)
6. Li, N., Verma, H., Skevi, A., Zufferey, G., Blom, J., Dillenbourg, P.: Watching moocs together: investigating co-located mooc study groups. In: Distance Education (ahead-of-print), pp. 1–17 (2014)
7. Strijbos, J.W., Martens, R.L., Jochems, W.M., Broers, N.J.: The effect of functional roles on perceived group efficiency during computer-supported collaborative learning: a matter of triangulation. Computers in Human Behavior **23**(1), 353–380 (2007)

Doctoral Consortium Paper

Promoting Self-regulated Learning in an Intelligent Tutoring System for Writing

Laura K. Allen[✉] and Danielle S. McNamara

Learning Sciences Institute, Department of Psychology,
Arizona State University, Tempe, AZ 85287, USA
{LauraKAllen,DSMcnama}@asu.edu

Abstract. The Writing Pal (W-Pal) is an intelligent tutoring system that was developed to improve students' writing proficiency; however, it remains relatively unclear whether and how this system promotes self-regulated learning. In previous studies, we have begun to investigate the *characteristics* of students' self-assessments, as well as whether interactions with W-Pal can lead to more accurate self-assessments and better writing performance. Here, we propose a series of three experiments that will test whether and how W-Pal can be used to enhance students' self-regulated learning strategies and, consequently, influence their writing habits and the overall quality of their essays. These studies will examine the role of self-assessment in the writing process, and investigate how explicit instruction on writing criteria and self-regulated learning strategies can improve students' writing processes and, ultimately, their writing proficiency.

Keywords: Intelligent tutoring systems · Self-assessment · Self-regulated learning · Metacognition · Writing · Automated writing evaluation

1 Introduction

Computer-based writing instruction provides students with *deliberate* practice on their writing. These systems rely on automated essay scoring engines to assign automated holistic scores and relevant feedback to submitted essays [1]. Previous research on these systems has emphasized the *accuracy* of the summative feedback (i.e., the essay scores), as well as the efficacy of the system to improve students' essay scores immediately after receiving feedback [1-2]. Considerably fewer studies, however, have investigated the impact of these systems on students' ability to regulate their own learning. In particular, it is relatively unknown whether these systems can teach students to better evaluate their performance, and adapt their learning strategies and processes in response to these evaluations. It is ultimately these self-regulated learning (SRL) strategies that we hypothesize will lead to greater long-term learning benefits from these systems. In this paper, we propose a series of three experiments that will test *whether* and *how* computer-based writing instruction can be used to enhance students' SRL processes and, consequently, influence their writing habits and the overall quality of their essays.

© Springer International Publishing Switzerland 2015
C. Conati et al. (Eds.): AIED 2015, LNAI 9112, pp. 827–830, 2015.
DOI: 10.1007/978-3-319-19773-9_125

Azevedo (2005) has argued that models of SRL should be used to guide the development of computer-based learning environments [3]. This is because learners who are *self-regulated* are actively engaged in their own learning processes – they consistently monitor their own performance and, in response to these evaluations, they adapt their learning strategies [3-4]. The aim of our research is to expand upon this notion within the context of the *writing* domain. Our proposed research is guided by Winne and Hadwin's (1998) information processing model of SRL [5]. This model has been proposed as an important framework to consider within research on computer-based learning environments, and educational environments more broadly [6].

Although SRL constructs have been largely understudied within the context of computer-based *writing* instruction, they have been successfully incorporated within learning environments for other domains. MetaTutor, for instance, is a hypermedia learning environment, which was developed to provide students with instruction on SRL processes within the domain of biology [7]. Similarly, Betty's Brain is an environment that reinforces students' SRL skills (e.g., self-monitoring and self-assessment) while they are learning about science topics [8]. Overall, the success of these systems, along with theoretical models of SRL, have provided us with a strong foundation with which to incorporate SRL within computer-based writing instruction.

2   Previous Research

The context of our previous and proposed research is the Writing Pal (W-Pal), an intelligent tutoring system (ITS) that was developed to improve students' writing proficiency [2, 9]. In recent work with the W-Pal system, we have begun to consider the role of SRL in the teaching and practice of writing processes. First, we have examined the *accuracy* and *characteristics* of students' self-assessments by investigating differences between students' and teachers' criteria for high-quality writing [10]. In one study, students wrote and self-assessed essays, which were subsequently rated by their teachers. Natural language processing tools were then used to calculate the linguistic characteristics of the essays. Students tended to overestimate their scores on the essays and their self-assessments were systematically related to fewer and different linguistic properties of the essay than the ratings provided by their teachers.

The results of this first study suggested that students were inaccurate in their self-assessments of performance. This is a significant issue because students' ability to *accurately* self-assess their own work has been cited as a key factor in promoting durable, long-term learning [11-12]. Students engage in performance evaluations for the purpose of establishing and maintaining their learning goals [13]. Consequently, students who are more accurate at self-assessing perform better on learning tasks and are better able to retain the material [12]. In response to these findings, we conducted an additional study where we examined the degree to which W-Pal promoted increases in the accuracy of students' self-assessments [14]. Results indicated that W-Pal training led to increases in self-assessment accuracy and essay scores over time.

Overall, this past research provides a strong foundation on which to develop computer-based writing instruction that promotes SRL processes. Future studies are needed, however, to provide more detailed information about the best methods for promoting these SRL processes, as well as how to specifically tailor this instruction based on students' strengths and weaknesses.

3   Future Research Plans

We propose and seek advice regarding three experiments that aim to deepen our understanding of SRL, particularly with respect to computer-based writing instruction.

Results from our previous research [14] suggest that engaging in self-assessment and deliberate writing practice helps students to improve their self-assessment accuracy and, consequently, their writing performance. However, the specific role that the act of monitoring (i.e., self-assessing) had on these improvements remains unclear. In *Study 1*, we will directly test the effects of self-assessment on the writing process. Our specific aim will be to examine whether prompting students to self-assess before they receive feedback and revise their essays will have an impact on the quality of their revisions. Our hypothesis is that by explicitly engaging in a performance evaluation task, students will be better able to "uptake" the system feedback. Study 1 will be a between-subjects experiment, wherein all students will compose an essay, receive feedback, and revise the essay. Half of the participants will self-assess before receiving feedback and engaging in revision, and half will not. We will investigate differences in the *types* of revisions made by students in each condition (i.e., surface-level or discourse-level), as well as score changes between original and revised essays.

In *Study 2*, we will investigate whether the self-assessment process can be enhanced through explicit instruction on the criteria used to assess quality writing. Winne and Hadwin (1998) claim that an important component of SRL is for learners to have knowledge of the task *standards* [5]. This affords learners the ability to compare their own performance to those standards and, when necessary, adapt their learning processes. Our aim will therefore be to examine whether students who are provided with explicit instructions regarding the grading rubric will provide more accurate self-assessments of their essays, compared to students who simply engage in a self-assessment and writing practice task. This will be a between-subjects experiment with two conditions. Half of the participants will be given the essay rubric along with detailed information regarding the specific components of this rubric; the other half of the students will not. Our hypothesis is that students who receive this instruction on the rubric will provide more accurate self-assessments and engage in more productive revision processes. We will also separately investigate the impact of this instruction on the different components of the rubric (e.g., grammar, cohesion, organization).

Our final aim in *Study 3* is to use the information learned from Studies 1 and 2 to develop an essay assessment module within the W-Pal system. In this module, students will be taught about the criteria for quality writing and be given examples and demonstrations on how to use these criteria to assess essays. Additionally, students will be taught SRL strategies for monitoring their own performance during and after the writing process. Thus, the aim of Study 3 will be to determine whether interacting with this module will increase the quality of students' writing compared to students who are not provided with this instruction. Additionally, we will investigate differences in students' revision habits and the accuracy of their self-assessments.

In general, this proposed work has implications for W-Pal, as well as for educational research in general. With respect to W-Pal, these studies will inform future modifications to the system directed at enhancing students' SRL processes. Ultimately, promoting SRL during the writing process is expected to lead to more substantial improvements in long-term writing proficiency. More broadly, this project will offer significant contributions to the AIED community by providing a deeper understanding of how SRL processes can be promoted in computer-based learning environments.

References

1. Warschauer, M., Ware, P.: Automated Writing Evaluation: Defining the Classroom Research Agenda. Language Teaching Research **10**, 1–24 (2006)
2. Roscoe, R.D., Snow, E.L., Allen, L.K., McNamara, D.S.: Automated Detection of Essay Revising Patterns: Application for Intelligent Feedback in a Writing Tutor. Technology, Instruction, Cognition, and Learning (in press)
3. Azevedo, R.: Using Hypermedia as a Metacognitive Tool for Enhancing Student Learning? The Role of Self-Regulated Learning. Educational Psychologist **40**, 199–209 (2005)
4. Zimmerman, B.J., Schunk, D. (eds) Self-Regulated Learning and Academic Achievement: Theoretical Perspectives. Lawrence Erlbaum, Mahwah (2001)
5. Winne, P.H., Hadwin, A.F.: Studying as self-regulated learning. In: Hacker, D.J., Dunlosky, J., Graesser, A., (eds.) Metacognition in Educational Theory and Practice, pp. 277–304. Lawrence Erlbaum, Hillsdale
6. Greene, J.A., Azevedo, R.: A Theoretical Review of Winne and Hadwin's Model of Self-Regulated Learning: New Perspectives and Directions. Review of Educational Research **77**, 334–372 (2007)
7. Azevedo, R., Witherspoon, A., Chauncey, A., Burkett, C., Fike, A.: MetaTutor: A Meta-Cognitive Tool for Enhancing Self-Regulated Learning. In: New Science of Learning, pp. 225-247. Springer, New York (2010)
8. Leelawong, K., Biswas, G.: Designing Learning by Teaching Agents: The Betty's Brain System. International Journal of Artificial Intelligence and Education **18**, 181–208 (2008)
9. Allen, L.K., Crossley, S.A., Snow, E.L., McNamara, D.S.: Game-Based Writing Strategy Tutoring for Second Language Learners: Game Enjoyment as a Key to Engagement. Language Learning and Technology **18**, 124–150 (2014)
10. Varner, L.K., Roscoe, R.D., McNamara, D.S.: Evaluative Misalignment of 10th-Grade Student and Teacher Criteria for Essay Quality: An Automated Textual Analysis. Journal of Writing Research **5**, 35–59 (2013)
11. Dunlosky, J., Hertzog, C., Kennedy, M., Thiede, K.: The Self-Monitoring Approach for Effective Learning. Cognitive Technology **10**, 4–11 (2005)
12. Dunlosky, J., Rawson, K.A.: Overconfidence produced underachievement: Inaccurate Self Evaluations Undermine Students' Learning and Retention. Learning and Instruction **22**, 271–280 (2012)
13. Dunlosky, J., Ariel, R.: Self-regulated learning and the allocation of study time. In: Ross, B., (ed.) Psychology of Learning and Motivation, pp. 103-140 (2011)
14. Allen, L.K., Crossley, S.A., Snow, E.L., Jacovina, M.E., Perret, C., McNamara, D.S.: Am I wrong or am I right? gains in monitoring accuracy in an intelligent tutoring system for writing. In: Proceedings of the Artificial Intelligence in Education Conference (2015)

Exploring Missing Behaviors with Region-Level Interaction Network Coverage

Michael Eagle[✉] and Tiffany Barnes

Department of Computer Science,
North Carolina State University, Raleigh, USA
{mjeagle,tmbarnes}@ncsu.edu

Abstract. We have used a complex network model of student-tutor interactions to derive high-level approaches to problem solving. We also have used interaction networks to evaluate between-group differences in student approaches, as well as for automatically producing both next-step and high-level hints. Students do not visit vertices within the networks uniformly; students from different experimental groups are expected to have different patterns of network exploration. In this work we explore the possibility of using frequency estimation to uncover locations in the network with differing amounts of student-saturation. Identification of these regions can be used to locate specific problem approaches and strategies that would be most improved by additional student-data, as well as provide a measure of confidence when comparing across networks or between groups.

1 Introduction

Data-driven methods to provide automatic hints have the potential to vastly reduce the cost associated with developing tutors with personalized feedback. Modeling the student-tutor interactions as a complex network provides a platform for researchers to generate hint-templates and automatically generate next-step hints [6]; the interaction networks also work as useful visualization of student problem-solving, as well as a structure from which to mine the high-level approaches of students in problem-solving environments [2]. Data-driven approaches require an uncertain amount of data collection before they can produce feedback, and it is not always clear how much is needed for different environments. Eagle et al. explored the structure of these student interaction networks and argued that networks could be interpreted as an empirical sample of student problem solving [3]. Students who are similar in problem-solving approach would also be represented in the same parts of the interaction network.

There are two questions this work will explore. The first, how much of the network is not yet observed that we would expect to see with additional data? This is important as the missing parts of the network represent missing student behaviors. A global metric for network coverage would be valuable evidence for the validity of automatically generated hints as well as for a visualizations representation of student behaviors. The second, where within the network would

© Springer International Publishing Switzerland 2015
C. Conati et al. (Eds.): AIED 2015, LNAI 9112, pp. 831–835, 2015.
DOI: 10.1007/978-3-319-19773-9_126

we expect these missing behaviors to be? Students do not traverse the problem-space uniformly which results in some regions of the network to have higher exploration than others. A metric of region-level coverage would identify locations of high or low confidence for hinting and visual representation of student behaviors.

1.1   Interaction Networks

An *Interaction Network* is a complex network representation of all observed student-tutor interactions for a given problem in a game or tutoring system [3]. To construct an Interaction Network for a problem, we collect the set of all solution attempts for that problem. Each solution attempt is defined by a unique user identifier, as well as an ordered sequence of interactions, where an interaction is defined as {initial state, action, resulting state}, from the start of the problem until the user solves the problem or exits the system. The information contained in a *state* is sufficient to precisely recreate the tutor's interface at each step. Similarly, an *action* is any user interaction which changes the state, and is defined as {action name, pre-conditions, result}. Regions of the network can be discovered by applying network clustering methods, such as those used by Eagle et al. for deriving maps high-level student approaches to problems [2].

Creation of adaptive educational programs is expensive, intelligent tutors require content experts and pedagogical experts to work with tutor developers to identify the skills students are applying and the associated feedback to deliver [5]. Stamper and Barnes' Hint Factory approach automates some of the intelligent tutoring system development and generates a next-step Hint Policy by modeling student-tutor interactions as a Markov Decision Process [6]. This has been adapted to work with interaction networks by using a value-iteration algorithm [1] on the states [3]. We define a state, S to be *Hintable* if there exists a path on the network to a goal-state starting from S. We define the *Hintable* network to be the induced subset of the interaction network containing only *Hintable* states.

1.2   Good-Turing Network Estimation

In this work, we are presenting a new method for estimating the size of the unobserved portion of a partially constructed Interaction Network. Our estimator makes use of Good-Turing frequency estimation [4]. Good-Turing frequency estimation estimates the probability of encountering an object of a hitherto unseen type, given the current number and frequency of observed objects. It was originally developed by Alan Turing and his assistant I. J. Good for use in cryptography efforts during World War II. Gale and Sampson revisited and simplified the implementation [4]. In its original context, given a sample text from a vocabulary, the Good-Turing Estimator will predict the probability that a new word selected from that vocabulary will be one not previously observed.

The Good-Turing method of estimation uses the frequency of frequencies for the sample text in order to estimate the probability that a new word will be

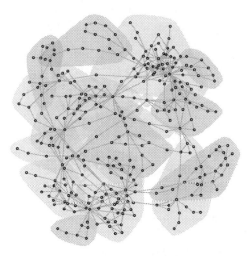

Fig. 1. An interaction network with regions of high coverage highlighted in light blue and regions of low coverage highlighted in orange. The low coverage regions of the network require more data before coverage could reach a IN_C level above 90%.

of a given frequency. Based on this distribution, we calculate the probability of observing a new word in the vocabulary based on the observed probability of observing a word with frequency 1. Therefore, the expected probability of the next observation being an unseen word P_0 is estimated by: $P_0 = \frac{N_1}{N}$. Where N_1 is the total number of words occurring with frequency 1, and N is the total number of observations.

In order to use Good-Turing Frequency Estimation we model the interaction network and the individual interactions as follows. Each problem-solving student-tutor interaction, I, is an opportunity to observe either a new state. If a state, S, has been previously observed than its frequency is incremented. Rather than add additional student-data one interaction at a time, we add a set of interactions that make up a single student's work within a problem at each step. Our version of P_0 is the probability of encountering a new state (a state that currently has frequency 0,) on an interaction, which we define as IN_0. We will use IN_0 to refer to the proportion of interactions expected to result in as yet unobserved (conceptually, "zero frequency") states. Its complement, $1 - P_0$ is therefore the probability of an interaction resulting in a previously observed state. We will denote this as $IN_C = 1 - P_0$, and use this value as an estimate of the network coverage, which can also be described as the proportion of observations resulting in previously observed ("non-zero frequency") states.

2 Discussion

Figure 1 shows the results of a preliminary analysis on an interaction network based on student-log data from a tutoring environment. For each region we calculated values of network coverage, IN_C, and have highlighted regions of the network which have values below 90% coverage. Good-Turing Estimation works well in the contexts of interaction networks. Our network coverage metric IN_C allows a quick and easy to calculate method of comparing different state representations, as well as quantifying the difference. New methods for improving automatic hint generation can target these low-coverage areas of the network, such as asking for instructor input on specific regions or by starting advanced students in these regions in order to observe their paths out.

We were also able to interpret this metric as measure of the proportion of the network not yet observed IN_0. On a high-level this value alone is a useful metric for the percentage of times a new student-interaction would result in a new state. The IN_0 score for the hint-able network, the subset of the network where next-step hints are available, is likewise a measure for the probability that a student will "fall off" of the network from which we can provide feedback. We expect that guiding some groups of students towards regions with higher proportions of hint-coverage will improve student performance.

Our network estimators also have implications given our previous theories on the network being a sample created from bias (non-random) walks on the problem-space. We expect that more homogeneous samples of bias-walkers will have smaller networks and reach high coverage faster than heterogeneous samples. We revisited [2], where two groups were shown to have different problem-solving approaches. The preliminary results of region-level coverage suggest that coverage is highest in regions dominated by one group over the other.

Future directions for this research include general improvements to the network clustering algorithms which generate the regions. Regions which have low coverage might not be worth separating from their parent region for visualization or high-level hint generation processes. Alternatively, using the IN_0 measurement to predict next-step "fall off" we could estimate the "risk" of different network regions. The local and global measures of network coverage can help identify problematic regions in interaction networks which could harm hint production; they also provide a metric to evaluate new, "cold start" problems and make sure that enough data has been collected in order produce hints to multiple problem solving approaches.

References

1. Bellman, R.: A markovian decision process. Technical report, DTIC Document (1957)
2. Eagle, M., Barnes, T.: Exploring differences in problem solving with data-driven approach maps. In: Proceedings of the Seventh International Conference on Educational Data Mining (2014)
3. Eagle, M., Hicks, D., III, P., Barnes, T.: Exploring networks of problem-solving interactions. In: Proceedings of the Fifth International Conference on Learning Analytics and Knowledge (LAK 15) (2015)

4. Gale, W.A., Sampson, G.: Good-turing frequency estimation without tears*. Journal of Quantitative Linguistics **2**(3), 217–237 (1995)
5. Murray, T.: Authoring intelligent tutoring systems: An analysis of the state of the art. International Journal of Artificial Intelligence in Education (IJAIED) **10**, 98–129 (1999)
6. Stamper, J., Eagle, M., Barnes, T., Croy, M.: Experimental evaluation of automatic hint generation for a logic tutor. International Journal of Artificial Intelligence in Education (IJAIED) **22**(1), 3–18 (2013)

Educational Technologies to Support Linguistically Diverse Students, and the Challenges of Classroom Integration

Samantha Finkelstein[✉]

Human Computer Interaction Institute, Carnegie Mellon University, Pittsburgh, PA, USA
slfink@cs.cmu.edu

Abstract. Though one of the main benefits of educational technologies is their ability to provide personalized instruction, many systems are still built with a one-size-fits-all approach to culture. In our work, we've demonstrated that there may be learning benefits when technologies use the same non-standard dialects as students, but that educators are likely to be initially resistant to technologies that bring non-standard dialect practices into the classroom. Based on what we have uncovered about teachers' needs and expectations regarding this type of classroom technology, our future work will investigate how systems designed to align with these needs may be able to support both students and teachers in this complex educational problem and promote a positive classroom culture.

Keywords: Dialect · Classrooms · Teachers · Culture · AAVE

1   Introduction

Although often unintentional, learning materials (whether physical or virtual) are typically designed to align with a group's dominant cultural practices, such as their language expectations [2]. Though language variation is exceedingly common in today's multi-cultural classrooms, learning environments often only explicitly value contributions in Standard American English (SAE) [4, 1]. While fluency with SAE undeniably provides speakers with important opportunities for cultural capital and class mobility, evidence suggests that when learning environments leverage students' non-dominant language practices, these students may benefit from improved academic performance, self-efficacy, classroom engagement, and even acquisition of SAE [see 4]. This is particularly true for students who are speakers of stigmatized dialects, such as African American Vernacular English (AAVE). Unfortunately, many well-intentioned educators ban students' non-dominant language practices from the classroom, with some even publicly shaming their students for their use of "Bad English." Some researchers propose that this negative classroom culture surrounding non-standard dialect use may be perpetuating the achievement gap that exists between Euro-American and African American students [1].

One of the key benefits of educational technologies are their abilities to offer individualized instruction to students, and as such, these systems may be able to play a role in supporting culturally-underrepresented students by taking culture into consideration.

© Springer International Publishing Switzerland 2015
C. Conati et al. (Eds.): AIED 2015, LNAI 9112, pp. 836–839, 2015.
DOI: 10.1007/978-3-319-19773-9_127

Ultimately, however, teachers are the experts of their own classrooms, and only they, not the technology, can be the agents of change. If these systems are effectively designed in line with teacher needs, though, evidence suggests that a "pedagogical evolution" is possible, whereby teachers may grow to reflect on their own teaching practices and may ultimately adapt their beliefs to align with these systems in positive ways [2].

In our research, we investigate two primary questions: (1) what are the impacts of a technology that can leverage students' non-standard language practices on their learning, self-efficacy, and language use; and (2) how does the integration of this type of technology into the classroom impact teachers' ideologies about and behaviors around their students' non-standard language use? In this paper, I describe our previous work on the impact of a technology that spoke with students using different dialect patterns, as well as the results of our investigations about the existing classroom context. I additionally describe how these results have guided our design of a classroom technology that we believe may be able to serve as an *object to think with* for teachers and students, and outline our plans for analyzing how this system may impact students, teachers, and the overall classroom culture.

2   Impacts of Dialect use in an Educational Technology

We worked with 29 AAVE-speaking African American 3rd graders to investigate the impact of different dialect use patterns on students' performance. We designed a "distant peer paradigm" where students were told they would be listening to and recording social talk and science examples for another student in another school, "kind of like a pen pal." Students heard the technology use one of three dialect patterns: (1) SAE for both social talk and the science talk, (2) AAVE for both social talk and science talk, or (3) AAVE for social talk and SAE for science talk. Students' pre- and post-science recordings were annotated for the number of "strong science arguments," which were ideas that included a hypothesis, evidence, and reasoning. Students' recordings were additionally annotated for AAVE features, and their prosodic features were analyzed for volume, pitch fluctuation, and speed, which may act as proxies for engagement. An ANOVA revealed that dialect had a significant impact on students' science performance (f(2,20) = 6.89, p<.01. Post-hoc analysis with a Tukey test revealed that there is a significant difference between the post-test scores of the children who worked with the SAE-only system (M = .86, 95% CI = .86 – 1.5) and those who worked with the AAVE-only system (M = 3.1, 95% CI = 2.0 – 4.3), p = .02. Partial-eta squared analyses revealed that the effect of this interaction is substantial at η_p^2 = .43, and the cohen's d was revealed to be *very large*, at 2.01. Additionally, we found that all students used AAVE features to some extent, but there was no difference between students' dialect use based on condition (p > .05). However, students who were speaking to an AAVE-speaking character produced speech themselves that was faster (p > .005), louder (p < .05), and had more pitch fluctuation (p < .005). These results demonstrate that there may be benefit to students when technologies are able to provide instructional materials in their native dialects, and that these interventions (albeit, after one exposure) do not promote the students to use more of the non-standard dialect themselves.

3   Understanding the Current Classroom Context

Our next steps were to understand the existing classroom context surrounding students' dialect use such that we would be able to design a system that could effectively work alongside teachers to support students. This work involved classroom observations and experimental investigations to understand students' dialect use as well as their implicit and explicit language ideologies. We additionally worked with teachers on participatory design activities to understand what they would expect and need out of an intervention. This paper will focus on the participatory design activities.

We worked with 15 teachers across local public and charter schools on two sets of participatory design activities that included classroom observations, semi-structured interviews, story boarding, and a guided participatory design activity we designed based off of our initial findings. We first spoke with teachers about their students' use of dialect in the classroom, and then invited them to draw ideas for technologies they *would* and *wouldn't* want in their classrooms to address the issues they discussed. Overwhelmingly, teachers designed technologies that served a similar role to the one that they already played in the classroom, such as correcting students' use of dialect as soon as the system detected dialect use. However, a theme across each of these sessions was the potential benefit of the technology acting as a *peer* rather than another *teacher*. As one participant said, "If it's another kid, then, well, that character can tell the kid stuff about how to talk that I can't, because I don't speak that way." We then created a guided activity to tease apart the issues teachers brought up by separating them out explicitly over each of the separate components of educational technologies, such as input, output, and embodiment. Through this process, educators demonstrated an evolution of their beliefs surrounding students' dialect. For example, while early on in these sessions teachers appeared to be completely against the use of AAVE in a technology (e.g., "Students need to be hearing the standard – that's just the way it is,") teachers seemed to demonstrate more nuance by the end of our design session. For example, as one participant said, "I don't want to enforce slang… but I don't want to continue to frustrate them. If it can [use AAVE to] help the students to feel comfortable with the standard, then okay, let's keep it moving," There was also some consensus that if it helped students, a technology could use AAVE with students when they were first learning new material, but that it should work with them to help them *translate* their final answer into SAE.

4   Next Steps: Impact of the Technology on the Classroom Culture

Based on the results of our work so far, we have iterated on the design of a virtual peer technology, Alex, that can collaborate with students on open-ended science problems. Alex collaborates with the student using typical accountable talk moves, such as providing counter-examples, asking if the student agrees or disagrees, etc. After they have reached some conclusions, Alex asks the student to practice their final presentations for their teachers, and they take turns asking and answering questions about the task and then finally presenting their ideas in a longer presentation. We have designed two versions of this system: one that speaks in SAE the whole time, and another that collaborates with the student in AAVE and then switches to SAE for the presentation practice. While currently an experimenter controls the agent as a Wizard of Oz (WoZ), we are preparing to pilot versions of the technology that would allow one or more students to control the agent's language and behavior while one or more students respond. This Child-Controlled Wizard of Oz (ChiCoWoZ) would serve to both allow the system to exist within a classroom without the use of an experimenter, while also providing the students with a tangible system through which they would be able experiment with dialect. We will continue to iterate on the design of ChiCoWoZ through pilot studies with students, family focus groups, and teacher interviews.

Once the system is designed, our next step will be to work with ten $3^{rd} - 5^{th}$ grade 100% African American classrooms. Half of the classrooms will be given the version of the agent that only speaks using SAE, and the other half will be given a version that speaks both AAVE and SAE. The system will be in the each classroom for two months, with students using the system at least once per week (or more, if the teacher chooses). We will measure our student participants' language ideologies, dialect use, and science reasoning before and after the intervention. We will measure our teacher participants' language ideologies toward AAVE, as well as the way that the teachers talk with their students about their classroom language expectations. This investigation will build off of our existing work by demonstrating the potential ways in which the dialect use in a classroom technology may impact not just students' learning with a system, but the overall classroom culture. More broadly, as there are culturally based decisions inherent in all classroom technologies, this work will help us understand the potential social impacts of the systems we as a community send off into the wild.

Acknowledgments. Many smiles to the ArticuLab, HCII, and the Graduate Training Grant # R305B090023 from the US Department of Education (IES).

References

1. Atkinson, J.L.: Are We Creating the Achievement Gap? Examining How Deficit Mentalities Influence Indigenous Science Curriculum Choices. Cultural Studies and Environmentalism, 439–446 (2010)
2. Ertmer, P.A., Ottenbreit-Leftwich, A.T.: Teacher technology change: How knowledge, confidence, beliefs, and culture intersect. Journal of research on Technology in Education **42**(3), 255–284 (2010)
3. Henderson, L.: Instructional design of interactive multimedia: A cultural critique. Educational technology research and development **44**(4), 85–104 (1996)
4. Siegel, J.: Keeping creoles and dialects out of the classroom: Is it justified. Dialects, Englishes, creoles, and Education, 39–67 (2006)

Developing Self-regulated Learners
Through an Intelligent Tutoring System

Kim Kelly[✉] and Neil Heffernan

Worcester Polytechnic Institute, Worcester, MA, USA
kimkelly915@gmail.com, nth@wpi.edu

Abstract. Intelligent tutoring systems have been developed to help students learn independently. However, students who are poor self-regulated learners often struggle to use these systems because they lack the skills necessary to learn independently. The field of psychology has extensively studied self-regulated learning and can provide strategies to improve learning, however few of these include the use of technology. The present proposal reviews three elements of self-regulated learning (motivational beliefs, help-seeking behavior, and meta-cognitive self-monitoring) that are essential to intelligent tutoring systems. Future research is suggested, which address each element in order to develop self-regulated learning strategies in students while they are engaged in learning mathematics within an intelligent tutoring system.

1 Defining the Problem

Intelligent tutoring systems (ITS) are designed to provide independent learning opportunities for students. Learning occurs through hints, tutoring, scaffolding and correctness feedback. A great body of research exists surrounding types and timing of feedback (Keher, Kelly, & Heffernan 2013) and tutoring that have been found to improve student outcomes. As a classroom teacher I have used several different ITS with students to help them learn mathematics. Over the years, I have seen many students benefit from these systems. However, I have also witnessed students struggling to use the systems and who fail to learn, despite all of the assistance provided. Addressing this failure serves as the basis of my dissertation. For an ITS to achieve maximum results, the students using the system must be good self-regulated learners. My proposed research attempts to use an ITS to help students develop self-regulating strategies, while students are learning the desired content.

Zimmerman and Campillo (2002), suggest that self-regulated learning is a three-phase process. During the *Forethought Phase*, students engage in a task analysis, which includes goal setting and strategic planning. Self-motivational beliefs, including self-efficacy (Schunck, 1991 & Dweck, 2006), outcome expectations, task value/interest (Pekrun, 2006), and goal orientation also play a significant role in this phase as they have been found to positively affect student learning. During the *Performance Phase*, students demonstrate self-control by employing various task strategies and help-seeking behaviors. Self-observation, which includes meta-cognitive

© Springer International Publishing Switzerland 2015
C. Conati et al. (Eds.): AIED 2015, LNAI 9112, pp. 840–843, 2015.
DOI: 10.1007/978-3-319-19773-9_128

self-monitoring, is also crucial. During the final phase, *Self-Reflection*, students engage in self-judgment and self-reaction.

2   Related Work

To help develop self-regulated learners, these components must be explicitly taught. However, some aspects are seemingly more relevant than others when interacting with an ITS. Specifically motivational beliefs (forethought phase), help-seeking behavior (performance phase), and meta-cognitive self-monitoring (self-reflection phase) can all be addressed within the structures of ITSs.

2.1   Motivational Beliefs

One aspect of the first phase of self-regulated learning is motivation. Students who are strong self-regulated learners have high self-efficacy. Schunk (1991) defines self-efficacy as "an individual's judgment of his or her capabilities to perform given actions." A student's belief that they are capable of learning can be influenced by a growth mindset (Dweck 2006). Some of my earlier research, using teacher-created motivational videos, attempted to create a growth mindset in students while they were completing math homework inside of an intelligent tutoring system (Kelly et al. 2013a). While the minimal intervention failed to show changes in student self-reports of mindset, there was a significant increase in the perception of task value and homework completion rates as a result of a video inspired by Pekrun (2006). In addition to improving self-efficacy, increasing task value/interest is important to developing self-regulated learners. The protocol employed in my initial study is promising and a more sophisticated intervention will be explored to further increase motivation.

2.2   Help Seeking Behaviors

Intelligent tutoring systems provide many different structures to support student learning. One such structure that I have explored is correctness-only feedback. I found that this simple support provided by an ITS during a homework assignment was found to improve student learning significantly compared to traditional paper and pencil homework that did not provide immediate feedback (Kelly et al. 2013b). Yet research has shown that many students do not effectively take advantage of these features. Aleven et al. (2003) explores ineffective help use in interactive learning environments and suggests that there are system-related factors, student-related factors and interactions between these factors that impact help-seeking behaviors. In one of my recent studies, I found that there are students who, despite access to the same instructional supports, do not successfully take advantage of them and therefore do not learn (Kelly, Wang, Thompson, & Heffernan 2015). This has resulted in a phenomenon called wheel spinning (Beck & Gong, 2013), where students persist without making progress towards learning. I hypothesize that wheel spinning is in part a result of ineffective help-seeking behaviors. To address students' inability to effectively engage in in help-seeking behavior, prior research has integrated the Help Tutor with a commercial math tutoring system and found that students can learn help-seeking behaviors (Roll, Aleven, McLaren, Keodinger 2011). Therefore, I propose a study that would advance this line of research providing direct interventions to teach students the necessary help-seeking behaviors to become self-regulated learners.

2.3   Meta-Cognitive Self-monitoring

Elements of meta-cognition, are evident in all three phases of self-regulated learning. For example, goal setting is prominent in phase one. Other elements, like self-monitoring, are evident in multiple phases. Self-monitoring involves students becoming aware of their performance and judging their knowledge. This is sometimes referred to as metacognitive knowledge monitoring (Isaacson & Fujita, 2006). In phase two, while students are participating in a learning task, they must monitor what they are learning. Students who are strong self-regulated learners will seek feedback to easily monitor their progress. I surveyed my students to better understand their perception of feedback. High performing students claimed that the immediate feedback provided by an ITS caused frustration, but was also beneficial to their learning. (Kelly 2013b). They were able to identify their mistakes and learn from them. To help all students recognize the importance of monitoring their learning, I propose a study to show the benefits of providing students feedback along with progress monitoring.

Self-monitoring continues into the third phase of self-regulated learning. During this reflection stage, students assess their success or failure. Strong self-regulated learners may challenge themselves in some way to confirm their success. A willingness to seek out challenges ties back into the growth mindset that is addressed in phase one. Students who believe that intelligence is fixed will often shy away from challenges for fear of failure, whereas students with a growth mindset view challenges as opportunities to learn more (Dweck 2006). Therefore, to encourage all students to seek out challenges as a method to self-monitor, I propose a study where growth mindset messages are embedded in ITS and opportunities for students to choose challenging problems are provided.

3   Contribution

Intelligent tutoring systems rely on independent learning practices to effectively teach students. For example, students must use available hints and tutoring to navigate new material. However not all students successfully learn when using an ITS. Some early research suggests that these students are those who struggle with self-regulated learning. The field of psychology has studied self-regulated learning for more than a decade, resulting in many ideas that can improve instruction. Some ITS have incorporated features to help students who lack self-regulated learning strategies, like automatically detecting when a student is frustrated (Baker et al. 2008) and providing additional assistance when a student is failing. However, little research has explored how technology can actually promote self-regulated learning. By integrating the capabilities of intelligent tutoring systems with the vast knowledge of self-regulated learning, the proposed research seeks to teach students how learn effectively. By addressing specific aspects of self-regulated learning, ITS can actually teach students how to learn while teaching them content.

References

1. Aleven, V., Stahl, E., Schworm, S., Fischer, F., Wallace, R.: Help Seeking and Help Design in Interactive Learning Environments. Review of Educational Research **73**(3), 277–320 (2003)
2. Baker, R., Walonoski, J., Heffernan, N., Roll, I., Corbett, A., Koedinger, K.: Why Students Engage in "Gaming the System" Behavior in Interactive Learning Environments. Journal of Interactive Learning Research **19**(2), 185–224 (2008)
3. Beck, J.E., Gong, Y.: Wheel-spinning: students who fail to master a skill. In: Lane, H., Yacef, K., Mostow, J., Pavlik, P. (eds.) AIED 2013. LNCS, vol. 7926, pp. 431–440. Springer, Heidelberg (2013)
4. Dweck, C.: Mindset. Random House, New York (2006)
5. Isaacson, R.M., Fujita, F.: Metacognitive Knowledge Monitoring and Self-Regulated Learning: Academic Success and Reflections on Learning. Journal of the Scholarship of Teaching and Learning **6**(1), 39–55 (2006)
6. Kehrer, P., Kelly, K., Heffernan, N.: Does immediate feedback while doing homework improve learning. In: Boonthum-Denecke, Y. (eds.). Florida Artificial Intelligence Research Society Conference, FLAIRS 2013, pp. 542–545. AAAI Press (2013)
7. Kelly, K., Heffernan, N., D'Mello, S., Namias, J., Strain, A.: Adding teacher-created motivational video to an ITS. In: Florida Artificial Intelligence Research Society, FLAIRS 2013, pp. 503–508 (2013a)
8. Kelly, K., Heffernan, N., Heffernan, C., Goldman, S., Pellegrino, J., Soffer Goldstein, D.: Estimating the effect of web-based homework. In: Lane, H., Yacef, K., Mostow, J., Pavlik, P. (eds.) AIED 2013. LNCS, vol. 7926, pp. 824–827. Springer, Heidelberg (2013)
9. Kelly, K., Wang, Y., Thompson, T., Heffernan, N.: Defining Mastery: Knowledge Tracing Versus N-Consecutive Correct Responses. Submitted to Educational Data Mining (2015)
10. Pekrun, R.: The control-value theory of achievement emotions: Assumptions, corollaries, and implications for educational research and practice. Educational Psychology Review **18**(4), 315–341 (2006)
11. Roll, I., Aleven, V., McLaren, B., Keodinger, K.: Improving students' help-seeking skills using metacognitive feedback in an intelligent tutoring system. Learning and Instruction **21**, 267–280 (2011)
12. Schunk, D.H.: Self-efficacy and academic motivation. Educational Psychologist **26**, 207–231 (1996)
13. Zimmerman, B.J., Campillo, M.: Motivating self-regulated problem solvers. In: Davidson, J.E., Sternberg, R.J. (eds.) The nature of problem solving. Cambridge University Press, New York (2002)

Building Compiler-Student Friendship

Zhongxiu Liu$^{(\boxtimes)}$ and Tiffany Barnes

North Carolina State University, Raleigh, NC 27695, USA
zliu24@ncsu.edu

Abstract. Previous studies have shown that compilers positively influence students when they are designed to build connections with students. In this paper, I propose to study the use of a friendly compiler for young novice programmers. This study involves designing compiler messages that incorporate a friendship model. The goal is to make students view compiler as a friend, instead of as an error-picking authority. I hypothesize that a good compiler-student relationship will change students' attitude, self-efficacy and motivation towards programming, as well as change students compilation behaviors.

1 Introduction

The relationship between students and their peers or teachers influences many aspects of learning. Liem et al. [9] found that a good peer relationship has a positive effect on learning outcomes, mastery, and students' self-efficacy. More specifically, Bickmore and Picard [2] found that a safe communication climate, characterized by support, openness, trust and mutual respect, positively influences students' self-efficacy. In Will et al. [10] study, teachers' verbal immediacy was found to be positively associated with learning.

Traditional compilers are not usually designed with the goal of building a relationship with the users. This may hinder novice programmers. Kinnunen [7] found that novice programmers frequently reflected on their own incapability when encountered difficulties. Traditional compilers repeatedly tells students what they have done wrong, which could anguish the feeling of personal failure. Bosch et al. [3] found boredom as one of the most common emotions experienced by first-time programmer, and was negatively correlated with debugging and programming performance. I believe that traditional compilers contribute to boredom, because they do not convey the warmness, happiness or willingness to engage students in their conversations.

Previous research has shown promising results when programming environments are designed to build connections with students. Lee and Ko [8] designed a game where students used a gamified programming language. In the experimental group, the compiler was represented as a fallible and self-blaming robot character. The study found that students in the experimental group completed more tasks, and were more likely to state that they "want to help the robot succeed". Boyer [4] added a dialog-based tutor to a Java programming task. The tutor read the compilation messages, and conducted conversations with students

© Springer International Publishing Switzerland 2015
C. Conati et al. (Eds.): AIED 2015, LNAI 9112, pp. 844–847, 2015.
DOI: 10.1007/978-3-319-19773-9_129

based on a corpus of real student-tutor dialogues. The study found that praise, reassurance, and dialogues with positive cognitive feedback increased students self-confidence with programming. However, these studies only evaluated designs that add to a specific programming environment and tasks. They did not develop a general purpose compiler or focus on adapting to more diverse programming activities.

2   Research Methodology

My research will focus on building a compiler-student friendship through the design of user-friendly compiler messages. I will investigate the following research questions: Will a friendly compiler change students' attitudes towards programming, such as self-efficacy, motivation and interest level? Are there differences in task completion, and compilation behaviors between groups? Moreover, as prior studies by Arroyo et al. [1] and by Evans and Waring [6] showed, females are more likely to be positively affected by affective and positive feedback. Thus I will also investigate whether a more affective compiler has larger affect on female students.

2.1   Compiler Design

Duck [5] defined relationship with friends as a list of provisions that we expect from friends.

- Provision1: Belonging and a sense of reliable alliance. The existence of a bond that can be trusted to be there for a partner when they need it.
- Provision2: Reassurance of worth and value, and an opportunity to help others.
- Provision3: Emotional integration and stability. Friendships provide necessary anchor points for opinions, beliefs and emotional responses.

Table 1 illustrates my approach to incorporate the three provisions into the friendly compiler design targeted for middle school students. For each provision, I explain how it can be interpreted in the context of programming, and give an example of a traditional compiler message in comparison to a friendly compiler message that incorporates the provision.

2.2   Experimental Design

To evaluate my design, i will use BlueJ, a free and open-source Java environment designed for novice programmers. Middle school students who have limited knowledge about programming will be randomly split into a control group, where they will use a traditional compiler, and an experimental group, where they will use the friendly compiler. Students will complete programming tasks. These groups will be assigned via balanced random assigment, but will be controlled for gender and incoming competence.

Table 1.

Interpretation	Traditional Compiler Message	Friendly Compiler Message
Convey the idea that the student and the compiler are in a team to solve programming tasks together	P.java:13:';'expected	I helped you find missing ';' on line 13. Lets work together and make this program runs.
Express to students that they are the compilers trustworthy friends, and the compiler needs students' help in order to compile	P.java:13: cannot resolve symbol	Sorry, I'm designed to be syntax sensitive. I need your help fixing a symbol I don't understand on line 13
a) respond to students success b) tell students that their mistakes are understandable c) show appreciation for the effort paid by the students	a)compilation successful b)';'expected (same errors happened several times before) c)';'expected (after several compilation errors in a row)	a)Great we made it! b)I found missing ';'. This is a common error even for expert programmers c)I found a missing ';'. I know debugging needs hard work. Thanks for all the effort you've been put to help me compile!

Before starting the programming activity, both groups will be given pre-questionnaires that ask about their programming experience, their opinions about programming and compilers, and their self-efficacy and motivation levels. During the programming activity, students from both groups are allowed to ask for help from observers, but each type of help will be recorded. BlueJ will be instrumented to log data at each compilation. The logged data will include the programming task's level, the time of the compilation, the corresponding source code, the compiler's output messages, and the wait-time before the student starts the next interaction with BlueJ. After the programming activity, students will be given post questionnaires include the same questions as the pre-questionnaires.

2.3 Evaluation

My evaluation will test the below hypothesis: a friendly compiler will:

- Improve students' self-efficacy and motivation in programing.
- Cause higher interest in and affection towards programming and the compiler?
- Help students persist through debugging. Thus, students will complete more tasks before giving up
- Cause difference in compilation behaviors. Students with friendly compiler will compile more frequently, and resume interactions with programming environment faster.
- Have stronger effect on female student for one or more of the above hypothesis

3   Conclusion

This study focuses on the re-design of a compiler that will build friendships between itself and novice programmers. A controlled study will be used to investigate how a friendly compiler affects students attitudes, self-efficacy and motivation towards programming, as well as their compilation behaviors.

I would like advice on the evaluation of students psychological attributes. My plan involves a questionnaire to collect students attitude toward programming and compiler, self-efficacy and motivation. I would like to be advised on the design of survey questions or alternative approaches that can help me collect information that best reflects students opinions.

Secondly, I would like to be advised on the design of my friendly compiler messages. The design of the compiler messages is highly subjective. What methodology should I use to create these messages to verify it well incorporates provisions goals, and well fits into the context of programming feedback?

References

1. Arroyo, I., Woolf, B.P., Cooper, D.G., Burleson, W., Muldner, K.: The impact of animated pedagogical agents on girls' and boys' emotions, attitudes, behaviors and learning. In: Proceedings of the Eleventh IEEE International Conference on Advanced Learning Technologies, pp. 506–510 (2011)
2. Bickmore, T.W., Picard, R.W.: Establishing and maintaining long-term human-computer relationships. ACM Transactions on Computer-Human Interaction 12(2), 293–327 (2005)
3. Bosch, N., D'Mello, S., Mills, C.: What emotions do novices experience during their first computer programming learning session? In: Lane, H.C., Yacef, K., Mostow, J., Pavlik, P. (eds.) AIED 2013. LNCS, vol. 7926, pp. 11–20. Springer, Heidelberg (2013)
4. Boyer, K.E., Phillips, R., Wallis, M.D., Vouk, M.A., Lester, J.C.: Investigating the role of motivation in computer science education through one-on-one tutoring. Computer Science Education 19(2), 111–136 (2009)
5. Duck, S.: Understanding Relationships. Guilford Press, New York (1999)
6. Evans, C., Waring, M.: Student teacher assessment feedback preferences: The influence of cognitive styles and gender. Learning and Individual Differences 21(3), 271–280 (2011)
7. Simon, B., Kinnunen, P.: Experiencing programming assignments in cs1: the emotional toll. In: Proceedings of the Sixth International Workshop on Computing Education Research, pp. 77–86 (2010)
8. Lee, M.J., Ko, A.J.: Personifying programming tool feedback improves novice programmers' learning. In: Proceedings of the Seventh International Workshop on Computing Education Research, pp. 109–116 (2011)
9. Liem, A.D., Lau, S., Nie, Y.: The role of self-efficacy, task value, and achievement goals in predicting learning strategies, task disengagement, peer relationship, and achievement outcome. Contemporary Educational Psychology 33(4), 486–512 (2008)
10. Witt, P.L., Wheeless, L.R., Allen, M.: A meta analytical review of the relationship between teacher immediacy and student learning. Communication Monographs 71(2), 184–207 (2004)

Toward Combining Individual and Collaborative Learning Within an Intelligent Tutoring System

Jennifer K. Olsen[1(✉)], Vincent Aleven[1], and Nikol Rummel[1,2]

[1] Human Computer Interaction Institute, Carnegie Mellon University, Pittsburgh, PA, USA
{jkolsen,aleven}@cs.cmu.edu, nikol.rummel@rub.de
[2] Institute of Educational Research, Ruhr-Universität Bochum, Bochum, Germany
nikol.rummel@rub.de

Abstract. Collaborative and individual learning appear to have complementary strengths; however, the best way to combine these learning methods is still unclear. While previous work has demonstrated the effectiveness of Intelligent Tutoring Systems (ITSs) for individual learning, collaborative learning with ITSs is much less frequent – especially for young students. In this paper, we discuss our prior and future work with elementary school students that aims to investigate how to best combine individual and collaborative learning using their complementary strengths within an ITS. Our previous findings demonstrate that ITSs are able to support collaboration, as well as individual learning, for this population. In addition, we propose future research to understand how to best combine individual and collaborative learning within an ITS.

Keywords: Problem solving · Collaborative learning · Intelligent tutoring system

1   Introduction

While Intelligent Tutoring Systems (ITSs) have mostly been used to successfully support individual learning [5], some previous work has also demonstrated success supporting collaborative learning - especially for older students [6]. Although collaborative learning has been studied more extensively outside of ITSs, there is no consensus on the effectiveness of collaboration compared to individual learning [1]. While they appear to have complementary strengths, it is not clear in what ways collaborative and individual learning are complementary and how best to combine them. Previous work with older students has found that students who worked collaboratively on conceptual tasks outperformed those who worked individually with the opposite results for procedural tasks [2]. Because of the developmental differences in younger learners, the question remains if the same results, that individual and collaborative learning are complementary for different knowledge types, will generalize to elementary school students. In addition, it remains an open question how collaborative and individual instructional methods can best be combined using an ITS.

To understand how collaborative and individual learning are complementary and how they can best be combined in ITSs, we have three research questions: *(1)* Is it feasible to support collaboration for elementary school students using ITSs, *(2)* do

C. Conati et al. (Eds.): AIED 2015, LNAI 9112, pp. 848–851, 2015.
DOI: 10.1007/978-3-319-19773-9_130

collaborative and individual learning have different strengths with conceptual and procedural knowledge, and *(3)* is a combination of the two learning methods better than either one alone and in what combination? In this paper, we present our previous research, which has begun to address the first two research questions, and our future research, which aims to address the second and third research questions.

2   Prior Research

2.1   Authoring Collaborative ITSs

To facilitate the studying of collaborative and individual learning, we expanded Cognitive Tutoring Authoring Tools (CTAT) to supporting the authoring of collaborative environments [4], which ITS authoring tools rarely do. The collaborative version of CTAT allows for the standard ITS support (step-level guidance, correctness feedback, next-step hints, and error-specific feedback) as well as embedded collaborative scripts tied dynamically to the problem state to provide support for collaborative learning. For collaborative tutors, the authoring tool supports synchronous, networked collaboration where students can sit at their own computer with a shared problem view that can be differentiated for each student through different error messages, hints, problem information, and actions the student can take.

This enhanced version of CTAT supports a range of collaboration script features such as the use of roles, cognitive group awareness, and unique information that can be combined within a problem. The collaboration features can be authored through the combination of displaying different information for different members of the group and by disabling steps for different members of the group so only one student can take an action. An example is provided in Figure 1 where cognitive group awareness, group members have information about other group members' knowledge, information, or opinions, was supported by allowing students to each express their opinion about an answer before having them provide a group answer. The extension of CTAT allows for flexibility in supporting a range of collaborative and individual problem types that has not often been afforded in previous ITS authoring tools. By using an ITS to support collaboration, we are better able control the learning environment and the features of collaboration that make learning in groups successful.

2.2   Methods and Results

In our prior work, we conducted a pull-out study designed to investigate if a collaborative ITS could effectively support elementary school students in learning (our first research question) and how the complementary aspects of collaborative and individual learning apply to conceptual and procedural knowledge (our second research question) [3]. In the study, 81 4th and 5th grade students worked on equivalent fractions through an ITS in a 2x2 between subjects design. Each teacher paired the students participating in the study based on students who would work well together and had similar, but not equivalent, math abilities. The pairs were then assigned to either work collaboratively or individually and on either a procedurally-oriented or a conceptually-oriented problem set. When the students were collaborating, they sat at separate computers and talked through Skype (audio only). The collaboration was supported through the collaboration features described above (see example in Figure 1).

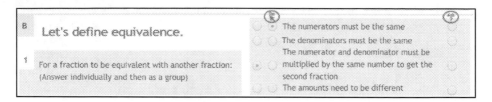

Fig. 1. Students have the opportunity to answer the question individually before seeing their partner's answer and answering the question as a group

To test our hypothesis that students working collaboratively have higher learning gains than students working individually when working on tutor activities targeting conceptual knowledge, we conducted two repeated-measures ANOVAs (conceptual and procedural test items). For the conceptual items there were pre/post learning gains, $F (1, 39) = 4.23$, $p = .046$, and on the procedural test items there were marginal learning gains, $F (1, 39) = 4.00$, $p = .053$. There was no interaction between the conditions. To evaluate our hypothesis that students working individually on tutor problems targeting procedural knowledge have higher learning gains than students working collaboratively, we again conducted two repeated-measures ANOVAs. There were no pre/post learning gains and no interaction between the collaborative and individual conditions. In this study, we found that students had equivalent learning gains in the collaborative and individual conditions showing that a collaborative ITS can effectively support learning with elementary school students. In this experiment, the students were in a lab-like setting, which is less ecologically valid than the classroom, and worked with the tutor for a short period of time. The future works aims to address these limitations as well as build upon the study.

3   Future Work and Conclusion

There are a number of social and academic benefits for collaborative learning among older students [1], but there is little work investigating these concepts among elementary students. As a first step, we investigated the effectiveness of a collaborative ITS among elementary school students in a controlled setting. Our next steps will be to investigate the plausibility of these systems in real classrooms. These studies will allow us to investigate the constraints of collaborative ITSs in real classrooms, as well as allow us to understand the collaborative behaviors this system elicits while we investigate the complementary benefits of both individual and collaborative learning. For our future work, we will conduct two classroom experiments in several local elementary schools. The first classroom study will address our second research question of what the complementary strengths are of collaborative and individual learning through a 2x2 design comparing collaborative and individual learning for both conceptual and procedural knowledge. By conducting the study in the classroom and over a week, we will be able to address some of the limitations with the pull-out study.

The second classroom study will be a 4-condition experiment to understand how collaborative and individual learning can best be combined and if the combination is better for learning than either method alone. For the experiment, there will be two conditions in which the students will only work individually or collaboratively. In the remaining two conditions, students will have a combination of individual and collaborative work. One combination will be in line with the complementary strengths of individual and collaborative learning while the other condition will be against. These combinations of strengths will be determined from the outcome of the previous classroom experiment. In addition to analyzing pre/post-test gains on a test of fractions knowledge, we will collect both tutor log data and audio transcripts during the intervention to provide insights into the collaborative learning processes.

Our work aims to demonstrate an effective combination of individual and collaborative learning within an ITS. We have contributed to previous research by extending ITS authoring tools to be able to flexibly support both collaborative and individual problem types, as previous systems have primarily focused exclusively on individual learning. Finally, although work with collaborative ITSs have primarily focus on middle grades and older, we have demonstrated that these tools are also effective for elementary students. Our future work will add to this understanding of collaborative and individual learning processes within an ITS, and how these instructional methods can be combined to support young learners effectively within an ITS.

Acknowledgments. We thank the CTAT team and Daniel Belenky for their help. This work was supported by Graduate Training Grant # R305B090023 and by Award # R305A120734 both from the US Department of Education (IES).

References

1. Lou, Y., Abrami, P.C., d'Apollonia, S.: Small group and individual learning with technology: A meta-analysis. Review of Educational Research **71**(3), 449–521 (2001)
2. Mullins, D., Rummel, N., Spada, H.: Are two heads always better than one? Differential effects of collaboration on students' computer-supported learning in mathematics. Int'l Journal of Computer-Supported Collaborative Learning **6**(3), 421–443 (2011)
3. Olsen, J.K., Belenky, D.M., Aleven, V., Rummel, N.: Using an intelligent tutoring system to support collaborative as well as individual learning. In: Trausan-Matu, S., Boyer, K.E., Crosby, M., Panourgia, K. (eds.) ITS 2014. LNCS, vol. 8474, pp. 134–143. Springer, Heidelberg (2014)
4. Olsen, J.K., Belenky, D.M., Aleven, V., Rummel, N., Sewall, J., Ringenberg, M.: Authoring tools for collaborative intelligent tutoring system environments. In: Trausan-Matu, S., Boyer, K.E., Crosby, M., Panourgia, K. (eds.) ITS 2014. LNCS, vol. 8474, pp. 523–528. Springer, Heidelberg (2014)
5. VanLehn, K.: The relative effectiveness of human tutoring, intelligent tutoring systems, and other tutoring systems. Educational Pyschologist. **46**(4), 197–221 (2011)
6. Walker, E., Rummel, N., McLaren, B.M., Koedinger, K.R.: The student becomes the master: integrating peer tutoring with cognitive tutoring. In: Proceedings of the 8th International Conference on Computer Supported Collaborative Learning, pp. 751–753 (2007)

Motivating Learning in the Age of the Adaptive Tutor

Korinn Ostrow[✉]

Worcester Polytechnic Institute, 100 Institute Road, Worcester, MA 01609, USA
ksostrow@wpi.edu

Abstract. My research is rooted in improving K-12 education through novel approaches to motivation and individualization via adaptive tutoring systems. In an attempt to isolate best practices within the science of learning, I conduct randomized controlled trials within ASSISTments, an online adaptive tutoring system that provides students with immediate feedback and teachers with powerful assessment. This paper examines two facets of my research: the optimization of feedback delivery and the provision of student autonomy. For each tenet, the basis for research is examined, contributions thus far are presented, and directions for future work are outlined.

Keywords: Motivation · Learning · Feedback · Choice · Adaptive tutoring

1   Research Focus

The U.S. Department of Education's National Educational Technology Plan supported the idea that technology will play a key role in delivering personalized educational interventions [10]. Adaptive tutoring systems are beginning to foot that bill in classrooms around the nation, providing interactive learning environments in which students can excel while teachers can maintain organized, data-driven classrooms. Yet there remains a severe lack of research regarding the effectiveness of online learning systems for K-12 education [11]. My research acts on this deficit, by conducting randomized controlled trials within ASSISTments, an online adaptive tutoring system, to identify best practices while striving to enhance educational content, its delivery, and the overall user experience.

Specifically, my work employs diverse and novel approaches to improve student motivation and performance within the context of adaptive tutoring. This paper examines two of the primary tenets of my research: optimizing feedback delivery and providing students with the perception of autonomy. In the following sections, I present reasoning for each focus, discussing problems inherent to the state of the art. I then propose my research goals as solutions, noting my contributions thus far and outlining future directions.

© Springer International Publishing Switzerland 2015
C. Conati et al. (Eds.): AIED 2015, LNAI 9112, pp. 852–855, 2015.
DOI: 10.1007/978-3-319-19773-9_131

2   Enhancing Motivation and Performance Within ASSISTments

2.1   Optimizing Feedback

Problem: Disengagement With (and Maladaptive Usage of) Feedback.
One of the most compelling aspects of adaptive tutoring systems is their ability to provide students with feedback at critical moments to optimize learning gains. Within the ASSISTments platform, both questions and feedback have traditionally been presented using rich text. A variety of tutoring strategies allow for the provision of feedback on demand (i.e., hints), automatically upon the student's incorrect response (i.e., scaffolding problems), or tailored to a common wrong answer (i.e., bug messages). Across most problems in the system, the final piece of feedback provides the correct answer, allowing the student to move forward in their assignment. Regardless of how or when feedback is provided, students frequently disengage from the content. In some cases, the feedback is too dense, too simplistic, or otherwise boring. In other cases, students are deterred from the appropriate use of feedback because the system records binary correctness on their first attempt or action when solving a problem. This can create an environment in which students avoid feedback due to the potential for penalization, or instead, overuse feedback if they have already lost credit (i.e., jumping to the answer rather than reading through a series of hints). Disengaging feedback and maladaptive practices surrounding the use of feedback reduce the likelihood of robust learning.

Proposed Solution: Enhancing Feedback through Video and Partial Credit.
To conquer stale feedback, the power of adaptive tutoring platforms should be harnessed to present feedback in a more engaging manner. According to Mayer's multimedia principles for the optimal design of e-Learning environments, it is possible to use hypermedia elements (i.e., video) to promote active learning while reducing cognitive load [1]. Still, systems that make use of video tend to do so in a manner that resembles lecturing (i.e., Khan Academy) rather than content specific feedback. Within my work, a novel approach is taken to embed brief (15-30 second) video snippets as feedback within the ASSISTments platform. Further, data mining has revealed that partial credit scoring would help to alleviate the maladaptive usage of feedback, serving to motivate student performance while simultaneously offering teachers a more robust view of student knowledge.

Contributions & Plan for Advancement.
My early work presented a randomized controlled trial comparing video and text feedback within the realm of middle school mathematics [5]. Results suggested a significant effect of video feedback, showing enhanced performance on questions following adaptive video tutoring, as well as increased efficiency in problem solving. Further, the majority of students self-reported video as a positive addition to their assignment. This study was the first of its kind to explore the potential for replacing text feedback within ASSISTments. Additional research has since investigated the specific elements of feedback delivery (i.e., audio, graphical, textual) using motivational feedback delivered via a

pedagogical agent [7]. To investigate realigning maladaptive feedback usage, my work has incorporated data mining approaches to develop and refine multiple models of partial credit scoring [3, 4].

Results promoting the effectiveness of video have inspired an influx of video content into the ASSISTments platform, providing endless opportunities for additional research. A group of studies are currently underway, examining research questions including, "What aspects of feedback delivery make the medium most engaging?", "Do older students with stronger reading ability react negatively to video feedback?", and "Does the effect of video differ across content domains?". Further, this work inspired investigations into the potential for crowd-sourcing feedback from teachers and students through simple screen capture technology via tablets or smartphones. Students will be able to record messages to help their peers, and teachers will be able to reach multiple students through focused feedback simultaneously. Next steps for the ASSISTments platform include the development of a contextual K-armed bandit algorithm that will learn how and when to provide optimal feedback for each student.

2.2   Promoting Student Autonomy

Problem: Tutoring Systems Fail to Consider Student Preference.
While adaptive tutoring systems offer a variety of features for personalization and individualization, few allow students to invest in their learning process. ASSISTments is built largely around assessment, putting teachers in control of assignments and leaving students with little say (a traditional approach to education). However, the platform offers untapped opportunities to examine the motivational effect of choice.

Proposed Solution: Instill the Perception of Autonomy.
Choice is an intrinsically motivating force [8] that has the potential to boost subjective control, or a student's perception of their causal influence over their learning outcomes [9]. By providing students with simple choices at the start of an assignment, it may be possible to enhance expectancies regarding performance and thereby enhance achievement emotions and motivation [9]. Considering the control-value theory within the realm of adaptive tutoring systems for math and science content, instilling autonomy may also help to ameliorate female dropout in STEM fields [2].

Contributions & Plan for Advancement.
A pilot study was conducted to investigate allowing student choice within ASSISTments [6]. In a 2x2 factorial design, students were randomly assigned to experience 'choice' or 'no choice' crossed with feedback medium (video or text). Results suggested that even if feedback was not ultimately utilized, students who were prompted to choose their feedback medium significantly outperformed those who were not. These findings inspired a significant infrastructure addition to the ASSISTments platform: If-Then path navigation. This feature will allow for the vast expansion of research in this area, allowing for investigations of how and when it is most appropriate to instill autonomy.

The If-Then structure is currently being used to conduct scaled-up replications of this work in additional content domains. If previous results are replicated, these findings may prove groundbreaking for the adaptive tutoring community by promoting a simple approach to enhancing student motivation and performance. The future of this work will also consider more persistent user variables through a feature that is currently in production for the ASSISTments platform. Essentially, researchers and teachers will be able to base assignments adaptively around student characteristics, preferences, or past performance, allowing for powerful levels of personalization.

Acknowledgements. Funding for my work has been granted by: GAANN (P200A120238), ONR (N00014-13-C-0127), and PIMSE (NSF DGE-0742503). Thanks to S.O. & L.P.B.O.

References

1. Clark, R.C., Mayer, R.E.: e-Learning and the science of instruction: proven guidelines for consumers and designers of multimedia learning. Pfeiffer, San Fran (2003)
2. Frenzel, A.C., Pekrun, R., Goetz, T.: Girls and mathematics – A "hopeless" issue? A control-value approach to gender differences in emotions towards mathematics. Eur. J of Psych of Ed. **22**(4), 497–514 (2007)
3. Ostrow, K., Donnelly, C., Adjei, S., Heffernan, N.: Improving student modeling through partial credit and problem difficulty. In: Russell, Woolf & Kiczales (eds) Proceedings of the 2nd Annual Meeting of the ACM Conf on Learning at Scale, pp. 11–20 (2015)
4. Ostrow, K., Donnelly, C., Heffernan, N.: Optimizing partial credit algorithms to predict student performance. In: Submitted to the 8th Int Conf on EDM (Under Review)
5. Ostrow, K.S., Heffernan, N.T.: Testing the multimedia principle in the real world: a comparison of video vs. text feedback in authentic middle school math assignments. In: Stamper, J., Pardos, Z., Mavrikis, M., McLaren, B.M.: (eds.) Proceedings of the 7th Int Conf on EDM, pp. 296–299 (2014)
6. Ostrow, K., Heffernan, N.: The Role of Student Choice within Adaptive Tutoring. To be included in Conati, Heffernan, Mitrovic & Verdejo (eds) Proceedings of the 17th Int Conf on AIED (In Press)
7. Ostrow, K.S., Schultz, S.E., Arroyo, I.: Promoting growth mindset within intelligent tutoring systems. In: Gutierrez-Santos, S., & Santos, O.C. (eds) EDM 2014 Extended Proceedings: NCFPAL Workshop, pp. 88–93. CEUR-WS (1183) (2014)
8. Patall, E.A., Cooper, H., Robinson, J.C.: The Effects of Choice on Intrinsic Motivation and Related Outcomes: A Meta-Analysis of Research Findings. Psychology Bulletin. **134**(2), 270–300 (2008)
9. Pekrun, R.: The Control-Value Theory of Achievement Emotions: Assumptions, Corollaries, and Implications for Educational Research and Practice. Educational Psychology Review **18**(4), 315–341 (2006)
10. U.S. Department of Education, Office of Educational Technology. Transforming American Education: Learning Powered by Technology, Washington, D.C. (2010a)
11. U.S. Department of Education, Office of Planning, Evaluation, and Policy Development. Evaluation of Evidence-Based Practices in Online Learning: A Meta-Analysis and Review of Online Learning Studies, Washington, D.C. (2010b)

Creating Data-Driven Feedback for Novices in Goal-Driven Programming Projects

Thomas W. Price[(⊠)] and Tiffany Barnes

North Carolina State University, Raleigh, NC 27606, USA
{twprice,tmbarnes}@ncsu.edu

Abstract. Programming environments that afford the creation of media-rich, goal-driven projects, such as games, stories and simulations, are effective at engaging novice users. However, the open-ended nature of these projects makes it difficult to generate ITS-style guidance for students in need of help. In domains where students produce similar, overlapping solutions, data-driven techniques can leverage the work of previous students to provide feedback. However, our data suggest that solutions to these projects have insufficient overlap to apply current data-driven methods. We propose a novel subtree-based state matching technique that will find partially overlapping solutions to generate feedback across diverse student programs. We will build a system to generate this feedback, test the technique on historical data, and evaluate the generated feedback in a study of goal-driven programming projects. If successful, this approach will provide insight into how to leverage structural similarities across complex, creative problem solutions to provide data-driven feedback for intelligent tutoring.

1 Introduction

Novice programming environments such as Scratch, Snap, Greenfoot, Alice and App Inventor have shown promise in classrooms and informal learning settings, with evaluations demonstrating improved student grades, retention and interest in computing [2]. These environments motivate students by connecting with their interests, such as games, stories and simulations [6]. However, even in environments designed for novices, programming can still be very difficult for students to learn. Tutorials can guide students, and teachers can help them when they get stuck, but at home, in informal learning environments, or in overcrowded classrooms, teacher help may not always be available. An Intelligent Tutoring System (ITS) for programming could bridge this gap by providing feedback and guidance, helping students continue when they are unsure how to proceed. Such advice would be quite valuable in these project-driven programming environments, especially for novices whose teachers may not be expert programmers.

While feedback could be hand-authored for a programming ITS, the process is very time consuming. Data-driven feedback is an alternative approach that uses programs written by previous students to provide guidance to new students with similar programs. The Hint Factory [5] and similar data-driven techniques have been successfully applied to the domain of programming [1,4]. However, its

© Springer International Publishing Switzerland 2015
C. Conati et al. (Eds.): AIED 2015, LNAI 9112, pp. 856–859, 2015.
DOI: 10.1007/978-3-319-19773-9_132

application is generally restricted to small, well-structured problems with easily evaluated goals, for example converting the index of a playing card (0-51) to a string representation (e.g. "7H" for the 7 of hearts).

By contrast, goal-driven projects, such as programming a game, story or simulation, require solving multiple, loosely ordered and interdependent subgoals. Such projects may be defined by a set of instructions (e.g. a tutorial), which outline these goals, but the student is given room to make design choices within the framework of the instructions. Further, evaluation of these goals may be a somewhat subjective process. The ill-defined and open-ended nature of these projects pose a challenge for current data-driven methods. Our goal is to adapt current methods to overcome these challenges.

Our research questions are as follows. Can data-driven feedback in goal-driven programming projects:

1. Be generated such that feedback is available in the majority of situations
2. Increase student performance in the environment
3. Improve students' self-efficacy with regards to programming

2   Subtree-Based State Matching

Hint-Factory-style data-driven techniques represent a problem as a space of possible states [5]. All students start in the same state and attempt to find a path to some goal state. Solution paths from previous, successful students are combined to form a network, and each state is assigned a value, approximating the likelihood of a student reaching a goal from that state. When a new student requests help, the system matches the current state of that student to a state in the network and suggests a path that will lead to a goal state.

In programming, the most straightforward representation of a student's state is the program itself, though other representations have been proposed (e.g. [1]). Two students are unlikely to have exactly matching programs, however, making it difficult to generate feedback. This problem was recognized by Rivers and Koedinger, who addressed it by transforming programs into Abstract Syntax Trees (ASTs) and performing canonicalization to increase the probability of overlapping states [3]. They also connected states in the network which had at least 90% similarity [4], creating additional paths to the goals states. If no existing path is found, path construction can be applied to generate a new path to a goal state. These techniques have been effective with small, well-structured problems. However, our preliminary results on goal-driven projects suggest that the resulting state space is much more sparse and resistant to canonicalization.

We therefore propose a subtree-based state matching approach that will isolate and match relevant sections of code, rather than entire programs. Like Rivers and Koedinger, we represent a program as an AST. When a student requests help, we isolate the subtree that encompasses their most recent actions. For instance, a student might be working only on code within a specific for-loop, and so we identify the subtree that is the body of that loop. Rather than finding an entire state which matches the student, we look for any states with a matching subtree and find advice that applies within that subtree. If multiple matches are found, we can look outside the subtree to determine which state is the closest match. If no exact matches are found, we can still apply previous techniques (e.g. path construction) to the subtrees.

For example, consider a student trying to implement code that will move a game character to a random position on the screen. In the previous section, this student added some extra code, which makes her current program state dissimilar from any previously observed state. However, the random movement logic is encompassed within a subtree. By isolating this subtree, we can still match her to the movement logic of a previous student who completed that goal.

3   Current Progress

We have already collected log and survey data from middle school students completing an hour-long goal-driven project, in both a block-based and textual programming environment. Students employed variables, loops and conditionals to create a simple Whack-a-Mole style game, where the objective is to click on a sprite as it jumps around the screen to win points. Our results indicate that students perform significantly better using a block programming interface, spending a larger portion of their time on-task, and completing more goals in less time. Therefore, since students can do more work in less time, and blocks prevent some kinds of errors, we will focus on block-based environments.

We constructed a network from the collected program logs to analyze the potential for applying current data-driven techniques. We applied strong canonicalization to the programs, removing all program-specific variable names and standardizing statement ordering, to achieve as much overlap between programs as possible. Even then, over 92% of the observed states were unique, confirming the intuition that open-ended, goal-driven tasks naturally have sparse state spaces. Further, states from different students were very dissimilar, even when they were pursuing the same subgoal, making it difficult to construct additional paths, as in [4]. However, inspection of the data revealed that even very dissimilar program states still contained similar or identical sections of code. For example, some students who had different solutions to one subgoal of the activity, had a similar solution to another subgoal. This suggests that the subtree technique would be successful with this data, which we seek to verify in future work.

4   Future Work

We plan to use the data we have already collected to evaluate the feasibility of our approach, specifically our ability to generate on-demand feedback in the form of hints. We will implement the subtree state matching algorithm and adapt the Hint Factory to generate hints from matching subtrees. We will use a technique called a Cold Start analysis to predict how much data will be necessary to provide hints to students at least 50% of the time, which is our goal. If too much data is required, we can modify the algorithm to increase hint availability (at the cost of applicability) by matching subtrees containing only a student's most recent action, rather than a set of recent actions. We will then determine which programming constructs we want to focus on and create a goal-driven project that incorporates them.

Our evaluation will target middle school students, and will be in two parts. First we will collect data from a group of students as they complete the project, who will serve as a control group. We will then use this data to generate hints and modify the programming environment to provide them on-demand. We will perform a second data collection using the hint-enabled environment, otherwise identical to the first. We will collect log data to determine how often feedback was available when requested. We will evaluate how well each group performed, as measured by the number of subgoals completed and the time required for completion. We will also measure how students' self-efficacy with regards to computing changed after completing the exercise, using a validated pre- and post-survey. We hypothesize that the hint group will outperform the control group and demonstrate higher self-efficacy.

The work proposed here leaves some open questions, which will need to be addressed. While subtree-based state matching will allow us to generate feedback in more states, the quality of the feedback will need to be evaluated. What impact will statements outside of a matched subtree have on the applicability of the generated feedback? When evaluating the technique, how complex should the goal-driven project be, and what programming concepts should it cover? What other measures could be used to evaluate the impact of the hints?

The work proposed here will represent a significant advance for automated feedback generation, expanding its application to open-ended design tasks, such as goal-driven projects. It lays the groundwork for a programming ITS capable of aiding students with programming at a novice level and beyond.

References

1. Hicks, A., Peddycord III, B., Barnes, T.: Building games to learn from their players: generating hints in a serious game. In: Trausan-Matu, S., Boyer, K.E., Crosby, M., Panourgia, K. (eds.) ITS 2014. LNCS, vol. 8474, pp. 312–317. Springer, Heidelberg (2014)
2. Moskal, B., Lurie, D., Cooper, S.: Evaluating the effectiveness of a new instructional approach. ACM SIGCSE Bulletin 36(1), 75–79 (2004)
3. Rivers, K., Koedinger, K.: Automatic generation of programming feedback: a data-driven approach. In: The First Workshop on AI-supported Education for Computer Science (AIEDCS 2013) (2013)
4. Rivers, K., Koedinger, K.R.: Automating hint generation with solution space path construction. In: Trausan-Matu, S., Boyer, K.E., Crosby, M., Panourgia, K. (eds.) ITS 2014. LNCS, vol. 8474, pp. 329–339. Springer, Heidelberg (2014)
5. Stamper, J., Eagle, M., Barnes, T., Croy, M.: Experimental evaluation of automatic hint generation for a logic tutor. Artificial Intelligence in Education (AIED) 22(1), 3–17 (2013)
6. Utting, I., Cooper, S., Kölling, M.: Alice, Greenfoot, and Scratch-a discussion. ACM Transactions on Computing Education (TOCE) 10(4) (2010)

Towards Multimodal Affective Detection in Educational Systems Through Mining Emotional Data Sources

Sergio Salmeron-Majadas[✉], Olga C. Santos, and Jesus G. Boticario

aDeNu Research Group, Artificial Intelligence Department,
Computer Science School, UNED, C/Juan Del Rosal 16 28040, Madrid, Spain
{sergio.salmeron,ocsantos,jgb}@dia.uned.es

Abstract. This paper introduces the work being carried out in an ongoing PhD research focused on the detection of the learners' affective states by combining different available sources (from physiological sensors to keystroke analysis). Different data mining algorithms and data labeling techniques have been used generating 735 prediction models. Results so far show that predictive models on affective state detection from multimodal-based approaches provide better accuracy rates than single-based.

Keywords: Artificial intelligence · Affective computing · Data mining · Human-computer interaction · Adaptive systems · User modeling · Machine learning · Multimodal approach · Sensor data

1 Theoretical Framework

In the last two decades, the e-learning field has emerged widely. Among its benefits, adaptation is one of the most researched nowadays. Many works focus on detecting failure or success leading patterns in students in order to take part when needed. Data mining is one of the most common approaches used in that pattern search (with an increasing number of educational data mining and learning analytics researchers involved). As to how to cater for those adaptive features, recommender systems have been usually selected as a sensible approach [1]. An important part of these systems is the user modeling, the method to let the system know the state of the learner in order to decide if a reaction is needed and why. The construction of a good and precise model is a key point in order to allow the system to know the learner in detail and decide an appropriate intervention if needed [2].

This model is desired to take into account all the learner information that may have any influence on her learning performance, being able to detect when some aspect should be revised to improve the learner results. Commonly, performance indicators have been the ones considered to evaluate the advance of the learner on her tasks, but psychologist have found that there are other factors that may have an important role on learners' effectiveness, being one of these the affective dimension of the learner. This issue has been detected and studied for many years, but rarely has been taken into account, neither in face to face teaching nor in e-learning environments. For that reason and thanks to the progress on affective computing field, research in online education is increasingly focused on taking advantage of learners' emotions [3].

© Springer International Publishing Switzerland 2015
C. Conati et al. (Eds.): AIED 2015, LNAI 9112, pp. 860–863, 2015.
DOI: 10.1007/978-3-319-19773-9_133

Many works have appeared during the last years to propose different ways and data sources to perform emotion detection [4]. Most of them focus on the evaluation of a single data source and are performed in non-educational contexts. In this respect, some works dealt with some context-related difficulties such as the low frequency and intensity of the emotions experienced in educational.

The approach followed in the emotion detection field usually relies on the use of supervised learning approaches, which needs a set of labeled data in order to train a model. This data labeling process is one of the many problems to be faced in this direction. Emotion labeling is usually performed by the participant, via lists of emotions or numerical scales of emotion dimensions like the Self-Assessment Manikin (SAM) or by an external annotator with experience in emotional or educational aspects (such as psychologist or e-learning teachers). These labelings have been performed (as shown in fig. 1). Whatever the labeling approach is, there is always a subjectivity component that may affect the model training task. Other open issues in this field include the different nature of the signals proposed in literature, being necessary many different ways of preparing the data to be processed.

Grounded on the existing and more recent approaches [5] to deal with the aforementioned issues, the hypothesis of this research poses that the use of data mining techniques on multimodal data sources can improve the accuracy rates of emotion detection obtained from a single data source .

2   Proposed Approach

The proposed approach relies on the use of data mining techniques in order to model the learners' affective state from the information collected from diverse input data. So far we have considered physiological information (heart rate, skin conductance, temperature and breath), sentiment analysis on learners' emotional reports (counting positive and negative terms) and interaction behavior with the mouse and keyboard. Detected affective states can be used by other components to generate personalized affective-based feedback. In particular, a large scale experiment was carried out involving 75 participants, where, while being sensed and recorded, they had to solve a series of mathematics problems. Data collected was preprocessed generating different indicators depending on the data source. From the physiological signals, user relative variances were calculated, while from mouse and keyboard tracking, some indicators as the typing speed or the mouse speed were extracted. After that, different data mining techniques and different data labelling approaches with different data sources combinations were tested. Partial results were reported in [6], applying machine learning techniques in an incremental way, considering a subset of the collected input sources, and [7], considering exclusively keyboard and mouse interactions.

Performing all the possible permutations between different combinations of data sources used in the experiment, the data mining algorithms and the data labelling approaches, 735 predictive models were generated using different data mining algorithms (see Figure 1). Most of the highest accuracy models obtained over each data labelling approach (17 out of 21) were those combining different data sources, which makes the multimodal research a plausible way to continue working in. Other works performed have focused on exploring the correlation between mouse interaction (computing 96 mouse indicators), keyboard usage (computing 42 keyboard indicators) and the participants' affective states reported using the SAM scale [7]. Results from the analysis of data processed from 17 participants suggest that these indicators could be useful in detecting affective states automatically in a non-intrusive and low cost way from changes in their behavior during the interaction with the e-learning platform. In all the works carried out, many open points have been differently approached, such as the data labelling process, the learning scenario and tasks proposed or the infrastructure developed, being these points still to be further researched.

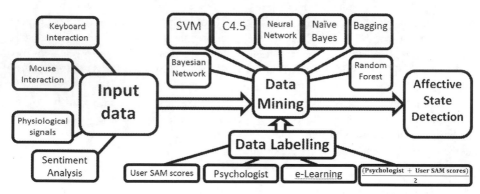

Fig. 1. data sources, data labelling techniques and data mining algorithms used.

3   Expected Contributions

Due to the wide variety of data sources proposed in literature and the current ways to access to learning platforms are using a wide variety of interaction devices, different data sources from interaction behaviors can be used to get affective information from the learner. Multimodal approaches allowing the expansion of affective data usage in learning environments is becoming a clear research spot, but not only access configurations or measuring devices have to be taken into account but also the methodological aspects of the orchestration needed to get closer to this goal. These methodological aspects concern many components of the information extraction process, where this research is focusing, studying the influence of the data labeling used (comparing different approaches and combinations of them), time (time window used, computational time needed, system reaction time), data combination (features proposed, combination methods, etc.) and data analysis (machine learning techniques, model explicitness, computational resources needed, etc.) on the accuracy rates when detecting emotions. Data mining techniques will be used to perform an individual analysis for each data source and another analysis over the outcomes from the single data source processing to detect the best way to combine every data source available.

4   Forthcoming Steps

Many data sources have already been analyzed, and their data has been used to evaluate some data mining techniques, but new ways of combining the data have to be tested as other data sources also have to be tested. The way to extract information and store it to be used by other components (e.g. recommender systems) is something also to be faced, looking for a standard-based way to store this affective model.

Other issue to take into account is to evaluate the dependency between the model generated and the activities performed. Different activities usually require different ways of interacting with the devices, so the impact of different variables on the user model adaptation should be observed. Other variables to be taken into account include possible special needs the user may have, user's skill with the device, etc.

Acknowledgments. Authors would like to thank the Spanish Ministry of Economy and Competitiveness for the support to the project TIN2011-29221-C03-01. Sergio Salmeron Majadas acknowledges the FPI grant BES-2012-054522.

References

1. Santos, O.C., Boticario, J.G.: Practical guidelines for designing and evaluating educationally oriented recommendations. Comput. Educ. **81**, 354–374 (2015)
2. Romero, C., Ventura, S.: Data mining in education. Wiley Interdiscip. Rev. Data Min. Knowl. Discov. **3**, 12–27 (2013)
3. Ahn, H., Picard, R.W.: Affective cognitive learning and decision making: the role of emotions. In: The 18th European Meeting on Cybernetics and Systems Research (EMCSR 2006), pp. 1–6 (2006)
4. van den Broek, E.L., Lisý, V., Janssen, J.H., Westerink, J.H., Schut, M.H., Tuinenbreijer, K.: Affective man-machine interface: unveiling human emotions through biosignals. In: Fred, A., Filipe, J., Gamboa, H. (eds.) BIOSTEC 2009. CCIS, vol. 52, pp. 21–47. Springer, Heidelberg (2010)
5. Baker, R.S., Ocumpaugh, J.: Interaction-Based Affect Detection in Educational Software. Oxf. Handb. Affect. Comput., 233 (2014)
6. Santos, O.C., Salmeron-Majadas, S., Boticario, J.G.: Emotions detection from math exercises by combining several data sources. In: Lane, H., Yacef, K., Mostow, J., Pavlik, P. (eds.) AIED 2013. LNCS, vol. 7926, pp. 742–745. Springer, Heidelberg (2013)
7. Salmeron-Majadas, S., Santos, O.C., Boticario, J.G.: An Evaluation of Mouse and Keyboard Interaction Indicators towards Non-intrusive and Low Cost Affective Modeling in an Educational Context. Procedia Comput. Sci. **35**, 691–700 (2014)

Promoting Metacognition Within a Game-Based Environment

Erica L. Snow[✉], Matthew E. Jacovina, and Danielle S. McNamara

Department of Psychology, Arizona State University, Tempe, AZ 85287, USA
{Erica.L.Snow,Matthew.Jacovina,Danielle.McNamara}@asu.edu

Abstract. Metacognition refers to students' ability to reflect upon what they know and what they do not know. However, many students often struggle to master this regulatory skill. We have designed and implemented two features to promote metacognition within the game-based system iSTART-2. These two features have been tested and shown to have positive impacts on students' ability to reflect upon their performance. Future work is being planned to further explore the most effective way to implement these features and the ultimate impact they have on learning outcomes. We are seeking advice and feedback on the methodology and metacognitive feature design that will be included in a series of follow-up studies. The implications of this work for both iSTART-2 and the AIED field are discussed.

Keywords: Metacognition · Game-based learning · Self-assessment · Design

1 Introduction

Students' ability to reflect upon what they know and what they do not know is often referred to as metacognition [1]. Metacognition is a regulatory skill that has been shown to be critical for academic and professional success [2]. However, many students struggle to effectively (and accurately) assess and reflect upon their learning and cognitive processes. Consequently, researchers have begun to develop various interventions and techniques designed to stimulate metacognition during learning tasks. These interventions often enable students to gain experience in reflecting upon what they know and how to behave while engaged in a learning task [3]. For instance, a common technique used to promote metacognition is prompted self-assessments. These instructional tools are designed to prompt students to reflect upon the assignment while objectively critiquing the quality of their own work [3]. Another technique includes the use of prompts designed to alert students to sub-optimal performance during a learning task [4]. Similar to self-assessments, the goal of performance prompts is to provide students with the opportunity to reflect upon their own performance and the learning task.

Recently, researchers have argued that metacognitive support techniques should be embedded within adaptive environments to enhance metacognition skills, which may ultimately lead to long-term learning outcomes [5]. Hence, the goal of the proposed work is to develop and test metacognitive interventions embedded within the game-based reading comprehension system, iSTART-2 (Interactive Strategy Training for

© Springer International Publishing Switzerland 2015
C. Conati et al. (Eds.): AIED 2015, LNAI 9112, pp. 864–867, 2015.
DOI: 10.1007/978-3-319-19773-9_134

Active Reading and Thinking; [6]). Previously, we have conducted two experiments designed to test two features embedded within iSTART-2 that indirectly promote self-reflection during learning tasks [4]. However, these experiments have been conducted separately and in isolation of each other. We propose to test these features in conjunction with each other to examine how they might interact to enhance metacognition and motivation within a more complete version of the iSTART-2 system. In this paper, we propose (and seek advice about) a series of experiments that will assess the effectiveness of these metacognitive features in prompting self-reflection, and in turn, their effects on motivation and learning outcomes.

1.1   iSTART-2

The Interactive Strategy Training for Active Reading and Thinking-2 (iSTART-2) is a game-based intelligent tutoring system (ITS) designed to improve students' reading comprehension abilities by instructing them on five self-explanation strategies (comprehension monitoring, paraphrasing, prediction, elaboration, and bridging; [6]). iSTART-2 is divided into two sections: lesson videos and game-based practice. The lesson videos provide students with information about self-explanation and comprehension strategies to improve their explanations. In the game-based practice interface, students can interact with a series of games designed to provide the opportunity to practice writing self-explanations or identifying the stratgies that they had just learned (for more info see [6]).

2   Previous Research

We have developed and independently tested two features designed to promote metacognition within iSTART-2. Both of these features (described below) are designed to prompt students to reflect upon their own performance and learning processes.

The first feature that we developed and embedded within iSTART-2 is *a performance- threshold feature*. The performance-threshold feature is incorporated within the practice games of iSTART-2. That is, after students complete each game play, their average score within the game is compared to an experimenter-set threshold. If this threshold is not met, students are presented with a message that explicitly informs them that their performance is low (promoting self-reflection) and that they will be transitioned to a remedial activity where they can receive more nuanced and direct strategy instruction. This feature is thus designed to indirectly support metacognition by presenting students with performance information. Previous work has shown that the performance-threshold feature has had a positive impact on students' self-explanation quality [4]. Specifically, after students are told of their low performance, they showed significant improvements in self-explanation quality during the following game-play, regardless of whether they received the additional instruction.

In addition to the performance-threshold feature, we also separately designed and implemented a *self-assessment feature* within the game-based practice in iSTART-2. This feature is designed to provide students with an opportunity to reflect upon and assess their performance. The embedded self-assessments prompt students to assess the quality of their self-explanations before receiving any feedback from the system. Across two texts, students using the self-assessment feature consistently overestimated their performance within iSTART-2. Thus, the self-assessment feature does not appear to enhance students' understanding of the task or their performance. Interestingly though, the degree to which students overestimated their performance varies as a function of prior domain knowledge. Thus, high ability students tended to be more closely aligned with the system than low ability students.

3   Future Research Plans

The two studies conducted thus far have provided insights on promising future directions as well as limitations that need to be addressed. We propose, and seek advice about, three experiments designed to enhance our understanding of how these metacognitive features may be improved and ultimately impact students' learning outcomes.

In *Study 1*, we will explore how the effects of the experimenter-set threshold on motivation and learning depend on individual differences. In a sense, we will be asking if *different students need different performance thresholds*. Currently, the performance-threshold feature uses a set performance threshold. The goal of Study 1 will be to determine the extent to which the effects of the threshold depend on prior ability levels. For instance, it is our hypothesis that different thresholds are likely necessary to avoid disengagement and frustration; indeed, lower ability students may benefit from thresholds that are relatively easier to achieve, as they may be perceived as a more manageable goal. To test this hypothesis, we will conduct a between-subjects experiment where students are randomly assigned to one of three conditions, each of which includes a different performance threshold. With this design, we will examine how various thresholds interact with individual differences to influence learning and motivational outcomes.

In *Study 2*, we will examine the frequency that students should be asked to self-assess within the iSTART-2 interface. In our previous work with self-assessments within iSTART-2, students were asked to self-assess their performance after each self-explanation. However, this may appear redundant to students and subsequently promote "gaming behavior" in which students click through this task thoughtlessly. Therefore, in Study 2, we will conduct a between-subjects experiment that manipulates the frequency that students are asked to self-assess (i.e., after every two target sentences or after every completed text). This will afford the opportunity to examine and identify how *varying the frequency of self-assessments influences learning outcomes and metacognitive awareness* within iSTART-2.

Finally, in *Study 3*, information gleaned from Studies 1 and 2 (optimal thresholds and self-assessment frequencies) will be used to guide a 2 (threshold vs. no threshold) x 2 (self-assessment vs. no self-assessment) between-subjects experiment. The goal of Study 3 will be to examine *if and how these two metacognitive features interact to influence learning outcomes and self-reflection ability*. It is our hypothesis that the two features promote metacognition at different levels. For instance, self-assessments may prompt students to reflect upon their performance at a more local level (e.g., each self-explanation they generate). By contrast, the performance-threshold feature may promote more global metacognitive reflections regarding their approach to the task (e.g., what strategy they used) rather than localized activity embedded within the task. Thus, the combination of these two features may prompt students to reflect on the task as well as how it fits into their overall learning goals.

4   Contributions

The proposed work has both local and global implications. Locally, the development and implementation of features designed to promote metacognition will improve the effectiveness and pedagogy of the iSTART-2. Currently, iSTART-2 does not explicitly promote metacognition within the game-based practice. Thus, the inclusion and testing of these features may improve the system feedback and guide the content to which students are exposed.

Globally, this project will contribute to the AIED community by enhancing our understanding of how metacognition can be supported and ultimately influence learning outcomes. Metacognition is of growing interest within the community, and researchers are beginning to develop and test interventions that promote this regulatory skill. However, more work is needed to decipher what intervention or combination of interventions is most effective at promoting self-reflection during learning. The features studied in this project are not tied to the specific context of iSTART-2 and thus can be implemented in a variety of educational systems. Although the current work is designed to test features that promote metacognition for the iSTART-2 system, this work is driven by the overarching goal of gaining a better understanding of students' learning processes.

References

1. Flavell, J.H.: Metacognition and cognitive monitoring: A new area of cognitive–developmental inquiry. American Psychologist **34**(10), 906 (1979)
2. Pintrich, P.R.: The role of metacognitive knowledge in learning, teaching, and ASSESSING. Theory into Practice **41**(4), 219–225 (2002)
3. Falchikov, N., Boud, D.: Student self-assessment in higher education: A meta-analysis. Review of Educational Research **59**, 395–430 (1989)
4. Snow, E.L., et al.: Promoting metacognitive awareness within a game-based environment. Paper submitted to the 2015 Artificial Intelligence in Education Conference (in press)
5. Roll, I., Aleven, V., McLaren, B.M., Koedinger, K.R.: Improving students' help-seeking skills using metacognitive feedback in an Intelligent Tutoring System. Learning and Instruction **21**(2), 267–280 (2011)
6. Snow, E.L., Allen, L.K., Jacovina, M.E., McNamara, D.S.: Does agency matter?: Exploring the impact of controlled behaviors within a game-based environment. Computers & Education **26**, 378–392 (2014)

Negotiation-Driven Learning: A New Perspective of Learning Using Negotiation

Raja M. Suleman[✉], Riichiro Mizoguchi, and Mitsuru Ikeda

School of Knowledge Science, Japan Advanced Institute
of Science and Technology, Nomi, Ishikawa, Japan
{suleman,mizo,ikeda}@jaist.ac.jp
http://www.jaist.ac.jp

Abstract. Negotiation mechanisms used in the current implementations of Open Learner Models are mostly position-based and provide minimal support for learners to understand why their beliefs contradict with that of the system. In this paper, we propose the paradigm of Negotiation-Driven Learning with the aim to enhance the role of negotiations in open learner models with special emphasis on affect, behavior and metacognitive abilities of the learners.

Keywords: Intelligent tutoring systems · Open learner models · Negotiation · Metacognition · Affect · Learner behavior · Interest-based negotiation

1 Introduction

Open Learner Model (OLM) [1] was introduced in Intelligent Tutoring Systems (ITS) to involve learners further in the learning process. OLMs provide learners with the opportunity to view and edit their Learner Models (LM). Allowing the learner to edit their LM results in scenarios where the learner's belief about their own knowledge is different from that of the system. Such events trigger an interrupt where the system tries to negotiate the changes made by the learner in an effort to remove this difference of beliefs. The underlying principle of the negotiation in OLMs is to test whether the learner can justify the change they made to their LM.

Although this strategy of OLMs has shown to produce significant learning gains, the negotiations in OLM follow a very Position-Based Negotiation (PBN) [4] approach, since the dialogues primarily focus on the *"positions"* held by the learner. This strategy of negotiation is often challenging because as the negotiations advance, the negotiating parties become more and more committed to their positions and without any information about why a certain position is held by the learner, any agreement that is reached produces unsatisfactory results.

Improving the metacognitive abilities of the learner has always been a key role of OLMs, however the current OLMs rarely scaffold the metacognitive processes.

© Springer International Publishing Switzerland 2015
C. Conati et al. (Eds.): AIED 2015, LNAI 9112, pp. 868–872, 2015.
DOI: 10.1007/978-3-319-19773-9_135

Since the system is actively involved in testing the learner about their knowledge, how they are reflecting or evaluating themselves is mostly left on the part of the learner.

1.1 Problem Definition

OLMs use a strict negotiation protocol which limits the system's ability to cater for a vast array of learner inputs. More often than not learner utterances & behaviors have little or no implications on the system's strategy which limits its ability to provide adequate scaffolding to engage the learner in a deeper learning dialogue.

2 Related Work

Most OLMs have deployed PBN as a negotiation strategy to resolve the conflicts. Mr.Collins [3] and STyLE-OLM [3] use a close-ended questioning approach where the learner is confined to a menu-based interface. They are allowed to challenge the system, and the system engages the learner in only directed-questions related to the domain knowledge. CALMsystem [3] provides a chatbot facility in order to engage the learners more actively. The dialogue functionality provided to the learner is a choice-based system where the system offers the learner the ability to choose from a predefined set of choices primarily focusing on learner's domain knowledge. Interest-Based Negotiations (IBN) [2] have been shown as a good alternative to PBN. IBN sees the negotiating parties as allies working for a mutual gain, hence allows each party to seek underlying interests of the other party in order to reach a mutually beneficial agreement. AutoTutor [5] is an ITS that does not use the OLM, and provides a Natural Language dialogue to interact with the learner. This natural dialogue ability has shown to promote learner engagement resulting in positive learning gains. Research has shown that a learner's affective and behavioral states play a vital role in their overall learning experience [6]. An approximate understanding of these states can allow the system to engage learners more effectively. The terminology of "caring systems" encompasses such systems which are meta-affectively and meta-cognitively aware.

3 Negotiation-Driven Learning

This paper proposes a learning paradigm of Negotiation-Driven Learning (NDL) which aims at enhancing the role of negotiations in OLMs to facilitate constructive learning. When a learner is involved in a learning exercise, they are not only learning something new, but they are also implicitly involved in learning how to learn. NDL aims at encouraging learners to use these skills more actively and effectively. We believe that when a learner negotiates their LM with the system, they are actively involved in a dialogue, intrinsically motivated to justify their claim, hence more likely to conceive new knowledge. This provides an excellent opportunity to engage the learner in metacognitive-guided learning, where they build knowledge by actively using and enhancing their cognitive and metacognitive skills.

3.1 Proposed System

Unlike most OLM implementations, NDL allows learners to interact with the system in a Natural Language environment. The system engages the learner in a mixed-initiative dialogue session where both the learner and the system can ask and provide justification for their answers. Both parties have the capability to challenge any justification and ask for further information.

Engaging the learner in self-reflection and evaluation during and after the dialogue session trains them to use these skills more actively. NDL deploys the strategy of repetition to reinforce such skills in a learner. Encouraging self-assessment has been shown to have positive effect on learner's metacognitive abilities.

3.2 System Architecture

IBN is more suited for NDL since it allows for the parties to share information that was not available at the start of the negotiation. In order to automate the IBN in NDL, extend the model of Interest-Based Negotiation Automation [7] with the following functional components:

- *State Engine*: It generates the State Model (SM) for the learner by translating learner inputs to the corresponding affective, behavioral and metacognitive states.
- *Reasoning Engine*: uses the information from the SM in conjunction with the LM in order to select the next system move with the maximum utility. The *Context_Analyzer* submodule articulates the current context.
- *Plan Base*: holds the different negotiation moves available to the system according to the current context.
- *Dialogue Engine*: this is the core module for providing a Natural Language interface to the learner. NDL does not require a complete NLP understanding as we are interested in the concept-level cognition of the learner's input. To accomplish this, the DE consists of submodules which include; i) *Concept_Classifier*: uses a minimum-distance matcher to return a list of concept identifiers that most closely match the learner input. ii) *Normalizer*: manages stemming and spell checking for the learner input. iii) *History_Manager*: stores information about the concepts used by the system and the concepts

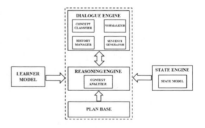

Fig. 1. Extended Interest-Based Automated Negotiation Agent

expressed by the learner. This information is passed to the RE, which uses it to classify the current context. iv) *Sentence_Generator*: uses the concepts identified along with the current context to generate a list of possible utterances of the system. These possibilities are matched with the library of template phrases and the best matching phrase is selected to generate sentences automatically.

4 Conclusion and Future Work

In this paper we proposed a paradigm of Negotiation-Driven Learning which follows the notion that learning is maximized by learner participation by exploiting opportunities provided by negotiation in OLM contexts. NDL finds its roots in the theory of repetition in learning. Continuously engaging learners in dialogue that encourage them to utilize their metacognitive abilities allows them to use such abilities more efficiently over time. Providing an NL interface to learners can ease the communication process but adds to the overall complexity. To minimize this complexity, we use the minimum-distance classifier which has been widely used for pattern recognition because it is simple and fast as compared to other complex classifiers.

Current Status: In order to realize the envisioned dialogues in NDL, a Wizard-of-Oz experiment was conducted. The goal of this experiment was to collect data in scenarios which require complex interactions between the learners and the system. The information we have gathered in the experiment has allowed us to generate rules that will power the automatic sentence generation by merging the template phrases with the concepts and context of the current interaction. We are currently acquiring rules for handling dialogues in the collected dialogues.

Future Work: Since in NDL, a dialogue is not based solely on the domain knowledge of a learner, therefore we believe that such a dialogue will have deeper implications on a learner's ability to transfer their learning skills to other domains. In order to test our hypothesis, we plan to evaluate NDL by testing the transferability of a learner's skills to a different domain.

References

1. Bull, S., Pain, H.: 'Did I Say What I Think I Said, And Do You Agree With Me?': Inspecting and Questioning the Student Model. In: Greer, J. (ed.) AIED 1995, Charlottesville VA, AACE, pp. 501–508 (1995)
2. Miao, Y.: An intelligent tutoring system using interest based negotiation. In: Control, Automation, Robotics and Vision, ICARCV (2008)
3. Bull, S., Vatrapu, R.: Negotiated Learner Models for Today. In: ICCE (2012)
4. Fisher, R., Ury, W.: Getting to Yes: Negotiating Agreement without giving in. Penguin Books, New York (1983)

5. Graesser, A. C., Lu, S., Jackson, G. T., Mitchell, H., Ventura, M., Olney, A., & Louwerse, M. M.: "AutoTutor: A tutor with dialogue in natural language". Behavior Research Methods, Instruments, and Computers 36(2), 180–193 (2004)
6. Du Boulay, B., et al.: Towards systems that care: a conceptual framework based on motivation, metacognition and affect. International Journal of Artificial Intelligence in Education **20**(3), 197–229 (2010)
7. Tao, X., Miao, Y., Shen, Z., Miao, C.Y., Yelland, N.: Interest Based Negotiation Automation. In: Huang, D.-S., Li, K., Irwin, G.W. (eds.) ICIC 2006. LNCS (LNBI), vol. 4115, pp. 211–222. Springer, Heidelberg (2006)

Supporting K-5 Learners with Dialogue Systems

Jennifer Tsan[✉] and Kristy Elizabeth Boyer

Department of Computer Science, North Carolina State University,
Raleigh, NC, USA
{jtsan,keboyer}@ncsu.edu

Abstract. Interactive learning environments have been built to support various audiences from preschool to university students. However, it is not yet known how to bring the great promise of tutorial dialogue systems, which engage students in rich natural language, to bear for young learners such as those in grades K-5. This doctoral consortium paper presents our goal of developing a dialogue system in the form of an interactive spoken dialogue agent with embedded assessment to support K-5 students in learning computer science. It discusses the challenges faced so far and how we plan to solve those challenges to bring individualized dialogue systems technology to young learners.

Keywords: Spoken dialogue · Virtual agent · Assessment

1 Introduction

As technology advances, dialogue systems are becoming more versatile with respect to their functionalities. Systems such as personal assistants on mobile devices and in video games are used daily, whether the goal is to complete a practical task or to have fun. Dialogue systems have also begun to find a place in schools where they are useful to university and high school students in their studies. Researchers are realizing that intelligent systems also have the potential to help children as young as preschoolers [3]. Learning in a classroom environment can be difficult as students often struggle with grasping concepts and mastering skills. Not only would students benefit from individualized scaffolding, but by embedding assessments into our intelligent systems we can help teachers know when students need help. We propose to build a tutorial dialogue system for elementary (primary) school students learning basic computer science concepts. Through dialogue systems, we can help students make the most of their education by building tools to better support their needs. Our work will be one of the few spoken dialogue systems for K-5 (ages 5-11) students and may be the first dialogue system with embedded assessments for this age group.

2 Related Work

This section presents a literature review of intelligent systems and conversational systems that have been built for, and piloted with, children in fifth grade and below.

© Springer International Publishing Switzerland 2015
C. Conati et al. (Eds.): AIED 2015, LNAI 9112, pp. 873–876, 2015.
DOI: 10.1007/978-3-319-19773-9_136

Marni is an animated conversational agent that helps young elementary students learn how to read [1]. Marni has interacted with approximately 1500 kindergarten through second grade students in control and experimental group classrooms. In one study, kindergarten and first grade students had greater learning gains when interacting with Marni compared to the control condition in single-word reading and letter identification. Later, Marni was adapted into a spoken dialogue tutoring system to aid upper elementary students in learning science concepts [2]. Marni uses a strategy called *Questioning the Author*, a strategy that directs students to challenge the authors' text, which helps them better understand the content by forming counterarguments. Marni is supplemented by illustrations, as well as both non-interactive animations and interactive animations. Although the authors did not report whether there were learning gains, they reported a word error rate (WER) of 27.1%, a concept recall of 0.86, and a concept precision of 0.90, suggesting that content word recognition was very accurate. Students reported a positive experience with Marni and students in low-performing schools felt Marni was helpful.

Another spoken dialogue system is Project LISTEN's Reading Tutor [6] which, like the early version of Marni, was built to help elementary students learn how to read. In a study over seven months, one group of students between first and fourth grades spent 20-25 minutes completing sustained silent reading (SSR) while the other group read with the Reading Tutor. There were 90 students in the SSR condition and 88 in the Reading Tutor condition. Various pre- and post-tests were given to the students to measure their learning gains. The authors found higher learning gains for the students in the Reading Tutor condition in many skills including Word Identification, Reading Comprehension, and Written Spelling. There was not a case where the SSR students learned more than the Reading Tutor students.

Axelsson, et al. describe a mathematics game with a teachable agent (TA) that supports preschoolers in understanding the meaning of numbers [3]. The authors conducted a study in which some students played the game that had the TA while others played the game without it. They found that the students were engaged with the game regardless of whether the TA was present or not. This suggests that the TA does not hinder preschoolers' engagement in an educational game. In addition, the authors tested the students' "theory of mind," the understanding that each individual has a different set of knowledge, and students without a fully developed "theory of mind" successfully interacted with the TA.

Developing spoken dialogue systems for young children can be difficult for many reasons: children often mispronounce words, are more spontaneous, and may find systems frustrating when misinterpreted. The ALIZ-E project produced a spoken dialogue system for young children embodied in a Nao robot [4]. The authors ensured that the natural language interpretation was robust; they trained their acoustic model on a corpus of children's speech, developed language models to recognize predefined quiz questions and answers, and implemented a fuzzy matching technique to increase the accuracy of quiz question recognition. Their dialogue manager allows users to navigate across sub-dialogues rather than remain confined in one sub-dialogue [5]. They conducted a study of the system with 19 children between the ages of 5 and 12 interacting with the Nao in one-on-one sessions for a maximum of three hours.

The average WER was 38%; improvements in automatic speech recognition (ASR) accuracy may improve the quality of the conversations.

We plan to build upon this prior work by creating a dialogue agent to support young children learning computer science. Based on prior work, we will incorporate the following design principles into the process of building our intelligent system: it will employ language models trained on a corpus of children's speech to increase ASR accuracy and concept accuracy; it will have an expressive child's voice with varied dialogue output to increase engagement; it will use pedagogical strategies such as Questioning the Author to assess students' understanding.

3   Preliminary Results

Our ultimate goal is to develop a dialogue system that supports young students in learning essential computer science concepts. We have already collected preliminary results in developing domain content for implementation within our intelligent agent. To date we have developed new 4th and 5th grade computer science curricula.

The 5th grade class based upon our preliminary work has completed two iterations during the 2014-2015 school year. The curricula was developed based on CS Principles. During each iteration, we collected data from students after receiving consent. We interviewed the students at the beginning and end of the course and collected data including videos of class participation and screen recordings of them programming. The interviews include questions about the students' motivation for taking the class, previous experiences in computer science, current attitude toward computer science, and attitude towards the class. Finally, we collected brainstorming documents from project work such as conditional trees and storyboards.

We are analyzing the data we have collected from the first two quarters of the fifth grade class. We would like to determine how much the students learned. These findings will be used to inform the design of the intelligent agents.

One challenge we faced during the pilot of the class is properly assessing the students on their knowledge and concept understanding. Each class runs for 45 minutes and students often face difficulties completing the task within the given timeframe. Depending on the activity, the students work individually, in pairs, or in groups. Although we are able to observe the students and make subjective inferences on how well they grasp each concept, we would like a formal assessment to better pinpoint their understanding. We propose the use of embedded assessment techniques within the agent to assess students' learning.

4   Project Proposal

We propose an animated virtual agent within a spoken dialogue system as a mobile app for young students for support and assessment of computer science learning. The agent will be designed to appear similar in age to the students and will converse with the students as a peer; this interaction is more natural to children than speaking to an investigator. Our overarching research questions are as follows:

- How can we build embedded assessment to measure elementary students' comprehension of a subject using an animated virtual agent?
- Which spoken dialogue strategies can be successfully used as embedded assessment techniques to assess elementary students' knowledge?

We will begin by building a simple dialogue system that will implement a Wizard-of-Oz approach. This app will converse with the children about computer science. The system's utterances will be generated by a wizard based on the system's ASR. During the study we will record the children's speech, the ASR interpretation of the speech, and the wizard's response to the interpretations. The first iteration will allow us to refine the techniques that evaluate the students' knowledge, and understanding via embedded assessment. Techniques we will use include self-explanation, and having the student and system quiz each other. This iterative cycle of research and development is expected to yield significant insight into how very young learners reach an understanding of computer science through interaction with a virtual agent. Moreover, the research results will shed light on dialogue strategies and embedded assessment approaches for these very young learners.

Acknowledgements. This work is supported in part by the Wake County Public School System.

References

1. Cole, R., Wise, B., Vuuren, S.V.: How Marni Teaches Children to Read. Educational Technology **47**(1), 14–18 (2006)
2. Ward, W., Cole, R., Bolaños, B., Buchenroth-Martin, C., Svirsky, E., Vuuren, S.V., Weston, T., Zheng, J., Becker, L.: My Science Tutor: A Conversational Multimedia Virtual Tutor for Elementary School Science. ACM Transactions on Speech and Language Processing **7**(4), 1–29 (2011)
3. Axelsson, A., Anderberg, E., Haake, M.: Can preschoolers profit from a teachable agent based play-and-learn game in mathematics? In: Lane, H., Yacef, K., Mostow, J., Pavlik, P. (eds.) AIED 2013. LNCS, vol. 7926, pp. 289–298. Springer, Heidelberg (2013)
4. Kruijff-korbayov, I., Cuayahuitl, H., Kiefer, B., Schroder, M., Cosi, P., Paci, G., Sommavilla, G., et al.: Spoken language processing in a conversational system for child-robot interaction. In: Proceedings of INTERSPEECH, pp. 33–40 (2012)
5. Cuayahuitl, H., Kruijff-korbayov, I.: An interactive humanoid robot exhibiting flexible sub-dialogues. In: Proceedings of NAACL-HLT, pp. 17–20 (2012)
6. Mostow, J., Nelson-Taylor, J., Beck, J.E.: Computer-Guided Oral Reading versus Independent Practice: Comparison of Sustained Silent Reading to an Automated Reading Tutor That Listens. Jl. of Educational Computing Research **49**(2), 249–276 (2013)

Sharing Student Models That Use Machine Learning

Benjamin Valdes[(⊠)], Carlos Ramirez, and Jorge Ramirez

Tec de Monterrey Campus Estado de Mxico,
Carr. Lago de Guadalupe Km. 3.5, 52926 Atizapan de Zaragoza, Mexico
bvaldesa@itesm.mx

Abstract. Sharing student models has long been a problem of interest for the AIED community. Current proposals can use student models that use machine learning, but can't modify them. We propose a multi-agent architecture for decoupled student models that enables machine learning components to: train with different data, choose what data is more reliable, and to compensate in case its sources of information are missing. The architecture uses a fragmented user model approach. The expected contributions are the architecture for sharing student models and its implementation, guidelines for decoupling or extracting implemented models from intelligent tutoring systems and intelligent learning environments, and an analysis of the portability of current state of the art student models.

1 The Problem of Sharing Student Models

Sharing student models SM has long been a problem of interest for the AIED community [5,6,11,12]. By sharing we mean re-utilization of implemented SM. Despite the research in the area there is still little reuse of SM. Traditionally, most Intelligent Tutoring Systems ITS and Intelligent Learning Environments ILE have been built in one of the 3 ways:

1. Complete implementation with no re-utilization. Which demands a significant amount of work, but continues to be done by researchers who do not have access to authoring tools or finished tutors which they can extend.
2. From authoring tools. Which limits the flexibility of the student model to the preconceived shell of the tool (see [8] for a survey).
3. As an extension to previous ITS or ILE [1], which implies that the model can only be used with that ITS.

Approaches which are becoming popular are:

1. The reimplementation of SM in other systems, like those used in the area of affective modeling [10].
2. Standalone models from the area of Educational Data Mining EDM. These are models which have not been integrated into any ITS or ILE.

© Springer International Publishing Switzerland 2015
C. Conati et al. (Eds.): AIED 2015, LNAI 9112, pp. 877–880, 2015.
DOI: 10.1007/978-3-319-19773-9_137

In theory most SMs could be decoupled since ITSs should have modular architectures [9]. In practice ITS are implemented as closed environments, i.e., the tutor, the student model, and the application are tightly coupled. By tightly coupled we mean that parts of the system have dependencies that complicate modularization. If an ITS developer would like to use the tutor to provide assistance in another application, or use the student model to generate a diagnostic in a different environment, a significant amount of work would be needed; that is, if it could be done at all.

We now present the most flexible approaches to share student models. Ritter and Koedinger [11] developed Plug-In tutor agents, which is an architecture for embedding reusable agents in traditional software to generate adaptive behaviors. Vassileva, Mccalla and Greer [12] developed I-help, a multi-agent multi-user system, where each user has its model represented by a group of agents, i.e., a fragmented student model. The agents in the system share the information of the student to perform matches between students and learning tools. Heckmann [5] proposed and developed a ubiquitous user modeling system, which creates a semantically organized repository of user models, and queries it using inference engines to generate views which could be presented as situational models. Lorenz [7] proposed an agent based architecture for integrating ubiquitous user model, the approach is similar to [5] in its goal, but it uses the approach of [12]. Carmagnola and Dimitrova [2] developed a series of algorithms to share user model information and preserve the models semantic attributes, i.e., context. The approach requires previous definition of the semantic properties in Resource Description Format RDF tags. Cena and Furnari [3] propose an approach similar to [5], where a centralized server semantically manages user models to present them as web services. Several of these proposals mention machine learning, but they do not contemplate aspects such as training or tuning the models. The ones that mention machine learning assume that SM wont be updated, or that they will be updated in their external native systems [5]. This means that the models will remain coupled within their ITS or ILE, will not be able to train with other data, and will constantly depend on the original system for access. In other words, the model is not shared, it is only queried. Machine learning is important because the models that are more likely to be reused use machine learning.

A system for sharing user models should be able to:

1. represent models from heterogeneous sources without losing information [2,5,12].
2. be distributed, i.e., not be restricted to a central location [2,5,6,12].
3. connect with other systems for it to be reused [2,5,11,12].
4. represent advanced modeling techniques (machine learning) [12].
5. have mechanisms to modify the on going models [5].
6. compensate when some of its models are missing [5,12].
7. store fragmented SM, i.e., allow for several models representing different parts of the student to work together [2,12].

2   Proposed Solution and Methodology

Our proposal is to:

- create a multi-agent architecture where decoupled SM can search for the resources to train/update itself. The architecture would use a fragmented user model approach where each student model would be encased in an agent similar to [12]. In our approach every model is a black box. The agent that encases the model is responsible for finding and obtaining training sources for its model through a blackboard architecture, answering queries made to the model, and updating its current status in the blackboard. The interfaces between the models and the systems are the agents? intercommunication protocols.
- to implement the architecture using an well known open standard (FIPA), so it can connect with external applications through agent communication protocols or web services. To implement the agent architecture Java Agent Development Environment (JADE) is used because the framework already incorporates FIPA communications protocols.
- to analyse which types of SM (a review can be found in [4]) can be shared through my approach and what are the trade-offs involved. It is our belief that SM with less domain dependence will be easier to decouple than domain dependent SM. By domain we mean academic concepts and knowledge, for instance math or physics. Affect, motivation, and engagement models present a higher domain independence than constraint, skill, and sequential models, because the first are related with personal traits and the second with abstract definition defined in a collective way i.e. consensus. It should be said that complete domain dependence in SM is very rate.
- to develop an easy to use system for other authors to replicate their models so they can be used by other environments.

3   Contribution(s) of the Research

The two expected contributions to the AIED community are:

- The architecture for sharing SM including those that have machine learning components. This would include re-implementation guidelines as to how to decouple SM from their ITS or ILE, as well as the interaction protocols between the agents design for choosing the better source of information.
- A study of the portability of current SM. Which will allow better understanding of what can be shared or reused in intelligent software for education.

4   Plans to Advance the Research Program

We have already finished our study of student model portability, from which we are selecting models to attempt to integrate. We have implemented a prototype of the architecture using the Java Agent Development Environment (JADE), and we are currently extracting SM from existing software and reimplementing them into our system. From this, we are learning what other traits are desirable in SM to make them more shareable, and what modifications the system requires. We work in an iterative loop and document it, to extract from there the guidelines for decoupling SM. We plan to test the system with 3 different SM as a proof of concept, and to run simulated tutors to measure system performance. We aim to release the implemented architecture online, so other researchers can access the models we have re-implemented and upload their own models as well.

References

1. Beck, J.E., Woolf, B.P.: Reasoning from data rather than theory. In: Proceedings of the Thirteenth International Florida Artificial Intelligence Research Symposium, Florida (2000)
2. Carmagnola, F., Dimitrova, V.: An evidence-based approach to handle semantic heterogeneity in interoperable distributed user models. In: Nejdl, W., Kay, J., Pu, P., Herder, E. (eds.) AH 2008. LNCS, vol. 5149, pp. 73–82. Springer, Heidelberg (2008)
3. Cena, F., Furnari, R.: A model for feature-based user model interoperability on the web. In: Kuflik, T., Berkovsky, S., Carmagnola, F., Heckmann, D., Krüger, A. (eds.) Advances in Ubiquitous User Modelling. LNCS, vol. 5830, pp. 37–54. Springer, Heidelberg (2009)
4. Desmarais, M.C., Baker, R.S.J.D.: A review of recent advances in learner and skill modeling in intelligent learning environments. User Modeling and User-Adapted Interaction **22**(1–2), 9–38 (2011)
5. Heckmann, D.: Ubiquitous User Modeling, vol. 297. IOS Press (2005)
6. Kobsa, A.: Generic User Modeling Systems. User Modeling and User-Adapted Interaction **11**, 49–63 (2001)
7. Lorenz, A.: Agent-based ubiquitous user modeling. In: Ardissono, L., Brna, P., Mitrovic, A. (eds.) UM 2005. LNCS, vol. 3538, pp. 512–514. Springer, Heidelberg (2005)
8. Murray, T.: Authoring Intelligent Tutoring Systems : An Analysis of the State of the Art. International Journal of Artificial Intelligence in Education **10**, 98–129 (1999)
9. Nwana, H.S.: Intelligent tutoring systems: an overview. Artificial Intelligence Review **4**(4), 251–277 (1990)
10. San Pedro, M.O.Z., Baker, R.S.J., Gowda, S.M., Heffernan, N.T.: Towards an Understanding of Affect and Knowledge from Student Interaction with an Intelligent Tutoring System. In: Lane, H.C., Yacef, K., Mostow, J., Pavlik, P. (eds.) AIED 2013. LNCS, vol. 7926, pp. 41–50. Springer, Heidelberg (2013)
11. Ritter, S., Koedinger, K.R.: An architecture for plug-in tutor agents. Artificial Intelligence in Education **7**(3–4), 315–347 (1996)
12. Vassileva, J., Mccalla, G., Greer, J.: Multi-agent multi-user modeling in I-Help. User Modeling and User-Adapted, 179–210 (2003)

Workshop Abstracts

2nd Workshop on Simulated Learners

John Champaign[1] and Gord McCalla[2]

[1] University of Illinois at Springfield, Springfield, IL
[2] University of Saskatchewan, Saskatoon, SK, Canada
https://sites.google.com/site/simulatedlearners/

1   Workshop Goals and Themes

This workshop, a follow-up to the successful first Simulated Learners workshop held at AIED 2013, is intended to bring together researchers who are interested in simulated learners, whatever their role in the design, development, deployment, or evaluation of learning systems. Its novel aspect is that it isn't simply a workshop about pedagogical agents, but instead focuses on the other roles for simulated learners in helping system designers, teachers, instructional designers, etc.

As learning environments become increasingly complex and are used by growing numbers of learners (sometimes in the hundreds of thousands) and apply to a larger range of domains, the need for simulated learners (and simulation more generally) is compelling, not only to enhance these environments with artificial agents, but also to explore issues using simulation that would be otherwise be too expensive, too time consuming, or even impossible using human subjects. While some may feel that MOOCs provide ample data for experimental purposes, it is hard to test specific hypotheses about particular technological features with data gathered for another purpose. Moreover, privacy concerns, ethics approval, attrition rates and platform constraints can all be barriers to this approach. Finally, with thousands of learners at stake, it is wise to test a learning environment as thoroughly as possible before deployment.

Since this is a follow-up to the 2013 workshop, we build on some of the ideas that emerged there (see proceedings at: http://goo.gl/12ODji).

The workshop explores these and other issues with the goal of further understanding the roles that simulated learners may play in advanced learning technology research and development, and in deployed learning systems.

© Springer International Publishing Switzerland 2015
C. Conati et al. (Eds.): AIED 2015, LNAI 9112, p. 883, 2015.
DOI: 10.1007/978-3-319-19773-9

4th Workshop on
Intelligent Support for Learning in Groups

Ilya Goldin[1], Roberto Martinez-Maldonado[2], Erin Walker[3],
Rohit Kumar[4], and Jihie Kim[5]

[1] Center for Digital Data, Analytics, and Adaptive Learning, Pearson, USA
[2] School of Information Technologies, University of Sydney, Australia
[3] Computing, Informatics, and Decision Systems Engineering, Arizona State University, USA
[4] Raytheon BBN Technologies, USA
[5] Software R&D Center, Samsung Electronic, South Korea
ilya.goldin@pearson.com, roberto@it.usyd.edu.au,
erin.a.walker@asu.edu, rkumar@bbn.com, jihie.kim@gmail.com

Technological advances in the use of artificial intelligence in education (AIED) over the past two decades have enabled the development of highly effective, deployable learning environments that support learners across a wide range of domains and age groups. Alongside, mass access to and adoption of modern communication technologies have made it possible to bridge learners and educators across spatiotemporal divides. Students can now collaborate using educational technology in ways that were not previously possible.

Intelligent tutoring systems seek to individualize each student's learning experience, but this need not imply a solitary experience. Research on computer-supported collaborative learning (CSCL) has revealed the pedagogical benefits of learning in groups, as well as how to structure the activity to lead to productive interactions. A variety of recent systems have demonstrated ways in which an adaptive learning environment can benefit from the presence of multiple learners. Similarly, students using CSCL systems have been shown to benefit from the introduction of adaptive support. It is of high relevance to the AIED community to explore how AI techniques can be used to support collaborative learning, and how theories of how students learn in groups can inform the design of adaptive educational technologies.

The goal of this series of workshops is to gather the sub-community of AIED researchers interested in intelligent support for learning in groups with learning scientists to share approaches and exchange information about adaptive intelligent collaborative learning support. We invite discussion on how the combination of collaborative and intelligent aspects of a system can benefit the learner by creating a more productive environment. Over the past few years, the AIED research community has started investigating extension of the fundamental techniques (student modeling, model-based tutors, integrated assessment, tutorial dialog, automated scaffolding, data mining, pedagogical agents, and so on) to support collaborative learning. We aim to explore ways that the current state of the art in intelligent support for learning in groups can be informed by learning sciences research on collaborative learning principles.

© Springer International Publishing Switzerland 2015
C. Conati et al. (Eds.): AIED 2015, LNAI 9112, p. 884, 2015.
DOI: 10.1007/978-3-319-19773-9

Workshop on Developing a Generalized Intelligent Framework for Tutoring (GIFT): Informing Design Through a Community of Practice

Benjamin Goldberg[1], Robert Sottilare[1], Anne Sinatra[1],
Keith Brawner[1], and Scott Ososky[1,2]

[1] U.S. Army Research Laboratory, Orlando, FL 32826
[2] Oak Ridge Associated Universities, Oak Ridge, TN 37830
https://giftutoring.org/

1   Workshop Goals and Themes

The purpose of this workshop is to examine current research within the AIED community focused on improving adaptive tools and methods for authoring, automated instruction and evaluation associated with the Generalized Intelligent Framework for Tutoring (GIFT). As GIFT is an open source architecture used to build and deliver adaptive functions in computer-based learning environments (Sottilare, Brawner, Goldberg & Holden, 2013), this workshop aids in gathering feature requirements from the field and addressing issues to better support future users.

The topics of interest highlight current research conducted within the GIFT community (i.e., 400+ users in 30+ countries) across three themes: (1) modeling across affect, metacogntion, teams, and experts; (2) tutorial intervention through communication, guidance, and sequencing; and (3) persistence functions of intelligent tutoring associated with compctency modeling and social media. Each theme will be comprised of short papers describing capability enhancements to the GIFT architecture, the motivation behind the described work, and considerations associated with its implementation. Paper presentations are organized to provide attendees with an interactive experience through hands-on demonstrations.

For attendees unfamiliar with GIFT and its project goals, this workshop exposes those individuals to the GIFT architectural structure, enabling participants to learn how to construct original functions, and how the framework can be applied to their own research. The intent is to engage the AIED community in an in-depth exploration of the various research topics being investigated and the potential leveraging and collaboration that a community framework such as GIFT affords.

Reference

1. Sottilare, R., Brawner, K. W., Goldberg, B., & Holden, H. (2013). The Generalized Intelligent Framework for Tutoring (GIFT). In C. Best, G. Galanis, J. Kerry & R. Sottilare (Eds.), *Fundamental Issues in Defense Training and Simulation* (pp. 223-234). Burlington, VT: Ashgate Publishing Company.

© Springer International Publishing Switzerland 2015
C. Conati et al. (Eds.): AIED 2015, LNAI 9112, p. 885, 2015.
DOI: 10.1007/978-3-319-19773-9

Learning Analytics for Project Based and Experiential Learning Scenarios

Rose Luckin[1], Manolis Mavrikis[1] and Daniel Spikol[2]

[1] The London Knowledge Lab
UCL Institute of Education London
[2] Malmö University
r.luckin@ioe.ac.uk

The migration of technology from the desktop to the wider learning environment provides the opportunity to collect data about learners' interactions with a greater bandwidth of learning resources. Smart phones, tablets and technologies embedded in the fabric of the environment are now commonplace in educational settings. In parallel with these developments, there has been great progress in developing the techniques that can be applied to the large amount of data that is generated to analyse learning interactions. The use of this kind of learning analytics offers the potential for the design of novel feedback and scaffolding to support project based and experiential learning that involves multiple technologies. These learning activities can be centred on physical computing projects and other hands-on type projects. The AIED community has a long history of designing systems that offer timely interventions to learners to support their interactions; it has also much to offer to those interested in the potentials obtained by large data sets, ubiquitous technologies and learning analytics. The presentations and discussions at this workshop tackle issues that are at the heart of the AIED community's interest.

The workshop will be structured according to 5 themes and will consist of a combination of short presentations, identified through paper submissions, and facilitated discussion. The themes are as follows:

- Theoretical Foundations
- Technologies
- Research Methods (including considerations for Privacy and Ethics)
- Learning Analytic techniques and visualizations
- Using learning analytics to scaffold students' learning.

Format of the Workshop

The format of the workshop will be organized around questions emerging from the 5 themes that will be followed by lively discussions during the workshop (rather than a small conference or symposium). This involves online discussions on the papers before the workshop and very short presentations of the submitted papers at the first half of the workshop. This is followed by group discussions ensuring that all participants can have a direct impact in addressing the workshop themes and questions.

© Springer International Publishing Switzerland 2015
C. Conati et al. (Eds.): AIED 2015, LNAI 9112, p. 886, 2015.
DOI: 10.1007/978-3-319-19773-9

6th International Workshop on Intelligent Support in Exploratory and Open-Ended Learning Environments

Manolis Mavrikis[1], Gautam Biswas[2], Sergio Gutierrez-Santos[3],
Toby Dragon[4], and James Segedy[2]

[1] London Knowledge Lab, UCL Institute of Education, University College London
[2] Electrical Engineering and Computer Science, Vanderbilt University
[3] London Knowledge Lab, School of Computer Science, Birkbeck
[4] Department of Computer Science, Ithaca College, US
m.mavrikis@lkl.ac.uk

By encouraging interaction, exploration and experimentation in environments that directly represent the domain to the learner, Exploratory Learning Environments (ELE) adhere to constructivist theories of learning that emphasise learners' control to construct their own understanding. More generally, Open-ended Learning environments (OLEs) offer students opportunities to take part in authentic and complex problem-solving and inquiry learning activities. This could be by providing a learning context and a set of tools for (i) seeking and acquiring knowledge and information, (ii) applying that information to a problem-solving context, (iii) assessing the quality of the constructed solution, (iv) evaluating and reflecting on their overall approach, and (v) assessing and enacting cognitive and metacognitive processes.

However, there are several factors that prevent appropriate learning within an exploratory learning environment. The structure of the activity sequences and the level of support by teachers, peers, technologies are crucial determinants of learning. This is particularly true in domains where knowledge is not a directly observable outcome of a situation under exploration (e.g. simulators) but is externalised by cognitive tools in the environment. There has been a lot of work in the learning sciences literature about support for learning in exploratory environments, but developing the technology to support these learning processes still faces several impressive challenges that the community is only beginning to address.

The papers submitted to the workshop address challenges that are relevant to the broad and interdisciplinary AIED and EDM community. This workshop builds on the work done in several editions of the Intelligent Support in Exploratory Environments[1] workshop and the Scaffolding in Open-Ended Learning Environments in AIED 2013. One our website http://link.lkl.ac.uk/iseole15 you can find more information and previous papers on the following illustrative topics: Pedagogical Strategies, Classroom integration, Learning analytics for teachers, EDM approaches, Learner Modelling and Open Learner Modelling, Support for Collaboration and Group Modelling, Authoring tools for feedback, Innovative frameworks or techniques for support, which we will address in the context of Exploratory and Open-Ended environments.

The format of the workshop is based on a question-oriented organisation around open problems raised by the papers accepted for the workshop.

---

[1] The proceedings from this and previous workshop are available at http://link.lkl.ac.uk/isee

© Springer International Publishing Switzerland 2015
C. Conati et al. (Eds.): AIED 2015, LNAI 9112, p. 887, 2015.
DOI: 10.1007/978-3-319-19773-9

6th International Workshop on Culturally-Aware Tutoring Systems (CATS2015)

Ma Mercedes T. Rodrigo[1], Emmanuel G. Blanchard[2],
Amy Ogan[3], and Isabela Gasparini[4]

[1] Ateneo de Manila University, Philippines
mrodrigo@ateneo.edu
[2] IDÛ Interactive, Montreal, Canada
ebl@idu-interactive.com
[3] Carnegie Mellon University, USA
aeo@cs.cmu.edu
[4] University of Santa Catarina State (UDESC), Brazil
isabela.gasparini@udesc.br

Culture has a profound effect on the way people interact with, react to, think and feel about knowledge, symbols, situations, etc. Yet it is underestimated in AIED research. Most of the currently influential learning systems have indeed been created by and for developed world contexts and with Western cultural perspectives in mind. However in recent years, more and more opportunities to design, develop, and deploy educational software for and in different contexts have emerged. This state of affairs naturally leads to broader questions. What features of culture are important to consider in the design process? Can software designed and developed in a specific cultural context transfer to other parts of the world and remain effective? The answers to these questions remain unclear although a growing body of research suggests that the use of AIED systems across cultural contexts results in variations of the knowledge acquisition process.

Over the last seven years, Culturally-Aware Tutoring Systems (CATS) workshops have been organized in conjunction with ITS2008, AIED2009, ITS2010, AIED2013, and ITS2014. The series is a venue for researchers to reflect on the universality of their work. CATS2015 thus proposes to discuss culture and AIED from five perspectives:

1. Developing both pedagogical strategies and system infrastructure mechanisms that incorporate cultural features to enculturate AIED systems;
2. Designing acquisition-oriented CATS, i.e. AIED systems to teach cultural knowledge and intercultural skills;
3. Designing adaptation-oriented CATS, i.e. AIED systems that can be personalized overtly or automatically based on users' cultural profiles;
4. Considering human features that are connected with the learning process, and that are culturally-sensitive, e.g. affect, behavior, cognition, or motivation; and
5. Considering cultural biases in the AIED research cycle.

In addition to describing the current state of the art in these domains, the workshop intends to engage participants in working to expand the reach of AIED research to a greater global audience, including those disadvantaged due to a lack of resources or other obstacles.

© Springer International Publishing Switzerland 2015
C. Conati et al. (Eds.): AIED 2015, LNAI 9112, p. 888, 2015.
DOI: 10.1007/978-3-319-19773-9

Workshop on Les Contes du Mariage:
Should AI Stay Married to Ed?

Kaska Porayska-Pomsta,[1] Gord McCalla[2], and Benedict du Boulay[3]

[1] University College, London, WC1H 0AL, UK
[2] University of Saskatchewan, Saskatoon, SK S7N 5A5, Canada
[3] University of Sussex, Brighton, BN1 9QJ, UK
www.sussex.ac.uk/Users/bend/aied2015/

At its origin, the field of Artificial Intelligence in Education (AIEd) aimed to employ Artificial Intelligence techniques in the design of computer systems for learning. The 25th anniversary of the IJAIEd is a good opportunity to interrogate the aims and aspirations of the field, its past and current achievements, while the AIED conference constitutes a timely forum for such an interrogation. This workshop explores questions such as:

- What is and what should be the role of AI in Education and conversely of Education in AI? Specifically, in the early days of AIED there seemed to be lots of AI in AIED, but now AI is more often a placeholder for any kind of advanced technology.
- What is and what should be the motivation of AIEd as a field? Supporting learning has been considered a great "challenge domain" for AI in that many of the big AI questions must be answered, at least to some extent, to build a sophisticated learning environment. But, it seems that the ideas generated in AIED are neither influencing AI nor Education in any serious way. Why not?
- What is and what should be the balance of respective contributions to AIED from AI and Education as distinct fields of research and practice? Both fields have well-established methodologies and practices, but the extent to which these are cross-fertilising under AIED is not clear.
- A related question relates to the extent to which the results of AIEd research are meaningful to real educational practices? Does the community even care?
- What are the future directions for the field that could justify and maintain its unique identity? How does AIED differ from related disciplines such as Learning Sciences, ITS, and CSCL? Or are these just labels for essentially the same research discipline?

© Springer International Publishing Switzerland 2015
C. Conati et al. (Eds.): AIED 2015, LNAI 9112, p. 889, 2015.
DOI: 10.1007/978-3-319-19773-9

International Workshop on Affect, Meta-Affect, Data and Learning (AMADL 2015)

Genaro Rebolledo-Mendez[1], Manolis Mavrikis[2], Olga C. Santos[3],
Benedict du Boulay[4], Beate Grawemeyer[5], and Rafael Rojano-Cáceres[1]

[1] Facultad de Estadística e Informática, University of Veracruz
[2] London Knowledge Lab, UCL Institute of Education, University College London
[3] aDeNu Research Group. Artificial Intelligence Department, UNED
[4] School of Science and Technology, University of Sussex
[5] London Knowledge Lab, School of Computer Science, Birkbeck
grebolledo@uv.mx, m.mavrikis@ioe.ac.uk, ocsantos@dia.uned.es,
b.du-boulay@sussex.ac.uk, beate@dcs.bbk.ac.uk, rrojano@uv.mx

1   Workshop Description

Emotions and affect play an important role in learning. There are indications that meta-affect (i.e., knowledge about self-affect) also plays a role. There have been various attempts to take them into account both during the design and during the deployment of AIED systems. The evidence for the consequential impact on learning is beginning to strengthen, but the field has been mostly focused on addressing the complexities of affective and emotional recognition and very little on how to intervene. This has largely slowed down progress in this area.

Research is needed to better understand how to respond to what we detect and how to relate that to the learner's cognitive and meta-cognitive skills. One goal might be to design systems capable of recognizing, acknowledging, and responding to learners' states with the aim of promoting those that are conducive to learning by means of tutorial tactics, feedback interventions, and interface adaptations that take advantage of ambient intelligence, among others. Therefore, we need to deepen our knowledge of how changes in learners' affective states and associated emotions relate to issues such as cognition and the learning context.

The papers submitted to the workshop address issues that bridge the existing gap between previous research with the ever-increasing understanding and data availability. In particular, these papers report progress on issues relevant to the broad and interdisciplinary AIED and EDM communities. AMADL 2015 workshop raises the opportunity to bring these two communities together in a lively discussion about the overlap in the two fields. To achieve this, we explicitly address and target both communities, as indicated by the workshop's organizers background and the programme committee set up. This workshop builds on the work done in affect related workshops in past AIED conferences, such as Modelling and Scaffolding Affective Experiences to Impact Learning in AIED 2007. The format of the workshop is based on presentations, demonstrations and discussions according to themes addressed by the papers accepted for the workshop.

© Springer International Publishing Switzerland 2015
C. Conati et al. (Eds.): AIED 2015, LNAI 9112, p. 890, 2015.
DOI: 10.1007/978-3-319-19773-9

Industry Track Papers

TutorGen: A Carnegie Mellon Start-Up for Providing Adaptive Learning at Scale

Ted Carmichael[1], Mary Jean Blink[1], and John C. Stamper[1,2]

[1] TutorGen, Inc., Wexford, PA, USA
{tcarmichael,mjblink}@tutorgen.com
[2] Carnegie Mellon University, Pittsburgh, PA, USA
jstamper@cs.cmu.edu

1   Products and Services

TutorGen works at the intersection of the Educational Systems, *Big Data,* and Computer Science to enhance student learning and support teacher and administrator assessment and management of student learning. We are engaged in three distinct markets: K-12, Higher Education, and Corporate/Government Training. Penetration of these markets varies greatly as the point of entry differs in each market. Ultimately, the end-user of our systems is the *learner*, but the learner is not the only beneficiary. We provide value along the value-chain, from the software developer, content developer, instructor, educational administrator, and ultimately the learner. The extensive analytical tools we are developing help content and software developers analyze the results of their systems and content to identify potential improvements and ensure accurate skill tracking. Further, visualization tools are provided to instructors and administrators to track the effectiveness of student learning and provide opportunities for input based on specialized knowledge of particular student populations.

2   Corporate Background

TutorGen (http://www.tutorgen.com) is a Carnegie Mellon University startup established in 2012 by Dr. John Stamper to make adaptive learning widely available regardless of the domain or industry segment. By combining development both internally and through strategic partnerships with academic institutions and research organizations, TutorGen works to develop systems that translate published results into marketable products and services. We are building the company as a lean startup working to develop commercial products through various small business funding opportunities (SBIR/STTR), providing consulting services in our areas of expertise, and participating in various related development and research projects. There are currently two Phase I grants underway and a Phase I and Phase II grant under review.

© Springer International Publishing Switzerland 2015
C. Conati et al. (Eds.): AIED 2015, LNAI 9112, pp. 893–894, 2015.
DOI: 10.1007/978-3-319-19773-9

3   Innovation – SCALE: Student Centered Adaptive Learning Engine

SCALE, TutorGen's flagship product, is an NSF-funded project for building a system that will provide a personalized learning experience for students using educational software. This technology can learn from the students themselves and improve over time using data-driven methodologies and a human-centered approach. SCALE has been successfully prototyped and is currently in the full development stage.

While it is known that personalized educational software is more effective, it is rarely implemented due to traditionally high costs of content development. The established players in our three target sectors do not widely provide adaptive functionality because of the difficulty and costs inherent in the development process, as this requires experts to understand not only the subject material, but also the underlying processes used to give help and feedback. Further, there has been little crossover of adaptive capabilities or student models from one ITS to another, even in the same domain. Each ITS therefore has required a custom approach, adding to development costs. TutorGen's previous research and Phase I SCALE project have shown that the development of intelligent tutors can be streamlined by using available data collected from students solving problems. Large data repositories such as the Pittsburgh Science of Learning Center (PSLC) DataShop have been created to store and analyze these data. Data-driven methods applied to these data repositories can enable the rapid creation of new intelligent tutoring systems, making them accessible for many more students. TutorGen's work in the automatic discovery of student models and intelligent tutoring capabilities lay the foundation for TutorGen's SCALE solution.

TutorGen's SCALE will include the following key components (1) – (5):

(1) **Databases, DataConnector Adapter,** and **DataConnector Library:** Allow developers of educational software to easily connect to SCALE for data logging.

(2) **Tutor Engine:** Uses educational data mining on logged data to automatically generate student models, or improve existing ones.

(3) **Problem Selection / Hint and Feedback Handler:** Uses student models to dynamically select students' next problems to minimize time needed to master skills. Provides context specific, just-in-time hints for multi-step problems through the ITS.

(4) **Assessment and Support Tools:** Allows educators to view students' progress as well as annotate, improve, and/or customize the student models.

(5) **Developer Improvement Interface and Tools:** SCALE provides an interface for developers of the educational technology to improve their systems by identifying areas where the data does not fit the models or not enough data is being collected.

SCALE provides machine learning techniques and algorithms, based on award winning, cutting edge research, that dramatically reduce the cost of development and thereby allow the widespread implementation of truly adaptive computer-based training.

Differentiation and Mastery Learning in Practice: Metrics and Visualizations for Cognitive Tutor Algebra

Stephen E. Fancsali, Ambarish Joshi, and Steven Ritter

Carnegie Learning, Inc.
437 Grant Street, 20th Floor
Pittsburgh, PA 15219, USA
{sfancsali,ajoshi,sritter}@carnegielearning.com

Abstract. We provide metrics and visualizations to illustrate learner progress through mathematics curricula in real-world classrooms that, to greater and lesser extents, allow for the differentiation affordances provided by the Cognitive Tutor intelligent tutoring system to guide that progress.

1 Carnegie Learning and Cognitive Tutor

Carnegie Learning is a leading developer of research-driven, blended curricula for mathematics. Its flagship software, the Cognitive Tutor (CT) intelligent tutoring system (ITS) [1], is used by over 600,000 learners each year in grades 6 through 12 in the United States and abroad, as well as increasingly by higher education learners. CT atomizes mathematics content knowledge in domains like algebra into fine-grained knowledge components (KCs) or skills and probabilistically models learner progress to mastery of KCs as they work multi-step problems in the ITS using a framework called Bayesian Knowledge Tracing (BKT) [2]. CT implements mastery learning (e.g., [3]) by requiring learners to demonstrate mastery of a particular set of KCs by practicing them on adaptively presented problems in each topical section of mathematics course content (comprising broader curricular units, which comprise course modules).

2 Differentiation via Mastery Learning

CT differentiates instruction for learners in a particular mathematics class; students are likely to master mathematics skills at their own pace, and CT provides for efficient instruction and practice that does not "waste" time on skills learners already know. However, CT is used in real-world classrooms in a variety of ways, some of which may not take advantage of such affordances for genuine differentiation. Teachers, for example, may feel uncomfortable with learners in a computer lab all working on different units of mathematics content, despite the fact that this might be a natural situation and beneficial for learning, given different rates at which students learn.

© Springer International Publishing Switzerland 2015
C. Conati et al. (Eds.): AIED 2015, LNAI 9112, pp. 895–896, 2015.
DOI: 10.1007/978-3-319-19773-9

3   Visualization and Metric

Fig. 1 illustrates elements of differentiation in two classes that use Carnegie Learn-ing's CT-based product for middle school math, MATHia. The graph on the left rep-resents a class that is not especially differentiated with respect to learners progressing (represented by usage hours) through course modules (represented by different col-ors); learners are in roughly one to four different course modules in a given week, most likely because an instructor seeks to keep learners "on the same page." The class on the right is highly differentiated with learners in many different course modules in a given week. While these visualizations provide an intuition that one class is better differentiated than the other, empirical error rates (median error rate per problem per hour over the academic year) (Fig. 2) are consistent with expectations provided by [1]: less differentiated learners have greater variability in error rates (red) compared to the relatively constant error rate (blue) observed in the differentiated class. As learn-ers progress through adaptively presented material of appropriate difficulty, we expect a relatively constant error rate. On-going research explores such visualizations and metrics to assess differentiation in real classrooms and to help teachers and stakehold-ers understand the importance of such differentiation.

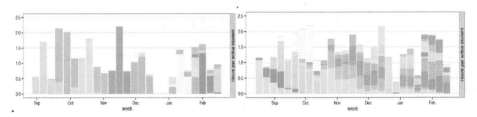

Fig. 1. "Blocked" class (left) with little differentiation vs. "Waves" class (right) with extensive differentiation. Colored blocks represent usage time in different course modules.

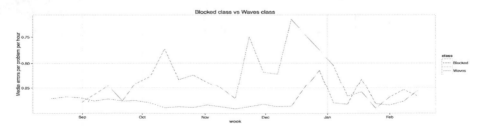

Fig. 2. Error rates (median error per problem per hour) for "Blocked" (red) & "Waves" (blue) classes over academic year

References

1. Ritter, S., Anderson, J.R., Koedinger, K.R., Corbett, A.: Cognitive tutor: Applied research in mathematics education. Psychonomic Bulletin & Review 14, 249–255 (2007)
2. Corbett, A.T., Anderson, J.R.: Knowledge tracing: Modeling the acquisition of procedural knowledge. User-Modeling and User-Adapted Interaction 4, 253–278 (1995)
3. Bloom, B.S.: Human characteristics and school learning. McGraw-Hill, New York (1976)

SMARTICK: Adaptive, Online, One-Pace-Fits-All System

Miguel Ángel Monje, Adriano Pezzi, Tania Alonso, and Javier Arroyo

Smartick
miguel@pajarita.org,
{adriano.pezzi,tania.alonso,javier.arroyo}@smartick.es

Abstract. Smartick is an online Math learning method, adaptive to levels and needs of individual students from 4 to 14 years old, regardless of their curricular age or achievement. Thus, Smartick develops through daily sessions of 15 minutes the mathematical competence of each student as well as the related cognitive training. It can be used both at school and home.

1 Introduction

Our interest started with the need to increase achievements in math, attention, memory, reasoning skills, willpower and motivation onto disliked subjects and reduction of extra-school supplementary costs. As for school teachers, we aim to help tackling the issue of student diversity in knowledge and capabilities at all levels. In addition, following the guidelines1 of the EU policy makers, reducing the UE 22% of students with low math performance is one of our priorities, as well as satisfying future demand of high capabilities job based on technical skills. Since Smartick kicked off, we registered several strategies and solutions, and developed an online (PC or tablet) math learning method consisting of daily sessions of 15 minutes, with real time adaptive content for each student, based on the individual capability and behavior, enabling thus an individualized learning experience.

2 Innovation and Capabilities

Smartick focuses on mental calculation skills' improvement along with transversal logic and problem solving capabilities. Through short daily effort at maximum concentration, the student receives instant feedback, following Lev Vygotsky's (1978) on Zone of Proximal Development and B.F. Skinner's (1961) research on operant conditioning, as well as recent research (Siyepu, 2013 and Roth, 2014) in that line, those for which immediate and regular reinforcement is critical to maintain student's interest and foster learning effectiveness.

Smartick Maths tackles effectively some major issues, especially within elementary education: a) Math teaching/learning, in Europe, has shown unable to keep pace with other countries' improvements, as shown in the latest PISA report, with the EU average falling behind the OECD average. b) There is a high variability of students'

© Springer International Publishing Switzerland 2015
C. Conati et al. (Eds.): AIED 2015, LNAI 9112, pp. 897–898, 2015.
DOI: 10.1007/978-3-319-19773-9

knowledge levels within any classroom. Current teaching methods proved unable to address diversity. c) Math is often inadequately taught and therefore commonly regarded as the most disliked subject, handing students onto teacher's own motivation and capacity. Our adaptive method is based on an algorithm that measures behavioral variables: difficulty, time, effectiveness of exercise, socio-demographic variables, motivation, and willpower. Firstly, this allows us profiling through unsupervised segmentation based on neural networks and later to create an algorithm that adapts teaching, based on both artificial intelligence techniques and classical statistic. On the other hand, Smartick together with the Neuroscience Department of the University of Granada is studying on one hand whether there is relation between the cognitive and math performance profile, and on the other hand, whether we can improve math performance through game-based cognitive training and the way this happens.

3 Impact of Smartick and Corporate Background

The results achieved so far on over 5.000 students (both at home and school) show an improve- ment in 64% higher achievement in math within two years. Children increase their attention and reasoning skills through game-based activities adapted to each age and student profile. An en- couragement to advance in math and technological subjects was also shown. Parents even re- duce costs since Smartick is 60% cheaper than mainstream competitors. School teachers are highly satisfied with our method as 35% of pupils move ahead of school curriculum. Additionally, real time feedback improves information quality for teachers with an user-friendly interface to track student achievements addressing personalized learning within classroom diversity. Since Smartick started its commercial activity in September 2011, it has hired over 20 employees (Mathematicians, Engineers, Psychologists, Teachers and Educators), and more than 5.000 students (in more than 35 countries) with a 200% annual growth. It has revenues over €1M and expect to reach €10M in 3 years time.

References

1. Vygotsky, L. S. (1978). Mind in society: The development of higher psychological processes. Cambridge, MA: Harvard University Press.
2. Skinner, B. F. (1961). Why we need teaching machines. Harvard educ. Rev., 31, 377-398.
3. EACEA/Eurydice, 2011d. Mathematics education in Europe: Common challenges and National Policies. Brussels: Eurydice. Retrieved March 02, 2015, from http://eacea.ec.europa.eu/education/eurydice/documents/thematic_reports/132en.pdf
4. Siyepu, S. (2013). The zone of proximal development in the learning of mathematics. South African Journal of Education,33(2), 1-13. Retrieved March 02, 2015, from http://www.scielo.org.za/scielo.php?script=sci_arttext&pid=S0256-01002013000200011&lng=en&tlng=en.
5. Roth, W.M. (2014). Zone of proximal development in mathematics education. In S. Lerman (Ed.), Encyclopedia of Mathematics Education (pp. 647-650). Springer Netherlands.

Difference Engine and Learning Objects, Inc.

Jon Mott, PhD and Rob Nyland

Learning Objects Inc.
1528 Connecticut Avenue NW
Washington, DC 20036
jmott@learningobjects.com

Abstract. We provide an overview of Difference Engine, a modular and configurable personalized learning platform designed to support learner achievement of goals.

1   Products and Services

Difference Engine is Learning Objects Inc's personalized learning platform. It is modular, configurable "operating system for learning" that is architected from the ground up to support learner achievement of goals. Based on clearly defined goals (including goal hierarchies and taxonomies) and assessments and learning aligned with those goals, Difference Engine powers a variety of personalized, adaptive learning experiences.

These experiences range from personalized courseware that adjusts for prior learning, adaptive high-stakes test preparation applications that dynamically update to account for learner progress toward mastery goals, and personalized degree programs based on competency-based education models.

Difference Engine enables learners to progress effectively and efficiently toward the achievement of their goals. It also empowers teachers and mentors—informed by real-time learner data analytics—to intervene just in time and in the right ways to enhance the learner experience.

2   Corporate Background

Difference Engine is the "powered by" brand behind solutions provided by leading colleges and universities, textbook publishers, and non-profit organizations.

Learning Objects Inc. is a privately-held, Washington DC-based company founded in 2003.

Notable clients include: Elsevier, Carnegie Learning, CUNY, and Lumen Learning
Platform Website: http://difference-engine.com
Corporate Website: http://www.learningobjects.com

© Springer International Publishing Switzerland 2015
C. Conati et al. (Eds.): AIED 2015, LNAI 9112, pp. 899–900, 2015.
DOI: 10.1007/978-3-319-19773-9

3   Innovation

Difference Engine is built on sound learning science and practices. Key examples and innovations include:

- A "backwards design" architecture centered on learner outcomes and evidence thereof
- Contextual social learning activities and tools
- Authentic assessment, including rubric-based assessments of artifacts
- Real-time learner dashboards to inform instructor, mentor, and instructional designer decisions to optimize individual tutoring, cohort instruction, and courseware improvement
- Implementation of industry standards for system integration and data aggregation (most notably LTI and Caliper)
- IRT-based probability estimates of student performance to drive students to activities in their ZPDs
- Spaced repetition activities on learners individualized plans to account for the forgetting curve

4   Evaluation

One of Difference Engine's key products is Elsevier Adaptive Quizzing, an adaptive quizzing product designed to help students study for high-stakes examinations. Elsevier recently completed an informal survey of EAQ users. Some of the top-level findings include:

- The greatest benefit of EAQ as seen by students was the ability of the tool to help them monitor their personal progress
- 79% of the students survey would recommend EAQ to incoming students in their program
- Nearly 60% of students indicated that the use of EAQ boosted their grade by as much as 30%

Elemental Path: Industry and Innovation Report

Arthur Tu

arthur@elementalpath.com

1 Products and Services

Elemental Path is an NYC-based tech company in the connected smart toys market. Our line of conversational smart toys, Cognitoys, targets early childhood learning and entertainment with emphasis on the development of procedural, reasoning and behavioral skills starting at the age four.

2 Corporate Background

Elemental Path (See: http://www.elementalpath.com) was founded in August 2014 after winning the IBM Watson Mobile Developer Challenge and has since established a partnership with IBM. Elemental Path currently has a team of ten including co-founders Donald Coolidge (business strategy), JP Benini (systems architecture), Arthur Tu (educational technology); Chief Operating Officer Bernard Stolar (former CEO of Mattel); Advisors Calvin Chu (former TechStars/RGA Director) and Michael Rinzler (co-founder Wicked Cool Toys) and employees.

The company launched a Kickstarter campaign in February 2015 that received strong backing as well as media coverage. Cognitoys are expected to be publicly available in Q4 2015. See more on Cognitoys website: http://www.cognitoys.com.

3 Innovation

In overview, a conversational smart toy that holds intelligent conversations with young children is in itself a novelty. Many speech-enabled technologies such as Siri of Apple, Echo of Amazon and Cortana of Microsoft, are naturally language query engines that have little to no regard for continuous discourse or instructional scaffolding. Suffice to say, these products do not facilitate knowledge acquisition. Conversational toys of equivalent NLP capacity are practically nonexistent. As far as intelligent tutoring systems are concerned, young children often go off-task while working with a computer-based learning interface without gaming or role-play components. Thus, there is a compelling reason to create a connected smart toy to bridge natural language dialogue management with model-tracing and example-tracing instructional technologies to deliver an interesting and engaging learning experience for early childhood.

Elemental Path's Cognitoys are a platform built specifically to address this challenge of creating conversational agents in physical toys that blend learning into highly personalized conversations.

© Springer International Publishing Switzerland 2015
C. Conati et al. (Eds.): AIED 2015, LNAI 9112, pp. 901–902, 2015.
DOI: 10.1007/978-3-319-19773-9

For example, a child may engage by asking Cognitoy to tell the story of Snow White. After story-telling, the toy may ask the child questions pertaining to details of the story (e.g. how many dwarfs did Snow White meet?). A child may stray away from the conversation and begin talking about cats. Subsequently, the toy handles the new conversation by asking the child how many legs a cat has. The child answers with "four". The toy then determines the appropriate level of math based on age an decides engage the child in a multiplication-by-counting by asking how many legs do five cats have in total. If the child responds incorrectly, the toy then guides the child through a scaffolded process of performing counting-by-four as a way to multiply. If the child succeeds in precisely demonstrating the skill, the toy will increase the difficulty of instructions by locating a relevant, more challenging goal. Additionally, if the child exhibits overwhelming off-task behavior, the toy is equipped to re-engage by either resuming the conversation about Snow White, or initiating a new learning exercise such as finding words that rhyme with "cat" or "leg". The toy will seek to reinitiate math instructions later.

The approach that Cognitoys takes is a hybrid conversational system that employs both non-finite-state, rule-based dialogue management (like RavenClaw/Olympus), and model-tracing (like ACT-R) and example-tracing instructions (like CTAT). Rule-based dialogue management allows flexible continuation of casual, themed conversations; whereas instructional tracing engine uses content of interest to the student collected through casual conversations to dynamically personalize assessments and instructional scaffolding without compromising the integrity of instructional designs. Such approach enables Cognitoys to optimize a child's learning experience by creating and managing educational conversations that continually stimulate student interest in real-time.

Small Improvement for the Model Accuracy – Big Difference for the Students

Michael V. Yudelson and Steve Ritter

Carnegie Learning, Inc.

1 Company Profile

Carnegie Leaning began as a start-up from Carnegie Mellon University in 1998. An in-dependent company now, it produces and sells math tutoring software – the Cognitive Tutor, math text books, and professional development in the United States and abroad. It is estimated that some 650,000 students are using Cognitive Tutor products every year. Carnegie Learning's Cognitive Tutor has always been a product tightly connected to cutting-edge research in the area of cognitive psychology and human-computer interaction.

2 Cognitive Tutor Innovation

The core of Cognitive Tutor is the skill model of the math curriculum. The model is used to track students' progress and to drive personalized problem selection. Over the years, the parameters of the skill model were revised several times by cognitive scien-tists. In general, when models of student learning are considered, primary attention is given to the accuracy. The practical effects of using an alternative model or a differently parameterized in stance of a model are often overlooked. When student model defines how the system functions (e.g., problem sequencing), these effects should, arguably, come first.

In this report, we talk about comparing three parameter instances of Cognitive Tutor cognitive model. We introduce an algorithm that, given the data and the model parameters, computes the work students might save (in terms of number of problems and time) and extra work students would need to master the material. We show that, although in terms of accuracy the three model instances do not differ much, the projected student work load differs significantly.

3 Method

We use a data set collected by Carnegie Learning's Cognitive Tutorsin 2010. Included in this dataset, are student transactions resulting in the skill updates. After retaining students who completed atleast two units of content, we have got 86,361,054 records of 56,046 students from 326 schools practicing 3,760 skills.

© Springer International Publishing Switzerland 2015
C. Conati et al. (Eds.): AIED 2015, LNAI 9112, pp. 903–905, 2015.
DOI: 10.1007/978-3-319-19773-9

The algorithm for computing time savings is similar to the one used in [1]. Given the data and the cognitive model parameters, we simulate the computation of the cognitive model values. The central value is the probability that the skill is mastered. Once it reaches 0.95 the Cognitive Tutor stops issuing practice problems for that skill. Once all of the skills in the curriculum section are mastered, student is allowed to proceed to the next section. When all of the problems of the section are exhausted, but not all skills are mastered, the student is promoted to the next section.

Table 1. Model comparison. Time (hh:mm) and problems are given per student

Model	Accuracy	Time saved	Time extra	Problems saved	Problems extra
BKT Shipped	0.771687	00:03	00:50	2.15	19.13
BKT EM	0.817828	01:09	00:50	41.53	19.17
BKT GD	0.807074	01:43	00:24	50.87	10.67
BKT GD Lag	0.819358	00:38	01:02	22.44	25.55

In the simulation, we consider student activity by blocks corresponding to problems. If, after solving a problem, all the skills are considered mastered but there are more problems in the data, all of them are considered *saved* problems under the model in question. The time student spent solving them is also considered as *saved*. If we ran out of student data but, as per the model, not all the section skills were mastered, we computed projected number of extra problems and the time necessary using a heuristic. For all unmastered skills, we computed the number of successful attempts it would require to take it to the mastered level and selected the highest value. We used this value as the number of extra problems necessary to complete the section. We multiply the number of extra problems by the average problem length in this section to get the extra time.

4   Results

Table 1 is a summary of our model comparisons. Here, we list both the model accuracy as well as number of problems and the time. Together with the fit models, we list results for the parameters that were shipped with the product. Projections could show savings and extra work simultaneously: students can save time on some sections, but require more work on others. Also, due to teacher ability to move students ahead in the curriculum and occasional adjustments of the initial masteries as a result of the pre-test, the extra time could be inflated.

As we can see, the differences in accuracy between the fit models BKT EM, BKT GD, and BKT GD Lag are quite small – all close to 1%. In this set, BKT GD fit model has the lowest accuracy. At the same time, it's projected saving are the highest and extra requirements are the lowest.

Reference

1. Yudelson, M., Koedinger, K., Gordon, G. (2013) Individualized Bayesian Knowledge Tracing Models. In: Lane, H.C., and Yacef, K., Mostow, J., Pavlik, P.I. (eds.) Proceedings of 16th International Conference on Artificial Intelligence in Education (AIED2013), Memphis, TN. LNCS vol. 7926, (pp. 171–180).

Conversation-Based Assessments
at Educational Testing Service

Diego Zapata-Rivera, Blair Lehman, and Tanner Jackson

Educational Testing Service, Princeton, NJ 08541, USA
{dzapata,blehman,gtjackson}@ets.org

Abstract. Work at Educational Testing Service seeks to adapt technologies and techniques originally developed for Intelligent Tutoring Systems to create innovative assessments. In this paper, we describe current work on conversation-based assessments that involve students holding natural language, adaptive conversations with virtual agents. This new assessment has been developed for a variety of domains such as science inquiry, formulating and justifying arguments, and reading, listening, and speaking skills for English language learners.

1 Introduction

Educational Testing Service (ETS) develops, administers and scores more than 50 million assessments annually in many locations worldwide. ETS does research in areas such as: natural language processing applications, reliably and validly measuring personal skills, understanding and enhancing teaching, understanding teacher effectiveness, integrating assessment and classroom instruction, and developing and improving assessment of adult literacy.

One of these areas of research involves work on adapting technologies and techniques originally developed in areas such as Intelligent Tutoring Systems (ITS) and Artificial Intelligence in Education for the creation of innovative, conversation-based assessments (CBAs). These CBAs build on advances in dialogue systems [2, 4] and assessment design methodologies [3] to inform the design of interactions in which the student holds a natural language conversation with artificial agents (e.g., a virtual teacher and a virtual peer) to solve a particular problem. This process is aimed at producing evidence of students' knowledge and skills that is difficult to assess with traditional assessment tasks. This type of interactive assessment is also hypothesized to be more engaging than some traditional assessments. In addition to conversations with artificial agents, these prototypes may include other types of tasks such as interactive simulations, multiple-choice and constructed response questions. Several prototype CBAs have been developed to measure skills in various domains including: science inquiry [6], formulating and justifying arguments [5], and reading, listening, and speaking skills for English language learners [1].

In each of these domains CBA allows for precise diagnosis of students' knowledge and misconceptions through adaptive conversations. Each conversation begins with a main question (e.g., *Do you agree with Art's prediction? Why or why not?*) and then

C. Conati et al. (Eds.): AIED 2015, LNAI 9112, pp. 906–907, 2015.
DOI: 10.1007/978-3-319-19773-9

branches into different conversational paths based on the quality of the student response to that main question. If a student responds with a partially correct answer, for example, one of the agents may ask follow-up questions to get more information (e.g., *Why do you think that?*). In other instances, a student response may trigger a sub-conversation that takes the student through a series of specific questions to determine which components of the construct are known. These adaptive conversations provide students the freedom to answer in their own words, while still allowing for assessment questions that precisely target student knowledge.

Current research in this area involves exploring issues such as the kind of evidence that can be collected by varying the types and source (e.g., teacher vs. peer) of questions, and exploring the emotional states that students experience in these types of environments. These research areas are of special interest for assessment purposes since the quality of student responses may be influenced by aspects of the environment that may not be part of the construct that is being measured. Various large-scale studies are underway to explore additional validity and reliability issues. Finally, this work has resulted in the creation of authoring tools and automated testing facilities that have the potential to support the creation of ITSs [7].

References

1. Evanini, K., So, Y., Tao, J., Zapata, D., Luce, C., Battistini, L., & Wang, X.: Performance of a trialogue-based prototype system for English language assessment for young learners. Proceedings of the Interspeech Workshop on Child Computer Interaction (WOCCI 2014), Singapore (2014)
2. Graesser, A. C., Person, N. K., Harter, D.: The Tutoring Research Group: Teaching tactics and dialogue in AutoTutor. Int. J. of Artificial Intelligence in Education 12, 257-279 (2001)
3. Mislevy, R.J., Steinberg, L.S., Almond, R.G.: On the structure of educational assessments. Measurement: Interdisciplinary Research and Perspectives. 1, 3-62 (2003)
4. Susarla, S., Adcock, A., Van Eck, R., Moreno, K., Graesser, A.C.: Development and evaluation of a lesson authoring tool for AutoTutor. In: Aleven, V., et al. (eds.) AIED 2003 Supplemental Proceedings, pp. 378–387 (2003)
5. Song, Y., Sparks, J., R., Brantley, J. W., Jackson, T., Zapata-Rivera, D., & Oliveri, M. E.: Developing Argumentation Skills through Game-Based Assessment. In Proceedings of the 10th Annual Game Learning Society Conference, Madison, WI (2014)
6. Zapata-Rivera, D., Jackson, T., Liu, L., Bertling, M., Vezzu, M., & Katz, I. R.: Science Inquiry Skills using Trialogues. 12th International conference on Intelligence Tutoring Systems. 625-626 (2014)
7. Zapata-Rivera, D., Jackson, G.T., & Katz, I.: Authoring conversation-based assessment scenarios. To appear in X. Hu & A. Graesser (Eds.), Design Recommendations for Adaptive Intelligent Tutoring Systems (Volume 3) (in press).

Interactive Events

The Development of Reading Comprehension Lessons in AutoTutor for the Center for the Study of Adult Literacy

Whitney O. Baer, Zhiqiang Cai, Qinyu Cheng,
Qiong Yu, D. Patrick Hays, and Arthur C. Graesser

Institute for Intelligent Systems, University of Memphis, Memphis, TN
{whitney.baer,zhiqiang.cai,qinyucheng711,
watermelonqyu,art.graesser}@gmail.com, dphays@memphis.edu

Abstract. The Center for the Study of Adult Literacy (CSAL) seeks to improve our understanding of ways to advance the reading skills of adult learners. Our web-based instructional tutor uses trialogues in the AutoTutor framework to deliver lessons in reading comprehension. We have found a way to manipulate proven comprehension strategies to fit the daily tasks of approaching the written word. With the added demand for digital literacy skills in today's world, it is important that adults with low reading ability experience learning on an online platform.

Keywords: Adult learner · Literacy · CSAL · AutoTutor

1 System's Purpose

The Center for the Study of Adult Literacy (CSAL) is a national research center committed to understanding the reading-related characteristics that are critical to helping adult learners reach their reading goals and to developing instructional approaches that are tailored to adult learners' needs and interests. Adults who struggle with reading have an extremely varied set of abilities and experiences. Many of them have difficult life circumstances which dictate their ability to attend classes regularly (Greenberg, 2008). Adopting a web-based instructional tutor allows for individualization of instruction, increased engagement, and the opportunity to acquire digital skills.

2 Significance of the Approach Implemented

Our computer-based program is CSAL AutoTutor, an intelligent tutoring system delivered online. Our web-based series involves two animated conversational agents, 35 curriculum scripts, semantic evaluation of student contributions, adaptive conversational trialogues (Graesser, Li, & Forsyth, 2014), and electronic documents to be read. Each AutoTutor lesson includes a short review video of the didactic instruction, exercises based in practical topics to assess understanding of the instruction, and

© Springer International Publishing Switzerland 2015
C. Conati et al. (Eds.): AIED 2015, LNAI 9112, pp. 911–912, 2015.
DOI: 10.1007/978-3-319-19773-9

independent reading using web-based texts from our repository. We are developing a repository of 6,000 web-based texts categorized into different theme topics (such as health, family, work, etc.) and ease of reading. To aid us in selecting appropriate texts for the repository and the lessons, we use metrics from a computer system called Coh-Metrix (e.g., Graesser, McNamara, 2011). This system allows us to scale texts on a large number of components of language and discourse.

One challenge of designing the lessons is determining the level of complexity in computer interaction that is suitable for the learner population (Graesser et al, in press). We want to provide an experience that allows the learner to practice new digital skills while emphasizing the comprehension strategies that are the focus of our lessons.

3   Experiments with Users

Early testing has demonstrated that adult learners are eager for the opportunity to use a computer and are capable of successful interactions with text and media – especially when the interactions are modeled by agents (Graesser, McNamara, 2010). Additional experiments have been conducted with college students at the University of Memphis to analyze boredom, gender of the agents, usability of the system, and modes of feedback. In January 2015, we began feasibility studies of the entire curriculum with forty learners in Atlanta and Toronto.

Acknowledgements. CSAL is funded by the Institute of Education Sciences, US Department of Education (Grant R305C120001).   Any opinions, findings, and conclusions or recommendations expressed in this material are those of the authors and do not necessarily reflect the views of IES.

References

1. Graesser, A.C., Baer, W., Feng, S., Walker, B., Clewley, D., Hays, D., Greenberg, D. (in press). Emotions in Adaptive Computer Technologies for Adults Improving Reading. Emotions, Technology, Design, and Learning: Communications, for, with, and through Digital Media. San Diego: Elsevier.
2. Graesser, A. C., Li, H., & Forsyth, C. (2014). Learning by communicating in natural lan-guage with conversational agents. Current Directions in Psychological Science, 23, 374-380.
3. Graesser, A.C., & McNamara, D.S. (2010).   Self-regulated learning in learning environments with pedagogical agents that interact in natural language.   Educational Psychologist, 45, 234-244.
4. Graesser, A.C., McNamara, D.S., & Kulikowich, J.M. (2011). Coh Metrix: Providing multilevel analyses of text characteristics. *Educational Researcher, 40,* 223-234.
5. Greenberg, D. (2008). The challenges facing adult literacy programs. Community Literacy Journal, 3, 39-54.

The Collaborative Logical Framework: Approach and Improvements Based on Instructors' and Learners' Needs

Mario Chacón-Rivas[1], Olga C. Santos[2], and Jesus G. Boticario[2]

[1] TEC Digital, Instituto Tecnológico de Costa Rica, Cartago, Costa Rica
[2] aDeNu Research Group, Artificial Intelligence Department, Computer Science School, UNED C/ Juan del Rosal, 16. Madrid 28040. Spain
machacon@itcr.ac.cr, {ocsantos,jgb}@dia.uned.es
http://adenu.ia.uned.es

Abstract. Intelligent and user friendly support to instructors and learners through e-learning platforms is crucial to get the best benefit of collaborative learning. In this sense, the Collaborative Logical Framework (CLF) developed by the aDeNu research group at UNED has been improved from the usability and modelling viewpoints and integrated into the dotLRN instance running at Instituto Tecnológico de Costa Rica (TEC). On one side, the visual and navigational architecture was redefined with usability techniques (card sorting, paper prototyping, wireframes, eye-tracking). On the other side, the associated Tracking and Auditing Module (TAM) developed for dotLRN was extended to compute more specific events.

1 Introduction and Background

Collaborative learning assessment is a difficult task for instructors when no tools are available to support and validate the process of interaction and collaboration. This turns into a real challenge in distance education provided through current e-learning environments. Here, there are many spread learners' interactions in forums, chats, and other collaborative support tools, which are to be analyzed in order to assess collaborative learning. To alleviate this problem and provide a more encouraging collaborative learning framework, aDeNu has proposed the so called Collaborative Logical Framework (CLF) [1]. Up to now, some implementations have been carried out in dotLRN and Moodle platforms.

The CLF is based on three consecutive stages: (1) *individual stage*: learners work individually to solve a given problem and publish their solution; (2) *collaborative stage*: learners are given access to the solutions from their peers in the previous stage and asked to comment and rate them, as well as to modify their own solution taking into account the comments received; (3) *agreement stage*: in accordance with learners´ activity (i.e., through tracking and modeling learners´ interactions), the system chooses one moderator in each group, who has to produce a consensual solution based on the collaborative participation of group mates (in a similar way as in stage 2). As a result, the final solution shows the agreement and the collaboration that took place.

© Springer International Publishing Switzerland 2015
C. Conati et al. (Eds.): AIED 2015, LNAI 9112, pp. 913–914, 2015.
DOI: 10.1007/978-3-319-19773-9

Interactions carried out by the participants along the different CLF stages within the *CLF Interactive Module* are collected and used by the *CLF Learning Module* to compute, with machine-learning techniques, collaboration indicators that are included in the *Learner Model*. This information can be used by the *Adaptive Module* that generates personalized recommendations to support students during the collaboration.

2   CLF Improvements Based on Users' Needs

Formative evaluations of the CLF implementation in dotLRN have raised several open issues (see [1]). In particular, some usability issues were identified, such as the need to reduce unnecessary navigation steps and present information more clearly on the user interface. Following a usability analysis, a redesign process of the user interface (involving 40 learners and 3 instructors) has been carried out by TEC based on a visual architecture analysis and card sorting techniques. In addition, paper prototyping was used to get insights from users, and wireframes were produced to optimize the space and prioritize contents and functionalities. Proposed designs were validated with eye-tracking techniques. These improvements aim to encourage and get a better engagement of instructors and learners when carrying out the CLF collaborative tasks.

In addition to that, the tracking capabilities of dotLRN TAM [2] have also been improved allowing to track events in folders and portlets. Additionally, the creation of events to be tracked on communities is done automatically. From the users' point of view, the goal here is to enrich the collaborative indicators to be used in monitoring and predictive assessment by considering more detailed collaboration data.

These improvements are used in TEC's Master degree courses, so instructors can create CLF activities, reuse and share them with other instructors. These activities can also be associated to assignments in the e-learning platform (i.e., dotLRN). In this way, instructors can check the collaborative indicators automatically computed in the CLF and the partial grades of students, as well as the log activities during the whole collaborative process. Once assignments are graded, the final result is automatically recorded in the course grading application.

The big challenge here consists in encouraging instructors in using this new kind of collaborative activities which are meant to engage learners in their learning while supporting collaborative learning management and assessment processes.

Acknowledgements. This work has been partly supported by the Spanish Ministry of Economy and Competitiveness (Project MAMIPEC: TIN2011-29221-C03-01).

References

1. O. C. Santos and J. G. Boticario. Involving Users to Improve the Collaborative Logical Framework. In The Scientifc World Journal, vol. 2014, pp. 1–15, 2014.
2. J. Couchet, O. C. Santos, E. Raffenne, and J. G. Boticario. The tracking and auditing module for the OpenACS framework. In 7th OpenACS and. LRN Spring Conference, Vienna, Valencia, Spain, 2008.

ReaderBench: The Learning Companion

Mihai Dascalu[1], Larise L. Stavarache[1], Philippe Dessus[2],
Stefan Trausan-Matu[1], Danielle S. McNamara[3], and Maryse Bianco[2]

[1] University Politehnica of Bucharest, Computer Science Department, Romania
{mihai.dascalu,stefan.trausan}@cs.pub.ro,
larise.stavarache@ro.ibm.com
[2] LSE, Univ. Grenoble Alpes, France
{philippe.dessus,maryse.bianco}@upmf-grenoble.fr
[3] LSI, Arizona State University, USA
dsmcnama@asu.edu

Abstract. Continuous progress tracking in terms of automated essay scoring, assessment of reading strategies, and evaluation of learners' involvement in collaboration groups represents a key component in technology-scaffolded learning. Our educational software, *ReaderBench* [1, 2], is based on current research in the automated essay scoring field (*E-rater*, *iSTART*, *Coh-Metrix*), but provides an integrated approach centered on cohesion. *ReaderBench* supports both tutors and students, affording automated evaluations of reading strategies, course materials selection, and CSCL collaboration. *ReaderBench* has been designed to flexibly allow multiple configurations for various educational scenarios and languages (English, French, and Italian).

1 *ReaderBench's* Purpose

ReaderBench targets both tutors and students by providing a fully functional learning model approach including invidual and collaborative learning methods, cohesion-based discourse analysis [2], dialogical discourse model [3], textual complexity evaluation [1], reading strategies identification [4], and participation and collaboration assessment [5]. By using natural language processing techniques, the main purpose of this framework is to bind traditional learning methods with new trends and technologies to support computer supported collaborative learning (CSCL). *ReaderBench*, by design, is not meant to replace the tutor, but to scaffold both tutors and learners by enabling continuous assessment, self-assessment, collaborative evaluation of individuals' contributions, as well as the analysis of reading materials to match readers to their appropriate class level text.

Overall, *ReaderBench* is a fully functional automated software framework, designed to be an educational helper for students and tutors. The system makes uses of text-mining techniques based on advanced natural language processing and machine learning algorithms to design and deliver summative and formative assessments using multiple data sets (e.g., textual materials, behavior tracks, self-explanations).

© Springer International Publishing Switzerland 2015
C. Conati et al. (Eds.): AIED 2015, LNAI 9112, pp. 915–916, 2015.
DOI: 10.1007/978-3-319-19773-9

2   Outline and Experiments

From a learner's perspective, *ReaderBench* can act as a Personal Learning Environment (PLE) that incorporates: a) *individual assessment* of textual materials making use of the textual complexity metrics (semantics, morphology, surface factors integrated by support vector machines) that reflect the textual organization and structure of reading materials [1]; b) *comprehension prediction* by identifying reading strategies employed by students in their self-explanations or by automatically evaluating student summaries [4]; c) *collaboration* and *participation evaluation* in CSCL conversations based on cohesion graphs and on Bakhtin's dialogism [5].

In the first representative experiment, French students aged between 8 and 11 years old (3rd–5th grade) explained what they understood from two French stories comprised of about 450 words, resulting in 149 summaries and post-test examinations used to assess their comprehension of the reading materials [4]. As expected, paraphrasing, control and causality strategies were more reliably identified than information stemming from students' experience, whereas comprehension was reliably predicted by using the identified reading strategies from learner's self-explanations or from the textual complexity factors extracted from their summaries [4].

A second experiment included 110 4th year undergraduate 1st year master students asked to manually annotate 3 chat conversations [5]. We opted to distribute the evaluation of each conversation due to the amount of time required to manually assess a single discussion. In the end, based on an average of 33 annotations per conversation, the overall results indicated a reliable automated evaluation of both participation (ICC = .97 Rho = .84) and collaboration (ICC = .90; Rho = .74) [5].

Acknowledgements This research was partially supported by the ANR DEVCOMP 10-BLAN-1907-01 and the 2008-212578 LTfLL FP7 projects, by the NSF grants 1417997 and 1418378 to Arizona State University, as well as by the POSDRU/159/1.5/S/132397 and 134398 projects.

References

1. Dascalu, M., Dessus, P., Bianco, M., Trausan-Matu, S., Nardy, A.: Mining texts, learners productions and strategies with ReaderBench. In: Peña-Ayala, A. (ed.) Educational Data Mining: Applications and Trends, pp. 335–377. Springer, Switzerland (2014)
2. Dascalu, M.: Analyzing discourse and text complexity for learning and collaborating, Studies in Computational Intelligence, Vol. 534. Springer, Switzerland (2014)
3. Dascalu, M., Trausan-Matu, S., Dessus, P., McNamara, D.S.: Dialogism: A Framework for CSCL and a Signature of Collaboration. In: CSCL 2015. ISLS, Gothenburg (in press)
4. Dascalu, M., Dessus, P., Bianco, M., Trausan-Matu, S.: Are Automatically Identified Reading Strategies Reliable Predictors of Comprehension? In: ITS 2014, Vol. LNCS 8474, pp. 456–465. Springer, Honolulu, USA (2014)
5. Dascalu, M., Trausan-Matu, S., Dessus, P.: Validating the Automated Assessment of Participation and of Collaboration in Chat Conversations. In: ITS 2014, Vol. LNCS 8474, pp. 230–235. Springer, Honolulu, USA (2014)

Talk, Tutor, Explore, Learn: Intelligent Tutoring and Exploration for Robust Learning

Beate Grawemeyer[1], Sergio Gutierrez-Santos[1], Wayne Holmes[2],
Manolis Mavrikis[2], Nikol Rummel[3], Claudia Mazziotti[3], and Ruth Janning[4]

[1] London Knowledge Lab, Birkbeck, University of London, UK
{beate,sergut}@dcs.bbk.ac.uk
[2] London Knowledge Lab, Institute of Education, University College London, UK
{w.holmes,m.mavrikis}@ioe.ac.uk
[3] Institute of Educational Research, Ruhr-Universität Bochum, Germany
{nikol.rummel,claudia.mazziotti}@rub.de
[4] Information Systems and Machine Learning Lab, University of Hildesheim, Germany
janning@ismll.uni-hildesheim.de

Abstract. It is widely acknowledged that many children have difficulty learning fractions. Accordingly, we are developing the iTalk2Learn system (www. italk2learn.eu), which aims to facilitate the robust learning of fractions by children in primary and early secondary education. The iTalk2Learn system integrates structured, practice-based tasks with exploratory, conceptually-oriented tasks, and intelligent affect-aware support. The system focus seson natural interaction via intuitive user interfaces, which includes speech recognition, and speech production.

1   Introduction

iTalk2Learn is a learning platform for children aged 8-12 years old who are learning fractions. It combines structured tasks from pre-existing intelligent tutoring systems with more open-ended tasks in an exploratory environment developed by the project. The platform is designed to detect children's speech in real time, which, together with the children's interactions, is analysed in order to provide adaptive and affect-aware support.

2   The iTalk2 Learn system

2.1   Combining Structured and Exploratory Learning Environments

We have designed and implemented a novel exploratory learning environment for fractions, Fractions Lab, that allows students to explore different representations of fractions while they engage with a wide variety of guided fractions tasks. The platform monitors the children's interaction and speech, which is analysed in order to provide two-dimensions of task-dependent feedback [1] and affect-aware task independent support [2]. The children's interaction and speech are also used to determine the individual child's learning path, either presenting them with more- or less-challenging

© Springer International Publishing Switzerland 2015
C. Conati et al. (Eds.): AIED 2015, LNAI 9112, pp. 917–918, 2015.
DOI: 10.1007/978-3-319-19773-9

exploratory tasks, or switching to mapped tasks from pre-existing practice-based Intelligent Tutoring Systems.

2.2   Speech and Learning

It is well known that encouraging students to reect aloud on their learning helps support that learning. Accordingly, the iTalk2Learn system asks students to reflect aloud on their strategies as they engage with the tasks. In addition, the automatic speech recognition uses novel techniques to draw inferences about the students' affective states while they engage with the learning situation (which in turn is used to determine appropriate support and learning paths). Additional input for affect detection comes from prosodic cues in speech. A perceived Task Difficulty Classifier (pTDC) uses raw speech data to determine whether students are under-, over-, or appropriately challenged [3].

2.3   Intelligent Support

Based on the students' interaction with the learning environment as well as the result of the speech recognition and pTDC, the intelligent support classifies the affective state of the student. This is used to adapt feedback, which aims to enhance a student's affective state, in order to enhance the learning experience. The adaptation is based on a dynamic Bayesian network [2], which is trained with data gathered from several Wizard-of-Oz studies where the effect of feedback on students' affective state was investigated [4].

3   Conclusion

We have developed a novel adaptive system, which is able to facilitate robust learning, by combining structured and exploratory learning. It enables natural interaction through speech, which is used to detect the affective state of the student. This is then used to adapt feedback according to the affective state.

Acknowledgments. This research has been funded by the EU in FP7 in the iTalk2 Learn project(318051).

References

1. Holmes, W., Mavrikis, M., Hansen, A., Grawemeyer, B.: Purpose and Level of Feedback in an Exploratory Learning Environment for Fractions. In Proc. AIED 2015 (2015)
2. Grawemeyer, B., Mavrikis, M., Holmes, W., Guti_errez-Santos, S.: Adapting Feedback Types According to Students' Affective States. In Proc. AIED 2015 (2015)
3. Janning, R., Schatten, C., Schmidt-Thieme, L.: Feature Analysis for Affect Recognition Supporting Task Sequencing in Adaptive Intelligent Tutoring Systems. In Proc. EC-TEL 2014 (2014)
4. Grawemeyer, B., Mavrikis, M., Holmes, W., Hansen, A., Loibl, K., Gutiérrez-Santos, S.: Affect Matters: Exploring the Impact of Feedback during Mathematical Tasks in an Exploratory Environment. In Proc. AIED 2015 (2015)

Reasoning Mind Genie 3: Interactive Demonstration

Victor Kostyuk, Leigh A. Mingle, and Kevin Mulqueeny

Reasoning Mind, Houston, TX
{Victor.Kostyuk,Leigh.Mingle,
Kevin.Mulqueeny}@reasoningmind.org

Abstract. Reasoning Mind Genie 3 is a recently developed intelligent tutoring system that simulates a small-group tutoring session. Elements of the system's design include interactions with peer and tutor pedagogical agents, embodiment and attention-focusing to reduce cognitive load, precise synchronization of voiced speech and on-screen movement, and complementarity rather than duplication of speech and on-screen text. The system is used to closely model the daily instructional practice and pedagogical decisions of expert classroom teachers. A pilot of the system in 2013-2014 showed promising results on a curriculum aligned assessment and an independent assessment (ITBS), and quantitative observations of student behavior and affect revealed a high percentage of time spent on-task and in engaged concentration.

Keywords: Intelligent tutoring systems · Mathematics education · Pedagogical agents · Demonstration

1 Purpose and Significance

The Reasoning Mind Genie 3 intelligent tutoring system was developed to reproduce the learning experiences of students in classrooms of expert teachers delivering a coherent middle school mathematics curriculum [1]. This is done by modeling the lesson activities and pedagogical decisions of an expert teacher in a flexible virtual classroom environment. This environment consists of a central work area – the whiteboard – and four character avatars: a tutor agent, two peer student agents, and the avatar of the student using the system. The tutor character is used to model the teacher: it delivers instruction, provides scaffolding and help, asks frequent questions (mostly of the real student, sometimes of a virtual peer), assigns quizzes and exams, etc. Peer characters are used to model common misconceptions (allowing the student to evaluate and correct mistakes, thus "helping" the peer character), demonstrate positive attitudes to learning, work cooperatively with the student on problem solving, engage in simulated competition, and provide encouragement and help when the student makes mistakes. All characters are voiced by human narrators, and speak in a direct, informal manner.

Each character has a marker which they use to write on the whiteboard and point to objects as they talk about them. For example, if the tutor says "And now, let's simplify the right side of the equation," while the equation $27=3x+6+5x$ is on the

© Springer International Publishing Switzerland 2015
C. Conati et al. (Eds.): AIED 2015, LNAI 9112, pp. 919–920, 2015.
DOI: 10.1007/978-3-319-19773-9

whiteboard, the tutor's marker will point to 3x+6+6x when the tutor says the word "right". This closely mirrors the pointing action and body language of classroom teachers, and it's designed to minimize the extraneous cognitive load associated with searching for the visual object corresponding to the spoken words [2]. Marker movements and the appearance and erasure of text is precisely timed to coincide with the appropriate words spoken by the tutor or peer characters. Additionally, as in a real classroom, most instruction and interaction is verbal – only key definitions, rules, problems, solutions, and questions to the student are displayed. As far as we are aware, Genie 3 is unique in having a rich multimedia environment with multiple pedagogical agents designed to closely simulate classroom instruction.

A previous iteration of Reasoning Mind's intelligent learning system, Genie 2 [3], is used in thousands of elementary classrooms annually, and over the next five years, we plan to have a comparable number of middle school students using Genie 3 as their core mathematics program. Preliminary results of the Genie 3 system are encouraging. In a small-scale pilot in 2013-2014, students in three districts across Texas used Genie 3 as their core 6th-grade curriculum. Those students showed significantly better performance on a curriculum aligned assessment [1] and on the Iowa Test of basic Skills [in preparation] than a matched comparison group, and quantitative observations using the Baker Rodrigo Ocumpaugh Monitoring Protocol [4] showed higher rates of on-task behavior and engaged concentration, and lower rates of boredom, than in the comparison classrooms [5].

2   Demonstration Details

The demonstration consists of a fully-interactive set of three 6th-grade lessons and an exam lesson. It can be accessed at http://grade6demo.rmcity.org/ using any Flash-capable browser.

References

1. Kostyuk, Victor, Mingle, Leigh A., & Mulqueeny, Kevin. (under review) Reasoning Mind Genie 3: Creating a next-generation intelligent tutoring system with research-based design principles.
2. Mayer, R. E., & Moreno, R. (2003). Nine ways to reduce cognitive load in multimedia learning. *Educational psychologist, 38*(1), 43-52.
3. Khachatryan, George A., et al. "Reasoning Mind Genie 2: An Intelligent Tutoring System as a Vehicle for International Transfer of Instructional Methods in Mathematics." *International Journal of Artificial Intelligence in Education* 24.3 (2014): 333-382.
4. Ocumpaugh, J. (2012). *Baker-Rodrigo Observation Method Protocol (BROMP) 1.0. Training Manual version 1.0.* Technical Report. New York, NY: EdLab. Manila, Philippines: Ateneo Laboratory for the Learning Sciences.
5. Mulqueeny, K., Mingle, L., Kostyuk, V., Baker, R.S., & Ocumpaugh, J. (under review). Improving engagement in an e-learning environment.

Online Assessment of Negotiation Skills through 3D Role Play Simulation

Daniela Pacella[1], Andrea Di Ferdinando[2], Elena Dell'Aquila[1], and Davide Marocco[1]

[1] Plymouth University, Plymouth, UK
{daniela.pacella,e.dellaquila}@plymouth.ac.uk
davide.marocco@gmail.com
[2] AIDVANCED Srl, Rome, Italy
andrea.diferdinando@aidvanced.com

Abstract. The lack of standardised technological tools to assess psychological characteristics allows traditional tests to be still widely used, though these tests require double processing and expensive procedures. ENACT is both a serious game for a standardised assessment of the user negotiation skills and an Intelligent Tutoring System, which makes use of the data collected during the interaction in order to generate a tailored environment for the user to experience and improve their skills and be guided through learning.

Keywords: Serious games · e-learning · Artificial Intelligence · Intelligent Tutoring Systems · Negotiation

1 Methodology and Implementation

In the actual e-learning and serious game context, what emerges is the lack of standardised technological tools to assess psychological characteristics and deficits.

The European Project ENACT (Enhancing Negotiation skills through on-line Assessment of Competencies and interactive mobile Training) aims at developing a 3D environment where users can:

1. Receive scientific, standardised profiles of their negotiation skills in a handy way;
2. Be guided through learning by an integrated Intelligent Tutoring System.

The ENACT platform consists of an assessment and a training environment. The assessment is composed of 8 scenarios, in which the user deals with a structured virtual agent, standardised on Rahim and Bonoma's [1][2] model of negotiation. This model differentiates four styles upon two dimensions, concern for self and for others:

1. Integrating (high concern for self and others)
2. Obliging (low concern for self and high concern for others)
3. Dominating (high concern for self and low concern for others)
4. Avoiding (low concern for self and others)

The training environment, which begins at the end of the assessment session, makes use of all the data and profile scores collected in the previous environment to

C. Conati et al. (Eds.): AIED 2015, LNAI 9112, pp. 921–922, 2015.
DOI: 10.1007/978-3-319-19773-9

build an intelligent and responsive environment which is suited to the user's needs. Artificial Intelligence is used in this context for two main purposes:

1. Generating an adaptive virtual agent initialised according to the user profile;
2. Finding correlations among user behaviour and negotiation profiles.

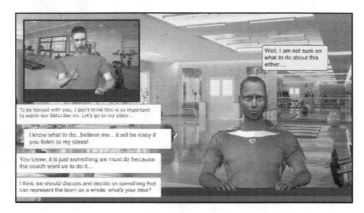

Fig. 1. Screenshot of the current platform interface of the assessment session (demo version)

Fig.1 shows the platform GUI. For each interaction, the user (the game character on the left) is asked to select a sentence on the four proposed, which is correlated to a specific gesture and face expression. Preliminary data on the beta version of the platform were collected at Plymouth University in September 2014. 152 subjects, of which 72 in the age 6-10 and 79 between the age of 11 and 60 (mean age ≈ 20.6, 41 males and 38 females) tested the game, and the latter were asked to complete a questionnaire about the game. The average rating for each of the question never scored below 3.5 on a 5 points Likert scale except for two questions, one regarding the realism of the conversations and one concerning the game graphics which scored a mean of 3.4 and 3.3. 93% of the subjects answered that they would play the game again.

The distinct contribution that we would like the ENACT Platform to give to the serious game and e-learning community is based upon the importance of the gamification of standardised psychological tests. We also wish to underline the importance of the validation that we want to achieve inside the ENACT Platform that will give a scientific based reliable profile easily accessible within all modern devices. The platform is still under development, and a demo can be found at **http://enactgame.eu**.

References

1. Rahim, M.A., Bonoma, T.V.: Managing organizational conflict: A model for diagnosis and intervention. Psychological Reports, vol. 44, pp. 1323-1344 (1979).
2. Rahim, M.A.: A Measure of Styles of Handling Interpersonal Conflict. Academy of Management Journal, vol. 26, pp. 368-376 (1983).

MEMORAe: A Web Platform
to Support Collaborative Annotation

Atrash Ala, Abel Marie-Hélène, and Moulin Claude

Sorbonne universités, Université de technologiede Compiègne, UMR CNRS 7253,
laboratoire HEUDIASYC, Centre de recherché Royallieu, CS 60 319, 60 203
Compiègne cedex –F rance
{ala-aldin.atrash,marie-helene.abel,claude.moulin}@utc.fr
http://www.hds.utc.fr

Abstract. We present MEMORAe, anontology-based web platform And show how it supports collaborative annotation.

Keywords: Collaborative Annotation · Web Platform · Ontology · Semantic Web

1 Work Context

According to us, the annotation is the "transcription of an idea that has a particular target (the annotated data) and a body (the data annotating the target) which somehow says something about the target". We consider that it must be possible to annotate the resource itself or any part of it. When the annotation is shared between collaborators who have access to the target resource, we call it a collaborative annotation. Despite the multiplicity of the platforms that support collaborative annotation, they all share a common limitation which is the restricted ability to share / retrieve annotations because they are embedded into resources [1]. In order to overcome this limitation, we consider the annotation as being a resource in its own right.

2 MEMORAe Web Platform

MEMORAe is a web platform[1] which is developed using web 2.0 technologies and based on MEMORAe-core 2 semantic model. It is an ontology model which is built using OWL (Web Ontology Language) and uses semantic web standards (foaf, sioc, bibo, oa[2]). The platform aims to facilitate knowledge sharing within organizations. All types of resources are indexed by one or more concepts of a semantic model shared among all users and representing the shared vocabulary of an organization. The platform presents a semantic map which is the graphical representation of this model. This semantic map is built by importing the ontology file into the platform. In order to

---

[1] A video demo could be found at: http://goo.gl/UbIs7x
[2] oa stands for Open Annotation: http://www.w3.org/ns/oa

© Springer International Publishing Switzerland 2015
C. Conati et al. (Eds.): AIED 2015, LNAI 9112, pp. 923–924, 2015.
DOI: 10.1007/978-3-319-19773-9

retrieve the resources indexed by a particular concept, the user choses the desired indexing concept from the semantic map. The sharing spaces of the user could be viewed in parallel while navigating through the semantic map. The user of the platform can annotate resources including documents, notes, other annotations, etc. There is also a possibility to annotate the concepts of the semantic map. There are two ways to access the annotations. The first is when opening the annotated resource. The second way is directly through the resources list of the the sharing space. When opening an annotation, the user has the ability to access the annotated resource.

The outline of the demo will start by a brief explanation of the web platform's purpose. Then, the different interfaces of the platform will be explained. Next, an indexing concept from the semantic map will be chosen in order to share resources and index them. These resources could be: documents, web links, notes, etc. After adding these resources, a particular resource will be chosen in order to annotate it. The key point of the demo is to show how this annotation is accessible either when opening the annotated resource or in the resources list like any other previously added resources.

3   Discussion

A recent test of the platform took place at the department of computer science at the Université de Technologie de Compiègne. The students were following a course in "The Techniques of Modeling, Capitalization, and Knowledge management". The test lasted three months (October to December 2014). The students had to perform a "technology watch" [3]about a particular topic. It's main purpose is to build an ontology of this topic. This ontology is used to produce the semantic map. The construction of this map was a part of the learning process. The students then started to capitalize and exchange knowledge around this map within MEMORAe web platform (sharing notes, annotations, etc.). At the end of the semester (January 2015), an anonymous questionnaire was organized to get the students' feedback. Considering annotations as information resources, 80% of the students indicated that they were interested by the annotations added by the others. The resource list shows the annotations. As the annotations are also linked to their targeted resource, it is possible to open this resource itself from one of its annotations.

Two other annotation functionalities are under development: multi-target and multi-author annotations.

References

1. Su, A. Y., Yang, S. J., Hwang, W.-Y., and Zhang, J. (2010). A web 2.0-based collaborative annotation system for enhancing knowledge sharing in collaborative learning environments. Computers and Education, 55(2):752766.

---

[3] The "technology watch" consists of gathering the latest technologies and their commercial availability

Soft Computing for Learner's Assessment in SoftLearn

Borja Vázquez-Barreiros, Alejandro Ramos-Soto, Manuel Lama, Manuel Mucientes,
Alberto Bugarín, and Senén Barro

Centro de Investigación en Tecnoloxías da Información (CiTIUS)
Universidade de Santiago de Compostela, Spain
{borja.vazquez,alejandro.ramos,manuel.lama,
manuel.mucientes,alberto.bugarin.diz,senen.barro}@usc.es

Abstract. This paper describes the contributions of the SoftLearn platform to key issues in learning analytics, as i) discovery of the learning path that students follow in a course and ii) provide interpretability of graphs in dashboards

1 System's Purpose

SoftLearn is a process mining-based platform that identifies and highlights all the content generated by the learners during the course, enabling teachers to improve the learning paths as well as the evaluation process for each of the learners. Moreover, SoftLearn has an intuitive graphical interface that has been specifically developed to evaluate both the learning paths and the data generated during the learning activities, to automatically build natural language reports describing the most relevant facts about them, and to visualize statistics regarding the learning process of the students.

2 Significance of the Approach

The development of SoftLearn was designed to support the teachers in the learners' tracking and assessment. Hence, it enables the access to information related to both the sequence and timing of the student work, thus allowing a better understanding of both the students' behavior and their activity patterns during the course. It also provides graphical and textual reports regarding the students' activity and impact during the course. Two novelties distinguish SoftLearn from other learner's assessment tools:

— **Process Learning Discovery**. ProDiGen [1] is a process discovery algorithm. Its purpose is to discover the workflow that represents the learning path followed by the learners. In order to guarantee feasible evaluations of the learning paths, it retrieves *complete* and *precise* solutions, i.e., models explaining only what the students did. Last, but not least, it retrieves *simple* learning models.
— **Automatic Textual Reporting**. The dashboard includes a service that provides automatically generated natural language reports [2] built from every student activity data. This service is based on linguistic description techniques adapted from the fuzzy sets field and natural language generation (NLG) tools.

© Springer International Publishing Switzerland 2015
C. Conati et al. (Eds.): AIED 2015, LNAI 9112, pp. 925–926, 2015.
DOI: 10.1007/978-3-319-19773-9

3   Outline

The graphical user interface of SoftLearn [3] allows teachers to (i) understand the learner behavior through the visualization of the learning paths followed by the learners and (ii) also facilitates the evaluation of the learning activities carried out by learners during the course. This graphical user interface is divided in three sections: (i) the Workflow Analytics section, where the learning paths are displayed and where the teacher can evaluate both the learning data generated by the students –through a defined rubric by the teacher– and the students' behavior; (ii) the Dashboard section, which provides different statistics about the students in both a graphical and textual form; and (iii) the Content of the course, where all the data generated in the course are showed in a table in order to provide a easy access to specific learning activities.

4   Experiments

To evaluate the benefits of the SoftLearn tool for students' assessment, we have conducted an experiment with two teachers of the subject Educational Technology of the University of Santiago de Compostela. The subject uses the open source platform ELGG which integrates an individual space and also a social network with forums, blogs, microblogging, a personal wall, calendar, favorites and pages. The assessment of the students' behavior is *extremely time consuming*, given the number of students (60 in this course) and the amount of documents associated to each personal space. In this experiment, we have studied the time invested to evaluate these 60 students involved during the learning process. The results of the teachers' assessment set a time saving of 54%. This time saving occurs because the tool eases the reading of the contributions of the students through a better and more accessible overall display.

Acknowledgments. This work was supported by the Spanish Ministry of Economy and Competitiveness under the projects TIN2011-22935 and TIN2011-29827- C02-02 and by the European Regional Development Fund (ERDF/FEDER) under the project CN2012/151 of the Galician Ministry of Education.

References

1. Vazquez-Barreiros, B., Mucientes, M., Lama, M.: Prodigen: Mining complete, precise and minimal structure process models with a genetic algorithm. Information Sciences 294 (2015) 315–333.
2. Ramos-Soto, A., Bugarin, A., Barro, S., Taboada, J.: Linguistic descriptions for automatic generation of textual short-term weather forecasts on real prediction data. IEEE Transactions on Fuzzy Systems, 23(1) (2015) 44–57.
3. SoftLearn demo. http://tec.citius.usc.es/SoftLearn/Demo.html. Retrieved: Mar., 9th, 2015.

Author Index

Printed in the United States
By Bookmasters